World Wide Web Quick Reference

The World Wide Web (Web) is a system for providing and accessing information and resources through interoperating computer hardware, software, and networks worldwide.

Software programs called Web browsers (or clients) run on a user's computer and access information on remote Web servers.

Web Information expressed in hypertext lets authors associate one resource with another through a link (indicated by highlighted text or hotspot). Links within hypertext can be to other hypertext documents or to network information servers such as Gopher, FTP, and Telnet. Extensions for multimedia (hypermedia) enable some browsers to access sound, graphics, and movies, as well as text. The figure illustrates some relationships among two popular browsers (Mosaic and Lynx), servers, and hypertext.

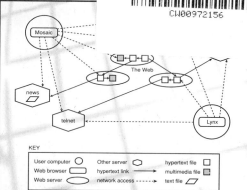

KEY		
User computer ○	Other server ⬭	hypertext file ▢
Web browser ▭	hypertext link →	multimedia file ▢
Web server ⬭	network access ----→	text file ▱

Key Online Web Resources

General Information
Web Overview:	http://www.w3.org/
Web FAQ:	http://sunsite.unc.edu/ boutell/faq/www_faq.html

Accessing The Web—Web Via a Client
Web Client's List:	http://www.w3.org/hypertext/ WWW/Clients.html
NCSA Mosaic Home:	http://www.ncsa.uiuc.edu/SDG/ Software/Mosaic/ NCSAMosaicHome.html
Lynx home page:	http://www.cc.ukans.edu/ about_lynx/about_lynx.html

Accessing the Web—Web via Telnet
Switzerland:	telnet telnet.w3.org
Finland:	telnet info.funet.fi
Israel: log in as	telnet vms.huji.ac.il; www
New Jersey, USA: log in as	telnet www.njit.edu; www
Kansas, USA: log in as	telnet ukanaix.cc.ukans.edu; www
Web via e-mail:	mail agora@mail.w3.org;

Providing Web Information
Server Software:	http://www.w3.org/hypertext/ WWW/Daemon/Overview.html

JumpStation:	http://oneworld.wa.com/ htmldev/devpage/dev-page.html
Web Weavers:	http://www.nas.nasa.gov/NAS/ WebWeavers/
CyberWeb:	http://www.stars.com/

Exploring The Web
Virtual Tourist:	http://wings.buffalo.edu/ world/
CERN Virtual Library:	http://www.w3.org/ hypertext/DataSources/ bySubject/Overview.html
EINet Galaxy:	http://www.einet.net/ galaxy.html
Yahoo:	http://www.yahoo.com/
Web Spiders:	http://web.nexor.co.uk/mak/ doc/robots/robots.html

Web Discussion
http://www.halcyon.com/grant/web-groups.html/

Announcements
news.comp.infosystems.announce

Internet Reference
http://www.rpi.edu/Internet/Guides/decemj/icmc/ top.html

Merit: ftp:/ftp.merit.edu/

Tips

Netscape users
- Use bookmarks to save interesting URLs; select Bookmarks / Add Bookmark
- Set the expiration time for your global history list; select Options / Preferences / Link Styles

Mosaic users
- Use the hotlist to save interesting URLs; select Navigate / Add Document to Hotlist
- To look at your hotlist, select Navigate / Hotlist
- When surfing, turn off image loading to avoid long downloads; select Options / Delay Image Loading
- Periodically clear your global history; select Options / Clear Global History...

Lynx users
- Use bookmark file to save interesting URLs; to add, press key a; to view, press key v
- To get help, press key ?

Information providers
- Planning: Define the purpose and information content to meet your users' needs.
- Analysis: Research other webs; continuously evaluate your web's value and usage.
- Design: Shape information for usability: Cue user to web purpose, status, and how to operate. Avoid long downloads for users (minimize inline graphics, break up large pages).
- Implementation: Check HTML files in multiple browsers.
- Maintenance: Keep links fresh. Frequently check and maintain.
- Development: Publicize your web appropriately; seek improvement and advice.

Praise for *The World Wide Web Unleashed...*

"*The World Wide Web Unleashed* is an impressive armchair traveler's guide to the Web."
—David Angell, *PC Magazine*

"*World Wide Web Unleashed* makes a great reference for any Web user.... Authors John December and Neil Randall provide effective, time-saving Web-surfing strategies, and if you're thinking of trying your hand at a Web page for your business, the book includes plenty of design tips and examples that show what works and what doesn't."
—David W. Methvin, *Windows Magazine*

"Run to your favorite bookseller and buy a copy of *The World Wide Web Unleashed*....This is a weighty tome and an incredibly rich source of useful information for WWW users and information providers—including several chapters on HTML. A winner!"
—Howard Harawitz, *HTML Assistant Newsletter*

"With this book December and Randall have made an important contribution to the development of the Web. Though by no means the last word on Web weaving, it is the first thorough, intelligent discussion of the topic. If you're interested in developing content for the Web, this book is a must buy."
—Bettina Vitell, *Internet Gazette & Multimedia Review*

"An exhaustive look at the hypertext system that has revolutionized the Internet. Co-author John December is well-known for his incredibly comprehensive guides to Internet resources; this book is no different....*The World Wide Web Unleashed* can be widely recommended as a very thorough introduction to the medium."
—John Maxwell, *Duthie Books News*

"For those of you searching for a good source of info about the WWW, Web browsers, and Web page design, check out *The World Wide Web Unleashed*.... It is an exceptionally good guide to the Web."
—Michael McDonald

"This is the most complete work on the World Wide Web that I have seen to date. It definitely contains more information than other works on the topic."
—Robert M. Slade

"*The World Wide Web Unleashed* is a guide for becoming a surfer on the Internet though the use of the World Wide Web interface.... I highly recommend this book for serious World Wide Web users."
—Angela Ambrosia, *The Forum*

The World Wide Web

UNLEASHED 1996

sams
net

201 West 103rd Street
Indianapolis, IN 46290

John December
Neil Randall

To my family, friends, and everyone on the Net
—John December

To my father, Jacob Lloyd Randall (1918–1994)
—Neil Randall

Copyright © 1995 by Sams.net Publishing

THIRD EDITION

International Standard Book Number: 1-57521-040-1

Library of Congress Catalog Card Number: 95-74792

98 97 96 95   4 3 2 1

Interpretation of the printing code: the rightmost double-digit number is the year of the book's printing; the rightmost single-digit, the number of the book's printing. For example, a printing code of 95-1 shows that the first printing of the book occurred in 1995.

Composed in AGaramond and MCPdigital by Macmillan Computer Publishing

Printed in the United States of America

Trademarks

President, Sams Publishing	*Richard K. Swadley*
Publisher, Sams.net Publishing	*George Bond*
Marketing Manager	*John Pierce*
Managing Editor	*Cindy Morrow*

Acquisitions Editor
Mark Taber

Development Editor
L. Angelique Brittingham

Production Editors
Kitty Wilson
Mary Inderstrodt

Editors
Kimberly K. Hannel
Joe Williams

Editorial/Graphics Coordinator
Bill Whitmer

Formatter
Frank Sinclair

Technical Reviewers
James A. Armstrong
Sam Kimery
James Pitkow

Cover Designer
Tim Amrhein

Book Designer
Alyssa Yesh

Page Layout
Carol Bowers, Charlotte Clapp,
Mary Ann Abramson,
Terrie Deemer, Louisa Klucznik,
Ayanna Lacey, Steph Mineart,
Casey Price, Andrew Stone,
Tina Trettin, Susan Van Ness,
Mark Walchle, Colleen Williams

Proofreading
Georgianna Briggs, Mona Brown,
Michael Brumitt, Charlotte Clapp,
Mike Dietsch, Kevin Laseau,
Paula Lowell, Brian-Kent Proffitt,
Nancy Price, Erich J. Richter,
SA Springer

Indexer
Greg Eldred

Overview

Contents

Part IV Exploring the Web

Part V Weaving a Web

Part VI   Setting Up and Administering a Web Server

Acknowledgments

Like the intertwining tendrils of the Web, my debt of acknowledgment spreads far and deep.

For the book itself, I thank Mark Taber and the team at Sams.net Publishing who've given me professional support as well as the freedom to shape my ideas. I thank everyone whose web I've used as an example in this book for their kind permission and for taking the time to answer my questions about their applications. In my writing, I relied on many tools and information sources to research and understand the Web, including Brian Pinkerton's WebCrawler, EINet's Galaxy, the Web Catalog at Centre Universitaire d'Informatique, Richard Bocker's Planet Earth, and the many other tools I describe in the chapters of Part III in this book.

I'd like to thank those who have helped me in my Net adventures and enriched my work by helping it become known and increasing the feedback I receive about it, including Harley Hahn, Oscar Nierstrasz, Brendan Kehoe, Ellie Cutler, Gleason Sackman, Kevin Savetz, Neil Randall, Lou Rosenfeld, and Kevin Hughes. I acknowledge the influence of pioneers in explaining the Internet, Brendan Kehoe and Ed Krol. I thank my fellow Net information surfers—Scott Yanoff, Simon Gibbs, Martin Koster, Richard Bocker, John Makulowich, and the many others whose work continues to contribute to my understanding.

There are many people at Rensselaer Polytechnic Institute who have helped me in my studies. The faculty of the Department of Language, Literature, and Communication have directly or indirectly assisted me in many ways. I thank my dissertation advisor, Robert Krull, for understanding why I would take a summer to work on a book. I thank Teresa Harrison and Tim Stephen for their continued guidance in my scholarly growth. I owe a debt of gratitude to Roger Grice for helping me learn about the information development processes and to Elizabeth Keyes and Patricia Search for giving me insights into visual aspects of information layering and structuring; these concepts influenced the weaving methodology I present in Part V. My fellow graduate students in the department have been a source of fun and support. I thank Laura Gurak and Emilie Gould for their help in understanding computer-mediated communication. The staff at Rensselaer's Information Technology Services runs a superb Web server, and I thank the RPInfo team for allowing me to contribute information to it.

My work and understanding of the Web itself, as represented in this book, has been influenced and guided by all those whom I've interacted with in my Net activities. I thank the people whose works I include in my CMC Information Sources list. *Computer-Mediated Communication* magazine's staff and everyone participating in the Computer-Mediated Communication Studies Center continue to help me learn. I thank my students in workshops and courses I've taught at the University of Wisconsin-Milwaukee and Rensselaer Polytechnic Institute, whose questions about computers prompted me to think about the needs of new users. I thank everyone on the Net—without you, I'd have a lesser world to explore.

—John December

As always, there are too many people to thank. So I will restrict this list to those who truly contributed.

My deepest gratitude to

My wife, Heather, for putting up with my sleepless nights, my battles with my computer, and all the little problems that go with doing a book—and the absences

My daughter Catherine, for her persistence against substantial odds

My daughter Michelle, for her laughter and her skill with people

John December, for sharing the book in the first place, and for his work in making the Web a worthwhile place to be

Carrie Pascal, for pitching in when I needed it most, and for being an accepting friend

Mark Taber, for his unbelievable patience, for which I have both admiration and appreciation

Dave Goodwin, for his constant encouragement

Keith McGowan, for his uncomplaining assistance

Karin Trgovac, for agreeing to help with the second edition and then carrying through with little guidance

The hundreds of creators and developers of the Web and its tools, for obvious reasons

—Neil Randall

About the Authors

Lead Authors

John December (john@december.com, http://www.december.com/) is a candidate in the Ph.D. program in Communication and Rhetoric at Rensselaer Polytechnic Institute in Troy, New York. He has taught courses in computer science, creative writing, expository writing, and technical communication, and conducted Internet training workshops. Prior to studying at Rensselaer, John earned an M.S. in computer science from the University of Wisconsin-Milwaukee, an M.F.A. in creative writing (Poetry) from The Wichita State University, and a B.S. in mathematics from Michigan Technological University. From 1985 to 1989, he worked as a software developer for the Boeing Company. His poetry has appeared in literary magazines including *Mid-American Review, Sou'wester, Passages North,* and others. Known on the Net for his list of information sources about the Internet and Computer-Mediated Communication, he's also written papers, articles, and book chapters about the Internet and is publisher and editor of *Computer-Mediated Communication Magazine.*

Neil Randall (nrandall@watarts.uwaterloo.ca) teaches English at the University of Waterloo in Waterloo, Ontario, Canada. He offers courses in professional writing and rhetorical theory, and conducts research in issues surrounding the Internet, computer-mediated communications, and other technological issues. He is the author of *Teach Yourself the Internet: Around the World in 21 Days* (Sams Publishing, 1994) and co-author of *Plug-n-Play Internet* (Sams, 1995). He has published articles and reviews in several computer magazines, including *PC Computing, The Net, CD-ROM Today, Windows, Compute, Amiga World, PC Gamer,* and *Computing Canada.* He writes a weekly newspaper column dealing with computers and has published several related newspaper features.

Contributing Authors

Thomas Boutell (boutell@netcom.com) keeps the frequently asked questions list (FAQ) for the comp.infosystems.www.* newsgroups and has written a number of other Web-related gimcracks. He became involved with the Web while at Cold Spring Harbor Labs, a biology research laboratory on the East Coast, and has since moved to Seattle where he works for a new firm, Progressive Networks. You can find his home page at the URL http://sunsite.unc.edu/boutell/index.html.

Andrew Dinsdale (aa293@detroit.freenet.org) is an Internet Communications Specialist for DataServ, Inc., a technology integration firm serving the K-12 community. He writes and maintains The Commercial Use (of the Net) Strategies home page, he developed the Web pages for Diversity University MOO, and he contributes to John December's Web-based Computer-Mediated Communication Studies Center.

Laura Lemay (lemay@lne.com, http://www.lne.com/lemay/) is a technical writer in northern California who has been a prolific user of and contributor to the Internet for close to eight years. She is the author of the best-selling *Teach Yourself Web Publishing with HTML in a Week* (Sams Publishing, 1994), and *Teach Yourself More Web Publishing with HTML in a Week* (Sams, 1995).

Carrie Pascal is a project manager in the multimedia products group at Microsoft Corporation. She received her B.A. degree in English and Computer Science at the University of Waterloo, and is currently planning a book about the Web as an advanced communications medium.

James Pitkow (pitkow@cc.gatech.com) is a graduate researcher with the Graphics, Visualization, and Usability (GVU) Center at Georgia Tech's College of Computing. He initially conceived, developed, and deployed the GVU WWW User Survey.

Brandon Plewe (plewe@acsu.buffalo.edu, http://wings.buffalo.edu/~plewe/) is Assistant Coordinator of Network Information Services at the State University of New York at Buffalo. He has an M.A. in Geography from SUNY/Buffalo. Besides managing the University's CWIS, he has built several geography-related services on the WWW, including the Virtual Tourist.

Adrian Scott (scotta@rpi.edu) is the founder of Scott Virtual Theme Parks (http://www.virtpark.com/theme), one of the premiere VRML content companies.

Karin Trgovac (ktrgovac@sunee.uwaterloo.ca) is responsible for the Graduate Student Database and the World Wide Web pages for the Electrical and Computer Engineering department at the University of Waterloo. Her home page resides at http://coulomb.uwaterloo.ca/.

David Woolley (drwool@freenet.msp.mn.us) created one of the first computer conferencing systems, PLATO Notes, the model for such conferencing software as Lotus Notes, DEC Notes, and the tin newsreader. Today he is a software designer, consultant, and writer in Minneapolis. He is also the lead system designer for the Twin Cities Free-Net, a Web-based community network (http://freenet.msp.mn.us:8000/).

Introduction

Seldom in human history have people adopted a communications technology so widely and rapidly as Internet users have chosen the Web. Begun in 1991 by developers at the European Laboratory for Particle Physics (CERN) in Geneva, Switzerland, the World Wide Web started as a way to organize and link related information. Through presentations and demonstrations, the CERN team taught others about their system, and Web use grew among members of scientific communities, researchers, and users of the Internet.

By 1993, the creators of graphical interfaces to the Web like Mosaic had developed a "look and feel" that fueled the Web's popularity even more. By late 1993, the Mosaic browser used with the Web was hailed by John Markoff in the *New York Times* as the "killer app" of the Internet itself. Through its easy-to-use interface, Mosaic revealed a seamless interplay of networked information, a treasure-trove of resources growing more rapidly than the exploding Internet itself.

Some people view the Web and its browsers as a harbinger of an "Information Superhighway." However, the reality of the Web doesn't match the images of a future with 500 TV channels or stereotypes of "hackers" and online subcultures. Instead, the Web exists now and offers opportunities for communication unparalleled in history. As a tool for human expression, the Web displays all the foibles, foolishness, and cacophony people seem destined to create. The Web also has the potential for human brilliance, for fostering sparks of interaction among people that grows into knowledge, perhaps leading to wisdom.

Why This Book?

If you are curious about what global networks may offer, or if you are an experienced Internet traveler, this book gives you information that will help you unleash the power of the World Wide Web. You will learn what the Web is, how to connect to it, how to move through its information spaces, what people do on the Web, the fundamentals of weaving your own web, and what issues the Web and its users face for the future.

- If you are new to computer networks, this book will guide you through the basics of the Web and offer you a reference for future growth.
- If you are in commerce, government, or education and are considering Web-based information and connections among people, this book will expand your awareness of what can be done.
- If you are an experienced Internet traveler, this book will open new insights into the structure and evolution of information spaces.
- If you are an educator, this book can help you define the Network literacy that is right for your students.

- If you are an information publisher, this book presents a method for weaving a web to meet your users' needs.
- If you are in industry, this book will open new avenues for disseminating research, connecting employees, and reaching customers.
- If you are considering the Web as a way to create a community, this book will give you skills in web weaving as well as describe examples of community information systems.
- If you train people to use the Internet or Web, this book will give you a valuable selection of topics to cover and teach.
- If you want to learn how to establish Web servers, this book will give you an overview of software for several platforms.

Gain an Overview of the Web

The Web itself is a world-wide collection of interconnected hardware, software, and networked systems. Part I of this book delves into the Web's development, history, and basic operation. You'll gain an understanding of the Web in the context of hypermedia and survey the Web in a whirlwind tour of some of its major features.

Find Out How to Connect to the Web

Part II introduces you to the browsers, tools, and connections necessary for you to experience the Web. You'll gain an understanding of the nuts-and-bolts issues of browsers and connecting to the Web, see the variety of browsers available for accessing the Web, and understand the add-ons necessary for multimedia experiences.

Learn How to Navigate the Web

While browsers present a coherent, seamless view into the Web, the problem of making sense of what you find remains. What is important? How does a user find something? Part III presents a full spectrum of skills for using the Web for information discovery and retrieval. You'll learn how the Web's information spaces interconnect, how to use a browser, and all about the many network protocols Web browsers can access. You'll develop skills in navigating and searching for subjects, keywords, and information spaces, and learn how to "surf."

Raise Your Awareness of What the Web Offers

In order to use the Web effectively and also consider how you might contribute your knowledge to it, you need to develop an awareness of the possibilities for Web expression. Part IV surveys dozens of uses in many areas, providing an extensive tour of information and communication applications of the Web. The chapters survey exemplary applications and describe details of the expressive possibilities they offer. You will increase your knowledge of what is "out there" now, with emphasis on the variety and ingenuity of expressions in commerce, entertainment, education, scholarship, research, science, technology, communication, publishing, government, and communities.

Learn How to Weave a Web of Your Own

Just as forming symbols is just one part of the task of writing, there is more to weaving a web than creating files of hypertext markup language code. Part V explains the basics of the hypertext markup language within the context of a method for weaving webs. This web-weaving method includes processes for planning, analysis, design, implementation, and development (including publicity) of webs for organizations or individuals, with practical advice on how to serve the needs of a target audience and organize and shape information.

Learn to Administer Servers

It's one thing to weave a web, but quite another to make it available to the world. To publish HTML pages created by individuals in your organization, you either need to set up and administer your own World Wide Web server or rent space on a server administered by someone else. If you decide to do it yourself, Part VI offers an introductory look at the fundamentals of server installation and administration, with guidelines and suggestions for several areas of concern.

Consider Issues for the Web's Future

Finally, we examine some issues important to the future of the Web. Included in Part VII are essays that look at the commercial future of the Web, challenges for information providers and society, the development of communication systems, and the trends in networked information and Web uses.

Unleash the Power of the Web

Perhaps you have heard the term "Information Superhighway." If you have, you might have wondered what it could mean. While not a fulfillment of all the hype associated with this term, the Web today offers an astounding collection of networked information with the potential to become even more extensive and valuable.

The constant growth of the Web creates an important need to gain insight into its tangle of links. As the Web rapidly becomes *the* destination for graphical interfaces to the Net, the focus of user training and the preferred method for perceiving the Net will become the Web. This book aims to unleash the Web's potential by giving you knowledge and skills, introducing expressive possibilities, and providing you with the understanding necessary to take part in the Web's communications revolution.

Typographic Conventions Used in This Book

The term *Web* refers to the global collection of all publicly accessible World Wide Web servers. In lowercase, *web* refers to a collection of hypertext that exists locally on one of these servers. In other words, you can weave a web and connect it to the global Web.

The names of Internet protocols are capitalized when used within the text (for example, Gopher, FTP). In examples of computer interaction or when shown in a Web browser, these terms are presented in lowercase.

Internet addresses, commands, and directory and filenames are set in `monospaced type` to set them off from the rest of the text and clarify, for example, where an address ends and where the rest of the sentence begins.

The World Wide Web Unleashed SUPPORT WEB

For updates to this book, sample Web pages demonstrating good design, and links to Web applications, interesting Web sites, and Web pages maintained by the book's authors, be sure to visit the **World Wide Web Unleashed Support Web** at URL `http://www.rpi.edu/~decemj/works/wwwu.html`

PART

I

Introduction to the World Wide Web

The World Wide Web: Interface on the Internet

1

by
Neil Randall

For any number of historical reasons, the Internet has emerged as a huge, rich source of information accessible only via a series of not-so-friendly interfaces. The basic commands for Telnet, FTP, Archie, WAIS, and even e-mail are powerful but nonintuitive, and the rapid growth of the Internet's user base has resulted in an increasing number of users who have neither the patience nor the desire to learn the intricacies of these interfaces.

Even those who know them, however, are aware that easier systems can very quickly result in greater productivity, an awareness that has spawned such eminently usable tools as the popular Gopher. But Gopher is limited as an information source by the restrictions of its display; a gopher is primarily a table of contents through which users read or download files—and tables of contents are useful for some but by no means all types of information reservoirs.

Enter the World Wide Web. Conceptualized not long after Gopher itself, the Web began life as a project designed to distribute scientific information across computer networks in a system known as *hypertext*. The idea was to allow collaborative researchers to present their research complete with text, graphics, illustrations, and ultimately sound, video, and any other means required.

Important ideas within or across publications would be connected by a series of hypertext links (or just *hyperlinks*), much like the information displays made both possible and plentiful through the Macintosh's famous Hypercard program and similar interfaces available on the NeXT, Amiga, X Window, and Microsoft Windows platforms. Users would be able to traverse Internet documents by selecting highlighted items and thereby moving to other, linked documents; and in the case of graphical displays, they would see these documents complete with graphics and other multimedia elements.

The World Wide Web project has made possible the idea of accessible and attractive interfaces on the Internet. Using the Web requires an Internet account and a piece of software known as a World Wide Web client, or browser, and it is the browser's task to display Web documents and allow the selection of hyperlinks by the user.

A few browsers exist that require only text-based displays, the most popular of which is the UNIX program Lynx (now available for DOS machines as well). Most, however, run atop graphical user interfaces such as X Window, Macintosh, Microsoft Windows, NeXTStep, and Amiga. The most popular browsers released to date are Mosaic and Netscape (available for several of these platforms), but many others exist and/or are in development, both as freeware and as commercially available programs.

With a graphical Web browser, you see formatted documents that contain graphics and highlighted hyperlinks. These browsers let you navigate the Internet not by entering commands, but rather by moving the mouse pointer to the desired hyperlink and clicking. Instantly, the World Wide Web software establishes contact with the remote computer and transfers the requested file to your machine, displaying it in your browser as another formatted, hyperlinked document. You can "surf" the Web by hopping from hyperlink to hyperlink without delving deeply into the contents of any particular document, or you can search the Web for specific documents with specific contents, poring over them as you would a book in the library.

But what *is* the World Wide Web? Where did it come from, and why is it so popular and so potentially important? It is clearly a system of both communication and publication, but how does it work and what can we expect in its future?

These are the questions answered briefly in this chapter and the next four, and examined through a tour in Chapter 6, "The World Wide Web: A Guided Tour." More importantly, however, they're questions explored over the thousand pages of this book, across hundreds of documents on the Web itself, and in magazines, journals, and research reports the world over. The Web is among the most rapidly adopted technological entities of a century that has seen many, and understanding it might be crucial for understanding the next century.

Let's get started.

The Concept of the World Wide Web

The Internet, it is said, is in need of a "killer app." It needs one tool, one program, one application that will take it from being a much-hyped but difficult-to-use linking of computers around the world to being a highly informative, highly usable database and communications tool. The spreadsheet was the killer app for PCs a long time ago, but so far the Net doesn't have one. Some have given "killer app" status to the immensely popular program called Mosaic (see Chapter 10, "NCSA Mosaic," for a lengthy discussion of Mosaic's potential as a killer app), but Mosaic still has its difficulties and its limitations. The same holds true for the equally popular Netscape Navigator (detailed in Chapter 11), which has also been touted as a killer app, and for all the various alternative and commercial Web browsers that have hit the market over the past year. The true killer app of the Internet remains somewhere around the corner, and nobody knows if just *one* killer app can handle the Internet's complexity. Until we have one, we simply won't know.

What the Internet does have, however, is a killer *concept*—and the name of that concept is the World Wide Web. In only a few short years of existence, the Web has captured the imagination of data searchers and information surfers alike. Its popularity isn't difficult to understand: The World Wide Web provides the technology needed to offer a navigable, attractive interface for the Internet's vast sea of resources, in much the same way that the toolbar on a word processor screen obscures the intimidating codes that actually comprise the program. Given the Net's history of nearly impenetrable commands and procedures, and the trend in today's software to hide complexity behind usable interfaces, this capability is essential if the Net is to become a mainstream set of applications.

But it's important to realize that the Web is a *concept*—not a program, not a system, and not even a specific protocol. It might be more accurate, in fact, to call it an interface, but even that wouldn't be quite right. The most accurate terminology might be meta-interface—an interface that incorporates other interfaces—but words with "meta" as a prefix went out of favor sometime during the early nineties. Calling it a tool would be far too restrictive, and calling it a set of applications and interfaces would be reasonably accurate but incredibly clumsy. So let's just stick with "concept," because that's as close as we might be able to get.

The Conceptual Makeup of the Web

Calling the Web a *concept*, however, doesn't answer the question of what the World Wide Web actually is. Technically, the Web is nothing more than a distributed hypermedia system (at least, that's what its designers call it, as explained in Chapter 5, "Putting It All Together with the Web"), but *distributed hypermedia system* is surely no more understandable a term than *concept* itself.

The next four chapters examine the variety of systems that constitute the World Wide Web, of which there are, primarily, three:

- The first is *hypertext*.
- The second is *the Internet* itself.
- The third is that most overused of 1990s terms, *multimedia*.

Important to keep in mind, however, is that the Web is truly a convergence of these systems, in a way that renders the whole much greater than the sum of the parts.

Right now, though, let's concentrate on defining the World Wide Web, or at least providing a definition that helps understand both its past and its future. To do so, we must turn to the three ideas mentioned above: hypertext, the Internet, and multimedia.

Hypertext is an idea that was introduced way back in the seventies by the sometimes visionary, sometimes flaky, and always provocative Ted Nelson. Hypertext is discussed in Chapter 3, "Hypertext," but the idea is deceptively simple. A hypertext document is one that provides clearly visible links to other documents; and in a hypertext computer environment, selecting a link in one document moves you directly to the other. Nelson's idea was to link all the world's information in a huge hypertext system. The World Wide Web is closer than any other system so far to accomplishing that idea, even though it remains a long, long way from fulfilling Nelson's vision.

The second system inherent in the Web's design is the Internet. Covered more comprehensively in Chapter 2, "The Internet," and in fact through a large array of books on the shelves of libraries and bookstores right now, the Internet is a global system of networked computers that allows user-to-user communication and transfer of data files from one machine to any other on the network.

The Net is the basis of the fictional *matrix* or *web* found in the science fiction of such authors as William Gibson and Bruce Sterling, and the basis, as well, of the Clinton administration's much-hyped information superhighway (or, more properly, Global Information Infrastructure). The World Wide Web, in fact, is the closest thing we have now to approximating any of those fictional or semi-fictional technologies.

It's important to note, however, that *the Web as a system does not require the Internet*. In fact, a distributed information system based on the Web can be constructed on *any* local-area or wide-area network, and in fact such systems are being developed all the time.

But the first two words in *World Wide Web* are "world wide," so it makes little sense to talk about the Web without basing it in the world-wide networking—and the only (relatively) open (relatively) world-wide network now available is the Internet. As a result, we'll build the Internet into our definition.

Even so, it's useful to keep in mind that the World Wide Web is *not* the Internet. As the focus of popular and media attention moved over the past year and a half from e-mail and newsgroups to the Web and, in particular, Mosaic and Netscape, the perception seemed to emerge that the Web and the Net were synonymous. Today's Web clients can perform FTP, Gopher, and even Usenet access, so it's tempting to see them as the Net's primary interface. But these technologies are in fact separate from the Web itself, even though they're increasingly becoming usable through Web interfaces. Electronic mail remains the biggest hold-out—most browsers let you send mail but none offers a truly integrated mail reader—and other Net technologies require proxies and/or gateways to make them work at all. Even the technologies that are included in browsers are usually better accessed through a program dedicated to their use, so it's not even fair to say that the Web is the best means of working with the entire Net. Still, what can't be denied is that the World Wide Web has become the most famous Internet item, and certainly the most popular.

So far, we've looked at hypertext, and we've drawn in the Internet. Good, but not good enough. There's another concept involved as well: *multimedia.*

Again, multimedia is explored more fully in a short while (Chapter 4, "Multimedia," to be exact), but for now let's just say that, as its name suggests, multimedia combines various presentational technologies in an effort to appeal to as many senses as possible. (Actually, the word should be multimedi*um*—like multipart, multisession, multigerm, and multilane—but we'll let the linguists battle over that one.)

Put a bit more simply, multimedia draws on graphics, sound, animation, and video to create a full, rich computing experience. And for the first time, through browsers such as Mosaic, Cello, MacWeb, Netscape, and Viola, the World Wide Web offers a multimedia experience for Internet users.

Although certainly in need of further development, the Web already lets information presenters place graphics, sound, and video within the page, and users with a direct, high-speed connection can download them quickly enough to feel as if they're participating in full multimedia. With a 14.4Kbps modem, the download process is far too slow; but within the next couple of years, high-speed access should be much more available and affordable. The important point is that the groundwork has been laid.

So what is it, then? Let's try this: *The World Wide Web is a convergence of computational concepts for presenting and linking information dispersed across the Internet in an easily accessible way.*

Does this help? Well, maybe. Other definitions of the Web tend to use phrases such as "network information delivery system" and "distributed information system"; but no matter how technically accurate these definitions are, they just don't seem very useful, because every term with them needs an individual definition as well. Arguably, so does the rather vague *concept* in our own definition, but we know enough about the word *concept* not to need a firm definition. *Concept* is uncertain, volatile, and difficult to grasp, but so is the Web itself—not as a definable computer technology, but rather as a combination of its specifications and its uses. Using the term *concept* might seem like an author's unnecessary avoidance, but anything more precise would almost certainly be outdated within months.

In its initial proposal (discussed in Chapter 5), the Web was simply termed "a hypertext project," but it clearly became more than that. What our new definition attempts to do is explain that the Web is a cleverly designed collection of interesting concepts, and allow for the very real possibility that other concepts will soon merge with it.

In fact, this is already happening. Technologies such as WAIS (Wide Area Information Servers) and Archie (the long-lived search engine) are already being programmed into Web-based search tools, and this means that some of the Internet's techniques are already becoming integrated into the Web's conceptual framework. The most successful technologies are those that make their individual components transparent; in the case of the World Wide Web, this seems to be happening early in its history.

The Web contains the technologies necessary to give the Internet a pretty face. Web browsers that take full advantage of these technologies make the Internet easier to use. It's not hard to see where in the history of computing these two crucial ideas—attractiveness and usability—came from. Essentially, the Web and its browsers have done for the Internet in 1994 what the Macintosh did for the personal computer a decade earlier. There were problems with the first Macs from a technological standpoint, and they were written off as toys by the business and computing communities, but they hung on and thrived on the strength of their interface.

Simply put, people could use Macintoshes easily, and that's something that was never true of the IBM PC or its mainframe predecessors. The Mac hid the difficulties of command-line computing under a bunch of objects you could click on with a funny-shaped thing called a mouse, and in doing so it opened computing to the masses. When Microsoft released Windows 3.0 some years later with the iconic, graphical, point-and-click interface (which had originally been developed by Xerox), the masses indeed took over.

Ten years later, graphical World Wide Web browsers such as Mosaic, Netscape, WinWeb, and MidasWWW offer an interface that has its technological problems, that oversimplifies some important Internet procedures, and that has been called a toy for people who want to glide over the Net rather than delve into it. But just like the Mac, it has thrived because of its interface, and at this time it threatens to overtake all other Internet use, perhaps even the most important Internet tool, electronic mail.

Actually, this comparison between the Mac and the Web isn't quite precise, because although the Mac offered just one interface, the Web itself allows all kinds. Its most important interface, however—the graphical, multimedia, point-and-click system offered by Cello, Mosaic, and others we'll examine in Part II, "Web Browsers and Connections," is attractive for precisely the same reasons as the Mac and Windows. No matter what its detractors might argue, the World Wide Web offers the Internet to the masses, and that's its true power. No longer do people have to master the vagaries of FTP and Archie and WAIS searching (although the Web's own search procedures demand considerable practice themselves), and as the Web develops it should fully incorporate e-mail, newsgroups, telnetting, and other technologies as well.

Different front ends to the Web will compete for our attention—currently we have Lynx, Viola, Cello, MacWeb, WinWeb, InternetWorks, and others—but the principle will remain the same: Link the information, let the users follow whatever path they choose, and when they reach their destination, let them do with the information whatever they please.

Given all this, it's easy to see why the term "World Wide Web" has become, for many people (including those who actually know better) synonymous with the term "Internet." In fact, it's the potential of the synonymity that makes this book possible in the first place. If you want to master the Internet through the mid- to late nineties, you can't possibly do so without mastering the Web as well. Web sites are popping up everywhere, Web designers and technicians are being hired and deployed, and the Web has even become an add-on for the planet's two most popular word processing packages. Quite literally, it's become unavoidable.

This book is already in its third edition, but the Web itself is still in its early stages of development. Even so, what's become clear since the time this book initially appeared is that paying attention to the World Wide Web is crucial, for casual users as well as professionals. The Web stands poised to become the basis for the revolution in information and connectivity we've all read about but are still waiting to see. You can browse it, search it, and add your own information to the swiftly expanding sea of Web materials. In many ways, it's there for the taking. Already, the Web has begun to change the face of marketing, customer service, business transactions, education, travel, publishing, information dissemination, and collaborative research. What the Web changes in the future is largely up to us. That, so far, is what makes it so fascinating.

The Internet

2

by Neil Randall

Even though the World Wide Web as a system can operate on any computer network, the Web as we know it is nothing without the Internet. In order to understand the Web's importance, in fact, it is necessary to understand the tools, the fundamentals, and even the history of the Net. But a book about the Web is no place for a fully comprehensive look at the Internet; instead, we'll examine the aspects that are especially pertinent for anyone who wants to know about the Web.

A Very Brief History of the Internet

It's been said often, but it bears repeating once more: The Internet was originally conceived by the U.S. military as a means of ensuring a workable communications system in the event of a strike by enemy missiles or forces. It was the sixties, after all, at the height of the Cold War, when the fear of Soviet attack guided all kinds of military projects. If one central communications location was bombed out of existence, the military wanted to make sure that surviving locations could still talk to one another, and that no communication would be lost.

Because the original network was developed by the Advanced Research Projects Agency of the U.S. military, it was given the name ARPAnet. Eventually, however, as increasing numbers of research institutes and research universities connected themselves to the network, ARPAnet came to handle only this kind of research data while a second network, MILnet, looked after military communications. In the 1980s, the National Science Foundation established NSFnet, linking a half-dozen supercomputers at an extremely high speed that has since been made higher still. NSFnet eventually took over the Internet (as it was now being called) from ARPAnet, and in 1991 the U.S. High Performance Computing Act established the basis for the National Research and Education Network (NREN). NREN's goals are to establish and maintain high-speed, high-capacity research and education networks, while helping to develop commercial presence on the Internet as well.

This last point is immensely important for the World Wide Web, which is rapidly being adopted as a medium of choice for businesses in North America and, increasingly, around the globe. During the Internet's early years, commercial activity was severely constrained by the NSF's "Acceptable Use Policy" (AUP), which directly disallowed any for-profit activities. The AUP has changed somewhat, but more importantly the Internet has taken on different forms and different policies. Although it's not actually stated anywhere, commercial activity is now very much accepted on the Net. Whether or not General Motors will begin to sell its vehicles over the World Wide Web remains to be seen, but already the Web is being used for product ordering and product support—and by very sizeable corporations, too.

The Internet has changed so much, in fact, that during the first half of 1994 the number of domain names for commercial organizations (the com domain) overtook those for educational institutions (the edu domain). In the month ending June 25, more than 1,300 new commercial (com) names were registered with the Internet, and the following month saw an additional 1,700. That's a 30-percent jump in just one month! By January 1995, the number of commercial domains had risen past 30,000, with a monthly growth rate of over 10 percent (and average monthly growth closer to 13 percent). And these businesses aren't just moving onto the Net to do research or e-mail, either; they're there because the Internet offers enormous commercial potential. If you want to examine the statistics yourself, as well as a great deal of additional commercial Internet information, check out the Internet Infohaus pages at `http://www.fv.com/access/by-seller/Internet_Info` and see what the Net has done recently.

To be sure, the Internet is still primarily a research and academic network, at least from the standpoints of creative use and extent of use. There's an enormous amount of activity happening in the educational field as well (with the K–12 area burgeoning), and a great deal involving community and nonprofit issues. That's almost certain to change, however, over the second half of the 1990s. The only question now is whether or not governmental legislation will stop the Internet's amazing growth, and the jury is still very much out on that one. Even here, however, we see the immensity of the Net. It's almost pointless to use the phrase "governmental legislation," because that leads to the other questions, "Which government?" and "Which legislation?" Still, the roles of governments around the world have yet to be determined, so the questions must continue to be asked.

A Very Basic Knowledge of the Internet

To understand the World Wide Web fully, it's essential to know a few significant Internet issues. Actually, the more you know about the Net, the better you know the Web as well, despite the fact that one of the Web's primary functions is to hide from users the difficulties regarding the interfaces of the Internet's tools. The Web is an important layer of functionality and accessibility riding atop the Net; but without the Net and its horde of concepts, the Web would simply be impossible. You can't have one without the other.

Some of the major terms and concepts associated with the Net are explained in this section. Arguably, you should know them well before even beginning your Web explorations; but as software such as Mosaic, Netscape, Cello, and MacWeb becomes increasingly popular, this is a bit like asking Windows users to keep their DOS commands in mind. It's just not going to happen. What will unquestionably happen, however, is that things will go wrong while you're cruising the Web, and without a good background knowledge of the Net you may not know what happened or how to proceed.

Domain Names

Every computer on the Internet has an Internet Protocol (IP) address associated with it. IP addresses have four parts, and a typical address looks like this: `198.43.7.85` (that is, four items all separated by periods). Happily, as a World Wide Web user you really don't need to know much about IP addresses, except possibly for getting connected to the Internet in the first place.

What you need familiarity with, however, is the Internet's domain name system (DNS). If you have an Internet account, you're already familiar with DNS: your userid, which originally looked like so much gibberish, contains the domain name for the computer on which your account exists. The U.S. president's e-mail address is `president@whitehouse.gov`, which contains the *domain name* `whitehouse.gov` and the *username* `president`. The domain itself is `gov`, which tells you that it is a government organization (big surprise), while the *subdomain*, `whitehouse`, tells you which part of government organization this address is attached to (again, big surprise).

Not all domain names are as easy to remember as the president's. Mine, for instance, is `nrandall@watarts.uwaterloo.ca`, which when analyzed reveals the following: my userid is `nrandall` (which at least is a whole lot more obvious than some people's userids), and my account is on a machine called `watarts` (the Arts faculty computer system) at the subdomain `uwaterloo` (the University of Waterloo), in the domain `ca` (which stands for the country Canada).

John December, this book's coauthor, has the address `decemj@rpi.edu`, which is also quite simple. His userid is `decemj`, the subdomain is `rpi` (Rensselaer Polytechnic Institute), and the domain is `edu`, which signifies an educational organization. In your Internet travels, you'll encounter much more complex domain names as well.

Notice the discrepancy between the domain field of my address (`ca`) and John's (`edu`). Mine points to a domain location, his to a domain type. The general rule of thumb is this: If a country code is *not* specified, assume the site is in the United States. There is in fact a domain code for the United States—not surprisingly, it's `us`—but it's rarely used. Similarly, a Canadian or Japanese university could use the `edu` domain suffix, but that also is rare. The exceptions to this, generally, are found in the `net` and `org` domains, and often `com`, where countries are often unspecified.

Table 1.1 lists the U.S. domains, and Table 1.2 shows some of the many international domains. For a fuller discussion of domain names and a longer list of international domains, see a book such as *The Internet Unleashed 1996* (published by Sams.net), in the same series as the book you're now reading.

Table 2.1. Domain types (usually associated with U.S. addresses).

Abbreviation	Meaning
com	Commercial organizations
edu	Educational institutions
gov	Governmental organizations (except military)
mil	Military organizations
net	Network and service providers
org	Organizations other than those listed above

Table 2.2. A sampling of international domains.

Abbreviation	Meaning
ar	Argentina
au	Australia
at	Austria
be	Belgium
br	Brazil
ca	Canada
cl	Chile
cn	China
cr	Costa Rica
cu	Cuba
cz	Czech Republic
dk	Denmark
ec	Ecuador
eg	Egypt
fi	Finland
fr	France
de	Germany
gr	Greece
hk	Hong Kong
hu	Hungary
in	India
ir	Iran
iq	Iraq
ie	Ireland
il	Israel
it	Italy
jp	Japan
kp	North Korea
kr	South Korea
kw	Kuwait
ly	Libya

continues

Table 2.2. continued

Abbreviation	Meaning
my	Malaysia
mx	Mexico
nl	Netherlands
nz	New Zealand
no	Norway
pa	Panama
pe	Peru
pl	Poland
pt	Portugal
pr	Puerto Rico
ro	Romania
su	Russia
lc	St. Lucia
sa	Saudi Arabia
sn	Senegal
sg	Singapore
sk	Slovakia
sl	Slovenia
za	South Africa
es	Spain
lk	Sri Lanka
se	Sweden
ch	Switzerland
sy	Syria
tw	Taiwan
th	Thailand
tr	Turkey
ua	Ukraine
ae	United Arab Emirates
uk	United Kingdom
us	United States

Abbreviation	Meaning
va	Vatican
ve	Venezuela
vn	Vietnam
zr	Zaire

Domain names affect your use of the World Wide Web in several ways. First, you're very likely to encounter something like a "DNS Lookup Error"; essentially, this means that the domain name server on your local computer couldn't translate the name you typed into a legitimate IP address. Practically speaking, it means that the requested file isn't available because the domain name portion of the URL was unrecognizable, or it means that the domain itself no longer exists (less likely). The domain name system was one of the most important individual developments of the Internet, and as a result the domain name server is something we could scarcely do without.

Next, the domain name is, in effect, part of the entire filename itself, and you'll find yourself typing domain names plus filenames whenever you request a specific URL address. URLs, or Universal Resource Locators, contain the specific instructions for your Web browser to find and retrieve the file you specify. Clicking a highlighted hyperlink in a Web document automatically activates the retrieval process (and effectively hides the URL address of the document from you), but Web browsers also let you type the URL manually.

Third, by learning domain names you can get a good sense of where you're going on the Web. In most browsers, if you rest the cursor over a hyperlink, the URL associated with that link will appear on the status bar at the bottom of the screen. This is often worth trying, since it will give you a good idea if you want to activate the link at all. You might know, for instance, that a particular site is extremely busy at 2:00 p.m. EST, so why bother aggravating yourself by clicking a link to that site? Scan the URL and then try someplace else. The link information can tell you immediately whether the link exists on an educational site, a commercial site, a governmental site, or something else—and this often affects your browsing strategy.

UNIX Filenames

If you want to understand the Internet thoroughly, you *must* develop a knowledge of UNIX. For a variety of reasons, mostly having to do with its strong flexibility and its excellent networking and multiuser capabilities, UNIX has become, in essence, the operating system of the Internet—and, in fact, all other operating systems must be customized to work with UNIX when they hook into the Net. For the time being, at least, there is no mask over the Net that makes UNIX invisible, although commercial service providers such as America Online are working hard to develop such masks.

To build a World Wide Web site, a good knowledge of UNIX is essential. To simply use the Web, however, you need to know only a tiny portion of it. An increasing number of Web users do their browsing through Macintosh or Microsoft Windows machines, and for them a very limited knowledge of UNIX is necessary. Except for one detail, in fact, they can largely do without its understanding.

That one detail is filenames. It's possible to cruise the Web without ever typing in a UNIX filename, but only if you do your browsing exclusively by clicking hypertext links. At some point, however, you're almost guaranteed to come across an e-mail message or another document that gives you a URL (Uniform Resource Locator) address, and this almost always represents, or at least contains, a UNIX-like filename. (Actually, the URL isn't a UNIX filename; it's a standard format. But URLs tend to look very much like UNIX filenames, and understanding the filename structure will help you locate specific documents.) In every major browser, you can enter that address to move directly to that page, but if you're not exactly precise in your typing, you'll find yourself unable to get there. That's because of UNIX's complex filename structure.

Unlike, say, DOS filenames, UNIX filenames have virtually no length restriction. If you want to name a file `This_is_an_incredibly_cool.file.man`, go ahead. Of course, conventions do exist (otherwise nobody would be able to find anything), but there's nothing at all like the 8.3-character filename structure of DOS. That's the first thing to keep in mind.

Secondly, UNIX filenames are case sensitive. The files `OJSimpson.gif`, `OJsimpson.gif`, and `ojsimpson.gif` are all entirely different files. This is something that DOS users typically have considerable difficulty getting to handle efficiently, because DOS is completely case insensitive. (Many would argue that it's insensitive in lots of other ways, but that's beside the point here.) You'll find lots of UNIX filenames that combine lowercase, uppercase, numbers, and other symbols, and you *must* type them exactly. One particular symbol that appears in many filenames is the tilde (~), for which you might have to search on your keyboard.

Finally, the URL addresses you see will show the complete directory structure for the file. UNIX directories are very much like DOS's, except that they're separated by a forward slash (/) rather than a backslash (\). Here's a typical UNIX filename, for example: `/u2/ojsimpso/projects/dev_tools/tapp/mango_leaf.tiff`. This simply means that the file `mango_leaf.tiff` can be found in the directory `tapp`, which is a subdirectory of `dev_tools`, which is in turn a subdirectory of `projects`, which is located in the `ojsimpso` subdirectory of the `u2` directory. Maybe this isn't difficult to read, but it's awfully tricky to type.

On the Web, you'll find this in URL addresses. As already mentioned, these can be typed manually into the Open URL (or similar) dialog box in Web browsers. The following, for example, is the URL to type in when you want to access the support page for *The World Wide Web Unleashed:*

`http://www.rpi.edu/~decemj/works/wwwu.html`

To access the Web site for Sams.net Publishing itself, type the URL:

```
http://www.mcp.com:80/sams.net/
```

Similarly, if you want to access the Table of Contents page for John December's well-known Internet Tools Summary, type in the following URL:

```
http://www.rpi.edu/Internet/Guides/decemj/itools/toc2.html
```

In all these cases, you're essentially telling your Web browser to connect to the remote server (that is, the computer where the document resides) and retrieve the specified file. Because you've done this using HTTP (HyperText Transport Protocol), the Web's standard and exclusive protocol, the file will be displayed as hypertext, complete with selectable hyperlinks. Note that two of the files have the extension `.html`, the standard for a page coded in HyperText Markup Language (HTML), which is explained in detail in Part V, "Weaving a Web." The Sams.net Publishing URL does not contain a filename. One exists, however, but it's a default filename that HTTP assumes if you don't actually specify one.

FTP—File Transfer Protocol

FTP is both a protocol and a program. As a protocol, it has been around almost as long as UNIX itself, and its function is to ensure a common standard for moving files from one computer to another across a network. As a program, FTP accomplishes these transfers. It enables you to enter file directories on remote machines and retrieve files from those machines or place files in those directories. A full FTP implementation offers a suite of file utilities such as creating directories and renaming and deleting files. Although you can access FTP sites by having an account with a password, the most widely used FTP type for casual users is called *anonymous FTP*; FTP software can be set to allow access to users who offer the word anonymous as a login name and their e-mail address as a password.

The World Wide Web makes extensive use of FTP. First, some sites do not have HTTP software in place, so to make their information accessible across the Web they place their HTML documents on FTP servers instead. Second, Web clients such as Lynx, Cello, and Mosaic make FTP connections and perform FTP downloads of files—but not uploads. In the case of sites containing graphics, sound, or video files, many are currently available via FTP only, either through anonymous FTP directly or through Gopher FTP access. FTP access is so common on the Web that you're unlikely to spend more than a few minutes cruising before you encounter an FTP transaction.

Figure 2.1 shows an FTP site as displayed through Mosaic.

FIGURE 2.1.

FTP site in Mosaic, showing extended parsing (includes file sizes).

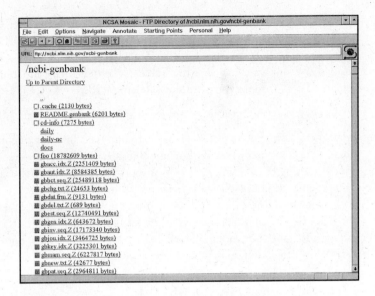

Gopher

Gopher is the best-known interface for the Internet. Developed by the University of Minnesota, Gopher is in fact very much like the World Wide Web, offering a friendly face on such difficult tools as FTP, Telnet, Archie, WAIS, and Veronica. The main difference is that Gopher is not a hypertext environment. The most common gopher client programs present information in numbered lists instead of hyperlinked documents, with different indicators for different kinds of files (such as text, sound, and search dialogs). Gopher software for graphical user environments such as X Window, the Macintosh, and Microsoft Windows typically offers the same lists with icons replacing the numbers. The icons offer information as to the type of file or directory you're accessing.

Gophers are directly accessible through the World Wide Web. Often this access is presented in the link itself, but you can use your browser to move to a particular gopher by specifying the gopher:// prefix when you enter a URL address (for example, gopher://cscns.com). This yields the gopher directory, each item representing a selectable Web link.

Figure 2.2 shows a typical gopher directory listing as seen on the Web.

FIGURE 2.2.

Gopher directory displayed in Mosaic.

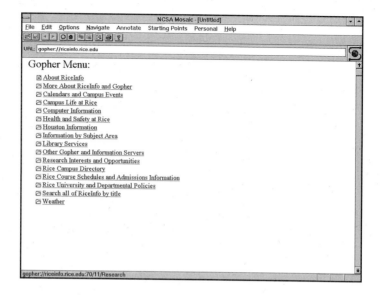

Electronic Mail

It's hard to be on the Internet and not know about electronic mail, but it's easy to overlook the fact that the World Wide Web is mail-enabled to a certain extent. You're not going to find a rich, full-featured e-mail package on the Web, at least not yet, but e-mail plays an important role in the Web's design. Through the use of HTML forms, you can have the readers of your pages submit mail to your address, and users of most browsers can mail directly from within that browser. (XMosaic, Netscape, Cello, and MacWeb are just a few such examples.)

Undoubtedly, the use of e-mail in the design of Web pages will increase in both usefulness and frequency. There is one main reason for this: The Web itself is primarily a public medium, whereas e-mail is primarily a private medium. In order to make full use of the Web even now, you often have to boot up your e-mail program and fire off messages to addresses you discover while browsing Web pages. At some point, a Web browser will probably need to include a strong e-mail feature if it is to be considered complete. Figure 2.3 shows the basic e-mail program contained within Cello.

Over the next few months, several browsers promise extended e-mail capabilities. InternetWorks, in beta format as of this writing, contains a separate messaging system that allows mail to be sent from the browser but also received through a full-featured e-mail program. It also handles Usenet newsgroups in this fashion, although other browsers handle them completely internally.

FIGURE 2.3.

Cello's electronic mail feature.

Cello WWW Browser
File Edit Search Configure Jump Bookmark... Help
The CBC Radio Trial

CBC ⊕ SRC

The CBC Radio Trial

It is being conducted by the Canadia...
the Communications Research Centr...
Branch of Industry Canada.

Currently, this section contains:

- more information abou...
- a list of CBC Radio prog...
- a list of transcripts ava...
- program listings for th...
- sample radio programs
- Daily News Broadcasts - International and Domestic
- Radio Canada International - Information and Schedules
- NEW: Illustrated Audio - Technology for synchronized sound and image presentations

Mail message

To: decemj@rpi.edu
From: nrandall@watarts.uwaterloo.ca
Subj.: Cello's mail feature

Send
Cancel

Message :

John,

The mail feature in Cello works well from within the program itself. Make sure to specify your mail servers from the Configure menu, though.

Thanks,
Neil

http://debra.dgbt.doc.ca/cbc/cbc.html

Usenet

Usenet has been in existence for a number of years, as the network through which users communicate in newsgroups. For some Internet users, in fact, Usenet and electronic mail are everything the Net has to offer. Usenet is the focus of any number of Internet stories in the popular press, as newsgroup users appear in stories about online romance, online harassment, the assisting of the unfortunate, and the corruption of the innocent as well. It's a very, very popular tool.

Web browsers are offering increasingly sophisticated hooks into Usenet, including graphically rendered subject threads and the ability (begun in Netscape) to follow threads and post new messages. By now it's clear that browser design intends to take Usenet fully into account, to the extent that it's possible to do most of your newsgroup activity through the Web already. Many Web pages refer to Usenet groups as sources of additional information, so it remains important to know of their existence and their use. Keep in mind, though, that today's Web browsers, no matter how capably they handle newsgroups, are no substitute for a dedicated newsreader program for anyone who works extensively with Usenet. That could change soon, however.

Wide Area Information Servers—WAIS

WAIS is an extremely useful tool that generates, and allows you to search through, a huge range of databases stored on the Internet. These databases in turn point you to locations on the Net that hold documents containing the keywords you've searched for. Among WAIS's most useful features are its relevance rating of documents—1,000 means a direct hit; 100 means a marginal hit—and its ability to build, through a process called "relevance feedback," from one search to another. In other words, you can keep narrowing the search until you find exactly what you want.

The World Wide Web works through WAIS gateways to offer full keyword searching. Several pages feature WAIS searches, and in fact they've become almost the standard for finding specific titles or headings throughout the Web. Typically, WAIS searches on the Web are combined with the HTML feature called *forms*—boxes that you fill in by typing text and then you execute by clicking a button. Fully developed forms allow highly specific searches, and in some cases you can even select the areas of the Net you want searched.

The interesting part is that you often don't know that you're entering a WAIS search. As with other Internet tools, the Web has essentially co-opted the WAIS process, incorporating it into the browsers so that users can access it almost transparently.

Figure 2.4 shows a search form at the top of the screen, and the results of the WAIS search throughout the rest. Notice the relevance ratings beside the items, and note also that each item is a hyperlink to another site or document.

FIGURE 2.4.

Filling in a search form in Mosaic.

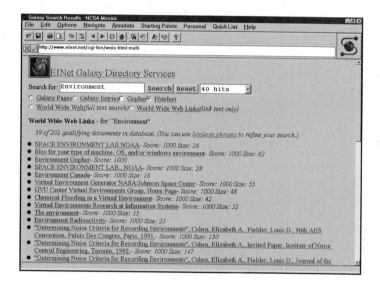

Integration

These aren't the only tools accessible through the World Wide Web. Archie, Veronica, Hytelnet, and a host of others appear in Web pages from a variety of sources, and in many cases the very existence of the Web makes these tools more usable than before. None of this suggests, however, that the Web makes other manifestations of these tools obsolete. As with the newsreading capabilities of the current crop of browsers, the Web's use of the Internet's most important tools is often at least somewhat limited. If you need extensive features on any of these tools, you're likely better off looking elsewhere. For many users, however, the Web's versions of the tools are sufficiently capable.

Remember that the point of the World Wide Web is to offer access to the resources available on the Net. To this end, it has been designed not to replace the existing tools, but rather to integrate them into one appealing and highly usable program, taking advantage through the browsers of the graphical user interface of today's machines.

There will always be those who prefer the command-line version of FTP, the richness of the feature set of a full Gopher client, and the multiple capabilities of a text- or graphics-based e-mail package. At this point, there seems little chance that any Web browser will ever fully substitute for these. Increasingly, however, the Web will integrate the Internet's tools into its structure to the degree that, for many people, the Web may well *become* the Internet. Not everyone likes that thought, but not everyone likes GUIs, voice-mail, or audio CDs, either. The point is that it's going to happen, and for anyone wishing to stay on top of the Internet, the Web will be an essential and unavoidable concept.

Fortunately, that's far from a bad thing. The Web has received its share of praise and criticism alike, but nobody denies the importance of providing solid, usable access to Internet resources. Personal computers themselves took off when their user interfaces stopped trying to emulate something out of code-level hell, and the Internet as an information provider began its rise when Archie made things findable and Gopher let you get to them. When high-speed access becomes commonly available, there's every reason to suspect that the Web will continue its trend toward becoming the most commonly accessed Internet tool—or *toolkit*—of them all.

Hypertext

3

by
Neil Randall

Hypertext is one of those ideas that appeared; rose to prominence by being written about, hyped, and otherwise touted as either a savior or a destroyer; and then seemed to fade away as its promise gave way to the difficulty of actually applying it to anything, or more particularly, developing things that it was worth applying to in the first place.

There have been several such ideas in computing, and in some cases the idea has simply been forgotten. But over the years since its introduction, hypertext joined two other concepts, artificial intelligence and speech recognition, in simply refusing to go away. These three ideas were so strong that despite their initial fading, they have begun to reassert themselves in a potentially very big way. Among the three, hypertext has been the most fully developed, at least from the standpoint of people being able to sit at their computers and use it.

The concept of hypertext is disarmingly simple: Use the computer's storage and searching capacity to link documents together and thus enable users to jump instantly from one piece of information to the next.

A *hypertext* is a series of documents, each of which displays on the screen a visible link to at least one other document in the set. The link is usually highlighted, either by boldfaced text, reversed text, differently colored text, or underlining. The user "navigates" through a hypertext by selecting these links, typically using either the keyboard or the mouse (although joysticks and touchscreens are certainly possible). The link leads to another document, which in turn offers links to additional documents, and so on. After following five or six links, in fact, the user might not be able to find the way back to the original document, a phenomenon known as becoming "lost in hyperspace."

It's not difficult to see how the concept of hypertext came about. Here's an example. Most of us have read books containing footnotes that contain references to other books. Often—probably because the grass is always greener on the other side—the book mentioned in the footnote sounds more interesting or relevant than the one we're reading. Wouldn't it be nice to simply point to the footnote and magically find that book in our hands?

Essentially, that's what hypertext enables us to do. In a well-constructed hypertext, any significant reference is shown as a link; select that link, and you're suddenly reading the linked document. If the hypertext is indeed well constructed, the new document will provide a link back to the original document, but often links go only one way. This might be the fault of the hypertext's author, or—in the case of the World Wide Web—of the sheer size of the hypertextual undertaking. Not everything can be linked to everything else.

Vannevar Bush and Ted Nelson

Two names come to mind when considering the origin of hypertext. The first is Vannevar Bush, who way back at the beginning of computer technology (in the July 1945 issue of the *Atlantic Monthly*) published a landmark essay entitled "As We May Think." The other is Ted Nelson, whose fanciful book *Computer Dreams*, published in the late seventies, offers a view of easily accessible information that is still a long way from being in place.

Bush's article has been used to cite the origin of everything from artificial intelligence to multimedia. In fact, it presaged both of these, but neither in particular. Bush was concerned primarily with bringing to the public mind the idea that computers were similar in some respects to the human mind, and that it therefore might be possible to program them to emulate the human mind. Along the way, his article discusses the nature of the dissemination of information, and although hypertext *per se* doesn't appear in his work, the idea of accessible, computer-organized information speaks quite loudly. Most importantly, however, Bush offered one of the first explorations of computer technology in relation to human thought processes and human information needs, and thus it remains an essential paper.

Nelson thought of computers in anthropomorphic terms long before most people did, and long before the technology suggested the possibilities. *Computer Dreams* is a lot of things to any number of people, but its primary, ongoing usefulness is its introduction of the idea that through computer technology we will have access to all the information in the world. Nelson has been alternatively praised and scorned, but through a host of changes in the computer field he has consistently maintained his vision of an information-centered, information-accessible world. His own attempts to realize this world is the Xanadu project which, depending upon whom you listen to, is either just around the corner or completely unrealistic. We're not about to make predictions here.

What Nelson did, however, was introduce the term *hypertext*. He envisioned a system of information access not much different from what we have today, and there's little doubt that he must cruise the World Wide Web with a knowing smirk and an attitude of "I told you so." He also, however, almost certainly wonders why it doesn't work better than it does. What he had in mind seemed somehow much simpler.

HyperCard and Hypermedia

There's little point in trying to track down the first hypertext application for personal computers. There is, however, a valid reason to point to the first mass-audience program to allow hypertext creation. That program is HyperCard, which at one point was packaged with every new Macintosh on the shelf.

HyperCard gave cheap, easy hypertext-creation facilities to anyone who owned a Mac. Shortly after its introduction, HyperCard "stacks" began to appear, and as the Mac sold well to the artistic and educational communities, these stacks ranged in subject matter across a broad sphere of human knowledge and experience. Moreover, the stacks were usually made available at no charge, through bulletin boards and other online services, which meant that Mac owners had access to a huge range of hypertext-based information packages. And because HyperCard allowed stack programmers to include graphics and eventually sound and even video, it gave popular birth to a revised concept, *hypermedia*.

Hypermedia extends hypertext in two ways. First, it incorporates multimedia (see Figure 3.1) into hypertext documents. Second, it allows graphic, audio, and video elements—rather than just text elements—to become links to other documents or multimedia elements. In other words, with hypermedia you aren't just linking text anymore; you're linking anything the readers can see to anything the author wants them to know. A text link to the Apollo 11 moon landing, for example, might send readers to a text document describing the landing, to a graphic representation of the landing, to a short sound bite of the crew declaring, "The Eagle has landed," or to a video showing Neil Armstrong descending the ladder toward the moon. In turn, this link can offer links to other text, graphic, audio, or video elements as well. The combinations are practically unlimited. With the World Wide Web, hypermedia explodes, because any of these elements can also be linked to documents and elements that exist on a computer halfway around the world. But we'll get to that.

Figure 3.1 shows a hypermedia screen from Microsoft Complete Baseball, a CD-ROM product for Windows.

FIGURE 3.1.

Joe Carter's famous winning home run during the 1993 World Series.

Help Systems

One of the most prevalent and noticeable uses of hypertext has occurred in the help systems for Microsoft Windows and the Macintosh. The Windows help system, for example, has employed hypertext technology for several years, to the extent that the CD-ROM versions of its software base their entire online documentation system around a usable hypertext model. Figure 3.2 shows the hypertext structure of the help system for Word for Windows 6.0, a word processing program, whereas Figure 3.3 demonstrates a similar structure in the help system of Procomm for Windows 1.0, a communications package.

FIGURE 3.2.

A multipart hypertext screen from Word for Windows 6.0.

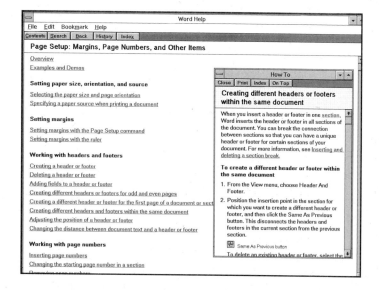

FIGURE 3.3.

A hypermedia graphics display from Procomm for Windows 1.0.

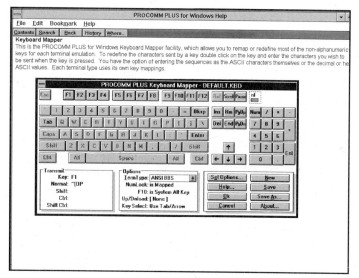

Each link is displayed as an underlined text string or a portion of a graphic. Click on the link, and you're taken to another section of the help system, from which you can click on links to still other sections, or back to the original section. The help system is extremely large in many programs, and these links make it easy to navigate through the descriptions and instructions. For many users, these hypertext systems are easier to use than the printed manuals because related topics can be accessed quickly. They're simply more effective than the paper-based "see also" instruction.

If you've used the Windows or Mac help system, you'll recognize Mosaic's, Cello's, or Netscape's interface instantly. Click on the underlined links, or sometimes on the graphic, to move to a related document or a portion of the same document. It's quick, it's effective, and it's satisfying. But there's one crucial difference: Unlike the help system, these documents are scattered around the world.

Actually, there are help systems that exist entirely on Web documents. The help menus in NCSA Mosaic and Netscape Navigator (all versions of both) lead you among documents stored on, respectively, NCSA's systems in Illinois (`http://www.ncsa.uiuc.edu:8001/`) and Netscape Communications' systems in California (`http://home.netscape.com/home/online-manual.html`). As long as your Internet connection is fast enough, accessing help this way isn't much different from accessing it on your Mac or PC. It's safe to say that we can expect to see many more software manuals available on the Web, especially for network-based software.

CD-ROM

Hypertext and hypermedia have flourished on CD-ROMs, and here we see a direct conceptual link to the idea of accessing information on the Net. CD-ROMs offer enormous storage capabilities (currently about 650MB), and in one sense that's what the Internet offers as well. The challenge for the designers and developers of both is to make all of those megabytes accessible in a user-friendly way. Enter hypertext, with its click-and-find mouse controls.

There are clear similarities between CD-ROM publishing and World Wide Web publishing. Both concepts are proliferating, yet both are very much in their infancy. Both offer the user access to a huge range of detailed information. And both are basing their future around the potential of multimedia, although in this regard CD-ROM has a clear and inevitable lead. A CD-ROM can be tailored to the hardware specifications of only one computer type, after all, whereas the Web is forced to struggle with the conflicting standards of many.

Like the Internet, a typical CD-ROM consists of a huge number of individual files. These are linked together through the construction of the various programs on the disc, but in the case of information-based CD-ROMs such as encyclopedia and reference tools, users must be presented with a wide range of links for their own individual use.

A product such as Microsoft Bookshelf, for instance—the popular collection of dictionary, thesaurus, mini-encyclopedia, quotation book, and other writing tools—uses hypertext to enable users to maneuver from topic to topic and word to word. Similarly, Compton's Interactive Encyclopedia uses hypertext extensively to link references and ideas among the topics, making the CD-ROM much more easily cross-referenced than a corresponding paper-based encyclopedia.

But these products (and a large and growing number of similar packages) don't just offer text links; also available are hyperlinks among graphic images and audio and video presentations. The best CD-ROMs are full hypermedia systems, as are the most entertaining (if not necessarily the best) World Wide Web sites.

In the next few years, we will see a further convergence of multimedia technologies. As CD-ROM access speeds increase, for example, Web sites themselves—minus perhaps the actual server software—could easily be stored on this inexpensive storage technology, offering full multimedia to Web users with high-speed Internet access. Already under development is the MBONE, a collection of technologies designed to allow real-time video and audio over the Web, and this is even a step beyond the static storage of CD-ROM. You might find a video clip of a portion of a Rolling Stones concert on a CD-ROM, for example, but the Stones actually played live over the MBONE during their 1994–1995 world tour (from all accounts, they got at least some satisfaction).

Assuming high-speed access and effectively unlimited bandwidth, there are no restrictions on the multimedia capabilities of the World Wide Web, but those two assumptions are far from being a reality. Most people, remember, access the Web with a 14.4Kbps modem or even less, and only widespread ISDN lines (with 128Kbps speeds), coupled with exceptional data-compression technologies, could allow the Web to accomplish its multimedia potential.

The point, though, is that hypermedia is a reality even now, and it promises to encompass a significant percentage of the Web's future. Click-and-retrieve is the best our interface designers and usability experts have managed to come up with so far, and hypermedia as it now exists is based precisely on this interface. The Web as it's now constructed is dominated by point-and-click hypertext and hypermedia, and so much design effort (not to mention so much money) is now being poured into making the most of that dominance that it's not likely to change in the near future.

Multimedia

4

by
Neil Randall

The World Wide Web is not necessarily a multimedia environment. The original CERN browser, as seen in Figure 4.1, showed only text because it was designed for terminals that were incapable of displaying graphics. A subsequently released Web browser, the well-known Lynx (see Figure 4.2), is similarly without graphics. Even with the popularity of Netscape and Mosaic today, many users still browse the Web in text-only mode.

FIGURE 4.1.

The original CERN browser, with its access via numbers.

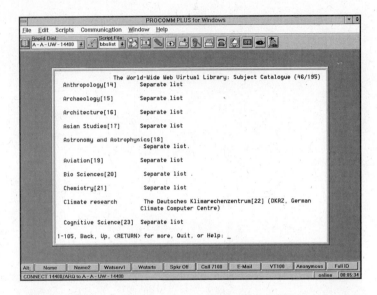

FIGURE 4.2.

Lynx, the popular arrow-key browser.

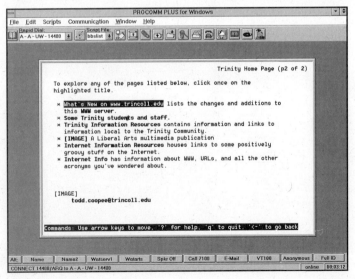

Not until the availability of the later graphical browsers did the Web's multimedia potential demonstrate itself. Mosaic took the early lead in the graphical browser race, of course, and Netscape has captured more than its share of the market lately, but others, such as Cello (for Windows) and MacWeb (for the Mac), are also multimedia capable. Yet in order to understand how these browsers are affecting the concept of exploring the Internet itself, it's helpful to look briefly at the history of multimedia computing, especially as it developed on personal computing systems.

The basic point about multimedia is simple: Barring physical disabilities, we experience the world as a combination of sensory perceptions. So if the world offers visual and auditory information, why can't computers? Presumably computers will one day build in tactility (it is happening already), smell (other than the fried power supply), and taste (edible floppies?). When that happens, we'll have multimedia that goes beyond simply the audio-visual. For now, though, computing is restricted to the visual and audio capabilities offered by movies and television, and it is of these two phenomena that multimedia computing is trying to take advantage.

The Limitations of Text

In the world of computing, anything over 5 years old is very old, anything over 10 years old is ancient, and anything older than that is grounds for both nostalgia and disbelief. It's hard to fathom, when we see computing in the mid-nineties, that the whole idea of graphics on computers was once considered pointless, counterproductive, and to be avoided at almost all costs. Sure, graphics had their use, but only for such applications as medical and other scientific research, and maybe professional publishing. But graphics on a personal computer? Especially one used in business? Not a chance.

When the IBM PC first shipped in the very early eighties, it offered a text-only display, because that's all a serious computer user needed (according to IBM, that is). Nor was color important, or even desired; the first monitors were monochrome, although there was sometimes a choice between green and amber. Text was all that mattered, because the only perceived uses of business computing were programming (which remains largely text-oriented), word processing (which by definition uses text), spreadsheeting (numbers only), and database management (names, addresses, product numbers, and so forth). Color was merely a distraction; graphics more of one.

Actually, there's more to it than this. In the early eighties, color displays were prohibitively expensive for use with personal computers. But it didn't take long for the lack of color to be deemed a plus among business, academic, and educational users, or for color displays to be denounced as toy-like. Some of this attitude was the result of sour grapes, of course, but color became officially, in some cases, a thing to be avoided.

To be sure, there's still an argument here. You don't need a graphical word processor to write a book (unless you're formatting it yourself, which is a rarity), and you don't need a graphical database-management program to keep track of your sales contacts or do relational searches. In fact, most graphical products are considerably slower than their text-only counterparts. But text has its limitations, and this is something the PC line has been trying to compensate for over the past decade. Text-only systems simply ignore the fact that information can be provided more effectively in other ways.

Graphics

As any blind or near-blind person can tell us, the world is a visually oriented place. But it took a while for graphics to be accepted on computers for a number of interesting reasons. At first, the hardware didn't exist to support them. But even when graphics became technically feasible, corporate computing cast a dim view on them. Why? Because they weren't seen as necessary.

This might seem strange, but it doesn't take much to see a general bias against graphical representations of material in Western culture. The printed page has long been our most prolific and accepted medium for disseminating important information, and since the invention of the printing press the printed page has been dominated by text. Go to any library—especially an academic library—and browse through the shelves. Very few books have illustrations, and many that do have only technical drawings. When was the last time you read an illustrated novel?

It didn't help, of course, that the first popular graphics-intensive computer programs were games. North American society has always been phobic about games, objecting to their use in education and utterly forbidding them in the workplace. (There's a fascinating irony here on the pursuit of happiness theme, but never mind.) So as computer graphics became increasingly associated with computer games, the entrenchment toward text-only computing became more concerted.

The biggest culprit was the Commodore 64. Although it wasn't the first computer to offer graphics and sound at a reasonable price—the Apple II could do so with enough add-ons, and the Atari 800 offered arguably better results—the 64 became a huge mainstream hit in the early eighties and made the equation of multimedia and games even stronger. Here was a machine that was compact, inexpensive, and advertised extensively on television; and it displayed graphics, played sound, and even offered reasonably good color. Add these things to the fact that it appealed to home users and kids, and the consensus grew that it was nothing but a toy. I wrote two books and a doctoral thesis on my Commodore 64, but I never managed to convince a single IBM-PC user that it was a computer worth having.

While the 64 crested the wave of its popularity, the IBM PC slowly began to add graphics. The first kick at the can was CGA, with its four ungodly colors and its total ineptness at animation. Next came EGA, slightly better at 16 colors, but animation was still next to impossible. By the time VGA was introduced, the Atari ST and Commodore Amiga were offering tons of colors and smooth animation, but primarily for these reasons they, too, were considered toys (or, at best, things that graphics specialists bought).

# Chapter 4

NOTE

I must emphasize, by the way, that I've owned and liked an Apple II, an Atari 800, a Commodore 64, an Atari ST, a Commodore Amiga, a Macintosh, and several PCs (just so the rest doesn't sound overly prejudiced in any way).

The machine that began to signal the acceptance of multimedia was the Macintosh. This is somewhat ironic, as the original Mac had a teeny-tiny monochrome monitor and very little sound to speak of; but because it was seen as a machine for serious artists and, more importantly, serious publishers, it quickly gained a following. Quite simply, it brought a new paradigm to computing in the form of the graphical user interface (GUI), originally developed by Xerox's Palo Alto Research Center. Because of the Mac's GUI, graphics entered the realm of business computing—not instantly, perhaps, and certainly not without detractors, but they entered nevertheless. As soon as business and government organizations saw how quickly users learned the Mac's interface, and how eager computer nonexperts were to use it, they started buying them, which is something that didn't really happen with the ST and Amiga, both of which had similar interfaces and better multimedia capabilities. Apple was able to market its graphics well, and once the publishing industry adopted the machine, graphical computing was here to stay.

This is not to say that everyone thought GUIs were great. In fact, many people still don't. And, to be sure, the first Macintosh users put out some of the worst-looking documents ever found on Earth, complete with multiple fonts, overly cutesy clip-art, and typographic emphases that would have made any high school newspaper blush in embarrassment. What became important, however, was the concept of direct graphic control. Yes, you could tell WordStar and WordPerfect how to set up your page, but with MacWrite you could see without printing exactly what your decisions would yield. This capability became known as WYSIWYG (what you see is what you get), meaning that you could see on the screen what the printed version would look like.

But—and this is important—the Mac's universe was very much print oriented. That's why its original screen was black on white; after all, isn't that what a printed page looks like? Although the Mac offered the capability of multimedia, its focus remained squarely on print, which was simply another reason its acceptance began to grow. More importantly, though, it offered a point-and-click interface, with icons that hid program names and mouse procedures that replaced typing. Where the command-line interface relied on users' memories, the GUI relied only on their ability to recognize. That, by itself, made computing available to the masses.

The graphical interface caught on so well that operating-system leader Microsoft, never having been known for innovation, decided to create one of its own. After a couple of mediocre efforts, and despite the appearance of demonstrably better interfaces such as GeoWorks, Microsoft Windows 3.0 brought graphical computing to the Intel 80x86 platform (Intel processors or clones run all machines known as IBM compatibles, or simply PCs), and it brought multimedia with it (although DOS-based multimedia had already arrived in the form of games). Windows is now dominant among developers of software for personal computers, a fact that many industry pundits feel is especially unfortunate, partly because Windows is not an operating system *per se*, but rather a graphical shell that sits atop DOS, a relatively weak operating system to begin with. This will change with the release of Windows 95, which by most accounts is an operating system in its own right and does away with DOS except for compatibility reasons, so perhaps developing for Windows will no longer initiate the kind of "necessary evil" response seen thus far in this GUI's history.

Sound and Music

The original IBM PC was no more interested in sound than it was in graphics. It had sound, but this sound was simple, to-the-point, and efficient. If you did something wrong, the computer beeped. In fact, PCs and their clones still beep today: They beep when you turn them on (one beep means the machine's okay, two mean your day's ruined), and they beep when you try to do something DOS doesn't like. It works, it's effective, and it's extremely annoying.

Acceptable sound for personal computers began to appear in the early eighties. Expansion cards for the Apple II offered reasonable sound effects for that machine, while the Atari 800 and the Commodore 64 made music and sound easy to program and effective to use. The Amiga introduced the idea of a dedicated sound chip, and the ST became a favorite of musicians because of its built-in MIDI port. The Macintosh started with very limited sound, but as new models appeared so did improved music and sound capability until the Mac, too, became a musicians' favorite.

Once again, it was the Mac that made this multimedia feature acceptable for the business and non-artistic audience. The reason, quite likely, was that the Mac, unlike the Amiga and the ST, wasn't a good game machine, a point that business buyers determined a good thing rather than bad. By contrast, the Atari 800 and the Commodore 64 were seen by the corporate computing folk as nothing *but* game machines, and the ST and the Amiga, with their Atari and Commodore names attached, quickly became labeled as game machines as well, driving their very devoted user base straight up the wall. People who owned Macs could be taken seriously, even with their mice and icons; people who owned STs and Amigas were primarily seen as game players, even though technically their systems were superior to the Mac in certain important ways—unfair, certainly, but that's the way it happened.

For multimedia computing, sound has been an even harder sell than graphics. Except for business presentations, perhaps, where effective music, digitized speech, and carefully chosen sound effects might help make the point, there seems to be little value to giving a computer the capability to make sounds. In crowded, open-concept offices, graphics don't impose on a neighbor's work, whereas sound without headphones creates a distraction. Not until the concept of business audio caught on in the early nineties, in fact, was sound considered something to be treated seriously. Even so, its uses remain limited.

But sound is an important feature of multimedia because movies and television, on which multimedia is based, make extensive use of it. Multimedia attempts to mimic both these media (which are themselves multimedia), and sound has attained new importance in related technologies such as the CD-ROM.

Animation and Video

Back in the late seventies, a very simple, very addictive game called Pong appeared on television screens. Actually, it had already been available in arcades, but when it hit the home screen it revolutionized, in its own way, what people did with their TV sets. Pong's graphics were far less sophisticated than those of even the worst TV show (or today's worst video game), but for the first time people could control what was displayed on the screen. Turn the knob one way, and the bar went up; turn it the other way, and it moved down. You could even put a "spin" on the "ball," so Pong quickly became a game of at least some appreciable skill.

A decade and a half later, Pong is small potatoes. Now our TV sets sport video games with graphics realistic enough to be considered by some to be dangerous for young viewers (Mortal Kombat is one such product, while Donkey Kong Country is a *tour de force* of computer animation), and our computer screens offer not only rich animation but equally rich, full-color video. The result has been a growing convergence of the computer with the television, a process that designers have been engaged in ever since computer graphics became a reality.

Animation and video are two separate technologies, but their effects are similar. They offer movement on the computer screen, something that just doesn't happen with spreadsheets or word processors. More importantly, they offer the movement of things that look like people, or at least objects people recognize. In other words, animation and video make computers part of the experience of seeing the world, which all but the sight-impaired rely on every day of their lives. That's what's made the motion picture so fascinating from its beginnings, and what transformed television into the most important (for better or worse) appliance in our houses.

To that end, however, video is significantly better received than animation. Animation is associated with cartoons, and is a drawn representation of the motion we see with our eyes. Video, by contrast, although still only a representation, looks so much like the world we see around us that we've come to accept it as an extension of that world. Put a video camera on someone and the results are called "realistic"; do an animation of someone and people will usually only smile and say, "Pretty good." For general acceptability, video wins hands down.

What's the importance of video to the World Wide Web? If the Internet is an information dissemination system, after all, what does video have to do with it? First, and very simply, video is an extremely important means of conveying information. Just think, for example, of the Apollo 11 mission in 1969, and the effect the video feeds of the moon landing and moon walk had on us. Had the cameras been unavailable, would we have huddled around the radio listening to the sound of it all? Not likely, given the centrality of video in our lives. More recently, think of the

TV coverage given to the O.J. Simpson arrest, that famous (and interminable) overhead view of the multitude of police cars following the van. Would anyone have paid attention to it on radio? Hardly. The only drama the situation presented was the result of the video feed. As a final example, consider the most recent California earthquake disasters. Without video, the extent of the disaster would have been invisible and almost meaningless to anyone not in the immediate area. In all three cases, video provided evidence, and that was what the situation demanded.

Everybody knows that video can be fabricated. Fabrication, in fact, is the central art form of cinematic special effects. But there's something about video that engages the totality of the senses, much more than audio could hope to do. It could be related to concentration; although it's eminently possible to be doing something visual while listening to the radio, it's almost impossible to accomplish any kind of complex task while watching television. That's why people think nothing of telling you to keep quiet while they're watching TV, but these same people will think nothing of showing you things while you're listening to your favorite symphony. It's also why most people have a very hard time listening to music without simultaneously doing something else, but can watch a movie intently with nothing able to block it out.

Video, in other words, is a crucial technology for information designers whose goal is to fully engage, inform, and entertain. Given that the World Wide Web intends to fulfill all three design goals, its use of video will almost certainly become paramount. There's a catch, however: High-quality video requires high-speed access, and that's something very few people currently have. By the last third of this decade, however, high-speed access should be a given, and Web designers will have the technologies they need to offer full, rich, visually oriented information.

Games

Nothing has pushed the envelope of multimedia technology more than computer games. Since their inception, games have incorporated graphics, sound, and a variety of interactive interfaces, all in an effort to make computer entertainment more enjoyable. Whereas it's been possible for a computer application such as a database program to be acceptable for its underlying technological excellence rather than its appearance and interface, games have been reviewed and bought according to their sensory appeal and their combined ease and realism of play.

The difference between games and applications, of course, is function. If an application is worth using for whatever reason, what it looks like and how easily it handles doesn't matter all that much. Users can be persuaded and even ordered to learn the software because it's good for them or for the company. For games, however, the good-for-you argument doesn't hold. Nobody believes that mastering Wing Commander or Betrayal at Krondor is about to do anything useful for them; they play these games to be solidly entertained. For this reason, multimedia and interface design make all the difference in the world. Offer an exceptional graphics display, superb sound effects, and an interface that makes the experience painless, and you have a possible winner. Offer anything less, and your chances are next to nil.

What does the World Wide Web have to do with games? For one thing, games are starting to appear on the Web, and as access becomes faster and demands stronger, better and more complex games will make their appearance as well. At first, as was the case with the early computers, any game will be happily played simply because it's an experience different from searching databases. Soon, however, designers of Web-based games will be forced to incorporate the best features of disk- and CD-ROM–based games, especially if they expect anyone to play them. The Web offers the possibility of games with exciting multi-player potential, with players the world over, but by telnetting to MUD (multi-user dungeon/dialog) sites, Net users can already get such games. What Web game designers must concentrate on is a combination of world-wide multi-player games with top-notch multimedia capabilities and equally strong interfaces.

There's more, though. As the designers of mainstream computer applications found out, there's a lot to be learned from the people who design computer games. Multimedia tutorials, context-sensitive help, simplified interfaces, and full "customizability" are products of the computer-game world, and they've found their way into today's graphically based application packages. Designers of Web sites can make full use of these and other capabilities as well. The potential for the convergence of solid game design and solid educational design is especially exciting on the Web, and business applications have even stronger potential. A Web-based store, for instance, is essentially a simulation of a store, and designers can make use of the basics of simulation games to help them establish a usable site that invites users to return.

Games continue to push multimedia. If you're a Web designer, ignore them at your own risk.

CD-ROM

CD-ROM threatened to take off as early as the late eighties, but 1993 proved to be its true year of acceptance. Before '93, Mac users had a fair portion of CD-ROMs to choose from, but the emergence of (reasonably) easily installed DOS-based upgrade kits in 1992 made the CD-ROM publishers sit up and take additional notice. The result was the beginning of a flood of products in 1993, with the flood showing every indication of becoming a tidal wave in 1995 and beyond. In fact, the 1995 edition of Meckler's *CD-ROMs in Print* is nothing less than a tome, and quite sobering for those who might have thought they knew the CD-ROM world quite well.

The reason for this growing acceptance is quite simple. Because of its strong storage capabilities (650MB per disc), CD-ROM lets designers make extensive use of sound, music, graphics, animation, and especially video. For the first time it was possible to offer reference works and education and entertainment products that featured a worthwhile smattering of all these technologies. Some products, in fact, became so large that they needed more than one CD-ROM to contain them. One example is the famous space simulator, Wing Commander III, which ships on three discs and boasts full multimedia video clips featuring actors Mark Hamill and John-Rhys Davies. With the blending of technologies on these packages, CD-ROM became the first stepping stone to the much-hyped, fully interactive information superhighway.

As shown earlier in this chapter, CD-ROM is similar to the World Wide Web in many ways. This is nowhere more apparent than in the inherent multimedia design of the two. In fact, it's easy to see how CD-ROMs might replace hard disk storage of Web sites in the near future. With multimedia files taking up enormous amounts of hard disk space, and with recordable CD-ROM in place and dropping in price, it only makes sense that site owners will want their multimedia pages—or at least the multimedia portions of those pages—on inexpensive CD-ROM storage.

But the full relationship between these multimedia elements and the development of the World Wide Web will simply have to wait until the next chapter.

Putting It All Together with the Web

5

by
Neil Randall

The Internet, hypertext, and multimedia—three important technologies of the nineties. Bring them all together, and you have the World Wide Web.

The Web is a by-product of the Internet, created because of the Internet's overwhelming size. There is so much information available across the computers and networks that make up the Internet that finding and actually using it is very, very difficult. We live in an age of information, but keep in mind that information—as its name implies—is *formed*. Having access to huge amounts of information is part of the Internet's charm, but perhaps only a small part; more significant is being able to find, view, and make use of this information. The World Wide Web, more than any other Internet concept, allows this to happen.

The first secret of a good Internet browser is making it possible for the user to navigate the Net without having to know, remember, or write down the lengthy and clumsy addresses and filenames that the Net and UNIX need to operate. The second secret is providing not just links from information source to information source, but links that are contextually related.

The Web does both, and this makes it different from any other browsing technology. Gopher, for example, offers a highly usable system of navigation, but its links are primarily to sites, not to contextually related documents or (as the Web makes possible) specific sections of documents. When you enter a Gopher directory, you see a wide range of possibly important information, but you can spend considerable time searching for exactly the document—and exactly the section of the document—you need. A well-constructed, Web-based hypertext can make all of this seamless, although it must be noted that most Web documents remain far from this ideal.

Through the use of hypertext, the Web can provide access to mountains of information in a very usable way. The primary reason, quite simply, is that the information (or, rather, the links to the information) is provided in a manner with which readers of the language are familiar.

Tables of contents, headings, paragraphs, lists, and graphic elements make up the pages of books, magazines, and newspapers, and these are the essential elements in an HTML (World Wide Web) page. Gopher's limitation is that it is exclusively list-oriented, while FTP's limitation is that it provides not just lists, but lists of obscure filenames.

Both seem computer-ish, and since the release of the Macintosh "computer-ish" is something computers aren't supposed to be. The Web provides a booklike layer on top of the Net, albeit a book with the less-linear capabilities that hypertext and other computer-ish systems offer, and books with their printed pages remain the most efficient and perhaps the most usable information-presentation system we have in place.

A half-millennium of the printed page is not about to be outdone by 15 years of the scrolling screen, and that's what makes the Web so instantly usable. Its usability will only be enhanced, although its efficiency might not be, as it moves toward integrating the multiple media of print with the multiple media of film and television.

History of the Web

The World Wide Web dates back to March 1989. In that month, Tim Berners-Lee of Geneva's European Particle Physics Laboratory (which is abbreviated as CERN, based on the laboratory's French name) circulated a proposal to develop a "hypertext system" for the purpose of enabling efficient and easy information-sharing among geographically separated teams of researchers in the High Energy Physics community.

The three important components of the proposed system were the following:

- A consistent user interface
- The ability to incorporate a wide range of technologies and document types
- Its "universal readership," that is, anyone sitting anywhere on the network, on a wide variety of different computers, could read the same document as anyone else, and could do so easily

Over a year later, in October 1990, the project was presented anew, and two months later the World Wide Web project began to take shape. Work began on the first line browser (called www), and by the end of 1990 this browser and a browser for the NeXTStep operating system were well on the way. The major principles of hypertext access and the reading of different document types had already been implemented.

In March 1991, two years after the presentation of the original proposal, the www line-mode browser saw its first (limited) network use. Two months later, www was made available more extensively at CERN, and the Web was effectively off and running. That summer saw seminars about the Web, and announcements were posted to relevant newsgroups. October 1991 brought the installation of the gateway for WAIS searches (a crucial development for the Web's future as a search as well as a browsing tool), and shortly before the end of 1991 CERN announced the Web to the High Energy Physics community in general.

Essentially, 1992 was a developmental year. The www browser was made available via FTP from CERN, and the Web team presented the Web to a variety of organizations and audiences, but it was the software-development efforts of that year that would make it a vitally important time. In January 1993, 50 Web servers were in existence, and at that time the Viola browser was made available for the X Window System. Viola was the early leader in Web browsing technology, offering the first glimpse of the graphical, mouse-based hypertext system originally conceived by the Web proposal.

The Web was on its way. But two other browsers saw daylight at the beginning of 1993, and these proved the most important. CERN's Macintosh browser brought the Mac into the WWW game, and at the same time the Internet community saw its first glimpse of Mosaic. In February 1993, the first alpha version of X Mosaic (Mosaic for X Window) was released by NCSA (the National Center for Supercomputing Applications in Champaign, Illinois); it was developed by Marc Andreesen, whose name ranks behind only Berners-Lee's in media popularity surrounding the Web.

In March of 1993, WWW traffic clocked in at 0.1 percent of total Internet backbone traffic. Six months later, the Web began to demonstrate its potential by expanding to a full one percent of backbone traffic. That tenfold increase became practically the norm for Web access increases, continuing into 1994.

The same tenfold increase was evident in the number of Web servers, which by October 1993 had increased to approximately 500. By the end of 1993, the Web project was beginning to receive technical awards, and articles on the Web and Mosaic (the two were already becoming inextricable) began to appear in publications as prestigious as *The Guardian* and *The New York Times*. By early 1994, in fact, the Web/Mosaic combination had begun to attract the sort of media hype that can both make and break a technology. 1993 also saw the release of Cello, an alternative browser developed by the Legal Information Institute at Cornell University, for users of Microsoft Windows.

1994 saw several important developments. First, work expanded on the development of "secure" Web access, the kind of security needed if real corporate work were to take place across the Web, and if users were ever to provide such details as credit card information.

Second, the licensing of Mosaic to commercial developers took hold, and even lesser-known browsers such as Cello were seeing licensing potential. NCSA's development of Mosaic took a turn with the departure of Andreesen and others to form the Mosaic Communication Corporation (now Netscape Communications Corporation), and the first international World Wide Web conference took place in Geneva.

In July 1994, CERN began to turn over the Web project to a new group called the W3 Organization, a joint venture between CERN and MIT (the Massachusetts Institute of Technology) to develop the Web further. The transition had several purposes, but primary among them was that the project had outgrown — by a long shot — the ability of CERN to deal with it. The Web was obviously becoming the heart of the information-providing function of the Internet, and the responsibility for its development and growth required more resources (both financial and human) than a single research laboratory could muster.

Over the course of a few months in 1994 and early 1995, this development venture was transformed into a collection of organization and expertise called The World Wide Web Consortium. Led by Web founder Tim Berners-Lee, the Consortium operates with funding from membership: Full members pay $150,000, whereas affiliate members pay a tenth that amount to join. In April 1995, MIT was joined by the French National Institute for Research in Computer Science and Control (INRIA) as co-host of the Consortium. CERN remains an important collaborator.

Accessing the Consortium's Web site (`http://www.w3.org/`) lets you see the organization's official statements. Especially noteworthy are the purposes and goals, stated as follows.

The purposes of the Consortium are

- To support the advancement of information technology in the field of networking, graphics, and user interfaces by developing the World Wide Web into a comprehensive information infrastructure
- To encourage the industry to adopt a common set of World Wide Web protocols
- MIT/LCS and INRIA's role is to provide the vendor-neutral architecture, engineering, and administrative leadership necessary to

    Design a common World Wide Web protocol suite

    Develop a publicly available reference code

    Promote the common protocol suite throughout the world

    Encourage the industry to create products that comply with the common protocol suite

The primary difference between these purposes and goals and those of the original WWW project is that these are not specifically aimed at one research community, and they actively encourage commercial support and development.

Also since 1994, the World Wide Web series of conferences has become internationally important. The Consortium is frequently involved in these conferences, which draw together researchers and practitioners in business, universities, and governments. Information about the conferences can also be found at the W3 Web site.

The Web has boomed. It continues to boom. This book is testament to the explosion.

Original CERN Proposal

The original proposal from Tim Berners-Lee outlining the World Wide Web project—actually, a revamped proposal from a little later than the original—is available on the Web itself, at the URL `http://info.cern.ch/hypertext/WWW/TheProject.html`. As a document predicting the future of a computing resource, it's more than a worthwhile read. As a document outlining a proposed long-term project incorporating both existing and still-to-be-developed computer technologies, a vision of what the World Wide Web could become, it's essential. Nowhere does the proposal suggest that the Web might become as important as it has, but perhaps this is inevitable. Few important inventions have ever had their full effects predicted accurately.

The title of the proposal was "WorldWideWeb: Proposal for a HyperText Project." Note, first of all, that the words "world," "wide," and "web" were, at this stage, joined together as a single word, a usage that is maintained in some instances today but not to a significant degree. But note, also, that the whole venture is described simply as "a HyperText project," not at all as the kind of global networking multimedia concept the Web has become.

Early in the proposal, the authors offer a word about the need for their system: "There is a potential large benefit from the integration of a variety of systems," they state, "in a way which allows a user to follow links pointing from one piece of information to another one. This forming of a web of information nodes rather than a hierarchical tree or an ordered list is the basic concept behind HyperText." Already we have here the word "web," and just as significantly "web" only a couple of words away from "information." The way the Web was perceived is essentially the way it was delivered.

The following passage takes the concept still further. I quote it at considerable length here because it remains one of the clearest statements about hypertext, hypermedia, and the Web that exists. It also points out two important facts: Hypertext nodes were seen as being on different machines and different networks, and hypermedia possibilities were part of the original concept:

> The texts are linked together in a way that one can go from one concept to another to find the information one wants. The network links are called a web. The web need not be hierarchical, and therefore it is not necessary to "climb up a tree" all the way again before you can go down to a different but related subject. The web is also not complete, since it is hard to imagine that all the possible links would be put in by authors. Yet a small number of links is usually sufficient for getting from anywhere to anywhere else in a small number of hops.

> The texts are known as nodes. The process of proceeding from node to node is called navigation. Nodes do not need to be on the same machine; links may point across machine boundaries. Having a world wide web implies some solutions must be found for problems such as different access protocols and different node content formats. These issues are addressed by our proposal.

> Nodes can in principle also contain non-text information such as diagrams, pictures, sound, and animation. The term hypermedia is simply the expansion of the hypertext idea to these other media. Where facilities already exist, we aim to allow graphics interchange, but in this project, we concentrate on the universal readership for text, rather than on graphics.

It's tempting to copy the entire proposal and go through it in detail, but that's neither practical nor necessary. However, the original goals set by the designers remain of interest today. These, too, appear quite early in the document.

It (the project) will aim:
- To provide a common (simple) protocol for requesting human readable information stored at a remote system, using networks;
- To provide a protocol within which information can automatically be exchanged in a format common to the supplier and the consumer;

- To provide some method of reading at least text (if not graphics) using a large proportion of the computer screens in use at CERN;

- To provide and maintain at least one collection of documents, into which users may (but are not bound to) put their documents. This collection will include much existing data (This is partly to give us firsthand experience of use of the system, and partly because members of the project will already have documentation for which they are responsible.);

- To provide a keyword search option, in addition to navigation by following references, using any new or existing indexes (such as the CERNVM FIND indexes). The result of a keyword search is simply a hypertext document consisting of a list of references to nodes which match the keywords;

- To allow private, individually managed collections of documents to be linked to those in other collections;

- To use public domain software wherever possible, or interface to proprietary systems which already exist;

- To provide the software for the above free of charge to anyone.

The project will not aim:

- To provide conversions where they do not exist between the many document storage formats at CERN, although providing a framework into which such conversion utilities can fit;

- To force users to use any particular word processor, or mark-up format;

- To do research into fancy multimedia facilities such as sound and video;

- To use sophisticated network authorization systems. Data will be either readable by the world (literally), or will be readable only on one file system, in which case the file system's protection system will be used for privacy. All network traffic will be public.

Little of this needs commentary. It is clear, unambiguous, and important. But it's instructive to read the first and last bullets, the intention to provide a publicly accessible protocol and the insistence that all traffic will be public, and the sheer lack of importance to the project of sound or video, which since that time have become of increasing significance. Clearly, the ideas behind the Web were in place early, but the Web was not seen as the killer concept it has become. Either that, or the authors of the proposal realized what would happen and kept quiet about it, realizing that academic institutions are rarely impressed by inventions with mass appeal.

After these introductory passages, the proposal establishes definitions for browsers and servers, sets milestones, argues the need for personnel, and so forth. There is surprisingly little hard detail on any of these items, but it's also clear that little was necessary. The concept itself drove the proposal, and the only thing at all surprising is that the project wasn't put into place until more than a year later.

How the Web Works: HTTP

Part VIII, "Whither the Web: Trends and Issues," offers a detailed explanation of how the World Wide Web operates. Here, we'll take a very brief look at the interactions between the Web server and Web documents or other Internet protocols such as Gopher or FTP, partly for interest and partly because even a short background is helpful when examining Parts II, III, and V.

The most interesting part of the way the Web works is its simplicity. Of course, that might be why it's as powerful as it is. You'd expect a technology like this to have the complexity commensurate with its capabilities, but in fact it doesn't. In fact, as the Web document prepared by CERN (http://info.cern.ch/hypertext/WWW/Protocols/HTTP/HTTP2.html) tells us, the transaction takes place in four basic phases, all part of the underlying HTTP (HyperText Transfer Protocol):

- Connection
- Request
- Response
- Close

In the connection phase, the Web client (for example, Mosaic, Cello, or Lynx) attempts to connect with the server. This appears on the status line of most browsers in the form Connecting to HTTP server. If the client can't perform the connection, nothing further happens. Usually, in fact, the connection attempt times out, yielding an explanatory message saying so.

Once the connection to the HTTP server is established, the client sends a request to the server. The request specifies which protocol is being used (including which version of HTTP, if applicable), and it tells the server what object it's looking for and how it wants the server to respond. The protocol can be HTTP, but it can also be FTP, NNTP (network news transfer protocol), Gopher, or WAIS (the Z39.50 protocol). Included in the request is the *method*, which essentially is the client's command to the server. The most common method is *GET*, which is basically a request to retrieve the object in question.

Assuming the server can fulfill the request (it sends error messages if it can't), it then executes the response. You'll see this phase of the transaction in your browser's status line, usually in the form Reading Response. Like the request, the response indicates the protocol being used, and it also offers a *reason line*, which appears on the browser's status line. Depending on your browser, you'll see exactly what is going on at this point, usually represented by a Transferring message.

Finally, the connection is closed.

At this stage, the browser springs into action again. Effectively, it loads the requested data and displays it, or it saves it to a file or launches a viewer. If the object is a text file, the browser will display it as a nonhypertext ASCII document. If it's a graphic image (such as a GIF file), the browser will launch the graphics viewer specified in its configuration settings. If it's a sound or video file (AU, WAV, MPEG, or other), the browser will launch a similarly configured player. Depending on the type of method specified in the request, the browser might also display a search dialog box.

Usually, however, the browser displays an HTML document. These are the documents that show the graphics, links, icons, and formatting for which the Web has become so famous.

How the Web Works: HTML

HTML is a simplified derivative of SGML, or Standard Generalized Markup Language, which is a code used to make documents readable across a variety of platforms and software. Like SGML, HTML operates through a series of codes placed within an ASCII (that is, text) document. These codes are translated by a World Wide Web client, such as Lynx, Mosaic, Cello, Viola, or MacWeb, into specific kinds of formats to be displayed on the screen, and on which the user can (in some cases) act.

These items include links, lists, headings, titles, images, forms, and maps. As you might expect, the longer HTML stays around, the more complex it is becoming. The original HTML allowed only text, and later inline images (graphics that appear on the document) and various types of lists and link types were added, but not until HTML+ were such elements as fill-in forms and clickable maps possible. Not surprisingly, HTML 2.0 promises even more variety, to the extent that HTML might well possess enough features to make serious documentation design possible.

The documents you see on your World Wide Web browser are usually HTML documents. True, the Web can display ASCII files, but they're just plain text files that can be downloaded and opened in any text editor. What makes an HTML file worthwhile is the browser's interpretation of its formatting codes—a link appears as a highlighted item, a list appears with associated bullets or numbers, and a graphic appears as the picture it represents. In other words, the World Wide Web would be nothing without HTML.

But HTML is limited; some would say extremely so. Even with HTML+, for example, it's barely possible to place graphics where you want them, and simple items like font selection are constrained as well. Nothing in HTML even approximates the sophistication of the desktop publishing capabilities of today's word processors, and it's a long, long way from offering the design tools of a desktop publishing package like PageMaker or QuarkXPress. The Web in its current state is still well short of the interest of professional page designers, and as a result many of the pages we see are amateurish, garish, or just downright ugly.

Accessing the Web

The World Wide Web can be accessed through both direct and indirect Internet connections, and through a variety of clients (browsers). Part II, "Web Browsers and Connections," examines the types of connections and how to acquire them, as well as the variety of browsers currently available. Here I'll simply outline the possibilities in a brief explanation of the issues you'll need to consider about Web access.

Indirect and Direct Internet Connections

There are two main types of Internet connection: *indirect* and *direct*. Both types can make use of either modems or existing network cards, and both types range in price from free through very expensive. There are also other ways of describing Net connections (Internet books differ widely on access descriptions), but these two are as effective as any.

The crucial difference between indirect and direct connections is this: With a *direct connection*, your computer is an individual node on the Internet (or, in some cases, a simulated node). With an *indirect connection*, your computer is simply a terminal on a computer or on a network that is itself an individual node on the Internet.

With a direct connection, your computer has its own IP address (see Chapter 2, "The Internet") and can be established as a server for FTP, Gopher, News, or the World Wide Web. In turn, you can use software to bring mail and software directly to your computer. Direct access is often necessary if you want to use programs such as Mosaic for Windows or Netscape for Macintosh, as well as the other graphical software available for these machines. It is possible to access this software through some other connection tools, such as PC packages that connect to X Window servers, but for many users direct access is the only means available.

With an indirect connection, by contrast, you are given disk space and access time on another computer. When you receive mail, the mail stays on that server, and when you transfer files they are stored on that server as well. (You can download this information to your own computer through a variety of means, but that's a separate activity entirely.) With an indirect connection you can't normally use graphical software such as a Web browser, and instead you must rely on the text-based browsers that your server can run.

A Summary of World Wide Web Browsers

Mosaic and Netscape are the most famous Web browsers, but there are many others. Most will be treated in detail in Part II. This section summarizes a selection of them according to their applicable computer platforms. Note that these are the freely available browsers; commercial browsers have been released and are increasingly available. Note also that NCSA Mosaic and Netscape Navigator are technically free only to educational users or as evaluation units, and that they must be licensed for corporate use.

UNIX Clients

Not surprisingly, given the importance of UNIX to the Internet, browsers for UNIX systems have been available the longest and are the most plentiful. Here are some of them.

Text-Mode UNIX Browsers (Nongraphical)

- CERN's Line Mode Browser—Available for any text-based terminal on the Net, the Line Mode Browser uses a numeric interface.
- Lynx—A full-screen browser for VT100 (or compatible) terminals, Lynx uses the cursor keys for navigation.

Graphical-Mode UNIX Browsers

- NCSA Mosaic for X—The most famous client of them all, X Mosaic requires X11/Motif to run, and is full featured and extremely well supported.
- Netscape Navigator for X—The client that appeared in 1994 and took the browser world by storm.
- ViolaWWW—Now unsupported, Viola was one of the first graphical browsers.
- Chimera—A browser with an X/Athena interface, Chimera supports both inline images and HTML forms.

Apple Macintosh Clients

- NCSA Mosaic for Macintosh—Released shortly after the original X version, Mac Mosaic offers similar features.
- Netscape Navigator for Macintosh—Released concurrently with Netscape for X and Netscape for Windows, this browser gained instant popularity.
- Samba—Developed by CERN, this client offers basic Web browsing.
- MacWeb—A full-featured client from EINet, MacWeb promises full future support.

Microsoft Windows Clients

- NCSA Mosaic for Windows—The fastest-growing Web client, Windows Mosaic is being licensed by several commercial interests.
- Netscape Navigator for Windows—Extremely popular, and also being licensed by commercial interests.
- Cello—The product of Cornell's Legal Information Institute, Cello offers Windows users a different look and feel.
- WinWeb—This is the Windows version of MacWeb (see above), offering a good but limited subset of its Mac counterpart.

Other Platforms

- NeXTStep WWW Browser-Editor—Available for the NeXTStep operating system, this browser offers both browsing and editing capabilities.

- WWWVM—For VM systems, WWWVM is a full-screen, text-only browser.

- Amiga Mosaic—Although not developed by NCSA, the Amiga version of Mosaic offers similar features.

- Web Explorer—Not free, actually, but freely available for OS/2 users from the IBM Network.

Uses of the Web

The remainder of Part I and the whole of Part IV, "Exploring the Web," offer glimpses into the wide range of activities currently underway across the World Wide Web. Part IV categorizes existing Web pages according to topic, but that's not the only way to understand what's going on throughout this important global resource. Listed here are the types of tasks being undertaken on the Web, not according to subject matter but rather according to what is being attempted.

Graphical Design of Information

For a long time, book publishers have known the importance of graphical design. So have computer users, of course, as anyone with a word processor and a set of fonts is well aware. Over networks, however, information has been presented largely as unformatted ASCII, primarily because there were few choices. (ASCII has been an extremely valuable "lowest common denominator," but it is limited.) Exceptions have existed on the Mac, of course, which has had built-in networking since its inception, and more recently on platforms such as NeXTStep, OS/2, and Windows. But over the Internet and other wide area networks, text has been the dominant mode of presentation.

The Web changes that. At least, it changes it if you consider a graphical browser as a default, which is clearly what's happening. Suddenly, information at remote sites can be presented in graphical format, complete with font choices and incorporated drawings, photographs, and other multimedia elements.

The results might have their downside—along the lines of trivial, unnecessary information presented solely because it's possible—but the plus side of the ledger is far more likely. Graphical elements offer different kinds of information, and information providers are researching precisely what that means. We are beginning to see strong uses of charts, diagrams, illustrations, tables, graphics, photographs, maps, flowcharts, and all other kinds of graphical representations as the Web's capabilities increase, and this can only mean an increase in the comprehensibility of the information. Of course, it all has to be done right, but that's another issue. The fact that it's possible means that those who care about their information will figure out how to do it.

This doesn't mean that HTML in its current incarnation allows anything like full graphic design. But as HTML 3.0 moves into full acceptance, and as Web clients begin to display fully formatted word processing and desktop publishing files, it almost undoubtedly will. At that point, we should begin to see exceptionally strong designs.

Dissemination of Research

Dissemination of research was, of course, one of the original purposes of the Internet itself, and more particularly of the Web project at CERN. Today, the Web is being used for this purpose to a certain degree, but perhaps more importantly—for the sake of its mass acceptance, at least—it's being used to make research findings available to the general public. The sheer amount of research available through diligent Web searching is staggering, and much of it is presented so that it's as easily understandable as possible.

This is an important development. As more publicly funded research agencies are called upon to account for their expenditures and activities, they are being forced to come up with increasingly creative ways of making their work known to the public. But booklets and pamphlets distributed through direct mailings are expensive and usually ignored, so getting the word out is difficult.

What better way than the Web? Through a well-designed HTML page, an organization can now demonstrate its activities graphically and comprehensibly, and these pages can be updated inexpensively and frequently as a means of continuing to foster public interest. Organizations like NASA are making extensive use of this kind of public dissemination, and we can expect others to do so as well. Among other things, it's a way of making research timely, enjoyable, and interactive.

Browsing and Ordering of Products

We're already beginning to see product ordering available through the Web, even though discussions continue as to its security for such activities as credit card use. In the near future, "secure" Mosaic will find a variety of releases, and when that happens, expect to see a flurry of Web shopping centers opening. Until then, you can find a considerable variety of products to order on the Web, ranging from flowers to books to music CDs.

What's the appeal? Very simply, this is home shopping at its most interactive. Unlike home-shopping TV stations, you don't have to sit through 15 descriptions of cubic zirconium rings and bracelets in order to find that elusive Wayne Gretzky undershirt you've been looking for. Shopping on the Web is more like walking into a shopping mall, and in fact *mall* is the name given to many current Web offerings. Just click the shop you want, turn on the inline graphics to see a picture of the product you're looking for, then go to the order forms page to do the actual ordering.

Client and Customer Support

The World Wide Web's potential for client and customer support is extremely strong. Already, companies like Hewlett Packard and Digital Equipment Corporation are using the Web to make available to their customers such items as technical documents, software patches, and frequently asked questions. The benefits of this approach are obvious. Customers with Web access can take care of their own information needs, resulting in less strain on the supplier's support staff and, quite likely, an improved reception of customer service on the customer's part.

The only danger to this approach is the possibility that the Web will be used as a substitution for person-to-person support. But that's not a danger at all if the Web site offers everything the customer needs, and in many cases that might well be the case. Consider, for example, the possibility of Web-based tutorials offering step-by-step installation procedures for a new piece of equipment, or for that matter how to program your VCR. If it's well designed, it will be better than a tech support phone call because it shows, rather than tells, the customer what to do.

Of course, HTML forms can also be used to provide feedback and questions on products, and these can be posted as well. The idea is to have a place where customers can feel they haven't been forgotten, and where they can learn from the experiences of other customers as well. That's what we're starting to see.

Display of Creative Arts

For some reason, people in the creative arts are often perceived as traditionalists, stodgy and resistant to new technologies. Yes, there are some of those. But throughout history artists have been among the first to adopt new technologies to their own purposes, as witnessed by everything from the printing press to MIDI. And there's every indication that the artistic community is seeing the World Wide Web as yet another medium that they can exploit in order to present their work and link up with other artists.

Already we have online galleries featuring new visual art, collaborative artistic efforts of a kind not previously possible, and presentations of artwork that outsiders are asked to evaluate. Examples of creative writing are springing up all over the Web, including some interactive stories and illustrated texts as well. There are even some preliminary attempts at Web-based drama.

The Web offers artists a couple of very important features. First, it allows an inexpensive way of mounting work. As long as the site is in place, the rest is up to the artist, in a way that differs considerably from standard galleries or the inevitable street corners. Second, everyone posting art on the Web has a built-in global audience, and that's something about which artists can usually only dream. Obviously, there are media that will never be entirely suited to Web presentation, but if today's efforts are any indication the Web, all by itself, could lead to a kind of renaissance in both the amount of artwork publicly available and the ability of a mass audience to access and appreciate it.

The Future of the Web

For any technology, it's impossible to predict the future. No sooner are the predictions made than the technology develops unexpected adherents and unforeseen uses. This was the case with gunpowder, with television, with computers, and now with multimedia, online services, and the Internet itself. But trends count for something, and the Web has revealed nothing if not a series of trends toward future use. Here are some, presented as ideas to be explored:

■ **Full-scale publishing**

A wide range of publishers have already appeared on the Web. Some have presented samples of publications; others have presented full texts. In the future, there's every reason to expect full publishing efforts on the Web, everything ranging from children's books through advertising-laden magazines. New approaches to design and new accesses to advertisers' wares will have to be considered, but the potential is certainly there. Watch also for newsletters and magazines that will be partially accessible publicly and fully accessible with subscriptions and associated account assignments.

■ **Voting**

Well, why not? With fill-in forms establishing themselves as perhaps the most important single advance in Internet-based technology, and with the White House and other governments turning to the Net for information dissemination of a variety of kinds, it seems only a matter of time until the Web can be used for voting—maybe not in a presidential election, at least for a while, but certainly for other purposes. Of course, all of this demands common access to huge numbers of people, but the Web need not be the only voting medium. If the idea is to get more people voting on public issues, why not use all public media?

■ **Live interactive entertainment**

Yes, we have television. But television is presentation only, not interaction, and here the Web can make a difference. Why not comedy routines in which Web users participate in skits and jokes? Why not dramatic pieces in which Web users influence the outcome? How about real-time role-playing games? And so on. True, there's a stretch of the imagination to some of this, and all of it has been hyped in the past, but the potential is now global, and that will make a difference.

■ **News**

The problem with CNN or any other continual news supply is that the news we get is the news they decide we'll get. No matter how comprehensive and fair-minded the programmers might be, we end up hearing a whole slew of news stories we're not interested in, and too little about stories we want to know more about. Here the Web's possibilities are enormous. How about fully customizable news packages, so that if we want to focus on Rwanda, or the Middle East, or a flood or earthquake area, or for that matter the qualifying games among African teams for the 1998 World Cup, we can get the text, audio, and video of whatever subject we want.

■ **Distance education**

Obvious, maybe, but no less important for being so. For decades, universities and colleges have been looking for ways of offering courses to students who don't have access to the campus (usually because of physical distance). The Web is beginning to see activity in this regard, and this activity will increase dramatically over the next few years. Watch for full university-level courses to be offered over the Web to all registered students (and perhaps others as well), complete with real-time seminars and exams, and professors' visiting hours. Much more interactive than the audio- or videotaped lectures of today's correspondence courses, Web-based distance education courses will very much be the next best thing to being there. Maybe even better, if it's done right.

■ **Distance presentations**

Organizations with high-speed Internet connections might well consider offering multimedia presentations over the Web. These need not be real-time presentations, which eliminates some of the problems presented by desktop conferencing, and they offer the benefit of eliminating travel and accommodation costs, as well as downtime costs, for presentation attendees. Presentations can take full advantage of the Web's multimedia and networking capabilities, and the HTML pages can be quickly redesigned and updated as a result of the presentation. Another benefit is that the presentation can offer links to other information sources, all of which will be updated by the site being linked. The presentation will thus always be up-to-date.

There are other applications: scheduling, interpersonal communication, meetings and conferences, you name it. But the Web is far from the only technology whose future points toward these possibilities, and it remains to be seen if it will overtake, fall behind, or simply incorporate all the rest. What's certain is that the Web is extremely flexible, and that its capabilities haven't begun to be explored. The remainder of *The World Wide Web Unleashed 1996* shows you the present and speculates on the future.

The World Wide Web: A Guided Tour

6

by
Neil Randall

The question is what would a tour of the World Wide Web consist of? Would it consist of a look at a variety of the possibilities for page design and information presentation? An attempt to show the changes in the look and feel of the Web over time? A look at the different categories of Web pages, acting as an introduction to Part IV "Exploring the Web," of *The World Wide Web Unleashed*? Or would it simply take a bunch of random Web pages, make sure they look either pretty or rich, and throw them together under the idea of judge-for-yourself?

No. A tour of the World Wide Web should be, quite simply, a tour of the world.

Not an extensive tour. That would take page after page of fascinating description, evaluation, and screen displays, and wouldn't be nearly as enjoyable as doing it yourself in the first place. Instead, this tour should touch on the many nations, people, and designs that make up the Web, focusing not on the technology or the sheer amount of information, but rather on the fact that the Web is, indeed, worldwide.

That's been the exciting part, after all. Yes, there's an unbelievable wealth of resources out there on the Web, just waiting for you to click and claim them; but for the first few years of the Web's existence, what's truly inspiring is watching the Web become a global tool. In early 1994, it seemed that every week someone in a new country was providing Web information, and the first click on a hyperlink leading to that country was actually exciting. If you're just getting started on the Web, that excitement might still be there.

That's why we've chosen the world tour as a starting point. We'll get to business, education, entertainment, and all the other attractions later—because they all have their necessary place. But for now, sit back and pretend it's the first time on the Web—and just grab the mouse and let fly.

> **NOTE**
>
> The bulk of this chapter consists of screen shots from the Web itself, using a wide range of World Wide Web browsers. The URL (address) of the Web site is shown in square brackets after the caption for each figure, and this URL is preceded by the name of the browser used for that shot.

The Virtual Tourist

Any time you want to find points on the Web by what country they reside in, Brandon Plewe's Virtual Tourist is a superb place to begin. An immensely popular site practically since the Web first supported clickable graphics, the Tourist (shown in Figure 6.1) consists of a series of imagemaps of the world, the continents, and then the countries. To find your way to sites in various parts of the globe, click the maps where you want to go. For the first few clicks, you'll remain on the server at the University of Buffalo, but before long you'll be elsewhere in the world, marveling at what's out there.

NOTE

We were so impressed with Brandon's use of imagemaps in the Virtual Tourist, we asked him to write an entire chapter on the subject for this edition of *The World Wide Web Unleashed*. See Chapter 36, "Creating Imagemaps."

FIGURE 6.1.

The Virtual Tourist, X Mosaic—`http://wings.buffalo.edu/world/`*.*

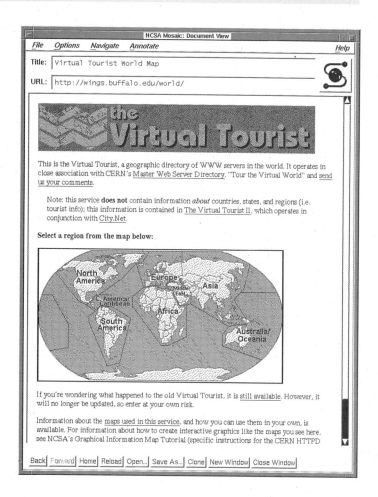

Clicking the European continent on the World map takes you to the European map shown in Figure 6.2. You could have chosen anywhere, but Europe is a good starting point for a very particular reason: The World Wide Web had its origins in Europe, at a high-energy physics laboratory called CERN, in Switzerland. So start there (you have to start somewhere), although you won't follow the geographical development of the Web as you tour.

FIGURE 6.2.

The European map from the Virtual Tourist, http:// wings.buffalo.edu/ world/europe.html.

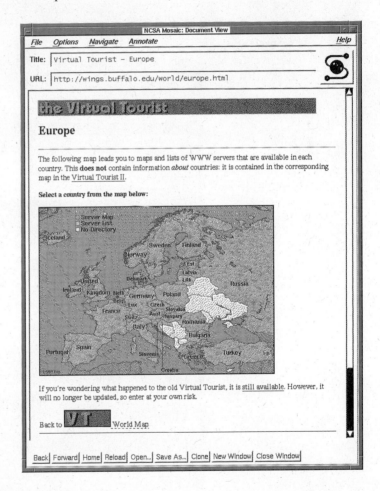

Switzerland

From this map, it's on to Switzerland itself. Clicking the country of Switzerland from the European map retrieves the Web site shown in Figure 6.3. Yet another imagemap (you won't be seeing all of these as we do your circumnavigation), this one gives you a colorful series of links to a host of Swiss Internet sites, most of which are accessible by scrolling down this long page.

FIGURE 6.3.

The imagemap for Switzerland, direct from a Swiss computer, XMosaic— http://heiwww.unige.ch/switzerland/.

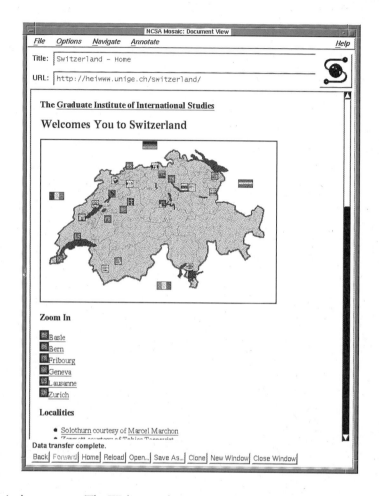

For now, though, scrolling isn't necessary. The Web started at CERN, the European Laboratory for Particle Physics in Geneva, so all you need to do is locate the Geneva site on the map and click directly on it. Doing so takes you to an even smaller-scale map, this time of Geneva and its surrounding territory (not shown here), where the first hyperlink is to this laboratory. The URL (Universal Resource Locator, or simply address) for this page is http://www.cern.ch/; it tells you in the first line that CERN is the birthplace of the World Wide Web. This link is shown in Figure 6.4.

Moving the cursor to the "birthplace of the World Wide Web" hyperlink gives the cursor a different look (such as a changed arrow in UNIX or a pointing finger in Windows). As soon as it changes to that shape, you can click the mouse button and activate that link. In more technical terms, you're telling the browser to retrieve the file located at the URL for that link. This process is known by many users as *jumping*. In this case, the link retrieves a page at http://www.cern.ch/CERN/WorldWideWeb/WWWandCERN.html (not shown here) explaining that CERN has practically removed itself from the World Wide Web project, having turned it over to INRIA in France and MIT in the U.S.

FIGURE 6.4.

The CERN home page, with link to World Wide Web, Netscape for UNIX—
`http://www.cern.ch/`.

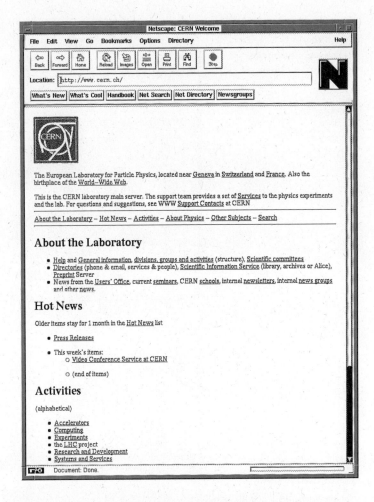

Only five hyperlinks are available from this page, one to INRIA itself. Now, this tour is about seeing the world rather than about finding out what's happened to the World Wide Web project, but France isn't a bad place to go next. So why not click the INRIA link and leap across the border?

France

As Figure 6.5 demonstrates, by the language of the links alone, you're now at a computer in France. Actually, you're not actually *at* the computer; you've downloaded a document *from* a French computer. In any case, you've made contact with a French machine, which is what it means to tour the world on the Web.

The language of the links isn't how you know you've reached France. The URL is shown just below the toolbar in the Netscape for UNIX browser; the URL reads `http://www.inria.fr`. The `fr` stands for France; you can often tell which country you've connected to by looking at the end of the URL. In Figures 6.3 and 6.4, the `ch` stood for Switzerland. (English isn't mandatory.) You'll see several other country codes as you tour.

FIGURE 6.5.

The INRIA home page, with colorful icons to other sites. Netscape for UNIX—
`http://www.inria.fr/`.

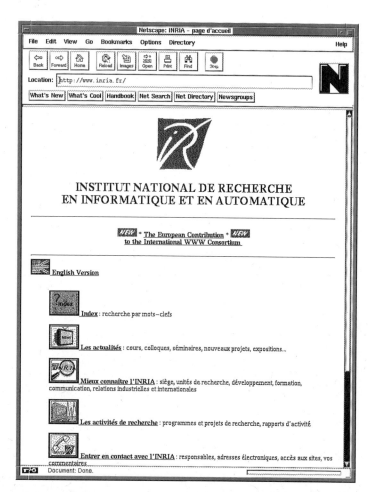

So far, you've seen two ways to move from country to country. The Virtual Tourist makes this kind of touring obvious, but it's equally possible to find links to Web sites from within Web pages. From this point on, we'll take less time to get to where we wish to go. Instead of moving laboriously from page to page (which is certainly possible), we'll simply make the leaps and examine the resulting pages. Many of these will be accessed from the Virtual Tourist, which is always a worthwhile place to begin.

Now that you've seen the scholarly side of things, it's time to leave the labs and head out into the France you'd *really* like to visit, the one with the Eiffel Tower and the vineyards. To do so, head back to the Virtual Tourist, and work your way through the map of Europe and into the map of France at `http://wings.buffalo.edu/europe.html`. From there, click France, and eventually you'll get to the tour of Paris, complete with the Eiffel Tower, at `http://www.cnam.fr/louvre/paris/hist/tour-eiffel.html` (see Figure 6.6). This is part of an historical tour of Paris, and it leads directly to the famous art museum Le Louvre.

FIGURE 6.6.

The Eiffel Tower in the Tour of Paris, X Mosaic— `http://www.cnam.fr/ louvre/paris/hist/ tour-eiffel.html].`

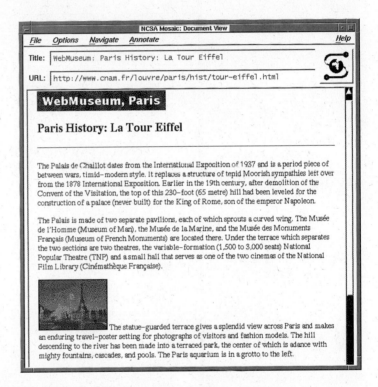

Spain

Now head southwest, across the Spanish border. The visit in Spain doesn't need to go further than the map of Internet resources shown in Figure 6.7. This is an impressive page, complete with a 3-D sculpted title, map, and icons. The country code of the URL (es) tells you that you've connected with a Spanish computer; it's obvious how you get from here to anywhere else. Of particular interest are the links to Madrid and Grenada, but others are well worth trying.

FIGURE 6.7.

The Internet Resources map of Spain, Netscape for Windows—`http://www.uji.es/spain_www.html.`

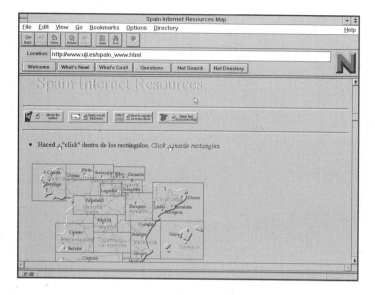

United Kingdom

Across the water to the north is the United Kingdom; in particular, you come to Oxford, one of the most renowned locations in the country. The Oxford Information page, shown in Figure 6.8, offers all kinds of information about Oxford, the university, and the surrounding territory. Not only can you visit museums and libraries, you can head for the pubs and retrieve a fascinating document called "The Aliens' Guide to Oxford." You could spend hours at this one site alone, but you have other places to visit.

FIGURE 6.8.

The Oxford, UK, home page, Netscape for Windows—`http://www.comlab.ox.ac.uk/archive/ox.html.`

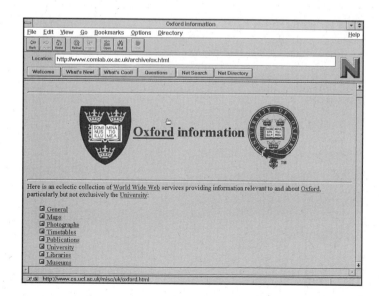

Netherlands

Across the channel from the UK, you come to the Netherlands, where the Web was useful as an information tool during the flooding in February of 1995. In particular, you'll stop on the west coast, at the home page for Erasmus University in Rotterdam (see Figure 6.9). The Netherlands has been active on the Internet for a long time, and the number and strength of their resources demonstrate this. This particular home page is useful without being spectacular, and there are many such pages across the Web.

FIGURE 6.9.

*Rotterdam's Erasmus
University home page,
Netscape for Windows—*
`http://www.eur.nl/`.

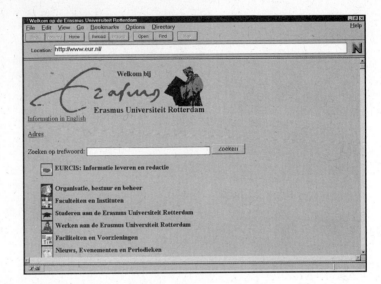

Norway

Surfing quickly over the North Sea takes you to Norway, a country that, with the rest of Scandinavia, has been actively involved in Internet activities since the early days. Figure 6.10 shows the Oslonett Marketplace (the tour has gone far enough for us to do a little shopping), with its host of commercial sponsors—both local and global. A visit to the Norwegian home page is well worth your time, but the glories of Sweden beckon.

FIGURE 6.10.

The Oslonett Marketplace in Norway, Mosaic for Windows—`http://www.oslonett.no:80/html/adv/advertisers.html`*.*

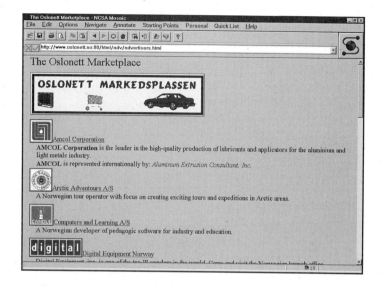

Sweden

It's always nice to find a site that won't be out of date the minute this book hits the shelves, especially when it's well-designed and informative. Stockholm has been named (by the European Union) the European cultural capital for 1998, and the city's "Webmasters" have established a rich, colorful page to detail how it got there and what to expect if you visit. If you have no interest in a gorgeous city with superb theater, food, and, well, other attractions, don't bother using this page as a basis for a real-world visit.

FIGURE 6.11.

Stockholm, the cultural capital of Europe 1998. Mosaic for Windows—`http://www.sunet.se:80/stockholm/kultur98/kulturhuvudstad98.html`*.*

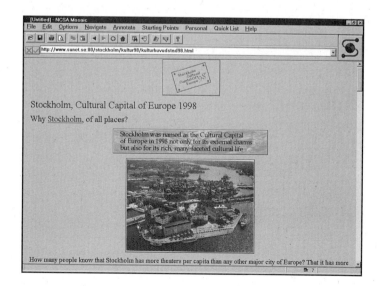

Russia

Despite Finland's strength in Internet and World Wide Web activity, we can't visit everywhere. So we'll skip right past the land of the reindeer and into Russia, which is showing Internet activity despite its woeful economic state. Figure 6.12 shows the home page for St. Petersburg (formerly Leningrad, but St. Petersburg before that), complete with commercial sponsorship and, impressively, a Web version of the city's major English language newspaper. Interestingly, the country code for Russia is now ru, but many of its servers still bear the earlier country code, su (Soviet Union).

FIGURE 6.12.

St. Petersburg home page. Mosaic for Windows—
http://www.spb.su:80/.

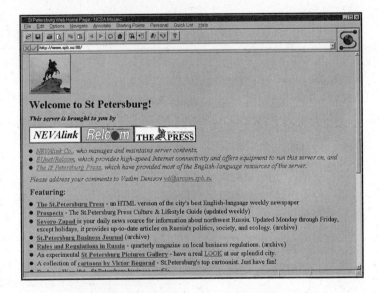

Germany

Once again skipping over a country with a growing Internet presence (Poland), you come to Germany—in particular, the capital of unified Germany, Berlin. Available from the Berlin home page are links to a number of good graphics files, as well as substantial information about the city's history, politics, and commerce. You can also begin exploring Germany's extensive collection of Web sites from here, many of which are in the German language. (See Figure 6.13.)

FIGURE 6.13.

The home page for Berlin, Germany. Cello—`http://www.chemie.fu-berlin.de/adressen/berlin.html`.

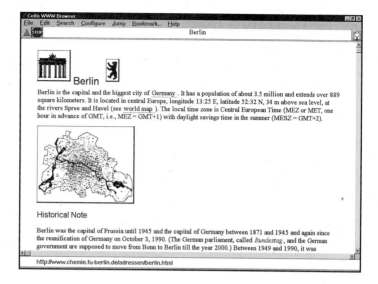

Italy

Working your way down central Europe, you'll find yourself in Italy, where Net and Web activity has been extremely strong. By now you might need some good, solid news, so pick up a newspaper and see what's going on. Figure 6.14 shows a typical daily issue of *il manifesto,* with print just a bit too small to read. Italian Web activity includes an excellent range of tourist, research, and cultural activity, with many pages—as you might expect—in Italian.

FIGURE 6.14.

il manifesto *home page in Italy. Netscape for Windows—`http://www.mir.it/oggi/`.*

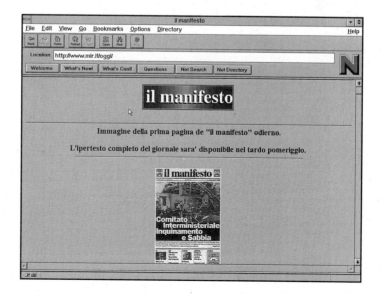

Greece

Across the Adriatic lies Greece, where you'll sail to now. With no time to stop and visit (yeah, right—like you would bypass Greece in real life), just take a look at the imagemap shown in Figure 6.15. Greece isn't exactly swarming with World Wide Web sites, but there's a start. Many countries in the Eastern areas of Europe are in roughly this position.

FIGURE 6.15.

The information map for Greece. Cello—http://www.ntua.gr/local/greece.html.

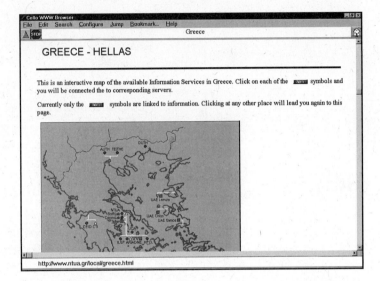

Turkey

It's not far from Greece to Turkey (as Agamemnon and Achilleus found out a wee while ago), and the two countries are fairly similar as far as their World Wide Web participation is concerned. Although not shown here, Turkey has a well-designed information page about Izmir, and there are worthwhile picture tours of the country as well. Interestingly, there's a good selection of material *about* Turkey, especially archaeological documents, in some Australian Web pages, but that's not really what we're after. For other good Turkish material, locate the pages for the Middle East Technical University (METU) as well.

Israel

Also in the Middle East is Israel, where you'll see a significant degree of Internet activity. Although only relatively recent in placing information on the Net, and even more recently on the Web, enough interesting Web sites exist in Israel to make the Web trip more than worthwhile. A top service provider, Macom Networking, operates a server in Jerusalem wherein lies an immensely useful home page, shown in Figure 6.16. From here you can link to the Tel Aviv Museum of Art, the children-oriented Peace in Pictures Project, the Israel Democracy Institute, and if you're into somewhat less significant material, the Israeli Linux Users Web site.

FIGURE 6.16.

The Macom Networking home page, with strong graphical design. Netscape for Macintosh—http://www.macom.co.il/index.html.

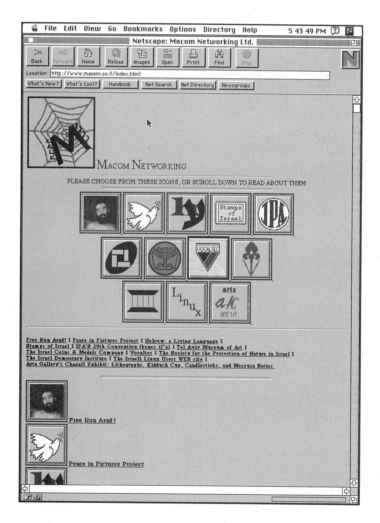

South Africa

Moving way down south, across the equator and into the next hemisphere in fact, you arrive in South Africa. The country's Internet activity is recent, but there appears to be sufficient Internet access to make an impressive start. The main page for Cape Town appears in Figure 6.17, where you'll discover that the city is a contender for the Olympics in 2004. Unfortunately, there's not much else here to see, beyond some very good graphics. What's more useful is the link at the bottom of the page to the Internet provider, Aztec. From there, through a series of audio files, you can even learn to sing the national anthem of South Africa.

FIGURE 6.17.

The Cape Town home page, with links to image downloads. MacWeb—
`http://`
`www.aztec.co.za/`
`aztec/capetown.html.`

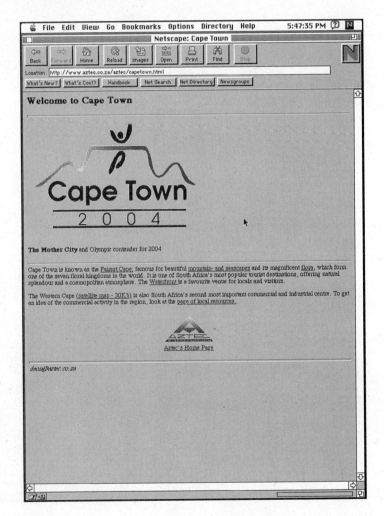

Malaysia

It's a long way from South Africa to Malaysia, fully across the Indian Ocean and other waters, but with the help of the Web you can make it in mere minutes, maybe even seconds. You'll land at a Malaysian information page (see Figure 6.18), operated on a Malaysian server by the government. From here you can get a considerable amount of basic information about Malaysia; if you have the patience and the disk space (a quarter megabyte's worth), you can download and listen to the national song. One link takes you to information and pictures about Kuala Lumpur, and other links to further information sources.

FIGURE 6.18.

Malaysia network information page. MacWeb—
`http://mimos.my/doc/`
`msia.html`.

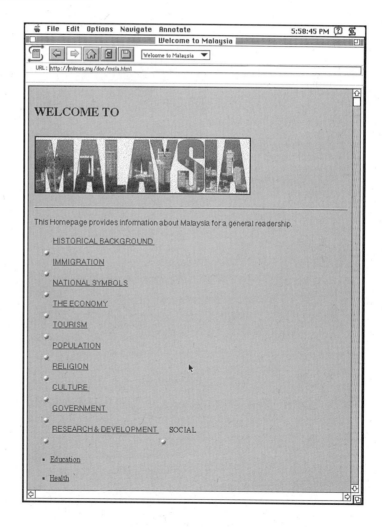

Thailand

Just in case you thought High Performance Computing Centers existed only in countries normally associated with a long history of technological bravado, take a look at Thailand's NECTEC pages, shown in Figure 6.19. Here you can find information about computing projects underway in Thailand. If you click the link to NECTEC's home page, you'll find a wide range of additional Web activity in this country, as well as information about its locales.

FIGURE 6.19.

High Performance Computing Center in Thailand. MacWeb—
`http://
www.nectec.or.th/
bureaux/hpcc/
home.html.`

Korea

Korea has demonstrated a very real strength on the Net in general and the Web in particular recently, and the number of Web sites continues to grow quickly. To get a good sense of what's available, and to see a page kept by someone who cares, fire up the Korean Web information page displayed in Figure 6.20. Not only does this site distinguish between types of organizations and delineates which sites are new, it also uses a distinctive special bullet system to tell you if the site is working well or poorly. The happy face, as you might expect, means things are fine.

FIGURE 6.20.

List of Korean Web sites available. Air Mosaic for Windows—`http://ara.kaist.ac.kr/ahmlhs/HTML/Korea/www_in_korea.html`*.*

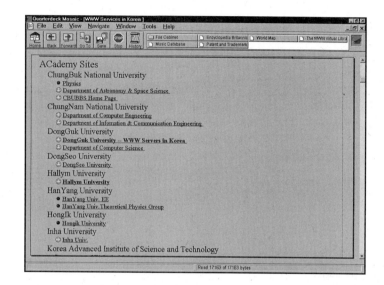

Singapore

Singapore has developed an extremely impressive World Wide Web presence. In fact, its famous Singapore Online Guide was one of the first extensive tourist information pages anywhere. With the exception of Australia, this country is probably the best represented of all Pacific area nations on the Web, especially since Japan got off the mark quite late. The Online Museum of Singapore Art and History (see Figure 16.21), maintained by the government of Singapore, offers a small glimpse of the Web sites in store for you in the country.

FIGURE 6.21.

Home page for the Online Museum of Singapore Art and History. Air Mosaic for Windows—http:// www.ncb.gov.sg/nhb/ museum.html.

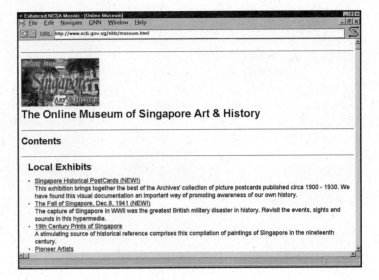

Australia

Australia has been a hotbed of Internet activity since the early days of international participation and remains one of the primary providers of Gopher sites. Their World Wide Web offerings are becoming increasingly impressive as well, and there's no better place to start than the two-designer creation shown in Figure 6.22.

FIGURE 6.22.

Guide to Australia, and to many other Pacific Rim sites. NCSA Mosaic for Windows—http:// www.csu.edu.au/ education/ australia.html.

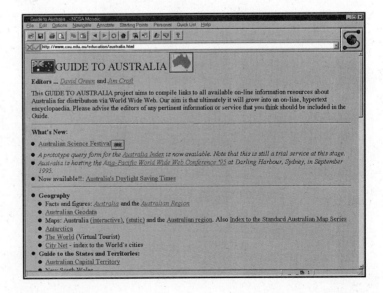

China

Despite what you might have heard, Internet activity is alive and reasonably well in China. The Web isn't exactly thriving, but as Figure 6.23 demonstrates, there are some sites worth seeing. This one is especially interesting, of course, because of its multiple languages.

FIGURE 6.23.

Home page for Beijing University of Chemical Technology. InternetWorks—`http://www.buct.edu.cn/`*.*

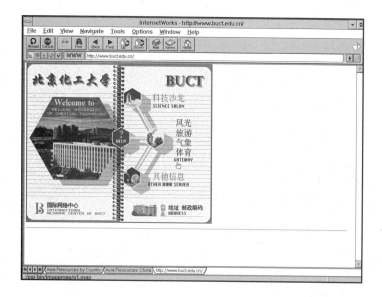

Japan

Although Japan came to the Internet community—particularly the World Wide Web community—surprisingly late, their Web contributions over the last year and a half demonstrate that they're in it for the long haul and the big time. Figure 6.24 shows the home page for the Center for Global Communications at the International University of Japan, a research site that offers extensive information about its activities. This is only one of many Japanese pages, however, and with Netscape and other browsers you can see them in Japanese itself. Stay tuned to Japan, as always, for future Internet activities.

FIGURE 6.24.

The Global Communications Home Page from Japan. Prodigy Web Browser—http://www.glocom.ac.jp:80/index.html.

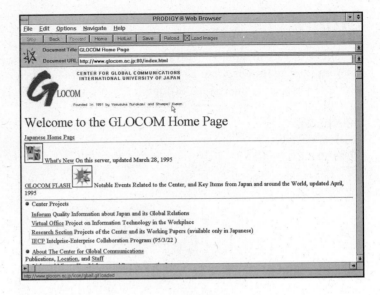

Hawai'i

Obviously, Hawai'i is part of the United States, but we've given it a separate look for two reasons. First, it's a nice landing spot across the Pacific from Japan. Secondly, and somewhat more significantly, Hawai'i is one of the leaders in Internet activity, with an extensive commitment to statewide networking and many exciting World Wide Web sites. Figure 6.25 shows the Weather and Surf page from the University of Hawai'i (UHINFO), from which you can get infrared graphics downloads and all sorts of information you need to plan that surfing outing you're ready for by now.

FIGURE 6.25.

The Surf and Weather page from the University of Hawai'i. Prodigy Web Browser—http://www.hawaii.edu/News/weather.html.

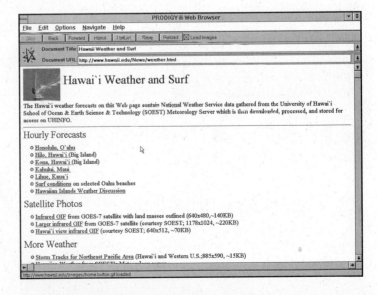

Chile

From Hawai'i it's off to the southeast coast of South America, where the Chileans have been offering some impressive World Wide Web documents. As you'd expect, most of the pages are not in English—something that will probably become more dominant around the world as the Web proliferates. Figure 6.26 shows the home page for Universidad Técnica Federico Santa María in Valparaiso, from which you can get information about the university, links to other Chilean Web servers, and a range of other information.

FIGURE 6.26.

Home page of a Chilean university. InternetWorks for Windows—`http://www.inf.utfsm.cl/`.

Brazil

Figure 6.27 shows the Rio de Janeiro home page in Brazil. Actually, this is the English version of the page, whereas most Web pages coming out of Brazil are in Portuguese instead. What's interesting here is the level of graphics quality and the degree to which the page is selling the city to those who fire it up. Somehow, Rio doesn't seem like a very hard sell, especially since, as I write this, it's snowing in April where I live.

FIGURE 6.27.

Home page for Rio de Janeiro, the "marvelous city." `http://www.puc-rio.br/english/mapario.html`.

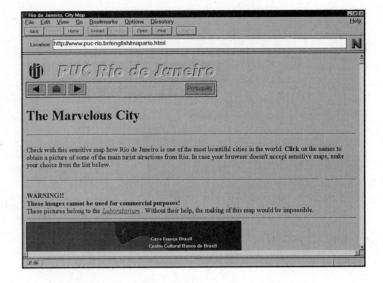

Mexico

Mexico got a bit of a slow start in its quest for Internet perfection, but the number of sites is growing continually. Figure 6.28 shows the home page for a Mexican service provider—which quite naturally is in Spanish.

FIGURE 6.28.

Mexican home page offers a look at Internet service in that country. The "other points of interest" link is well worth visiting. InternetWorks— `http://www.spin.com.mx/`.

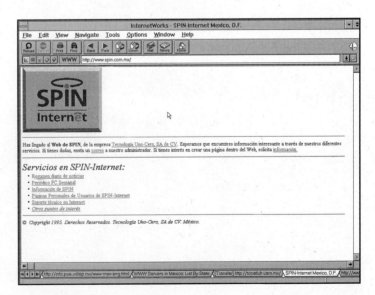

California

It's extremely well known by now that California (with a little help from Utah) is the place where the Internet got its start; so we'll visit the educational institution where the first Internet protocols were put into place. UCLA's Web site has much to offer, including a virtual tour of the campus. (See Figure 6.29.)

FIGURE 6.29.

*Home page for the University of California at Los Angeles, with opening imagemap. NCSA Mosaic for Windows—*http://www.ucla.edu/*.*

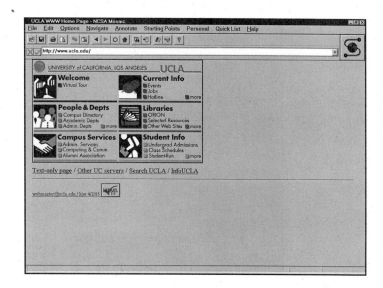

Canada

Canada wasn't far behind the United States in developing and sustaining an Internet presence, and they've been equally quick at a World Wide Web presence as well. There are information maps to the ten provinces and the two territories, while the federal government has implemented a number of programs to hasten Canada's leap into the whole superhighway arena. Many Quebec-based pages are in French, and every province has pages to promote their locations and their wares. Figure 6.30 shows the home page for the government of the Atlantic province of New Brunswick, with its contents designed as an information binder.

FIGURE 6.30.

The Government of New Brunswick home page. WinTapestry—http:// www.gov.nb.ca/.

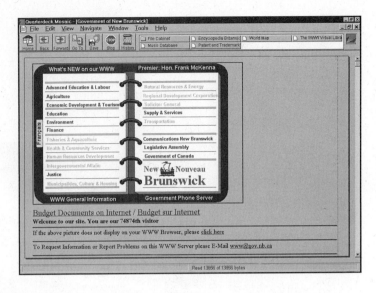

White House

Moving back down into the United States, we come to the site of the best-known dwelling in North America--the White House. From here you can send comments to the president or vice-president of the United States, and you can retrieve hordes of documents (many of which are from the current day). You can take a photo tour of the building, and you can even get a photo album of the first family doing real-life things. Nice, if a bit modem-unfriendly with the huge opening graphic. (See Figure 6.31.)

FIGURE 6.31.

The White House home page. WebExplorer for OS/2—http:// www.whitehouse.gov.

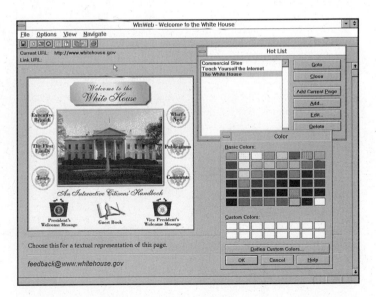

MIT

The world tour concludes with a visit to the Massachusetts Institute of Technology, better known as MIT. Why disembark here? Well, you started at CERN in Switzerland, the birthplace of the World Wide Web, so it makes sense to stop at MIT, where the Web and its founder, Tim Berners Lee, currently reside. MIT is working with CERN and the European INRIA to develop the Web project beyond its current stages, and currently much of the "official" research is being undertaken and/or supervised from this site. Figure 6.32 shows the page of information about the consortium, including links to the Laboratory for Computer Science at MIT.

FIGURE 6.32.

Information page for the W3 Consortium. WebExplorer for OS/2—http:// www.w3.org/hypertext/ WWW/Consortium/.

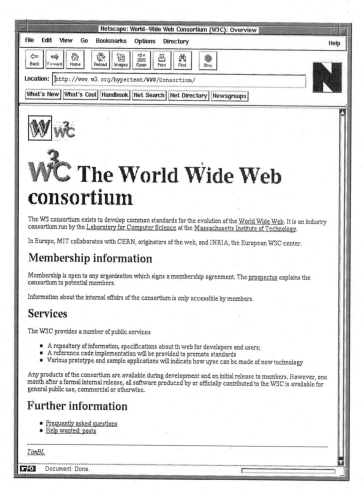

That's it. You started in Switzerland, moved around Europe, went south into Africa and east to Southeast Asia, and then went through China and Japan and across the waters to Hawai'i. From there, you traveled southeast to Chile, came northeast through Rio de Janeiro and then into Mexico, and moved through California and across the North American continent to New Brunswick. It was only a quick jaunt from there to the White House, and you ended where the Web project flourishes, at MIT in the heart of New England.

And you did it all without leaving the computer and the comfy chair you happen to be sitting in. That's the kind of power the World Wide Web offers, and as page designs, connections, and technologies improve further, a journey like this could easily become at least a fraction as good as the real thing. As it is, it's exciting, and it remains fascinating even when you think you're used to it. To connect to computers around the world on any given day of any given week, with very few restrictions and for some very real information, can never be anything less.

Welcome to the World Wide Web.

PART

II

Web Browsers and Connections

World Wide Web Browsers: An Introduction and Gallery

by
Neil Randall

In order to use the World Wide Web in any meaningful way, you need a piece of software called a *browser*. Actually, the technical name for such programs is a *client*, in keeping with the standard Internet paradigm of client and server (just as the Gopher program you regularly use is called a Gopher client because it allows you to use a Gopher server). However, over the brief course of the Web's history, the programs that allow access to its resources have come to be called browsers more often than clients, because browsing is precisely what most Web users seem to do.

Whether the Web was originally designed to be "browsed" rather than "engaged" is not the point, even though many groups do indeed engage it fully without becoming sidetracked in the process. The Web has become equated with browsing in much the same way that cable TV has become associated with channel-surfing.

The difference between browsing the Web and engaging the Web is important. As an analogy, consider what happens when you enter a library. If you're conducting serious research, you engage the library's resources—its books, its catalogs, its reference tools, its librarians—to help you locate the material you need and to deepen your understanding of the topic under research. But we've all entered libraries wherein, even if we intended to conduct intensive research, we ended up traversing the shelves, finding books with interesting titles, reading the first few paragraphs of a couple dozen of them, and never coming any closer to our stated research goal. Indeed, such an experience can prove more gratifying than the research would have been, even if the time could hardly be called productive. This last method is popularly known as browsing the shelves, and it remains one of the most enjoyable things that can happen to you among shelves of books.

Browsing the World Wide Web is much like browsing a library. The Web is filled with documents—some are highly detailed and extensively researched, some are slick and dazzlingly presented, some are merely signposts on the way to something more useful, and some are the products of amateurs who suddenly have a new way of telling the world about their hobbies. In other words, the Web is a library, and it offers all the variety, all the excitement, all the work, and all the inconsistency that a real library offers.

If you know where you're going on the Web, if you're part of a group that places material on the Web so that others can find it and use it, or if you use the Web to help you in your scholarly research, your business dealings, or your scientific collaboration, you don't browse the Web— you *engage* it.

But if you're like the new wave of Web users, who see an interesting hyperlink and immediately click, and then find another interesting link and click again, moving from document to document and computer to computer and possibly never returning to the document from which they started, you're not engaging the Web, you're *browsing* it. Neither activity is inherently right or wrong. Both are common, and designers of client software have come to realize this. (There is, of course, an increasingly significant middle ground.)

The most famous single client program in Internet history is *Mosaic*. Arguably, Mosaic has done more to bring public awareness of the Internet than all the e-mail flame wars and all the banned newsgroups in existence. Yet Mosaic is nothing more than one of many Web clients (browsers), and its popularity has now been eclipsed by the Netscape Navigator. But even Netscape is nothing more than yet another Web client; it is client software that feeds off the thousands of World Wide Web servers, and its only real function is to display the documents it finds in a manner befitting the Web's standards. It's the World Wide Web itself—not Mosaic or Netscape—that the mainstream magazines are actually writing about.

This is not to take anything away from these two famous browsers. This book, in fact, offers a long, detailed look at Mosaic and Netscape, giving them each an entire chapter (Chapters 10 and 11, respectively), while relegating all the other available browsers to Chapters 12 and 13 that are not only shorter but designed expressly to compare these other Web clients with their headline-making cousins. The reality is that most people who use the Web use Mosaic or Netscape, and many of those who don't probably use Lynx because they don't have graphical access. The fact that Mosaic and Netscape exist for the three most important platforms—X Window, the Apple Macintosh, and Microsoft Windows—is almost sufficient to explain their popularity.

But they're not the only clients in existence, not by a long shot. Nor was Mosaic the first, not even for a graphical environment, nor will Netscape be the last. Mosaic is nothing more than a World Wide Web browser that did the things that people wanted from a browser and that appeared at exactly the right time, neither too early for anyone to know what it was all about nor too late to take center stage when center stage was waiting to be taken. Netscape is nothing more than a browser that took Mosaic's best ideas and supplemented them with better modem usability and more appealing documents design possibilities.

If you want to understand the World Wide Web thoroughly, there are other client names to get to know. For UNIX itself, there's *Lynx* and the *CERN Line Browser* (or *www*). For X Window, find out about *Viola*, *MidasWWW*, *Chimera*, and *tkWWW*. For the Apple Macintosh, you'll want to know about *MacWeb* and *Samba*. For Microsoft Windows, your alternatives are *Cello*, *WinWeb*, and a growing number of commercially available Web clients, including *Air Mosaic*, *WebSurfer*, *InternetWorks*, and *WinTapestry*. There are browsers for VMS, NeXT, OS/2, and the Amiga as well. These are all Web browsers with their own personalities, their own feature sets, their own strengths, and their own weaknesses. They have the curse of being continually compared with Mosaic and Netscape, but the comparisons, in many cases, prove to be positive. Any one of them might be perfect for your needs.

This chapter of *The World Wide Web Unleashed* gives you a brief tour of a tiny portion of the Web, and it does so through many of the browsers that are covered in detail in Chapters 10-13. You'll see that each of the browsers looks different from the rest (although some are extremely similar), that each has its peculiar icon or button set and perhaps its own way of displaying hyperlinks and other document characteristics, and that each can be either inviting or off-putting, depending entirely on your preferences for what a browser/client is supposed to do.

As you look at them here, keep in mind the function of all clients: to retrieve and display documents from the Web servers around the world and to enable you to change the displays to suit your needs and to bookmark your activity so that you can return to Web locations of importance to you. And even if you're fully committed to one of the browsers before you start, or utterly repelled by another one and refuse to try it, you should give each browser a quick glance. They're not all here; only X Mosaic and Netscape for UNIX are covered for the X Window platform (although others are covered in Chapter 13), and Amiga Mosaic and several of the Windows commercial browsers don't appear here either. (See Chapters 13 and 12, respectively.) What *are* here are some of the best-known and most-representative browsers, including four for UNIX, four for Apple's Macintosh, and four for Microsoft Windows.

UNIX Browsers

The first Web clients appeared on the UNIX platform, so we'll start our tour with them. In fact, these clients weren't at all like the famous browsers of today. Because most computers were incapable of displaying graphics (graphically capable monitors and video cards were prohibitively expensive), the first Web clients were text-only. One of them, Lynx, survives today for users without graphical access, but despite its excellence it has been completely overshadowed by the likes of Mosaic and Netscape. Here we'll see both types of browsers, text-based and graphics-based, and it will be easy to see why the latter have become so popular.

CERN Line Browser

The first browser available for the World Wide Web was originally called *www*, but today it's known as *The CERN Line Browser*. Figure 7.1 shows essentially what the browser looks like, displaying the well-known subject catalog from the Virtual Library, a collection of hyperlinks to Web and Internet resources. Note that there are no graphics—nor will there ever be. This is a text-only client, and it was created purely to demonstrate that hyperlinks could work on a wide-area network system.

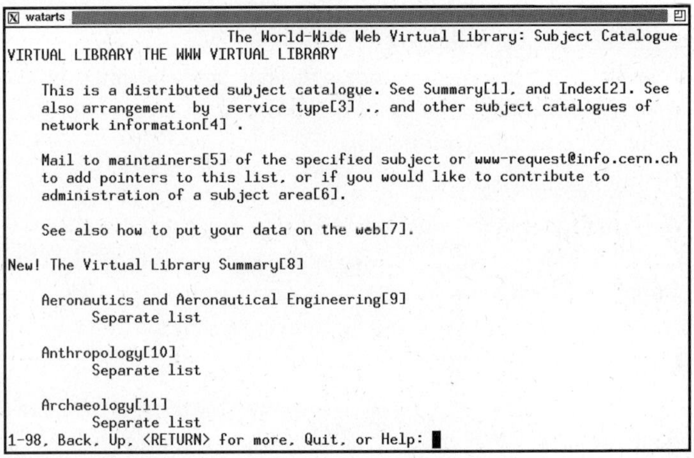

FIGURE 7.1.

The CERN Line Browser, displaying the Virtual Library.

```
X watarts                                                                    回
                                 The World-Wide Web Virtual Library: Subject Catalogue
VIRTUAL LIBRARY THE WWW VIRTUAL LIBRARY

      This is a distributed subject catalogue. See Summary[1]. and Index[2]. See
      also arrangement by service type[3] .. and other subject catalogues of
      network information[4] .

      Mail to maintainers[5] of the specified subject or www-request@info.cern.ch
      to add pointers to this list. or if you would like to contribute to
      administration of a subject area[6].

      See also how to put your data on the web[7].

New! The Virtual Library Summary[8]

      Aeronautics and Aeronautical Engineering[9]
            Separate list

      Anthropology[10]
            Separate list

      Archaeology[11]
            Separate list
1-98. Back. Up. <RETURN> for more. Quit. or Help: █
```

Note the parenthesized numbers appearing at various points in the document (11 in all on this screen). These are the hyperlinks. You don't click on them, however; your mouse won't work with this browser. Instead, you decide which one you want, and then you type that number and press Return. Off you go, across the Web to the linked document. Or you can press the Return key and go down several screens, finding the subject area you want. In Figure 7.2, one possible choice from the Virtual Library—Plasma Physics—offers a separate list of its own.

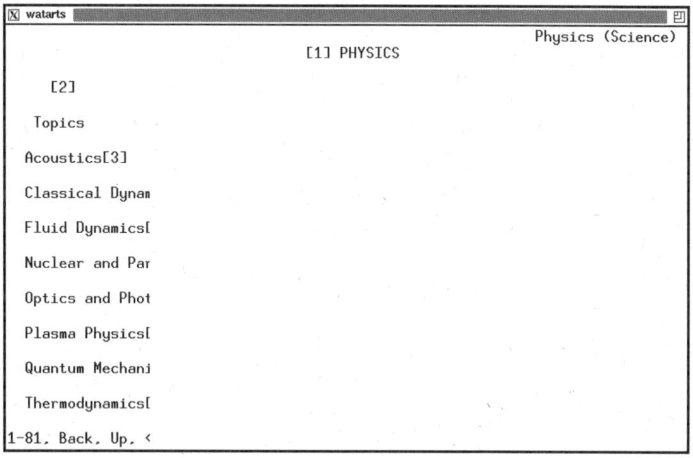

FIGURE 7.2.

The CERN Line Browser, displaying a physics-related list.

```
 X  watarts                                                              回
                                                            Physics (Science)
                                  [1] PHYSICS

      [2]

     Topics

   Acoustics[3]

   Classical Dynam

   Fluid Dynamics[

   Nuclear and Par

   Optics and Phot

   Plasma Physics[

   Quantum Mechani

   Thermodynamics[

1-81, Back, Up, <
```

Even though the Line Browser doesn't display graphics, it's hardly useless. In fact, it's preferable for some kinds of research because there's less chance of becoming sidetracked into areas you had no intention of visiting. Figure 7.3 shows the result of finding a scientific paper on the Web, something CERN users would routinely do.

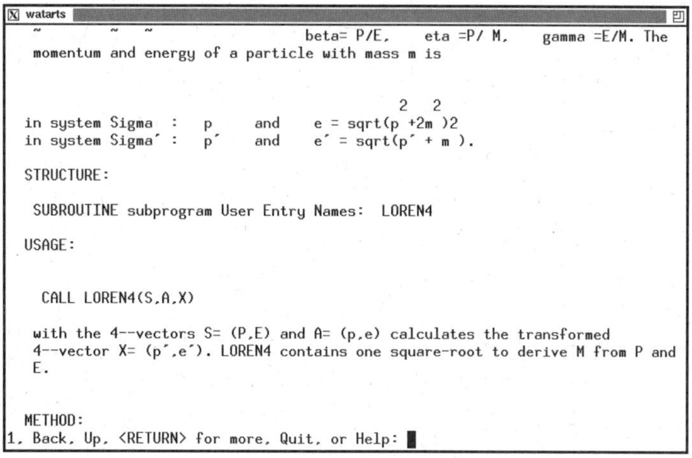

FIGURE 7.3.

The CERN Line Browser after loading a scientific paper stored on a Web server.

```
 X  watarts                                                              回
  ~         ~     ~                  beta= P/E,     eta =P/ M,    gamma =E/M. The
     momentum and energy of a particle with mass m is


                                             2   2
    in system Sigma  :   p     and    e = sqrt(p +2m )2
    in system Sigma' :   p'    and    e' = sqrt(p' + m ).

    STRUCTURE:

     SUBROUTINE subprogram User Entry Names:  LOREN4

    USAGE:


      CALL LOREN4(S,A,X)

    with the 4-vectors S= (P,E) and A= (p,e) calculates the transformed
    4-vector X= (p',e'). LOREN4 contains one square-root to derive M from P and
    E.


    METHOD:
1, Back, Up, <RETURN> for more, Quit, or Help: █
```

Anything text-based works just fine on this browser. Figure 7.4 shows the results of maneuvering through a movie database on the Web, displaying a series of links to the archives of one particular movie-oriented newsgroup on the Internet. It may not look pretty, but the browser serves its purpose nonetheless.

FIGURE 7.4.

The CERN Line Browser with links to newsgroup archives.

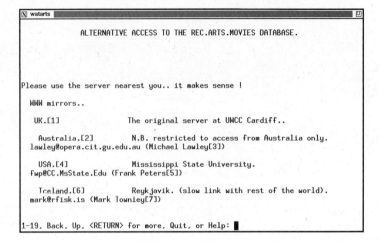

Please use the server nearest you.. it makes sense !

```
ALTERNATIVE ACCESS TO THE REC.ARTS.MOVIES DATABASE.



Please use the server nearest you.. it makes sense !

  WWW mirrors..

  UK.[1]                   The original server at UWCC Cardiff..

   Australia.[2]         N.B. restricted to access from Australia only.
lawley@opera.cit.gu.edu.au (Michael Lawley[3])

   USA.[4]              Mississippi State University.
fwp@CC.MsState.Edu (Frank Peters[5])

   Iceland.[6]            Reykjavik. (slow link with rest of the world).
mark@rfisk.is (Mark Townley[7])

1-19, Back, Up, <RETURN> for more, Quit, or Help:
```

Lynx

Like the Line Browser, Lynx is a text-only Web client, incapable of displaying graphics or other multimedia elements, although you can configure Lynx to display graphics with an external file viewer. What makes Lynx so interesting—and so usable—is that it makes full use of the VT-100 terminal standard to let you navigate the Web by using little more than the arrow keys, the space-bar, and the Return key. As Figure 7.5 shows, the hyperlinks in Lynx (here from the EINet Galaxy listing) appear as bold-faced items, and when you move your cursor across them, they take on a reverse-video appearance. Move to one, press the right-arrow key, and you're on your way to that particular destination.

Moving through the Web via Lynx, we come to list after list of selectable links. As Figure 7.6 demonstrates, Lynx uses asterisks in place of bullets, and a page such as this one is every bit as readable as the same page in a graphical browser. Here we've entered a list dealing with environmental issues, and we've decided to choose an item about "going green."

Choosing this item takes us to the list shown in Figure 7.7. This is primarily a text page, and Lynx displays it clearly and without difficulty. Unfortunately, it can't display the inline image beside item 12, noting it merely as [IMAGE] and making us wonder what that image might be. This is Lynx's biggest drawback: For displaying only text it's fine, but as soon as the image place-holders begin to appear, the client loses some of its appeal. This is an important point, as more and more Web pages become built around their graphic components.

FIGURE 7.5.

The Lynx client, showing reverse video on the currently selected hyperlink.

FIGURE 7.6.

Lynx with a full list of hyperlinks.

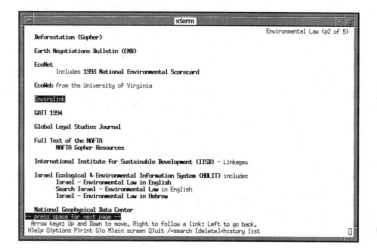

Figure 7.8 shows one area in which Lynx is graphically capable. Taken from a server in Norway, this page contains two downloadable graphics featuring the Oslo City Hall. Lynx displays the size of the graphics and lets you download them to your hard disk. In this way, it's little different from any of the graphical browsers, which also require an external viewer to see noninline graphics.

FIGURE 7.7.

Lynx displaying a text page, with one undisplayable image placeholder.

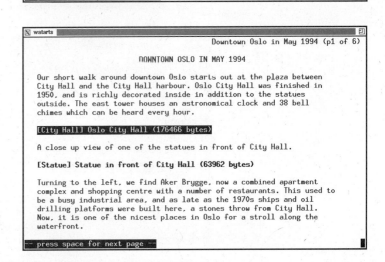

```
Ⓧ watarts                                                               囘
                                               Jalan Hijau: 40 Tips (p3 of 7)
9. Use cloth towels in the kitchen instead of paper towels. They can
be re-used after washing.

10. If your fridge is set too cold and many are 5% colder than they
need to be - then it's using 25% more electricity. Check it.

11. Always wait until you have a full load before using the washing
machine. This saves both water and energy.

ON THE ROAD

[IMAGE] 12. Cars are polluters. Limit the use of the car through
car-pooling. Take turns to fetch children to and from school, music or
sports or to drive to work.

13. Have one day a week or month - when you leave the car at home and
take public transport or walk when its a short journey - it's
healthier! If you must drive, then maintain your car well. A
well-tuned car with clean filters uses 9% less petrol and that means
less pollutants in the air.

14. Use unleaded petrol whenever possible & help keep the air clean.
-- press space for next page --
```

FIGURE 7.8.

Lynx displaying downloadable graphics files from a Norwegian site.

```
Ⓧ watarts                                                               囘
                                               Downtown Oslo in May 1994 (p1 of 6)
                        DOWNTOWN OSLO IN MAY 1994

Our short walk around downtown Oslo starts out at the plaza between
City Hall and the City Hall harbour. Oslo City Hall was finished in
1950, and is richly decorated inside in addition to the statues
outside. The east tower houses an astronomical clock and 38 bell
chimes which can be heard every hour.
 [City Hall] Oslo City Hall (176466 bytes)

A close up view of one of the statues in front of City Hall.

 [Statue] Statue in front of City Hall (63962 bytes)

Turning to the left, we find Aker Brygge, now a combined apartment
complex and shopping centre with a number of restaurants. This used to
be a busy industrial area, and as late as the 1970s ships and oil
drilling platforms were built here, a stones throw from City Hall.
Now, it is one of the nicest places in Oslo for a stroll along the
waterfront.

-- press space for next page --
```

X Mosaic

The next UNIX Web client examined in this chapter is NCSA Mosaic for the X Window System, better known simply as Mosaic, or, for our purposes, X Mosaic. Unlike both the CERN Line Browser and Lynx, X Mosaic is a graphical Web client—one that uses a graphical user interface (Motif in this case) to display Web documents in a formatted manner. Although X Mosaic is capable of showing inline graphics, even a page such as the EINet Galaxy listing in Figure 7.9

shows the effects of formatting. Headings are clear and bold-faced, while each hyperlink demonstrates an equally clear highlighting technique (underlining). Other elements of the program display attractively as well, from the sculpted navigation buttons at the bottom of the screen to the signature spinning globe icon at the top.

FIGURE 7.9.

X Mosaic screen showing a list of hyperlinks.

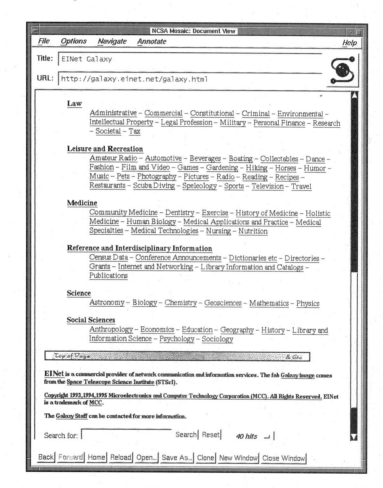

The screen illustrated in Figure 7.10 is an example of why most users prefer graphical browsers. Neither Lynx nor the Line Browser, whatever their other strengths, could display the inline image shown here as the graphic of Jupiter. Unfortunately, this book is not in color, or this page (and many of those that follow) would show this and the other graphical browsers to an even greater advantage.

FIGURE 7.10.

*X Mosaic screen displaying
an inline image.*

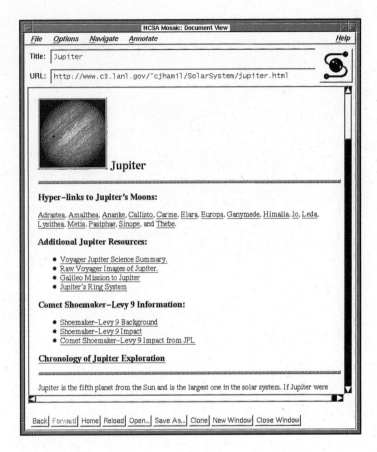

Increasingly, access to graphical browsers is being taken for granted by page designers. Such is the case with the Sense and Perception tutorials shown in Figure 7.11. The importance of graphics would become even more evident if you were to follow the links further. The small icon at the bottom of this page is admittedly gratuitous (another clear tendency in Web page design), but it too, has its design appeal.

FIGURE 7.11.

X Mosaic screen showing inline graphic and smaller icon.

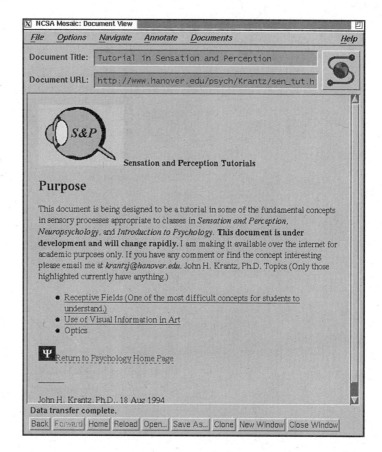

By the time you reach the screen pictured in Figure 7.12, you will see how extensively graphics are figuring in to Web page design, perhaps especially in the entertainment-oriented sites. This page is from Switzerland (as evidenced by the .ch in the domain name from the Document URL box), and it offers an entire collection of small inline images. These images, as the page outlines, are actually introductory shots to short videos, which can be displayed by X Mosaic if you've set up the necessary external players properly. (See Chapter 12, "More Browsers for Microsoft Windows.") Note, however, that these video files are *huge*. One is 23MB in size, and even that won't be a long video. (23MB, by the way, would take more than eight hours to download across a 14.4Kbps modem connection.)

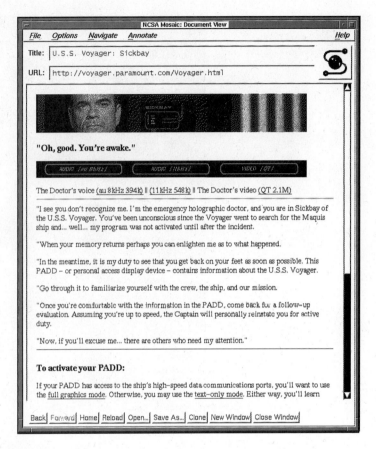

Netscape for UNIX

The last of the UNIX-based Web clients we'll look at is Netscape for UNIX. Netscape, like Mosaic, is available for all three platforms covered here, but unlike Mosaic this newer browser offers an almost completely consistent user interface across the platforms. As we move into the Netscape version for the other two platforms, you'll see how closely the three Netscapes match.

Figure 7.13 shows Netscape for UNIX displaying the Virtual Tourist page and its famous imagemap of the globe. At the top of the screen is the browser's large, easy-to-read toolbar, as well as a series of six "directory" buttons, immediately below the Location box, that lead you to pages controlled by the Netscape team. The toolbar and directory buttons appear identically on all three versions of the product.

FIGURE 7.13.

Netscape for UNIX displaying imagemap.

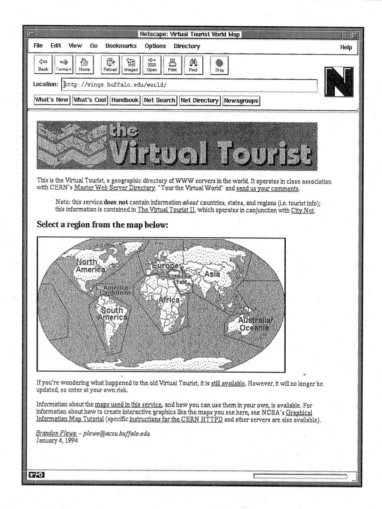

Figure 7.14 shows Netscape's capability to display even an unremarkable page quite professionally. It also shows a welcome feature, the status bar at the bottom of the page. On the bar is an icon of a broken key, which shows the page isn't "secure." (See Chapter 11 for a lengthier discussion about Netscape and security.) Beside the key, there is a truly useful item: a percentage bar showing the time remaining to download the document. After a few times seeing this, you'll wonder how you got along without it.

Finally, there is Netscape's most noted feature, its capability to display non-standard HTML tags (such as formatting code). The graphic at the top of Figure 7.15 is centered, and centering isn't part of the official HTML specifications (although it will be soon). Netscape has encouraged the designers of Web pages to spruce them up to the point that they're beginning to look like professional designs rather than thrown-together clumps of information, but not everyone on the Web has welcomed this feature. Many technical people feel that the standards should be adhered to, in the interest of ensuring that all browsers work with all pages. Still, Netscape tags continue to gain in popularity (even the latest Mosaic, 2.0 beta 4, offers centering and other details), so they're not likely to go away.

FIGURE 7.14.

Netscape for UNIX displaying document security and time bar at bottom.

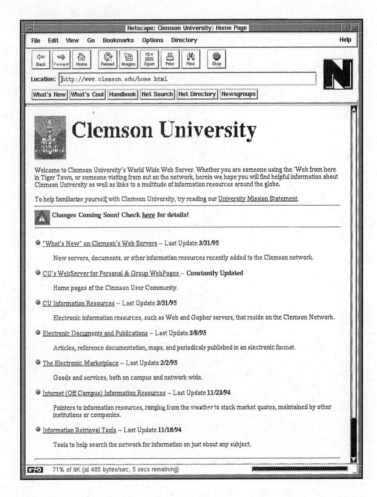

FIGURE 7.15.
Mastercard site in Netscape showing centered graphics.

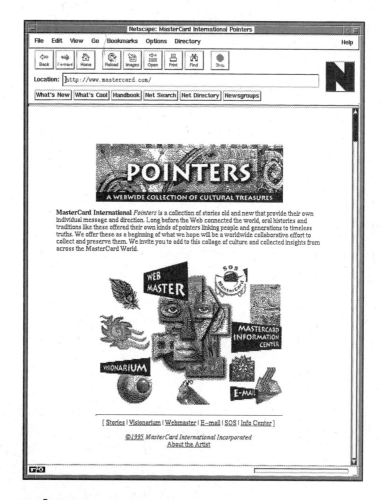

Apple Macintosh Browsers

Four browsers are available for the Macintosh environment, and all four are discussed here.

Samba

The first Macintosh browser is Samba, originally known as MacWWW, developed by the same people who brought us the CERN Line Browser. There are similarities between Samba and the Line Browser, which is to be expected given the fact that both were released shortly after the World Wide Web project began, and both were probably intended to demonstrate how clients might be constructed. Figure 7.16 shows a typical list in Samba.

FIGURE 7.16.

Samba screen showing Hong Kong listing.

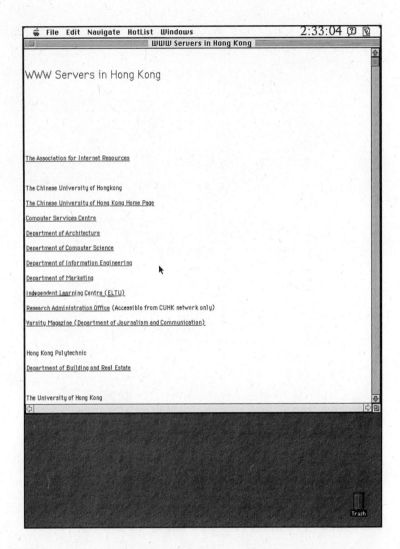

As you move from document to document in Samba, you open new windows. Figure 7.17 shows the result of a series of two accesses past the screen shown in Figure 7.16. (And there are other windows hidden behind these.) The result is a fairly messy screen and, in this case, an unattractive document appearance, as well.

FIGURE 7.17.

*Samba screen showing
multiple open windows.*

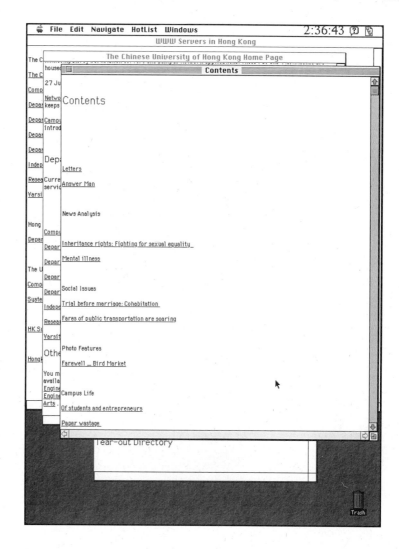

Taken to an extreme, the number of open documents, and their continually changing sizes, renders Samba in some ways unusable. Still, it's a Web browser, and extensive double-clicking enables you to reach the site displayed in Figure 7.18, a text screen that looks as clear as anything we've seen in this browser.

FIGURE 7.18.

*Samba screen showing
pure text document.*

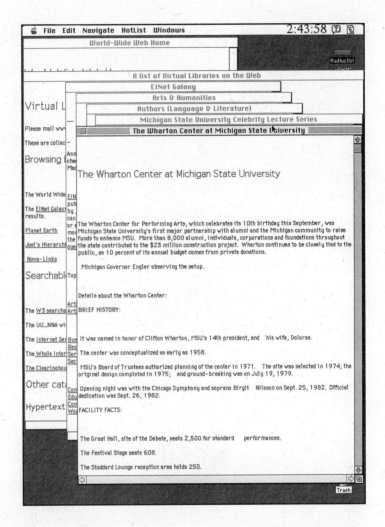

When all the windows are ordered properly, the Samba screen doesn't look all that bad, and it's easy to see where you've been. Figure 7.19 shows a screen with many open documents, and in fact resembles a graphical Gopher browser rather than a Web browser.

FIGURE 7.19.

Samba screen showing ordered multiple documents.

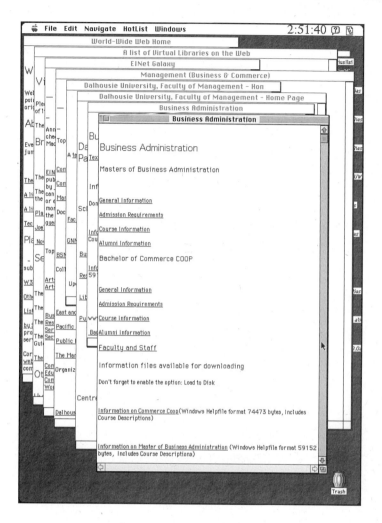

Mac Mosaic

The second Macintosh Web client to appear was NCSA Mosaic for the Apple Macintosh, better known as Mac Mosaic (or just Mosaic, if you're exclusively a Mac user). This is, of course, the Mac counterpart to X Mosaic, and in many ways the two browsers are alike. However, the appearance of the Mac Mosaic screen, as shown in Figure 7.20, is significantly different, reflecting the fact that different programming teams are in charge of the different versions. Note the icon bar at the top of Figure 7.20, which replaces X Mosaic's button bar (which was at the bottom). Other differences are evident as well.

FIGURE 7.20.

Mac Mosaic screen showing icon bar and history window.

If this book were in color, the Oregon map displayed in Figure 7.21 would be nothing short of eye-catching. As it stands, it's a good demonstration of the kind of "clickable" map finding its way into an increasing number of Web documents. (More such maps appear later in this chapter.) By clicking one of the cities displayed in outline font, you are taken to a document elsewhere on the Web that contains information about that city. Unfortunately, a graphic such as this takes a long time to transfer if you have a slow Internet connection.

FIGURE 7.21.

Mac Mosaic screen with an example of a "clickable" map.

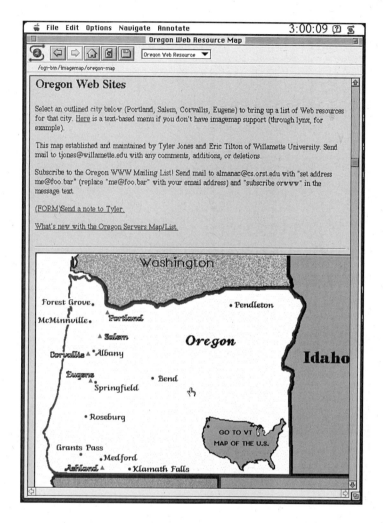

More and more, graphic images are dominating Web documents. The page shown in Figure 7.22 contains not only a striking opening graphic, but creative iconic use as well in the display at the bottom. To maneuver to any of these documents, you need only click the appropriate icon. This is highly attractive, but possibly unnecessary, and almost unusable by modem connections.

FIGURE 7.22.

Mac Mosaic screen showing extensive use of inline graphics.

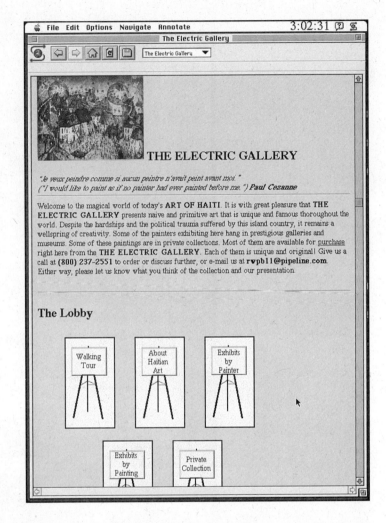

Figure 7.23 is simply a beautifully designed document. By clicking the musical notes icon you can hear a tune (as long as your Mac and your Mac Mosaic program are configured to play sound files), and each item has its own attractive icon. Expect more such pages as high-speed access increases in the near future.

FIGURE 7.23.

Mac Mosaic screen showing the effects of strong page design.

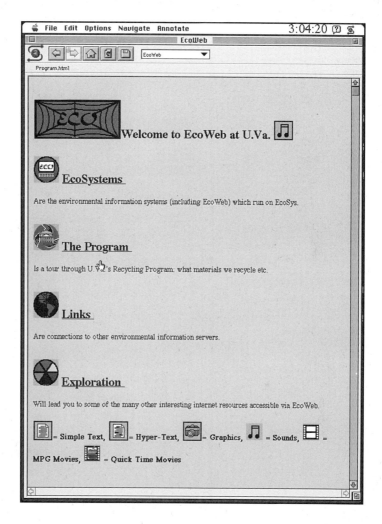

MacWeb

Released soon after Mac Mosaic, MacWeb made some very significant early strides but, upon the release of Netscape, it began to fall a bit behind in popularity. Figure 7.24 shows that MacWeb is very similar to Mac Mosaic in appearance and is fully capable of displaying whatever graphics the Web designers choose to throw at it. The page is from Cornell University's Kids on Campus selection, one of the most creative uses of the clickable graphic on the Internet. As you'd expect, however, it's hopeless for modem users.

FIGURE 7.24.

MacWeb screen showing fascinating graphic design.

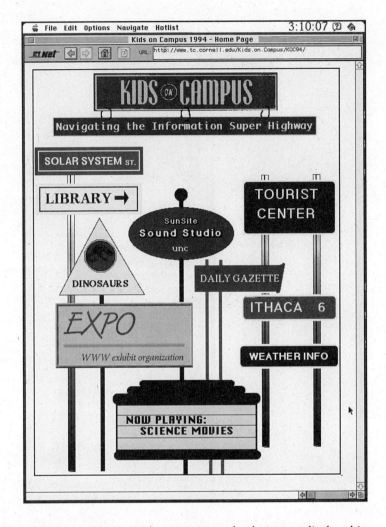

By following a few links from the signs in Figure 7.24, you arrive at the document displayed in Figure 7.25. Each colorful icon leads to a related video, which MacWeb can show if it is configured to use the appropriate external viewer. Note, by the way, how much screen "real estate" MacWeb gives to the actual document; considerably more than Mac Mosaic, in fact.

FIGURE 7.25.

MacWeb screen displaying links to playable videos.

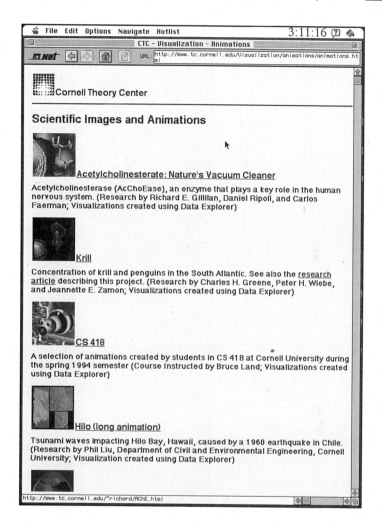

Changing the background color of MacWeb is extremely easy, and in Figure 7.26 it is changed to gray. The page itself is from an excellent collection called The Jerusalem Mosaic; the domain name in the URL box shows the il Israel address, meaning that we've transferred the file from Israel itself. There's an increasing number of such informative documents finding their way onto the Web.

FIGURE 7.26.

MacWeb screen showing a document from Israel.

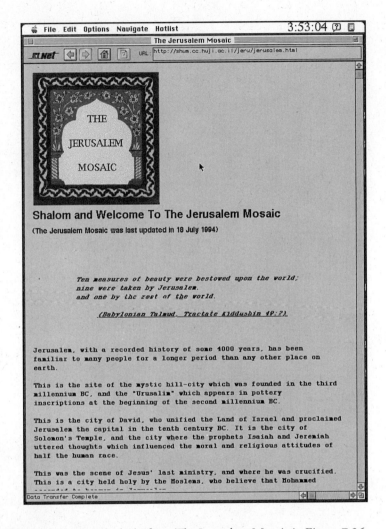

Figure 7.27 shows a document further along the links from The Jerusalem Mosaic in Figure 7.26. Here you can see MacWeb's strong display of inline graphics, both in the picture and the icons at the bottom. Bookmarking the site is possible by simply selecting the Hotlist menu at the top of the screen.

FIGURE 7.27.

MacWeb screen showing document formatting.

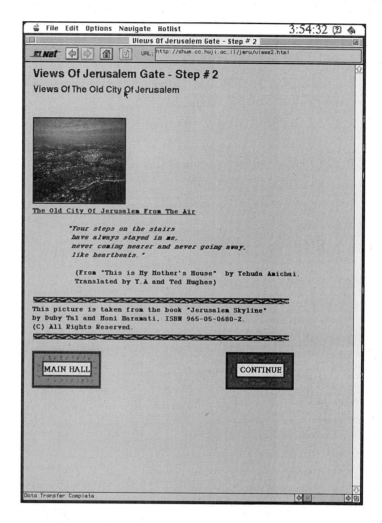

Netscape for Macintosh

The most recent Macintosh Web client, and quickly becoming the most popular, is Netscape for Macintosh. As Figure 7.28 demonstrates, there's not much difference between the UNIX and the Macintosh versions of this browser, except of course the difference in appearance between the two platforms.

FIGURE 7.28.

Netscape for Macintosh screen, showing identical user interface to UNIX version.

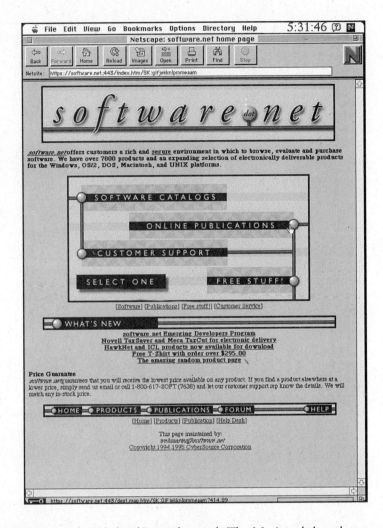

Netscape's popularity on the Macintosh isn't hard to understand. The Macintosh has always attracted artists or would-be artists, and Netscape's non-standard HTML tags allow a greater degree of Web artistry than do other programs. Figure 7.29 shows a bookmark list in front, but the Web page behind demonstrates the centering and backgrounds feature Netscape offers. In this case, it's a bit much, perhaps, but the graphical possibilities are endless.

FIGURE 7.29.

Netscape's centering and colored backgrounds option.

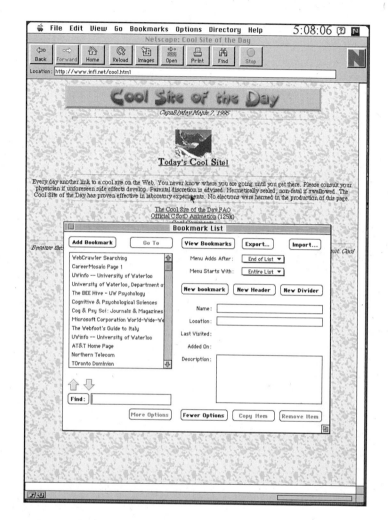

Microsoft Windows Browsers

Although World Wide Web clients for Microsoft Windows have been the last to appear, they've gone a long way towards catching up to the rest. Four are currently available for the price of a download, and two of these are of primary quality. Furthermore, commercial browsers are now making their appearance as Internet providers begin to tap the vast Windows-user base.

Cello

We'll start our Windows browser tour with Cello, the favorite of quite a few Windows users, which is available from Cornell University's Legal Information Institute. Cello easily handles graphical maps, and that it offers substantial screen space to its documents. This page is The Virtual Tourist, which features a clickable map of the world (and, through the insets, regions as well).

Cello's extraordinary clarity of image is apparent. Of course, it helps that the map itself is attractive and crisply designed, but the browser has to be able to display it, and do so quickly. Cello does this, and if this book were in color, you'd notice even more about the browser's capabilities.

If Cello were capable of displaying Japanese characters (it's not, but neither is Windows Mosaic, described forthwith), we could get even more information. As it stands, this page is clear and informative, and Cello can be configured with an external viewer to play the long sound file displayed near the top. Note also the attractive bullets that come as a Cello default.

FIGURE 7.30.

Cello screen demonstrating default sculpted bullets.

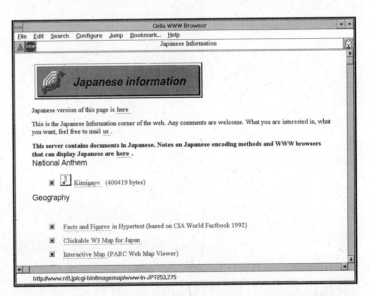

We return to a map display for Figure 7.31, not so much to demonstrate a Cello feature as an intriguing page design. From Xerox PARC (from which comes the graphical user interface concept itself) is a map that, when clicked, zooms in to reveal a closer display. Notice the rivers and political boundaries shown in the map, again rendered crisply by the browser.

FIGURE 7.31.

Cello screen showing innovative map design from Xerox PARC.

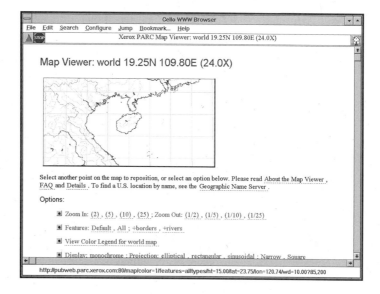

Windows Mosaic

With Figure 7.32, we move to NCSA Mosaic for the Microsoft Windows system, known for our purposes as Windows Mosaic. This program is in high demand among Windows users, although it consumes considerably greater system resources than Cello and, in its latest version, requires the large and not easily available Windows 32-bit extensions in order to run. Still, its popularity is established, and it remains to be seen if the commercial clients will cut into that popularity.

Figure 7.32 shows the City of San Carlos home page in Windows Mosaic. (This illustrates how the latest version of the browser offers substantially more screen real estate than before.) More and more cities and towns are developing Web sites as a means of promoting themselves to the outside world.

Countries, too, are making themselves known on the Web. Figure 7.33 displays the Singapore government's clear, attractive, and well-organized "online guide," which Windows Mosaic renders well. As you travel the Web, you'll realize that document writers tend to test their designs exclusively on Mosaic, since some pages display better on it than on Cello or WinWeb.

An appealing logo graces the screen in Figure 7.34, and the page is one of many on the Web that offers extensive reading. No specific Windows Mosaic features are shown here, but note that the URL display shows the address only, while the document title appears on the title bar at the top (which is a peculiar feature of Microsoft Windows). Only in the most recent version of Windows Mosaic does the document title *not* appear with the URL address.

FIGURE 7.32.

Windows Mosaic screen showing a city's home page.

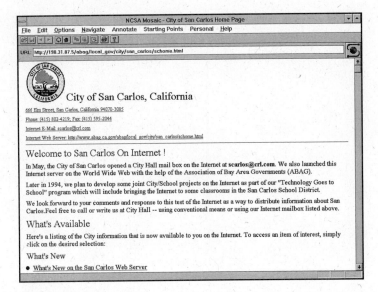

FIGURE 7.33.

Windows Mosaic, showing Singapore Online Guide.

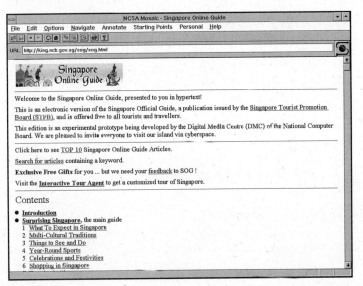

Figure 7.35 demonstrates another extremely creative and appealing page design. This one comes to us from the U.K., and everything from its logo to its individual icons is innovative. Windows Mosaic displays it very well indeed. In the menu line of Windows Mosaic is a Personal menu that is entirely customizable from the program's menu editor utility.

FIGURE 7.34.

Windows Mosaic screen showing large inline graphic logo.

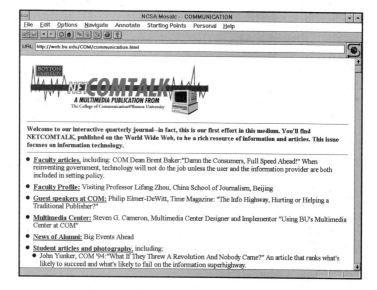

FIGURE 7.35.

Windows Mosaic, showing superb Cyber-Town home page.

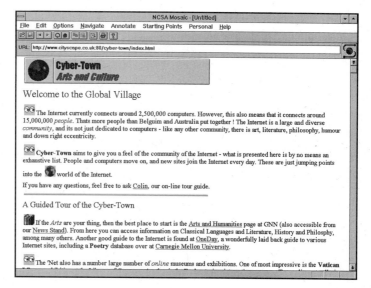

WinWeb

The final browser in our tour is WinWeb, the Windows counterpart to MacWeb. Unfortunately, this client shows many of the typical signs of a first release. As Figure 7.36 illustrates, the browser displays text pages clearly, but the nonunderlined links show up poorly on monochrome displays (which, admittedly, are uncommon among Windows users).

FIGURE 7.36.

WinWeb screen showing small bullets and good alignment.

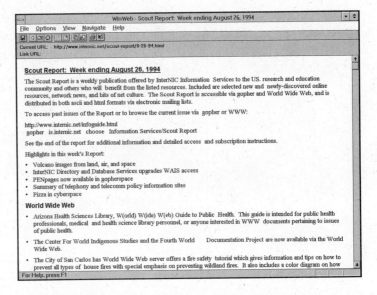

Figure 7.37 demonstrates that WinWeb is fully capable of displaying large graphic images. Unfortunately, in its first version it doesn't recognize that the two bold-faced Information lines are actually links, something that renders several Web pages useless. The icon bar is much like Windows Mosaic's, but expected menu items are missing. The page, incidentally, promises some interesting material in the future.

FIGURE 7.37.

WinWeb screen showing unrecognized hyperlinks.

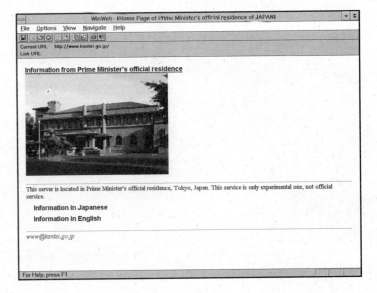

Another demonstration of WinWeb's graphic capability appears in Figure 7.38. Of more interest, however, is the page itself, which is part of a series of pages devoted to the city of Des Moines, Iowa. The graphics here are small versions of huge files that you can download, which together make up a full map of the city. Of course, you could buy one for about three bucks when you get there, but....

FIGURE 7.38.

WinWeb screen with large downloadable graphics.

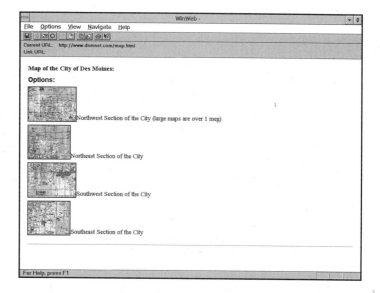

We close our tour of Web clients appropriately, by showing the kind of page that will almost certainly become increasingly visited as the average age of Web users continues to fall. *Vibe Magazine*, perfectly displayed by WinWeb as shown in Figure 7.39, is one of many pages designed to appeal to the twenty-somethings. There's concern among the older Webbers that this kind of page (and the even more elaborately graphic pages available elsewhere) are simply using up valuable bandwidth. But this page demonstrates that part of the Web's future—a large part, perhaps—lies in entertainment rather than research, and it will be increasingly important for Web client software to be able to handle the challenge.

Besides, I wanted to show the only guy in the world with a smiley for a name.

FIGURE 7.39.

Vibe Magazine displayed on WinWeb.

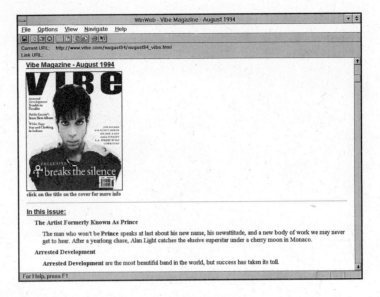

Netscape for Windows

Netscape for Windows looks much like Netscape for X and Netscape for Mac, and once again it's quickly overtaking all other browsers in both hype and popularity. Figure 7.40 shows the non-standard Netscape tags in full gear, with differently aligned graphics on the page, along with a colored and patterned background. It's this kind of design that is making people turn to Netscape as the browser for which they develop their pages.

FIGURE 7.40.

Netscape Communications' Galleria, showing alignment and background tags.

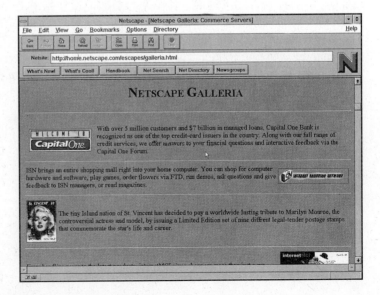

Another popular feature of Netscape is its capability to display newsgroups and to let you read and post news messages. Figure 7.41 shows the hierarchically arranged messages in one newsgroup; selecting any of them will bring up the screen for reading and replying. The imagemap buttons above the newsgroup title let you post to the newsgroups and subscribe and unsubscribe—to the extent that many people won't need any other news reader.

FIGURE 7.41.

Netscape's newsgroup feature, with control buttons at top of page.

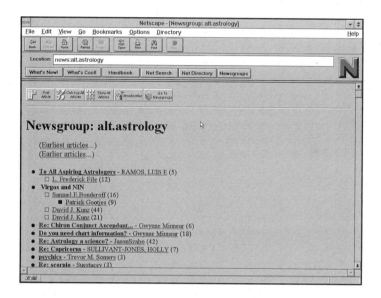

Finally, Netscape's tags appear again in the Cool Site of the Day page, shown in Figure 7.42. Here we see centered graphics, but we also see another non-standard, but popular, Netscape tag: thick rules. The horizontal lines are thicker and shorter than usual, and Netscape allows you to control both.

FIGURE 7.42.

Netscape for Windows showing horizontal rule tags.

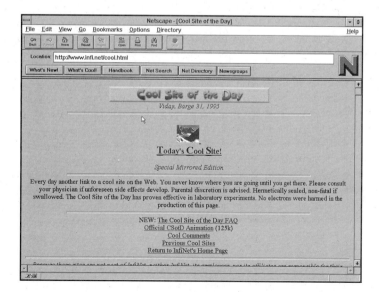

Summary

The browsers covered in this chapter aren't the only ones available; they're not even the only browsers covered in this book. Still, they give a good indication of the quality and variety of Web clients you can download from the Internet at no cost—which is probably the greatest deal in computing history. And since they're so cheap, why bother using just one? Download them all, install them, and give 'em a whirl. If you're like many people, you'll end up flitting from one to the other depending on what you want to do that particular day. And that's hardly a bad thing.

Getting Connected: Accessing the Web

8

by
Neil Randall

To connect to the World Wide Web, you need an Internet account. That's probably the most obvious thing this book will say, but it needs to be said anyway. The Web is on the Net, and although you could structure a purely local one, or even a company-wide one, it wouldn't be a *world-wide* web. And that's the whole point.

So how do you get an Internet account? There are several ways, many of which are covered briefly in this chapter. (For a much more thorough account, pick up a companion book, *The Internet Unleashed 1996*, from Sams.net Publishing.) See also Appendix A "Web Reference," which lists Internet service providers in a variety of regions.

Your main choice, however, lies in accessing the Web from within the local area network (LAN) in your organization, or through an Internet service provider via modem. A third choice, only beginning to appear, is to use a commercial online service—CompuServe, America OnLine, Prodigy, and so on—as a gateway into the Net (in fact, Prodigy and CompuServe already offer full graphical access to the Web), or you can use a local bulletin board system (BBS), many of which now offer good Internet access. Other higher-priced choices are available as well, but you aren't likely to establish access through these on your own. Access through large organizations generally falls into this category.

The basic principle of LAN access is this: Your computer is part of an organization's network, in which all computers are wired to each other through a series of hubs and routers and other networking hardware and software. That LAN, in turn, is connected to the Internet, usually through a high-speed line that links either directly to the Internet backbone or, more commonly, to an Internet service provider, which in turn links to a regional hub, and thence to the backbone. Certainly, that's a simplified version of the internetworking chain of being, but for our purposes here, it's workable. (This is a *Web* book, remember, not a networking book.)

Connecting through a modem offers two main varieties of connection. The first is to dial into your organization's LAN (called a *dial-in* or *remote* session), and then, through the LAN, into the Net itself. The second, which is becoming increasingly popular and important, is to use a connection to an Internet service provider, which is in turn connected to the Internet.

Actually, the two varieties aren't all that different; in both cases you're moving through one computer—or set of computers—to get to the Internet, but in the latter instance you don't need a LAN account in the first place. In other words, going directly to a service provider makes Internet access possible for anyone with a computer and a modem, not just those who are already hooked up to a network in their office.

Using one of the commercial services (or a local BBS) for Internet access is a strong possibility, especially if you already have an account with one of these services. In general, however, full Net access is more readily available, and often cheaper, through a commercial Internet provider. Still, the commercial providers are working extremely hard to establish full Internet access and offer that access to their subscribers, as it has become apparent to them that their subscribers will settle for nothing less. Being on *a* network isn't nearly as important, it would seem, as being on *the* network.

NOTE

Even more in its infancy is Internet service through your cable TV (CATV) provider. This is an extremely promising category of service because it has the potential to offer high-speed access to any home that has access to cable, and that means millions of potential users. The CATV providers also promise super high-speed access for organizations and corporations. Still, this is a beginning service offering, so again this chapter deals only briefly with it.

Other access possibilities beckon, such as the long-awaited and now-appearing ISDN (available in an increasing number of regions at a variety of prices), and the full fiber-optic networks beyond. But this book is concerned with what's here now, so neither CATV nor ISDN will be treated. For the future of the Web, however, these technologies will be crucial. It's impossible to exaggerate the importance of ultra high-speed access to the needs of true multimedia environments.

Access Through a Local Area Network

If you have a computer at work, and you're part of a local area network (usually this means you can send e-mail and perhaps exchange files with your coworkers), you might already have Internet access. Check with your systems or computer services group (often called IS or MIS), and ask them if this is the case.

Increasingly it is, and you might as well take advantage of it. Of course, you'll likely need to go through various channels to establish Net access, but maybe not. Maybe you've been connected all along, and you just haven't known it. If you find out that your organization isn't on the Net, and you're convinced they should be, then make the inquiries you can, request that it be looked into (there are usually standard internal procedures for this sort of request), and do your best to interest others. A good grasp of office politics might be invaluable here.

The point is that you can't establish LAN access to the Net by yourself, unless of course you have absolute authority in systems issues. (This book assumes that you don't.) Internet access for an organization is expensive, and approval for it must go through the same channels as approval for any other significant expenditure. Chances are, however, that even if your firm isn't on the Net, it's researching the possibilities, and if it's possible you might want to get involved in this process.

If your organization is on the Net but your department is not, and you know very well that your supervisor won't even consider it unless there's a very good reason (they're touchy this way), consider putting together a presentation and even a demonstration of how the Net will help you and your fellow department members. There are a couple ways of doing this.

The easiest is to use *The World Wide Web Unleashed 1996* and its companion book *The Internet Unleashed 1996* as a basis for the presentation, pointing out how important the Net and the Web have become to business and research activities of all kinds. (Doing so would also demonstrate your commitment to this book and the series in which it resides, thereby making its authors incredibly proud.)

Of course, there is a large array of Internet books on the shelves of your local bookstore, and many of these will help you as well. Among the most notable are Mary Cronin's *Doing Business on the Internet* and *The Internet Business Guide* by Rosalind Resnick and Dave Taylor, which offer case studies and advice for Internet business activity. And there are business and research chapters in many of the other Internet books as well. Similarly, my own *Teach Yourself the Internet: Around the World in 21 Days* offers two chapters on business-related activity, and points to a number of Net sites dealing with research ventures as well. Another suggestion is to pick up copies of magazines that cover the Internet. *Internet World* is the oldest of these, but *Online Access* has developed a primarily Internet slant, *NetGuide* offers a slick and wide-ranging perspective, *NetSmart* caters to the professional user, *The Net* looks to novice users, and the extremely trendy and often superb *Wired* demonstrates the Net's role in a larger cyberspace. Business magazines themselves are offering business-oriented glimpses of the Net and the Web, with *Business Week*, *Inc* (and the offshoot *Inc Technology*), *Fortune,* and others picking up the theme. The major computer magazines have also been offering extensive features about the Net; among them are *PC Magazine, PC/Computing, MacWorld, PC World, Windows Sources, Byte, Windows, MacUser, Open Systems,* and so on.

The other way, if you're really serious about all this, is to take the initiative and get yourself an Internet account from a local service provider. Once it's established, you can use the Net for a few weeks, bookmarking and taking screen shots of the most useful sites and services for your organization. Then, put together a formal presentation using the screen shots (converting them to slides, for instance), your computer and modem, and your account. If it works, and your supervisors listen, you might even be able to recoup your expenses for all of this. Sure it's work, but if you want to be on the Web you might have to expend a fair bit of effort to get there. Not all companies see the benefits of the Internet itself, let alone the Web portion of it.

And remember, getting on the Net doesn't immediately imply Web access. Many firms have e-mail access to the Net, and sometimes Gopher and (restricted) newsgroup access, but Web access requires different software and different goals. When putting together your argument, concentrate on the Web's benefits; if you can't convince yourself, you're certainly not going to convince anyone else. Get into your browser, select your sites carefully, and then show them to the people who can sign the forms.

Still another consideration comes with getting graphical Web access rather than just terminal-based Web access. If you're enchanted by the multimedia capabilities of Netscape, Mosaic, Cello, or WinWeb/MacWeb, and that's what you want to establish through your LAN, you won't be satisfied with even the best text-mode browser, Lynx. (See Chapter 9, "Non-Graphical Web Clients.") It's very capable, but it isn't nearly as pretty. Keep this in mind as you prepare your presentation and demonstration of the Net.

Access Through a Modem

If you're on the Net through a LAN at work, often that LAN is accessible via remote dial-in through a modem. If so, it's possible, as long as both your computer and the LAN have the right software installed, to link to the LAN via modem and access the Internet in that way. This set of connections is far beyond the scope of this book; but again, contact your systems group and find out if this kind of access is in place and, if not, how you might get it established.

Often, such a connection will make your computer a terminal on that network, and you'll be restricted to a text-based "shell" account that lets you send and receive e-mail, exchange files, and (sometimes) read newsgroups. A well-stocked computer will also provide text-based Gopher programs and other Internet tools, and you might also have access to Lynx or another nongraphically based Web browser. Many colleges and universities offer this type of dial-in shell access.

The other kind of modem access is becoming more and more popular as local Internet service providers increase in number. With this method, anyone with a computer and a modem can contact the service provider, establish an account for (usually) a monthly fee, and connect to the Internet whenever and for as long as it suits you. If you've ever had an account on CompuServe, Prodigy, America OnLine, or any other commercial online service, you'll recognize this model.

The difference is that the commercial services are based around one proprietary computer, whereas an Internet account lets you wander around the world's computers. Even this distinction is lessening somewhat, however, as the commercial services scramble to connect their own members to the Net. Leading the way are Delphi, Prodigy, and America OnLine, but the others will certainly follow suit. In the mid-nineties, the Net is hot stuff.

As you might expect, different Internet providers offer different pricing structures and different types of connections. Increasingly, however, one particular model seems to be gaining dominance. Here, you pay a setup fee to establish an account, and then you pay a flat monthly rate for the type of access you need. Typically, this monthly fee gives you a certain number of access hours, and if you're logged on for more than this number you pay a (relatively) low hourly rate.

Because you want to access the World Wide Web and not just e-mail and newsgroup services, be sure to ask your provider what category of service you'll need. Almost always, this will mean SLIP or PPP dial-in service, or a higher-speed service that doesn't involve modems at all. These higher-speed services usually mean dedicated lines, and are priced for organizations rather than individuals. Normally, a dedicated line will be connected to the organization's internal LAN, in which case see "Access Through a Local Area Network" in the preceding section.

> **NOTE**
>
> One type of high-speed service is in place now and will almost certainly plummet in price in the near future. This is ISDN, the long-awaited digital service from telephone companies, and several companies now offer it. At least one U.S. telephone company, Pacific Bell, promised ISDN services to any Californian who wants it by early 1995. The problem with ISDN is, first, that it's only sporadically available and, second, that it's difficult to set up. Wait until prices in your area drop below $50 a month (already in place in some areas), and until your phone company offers a complete connectivity package, including add-on board for your PC or Mac. These, too, are coming.

SLIP and PPP are the most common protocols for dial-in accounts that support graphical interfaces. *SLIP* (Serial Line Internet Protocol) is extremely popular for PC users, although it's certainly available for anyone with a UNIX station in their home and for Macintosh users as well. More common for Mac users is *PPP* (Point to Point Protocol), a newer protocol that offers more security and a more stable connection through a technique known as handshaking. PPP is becoming the protocol of choice for Microsoft Windows-based PCs as well.

PPP is becoming the *de facto* standard even though new versions of SLIP are appearing (particularly CSLIP). The reason? First, it's more secure, and arguably more stable. Second, Windows 95 ships with Microsoft PPP and a TCP/IP stack, and for better or for worse—and many would say worse—where Windows goes, so goes the PC user and PC standards. Even the standard shareware TCP/IP package, Trumpet WinSock, began supporting PPP in 1994.

Most services offer both SLIP and PPP as part of the basic package. This is important, because if you want to use a modem to use graphical applications such as Mosaic or Cello, you need such a connection. In effect, both SLIP and PPP make it possible for your computer to be an independent "node" on the Internet (see "Indirect Versus Direct Access," later in the chapter), a requirement for using these packages. In a way I keep thinking must sound extremely condescending (but nobody's ever complained), I like to explain to people that SLIP access lets you "slip through" your service provider and directly into the Net. It isn't technically true, but it sure beats trying to explain what Serial Line Internet Protocol means. So far, only one listener has audibly groaned.

Not only do most providers offer SLIP or PPP connections, they also provide you with the software you need to give your own computer SLIP or PPP capabilities. The thing to keep in mind is that your machine and the one you're dialing into must *both* be SLIP- or PPP-enabled. You can buy or download all the SLIP/PPP software in the world, but you still won't be able to access the Net through them if the machine you're dialing into can't handle those protocols. That's why it's important to check what the providers have to offer, and how easy they make it for you to enable your own computer to make these kinds of connections.

In many cases, and increasingly, the service providers don't just provide SLIP/PPP, they also provide a full suite of graphically oriented Internet programs. Common among them are Eudora, the well-known e-mail package for both Windows and Macintosh; both a Gopher program and a newsgroup package with a graphical interface; an FTP package; and—almost inevitably—the version of Mosaic or Netscape your computer needs.

If these aren't provided, as soon as you have your connection you can download them to your machine using your FTP program, or you can get them on disk from a friend, from a computer store (try the shareware and freeware section), from a users' group, or inside any number of current Internet books available in your bookstore. With your SLIP/PPP connection in place, you can install these packages and, sometimes with a bit more configuration, run them without trouble.

In some cases, and increasingly, the service provider will include a suite of Internet tools with your account subscription. For example, one such service—Netcom—makes available a well-designed package called NetCruiser, which includes all of the expected tools plus a World Wide Web browser that combines the functionality and appearance of both Mosaic and Cello. Another service, New York's The Pipeline, offers a full suite of tools, including its own (very capable) Web browser, as a front end to its service. Other providers will inevitably follow suit, but make sure that the access you receive lets you download and use other software as well. In other words, before you sign on the dotted line, be certain that your service provider isn't offering some kind of proprietary service, because that's not what the Internet is all about. If you have no interest in being bothered with SLIP or PPP connections, however, proprietary service will quite likely suit you just fine. This, in fact, is what Netcom and Prodigy offer now.

Recognizing the difficulty in getting connected to the Internet, plus the desire for many people to have World Wide Web access specifically, at least one software vendor has shipped a package designed solely to give new users WWW access. Spry, Incorporated, producers of the Air series of LAN-based applications as well as the well-known Internet in a Box, offer an inexpensive solution called Mosaic in a Box. This package, which retailed for $49.95 when this was written, connects users to the World Wide Web through the CompuServe network. Spry's software is at the center of CompuServe's Internet division, which is why this network is available, and Air Mosaic gives you an Internet account through that network. Using the Web this way isn't exactly cheap, though. You pay $9.95 per month for three free hours, then an additional $2.95 per hour after that. Still, it's an easy and worthwhile way to get started.

Access Through a Commercial Online Service or BBS

Bulletin Board Systems (BBSs) are computers into which users with accounts can dial through a modem. They've been around almost as long as modems have existed, as enterprising or just plain energetic computer owners have long wanted to make it easy for other computer owners to communicate with each other and share programs and other files. Local BBSs are typically run by one person (called a *sysop*, or system operator), and the BBS stays in existence only as long as the sysop's energy lasts. Some BBSs have continued for years; others disappear after a few months. To find the phone numbers for local BBSs, check in your newspaper's want ads or at your local computer store.

Larger BBSs are run by several people, and are often either nonprofit or low-profit ventures. Some of them now offer Internet connections, with an increasingly impressive range of features. Again, check with your local computer store for numbers about accessing to these BBSs, or pick up the computer newspapers you'll often find free or cheap at these stores. Try them out, but in many cases be prepared to give them your credit card number. (This is quite safe usually, but many people are hesitant.)

The largest BBSs of all are the commercial online services. The granddaddy of these is CompuServe, but many others have entered the fray. Some of the best-known, in alphabetical rather than chronological order, are America OnLine, BIX, Delphi, GEnie, and Prodigy. All of these services are in the process of making Internet access available to their customers on a variety of levels, but the process is proving to be long and difficult. Delphi and BIX offer the most complete service so far, and America OnLine is the most user friendly.

At the December 1994 Internet World trade show and convention in Washington, D.C., all of the major commercial services were trumpeting full Internet access at some point in 1995. What's appealing about the idea of accessing the Net through CompuServe, America OnLine, Prodigy, and the like is that you won't have the installation and configuration woes currently experienced by those who buy even the most user-friendly Internet connection software. Books are now appearing that offer full working versions of such programs as NetManage Chameleon, for example (*Plug-n-Play Internet*, a Sams book by Neil Randall and Celine Latulipe, is one of them), but although this is probably the easiest way of getting an account and getting onto the Net with a SLIP or PPP connection, it's still open to errors, incompatibilities, and just plain bad experiences. Anyone who has used Prodigy's World Wide Web browser already knows how nice it is not to have to worry about setting up your domain names and IP addresses; and in fact, Prodigy users who've never bought an account through an independent Internet service provider wouldn't even know what these problems mean.

Net purists might suggest that the level of newbie ignorance will simply increase as a result of this easy access, but I simply don't see that as a valid argument. Wasting gray matter trying to get your Internet connection working might be the kind of trial by fire some technically oriented people would classify as a good thing, but my idea of perfect software is software that is 100 percent transparent to the user. As soon as the technology itself makes its presence felt, the concern is with that technology, not with whatever the technology is supposed to enable you to accomplish. Users shouldn't have to concern themselves with domain name servers when they access the Web any more than they should have to rewire their toasters when they want a piece of toast. That ideal is still a fair ways off, but by the end of 1995 the commercial providers will be closer than anyone else to attaining it. More power to them.

A more serious concern behind connections through commercial services is this: The services take but don't give back. Why, the argument goes, should those people get access to the Internet's riches when Internet subscribers don't get access to their materials in return? This is obviously a point of fair play, and unless the commercial services address it the number of flames directed at their subscribers will only increase. There's another side to this point, however: Assuming that the commercial providers pay money for Internet access, and that part of their subscribers' fees goes toward meeting this debt, then the Internet gains from these new members whether or not resources are offered in return. And besides, Internet members don't lose any of their existing resources just because another service is hooked in. Nobody demands that a new corporation getting onto the Net make its data files available to long-time Netters, so why should AOL or CompuServe make theirs available? The argument continues, and will undoubtedly do so for some time.

From the standpoint of using the Internet, the problem with some of these services is twofold. First, on the practical level, they cost a lot. Although they advertise their wares at a very low monthly rate (anywhere from about $4.95 through $9.95), that doesn't always get you very much. Check carefully to see how much you'll actually be paying for Internet access. As a rule of thumb, it's almost *always* cheaper to go with a local Internet provider, but if you're a member of one of these services, find out what it has to offer.

The second problem is a little harder to specify. If the goal of the online service is to open a door-way to the Internet for its customers, and then to let them explore the Net in all its positive and negative aspects, then fine. But if it is trying to establish the Net as just another addition to its service, less fine. Accessing Gopher through America OnLine, for example, gives nothing of the overwhelming scope of Gopherspace; instead, it simply feels as if you've launched into yet another AOL application. To appreciate what the Net—and hence the Web—has to offer, it's crucial (in my mind, at least) to understand that you're actually switching from computer to computer to computer, all over the world, to access your data and explore what people want you to see. Localize it, and the whole thing starts to mean very little.

Delphi

As of late March 1995, Delphi Internet remained the only service to offer full access. But Delphi's access won't appeal to everybody: The user interface is nongraphical (even InterNav, its Microsoft Windows shell, is only marginally graphical), and hooking into the World Wide Web in this manner is less than ideal. For a look at nongraphical Web browsers, see Chapter 9; if you like the no-nonsense speed of these programs, by all means give Delphi a shot. Even this is temporary, however; in March 1995 Delphi announced that it had licensed Netscape Navigator (detailed in Chapter 11, "Netscape Navigator") as its primary graphical interface for the Net (and, obviously, its primary Web browser). Delphi's Internet access has been impressively complete for months, and using Netscape will make it more complete and far more attractive to use.

Prodigy

The first graphical World Wide Web access available through a commercial online service comes from Prodigy. Given Prodigy's history of being a less "serious" service than either CompuServe or even AOL, this is somewhat surprising, but the fact remains that early in 1995 Prodigy users were given a full-featured Web browser to use directly from their accounts. If you join Prodigy, you need only click the Internet button (or Jump: Internet), and you'll see quick-and-easy instructions for downloading your browser (installation is automatic and virtually flawless). After you have it, you need only enter the Internet area whenever you wish, and then surf the Web to your heart's content. Given that the browser can access FTP and Gopher sites as well as Web sites (as all browsers can), and that Prodigy subscribers already have newsgroup access, this effectively means that if you're a Prodigy member you have the entire Net at your disposal. Such is the power, incidentally, of the World Wide Web itself.

America OnLine

AOL is among the fastest growing commercial services, and it comes complete with an extremely accessible and easy-to-use graphical interface. That interface, in fact, is part of what's been slowing up AOL's full access to the Net. Whereas Delphi offered a rudimentary Gopher browser, AOL ensured that Gopher access was built into the interface and search requirements guaranteed by the rest of its interface. The same holds for Usenet access and for electronic mail as well. The point is that AOL is striving to maintain a consistent interface across its service and onto the Net, and as the last several months have shown, especially to Microsoft Windows users, the Internet seems to resent having a single interface spread on top of it. AOL has acquired Booklink Technologies' superb InternetWorks integrated package (see Chapter 12, "More Browsers for Microsoft Windows," for details about this program), and they've also licensed Enhanced NCSA Mosaic from Spyglass. It'll be interesting to see what AOL subscribers get as a standard browser when Web access on AOL finally kicks in. In the meantime, AOL users have access to Usenet, e-mail, Gopher, and FTP, so the Web is the only major issue that remains. AOL subscribers, meanwhile, continue to be prejudiced against on Usenet, a practice that can only be described as blatantly offensive.

CompuServe

CompuServe has been in the lead as a commercial online service for so long that its paucity of Internet tools is somewhat surprising. Simply put, there isn't much Internet activity you can do through CompuServe that would justify subscribing for the sake of connecting to the Net. As a commercial service CompuServe remains excellent, with a huge array of topic-oriented forums, a wealth of software available for download, and a solid e-mail system, but for Internet access you're much better off with Prodigy, Delphi, or America OnLine. This will change, however, during the course of 1995 and 1996, because in March of 1995 CompuServe acquired Spry, Incorporated, publishers of the popular Internet in a Box software suite. Spry's software will provide the basis for CompuServe's Internet Division, all of which means that getting onto the Web through CompuServe means using Spry's Air Mosaic (in one version or another) as well as other Spry tools. (CompuServe's name for the access is NetLauncher.) Interestingly, CompuServe's service is dial-up PPP, which means you'll be able to use whatever Web browser you want (Prodigy users, for example, are restricted to the company's own browser). All of this is welcome news for CompuServe subscribers, who until now have been waiting for their provider to make an important Internet move. Unfortunately, Internet access through CServe is quite expensive (as much as U.S. $4.80 per hour as of this writing), but it is quite easy to use as well.

GEnie

As a commercial service, GEnie seemed to take a beating when America OnLine hit the wires. Still, over the past year it's revamped its interface into a graphical one, hiding its once-obscure system of pages and moves behind the point-and-click ease to which we've all become accustomed. The problem is that GEnie still offers very limited Internet access, a fact the service promises to change during 1995 (which will be a huge year for the relationship between online services and the Net, if all of the promises come to pass). World Wide Web browser access will become available, as will newsgroup and all other Internet access. Given GEnie's already-proven strength in strong discussion groups (roundtables), it's doubtful that newsgroup service will have much impact on its subscribers. They already have more than they can handle at home. Access to the Web, however, will become a crucial aspect of this service, and if they keep costs reasonable it should help increase the subscribership. Like AOL, however, GEnie continues to take its customers' flack about not being able to ship its Internet software at the promised time.

Indirect Versus Direct Access

Let me state off the top that Internet access is categorized differently by different people. Sample a bunch of Internet books at your local library, and you'll run into terms like *dedicated access, dial-up access, remote access, terminal access, SLIP/PPP access,* and any number of others.

Because *The World Wide Web Unleashed 1996* isn't, once again, a comprehensive guide to the Internet itself, but rather to that portion of the Net known as the Web, my goal is to simplify these details as much as possible without losing their essential characteristics. For that reason, I'll categorize the major access types as *indirect* and *direct.* These are terms that are coming more and more into prominence, and although they might not be quite as technically accurate as some of the others, they're more than useful enough for our purposes. And from the standpoint of the Mac and Windows users acquiring commercial Net accounts, a group that is growing in size perhaps more than any other, this distinction is the only one that's really necessary.

Indirect Access

Indirect access means that your computer is not directly attached to the Internet. Instead, it is one of many terminals connected to another computer, which is itself attached to the Internet. As a mere terminal, your computer does not have its own IP address, and you cannot perform tasks such as FTPing a file—or downloading e-mail—directly to your hard drive. In other words, your computer is *not* a node on the Internet, and this restricts your activity and your environment to whatever the directly connected computer allows.

Often, this restriction means that you operate from a UNIX *shell* environment. UNIX, the operating system that forms the *de facto* basis of the Internet, is an immensely powerful and flexible operating system, but its shell environments are difficult for a novice to master and do not provide the graphical interface to which many personal computer users have grown accustomed. In fact, UNIX has several graphical environments available—X Window being the one we'll see most often in this book—but a typical shell environment offers only a command-line interface, and an often cryptic one at that.

One of the great benefits of indirect access through a UNIX shell environment or any other form of indirect access is that you don't have to worry about finding and downloading new software, nor, in fact, do you have to concern yourself with the computer's operation at all. E-mail packages such as Elm or Pine will be upgraded by the systems people as they become available, as will such essential Internet browsing tools as Gopher. A well-stocked indirect environment will provide you with a host of powerful Internet tools such as an excellent mailer, the most up-to-date Gopher client, a variety of Telnet and perhaps FTP possibilities, and two or three newsgroup packages, to name some of the more important features. Your only task is to use these tools, not to maintain them on your own.

The major disadvantage of indirect access is that you often can't use the important graphical tools such as Mosaic, Cello, and MacWeb. And those are the tools that are making the most noise. Note that this isn't necessarily the case across LANs, but it is certainly the case for home computer users who purchase an account from a commercial Internet provider. For these users, only direct access is a useful choice.

Direct Access

Direct access means that your computer has its own IP address and is an independent node on the Internet. In effect, you have become another statistic on the Net, one more computer added to the hordes already there. (As a terminal with indirect access, your personal machine wasn't even this significant.) If you wish to establish your computer as an FTP site or, indeed, a World Wide Web site, you can do so. In the latter case, as this book will make clear, you need to do more work than just establishing an IP address, but the point is that it can be done. With indirect access, it can't.

With a direct-access Internet account, you FTP files to your own hard disk, rather than to the server's, and your e-mail can appear on your own hard drive as well—again, rather than on the server's. If you create a Web page and store it on your hard drive, you can load it into a browser, click on the links, and be transported to the linked site. With indirect access, by contrast, you typically have to place such a page on the server, because your own machine isn't accessible. Furthermore, although it's true that you're suddenly responsible for maintaining your own Internet software tools, you also have full control over which programs you download, install, and run. If you see an announcement for a new piece of software, or an upgrade to one you already have, simply FTP it to your hard drive, follow the installation procedure, and let it fly. Of course, if there are serious bugs in the software (or even a virus), that's your problem and not the systems group's, but such is the price of independence.

Most importantly from the standpoint of users with modem access, direct access means being able to use the graphical tools under constant development for environments such as Windows and the Macintosh. No longer restricted by the text-based interfaces of the UNIX shell, you now have access to e-mail, newsgroup, Gopher, FTP, Archie, WAIS, IRC, and World Wide Web packages that are fully capable of making use of your graphical environment. From a Web user's perspective, this means that you are able to experience, use, and contribute to the Web in all its multimedia glory.

In fact, as mentioned earlier, this strict demarcation between indirect and direct access isn't completely accurate from a technical point of view. As just one example, SLIP/PPP access gives you your own IP address and the full use of multimedia tools for your environment, but you're not really directly connected to the Net. You're still dependent on a server that is in turn directly connected, and SLIP/PPP in effect only *simulates* a direct connection. (If you don't believe you're not directly connected, try logging in when the server is down for maintenance.) But the results are the same, so who cares? Your machine has a unique IP, you have substantial control over your Internet environment, and you use a multimedia Web browser—which is, after all, the point.

Non-Graphical Web Clients

9

by
Carrie Leigh
Pascal

The overall appeal of the Web derives largely from its graphics capabilities. People enjoy the Web because it is a user-friendly gateway to the Internet that offers appealing, colorful graphics that are more aesthetically pleasing than standard font text. However, not everyone can access graphical browsers, not everyone has the patience to wait for large GIFs to download, and not everyone cares that much about aesthetics. A number of non-graphical browsers, mostly for UNIX, have been developed by members of the Web project. For the most part, these browsers were not designed solely for users to interact with the Web; they were designed to be self-contained hypertext systems, to be test tools for code libraries, or for other purposes. However, they provide Web access (some more fully than others), and they are quite speedy because they transfer only text. No fancy stuff here.

In this chapter, I discuss two non-graphical browsers in detail: Lynx and the CERN Line Mode Browser. Both run on UNIX and VMS. (A version of Lynx exists for DOS as well.) Both provide full access to the Web. Lynx is a full-screen interface that uses mostly arrow keys to navigate. The Line Mode Browser is a command-line interface wherein the user types commands to navigate. These two browsers are the two most comprehensive non-graphical browsers available.

Of course, the general trend in Web navigation favors the popular graphical apps (primarily Mosaic and Netscape), and as the Web increases in popularity and gains prominence, the non-graphical browsers will fade into obscurity. However, they are out there, and some of them are quite good. At the very least, they're worth knowing about for those times when a graphical system is not available.

Lynx

Lynx is a non-graphical, hypertext World Wide Web client for users running cursor-addressable displays. It provides users with full access to the Web, allowing them to navigate and select hypertext links with cursor keys. Lynx currently runs on UNIX, VMS, and DOS. While Lynx is primarily used to access information on the Web, it can also be used to build information systems intended for local access (for example, campuswide information systems). Lynx can also be used to build systems isolated within a single Local Area Network (LAN), which might prove useful in a small business environment.

Lynx was developed by Lou Montulli, Charles Rezac, and Michael Grobe of the University of Kansas. Garrett Blythe developed DOSLynx and now contributes to the Lynx effort as well, along with Jeff Porter, Craig Lavender, and Ravikumar Kolli. Originally designed for the purpose of building a self-contained campuswide information system at the University of Kansas, Lynx was eventually expanded to include many Internet resources. It now contains Gopher servers, it allows Telnet connections, and it provides users with full access to all Web servers. The current stable version of Lynx (Version 2.3.7 as of March 1995) includes all Web libraries, allows users to switch on the fly to HTML mode, and supports interactive fill-in forms. Lynx's original design included a native hypertext document format, but as the popularity of HTML grew, the native format was phased out and replaced with the *real* HTML. Lynx is a full-featured Web browser, but it has limited display capabilities. It replaces all Web graphics with the word [image] in square brackets ([ ]). It is currently available free for non-commercial use, with plans for commercial licensing in the works.

Even though Lynx's popularity has been almost completely superseded by that of Mosaic, Netscape, and the other graphical browsers, those who use the Web as a means of moving quickly from one information source to another realize that Lynx is, in many ways, their best bet. It's much faster than graphical browsers, it requires only a shell account with a VT100 terminal in order to run (and is therefore often cheaper to use than the others), and it does a very good job of cutting through the Web's clutter. If you need speed, go with Lynx.

Where to Get Lynx

You can access the Lynx files needed to run the browser via anonymous FTP to

`ftp2.cc.ukans.edu`

The files are located in

`/pub/lynx`

To receive information about Lynx and notification of Lynx updates, subscribe to the Lynx mailing list by sending mail to `listserv@ukanaix.cc.ukans.edu`. Leave the subject line blank, and in the body of the message type `subscribe lynx-dev` *your_name*, where *your_name* is your full name (and not your e-mail address).

Getting Started

All instructions contained in this and subsequent sections assume the user is working with UNIX.

To execute Lynx, type `lynx` at the command prompt. If you are using UNIX and you pick any old file in one of your directories and type `lynx` *myfile* at the UNIX prompt, Lynx will execute with your file as the default opening file. There will not be any hypertext links, and you will not be able to jump anywhere with your cursor keys, but you can still view your file and apply Lynx paging commands to it. (See "Navigating in Lynx," later in this chapter, for a description of paging commands.) Lynx will actually read any file with any extension, but it will only recognize hypertext links in a file with the extension .HTML (provided that the file contains the proper linking syntax).

To run Lynx with an HTML file that you have created, simply type the following from a UNIX prompt:

`lynx myfile.html`

or

`lynx /home/mydir/myfile.html`

Provided that your HTML file contains correctly specified Uniform Resource Locators (URLs) and is built in syntactically correct HTML, you can begin navigating the Web with your file as the starting point.

You may also wish to run Lynx with a remote file; that is, with a specific Web page, perhaps, or a Gopher site. You may do this as long as you know the URL of that page. The format is

```
lynx protocol://host/path/filename
```

The individual components of this format are as follows:

protocol:	identifies the communications protocol used by the server you are accessing (for example, HTTP, Gopher, FTP, or WAIS)
host:	specifies the Internet address of the computer system on which the server you want to access is running
path and `filename`:	identify the directory path and file of interest

If, for example, you want to execute Lynx with NASA's home page, you could type:

```
lynx http://www.gfsc.nasa.gov/NASA_homepage.html
```

Lynx comes up as shown in Figure 9.1.

FIGURE 9.1.

The NASA home page in Lynx.

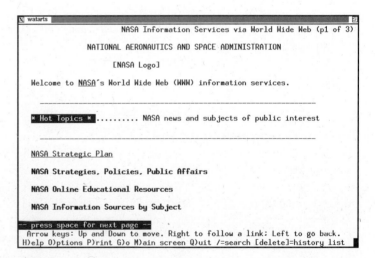

You can also access a specific Web page once in Lynx by simply typing the letter g. You will be prompted for `filename` or URL to open, at which point you would enter the protocol, host, path, and/or filename.

You might want to configure Lynx to execute with the same page all the time. To do so, you must set your home environment variable in UNIX. If you are running ksh, type the following at your UNIX prompt:

```
export www_home=http://www.gfsc.nasa.gov/NASA_homepage.html
```

If you are running csh, type

```
setenv www_home http://www.gfsc.nasa.gov/NASA_homepage.html
```

NOTE

You may replace the preceding HTTP addresses with whatever page you would like.

Once your home-environment variable is set, when you execute the Lynx command, it will open with whatever page you specified. You can always reset your environment variable by retyping the preceding command and replacing the URL with a new one. If you choose neither to set a home-environment variable nor to specify a URL or a filename when you execute the Lynx command, Lynx will run with whatever default file was chosen by the administrator of your system.

Leaving Lynx

To exit Lynx, simply type q. You will be prompted for confirmation, so type y to confirm and n if you change your mind. To exit without being prompted for confirmation, type Q or Ctrl+d.

Navigating in Lynx

You may use arrow keys and/or the numerical keypad to navigate in Lynx. Do not try using your mouse; it will not work, and it may confuse things somewhat. In some UNIX windows, you can always select text with your mouse and change it to reverse video. Doing so while in Lynx, however, may lead you to believe that the text you have selected is a hypertext link, because selected links in Lynx are also represented in reverse video.

The following paragraphs describe how to navigate with the arrow and keyboard keys, and indicate the numpad equivalent in parentheses. See also the Commands section for a list of all Lynx commands.

One web page may consist of more than one screen. To scroll through a web page with multiple screens, use the plus (+) key (or numpad 3) to move forward one screen, and use the minus (–) key (numpad 9) to move backward one screen. To move from link anchor to link anchor (the highlighted text), use the up or down cursor arrows (numpad 8 and 2, respectively). Do not use the left or right arrow keys to move from anchor to anchor, even if there are multiple links in one line of text. The left and right arrow keys (numpad 4 and 6, respectively) are used to move back and forth between Web pages. That is, they are the equivalent of the Back and Forward commands in Mosaic. Additionally, you may use numpad keys 7 and 1 to return to the top of the current web page or to skip to the bottom.

Link anchors in Lynx will vary depending on your monitor. On a plain, black-and-white monitor, they are represented in bolded text, and they change to reverse video when selected. Your monitor, of course, may be slightly different. Once you have selected a link with your cursor keys, hit Return or the right arrow key to jump to the destination indicated by the link.

Other keyboard commands may help you chart the web through Lynx. Lynx keeps a list of each site you have visited. You may access this "history list" with the Backspace or Delete keys. You can then scroll through the list and revisit any site by selecting it (again, with your up and down cursor keys) and by hitting Return or Enter. Inside the history list, you can also type m to return to the first site you visited.

You might notice on occasion that when you jump to a certain site, the data transfer is extremely slow. This may happen for a number of reasons, but if you do not like staring at the screen while twiddling your thumbs, you can always halt a data transfer by typing z. This will stop the transfer completely and will leave you at the site from which you attempted the hypertext jump.

Once in a while, you may encounter a binary file in the course of your navigation. You cannot view binary files onscreen in Lynx, but you will automatically be prompted to either download the binary file or to cancel the operation altogether. If you select d for download, Lynx will transfer the file into a temporary location and offer you a list of options (again, depending on your system setup). The one default option is save the file to a disk.

You may also select a link that transfers you to a secure site, meaning you will need authorization to access the site. In such cases Lynx will prompt you for your userid and password. If all information is correctly supplied, you will then gain access to the requested site. You only need do this once for each site. Lynx automatically sends your userid and password to the secure server for later use.

To print, mail, or save a document, type p anywhere inside Lynx. The options you receive will depend on the way your system has been set up. You should be able to save the page to a file in any of your directories, print the file, and mail the file to yourself.

Online help is available from anywhere within Lynx. Simply type ? or H to access a list of help topics. The Help page shown in Figure 9.2 appears.

FIGURE 9.2.

Lynx Help.

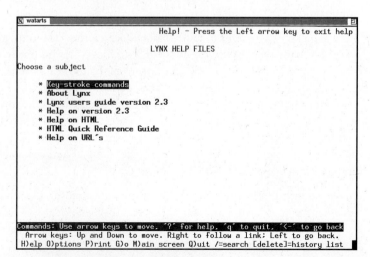

You may also wish to view the online User's Guide. This is available at `http://www.cc.ukans.edu/lynx_help/Lynx_users_guide237.html`.

Lynx Commands

The following is a full list of Lynx commands and their functions. Some of these commands were described in the "Navigating in Lynx" section.

Key Command	Function
↑(numpad = 8)	Move back one link.
↓(numpad = 2)	Move forward one link.
←(numpad = 4)	Move back one page.
- (numpad = 9)	Move back one screen.
+(numpad = 3)	Move forward one screen.
spacebar	Move forward one screen.
numpad 7	Jump to the top of the current page.
numpad 1	Jump to the end of the current page.
/	Enter a search string for the current page.
\	Toggle to view the HTML format of the current page.
=	View details about the current page (owner, URL, size, and so on).
!	Spawn your default shell (disabled for anonymous users).
Backspace	Access the history list.
?	Access online help.
a	Create a bookmark for the current page.
b	Jump to the top of the current page (same as numpad 7).
c	Send a comment to the owner of the current page (if an owner exists).
d	Download the current page onto your machine.
e	Edit the current page if the editor has been defined through Options and if the page is local.
g	Select a URL to open. (You must know the full address of the URL: protocol, host, path, and/or filename.)
h	Access online help.
i	Access a Web index, the contents of which depend on your system setup.

continues

Key Command	Function
m	Return to the first page you visited during the current session.
n	Search a non-indexed document for keywords.
o	Access the Options menu.
p	Print, mail, or save a file.
q	Leave Lynx with confirmation.
Q	Leave Lynx without confirmation.
r	Remove a bookmark.
s	Search an indexed document.
u	Return to the previous document (same as numpad 4).
v	Access your personal list of bookmarks.
z	Abort the current transfer process.

Creating Bookmarks in Lynx

Perhaps while navigating the Web you will come across a page that you feel you will access often. If so, you may bookmark the page and then access it by calling up your bookmark file and selecting it. Lynx allows you to bookmark in two ways: You can mark an entire document, or you can mark only the link currently selected on the page.

You must have a bookmark file on your machine to create bookmarks. (In UNIX, simply create a file titled bookmark_home or something similar in one of your directories.) In Lynx, set your bookmark option to the name of the bookmark file you created. To do so, type o to access the options screen, and type the bookmark filename in the bookmark field. Press Return (so that Lynx will accept the new setting), and then type r to exit the options screen and return to your current page. You may then type a to create a bookmark. You will be prompted with the following:

```
Save D)ocument or L)ink to bookmark file or C)ancel? (d,l,c):
```

Select d to save a link to the document you are currently viewing or l to save the link that is currently selected on the page. Selecting c will cancel the bookmark operation without saving anything.

To call up your list of bookmarks, simply type v from inside Lynx. The list of bookmarks you have created will appear, and you may select any of them with your cursor keys.

To remove a bookmark from your personal list, select the bookmark (after having typed v to view the list), and type r. The bookmarked page will no longer appear in your list.

Filling in Forms in Lynx

Lynx now supports HTML forms, interactive documents that you can fill in and submit to the service provider. Forms are used to gather and store data, and on the Web they are used for functions ranging from ordering merchandise to participating in surveys and providing feedback.

An HTML form consists of text-entry fields, checkboxes, buttons, and listboxes. When you encounter a form in Lynx, you will be asked to enter data as follows:

Text-entry fields: These are displayed as a row of underscores that comprises the length of the field ("_____"); you simply type over the underscores, using the backspace key to correct errors. Text that is longer than the length of the field will be truncated.

Checkboxes: These are displayed in parentheses in Lynx. To check a box (an asterisk will appear between the parentheses), press the right arrow or Return key.

Buttons: Buttons are displayed the same way as links. To "push" a button, press the right arrow or Return key.

Listboxes: A listbox is displayed with one list item shown in parentheses ("listitem___"). To view the whole list, press the right arrow or Return key. To select an item in the list, use the up or down arrow key and press the right arrow or Return key when you reach the item you wish to select.

To move around the form, use the standard Lynx navigation keys. To move from field to field, use the Tab key. When you have completed filling in your electronic form, you will generally be asked to select a Submit button; do so by moving the cursor to the Submit button's location and then pressing the right arrow or Return key.

Refreshing Your Display

At times you may wish to reload your current URL, in case of strange errors that may be caused by your operating system, or by interruptive messages. To reload the file you are viewing, press Ctrl+l or Ctrl+w.

Setting Options in Lynx

You may configure a number of options in Lynx. To do so, select o from inside Lynx, and a screen listing configurable options appears, as in Figure 9.3.

FIGURE 9.3.

Lynx Options page.

```
watarts
                         Options Menu

  E)ditor                         : NONE
  D)ISPLAY variable               : NONE
  B)ookmark file                  : NONE
  F)TP sort criteria              : By Filename
  P)ersonal mail address          : NONE
  S)earching type                 : CASE INSENSITIVE
  C)haracter set                  : ISO Latin 1
  V)I keys                        : OFF
  e(M)acs keys                    : OFF
  K)eypad as arrows
         or Numbered links        : Numbers act as arrows
  U)ser mode                      : Novice




  Select first letter of option line, '>' to save, or 'r' to return to Lynx.
  Command:
```

The options are as follows:

Editor	Select the editor you wish to use when editing browsable files and sending mail or comments. Specify the file path name of the editor when possible.
Display variable	Available only on UNIX displays and relevant only to X Window users. This variable is picked up automatically from the environment if it has been previously set.
Bookmark file	Specify the filename and location of your personal bookmark file.
FTP sort criteria	Specify how files should be sorted within FTP listings. Current options include: by filename, by size, by type, and by date.
Personal mail address	Specify your mailing address. This will be used when you send files to yourself and will be included as the "From:" address when you mail comments.
Searching type	Specify whether searches should be case sensitive or case insensitive. This affects only searches performed within Lynx.
VI keys	If ON, then lowercase h, j, k, and l will map to the left, down, up, and right arrow keys respectively.
Emacs keys	If ON, then Ctrl+p, Ctrl+n, Ctrl+f, and Ctrl+b will map to left, down, up, and right arrow keys respectively.
Keypad as arrows or numbered links	Allows the options to navigate with arrow keys or to number every link and then to select a link by typing its corresponding number.
List Directory Style	Select the file/directory representation: Mixed Style (files and directories listed together in alphabetical order), Directories First (files and directories separated into two alphabetical lists, with

	directories listed first), or Files First (files and directories in two alphabetical lists, with files listed first).
User mode	Choose between Novice (displays two lines of help at the bottom of the screen), Intermediate (turns off the help lines), and Advanced (displays the URL of the currently selected link at the bottom of the screen).
Local execution	If local execution is *not* activated by scripts or links created by the system administrator, this option allows you to choose Always Off (local execution scripts will never be executed), For Local Files Only (scripts will only be executed if they reside on your machine), and Always On (local execution scripts will always be executed).

Lynx is a powerful tool for anyone accessing the Web with a system that cannot handle the multimedia capabilities of the graphical browsers discussed in Chapters 10, "NCSA Mosaic," and Chapter 11, "Netscape Navigator." It has been refined over time to become a thoroughly enjoyable system to use for browsing, and in some cases it can actually be more efficient than other Web clients. If you use the Web for access to documents that do not rely on graphics, or indeed to download documents from FTP sites, you have little need for multimedia. In fact, for that type of access requirement, graphics and other peripheral elements can actually be distractions. Lynx is a program well worth considering for specific kinds of access, or simply to find out if the World Wide Web is of use to you in your work.

CERN Line Browser

The CERN Line Mode Browser (sometimes referred to as www) is a character-based World Wide Web browser, developed for use by anyone with a dumb terminal. Currently used mainly as a test tool for the CERN Common Code Library, it was developed by Tim Berners-Lee, one of the original creators of the Web at the European Particle Physics Lab (CERN); Nicola Pellow from Leicester Polytechnic in the UK; and Henrik Frystyk, a student from Aalborg University in Denmark. www is not often used, ironically, as a World Wide Web browser; rather its usefulness is derived from running it as a background application or from a batch job. It also provides a variety of possibilities for data-format conversion and filtering.

Although Lynx is the most comprehensive character-based browser, you may wish to have a look at www. It currently runs on UNIX, VMS, and VC/VMS. Its current version, 3.0, has been stable at least since February 1995. To view a demo, Telnet to `telnet.w3.org`. No username or password is required.

Where to Get the CERN Line Browser

The Line Mode Browser is available via anonymous FTP to `ftp.w3.org`. The files you need are located in `/pub/www/src`.

Starting the Line Mode Browser

The following directions to start the Line Mode Browser assume you are using UNIX.

To access the Line Mode Browser, type

www

at your operating system command prompt. With no options, the Line Mode Browser executes with the system default page, /usr/local/lib/WWW/default.html, which was likely set up by your system administrator. You may specify a number of options, a document address, and/or a list of keywords as arguments to your www command. Some of these arguments are outlined forthwith. For a complete listing, see the Line Mode Browser online documentation (URL: http://info.cern.ch/hypertext/WWW/LineMode/Defaults/QuickGuide.html).

Options

-h *hostname*	Establishes a Telnet connection to the remote host specified. This implies a secure mode of execution where all references to the local file system are cancelled.
-n	Non-interactive mode. This outputs the formatted document to the standard output (already set up), then exits.
-v	Verbose mode. Provides a status line in the browser that indicates the program's attempts to read data in various ways. You can also set this from within the browser. See the Commands section.
-o *filename*	Redirects output to a specified filename.
-l *filename*	Writes a list of visited sites to a specified log filename.
-p *n*	Where *n* is a number, specifies the page length in lines. Default is 24.
-w *n*	Where *n* is a number, specifies the page width in columns. Default is 78, 79, or 80 columns, depending on your system.

Document Address

If you specify a document address, the argument is the hypertext address of the site at which you want to start browsing. If, for example, you wanted to call up the Line Mode Browser with NASA's home page, you could type

www http://www.gfsc.nasa.gov/NASA_homepage.html

The program would run as shown in Figure 9.4.

FIGURE 9.4.

The NASA home page in the Line Mode Browser.

```
X| watarts                                                              2|
1-34, Back, Up, <RETURN> for more, Quit, or Help: 14
                                    NASA Information Services via World Wide Web
                   NATIONAL AERONAUTICS AND SPACE ADMINISTRATION


   Welcome to NASA's World Wide Web (WWW) information services.

   \
 * Hot Topics *  [1]......... NASA news and subjects of public interest

   \
 NASA Strategic Plan[2]

    NASA Strategies, Policies, Public Affairs [3]

 NASA Online Educational Resources[4]

    NASA Information Sources by Subject [5]

   \
 NASA Centers (click on a center's name for its home page):[6]
 Or see: list of NASA center home pages[7].

   \
1-19, Back, Up, <RETURN> for more, Quit, or Help: █
```

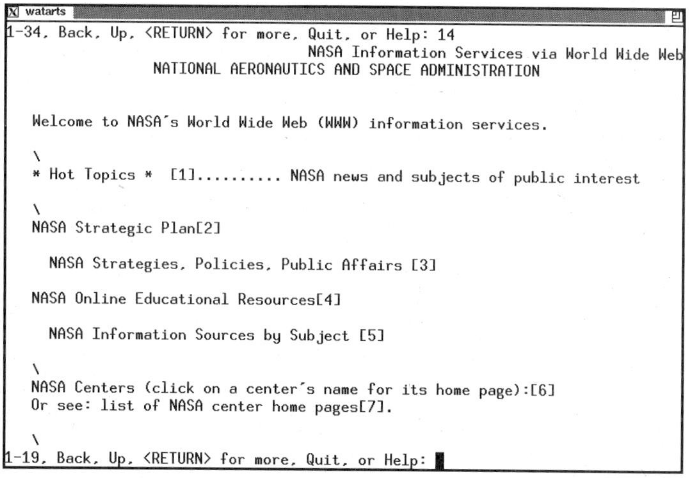

Keywords

If you referenced an index as your document address, any words following the document address will be read as keywords and the browser will search the index for those words. Note that this only works on indexed documents.

Leaving the Line Mode Browser

To exit the Line Mode Browser, type quit or q, exit, or e from inside the program. All Line Mode Browser commands are case insensitive, so the above may be upper- or lowercase. You will not be prompted for confirmation.

Navigating in the Line Mode Browser

The CERN Line Mode Browser (www) shows a screen of information and has a command line at the bottom of that screen. From this command line, you may tell the browser to jump to a specific destination, to move forward, to go back, to go home, to get help, to print, and to perform a host of other commands. Each hypertext link has a number next to it in parentheses; to access the site at the end of that link, type the corresponding number at the command line and hit Return or Enter. If one Web page has multiple screens on your display, you may press the Return key to move forward one screen. For many of the text commands (meaning you must type a text string at the command line, followed by a hard return), abbreviations are available. For example, to jump back to the previous site visited, you may type back, or b.

To move to the top of a Web page, type top. To move to the bottom, type bottom. The Line Mode Browser is case insensitive, so to execute the bottom command, for example, you may type BOTTOM, bottom, bo, or BO, among others. (Note, however, that you cannot type b for bottom, because that abbreviation is reserved for the back command.) Type up to scroll up one screen in a page, and down to scroll down (the equivalent of pressing the Return key, as described above). Pretty simple so far. As described, type back to jump back to the previous site you visited.

To return to the first document you read, type home. To access a specific site, type go followed by the URL of that site. If you type go and do not specify any parameters, then the Line Mode Browser will jump to the screen in your system default page, likely stored in /usr/local/lib/WWW/ default.html. The command list provides a list of all document titles and corresponding numbers for the hypertext links on the current page. Where no title is available, the document's URL is used. If you type source list, you will receive a list of URLs only (and their corresponding numbers). For example, Figure 9.5 shows part of the list of the World Wide Web Virtual Library, without using the source command.

FIGURE 9.5.

List for the WWW Virtual Library.

```
[X] watarts                                                                    [P]
[54] http://euclid.math.fsu.edu/Science/math.html
[55] http://golgi.harvard.edu/biopages/medicine.html
[56] http://www.met.fu-berlin.de/DataSources/MetIndex.html
[57] http://info.cern.ch/hypertext/DataSources/bySubject/Overview.html#ove12
[58] http://www.comlab.ox.ac.uk/archive/other/museums.html
[59] http://www.oulu.fi/music.html
[60] http://www.mth.uea.ac.uk/ocean/oceanography.html
[61] http://info.cern.ch/hypertext/DataSources/bySubject/Overview.html#ove13
[62] http://info.cern.ch/hypertext/DataSources/bySubject/Overview.html#ove14
[63] http://info.cern.ch/hypertext/DataSources/bySubject/Physics/Overview.html
[64] http://info.cern.ch/hypertext/DataSources/bySubject/politics/Overview.html
[65] http://info.cern.ch/hypertext/DataSources/bySubject/Overview.html#ove15
[66] http://info.cern.ch/hypertext/DataSources/bySubject/Overview.html#ove16
[67] http://www.cis.ufl.edu/~thoth/library/recreation.html
[68] http://info.cern.ch/hypertext/DataSources/bySubject/Overview.html#ove17
[69] http://info.cern.ch/hypertext/DataSources/bySubject/Overview.html#ove18
[70] http://www.pitt.edu/~cjp/rees.html
[71] http://freethought.tamu.edu/
[72] http://coombs.anu.edu.au/WWWVL-SocSci.html
[73] http://www.atm.ch.cam.ac.uk/sports/sports.html
[74] http://www.stat.ufl.edu/vlib/statistics.html
[75] http://www.bgsu.edu/~jzawodn/ufo/
[76] http://info.cern.ch/hypertext/DataSources/bySubject/Virtual_libraries/Overv
iew.html
[77] http://info.cern.ch/hypertext/DataSources/bySubject/coordination.html

1-77, Back, Up, <RETURN> for more, Quit, or Help: █
```

The recall command presents you with a numbered list of the sites you have visited throughout your session. If you wish to revisit one of those sites, type recall followed by the list number of that site, and then press the Return or Enter key. A recall list looks something like Figure 9.6.

To print the current page, type print at the command line. This command will print the document without any numbered references. Output is piped to the command defined by the environment variable WWW_PRINT_COMMAND (lpr by default). You can set your environment variable in UNIX, the syntax depending on whether you are using csh or ksh. For details, see the online documentation for the Line Mode Browser. (URL: http://info.cern.ch/hypertext/WWW/LineMode/ Defaults/QuickGuide.html).

Help in CERN's Line Mode Browser is available by typing help at the command line. The context-sensitive list of commands that appears depends on the version you are using and the hypertext address of the document you are currently reading. The screen you access presents other information besides the commands and their definitions. You can figure out the version number of the Line Mode Browser you are using, and you can view the URL of the current page.

Note that not all commands appear in every help screen because of the Help utility's context sensi-tivity.

FIGURE 9.6.

Recall command with the Line Mode Browser.

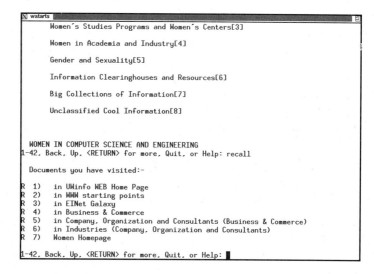

```
X watarts
      Women's Studies Programs and Women's Centers[3]

      Women in Academia and Industry[4]

      Gender and Sexuality[5]

      Information Clearinghouses and Resources[6]

      Big Collections of Information[7]

      Unclassified Cool Information[8]



   WOMEN IN COMPUTER SCIENCE AND ENGINEERING
1-42, Back, Up, <RETURN> for more, Quit, or Help: recall

   Documents you have visited:-

R  1)    in UWinfo WEB Home Page
R  2)    in WWW starting points
R  3)    in EINet Galaxy
R  4)    in Business & Commerce
R  5)    in Company, Organization and Consultants (Business & Commerce)
R  6)    in Industries (Company, Organization and Consultants)
R  7)    Women Homepage

1-42, Back, Up, <RETURN> for more, Quit, or Help: █
```

List of Line Mode Browser Commands and Other Functions

CERN's Line Mode Browser contains a wide range of commands, many of which are not obvious. Most are shown here.

Line Mode Browser Commands

The following is a fairly comprehensive list of Line Mode Browser commands, including all the commands you will need while navigating. Some of these were described in the "Navigating in the Line Mode Browser" section. It is interesting to note that the Line Mode Browser currently does not allow you to abort a data transfer if it is too slow, as do Mosaic, Cello, and Lynx. This is one of the proposed upgrades for the next version, however.

Command	Definition
! command	Executes a shell command from inside www by typing ! followed by the command.
> filename	Saves the current document to a file specified by filename.
>> filename	Appends the current document to a file specified by filename.
Back	Moves back one page.
cd	Changes directory from inside www.

continues

Command	Definition
Down	Scrolls down one screen (you can also press the Return key to do this).
Exit, Quit	Leaves www.
Find *keyword*	Only works on indexed documents, looks for the keyword you specify. Find will be an option listed at your prompt when it is available for use.
Go *URL*	Jumps to the URL you specify.
Help	Accesses the main help screen, which tells you the version number of the www you are using, the URL of the current page, and a list of all command-line commands.
Home	Returns to the first page you visited.
List	Lists all titles and corresponding link numbers for the links in the current document; where no title exists, lists the URL. Typing source list will provide you with a list of URLs and link numbers for the current document.
Manual	Jumps to the main page of the online documentation for www.
Next	Jumps to the site of the next pointer of the menu from which you made your last selection. See the next page for details.
number	Jumps to the site corresponding to the number on the screen.
Previous	Same as Next, but for the previous item in the list of pointers.
Print	Prints the document. Specify the destination with your *WWW_PRINT_COMMAND* environment variable.
Quit, Exit	Leaves www without confirmation.
Recall	Produces a numbered list of all the sites you have visited in the current session.
Recall *number*	For example, type recall 5 to revisit site number 5 in your recall list.
Refresh	Refreshes the screen to the way it appeared when you first accessed it. (Note: This command is not very useful.)
Source	Followed by another command, causes raw source data to be generated for that command without any MIME headers wrapped around it. You can use this with print, >, >>, and list.
Top	Jumps to the top of the current page.
Up	Moves up one screen.
Verbose	For maintenance purposes, produces messages during data-transfer processes.

Using *Next* and *Previous* with the Line Mode Browser

Next and Previous are useful commands when you are browsing through documents with a menu of items from which to choose, and you would like to explore each menu item in full. If, for example, you are reading the list of items in the World Wide Web Virtual Library (URL: `http://info.cern.ch/hypertext/DataSources/bySubject/Overview2.html`), you will come across the following subset of items:

```
Anthropology [10]
Archaeology  [11]
Architecture [12]
```

You may select [11], read about Archaeology, and then decide to move on to [12]. You may do so without first returning to your menu and then selecting [12]; simply type next at the command line while in the Archaeology page and you will jump to the Architecture page. Previous works the same way, but for the previous site, so typing previous would take you to the Anthropology page.

Performing Keyword Searches with the Line Mode Browser

You may perform a keyword search in the Browser with indexed documents. If a document is indexed, then the command find appears in your prompt as one of your choices. To search for a keyword, type find *keyword* followed by Return, or keyword *keyword* followed by Return. If your keyword or keywords does or do not conflict with existing commands, you may omit the word find and the program will automatically interpret your command as keywords to search.

Customizing the Line Mode Browser

You may customize the Line Mode Browser from your shell prompt. Some of the customization features include setting the WWW_HOME environment variable, setting the WWW_PRINT_COMMAND (UNIX only) environment variable, and creating aliases for some commands. To learn how to set these variables, see the "Customizing www" section of the online manual (URL: `http://info.cern.ch/hypertext/WWW/LineMode/Defaults/QuickGuide.html`). To access the documentation inside www, type manual at the command-line prompt.

Although it works, and its historical value is undeniable, the Line Browser is a relatively unappealing introduction to the World Wide Web. Not only does it not offer the Web's multimedia features, its navigation system offers none of the ease, or even the attractiveness, of Lynx. By all means, use it as a means of accessing necessary sites, but to experience the Web in anything approaching its full potential, you should use the Line Browser as a temporary tool only.

Other Non-Graphical Browsers

Lynx and CERN Line Mode are the two most comprehensive non-graphical World Wide Web browsers. Others, of course, have been developed for different platforms, often by hackers wanting to create a new interface for the Web. Many of the non-graphical browsers available never made it past their respective beta releases. Some are undergoing continued development, some have been scrapped altogether, and most are rarely used. Such browsers include Emacs W3 Mode, Rashty's VMS Client, and Tom Fine's PerlWWW. Only the Emacs browser will be discussed here.

Emacs W3 Mode

Author:	William Perry (wperry@spry.com) (wmperry@spry.com)
Status:	Version 2.20
Platforms:	UNIX on tty or X Window, NeXTStep as native NeXTStep app, Windows (3.1, 3.11, NT, Win95) as a native Windows app, Mac System 7.x, Amiga, VMS, DOS, DOS+DesqView/X
Availability:	Anonymous FTP from ftp.cs.indiana.edu /pub/elisp/w3/w3-2.1.102.tar.gz

The Emacs World Wide Web Browser enables the user to browse the entire Web, as long as he or she has Emacs or a subset thereof installed. This browser is compatible with Mosaic in that you can share a hotlist file (a file containing URLs of frequently visited sites) between the two applications. You can also share a global history file and a personal annotation directory. It is a highly portable browser, but note that its ability to run on all the platforms listed above depends on the version of Emacs installed on each of the platforms. To make full use of the Web with the Emacs browser, you need the following emacs packages: nntp for news reader, ange-ftp or efs for accessing files over FTP, Gopher (optional), HTML-mode (if you intend to use the group or personal annotation support), and mailcrypt (if you plan to access Web pages that require PGP/PEM encrypted requests).

According to the browser's author, William Perry, Emacs W3 is still being actively developed and improved. The current version, 2.20, includes support for HTML 3.0 and support for style sheets. Development to support tables is also ongoing.

NCSA Mosaic

10

by
Neil Randall

Anatomy of a Killer App

Unless you've been hiding under an extremely large rock for the past year and a half, you can't have avoided hearing something about Mosaic. The subject of almost as much media hype as the Internet itself, Mosaic has been called—and with some justification—the Internet's first "killer app." Articles about it have appeared in everything from *The New York Times* to *Wired*, and it's made several appearances on CNN and other TV networks with high-tech interests. To be quite honest about it, its extreme popularity is the reason this book was published in the first place.

Over the past six months, Mosaic's hold on the world of the Web has been challenged, perhaps even eclipsed, by the release of the Netscape Navigator (covered in Chapter 11, "Netscape Navigator"). But even though Mosaic has one group of adherents and Netscape a different (and equally vocal) group, the fact remains that both programs do the same thing: They display Web pages in an attractive, graphical manner. No matter which of the two browsers you use, or even if you use a less popular one such as MacWeb, InternetWorks, WebExplorer, or HotJava, the point is identical. Out there on thousands of the world's computers resides a huge number of fascinating multimedia documents, all waiting for you to point your Web browser in their direction.

Still, Mosaic and Netscape currently rule the roost, and this book distinguishes them from the rest because of their immense popularity. More importantly, they're distinguished because *both* have been called "killer apps." Netscape, indeed, has been called a "Mosaic killer," but so far the older browser's death has been greatly exaggerated and, to judge by its licensing accomplishments, utterly untrue. Together, however, they might well deserve the epithet "killer app," because both offer reasons, all by themselves, for people to get an Internet account in the first place. The remainder of this introduction discusses the whole idea of the phrase "killer app," applying that term to these two browsers together.

So what's a killer app?

A *killer app* is a computer application, or program, that capitalizes on the strengths of a computer system and applies those strengths to fill a user need, and it does both so well that the user community feels the application has become essential to their professional or personal lives. If it is truly a killer app, it not only raises these expectations; it fulfills them as well. The result is the lifting of a barrier between user and technology, and inevitably the app becomes identified *with* that technology. The app and the technology become, in many ways, one and the same, and the existence of the app eventually alters the activity it was initially designed to support.

Sounds good, but what does it mean...?

The first killer app for personal computers was Visicalc for the Apple II. Visicalc was the first spreadsheet program, and its design stemmed from what now seems an obvious link between the mathematical power of computers and the mathematical needs of people who work with numbers. When the IBM PC was introduced in the early eighties, Visicalc gave way to Lotus 1-2-3, originally an integrated package (hence its name), but eventually only a spreadsheet program.

Lotus 1-2-3 was one of two killer apps for DOS (we'll get to the other in a minute), and it can be called a killer app because it was so successful at giving PC users the tools they thought they needed that it became the catalyst for change in the kinds of tasks they were being asked to perform. In other words, Lotus 1-2-3 changed the nature of jobs, even careers, and inevitably it changed the way companies did business. Doubt it? Try offering a financial forecasting model to your clients, telling them that because you did it by hand any changes would take a couple of days to process. In fact, try putting the financial forecasting model together in the first place without using your spreadsheet program.

Visicalc and—much more widely—Lotus 1-2-3 brought personal computers into the business mainstream, changing some of the functions and tasks of business in the process. They did it so well, in fact, that people began to believe that there was no other way of accomplishing these functions and tasks. Realistically, your spreadsheet program does nothing that you couldn't do by hand, or at the very least with adding machines and sliderules. What it does is make it easier, more easily alterable, and much, much faster.

The other essential killer app of the eighties was WordPerfect. Yes, word processing has been a killer *category* in every personal-computing environment—MacWrite and soon afterward Word on the Macintosh, for instance—but WordPerfect became as crucially important to business as Lotus 1-2-3. It actually went quite a bit beyond the impact 1-2-3 had, extending into the academic world, into governments, and into people's personal lives as well. In fact, people stopped asking, "Do you know word processing?" and started asking, "Do you know WordPerfect?" And because of its capabilities—its formatting, macros, and editing tools—it changed the way documentation (and all other writing) took place. I hate to use the phrase *paradigm shift*, but it probably applies to WordPerfect.

If there was a killer app for the Macintosh, it was Aldus PageMaker. Because the Macintosh was hyped from the beginning as a friendly computer that helped you create attractive publications on-screen and then print them exactly as they appeared (I realize WYSIWYG was never quite *this* smooth), the move to professional page design with PageMaker was a natural transition. This program catapulted the Macintosh into prominence in a previously nonexistent category of computing (desktop publishing), and businesses began to change the way they worked as a result. PageMaker sold Macs the way Visicalc sold Apple IIs and 1-2-3 and WordPerfect sold PCs. The only reason PageMaker is more difficult to consider as a killer app is that serious competition not only quickly developed (as it did with 1-2-3 and WordPerfect) but also quickly managed to gain ground (as was not the case with the others). Still, the idea is the same.

Killer apps fulfill both existing needs and needs that users didn't know they had, but which they develop as a result of using the app. For the Internet, the need was simple: It was wild and chaotic, and it needed an interface that the masses could handle. As long as the Net was under the control of the command-line vagaries of Telnet and FTP, it wasn't going to happen. The first application that came close to killer-app status was Gopher, which effectively offered that comfortable interface and became the accepted means of disseminating information across a broad spectrum of platforms and categories. But from the perspective of mass media acceptance,

---

Gopher had one significant limitation. In an age when information is in many ways equated with the combination of sound, video, graphics, and text, Gopher's nonmultimedia, never-ending table of contents (which in many ways it is) didn't quite cut it. Using Gopher is a lot like using a library, and although a library is immensely useful for many things, for better or for worse it doesn't have mass appeal.

Enter Mosaic. Like Lotus 1-2-3 and WordPerfect, it was far from the first in its genre. Lotus had Visicalc before it, WordPerfect had WordStar before it, and Mosaic had the CERN line browser before it and others in the works. What Mosaic did, like the killer apps before it, was to become so popular that people began to associate the program with the genre. Part of the reason was simply that Mosaic began life as a good program and developed well from there, with frequent upgrades and intelligent interface and technology decisions.

A great deal, however, had to do with the fact that it captured its underlying technology—the World Wide Web—almost perfectly. Its by-now classic "spinning globe" icon showed people graphically that they were connecting not just to a computer but to the world, and its display had the features that the World Wide Web was designed to have from its inception. The fact that a Macintosh version was available early in the game also helped considerably, because there was almost no competition whatsoever in this arena. Mosaic came to Microsoft Windows soon afterward. The program became ubiquitous, and—again for better or for worse—became for many users another name for the World Wide Web.

So was Mosaic the Internet's first killer app? To a degree, yes. It had the publicity, it had the brand-name status, and it fulfilled—and continues to fulfill—a considerable portion of the Web's great promise. It has even become a business application, as every killer app inevitably becomes. Users are designing information and sites specifically for it, and all other Web browsers are striving for compatibility with it. All the signs are there.

But Mosaic hasn't quite reached killer app status, because it can't perform all Internet functions. Its Gopher and FTP capabilities are still rudimentary, even after many alpha releases, as are its newsgroup and e-mail functions (which many see as the two major Net applications). In fact, because most people would classify e-mail as the true killer app of the Internet (I don't, because e-mail is a killer app on LANs as well, and is therefore more accurately networking's killer app), Mosaic doesn't even come close from that perspective. But Mosaic did what no other Internet application was able to do: It got people by the thousands onto the Net precisely so they could use this single program.

What Netscape has done is up the ante. Mosaic users quickly realized they had to FTP the software, struggle with installation, and put up with crashes and other bugs simply because this program was far and away the best game in town. Commercial versions of Mosaic (based on the original NCSA version) then hit the market and solved most of these problems, but they cost money and were seen by many as not being the real thing. Then Netscape came along, and it brought with it two important factors. First, it was easy to install, easy to use, and—wonder of wonders—easy to configure. Second, it was designed by the same person and team who designed Mosaic in the first place, and that gave it instant credibility. For many, in fact, Netscape became Mosaic as it should have been.

Netscape's appearance on the scene caused a different kind of stir from Mosaic's. What users saw in Netscape was a product that would take the Web several steps further. Modem users finally had a product that obviously dealt with their slower access problems. HTML authors saw the browser as an opportunity to design pages with much greater sophistication. And Web surfers saw these designs grow increasingly impressive by the week, reaching the point when all pages on the Web finally stopped looking alike. Netscape turned the Web—at least partially—into a design arena, and suddenly Web publishing took on a different dimension. In the process, it added greater capability to read and post to newsgroups, a somewhat better connection to e-mail, and stronger support for other Internet functions such as Gopher and, to a lesser degree, FTP.

So are Mosaic and Netscape together a killer app? Maybe. But what matters is that the World Wide Web continues to ride its wave as a "killer concept," as we discussed back at the beginning of this book. Perhaps the idea of a killer app for the Internet no longer truly applies; nevertheless, Mosaic and Netscape are hauling in Internet users in numbers never before seen, so we might as well grant these two programs the status of "joint killer app" for the time being.

Before We Begin

The three Mosaics covered here are the NCSA versions only. Several software publishers have released or are preparing commercial versions of Mosaic, some of which are covered in Chapter 12, "More Browsers for Microsoft Windows." A freeware Mosaic for the Amiga computer, Amiga Mosaic or AMosaic, is covered in Chapter 13, "More Browsers for X Window, Macintosh, and OS/2," because it is not an NCSA release.

This chapter does *not* treat installation or configuration in great detail. Especially for X Window users, configuration is rarely out-of-the-box standard, and there's no way whatsoever to deal with all the possibilities here. Things are much easier for Windows users, and easier still for Macintosh owners; general installation and configuration issues will be outlined for all versions.

Mosaic for X, Macintosh, and Microsoft Windows: The Common Features

Figures 10.1, 10.2, and 10.3 show the three main Mosaics—X, Mac, and Windows. You might want to refer to these figures as you read this chapter.

The Document View Window

The most important portion of the Mosaic screen, the *document view window,* holds the file you're currently viewing. Usually this file is in HTML format, and Mosaic interprets it accordingly, displaying it as a series of headings, lists, graphics, forms, and highlighted links. When Mosaic finds a text file, it displays the file in an unformatted manner.

FIGURE 10.1.

NCSA Mosaic for X Window.

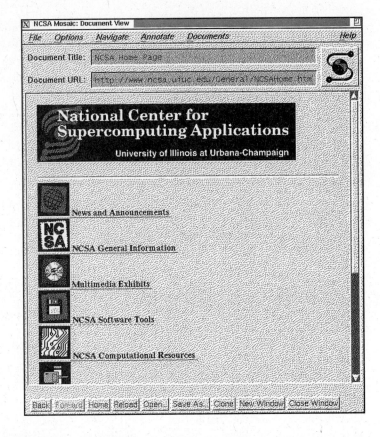

There's little difference in this window across the three computing platforms. And that, as much as anything else, demonstrates why the World Wide Web is so important to computing. Write an HTML document, and any browser on any platform can effortlessly display it. What other programs offer interchangeability of document types across this many platforms? Few at best, and fewer still when the documents become complex. True, this is a Web feature, not a Mosaic feature, but again it's something that the press has attributed to this popular program. (Become popular, it seems, and everything gets credited to you.)

The Spinning Globe

Mosaic's trademark is the spinning globe. Whenever Mosaic attempts to access a URL, the globe spins and lights travel along the arms of the icon. This means absolutely nothing for the program's functionality but serves a surprisingly important purpose for the user. First, the globe looks sharp; it's an icon that exactly suits the purpose of the program itself, and designs that strong are hard to find even in an icon-laden world. Second, the globe tells the user that something's actually happening—that Mosaic is trying to make connections. The more important information in this regard resides on the status bar, but the spinning globe offers reassurance and demonstrates activity.

FIGURE 10.2.

NCSA Mosaic for the Macintosh.

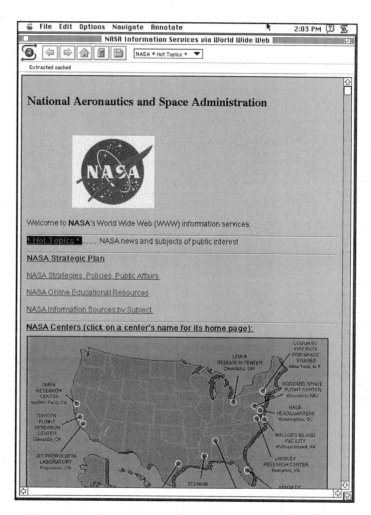

All three versions of Mosaic feature the spinning globe. On the X and MS Windows versions it lives in the top-right corner. For the Macintosh, it's on the left. A few other cosmetic differences exist.

FIGURE 10.3.

NCSA Mosaic for Microsoft Windows.

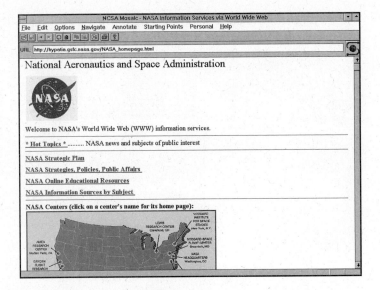

Actually, the globe serves two other functions. On all versions, clicking the globe while it's spinning stops—or at least attempts to stop—the current activity. This doesn't always work, especially when Mosaic is engaged in activities such as FTP. And it works less well in general on the MS Windows version than the X version. But for the most part it will do as it's supposed to. The other function exists with the Mac version, in which the globe encloses different icons depending on the function it's performing, whether that function is loading a document, performing an FTP download, or something else. The icon changes each time.

The Status Bar

At the bottom of the document view window is the *status bar* (called the *status line* in X Mosaic). Like all status bars, its function is to display a status, and in Mosaic's case it displays two important items. When you move the cursor to a hypertext link, the status bar reveals the link's URL address. Then, when you click on the link, the status bar displays the progress of the transaction, a running count of the number of bytes being transferred, the total number of bytes in the document being transferred, and the percentage of the download completed.

Both features are immensely useful. By noting the URL before selecting the link, you can often determine whether you want to make the jump. If the link is to a computer on another continent, for example, and you know it's the middle of a business day in that country, you'll know in advance that the connection will probably be slow. As a result, you might not select the link at all. Similarly, as you become experienced with Web access, you'll recognize some URLs on sight; and because you already know what's at the other end, you can stop yourself from clicking to avoid lengthy or repetitive downloads.

Equally useful is the transaction- and download-progress indication. This indicator tells you that you're actually making progress (something the spinning globe should relay but often doesn't), and the size of the download guides your decision to keep it going or simply click the globe and forget about it. Especially with a low-speed connection, having this information can make the difference between information gathering and simply wasting time.

The Vertical Scrollbar

On the right side of the document view window is the vertical scrollbar. Like the vertical scrollbar in any application, it tells you that the document is larger than the screen in front of you. You use the scrollbar, of course, to access the rest of the document.

This seems like a minor feature and an obvious one, but as it turns out it's quite important. Many HTML documents are extremely large, and many contain inline graphics that take up considerable downloading time. Whereas the status bar lets you know that information is still loading (during download), the scrollbar becomes the major tool for making use of the entire amount of information being presented. In fact, as you browse the Web, you'll find yourself clicking the scrollbar every bit as often as on the links themselves.

The scrollbar also points out a design consideration for HTML page designers. There's nothing more frustrating when using Mosaic than seeing progress being made on the status bar for information that the screen doesn't show and that you can't access without the scrollbar. To an extent it's a good thing, because it shows that the information is extensive, but watching a long or image-laden page load can be excruciating, especially on a slower connection. It's something to keep in mind, especially for pages that are specifically designed for browsing by home users.

The URL Display

Prominently featured at the top of the document view window is the *URL display*. This display consists of two parts, the Document Title and the Document URL (except in Mosaic for MS Windows, which offers the Document URL only and places the title in the standard window title bar). Although the URL display can be toggled off, you'll quickly find it to be among the most useful features of the software.

One of the elements of a typical HTML page is the formally designated title. This is what Mosaic displays in the Document Title box (the MS Windows version places it in the window's title bar). Although it's redundant for short HTML documents (the title is normally repeated as the first heading on the page; in fact, some HTML editors do this automatically), the title is extremely useful when viewing long documents. As you scroll down below the first page, the first heading disappears, and you'll often find yourself glancing at the Document Title box to refresh your memory of what document you're actually viewing. The Document Title box offers one other use: Its text is the title stored when you add the page to the hotlist or, in Windows Mosaic, when you add the page to a specific menu.

The Document URL box reminds you of exactly what document you've transferred to your machine. This is useful for reminder purposes; and, once again for hotlisting, this is the URL that goes into the hotlist. But on recent Mosaic releases this box is useful for one other thing as well: It's editable. If you're viewing one document, and you know the URL of the next one you want to view, you can click in the URL box, type the URL, and hit the Enter key. This is especially useful for documents you're familiar with that have similar URLs to the one you're currently viewing, because rather than search for a link you can simply change the desired section of the URL address and gain access to the next document that way.

The Navigation Buttons

All versions of Mosaic have navigation buttons, although they're in a different place in each version. Mac Mosaic offers navigation arrows on the icon bar at the top of the document view window; Windows Mosaic offers similar arrows on the toolbar (again at the top); and X Mosaic features text buttons, not arrows, and places them at the bottom. The function of the buttons in all versions is identical, however. The left arrow (or X's Back button) takes you to the previous page, the right arrow (or X's Forward button) takes you to the next page (that is, where you originally moved to from this page), and the house icon (or X's Home button) loads your specified home page.

The home page is yours to decide. At one point, NCSA released Mosaic with the home page specified as one of their own, but recent Mosaic releases have stopped this practice, and for good reason. Because Mosaic was so popular, the NCSA server quickly became severely overloaded. Every time users loaded the Mosaic program, it would launch the NCSA home page, and even though this is alterable, NCSA forgot to consider that many users, especially Windows and Macintosh users, either wouldn't bother to change the home page or wouldn't know how. Now it's up to you to specify your home page, and whichever one you choose becomes the page where the Home button takes you.

The arrow buttons (or X's Back and Forward buttons) seem entirely straightforward, but in fact they can be confusing. When you move from page A to page B, the back arrow returns you to page A. If you then press the Forward button, you'll move to page B once again. This is fine, but it gets strangely complex, as sometimes it's not exactly clear where the Forward button will actually take you. The principle is this: The Back button backs you up along the path you've traveled (and it keeps in mind if you've jumped back and forth a few times, so you could easily see the same document keep reappearing), whereas the Forward button returns you to the document that preceded the current document.

Loading URLs and Local Files

Clicking on hyperlinks is one method of moving from document to document, but there's another. In the File menu of every version are two items, Open URL and Open Local (Open Local File in Windows Mosaic). The first of these lets you type in the URL address of the document you wish to load. The second (see Figures 10.4, 10.5, and 10.6) lets you load a file from a local disk into Mosaic.

Alternatively, you can copy and paste the URL in all three versions, although the method by which you do so will vary. UNIX's universal copy-and-paste (left and middle or left and right mouse buttons) will work, as will Ctrl (or command)+C and Ctrl (or command)+V from the Windows and Mac versions, respectively.

One annoying aspect of actually typing the text occurs when you attempt to connect to a site whose URL you've mistyped. Mosaic informs you that it cannot find the site but then does not keep the typed address in its Open URL box. Unfortunately, you are then forced to retype the entire address (more carefully this time), truly a trying experience.

FIGURE 10.4.

*Loading local files
in X Mosaic.*

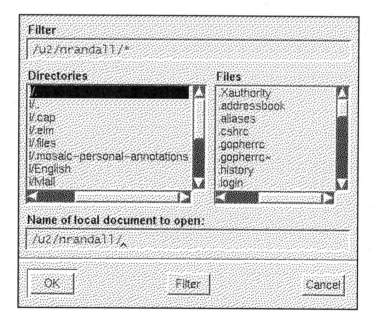

FIGURE 10.5.

*Loading local files
in Mac Mosaic.*

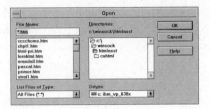

FIGURE 10.6.

*Loading local files in
Windows Mosaic.*

The purpose of Open URL is straightforward. Often through mailing lists or newsgroups, you'll hear of interesting new Web sites to visit, and you'll be given the URL address in the message. Type that address into the Open URL box, and Mosaic will make the connection and load the document exactly as if you'd clicked on a hyperlink.

If you store HTML files on your local drive, you can load them into Mosaic through the Open Local feature. This is a highly useful feature if you're writing HTML code and want to test the appearance and functionality of a page, or when software authors provide HTML files with their software. You can also save retrieved documents as HTML files to your local drives—a good idea for long documents that don't change frequently—and then load them locally.

Saving Files

In the File menu of every Mosaic version is a Save As feature. With this feature, you can save the currently displayed file onto your local disk in one of several formats. The difference in format points to the difference in platforms. X Mosaic allows you to save in plain text, formatted text, PostScript, or HTML format. The options for both Mac Mosaic and Windows Mosaic are text and HTML.

There are several good reasons for saving a file, but the main one is to have the information readily available without having to go out into the Net and find it every time you want to see it. This feature will become increasingly important in the future, as full documents begin to be provided over the Web, but for now the primary interest lies in capturing text files and HTML files to disk. In the case of HTML files, having long files available locally means you can load them into Mosaic instantly (through the Open Local option) without worrying about the destination connections (although the hyperlinks are still dependent on those connections). You can also use them as a basis for your own HTML files.

One warning, however, is that saving HTML documents does not save the corresponding inline graphics (which remain on the remote server). If you load the document from your local machine with inline images toggled on, Mosaic will go onto the Net to find the image files. This can take a great deal of time.

All Mosaics offer another way of saving files to disk: the Option menu's Load to Disk option (or Load to Local Disk in X Mosaic). When Load to Disk is toggled on and you click a hyperlink, the incoming file is saved on your local disk rather than being displayed in the document view window. There are several useful functions for this feature. First, if you know you want to capture a file but you don't actually need to see it, you can turn on Load to Disk and click the link to transfer the file without losing the file currently displayed. Second, in the case of links to graphic, audio, or video files (or such items as PostScript or other special-format files), Load to Disk lets you store the file and does not activate the viewers of players that would otherwise be necessary.

Printing

Several months ago, I got into a discussion in a Cello mailing list about Cello's and Mosaic's relative strengths for printing. The point I made at the time was that, given the nature of hypertexts, I couldn't understand why anyone would want to print from one of these programs in the first place. I seemed to be in the minority, however; in fact, I was shouted down quite energetically.

Given the attention by Mosaic's designers to ensuring that the print functions work, I now know that people want to print Mosaic screens, even if they're hypertext documents and therefore don't function well as printed documents. People want to print out documents page by page as they find interesting ones, and all three Mosaics allow you to do this. In all versions of the program, you can print the document as you like, with each individual version adhering to the standards of that system. Windows Mosaic offers a Page Preview option, for example, whereas Mac Mosaic includes the standard Mac Page Setup feature. X Mosaic allows you to print in plain-text, formatted-text, PostScript, or HTML format.

The argument I was given about printing Web pages is that otherwise you can't examine them in a different location or show them to others (at a meeting, for example). This, of course, is quite true. But I maintain that, in general, printing a Web page is counterproductive to what that page is trying to accomplish. First, it eliminates the hypertextual concept of the Web environment. Second, it's extremely rare that one or even a series of a dozen pages can convey the flavor of what Web access is truly like.

Printing does make sense for pages that are primarily text and hence are less likely to be read as you browse past, and which contain no hypertext links.

Viewing the Document Source

If you're interested in learning to write HTML documents for publishing on the Web, Mosaic's document source feature is invaluable. Available across all platforms, the View Source (or Document Source in Windows Mosaic) feature brings up a separate window that shows the HTML source code for the displayed document in all its tagged glory.

Although you might not care how the document you're looking at was actually constructed, as an HTML writer you can make extensive use of this code by simply borrowing ideas you find useful. Especially in the case of the construction of forms and other complex objects, it's much easier to alter code that you already know works well than to develop the form or map entirely from scratch.

From the Document Source window, you can copy specific sections or save the entire file to your local disk. At this stage in Mosaic's development, you can't edit the code and apply the edits to the currently loaded document, but that feature, apparently, is under development. This will be an extremely useful feature for HTML document designers, because they will be able to see, instantly, the results of making changes. As it stands, just being able to access the HTML source is a supremely useful feature, but NCSA would do well to develop it even further to better assist designers.

Finding Text in the Current Document

Web documents can be long. In fact, some require you to scroll down seemingly forever, or to hit the Page Down key as many as 10 times. Although such documents can be criticized as being way too long for good usability, they exist and aren't likely to disappear soon. Furthermore, some documents are necessarily long because they're used as ongoing archives and are updated weekly or even daily. NCSA's What's New page is one such document, and by the time the end of the month comes (at which point a new archive is begun for this page), the document is several screens in length. Of course, loading a long ASCII document into a Mosaic window can result in a multiscreen reading as well.

To compensate for this inevitability, Mosaic includes a feature for finding text strings in the current document. This feature is found in different places, and is of varying quality in the three versions. In X Mosaic the feature is called Find in Current, and is found in the File menu, whereas in both Mac Mosaic and Windows Mosaic the item is called Find and is part of the Edit menu. Nor do all three sport the same internal features. Mac Mosaic offers a Context Sensitive search and a Search Backward option (extremely useful), whereas Windows Mosaic offers neither of these but has a Find Next option. Whatever the case, the point is that for many documents the Find command is important, and as HTML documents grow in size and complexity, this feature will become crucial.

In fact, Mosaic's designers could profitably expand this feature. Why not allow a search for HTML codes, heading types, list types, map locations, specific file types, or partial URL addresses (within links), and other options? All of these would be useful, particularly as HTML increases in usage.

Hiding or Displaying Document View Features

As mentioned, Mosaic on all platforms displays the URL address (and, in two cases, the document title at the top of the viewing window), and a status line and navigation buttons elsewhere. The problem with these items, for users who aren't fortunate enough to have full-page or other workstation-sized monitors, is that they take up room on the screen that might better be used for a more complete view of the loaded document. This is especially true for MS-Windows users who use 14-inch VGA monitors (and there are still lots of them around), and nearly as true for Mac Classic users as well. Even with higher-resolution displays, however, such as Windows SuperVGA mode or on a larger Mac monitor, the amount of document information actually on the screen is sometimes limited. It's even worse when all of the various Mosaic features are present as well.

Mosaic enables MS-Windows and Mac users to customize the appearance of their screens by giving them the option to hide certain elements. These toggles are contained in the Options menu of each program. For Mac Mosaic, the commands are Hide URLs and Hide Status Messages (which then become "Show" commands in the same menu). The similar commands in Windows Mosaic are Show Current URL and Show Status Bar (turning these items on puts a checkmark beside them). Windows Mosaic also offers a Show Toolbar option, which lets you get rid of the status bar as well, leaving all control to the menu items.

Of all these features, I find the status bar the most difficult to be without, for reasons stated in the section titled "The Status Bar," earlier in this chapter.

Toggling Off Inline Images

The graphics images built into an HTML document are known as *inline images*. These images are actually separate files, loaded into the HTML page by the specific command that appears on that page. (See Part V, "Weaving a Web," for details.) Almost invariably, each of these files is larger—often much, much larger—than the HTML file itself, and therefore loading the images significantly increases the time it takes to load the document into Mosaic. As Mosaic and HTML become more popular, more graphics-oriented documents are appearing, and these can take as much as 10 full minutes to load for users with modem connections. Even with high-speed access, sometimes there's simply no point using the bandwidth to load graphics, especially if you're linking to a page only for the purposes of using it as a jump station to another page.

For this reason, the designers of Mosaic offer a toggle switch that enables you to turn off the loading of inline graphics. X Mosaic stores this switch in its Options menu and calls it Delay Image Loading. Mac Mosaic's version of this command is also in the Options menu and is named Auto-Load Images. In Windows Mosaic, the option is called Display Inline Images and is contained in the General tab of the Preferences dialog box. When Mosaic loads, it has these features on by default; by changing the Preferences dialog box, you can specify that you want it to load with the toggle off. This is an extremely useful switch, especially given the tendency of recent HTML documents to use multiple graphic images.

If you enter a page with inline images off, and you want to display the same page complete with images, you can toggle inline images on and use the Reload command in any of the three versions. (See the next section for details.) Unless you want to see *all* of the images, however, this isn't necessary. Often you need to check out only one or two, in which case Mosaic offers a solution. In X Mosaic and Windows Mosaic, moving the cursor over the image symbol and clicking the right mouse button (far left button for unaltered X systems) commands Mosaic to load that specific image file. Mac Mosaic users accomplish the same thing by moving the cursor over the icon and simply clicking with the mouse's only button. Although this feature isn't immediately apparent when you start using Mosaic, it's a highly useful one to know as you make your way across the Web.

Reloading Documents

All versions of Mosaic offer the possibility of reloading the current document. Called Reload Current in X Mosaic's File menu, Reload in Windows Mosaic's Navigate menu, and Reload in Mac Mosaic's File menu, this feature does the same thing as if you'd clicked on a hyperlink featuring your current location. Each version also sports an icon in its toolbar or icon bar that lets you accomplish the same thing.

There are three reasons to reload a document. First, if you've been using Mosaic without automatically loading inline images and you discover you want to see your current document's images, you can toggle the image feature on and then reload the document, thereby revealing the images. Second, if the Mosaic browser has somehow garbled the current document (not surprisingly, this isn't all that uncommon with Windows Mosaic), reloading will restore its appearance. Third, if you're creating your own HTML files, reloading the image lets you see the effects of the changes you're making as you go along. Some HTML editors do this for you, but if you're creating images using a text editor (such as UNIX's vi or Pico, or MS-Windows Notepad), using Reload is obviously much faster than using the Load Local File option all the time.

Loading the Home URL

The *home URL* is the URL address you specify using Mosaic's configuration tools or by editing the configuration files. Once it's specified, you can move immediately to that URL address by clicking the Home button in X Mosaic or the Home icon in Mac Mosaic and Windows Mosaic, or by selecting the Home command from the Navigate menu of all three Mosaics. Click once, and you're home (and you thought Dorothy and Toto had it easy).

This command seems almost pointless at first, but in fact it comes in handy quite often. After working your way around the Web for a while, you'll almost certainly find yourself reading pages you had no intention of reading, with no real idea of where you might be (nor do you necessarily care). If your home page is a useful one—and you should make sure that it is—it is a jumping-off point to a host of other sites, and getting back there with one click can save you the time it would take to type the URL address in the Open URL dialog box, or even to fire up the History list or Hotlist and find it from there. It's an obvious feature, but a good one.

Configuring Fonts

Although HTML itself controls much of how a document appears when loaded into your browser, Mosaic lets you customize at least one significant feature: fonts. In all versions, you can specify the font that displays for each heading level and for menus, directories, and other document items that Mosaic displays. These items are put in place by the author of the HTML document, but how each is actually displayed is up to you with this customizable Mosaic feature. All versions contain the Fonts feature in the Options menu.

X Mosaic's font-configuration system is the least involved of the lot, offering a choice of three varieties of four different fonts. Mac Mosaic's system is the most intricate, with a full dialog box containing several strong options. Windows Mosaic's font system exists entirely in one cascaded menu, each option of which yields a separate font dialog box. The different font-configuration systems are covered under their respective versions in the corresponding section later in this chapter.

Being able to configure fonts is as important for Mosaic as it is for any other program, and more important than for many. Much of Mosaic's power—the World Wide Web's power, actually—resides in the usefulness and attractiveness of document appearance, and tailoring this appearance precisely to your liking means that the Web succeeds even more than it was designed to do. For easy reading and browsing, and for showing the Web to other users, font configuration makes a great deal of difference.

The History File

All versions of Mosaic assist you in returning to a document you've previously visited during the current session. Called the History list in Mac Mosaic and Windows Mosaic, and Window History in X Mosaic, this feature keeps track of where you've been on your Web travels. By calling it up, you can return to any of these places by clicking the document you wish to revisit.

Actually, it's not quite as simple as that. Mosaic's history feature works well, and is essential if you do any amount of browsing and returning during your Web sessions, but it's not quite as straightforward as it seems. Each browser has its own logic for which document references it stores, to the degree that switching from version to version (as many people do) can be fairly confusing. This feature isn't even in the same place in all versions: It's in X Mosaic's and Windows Mosaic's Navigate menu, but it's part of the icon/URL area, as a pull-down window, in Mac Mosaic. Furthermore, X Mosaic offers not just one but two forms of document history. The standard form, Window History, displays the URLs visited during the current Mosaic session, but the Global History feature keeps track of all URLs you've ever visited, in all the time you've used Mosaic, either currently or in the past.

The Hotlist

Navigating the Web productively means keeping track of where you've been so that you can return to the most important (or most desired) documents you've visited. In computer terminology, such a process is known as *bookmarking*; but Mosaic doesn't use this term, even though other browsers (Cello, for instance) and other Internet programs or program types (such as Gopher) do so very usefully. But Mosaic is nothing if not individualistic, and it refers to its bookmarking item as the *hotlist*.

When you add a document to Mosaic's hotlist, you're recording that document's URL address and title so that you can easily access it again. Every version of Mosaic treats the hotlist concept entirely differently, and each of the following individual sections deals with hotlisting in greater detail. Windows Mosaic, for instance, actually has two bookmarking features. One is the hotlist, which is accessible from the Open URL command of the File menu, and another, far more powerful, is this version's exceptional Menu Editor, accessible from the Navigate menu.

It is impossible to overestimate the importance of bookmarking to any Internet browsing tool. Similarly, it is impossible to overstate how much a well-designed bookmarking system adds to the value of a browsing program, and to the use of the Web in general. Mosaic's hotlisting is strong, but with the possible exception of Windows Mosaic's menu editor system, it could be better.

Annotating Documents

Not only is bookmarking important, but so is the ability to comment on sites you've visited. For your own browsing, and to help or guide the browsing of others on your network, noting a document's significant content or features saves hours of cumulative time going over the same ground again and again. Wasting unnecessary time this way is one of the Web's very real dangers.

Mosaic solves the problem by letting you annotate any document you're currently visiting. By *annotating*, you essentially attach a sticky note to the document, so when you return to the document, or another person on the network visits the site, this sticky note calls out, "Read me first." Once again, each version of Mosaic handles the feature differently, and all are dealt with in the individual sections later in this chapter. To date, in addition, only the X Window and Macintosh versions allow both text and audio annotations (the MS-Windows version will surely follow, even though annotation is far weaker in this version than the others so far), and only the X Mosaic version lets you use HTML formatting to make the annotations more noticeable.

An extremely important feature, annotations must become more powerful if they are to realize their full capability, especially across a workgroup.

Caching Documents

Because Web pages are loaded from a remote computer, not your own, they can often take a fairly long time to load. That's because retrieving them depends on so many factors: the speed of your connection, the status of the remote machine and its network (other network activities take priority over your trying to download a page), and (if you're working from LAN connection) the status of your own network as well. For modem users, retrieving a Web page is never as fast as one would like, but even with high-speed connections it can become tedious.

The problem comes when you're working with several Web documents and keep returning to one or two of them repeatedly. The last thing you want to have happen every time you want to access a document is for Mosaic to head out into the Net, find the document, make the

connection with the remote server, and download the page. Fortunately, the program offers a feature called *document caching*, designed precisely to avoid this problem. Mosaic keeps the last few documents (you can specify how many, or at least how many bytes) in your local system's memory, reloading them instantly when you request them via the history list, the navigation buttons, or a hyperlink. Essentially, Mosaic checks locally for the existence of a document before sending the HTTP request out to the network.

This feature is not only useful—it's indispensable. In the case of X Mosaic and Mac Mosaic, you can run multiple windows of the program, meaning that you can keep one window with a base document while you browse with the other, but even here the caching system is useful. You don't want separate windows for all frequently accessed documents (things would get extremely cluttered extremely quickly), and caching prevents this from being necessary. Windows Mosaic does not support multiple windows, so caching is simply a necessity if you're going to get anything done at all.

World Wide Web Starting Points

The Web is a big place, and it's getting bigger by the hour. As a result, it's impossible for new Web users to figure out where to begin. Mosaic solves this problem by including a collection of useful and popular Web sites (the two aren't necessarily one and the same) that serve as starting points. By the time you've worked your way through even a few of these sites, you'll have both a sense of where you want to be and a hotlist file to take you back to the most interesting spots.

The starting points appear differently in the three versions. In X Mosaic and Mac Mosaic, they're in the Navigate menu, whereas Windows Mosaic ships with two menus, Starting Points and Personal, both of which feature various sites. The menu items for X Mosaic are Internet Starting Points (a collection of interesting sites) and Internet Resources Meta-Index (a series of Web-based directories and indexes). In Mac Mosaic, these are called Network Starting Points and Internet Resources Meta-Index. Windows Mosaic's much-different version of this idea includes two separate top-level menus with all of these sites, including important Gopher, FTP, and search sites as well.

It's hard to imagine getting started on the Web without these sites, and some of them you'll use repeatedly no matter how long you've been at it. But it's also hard to imagine users sticking with these and not developing a much more useful hotlist instead.

Help

Mosaic is easy to use—so easy, in fact, that there seems absolutely no reason to have complete documentation for the program. For many users, though, the documentation will never be necessary, because everything they need to know is included in one basic instruction: "click the links." Still, as with just about any program, there's more to Mosaic than just clicking the links—as this chapter should, by now, have demonstrated. And not all of Mosaic's menu commands are instantly recognizable, especially at first (Load to Disk and Group Annotations, for instance). Thankfully, there's help available.

There isn't, however, local help. When you access the documentation from Mosaic's help menu, no matter which version you're using, you aren't asking for a help system to be loaded from your local hard disk (as you would for a spreadsheet program, for instance). Instead, you're asking Mosaic to connect with the NCSA server and display the appropriate user manual. In other words, help exists elsewhere.

Windows Mosaic and Mac Mosaic users have a bit of an advantage here. Although there was no help system in place (the documentation wasn't ready) until very recently, NCSA has packaged the Windows Mosaic help system in a `.zip` file that you can download and install to your local disk. This means you can use Mosaic and its help system more quickly and even offline. The same exists for the Mac documentation, which is available as a Common Ground document (NCSA also provides a Common Ground mini-viewer), as well as a compressed `tar` archive.

Mosaic help is useful for any of the program's features. It's also useful in that it provides links to HTML documentation, in case you're interested in constructing your own Web pages. But local help should be the rule, not the exception. And no, you can't just download and save all the individual pages, because the inline graphics don't come with them.

Mail Technical Support

After you've used Mosaic for a while, you'll almost certainly discover some things you wish worked a bit differently, or you'll realize that you could do with some features that just aren't available. If so, you'll appreciate the Mail Developers feature, in the Help menu of Mac Mosaic and Windows Mosaic and the File menu of X Mosaic.

With this feature, you can send e-mail to the people who are continually upgrading your version of Mosaic. Don't expect a response, though, other than a canned one. What's supposed to happen is that NCSA's programmers store your suggestions, adding them to a Wish List or a Bug List that you can see by calling up the home pages for your version of Mosaic. Whether or not this actually happens is anyone's guess, but try it if you want. More importantly, this feature demonstrates Mosaic's potential to work with electronic mail features, and that's something you can make use of when developing your own HTML documents.

Send E-Mail

You can send electronic mail messages from any of the three Mosaics. The feature is selectable from the File menu, and doing so yields the Mail window, in which you can type the recipient's name and the message. You can also include a *signature*—that is, a piece of boilerplated text that you append to all messages—but you can't send file attachments. As with practically all browsers, you can only send e-mail, not read it.

Multimedia Capabilities

All three Mosaics offer multimedia capabilities. Inline graphics can be built into HTML pages, and other graphics can be specified as downloadable files. In addition, Mosaic can play both sound files and video files. Unfortunately, Mosaic doesn't ship with the viewers or players necessary to make use of these files. Instead, you must buy or download the necessary software, then configure Mosaic to load the programs whenever the specific file type is downloaded. See the individual section following for details on configuring each version of Mosaic. (See Chapter 12, "More Browsers for Microsoft Windows," for a detailed discussion of acquiring and configuring add-on viewers and players.)

So far, the use of these features is limited, and for the most part video and sound are cosmetic features only. Typically, these files are huge, so unless you have a high-speed connection you won't want to bother with them. As the Web develops, however, and HTML designers find new ways to work with sound and video, they'll become increasingly important. By that time, versions of NCSA Mosaic will likely ship with built-in viewers and players, as commercial versions of Mosaic already do.

Configuration Options

Mosaic is extensively configurable. You can specify a wide range of viewers and players to handle graphics, sound, video, and special-format file types. In addition, you can determine which fonts will display which headings and feature formats. Hotlists are obviously configurable, but at least one version of Mosaic—Windows Mosaic—also lets you configure the hotlists as top-level (and cascading) menus. Furthermore, you can set Mosaic's appearance, including background color; color and style of hyperlink; whether or not URL displays, status bars, or icon bars are visible; and so forth. And you can set your home page and tell Mosaic whether or not to retrieve that page as the program loads.

The trick is to search the menus and the help documents for ways of configuring Mosaic to suit your needs exactly, experimenting to give it precisely the right feel. For some features, viewers and players for example, configuration is necessary for Mosaic to work properly. For most, however, you're simply setting your preferences, but these are extremely important for the way in which you use Mosaic and hence the Web itself.

NCSA Mosaic for the X Window System

FTP Site: `ftp.ncsa.uiuc.edu`

Directory: `/Mosaic/Unix/binaries/2.6b/`

Filenames: `Mosaic-sun.2.6b1.Z` (Sun 4, SunOS 4.1.x)

`Mosaic-sun-lresolv.2.6b1.Z` (Sun 4, SunOS 4.1.x, no DNS)

`Mosaic-sgi.2.6b1.Z` (Silicon Graphics, IRIX 4.x)

`Mosaic-indy.2.6b1.Z` (Silicon Graphics, IRIX 5.x)

`Mosaic-ibm.2.6b1.Z` (IBM RS/6000, AIX 3.2)

`Mosaic-dec.2.6b1.Z` (DEC MIPS Ultrix)

`Mosaic-alpha.2.6b1.Z` (DEC Alpha AXP, OSF/1)

`Mosaic-hp700.2.6b1.Z` (HP 9000/700, HP/UX 9.x)

The X Window version of NCSA Mosaic was the first of the three, and in some ways it remains the most extensively developed. It is unique in the following areas:

- It offers four different file formats in its Save As, Mail To, and Print options: formatted text, plain text, HTML, and PostScript.
- It uses a button bar rather than an icon bar for navigation and other commands.
- It maintains a global history of all documents you've ever visited (as does Mac Mosaic).
- It offers a Reload Images command to bypass the usual cached images.
- It lets you refresh a current document from memory rather than fully reloading.
- It enables audio annotations (as does Mac Mosaic).
- It enables retrieval of selected images with the left mouse button (as does Windows Mosaic).
- It gives you capability to flush the image cache to retrieve system memory.
- It features an advanced cut-and-paste mechanism that preserves formatting.
- It offers *Common Client Interface* (CCI), which allows external applications to communicate with running sessions of Mosaic via TCP/IP protocol.
- It offers support for HTML tables.

File Menu

New Window

If you want to keep your current document open as a base, and start browsing from a new Mosaic window, select New Window. Your default home page will be loaded into the new window, and you can go from there. You can open as many new Mosaic windows as you want, but beware of clutter.

Clone Window

This is the same as New Window, except instead of loading your home page, Mosaic creates a new window that contains the same document as the one you were looking at when you selected the option. Very useful for working through a series of linked documents when you need to refer back to one.

Open URL

This command opens a dialog box in which you enter the full URL address of the document or site you want loaded. (See Figure 10.7.) Keep in mind that you must start the URL with the protocol type, which will often be http:// but might also be gopher://, ftp:/, or any other valid URL address. The important thing is that you enter the *complete* address, or you'll find yourself redoing it until you get it right.

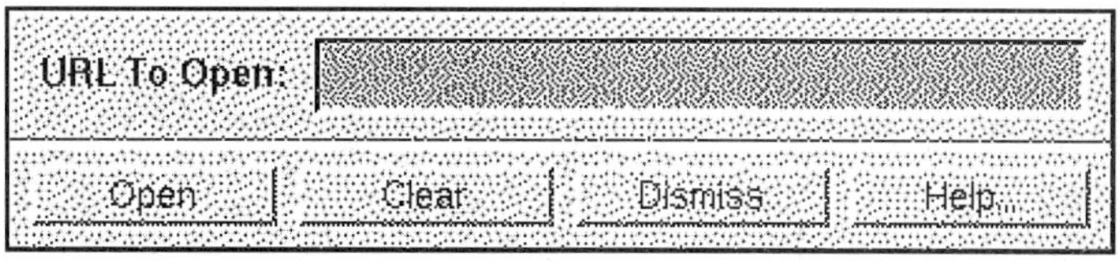

FIGURE 10.7.

X Mosaic's Open URL dialog box.

URL To Open:

Open   Clear   Dismiss   Help...

Open Local

This command lets you load a file from your local hard disk (or local network disk) into Mosaic. The command presents you with a standard X Window dialog box, from which you select the directory and file you wish to load. X Mosaic includes a Filter item to help you ascertain that this is the correct file, after which the OK button loads it.

Reload Current

Reload Current retrieves the current file from its remote (or local) server, and it's used either to display any changes you've made to the HTML code since you originally loaded it, or to display inline images if you had them toggled off for the original retrieval. One thing to keep in mind is that images, if they were originally loaded, are not loaded again; they're grabbed from the image cache. If you want to redisplay images, select Reload Images instead.

Reload Images

When you reload a document (see Reload Current), the inline images are taken from the document cache, not reloaded from the source. Sometimes, however, you need to load new versions of the image; in this case, select the Reload Images command. This will flush out the cached images and cause a full reload from the server, including all images.

Refresh Current

If something goes wrong with your document's appearance, Refresh Current redisplays it with the original data intact. It doesn't actually reload the document but rather recaptures the code that resides in memory.

Find in Current

Particularly in long Web documents, it's handy to be able to search for specific strings of text. This command enables you to do so. This is a perfunctory search mechanism only, with options for a duplicate search but little else. (See Figure 10.8.) In the case of extremely long documents with complex search needs, it's not highly useful.

FIGURE 10.8.

X Mosaic's Find in Current dialog box.

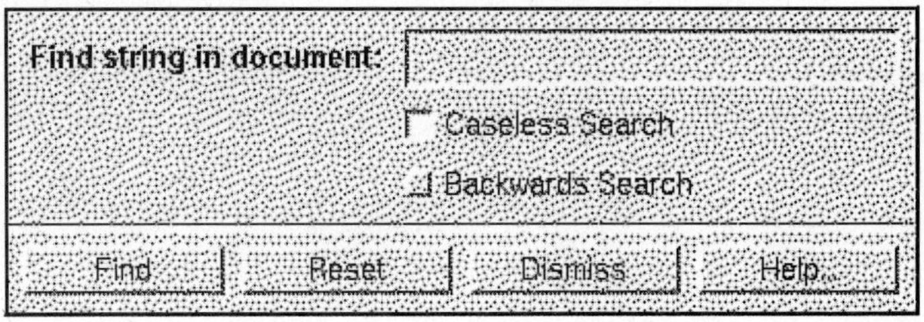

Find string in document:

☐ Caseless Search
☐ Backwards Search

| Find | Reset | Dismiss | Help |

View Source

This command opens a separate window that displays the source code for the currently displayed file. When you invoke this command, the document that displays contains HTML coding features, letting you see how the document was actually constructed. It's immensely useful if you're developing your own HTML documents, because it helps you imitate good ideas you see.

Save As

When you want to save the currently displayed document as a file to your local disk, this is the feature to use. You are shown an X Window dialog box that lets you select the directory and enter the filename, and you can save the document in one of four formats: HTML, PostScript, or plain or formatted text. This feature is more convenient than Load to Local Disk.

Print

This command yields the Print Document window (see Figure 10.9), with which you can print the displayed file to the printer you choose. As with Save As, you can print in plain text, formatted text, PostScript, or HTML format.

FIGURE 10.9.

X Mosaic's Print dialog box.

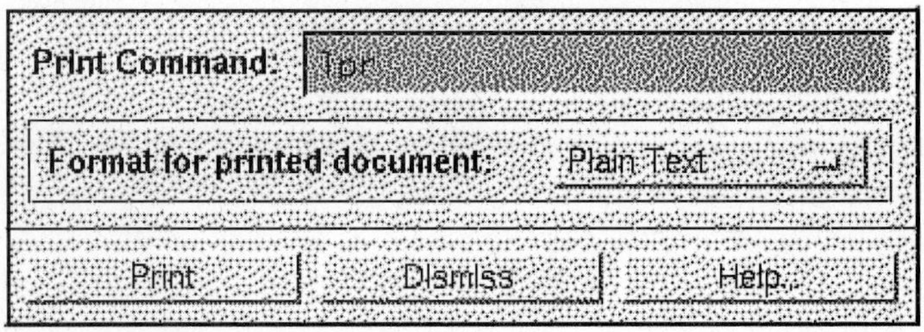

Print Command: lpr

Format for printed document: Plain Text

| Print | Dismiss | Help |

Send Email

If you want to send e-mail without loading a separate program, the Send Email command lets you do so. (See Figure 10.10.) This is a limited e-mail program, but it's more than adequate for sending most messages. You cannot read e-mail through this program, however.

FIGURE 10.10.

X Mosaic's Mail To dialog box.

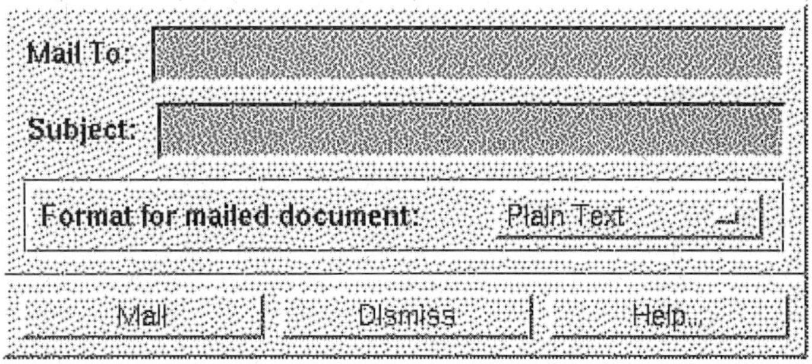

Close Window

With the New Window and Clone Window commands, your X Mosaic session can quickly become next to unwieldy. Close Window lets you get rid of the currently displayed document, leaving the others open. If only one document is loaded when you select Close Window, X Mosaic shuts down without asking your permission; use this feature carefully.

Exit Program

After you confirm that you really want to exit the program, X Mosaic closes all windows and removes itself from memory.

Options Menu

Fancy Selections

X Mosaic lets you cut and paste material from document to document (and to documents in other programs). Fancy Selections—surely one of computerdom's more ambiguous and initially meaningless command names—maintains the formatting of the selected text in order to duplicate its appearance as much as possible in the destination document. With this command toggled off, only the text itself is copied.

Load To Local Disk

With this command toggled on, you're presented with a Save Binary File dialog box whenever you click on a hyperlink or access the navigation buttons. This is useful for downloading files such as graphics, sound, and video, which have a separate hyperlink for the FTP function. For capturing the HTML document itself, use Save As instead.

Delay Image Loading

This toggle switch lets you turn off the automatic loading of inline images. It's especially useful for users with modem connections, to avoid long transfer times, but it's also useful if you're looking for information around the Web and don't care about the graphics with which you might be presented. This is a vital feature.

Load Images in Current

Often, when you've turned inline images off, you'll come across a document whose graphics are crucial to its comprehension. If such a document appears, rather than turning on images and reloading the document, select Load Images in Current, which keeps the existing document in memory but accesses the server to transfer all the inline images.

Reload Config Files

This command causes all configuration items to be reloaded, so that X Mosaic is fully aware of all associations and extensions. It's also useful if you alter a file association or other viewer/player information, so you don't have to exit Mosaic and then reload.

Flush Image Cache

Inline images are cached in memory to save retrieval time if you reselect the document in which they originally appeared. They can be large files, however, and you'll quickly accumulate many of them in memory. Flush Image Cache clears this memory for other purposes.

Clear Global History

X Mosaic maintains a list of all Web documents you've visited, not just in the current session but throughout your entire browsing career. This information is kept in a file called `.mosaic-global-history`, a dot (hidden) file in your home directory. Whenever you retrieve a document, X Mosaic checks this file to see if you've been there before, and from this check it determines whether the links on the retrieved page are shown as previously viewed or still unviewed. Clearing this lets you start over, although bear in mind that it also clears the current session's history as well.

Fonts

This command lets you choose which of four fonts you want to use to view documents (Times, Helvetica, New Century, or Lucida Bright), and the size and style of these fonts as well. Note that these fonts apply to all heading levels.

Anchor Underlines

With this command, you choose the way a hyperlink is underlined. Your choices are default underlines; no underlines; or light, medium, or heavy underlines. With no underlines, the color of the hyperlink is the only way of knowing that a hyperlink exists, so this selection is not recommended for monochrome displays.

HTTP 1.0 Encryption

This feature has yet to be implemented as of version 2.5, but in the future it will support PEM and PGP encryption schemes for assisting document privacy.

Navigate Menu

Back

This command takes you back to the document that appears immediately before the current document in the Window History. Usually it's where you were last—but not always, and especially not when you used the History Window to access the current document.

Forward

Forward takes you to the document that preceded the current one. It differs from Back in that it doesn't use the Window History as its basis, so you can use it to toggle back and forth from one document to another over and over again; confusingly named.

Home Document

This command retrieves the document specified in your configuration file as your "home" document and loads it into Mosaic. Convenient for finding your way out of a hopeless navigation maze.

Window History

This important command yields the Window History window, which displays the title of every document you've viewed in your current X Mosaic session. From here you can return instantly to any document in the list, without having to backtrack using the navigation buttons.

Hotlist

By invoking the Hotlist command, you bring up the Hotlist View window (see Figure 10.11), which shows the documents you've bookmarked to this point. Click the document you want to retrieve, then on Go To, and Mosaic will connect with the remote server and perform the download. From this window you can also add new documents, or delete documents you no longer want bookmarked. You can edit the name and URL of a URL entry, copy an entry and later paste it with the Insert command, and insert URLs and list entries. The Up button moves you up one level in the hotlist hierarchy, and the Save button enables you to save the current hotlist to an HTML file.

FIGURE 10.11.

X Mosaic's Hotlist dialog box.

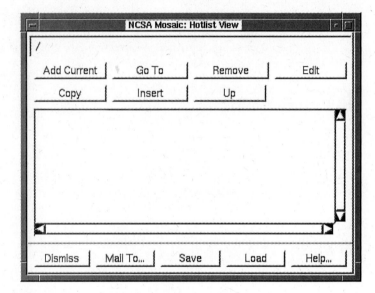

Add Current to Hotlist

When you arrive at a document you want to bookmark, selecting this command adds the document to your hotlist. From then on, you can access the document using the Hotlist View window.

Internet Starting Points

This command is actually a bookmark; invoking it retrieves an NCSA-prepared document called Internet Starting Points, which offers hyperlinks to a rich variety of information pages throughout the Internet.

Internet Resources Meta-Index

Similar to Internet Starting Points, this command is a link to a bookmarked page. It retrieves an NCSA-prepared document with hyperlinks to a variety of indexes, directories, and collections of information on the Net.

Annotate Menu

Annotate...

When you want to make comments about a document you've retrieved, for the sake of your future browsing or the browsing of colleagues, the Annotate command lets you do so. (See Figure 10.12.) You enter the comments in the Annotate window that results from selecting this command, and X Mosaic adds a hyperlink on the current page that, when clicked, reveals the comments. You can add as many annotations as you want. Note that you can type in your annotation and/or include an existing file for yourself or colleagues to read. The Commit button sets the annotation in place.

FIGURE 10.12.

X Mosaic's Annotate dialog box.

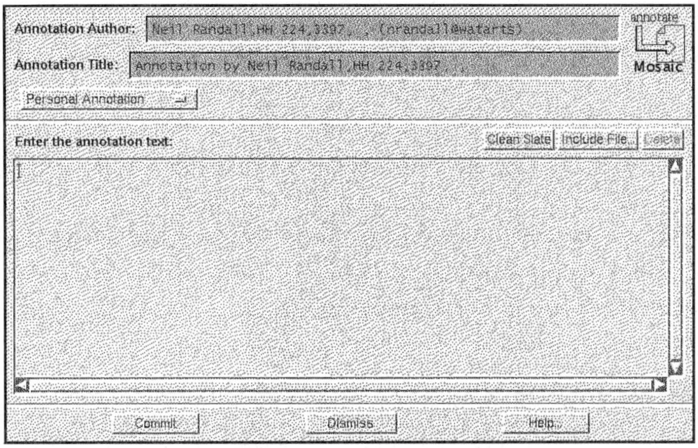

Edit This Annotation

When reading an annotation, this command lets you alter the annotation by adding text or appending a file to it.

Delete This Annotation

Rather obviously, this command deletes the currently visible annotation.

Help Menu

About

Here you find standard About material, including version number, resource hyperlinks, developer information, and so forth.

Manual

This command retrieves the online X Mosaic user manual from the NCSA server.

What's New

Invoking the What's New command retrieves NCSA's famous What's New With NCSA Mosaic and the WWW page, a regularly (weekly or even daily) updated page showing new resources for Web users. Why it's here and not in the Navigate menu with the other NCSA pages is anyone's guess.

Demo

This command retrieves the NCSA Mosaic Demo Document, with hyperlinks to a variety of different types of pages, including audio and video demonstrations. As with What's New, it belongs in the Navigate menu, but for some reason it isn't.

On Version 2.5

This tells you which version of X Mosaic you're using (2.5, in this case), and retrieves a file from NCSA that lists changes from previous editions and states when the next version is scheduled for release.

On Window

An actual Help screen, On Window gives you information about hotkey commands, menu items, and the parts of X Mosaic's screen.

On FAQ

This command yields a document offering hyperlinks to Frequently Asked Questions about X Mosaic. If you're having a problem with the program, someone else has probably had it already, and the solution might well be found here.

On HTML

From here you retrieve a series of Web documents outlining the HyperText Markup Language (with which Web pages are constructed), with links to tutorials, examples, and other HTML reference documents.

On URLs

On URLs opens a hyperdocument dealing with Uniform Resource Locators—how they work and what they mean.

Mail Developers

This command opens a rudimentary e-mail window designed exclusively for sending comments, problems, complaints, bribes, and threats to X Mosaic's developers. It automatically includes your e-mail address (as long as you've set it up in the configuration file), and clicking on Send transmits the message. Don't expect a personal response, though; your comments will be logged, but you'll get something along the lines of, "Dear Occupant, we appreciate your ...." How deep the appreciation actually runs is unclear.

NCSA Mosaic for the Apple Macintosh: Features and Menus

FTP Site: ftp.ncsa.uiuc.edu

Directory: /Mosaic/Mac

Filenames: NCSAMosaic200B9.hqx

NCSAMosaic200B9.hqx (Power Macintosh)

Mosaic for the Macintosh was released second to X Mosaic, and its developers have spent a great deal of time developing the program to take advantage of the Mac's strengths and idiosyncrasies. Mac Mosaic's unique features include

- An extensive hotlist-editing dialog box
- Audio annotations
- The capability to display external graphics as inline graphics
- An easily accessible document history (from the icon bar)
- An extensive and highly usable Preferences configuration box
- An extremely usable (and powerful) Styles dialog box

File Menu

New Window

If you want to keep your current document open as a base and start browsing from a new Mac Mosaic window, select New Window. Your default home page will be loaded into the new window, and you can go from there. You can open as many new Mosaic windows as you want, although beware of clutter.

Clone Window

This is the same as New Window, except instead of loading your home page, Mosaic creates a new window that contains the same document as the one you were looking at when you selected the option. Very useful for working through a series of linked documents to which you need to refer back.

Open URL

This command opens a dialog box in which you enter the full URL address of the document or site you want loaded. (See Figure 10.13.) Keep in mind that you must start the URL with the protocol type, which will often be http:// but might also be gopher://, ftp://, or any other valid URL address. The important thing is that you enter the *complete* address, or you'll find yourself redoing it until you get it right.

FIGURE 10.13.

Mac Mosaic's Open URL dialog box.

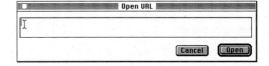

Open Local

This command lets you load a file from your local hard disk (or local network disk) into Mosaic. The command presents you with a standard Macintosh dialog box, from which you select the directory and file you want to load.

Reload

Reload retrieves the current file from its remote (or local) server, and it's used either to display any changes you've made to the HTML code since you originally loaded it, or to display inline images if you had them toggled off for the original retrieval. One thing to keep in mind is that images, if they were originally loaded, are not loaded again. (They're grabbed from the image cache.)

Close

With the New Window and Clone commands, your Mac Mosaic session can quickly become unwieldy. Close lets you get rid of the currently displayed document, leaving the others open.

Save As

When you want to save the currently displayed document as a file to your local disk, use this feature. You'll be shown a Macintosh dialog box that lets you select the directory and enter the filename, and you can save the document in either text or HTML format. (See Figure 10.14.)

FIGURE 10.14.

Mac Mosaic's Save As dialog box.

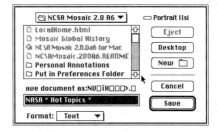

Page Setup

This command brings up the standard Macintosh Page Setup dialog box, from which you can specify the format of the pages as you want them printed.

Print

From this command, you can print the Mac Mosaic document you're currently reading. It will appear on paper as it appears on-screen, tailored by your specifications in the Page Setup command.

Quit

Invoke this command to exit Mac Mosaic. (Okay, so it's obvious.)

Edit Menu

Can't Undo/Undo

This is the standard Macintosh command for taking back your last action. If it's dimmed and says Can't Undo, you can't take the last action back.

Cut

This command lets you cut text from various dialog boxes, such as Annotations. You can't cut text from a Mosaic document itself.

Copy

When you select a block of text with the mouse, you can use this command to copy the text into the Mac's Clipboard. Keep in mind, however, that only text is copied. Inline images are not.

Paste

This is the Mac's standard Paste command, useful in the URL box, dialog boxes, and text fields. You can't paste text into a Mosaic document on-screen.

Clear

This command deletes the text you've currently selected, but it does not modify text in a document in the document view window.

Find

Choosing the Find command brings up Mac Mosaic's Find window (see Figure 10.15), which offers the ability to search for case-sensitive text, to search backward from the current position, and to perform a wraparound search to include the entire Mosaic document. To let you know that it has found the search key you entered, Mosaic highlights the first instance of the key.

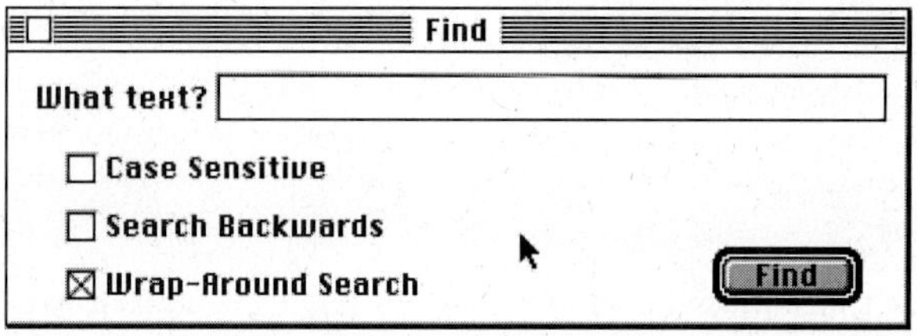

FIGURE 10.15.
Mac Mosaic's Find dialog box.

```
┌──────────────────────────── Find ════════════════════┐
│  What text? [                                      ]  │
│                                                       │
│    ☐ Case Sensitive                                   │
│    ☐ Search Backwards           ▶                     │
│    ☒ Wrap-Around Search              ( Find )         │
└───────────────────────────────────────────────────────┘
```

Find Again

After you've initiated a search, Find Again locates the next occurrence of the most recently specified text string.

Show Clipboard

This command, not surprisingly, yields a window that displays the current contents of the Mac's Clipboard.

Options Menu

Hide URLs/Show URLs

With this item you can toggle the URL display on and off. The main reason for wanting to do this is to maximize the screen space devoted to the Mosaic document itself, which is especially important for smaller monitors.

Hide/Show Status Messages

This command toggles the status message area on and off. Again, the main reason is to save display space and processor usage.

Use This Page for Home

This aptly titled command saves the current page as your home page; the next time you invoke Mosaic it will automatically load the page as your new home page.

Load to Disk

When you find a graphic, sound, or video file within a document (you can tell by the file extension of the file when you move the cursor over it), or when you want to download an HTML, text, or other type of file to your hard disk, toggle on Load to Disk and then click the hyperlink. You'll be presented with a File Save dialog box, at which point you can specify directory and filename. The document will *not* load into Mosaic's main window.

Auto-Load Images

This command toggles automatic loading of inline images on and off. With slow connections (such as modems of any speed), it's a good idea to turn this off by default, toggling it on only when you find a page where the images actually matter.

Use Mac Temporary Folder

This command lets you specify how to store temporary files, which Mac Mosaic uses quite extensively. If Use Temp Items is not toggled on, these files are stored in the system folder (and deleted when Mac Mosaic exits). When checked, the feature stores temporary files in whatever folder you specify.

Remove Temp Files

This command deletes all temporary files, no matter where you've stored them with the Use Temp Items command.

Flush Cache

Mac Mosaic stores document and image information in a memory cache. This command clears out the cache, releasing that memory to the system. During long sessions and with limited RAM, use of this command is highly important.

Enable/Disable View Source

When enabled, this command allows you to view the HTML source code of a document if you select View Source from the File menu.

Preferences

This is an extremely important command, because it enables you to set the configuration for your Mac Mosaic program. From the resulting dialog box (see Figure 10.16) you can specify the default home page, your name, your e-mail address, the colors of the hyperlinks and an underlining style for them, the Temp directory (see Use Temp Items above), and details about the local newsgroup server and a WAIS gateway (used for WAIS searches). From here you also configure the external viewers used by Mac Mosaic to automatically play sound and video files and display documents with specific formats (such as PostScript files). Be sure to spend time learning your way around this dialog box.

FIGURE 10.16.

Mac Mosaic's elaborate Preferences dialog box.

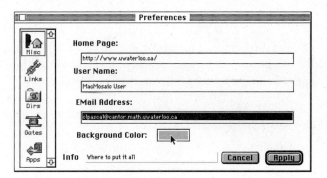

Styles

This command yields the Styles dialog box, as shown in Figure 10.17. Fairly complex, this box lets you set the appearance of the documents that load into Mac Mosaic's main window, enabling you to specify a different font and style for each heading and formatting type. You can also control the global appearance of styles from this box. As with Preferences, this dialog box helps you customize Mac Mosaic to your liking.

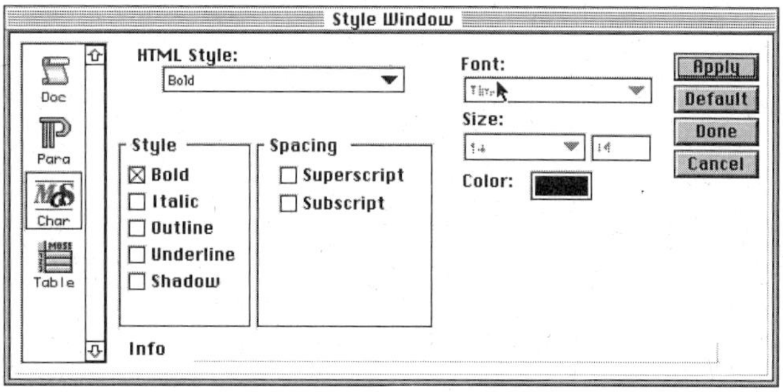

FIGURE 10.17.

The Mac Mosaic Styles dialog box.

Navigate Menu

Back

Choosing this command takes you back to the previous document. Hardly surprising.

Forward

This command takes you to the next document in the history list.

Home

This command retrieves the document specified in your configuration file as your "home" document and loads it into Mac Mosaic. Convenient for finding your way out of a hopeless navigation maze.

Hotlist

Mac Mosaic's Hotlist Interface menu is a hierarchical menu that enables you to bookmark documents you want to revisit in the future. From this menu you can create a new hotlist or open an existing one, save the current hotlist, or edit your hotlists. The Edit subcommand brings up the Hotlist dialog box, which enables you to delete and rename menu items, or give them new URL addresses.

Add This Document

This command adds the currently displayed document title to the hotlist menu itself, making it readily available from that menu.

Network Starting Points

This command is actually a bookmark: Invoking it retrieves an NCSA-prepared document called Starting Points for Internet Exploration, which offers hyperlinks to a rich variety of information pages throughout the Internet.

Internet Resources Meta-Index

Like Internet Starting Points, this command is a link to a bookmarked page. It retrieves an NCSA-prepared document with hyperlinks to a variety of indexes, directories, and collections of information on the Net.

NCSA Demo Page

This command retrieves the NCSA Mosaic Demo Document, with hyperlinks to a variety of different types of pages, grouped by "Exemplary Applications Categories" such as Arts and Humanities; Scientific, Technical and Professional Information; and Industry, Business and Publishing.

NCSA What's New Page

Invoking the What's New command retrieves NCSA's famous What's New With NCSA Mosaic and the WWW page, a regularly (weekly or even daily) updated page showing new resources for Web users.

NCSA Mosaic for Mac Home Page

This command takes you to NCSA's main page for the Macintosh version of Mosaic.

NCSA Mosaic for Mac Features

With this command you retrieve an NCSA-prepared page listing the features and known bugs in the current version of Mac Mosaic.

Annotate Menu

Text

When you want to make comments about a document you've retrieved, for the sake of your future browsing or the browsing of colleagues, the Annotate command lets you do so. You enter the comments in the Annotate window that results from selecting this command, and Mac Mosaic

adds a hyperlink on the current page that, when clicked, reveals the comments. You can add as many annotations as you want. Note that you can type in your annotation and/or include an existing file for yourself or colleagues to read. The Commit button sets the annotation in place.

Audio

If your machine is equipped with sound-recording equipment, you can record an audio annotation using this command. As with Annotate, Mac Mosaic will show the annotation as a hyperlink on the current page. (See Figure 10.18.)

FIGURE 10.18.
Mac Mosaic's Audio Annotate dialog box.

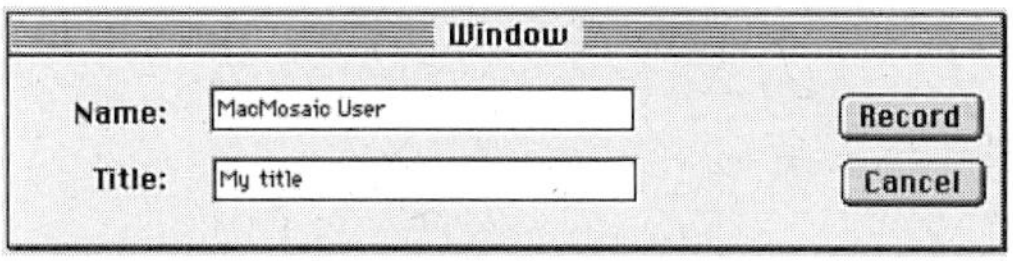

Edit Annotation

When reading an annotation, this command lets you alter the annotation by adding text or appending a file to it.

Delete Annotation

Rather obviously, this command deletes the currently visible annotation.

Balloon Help Menu

About Balloon Help

Here you get typical Macintosh information about Balloon Help.

Show Balloons

Obviously, this command lets you toggle balloon help, but as Mac Mosaic doesn't offer balloon help messages there's not much point.

Mail Developers

This command opens a rudimentary e-mail window designed exclusively for sending comments, problems, complaints, bribes, and threats to Mac Mosaic's developers. It automatically includes your e-mail address (as long as you've set it up in the configuration file), and clicking Send transmits the message. Don't expect a personal response, though; your comments will be logged, but you'll get something along the lines of, "Dear Occupant, we appreciate your...." How deep the appreciation actually runs is unclear.

Mac Mosaic Documentation

This is a hotlist item to NCSA's online documentation about Mac Mosaic.

HTML Help

From here you retrieve a series of Web documents outlining the HyperText Markup Language (with which Web pages are constructed), with links to tutorials, examples, and other HTML reference documents.

URL Help

URL Help opens a hyperdocument dealing with Uniform Resource Locators, how they work, and what they mean.

FAQ

This command yields a document offering hyperlinks to Frequently Asked Questions about Mac Mosaic. If you're having a problem with the program, someone else has probably had it already, and the solution might well be found here.

NCSA Mosaic for Microsoft Windows

FTP Site: `ftp.ncsa.uiuc.edu`

Directory: `/Web/Windows/Mosaic`

Filenames: `mos20B4.exe` (most Windows machines)

> **NOTE**
>
> To run versions of Win Mosaic above 2.0alpha2, which means anything recent, you must have the Win32 extensions installed (they're already in Windows 95 and Windows NT). These are available from the NCSA site as file `w32ole.exe`, in the same directory as Mosaic itself.
>
> Mosaic for Windows is an immensely popular program among Windows users with Internet access, which is almost certainly the fastest-growing user group. Some of Windows Mosaic's features include:

■ Full-featured hotlist editor that lets you create top-level menus for hotlist access

■ Print Preview option to see what the document will look like on paper

■ Extended FTP Parsing command for fuller FTP directory listings

■ Access to newsgroups for one-stop reading

File Menu

Open URL

This command opens a dialog box in which you enter the full URL address of the document or site you want loaded. Keep in mind that you must start the URL with the protocol type, which will often be `http://` but might also be `gopher://`, `ftp:/`, or any other valid URL address. The important thing is that you enter the *complete* address, or you'll find yourself redoing it until you get it right. Rather than pulling up the URL dialog box, however, you can also type the URL straight into the URL box at the top of the screen.

Open Local File

This command enables you to load a file from your local hard disk (or local network disk) into Mosaic. The command presents you with a standard Windows dialog box, from which you select the directory and file you want to load.

Save As

With this command you can save the currently displayed document to your hard drive as an HTML file (`.htm` extension).

Save As Text

Saves the current document as a text file, with no HTML tags and no hyperlink information. Very useful if the content is the information you actually want.

Print

With this command, you can print the current document. As with all MS-Windows programs, however, what you see is not necessarily what you get. To get exactly formatted printouts, you'll need to keep your font choices appropriate to your printer and your system's configuration.

Print Preview

This displays a preview of what the printed page will look like.

Print Setup

This command simply yields the standard Windows Print dialog box.

Newsgroups

If you've configured and subscribed to newsgroups in the Preferences dialog box (see the Preferences heading in the Options menu section), you can read your subscribed newsgroups directly in Mosaic. While reading newsgroups, you can respond to the writer of the message through Mosaic's Send Email command. As of 2.0beta4, Mosaic's newsreading capabilities aren't as strong as Netscape's, however (see Chapter 11 for details on Netscape).

Send Email

This command opens a rudimentary e-mail session from which you can send a message. You can include the URL of the currently loaded document in this message, and you can also send the text of that document.

Document Source

Document Source brings up a separate window showing the source code of the currently displayed document. If the document contains HTML formatting, all HTML codes will be displayed in full. You can save this source file to your hard drive or copy some or all of the file to the clipboard. It's extremely useful for HTML developers, who can study other people's work for inspiration and judicious borrowing.

Exit

This command removes Windows Mosaic from memory (the computer's, not yours).

Edit Menu

Copy

If you've selected text with the mouse, Copy will copy the selection to the Windows Clipboard. You can copy selections from the document itself, from the Document Title and URL fields, from the Document Source window, and from any other window in which you enter text manually.

Paste

With the Paste command you can paste text into any field into which you can type characters, including the URL box at the top of the viewing area.

Find

This command enables you to locate specified text strings within a document, and includes a Match Case option for case-sensitive searches and a Find Next command. Find does not actually highlight the string in the document when it is found, so it's not quite as useful as it might be.

Select All

With this command, you can select the entire text (including links, but not their associated information) of the document.

Options Menu

Show Toolbar

This command, when checked, displays Windows Mosaic's toolbar. Uncheck it if you want to save screen space for the main document.

Show Status Bar

When unchecked, Show Status Bar hides the status bar at the bottom of Windows Mosaic's screen. Unless you're really desperate for screen space, leave it on, because it conveys extremely useful information.

Show Current URL

This command lets you show or hide the URL display.

Presentation Mode

Presentation mode (called *Kiosk mode* in some browsers) displays your Web pages without any of the surrounding windowing features. In other words, you see the document itself, as well as the vertical and horizontal scrollbars. The title bar, toolbar, status bar, and spinning globe are all hidden. The purpose of Presentation mode is to see more of the document, and also to give users access to the Web but not to the menu or icon features within Mosaic.

Preferences

Back in the good old days, which in Web terms means about eight months ago, the only way to configure Win Mosaic was to open the mosaic.ini file in a text editor and laboriously edit line by line. No longer! Now Win Mosaic comes with a powerful Preferences dialog box, complete with tabs that lead you from topic to topic (with several configuration items within each topic screen). There are several different tabs: General, Viewers, Services, Proxy, Tables, Anchors, Font Styles, and Caching.

From the General tab, you can specify which elements of the Mosaic window you want to display (URL bar, status bar, tool bar, and so on). You can also specify your home page here, select the background color, toggle inline images on or off, display 3-D horizontal rules (that is, the lines that run across the Mosaic page), and display bullets as circles or dashes. The Viewers tab enables you to configure the external programs needed to display or play certain document types found on the Web (such as sound and video files). From the Services tab you can set the necessary information for e-mail use, as well as FTP and newsgroup sessions. The Proxy tab lets you identify HTTP, FTP, WAIS, and Gopher proxy servers, useful if your system operates behind a network firewall. You simply specify the proxy gateway (get this information from your systems administrator), and Mosaic will retrieve documents through that gateway.

The Tables tab allows you to configure settings for the HTML tables that are starting to appear on the Web. The Anchors tab offers configuration settings for the hyperlinks that appear in your documents, deciding on color and whether or not the links are underlined. From the Font Styles tab you can assign fonts to the various document-display elements, such as headings, anchors, and list items. Finally, the Caching tab lets you specify the number of documents you want cached, as well as the location and size of the cache.

Navigate Menu

Back

This command takes you back to the previous document, unless that document was one you selected from the History window in the Navigate menu, in which case you'll return to the last document you actually retrieved from a server.

Forward

This command moves you forward along the path of documents you originally navigated.

Reload

Windows Mosaic's Reload command reloads the current document into the Document View window. It's useful if the screen becomes garbled (hey, this *is* Windows), or if you have Display Inline Images toggled off and you come across a document whose images you'd like to see.

Home

Selecting this command takes you directly to the Home page specified via the Preferences dialog box in the Options menu.

History

The History command opens the NCSA Mosaic History window, from which you can jump to a document you visited during that session. Windows Mosaic does *not* maintain a global history file like X Mosaic.

Add Current to Hotlist

This features adds the title and URL address of the currently displayed document to the current hotlist.

Hotlist Manager

One of Windows Mosaic's most useful design features, the Hotlist Manager, enables you to not only bookmark items, but to also place them inside menus and submenus of your choice for future access. With the Hotlist Manager you can add top-level menus (those that appear on the menubar), and submenus within those menus. You can also edit document titles and change the current hotlist. Note that Hotlist Manager completely replaces the superb Menu Editor of previous Win Mosaic versions, and the jury's still out as to which is the better concept.

Annotate Menu

Annotate

When you want to comment on a particular document, either for your own reference or that of colleagues, selecting the Annotate command brings up a dialog box that lets you do so. Windows Mosaic will then display the fact that an annotation exists at the bottom of the current page whenever it is accessed in future. This feature is less useful in Windows Mosaic than in either of the others, however, because it is far more limited in function, and Windows Mosaic does not allow audio annotations.

Edit Annotations

This command yields the Annotate dialog box so you can edit the entry.

Delete This Annotation

This command deletes the selected annotation.

Starting Points Menu

Starting Points Document

This command is actually a bookmark; invoking it retrieves an NCSA-prepared document called Starting Points for Internet Exploration, which offers hyperlinks to a rich variety of information pages throughout the Internet.

NCSA Mosaic Demo Document

This command retrieves the NCSA Mosaic Demo Document, with hyperlinks to a variety of different types of pages, including audio and video demonstrations.

NCSA Mosaic's What's New Page

Invoking the What's New command retrieves NCSA's famous What's New With NCSA Mosaic and the WWW page, a regularly (weekly or even daily) updated page showing new resources for Web users.

Mosaic for Microsoft Windows Home Page

This command takes you to NCSA's main page for the Windows version of Mosaic.

World Wide Web Info

This submenu contains hotlisted links to pages dealing with the World Wide Web project itself.

Home Pages

Windows Mosaic ships with a wide range of prehotlisted home pages of various institutions. This submenu gives you instant access to any of them.

Gopher Servers

From this submenu, you can access a range of useful Gophers through Windows Mosaic. Several are included.

Finger Gateway, Whois Gateway

These commands access the gateways for `Finger` or `Whois` commands, as specified in your Preferences dialog box.

Other Documents

This submenu includes a hotlist of interesting Web documents.

Help Menu

Online Documentation

Selecting this command retrieves the NCSA-prepared documentation for Windows Mosaic.

FAQ Page

This command yields a document offering hyperlinks to Frequently Asked Questions about Windows Mosaic. If you're having a problem with the program, someone else has probably had it already, and the solution might well be found here.

Bug List

This command loads a document dealing with known bugs in the current version of Windows Mosaic. Quite revealing.

Feature Page

Selecting this command gives you a page of new features in the current version of Windows Mosaic.

About Windows Mosaic

This pulls up a standard information box that contains the version number, copyright info, programmers' names, and an e-mail address to which you may send comments or questions.

Mail Technical Support

This command opens the e-mail window with the address already filled in. It's designed exclusively for sending comments, problems, complaints, bribes, and threats to Mosaic's developers. It automatically includes your e-mail address (as long as you've set it up in the Preferences dialog box), and clicking Send transmits the message. Don't expect a personal response, though; your comments will be logged, but you'll get something along the lines of, "Dear Occupant, we appreciate your…." How deep the appreciation actually runs is unclear.

Summary

This chapter provides an introduction to Mosaic in its X Window, Apple Macintosh, and Microsoft Windows formats, and compares the strengths and weaknesses of each. Full books on Mosaic are beginning to appear, and if you want to use this software to its greatest capacity, including a full and specific configuration, you're advised to give one of these books a try.

Or maybe not. Mosaic is anything but a difficult program. Like all the graphical browsers, once it's up and running it's next to effortless to work with. You can easily explore the Web, create your hotlists, and download files as you like, without ever bothering to study a help file. The important points to keep in mind are: first, Mosaic has its share of instabilities; and second, when Mosaic doesn't work right it could be the fault of either the program or the Web itself. Mosaic is, in fact, like every other Web browser in this respect.

Netscape Navigator

11

by
Neil Randall

When the first edition of *The World Wide Web Unleashed* went to press, a company called the Mosaic Communications Corporation was working on a new WWW browser that went by the code name Mozilla. It was well known by that time that MCC was formed by Jim Clark, former head of the graphics workstation innovators Silicon Graphics, Inc., and that Clark had enticed several of NCSA Mosaic's chief programmers away from NCSA itself. Among these programmers was Marc Andreesen, who was already well known on the Web for having designed and programmed the first version of Mosaic.

Unfortunately, as we closed the book, MCC had yet to release even the earliest beta of their Web browser. If they had, we would have stopped the presses and featured it right then and there. From its earliest available incarnation, Netscape (as it was instantly known) offered modem users something they hadn't yet seen in a World Wide Web browser: usability and slow-speed consideration. Within months, MCC changed its name to the Netscape Communications Corporation, Netscape became the Netscape Navigator, and Marc Andreesen had created yet another World Wide Web phenomenon. The Netscape Navigator (called both "Netscape" and "Navigator" from here on out—Web users call it by both names) continues to lead the flock in features, price, and usability, and has become, for a great many Web users both novice and veteran, the browser of choice.

Figures 11.1, 11.2, and 11.3 show the three nearly identical versions of the Netscape Navigator—UNIX, Windows, and Macintosh.

As the second edition of *The World Wide Web Unleashed* went to press, the battle between Mosaic and Netscape for the position of primary World Wide Web client shifted into high gear. Netscape landed some important licensees, and the Navigator will appear in future versions of WordPerfect, as the Web tool for InternetMCI and Delphi Internet, and bundled with various hardware platforms. NCSA Mosaic, whose licenses are handled by Spyglass, Inc., licensed well over 20 million copies of the famous browser, but their most important license might well be with Microsoft, who apparently intends to include it in Windows 95 and in the best-selling Microsoft applications. Among users who download their browsers free from the Net, Netscape seems to have the advantage, and many educational institutions are shifting to it as their chief browser. The next year will almost certainly be fascinating.

FIGURE 11.1.

A typical page in Netscape Navigator for UNIX.

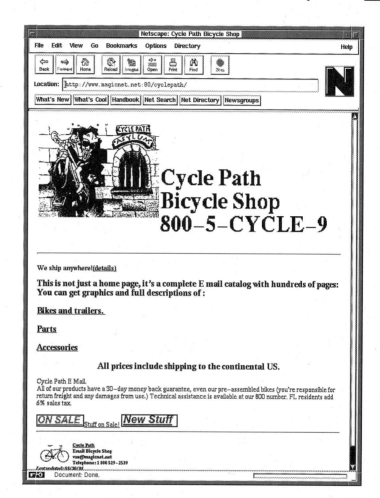

FIGURE 11.2.

A typical page in Netscape Navigator for Windows.

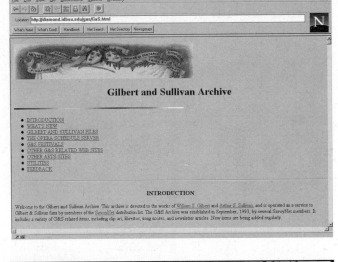

FIGURE 11.3.

A typical page in Netscape Navigator for Macintosh.

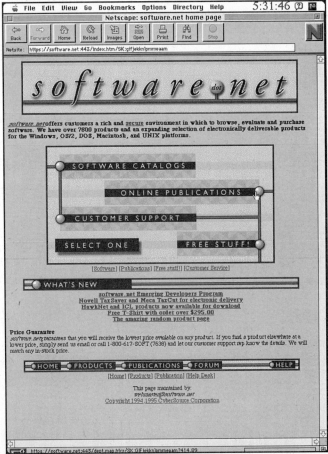

Major Features

Netscape wouldn't have become so popular so quickly if it hadn't included a number of features distinguishing it from other browsers on the market. Many of these features are being built into other Web clients in the wake of Netscape's success, but the Navigator is showing its versatility by adding even more features with each new release. Listed here are several of the most important enhancements Netscape brought to its users, in addition to some that have only recently appeared.

- **Caching of retrieved pages to disk**

  Although it's quickly becoming the standard in Web clients, effective disk caching of retrieved files was first popularized by Netscape. What this means is that Netscape stores a specified quantity of Web pages you've downloaded in your recent sessions, then loads them from your hard drive rather than retrieving them across the Internet when you next access that site.

  Disk caching is hardly a new idea. X Window versions of Mosaic have used it in the past, as have commercial online services such as America Online and Prodigy. AOL, in fact, made quite a stir with the feature, suddenly allowing nearly instant access to previously visited areas of their service. And that's the point of disk caching: If you access a site or page you've already visited, the components will load from your hard disk rather than from the remote machine. The result is much faster loading and much less network traffic.

  The problem with early versions of Mosaic for the Macintosh or Microsoft Windows, especially for modem users, was that it was nearly impossible to see the Web consistently in all its graphics glory. It simply took too long to download all those graphics from all those sites. Early in its design, Mosaic allowed memory caching, which meant that revisiting a site was much less time-consuming than visiting it the first time, but memory caching only worked for the current Web session. When you shut down Mosaic, then loaded it later and entered a previously visited page, the page took as long to appear as it had the first time.

  Disk caching stores the last so-many kilobytes of documents on your hard disk, in effect acting as a permanent memory cache. The advantages, as mentioned above, are greater speed and lessened network traffic. The disadvantage, and there's only one, is that the cache uses hard disk space. But given the decreasing cost of hard drives—less than half a buck a megabyte these days—it makes much more sense to clog your hard disk than your network. You can set Netscape to cache as much or as little as you want, so if you're a frequent Web user you might even consider buying a hard drive solely for your Web use. It's certainly an option, and for some people a valid one.

- **Access to links as documents are being retrieved**

  Again, this feature is becoming standard in Web browsers, but Netscape was the first to put it into operation. When earlier browsers retrieved documents from remote machines, they appeared in the browser window only after the download was complete. At 14.4Kbps, any page larger than 50KB took a considerable amount of time to retrieve, and if you had graphics toggled on the wait was much longer. Netscape displays its documents as they're downloading, and the links or image elements you see on the screen are fully active as soon as you see them. This means that you don't have to wait for the entire page to download before clicking on a hyperlink or imagemap. When you click, Netscape stops the current download and begins to retrieve the documents associated with the link.

This is an incredibly important technology. At this point in the Internet's history, most Web users are using 14.4Kbps modems or even slower, and many are using over-crowded—thus slow—local area networks (schools especially fall into this category). These two groups, but especially the first, find in Netscape a browser that recognizes their needs, and therefore they tend to flock to it. This fact affects such things as the possibility of doing business on the Web as well. If the Web is to become a potent sales medium, businesses will need the largest possible number of potential buyers. If 14.4Kbps-modem users can now traverse the Web relatively painlessly, they're much more likely to experiment with the idea of over-the-Web purchases, simply because they don't experience as many frustrations about getting into sites. This feature is also important technologically, because there'll be less traffic over the Internet itself, or at least less unwanted traffic. Downloading a 200KB page that you end up not even looking at is a waste of the Internet's resources; stopping it in progress by moving somewhere that interests you is a much better use of those same resources.

A related Netscape feature is its loading of inline images in layers. Instead of waiting for the image to download completely and then display, Netscape lets you see the image as it's downloading. You can tell very early if you'll want to see the full image, and if you don't you can click the Stop button and not bother with it. Again, this is an important attraction for modem users who want to know what sorts of images are out there but who certainly don't need to see them all in detail.

Figure 11.4 shows how Netscape allows access to hyperlinks while graphics are being downloaded.

■ **Support of non-standard (Netscape) tags**

From its first release, Netscape was built to display standard HTML pages, but also to display enhanced HTML *tags*, or features, that had not yet been set as standard by the Internet standards groups. This caused a significant furor among Internet developers, especially those who work extremely hard to ensure that useful standards are continually being debated and introduced. Just as importantly, however, it also caused considerable excitement among both Web users and HTML designers, because suddenly the Web was a much more graphically appealing place to be.

Graphics and text could now be centered or right aligned. Horizontal lines (rules) across the page could be shortened and thickened for a nice graphic effect. Font changes within lines were possible. And so forth. With the release of Netscape 1.1 Beta 1, other impor-tant additions were introduced. Among these were the inclusion of backgrounds, so that document designers were no longer figuring out how many things you could do with gray.

FIGURE 11.4.

A partially loaded graphic in Netscape, with a cursor demonstrating an active hyperlink.

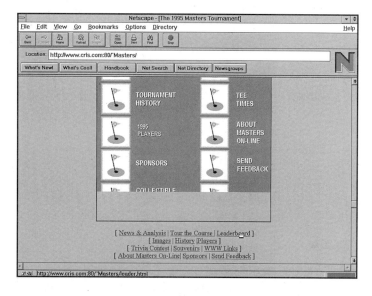

Figures 11.5 and 11.6 show some of the creative page designs made possible by the Netscape tags.

FIGURE 11.5.

Netscape (HTML 3.0) tags demonstrating multiple fonts and an aligned graphic.

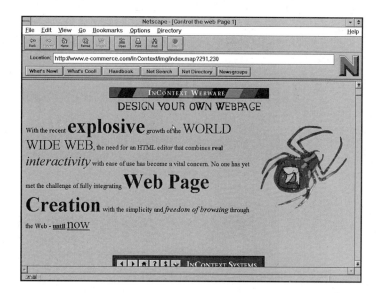

FIGURE 11.6.

A Netscape page showing the use of a background by the page designer (real color is salmon-ish).

However sympathetic we might be with those who insist on accepted and authorized standards, the fact remains that designers are picking up on the *Netscape tags*, as they've come to be called, quickly and with some very good (and often very bad) results. These tags are, in fact, based on the proposed HTML 3.0 standard, so it's not as if they've been invented out of thin air. In effect, the popularity of Netscape has made these tags *de facto* standards, for the very simple reason that users are demanding them and designers in increasing numbers are making use of them. They've become an important part of the Web, and there's every reason to suspect they're here to stay.

■ **Consistent features and interface across platforms**

There's very little difference between the interfaces for the X Window, Microsoft Windows, and Macintosh versions of Netscape. When you know one, you can use the others without delay. By contrast, the interfaces for the three versions of Mosaic have been substantially different across the platforms, to the degree that the three have had different feature sets. Obviously this isn't important if you have access to only one type of machine, but in organizations that typically have all three platforms, consistency matters a great deal.

■ **Full newsgroup reading and posting capabilities**

Web browsers have been able to access newsgroups for a while, but from its inception Netscape offered a strong newsgroup package. From within Netscape, you can read newsgroups, follow threads, post new articles, catch up full groups, send mail, and so forth. It's not as rich as a dedicated newsreader, but it's there, it offers a strong graphical appearance, and it works well. For many newsgroup readers, in fact for most, Netscape will be all they need.

■ **Built-in security capabilities**

The security of World Wide Web documents has been an issue almost since the Web's inception. Especially in the area of the transfer of sensitive and private data, such as credit card numbers for financial transactions, the Web has provided no security whatsoever. Netscape's designers certainly weren't the first people to think about the issue, but Netscape was the first browser to use its appearance to distinguish between secure and non-secure pages. When combined with security-enhanced World Wide Web servers (and especially with Netscape's own Netsite), the browser can warn you that you're about to send information across an insecure link, or it can tell you that you're entering a security-enhanced site. Inside a secure site Netscape's borders change color, and a key icon tells you you're dealing with a secured area. Security is unquestionably the most significant issue among Web professionals, including businesses on the Net, and Netscape offered a glimpse of the future the minute it hit the Net.

If you want to download and install Netscape right now, skip to the Installation section near the end of this chapter.

The Display

Obviously, everything you see on your screen during a Netscape session is part of the display, but for this section we'll look at everything but the menu bar. The menus will be dealt with in detail after a description of the visible windows and tools.

Content Area

By far the most important area of Netscape, and in fact of any Web browser, is the main window or, in Netscape parlance, the *content area*. This is where you see the information you've retrieved. This information can appear as HTML pages (the standard Web format) or as Gopher directories, FTP directories, or newsgroup listings. Netscape will also display downloaded graphics files in GIF or JPEG format, without need for an external program.

The actual material in the document in the content area depends entirely on the person/people who designed it and made it available. In addition, some of the elements on that page appear as designed by the authors. But you can change the appearance of a page significantly by using Netscape's customizing features, to the extent that fonts, background colors and images, and many other features will be different. For information on how to make these changes, see the details in the Options|Preferences menu (discussed in the next section).

Toolbar

Like any good GUI application, Netscape Navigator comes with a toolbar (shown in Figures 11.7, 11.8, and 11.9). Unlike many, though, this is a useful one, because it contains a limited number of icons, all of which are easy to read and understand. There are nine icons in all, none of them unusual to find in a Web browser, but as many as you'd typically want anyway. There's no way of altering the toolbar, however, so you're stuck with what the designers give you.

The Back icon reloads the previous document you visited. Officially, this is the previous document in the History list, which Netscape compiles as you work your way from site to site through the current session (there's no history of previous sessions). You can get the History list from the Go menu (discussed shortly) if you want to determine where the Back icon will actually lead you.

The Forward icon is a bit tricky, as it is in all Web browsers. Simply, the Forward icon retrieves the next document in the History list. The Forward icon isn't available (that is, it's grayed out) until you've either used the Back icon or retrieved a previous document through the History list itself (available from the Go menu). Once you've done either, the Forward icon is no longer grayed out, and its function is to move you ahead one page toward the end of the History list.

FIGURE 11.7.

The toolbar in Netscape for UNIX.

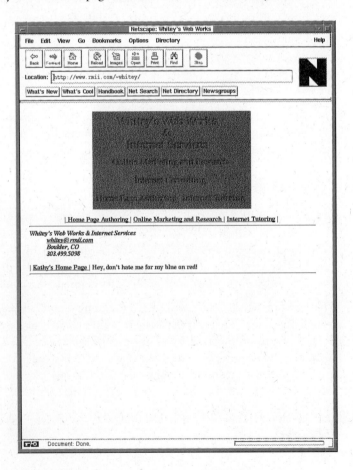

FIGURE 11.8.

The toolbar in Netscape for Windows.

FIGURE 11.9.

The toolbar in Netscape for Macintosh.

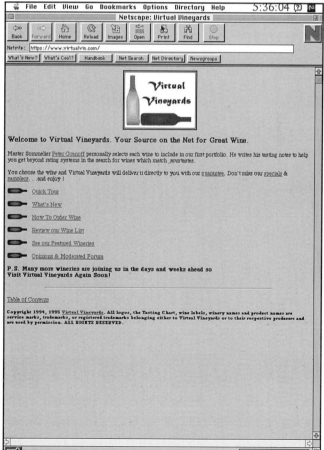

If all you've done is used the Back icon to go back one page, the Forward icon will return you to the page where you started. But let's say you have 10 documents in the History list, and you access the list to return to document #3 from, say, document #8. In this case, after you've re-called document #3, the Forward icon will take you to document #4. It's quite straightforward after a while, but many people find it takes some getting used to.

The Home icon takes you directly to your home page. By default, this is the home page for Netscape Communications, Inc. (`http://home.netscape.com/`), but you can change this URL to whatever home page you want by calling up the Styles dialog box in the Preferences area of the Options menu.

Clicking the Reload icon tells Netscape to find and retrieve the current page once again. This icon is useful if you're working with a dynamic page that changes frequently, and you've been in Netscape long enough that changes might have occurred. Reload replaces the page you're currently viewing with an updated version of the original source. Reload is also useful if you've had to Stop a retrieval part way through the download (by using the Stop icon). In this case, clicking on Reload will give the network another chance to bring the page across from the source.

The Images icon demonstrates Netscape's modem friendliness. As anyone who's toured the Web on a 14.4Kbps modem (or slower) knows, Web pages can be filled with hordes of large graphics that take forever to download. It's not unusual at all for a page to take 5–10 minutes to transfer, and since the design trend is toward more graphics rather than fewer, the Web will get even slower for those with modem access. The Images icon lets you start your Web sessions with the Auto Load Images feature turned off (accomplished through the Options menu or in the Preferences/Styles dialog box). Then, when you enter a site whose graphics you want to see, simply click on the Images icon and Netscape will reload the page complete with images. This isn't something that other browsers don't have; Mosaic has always allowed users to browse without images. But by placing the icon among the select few on the toolbar, Netscape demonstrates a direct nod toward modem usability.

With the Open icon, you can type the URL of a document you want Netscape to receive. You can achieve the same result by typing the URL in the location box and pressing Enter. The Open icon is identical to the File | Open Location menu item.

Netscape prints Web pages well, and the Print icon provides direct access to the printing features. A dialog box appears that lets you specify printing choices. This feature is identical to the File | Print menu item.

With the Find icon, you can search the currently displayed document for words or phrases. A dialog box appears, letting you choose the direction of the search and whether you want case sensitivity. Unfortunately, there's no provision for advanced searching, such as all cached documents. The Find feature can also be evoked from the Edit menu.

The most useful icon of them all, Stop lets you halt the document transfer currently in progress (it's also available in the Go menu as Stop Loading). You'll use this one often, especially if the page you're retrieving is taking too long, or if Netscape can't seem to make the connection with the remote host. When Netscape is performing network activity, the Stop button shows a bright red light. When you click on it, the light appears to shatter, letting you know it's stopped.

Netscape Icon

On the far right side of the toolbar is the Netscape icon. Its official name is *status indicator*, as it's one of the two elements on the Netscape display that show you the browser is actively on the network retrieving a document. When that activity is occurring, the icon pulses in and out, giving a 3-D effect of moving toward you and then pushing away from you. Its function is no different from Mosaic's spinning globe (see Chapter 10, "NCSA Mosaic"), or WebSurfer's crawling newt (see Chapter 12, "More Browsers for Microsoft Windows"), or any other by-now inevitable status icon. But it's useful, even if only to give you a clue that a transaction is transpiring. Often, in fact, you use this knowledge to stop a connection that doesn't seem to be going anywhere.

Location Box

Known as the *URL display* in other Web clients, this one-line box stretches across the toolbar, displaying the URL of the current document. You can type a URL directly into this box, followed by pressing Enter, in order to download a specific URL of your choice. This is exactly the same as using the Open Location dialog box in the File menu, except that the location box is often more useful because it enables you to edit the URL that's already in there. For instance, if your current URL is `http://www.company.com/products/Unix/workstations.html`, and you want to go to that company's home page, just click in the location box, erase everything in the URL beginning with "products" (leaving only `http://www.company.com/`), then press Enter. Presto: company home page.

Note that, when you access a Web page that's stored on a Netsite server (the server software available from Netscape Communications), the Location Box's name changes to "Netsite:".

Directory Buttons

Below the location box are the directory buttons. These are shortcut buttons to pages that take you to the same pages as those that appear in the Directory menu or Help menu. One leads to a What's New page, a second to a What's Cool page, a third to the Handbook, a fourth to newsgroups, and a fifth to Internet directories and search pages. These buttons can't be modified, unfortunately, nor can their related URLs be changed. So you'll probably end up not displaying them at all after a while (via the View menu).

Status Bar

The *status bar* runs along the bottom of the display and is one of the most important information areas of all. This bar tells you in comprehensible language what the browser is doing or attempting to do, something extremely important for serious and frequent network use. The bar also provides other useful information, including the security status of the document and the URLs of available hyperlinks on the currently loaded page.

To transfer a page across the Web to your computer, Netscape must perform several specific transactions. The status bar presents them as they occur. The first message you'll see is `Connect: Contacting host:xxx.xxx.xxx.xx...` (xxs signify the host computer's name). After the connection has been made, the status bar reads, `Connect: Host contacted. Waiting for reply....` Assuming that everything's worked okay this far (and remember that the connection might be hindered at either of these two points), you'll see the very welcome announcement, `Transferring data`. Next you'll see the document start to appear in the Netscape content area, while the status bar shows, `Document:Received xxx of xxxx bytes`" (xxs signify numbers). As the document continues to download, the numbers will change accordingly, until the number of bytes received equals the total number of bytes in the document. When that occurs, Netscape will either start loading the next document (often a graphic), or it will stop if there's nothing more to transfer. In the latter case, the status line will read `Done`, and the Netscape icon to the right of the status bar will stop its animation.

The status bar performs two other important functions as well. When you move the cursor over a hyperlink, the status bar will display the URL for that link. This information helps in your browsing strategies, as you'll often decide not to choose a hyperlink that experience tells you will take too long to retrieve (you can also avoid unwanted FTP accesses this way).

Finally, the status bar contains one of three indicators of the security status of the currently loaded page. The key, at the bottom left of the screen, lets you know whether the document is non-secure, secure, or mixed. For non-secure documents, the key is displayed as broken, on a gray background, whereas for secure documents the key is fully formed and the background is blue. The key has one "tooth" if it's a mixed security document, and two teeth if fully secure. In addition, non-secure documents (which are by far the most numerous kind) display a gray border around Netscape's content area, whereas mixed and fully secure documents place a blue border around this area. A third possible indication of security exists in the location box. If the URL begins with https rather than the standard http, the document you're reading is stored on a secure server.

Security was explained in the Major Features section of this chapter. Also explained there are the notification boxes that result from entering or leaving a secured or non-secured area.

Scrollbars

Two scrollbars are available—horizontal and vertical. The horizontal bar runs along the bottom of the screen, and for the most part won't be used at all, as Netscape reformats documents to fit the window's width anyway. The vertical scrollbar, however, running down the far right side of the content area, is something you'll use constantly. Most Web pages are longer than one screen, and you use the scrollbar to view higher or lower in the document. Keep in mind the standard trick for scrollbars: The arrows will scroll you slowly, while clicking in the bar itself above or below the location indicator will jump you higher or lower in far larger increments.

Newsgroups Screens

Through Netscape, you can perform most of your daily newsgroup reading and posting. The first step is to use Options | Preferences to set up the news host to which you have access (contact your Internet provider or systems administrator for this information); once this is in place, selecting Go to Newsgroups from the Directory menu will take you right in.

Figure 11.10 shows the opening newsgroup screen, Subscribed Newsgroups. From here you can access all newsgroups currently subscribed to, or you can subscribe to additional groups. To add to the subscription list, type the newsgroup name in the box labeled "Subscribe to this newsgroup."

FIGURE 11.10.

The Subscribed Newsgroups listing in Netscape.

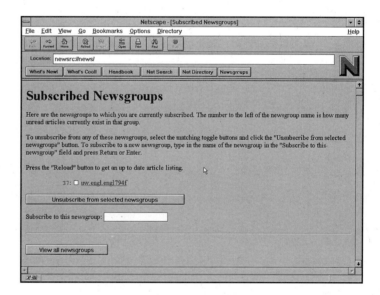

Alternatively, you can click the View all newsgroups button at the bottom of the screen (you might have to scroll down to see it) to call up a list of all available groups. Figure 11.11 shows the result of this action, a list of newsgroups or newsgroup hierarchies into which you can click further. Beside the available newsgroups is a checkbox; click on the newsgroups to which you want to subscribe, then on the Subscribe to selected newsgroups button at the bottom of the list (scroll to see it), and they'll be added to your subscription list.

As soon as you add newsgroups to your subscription list, Netscape returns an updated Subscribed Newsgroups page. Click on the newsgroup you want to read, and you'll be presented with a list of articles from that newsgroup. Figure 11.12 shows the results of clicking on alt.astrology.

FIGURE 11.11.

The full listing of newsgroups, showing both available groups and group hierarchies.

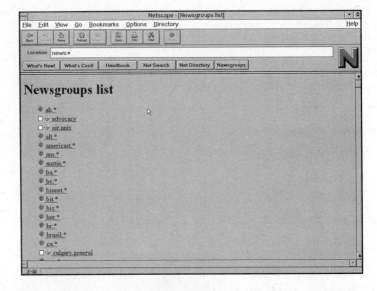

FIGURE 11.12.

A typical newsgroup listing in Netscape, showing articles and article "threads" (follow-up articles).

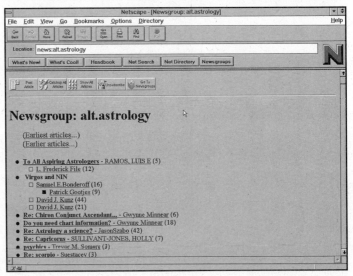

Only 100 articles out of the more than 4000 available are shown (you can increase or decrease the displayed number through the Options/Preferences screen). If you want to see additional articles, click on either the "Earlier articles" or "Earliest articles" links at the top of the listing (the links won't be there if no additional articles exist).

At the top of the page are five buttons:

■ **Post Article** lets you send a message to the entire newsgroup, with an entirely new subject. Generally speaking, you use this only if there's no discussion of this subject already in progress; if there is, use the Post Followup feature instead, which is available from within that particular thread (see Figure 11.13).

■ **Catchup All Articles** sets all articles in the newsgroup to the status of having been read. Whenever you click on an article to read it, Netscape automatically marks it as *read*, which means it won't appear next time you call up that newsgroup. The Catchup button tells Netscape to mark them all this way, even though you haven't actually read them. This is useful primarily when the number of articles is too high for you to bother with, or if you've read all you intend to read and want to get rid of the rest.

■ **Show All Articles** displays every single article available, whether or not it's been marked as read (but still only as many as you've specified in Options/Preferences). When all articles are displayed, this button becomes Show New Articles, which when clicked displays only the unread articles. Show New Articles is the default and is usually the only display you need.

■ **Unsubscribe** lets you remove a newsgroup from your subscription list. You can always get it back again by using the Subscribe function on the opening newsgroup screen.

■ **Go to Newsgroups** returns you to the Subscribed Newsgroups page displaying your current subscriptions. Use this when you want to start reading a different subscribed newsgroup.

Clicking on an article opens a new page with the details of that article displayed. Here you'll see the subject line (the same as appeared on the newsgroup page itself), the date the article was sent, the sender's e-mail address, the sender's organizational affiliation, the newsgroup(s) to which the article was posted (articles can be cross-posted to several groups), and a list of references. These are shown (slightly behind the Send Mail/Post News box) in Figure 11.13.

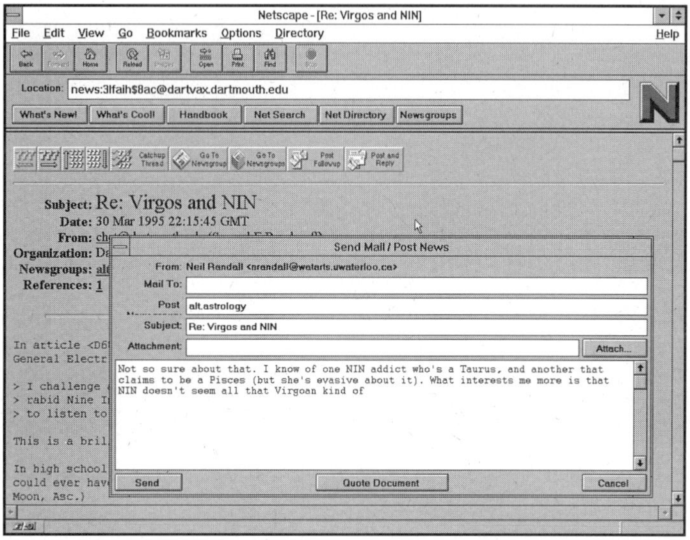

FIGURE 11.13.

A typical news message in Netscape, also showing the Send Mail/Post News box resulting from clicking on Post Followup.

Two points are worth noting here. First, you can send e-mail directly to the sender of the message by clicking on the sender's name in the From line. This is advisable if you have something to say to that person, but no need to involve the rest of the newsgroup (Netscape is to be commended for making this possibility so easy; newsgroups get bombarded by messages that would be much better sent as personal e-mail). Second, the References line lets you easily move among articles in that thread, taking you right back to the original if it's still available. Both items are highly useful.

Several buttons are available at the top and the bottom of the message page:

- **Left Arrow** takes you to the previous message in that particular thread. It's grayed out if you're already on the thread's first message.

- **Right Arrow** opens the next message in that thread. It's grayed out if you're already on the thread's last message.

- **Up Arrow** takes you out of that thread and into the article in the newsgroup list directly above the current article. It's grayed out if you're already on the first available article.

- **Down Arrow** takes you out of the current thread and into the article in the newsgroup directly below it. It's grayed out if you're already on the last available article.

- **Catchup Thread** marks all articles in that particular thread (only) as read. See Catchup All Articles, also in this list, for an explanation of how the Catchup function works.

- **Go to Newsgroup** (singular) takes you to the frontmost page of that particular newsgroup, letting you select a new thread for reading.

- **Go to Newsgroups** (plural) returns you to the Subscribed Newsgroups screen, where you can choose a different newsgroup to read.

- **Post Followup** opens the Send Mail/Post News box, letting you write a response to the current thread and post it to the newsgroup.

- **Post and Reply** opens the Send Mail/Post News box, letting you write a response to the current thread and post it to both the newsgroup and, as an e-mail message, to the original writer of the message you're reading.

Figure 11.13 displays the Send Mail/Post News box. In this example, Post Followup was selected, so the Mail To: field is blank. You can fill in any e-mail address here (you might want to send it to a friend or colleague, for instance), or you can just leave it blank. To write your message, type whatever you want in the message box. If you want to include text from the message you're reading, click on Quote Document, but trim it as much as possible (using the Delete key) in the interest of netiquette. Although it's possible to attach a document to a posting, this procedure is highly discouraged; people will hate you for it. When you've finished your message, click Send. Keep in mind before you do so that your message will be sent to thousands of people around the world.

The Menus

Despite the usefulness of the icons on the toolbar, most of your interaction with Mosaic will take place in the menus. From the menus you can load files, print documents, navigate, and customize the interface. You can also call up bookmarks and special locations, and you can tailor the appearance of the page.

File Menu

From the File menu, you control a number of file-oriented activities, as well as some others. True to GUI tradition, the File menu seems a bit of a catchall for commands that don't readily fit into any other menus.

New Window

You aren't restricted to only one document window in Netscape. When you choose File | New Window, you open an additional document window in which to conduct your browsing. The new window contains the same History list as the window from which it was started, but it loads the first document in that list. In other words, it's like starting from the beginning, but with the original session still active. An example of New Window is shown in Figure 11.14.

The nice thing about multiple windows is that you can navigate the Web in one direction in the first, and in an entirely different direction in the second and subsequent windows. This lets you use a particular Web page as a jumping-off point to several different locations, eliminating the need to backtrack continually to the first one.

Open Location

Fulfilling the same function as the Open icon, Open Location yields an extremely simple dialog box in which you can type a specific URL. It's functional, but that's all. Mosaic's is far more useful.

Open File

If you have an HTML file or a graphics file in GIF or JPEG format on your hard drive, you can load it into Netscape with the Open File command. You'll be presented with your system's standard File Open dialog box, from which you select the file you want to load. This is also useful if you receive an HTML file as an e-mail message or newsgroup posting; use your mailer to save the file to your hard disk as an HTML file (`.htm` in Windows), then load it into the browser with the Open File command.

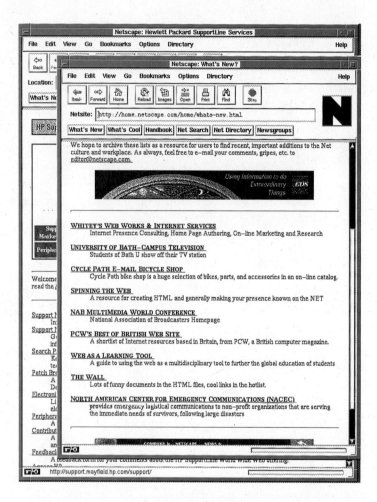

Save As

The counterpart to Open File, Save As lets you save the current document to your hard drive. You'll be presented with your system's standard File Save dialog box, in which you choose the file type and give it a name. Often the file type will be HTML (.htm in Windows), but in the case of graphics files (GIF or JPEG), you'll be given that extension as a Save default. If you access a site frequently, it's often a good idea to use Save As to capture the file to your drive, so you can load it from your hard drive rather than transferring it over and over again from the remote host.

This is especially true of directory sites, such as the EINet Galaxy or Yahoo, or What's New pages, such as the one prepared by NCSA.

Mail Document

With Mail Document, you can send an e-mail message from directly within the Navigator. Choosing this command yields the large Send Mail/Post News window, which you use exactly as you would a dedicated e-mail package. This window is shown in Figure 11.15. It offers the following fields:

- **Mail To:** Enter the e-mail address of the intended recipient. Unfortunately, there's no address book or aliasing system.

- **Post:** Post to a specific newsgroup. Note that it's much easier to do this with the newsgroup interface (also within Netscape).

- **Subject:** Enter the subject of your message here. By default, Netscape places the URL of the currently loaded document in the subject line, but you can change it to whatever you want.

- **Attachment:** The Attachment box lets you specify a file you want sent with the e-mail message. This feature is essentially the same as the attachment feature on any e-mail package, but it's nice to have this level of sophistication from within a Web browser. Clicking on the Attach button to the right of the dialog box yields the Mail/News Attachments dialog box, with which you can attach a specific document or, by clicking the File option radio button and then the Browse button, choose a file from your local hard drive to attach.

- **Message Box:** Type whatever you want. Or paste information from another file. Or include the text or HTML code from the currently loaded document by clicking the Quote Document button at the bottom of the window.

- **Send:** Not surprisingly, clicking this button sends the message and any attached file to the recipient.

- **Quote Document:** If you want to include the current document in the message box, click Quote Document. The file will appear as text, not as HTML, and each line will be prefaced with a > character to denote that it's a quotation. The message box will accept no more than 30,000 characters, however, so long documents are best left unquoted.

- **Cancel:** Obviously, choose this if you want to forget about sending the message. Netscape will ask you if you're sure you want to discard the message.

FIGURE 11.15.

Netscape's Send Mail/Post News window, showing the large message screen and file attachment button.

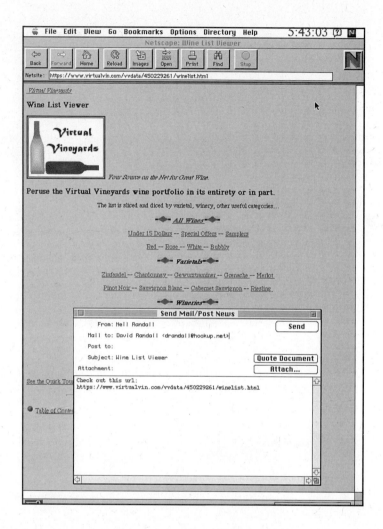

Document Info

If you're interested in the technical details of the document currently displayed in the Netscape content area, select File | Document Info. Here you'll find obvious details such as the Document Title and its Location (URL), but also information about when the file was Last Modified, its Encoding system, and its specific security details, especially the server certificate. Figure 11.16 shows the Document Information box for the Internet Shopping Network, a secure site.

Print

The Print command yields the Print dialog box that is standard for your particular system. You can print in various resolutions, and you can control your printer options as well.

FIGURE 11.16.

The Document Information window for a secure Web page.

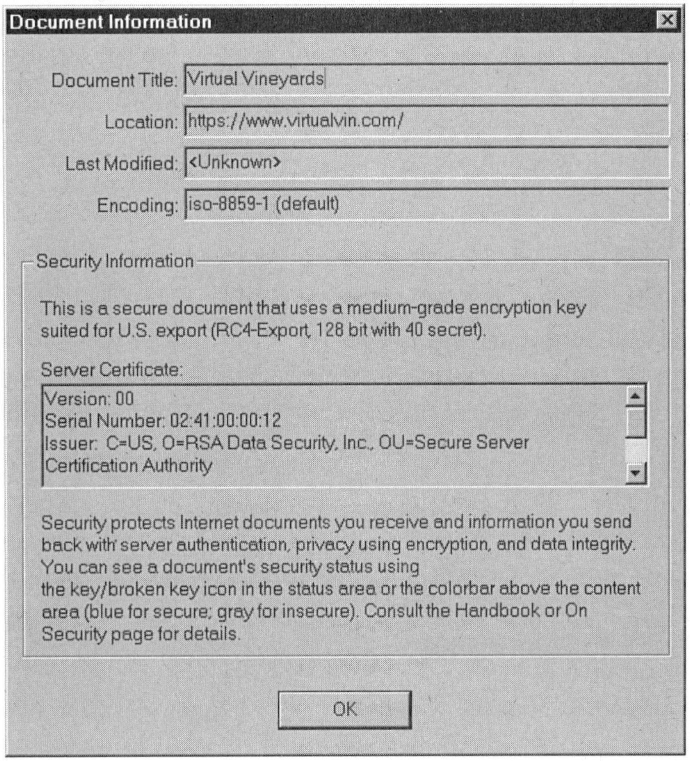

```
┌─────────────────────────────────────────────────────────┐
│ Document Information                                   ☒ │
├─────────────────────────────────────────────────────────┤
│                                                           │
│      Document Title: │Virtual Vineyards│                  │
│                                                           │
│           Location: │https://www.virtualvin.com/│         │
│                                                           │
│       Last Modified: │<Unknown>│                          │
│                                                           │
│           Encoding: │iso-8859-1 (default)│                │
│                                                           │
│  ┌─ Security Information ────────────────────────────┐   │
│  │                                                    │   │
│  │  This is a secure document that uses a medium-grade encryption key │
│  │  suited for U.S. export (RC4-Export, 128 bit with 40 secret). │
│  │                                                    │   │
│  │  Server Certificate:                               │   │
│  │  ┌──────────────────────────────────────────┐ ▲  │   │
│  │  │Version: 00                                 │    │   │
│  │  │Serial Number: 02:41:00:00:12               │ ▓  │   │
│  │  │Issuer: C=US, O=RSA Data Security, Inc., OU=Secure Server │
│  │  │Certification Authority                     │ ▼  │   │
│  │  └──────────────────────────────────────────┘    │   │
│  │                                                    │   │
│  │  Security protects Internet documents you receive and information you send │
│  │  back with server authentication, privacy using encryption, and data integrity. │
│  │  You can see a document's security status using    │   │
│  │  the key/broken key icon in the status area or the colorbar above the content │
│  │  area (blue for secure; gray for insecure). Consult the Handbook or On │
│  │  Security page for details.                        │   │
│  └────────────────────────────────────────────────────┘   │
│                                                           │
│                      ┌──────────┐                         │
│                      │    OK    │                         │
│                      └──────────┘                         │
└─────────────────────────────────────────────────────────┘
```

Print Preview

If you want to see what your page will look like before committing it to paper, choose Print Preview. A rendering of the printed page appears on the screen.

Close

The Close command closes the current document only. If you want to quit from the Netscape program completely, choose Exit.

Exit

Exit removes the Netscape Navigator from memory and lets you get some work done.

Edit Menu

The Edit menu in Netscape Navigator contains the standard Edit commands. There's nothing particularly notable here, except for the Cut, Copy, and Paste commands that actually work. For a long while, these commands didn't work in any browsers, especially Microsoft Windows versions.

Undo

The Cut command is available only within areas in which you can actually type. This includes the Location box, some of the dialog boxes, and the newsgroup and e-mail windows. Cut text is placed in your system's clipboard area for use in programs, dialog boxes, or other text areas that will accept it with the Paste command.

Copy

In Netscape, you can drag the mouse across text on the page in order to select it (it will be highlighted). At that point, you can select Copy to copy it, and then paste it into another program, such as a word processing document. You can also use the Copy command to copy text from box to box within the program, such as from message area to message area.

Paste

If you have text in the clipboard, you can paste it in several locations within Netscape. One of these is the message box in the Send Mail or Post to Newsgroups areas. Another is within the comments areas. A third, and an important one, is into the Location box. This is incredibly useful when you discover a URL in a newsgroup posting or an e-mail message (usually from mailing lists). You can copy the URL to the clipboard of your system, then position the cursor in the Location box (first erasing whatever URL is already there) and choose Edit | Paste. The URL will appear in the box, at which point pressing Enter will retrieve that page from the network.

Find

Identical to the Find icon on the toolbar, Edit | Find opens a simple dialog box that lets you search for text strings in the current document. Note that it won't search across documents, merely through the full length of the current one.

View Menu

The View menu has only four commands, all related to the document currently in the content area.

Reload

Like the Reload icon, the Reload command checks the source document of the current page for changes, then loads that page from Netscape's memory cache, updating text or images as necessary to make the page current.

Load Images

This is identical to the Images icon. If you currently have Auto Load Images (Options menu) toggled off, and you retrieve a page containing images (as most do), Netscape shows a placeholder where the image should be and activates the Image icon. If you then decide you want to see the images on the page, clicking on the Images icon will display them. You can accomplish the same task by toggling Auto Load Images back on and then clicking the Reload icon.

Refresh

Refresh does much the same as Reload, except that it doesn't connect with the original document to determine if any changes have been made. Instead, Refresh simply brings the page out of the cache and places it in the content area. It's primary function is to provide a fresh version of the page, necessary at times if certain elements have disappeared or have scrambled (which isn't supposed to happen, but sometimes it does). Refresh is not available in the Macintosh version.

Source

Choosing View | Source opens the View Source window (shown in Figure 11.17), which shows the HTML code present in the current document. Here you'll see all the HTML tags along with the text itself. One of the most popular uses of the View Source window is to make use of other designers' HTML code to construct your own Web pages; if you see code you want to try for yourself, simply use the Edit | Copy feature to select and copy the text you want, then paste it into your HTML editor program. You can't save text to disk directly from this window, but you can do so by using the File | Save command on the page itself.

FIGURE 11.17.

The View Source window, showing the HTML code of the currently loaded document.

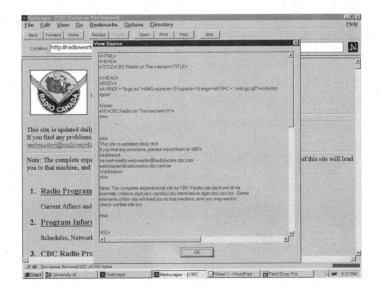

Go Menu

Given that navigation is at the core of Web use, the Go menu should be the most important of all. And it is, except for the fact that the first four items are also available as icons on the toolbar. What makes the Go menu indispensable is the list of current sites, through which you'll find yourself doing most of your returns to previously loaded documents.

Back

Like the Back icon, this command takes you one document back in the History list.

Forward

Identical to the Forward icon, the Go | Forward command is available only after you've either used the Back command or selected a previous document from the History list. Then, Forward will take you one document closer to the end of the History list, no matter how far you've actually gone backward in your travels.

Home

This command, like the Home icon, directly retrieves your home page. You can specify your home page within the Options/Preferences dialog box (see below); by default, the home page is the Netscape Navigator home page at Netscape Communications.

Stop Loading

This command is identical to the Stop icon. It simply stops the current network activity, giving you full command over the program again.

View History

Figure 11.18 shows a typical View History window, accessible through the Go | View History command. It lists the recently visited sites, with the most recent shown at the top. Three buttons are arrayed along the bottom. By highlighting an entry and pressing Go, you return to that document. By clicking on Create Bookmark, you place that URL in your Bookmarks listing (see the Bookmarks menu, discussed later). Close, of course, closes the window.

What sites are actually maintained in the History list is a bit difficult to determine. Essentially, as long as you keep selecting new links, without backtracking to a previously loaded page, the list will continue to grow. After you backtrack, however, the list truncates and re-starts from that point. This makes the history list far less useful than it might be.

FIGURE 11.18.

The View History window, showing the last few sites visited.

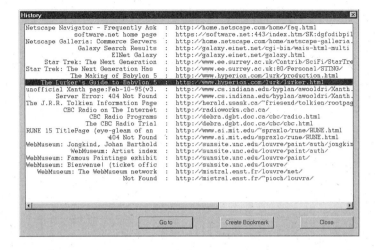

Current Sites List

At the bottom of the Go menu is another view of the History list, but let's call it the Current Sites list to give it more presence. This is an extremely useful feature of Netscape, one that is alone almost worth the price of admission. As you work your way around the Web, you'll want to get back to an earlier document. You can do so by using the View History window, but selecting the document you want from the Current Sites list is easier. Its problems are identical to those of the History list itself; that is, it maintains too few documents to be fully useful. Figure 11.19 shows a typical Current Sites list, residing at the bottom of the Go menu.

FIGURE 11.19.

Current Sites list in the Netscape Go menu.

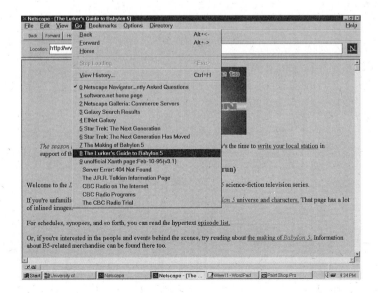

Bookmarks Menu

Netscape's bookmarking feature is extensive, flexible, and—for many users—overly confusing. Even those who like it a great deal acknowledge that using the full system takes a fair bit of effort, and that the bookmarking systems in other Web clients are generally easier. The complexity of Netscape's bookmarking area is somewhat surprising, given the browser's continual nods toward usability, but mixed with that complexity is a considerable degree of power. You can use this system to ensure that you'll find your way back to hordes of different Web sites sorted by any number of categories, to the degree that your browser becomes your primary information storage-and-retrieval tool for all of your Internet activities.

Add Bookmark

When you retrieve a page you want to bookmark, selecting Add Bookmark places the title and URL of that page in the Bookmarks list. Depending on how you have your Bookmarks list set, the page will be added into whatever organizational *folder* (called *headers* in Netscapese) you choose. (See the following section on View Bookmarks for details on setting the Bookmarks list.) As soon as you add a bookmark via this command, it is available both in the Bookmarks box and at the bottom of the Bookmarks menu. Bookmarks are saved to a separate file, which means they're available every time you load Netscape; they don't disappear when you exit the program, the way the Current Sites list does.

View Bookmarks

Selecting View Bookmarks yields the dialog box shown in Figures 11.20 (X Window), 11.21 (Windows), and 11.22 (Macintosh). Actually, only half of this box is displayed initially; the remainder appears when you click the Edit button, which is called More Options on the Mac version. From this extensive dialog box you control your entire bookmarking strategy, building new categories and new bookmark files as you see fit, and even creating a Web page that contains nothing but your own bookmarks.

The preceding figures show, in the bookmarks window on the left, both bookmarks and headers. The principle behind an effect bookmarking strategy is this: Keep your bookmarks sorted under usefully named headers (which act more or less like folders). You could have one header named "Business Sites," another named "Web Searching Pages," a third called "Interactive Games," and so on, up to as many as you want. If you choose to, you can even further categorize them by placing headers inside headers (that is, *nesting* them). Then, by placing each individual bookmark under the appropriate header, you can keep your Web sessions productive and efficient.

Unfortunately, doing all this takes time to learn, and even after you think you have it down there seems to be a fair bit of fiddling necessary. The problems are twofold. First, the feature doesn't support drag-and-drop, so you have to move your bookmarks one click at a time from one header to another. Second, when you simply choose the Add Bookmark item from the Bookmarks menu, it places the item into the currently selected header, and that can also be confusing. But, then, so can this explanation.

By default, all bookmarks are placed into the header called Top of Listing (which isn't actually a header at all; it's just the basic shell). They're also placed at the bottom of the Bookmarks menu, an extremely handy feature. After collecting about 20 bookmarks, you'll realize that the Bookmark dialog box, as well as the list of Bookmarks, is quickly becoming too cluttered. So it's time to start sorting.

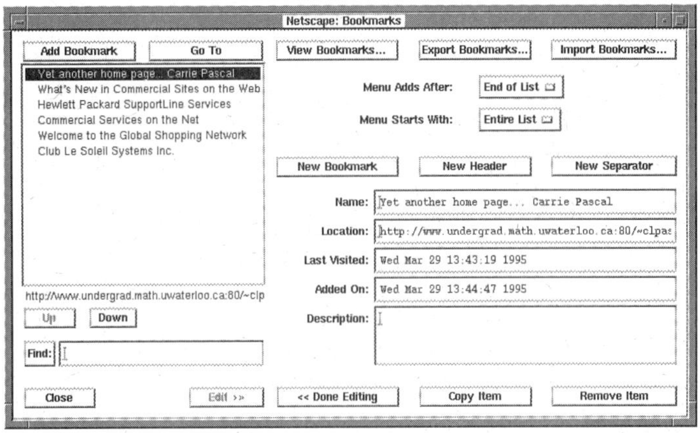

FIGURE 11.20.

The X Window version of Netscape's Bookmarks dialog box.

FIGURE 11.21.

The Microsoft Windows version of Netscape's Bookmarks dialog box.

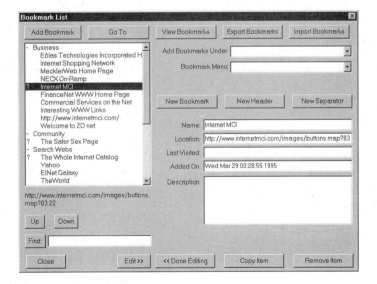

FIGURE 11.22.

The Macintosh version of Netscape's Bookmarks dialog box.

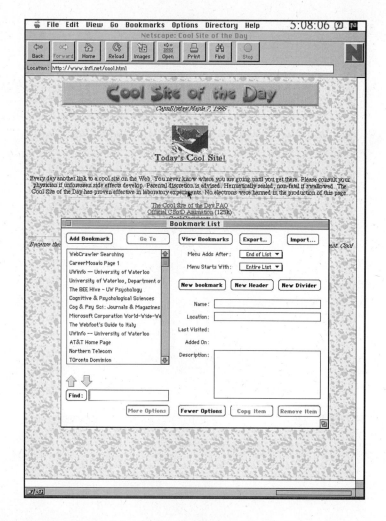

To do so, you need some headers, which you can create by clicking on the New Header button. "New Header" will appear in the Name field of the box (refer to Figures 11.20, 11.21, and 11.22 for the location of the various fields), and you simply type the name of your header ("Business," "Search Tools," whatever) in its place. After you've done so, well, nothing happens. There's no button labeled "Finished Adding," or anything like that. Instead, you either click on "Done Editing" (the label is even worse on the Macintosh—"Fewer Options"), or you click on any item in the Bookmarks area to the left. Your header will now appear in that window, with a minus sign (–) to its left.

Now it's time to place bookmarks under that header. If you're starting a session looking for items that will fit under a given header (let's say "Electronic Malls"), you can tell Netscape to place all bookmarks you locate under that header. Click on the down arrow beside the field named Add Bookmarks Under, and choose the header you want to use. Close the Bookmarks dialog box; then start browsing. Now, whenever you choose Add Bookmark from the Bookmarks menu, that URL will be placed under the Electronic Malls header.

If you have existing bookmarks that need to be sorted (and that's almost inevitable), you can move them under their respective headers, but the procedure is quite clumsy. First, choose View Bookmarks from the Bookmarks menu to yield the Bookmarks dialog box. Click the Edit (or More Options) button to open the dialog box fully, then start sorting. First, create the headers you want by clicking the New Header button, typing the header name, clicking the New Header button again, typing the next name, and so on until you have all the headers you want.

Now, click in the Bookmarks area to the left, on the first bookmark you want placed under a header. This will highlight it, and you'll immediately think you should be able to drag it to the appropriate header. Wrong. Instead, you must use the Up and Down buttons (arrows on the Macintosh) to move the bookmark up or down until it appears beneath the correct header (that is, the bookmark will be below the header and indented slightly to the right). You must do this with every single bookmark you want sorted. You can ease the pain somewhat by double-clicking on any headers that have items in them, thereby "closing" them (they'll have a plus sign [+] beside them), but if you close the header you do want you won't be able to add bookmarks to it until you re-open it by double-clicking. But it's only somewhat less annoying, and quite unnecessary.

After you have your bookmarks sorted, Netscape's bookmarking system shines. Figure 11.23 shows a Bookmarks dialog box with a fairly well-sorted list, and this one is now completely usable.

FIGURE 11.23.

The Netscape Bookmarks dialog box with bookmarks sorted under headers.

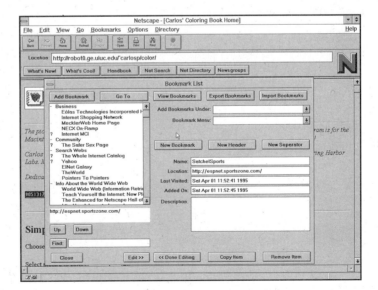

More importantly, the list appears sorted on the Bookmarks menu as well. The headers are all listed, with cascading window arrows leading to the sites bookmarked under those headers. This listing will quickly become the primary focus of your Web browsing, especially if you use the Web as a system for information discovery and retrieval instead of simply a tool for seeing what's out there.

If you want, you can tailor this bookmark listing even further by using the Bookmark Menu field in the Bookmarks dialog box. Here you can specify which header you want to appear in the Bookmarks menu, and that's the only one Netscape will show. If you're doing research on cancer issues, for example, and you have a header (or even a subheader) devoted to those sites, you can select it as the only header that will appear in the Bookmarks menu.

There are three other useful items in the Bookmarks dialog box. Clicking on the View Bookmarks button tells Netscape to display your bookmarks as an HTML page within the content area itself. Export Bookmarks lets you save your bookmarks as an HTML file (.htm in Windows), whereas Import Bookmarks lets you load any HTML file into your bookmarks file. Be careful, though, because it loads the entire thing, not just the URLs, but it can be a useful feature nevertheless.

Bookmark Listing

At the bottom of the Bookmarks menu, Netscape displays your bookmarks. Items with arrows to the right are headers and indicate a cascading menu with more information (bookmarked sites or sub-headers leading to further sub-menus). Expect this to become one of your most frequently accessed areas.

Options

The Options menu of Netscape lets you alter the appearance of the browser, and lets you input important information about yourself, your account, and your access to various servers.

Preferences

After you've spent 10 minutes or so navigating the Web in your first Netscape session, visit the Preferences area and adjust as much as you can. This is a central feature of all Web browsers, and Netscape's is different in its own ways but still similar in what it enables you to do. Some features of the browser won't work at all until you set some preferences, whereas others won't work the way you want them to work until you tell the program exactly how to perform.

When in the Preferences dialog box, use the arrow in the Set Preferences On bar at the top of the dialog box to select the item to configure. The dialog box's appearance and specific preference types are different depending on what platform you're using (X Window, Microsoft Windows, or Macintosh), but the items are essentially the same.

Window Styles (Styles)

In the Window Styles box (shown in Figure 11.24), you can select the appearance of the toolbar icons. They can appear as pictures and text together (the default), as pictures only, or as text only. To turn the toolbar off completely, use Options | Show Toolbar instead.

FIGURE 11.24.

The Window Styles panel from Netscape for UNIX.

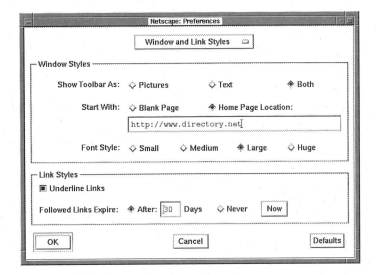

You use the Window Styles box to specify your home page as well. The default is Netscape Communications' main page, but you can replace this with whatever URL you like, including a local file. Once you've selected your home page, you need to tell Netscape whether or not you want to load that page when the program starts. Beside "Start With:" are two radio buttons: Blank Page and Home Page Location. Clicking the latter instructs Netscape to load your home page on startup, whereas clicking Blank Page opens the program with nothing in the content area.

For UNIX users only, the Window Styles area also lets you make font choices. Click Small, Medium, Large, or Huge to determine the font size for the content area. Windows and Macintosh users set fonts in the Fonts panel instead.

Link Styles (Styles)

This panel allows you to set how the hyperlinks will appear in your documents. You can have them underlined (default) or non-underlined, and you can specify how you want Netscape to handle Followed Links. *Followed links* are those hyperlinks you've already clicked on once; Netscape keeps track of these, displaying them differently from normal links, to help you navigate more efficiently in future sessions. You can specify that they are never to expire, or you can set a number of days for them to remain as followed links (30 is the default). If followed links are allowed to expire, they revert back to the same color as normal links after the specified time period. You can also choose to force your followed links to expire, useful if you want to start over or if you don't want other users to see where you've been.

Fonts (Fonts and Colors)

Available only in the Windows and Macintosh versions of Netscape, the Fonts panel lets you determine how fonts will display in retrieved Web documents. This is much less flexible, and much less easily understood, than the font-selection procedures in other browsers, because it's based on encodings rather than specific HTML tags. At any rate, your options are limited.

Each item in the "For the Encoding:" field has a proportional font and a fixed font associated with it. The default, Latin 1, uses Times (or Times New Roman) 12 point for the former, and Courier 10 point for the latter. You can change these by clicking on the respective Choose Font button, which yields a Font dialog box in Windows or a pop-up menu on the Mac.

The Default Encoding field sets the fonts for pages that don't specify an encoding. Select one of the options. The default for both areas is Latin 1, which seems to work quite well for most documents. The entire font-selection process, however, is almost diametrically opposed to Netscape's general level of usability, because most people simply won't have any idea to what "encoding" refers.

Colors (Fonts and Colors)

Available on Macintosh and Windows versions only, the Colors panel lets you make color choices, once again enhancing or altering the appearance of retrieved documents. The Windows version is displayed in Figure 11.25, the Macintosh in Figure 11.26.

Your first option is to let the retrieved document decide the background color of your display, or whether your background will always display no matter what the retrieved document includes. This is especially important as backgrounds become available as HTML tags; different pages will have different backgrounds, but you might not want your browser's appearance to change according to the whims of the page designer.

Next, you can tell Netscape the colors for normal links, followed links, and text. The defaults are blue, mauve, and black, respectively, but you can change each by clicking on the Choose Color button to the right (or the Color box on the Mac). If you choose a color, the Custom button will be checked automatically; if you uncheck it, default colors are used instead.

Finally, you can select a background for your Web pages. This can be a background color, which defaults to gray but can be changed to white or anything else you like. It also can be an image in GIF or JPEG format, which you select by clicking on the Image File radio button and then the Browse button. Select the file you want to use, then click OK in the Colors panel. All Web pages will be set against this background color or image unless they come with a background specification of their own. In this case your background will change, unless you've selected the Always Use Mine button in the Colors field at the top of the panel. Figure 11.27 shows Netscape for Windows with a graphics file loaded as a background.

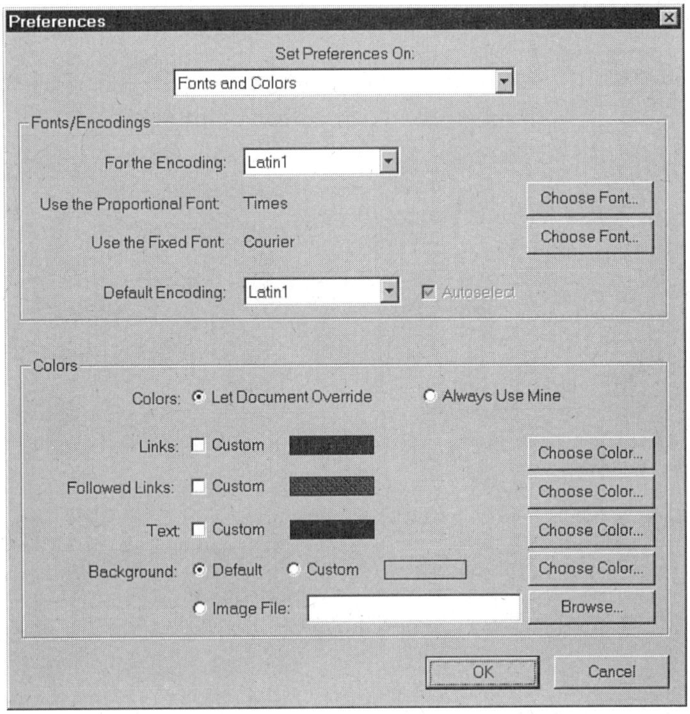

FIGURE 11.25.

The Fonts and Colors dialog box from Netscape for Windows.

Preferences	☒

Set Preferences On:

Fonts and Colors ▼

Fonts/Encodings

For the Encoding: Latin1 ▼

Use the Proportional Font: Times   [Choose Font...]

Use the Fixed Font: Courier   [Choose Font...]

Default Encoding: Latin1 ▼   ☑ Autoselect

Colors

Colors: ⦿ Let Document Override   ○ Always Use Mine

Links: ☐ Custom   [Choose Color...]

Followed Links: ☐ Custom   [Choose Color...]

Text: ☐ Custom   [Choose Color...]

Background: ⦿ Default   ○ Custom   [Choose Color...]

○ Image File: [Browse...]

[OK]   [Cancel]

Mail (Mail and News)

To send e-mail from Netscape's Send Mail/Post News feature, you must configure the browser from this panel. If you don't, Netscape will tell you to do so whenever you try to mail or post a message. In this panel you must include your Mail (SMTP) Server, information that is available from your Internet provider or systems specialist. This is the hard part. After that, just fill in your name (your real name, that is), your e-mail address (the full one with the @ sign and all the dots), and your organization (if you want). If you have a text file you want to use as a signature (that is, that will appear at the bottom of all of your messages), tell Netscape where to find it by clicking the Browse button.

News (Mail and News)

The News panel has only three entries. The first is your News (NNTP) server, which is available from your Internet provider or systems administrator. In the second field, you must tell Netscape where to find your newsgroup information file (typically named newsrc). Mac owners don't have this option, as newsrc is in the Netscape preferences folder with the system folder. Finally, you can specify how many articles you want Netscape to load into a news page. The default is 100, but you can raise or lower this number. Keep in mind that higher numbers show more articles, but they also take an increasing length of time to load.

FIGURE 11.26.

The Fonts and Colors dialog box from Netscape for Macintosh.

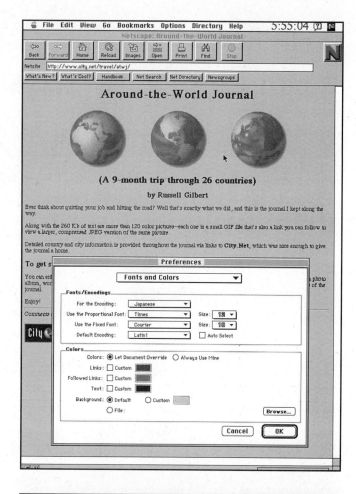

FIGURE 11.27.

Netscape's backgrounds feature, with a self-chosen graphics file.

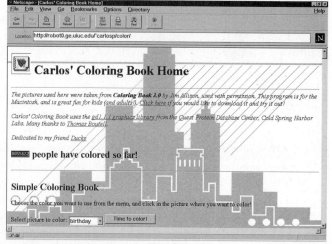

Cache (Cache and Network)

Document caching is among Netscape's most important features. In the current session, a certain number of documents you've already viewed are cached (stored) in your computer's memory (RAM); when you return to one of these documents, the browser loads it from RAM rather that sending out across the Internet to retrieve it. The result is an enormous savings in time. In addition, Netscape caches (stores) retrieved documents on your hard disk, so they are available locally when you revisit that site in a future session. Again, the result is a time savings.

You can set the memory cache as large or as small as you wish. The default is 2000KB (that is, 2MB), but keep your machine's memory capabilities in mind as you set this. The disk cache defaults to five megabytes on Windows and one meg on the Mac, and can also be set to accommodate your own hard drive capabilities. If you want to clear existing caches, click the appropriate button to the right of the panel. This allows you to start the caching process over again.

It's important to determine how often you want Netscape to verify the contents of cached documents. If a document is stored on your hard drive or in RAM, and that document has changed on the original host computer, you'll continually be working with an outdated page. You can tell Netscape to check for changes (that is, go out onto the Net and compare your page and the real one) either Once Per Session, Every Time you load the document, or Never. The first choice is a good compromise, because Every Time is often too slow and Never doesn't get you the updated version. Remember that you can use the Reload command to retrieve the original at any time.

Network (Cache and Network)

In the Network panel, you specify how you want your computer to interact with your network. There are only two choices: Connections lets you specify the maximum number of network connections you'll allow Netscape to make at any one time, whereas Network Buffer Size determines how much of your computer's memory you want to give over to connecting and transferring files. Use the defaults unless you have a good reason not to do so.

Supporting Applications (Applications and Directories)

Netscape can't do everything on its own. Some functions need to be turned over to other applications, so the Supporting Applications and Helper Applications panels let you do so. In Supporting Applications, you're assigning external programs for Telnet, TN3270 (a specific type of Telnet), and viewing document source (that is, when you use the View | Source command). If you don't have a Telnet program, you won't need one unless you come to a URL that begins with telnet:, but you probably have one anyway (they come with all Internet suites and are readily available as freeware). The same holds for the less frequent TN3270. The only reasons you'd want a separate View Source application is because Netscape's built-in viewer is limited in both size and capabilities. If you have a favorite text editor, specify that here.

Directories (Applications and Directories)

Here you specify the location of a Temporary Directory, which Netscape uses to store certain files and then automatically deletes them later. This is necessary, so make sure you specify one; the Mac and X versions have a Browse button to select a temporary folder. From this panel you also specify the directory where Netscape stores its bookmark file (bookmarks.htm). This is only important on Windows and X versions, because on the Mac this file is automatically stored in the Netscape folder inside the Preferences folder.

Images (Images and Security)

This panel offers two choices, and only one in the Mac version. The first choice, on X and Windows versions only, is to have Netscape dither images to match your system's colors as closely as possible, or to substitute colors to the closest available color. Dithering looks better, but substitution results in faster displays of images.

The second choice is to have Netscape display images while it's transferring them, or to wait until it's completed the transfer. The default is While Loading, because Netscape is set up for modem users, who want to see at least the start of each image as quickly as possible to know whether or not to click on another hyperlink or stop the transmission. After Loading can speed transfer times on high-speed networks.

Security (Images and Security)

With the Security panel, you configure Netscape to show pop-up alert windows when dealing with secure documents. By default, all choices are on, but if you don't need the alert (that is, you've trained yourself to read the key icon and the color of the content area border), there's no reason to leave them toggled on. The only exception might be the last choice, Submitting a Form Insecurely. If you submit your credit card information through a fill-in form, it's probably a good idea to have a reminder window pop up to tell you that you're dealing with insecure information.

Proxies

Most users won't have any need for this panel; if you're not sure, try to browse the Web and see if your access is blocked. If it is, your organization has possibly established a series of firewalls, which are designed as a security measure against external access to your system. If that's the case, the only way you can use Netscape is through your system's *proxy* software, which in effect (and as its name implies) carries your information for you, rather than letting your computer do so directly. The proxy software itself is secured by careful network administration; it's a bit like an intelligent bodyguard.

The Proxies panel enables you to specify proxy software and associated ports for each type of Netscape transaction: FTP, Gopher, HTTP, Security Sockets Layer, and WAIS. You can also specify the SOCKS Host, which allows the firewall to be bypassed (under the control of the systems specialists). You can also specify situations under which Netscape will bypass the proxy and communicate directly.

Helper Applications

Helper applications (called *viewers* or *players* by some other browsers) are programs that display or play specific kinds of files. As with Supporting Applications, the purpose is to extend Netscape's capabilities beyond those actually built into the program. Netscape will display GIF or JPEG graphics images, for example, and its latest versions have limited support for audio files, but it can't play MPEG, AVI, or MOV video files; it can't display PostScript or WordPerfect files; it can't automatically decompress ZIP or BinHex files; and so on. One way of handling these other file types is simply to save the file on your hard drive (right-clicking on a hyperlink brings up a menu that lets you do so), but then you have to manually fire up a separate application to make use of that file. Helper Applications enable you to tell Netscape to use specific external applications to interact with these file types.

Netscape's Helper Applications dialog box is quite detailed. (The UNIX dialog box is shown in Figure 11.28, the Mac's in Figure 11.29, and the Windows version in Figure 11.30.) Several file types are included in the File Type box, and you can click on any of these to specify what Netscape is to do with it. Figure 11.30, for example, demonstrates a specification for MPEG file types, which can have the extension mpeg, mpg, or mpe. The file type is highlighted, and the Launch Application radio button is activated. Clicking on that radio button allowed the MPEG viewer application to be specified, and it now appears, complete with its icon, at the bottom of the dialog box. The next time Netscape retrieves an MPEG file, it will automatically launch the MPEG viewer and play the video.

FIGURE 11.28.

The Helper Applications dialog box from Netscape for UNIX.

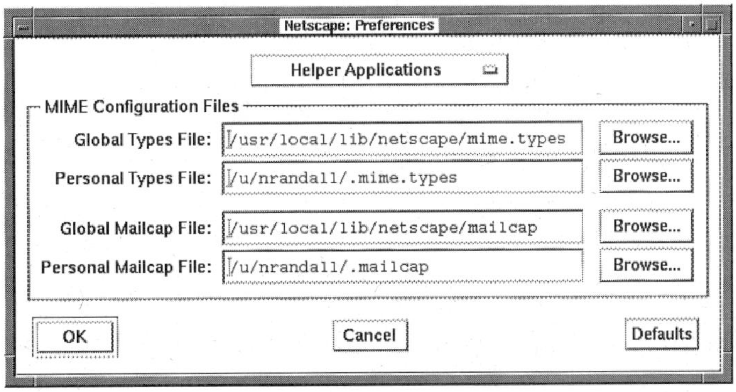

Netscape: Preferences

Helper Applications

┌─ MIME Configuration Files ─────────────────────────────

Global Types File: `/usr/local/lib/netscape/mime.types` Browse...

Personal Types File: `/u/nrandall/.mime.types` Browse...

Global Mailcap File: `/usr/local/lib/netscape/mailcap` Browse...

Personal Mailcap File: `/u/nrandall/.mailcap` Browse...

OK   Cancel   Defaults

FIGURE 11.29.

The Helper Applications dialog box from Netscape for Macintosh.

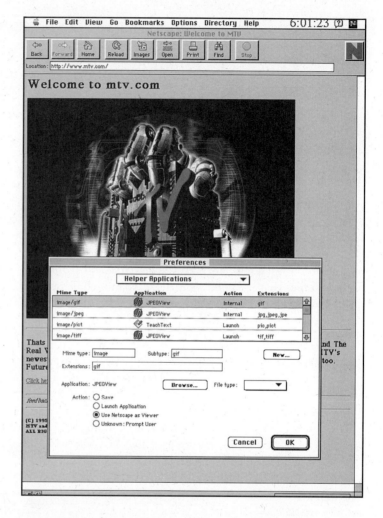

As you select each file type, Netscape will occasionally activate the Use Browser as Viewer radio button. This tells you that Netscape is capable of displaying or playing the file on its own. You still have the option of specifying your own application for that file type, however; you might have particularly rich multimedia software that Netscape's built-in sound player can't touch, or you might want text files all loaded into your word processor so you can deal with them in a more feature-filled program.

If you encounter a document type that is not included in the Helper Applications dialog box, you can add it to the list by clicking on the Add Type button. A resulting small dialog box lets you specify the file type and the subtype as well, and then places it in the File Type window. At that point you can highlight it and assign it to an external viewer just as you would any other file type.

FIGURE 11.30.

Netscape for Windows, configured to launch external MPEG player whenever it transfers an MPEG file.

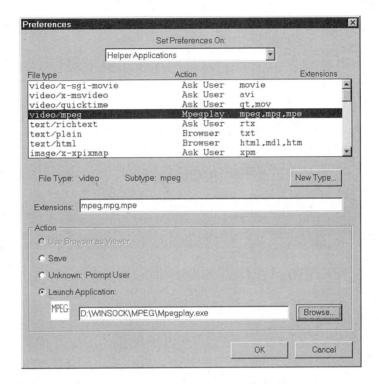

You can tell Netscape to display the file itself, or you can have an external application launch whenever the browser retrieves a specific file type, but there are two other options as well. The first is to have Netscape prompt you to Save a specific file type to your hard disk; this will launch the Save As dialog box for your system. The second is to click the radio button labeled Unknown: Prompt User, in which case Netscape will let you know that the file type is unsupported and allow you to perform whatever action you see fit.

Show Toolbar

The Show Toolbar option lets you toggle the toolbar on and off.

Show Location

The Show Location option lets you toggle the location box on and off.

Show Directory Buttons

The Show Directory Buttons option lets you toggle the directory buttons on and off (yes, I realize there's a pattern forming here).

Auto Load Images

Choosing Auto Load Images enables you to tell Netscape whether you want inline images loaded with the document. Because images typically take a fairly long time to load, you can navigate the Web much more quickly if they're off, even if you have a high-speed connection. Increasingly, however, Web pages are based on images, so don't expect to use this option all that often. Besides, as Netscape lets you stop a download, or access a link without waiting for the transfer to finish, this feature is much less necessary than it seems.

Show FTP File Information

When accessing FTP sites, a considerable amount of information about the files is available. Turning this option on (that is, placing a checkmark beside it) gives you all the information about the files. Turning it off gives you less information, but a much more readable page.

Save Options

As the name suggests, this feature saves all the options you've selected so they'll be in place next time you load Netscape.

Directory

The Directory menu lists several useful sites to help with your Web browsing. Choose them to get you going, or when you need to discover specific information or keep apprised of new developments on the Web.

Netscape's Home

This is the Netscape Communications Corporation home page. It's worth visiting once in a while to see if a new version of the Navigator has been made available.

What's New

This is Netscape Communications' page of new and interesting sites. Not as famous as NCSA's page, but frequently updated and always useful. Visit weekly.

What's Cool

This is Netscape Communications' collection of Web sites they consider "cool." Obviously the choices aren't necessarily the ones you'd select, but you're certain to find several sites worth visiting more than once here.

Go to Newsgroups

This item takes you to your newsgroups. You must have a news server specified in the Preferences dialog box in order for this item to work.

Netscape Galleria

This item opens a page listing sites that make use of Netscape's security-enabled Netsite Web server, and several with advanced Netscape HTML tags as well. If you want to see everything your browser has to offer, visit some of these locations.

Internet Directory

This is a listing of Internet directories, meta-pages, and subject listings from which you can browse the Web efficiently.

Internet Search

This page lists a wealth of Internet search tools, all of which are useful for specific purposes.

Internet White Pages

From here you can attempt to find the e-mail addresses of Internet users, but don't get your hopes up. The best way to get someone's Internet address is still by phoning them and asking.

About the Internet

From this page you can discover just about everything you've always wanted to know about the Internet itself.

Help Menu

Netscape doesn't ship with help files; instead, selecting an item from the Help menu launches the retrieval of a document from the Netscape host computer. In one way, this is an extremely useful thing, because Help pages can be continually updated. In another, however, it can lead to frustration, because the host isn't always available, and even when it is it can be quite slow.

If you want to use the Help files extensively, it's a good idea to retrieve them once and then save them as local files on your hard drive, using the File | Save As feature. Then, when you want Help, you can use File | Open File to read them.

About Netscape

This is a local file that tells you which version of Netscape you're running. It can be useful if you keep both a supported version (the latest non-beta) and an unsupported version (the latest beta) on your hard drive in different directories. This is a recommended procedure, by the way, whenever you deal with alpha or beta software.

Handbook

The Netscape Navigator handbook is a series of HTML files available from the Netscape home machine. It is, in effect, the program manual. It's not context sensitive, like most online manuals, but it contains all of the information you need to perform the tasks you want. Don't expect it to tell you everything, however; for most procedures it's fine, but for items like bookmarking it's not as clear as it should be. Still, it's a good resource. There's a separate version available for each release of Netscape, but many of the items are the same. Particularly worth reading, if you have a few minutes, is the heartwarming introduction (`http://home.netscape.com/newsref/manual/docs/intro.html#C0`), which shows, among other things, that Netscape is the product of human beings. Let's hope it survives the company's leap into Major Company status. Figure 11.31 shows the contents screen of the Handbook.

Release Notes

If you're curious about the features your new version of Netscape offers—or even your older version, for that matter—check out the Release Notes page. Here you'll find features added to the various releases (the page is an entire history of the product's progress), as well as known bugs that are being worked on by the developers. It's always good to check this page whenever you FTP a new version, even though most of the items are included in the README file that accompanies the software. Note that there's a separate Release Notes page for each version of the Navigator (including separate ones for beta releases). The index page (`http://home.netscape.com/home/help-on-version/`) will give you a table of contents for the various versions.

FIGURE 11.31.

Contents of the Netscape Navigator Handbook, from Netscape for Mac.

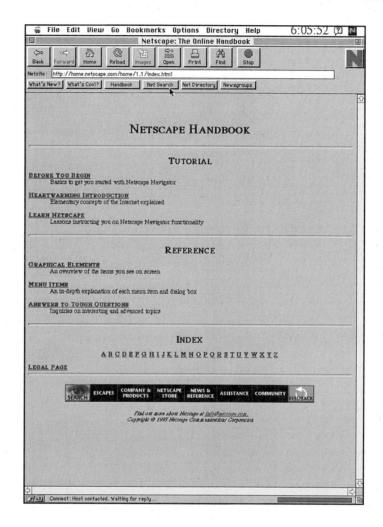

252

Frequently Asked Questions

As its name implies, this menu item takes you to the page of Netscape FAQs (`http://home.netscape.com/eng/mozilla/1.1/faq.html`). If you want to know your software completely, fire these up once in a while. You'll discover many things you already know, but a number more you probably don't. Note that there's a separate section here for each Netscape platform: X Window, Microsoft Windows, and Macintosh. This is an extremely informative page, and it's worth saving to your local hard drive. Figure 11.32 shows a partial list of these FAQs.

FIGURE 11.32.

The Frequently Asked Questions page from Netscape for UNIX.

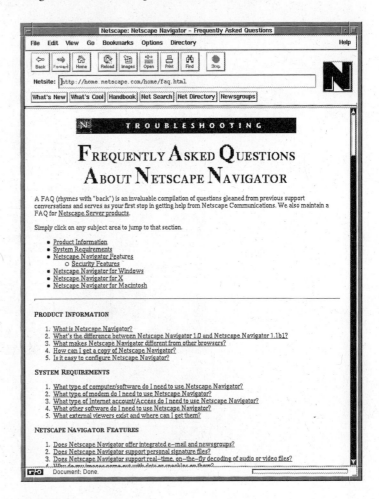

On Security

One of Netscape's strongest features, at least potentially, is its ability to offer an interface to secure documents and sites on the Web. This Help item (`http://home.netscape.com/info security-doc.html`) explains how your browser helps you distinguish between secure and non-secure pages (the correct word is probably "insecure," but why do a psychological number on a Web page?), and what it means to be entering a secure page in the first place. Extremely informative, this page gives a glimpse of what the Web will become. Figure 11.33 shows the alert window that accompanies a secure page, whereas Figure 11.34 shows a secure page with an unbroken key in the bottom-right corner.

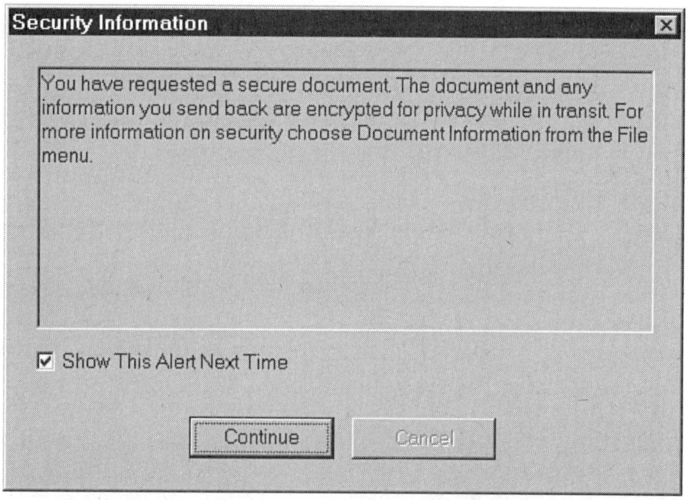

FIGURE 11.33.

The Alert window that results from entering a secured site in Netscape.

FIGURE 11.34.

A secure page in Netscape, with a blue border and an unbroken key icon.

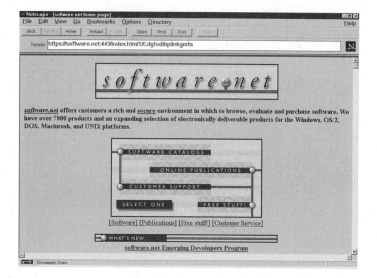

How to Give Feedback

The title of this item is a bit misleading, because the resulting page (`http://home.netscape.com/home/how-to-give-feedback.html`) is primarily an information guide to getting further information, purchasing the products, or reporting bugs to the development staff. There isn't a form that simply lets you tell the company what you like and dislike about the product, which the term "feedback" seems to suggest.

How to Get Support

This page (`http://home.netscape.com/home/how-to-get-support.html`) tells you what to do if you need technical support for your Netscape products. It also explains that, unless you pay the $39 licensing fee for the product, you're not entitled to technical support—which, after all, seems reasonable. As you might expect, you can also jump from this page to Netscape's "e-store" to actually buy their products (and, yes, you can do so over the Web through secured transactions), made possible by Netscape's Netsite Commerce Server.

How to Create Web Services

This page (`http://home.netscape.com/home/how-to-create-web-services.html`) is an excellent directory of sites where you can find out about creating HTML pages for your own Web publishing effort. It includes a link to Chris Tacy's always interesting *Off The Net* newsletter, which keeps you informed and up to date about Web happenings.

Installation

Installation of Netscape is quite simple on all three platforms. UNIX, of course, is the most complex of the lot, but even here the browser installs fairly easily on many systems. For the Mac and Windows, Netscape uses the standard installation procedures.

Netscape Navigator for X Window

Publisher: Netscape Communications Corporation

Version Reviewed: 1.1beta2

FTP Site: `ftp.netscape.com`

FTP Directory: `/netscape/unix`

FTP Filename: Several choices for varying UNIX platforms—all are `tar.Z` files

To install, FTP to `ftp.netscape.com` and retrieve the `tar.z` file that matches (or most closely matches) your computer and system. Next, move this file to a directory of your choice, wherever you want the program to reside. Enter that directory and uncompress the `tar.z` file by typing, typically, **uncompress xxxxxxxxx.tar.Z** (replace *xxxxxxxxxx* with the actual filename). Finally, type **tar xvf xxxxxxxx.tar** to complete the process. Netscape might run as is, but you should call up the README files and make adjustments to the configuration files and system setup. Some files might need to be moved to other directories, and you might need to attend to details specific to your network setup.

Netscape Navigator for Microsoft Windows

Publisher: Netscape Communications Corporation

Version Reviewed: 1.1beta2

FTP Site: `ftp.netscape.com`

FTP Directory: `/netscape/windows`

FTP Filename: `ns16-xxx.exe` or `ns32-xxx.exe` (xxx signifies current version)

To install, FTP to `ftp.netcom.com` and retrieve the .exe file. Note that the ns32xxx version works only on Windows NT or Windows 95, and not with Windows 3.1 or 3.11 with the Win32s extensions loaded. Create a temporary installation directory (`c:\tempinst` or something similar), and move the .exe file into that directory. Enter that directory from DOS or in Windows File Manager. In DOS, type the name of the file and press Enter. In Windows File Manager (or Windows 95 Explorer), double-click on the filename. Either action will uncompress the files into that directory. From within Windows File Manager (you can't do this from DOS), enter that directory—or choose Window | Refresh if you're already there—and double-click on `setup.exe`. Follow the screen prompts to complete the installation. When the program group appears, double-click on the Netscape icon to run the program. Note that you must be already running a Windows Sockets program for Netscape to work.

Netscape Navigator for Macintosh

Publisher: Netscape Communications Corporation

Version Reviewed: 1.1beta2

FTP Site: `ftp.netscape.com`

FTP Directory: `/netscape/mac`

FTP Filename: `netscape.sea.hqx`

Using Fetch or any other FTP program, FTP to `ftp.netcom.com` and retrieve the self-extracting file. If your FTP doesn't do so automatically, pick up the file and uncompress it by dropping it on your Unstuffit application. Finally, double-click on the Netscape icon to load the program.

The Future of Netscape: Navigator 2.0 Does It All!

As *The World Wide Web Unleashed 1996* went to press, Netscape Communications was on the verge of releasing version 2.0 of the Netscape Navigator browser. While it was far too late to include a full write-up of the features and capabilities of the new release, its appearance was far too important for us to ignore completely. Here, then, is a quick look at the new browser.

Calling Netscape 2.0 a *browser* is a bit of a misnomer, because with this release Netscape becomes an all-purpose Internet tool. As with all Netscape versions, 2.0 supports the most advanced Web page designs, but now there's much more. Built into Netscape 2.0 are advanced newsreader features, full e-mail retrieval, and technologies such as HotJava's "applet" capabilities. Netscape 2.0 wants to become your only necessary Internet program, and early indications are that it might just succeed.

And something else happened to Netscape just before we went to press. Netscape the company, that is, not Netscape the browser. In September 1995, Netscape Communications went public, and the stock market responded with a bang. The company was worth well over a billion dollars overnight, despite the fact that it had yet to post a profit, and despite that fact that, essentially, it was giving its products away.

What this tells you is exactly how hot the World Wide Web remains as we approach the end of 1995, the Web's second significant year of operation. With companies like Netscape, Microsoft, Quarterdeck, and any number of start-ups fighting for the right to claim market share for the most publicized software genre of our time, it's a safe bet that this popularity will continue unabated.

From all indications, Netscape Communications intends to rule the roost. Not only do they offer the most successful browser in the world, they keep improving on it at a speed that no other browser publisher has been able to emulate. Furthermore, with Netscape Gold (a more full-featured version of the basic browser) they're offering a fully WYSIWYG Web authoring environment. Their Web server software features strong security (despite a much-publicized security problem unveiled in September 1995), and is also available for free extended trial. Their high-end server packages offer full solutions for specific kinds of companies and organizations, and their determination to incorporate other technologies into their software—Sun's HotJava and Adobe's Acrobat being the two primary examples—bodes well for the future of their famous browser. As this text was being written, Netscape had just acquired Collabra Software, publishers of a highly regarded package of online collaboration software, so we can expect even more enhancements to Netscape as the months progress.

Netscape's home page resides at `http://home.netscape.com/`. It's worth your while to visit it at least once a week to see what's next on the World Wide Web horizon.

Netscape 2.0, the Browser

As a World Wide Web browser, Netscape 2.0 picks up where Netscape 1.1 and 1.2 left off. That is, it's the most capable browser available. Because Netscape is at the forefront of browser technology in most areas (and certainly most popular areas), if you want to see the immediate future of browsers, this is the one to get.

The Little Stuff

Figure 11.35 shows the new browser (Windows 32-bit edition). There are few visible changes from earlier versions, except that the toolbar, which was formerly between the menus and the Location box, is now the bottom element of interface tools. This makes sense, because the toolbar contains the navigation buttons and should therefore be most easily accessed. In fact, the toolbar can be detached completely from its default location. You can slide it to the right or left along its standard bar (in Figure 11.35 it's been moved away from its flush-left position), or you can pick it up and drag it anywhere on the screen.

FIGURE 11.35.

The Netscape 2.0 screen showing the new position of the toolbar.

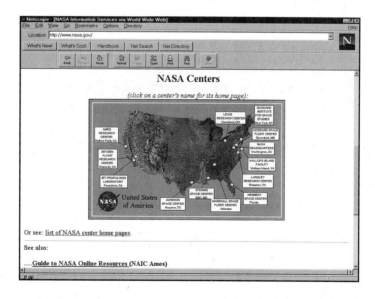

This version of Netscape offers support for "progressive" JPEG images. Simply, this means that JPEG-type images will load more quickly than before, letting you figure out earlier whether or not you want to load the whole thing. Netscape 2.0 will also decide automatically whether or not to smooth out images through "dithering"; before, you made that decision yourself. The result? More consistently high-quality graphics.

For Web authors, Netscape 2.0 offers several enhancements. The new font color tag lets you specify different colors for any font string on the document (including individual letters, if you wish). To see this in operation, go to `http://randall.uwaterloo.ca/~news2.htm` (not shown here because the book isn't in color). The phrase "Explore and have Fun!" at the bottom of the page is a different color from the rest of the text. The font color tag has specified "red." (The red in the image comes from the image itself and isn't the result of a tag.)

Also available to Web authors is the `DIV ALIGN` tag, an HTML 3.0 extension. `DIV ALIGN` lets you align text elements to the left, center, or right of the page. Until now you could center text, or you could align graphics, but this new tag gives you better control over your text. Also new are the `SUP` and `SUB` tags, which let you place superscripts and subscripts into your documents.

Web authors can now design hyperlinks that will open a new Netscape window automatically. This feature, called "targeted windows," is especially useful if you want people to experience your site without forcing them to leave the current page. When they click on a link, they'll get a new window, but the original will remain open for them to return to. You can also build in links to external sites this way, as a means of preventing the users from losing your site completely as they explore elsewhere.

Also supported are client-side imagemaps. They work the same as normal imagemaps (which are called "server side"), but you'll notice two differences.

First, they'll be faster, because clicking on an area of the map no longer means a message to the server, followed by a response to the browser, followed by a retrieval message to the URL in question. Since mapping information is stored with the document itself (that is, on the "client's side"), when the user clicks on an area the request will go directly to the desired URL.

The other difference is related to this one: Moving your cursor over the imagemap now reveals the destination URL rather than the meaningless set of x,y coordinates of the image itself. As a user, your choice of whether to click can be made more intelligently.

The Big Stuff

Four major new additions to Netscape 2.0 make this version the most capable and most state-of-the-art browser available: frames, inline plug-ins, Java applets, and the Netscape scripting language.

With frames, Web authors can place separate windows on the same page, each of which has its own URL and each of which can scroll independently of the main window. This offers, in effect, a complete user interface solution on any given page. A frame down the left side of the page might show, for instance, a scrolling list of the covers of the Sams.net books written by John December and Neil Randall—*World Wide Web Unleashed, Presenting Java, Teach Yourself the Internet.* Click on any one of them, and the main window will display the new URL without leaving the original listing, so the user can keep the idea of the page in mind. A third frame could offer other possibilities as well. It takes some programming, but it's a powerful addition.

Inline plug-ins lets developers add "live objects" to Netscape's basic functionality. Essentially, it means that Netscape 2.0 can now be used as a platform for viewing other document types. You can already automatically see JPEG or GIF graphics files, but now you'll be able to view Adobe Acrobat PDF documents, with their full slate of graphics components, and Macromedia Director presentations (with complete interaction). Also supported right off the bat are Apple QuickTime movies and RealAudio sound files. Look for other publishers to build in automatic support through inline plug-ins as well.

Java applets are small applications produced using the Java language developed by Sun Microsystems. There's a dedicated Java browser available—HotJava (`http://java.sun.com/`)—but Netscape 2.0 will handle these small programs as well. Java applets can be fully interactive, separate programs, with their own interfaces and purposes. They make the Web potentially much more than an information tool, and increase the possibilities of full interaction over the Web. See Chapter 43, "Java and HotJava," for more information on this important new technology.

Finally, there's the new scripting language. Effectively, you can create your own Netscape-run "programs" with this language, linking applets, plug-ins, multimedia, and many other information types. Again, this will improve the potential of information retrieval via the Web, and should quickly become a standard feature of new Web pages.

Netscape 2.0, the E-Mailer

Practically all Web browsers—and certainly all versions of Netscape—let you send an e-mail message directly from the browser itself. With version 2.0, Netscape now lets you receive e-mail as well. From the File menu, you can select the command Open Mail Window, and you'll be presented with the screen shown in Figure 11.36.

Although the e-mail package wasn't complete as this was written, it already demonstrated its potential convenience. You can create folders (top-left window), and while there is no message filtering mechanism, it's easy to move messages into one of these folders. The messages within the folder (such as the inbox) appear in the top-right window, and are accessed with a single mouse click.

The greatest convenience, however, is shown in the message window of Figure 11.36. If a URL appears in a message, it's shown as a hyperlink. Click on the hyperlink, and you'll call up the URL directly in the Mail window (this feature was implemented earlier by Wollongong's Emissary—`http://www.twg.com/`). No more cutting and pasting from e-mail program to Web browser, and pure convenience at your fingertips. E-mail addresses and newsgroups also appear as hyperlinked URLs.

FIGURE 11.36.

Netscape 2.0's e-mail screen, with URLs highlighted in the message window.

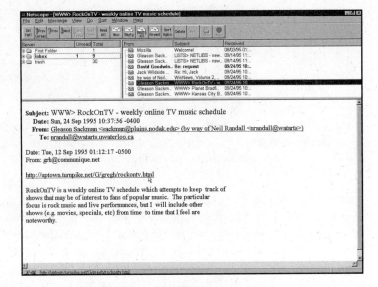

Netscape 2.0, the Newsreader

Earlier versions of Netscape provided a capable newsreader, but version 2.0 expands those capabilities considerably. The File menu contains an Open News Window command, which brings up the screen shown in Figure 11.37.

At the top left are the newsgroups available from your Internet provider; at top right are the messages themselves. The newsgroups are sorted into their hierarchies (`alt.*`, `comp.*`, and so on), and subsorted into their main categories (`comp.binaries`, and so on). These appear as easily accessed folders. Messages are threaded with threads clearly visible (although Figure 11.37 doesn't have any threads. The message itself appears in the message window in the bottom half of the screens. All windows can be sized.

Netscape 2.0's newsreader features are quite strong. Not as good as those of a dedicated newsreader, but close enough. The most important addition, however, is the automatic decoding and displaying of binary files. Shown in Figure 11.37 is a graphic of a cheetah, which was accessed by single-clicking the appropriate news message. No further decoding command was necessary; Netscape 2.0 simply did its thing and displayed the graphic.

This is extremely good news for those who view newsgroup graphics regularly (again, the feature was already implemented by Wollongong's Emissary). It's much worse news for anyone fearful of children seeing pornographic or other objectionable pictures on the Net. Clearly, this feature will need a parental control feature if Netscape isn't to be trashed by those with such concerns. It will be interesting to see if this is implemented in the final—or near future—release.

FIGURE 11.37.

Netscape 2.0's newsgroup reader showing a decoded binary image.

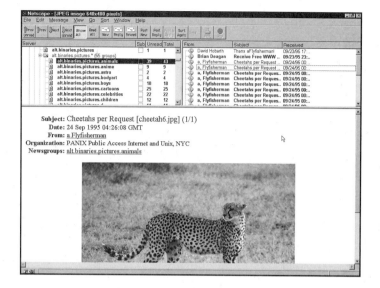

Netscape Navigator Gold 2.0

For Web creators, the big news is Netscape Navigator Gold 2.0, which wasn't available in any form as this was written. Navigator Gold 2.0 is an enhanced version of Navigator 2.0. It adds nothing less than full WYSIWYG creation and editing of HTML documents.

The September 1995 news release promised a true WYSIWYG editing environment, directly within the Navigator itself. In other words, you can see what your pages look like without having to switch programs and load the file. Also promised were cut-and-paste of text, graphics, and live objects directly into the document, and full support for frames, inline viewers, and form design.

If all these features are present, Navigator Gold 2.0 should prove to be the HTML editor to end all HTML editors. Added to their other newly announced product, LiveWire and LiveWire Pro, which provides a means of creating full online application systems, this product demonstrates a very promising commitment to the Web's future. Netscape Communications has its detractors, who claim that the company is destroying the purpose of the Web by straying from the original purpose of nonproprietary commands and tags, but nobody can deny that they intend to stay in front.

Summary

Netscape Navigator has become, in seemingly no time at all, probably the most popular Web browser of all. Use it once, and you'll see why. It's feature rich, it displays great variety in graphics, it suits modem users extremely well, and it's continually being updated and expanded by its developers. And because a free-trial evaluation copy is easily available over the Net itself, there's really no reason not to give it a try.

More Browsers for Microsoft Windows

12

by
Neil Randall

Whatever Microsoft Windows touches, it ends up dominating, always in quantity and sometimes even in quality. Nowhere has this proven more true than in the development of commercial World Wide Web clients, that is, those produced for sale by a software company. There's scarcely a commercial browser to be found for any other platform, and that includes the Macintosh—whereas for Windows a host has appeared in the past year. Despite the fact that the two most popular browsers—NCSA Mosaic (see Chapter 10, "NCSA Mosaic") and Netscape Navigator (see Chapter 11, "Netscape Navigator")—are downloadable at no charge on the Net itself, the commercial browsers seem to be selling just fine. But that's what happens when you have a platform as huge as Windows has become.

Four Windows browsers are available free via FTP: NCSA Mosaic, Netscape Navigator, Cello, and WinWeb. Of these, only the first two show signs of continual upgrading and enhancement. Cello continues to be available only in Version 1.1, as of this writing at least, whereas WinWeb has improved significantly over the past eight months but gets upgraded less frequently than its Macintosh counterpart, MacWeb. Then again, upgrading MacWeb makes more sense than upgrading WinWeb, because MacWeb has many adherents and faces far less competition. In the case of Cello, which is largely the work of one man and a small support team, Version 2.0 has taken so long that there's significant danger it won't find a significant body of users at all. That's too bad. When the first edition of *The World Wide Web Unleashed* went to press, the Cello upgrade was eagerly anticipated.

So far, there's no real reason for anyone to go out and actually buy a Web browser, unless it's part of a complete Internet suite. Both Mosaic and Netscape are excellent Windows products (although Netscape technically is free only for educational use or for evaluation), and Quarterdeck Mosaic, as just one other example, has been available in beta form through FTP. The only possible exceptions to this thinking are Booklink Technologies' InternetWorks, which offers a number of excellent enhancements, and Spry's Mosaic in a Box, which offers not only a stand-alone Web browser but full Web connectivity as well through the CompuServe network. (See Chapter 8, "Getting Connected: Accessing the Web," for details about Mosaic in a Box.) Several books about Mosaic include versions of Spyglass's Enhanced NCSA Mosaic, which has been licensed by Microsoft and might be placed in Windows 95 as well.

What's interesting is that Windows, which was the last of the three major graphical platforms (behind X and Macintosh) to have a full-fledged browser, now has more than the rest. More interesting still is the fact that the quality is consistently quite high.

Free Browsers

The most popular free browsers for Windows are, of course, Mosaic and Netscape (again, Netscape isn't free for every user). Two others, however, are available and reasonably well known. Cello is the oldest of the Windows browsers, whereas WinWeb is easy on system requirements and directly tied to the EINet Galaxy search engines. The latter two are worth downloading and trying for yourself.

CELLO

Publisher:	Cornell University's Legal Information Institute
Reviewed version:	1.01a
FTP site:	`ftp.law.cornell.edu`
FTP directory:	`/pub/LII/Cello/`
FTP filename:	`cello.zip`

Cello is the product primarily of one person, Thomas Bruce of Cornell University's Legal Information Institute. This is significant for a couple of reasons. First, it might signify the last time we ever see a groundbreaking piece of Windows-based Internet software designed by one person with a small support staff. Second, and more important for our purposes, it is the reason Cello has not yet seen its necessary major revision. Simply put, Tom is too busy with his real job.

Cello began life as a colorful browser that differed from Mosaic in several ways and in fact was available before Windows Mosaic. From its beginnings, Cello operated without the memory-hogging problems of its competitor, allowing users with SLIP access and slower processors (386-25s, for instance, or even 286s) to make use of a strong World Wide Web client program.

Figure 12.1 shows a typical Cello screen, displayed on a 14-inch monitor in 1024×768 resolution. Immediately apparent is the browser's inherent colorfulness. If this book were in color, you would see the main title of the document, The Virtual Tourist, in a bright red. The image map is similarly colored, and the entire effect of the page—as of all of Cello—is that it appears as a bright, accessible program.

FIGURE 12.1.

Cello, showing inline graphics and clean design features.

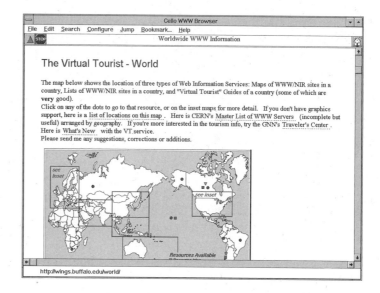

Cello ships this way, with the colors turned on, but you can change all of the fonts with its configuration program, including the colors, so this might seem like unfair praise. Windows Mosaic, by contrast, enables you to change fonts but not the colors of fonts—at least not even remotely easily—so let's let the point stand. If you want to truly customize the appearance of your Web documents, Cello makes it possible. You can have every text style in a different color, typeface, and font size if that's what you want; as long as you don't blind yourself, it's fine. Figure 12.2 offers a look at the font configuration dialog box, and as you can tell by the bottom-left corner, maroon is the color for first-level headings.

FIGURE 12.2.

Font dialog box from Cello, with color choices.

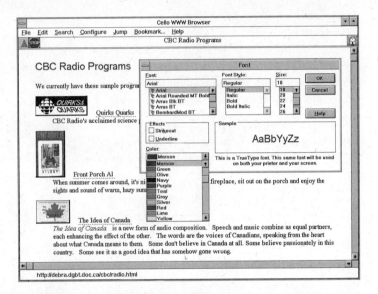

Despite the strengths of this sort of configuration feature, Figure 12.2 also demonstrates one of Cello's less attractive attributes, its underlining appearance. In fact, these dotted underlines alone have caused users to abandon the program for the more attractively highlighted Windows Mosaic, and although this seems a silly reason for switching, that's the nature of working with users of GUIs. It would be nice if Cello offered an underlining choice that meant something, but as the open Configure menu in Figure 12.3 shows, the options are to have Links Underlined Only either on or off. If they're off, Cello displays hyperlinks with dotted rectangles surrounding the word, also shown in Figure 12.3.

Still, the Configure menu makes it clear how easily configured this program is. The home page, download directory, background color (with full spectrum), e-mail address, mail relay, news server, and WAIS gateway can all be set from this menu, and you can even specify which Telnet program you want for those times when hyperlinks open Telnet sessions. Such features are similarly available in some browsers, but they aren't available at all through the Options menu of Cello's main Windows competitor. With this kind of interface consideration given to Version 1.0, the new version promises to be even easier to configure.

FIGURE 12.3.

The choices in Cello's Configure menu.

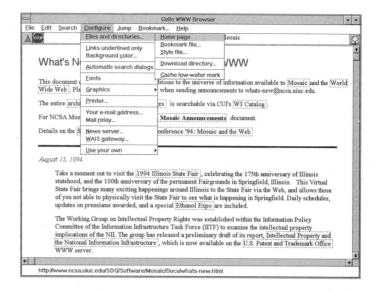

For a beginning Web user, Cello's bookmarking feature is among the easiest of any browser's to understand. For one thing, the feature is actually called Bookmarks, rather than the much less self-explanatory hotlists, and it has its own top-level menu name, surprisingly absent from the majority of browsers (surprisingly, because bookmarks on the Web are a constant application). Figure 12.4 shows the Bookmarks dialog box, which lists the bookmarks in alphabetical order and offers a full interface for dealing with them. From here you can dump the entire list to a file to produce an HTML page consisting solely of your bookmarks, you can jump to the bookmarked page, or you can copy the reference to the clipboard. When you find a document you want to bookmark, you use this dialog box to do so, clicking Mark Current Document. This command yields the small dialog box shown at the bottom of Figure 12.4, in which you can change the document's title to suit your own purposes.

Unfortunately, Cello's bookmarking system lacks some important features. It doesn't allow categorization, as does Windows Mosaic's Menu Editor. Instead, all bookmarks are lumped together (albeit in alphabetical order), and after a time they're difficult to locate in the list. Furthermore, you can bookmark only 50 entries, after which you have to dump the lot to a file and start over. This will be corrected in Version 2.0 (according to the designer), but for now it presents some very real difficulties.

Despite the lack of sophistication of this particular feature, Cello sports some features that its competition added only recently or indeed hasn't added yet. From before Version 1.0, Cello's Edit menu contained two items, View Source and View As Clean Text. View Source offers the same thing as the Document Source option in a variety of browsers, but only very recently in Windows Mosaic: the HTML-coded text version of the file. A very nice feature is View As Clean Text, which does the same thing but loads the document without the HTML tags. When you see a page that you actually want to read (rather than reformat or borrow HTML ideas from), this is an extremely handy feature. An example of the result of using the View As Clean Text feature appears in Figure 12.5. In fact, the text in the document looks like the text in the Cello window.

FIGURE 12.4.

Cello's bookmarking interface and Name your bookmark box.

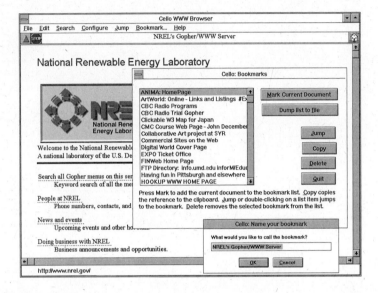

FIGURE 12.5.

The result of Cello's View As Clean Text feature.

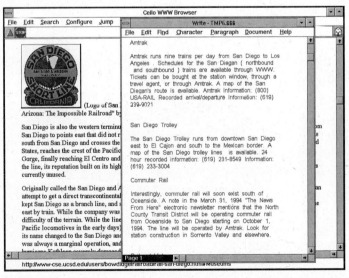

One area in which Cello shines is its inclusion of local help files. Most browsers don't offer help files, and the various versions of Mosaic have help systems available but only by retrieving files from the Net. Cello's help system ships with the program—the way all MS Windows programs ship—and because it's a hypertext system (again like all MS Windows help systems), getting accustomed to it is effortless. Figure 12.6 shows the help system's content screen. The links from here reveal a host of features that aren't obvious from just looking at Cello's structure, and they demonstrate quite nicely why *all* programs, no matter how self-evident they may seem, need a local help system. One such feature is near the bottom of this screen, information for users with low-speed connections. For these users, Cello offers a "peek" mode; if you hold the Control key when clicking a hyperlink, Cello loads only the first 4096 bytes (4KB) of the resulting file to let you know what's there. Also, because Cello doesn't display the destination URL when you pass the cursor over it, it offers a similar feature: Holding the Shift key while clicking the link brings up a small box showing the link's address.

FIGURE 12.6.

The Table of Contents from Cello's help system.

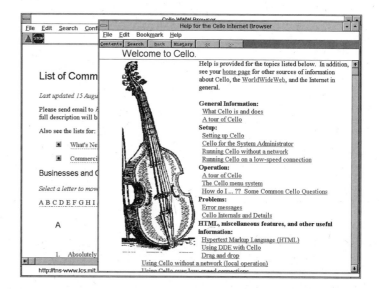

Perhaps the most useful section of the help system deals with writing HTML documents. Included here is the vast majority of HTML codes, their meaning and their usage, to the extent that anyone, beginner or experienced user, can learn here about writing HTML pages. True, there are more comprehensive HTML starter pages out on the Web, but the point is that they're *out* on the Web. Download Cello, and you have an HTML help system available at all times, without the need for actually logging in. As long as Cello is set not to retrieve a file from the Net as soon as it loads, you can use it as a local browser for testing your HTML pages as well.

Figure 12.7 shows one of the HTML pages, this one dealing with the various types of reference codes. Each is explained quite thoroughly, and several examples are available as well. Combine a page like this with Cello's View Source command from the Edit menu, and you have a powerful starting kit for HTML authors.

FIGURE 12.7.

The Anchor page from Cello's HTML reference section.

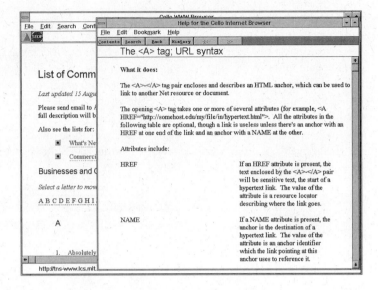

Finally, Cello offers a rudimentary e-mail front end. It appears in two places: in the File menu, where it's designed specifically to mail the current page to anyone on the Net; and in the Jump menu (see Figure 12.8), where it's a simple e-mailer for any purpose (not just to the program's developers, as it is in Windows Mosaic). Cello's e-mailer is hardly elaborate, and you can't receive e-mail through Cello, but as anyone who's done any evening-long browsing knows, it's nice not to have to load a separate e-mail package just to send off a quick note.

FIGURE 12.8.

Cello's built-in e-mail feature, here showing a meaningful exchange between hardworking authors.

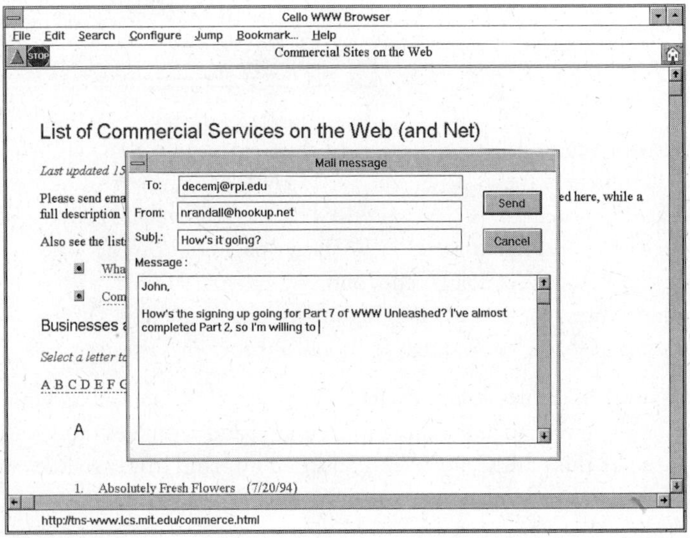

For Microsoft Windows users, Cello more than rewards you for the few minutes it takes to download. Version 1.0 is sleeker than Windows Mosaic as far as resource usage is concerned (a huge consideration for Windows systems), and Version 2.0 promises to provide even stronger competition.

A Look Ahead to Cello 2.0

Cello 2.0 is much different from the first Cello. You can open URLs—including Gopher, FTP, and Telnet locations—in one window or in several tiled or cascaded windows. The bookmarking feature has been expanded to include more bookmarks and easier access to them, and the history feature, although much the same, enables you to jump to a specific history URL in a separate window or store it as a bookmark. Most importantly, Cello 2.0 supports forms, imagemaps, and other advanced HTML features, something that inhibited Version 1.0 greatly. Figure 12.9 shows Cello's new look, complete with the Open URL box from the File menu.

FIGURE 12.9.

Cello 2.0, with cascaded windows and the Open URL dialog box.

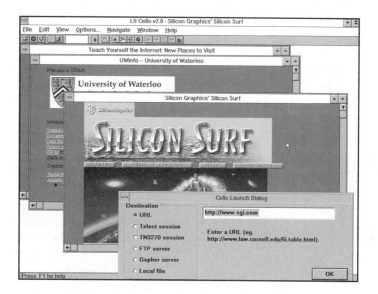

The hallmark of Cello 1.0 was simplicity, and in that simplicity, usability. That hallmark is sustained in this new version, with the capability to save pages as ASCII or .htm files as before and with simple, elegant features for selecting options (remember, Cello was one of the first Windows browsers to offer dialog-based options settings) and for launching mail messages. It remains elegant, even with its new capabilities.

Since the release of the first edition of *The World Wide Web Unleashed*, a great deal has changed in the Windows browser market, and Cello's survival is far from assured. When version 2.0 was first promised, in late summer or early autumn of 1994, there was room for it, with only NCSA Mosaic, WinWeb, and a couple of new commercial browsers to choose from. Now, however,

Netscape, a greatly enhanced Mosaic, and a slew of commercial servers are available, with some of them still free over the Net. It's doubtful if the release of Cello 2.0, no matter how good it might be, will be anything other than an unfortunately minor event. So goes life in World Wide Web development.

WINWEB	
Publisher:	MCC
Reviewed version:	1.0alpha2.2
FTP site:	`ftp.einet.net`
FTP directory:	`/einet/pc/winweb/`
FTP filename:	`winweb.zip`

Until very recently, Microsoft Windows users had two WWW clients to choose from: the famous Mosaic and the strong alternative Cello. In mid-1994, another browser became available, MCC's WinWeb 1.0, distributed through EINet, home of the well-known Internet resource site, the EINet Galaxy. If you think there must be a connection between WinWeb and MacWeb (discussed in Chapter 13, "More Browsers for X Window, Macintosh, and OS/2"), you're absolutely right. WinWeb is the Windows version of MacWeb, and many features are similar.

At first sight, WinWeb seems sparse. Its menus are small and few, and it seems to offer none of the user interface dazzle of either Windows Mosaic or Cello. Furthermore, it lacks some of the nicer features of both its competitors, one of which, you'll discover immediately, is the document loading status report on both Cello's and Mosaic's scroll bars. When you click a hyperlink in MacWeb, you get a box telling you the document is being loaded, and the icon changes to a connected serial cable (sorta cool), but there's nothing whatsoever to indicate that something's actually happening. If you've browsed the Web for any length of time, you know how crucial this information is. In fact, neither Windows Mosaic nor Cello offers *enough* information, and they provide at least some. One of WinWeb's very real strengths in this area is, however, that the progress box features a Cancel button that actually works, at least most of the time. It's more reliable than Cello's Stop button, and it works more frequently than clicking Windows Mosaic's spinning globe.

Figure 12.10 shows the appearance of a typical WinWeb page. As you can tell, the page looks very much like a stripped-down Windows Mosaic. The current URL address is displayed at the top, as is the URL of the selected link, and the tiny icons appear just beneath the menu bar. (WinWeb and Windows Mosaic, like many Windows programs, are not designed to change icon sizes for different screen resolutions, hence the practically unreadable icons.) The page itself displays quite well, except that selecting nonproportional fonts for the Normal text display often results in an inexact alignment. This is being worked on, according to WinWeb's home pages, for the next version.

FIGURE 12.10.

A typical WinWeb display, displaying inline graphics.

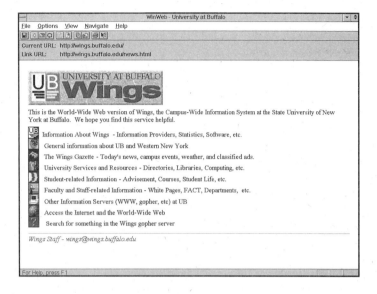

Much of WinWeb's configurability, as with early versions of Windows Mosaic, happens in its associated .INI file. However, WinWeb is quite customizable from within its menus, closer in this regard to Cello. Fonts, home pages, colors, and other attributes can be set from the menus easily and efficiently. Unfortunately, you can't configure nearly as much as you'd like from here, and the result is a browser that seems to offer its user the option of a simple appearance, but in reality seems to lack essential features.

Figure 12.11 shows WinWeb's font configuration menu. The program nicely combines its own specific styles menu with a fairly standard Windows font selector, but even here things are missing. Font changes are possible for more HTML headings and text types in both competing programs.

As Figure 12.12 demonstrates, WinWeb handles HTML forms. This might be the only thing that makes this browser worth more, for the time being at least, than Cello (which won't handle forms until the release of its Version 2.0). The comparison between WinWeb and Cello is inevitable, because both seek to gain market share from Windows Mosaic, and both are extremely kind to MS Windows' precious resources, compared to Windows Mosaic. WinWeb runs acceptably well on a 2MB Windows machine (inasmuch as *anything* will run acceptably these days with such little memory), and so will Cello. Windows Mosaic 2.0alpha6, by contrast, needs at least 4MB and actually works properly with 6MB or 8MB.

FIGURE 12.11.

WinWeb's font configuration system.

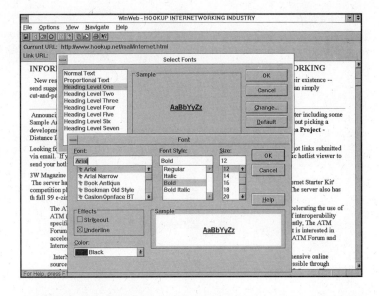

FIGURE 12.12.

An example of an HTML form in WinWeb.

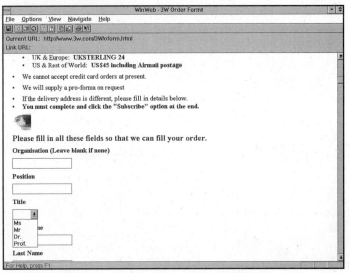

Another WinWeb usability decision appears to need reconsideration. In many Windows products (although in neither of the other Web clients), moving the cursor over the icon bar offers text help, often on the status bar, describing what that icon accomplishes. WinWeb gives you that information, but only after you've clicked on the icon. If you want to know what the circular arrow does, for instance, you won't find out until you've activated it. This is a little like pulling a trigger to discover what it does; you'll find out, but you might not like the results. (Incidentally, the circular arrow means Reload Document, a borrowing from Windows Mosaic that would have been much better changed to something more intuitive. Why copy someone else's poor design?)

Two aspects of WinWeb are, however, especially helpful. First, when you select the Load Images command from the Options menu and you return to a cached document that you originally loaded *without* images, WinWeb will *not* automatically load the corresponding images. This is a feature that Windows Mosaic and Cello could both profitably imitate. In those two browsers, it can be extremely frustrating to avoid image loading on a page you know is graphics heavy, then toggle graphics on for another page, and then return to the original page and watch the browser go out onto the Net and start transferring the images. WinWeb saves you this agony.

The other strong point is WinWeb's direct tie-in to the EINet Galaxy. Because it's a product of a team directly associated with the Galaxy, WinWeb has been built with a dialog box that enables you to search the Galaxy without actually entering the Galaxy's HTML page. Effectively, this means that WinWeb offers a built-in Internet search tool, something that's possible in the other two browsers only by accessing a search-specific Web site. Figure 12.13 illustrates the link to the Galaxy.

FIGURE 12.13.

WinWeb's search EINet galaxy dialog box.

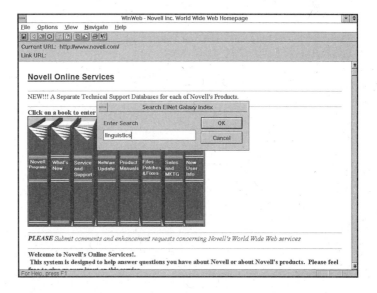

When the first edition of this book went to press, WinWeb was well on its way to becoming a strong, capable World Wide Web browser. After all, its Macintosh counterpart—MacWeb— had features and design strategies that ranked it close to Mac Mosaic, without requiring the huge dollop of systems resources. WinWeb was easy on Windows resources as well, and it could look to MacWeb for its feature set.

Unfortunately, WinWeb has received little attention from its designers. The version reviewed here was released in December of 1994, and there was no word at this writing that anything substantial was going to be done to the browser in the near future. As it stands, WinWeb is a decent browser, with a good link to a very useful search site (although the search dialog box needs expansion), but with all the other browsers now available for free use—especially Netscape and Mosaic—WinWeb has fallen seriously behind. Even if it is revised, the revision might be, like Cello's, too little and too late. Too bad.

SLIPKNOT WEB	
Publisher:	MicroMind, Inc.
Version reviewed:	1.08 beta
FTP site:	`ftp.netcom.com`
FTP directory:	`/pub/pb/pbrooks/slipknot`
FTP filename:	`slnot110.zip`

One of the most fascinating programs to appear since the first edition of this book has been SlipKnot, a graphical World Wide Web browser with a very real difference. That difference is significant: SlipKnot doesn't require SLIP or PPP access to offer the Web in all its graphics splendor. All you need is a good old dial-in UNIX shell account, and the Web can be yours.

The program is quite ingenious. Essentially, it's a Web browser that uses your shell account's existing resources. It taps into your text-oriented browser (preferably Lynx), offering in effect a graphics version of what you'd normally see. Instead of showing just a symbol for each graphic, however, it automatically transfers the file via XModem, YModem, ZModem, or even Kermit to the browser for display. You can set a login script to enter your account automatically, or you can use the included terminal program to log in manually and then enter the Web browser.

Figure 12.14 shows a typical Web page on the SlipKnot browser. The colors are fine, and although the page isn't resizable, it looks much like a standard Mosaic window. When you single-click a link, you're presented with a dialog box featuring the URL, which you can change or click again to start the transfer.

The secret to using SlipKnot is correct configuration. Figure 12.15 shows the detailed configuration dialog box, in which you explain exactly how your UNIX host works. Most of the defaults are fine, but SlipKnot gives you the option of changing whatever you must change.

By itself, SlipKnot can't display or process fill-in forms. If your UNIX browser is Lynx, however, the Forms menu from the browser temporarily takes you back to the SlipKnot terminal, which will automatically invoke Lynx, download the same document, and enable you to fill in the forms using the text-based browser instead (Lynx supports forms). The process is fast and slick, and it works well.

SlipKnot isn't as fast as some SLIP or PPP connections (although at times it's faster because of more direct network access), but speed isn't really the point. If you can't get a SLIP or PPP account—whether because you can't afford one or there isn't a provider in your area or you simply see no reason to have one—SlipKnot gives you the Web anyway. This Web client isn't perfect, but it's capable and a lot more colorful than Lynx or the CERN line browser. SlipKnot is a good choice that does exactly what it promises.

FIGURE 12.14.
SlipKnot WEB page showing CommerceNet's home document.

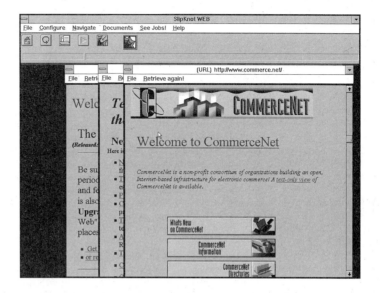

FIGURE 12.15.
SlipKnot's configuration dialog box, showing settings for the specific UNIX shell.

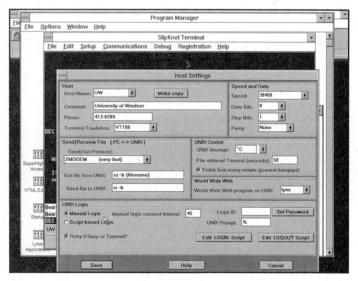

Browsers in Commercial Packages for Microsoft Windows

While the Internet continues to offer strong Web clients that are also free for the asking, commercially produced and distributed browsers have begun to make their appearance. This is a trend that will unquestionably continue, because the World Wide Web (in particular) and the Internet (in general) have become extremely hot property in the past six months. Discussed here are several commercially available browsers; AirMosaic from Spry, and the Web browser built into Netcom's NetCruiser software. Most, in fact, are part of a larger collection of Internet tools (although some are also available separately); this, too, is a trend that will continue for some time. Packages that feature software for Gopher, Telnet, FTP, e-mail, Finger, Archie, WAIS, and the Web will sprout like proverbial mushrooms through the next year or so, all of them trying to capture the market share that the Web's media popularity has created. Another trend is the integrated Internet package, which we also look at here.

AIRMOSAIC

Publisher:	Spry, Inc.
Reviewed version:	03.0A.06.07

Available either separately as Mosaic in a Box or as part of the Internet in a Box and the Air Series packages (all from Spry), AirMosaic is the first licensed version of NCSA Mosaic to hit the software shelves, and it's a good one. Windows Mosaic users will recognize immediately that AirMosaic offers essentially the same features as the latest freeware product from NCSA, without the need for downloading and installing the Win32 extensions (as Windows Mosaic 2.0 demands). Furthermore, AirMosaic offers several other new features that increase usability in some very important ways, even while sacrificing a bit of Windows Mosaic's richness.

Figure 12.16 shows the Virtual Tourist home page in AirMosaic.

FIGURE 12.16.

The AirMosaic screen featuring the clickable map in The Virtual Tourist's home page.

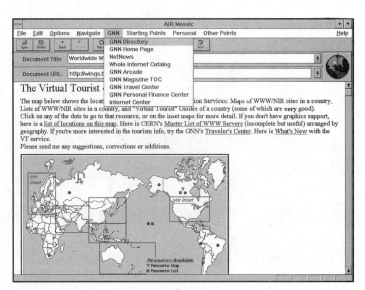

Also shown in Figure 12.16 is AirMosaic's built-in GNN menu for instant access to the popular magazine and information service. More of this kind of built-in reference can be expected as commercial publishers form links with well-known Internet sites.

Another strong feature of AirMosaic is its configuration menu system. Instead of asking you to edit the `mosaic.ini` file, as the NCSA version does, this browser contains a series of usable menus that enable you to perform the same functions. Figure 12.17 shows the main configuration menu and one of several adjoining submenus. For obvious reasons, this kind of configuration system is a good idea, especially for a product designed expressly for Internet newcomers.

FIGURE 12.17.

The configuration menus from AirMosaic.

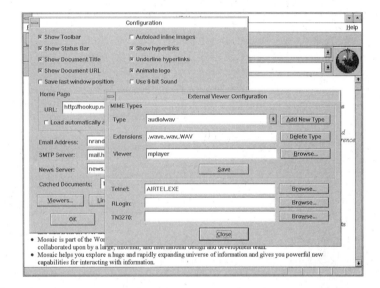

Although AirMosaic does not feature Windows Mosaic's excellent menu editor utility, it does enable you to import your existing hotlist menus directly from your `mosaic.ini` file. The import is quite easy, and the result is a series of menus like those you already have available. Strangely, however, creating new menus isn't included as a feature in AirMosaic as a stand-alone product, which means that non-Windows Mosaic users will have only the rather underdesigned hotlist feature AirMosaic offers.

Figure 12.18 shows a final AirMosaic strength, Kiosk mode. Designed expressly for use by libraries or institutions who want to allow Web browsing as a completely contained activity, without the possibility of configuring and toggling of features, Kiosk mode also makes the Windows screen show more of the document. It's useful, although after you're accustomed to the status bar and all the other usual options, Kiosk mode seems a bit flat.

FIGURE 12.18.

NCSA's What's New Page, shown in Kiosk mode.

> **What's New With NCSA Mosaic and the WWW**
>
> This document covers recent changes and additions to the universe of information available to Mosaic and the World Wide Web. Please follow these guidelines when sending announcements to whats-new@ncsa.uiuc.edu.
>
> The entire archive of NCSA What's New pages is searchable via CUI's W3 Catalog.
>
> For NCSA Mosaic news, see the new NCSA Mosaic Announcements document.
>
> Details on the Second International WWW Conference '94: Mosaic and the Web
>
> ---
>
> *August 15, 1994*
>
> Take a moment out to visit the 1994 Illinois State Fair, celebrating the 175th anniversary of Illinois statehood, and the 100th anniversary of the permanent Fairgrounds in Springfield, Illinois. This Virtual State Fair brings many exciting happenings around Illinois to the State Fair via the Web, and allows those of you not able to physically visit the State Fair to see what is happening in Springfield. Daily schedules, updates on premiums awarded, and a special Ethanol Expo are included.
>
> The Working Group on Intellectual Property Rights was established within the Information Policy Committee of the Information Infrastructure Task Force (IITF) to examine the intellectual property implications of the NII. The group has released a preliminary draft of its report, Intellectual Property and the National Information Infrastructure, which is now available on the U.S. Patent and Trademark Office WWW server.
>
> The U.S. Department of Energy's Office of Environment, Safety and Health has a new WWW server.
>
> The GRAF Lab at NASA's Johnson Space Center now has its server up and running. There is a lot of stuff there, mostly about Virtual Reality and related topics. The GRAF lab uses VR as a design tool for NASA's space station program; check it out!
>
> Sounds from Chaos in Chua's Circuit - References and Sound Examples contains on-line papers with sound examples and references of one of the most interesting chaotic systems. The variety of sounds generated by this system ranges from Bassoon and Clarinet like sounds all the way to quasi-white noise. An interactive version of the same system with a virtual reality interface was displayed as a VROOM exhibit at this year's SIGGRAPH'94 conference.
>
> At the intersection of U.S. Interstate Highways 81 and 64, just 2 hours from Washington, D.C., lies historic Staunton, Virginia, nestled between the scenic Blue Ridge Mountains and the Alleghenies in the heart of the Shenandoah Valley. Staunton's architectural ambience is nineteenth century (5 historic districts), and its personality, friendly. It is a hub for vacationers and travelers, offering access to attractions ranging from historic sites and museums to the broad-spectrum recreational opportunities of the national parks, forests, and resorts that surround it. It offers telecommuting and

WEB BROWSER FROM NETCRUISER

Publisher:	Netcom
Reviewed version:	1.52

The WWW browser shown in Figure 12.19 is one of a collection of Net programs that comes with the NetCruiser suite of applications from Netcom. As with Internet in a Box, this suite is designed to save users the trouble of going out onto the Net and downloading and installing the software they'll need. Unlike the Spry product, however, NetCruiser is tied exclusively into a service provider's operation. Without an Internet account with Netcom, you can't use this software.

The benefit to an approach like this is, of course, that it's an all-in-one solution for Net denizens who don't want to get involved in the download fever that assaults many of us. In addition, users receive software that is supported (and easily upgraded) and is tailored to their particular service. This all-in-one solution can be attractive for users who want to get on the Net without actually understanding the way it works, and such users will become dramatically more numerous over the next year or so.

NetCruiser's Web browser is more reminiscent of Cello than of Windows Mosaic. In fact, it shares one of Cello's negative attributes, the incapability to work with HTML forms (at least as of NetCruiser Version 1.4). In general, though, the browser works well, and it comes with a good base of usable features. During a document load, for example, on the right side of the status bar, the browser displays not only the number of bytes transferred so far, but also the total size of the file, and it does so for each inline image as well. Furthermore, instead of an Open URL dialog box, you simply type the desired address into the URL display at the top of the screen. As with

Internet in a Box, users don't have to worry about downloading and installing their own viewers and players; for the most part, they're installed and available right out of the package. The configuration menus, like the Spry product, provide instant access to the most important customization features. The main configuration box appears in Figure 12.20.

FIGURE 12.19.

The NASA home page in NetCruiser's built-in Web browser.

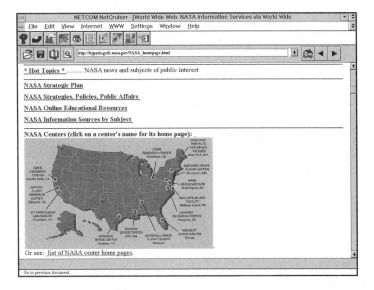

FIGURE 12.20.

The configuration dialog box from NetCruiser.

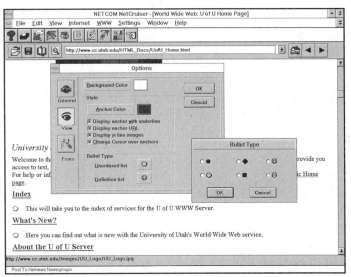

NetCruiser's browser displays cleanly and crisply, and it is easy to use. In its obvious nod to simplicity, however, it lacks some of the features found in the more extensive clients. Bookmarking is similar to Cello and just as limited. The history list works but is rudimentary (but then, so is

Windows Mosaic's). But items such as Load to Disk are very good (enabling you to save the current document to disk, rather than—as in Windows Mosaic and Cello—the next retrieved document), and the whole effort has a feeling of stability to it.

QUARTERDECK MOSAIC	
Publisher:	Quarterdeck
Reviewed version:	Beta Release 2

Quarterdeck Mosaic (QMosaic) is part of Quarterdeck's collection of Internet programs, which range from an HTML authoring tool (WebAuthor) to World Wide Web server software. To judge from both WebAuthor, which is commercially available, and QMosaic, which was still in beta at this writing, the software suite will be strong enough to withstand the pressure exerted by other commercial vendors. Quarterdeck's focus seems to be on maximum usability, and that can never hurt.

QMosaic looks different from almost every other Web browser. Its toolbar is large and presents its commands with equally large icons, and its orientation is more windows-based than most other browsers. What this means, quite simply, is that during your browsing of the Web you'll open a number of individual windows on your screen, each of which can be performing concurrent accesses to different Web, Gopher, or FTP sites. Although this tends to lead to an almost unmanageable number of windows on the screen if you're not careful, it also means that a well-planned Web session can be extremely productive.

Like InternetWorks, QMosaic is fully multithreading. This feature, which allows the concurrent downloads, practically guarantees that you won't be stuck, as you are in many browsers, watching your program trying in vain to access the link you clicked on. By launching three or four different concurrent accesses, you know that at least one or two will succeed. The result is, inevitably, a less frustrating and more productive experience.

For modem users, multithreading is quickly becoming essential. Even with a strong 28.8Kpbs connection, the Web is too slow. More and more pages feature large and multiple graphics, a point that makes clear the simple fact that most Web page designers work from high-speed connections. The browser can't solve the problem of designers who are insensitive to the needs of modem users (by far the largest group of Web users), but it can go a long way toward making the situation more tolerable. QMosaic's multithreading does just that. If you see that a site is graphics-heavy, you can continue to download it in the background while you launch as many other accesses as you want. It's quite possible, in fact, to have four or five graphics-dominant windows loading in the background while you do your real work (often with the graphics toggled off) in a maximized window in the foreground.

Figure 12.21 shows a typical multiwindow QMosaic session in progress. Visible along the top are the large icons (which you can hide or resize), and the individual session windows are shown in cascaded fashion in the main viewing window. The first window was retrieved using the

File/Open menu, which includes a URL helper to assist you in constructing URL syntax (including Gopher, FTP, WAIS, Mailto, and other URL types). The remainder were created by double-clicking hyperlinks or on items in the File Cabinet.

FIGURE 12.21.

Multiple cascaded windows in a QMosaic session.

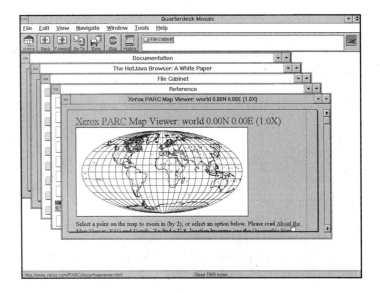

One of QMosaic's early problems, and one recognized by the developers, is that the number of windows can become overwhelming. If you single-click a hyperlink, as you do in most browsers, that window replaces the existing page with the hyperlinked page. If you double-click, however, QMosaic opens the linked page in a new window. Given that you also get a new window whenever you double-click an entry in your File Cabinet, where your most important sites are bookmarked, you can quickly get 10–15 windows on-screen, any number of which are actively retrieving documents. Expect some of this to change in later versions.

QMosaic's File Cabinet is a rich bookmarking feature. The file cabinet is a collection of folders, several of which come fully stocked with the browser itself. Figure 12.22 shows the File Cabinet open, shown here as a "tree" similar to Windows' File Manager. You can display the Cabinet as an icon list, as a text list, or as a Windows-like group of icons arranged in the window. By right-clicking, you can create new folders and new URLs.

A number of features stand out in QMosaic, including an easy configuration and preferences system. Two, however, merit special attention. By clicking the History icon (or selecting Window/Global History), you bring up the history feature, a separate window that shows you where you've been. There are two components to this window, each available via a clickable tab. The first is the global history, which keeps track of your browsing from session to session. The other is local history, which enables you to re-navigate that particular session's visited sites.

FIGURE 12.22.

QMosaic's File Cabinet, showing folders arranged as an icon tree.

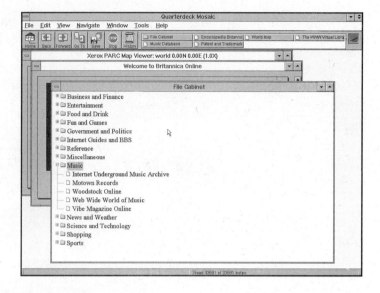

The other well-designed feature is annotations. When you choose Edit/Annotation, QMosaic yields the annotation window, in which you type whatever you wish. Doing so places a lowercase *a* in the annotation margin at the right of the appropriate window. Clicking that *a* yields the annotation as a yellow sticky note, which you or your colleagues can read and edit.

Figure 12.23 shows the history window at the left of the screen and a retrieved annotation on the right. It also shows, at the top of the screen, the Extra Hot Hotlist window on the toolbar, in which you can place several must-have hotlisted items, keeping them visible so that you can retrieve them with a click.

FIGURE 12.23.

QMosaic's history window, annotation feature, and Extra Hot Hotlist feature.

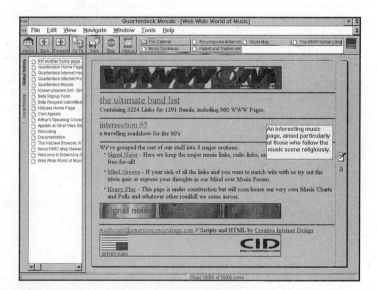

QMosaic is a browser to pay attention to. Designed expressly for Microsoft Windows, it makes strong use of the Windows interface. It's fast, usable, and feature-filled, with no real bad points.

WEBSURFER

Publisher:	NetManage, Inc.
Reviewed version:	4.1

WebSurfer is part of the popular Chameleon suite from NetManage. The full suite is widely available in software stores and has been packaged recently, complete with relatively easy access to Internet service providers, in several Internet books. One such book is *Plug-n-Play Internet*, which I recommend highly because I'm one of the co-authors (okay, I know it's a cheap plug...). WebSurfer itself is the Mosaic-based World Wide Web client, and it's fully functional and quite easy on system resources.

Figure 12.24 shows a Web page, complete with fill-in forms, as seen through the WebSurfer browser. The display isn't quite accurate in many instances in this version, but updates should take care of those difficulties. In fact, several facets of the entire Chameleon suite show signs of the package being initially rushed, but again the updates will correct any deficiencies. The major concerns of the designers and users alike, those of stability and robustness, are very much in evidence across the suite.

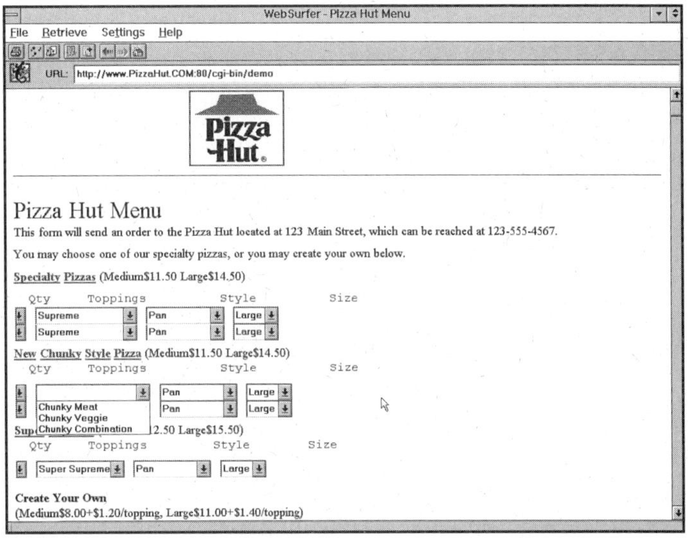

FIGURE 12.24.

WebSurfer's display shows its rough spots, but its support for forms is good.

WebSurfer doesn't give you access to hyperlinks while the page is downloading, as Netscape and other browsers do, but WebSurfer loads graphics as quickly as any other browser so this is not necessarily a problem. WebSurfer doesn't, however, give you any indication of the download's progress, so you really have no idea how long you must wait. This is a serious usability deficiency, one that the designers must address immediately if WebSurfer is to become a browser of choice. WebSurfer does support multithreading, however, so the downloading issue isn't quite as significant as it might be. It is, however, an annoyance at best.

Where WebSurfer stands out, however, is in its configuration systems. Figure 12.25 shows the Style Schemes dialog box, with its broad range of choices and its excellent view of existing styles. Similar dialog boxes guide all configuration items, and taken together they represent one of the most sophisticated configuration sets of all Windows browsers.

FIGURE 12.25.

WebSurfer's Style Schemes dialog box has perhaps the best font-management system of any browser.

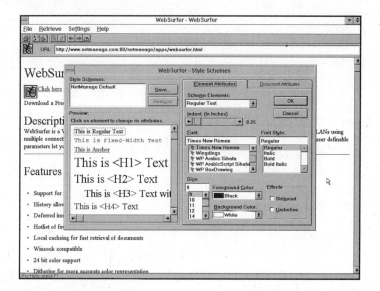

WebSurfer won't win any awards for prettiness or glitziness, but it's a solid product within a collection of equally solid but often unexciting products. If your idea is to get work done and not to delve into software's aesthetic side, WebSurfer, like the rest of the Chameleon suite, will serve you well.

Integrated Browsers

A new category of Web client is the *integrated browser* package. The purpose of these programs is to provide all Internet major functions—e-mail, newsgroups, Telnet, Gopher, FTP, and the Web—inside one easy-to-use program. Acquiring one of these programs spares you the need of loading individual programs to accomplish these functions. Whether integrated browsers become the all-in-one solution their designers claim, or are treated instead with the relative disregard of integrated productivity packages (ClarisWorks, Microsoft Works, and so on), remains to be seen.

INTERNETWORKS

Publisher:	Booklink Technologies (America Online)
Reviewed version:	Beta 7
FTP site:	`ftp.booklink.com`
FTP directory:	`/beta`
FTP filename:	`beta7.exe`

InternetWorks is the design of Booklink Technologies. Late in 1994 the company was acquired by the commercial service America Online, which was looking for a solid front end for its coming Internet access. Fortunately for Web users, InternetWorks was never removed from free FTP status; as of this writing, you can still download it and use it as is.

And "as is" is strong indeed. Behind InternetWorks is the idea of providing a Web browser that is as modem-friendly as possible, one that helps to solve two major problems. The first problem is keeping track of where you've been; the second is waiting for pages to be retrieved. Both are applicable to all Web users, but the second is especially crucial for those with 14.4 (or slower) modem access.

To speed access to Web pages and to significantly reduce the frustration of watching Web pages download, InternetWorks incorporates multithreading technology. Like Quarterdeck Mosaic, InternetWorks enables you to retrieve several pages simultaneously, thereby making full use of your modem (which is idle if it has to wait for responses from the remote computer). You can have dozens of pages being retrieved at once, but, practically speaking, you won't want to try more than six or eight. If you're using a 28.8Kbps modem, you won't usually be able to keep up with them anyway, and even at 14.4, retrieving more than eight pages leads to inefficiency and simply getting lost in what you're doing.

Still, InternetWorks is designed to prevent you from getting lost. Two features differentiate the program from practically all other browsers: the Tab List and the Card Catalog. As shown in Figure 12.26, the Tab List rides along the bottom of the screen, with the title of each open page (or sometimes the URL) occupying its own tab. In the lower-left corner are the Tab List navigation arrows, which enable you to scroll the Tab List either left or right (and in small chunks or big leaps). Click any tab, and that page appears in the viewer. This is InternetWorks' version of a windowing system, and it works well. The only problem is that the Tab List quickly becomes huge. That's where the Card Catalog comes in.

FIGURE 12.26.

*InternetWorks Card Catalog
screen, with Tab List
displayed along the bottom.*

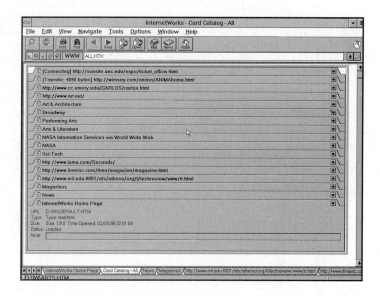

InternetWorks' Card Catalog, which occupies the main screen in Figure 12.26, gives you a quick and usable summary of currently loaded pages. Each page has its own line, with the icon type displayed to the left of the title (showing you the type of page), and an arrow at the far right. By double-clicking the title, you open the small status display (shown here with the last item), which tells you the URL, the type of page, and whether or not it's connecting to the remote site, transferring data, or already loaded. This information is shown in brief on the one-line entry as well; Figure 12.26 shows the top request trying to connect, the second transferring data, and the rest, which display only the title or the URL, already loaded and ready for viewing. Clicking the arrow to the right of any title displays that page in the main viewing window.

You can create your own customized catalogs as well. If you've been browsing extensively and have several Web, Gopher, and FTP sites open, using the Create Card Catalog feature (Tools menu) enables you to instantly create separate catalogs for each type of site. The catalog then appears as a separate entry on the Tab List. You can also move entries from one catalog to another, and you can sort each catalog by document type, by the order in which the pages loaded, or by title alphabetically. You can also delete individual items from each catalog.

Like all current browsers, InternetWorks makes no essential distinction between Web pages, Gopher sites, or FTP sites. But this lack of distinction is even more pronounced with this program than others (except for WinTapestry, reviewed later in this chapter). No matter what type of resource you access, it appears simply as another entry on the card catalog. If you click a downloadable file from an FTP site, InternetWorks either displays it in the viewing window (text files) or automatically activates the Save As dialog box (binary files). The idea is to make the Net as transparent to users as possible, and in that it succeeds quite well.

Although InternetWorks doesn't offer windowing per se, it does offer split panes. Figure 12.27 shows a horizontally split pane (you can split vertically instead), with one site in the top window and another in the bottom. The Tab List is the same for both windows. You click either window to make it active and then use the Tab List to access a different site in that window. This is another nod to navigability.

FIGURE 12.27.

Horizontally split panes in InternetWorks, with the common Tab List at the bottom.

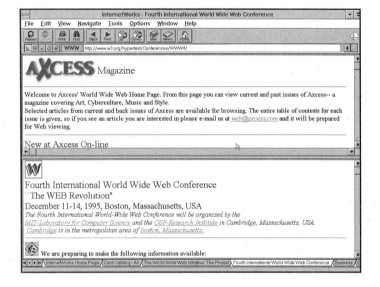

Two other features demonstrate InternetWorks' overall excellence. First, you can print Web pages in nicely organized columns, which makes them look different from their screen counterparts and lends them a unique attractiveness on paper. Second, and more importantly, the browser includes a feature called the InternetWorks Messaging System, which is a full-featured e-mail and newsgroup program. Although not strictly built into the browser, Mail and News are accessible via a single click on the icon bar, which launches the program. The e-mail program, shown in Figure 12.28, is richly detailed and highly usable, complete with file attachments of multiple types.

All in all, InternetWorks is a superb piece of software. As of this writing, InternetWorks had yet to be released commercially, but its beta versions are available through FTP and are well worth the download. The only downside of InternetWorks is that its presentation of HTML isn't quite as strong as that of Netscape or Mosaic; but other than that, InternetWorks gives you everything you need.

FIGURE 12.28.

The Send Mail feature in InternetWorks opens the Messaging System.

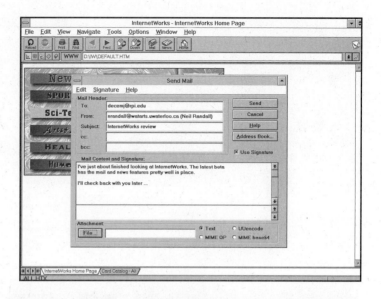

WINTAPESTRY

Publisher:	Frontier Technologies Corporation
Reviewed version:	1.67 (in Superhighway Access 4.0)

WinTapestry comes packaged with FTC's two major Internet suites, SuperTCP and Superhighway Access for Windows. SuperTCP is a full-featured package designed for use on a LAN connection to the Net (it includes an extensive set of X Window tools), whereas Superhighway Access is meant primarily for modem users. You can use Superhighway Access as your only Internet package, because it includes the necessary TCP/IP stacks and dial-up functions, as well as very capable e-mail, newsgroup, FTP, and Telnet apps.

WinTapestry is the package's Web browser and general Internet navigation tool. It offers a cross between the windowing features of Quarterdeck Mosaic (reviewed previously in this chapter) and the organizational capabilities of InternetWorks (reviewed previously in this chapter). In many ways, in fact, WinTapestry is the most navigable browser of any, because it comes pre-stocked with a wide assortment of bookmarks and because it uses a topic-oriented tabbed windowing system to enable you to move back and forth across the Web.

When you launch WinTapestry, you automatically open a window called the Internet Organizer. As shown in Figure 12.29, the Organizer is organized according to topic, and you can add your own sites to any topic and add new tabs (in topic or any other order). Clicking the tabs at the top of the Organizer takes you to the bookmarks associated with that topic, with each site listed by name and with an icon telling you which type of site it is. At the right of Figure 12.29 is the help screen showing some of the icon types.

FIGURE 12.29.

WinTapestry's Internet Organizer, with the help screen showing document icons.

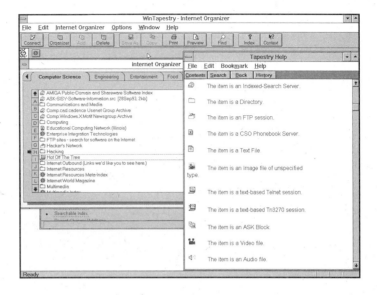

Notice that WinTapestry handles Telnet, FTP, CSO Phonebook, Gopher, and other types of retrievals. In this way, the program is perhaps the most flexible of all the browsers. Simply put, most people just don't need anything other than this browser, except for an e-mail package and a newsgroup program, which are covered in separate programs in the Superhighway Access box. It's an all-in-one integrated solution, although one that's received surprisingly little media attention.

One of WinTapestry's strongest features is its configuration dialog boxes. Figure 12.30 shows a typical configuration system, this one moving through the full browser configuration to choosing specific fonts for page display. There is a wide range of configuration dialog boxes of this type in the program, making it among the most easily and fully configurable of all packages.

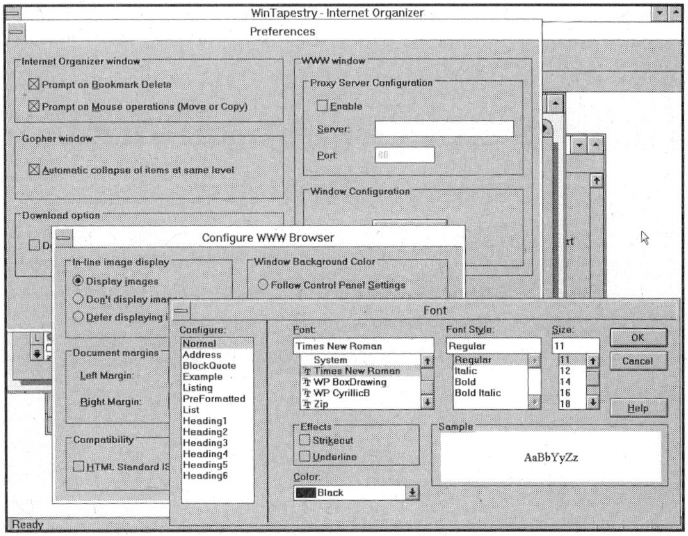

FIGURE 12.30.

WinTapestry's configuration dialog boxes, with a wide range of options.

Double-clicking any item in the Organizer starts the retrieval process and opens a new window. Within each window, hyperlinks act as they do in most browsers, with a single-click initiating the connection (double-clicking does nothing). WinTapestry doesn't support advanced Web features such as redirection and Netscape HTML tags, but it undoubtedly will in future iterations. WinTapestry fully supports fill-in forms, as Figure 12.31 demonstrates, and it allows easy Archie and WAIS searches as well. After downloading a file via FTP, you can launch it directly from within WinTapestry, as long as you have the file associations established for that file type.

FIGURE 12.31.

The White House Comments fill-in form in a WinTapestry window.

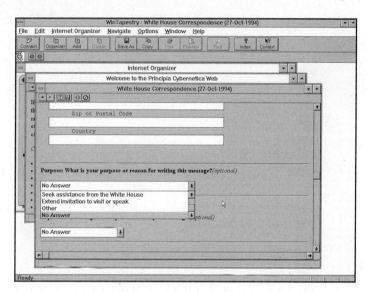

All told, WinTapestry is an extremely capable program and well worth consideration. WinTapestry seems to be an example, however, of a commercial Internet product that isn't getting the marketing attention it deserves, a problem that will only worsen as more and more products become available.

Commercial Online Services

As *The World Wide Web Unleashed, Second Edition* went to press, only one of the commercial online services offered a graphical Web client. Prodigy's Web Browser, in fact, was available in early 1995, while—as of the end of March 1995—even the aggressive America Online and the newly aggressive CompuServe hadn't promised an exact date for their browsers. By that time, Delphi Internet had just signed a licensing agreement with Netscape Communications to use Netscape Navigator as their browser of choice (their text-based browser isn't covered here), and

GEnie was still announcing full Internet access to take effect some time in April. With this book's third edition, the choices will be much more extensive, but as of this writing Prodigy's was the only one available.

PRODIGY WEB BROWSER

Publisher:	Prodigy Services Company
Reviewed version:	1.1b

Prodigy was the first of the commercial online services to offer a full-featured graphical browser as part of its regular service. Any Prodigy user can use the Prodigy Web Browser, as it's called, simply by clicking the Browse The Web button and downloading the update. Prodigy makes the whole process a no-brainer, with downloading and installing the Web browser all at the same time so you can start browsing the Web without even disconnecting from the service. This is the ease-of-use Windows users simply aren't accustomed to, but once you've been through the process, as well as through the browser's frequent upgrades, you'll be convinced that wrestling with configuration files, missing DLLs, and other Windows arcana is suddenly a little pointless.

The browser itself is good. As Figure 12.32 demonstrates, it displays graphics very well, and Figure 12.33 shows its equal strength in fill-in forms.

FIGURE 12.32.

This display of Digital Equipment's home page shows Prodigy's graphics capability. The imagemap is fully active.

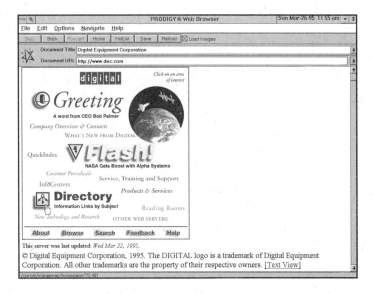

FIGURE 12.33.

This White House Comment form shows Prodigy's capability to display fill-in forms functionally and attractively.

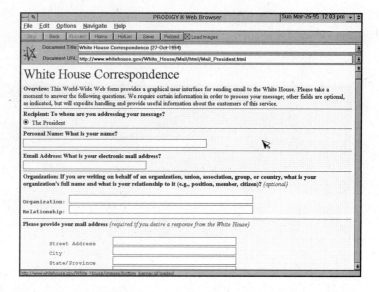

Prodigy's maximum modem speed, as of this writing, is 14.4Kpbs and has only recently upgraded from 9600bps, so loading pages takes a bit long, but the browser uses several techniques to make its use tolerable. Primary among these is the system—by now fairly standard—of caching Web pages to your hard drive. Everything you access is cached to a growing file on your drive, so that when you return to that page in a future session the page appears much more quickly than the first time. You can set the number of items to store from Prodigy's advanced options setup dialog boxes (shown in Figure 12.34), but if you're a frequent user of the browser you'll want to cache as many pages as possible. The browser is sophisticated enough to check automatically for updated versions of cached pages by comparing the date of the cached item to that of the live URL. You can adjust how frequently this checking occurs.

Other features of Prodigy's browser include a handy button on the toolbar to enable you to turn image loading on and off easily, an extremely usable dialog box for setting up multimedia viewers (a viewer for .GIF and .JPG files is included with the browser), a global history listing, and one of the most usable hotlist systems of any Web browser on the market. Click the HotList button at any time during your browsing, use the existing Main List or create any number of your own, click into the list of your choice, and then click the Add To Hot List button to add the item to that particular hotlist. You can re-title the site when adding it, or you can edit the title and URL later. It's as easy as Cello's original Bookmark feature but considerably more flexible.

Like all current WWW clients, Prodigy Web Browser displays FTP and Gopher sessions capably. In fact, the browser is the only FTP and Gopher access that Prodigy offers; not that this is an insurmountable problem, but the Web has never been the best place from which to perform Gopher or FTP. Still, Prodigy's browser is easy, quite full-featured, and in place. For graphical Web access, Prodigy users were given a quick leg up.

FIGURE 12.34.

Prodigy's Stage Setup dialog box enables you to set the caching and version-checking features.

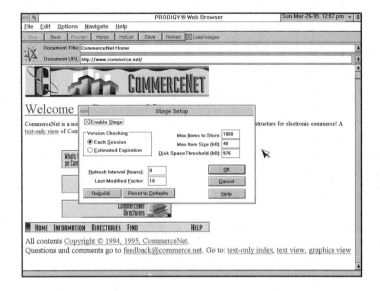

Summary

With the enormous number of Microsoft Windows users now joining the Internet community, the number of available browsers has predictably grown as well. Fortunately, the quality is quite high throughout the selection, with still more choices to come. The Windows browser category is clearly the one receiving the most developmental effort, and this effort has become fascinating to watch.

More Browsers for X Window, Macintosh, and OS/2

13

by
Neil Randall

Without question, Mosaic and Netscape are the most famous Web clients. They have made headlines; they're pictured in mainstream and computer publications alike; and they have come to be something of a synonym, in the public's mind and in the minds of many who should know better, for the World Wide Web itself. But equating Mosaic and Netscape with the Web is more or less analogous to equating your RCA ColorTrak TV with the production and distribution of television programming. The ColorTrak is the gizmo that brings the TV show into your family room, but it has nothing to do with production and distribution. They're two entirely separate technologies, even though, as with Web browsers, the one technology was developed specifically to display the other and make it accessible.

As mentioned before in this book (and as will continue to be mentioned in future editions), Mosaic and Netscape are *not* the World Wide Web. They are nothing more than two of several World Wide Web client programs, better known as *browsers*. All they do is display Web documents, just as many other programs do. Chapter 9 examines the text-based clients such as Lynx and the CERN line-mode browser, and Chapter 12 examines the explosion of browsers for Microsoft Windows. This chapter presents a selection of graphically based browsers for the other major platforms.

The fact that I've just spent the past couple of hundred words explaining that Mosaic and Netscape shouldn't be confused with the Web itself goes a fair ways toward describing the enormous selling job the designers of any other graphical Web browsers have on their hands. Making them available is one thing; getting people to actually use them is another. To a large extent, this is perfectly understandable. Because you can download Netscape or Mosaic from many sources, and because they work so well, why bother trying anything else?

If you're an OS/2 user, the answer is easy. You use WebExplorer because it's the only OS/2 browser widely available, and it's free with OS/2 Warp itself, as long as you join the IBM network (which is quite a good deal, actually). For Macintosh users, the answer is that, with only three significant browsers available, there's no reason not to add MacWeb to your library to see if you like it. For X Window users, the answer lies with the general desire of that community to experiment with new software, especially new freeware. There's nothing most UNIX junkies like better than well-written new software, and programs like MidasWWW and Viola provide just that.

The problem is that many of these browsers will never get a fair trial, at least not among a wide range of users. There are many users out there who will FTP, install, and use any Web browser that becomes available on the Net, just as there are many word processor users who will happily try any word processing package. But there are just as many of each group who want only the best-known, not even necessarily the strongest-featured, and who won't budge from their initial choice unless forced by some unlikely circumstance. The danger for browser designers is that they'll end up gaining adherents not from the installed base of Mosaic users, but rather from the users of a competing browser.

The point is that competing browsers exist, and each has its own specific strengths. It's important for any user of the World Wide Web to be aware of them, because although everyone concedes Netscape's and Mosaic's numerical superiority over all other graphical browsers combined, there's no logic whatsoever in declaring their technical superiority, or even their suitability-to-task superiority, until you've tried a few others.

Even in a much smaller program, you might discover a feature that Mosaic does not offer and that you simply can't traverse the Web without, especially after using that feature even once. Then there's the issue of desiring to avoid the mainstream, something that every critical user of anything eventually wants to do. The hype and the development dollars are all behind the Goliath; let's see what the Davids can do in the background with much less fanfare.

One thing must be said, however, before we look at the alternatives. Essentially, the Mosaics and Cellos and Sambas and Violas and MacWebs and Chimeras all do precisely the same thing: They display HTML documents inside a main viewing window, offering highlighted hyperlinks that, when you select them with your mouse, take you to another document on the Web. That's the purpose of a World Wide Web client program, and that's what all of these packages accomplish. The differences among them lie in their individual sets of features. Your choice will be based on appearance, usability, intelligence of design, and incorporation of features that help you use the Web exactly as you want. The browser you decide upon will be the one that most closely matches what you want it to do.

And one last thing: There's no reason to settle on just one browser. As long as you have room on your hard drive (these programs are relatively small, at least so far), get two or three, and try them all. That way you'll know the differences, and will probably discover that you use one browser for some purposes and another for other tasks. It's simply a matter of firing up the one that will serve the purpose you have in mind at any particular moment.

> **NOTE**
>
> Not all available browsers are discussed in this chapter. Only two X browsers are included, for example (MidasWWW and Viola), whereas Chimera and tkWWW aren't examined. Similarly, although Amiga Mosaic is dealt with at the end of the chapter, no browser for the NeXT system has a spot. Some of this has to do with my own familiarity with the software in question, some with the fact that not everything can be included, and some because they are not anywhere close to approaching widespread use. What are included are the most widely used of the alternative packages.

Browsers for the X Window System

World Wide Web client software for the X Window system has been under development since the inception of the Web project itself. The reason is obvious: The Web was designed as a multimedia information-dissemination system for use with GUI systems, X Window was the predominant GUI for UNIX workstations, and UNIX was the essential operating system underlying the Internet itself. Therefore, it made perfect sense for X Window developers to create their own client software—particularly at research institutes (where funding might be made available) and universities (which are typically flooded with UNIX hackers in the guise of both professors and students).

These are indeed the institutions Web clients have come from—until quite recently. Commercial versions of Mosaic, Netscape, Cello, and independent browsers are now being released or are under development, but before now all of the design and development impetus has come from the research labs. Again, this makes sense, given that the Web itself is a product of a university research group.

What makes the X clients so appealing is that they run on workstations that typically have large screens and high-speed access. As a result, they show a large amount of information by default, and they do so quickly. What makes them less appealing is the difficulties with installation and configuration that accompany any UNIX or X program running on a local or wide area network, difficulties that put these programs out of the reach of casual users. And, quite simply, most people don't have X stations on their desks at home, which means that the audience for these clients will always be larger organizations.

If you use X Mosaic or Netscape for UNIX, you owe it to yourself to check out some of the alternatives. Each has its strengths; each is aware that it must offer something different from the leader; and each tends to be under the development of people who are, if nothing else, easier to get in touch with than the Mosaic and Netscape teams. That usually means more immediate support for problems, but it also means that you're dependent on a smaller team's (or even an individual's) sustained commitment to the project. Still, some superb offerings await.

MidasWWW

Publisher:	Stanford Linear Accelerator Center
Latest Version:	2.2
FTP Site:	`freehep.scri.fsu.edu`
FTP Directory:	`freehep/networking_email_` `news/midaswww`
FTP Filename:	`midaswww-2.1.tar.Z or your platform-specific file from /` `binaries/`

One of the ways for a program to compete with other programs is to provide enhanced features in specific areas, thereby distinguishing it from the rest. MidasWWW, developed over the past three years at the Stanford Linear Accelerator Center by Tony Johnson, offers precisely those sorts of enhanced features. This is a browser that looks sharp, works well, and demonstrates a strong commitment to user-interface considerations.

Figure 13.1 shows a sample Midas screen. There's little to note here, except that all of the expected Web components are in place, and especially that the screen's sculpted appearance is extremely strong. It's the kind of screen that instantly attracts, a highly important consideration for any Web browser.

FIGURE 13.1.

Midas screen showing links and inline images.

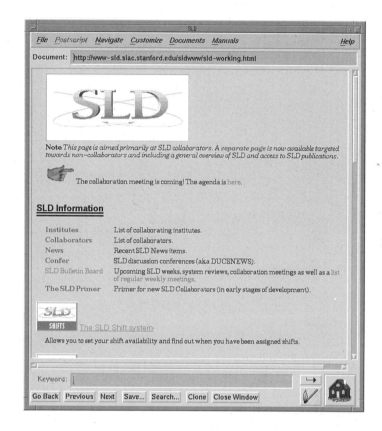

The user interface considerations show up practically everywhere. Figures 13.2 and 13.3 demonstrate Midas's ability to interact with Gopher and FTP servers. Of note in both instances are, first of all, the iconic differentiation among document or function types (notice the easy-to-understand See login messages link at the top of Figure 13.3), and, equally as important, the Open Gopher and Open FTP dialog boxes. In most Web browsers, you enter an FTP site either through a hyperlink or by typing in the full URL address in the Open URL dialog box. Midas gives you an interface that lets you forget about the URL syntax, and the FTP dialog box even includes a space for your username and password (extremely useful for changing login types).

FIGURE 13.2.

*Midas Gopher screen
showing the Open Gopher
Document dialog box.*

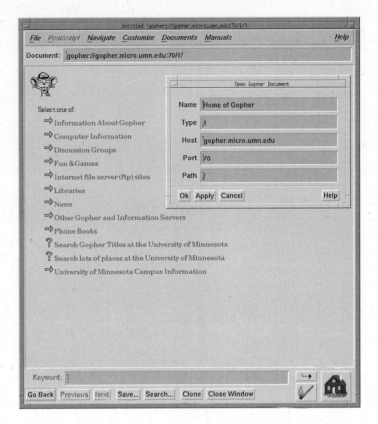

Another important interface consideration appears in Midas's configuration dialog boxes. Configuring Web browsers isn't fun at the best of times, but in the case of all versions of Mosaic (except Mac Mosaic), it's downright painful. Midas offers a series of configuration dialog boxes (see Figure 13.4) that make the whole process much simpler; they include printer setup, default Gopher page setup, and a range of options that are easily changed, either by clicking in the appropriate box or by using the slider controls to customize times and sizes. You can easily enable or disable document caching (shown), font styles and sizes, display of document title and URL, appearance of hyperlinks, and several other options without going through the tedium of editing your configuration files. Given the importance of customizing your Web client to serve your specific needs, this is a strong feature.

FIGURE 13.3.

Midas FTP screen showing the Open FTP Document dialog box.

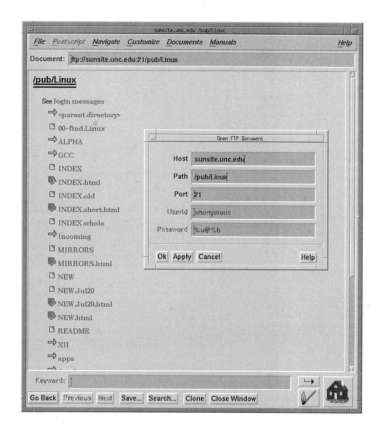

There are even more interface enhancements: Context-sensitive help is available through the On Context command in the Help menu. Clicking a hyperlink does what you'd expect, but holding down the mouse button on a link brings up a menu that enables you to choose between retrieving the document normally, downloading it to your local disk, or opening a new window and displaying it there. You can even just cancel the process, which is useful if you simply want to ensure that the hyperlink works. This is one of two significant features provided by Midas for HTML page designers; the other, shown in Figure 13.4, is an option that displays illegal HTML tags in documents. The next version of the program (3.0) promises the capability to edit HTML documents as well as view them.

FIGURE 13.4.

Illegal HTML tags option from MidasWWW.

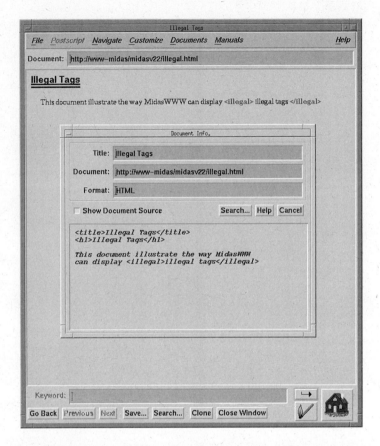

Midas offers a Visited Documents window that in many ways is much stronger than the history feature in any version of Mosaic. As Figure 13.5 shows, this window displays the titles of all of the documents you've visited this session, arranging them in a hierarchical order with the currently loaded document indicated by a large yellow dot. The hierarchical view is extremely useful, as it indicates where you can find items and enables you to load any of the documents into the main Midas window simply by clicking that document's name. But that's not all this window does. From the File menu in the window itself, you can save your current session as an HTML file, at which point you can load it from your local disk. This means that you can capture especially productive sessions and completely re-enact them, a useful design feature for those who navigate the Web frequently and who must do so efficiently.

FIGURE 13.5.

The hierarchical Visited Documents window from Midas.

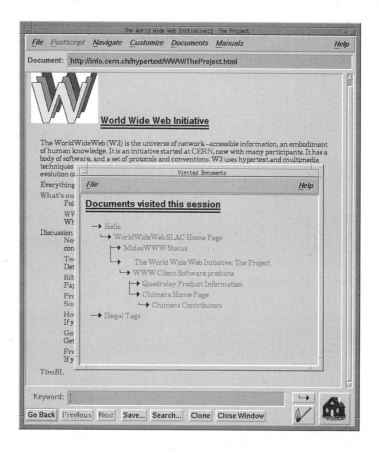

Whereas Mosaic and other browsers require that you install external viewers to view non-inline file types, Midas, like Netscape, displays many such files directly in its main window. In other words, the viewers are built in. Once again, this demonstrates user-interface consideration, because setting up external viewers is unnecessarily difficult even in the most easily configured browsers (such as Mac Mosaic). Not all file types are supported, however; to run sound files or video (MPEG) files, you still need an external viewer/player.

Because one of the design team's main reasons for developing Midas was to display scientific papers stored inside publication databases, Midas is especially strong at dealing with PostScript files. Figure 13.6 illustrates Midas's capability to display encapsulated PostScript documents (the tiger is such a document). Figure 13.7 shows how Midas handles multiple-page PostScript documents: It opens an HTML document showing the table of contents, from which you can select and view any of the individual pages. One such page, a PostScript document with the kinds of figures and scientific notation PostScript makes possible, is shown in Figure 13.8.

FIGURE 13.6.

Midas page showing a PostScript image.

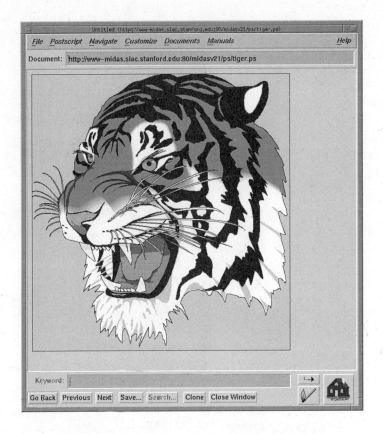

Finally, MidasWWW provides a Next/Previous feature in addition to the Back/Forward system found on virtually all Web browsers. Effectively, this feature lets you avoid backtracking over a whole series of documents you've already viewed by letting you go to the logical next or previous screen. This is especially useful for such activities as reading newsgroups, when you need to make your way to a specific point and not meander through the intermediate areas.

FIGURE 13.7.

HTML page displayed by Midas showing a table of contents for a PostScript document.

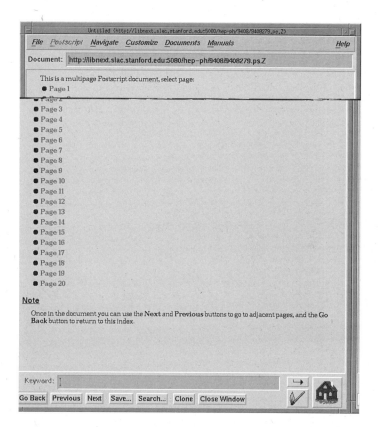

Midas supports forms (and offers a sculpted appearance to forms), and its menu structure contains all the items you'd expect. Although it does not support a global history feature, its navigation mechanisms and Visited Documents window make each session productive by helping you avoid the tendency to head off onto an undesired track. For anyone who needs to work extensively with PostScript or other types of files that don't load directly into Mosaic or other browsers, or for anyone who doesn't understand why most browsers require so much additional configuration, MidasWWW is a strong alternative.

FIGURE 13.8.

Individual PostScript page displayed directly in the Midas view window.

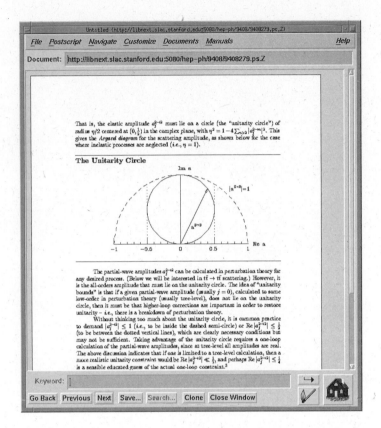

ViolaWWW

Publisher:	O'Reilly & Associates
Latest Version:	3.3
FTP Site:	ftp.ora.com
FTP Directory:	/pub/www/viola/
FTP Filename:	viola3.3.tar.gz

ViolaWWW was the first World Wide Web client available for X Window systems. It is a full-featured browser, albeit not quite as full-featured, from the standpoint of menu items, as either X Mosaic or MidasWWW. It features a Motif look and feel (sculpted icons, selectable text, all the standard features), it supports HTML fill-in forms, and is very good at displaying features of HTML 2.0 and 3.0 (such as tables). Indeed, a good Viola document can look like a published page, as illustrated in Figure 13.9. This document makes use of a specific advanced HTML tag,

<HPANE>, to create the columns. In fact, <HPANE> is not an older HTML standard, but as Figure 13.9 demonstrates, it should be. Because of Viola's origin as a language and programming tool rather than just a browser, it is capable of some functions that HTML itself does not incorporate.

FIGURE 13.9.

Viola screen featuring a document with columns and graphics.

The name Viola is an acronym for Visual Interactive Object-oriented Language and Applications. It is a toolkit that includes several features not found in current versions of HTML, and therefore can display document types and features that X Mosaic and MidasWWW cannot. If Viola were the standard browser, Web documents would be far richer in both appearance and function, but because it's not, few people are writing documents that take advantage of all of its features. Some of these features are demonstrated in the following pages.

Figure 13.10 shows a sample program built into Viola. This doesn't come as part of the Viola package but is included to show you how you can tailor Viola by engaging its programming capabilities. Doodle is a simple drawing program that appears in the main document window.

FIGURE 13.10.

Example of a program appearing in the document window.

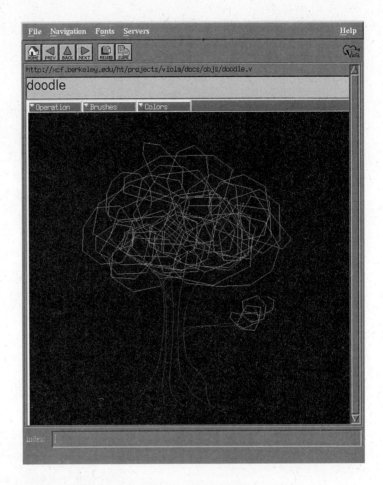

Another example of a Viola document consisting of a Viola-written program is shown in Figure 13.11. In effect, the program becomes embedded into the browser, to the degree that it includes its own interface and capabilities. Again, the secret here is using the Viola toolkit to program both the external program and the browser itself, with the results being an extremely rich environment. As mentioned previously, however, the problem is that this kind of program won't be readily available across the Web, because ViolaWWW is the only client that can take advantage of it, and its use is not widespread enough. For specific, customized functions within organizations, though, the possibilities are almost endless.

FIGURE 13.11.

Example of a Viola program embedded in a ViolaWWW window.

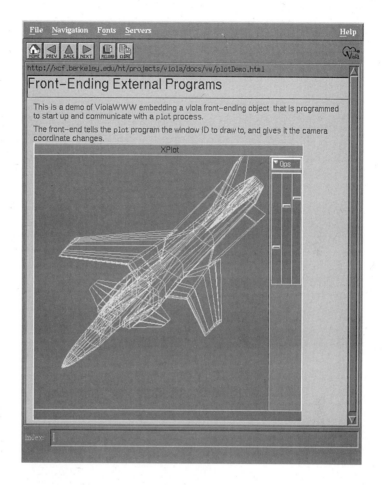

Figure 13.12 shows the main Viola window with a complex chart drawn into it. As is evident, Viola's is a relatively sparse interface, at least from external appearances. The Home button takes you to your default home page, Back takes you to the previous document and removes the current one from the history list, Previous does the same but leaves the current one available, and Next moves to the next document on the history list. At the bottom is the index line, where searches take place.

FIGURE 13.12.

The main Viola window, showing an icon bar at the top.

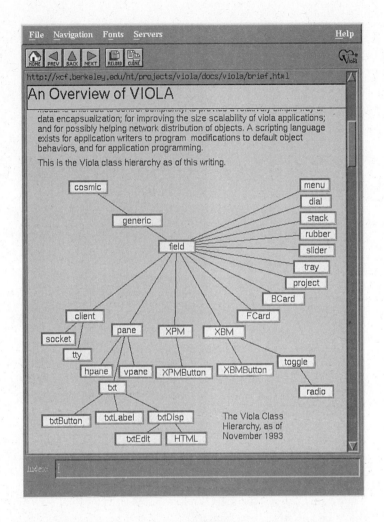

Of particular interest is the Clone icon. This icon opens a new window, called the Navigational Viewer, that shows the current document. Its purpose is to act as a launching pad for your Web browsing, and to that purpose it does not change as you use it. When you click on a hyperlink from the Navigational Viewer, the destination document is loaded into the main document window, not into the cloned one. The cloned window simply stays in place, waiting for you to select another item from it, which will then take over the main window. This is especially useful when working from long lists of sites (such as the NCSA What's New page or the EINet Galaxy), because you're not forced to return to that site (and hence often reloading the entire document) when you want to make a new selection.

Figure 13.13 shows Viola's support of forms. This example, like Figure 13.9, uses the <HPANE> tag in HTML to offer columns of buttons, and Viola-specific capabilities to offer sliding bars in the item selections and the doodle pad in the Signature box. The appearance of this form is superior to other forms found on the Web because of the browser's inherent capabilities. Again, however, the form in Figure 13.13 will not display on a standard browser.

FIGURE 13.13.

Fill-in form using Viola's programming capabilities.

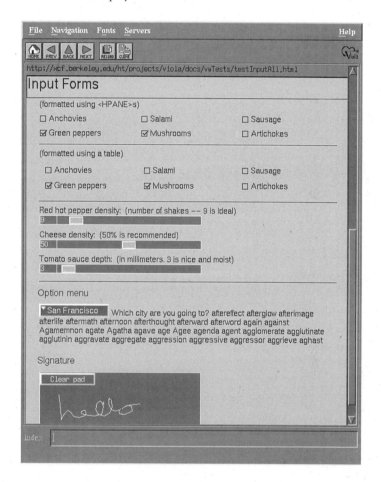

Viola thus offers a rich opportunity for sophisticated document creation. In addition, it features a source-code viewer and editor to help you work through HTML authoring. But as a browser for the World Wide Web as it exists today, with the reliance on much less sophisticated HTML documents, it is less useful than either X Mosaic or MidasWWW. In particular, its lack of a hotlisting (bookmarking) feature nearly incapacitates it, as bookmarking has become an absolute must for repeated Web navigation. After these features are added, as they will be shortly, this browser should see many advanced uses.

Actually, there are two versions of Viola, one that uses the Motif front-end and an older one that uses the XLib front end. Users capable of displaying Motif will want the former, because it features the polished and attractive interface sported by the other major X clients, but other than that the versions are generally the same. Some differences are as follows: In the XLib version, you can directly edit the URL display, but this option is unavailable in the Motif edition. An important feature of the XLib version is that it enables you to bookmark documents in three menus: Public, Local, and Private; the Motif version of Viola features a history list but not a bookmarking function. According to the designer, however, the two versions will become identical through the course of a few revisions.

Browsers for the Macintosh

Basically, Macintosh users are in the same position as Microsoft Windows users (see Chapter 12), at least as far as freeware browsers are concerned—they have NCSA Mosaic, Netscape Navigator, plus two other choices. What differs is the quality of those other choices, although even here there's a strange similarity. Windows users have Cello and WinWeb (both discussed in the following Windows section), whereas Macintosh users have Samba and MacWeb. Now, there's no way whatsoever that Samba can be reasonably compared with Cello; the latter is so far superior that it's hard to write about them in the same chapter of this book. But WinWeb, in its first incarnation, is distinctly inferior to its Macintosh sister program, MacWeb, so on balance the quality of browsers for the two user bases isn't all that far off. It seems reasonable to give Cello the nod over MacWeb, and WinWeb the definite nod over Samba, so it would seem that Windows users are, indeed, better off.

There are really only two choices for Mac users: Mosaic and MacWeb. Samba is described even by its own creators as "basic," and a quick look at it here will demonstrate the accuracy and honesty of that assessment. However, there's no need whatsoever for Mac users to feel impoverished. Mac Mosaic is smoother and more stable than its Windows counterpart, and MacWeb is far better than its Windows counterpart as well. The only area in which the Windows versions get the nod is in speed, but not dramatically so. None of this should surprise Mac owners in the least.

Samba

Publisher:	CERN
Latest Version:	1.03
FTP Site:	ftp.w3.org
FTP Directory:	/pub/www/bin/mac/
FTP Filename:	MacWWW_V1_03.sea

Samba, otherwise known as MacWWW, was the first available Web client for the Macintosh. Developed by the World Wide Web team at CERN, it is worth examining now only for historical interest, because it is underpowered by comparison to all other browsers in this book—arguably even less capable than the CERN line browser itself. There's nothing intrinsically *wrong* with Samba; it works, and it does everything it was apparently designed to do. It's just that it wasn't designed to do much, and in a year that has given Mac users both Mosaic and MacWeb, Web clients have to do a very great deal indeed. The program is scarcely worth the time it takes to download.

Figure 13.14 gives a good indication of what Samba looks like. As is evident, Samba does not replace the current document with a new document when you access a hyperlink. Instead, it opens a new window. The problem with this approach is that the screen becomes extremely cluttered very quickly. Again, however, Samba itself isn't really to be blamed for this. When they created a browser designed to support the Web in its early stages, the design team likely never envisioned the amount of Web activity, and the number of Web sites, now available to even the casual user. Samba was not designed to handle this level of activity.

Still, if you come to this program now, instead of graduating *from* it into something else, its limitations seem difficult to believe, even given its early introduction into the fray. There's no dialog box to allow font changes, for instance—something that's almost a constitutional right among Mac users of Web clients. In addition, you have to double-click on a link rather than single-click, which wouldn't be so bad except that a single click gives you an insertion point wherever you clicked on the link, giving the impression that the text of the link is editable (it's not). After you have double-clicked, there's no progress indicator telling you how much of the destination document you've transferred, how much remains to be transferred, or even if anything's happening at all. Nor is there any way to stop a transfer once it's begun.

Samba does not display graphics, as shown in Figure 13.15. Nor does it display bullets in lists. In fact, this is a graphical browser only because it is on the Macintosh platform and has its commands activated by a mouse, not because it has any connection with graphics *per se*.

FIGURE 13.14.

Samba with the home page and four additional windows open.

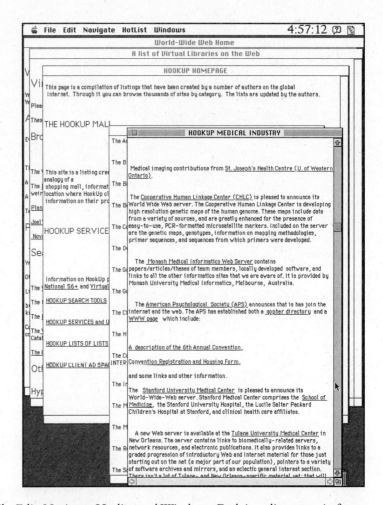

Samba's menus include File, Edit, Navigate, Hotlist, and Windows. Each is rudimentary in function. File contains the standard Mac items, but only Close, Save As (see Figure 13.16), Page Setup, Print, Quit, and Preferences actually do anything. Preferences enables you to specify your startup document and whether to underline your links (essential with a monochrome Mac), and that's pretty much it. The only possibility with the Edit menu is Copy, which you can also do by highlighting text in a document. (Of course, Windows Mosaic can't do this yet....)

FIGURE 13.15.

A separate window showing a graphical map (nonexistent) in Samba.

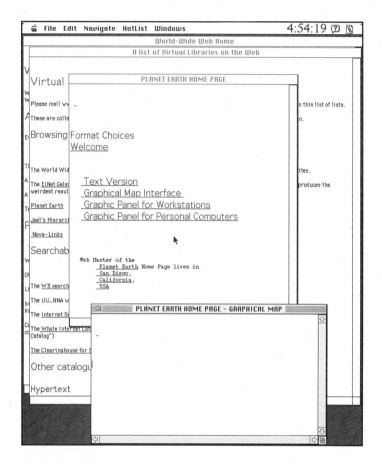

The Navigate menu sports the usual Back and Forward choices, but also includes Previous and Next. Next is a useful (but somewhat strange) command: If you proceed from Document A to Document B via hyperlink, and then click on Next, you'll be taken to the item from Document A that occurs below the link you chose first. Navigate also lets you open a document by URL, a feature that has become standard in all browsers.

318

FIGURE 13.16.

The Mac-standard Save As dialog box in Samba.

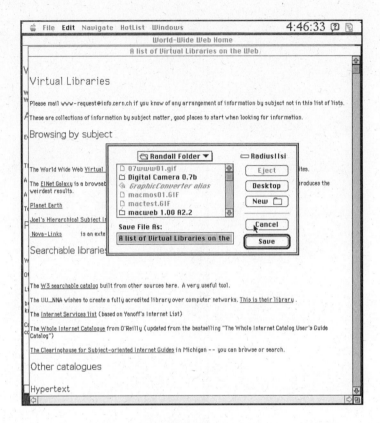

The Hotlist menu offers some built-in documents, and you can add the current document to that list or remove any already on the list. The Windows menu simply enables you to move from open window to open window. There's little more to report, except that instead of a permanent URL display, Samba features (from the Windows menu) the Current Document Identifier box shown in Figure 13.17.

Clearly, this is a browser of limited usefulness, and one that was overtaken so quickly by every other graphical browser that loading it today is almost like stepping back into the dark ages. Interesting, but only as a curiosity.

FIGURE 13.17.

The Current Document Identifier box in Samba.

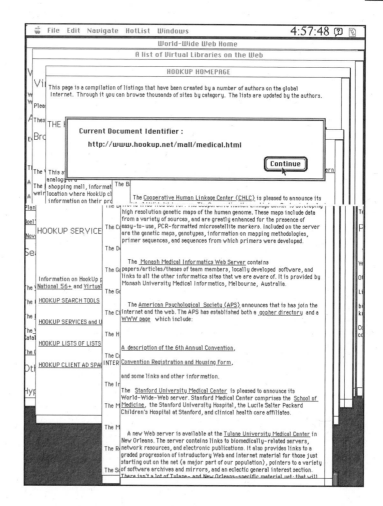

MacWeb

Publisher:	EINet
Latest Version:	1.00A2.2
FTP Site:	ftp.einet.net
FTP Directory:	/einet/mac/macweb/
FTP Filename:	macweb.latest.sea.hqx

MacWeb was the first World Wide Web client package available from EINet. (WinWeb was the second.) It's a highly capable browser, leaner than Mac Mosaic or Netscape for Macintosh (that is, requiring less RAM), and with a slightly larger amount of space given over to actual document display. (See Figure 13.18.) Dedicated Mac Mosaic or Netscape users will have little reason to switch, but if, like many, you're growing tired of being a walking advertisement for NCSA's or Netscape Communication's software, it's well worth a serious examination. Especially for the more casual Web user, it's not only good enough; it might be better than its more famous competitor, precisely because it doesn't have all the bells and whistles.

There's much to like in this program. You can import your Mosaic hotlists (assuming you're already using that program) either by opening them with the Open URL dialog box or by dragging and dropping them on the MacWeb icon. The URL display can be edited, which is extremely useful for specifying a follow-up URL to the one that is open now, but for which there is no link on the current page. MacWeb supports HTML forms fully (as shown in Figure 13.19), and its user interface is simply and cleanly designed. Furthermore, the status line displays the number of bytes already transferred and the total for the entire file (always a useful thing to know), and a direct link to the EINet galaxy gives you instant access to a wide range of Web documents.

FIGURE 13.18.

A typical MacWeb window, showing a large document display area.

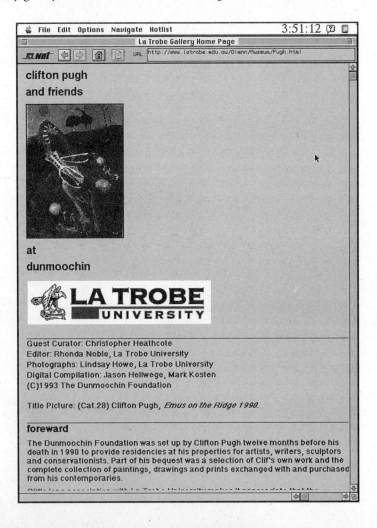

FIGURE 13.19.

MacWeb page showing support for HTML fill-in forms.

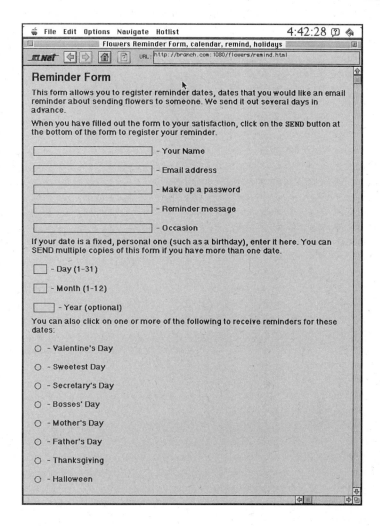

MacWeb can be configured entirely from within. The File menu, for example, features a Preferences item with which you can specify your default home page, your e-mail address, and the news host you want to use. Also available here are settings for the hotlist to open at startup and the default folder for temporary files. From the Format section of this dialog box (shown in Figure 13.20), you can specify whether to automatically load inline images into documents as you retrieve them, whether to collapse blank lines (this feature lets you get rid of excess white space on documents), what color you want the document window background to be, and how to handle character translation.

FIGURE 13.20.

The Format dialog box from MacWeb's Preferences menu.

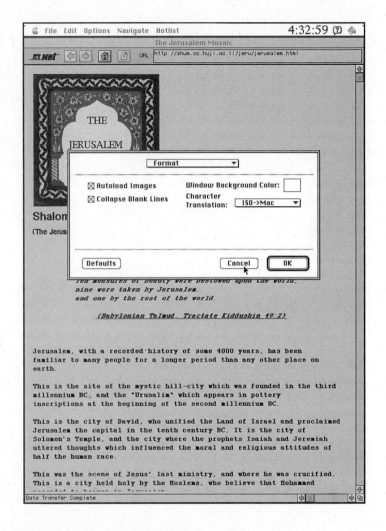

The rest of the configuration possibilities are found in the Edit menu. From here you can access three dialog boxes: Styles, Helpers, and Suffixes. Figure 13.21 shows the main Styles dialog box; the pull-down menu at the top of the box enables you to set the various elements of the page view. Of note is the Size Is Relative box at the bottom of the box, which enables you to adjust only the root style and have all other styles adjust themselves accordingly. It's similar to the Increase or Decrease All Fonts option found in other browsers.

FIGURE 13.21.

MacWeb's Styles dialog box.

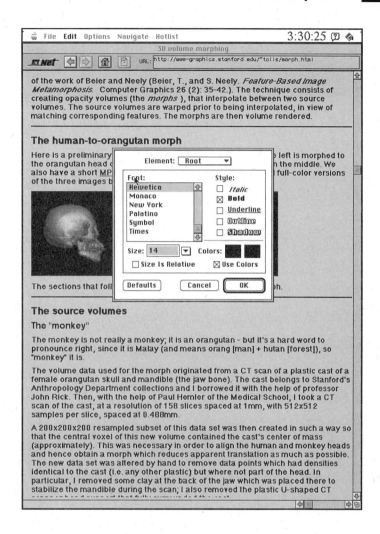

One of the other two configuration menus from the Edit menu is Helpers. As Figure 13.22 shows, this menu enables you to easily determine which tools (viewers or players) will handle which file types. Note that it's possible to set decompression software to handle FTPs of compressed files, an obviously useful feature.

FIGURE 13.22.

The Helpers dialog box from MacWeb.

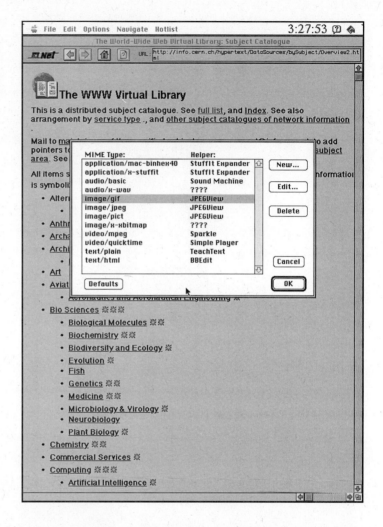

With these helpers in place, you can do all of the multimedia things with MacWeb that you can in any other browser. Shown in Figure 13.23 is a QuickTime movie playing through an external player, accessed simply by clicking the movie link in the document.

FIGURE 13.23.

A QuickTime movie playing on an external viewer from MacWeb.

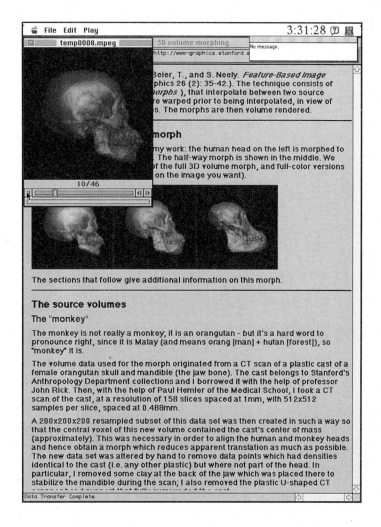

Like the other main Web clients, MacWeb can show you the HTML source code for the current document. As displayed in Figure 13.24, the source code appears in a separate window, from which you can select and copy text or save to a separate file. (Note the Save As dialog box in this figure as well.)

MacWeb's Navigate menu offers the usual choices, including Forward, Backward, and Home, which are also found as icons above the main viewing window. Also here are links to EINet and the EINet Galaxy, although strangely MacWeb doesn't offer the instant search of the Galaxy available in the much less capable WinWeb. There's also a link to the MacWeb home page, as you'd expect.

FIGURE 13.24.

The View Source window and Save As dialog box from MacWeb.

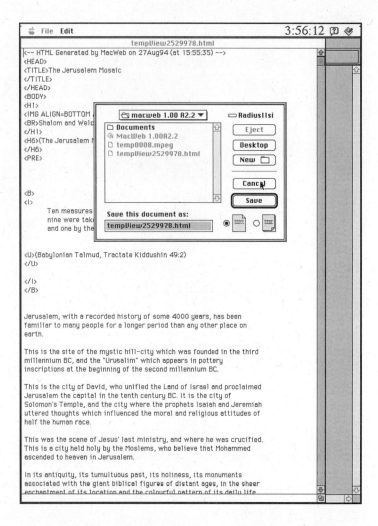

Hotlisting in MacWeb is practically identical to hotlisting in the Mac Mosaic version that preceded the most recent one. A separate Hotlist menu offers two items, Hotlist Interface and Add This Document. With the latter you add the current document to the Hotlist menu itself, whereas the former offers submenus that enable you to open stored hotlists, begin a new one, edit hotlist entries, and so forth. If you've come over from Mac Mosaic, you'll have no trouble picking up on this feature.

MacWeb's strengths make future versions of this program worth watching for. This is a real competitor to Mac Mosaic, a smaller, more concise program and one perfectly suited to staying loaded in the background as you work. One or two releases from now, it might well become the preference of many.

OS/2

If you're an OS/2 user, you can make use of any browser currently available for Microsoft Windows. The problem is that, despite claims to the contrary in the press, OS/2 runs Windows slowly unless it's tweaked to perfection, and most people have little idea how to do that. Besides, it feels a bit traitor-like to invoke Windows every time you want to do anything important in OS/2, so OS/2 users want native versions of their programs to perform the tasks.

At this point, the only choice is WebExplorer from IBM, which is free for anyone who uses OS/2 Warp and who joins the IBM Network. That's the bad news. The good news, and it's much better, is that WebExplorer is an excellent browser that fits the OS/2 operating system extremely well.

WebExplorer

Publisher:	IBM
Latest Version:	1.1
FTP Site:	N/A
FTP Directory:	N/A
FTP Filename:	N/A

If you've purchased OS/2 Warp, the brilliantly advertised operating system from IBM, you have all the Internet tools you need. OS/2 Warp (and the upcoming 3.0) ships with a full Internet package, and with a built-in program for establishing an Internet connection with the IBM Network. IBMNet is readily available with local phone numbers around the world; it's been well designed and is well supported, and compared to other commercial providers its rates and its capabilities are just fine. If you're not on the Net, and you use OS/2, by all means give this network a shot.

The Internet package consists of e-mail, Telnet, and FTP packages, as well as a dedicated newsreader and, most importantly for the purposes of this book, a World Wide Web browser named WebExplorer. WebExplorer doesn't actually ship with the operating system; instead, you can download it (at no charge for the connection) when you log onto the IBM Network for the first time.

WebExplorer, like the other programs in the IBM Internet suite, is continually being updated, and whenever you log onto IBMNet you're told if a new version is available. You are also asked if you want to download the new versions, and doing so automatically updates the individual programs. There's no FTPing, unzipping, or manually installing necessary; just click once and sit back and wait. You might have to reboot to set all of the changes, but even that's nicely taken care of by the software.

As far as the program itself is concerned, WebExplorer is a quite capable graphical World Wide Web client. It offers a fully interactive download feature—that is, page transfers are interruptable by stopping them or clicking on whatever links appear during the download—and it supports advanced HTML coding, including several of the better known (and somewhat controversial) Netscape tags. It's easy to set up (no SLIP/PPP to configure) and equally easy to configure (with excellent configuration dialog boxes), it contains several viewers for graphics and other multimedia files, and it's both fast and reliable.

One of WebExplorer's strongest features is WebMap, its unique history list. The WebMap feature creates a hierarchically organized HTML page that you can use to find your way to wherever you've been during that session. It's among the best history list features of any browser on the market, and by itself practically makes having OS/2 worthwhile.

There's really nothing to dislike about WebExplorer. It's strong, and it will get even better with development. The bookmarks feature could use greater sophistication to allow for stronger archiving of locations and pages, which is one possible minus, and people who want their browsers to integrate all Internet activity—including newsgroups and everything else—won't like the fact that WebExplorer is a very good Web browser but not an all-purpose tool. But as WebExplorer develops, it's safe to say that IBM will keep it close to the competition (at least, given its good start), so OS/2 users have little to fear.

It would be nice to see an OS/2 version of Mosaic and Netscape, and it would certainly be good to see shareware and freeware developments of OS/2 browsers. For now, though, WebExplorer more than serves the purpose.

Amiga Mosaic

Publisher:	SUNY Stony Brook
Latest Version:	1.3 beta
FTP Site:	`max.physics.sunysb.edu`
FTP Directory:	`/pub/amiga/amosaic/`
FTP Filename:	`Mosaic_1.3betaAS225r2.lha`

Web clients exist for other platforms, such as VMS and the NeXT. This chapter makes no attempt to cover every existing browser, however, so here I'll offer only one further example. Commodore's Amiga was one of the first true multimedia computers on the market, and by all rights it should have been a giant hit. But the company's ability to market its products seemed to start and end with the earlier Commodore 64, and the Amiga, despite huge initial hype, never got the audience it deserved. Much of that audience, indeed, opted for the (then) less capable Macintosh instead. Commodore itself folded recently, but rumors have the Amiga surviving with another company.

At any rate, Amiga owners have a Web browser to work with, and an interesting one at that. Called Amiga Mosaic, the program looks very much like the Mosaics covered in Chapter 10, "NCSA Mosaic," but this one is *not* distributed or developed by NCSA (which is why it's in this chapter, not the last one). It is the work of a team headed by Michael Fischer, a systems administrator at SUNY in Stony Brook, New York, and it demonstrates the kind of commitment Amiga owners seem to have had since the beginning to create software for themselves that no one else would make available.

As Figure 13.25 demonstrates, there's little to differentiate Amiga Mosaic from the official Mosaics, at least from an external perspective. Inside, of course, the program is significantly different, primarily because of a reliance (as is common in Amiga packages) on the Rexx programming language, which controls such features as hotlisting. Other small differences are apparent as well, including the omission of the spinning globe, but there's actually less apparent difference between Amiga Mosaic and X Mosaic (for example) than between, say, Mac Mosaic and Windows Mosaic.

FIGURE 13.25.

The Amiga Mosaic main screen.

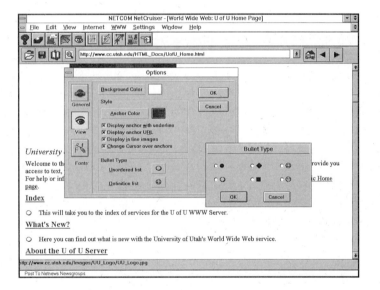

As you'd expect from an Amiga program, the color schemes and other visual elements of Amiga Mosaic are highly configurable. Anyone willing to work with a package like MUI (the MagicUserInterface) can make Amiga Mosaic look exactly as they want, virtually pixel by pixel. For that matter, anyone willing to work with Arexx can add interface and special functions to the program as well. Good Amiga hackers—and there are still hordes of them—will take an already strong browser and add whatever they like.

Summary

Although Microsoft Windows users are blessed with the largest number of World Wide Web browsers (and practically all the commercial ones), users of other systems have several to choose from. Chapter 43 examines the new X Window browser HotJava. Macintosh owners have three very good choices, and OS/2 users and Amiga owners, while they have only one substantial browser each, aren't suffering from lack of quality. The Web is a cross-platform phenomenon, and it's safe to expect even more good browsers to appear in the near future.

PART

III

Web Navigation Tools and Techniques

Web Structures and Spaces

14

by
John December

IN THIS CHAPTER

The first step in learning how to successfully navigate the Web is to understand the Web's structure and information spaces. Although Web browsers can enable you to use a "point and click" operation to move through the Web, knowing how online networks operate together can help you better understand the workings of Web navigation tools and the reasons behind navigation techniques discussed in later chapters. Moreover, with knowledge of the topology of global networks, you are more prepared for the changes and growth that will inevitably occur as global networks evolve (and possibly merge). This chapter will help you gain an understanding of how the Web relates to global information and communication networks. To begin our tour, we'll start from the widest possible context for computer communication—cyberspace—and then converge in closer and closer detail on the Web.

The Topology of Cyberspace

Cyberspace refers to the mental construct a person generates from experiencing computer communication and information retrieval. The science fiction author William Gibson developed this term to describe the visual environments in his novels. Gibson described worlds in which computer users navigate a highly imagistic global network of information resources and services.

The term cyberspace is used today to refer to the collection of computer-mediated experiences for visualization, communication, interaction, and information retrieval. You can think of cyberspace as the largest context for any activity done online or through computers. Examples of activities in cyberspace include a doctor using a virtual reality helmet for visualizing a surgical operation, a student reading a newspaper online, and a teacher presenting class materials through the Web.

You can think of cyberspace as consisting of a wide variety of global networks as well as non-networked systems for communication and interaction. For example, in the broad definition of cyberspace given previously, a person using a CD-ROM application on his or her computer can be considered to be interacting in cyberspace, although the computer the user has may not be connected to a global (or a local) communications network. These offline activities are one portion of cyberspace that are unreachable from the networked region of cyberspace (such as the Internet and other global networks).

Figure 14.1 summarizes two separate regions of cyberspace—offline and online. Since, by definition, the offline region involves no network communication (via a wire or wireless), there is a "wall" in cyberspace that separates activities in these two regions.

Since our journey to the Web will require us to go online, we'll turn our attention to the topology of the online region of cyberspace. In this online region, there are thousands of networks and systems worldwide that enable users to exchange information and communicate. These systems and networks may use different protocols, or rules, for exchanging information, and may use different conduits for transmitting messages (everything from copper wire to fiber-optic cable to satellites and wireless communication). These networks might also vary in size from room-sized Personal Area Networks (PANs) involving networked personal communications devices such as handheld digital assistants or personal identification medallions to world-sized Global Area Networks (GANs) such as the Internet. In between these two size extremes, rooms and buildings may be connected in Local Area Networks (LANs), cities in Metropolitan Area Networks (MANs), large organizations or regions connected in Wide Area Networks (WANs), or Region Area Networks (RANs). As technologies evolve, new possibilities open up for creating still more kinds of networks in online cyberspace.

FIGURE 14.1.

The regions of cyberspace.

Cyberspace Regions	
and sample activities	
Offline (no network connections)	**Online** (network connections)
Single–computer applications	Internet communication
Non–networked hypermedia	Commercial online services
Non–networked virtual reality	Dialup BBS
CD–ROM	Local or wide area networks

The Internet and the Web Within Cyberspace

Within the large context of global cyberspace, there are many computer networks that allow people to exchange information and communication worldwide. The Internet refers to one such system for global communication and information dissemination.

The term *Internet* refers to not just a single network, but a globally distributed collection of computer networks that all use the same set of rules (protocols) to exchange information. The Internet is cooperatively run and constitutes one of the largest systems for human communication ever created. The Internet itself supports a wide variety of applications that people use to exchange information:

- Gopher
- File Transport Protocol (FTP)
- Wide Area Information Server (WAIS)
- Telnet

Later chapters explore how you can use each of these information applications.

These Internet information applications are also the basis for information retrieval on the Web. In this way, you can think of the Web as being located "within" (or "on top of") the Internet.

The Web is not a computer network like the Internet. Rather, the Web is an application that uses Internet tools as its means of communication and information transport.

Since the Internet is so key to the Web's operation, a Web *navigator* (someone who uses the Web for information retrieval or communication) needs to know something about the Internet's place in online cyberspace.

The Internet as Common Ground

One key to navigating online cyberspace is to understand how communication might take place among the networks. Since each online network may use a different set of rules for communication, communication among networks is not necessarily automatic, simple, or even possible.

The Internet is a very popular network in online cyberspace, but it is not the only one. But because of its resources and large base of users, the Internet acts as a *common ground* for communication and activity, and many online networks have some way (either through gateways or other connections) for their users to reach the Internet.

The Internet uses a special set of protocols called TCP/IP, or "the Internet protocol suite," to exchange information. These protocols serve as the standard rules for the applications that are commonly used on the Internet for communication and information. For example, the Telnet application uses a special protocol for exchanging information on the Internet, as does the Internet Gopher application.

The Web utilizes these Internet protocols for communication. It is possible, however, to create Web communication that exists on stand-alone computer systems or on non-TCP/IP networks such as DECNET. Thus, the software of the World Wide Web can operate on computers without using the Internet (or any network) at all. However, for the purposes of this discussion, we will consider these non-networked applications of the Web to fall under the categorization non-networked hypermedia, in the offline region of cyberspace.

The Internet's role as *common ground* in online cyberspace draws other networks to make connections to it.

Commercial online services such as Prodigy, America OnLine, CompuServe, and Delphi provide users with access to global information systems. However, these commercial services may use different protocols for communication so that their users may not be able to directly access all the Internet protocols (or services on the other systems).

These commercial services may also provide graphical interfaces to their online services. These graphical interfaces, however, are not necessarily views of the Web.

However, many commercial networks offer a range of connections to the Internet. For example, Prodigy was the first commercial service to provide direct access for its users to Internet's Web. Other commercial services are expected to follow and provide greater connectivity to the Internet and the Web.

Just like users of commercial online services, users of other global networks can't easily access the Internet or Web. FidoNet is a network of personal computers worldwide that exchanges information by modems and phone lines. BITNET (Because It's Time Network) and UUCP (UNIX-to-UNIX Copy Protocol) are other networks used for exchanging information among users. Users of these networks can't directly access the Web (except in limited ways, such as through electronic mail interfaces).

Figure 14.2 shows the topology of online cyberspace, listing some major networks and gateways to the Internet.

FIGURE 14.2.

A topology of online cyberspace.

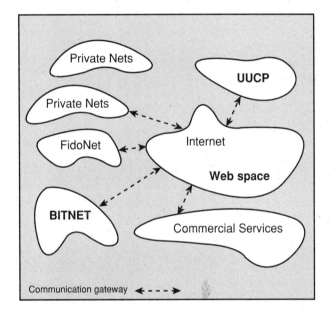

Gateways Among Networks

In many cases, there is no way to exchange information directly among the networks of cyberspace. For example, the world-wide system for exchanging banking transactions is not accessible from the Internet (for obvious security reasons). In other cases, there is some level of connection among these large networks. For example, BITNET and Internet users can exchange electronic mail through gateways built for that purpose. Similarly, many commercial services provide e-mail gateways from their services to the Internet. Figure 14.2 shows some of the electronic mail gateways (as dashed lines) that exist among the networks of cyberspace. Note how many global networks provide some connectivity to the Internet.

For Web navigators, the key to remember is that the Web can't be easily experienced except through direct Internet connectivity. Since not all networks have gateways to the Internet for all the protocols that the Web uses, it is often very difficult for a non-Internet user to make use of the Web.

TERMINOLOGY

When talking about cyberspace, the following brief definitions of its regions may be helpful:

The Matrix: The set of all networks that can exchange electronic mail either directly or through gateways. This includes the Internet, BITNET, FidoNet, UUCP, and commercial services such as America Online, CompuServe, Delphi, and Prodigy. This term was coined by John S. Quarterman in his book *The Matrix* (Digital Press, 1990).

The Net: An informal term for the Internet or a subset of the Matrix in context. For example, a computerized conference via e-mail may take place on a BITNET host that has an Internet gateway, thus making the conference available to anyone on either of these networks. In this case, the developer might say, "Our conference will be available on the Net."

The Web: Used in its strictest sense, *the Web* refers to all the documents on all Web servers worldwide. In a broader sense, The Web could be used to refer to all accessible hypertext-linked documents (on FTP and even Gopher servers). In still a broader sense, The Web could be considered to include all the collected resources that are accessible through a Web browser. This broad meaning, then, would include FTP space and Gopher space (see below). It would, however, be misleading to say, "We put the documents on the Web" when one has placed them only on an FTP server (as opposed to placing the documents on a Web server). Although FTP documents are accessible by Web browsers, the audience for the preceding statement might be misled to believe that the documents are on a Web server and perhaps in hypertext. A single Web server with its associated files can be called a web (with a small w). For example, you might say, "We're going to have to make a web to describe the new system." (Web refers to a single, local web.) In contrast: "We'll put the documents on the Web." (The term *"web"* refers to the global collection of publicly accessible webs and indicates the speaker's intention to make the local web widely known and publicly available.)

The Internet: The Internet is the cooperatively run, globally distributed collection of computer networks that exchange information via the TCP/IP protocol suite. The Internet consists of many internetworked networks, called *internets* (with a small i). An internet is a single network that uses the TCP/IP protocol suite, and some internets are not connected to the Internet.

FTP space: The set of all resources accessible through the file transfer protocol. These resources include directories of files and individual files that may be text or binary (executable files, graphics, sound, and video) files.

Gopher space: The set of all resources accessible through the Internet Gopher protocol. A Gopher is a system for organizing information in terms of menus. Menu items can be links to other documents or information services.

Usenet: This is not a network at all, but a system for disseminating asynchronous text discussion among cooperating computer hosts. Usenet is not limited to the Internet. Its origins are in UUCP systems, but Usenet is disseminated widely throughout the Matrix and beyond.

As a navigator of the Web, you need to keep Figure 14.2 in mind as a basic operational chart. Remember the following:

- Cyberspace consists of an offline region and an online region consisting of many different local and global networks.
- The Internet is a collection of networks in online cyberspace. Because the Web links Internet resources, the Web can be considered to be "located" within the Internet.
- Users of networks can exchange electronic mail or other information through gateways.
- Because most implemented gateways among networks are for electronic mail only, it is easiest to use the Web from the Internet.

When navigating the Web, you may encounter many references to non-Internet activities and other networks in cyberspace. Remember that these activities may not be directly accessible from the Internet. Eventually, gateways may be built from these other networks to support the protocols necessary for full Internet connectivity.

The Web Within the Internet

Now that we've examined the role of the Internet and Web as one part of the online region of cyberspace, let's examine the Web's role with the Internet itself. The power of the Web, as discussed in Part I, "Introduction to the World Wide Web," is that it links Internet resources through a system of hypertext.

From a user's point of view, the Web consists of resources on the Internet that are accessible through a particular Web browser. The Web connects these resources through hypertext written using the HyperText Markup Language (HTML). Files containing text marked using HTML are located on a Web server and available for Web browsers (clients) to access. The HTML file contains links to other Internet resources. For example, Figure 14.3 illustrates the connections among an HTML document to other Internet resources and sample relationships among the Web browser, information servers, and files located on the servers.

The resources shown in Figure 14.3 include a remote login to a host through the Telnet protocol, a link to a text file on an FTP server, a link to a menu on a Gopher server, and a link to another HTML document on another Web server. Thus, the Web links disparate resources scattered across the network.

FIGURE 14.3.
The Web within the Internet.

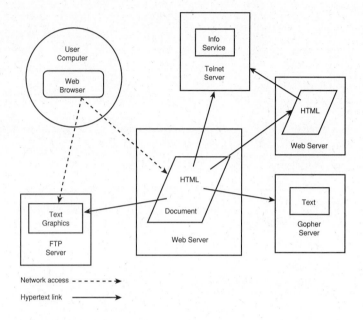

You can think of the "binding together" that the Web does for Internet resources in terms of the protocols that Web browsers can understand. Web browsers use the HyperText Transfer Protocol (HTTP) as a means to exchange hypertext written in HTML. HTTP is a protocol developed especially for the Web and was designed to operate quickly for hypertext jumps. Web browsers (discussed in detail in Part II, "Web Browsers and Connections,") can also access information according to other protocols, some of which are shown in Figure 14.3:

- *FTP:* A widely used protocol for transferring information (text, graphics, and video) across the Internet.
- *NNTP (Network News Transfer Protocol):* A protocol used for exchanging Usenet news.
- *Gopher:* A protocol for sharing information in the form of menus and documents.
- *Telnet:* A means to remotely log into a host on the Internet.

Information Spaces in the Web

Now that you've seen the Web's linking relationship with Internet resources, you can examine the structure of the spaces created by the Web's scheme for referring to resources.

Uniform Resource Locators

The basis for identifying resources on the Web is the Uniform Resource Locator, or URL. A URL consists of a string of characters that uniquely identifies a resource. You can think of a URL as a sort of "catalog number" for a resource. When you use a Web browser to open a particular URL, you will gain access to the resource identified by that URL.

The basic format for many URLs is as follows:

`scheme://host:port/path`

where

> `scheme` is one of the rules or protocols to retrieve or send information, such as FTP, NNTP, Gopher, and Telnet.
>
> `host` is the computer host on which the resource resides.
>
> `port` is a particular number that identifies the service you are requesting from the computer host; provided if the service is installed on a port different than the standard one for that service.
>
> `path` is an identification of the location of a resource on a particular computer host.

There are other variations in format that a Web navigator will encounter. All URLs, however, share the same purpose when used in a Web document: to identify a resource for linking within hypertext read by Web browsers.

WEB HYPERTEXT TERMINOLOGY

Although the concept of hypertext and its actual use in computer systems has been around a long time, terminology for Web-related hypertext elements is evolving, both in formal definitions and informal usage. The following terms are often used in talking about Web-based hypertext:

Page: Refers to a single sheet of hypertext (a single file of HTML).

Home page: Refers to a designated entry point for access to a local web. Also refers to a page that a person defines as his or her principal page, often containing personal or professional information.

Hotspot: The region of displayed hypertext that, when selected, links the user to another point in the hypertext or another resource.

web (lowercase "w"): A set of hypertext pages considered to be a single work, often located on a single server. In popular usage, is synonymous to "home page."

Web (uppercase "W"): The set of hypertext on Web servers worldwide; in a broader sense, all information available through a Web browser interface.

For example, here are some URLs (some of which are variations from the pattern shown previously) that show different forms a URL can take:

> `http://www.eff.org`   The Web server of the Electronic Frontier Foundation (EFF), an organization to advocate the civil liberties of online users. The EFF's home page leads to many other links in their web. This URL actually has no path specified. Only the host name, `www.eff.org` is listed. In this case, a default home page is retrieved as a result of accessing this URL.

`ftp://nic.merit.edu/documents/fyi/fyi_20.txt`   This is a text document that answers the question "What is the Internet?" written by E. Krol and E. Hoffman. This URL uses File Transfer Protocol and has a host name (`nic.merit.edu`) as well as a pathname listed (`documents/fyi/fyi_20.txt`).

`gopher://gopher.cic.net:2000/11/hunt`   This is the URL of a Gopher menu that presents information about a game called "The Internet Hunt" that helps players build their skills in navigating the Internet. This URL uses the Gopher protocol. The pathname given after the host, `gopher.cic.net`, identifies the menu entry for this particular resource. The `2000` following the host name is a port number.

`telnet://locis.loc.gov`   This is a Telnet connection to the U.S. Library of Congress's online catalogs and databases.

When a Web browser opens this URL, a Telnet session will appear (a session in which the user will log into a remote computer host).

`news:comp.infosystems.www.users`   This is the URL format to access Usenet news delivered according to the network news transfer protocol (NNTP).

This Usenet newsgroup name shown here, `comp.infosystems.www.users`, is a group devoted to discussing user aspects of WWW computer information systems.

`http://www.rpi.edu/~decemj/works/wwwu/contents.html#part3`   This is a URL to the support web for this book, to the section of the table of contents page for Part III.

Note that the `#part3` part at the end of the pathname for the file indicates that this URL points to a specific place within the file called an anchor.

`http://www.ncsa.uiuc.edu/SDG/Experimental/demoweb/marc-global-hyp.au`   This is an audio file (`.au` extension) located on a server demonstrating Mosaic's capabilities. This sound file, when accessed by a browser (provided that the user has the appropriate audio player software and hardware installed in the computer), will produce a voice greeting.

`http://uu-gna.mit.edu:8001/uu-gna/index.html`   This is the URL to the home page of the Globewide Network Academy, an organization dedicated to creating a fully accredited online university. Note that this URL has a port number (`8001`) specified by the developers of this page. The standard port number for HTTP access is 80; so when a port not equal to 80 is set, you should use it in the URL. If you leave off the port number, you will get the following error message:

```
Requested document (URL http://uu-gna.mit.edu/uu-gna/index.html) could not be
accessed.
The information server either is not accessible or is refusing to serve the
document to you.
```

KEY RESOURCES

For finding out more about URLs, see the following:

"Uniform Resource Locators." (`http://www.w3.org/hypertext/WWW/Addressing/URL/Overview.html`)

Andreessen, Marc. "A Beginner's Guide to URLs." (`http://www.ncsa.uiuc.edu/demoweb/url-primer.html`)

Theise, Eric S. (1994, January 7). "Curling Up to Universal Resource Locators." (`gopher://gopher.well.sf.ca.us/00/matrix/internet/curling.up.02`)

Information Spaces

URLs create information spaces on the Web in terms of the protocol used. For example, you can consider all FTP URLs to be in FTP space, the set of all servers publicly available for anonymous FTP. This space is just one region of the Internet's resources, but represents a vast repository of knowledge to which the Web can connect.

Not only does a URL identify the protocol used for the information, but a URL also often identifies the type of media represented by the resource. For example, the URL shown previously, `http://www.ncsa.uiuc.edu/SDG/Experimental/demoweb/marc-global-hyp.au`, is an audio file. Similarly, there are filename extensions for movies (`mpeg`) as well as many kinds of graphics (such as GIF, JPEG, and XBM) and text files (such as TXT, PS, and TEX). In this way, a URL can identify the sensory experience that a resource may offer. You can thus consider the information spaces in the Internet to be multimedia spaces. A good source of more information about multimedia is Simon Gibbs's "Index to Multimedia Information Sources," `http://viswiz.gmd.de/MultimediaInfo/`.

We'll cover techniques for using URLs and writing HTML in more detail in Part V, "Weaving a Web." As a Web navigator, remember that the URL is the basis for some tasks in Web navigation. You will use a URL to call up a specific resource in a browser and use URLs within HTML documents to link resources.

A PEEK AT HTML

In Part V, "Weaving a Web," you'll look at how to construct HTML documents. It might be helpful at this point, however, to get a glimpse of what an HTML file looks like. The output following this note is an example. The < and > symbols mark the start and end of tags that are used to identify components of the document.

In this example, I've included several kinds of URLs: HTTP, Telnet, electronic mail, Gopher, and Usenet news. Notice how the URLs are enclosed within <A HREF="URL">HOTSPOT</A> markers, where HOTSPOT is the part of the displayed text that will be highlighted in the displayed hypertext. Figure 14.3 shows how this HTML file is displayed in a Web browser. All the items marked labels between < and > are used to interpret the document for display.

```
<HTML>
    <HEAD>
    <TITLE>
        Telecommunications Resources
    </TITLE>
    </HEAD>
    <BODY>
    <H1>Selected Telecommunications Resources</H1>
    <HR>
    <UL>
<LI><A HREF="http://gozer.idbsu.edu/business/nethome.html">DELTA</A> Distributed
ELectronic Telecommunications Archive-teaching and learning about business
telecommunications and data
                communications
            <LI><A HREF="telnet://ntiabbs.ntia.doc.gov">NTIA</A>
    National Telecommunications and Information Administration (USA) <LI><A
HREF="ftp://ftp.ctr.columbia.edu/CTR-Research">Center for Telecommunications
Research</A> Columbia University,
                New York, NY
<LI>RITIM-L: Research Institute for Telecommunications and
                Information Marketing discussion list:
<A HREF="mailto:listserv@uriacc.uri.edu">Send email to listserv@uriacc.uri.edu, with
the Body: "sub RITIM-L YOUR NAME"</A>
<LI><A HREF="gopher://info.itu.ch">ITU</A> International Telecommunication Union, a
United Nations agency which coordinates telecommunications
<LI><A HREF="news:comp.dcom.telecom">The Usenet newsgroup
                comp.dcom.telecom</A>
    </UL>
    <HR>
<ADDRESS><A HREF="http://www.rpi.edu/~decemj/index.html">John December</A> (<A
HREF="mailto:decemj@rpi.edu">decemj@rpi.edu</A>) / 11 Feb 1995
    </ADDRESS>
    </BODY>
</HTML>
```

TIP

Since a URL is widely recognized as a standard way to refer to an Internet resource, you might use a URL as a resource descriptor in non-Web settings. For example, in citing a source in a bibliography, you can list the URL for the source if it has an online equivalent (or only an online version). For example:

Polly, Jean Armour. (1993, May 15). "Surfing the Internet: an Introduction." URL (ftp://nysernet.org/pub/resources/guides/surfing.2.0.3.txt).

If you have a Web home page, you might list its URL on your business card along with other telecommunications identifiers such as this:

Phone: (518)555-1212

E-mail: smith@foo.edu

Web: http://www.foo.edu/~smith/index.html

FIGURE 14.4.

Browser display of Selected Telecommunications Resources file.

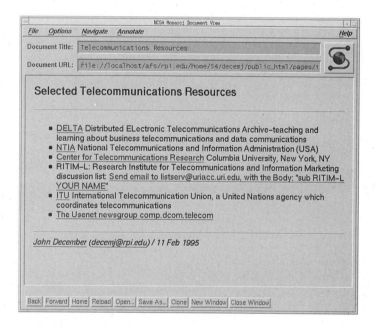

Navigator's Check

Your challenge as a Web navigator is to understand the topology of cyberspace and the way the Web links resources. With this knowledge, you can begin to gain skills using a Web browser and learn tools and techniques for navigation. Eventually, you will be able to use the Web to find useful information.

As a Web navigator, you'll need to remember the following:

- The Web is "located" on the Internet, and the Internet is just one of the networks in global cyberspace.
- The Web is a system for linking the vast resources of the Internet together through hypertext.
- The Uniform Resource Locator (URL) is the basis for Web references.

You can envision the Web as the glue that holds together many different kinds of Internet resources. These resources might be information services, multimedia documents, or other Web documents that in turn contain links to other resources. The power of the Web lies in the possibilities that its hypertext language, HTML, offers for providing expressive ways to present, organize, and link multimedia information distributed globally.

Browser Operations

15

by
John December

After you have a Web browser installed on your computer (as explained in Part II, "Web Browsers and Connections,") and have an idea of the general layout of cyberspace and the Web (explained in the previous chapter), the next step for you as a Web navigator is to learn to use the functions offered by your Web browser for navigation.

There are many browsers available to navigate the Web, offering graphical as well as text interfaces (as shown extensively in Part II). This chapter focuses on the commonalities and functions that many Web browsers offer and how these functions help you navigate the Web. This chapter surveys the needs of Web navigators and then explores the key browser operations of two popular graphical Web browsers—Netscape and Mosaic—as models.

A Web Navigator's Hierarchy of Needs

Whenever you navigate the Web using a browser, there will be many essentials you *must* have (like the ability to view documents and active links in hypertext). You'll also *want* an additional set of functions in a browser, such as a way to record items in a hotlist or having other access to charting features. These functions might not be essential for viewing the Web, but could be very useful for effective navigation. Finally, there are a range of functions that would be *nice* to have— for example, ways for you to change fonts and set other preferences in the browser. These "deluxe" functions can help make your journeys through the Web more enjoyable.

A Web navigator's needs, then, encompass a series of activities that can be arranged from the lower-level survival needs to the luxuries of Web navigation. This progression of needs, because it is arranged with the most basic needs first, often reflects a possible training sequence for a Web navigator who is learning how to use the Web for the first time. An experienced Web navigator (trained perhaps in another form of graphical Web browser) will often be able to very quickly adapt to a new Web browser (as long as the navigation functions previously learned are not "negative learning"—that is, actions that produce unexpected results in the new browser). This hierarchy of needs also might serve as a list of evaluation points that you can use to examine or evaluate a new Web browser.

The following subsections trace through a Web navigator's hierarchy of needs, highlighting how these needs are met by Web browser features (using Netscape and/or Mosaic as examples in some cases). This hierarchy of Web navigators' needs consists of seven levels:

1. Information display
2. Link activation
3. Movement
4. Information control
5. Interactivity
6. Options and feedback
7. Web actualization

Information Display

A Web browser's most essential function is to provide a visual, aural, or other sensory representation of a Web document, Net information file, or service to the user. When activated, either at the time the Web browser is started on the user's computer or as a result of the user selecting a network location, a Web browser displays information. For example, Figure 15.1 shows the information display in a Netscape (for X Window System) browser.

FIGURE 15.1.

An information display in the Netscape (for X) browser.

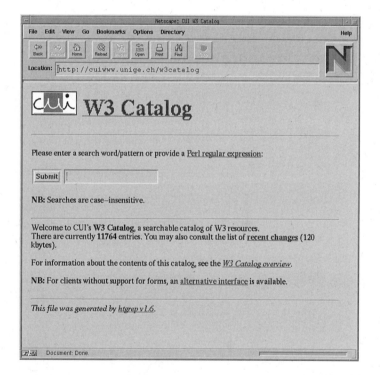

For the display in the Netscape browser, this page representation uses X Window System graphics to give visual information to the user. This information can also be in the form of ASCII characters (such as seen previously in Part II with Lynx or the CERN line-mode browser) or with other graphical variations (Netscape, Mosaic, Cello, and Prodigy's browser, for example). In all cases, though, the browser interprets the HTML (or other information format) so that the user can experience it. For sound, movies, graphics, or other sensory stimuli, the browser's connection to helper applications (see Part II) should call the proper multimedia player into action for appropriate sensory display.

Despite the potential that these multimedia communications can bring to the Web, the most popular form of communication on the Web remains visual, in the form of text and graphics. The elements of the visual displays of information include the following:

- The *text of the resource* (if any) will be displayed on the user's terminal or on a graphical area of the browser. In Figure 15.1, the display area is below and set off from the *control area* (that part of the browser that consists of user-selectable functions and options) of the browser. Other graphical browsers take a similar approach, often placing control areas just above the display window of the browser. (See Figure 15.2.)

FIGURE 15.2.

Arrangement of control and information features in browsers.

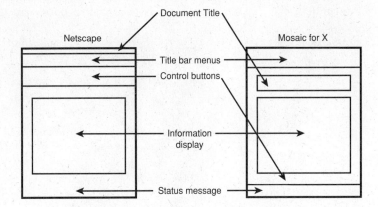

The *display area* is the part of the information display that changes, whereas the control area remains constant. In text-based browsers, the control functions accessible by the user are often keyboard commands; so an elaborate visual reminder of the options is not always in view of the user.

- The *hyperlinks* (if any) exist within the text of the resource. These hyperlinks are linked to other information, spaces, or services, and are indicated by hotspots within the text. Browsers identify these hotspots in a variety of ways—reverse-video, underlines, numbering schemes, or other markings or symbols to indicate the presence of a hypertext jump a user can select. For example, Figure 15.3 shows how hyperlinks are represented in CERN's line-mode browser. Each hotspot in the document is marked with a number in brackets.

FIGURE 15.3.

CERN's line-mode browser display showing numbering hotspots.

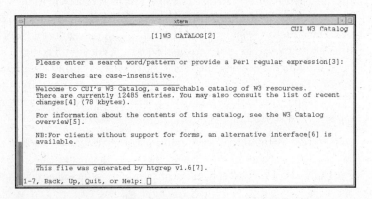

Representation of hotspots can also include graphical variations, such as shading, which indicate that the user has previously visited a resource.

■ *Special browser-provided symbols* for special features such as unloaded images or unloadable images (in the case of non-graphical browsers). These include, for example, the symbol that the Mosaic browser uses to show the presence of an inline image in a document that has not been reloaded (see Figure 15.14). Similarly, other graphic browsers, such as Netscape, display special symbols for unloaded inline images. For non-graphical browsers, inline images, of course, cannot be displayed. A non-graphical browser can, however, display a string of characters that the information provider defines within the HTML of the resource (using the ALT field of the IMG tag—see Part V, "Weaving a Web"). The non-graphical browser displays this character string instead of the image.

These visual elements—text, hyperlinks, and special symbols—are the fundamental needs for a Web navigator. The need for information display is the most basic need a Web navigator has. The information displayed is used to convey a universe of meaning on the Web—through text, graphics, symbols, and other hypermedia.

Link Activation

Although the display of information is a Web navigator's most basic need, without link activation—the ability to activate a hyperlink so that the browser displays the resource to which the link refers—the Web would not be a web at all, but just a set of information pages located on servers. Associative linking is the key to the unique way the Web helps people create meaning, and the ability to traverse these links is the next level in the hierarchy of needs for a Web navigator.

The fundamental idea of link activation is that a user can select one of the hyperlinks (if any) in the information display. This selection causes the browser to retrieve the resource specified by the selected link. This resource might be another document, an information service, a picture, a sound, or some other sensory stimulus. Once the user selects the link, of course, the resource must be retrieved (possibly from the user's own computer or possibly from a server on the Internet located across the world). After a resource is retrieved, a user's needs shift back to information display (as discussed previously).

There are a variety of ways a Web navigator can activate a hyperlink, and these ways vary according to the Web browser used. Graphical browsers usually employ a mouse-based scheme of point-and-click selection. For nongraphical browsers, keyboard commands or number selection (as shown in Figure 15.3) are frequently used. The essence of link activation involves a transaction between the user and the Web browser: Based on experiencing the information display, the user chooses a hyperlink to follow and conveys that choice to the browser. This process of viewing, choice, and link activation is the essence of Web navigation.

Movement

The first two categories of needs for a Web navigator—information display and link activation—could, theoretically, provide a Web navigator with all she or he needs to experience the Web. By following the links on the default home page of his or her browser, a Web navigator could follow links until reaching a "dead end"—that is, until a resource that has no hyperlinks is displayed in the browser. Without the ability of movement, however, a Web navigator, upon reaching such a dead end, would have to exit the browser and start all over to follow a different path! It would be possible to navigate the Web with this scheme, but it would be very unpleasant.

Movement, then, is the next level of Web navigators' needs. *Movement* is the ability to select a link from a set of previously visited resources or to move directly to a particular resource. Movement is key for a Web navigator to make good use of the Web and enables a Web navigator to be more flexible in following paths.

The most basic movement function is *back*. This function enables the user to reselect the resource that was displayed in the browser before the most recent link activation. The back function helps a user retrace his or her steps after reaching a dead end on the Web. Although this might seem to be a very simple procedure, a browser has to have a "memory" in order to support a back function, storing the URL of the currently displayed resource when the user chooses to activate a link. The capability to repeat the back function multiple times requires the browser to store a stack of previously visited locations. For the Mosaic and Netscape browsers, storing these locations from a nonlinear traversal of the Web into a linear data structure (stack) requires an algorithm that involves recording only certain past paths in the Web.

Another basic movement function is to *open* an arbitrary URL. Although a very popular way to view the Web is to make selections only from the available set of hyperlinks in the browser's information display, a user might want to go to a particular place on the Web. Without an open function to enable this, a Web navigator would be doomed to wander through only that portion of the Web connected to where he or she happened to have started. Theoretically, the entire global Web eventually can become connected through spiders (Chapter 19, "Spiders and Indexes: Keyword—Oriented Searching") and trees (Chapter 18, "Trees: Subject-Oriented Searching"), but it is possible for *floating islands* of hypertext to exist in the Web that are not listed in any spider database or Web tree, nor are connected via a link to any page of hypertext that is listed in the popular spiders or trees.

Although not as crucial as the back and open functions, a Web navigator often needs a *forward* function (implemented often in browsers for symmetry and completeness). A forward function enables the user to revisit resources that have been backed over from the operation of a back function. Figure 15.4 summarizes the back and forward relationships.

FIGURE 15.4.

Forward and back movement functions.

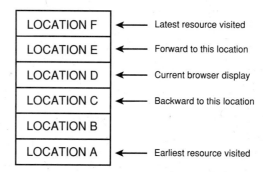

The key to using the back and forward functions with any particular browser is understanding the algorithm used to fill and flush the browser's memory stack that holds these locations. The user's experience of the Web could be (and most often would be) nonlinear, but most browsers use a linear stack method for storing locations in memory. (See the discussion of the "nipping" phenomenon in the section titled "Using Your Browser.")

Information Control

The navigator's needs discussed so far could give a Web navigator just about all the functionality he or she needs to encounter the Web fairly well. However, a Web navigator often desires a higher layer of needs that is related to the ability to control information. These information control needs arise from the imperfect nature of the Web. If network connections never failed, retrieval of data across the network was nearly instantaneous, and all Web pages were designed well, these information control needs would never arise. But the Web isn't perfect, so the Web navigator has to have ways to control information.

First, a Web user needs to be able to stop network information retrieval. Network information retrieval occurs when a user selects a hyperlink referring to a resource on a remote host. If that remote host is not operating, the browser will often *hang*—and keep trying and trying to retrieve the resource. Or, if the resource is huge, the browser will keep working away, retrieving the resource byte by byte. Unchecked, these retrieval processes could take a very long time and waste a great deal of network bandwidth. Faced with such a situation, a navigator needs to be able to request the browser to stop the retrieval. In Mosaic, the famous *spinning globe* serves this function. In Netscape, the stop sign icon does this. (Alternatively hitting Netscape's logo will stop this, but this action will send you to the browser manufacturer's [Netscape's] home page.) Nongraphical browsers sometimes have control sequences to enable this (the keyboard commands Ctrl+C or Ctrl+Q, for example).

Without the stop function built into a browser, a navigator's only alternative might be to kill the browser itself—either forcing a shutdown (killing its process on a UNIX workstation, for example) or completely powering down the system (or disconnecting the network connection). Without a stop function, the resource might eventually be retrieved or an error message returned, but the cost in terms of user time, bandwidth, and user frustration makes the stop function an important part of a navigator's needs.

Another information control need is related to the idea of stopping network information retrieval. This is the ability to control image loading. Controlling image loading is only an issue, of course, in graphical browsers, but it is closely related to the need for stopping network information retrieval. In most graphical browsers—such as Mosaic and Netscape—turning image loading off involves making a selection from the user controls of the browser. Once done, all inline images will be represented by an unloaded image symbol. By being able to control image loading, a navigator can avoid situations in which massive amounts of inline images are used on Web pages. Large amounts of inline images on a Web page can be as potentially crippling as a massive resource retrieved from a remote site. Unfortunately, the practice of including many inline images on a page is not uncommon on the Web. Therefore, the ability to turn these inline images off for more efficient Web navigation and specialized techniques such as surfing (see Chapter 21, "Surfing: Finding the New and Unusual") is crucial.

Just as the stop and turn-off-images functions are key to a Web navigator's ability to control the information, so too is the ability to make use of a (possibly large) resource displayed in a browser's information display. The Find function enables a user to search for character strings or patterns within the document text currently displayed in the Web browser. This find function often works similarly to functions found in word processors to search for the occurrence of a string in a document. Without this find function for a browser, a Web navigator must visually search for a string or keyword of interest in a document. Such a search is possible, but it also can be extremely laborious in long documents.

Interactivity

The next series of navigator needs starts to lean toward the nice-to-have category. The first of these is interactivity.

Interactivity includes the ability of the user to transmit specific information (beyond information about link activation choice) to a Web server or information provider. Interactivity includes a Web browser's capability to support the interactive Forms feature of HTML, imagemapping, as and electronic mail or other communication links among people or information services.

Forms enable a user to enter a response or select an option using interfaces designed through HTML. (See Part V on creating Forms; see Part IV for other examples of Forms.) Figure 15.5 shows a Forms interface to the CUI W3 Catalog, a useful place for looking up items on the Web. The user can enter a keyword or expression in the box. After the user selects the Submit button, a series of operations defined by the particular search engine used in the Form is activated to serve the user's response. Figure 15.5 shows the response to the search for the string cats in the W3 Catalog's database.

FIGURE 15.5.

An example of a Forms result.

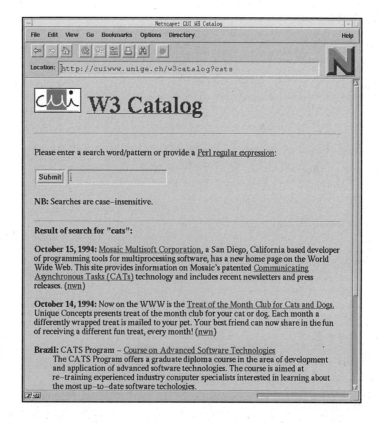

The interactivity enabled by Forms goes above and beyond the possibility for making selections from a given set of hyperlinks in a document. The example of Forms shown in the CUI W3 Catalog is a very powerful example of how effective forms can be in navigation. Not all Web browsers support Forms interfaces, but most new Web browsers nearly universally do (such as Mosaic and Netscape).

Another kind of interactivity is electronic mail. First, there are hyperlinks within displayed HTML documents that include URLs starting with mailto. When selected in a browser such as Netscape, a mailto link causes a pop-up window to appear. The example shown in Figure 15.6 results from selecting a hotspot containing the URL mailto:decemj@rpi.edu from within a document displayed in the browser.

FIGURE 15.6.

*An electronic mail session
(Netscape for X).*

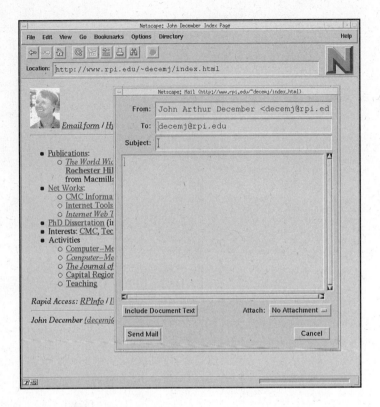

In nongraphical browsers such as Lynx, a text-based e-mail session results from selecting a `mailto` URL link. Mail links such as these can play a major role in fostering contact with other people on the Web, because they enable a seamless way to enter an electronic mail session—directly as a result of a hyperlink activation.

Another set of needs that are part of the interactivity category are security and privacy. A user's selections of what information to encounter on particular servers could become known. One way this could be done is as a result of the Web server software. Another is through people snooping in on the flow of data traffic through the network. If a user is not too concerned that others may discover what they view on the Web, though, this might not be much of an issue. Identifying which users access what pages on a server is not universally done, but some users might be sensitive to this.

Forms represent very large privacy and security issues for users. First, the Forms themselves often ask for very private personal or financial information (for example, credit card numbers). Security methods (such as encryption) might ensure the safer traversal of such information across the network. Users should always use caution, particularly when using insecure Forms. Systems for higher levels of security on the Web are evolving. Integrating these systems into browsers (visual schemes for security verifications such as in Netscape), as well as the explicit use of encryption methods, are what the user concerned with security and privacy should look for in browsers.

Options and Feedback

Although not essential for the navigation of the Web, options and feedback provide the user with a way to be more efficient and to customize the Web browser to his or her set of preferences. Options and feedback needs include a variety of features. First, we'll look at some basic options and feedback needs that most browsers support; then we'll look at some more esoteric options.

■ **Display options**

A Web navigator can move very efficiently if a Web browser readily displays the following information:

The Current Location URL: In graphical browsers, this is often displayed in a window labeled "Document URL" or "Location."

Hotspot URL: The user can view the complete URL of any particular hotspot in the browser display (usually in the status message area). This is an extremely useful capability for helping the user "look before leaping" into a resource. In graphical browsers, the user can usually do this by passing the cursor over the hotspot, causing the URL of the resource to be displayed in a message area of the browser. In some browsers (such as an e-mail Web browser, for example), the complete URL of each hotspot is displayed as a result of information retrieval.

Network retrieval status: Some indication of "what's going on" with regard to resource retrieval. For Mosaic, the spinning globe, in addition to a status message, accomplishes this. Netscape has an animated logo and also a status-line message.

■ **Navigation aids**

Hotlist (also called bookmarks): The ability to record resource locations on a list that is saved on the user's storage area or disk from session to session. The hotlist is the most effective way for a Web navigator to quickly record great finds on the Web. Most browsers support hostlists (such as Mosaic, Netscape, and Lynx), but public-access Web browsers (such as the agora@mail.w3.org e-mail browser or the telnet.w3.org access browser) cannot support such a list because the user doesn't have personal storage space from session to session.

Session history: This aid enables the user to access the history list used with the back and forward functions. This can help the user get back to somewhere he or she has been during the current session, without having to retrace steps or repeatedly select the back function.

Built-in directories: These are a set of hard-coded links available as selections within the controls of a particular Web browser. These built-in directories include quick links to Web pages. Often these pages are supplied by the browser manufacturer. (For example, Netscape's What's Cool button takes the user to a Netscape-supplied Web page.)

Annotations: Enables a user to create a message in text, audio, or some other medium that can be associated (in the user's browser) with a particular resource.

This annotation capability was included in Mosaic but never seemed to catch on among users. Netscape has an annotation option within its bookmark management system.

File management: this includes the full range of printing and saving files, opening local files, and reloading files.

■ **Visual aids**

Font changes: The user should be able to select the size (and often the style) of font for the display of text information. This is useful particularly for poor screen resolution (or less-than-perfect eyesight!).

Display refresh: The Web browser's graphical display might become corrupted because of a window overlap or some other problem. A "refresh" function enables the user to redisplay the browser without re-initiating the network information retrieval or reloading the current document.

Color changes: Options may be implemented in future browsers to enable a user to change the default background color (or link color).

Web Actualization

Not every Web browser is perfect. Every Web browser should meet the critical navigation needs, as outlined previously, for users. The aforementioned six categories of Web navigators' needs—for information display, link activation, movement, information control, interactivity, and options and feedback—might suffice to give the user all that he or she needs to navigate the Web well. However, Web navigators have a higher need to become so adept with their browser that they can seamlessly observe the vast panoply of networked information on the Web. Any Web browser is an interface, and as such, it may help or hinder, hide or obscure, or trivialize or exalt the world of the Web.

With an ideal browser, a user would feel that nothing intervened between himself or herself and the Web. In order to accomplish this, the user must be trained well in navigation techniques for the particular browser, as well as in general Web tools and techniques. (See the other chapters in this part of the book.) The browser, too, must have an inherently good design; otherwise, even the most adept users would grow impatient with it. Similar to the emergence of standard applications in word-processing software, so too will there probably emerge standard Web browsers whose interface will most elegantly and lucidly meet user needs. A well-designed Web browser is the essential first step in the process for a user to navigate the content of the Web.

Using Your Browser

Now that we've looked at a list of the needs of Web navigators, let's look in detail at how you might typically use your browser. Although there is no standard way to use a browser, here are some general guidelines:

- **Keep aware of all indicators.** You want to watch your browser carefully, particularly Mosaic's globe or Netscape's animated logo and the status-message line. Watch for these conditions: an endlessly spinning globe or an endlessly throbbing N, which could indicate that a network connection has hung (or is not presently reachable). Look at the status line to see what is happening. If the globe is spinning quickly, this usually indicates a good situation; that is, Mosaic is quickly retrieving the information you are seeking from the network.

  Huge files: If the globe keeps spinning and the status message line reports something like this:

  ```
  Read 1024 of 38000999000 bytes of data.
  ```

  you know you are going to be waiting a long time for that resource to come up. Consider clicking the spinning globe or the stop sign.

  Total freeze-up: If the globe is not spinning and the N is not throbbing, there is no message status line, and you can't get a response by clicking anything on the main panel, you should wait just a bit longer. For very large files, a browser needs some time to load the file in local memory (in which case the indicators would have stopped to signal the end of network data retrieval). If after a period of time (like 2-5 minutes) the browser still seems frozen, you should consider trying to close the browser window or killing the process running the browser. (You'll need some UNIX skill for this.)

- **Expect problems.** The nature of the Internet is that it is cooperative, vast, and complex. (See the sidebar later in this chapter titled "Top 10 Things to Keep in Mind When Navigating the Web.") As such, not all of the computer hosts that hold resources will be up and operating all the time. Also, machine names, resource names, and other identifiers that make up a URL can change. Therefore, you might run into situations in which you have a "stale" URL (one that no longer resolves to a resource). You also might have typed a URL incorrectly.

  The URL you click might not be to an existing resource. You will quickly find this out through an error message in Mosaic's display window, something such as

  ```
  404 Not Found
  The requested URL /foo.html was not found on this server.
  ```

  You either have a bad URL (recheck your typing if you entered it directly through the Open option) or the URL is no longer valid (has gone stale).

  The host name in the URL might no longer exist or is temporarily down. You'll see a message like the following:

  ```
  ERROR
  Requested document (URL http://foo.bar.com/foo.html) could not be accessed.
  ```

  The information server either might be not accessible or might refuse to serve the document to you. The host and document might exist, but there is some problem with file permissions of the document itself.

```
ERROR
Requested document (URL http://pass.wayne.edu/foo.html)
could not be accessed.
```

To deal with the these problems, the best things to do are the following:

1. Check the URL again to make sure there were no typographical errors if you had typed the URL in yourself.

2. Wait a bit; it might be that network connections or a host is temporarily down. Try again in an hour or a day.

3. Use spider searches (covered in Chapter 19) to try to locate the resource. Perform searches for portions of the URL or the title of the resource.

4. If you know the maintainer of the information, check to see if he or she knows the status of the resource.

■ **Use the Window History.** As mentioned in the previous list of browser operations, the Back and Forward buttons take you along the last encountered path through the Web during your current browser session. One way to help keep track of where you are in the window history is to use the Navigate | Window History... option to bring up the window history. Position this window on your display so that it doesn't overlap the browser main panel. It will stay up and help you keep track of where you have been. Remember, the window history is dynamic (unlike the global history file that serves as a complete record of your Web visits from session to session). The window history file will lose and gain items as you navigate the Web and contain entries only from your current session. For example, if you are currently in resource A and you follow a link in it to resource B, your history list will read

A
B

Then, if you take a link from resource B to resource C, your window history will be

A
B
C

Now if you go back to resource B (using the Back button) and then, instead of taking the link from resource B to C, you take another link to resource D, your history list will read

A
B
D

Resource C has been *nipped* from your window history list; it will be unreachable via the Back and Forward buttons. This is not too serious (because you can revisit C from a link in resource B), but keep in mind that this nipping can delete a whole branch of your voyage. Let's say that your window history lists reads

E

F

G

H

I

J

K

L

M

and you are presently in M. Suppose that you use your window history list to quickly go to resource F. You can do this by double-clicking the entry for resource F in the window history list. (You also could have gone to F from M by clicking the Back button seven times.) Now, let's say that at resource F, there's another link—to X—and you take it instead of selecting link G.

Your history list will then read

E

F

X

Everything from G, H, I, J, K, L, and M has been nipped off. This is no real problem, because you can certainly revisit G, H, I, and so on, but you won't be able to use the Forward button to do it from resource F.

■ **Act responsibly.** Your access to free, available resources on the Web depends on the thousands of people who invest their time, energy, and money providing information and maintaining machines. Don't abuse this tradition of shared gifts by overloading the network or repeatedly obtaining huge graphics or movie files, for example.

Remember, however, that you should feel free to explore. Web browsers work very efficiently. Most work in a connectionless fashion, by obtaining the resource you request by using the network connections and then *stopping*. For example, when you are at a particular site (you have opened a URL referring to a resource at that site), after the resource has been obtained over the network, you are not using time on that remote host. When Mosaic's globe has stopped spinning and Netscape's N has stopped throbbing, you are not using network bandwidth to retrieve information, so you can feel free to take your time to examine the information you have obtained. In fact, it is best to carefully look at what you obtain, so that you can best utilize the resources you are accessing without needlessly obtaining something you don't need.

■ **You'll encounter new things.** Advances in HTML and Web browsers will bring new kinds of interaction to your screen. Mosaic and Netscape support a capability called Forms that not all Web browsers support. With Forms, you can enter information into boxes and select controls (like buttons and checkboxes) that are similar to the controls in Mosaic. You'll find that the graphical user interface in Forms is very intuitive. Netscape supports the display of specialized HTML features such as BLINK. (See Part V.)

TOP 10 THINGS TO KEEP IN MIND WHEN NAVIGATING THE WEB

1. **Traffic may be heavy.** People are using the Internet and Web in increasing numbers, and popular Web servers can receive a very large number of *hits,* or browser accesses. When a Web server becomes overloaded, it may take you a very long time to retrieve a resource from it, or you might not be able to retrieve the resource at all (you'll get an error message instead).

   Web prime time for a server is typically during weekdays from 9 a.m. to 5 p.m. local time (business hours). Because of the large concentration of Web users and resources in eastern North America, the entire Internet and Web experiences heavy traffic during prime time for North America's Eastern Time zone. Some servers provide statistics or graphs showing their prime time. You can use these statistics to plan for the best time for you to access resources on a server.

2. **Servers can go down.** Web servers and the networks they use are subject to all the foibles of machines. Scheduled maintenance, unplanned hardware failures, and other unusual circumstances can all temporarily (or permanently) take a server offline. The most common reason for a server to go offline is for scheduled maintenance or for unscheduled bugs. A server experiencing very heavy traffic can also begin to *thrash* and slow down so much that it is essentially offline.

3. **The Net can go down.** Originally designed to withstand nuclear attack, the Internet is very robust, and can often survive earthquakes and natural disasters. The Net is still vulnerable to interruptions and service outages—particularly at the local network level (where a single "wire" may be the only bridge between a local area network and the larger Net).

4. **Resource names can change.** A good web designer should create a stable server name and use a stable, extensible system of filenames for resources he or she provides on the Web. (See Part V.) However, people developing Web resources sometimes must change server names or filenames. When this happens, the URL you have been using to access your favorite resource might no longer work. (A good information provider will provide a "file moved" pointer, but you might not get that.) If the filename changes, you might be able to use a shorter form of the URL to find the resource; for example, if the resource was at the URL

   ```
   http://www.foo.edu/~chris/projects/start/home.html
   ```

   and if this URL no longer works, you might try

   ```
   http://www.foo.edu/~chris/projects/
   ```

   or

   ```
   http://www.foo.edu/~chris/
   ```

   or even

   ```
   http://www.foo.edu/
   ```

to try to find the resource you were using.

If the Web server's name changes, you might consider looking up the server in the registry of servers at

```
http://www.w3.org/hypertext/DataSources/WWW/Servers.html
```

5. **Resources can disappear.** The dynamic nature of information on the Web means that things change often. Web information or resources can disappear for a variety of reasons. The person who was providing the resource might no longer have an account or might have moved. The resource might have gone out of date, and the information provider might have decided to discontinue it (delete it from the system). A good information provider should provide some helpful pointer if this happens. However, on the Web, nothing lasts forever.

6. **Resources can be HUGE.** A fundamental principle of good Web design (see Part V) is that you should never create resources that involve information transfers of gargantuan proportions. However, an extremely large file size may be unavoidable —for a large movie or graphics, for example. As a result, be wary of transfers that take an extremely large time, and be aware that these transfer times can be truly great in some cases. If you are paying by the minute for access to the Web, use judgment about what kinds of resources you choose to encounter. (You might want to avoid movie archives, for example.)

7. **Links can "break."** In conjunction with file and server names changing, links within documents can go stale (no longer be valid), and thus the hyperlinks in the web will break and no longer take you anywhere. This happens when a hotspot within a Web document includes a URL to a resource whose location has changed or that is temporarily or permanently unavailable. Therefore, within hypertext, expect stale links. Common places for links to grow stale include the archives of time-dependent information, such as the archives of a magazine or a what's-new service. When the developers of this information created the text, the links may have worked; but as time goes by, links on the Web inevitably go stale.

8. **Your senses might get overloaded.** The Web is an electronic feast, and you (or your equipment) can get sick consuming it. The Web's storehouse of text, images, sounds, movies, and information can easily overload the attention capacity of someone not used to encountering large amounts of networked information. At the same time, your Web browser, along with its associated helper applications, can often experience problems because of overloaded memory, unusual multimedia formats, or extremely large files. Your browser will crash sometimes, or your helper applications might not work.

9. **You may be shocked (or bored).** The Web isn't tame. You'll find text, images, and movies on the Web that will shock, provoke, or outrage you. You also might be astonished at the banality of some Web resources. Keep in mind that humans

are behind all the resources on the Web—humans have a tendency to sometimes be outrageous, say what they want, or intentionally try to shock others. You can see some amazing examples of "useless" Web pages at URL `http://www.primus.com/ staff/paulp/useless.htm`, Paul Phillips's collection of "America's Funniest Home Hypermedia."

10. **There might be typos!** If you encounter a URL in a printed publication, be wary. Typos often occur when a URL is transported from one medium to another. For example, a URL might be copied incorrectly by hand from a browser display onto paper. Transmitting a URL by voice is notoriously unreliable, particularly because of the difficulty in pronouncing sequences such as `://` and the long series of characters in a URL. Paper outlets for mass media often mangle a URL or a network address because editors may not understand the meaning of symbols such as @ or ~. An editor may translate an e-mail address like `president@whitehouse.gov` to `president.AT.whitehouse.gov` in print. The tilde (~) used in a URL also often gives editors and typesetters problems.

Techniques and Tips

After you've become familiar with operations that you can perform with your browser, the next step in navigating is to put these elements together to navigate well. This section lists specific tips and techniques for using your browser to increase your skills and develop your intuition into how to navigate the Web.

Interpret URLs

The URL given in the window near the top of Mosaic or at the Status Message area on the front panel can tell you many things about the resource to which it refers:

■ The URL can tell you what protocol was used to access the resource across the network. (See the discussion of URLs in Chapter 14, "Web Structures and Spaces.")

An example of when you might want to find URLs using a specific access method is when you want to find only Gopher resources about telecommunications. Therefore, you would want to watch out for Gopher resources by looking at the start of the URLs of the resources you encounter.

Table 15.1 can help you identify the protocol of the URL. We'll talk more about how each of these protocols operates in detail in the next chapter.

Table 15.1. Popular protocols.

Protocol	Name/Description
HTTP	Hypertext transfer protocol; you can expect to find HTML files and possibly other kinds of files at this URL. (Examine the filename ending for more clues.)
FTP	File transfer protocol; you can expect to find files and directories of files at an FTP site.
news	Usenet newsgroup, which indicates a series of postings (articles contributed by people discussing a particular topic, or newsgroup).
Telnet	Remote login; you can expect a pop-up window to appear that will (possibly) ask you for a login name and a password for entry to an information system. Typically, these information systems consist of menus and choices and are sometimes called bulletin board systems (BBSs).
Gopher	Gopher information (menu system); you can expect a series of menus and choices. You will be able to select menu items to reach other resources.
WAIS	Wide Area Information Server; a system of indexed databases.
mailto	Electronic mail; a link to an application that enables you to compose a message to be sent to an address via electronic mail. For browsers like Netscape, this e-mail application is built into the browser. Other browsers (like Mosaic) don't recognize URLs with this prefix.

For example, the URL `http://www.ncsa.uiuc.edu/demoweb/url-primer.html` uses the hypertext transfer protocol, which is the native protocol of the Web.

■ The URL can often tell you the format of the resource.

The URL `http://www.ncsa.uiuc.edu/demoweb/url-primer.html` has an ending of `.html`, which indicates an HTML document. (See Table 15.2 for a list of popular file and URL endings.)

Table 15.2. Popular file and URL endings.

Ending	Name
.html	HTML file (hypertext).
.ps	PostScript; "pretty printed" text with fonts and graphics.
.txt	Text.

continues

Table 15.2. continued

Ending	Name
`.tex`	TeX or LaTex; typesetting languages using a system of tags.
`?string`	The `?` indicates that this URL pointed to a query (a way of finding string within a document).
`#anchor`	This is a URL that points to an anchor (a specific place) within the document.

The file endings in combination with the protocol can give you a clue about what to expect at a given URL. However, these are just clues, not necessarily hard and fast rules, about what you will find. For example, an HTTP server does not always have just HTML files on it; it is possible to have text and other resources on such a server. Also, you can have HTML documents on an FTP or a Gopher server. The key to remember is that the protocol name of the URL and the file ending are clues to help you navigate, and can help you develop intuition about Web resources.

■ The document URL can tell you from what network host you are retrieving the information. This information is important if these things are true:

> You are trying to find a specific network host (in which case you are looking for an exact match in the host name).

> You are looking for a host in a particular geographic region.

> You are trying to find the "nearest" network host, in terms of network transfer speed and volume.

In any of these cases, first you can use the name of the host as a clue about all these concerns.

You can interpret a typical URL:

`http://www.uwm.edu/Mirror/inet.services.html`.

The machine name on which this information resides is `www.uwm.edu`. This name is connected with a particular institution. The last two parts of this name, `uwm.edu`, give a clue about what this institution is. The `edu` part tells that this is an educational institution. The `uwm` part tells that the initials of this university are UWM. If that is not enough to clue you into what university this is, you can use the UNIX `whois` command to find out. In a UNIX window, you can enter:

`whois uwm.edu`

and find out

```
[No name] (WISC-CSD1-MILW) UWM.EDU 129.89.7.2,129.89.6.2
University of Wisconsin, Milwaukee (UWM-DOM) UWM.EDU
```

This tells you that the URL shown in the preceding line is a resource on a machine at the University of Wisconsin at Milwaukee.

Table 15.3 lists a brief selection of the kinds of endings for Internet host names in mostly U.S. domains.

For international and other endings, see the URL `ftp://rtfm.mit.edu/pub/usenet/news.answers/mail/country-codes`.

Table 15.3. Popular Internet domain name endings.

Ending	Description
com	Commercial
edu	Educational
gov	Government
mil	Military
org	Nonprofit organization
net	Network administrative sites

Trying to find the "nearest" network host is a bit more complicated, and beginning or intermediate users might use a geographical rule of thumb for finding a machine that is closest, in network terms, to their own. This need arises in situations in which you are using a resource that might require a large amount of data transfer. To make this transfer easiest on the network and on yourself, you might find the machine that is closest to your own in terms of the network.

Naturally, those machines that are geographically close often are the best choice for connections, particularly when your choices are either a machine across the world or one across the street. However, this is not always the case because of the nature of the network topology and connections between your host and your target host.

Moreover, you might want to sometimes use a distant host in order to take advantage of off-peak usage of a machine. For example, if you are in New York and the current time is 11:52 a.m. on Saturday, it is 1:52 a.m. in the morning on Sunday in Australia—and probably machines in Australia are experiencing less network traffic. In this case, you might want to use an Australian machine rather than one in a busier region, particularly if the resource you are accessing requires a lot of processing by the remote host.

TRICK: FINDING LOCAL TIME

You can find the local time at an Internet domain name by using the UNIX Telnet command to port number 13 of that machine. For example, at the Internet domain `msoe.edu` (Milwaukee School of Engineering in Milwaukee, Wisconsin), the time can be obtained by entering this command at the UNIX window:

```
telnet msoe.edu 13
```

which gives

```
Trying 155.92.10.7 ...
Connected to msoe.edu.
Escape character is '^]'.
11-FEB-1995 19:25:21.66
Connection closed by foreign host.
```

At the domain aarnet.edu.au (Australia)

```
telnet aarnet.edu.au 13,
```

the time is

```
Trying 139.130.204.16 ...
Connected to aarnet.edu.au.
Escape character is '^]'.
Sun Feb 12 12:26:51 1995
Connection closed by foreign host.
```

The thing to remember is that, as a navigator, there are reasons why you might want to identify the institution sponsoring the machine on which a resource resides. You might want to know the machine's geographic location or local time, or the network route to that machine in order to choose the most efficient time or machine for routine or large volume access.

PINGING A REMOTE MACHINE

You might want to use the UNIX ping command to do some probing of the network to find a close machine. The routes to which the data is transferred could change all the time, but this pinging can give you a clue about how close a host is.

For example, from my machine in Troy, New York, I can ping a host in Milwaukee, Wisconsin, by entering this command in a UNIX window:

```
/usr/etc/ping -s uwm.edu
```

I get the output:

```
PING uwm.edu: 56 data bytes
64 bytes from 129.89.7.2: icmp_seq=0. time=856. ms
64 bytes from uwm.edu (129.89.7.2): icmp_seq=2. time=1877. ms
64 bytes from uwm.edu (129.89.7.2): icmp_seq=3. time=1751. ms
```

(I stop this pinging by entering the keyboard sequence Ctrl+C.)

Now if I ping a machine in Ithaca, New York:

```
/usr/etc/ping -s cornell.edu
```

I get the results

```
PING cornell.edu: 56 data bytes
64 bytes from cornell.edu (132.236.56.6): icmp_seq=0. time=92. ms
64 bytes from cornell.edu (132.236.56.6): icmp_seq=1. time=23. ms
64 bytes from cornell.edu (132.236.56.6): icmp_seq=2. time=28. ms
```

This shows me that my test data traveled most quickly back and forth to the Ithaca machine than the Milwaukee machine: 28–92 milliseconds round trip to Ithaca versus 856–1751 milliseconds round trip to Milwaukee.

Use the Hotlist Effectively

The hotlist is one of the most useful features that you will probably use in a browser (In Netscape and Lynx, the hotlist features are called bookmarks; we'll use the term *hotlist* in its generic sense here.) A hotlist gives you a basic means to create your own information library, and is one of the major ways that you'll be able to "record" your favorite spots on the Web. The things to remember about your hotlist are these:

- Your hotlist provides you with the fastest and most reliable way to record a Web location. Using your hotlist does not require cutting or pasting from the document URL window (although you could do this if you wanted to record URLs in a separate file), and there is no hand-copying of the URL onto paper (an unreliable way to record a URL anyway, particularly when it is a long one).

- Your hotlist gives you rapid access to your favorite Web locations. For example, Figure 15.7 shows the top of a hotlist. In the figure, SIMON HOMEPAGE is highlighted, so clicking the Go To button takes the user directly to that resource.

- Your hotlist accumulates until you change it. It is preserved from session to session in a file called .mosaic-hotlist-default (Mosaic) and .MCOM-bookmarks.html (Netscape) in your home directory. You can use the hotlist controls to add and remove items from your hotlist or edit the titles of the entries.

- Some browsers support fairly elaborate ways to manage hotlists. Figure 15.8 shows Netscape's bookmark system. This system includes ways to search your hotlist, divide it into sections, and annotate entries.

FIGURE 15.7.

A sample hotlist (Mosaic for X).

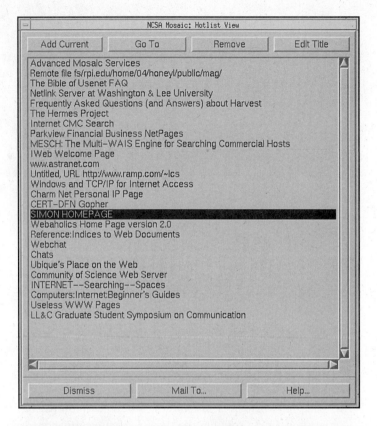

FIGURE 15.8.

Bookmark list (Netscape for X).

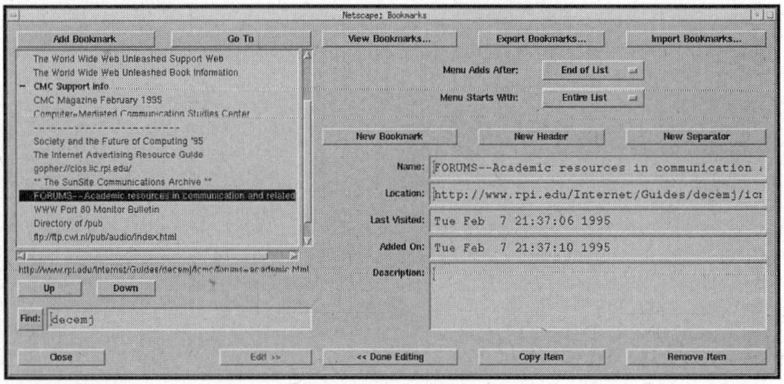

When you enter the currently displayed URL into your hotlist, the title added to the hotlist is the same as that in the <TITLE> text of the HTML file. Sometimes this title isn't descriptive, which is why you might want to consider changing it by using the hotlist management features of your browser.

For example, the entry at the top of the hotlist shown in Figure 15.7 is Advanced Mosaic Services, and isn't very descriptive. To remedy this situation, first use the hotlist facility of your Web browser to go to the entry. In this case, this entry is for a file describing how to implement imagemaps and Forms on the `www.rpi.edu` Web server. Use the edit title facility of your hotlist management system to change the entry to read `How to implement Imagemaps and Forms on www.rpi.edu`. Similarly, the entry in the hotlist reading, `Remote file afs/rpi.edu/home/04/honeyl/ public/mag/` could stand a revision so that the hotlist entry will be more descriptive.

Keep Your Hotlist Clean

Because the hotlist is so useful, you should not hesitate to add a beneficial document onto it. However, you will find that your hotlist can get very crowded. Every once in a while, you should go through your hotlist, rename the items to more meaningful names, and remove stale or unimportant links. Eventually, you'll want to use techniques of weaving your own web to create your own pages containing information about your favorite resources. (See Part V.) You can keeping your hotlist clean by following these general guidelines:

- **Keep junk off of it in the first place.** When you find a resource that you know is going to change or you have no interest in it, avoid placing it on your hotlist. This seems obvious, but new users often feel anxious about where they are within the Web, and the discovery of their hotlist gives them a feeling of being able to chart their way through the Web. This often results in very cluttered hotlists. (A cluttered hotlist might be called a *warmlist;* a totally junked hotlist might be called a *coldlist.*) New users should remember that a window history list is usually available on their browser.

- **Make sure you record "great" finds.** As a converse tip to the preceding one, if you find a resource that seems fantastic, be sure to record it on your hotlist. Sometimes a resource is so amazing, you end up going through it without remembering to put it on your hotlist. You might try to associate any feelings of amazement or excitement with the procedure for adding items to your hotlist. By recording great finds, you'll increase the "temperature" of your hotlist.

- **Transfer the truly great discoveries to another file.** As a matter of routine maintenance, go through your hotlist and record the URLs of critical resources to a separate file. Occasionally, an abnormal exit from a Web browser will corrupt or destroy your hotlist. Because your hotlist should be "hot," make sure that you occasionally back it up so you don't lose critical URLs. At the UNIX prompt, you can do the following:

  ```
  cp .mosaic-hotlist-default hotlist.11feb95
  ```

  or a "color coding" scheme such as:

  ```
  cp .mosaic-hotlist-default hotlist.red
  ```

  and then use a text editor to edit `hotlist.red` to include only your very best finds.

- **Share your hotlist.** There are ways that you can directly mail your hotlist to another person (in Mosaic, by using the Mail To... option on the hotlist pop-up window). There are also utilities to convert your hotlist file into an HTML file, which can then be easily browsed by others.

Use Your Global History

Each browser maintains a transcript of your initial visits to Web sites in a global history file. In Mosaic, this file is named .mosaic-global-history; in Netscape, it is called .MCOM-global-history. The lines with the file are formatted according to a URL and the date when you first visited the given URL. In Mosaic, the global history file

```
http://www.rpi.edu/Internet/Guides/decemj/text.html Sat Jun 25 10:46:08 1994
http://www.rpi.edu/~decemj/cmc/people.html Sat Jun 25 10:46:08 1994
http://bingen.cs.csbsju.edu/~jahoffma/letterman/paul.gif Sat Jun 25 10:46:08 1994
http://nistor.paed.uni-muenchen.de/ Sat Jun 25 10:46:08 1994
```

can give you clues about resources you have visited.

In Netscape, the history file

```
http://www.nd.edu/~mmiller    792374088
http://www.whitehouse.gov/White_House/Family/images/crop/family.gif    792373866
http://www.w3.org/hypertext/WWW/Icons/WWW/ListOfServers.gif    792388044
http://ftp.cac.psu.edu/~saw/genealogy.html    792373330
```

is more bewildering, because the visits aren't logged in a familiar format (showing the month, day, and year). Instead, the log shows entries in an integer code that don't easily translate to a date and time.

In Mosaic, you can see the URL and the time of your first encounter with it. If you visit a URL again, the new time will not be recorded. The global history list also serves as a database that Mosaic uses to shade hotspots you have already visited. This shading often puzzles new users who wonder how a Web browser remembers where they've been.

Use your global history file as another way to answer the question you might have: "I know I visited a really great site yesterday, but I can't remember the URL and I didn't place it on my hotlist." In this case, use a text editor to read your global history file in your home directory. Examine the dates (if possible) and the names of URLs for clues about your lost, great resource.

The global history file grows larger and larger as you visit more URLs, so you occasionally must purge it (or it will expand to fill your disk space!). Purge your global history in Mosaic by choosing Options | Clear Global History.... You will be given a chance to confirm this, and when you exit from Mosaic, the .mosaic-global-history file will be rewritten. In Netscape, use Options | Preferences | Styles | Link Styles to either purge your history file or set the date and time that entries will be purged.

Have a Backup (Terminal-Based) Browser

Although graphical Web browsers like Netscape and Mosaic are fantastic, they require a graphical windowing system to use. You might often find yourself in a situation where you don't have the necessary access to the network to run your graphical browser. In such cases, a navigator should be prepared. Find a line-mode browser (a good example is Lynx), and ask your system administrator to install it on your system or install it yourself. (See Part II.)

A terminal-based browser can work wonders when you are using your dialup account. Indeed, a terminal-based browser can be a quick alternative to Mosaic when you want to look at a file rapidly and you don't care about graphics. For example, the Selected Telecommunications Resources looks like Figure 15.9, as seen in Lynx.

FIGURE 15.9.

A lynx display of Selected Telecommunications Resources.

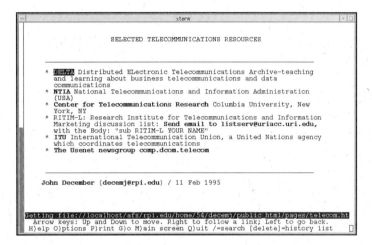

Although the Lynx display does not have all the graphical features of the Mosaic interface, it is a good alternative. You can go through the online Lynx documentation to discover how to use a Lynx hotlist and other similar options that Mosaic offers.

If you don't have a Web browser available and you need access to a Web resource, you can connect, via Telnet, to a Web server. This is generally not a good idea because it drags down the performance of this remote server. However, it may be your only alternative in certain situations. You can find the names of Telnet-accessible Web servers in the Web quick reference on the inside back cover of this book.

For example, you can connect with Telnet to www.njit.edu and login as www to use the New Jersey Institute of Technology's Telnet Web browser. You can also Telnet to telnet.w3.org as a way to access the Web.

If you find yourself on a desert island with no direct Internet access, you can reach the Web if you can reach the Matrix (perhaps through a cellular modem or the Amateur Radio Packet network). See URL http://www.tapr.org/tapr/html/pkthome.html. For information about e-mail access to the Web, send e-mail to agora@mail.w3.org with the message body HELP.

NOTE

Do not routinely use this Telnet access to the Web. Use it only for demonstration or limited purposes, because it degrades the performance of the server machine.

Frequently Encountered Navigation Situations and Their Solutions

A new Web navigator should be familiar with what functions a Web browser offers. Then, the navigator can integrate this knowledge with the tips and techniques given previously to solve common, real-world problems.

Here are some typical situations that you might encounter as a user of a Web browser. Following each situation is a discussion of how you might deal with the problem. These situations start out very simple and increase in complexity.

Situation 1: Your best friend tells you that there is a digital confession booth at `http://anther.learning.cs.cmu.edu/priest.html`.

Solution: Go to your computer, start up your Web browser, and use the Open URL function. Type in the URL of the confession booth and then click the Open button. Ideally (from the data efficiency standpoint, rather than for interpersonal reasons), your friend would have told you this via electronic mail, in which case you could have used a cut-and-paste method to put the URL directly in the URL To Open box. If the URL is transmitted orally, make sure to write it down correctly, and type it in the URL To Open box correctly.

Situation 2: You've just run across a great source, and you want to tell a friend about it.

Solution A: Send e-mail to your friend giving the URL exactly. Use a copy-and-paste technique to paste the URL into the letter.

Solution B: For Mosaic, the File | Mail To... option on Mosaic's front panel (Netscape: File | Mail Document). However, if your friend has a Web browser and the skills to use it, this is a less efficient solution because you are mailing the entire page rather than the reference to it. If your friend does not have a Web browser or the skills to use it, this might be the only alternative to getting the information to him or her.

Solution C (advanced): Put a reference to this resource on your home page, which requires Web weaving skills. (See Part V, "Weaving a Web.") Then tell your friend to open your home page.

Situation 3: You've just pulled up a great resource, a long list of network terms and their definitions. However, you're not looking up a particular term (in which case you could scroll down the alphabetical listing), but you want to see which entries use the `foo`.

Solution: Use File | Find In Current... (Mosaic) or Edit | Find (Netscape) to search for occurrences of `foo`. Use the caseless search option to locate occurrences of `FOO`, `Foo`, or `foo`.

Situation 4: You've absolutely no clue where you are. You're looking at a resource, but you can't remember how you got there or how to get back to a page you were at an hour ago.

Solution A: Bring up your window history file: Navigate | Windows History (Mosaic) or Go | View History (Netscape). Scroll through this list to see if what you want is there. This method is much faster than repeatedly pressing the Back button. Remember, that great page you have in mind might not be on your window history list because of the nipping process described previously. It will, however, be on your global history list. To look at your global history list, exit the Web browser (in order to rewrite the global history file), and then use a text editor to examine the clues about time, resource titles, and URLs.

Solution B (less efficient): Click the Home button, get back to your home page, and try to retrace your steps. This is unlikely to work because you have to trace your steps exactly (or somehow be able to find an alternate route to your lost location).

Situation 5: The URL you've been given to the resource at `http://www.foo.edu/~cookel/style/guide.html` doesn't work; you keep getting the error

`The requested URL /~cookel/style/guide.html was not found on this server.`

Solution A: The information provider might have moved the resource to some other location. Try to access information at a series of shorter versions of the same URL. Try the URL

`http://www.foo.edu/~cookel/style/`

If that doesn't work, try

`http://www.foo.edu/~cookel/`

If that doesn't work, you might not be able to find the resource even at

`http://www.foo.edu/`

because the tilde (~) in the URL before `cookel` is a clue that the information you seek is stored in an individual's account (the user `cookel`). If the URL to that person's "area" on the server, `http://www.foo.edu/~cookel/`, doesn't work, it may be that person no longer has an account. (See solution D for another solution.)

Solution B: Try a spider. Use one of the Web spiders (see Chapter 19) to search for keywords in the title of the resource (if known) or some keywords that identify the information it contains. If a spider has visited the new location of a moved resource, you should be able to find this location in the spider's database. Remember, you can't use the entire original URL as a search term (because it is wrong!), but you can use a portion of it (such as a style or guide), hoping that in its new location it will have a similar name.

Of course, if the resource is no longer anywhere on the Web or if no spider has crawled on the resource, you'll never find it through a spider.

Solution C: Try a tree. Use one of the many subject trees of the Web (see Chapter 18) to try to find the page you were looking for in the subject hierarchies. This would probably only work if the resource you are seeking is a fairly well-established source of information for that area. Personal or very specialized interest pages aren't likely to be listed in major subject trees.

Solution D: Piecing together clues from the URL `http://www.foo.edu/~cookel/style/guide.html`, we can notice that the `~cookel` part of the URL often indicates the login name for a user in a domain. The domain of that user might be `foo.edu` (the first part of the host name minus the `www` part). Therefore, we might try sending e-mail to the user `cookel@foo.edu` and ask if this resource has moved or is no longer available. Before mailing, you should try to finger `cookel@foo.edu` to see if that is actually an account on the `foo.edu` domain.

Navigator's Check

It is the function of every Web browser to meet or exceed a Web navigator's hierarchy of needs. A Web navigator's needs are for information display, link activation, movement, information control, interactivity, options and feedback, and Web actualization. The goal of every Web navigator in encountering a Web browser should be to learn the functions the browser offers to meet these needs.

Learning how to use a Web browser is just the start of a growing expertise a Web navigator accumulates. While navigating the Web, keep in mind the following:

- Your Web browser offers an array of built-in functions to help you navigate within hypertext, search through resources, and store URL references.

- Interpreting URLs can give you excellent insight into the kinds of resources available through hotlinks displayed in the browser.

- Click Mosaic's spinning globe or Netscape's stop sign to cancel network information retrieval. Know the equivalent function to stop network information retrieval on other browser types that you use.

- Use techniques to manage your hotlist, to keep it clean, and to periodically review its contents.

- Remember that the Web and Net can be chaotic and dynamic places. Be prepared for changes and surprises.

We'll cover the details of using resources on the Web for navigation in the following chapters. The next chapter looks at some destinations associated with the protocols of URLs. These protocols, as you saw in the previous chapter, create the many kinds of information spaces that the Web melds together.

At the Edge of the Web

16

by
John December

IN THIS CHAPTER

A navigator who knows what regions of cyberspace are reachable from a Web browser and knows how to use a browser for navigation can explore the Web well. In this chapter, we'll begin by navigating the "edges" of the Web: those Internet tools and resources that often are the destinations for the hypertext that makes up the Web but are not themselves provided through Web servers or made of hypertext.

We'll look at how these tools and resources link with the Web, we'll see how they look when viewed through a graphical Web browser, and we'll learn the basics of their operation.

What's at the Edge?

As we discussed earlier, the Web consists of hypertext that primarily links Internet resources. These resources can be multimedia information as well as searching tools and interfaces used to find and retrieve information. As we saw in Figure 14.3, hypertext files written in HTML "point" to many non-hypertext, Internet-based resources and tools. These tools and resources can be thought of as being at the "edge" of the Web. Figure 16.1 illustrates these relationships.

FIGURE 16.1.

The edge of the Web.

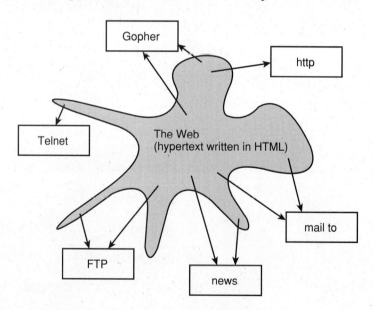

The Web's links reach into the information spaces created by Internet tools and protocols. For example, a link to the FTP resource `ftp://ftp.ctr.columbia.edu/CTR-Research` reaches into "FTP space," or the collection of all information on File Transfer Protocol sites. Similarly, `gopher://info.itu.ch/` reaches into "Gopher space" to a particular Gopher offering information about the International Telecommunications Union.

Mail links such as `mailto:listserv@uriacc.uri.edu` don't work with Mosaic 2.1, but they work in browsers such as Lynx or Netscape. This link essentially reaches into "mail space," or that portion of cyberspace that can be reached via electronic mail from the Internet (the region of online cyberspace known as the Matrix).

All these link into information spaces and then reach from the Web into other spaces. What happens when you go into these spaces? What does your browser look like? These are the questions we'll investigate in the following sections of this chapter. We'll encounter many "edges" of the Web, learning how these information spaces are used, how they look through a Web browser, and techniques and tips for navigating them.

FTP Space

File Transfer Protocol, or FTP, has long been used as a means to share information over the Internet. By using FTP, you can obtain files from remote computers—files of text, executable programs, graphics, movies, sound files—on a wide variety of subjects. Before the invention of Web browsers, the FTP procedure was done by hand, a process in which a user issued commands to a line-mode FTP interface. With a browser such as Netscape, your entry into FTP space will be seamless and effortless—it's just a matter of clicking on the hotspot of a hypertext document or menu entry in information systems such as Gopher. Despite this ease of access, however, a navigator needs to pay attention to what happens when entering FTP space. A navigator must learn how to move through an FTP site as viewed through a Web browser, and learn some tips and techniques for dealing with special situations that arise in FTP space. We'll also look at how you can search not just one FTP site but *thousands* of sites with a single tool called Archie. We'll begin our journey by going to a sample FTP site and looking around.

A Sample FTP Site: The Center for Telecommunications Research

Let's say that you want to find out something about telecommunications research. A good place to start is an academic center for such research at Columbia University in New York City, the Center for Telecommunications Research. The URL for their site is `ftp://ftp.ctr.columbia.edu/CTR-Research`. You might have obtained this URL from a friend and typed this link into your browser by hand, using the Open button on your Web browser. Or, you might have used the linking mechanisms of hypertext to follow a hotspot to this URL. Either way, once the Web browser has opened this URL, you will see the display as shown in Figure 16.2.

FIGURE 16.2.

The opening screen for a typical FTP site.

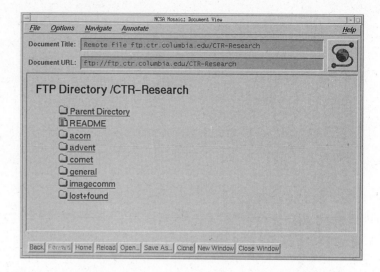

This opening screen for the FTP site that is shown here is typical. Let's discuss its features.

1. The document doesn't have a descriptive title in the Document Title box. This isn't the fault of the developers of this information; rather, it is a limitation of FTP sites as displayed in a Web browser. Unlike in the HTML file we looked at in Chapter 14, "Web Structures and Spaces," there is no way to designate a descriptive title from an FTP site for viewing through a Web browser. When FTP sites were invented, there was no consideration about how they would be viewed through a Web browser. (Refer to the technique described in Chapter 15, "Browser Operations," for how you can put a descriptive title on this information if you put it in your hotlist.)

2. There is a title across the top of the Mosaic display window that reads "FTP Directory/ CTR-Research." This tells you the location of this information on the host machine (ftp.ctr.columbia.edu). The fact that you are in a subdirectory on the host itself (the /CTR-Research part of the URL) lets you know that there are other directories "above" you.

3. There are symbols next to the list items. These give a clue about the file contents. The icon that looks like a folder is a directory of files. The icon that looks like a document is a single file (the README entry). Figure 16.3 shows other icons that you might expect to see at FTP sites using the Mosaic browser (or using Gopher in Gopher menus, as will be discussed later). In Netscape (or other browsers), these symbols may vary. For example, in Netscape, the search icon is a small binoculars symbol.

4. There are short names (rather than descriptive phrases) describing elements of the list. Because the entries in an FTP menu are the names of files or directories, the names are necessarily short. The entries themselves are all hotspots, underlined and highlighted to indicate that they are links to further information.

FIGURE 16.3.

Icons for FTP or Gopher sites. (Courtesy of Kevin Hughes.)

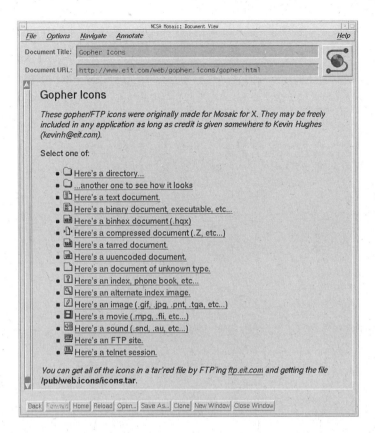

Navigating an FTP Site

Because of the restrictions on information representation in FTP sites (short names or few opportunities for putting phrases or terms on the entries in the lists), you need to recognize the conventions that well-organized FTP sites use. Understanding these conventions is crucial to navigating an FTP site efficiently.

Because the names in the list at an FTP site are so short, providers of information have recognized the need for more descriptive information and usually offer such a file that explains their site's offerings. The name of this file is often README, as is the case at the Center for Telecommunications Research FTP site. Often the list of entries will be very, very long. To place the README file in a more prominent position (the entries are usually listed alphabetically by default), a developer will capitalize the README filename or use a name such as 00README. There are many variations, but look for a file with a name with variations on README, INDEX, NOTICE, or ABOUT.

Because the README file is probably the best place to start at an unfamiliar FTP site, let's look at the README file from the Center for Telecommunications Research FTP site. When you place the cursor over the README file and click the left mouse button, the Mosaic browser appears as shown in Figure 16.4.

FIGURE 16.4.

README file for Center for Telecommunications Research site.

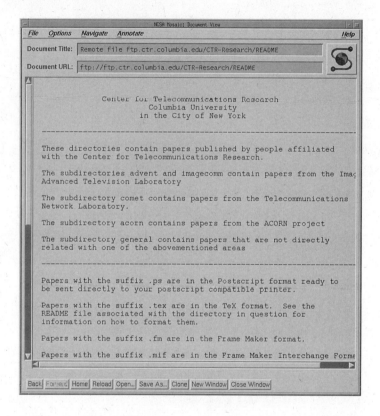

The Mosaic browser shows just the top of the README file's contents. The entire contents of the file are as follows:

```
Center for Telecommunications Research Columbia University
in the City of New York
------------------------------------------------------------------
These directories contain papers published by people affiliated
with the Center for Telecommunications Research.

The subdirectories advent and imagecomm contain papers from the Image and
Advanced Television Laboratory.

The subdirectory comet contains papers from the Telecommunications
Network Laboratory.
The subdirectory acorn contains papers from the ACORN project.
The subdirectory general contains papers that are not directly
related with one of the above-mentioned areas.

Papers with the suffix .ps are in the Postscript format ready to
be sent directly to your postscript compatible printer.
Papers with the suffix .tex are in the TeX format. See the
README file associated with the directory in question for
```

```
information on how to format them.
Papers with the suffix .fm are in the Frame Maker format.
Papers with the suffix .mif are in the Frame Maker Interchange Format.
For further information about the Center, you can contact the
center via the following methods:

E-mail: ctr-info@ctr.columbia.edu

Phone: (212) 854-2498 (9-5 EST5EDT)

Fax: (212) 316-9068

Snail-Mail:
CTR Information
Columbia University
Room 801 Schapiro Research Bldg.
530 W. 120th Street
New York, NY 10027-6699

Comments, questions, or problems to archivist@ctr.columbia.edu.
-Seth Robertson
seth@ctr.columbia.edu
```

The nice thing about this site's README file is that it gives you an overview of the site, tells you what to expect in each directory, and then gives you information about contacting the administrator of the site. These are all important elements of a README file. Not having this information is often the biggest obstacle in navigating an FTP site.

Let's go over the Center for Telecommunications Research (CTR) README file, picking out the major points you will need to know for navigation:

1. *The sponsoring institution or the individual providing the information:* You will often encounter FTP sites lacking this information, making it difficult to determine what institution or individual is providing the information (or even where the information is located) or the date when the information was posted. Without this orientation information, it is hard to make a judgment about the information's usefulness or reliability.

    In our CTR example, the sponsoring institution is listed directly at the top of the file and a snail mail (U.S. mail) address is shown at the bottom.

2. *The contents of subdirectories:* Often there are many subdirectories at an FTP site, and a good description of each is very difficult to maintain (because there are many information contributors at that site or simply a very large number of directories). Look for information in the README file that can give you clues to subdirectory contents. Ideally, the names of the subdirectories themselves will be descriptive. However, since the information providers are limited in naming directories and files, clues from the README file increase your efficiency in navigating an FTP site. In our CTR example, the README file describes the contents of the directories very well; it clarifies the meaning of directory names such as "comet" that might not otherwise yield a clue to their contents. Also, this README file does a very good job of describing the file extensions used in the information within the directories, explaining the file extensions such as .PS, .TEX, .FM, and .MIF. This is particularly important information, as a Web browser can't interpret all types of file formats.

3. *Further information:* You need to have a person to contact in order to direct questions or obtain other information, particularly if you have a problem with the information at the site. From the administrator's point of view, this contact is essential for catching errors and gaining input from users about the information. In our CTR example, a contact e-mail address is given for the person responsible for maintaining the information, so you can contact that person with further comments, suggestions, or questions.

Armed with the information from the README file, our experience of this FTP site can be much more efficient. We might have decided, based on the contents of the README file, that this site doesn't contain the information we want. If so, we can go on to other pursuits, rather than wasting time (and network bandwidth) trying to figure out if the information at the site fits our needs.

Having viewed the README file, we use the Back button on Mosaic's front panel to return to the front screen of this FTP site. (Refer to Figure 16.2.) By using the cursor and mouse, we can enter the subdirectories and encounter more information, each time using the same procedures as when we encountered the first screen. Use clues such as README or INDEX files as well as symbols next to list entries to gain clues about the information you are encountering. As you click entries in the FTP menu, the resources will appear in the Mosaic display window, or, in the case of specially formatted graphics, movies, or postscript files, an external viewer will appear displaying the information. If you have problems with obtaining a file using FTP, try a "manual method" of using a line-mode interface to FTP. You may run into some problems with formats. Your Web browser may not be able to display a file, or you may encounter a file for which you don't have the appropriate multimedia software to view it. See Part II, "Web Browsers and Connections," for more information about browsers and the multimedia viewers that go along with them.

Navigating FTP Space

We've looked at one example of an FTP site in detail to see what a typical site looks like and the basics of navigating within it. There are thousands of FTP sites across the world, and, unless the site is focused toward collections of information that you are very interested in, you won't want to browse each one to find something. Navigating FTP space (the collection of all information available at all publicly-accessible FTP sites in the world) is much easier than visiting each one. Tools have been developed to find files in FTP space. One such tool available on the Web is called ArchiePlex, a Web-based interface to a tool called Archie that can search the contents of registered FTP sites. The Archie software was developed by Peter Deutsch, Alan Emtage, Bill Heelan, and Mike Parker at McGill University in Montreal, Canada. A list of ArchiePlex gateways around the world is at http://web.nexor.co.uk/archie.html. An example ArchiePlex interface is in Figure 16.5.

By filling out the ArchiePlexForm and submitting it, you will get back (through the Web browser interface) a list of all files that match your search string. These files won't necessarily be all the files in the world, only those that are currently in the database on the Archie server you selected in the form. Remember that the string you want to match is a file or directory name at a site, not a descriptive word or phrase. Therefore, you should use short keywords or string patterns.

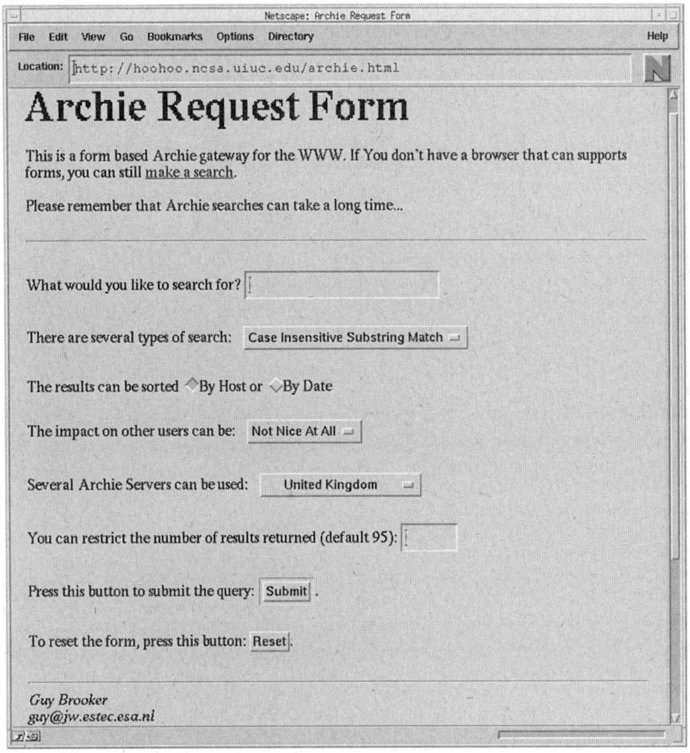

FIGURE 16.5.
ArchiePlexForm.

Archie is a marvelous searching tool for finding things in FTP space based on keywords. However, you might want to find an FTP site with a particular name. You could certainly try to guess what that name would be (often it is `ftp.site.domain`), but you might want to examine a list of sites where anonymous FTP access is allowed. In this case, Archie would not be as useful as such a listing of all FTP sites. Such a listing exists at `ftp://rtfm.mit.edu/pub/usenet-by-group/news.answers/ftp-list` or on the Web at `http://www.info.net/Public/ftp-list.html`.

By using this list, you'll be able to search for a particular FTP site based on its name. While an FTP site monster list is not necessarily comprehensive (because it is maintained by hand), it can serve as a valuable reference while navigating FTP space.

Gopher Space

Like FTP space, Gopher space has long been used as a means to share information over the Internet, and there are thousands of Gopher sites throughout the world. Similar to our earlier discussion of FTP space, we'll first look at a sample Gopher site and how to navigate it, then we'll look at how you can search Gopher space itself from the Web.

A Sample Gopher Site: The Minnesota Gopher

Gopher is an information system designed at the University of Minnesota, and it provides a very efficient way to organize information and provide it for other people to browse on the Internet. The term "Gopher" refers to the University's eponymous mascot, and also hints at the operation of the Internet Gopher itself—to "go for" information.

Just like FTP, Gopher was used before Web browsers became popular. Special software programs have been written, Gopher clients, that provide an interface to information on Gopher servers, just as Web clients (browsers) obtain information from Web server sites. There are even graphical browsers for Gopher, in addition to line mode Gopher clients. Your Web browser itself acts like a Gopher client when it encounters a Gopher "hole" (a Gopher site in Gopher space).

Let's look at the "mother Gopher," the original Gopher at the University of Minnesota, through Mosaic. The URL `gopher://gopher.micro.umn.edu/` refers to this Gopher. Figure 16.6 shows the Mosaic display of the Minnesota Gopher.

FIGURE 16.6.

The Minnesota Gopher.

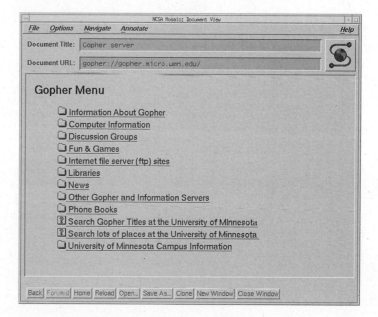

Let's discuss the features of the Minnesota Gopher:

1. Just as in the FTP site in the previous section, the title that shows up in Mosaic's Document Title box is just Gopher server. If you save a reference to this Gopher on your hotlist, you can consider using the hotlist's facilities for changing the title that appears on your hotlist.

2. The title in the Mosaic window is Gopher Menu, and, since it appears in large font in a prominent place in the menu, might be the first clue that you've entered a Gopher hole as you are navigating the Web.

3. The symbols in the Gopher are the same as those at FTP sites on the list shown in Figure 16.3. Just as at the FTP site, you can use these symbols for clues as to what appears beneath the link. In the case of Gophers, a file folder symbol will lead to another menu, and a symbol that looks like a page of text will lead to a document.

4. The Gopher menu has longer names than at the FTP site. This is because the Gopher information system allows for longer, more descriptive names in menu titles.

GOPHER ON MTV!

One of Gopher's claims to fame was that MTV Video Jock (VJ) Adam Curry (now no longer with MTV) wore a Gopher t-shirt on an MTV program. You can view a movie of this appearance as well as still pictures from the Information About Gopher menu selection from the front screen of the Minnesota Gopher.

Navigating a Gopher: the Minnesota Gopher

Because Gopher menu entries are more descriptive, you'll often find that you need fewer cues than at FTP sites to navigate them. These longer names mean that a Gopher URL can be a bit more unwieldy. For example, this is a Gopher URL:

```
gopher://gopher.tc.umn.edu/11/Information%20About%20Gopher
```

Since the menu entry names are more descriptive, navigating a Gopher requires fewer README file cues. However, you will still want to know

- The individual or institution providing the information and some information about the freshness of the information (the date it was last updated)

- What to expect to find at the Gopher site

- How to get more information, ask questions, or give feedback

The Minnesota Gopher fulfills these needs very well with its Information About Gopher menu entry. By selecting this link, you can browse an extensive directory of information about Gopher itself. A good place to find out more about Gopher itself is from the Frequently Asked Questions (FAQs) list for Gopher. The URL to the Gopher FAQ list is `gopher://mudhoney.micro.umn.edu/00/Gopher.FAQ`.

Besides a gold-mine of knowledge about Gophers, the Minnesota Gopher also is a good example of a Gopher-based, campus-wide information system for the University of Minnesota. By selecting "University of Minnesota Campus Information" from the front Gopher menu, you can examine a wide range of information about the university, from Academic Staff to the University of Minnesota Women's Center.

Just as at the FTP site, you'll encounter files and resources in a variety of formats. Unlike an FTP site however, you'll see some unique kinds of resources and connections at a Gopher site:

■ The question-mark icon (shown in Figure 16.3 to the left of "Here's an index, phone book, etc.") is a connection to a searching mechanism built into the Gopher itself.

For example, from the Minnesota Gopher's opening screen, you can select "Search Gopher Titles at the University of Minnesota." Your Mosaic display window will show a screen like the one in Figure 16.7.

FIGURE 16.7.

The Gopher search screen.

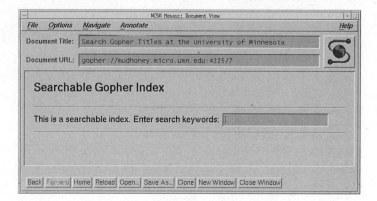

In the box provided, you'll be able to enter a keyword or phrase identifying information you want to find at the University of Minnesota. By entering the keywords and pressing Return, you'll generate a list of resources whose titles match the keyword or phrase you entered. A Gopher title is the phrase that appears on the Gopher menu. By using this search mechanism, you don't have to browse the complete tree of menus on the Gopher, but have all matching menus, documents, or other resources gathered together in a single list as a result of your search request. You can then select items from this list.

■ The Telnet icon (shown in Figure 16.3, the bottom of the list, to the left of "Here's a Telnet session") is a connection to a remote machine. You can see an example of this on the Minnesota Gopher by starting from the "front" of the Minnesota Gopher (Figure 16.6), selecting "Libraries" and then "Internet Accessible Libraries." You'll see the symbol for a Telnet session link next to an entry for "Libraries of the University of Minnesota Integrated Network Access."

By selecting a Telnet session link, you will cause a pop-up window to appear, independent of your Web browser, which brings you into a remote session with a remote computer. (If you are using a nongraphical Web browser such as Lynx, your browser's display will "transform" to the Telnet session shown in Figure 16.8.)

By selecting the "Libraries of the University of Minnesota Integrated Network Access," option on the page given by the URL shown in Figure 16.7, a pop-up window will appear as in Figure 16.8.

FIGURE 16.8.

Telnet access to the University of Minnesota Public Access Information Service.

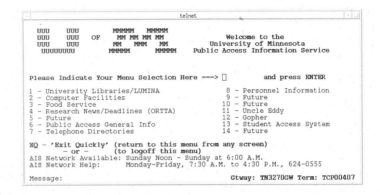

```
                                                      telnet
UUU      UUU          MMMMM    MMMMM
UUU      UUU    OF    MM MM MM MM                   Welcome to the
UUU      UUU          MM  MMM   MM              University of Minnesota
  UUUUUUUU            MMMMM    MMMMM        Public Access Information Service


Please Indicate Your Menu Selection Here ===> []        and press ENTER

1 - University Libraries/LUMINA            8 - Personnel Information
2 - Computer Facilities                    9 - Future
3 - Food Service                          10 - Future
4 - Research News/Deadlines (ORTTA)       11 - Uncle Eddy
5 - Future                                12 - Gopher
6 - Public Access General Info            13 - Student Access System
7 - Telephone Directories                 14 - Future

XQ - 'Exit Quickly' (return to this menu from any screen)
   - or -         (to logoff this menu)
AIS Network Available: Sunday Noon - Sunday at 6:00 A.M.
AIS Network Help:      Monday-Friday, 7:30 A.M. to 4:30 P.M., 624-0555

Message:                                   Gtway: TN3270GW Term: TCP00407
```

These Telnet sessions have their own peculiarities. (We'll discuss navigating Telnet space in the next section of this chapter.) However, the point to remember is that you may find links to Telnet space from Gopher space.

We've seen how navigating a Gopher is a bit easier than an FTP site because of the more descriptive names possible in the menu entries and the built-in search mechanisms for finding information at a particular Gopher.

Navigating Gopher Space

While an individual Gopher is easy to navigate, how do you navigate the thousands of Gophers spread throughout the world? Well, as you might suspect, it is far easier than exhaustively burrowing into every Gopher hole in cyberspace. Instead, there is a tool called Veronica that does for Gopher space what Archie does for FTP space: It searches out individual items on servers worldwide.

From the Minnesota Gopher's first menu, you can select "Other Gopher and Information Servers" and look for the menu entry "Search titles in Gopher space using Veronica." Selecting this entry puts you into a long menu of information as well as query menu entries (entries with a question mark) that allow you to do various kinds of searching in Gopher space. There are many options for this kind of searching, and a good document to consult to help you compose exactly the right Veronica query for you is titled, "How to Compose Veronica Queries." You can find this document in the "Search titles in Gopher space using Veronica" on the Minnesota (and many other) Gophers.

By using Veronica, you can obtain a list of entries in many Gophers that match your search specification, and you'll be able to browse the entries from a single Gopher menu, even though the entries themselves may be scattered across Gopher menus all over the world.

Besides Veronica's power to search Gopher space through keyword search patterns, you also can search Gophers by subject area. Subject-related Gophers have sprung up worldwide, growing with the popularity of Gopher itself. Because of the additional expressiveness offered by Gopher, it is often the preferred information delivery system for many organizations. A very fine collection of subject-related Gophers is called "Gopher Jewels," developed by David Riggins. A Web-based version of Gopher Jewels is at the URL `http://galaxy.einet.net/GJ/index.html`. The opening screen of this Gopher Jewels collection is shown in Figure 16.9.

FIGURE 16.9.

The Gopher Jewels collection.

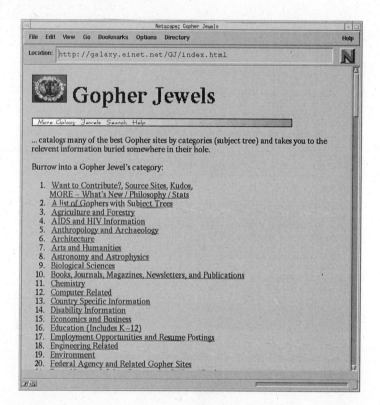

The Gopher Jewels collection gives you a subject-oriented view of Gopher space. This is particularly useful when you are looking for information related to a particular area of interest, and you don't necessarily know search terms to use. (If you did, you could use a Veronica search.) In addition, the Gopher Jewels collection also provides a way for you to search the document and directory titles of all Gophers in the collection. This Gopher Jewels search mechanism serves as a Veronica search localized to the Jewels region of Gopher space (Figure 16.10).

The keyword (via Veronica) and subject-oriented (via Gopher Jewels) navigation of Gopher space is useful, but there is still another way to search Gophers—geographically. From the front screen of the Minnesota Gopher, you can select "Other Gopher and Information Servers" to enter a geographically based tree of Gophers. In this way, you can attempt to locate a particular Gopher at an organization if you know its geographic location.

FIGURE 16.10.
The Gopher Jewels search screen.

Telnet Space

FTP space and Gopher space offered an elaborate and fairly uniform (as viewed through a Web browser) way of navigating. However, the links to Telnet connections from Web documents vary widely in terms of what happens when you enter them. The connection to a Telnet session is straightforward: You click on a hotspot, invoking a URL such as `telnet://downwind.sprl.umich.edu:3000`, which causes a pop-up window to appear that allows you to begin the login procedures to the remote computer. What differs is what happens after you select the hotlink and open the URL. There is no uniform arrangement of how a Telnet session on a computer can proceed, and you won't expect to see any of the icons shown in Figure 16.3. Let's look at a typical session, see how it works, and then talk about general navigating tips for individual sessions and Telnet space itself.

A Sample Telnet Session: The Weather Underground

The URL `telnet://downwind.sprl.umich.edu:3000` will take you to the Weather Underground, a public service offered by the College of Engineering at the University of Michigan in Ann Arbor. The National Weather Service data in the Weather Underground is courtesy of the National-Science-Foundation-funded UNIDATA Project and the University of Michigan. This service is quite useful for finding out current weather, earthquake, skiing, and other environmental conditions. After opening the above URL, a pop-up window will appear, as shown in Figure 16.11.

FIGURE 16.11.

The Weather Underground opening screen.

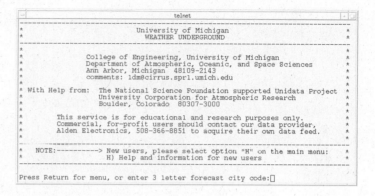

The service is very descriptive in its opening screen. As a new user, you should pay attention to how you can obtain help in a Telnet session. Usually, there is a selection for obtaining help. Look for this to familiarize yourself with the service so you can work efficiently with it. Given the information on the opening screen shown above, a user should probably go into the main menu and select the help for new users. When you press Return, the main menu is displayed as in Figure 16.12.

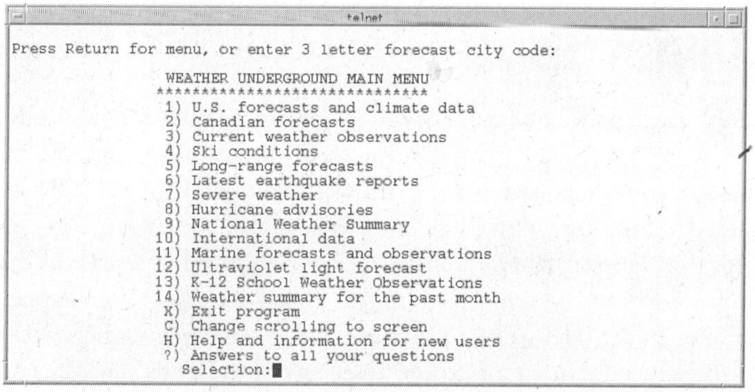

FIGURE 16.12.

The Weather Underground main menu.

This opening menu shows a common pattern of Telnet session menu selections by numbers or letters. This common arrangement will help you navigate most Telnet sessions rather easily. Note on this main menu there are two selections for help—the H selection new users were told to select and the ? selection. It is a good idea to select what you are told to at first—this will give you the introductory information that will help you work well with the interface. Selecting H, we see Figure 16.13.

This new user information describes typical navigation methods for Telnet sessions, including shortcuts for working with the interface. While built-in search mechanisms such as the one for searching titles at the Minnesota Gopher are not always available, the help files and the menu options should provide the user with the clues necessary to navigate a Telnet session. This weather service offers you a wide range of weather information. By using the simple menu interface, you can access current climate, weather, and earthquake reports from all over the world. For example, we can find out about a recent earthquake (Figure 16.14).

```
telnet
          INFORMATION FOR NEW USERS OF THE WEATHER UNDERGROUND
          ----------------------------------------------------

   Welcome to the Weather Underground! Through our host computer in Ann Arbor,
Michigan, we provide a variety of weather information through this menu-driven,
interactive program. Use of this service is free, as long as the information is
is for personal or educational use. Feel free to access the service as much as
you like, but be aware that during major weather events usage gets quite heavy,
and you may receive the following message:

   The Weather Underground is fully loaded. Try again later.

  The Weather Underground is limited to 100 simultaneous users, so you will
have to wait until someone else signs off before you can get on. Once you do
get on, please limit the duration of your session so that others may sign on.

BYPASSING THE MAIN MENU
-----------------------

   When first entering the Weather Underground, you will get the following
prompt:

   Press Return for menu, or enter 3 letter forecast city code:
   Press Return to continue, M to return to menu, X to exit:
```

FIGURE 16.13.
The Weather Underground help menu.

```
telnet
   **************************************************************
               Tsunami bulletin for 02/06/95
   **************************************************************
521
WEPA41 PHEB 060014
''''''''''
   Press Return to continue, M to return to menu, X to exit:
TSUNAMI BULLETIN NO. 001
PACIFIC TSUNAMI WARNING CENTER/NOAA/NWS
ISSUED AT 0014Z 06 FEB 1995

. . THIS IS A TSUNAMI INFORMATION MESSAGE, NO ACTION REQUIRED . .

AN EARTHQUAKE, PRELIMINARY MAGNITUDE 7.3 OCCURRED AT 2251 UTC
  5 FEB 1995, LOCATED NEAR        LATITUDE 38S      LONGITUDE 178E
IN THE VICINITY OF NEW ZEALAND
EVALUATION:        NO DESTRUCTIVE PACIFIC-WIDE TSUNAMI THREAT EXISTS.
                   HOWEVER, SOME AREAS MAY EXPERIENCE SMALL SEA LEVEL
                   CHANGES. THIS WILL BE THE FINAL BULLETIN ISSUED
                   UNLESS ADDITIONAL INFORMATION BECOMES AVAILABLE.
. . . NO PACIFIC-WIDE TSUNAMI WARNING IS IN EFFECT . . .
STOP

  Press Return for menu:
```

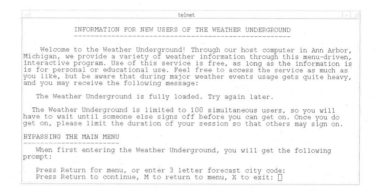

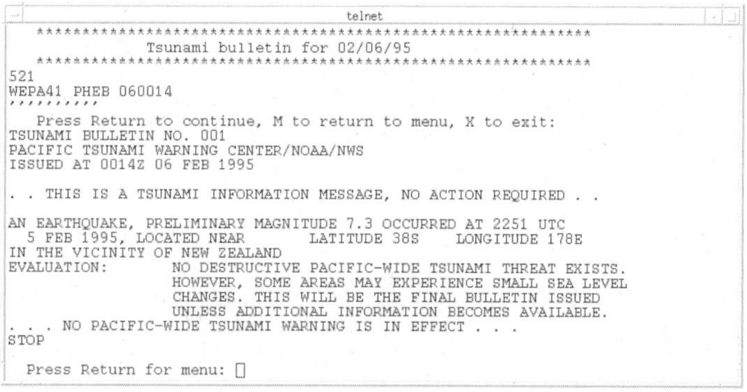

FIGURE 16.14.
The Weather Underground earthquake report.

Navigating a Telnet Session

The Weather Underground is a good example of a Telnet session because its menu and help system are typical. Here are some tips for navigating a Telnet session:

1. **Read the Screen.** It is a cardinal rule of user-interface design that the user will never read a screen :). However, reading the information on the screen and looking through the help files (at least the first time that you enter a Telnet session) can help you in the long run. Look for shortcuts to commands if you use a service frequently. Use the help information and the opening screens to get a quick idea of what the service offers.
2. **Press Enter.** Sometimes a Telnet session screen stops, particularly when you first start it. If this happens, press the Enter key on your keyboard.
3. **Set your terminal type.** Sometimes a Telnet session will ask you to set the type of terminal you are using. This is so that the session can send graphics or other information

to your terminal with the appropriate format. If you are asked a terminal type, unless you know it to be different, you can usually respond with `vt100` or `xterm` safely. If you encounter garbled graphics, log off the Telnet session and try another type.

4. **Quit via a command.** The best way to quit a Telnet session is by using the `exit` command provided by the session itself. Frequently this command is `quit`, `exit`, `end`, `stop`, `bye`, `logout`, or some other variation.

5. **Be courteous.** When you are using a Telnet session, you are actually "on" the remote computer—its processing power is devoted to waiting for your inputs and processing your responses. As such, obtain the information from a Telnet session as quickly and efficiently as you can. Sometimes, after a period of time without input from you, a Telnet session will terminate on its own. This is very different from a Web browser, in which you are not using the processing power of the remote computer once you've retrieved the resource across the network.

6. **Remember—you're independent.** Once your graphical Web browser (such as Mosaic or Netscape) spawns the pop-up window of the Telnet session, the browser itself is free to operate independently. This is a fairly useful feature in situations where you want to use the Telnet session's information as part of navigating with Netscape or Mosaic.

Navigating Telnet Space

Unlike Gopher space and FTP space, there are no tools to cruise through Telnet space and find all the Telnet hosts with particular menu entries. However, there is a wonderful catalog of many Telnet-accessible services on the Internet called Hytelnet. Developed by Peter Scott, Hytelnet organizes Telnet-accessible services by categories. You can use Hytelnet through Telnet itself, by entering the following command at your operating system prompt (assuming you have the Telnet program installed on your computer):

```
telnet access.usask.ca
```

and using `hytelnet` as the login name. From a Web browser, you can open the URL `telnet://access.usask.ca`. However, this Telnet session, like the sessions similar to the Weather Underground, creates a drain on the remote computer you are using. You should obtain a client program to most efficiently use Hytelnet. Mosaic acts as a client for you when you use the Web-based version of Hytelnet available at the URL `http://andromeda.einet.net/hytelnet/START.TXT.html`. The opening screen for this Web-based Hytelnet session is shown in Figure 16.15.

The opening screen of Hytelnet gives you access into a tree of menus that organize Telnet-accessible sites and resources into categories. A big category is library catalogs at many universities and public sites. The Web version of Hytelnet will guide you through the process of selecting a Telnet session. Eventually, you will reach the point where you will start a Telnet session. For example, selecting the Universidade de Sao Paulo from the world-wide libraries list, we see Figure 16.16 in the browser display window.

FIGURE 16.15.

Web-based Hytelnet.

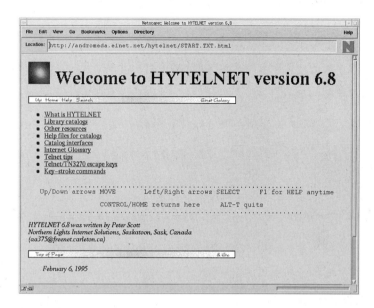

FIGURE 16.16.

Universidade de Sao Paulo Telnet connection.

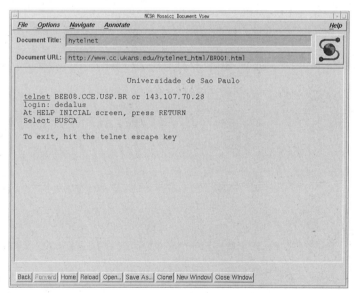

In the display above, the word telnet is a hotspot. If I put my cursor over the word telnet, I see telnet://bee08.cce.usp.br/ in the status message area of the browser main panel. This tells me that I've reached the edge of the Web-based version of Hytelnet. Clicking this Telnet link will cause a window to pop up with a Telnet session started at this remote host. From the Hytelnet screen shown in the browser window, I have further information to complete the connection, such as the login name I should use (dedalus) and how to get help during the session.

Although Hytelnet doesn't cover every conceivable Telnet session worldwide, it does represent the most comprehensive collection of Telnet connections in existence. Just as we searched FTP space with Archie and Gopher space with Veronica, we can search Hytelnet space also. Galaxy maintains a search service for the descriptions of Hytelnet entries for keywords or phrases at URL `http://andromeda.einet.net/hytelnet/HYTELNET.html` (Figure 16.17).

FIGURE 16.17.

Searching Hytelnet space.

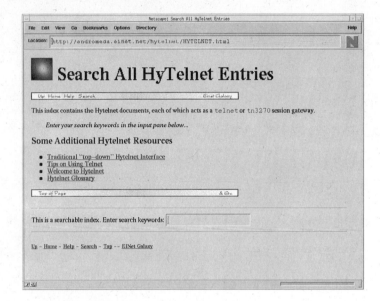

WAIS Space

WAIS stands for *Wide Area Information Server* and refers to a system for organizing information into databases that can be queried using a set of commands known as a Natural Query Language. There are many WAIS databases on a variety of topics that are accessible on the Internet. One view of WAIS space is by looking at the directory of all the known publicly accessible databases in the world in the directory of WAIS servers maintained by WAIS, Inc. (`http://www.wais.com/`), which provides commercial versions of WAIS software and services. Figure 16.18 shows a partial listing of these WAIS servers.

As shown in the list in Figure 16.18, the WAIS servers are identified by keyword names. Choosing the link for Environmental Guidance, we obtain Figure 16.19.

By entering a search query `acid rain damage` into the dialog box shown in the form in Figure 16.19, we can then obtain documents that match the WAIS query, as shown in Figure 16.20.

FIGURE 16.18.

A partial listing of a WAIS directory of servers. Copyright by WAIS, Inc. Printed by permission.

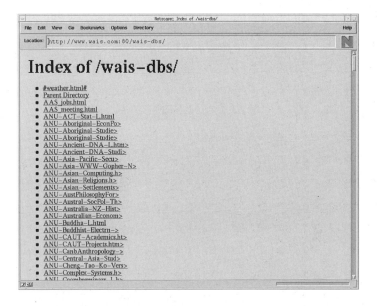

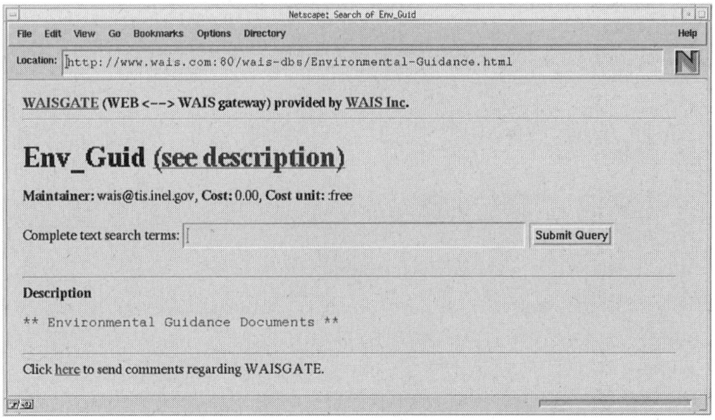

FIGURE 16.19.

The Environmental Guidance Database from WAIS. Copyright by WAIS, Inc. Printed by permission.

The value of this simple example is just a glimpse of what WAIS can offer. The "scores" listed with the documents retrieved as shown in Figure 16.20 have to do with how much WAIS "weighs" the document based on the algorithm used in the WAIS software. The goal is to give a higher score to documents that are likely to be most relevant to the user, based on the search command given.

FreeWAIS is a freely available version of WAIS. You can get information about FreeWAIS from the Clearinghouse for Networked Information Discovery and Retrieval (http://www.cnidr.org).

FIGURE 16.20.

Documents matching "acid rain damage" search from WAIS. Copyright by WAIS, Inc. Printed by permission.

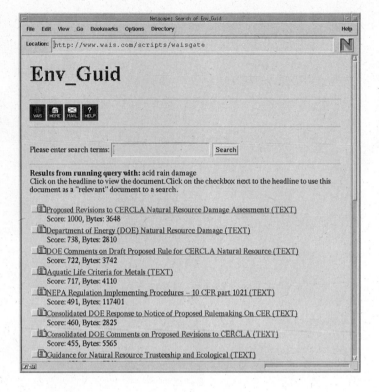

News Space

Usenet news is a vast space for communication accessible through Web clients and includes lively discussion among tens of thousands of people on thousands of topics. Usenet news itself is not confined to the Internet, but flows throughout the Matrix according to a cooperative distribution scheme. Usenet consists of thousands of discussion areas called newsgroups that are identified through a hierarchical naming scheme. For example, the newsgroup name rec.food.restaurants has three parts to it: rec stands for the recreational hierarchy, food indicates a subdivision within recreation, and restaurants qualifies this newsgroup further. Two other examples of recreational newsgroups are rec.gambling and rec.food.sourdough.

Tens of thousands of people read Usenet news daily for information or discussion on a wide range of topics. The culture of Usenet and the individual communities of people who participate in the newsgroups is quite complex. If you are a newcomer to Usenet, it is very important that you become aware of the culture, language, practices, and traditions of Usenet itself. It is not just a collection of hardware, software, and network feeds, but a vibrant society in which individuals contribute their opinions and engage in text-based asynchronous discussions. You can learn more about Usenet in the newsgroup news.announce.newusers, which is specifically designed to carry information for new users.

Usenet news has its own client programs, or newsreaders, that give a variety of interfaces for reading and contributing to the thousands of newsgroups. You can use Mosaic as your newsreader and browse Usenet newsgroups in hypertext fashion. To read a particular Usenet newsgroup (for example, `news.announce.newusers`) using a Web browser, you can use the `Open` function and enter the URL `news:news.announce.newusers`. The computer on which you are running your Web browser must have a Usenet server available for it to access, and this server must carry the particular Usenet newsgroup you are attempting to read. If this is the case, your Mosaic browser will appear as in Figure 16.21 when you open a URL for a newsgroup, for example `news:alt.fan.letterman`.

FIGURE 16.21.

A Usenet newsgroup displayed in Mosaic.

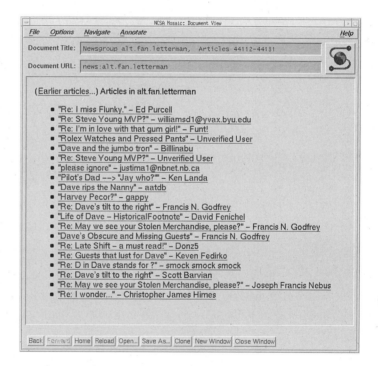

In Netscape, a Usenet newsgroup's articles are displayed showing the groups of related messages (called *threads* of discussion). Note how there are a series of indented threads of discussion in the newsgroup about David Letterman displayed in Figure 16.22. The display of the threads "BOBBY TESSEL BUMPED AGAIN!!!" and "The worst Guest of ALL time was…" help you follow discussion that is related to that subtopic within the Letterman group. In contrast, Mosaic displays a chronological list of posts, starting with the most recent posts first and providing you access to previous posts through the "Earlier articles…" link at the top of the page.

FIGURE 16.22.

A Usenet newsgroup displayed in Netscape showing threads.

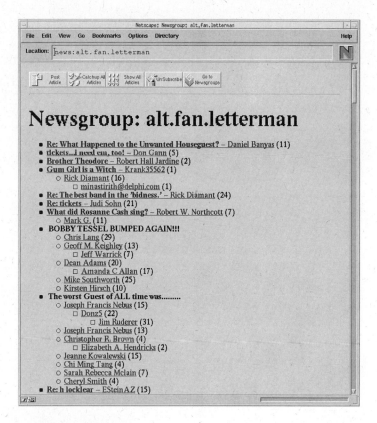

Navigating Usenet on the Web

Individual entries in a newsgroup are called articles, and each article is contributed or posted by someone to that newsgroup. On a Web browser display of a Usenet newsgroup, the article titles are highlighted. By clicking an article name, we can see the article's contents.

The article will contain links into articles for which the given article is a follow-up (response) and to any other newsgroups where this article has been cross-posted (contributed simultaneously to several groups). Using a Web browser, you can follow these links to the other articles or the other newsgroups where the article might be cross-posted. In this way, the Web browser interface to Usenet is fairly easy to navigate—you follow links just as in any other hypertext.

While navigating Usenet, keep these things in mind:

■ Orient yourself to the culture of Usenet. Use the articles in news.announce.newusers as a starting point. Then spend time observing the conversation before you consider contributing to any group.

■ You won't be able to access newsgroups that your local newserver doesn't carry. There are many regional hierarchies for Usenet news that contain newsgroups particular to one region, or specialized hierarchies that aren't necessarily distributed to your site. You'll get the error message No such group on your Mosaic display window if you attempt to access one of these newsgroups.

■ You won't be able to access articles that have expired. After a period of time set by your local Usenet administrator, the articles that reach a certain age (have been on the server for the given period of time) are deleted. It may happen that you find links in articles that refer to an expired article. If you follow such a link, you'll get an error message. Also, if you place a reference to an article on your hotlist, after a few weeks you might find that the article has expired, and you won't be able to read it again.

■ You won't be able to contribute an article to a newsgroup using Mosaic; instead, you'll have to use a special program on your operating system (a Postnews) program. With Netscape, however, you can post an article (Figure 16.23). Practice posting articles in a special "test" newsgroup, such as alt.test, so you don't irritate the regular readers of a newsgroup with your experiments. Also, it's a good idea to read the newsgroup's FAQ (Frequently Asked Questions) list before posting an article to the newsgroup.

FIGURE 16.23.

Posting a Usenet article with Netscape.

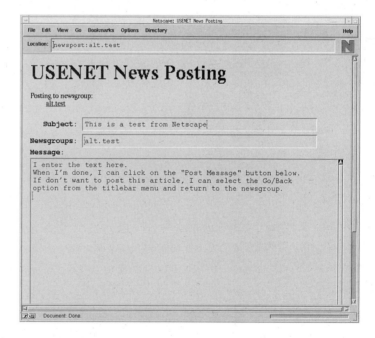

Figure 16.24 shows the article posted. Notice how Netscape's Usenet interface provides you with pushbutton access to popular newsreading functions in a control bar. Using this control bar, you can go to the previous or next articles, mark an entire thread as read, go to a particular newsgroup, go to a list of all your subscribed newsgroups, follow up to the post displayed, or reply directly to the sender of the post. These are the major newsgroup navigation functions, and Netscape's integration of them into its interface is a major accomplishment—transforming a Web browser into a people-to-people communications tool rather than just an information browser.

FIGURE 16.24.

A posted test article viewed with Netscape.

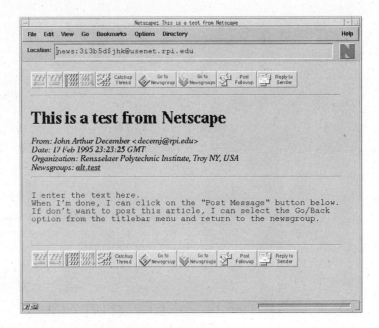

■ You won't find many of the news reading navigation features in some Web browsers, such as Mosaic, that are offered by other newsreaders. The Mosaic interface, despite its hypertext links among articles and newsgroups, is not very sophisticated as a newsgroup navigator. Netscape is quite a bit better. You'll find that other newsreaders such as trn, nn, xrn, or rn, may offer some features for rapidly scanning newsgroup contents that Web browsers don't provide. Netscape's interface, however, particularly in its display of threads (Figure 16.23) is fairly well done.

Looking at News Space

If you think of news space as all the unexpired newsgroup articles on all the servers in the world, you won't be able to search or navigate the entire space. Instead, you are limited to the newsgroups and articles that have propagated to the site where you are reading Usenet news. A handy list in hypertext; listing many newsgroups and a brief description of each is at http://www.w3.org/hypertext/DataSources/News/Groups/Overview.html. This list can help you navigate through the hierarchies of groups to find some that might interest you. However, this list, because it was originally prepared at a Swiss site, won't match the groups that might be available at your site, and it might not contain some new groups that have just developed. With these warnings in mind, a navigator can remember that the anarchy of Usenet is accessible at the edge of the Web, and that Mosaic offers some hypertext features for reading newsgroup articles.

In Netscape, you can pull out all the newsgroups with a particular starting string via a URL. For example, open the URL news:rec.collecting.* to retrieve all the recreational (rec) newsgroups having to do with collecting that you receive at your Usenet feed site (Figure 16.25). In Netscape, you can see a full list of newsgroups available from your server by opening the URL `news:*`.

FIGURE 16.25.

Usenet newsgroups
`rec.collecting`.

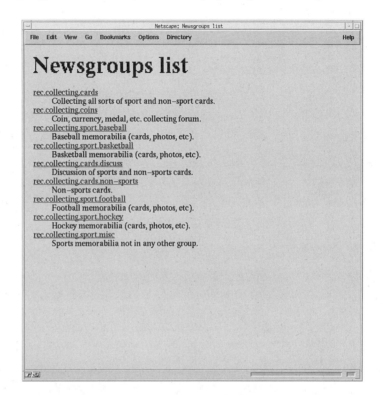

Mail Space: The Matrix

The set of all Internet or gateway-accessible e-mail addresses compromises a rich resource for communication. This space is called the Matrix, a term coined by John Quarterman. Using Netscape, you can make use of mailto URLs such as `mailto:listserv@uriacc.uri.edu`. Other Web browsers, such as Lynx, also recognize these URLs and allow you to enter a session in which you can send e-mail to anyone in the Matrix. Mosaic itself supports electronic mail interaction in some of the options accessible from its main panel (such as File | Mail To).

While there's no tool analogous to Archie for FTP space and Veronica for Gopher space for the Matrix, you do have some options to find out about e-mail-based discussion lists. A searchable index to discussion groups is located at the URL `http://alpha.acast.nova.edu/cgi-bin/lists`. Stephanie da Silva maintains a collection of Publicly Accessible Mailing Lists at the URL `http://www.NeoSoft.com:80/internet/paml/` that you can browse and search. You can access a WAIS-based index of academic e-mail conferences at the URL `wais://munin.ub2.lu.se:210/academic_e-mail_conf`. These lists will help you locate an e-mail-based conference or discussion. Neither service will allow you to search through the contributed electronic mail discussions or archives of discussions. These archives, if kept at all, are saved usually by a list administrator or a group of active members. Check with members of the list itself or its FAQ to see if such an archive exists.

Other Spaces

The previous tour took you through some of the most popular edges of the Web. New kinds of protocols and information systems which will offer you still other kinds of interfaces are being developed all the time. Internet-based activity that is not now directly accessible from the Web, such as MU*s (a family of real-time text conferencing systems, often involving social role playing), may develop Web gateways.

ENTERING FINGER SPACE

The finger protocol is used to retrieve information about a user with an account on a particular host computer. At the UNIX prompt, you can enter

```
finger decemj@rpi.edu
```

and find out about the person connected with this e-mail account. By including information in a file called .plan in your home directory and setting its permissions so that it is readable to everyone, you can create a service based on finger that provides information. A collection of Web-accessible, finger-based information services is collected at the URL

```
http://sundae.triumf.ca/fingerinfo.html
```

based on Scott Yanoff's finger info script. The Web-based version of finger info makes use of a way to obtain finger information using a Gopher client. Within a Web browser, you can open the URL gopher://rpi.edu:79/0decemj to see finger information for the user decemj on the host rpi.edu. By using this Gopher to finger trick, the Web-based finger info program offers a view into "finger space" at the edge of the Web.

Navigator's Check

Now that we've toured the major spaces at the edges of the Web, we can integrate our knowledge in some navigational charts. First, the map shown in Figure 16.26 gives you a rough idea of Network relationships in online cyberspace. The map shows the major spaces of cyberspace. You can see how the Matrix encompasses BITNET, UUCP, and many commercial services, as well as the Internet itself. Gateways make it possible to exchange electronic mail among networks, and other kinds of gateways among tools and protocols allow the flow of information from places such as FTP space or Web space to other networks and services.

Notice how the French communications system TeleTel (popularly know as Minitel, after the name for the actual hardware terminals used in the system) is approaching the Matrix and the Internet. The critical mass of users offered on the Matrix and Internet lures other networks to build gateways or connect directly to the Internet. (There is a gateway from the Internet that allows you to view Teletel activity at `http://www.enst.fr/~meunier/english/minitel/`.)

FIGURE 16.26.

Network relationships in cyberspace.

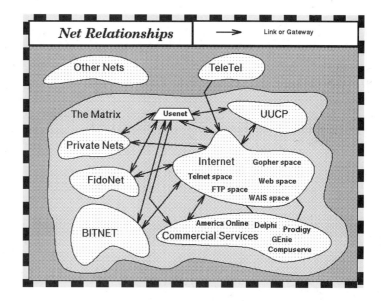

Figure 16.27 summarizes some client–server relationships on the Internet. Notice how the Web clients shown—Netscape, Mosaic, and Lynx—can be used to access a variety of servers. In this way, your Web browser takes the place of specialized clients that are designed to access one kind of server (such as a Gopher client to access Gopher servers). Notice how Web clients still don't give you access to some of the communication spaces on the Internet, such as MU* (multiple user dialogues—MUD/MUSH/MUSE) or IRC (Internet Relay Chat).

Finally, Figure 16.28 shows major information spaces of the Internet, including gateways among them and major subject and searching landmarks in these spaces. We'll explore these subject-oriented and keyword-oriented searching resources in the next chapters.

These charts show how the Internet is at the heart of global cyberspace and how the Web is at the heart of the Internet. Browsers like Netscape, Mosaic, and Lynx give you access to many of the major Internet information protocols and tools.

The maps shown here are like imperfect charts of the world drawn by early explorers; they represent only a snapshot of understanding and will require updating as new tools, information spaces, communication forums, and connections are developed.

FIGURE 16.27.

Client–server relationships in information spaces.

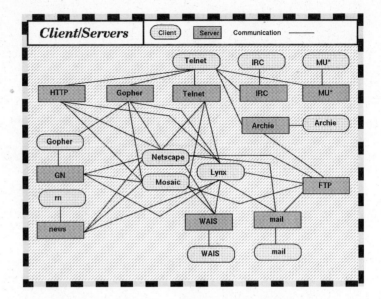

FIGURE 16.28.

Network information spaces showing landmarks.

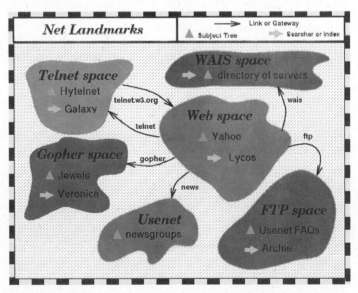

As a navigator, you'll need to create your own maps of cyberspace. Other maps can serve as general charts, a way of starting. You'll populate your actual experience of cyberspace with the astounding things you'll find and the people you'll meet. The next chapter presents an overview of navigating the Web, and this will be a stepping-stone for you to find out still more.

An Introduction to Web Navigating and Searching Techniques

17

by
John December

Navigating the Web requires a variety of information skills. Whereas in the previous chaper we examined techniques for navigating the edges of the Web, in this chapter we will look at techniques for navigating the Web itself. And just like FTP and Gopher, the protocol that is native to the Web—HTTP (hypertext transfer protocol)—creates information spaces that you can navigate in a variety of ways.

This chapter refers to concepts and terminology you will need to know in order to make use of the searching techniques that are covered in the chapters following this one. After exploring a sample Web page, this chapter presents an overview of ways to search the Web. Finally, this chapter discusses some important caveats for using (and understanding the limitations of) networked information.

A Sample Web Page: Window to Russia

A typical Web page presents a variety of information, possibly using a large variety of multimedia resources. Through a Web browser, a Web page is often very colorful and can have a pleasing layout and design. As such, a Web-based information system can be very appealing to people who want to find information on a particular topic.

We'll look at a particular Web page to illustrate features commonly found. The URL `http://www.kiae.su/www/wtr/` points to a Web page called Window-to-Russia and is a project of Relcom corporation to provide world-wide resources to information sources about and from Russia. The top part of the home page is shown in Figure 17.1, and the middle is shown in Figure 17.2.

The home page contains elements that you'll find on most Web home pages:

- A descriptive title that appears in the Document Title box on the Web browser main panel.
- A header that describes the sponsors and originators of the information.
- A short introductory text that tells the purpose of the server itself.
- A warning about special resources that may be required to use this information: Cyrillic fonts and the ability to read Russian.

- An appealing arrangement of the link choices, with small icons that help you gain an idea of what the links will retrieve. The icons used in the Russian home page are not standard; unlike the FTP and Gopher symbols (that the Web browser automatically supplies to FTP lists and Gopher menus), there is no standard for icons on Web pages. Developers use whatever they would like. From practice and convention, an arrangement of small icons is often used, rather than many large ones, because many large icons or pictures would require far more time to transfer over the network and slow down the retrieval of the entire page.

- The bottom of the Russian page (not shown in Figure 17.1) includes contact information for the developers of the page.

The preceding list illustrates the kinds of orientation information you should look for on a typical Web server. Although the list of icons and titles on the Russian server are typical, a linear arrangement (reminiscent of a Gopher list or an FTP list as shown in the previous chapter) is not necessary. The HTML language allows developers to be very creative in placing hotspots. A traditional arrangement such as that on the Russian server, however, is very effective for quickly summarizing the choices a user has for encountering the information.

FIGURE 17.1.

The Window-to-Russia home page. © 1994, Relcom Corporation, Eugene Peskin. Printed by permission.

FIGURE 17.2.

The Window-to-Russia home page. © 1994, Relcom Corporation, Eugene Peskin. Printed by permission.

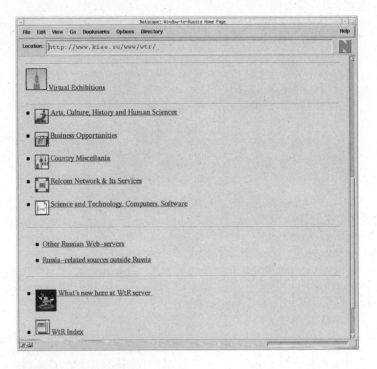

Navigating a Web Page

Now that we've covered the basic elements of a Web page, let's cover some of the basics of navigating the hypertext. The following is some general advice about navigating Web resources:

■ **Look at all your options:** From any Web page, notice what hotspots exist in the text and quickly pass your cursor over some of them, watching the Web browser's message status area for clues about what kinds of resources these links are tied to.

Are all the files at the same server? If so, you're looking at (possibly) a large collection of information, probably developed by the same person or organization. If not, you're probably looking at a page that points to resources not created by the author of that page. This distinction can help you evaluate the usefulness of the information for your purposes. For example, you might want to get the information directly from a particular source.

What kinds of file extensions are on the URLs? Graphics? Movies? You might be particularly interested in finding multimedia information. Passing the cursor over the hotspots on a Web page can help you identify these.

■ **Look beneath the surface:** As a follow-up to the previous point, you'll need to delve into a web in order to find out what is beneath. The file-extension names can give you clues, but only to a limited extent. An `.html` extension on a URL indicates an HTML file connected to the link. This HTML file could be the very treasure-trove you're looking for, or it could be a dead end.

■ **Look for orientation marks and guides:** Once you follow a link from one Web page to another, what have you found? What cues can you use to go back? On a page "beneath the surface" of another page, look for cues or links back to the home page. Of course, you can always use your windows history or your Back button to return to the home page, but developers of pages often provide a "home icon," repeated throughout the Web pages, that assists you in returning to the start. Moreover, developers will provide other kinds of more complex navigational links, including graphical information maps, that help you navigate a web.

For example, on the Russian server, under the "Virtual Exhibitions" link, there is a page with a variety of exhibitions on Russian culture and history. One such link is to the Moscow Kremlin. On the page describing the Moscow Kremlin online excursion, is the following sentence:

```
Begin the excursion. Alternatively, use Index to find
a particular place.
```

This statement is an excellent guide for choosing a way to encounter this information. The first highlighted phrase, `Begin the excursion`, gives a cue that the exhibits will be presented sequentially. The Index hotspot offers nonsequential access. When you click Index, the display shown in Figure 17.3 appears.

FIGURE 17.3.

The Window-to-Russia Kremlin tour index.

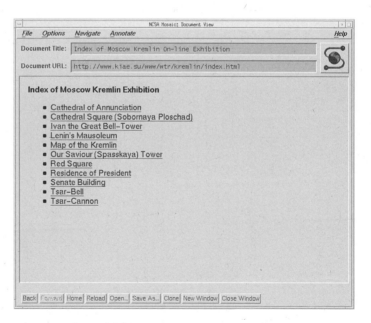

The Kremlin tour index is very useful because it gives rapid, random access to the whole exhibit. By looking for such indexes and guides on a Web page, you will be able to navigate them well.

- **Be aware of your window history:** Every time you take a different link from a Web page, your window history is renewed from that point on. (This is known as the "nipping" phenomenon.) Thus, a good way to explore a whole web is by following branches in a depth-first manner, going down a branch completely until you reach a page without further links and then backing up. This is not a perfect algorithm for finding every page. The layout of a web is not necessarily a tree in which the links among the pages branch out so that a complete tour of all the pages is easy; rather, a collection of pages can be connected in an arbitrary manner.

Figure 17.4 shows a sample web layout. Following the link from the home page to Page A, and then proceeding to D and F will help you tour that one branch. Returning to the home page from F can be as easy as clicking the Back button three times. If you go to Page B after this, your windows history file will "lop off" your trip down the A-D-F branch. Your global history file will still retain the time of your visit and the URLs of pages A, D, and F, however, so that the shading of the links on the home page for Page A will clue you in to your previous visit.

FIGURE 17.4.

A sample web layout.

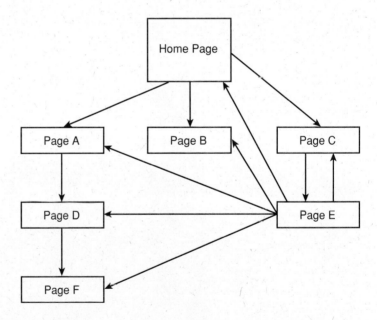

In Figure 17.4, notice also how Page E serves as a kind of index page, actually linking to all the other pages in the web. If, after visiting Page B and returning from the home page, you go to Page C and then Page E, you will find that all the hotspots on Page E are all shaded, as you've previously visited all the other pages. Your window history list will include Home Page, Page C, and Page E.

As you gain more experience in navigating a web, you'll find that the combination of your windows history used with observing the shading of previously visited links will help you explore a web. Diagrams for hypertext organization like that in Figure 17.4

might help you, although there is no current facility in Web browsers to generate such a diagram. Thus, the burden of providing a good orientation for the reader falls to the web weaver.

- **Use indexes when available:** It is important to remember that your goal in navigating a web like the Window-to-Russia home page is not to exhaustively search the entire web, but to choose the information you would like to see. Often a web will have its entire contents indexed in a searchable database. By entering keywords into the input window to the index, you'll get a list of links to pages on the web that match that keyword.

- **Read the text:** Just as many users don't read the text during Telnet sessions (because there often is a lot of it), so too do readers often skip over the text on Web pages. Instead they focus on the graphics or other features that draw the eye. It is important in navigating to skim through the accompanying text to find important navigation cues. For example, on the Russian page, the statement about Russian Cyrillic fonts could be very helpful when you want to read text later on in this web.

- **Give constructive feedback:** Many Web pages include the name and e-mail address of the administrator (often called the webmaster). If you find an error or a link that won't work and you're pretty sure it isn't a temporary problem, send a polite note to the web administrator. Similarly, if you find the organization of the information or links confusing, constructive feedback to the administrator (who may not be the information developer but might be able to give you the address of the developer) can help improve the usability of the information on the Web.

Finding What You Want: Ways of Searching

Now that we've talked about general ways of navigating a single web, let's turn our attention to the whole of the Web itself. Just as FTP space has Archie and Gopher space has Veronica, so too does the Web have analogous tools: spiders that help you find things using keyword searches. Moreover, just as there is a mega-list of all FTP sites and a geographical list of all Gophers, so too are there mega-lists and geographical lists of Web sites. The searching mechanisms on the Web, however, are more varied and complex than those for FTP and Gopher, and the variety of searching tools and resources gives you a range of ways to search for a resource that you want. The next chapters cover ways that you can search the Web, as follows:

- **Searching by subject:** Making use of hierarchically-arranged subject catalogs and trees.
- **Searching by keyword:** Utilizing spiders (things that crawl on the Web to find resources).
- **Searching by space:** By using lists servers in information spaces, using lists of Web sites arranged by geography, and searching directories of people in "home page space."
- **Searching by surfing:** Utilizing techniques, resources, and tools to help you locate new or unusual Web information as well as making serendipitous finds.

Because using the Web to locate information is truly an integrative activity that can combine several or all of the preceding techniques during the course of any one search, this part of the book includes a final chapter that integrates all these techniques in a single example.

Caveats About Networked Information

Although the Web is a treasure-trove, it is important to approach the vast resources it contains with some caution. We cannot carry the same expectations about accuracy, completeness, and reliability from the print world to the world of the Web. Moreover, we cannot apply print-based standards about the authorship or the completeness of a work when it is on the Web.

Origins of Our Expectations About Information and Publishing

We are a culture still relying largely on print to convey information, and our expectations about information accuracy and reliability are based on traditions evolving out of print traditions. The invention of the printing press was revolutionary in human history because it gave people who owned printing presses a way to widely disseminate their ideas. However, the relatively large expense of owning a press and printing multiple copies of a work limited the number of people who could engage in publishing. The scarcity of the printer's resources also caused the printer to make careful judgements about what to publish. This resource scarcity was one factor contributing to the traditions of editorial control over publishing. The development of the scientific method and scholarly traditions of peer review added onto this publishing control an additional layer of requirements for accuracy and completeness. While our culture and institutions have embraced these publishing traditions for centuries, the Web transforms them. The Web allows a person, equipped with the skills this book aims to convey, the power to be a printer as well as an instant, global publisher.

The Web transforms people into global information publishers like no other advance in human history. Desktop publishing has enabled the explosive growth of small presses, journals, and publications. However, a person with a desktop publishing system, while arrayed with the tools necessary for high-quality documents in terms of appearance, is limited in terms of reproduction and distribution. If someone writes a book and prints 100 copies of it on a laser printer, who would buy such a book and how would they find out about it? In contrast, a Web-based system of information can include multimedia graphics and interactive elements, and can be available to people with the right equipment (such as computers, Internet connections, and browser—which may be a very steep requirement). This Web-based approach might be far more successful in distributing a book or information. However, something has been lost in this process of self-publishing, and that something is the expectation about editorial control and selection that (paper) publishing institutions have.

On the Web, just about anyone can put out almost anything without any checks on its accuracy, completeness, value, or impact on the wider Net community. As a consumer of Web information, then, you will need to develop your skills in evaluating the accuracy, completeness, stability, and value of any information you find. You won't be able to use the attractive appearance of any Web resource as an indicator of quality or accuracy. You'll find most Web resources are offered in good faith with careful attention to detail and concern about accuracy. Moreover, Net-based information can actually can go through a very active peer review process in which users correspond with the information provider and offer comments and corrections. Not everything on the Web is junk, nor is everything accurate.

Things to Remember When Accessing and Using Net and Web Resources

There's no simple way to evaluate the value of Web information. You can use your own experience and judgement, rely on people you trust, or consult others who use the same information. Here is a checklist of some things to keep in mind when using Web resources:

■ **Net resources are not always accurate.** Just because you "read it on the Web" doesn't mean that something is true, just as seeing something on TV or reading it in the newspaper doesn't make it true. The appealing graphical display a Web browser gives to Net information, with fonts and well-formatted displays, may mislead a user to "feel" that the information is accurate. While there is certainly not any Web-wide conspiracy about spreading false information :), inaccuracies can have a way of propagating on the Net in particularly virulent ways. (See URL news:alt.folklore.urban for some discussions about how people can think something is true when it simply isn't.)

The key points to keep in mind about accuracy are as follows:

1. Can you trust the source? Is the provider of the information an expert in the field? The importance of this question depends on the kind of information you are looking for.

    For example, if you run across a list of "smileys" (symbolic shorthand for facial expressions) on the Web, you can consider if the author consulted other comprehensive and authoritative listings in the field. In the field of smileys, David W. Sanderson is the "Noah Webster of Smileys" (*The Wall Street Journal*) and has published a (paper) book as well as created a smiley server program containing a large amount of known smileys. On the other hand, you can probably judge a good smiley yourself. The determiner for your trust is your purpose—are you looking for a comprehensive list or just one good smiley?

2. Are there others who point to the same information or resource as a reliable source? Is the source you found a very odd occurrence in an obscure corner of the Web? If so, the information might have great value, or it might be just ramblings.

In any case, you might ask peers or practitioners in the field. If the source is often cited, you still should be critical—how reliable to you is the source of information for your purpose?

3. What do you know about the information's accuracy? For example, is the Frequently Asked Questions (FAQ) list for the Usenet newsgroup `alt.war.civil.usa` accurate? Does someone you know who is knowledgeable in the field consider it an accurate (although not necessarily complete) source of information? In general, Usenet newsgroup FAQs encounter a great deal of scrutiny by newsgroup participants, all of whom are interested in the field and many of whom practice professionally in the area of expertise. However, there will be errors and misinformation—the key is to check out how authoritative the source is considered for that field.

4. What is the original source of the information? For example, the Weather Underground gets its information from U.S. National Weather Service data and forecasts. This attests to a reliable, "official" source. In other cases, the source of the information might be a laboratory or a professionally-run server. However, you can't always expect "official" sources for Web-based information.

   A Web server is often set up by an administrator or technician as an experiment, with content provided haphazardly. One should not expect the Web server at `www.foo.edu` to always be the "official" voice of Foo University. Check for claims made on a Web page. Just because the page might include a graphic of the official University logo (which can be easily scanned in), the information it contains is not necessarily official. Generally, official servers have names like `www.foo.edu`, rather than `mickey.unix5.cs.foo.edu` (although it is not all that difficult to manipulate the name that appears on a server). Keep in mind that an official server will normally have a Web administrator assigned, with phone contact as well as e-mail contact information. And of course, the tone and organization of the information itself on the server will give you many clues about the "officialness" of the information.

■ **Net resources might even be illegal.** There are law firms that specialize in communications law that routinely cruise the Net looking for licensed commercial software available at FTP sites illegally, or illegally provided information and copyright infringements. Information that has high monetary value is not often placed on the Net for free. Therefore, be suspicious of sites that claim to have commercial software available for free, and be suspicious of information providers who give out copyrighted works without permission of the copyright owners. Many publishers of books, however, create support sites for samples of a copyrighted work as part of a marketing strategy—look for notices of copyright and ownership. As a consumer of information, respect these copyrights, as the traditions of intellectual property and copyright law encourage individuals to create more valuable works.

■ **Net resources are not always complete.** Information you find on the Web is not all that there is. For example, we'll see in the next chapters how you can find multiple collections of information on a particular subject in many different places on the Web and at the edges of the Web, yet still come up short for certain topics. Moreover, the Web itself isn't even close (yet) to containing the sum of all human knowledge! The holdings of even a modest university library far outstrip the Web in terms of completeness of coverage in many subjects.

■ **Net resources are not always peer-reviewed.** Information on the Web is often created by a sole author, without a formal process of peer-review. Peer-review processes have long been used in scientific communication to make sure information is accurate and complete, and that there are no errors of logic or presentation that devalue the work. Some Net-based information (for example, in peer-reviewed electronic journals) has gone through review processes as rigorous as for print-based publications. However, a great deal of Net-based information has not. Often, the review process is informal, such as in the case of Usenet newsgroups or a frequently-accessed information resource. You might contact the provider of the information and ask about any review done on the information or resource. It may be that they have more background information as well as an opinion on its value.

■ **Net resources are not a substitute for libraries (and librarians).** Some people, finding the Net and the Web a rich source of information, easily accessible through clicks of a mouse button, might ignore other means of gathering information. The Net is not a substitute for a library or a good reference librarian. (In fact, you'll find many good reference librarians are Net-savvy themselves.) The key to remember is to not assume that just because you've used all the methods described in this book for finding all the Web-accessible information on a subject, your research is complete. Your library may hold even more information.

Navigator's Check

We've seen the basic layout of a typical Web site and how to navigate it. While going through the Web, keep these points in mind:

■ An individual web usually offers many informational cues and navigation aids to help you use the information presented efficiently.

■ Your windows history can be a useful navigational aid; keep in mind the "nipping" phenomenon.

■ The chapters that follow will cover how you can search the Web by subject, keyword, space (information, geographical, people), and via surfing.

■ Be critical and cautious of the information you find on a network; it isn't always true.

Trees: Subject-Oriented Searching

18

by
John December

There might be situations in which you want to learn about a subject without necessarily having a precise idea of the specific topics you would like to study. You wouldn't necessarily want to use the keyword searching mechanisms, Archie and Veronica, to search FTP space and Gopher space, because you would not have a specific set of filenames or keywords to look for. Rather, you would want to locate collections that present broad categories of information organized according to subjects. You've already seen an example of a subject-oriented compilation in Gopher space (the Gopher Jewels collection). There are similar, Web-based collections of subject-oriented resources.

When you want to find collections of information or individual resources related to a particular subject, you'll need to seek out the many subject-oriented collections on the Web. There is no single source for subject-oriented information on the Web, although there are some very complete collections, and a few key places on the Web provide excellent jumping-off points.

This chapter outlines resources, tools, techniques, and tips that you can use to find subject-oriented information on the Web. Using subject-oriented searching methods alone probably won't help you find all the information you might need. Instead, consider subject-oriented searching as just one technique that you can use to search the Web. This chapter uses the metaphor of the tree as a way of providing a useful analogy for what you will explore during subject-oriented searching.

NOTE

The correct mathematical term for many Web information structures described here is *graph*. A graph is a structure of nodes (documents) and edges (links). A tree, in the mathematical sense, is a special kind of graph that branches similar to the way a real-life tree's branches grow upwards, without reaching back towards the ground or other branches. (There are no cycles in a mathematical tree.) The structure of most subject-oriented collections, however, is not always in the form of a mathematical tree. A Web-based collection can include arbitrary branching (not always just "growing" in one direction). However, this chapter uses the term *tree* in its more informal sense; understand that the Web-based trees can allow for branching in any direction.

The Web is full of trees—lists and directories of resources, many arranged hierarchically so that you can go down a series of selections to find what you want. Like the yellow pages of a phone book, the labels on the branches of these trees include subjects, topics, and subtopics.

As you look at techniques for searching these trees, remember that there is no single tree that organizes all subject-based information for the entire Web or Internet. You'll have to use a variety of techniques to seek out appropriate subject-oriented trees and use surfing techniques (covered in Chapter 21, "Surfing: Finding the New and Unusual") to keep abreast of other useful subject trees that pop up all the time.

The sections that follow introduce many of the most popular subject trees on the Web and at the edge of the Web. To help you follow this survey and to compare the trees, this chapter uses the environment as a sample subject for searching.

Resources for Subject-Oriented Searching

This book already discussed one very valuable subject-oriented tree, the Gopher Jewels Collection in Chapter 16, "At the Edge of the Web." The Gopher Jewels collection, based on Gophers, is at the edge of the Web (accessible through a Web browser, but not in hypertext itself). Because good subject-oriented trees attempt to collect information from the whole Internet, you'll find that there are few trees totally contained within the Web. Instead, most trees extend to the edges of the Web (and thus contain links to non-hypertext documents).

The WWW Virtual Library

CERN (Conseil Europeen pour la Recherche Nucleaire) is a center for high-energy physics research in Switzerland, the birthplace of the Web. Therefore, CERN's subject tree (the WWW Virtual Library, now hosted on `http://www.w3.org/`), an early outgrowth of the initial Web development, is a comprehensive source of subject-oriented information. The URL of the WWW Virtual Library is `http://www.w3.org/hypertext/DataSources/bySubject/Overview.html`, and the tree is mostly Web-based; that is, its branches and individual items reach into the Web fairly deeply, although eventually individual pages within the tree reach the edges of the Web.

Figure 18.1 shows the front page of the Virtual Library, showing the top-level organization. You'll notice that the subject breakdown is not necessarily along standard lines (such as a Library of Congress Subject division).

Navigating the Virtual Library is quite simple. You can get more specific in your search by following the tree's branches. You'll encounter more pages with lists of more specialized subjects and topics. This multiple-page approach, in which the tree is very tall (contains many levels of hierarchy) is common in Web-based trees. The entire tree itself is not hosted entirely on the host `www.w3.org`, but you'll encounter pages on many different hosts as you go deep enough into the tree. In this way, the Virtual Library represents a massive, collaborative effort to gather and present information on a wide range of subjects.

FIGURE 18.1.

The WWW Virtual Library.

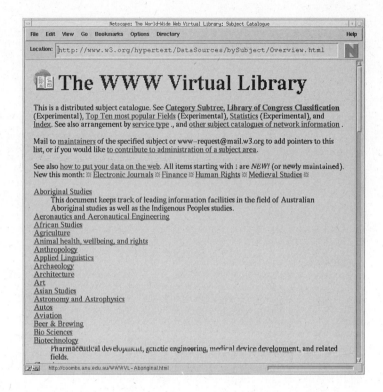

Let's use the example of seeking environmental information as a means to illustrate individual tree-offerings and to compare trees. The front page of the WWW Virtual Library has an entry for "Environment." Selecting this link, we obtain the page shown in Figure 18.2. Because the list is so long, the bottom portion is shown in Figure 18.3.

The Virtual Subject Library page for the environment is impressive. The multimedia guide at the bottom of the page defines the media formats you will find in the pages. Notice that the host for this page, `ecosys.drdr.virginia.edu`, is also the host for EcoWeb, a collection of resources devoted to local recycling and environmental concerns (Figure 18.4). This environment page is typical of Virtual Library pages—containing a rich set of links for topics and subtopics. We'll see how other trees offer similar collections, but their contents are different, as they grew independently.

FIGURE 18.2.

The WWW Virtual Library entry for Environment 1.

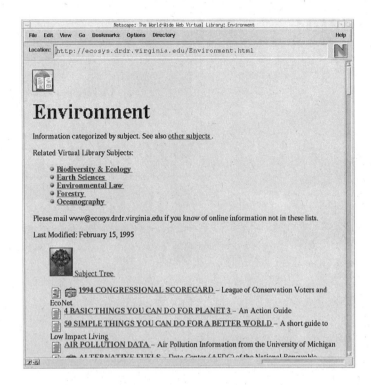

FIGURE 18.3.

The WWW Virtual Library entry for Environment 2.

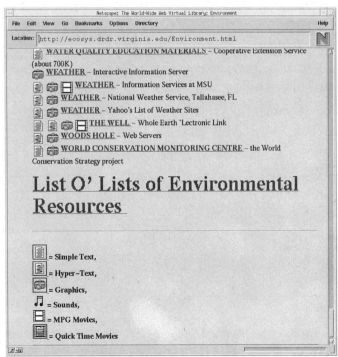

FIGURE 18.4.

Eco Web.

Yahoo

Yahoo is a very large collection of Web links arranged into a hierarchical hotlist. Created and maintained by David Filo and Jerry Yang, the Yahoo database (http://www.yahoo.com/) front page is shown in Figure 18.5.

Yahoo grew very rapidly over the winter of 1994–95 (Figure 18.6), with the number of files being retrieved daily reaching near one million by early February 1995.

FIGURE 18.5.

Yahoo Database front page. Copyright © David Filo and Jerry Yang. Printed by permission.

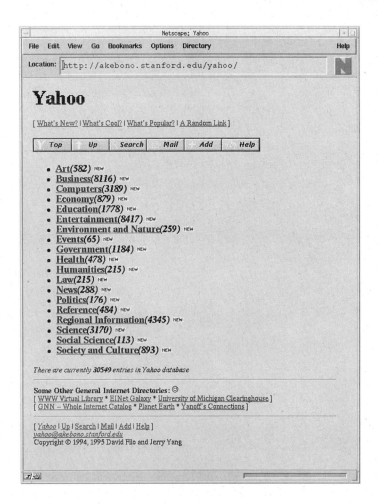

FIGURE 18.6.

Yahoo usage statistics (number of files retreived daily) from October 1994 through February 1995. Copyright © David Filo and Jerry Yang. Printed by permission.

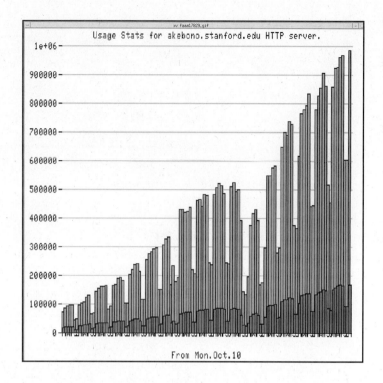

Yahoo's "What's New" pages have come to be one of the best places on the Web to encounter new information. Since user-suggested links are quickly added to Yahoo, the database gives a comprehensive list of Web resources. While not as conservative as the WWW Virtual Library or Galaxy, Yahoo serves the Web community well as a "fast cache" access point for Web information. Yahoo does have its limitations: The categories are not defined using a standard naming scheme, and the inclusion of items is not formally reviewed by experts in the particular category or topic.

Let's continue our search for environmental information into Yahoo. From Yahoo's front page, we can see "Environment and Nature" as one option. Choosing this link, we obtain Figure 18.7.

Figure 18.7 illustrates many of Yahoo's features:

- The title bar at the top of Yahoo pages allows you quick access to the top page, a search index for the whole database (discussed in the next chapter), as well as feedback (mail, suggesting links to add) and help.

- The database includes listings of individual documents and resources shown in regular-weight bold titles.

- Submenus of the current Yahoo subject division are shown as bold text with ( ) after the title, showing the number of links in that subdivision.

- Cross references to other Yahoo subdivisions are shown in bold text with an @ sign after the title.

- Entries that have been added during the current day are shown with a New icon beside them (or a text-equivalent [New] label).

- Subdivisions that include new entries have a New icon beside them.

FIGURE 18.7.

Yahoo Environment and Nature section. Copyright © David Filo and Jerry Yang. Printed by permission.

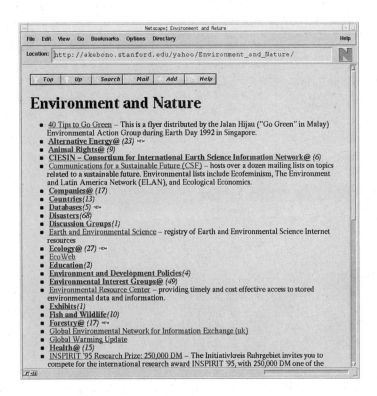

Notice that Yahoo's entries vary in the degree of annotation. Some entries include a detailed description, while some entries are merely a single link. Because the addition of new links is moderated by Yahoo developers, the items in the categories fit the subject matter represented. To understand the specialization possible in Yahoo, choose the Disasters subcategory from the Environment and Nature section. You'll get what is shown in Figure 18.8.

FIGURE 18.8.

*Yahoo Disasters section.
Copyright © David Filo
and Jerry Yang. Printed
by permission.*

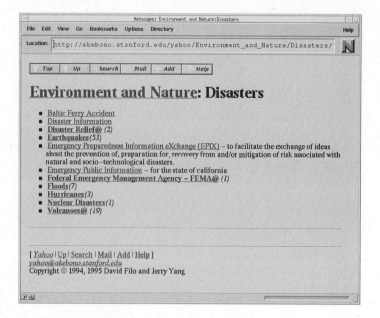

Galaxy from EINet

While the WWW Virtual Subject Library contains a great deal of links into the Web, the important thing to remember when searching trees is that you shouldn't rely on only one as a sole source for subject-oriented information.

Let's examine another subject tree, called Galaxy, developed by EINet, a commercial provider of network communication and services. While the WWW Virtual Library was essentially a non-commercial, cooperative venture, EINet's Galaxy is offered to the Web for free, courtesy of a commercial company. Galaxy enhances EINet's reputation as a provider of network information and communication services while also contributing a valuable public service to the Web community. Galaxy's URL is `http://www.einet.net/galaxy.html`, and its front page is shown in Figure 18.9.

Like the WWW Virtual Library, Galaxy's front page shows a hierarchical organization of subjects, arranged in broad subject categories listed alphabetically, with links from the front page to other pages containing further information. Unlike the Virtual Library, however, Galaxy provides a search mechanism for finding entries in the Galaxy web.

FIGURE 18.9.
EINet's Galaxy.

This search mechanism, located at the bottom of the front page (Figure 18.9) gives you a quick way to find information that might be buried deep within the Galaxy tree. For example, a user might not know from the front page which subject classification to follow for environmental information. A quick search using the search mechanism yields a link to a page for the environment located in the Community subdivision on the home page (which a user might not have seen upon first coming into Galaxy). The search page shows entry points to all searching methods available through Galaxy in Figure 18.10. The top of the environmental page is shown in Figure 18.11.

This environmental page contains a similar organization to the WWW Virtual Library's environmental page, with links to pages that further refine the subject area of the environment to specific topics (agriculture, air and water quality, ecosystems, and so on), as well as links to specific documents, directories, and collections.

FIGURE 18.10.

*EINet's Galaxy
search mechanism.*

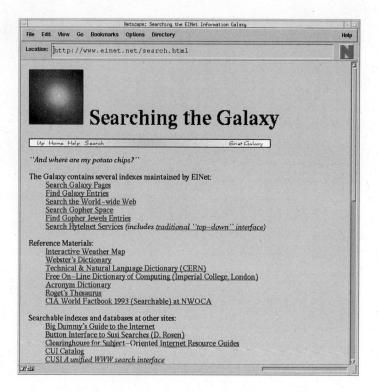

What sets Galaxy apart from the WWW Virtual Library page are its facilities for growing (for allowing users to fill out a form to add information to the page), as well as built-in searching mechanisms for gaining maximum reach into the Web space, Gopher space, Hytelnet entries, and WAIS indexes for terms related to the environment.

FIGURE 18.11.

EINet's Galaxy environmental page.

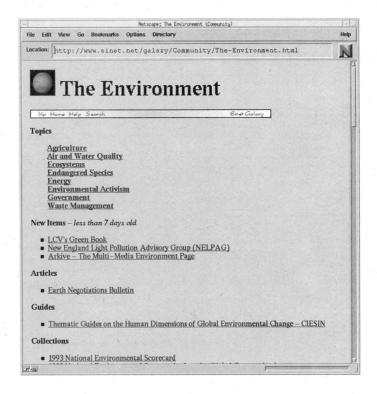

Figure 18.12 shows the "Search Results for Keywords" section of the page, with links to search results from the Web, Hytelnet menu entries, Gopher space, and WAIS indexes related to the keyword environment. The next chapter discusses keyword searching in detail.

FIGURE 18.12.

Search results for keywords.

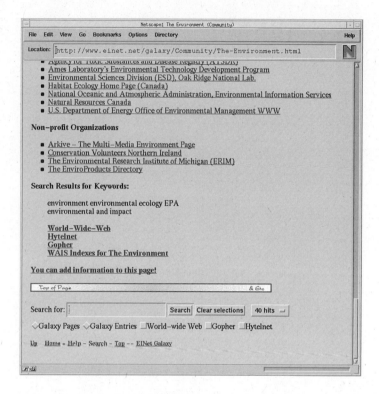

Galaxy's links to these search results are useful because they organize the results using WAIS (wide area information system) technology. WAIS technology retrieves documents based on a request from a user according to a system of indexes, and returns a list of documents to the user along with a "score" for each "hit" in the database, with a higher score indicating a greater relevance to the user's search request. This searching and scoring takes into account the user's search string (which might contain Boolean expressions or wild cards), as well as word frequency, density, and other characteristics of the texts in the database.

The "You can add information to this page!" link is also a valuable addition. It allows the user to enter a form (Figure 18.13) to add additional information (moderated by Galaxy developers) to Galaxy's database.

FIGURE 18.13.

EINet's Galaxy add information form.

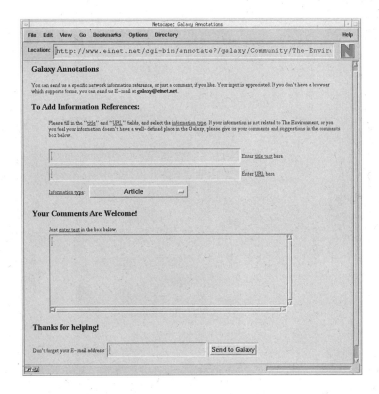

While subject trees such as the WWW Virtual Library welcome submissions via e-mail, Galaxy's forms-based facility makes it easy for someone to add information, and it helps the user supply all the necessary information for an entry into the subject tree.

The Whole Internet Catalog from O'Reilly

O'Reilly & Associates is an information publisher that has established a strong presence on the Internet through its Global Network Navigator (GNN) information system. The Whole Internet Catalog (WIC) portion of GNN is an extension of the resource section in Ed Krol's *The Whole Internet User's Guide and Catalog,* a paper-based book O'Reilly first published in 1992. Like Galaxy, the O'Reilly's WIC is a public service, supported by a commercial firm, extending O'Reilly's reputation as an information provider both on the Net and in its (paper-based) book publishing business.

Similar to the WWW Virtual Subject Library, GNN's WIC (`http://www.gnn.com/wic/newrescat.toc.html`), provides a tree structure showing various subjects on its front page (Figure 18.14).

FIGURE 18.14.

O'Reilly's Whole Internet Catalog.

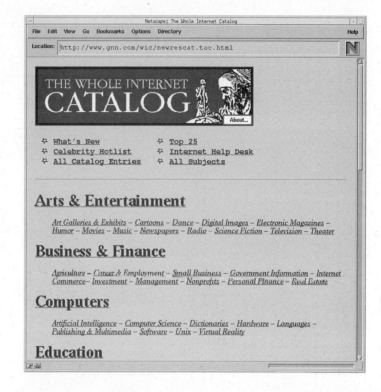

Continuing with the illustrative search for environmental information, select the Science link on the WIC front page and obtain a page listing many subjects within the field of science, including a link to Environmental Studies, shown in Figure 18.11.

The WIC's entries contain descriptive text underneath the links. For example, under the link for the 1994 National Environmental Scorecard, you can find text, written by people at GNN, describing what this resource offers.

Usenet FAQ Archives

The global asynchronous text communication system known as Usenet has grown very quickly over the years since its inception in 1979; Usenet is a project of two graduate students at Duke University: Jim Ellis and Tom Truscott. Today, Usenet newsgroups number in the thousands, covering a very wide range of topics on just about every human pursuit or subject imaginable. Participants in Usenet newsgroups contribute articles to ongoing discussions. These articles propagate through the Matrix (not just the Internet) for others to read and respond to. This process of discussion is ongoing, with some newsgroups experiencing hundreds of new articles per day. Since articles eventually expire (are deleted from the local systems on which they are stored), information within the individual articles can eventually be lost. Long-time participants in the newsgroup can often face the same questions and discussions from new users over and over again. It is from this need to transmit accumulated knowledge that the tradition of Frequently Asked Questions (FAQ) lists arose.

FIGURE 18.15.

O'Reilly's Whole Internet Catalog environment page.

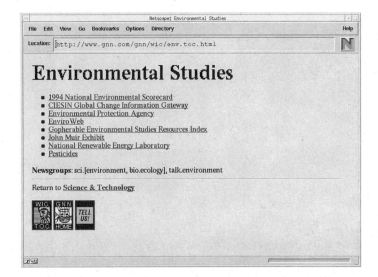

FAQ lists evolve out of newsgroup discussion. Sometimes one person decides to record the results of a discussion about a particular question and then periodically post this question again with its answer in the newsgroup. This way, longer lists of such questions and answers develop and are often reposted to the newsgroup for further comment, as well as an informational service to new readers. While periodically posted to the newsgroups, these FAQs often get lost in the hundreds of other articles or don't appear at the right time for new users to see. Therefore, a more static form of housing these FAQs developed at an FTP site on a machine at MIT. The machine, rtfm.mit.edu, holds these FAQs for newsgroups, making them available via anonymous FTP. The resulting list of FAQs covers a wide variety of subjects. The entire collection of Usenet FAQs can be found at the URL ftp://rtfm.mit.edu/pub/usenet/. A Web version of access to FAQs posted to the newsgroup news.answers is maintained by Tom Fine at http://www.cis.ohio-state.edu/hypertext/faq/usenet/FAQ-List.html and is shown in Figure 18.16.

FIGURE 18.16.
Usenet FAQs.

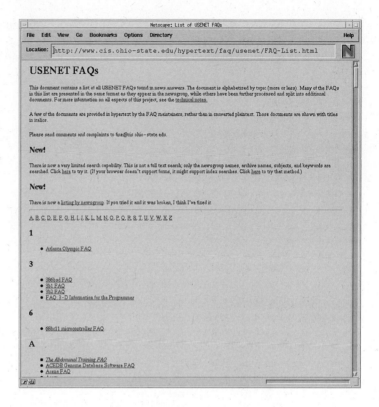

Usenet FAQs are generally in text form, although the collection shown in Figure 18.12 includes many that are in HTML. The information in the FAQs can often include very rich discussion of the field of study, as well as descriptions of other information and online resources. Because the newsgroup names are so specialized, Usenet FAQs are often very particular (and peculiar). For example, you can see a very specialized FAQ (listed in Figure 18.12) called Abdominal Training FAQ. Usenet FAQs are therefore very useful for finding very specific information on a particular topic.

Continuing the search for environmental information, scroll down the list of Usenet FAQs; but you won't find an entry for environmental information. Using the File / Find In Current… also yields no results. Going to FTP space, you can try the collection of all Usenet FAQs at `ftp://rtfm.mit.edu/pub/usenet`. Looking in the Usenet by newsgroup directory, you find a promising newsgroup, `sci.environment` and find that it contains several FAQs: "Ozone Depletion FAQ" (in four parts), and an "FAQ on Sea Level, Ice, and Greenhouses." These FAQs are very specialized and contain a great deal of information, including references to published, peer-reviewed articles on the subject. As mentioned previously, this specificity in FAQ coverage is typical of

Usenet—very complete on specific subjects, but not necessarily offering a comprehensive selection of subjects and topics.

The Clearinghouse for Subject-Oriented Internet Guides

While the Usenet FAQs provide a great deal of information on a variety of subjects related to newsgroups, another subject-oriented collection is at the University of Michigan. Developed by Louis Rosenfeld, the Clearinghouse for Subject-Oriented Internet Guides (Figure 18.17) provides a collection of guides in many areas outside of newsgroup subject divisions. Like the Usenet FAQs, the Michigan collection consists of subject-oriented guides. However, the Michigan collection's aim is to gather guides that help people discover further Internet resources, and thus is very useful for obtaining guides that help you locate information on the Internet.

The Clearinghouse is available through the Web at `http://www.lib.umich.edu/chhome.html`, as well as through Gopher and FTP. (URLs are given on the home page.) Although most of the guides are in text, some have HTML analogues, and others have no plain text equivalent. In the Clearinghouse, there is a wide variety of subjects represented in the humanities, social sciences, sciences, and multiple subjects.

FIGURE 18.17.

The Clearinghouse for Subject-Oriented Internet Guides. Courtesy of Lou Rosenfeld.

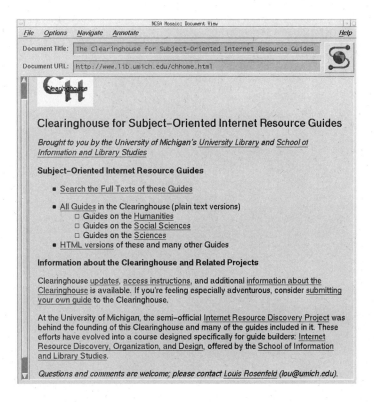

The Michigan Clearinghouse does have two guides about the environment, one by A. Phelps, and one by T. Murphy and C. Briggs-Erickson. The Phelps Guide includes a caveat that it is not intended to be a comprehensive guide but a representative guide of sources of information on the Internet. As such, it can be a useful introduction to finding other sources. The Murphy and Briggs-Erickson guide on the environment, mentioned in the Phelps Guide, gives a more comprehensive view of Net-based information, including listings of major environmental organizations and networks, resources for specific topics in the environment, regulations and standards, regional concerns, online library catalogs, and a further bibliography. Thus, the Michigan guides can be very useful in locating more resources on the Net.

The InterNIC Directory of Directories

The InterNIC (`http://ds.internic.net/`) is a network information center that is the result of National Science Foundation support. Two organizations provide directory and database services, and registration services. As part of the InterNIC Directory and Database Services (run by AT&T), The InterNIC Directory of Directories provides a catalog of information resources on the Internet. You can browse the Directory of Directories (Figure 18.18) or use a keyword search mechanism (Figure 18.19).

FIGURE 18.18.

InterNIC Directory of Directories (browse).

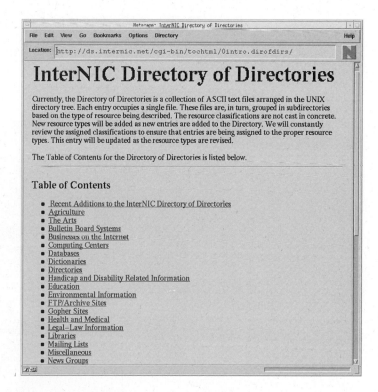

The subject coverage of the directory is far thinner than most other online subject trees, but the entries given usually represent fairly well-done sources of information, and the InterNIC Directory services actively work to make sure that the information in the directory is verified, kept up to date, and is presented using a standard information format (making searching and comparison of resources easier). Figure 18.20 shows the entries in the InternNIC Directory of Directories for environmental information.

FIGURE 18.19.

InterNIC Directory of Directories (search).

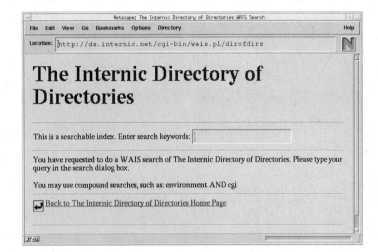

An Alternate View of the WWW Virtual Library: by the Library of Congress

One of the drawbacks of many Web-based subject trees is the classification scheme used. For very large trees, a poor scheme for categories and subcategories can drive the user down bewildering twists and turns (and cross-references). One attempt to use a more standard classification scheme is the WWW Virtual Library, arranged according to the U.S. Library of Congress Categorization scheme (as shown in Figure 18.21).

FIGURE 18.20.

InterNIC Directory of Directories—Environmental information.

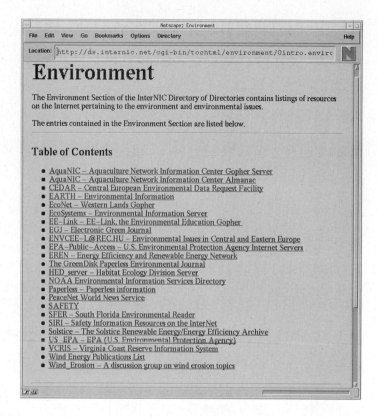

To find the WWW VL page on the environment, follow the link for "Geography. Anthropology. Recreation" from Figure 18.21 to arrive at the page in Figure 18.22.

FIGURE 18.21.

The World Wide Web Virtual Library: the Library of Congress classification.

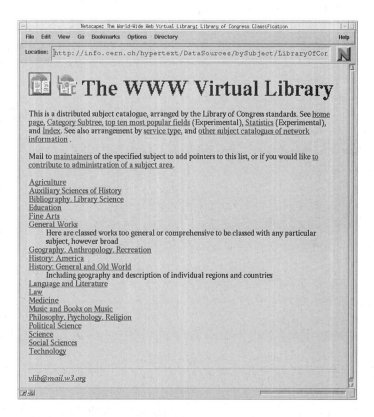

FIGURE 18.22.

The World Wide Web Virtual Library— Geography. Anthropology. Recreation.

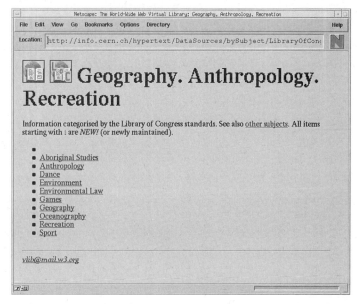

The link for environment from this page is the same as for the regular view into the WWW VL. The benefit of having the Library of Congress view as an alternative is that it conforms to a more commonly accepted standard for categorizing subject information.

Gopher Trees

Just as the WWW Virtual Library broke Web space into a subject-oriented tree structure, so too do various Gopher trees. We've already talked about the Gopher Jewels collection (`http://galaxy.einet.net/GJ/index.html`) in a previous chapter. There are other Gopher space subject trees available that aid in finding subject-oriented resources. The subject tree at URL `gopher://burrow.cl.msu.edu/11/internet/subject` provides a large variety of subject trees from many institutions, as well as Gopher links to the Michigan collection and Gopher Jewels.

To find a particular subject on the Gopher trees, you could investigate each Gopher tree separately. You could also use a Veronica search to find information about the environment. A good place to start if you want to use the tree-like method for searching is Gopher Jewels. There is an entry for Environment on the list at `http://galaxy.einet.net/GJ/index.html`, shown in Figure 18.23.

FIGURE 18.23.

The Gopher Jewels Environment page.

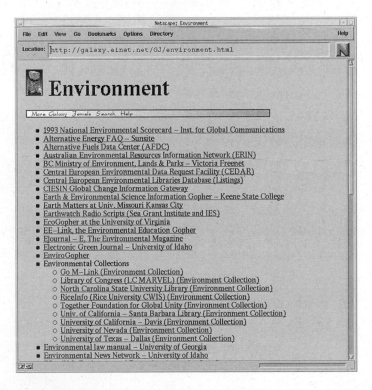

You can see that the Gopher Jewels page for the environment contains links to many Gophers, and some of the names should be familiar to you from your previous searches for environmental information.

Other Trees

On the Web, there are many other subject-oriented classifications of Net resources. In fact, the proliferation of subject-oriented trees has been so virulent that probably a tree of the subject trees will soon develop :). Here are some of the other Web-based trees that provide a way to search for subject-oriented information. (See also the Net Directory in Appendix C for more subject trees on the Internet.)

- Planet Earth Home Page, `http://white.nosc.mil/info.html`. Richard P. Bocker created this web that collects a wide variety of links on starting points ranging over many Net resources. Unlike other hierarchies, this one does not allow automatic additions to the menus and entries, although the developer accepts suggestions.

- CyberNet, `http://cybersight.com/cgi-bin/cs/s?main.gmml`. CyberNet is a commercial venture for providing alternative information, provided by Internet Marketing, Inc. The goal of these developers is to provide information that will attract viewers and then attract advertisers.

- DA-CLOD (Distributedly Administered Categorical List of Documents), `http://schiller.wustl.edu/DACLOD/daclod`. This is an effort to create a categorized database of links to subject-oriented information on the Internet. Like Galaxy and O'Reilly's WIC, the DA-CLOD project attempts to organize and gather subject-oriented information. Like Galaxy, it employs a method by which users add items to its database through a forms interface.

- Mother-of-all BBSs, `http://www.cs.colorado.edu/homes/mcbryan/public_html/bb/summary.html`. This is an interactive system for collecting subject-oriented information developed by Oliver McBryan. Users of this BBS can add items or create new directories on the bulletin board. The information and organization of this bulletin board is contributed and determined by users themselves.

- Tree of Gopher Trees, `gopher://burrow.cl.msu.edu/11/internet/subject`. This is a large collection of Gopher subject trees. This collection includes, for example, pointers to the Michigan Clearinghouse Gopher, as well as other subject trees.

- Joel's, `http://www.cen.uiuc.edu/~jj9544/index.html`. Joel's Hierarchical Subject Index (JHSI), is a project created by Joel Jones that collects and organizes information on the Internet based on a hierarchical division of knowledge. Although the contents of some of the tree's branches are sparse, the coverage of the structure itself is fairly ambitious.

Indexes

Besides Web sites that offer a series of pages to access information on the Web, there are some subject-oriented indexes that can give you jumping-off points to information on the Internet.

- The Meta-Index from UIUC (The University of Illinois, Urbana-Champaign (home of Mosaic) maintains a Meta Index at `http://www.ncsa.uiuc.edu/SDG/Software/Mosaic/MetaIndex.html`. This is the same list that you can obtain from the Navigate / Internet Resources Meta-Index through the Mosaic control panel. It gives you access into a list of indexes of Web resources.

- Scott Yanoff's list of special Internet collections is a popular view into the Net and Web. Begun as a list of just six items in 1991, it has continued its popularity. The hypertext version at `http://www.uwm.edu/Mirror/inet.services.html` can give you jumping-off points to subject-oriented information on a range of subjects. The list summarizes a wide variety of information and resources that are very useful for showing "what's out there" on the Net.

- My list of Information Sources for the Internet and computer-mediated communication at `http://www.rpi.edu/Internet/Guides/decemj/internet-cmc.html` is useful for finding sources of information about the Internet itself. Included in this guide are links to many subject-oriented collections and indexes, as well as resources discussed in this book.

Hand-crafted indexes such as the ones shown here have some value in guiding you to subject-oriented information, particularly if the index is well-organized and the author is well-versed in what is available on the Net. These indexes can give you a start in finding specialized subject-oriented trees.

Organizations and Individuals

While guides that are organized around subject classifications and lists are very useful, don't overlook other sources of subject-oriented information. Look for home pages of organizations and individuals who are experts in a particular area. Often, their pages will contain links to major sources of information for a particular area of study.

META CENTERS

The idea of gathering links to scattered Net resources into one Web page or a set of pages is behind an information structure called a *meta center*. A meta center is something much more than just another subject-oriented page. It gathers all commonly used information for a particular subject as well as background information, links to discussion groups on Usenet, and pointers to individuals and organizations with further expertise in an area. The best meta centers are collaboratively built, with contributions coming from experts in the field from all over the Net. A meta center is the following:

■ *Pan-organizational.* It doesn't represent just one organization's view point of a topic, but contains links and contributions from many major organizations and individuals that have capabilities in that area.

■ *Pan-protocol.* It is not restricted to gathering just Web or Gopher links, for example, but includes links to resources regardless of where they are, including references to e-mail-only, or off-Net connections such as phone numbers and bibliographies of print materials.

■ Develops original, authoritative resources. Its cooperating participants develop material that provides information to its participants and the Net community as a whole. Usenet newsgroups have been doing this a long time with the development of FAQs.

■ Supports multiple activities. It contains not just resource listings on a topic, but also white pages of individuals with expertise in that area, as well as lists of activities, connections to real-time and e-mail-based conferences, and other forums for participants to interact in detail about that activity. It may have online conferences, based on e-mail or the interactive Forms capability of HTML.

■ Is collaboratively developed. Not just the work of one individual or even a group of individuals in one organization, a meta center draws the attention of experts in the field, fosters their contributions to knowledge, and provides for a community "memory," through an online newsletter, magazine, or journal.

The last two qualities—activities involving discussion and collaboration—are what set aside a meta center from just a resource collection or a reference web page. After all, the power of the Web lies in the connections it fosters among people and the diverse activities and resources these people take part in creating.

Finding specific organizations and individuals with expertise in certain areas is part of keyword searching, covered in the next chapter. Often the links within resources you locate through the subject trees will contain links to organizations and people, and these links may reveal more relevant information.

Techniques and Tips for Subject-Oriented Searching

In wading through the vast amount of information available within subject trees on the Web, it is helpful to know some basic techniques for managing the information and finding what you want. As the illustrative discussion about environmental issues has shown, you can find a variety of pages dealing with a subject in several different subject-oriented trees. Glance back over the figures showing the results from the major trees: the WWW Virtual Subject library, EINet's Galaxy, and GNN's WIC. Notice how there is variation in what is presented, as well as some overlap. Also keep in mind that the composition of these pages changes frequently, so the figures shown in this book are more of a historical reflection than what is probably out on the Web right now. As you navigate the Web's trees to find what you want, keep these techniques in mind:

1. **Search broadly at first.** If you don't have the URL of what is considered to be an authoritative or standard source in a particular area, check the main subject trees listed previously (Virtual Library, Galaxy, Whole Internet Catalog, Usenet FAQs, Michigan's Clearinghouse, Gopher Jewels, and perhaps several of the other trees mentioned). Go down the tree until you find the page that contains your subject area. Save a reference to this page on your hotlist, and then go to the next tree. In this way, you can gather the pages within the trees referring to your area before you evaluate which page to look at in detail. In this way, you'll gain a broad view of the major collections in many spaces in the Web and at its edge. References to sources that appear in many tree collections often are the ones to look at first.

2. **Look for authoritative sources.** The "authoritative" source for information varies by the subject matter. For example, if you're looking for space-travel-related information, seek out NASA or other space-agency Web pages. You might use the subject-trees to find the general collections and background information, but then draw most heavily for your work from the most authoritative sources. The level of "authoritativeness" might not always include academic or scientific authority; you may be looking, for example, for an entertainment-oriented or nontraditional source. In this case, consider the more informal/alternative trees, such as CyberNet, that tend to be more open to new links such as Mother-of-All-BBS, or trees that have developed reputations for a broad range of informal resources, such as Yahoo.

3. **Travel lightly at first.** Save references (URLs on your hotlist) to promising documents before you download their entire contents to your local directory. Although the first source you find may seem like the most comprehensive, it might be that you later find you want just a particularly well-done, focused collection of information, perhaps just the contents of one link from one of your previous findings.

4. **Use tools.** Use the indexes offered by any of the trees—for example, the Galaxy's search mechanism. You'll employ keyword searching techniques also in looking for subjects. (See the next chapter for more information on keyword searching.)

5. **Look for major collections.** Look for a page that brings together as much of the subject information you seek in a coherent form, rather than saving URLs pointing to this same information scattered in bits and pieces across the Net. For example, you'll find many references and links to resources connected to the United State's High Performance Computing and Communications (HPCC) initiative. Rather than save links to this program that are scattered in many places, save a single link to the Web server to the entire HPCC project, http://www.hpcc.gov. Not all subjects will have a similar, unifying server for official information, but seek out major collections.

6. **Collaborate.** Don't underestimate the power of asking others who have looked for information in the subject area of your interest for help in finding Net resources. If a newsgroup that relates to the subject you are interested in doesn't have any information in its FAQ, ask in the newsgroup itself or ask one of the frequent contributors to the newsgroup.

7. **Start a collection.** If your subject area is so specialized that you don't find a collection of URLs on it elsewhere, start your own page on this subject. (See Part V, "Weaving a Web.")

8. **Follow clues.** Use your Web navigation skills and techniques to following links on pages to lead you to more information. For example, look for major indexes and listings and links to search engines. Often, page developers include these kinds of links as an afterthought, and they are not readily apparent. Look at the home page of the page developer. Often that person is an expert in the field.

9. **Keep cool.** Be patient in examining the Net, because information servers might go down temporarily, or you'll feel endlessly lost in information. Take a break from Net cruising, remembering to save URLs of places that seem key to your search.

10. **Be wary.** Be cautious about information and judge it critically. If you are doing a serious report or research, be very careful about using a Net resource as a reference. Apply the same level of critical perspective you would take toward printed sources and ask yourself if there is a more authoritative, paper-based source. If so, seek it out and use it.

11. **Be flexible.** Don't get stuck in any one server or web for too long, particularly if it doesn't seem to yield results. Try another information space (such as Gopher, Hytelnet, or discussion lists). If the subject-oriented approaches given previously don't work, try the keyword-oriented approaches discussed in the next chapter.

Navigator's Check

There are many subject-oriented trees on the Web and at the edge of the Web. A few major ones have established themselves as large collections of resources. These major trees are

- The WWW Virtual Library, `http://www.w3.org/hypertext/DataSources/bySubject/Overview.html/`.

- Yahoo (Yet Another Hierarchically Odoriferous Oracle) URL, `http://www.yahoo.com`.

- EINet's Galaxy URL, `http://www.einet.net/galaxy.html`.

- O'Reilly's Whole Internet Catalog URL, `http://www.ora.com`. (Use this URL as a front door to choosing the O'Reilly server closest to you.)

- Usenet FAQs URL, `http://www.cis.ohio-state.edu/hypertext/faq/usenet/FAQ-List.html`.

- Michigan's Clearinghouse for Subject-Oriented Guides to the Internet URL, `http://www.lib.umich.edu/chhome.html`.

- The InterNIC directory of directories URL, `http://ds.internic.net/ds/dsdirofdirs.html`.
- Gopher Jewels URL, `http://galaxy.einet.net/GJ/index.html`.
- Gopher Trees URL, `gopher://burrow.cl.msu.edu/11/internet/subject`.

Other subject trees vary in their coverage, tone, completeness, and organization:

- Planet Earth Home Page URL, `http://white.nosc.mil/info.html`.
- CyberNet URL, `http://cybersight.com/cgi-bin/cs/s?main.gmml`. Some handcrafted lists might help you with jumping-off points to find other resources:
- DA-CLOD (Distributedly Administered Categorical List Of Documents) URL, `http://schiller.wustl.edu/DACLOD/daclod`.
- Mosaic Meta-Index Navigate/Internet Resources Meta-Index URL, `http://www.ncsa.uiuc.edu/SDG/Software/Mosaic/MetaIndex.html`.
- Yanoff's List URL, `http://www.uwm.edu/Mirror/inet.services.html`.
- Information Sources URL, `http://www.rpi.edu/Internet/Guides/decemj/internet-cmc.html`.

Whether collaboratively built or built under the guidance of commercial organizations employing knowledgeable workers, the subject-oriented trees available for finding information won't lead you to all the information on a subject that you want. You'll find much information that seems worthless to you along with the nuggets that seem extremely valuable. The development, maintenance, and even the veracity and value of Web information can easily be called to question. You will find, however, that the explosive growth in Web-based and Net-based information will continue, along with (hopefully) advances in information quality.

Spiders and Indexes: Keyword-Oriented Searching

19

by
John December

If your goal is to find a specific piece of information and you are not necessarily interested in finding contextual or related information through a subject-oriented search of trees (see Chapter 18, "Trees: Subject-Oriented Searching"), your best bet is to use a *spider*. Spider is a term for a class of software programs that wander through the Web and collect information about what is found there. (Other terms used for these tools include *robots* or *wanderers*, but I'll use the term *spider* throughout this chapter.) Some spiders crawl the Web and record URLs, creating a large list that can be searched. Other spiders look through HTML documents for URLs and keywords in title fields or other parts of the document. The nice thing about spiders is that they are *automated*; after initial setup, and with proper care and feeding, they can industriously scour the Web, recording the patterns of the links and keywords in documents, creating a valuable database for users to query.

In this chapter, we'll look at what spiders do and how you can use them to find specific information on the Web based on searching for specific words or phrases in documents. There is no "super spider" that knows what is on the entire Web or that can find whatever you want. But you will see that many of the spiders that exist now can give you a very big start in locating what you want in the Web.

Introduction to Spiders

One of the challenges in making sense of any large body of information is how to find something specific within it. Books have indexes. If you have a file in your word processor, you can usually use the find command to search for a specific occurrence of a string. But before the development of search mechanisms, the Web was a tangle of links, branching and forking, an inscrutable mesh. To find resources, users of the Web had to use handcrafted lists and indexes—which were not always reliable, current, or complete. The situation was ripe for the development of automated mechanisms to index the Web's information spaces. Historically, there were precedents for automated programs to search information spaces—Archie and Veronica helped users make sense of the vast repositories of FTP space and trees of Gopher space long before the first spiders crawled out onto the Web. It should not be surprising, then, that Web developers created spiders and that Web users make use of spiders often.

Spider-Like Programs

We've already talked about some tools that behave in a similar way to spiders in other information spaces. Archie catalogs FTP space so that it can be searched easily. The product of an Archie search is a list of filenames and directories that match a keyword-search pattern. Similarly, Veronica traverses Gopher space, finding menu titles and documents that conform to a user's wishes. But Archie and Veronica do not crawl on the Web—at least in their original forms—so they do not search Web servers for documents and keywords. But their action is analogous to that of spiders. The following is a table that summarizes tools used to search spaces by keyword patterns.

Table 19.1. Keyword searching tools.

Space	Tool	URL to Web-Based Page
FTP	Archie	`http://web.nexor.co.uk/archie.html`
Gopher	Veronica	`gopher://veronica.scs.unr.edu/11/veronica`
Telnet	Galaxy	`http://www.einet.net/hytelnet/HYTELNET.html`
WAIS	WAISgate	`http://www.wais.com/directory-of-servers.html`
Web	Spiders	`http://web.nexor.co.uk/mak/doc/robots/robots.html`

Basic Spider Use

Spiders take advantage of the structure of the Web to automatically traverse its links to gather information. Spiders can "crawl" across links in one HTML document to another through a URL reference. Once at the next document, the spider can use the tagging structure of HTML to obtain key information about a document and its links. This *semantic*-carrying content of HTML is key to the success of powerful spiders. Veronica and Archie have nothing like it currently in FTP space and Gopher space. The combination of structure and language gives spiders an edge in being able to successfully index the Web.

Here's the basic procedure for using a spider:

1. **Open the URL of the spider's home page**.
2. **Enter a query string in the input area**. This query is usually implemented through a Forms interface. The form of the query itself could be just a set of keywords or the search facility could allow for search patterns or Boolean expressions. Other options in the query could allow for searching references, titles, or text within documents.
3. **Submit the query**. According to the size of the database, this query is usually processed interactively (right away) rather than "batched" to run at a later time.
4. **Access the results**. These results are usually in the form of a Web page, dynamically created by the spider. When the results are given interactively, the Web page will usually appear in your browser display window.
5. **Interpret the results**. The list of results returned might or might not contain what you are looking for. The usual form of the results is in the form of a list of page of hypertext containing links. You can look at the names of the URLs for clues about what they refer to, or open the URL itself.

Things to Look for in Spiders

While the process of using a spider is fairly straightforward, the question you need to consider about the results of any spider search is as follows: "Is this everything that is available on the Web about *X*?" The answer will not necessarily be a resounding "Yes," because you cannot be assured about the meaning of the actual results until you know more about the spider—its feeding and care, as well as how it handles search expressions.

The following are some things to consider when you're using a spider:

1. **How is the spider fed?** What is the process for a spider encountering new information? New resources at new URLs are developed all the time. While there are commonly accessed lists that contain such URLs, how does the spider find out about them—in other words, what is the spider's diet? Is it fed a selected set of the same "root" URLs, or is it given an amalgam of "fresh" URLs often? How does the spider find out fresh URLs (URLs that are not yet referenced in any existing Web document)? Can you "feed" the spider your own URLs? How does the spider eliminate "waste" (stale URLs) from its system?

2. **How often does the spider walk?** Since the Web and its documents change continuously, how often does the spider revisit sites and documents? Given its diet, how often does it execute its foray into the Web? The Worm (described later in this chapter) is a periodic walker, while Lycos (also described later) is a continuous walker.

3. **Is the spider caged?** Is the spider limited to a fixed set of Web servers or URLs and not allowed to wander away from these? Are there file types or special structures that the spider ignores?

4. **Can the spider leave the Web?** Most spiders in existence now stay strictly on the Web (that is, they only traverse Web servers and HTML documents). Some spiders can touch the edges of the Web (by looking through documents at FTP or Gopher sites, for example). Unless the text in Gopher or FTP space is structured into HTML, a spider uses it to find more documents to read. Thus, current spiders can only touch the Web's edges. Perhaps smarter spiders will learn how to read other information formats. Only then will spiders be able to leave the Web entirely.

5. **Does the spider behave well?** Is the spider responsible in its behavior (not overloading a single server, not dragging down the Web's performance as a whole, and identifying itself)? A well-behaved spider should not enter restricted areas or go onto a server if it is specifically forbidden. A spider should also walk slowly, with sleeps in-between its accesses, so that it doesn't overload a single server. A spider should ideally also walk during off-peak usage times on a server so that it doesn't disturb users.

6. **What does the spider know?** When the spider traverses the Web, what information does it record? Just URLs? Text in HTML hotspots? All the text in a document?

7. **How can you communicate with the spider?** What kind of searching patterns can you use to query its database?

Because of their automated nature, poorly behaved spiders can wreak havoc on the Web. If you want to create your own spider, get in contact with experienced spider developers to share technical and ethical information.

These are questions to keep in mind when using a spider. Not all of these questions are easy to answer, because the technical details involved in spider operation are developing and evolving rapidly. You might not be able to get all the answers to the preceding questions, even from the spider developers. The key is that you'll have to be flexible in trying alternative spiders and interpreting the results of what you find. The spiders we'll examine in the following subsections are currently being used widely on the Web to locate information. There will certainly be new ones developed, so you'll need to hone your skills in order to understand and use spiders.

A Gallery of Spiders

Unlike Archie and Veronica, which seem to have exclusive domain over their respective information spaces, spiders come in a variety of configurations with differing capabilities. In this section, I outline some of the most popular spiders that are currently available. Certainly, more spiders will be developed, and the spiders here will evolve.

Lycos

Lycos is a relatively young spider that rocketed to prominence on the Web during the winter of 1994–95 because of the comprehensiveness of its database. Lycos provides an easy-to-use interface to a vast portion of the Web. Lycos' home page (URL `http://www.lycos.com`) is shown in Figure 19.1.

FIGURE 19.1.

The Lycos home page. Copyright © 1995 by Carnegie Mellon University. All rights reserved. Courtesy of Dr. Michael L. Mauldin. Printed by permission.

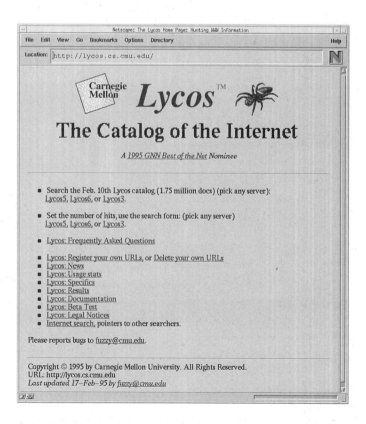

Dr. Michael L. Mauldin, a developer of Lycos, describes Lycos as a descendent of a program called Longlegs that was written by John Leavitt and Eric Nyberg. The term "Lycos" comes from the arachnid family *Lycosidae*, which are large ground spiders (the real-world kind) that are very speedy and active at night, catching their prey by pursuit rather than in a web. Lycos lives up to its name—rather than catching its "prey" (URLs on a server) in a massive single-server sweep, Lycos uses an innovative, probabilistic scheme to skip from server to server in Web space.

The secret of Lycos' search technique lies in random choices tempered by preferences. Lycos starts with a given URL and collects information from the resource (when present), including the following:

- The title
- Headings and subheadings
- The 100 most "weighty" words (using an algorithm that considers word placement and frequencies, among other factors)
- The first 20 lines
- The size in bytes
- The number of words

Lycos then adds the URL references in the resource to its queue. To choose the next document to explore, Lycos makes a random choice (among the HTTP, Gopher, and FTP references) with built-in "preferences" for documents that have multiple links into them (popular documents) and a slight preference for shorter URLs (to keep the database oriented to the Web's "top").

While many early Web spiders infested a particular server with a large number of rapid, sequential accesses, Lycos behaves. First, Lycos' random-search behavior avoids the "multiple-hit" problem. Second, Lycos complies with the standard for robot exclusion to keep unwanted robots off WWW servers, and it identifies itself as Lycos when crawling, so that webmasters can know when Lycos has hit their server.

With more than 3.3 million references in its database as of the start of April 1995, Lycos offers a huge database to locate documents matching a given query. This database grows all the time, as Lycos walks continuously on the Web. In fact, Lycos now offers multiple servers as entry points into its database. You can feed Lycos—there is a form in its web that allows you to register URLs in its database. A user can also "de-register" a URL by requesting it to be removed from Lycos' database. This "de-registering" function helps Lycos eliminate "waste," or stale, URLs.

The search interface to Lycos' databases provides a way for users to find documents that contain references to a keyword, and to examine a document's outline, keyword list, and excerpt. In this way, Lycos enables the user to determine if a document might be valuable without having to retrieve it. According to Dr. Mauldin, plans are in the works for other kinds of searching schemes. Another related project underway is called WebAnts (described forthwith), which is aimed at creating cooperating explorers, so that an individual spider doesn't have to do all the work of finding things on the Web or duplicate other spiders' efforts.

Searching the Web with Lycos

Let's use Lycos' search form (Figure 19.2) to find resources on the Web. First, we can select one of the search Form options from the Lycos home page (Figure 19.1). Notice that because of Lycos' popularity, the developers provide several machines to help run Lycos. Choosing one of the servers gives us the form in Figure 19.2.

FIGURE 19.2.

The Lycos search form.

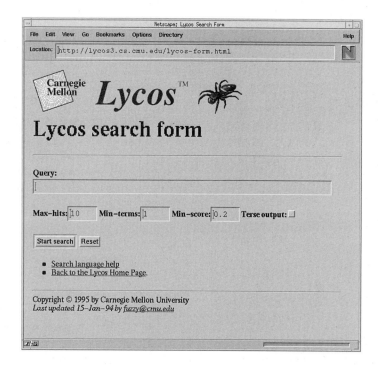

First, we fill in the Query box of the form. We'll start off with a very basic search and then examine how we can take advantage of Lycos' search language to fine-tune our search. Let's continue our search for environmental information and find resources that include references to "acid rain damage." We can enter this query in Lycos' Query box:

```
acid rain damage
```

The buttons under the box enable us to adjust the number of hits as well as to elect terse output. Let's leave these set to their default values for now. After clicking the Start Search button, we get the results shown in Figures 19.3 and 19.4.

FIGURE 19.3.

Lycos search results.

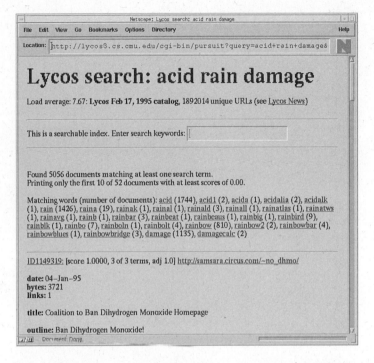

FIGURE 19.4.

Lycos search results.

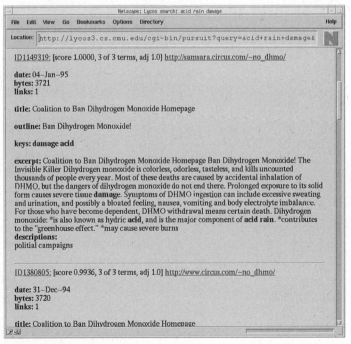

An important aspect of the Lycos results is that you can view information about the remote documents that match your query before you actually retrieve that remote document. This can help you be more selective about which documents to retrieve. The results Lycos gives you include (as shown in Figures 19.3 and 19.4):

- A Lycos Database ID number as a hyperlink. This link will take you to a database file for that particular document, showing the keywords, the text excerpt, as well as other information about the document that Lycos holds in its database.

- The URL as a link to the actual document. You can click on this hyperlink to request retrieval of the actual document or resource.

- The date the document data was gathered by Lycos.

- The size of the document in bytes.

- The title of the document as defined by the <TITLE> tag within it.

- An outline of the document as defined in the document itself (using header tags).

- An excerpt from the document. This is text that Lycos grabs as "representative" (according to its algorithm scheme of looking at the start of paragraphs and the start of the document itself).

- Descriptions. This is a list of the text that is used by others in describing links to this resource; if this section is long, it indicates that this resource is referenced in many other parts of the Web.

Based on the preceding information, you can make some choices about which resources Lycos has found meet your needs. Note that, of course, the resource might have moved or is no longer available since Lycos collected data about it. But the list Lycos produces can go a long way to helping you make sense out of the vast links of the Web.

Advanced and Specialized Searching with Lycos

We've used a very simple search example to show the basic operation of Lycos. Now let's focus on some more advanced and powerful searches to illustrate how you can use Lycos to untangle the Web. These examples reflect the state of Lycos' search interface as of February 1995; see the Lycos home page and documentation for the most current information.

Lycos Example 1: Finding Resources That Relate to a Specific Set of Keywords

This is the most basic kind of match. We've already seen how our query acid rain damage yielded us with a list of matching documents. The refinement we can make is to use a period (.) after the keywords to force an exact match on the words (notice that in Figure 19.3, the matches included words that had a prefix of rain, including rainbow, rainavg, and rainald. So our first refinement on our original search would be to force exact matches on our keywords:

acid. rain. damage.

Note that the order of the words is not important. Lycos will return those documents which match all of the three words with a higher priority. Eventually, Lycos' search interface should have an AND operator where you could force this condition for returning documents.

Lycos Example 2: Finding References to a Particular Home Page

Another example that illustrates the power of Lycos involves searching for Web resources that reference another page. For example, you might be interested in locating resources that contain references to your home page. To do this, simply perform a Lycos search on some key portions of the name of your home page's URL. For example, let's say your home page URL is as follows:

```
http://www.foo.edu/~chris/chrishome.html
```

Because Lycos indexes the URLs of the links on pages, we can query Lycos for documents that contain links in which your URL occurs. To find these, we simply need to give some keywords for a match. Based on the URL in the previous line, a good strategy might be to use the Lycos search query:

```
chrishome.
```

It would *not* have been a good idea to use the query chrishome. foo. as this would have returned all pages with *either* chrishome *or* foo in the URL references. Also, the search on chris would have returned many matches (which were not your home page). In other words, try to use a string in your home page's URL that uniquely (as much as possible) identifies it. If there is some over lap, you'll have to examine the Lycos results to weed out the pages that weren't referring to yours. If you have two "unique keys," you can use them both in your Lycos query.

Lycos Example 3: Using Negation

Lycos allows you to set a preference for reducing the score of documents returned by your query that contain a particular keyword. You indicate this preference by the minus sign (-) before the keyword. For example, you may be interested in all the information you can find about "wildflowers" but not on a particular server, alpha.com. Your query can be as follows:

```
wildflowers. -alpha.
```

Note that, you don't want to use the term -alpha.com because Lycos would understand this as -alpha. and all terms matching com—which would include all the commercial servers! Notice that the negation term means that the *scores* of the returned documents are reduced—you still may get documents returned that include references to "wildflowers" which also include references to "alpha," but, according to Lycos' scoring scheme, these documents should be lower on the returned list.

Lycos Example 4: A Typical "Deep Web" Search

As a final example, let's say that we want to find out everything about the acid rain damage that we can through Lycos. Here are the suggested steps:

1. Work during off-peak hours. Lycos is a very popular spider and tends to be busy during daytime work hours (8am to 5pm, Eastern Standard Time). Lycos offers a number of search servers, but if you intend to do a very deep search, your query might not be processed if Lycos estimates it would take too long.

2. Create a query that contains all of your keywords of interest. Remember that Lycos will return to you the documents that best match *all* your keywords first, then it will return documents that match *most* of them, then *some* of them, and so on. By having a good set of keywords to start, you'll be assured that you'll first get the most relevant documents (matching many of your keywords) as well as documents that match some of your keywords (leaving no corner of the Web unturned).

3. Bump up the "Max-hits" selection—increase this to a fairly large number if you truly want a "deep" scan of the Web (keeping in mind your consideration for other users— work off-peak; think carefully about which "deep" searches you need to do).

4. Get terse. Experiment with a small number of max-hits first (with the Terse mode OFF) and then do this same search with the terse mode ON. You'll find that the terse mode does give you quite a bit of information about the resources Lycos finds. If you agree, choosing the terse mode for a "deep" scan of the Web can save you a great deal of time, as Lycos won't have to return all the auxiliary information and text it does in non-terse mode.

5. Save your results in HTML. When you get some search results, you'll need to save the output (in HTML) to your own disk for examination later. You won't be able to save the output as a link on a hotlist, as the results are stored in a temporary file on Lycos' server. Use your browser's file management facility to save the results to an HTML file that you can examine in more detail.

The Harvest System

The Harvest Information and Discovery and Access System (`http://harvest.cs.colorado.edu/`) home page is shown in Figure 19.5. Harvest is more than just a spider; it encompasses an entire set of tools to manage information.

The Harvest System consists of a series of subsystems to create an efficient, flexible, and scalable way to locate information on the Internet and to provide for efficient use of information servers. Harvest is being designed and built by the Internet Research Task Force Research Group on Resource Discovery with support primarily from the Advanced Research Projects Agency, with other support from the Air Force Office of Scientific Research (AFOSR), Hughes, National Science Foundation, and Sun.

The philosophy behind the Harvest system is that it gathers information about Internet resources and customizes views into the information that is "harvested." According to developer Mike Schwartz, "Harvest is much more than just a 'spider.' It's intended to be a scalable form of infrastructure for building and distributing content, and indexing information, as well as for accessing Web information."

FIGURE 19.5.

The Harvest Information and Discovery and Access System home page. Courtesy of Dr. Michael F. Schwartz, Associate Professor of Computer Science at the University of Colorado–Boulder.

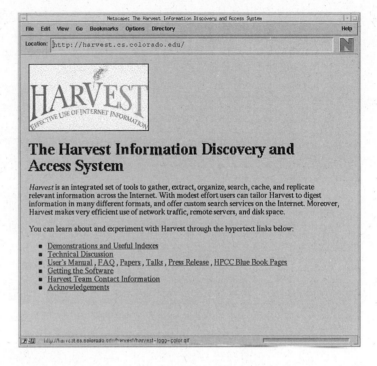

Harvest consists of several subsystems. A gatherer collects indexing information, and a broker provides a flexible interface to this information. A user can access a variety of collections of documents. One example of a broker of particular interest to Web navigators is the Harvest WWW Broker, which includes content summaries of more than 21,000 Web pages. This database has a very flexible interface, providing the user with the ability to make search queries based on author, keyword, title, or URL reference. While the Harvest WWW page database isn't yet as extensive as Lycos', its potential for efficiently collecting a large amount of information about Web pages is very great.

Other subsystems further refine Harvest's capabilities. Subsystems for Indexing/Searching provide ways for a variety of search engines to be used within the Harvest system. For example, a system called Glimpse supports very rapid space-efficient searches with interactive queries while a Nebula system provides fast searches for more complex queries. Another Harvest subsystem, a replicator, provides a way to mirror information the brokers have. An Object Cache system meets the demand for managing networked information by providing the capability to locate the fastest-responding server to a query.

A Sample Application for Keyword Searching: WWW Home Pages Harvest Broker

For Web navigators, the WWW Home Pages Harvest Broker is a very useful component of the Harvest system. The Harvest WWW Broker gives the user access to a large collection of Web pages (which is continuously being augmented) whose entire *content summaries* (not just anchor or other HTML tagged strings) have been indexed.

Let's use the Query interface to the Harvest WWW Broker (Figure 19.6) to find information to illustrate keyword searching techniques.

FIGURE 19.6.

Query Interface to the WWW Home Pages Harvest Broker.

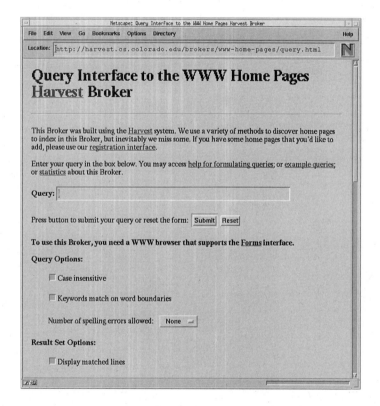

The query form to the Harvest WWW Broker involves a variety of options in a Forms interface (which are originally set to default options). At the simplest level, you could use the WWW Broker to query for the occurrence of particular keywords in Web pages, such as "environment." As an example, if I enter the keyword environment into the Query box and submit this request (leaving all the other options set to their default values), I obtain the results shown in Figure 19.7.

FIGURE 19.7.

Harvest WWW Broker search for Environment.

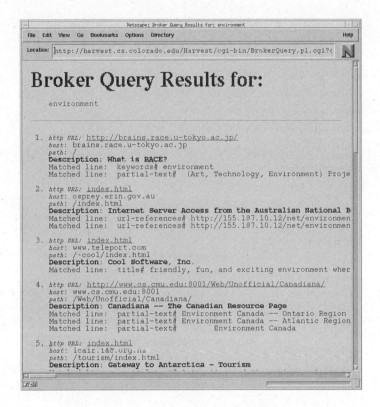

Using the Harvest WWW Broker involves a careful interpretation of the results. First, we need to keep in mind that we used a very simple search method (a single keyword), and second, we chose to keep the default options selected on the search form. Let's take a detailed look at our results shown in Figure 19.7:

- The matches are presented in an order based on the Broker's system for assigning weights to documents. The goal of this system is to present the documents that are most likely to match the user's query first. Therefore, the first items shown in Figure 19.7 are judged (by the broker) to be the best matches.

- The results show us the title of the documents returned, the matched lines (showing text or URL matches), the name of the host, as well as a hyperlink directly to the document. The benefit of this information is that the user can examine this information *before* accessing the actual document, perhaps narrowing down the decision of which documents to retrieve and thus saving the bandwidth (and time) of laboriously retrieving each matched document.

- The results are truncated to 50 matched lines (a default number that we could have changed on the form). This message shows that the results certainly don't exhaust the entire database of items matching the keyword search on environment.

After you examine the results, a good point to observe is that a search for a single keyword such as environment is not restrictive enough to be of great value in a database like the Harvest WWW Broker's. By taking advantage of the search language, we can be more selective, increasing the power of our search, making it more likely that we find more precisely what we want. Otherwise, we'll end up slogging through hundreds of Web pages that relate to the environment (which we might have better found using a subject-oriented search, as described in Chapter 18).

To narrow our search and take more advantage of the power of the Harvest WWW Broker, we first return to the search form (Figure 19.6). Instead of entering the single word environment, let's instead try to find more specific information that we might be looking for—on acid-rain damage, for example. To do this, we have to use the Harvest WWW Broker's search language (help and examples are available from links on the search form), to formulate the syntax of our query. Type the following in the Query box:

```
keywords: acid and rain and damage
```

The and conjunction connects keywords of interest and lets the Broker know that we're interested in Web pages that relate to that particular subtopic and contain all of the keywords listed. After clicking the Submit button and waiting, we get the results (top shown only) in Figure 19.8.

FIGURE 19.8.

Harvest WWW Broker search results for acid rain damage.

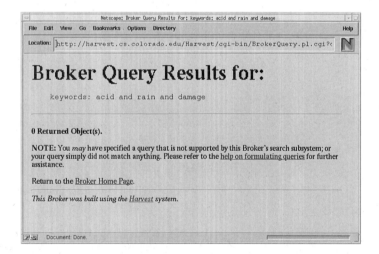

This Harvest Broker didn't find any matches for all three words. To find more matches, we need to revise our search criteria to be less restrictive, as follows:

```
keywords: acid and rain
```

This, unfortunately, also produces no results. Finally, we narrow our search to the following:

```
keywords: rain
```

We get more results. (See Figure 19.9.)

FIGURE 19.9.

Harvest WWW Broker search results for rain.

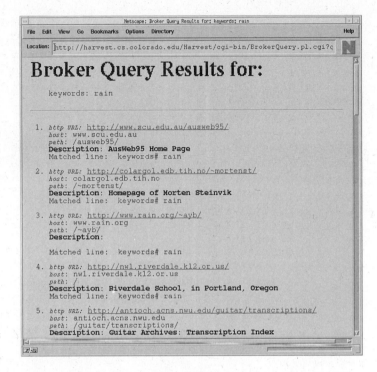

Unfortunately, we would expect the matches we did find for rain to be false (not leading us to results), because the keyword rain is missing from all of them (or the matches would have shown up in the previous search). Although this simple search didn't yield us results this time with the Harvest WWW Broker, the database of its home pages continues to grow.

Advanced and Specialized Searching with Harvest

We've used a very simple search example with Harvest to show its basic operation. Similar to the examples we looked at for Lycos, let's focus on some advanced and powerful searches to illustrate how you can use Harvest.

Harvest Example 1: Finding Resources That Relate to a Specific Set of Keywords

This is the most basic kind of match. We've already seen how our query acid rain damage didn't quite work out. We could have used a variety of options within the Harvest search language for other kinds of searching. We could have searched for

```
"acid rain" and damage
```

giving us the results of pages that included (as keywords) the phrase "acid rain" and also the word "damage."

We could have also used the capabilities to search titles of documents:

```
title: "acid rain"
```

Harvest Example 2: Finding References to a Particular Home Page

Just as you could use Lycos to locate references to a particular home page, you can do this kind of searching with the Harvest WWW Broker. Let's say your home page URL is as follows:

```
http://www.foo.edu/~chris/chrishome.html
```

We can query Harvest for documents that contain links in which your URL occurs. To find these, we simply need to give some keywords for a match. Based on the above URL, a good strategy might be to use the Harvest search query:

```
url-references: chrishome
```

Harvest's search language also allows a more specific search for a URL string such as the following:

```
url-references: ~chris/chrishome.html
```

The World Wide Web Worm

The World Wide Web Worm is one of the oldest spiders on the Web. Released in March 1994, the Worm was an early tool that was widely used to perform keyword searching on the Web. The innovation it represented earned it a "Best of the Web" award in 1994 for "Best Navigational Aid," as shown in the Worm's home page (URL `http://www.cs.colorado.edu/home/mcbryan/WWW.html`) in Figure 19.10.

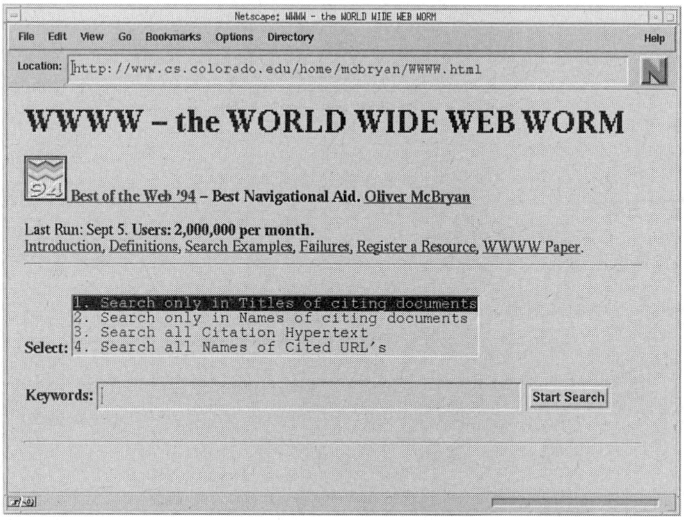

FIGURE 19.10.

The World Wide Web Worm home page. Courtesy of Dr. Oliver A. McBryan, Department of Computer Science, University of Colorado–Boulder.

The Worm, like Lycos and Harvest, provides users a flexible way to search for resources on the Web based on keywords or URLs. The Worm's database is periodically rather than continuously updated, however, so see its home page for the latest information about its latest walk on the Web.

> **NOTE**
>
> Don't confuse the World Wide Web Worm with a computer security term for a type of software program known as a "worm," which is intended to cause a computer system to crash. The World Wide Web Worm is benign.

Unlike Harvest and Lycos, the Worm isn't a database of all keywords in a document. Instead, the Worm saves text in `<TITLE>` tags, in hypertext hotspots (the text used in the HTML anchors), and the text of the URLs occurring in a document.

In all searches using the Worm, the keyword pattern must be exact (no wildcards currently implemented) and in the order of occurrence. The pattern is case-insensitive (will return a match for the string regardless of whether the letters are in uppercase or lowercase). The following are the options for searching:

1. Searching a list of all known Web pages (Web resources starting with `http` in the URL). This list includes the URL of the page and the title of the page, as given within the angle brackets used in HTML to designate a title (`<TITLE>...</TITLE>`). You can search this database by looking for keywords or strings within the URLs or within the title names.

2. Searching the database of HTML pages and links within them. The Worm keeps track of what documents cite other documents on the Web, so that you can search a database of these patterns. The arrangement of the database information is two-tiered: There are citing documents that contain references to cited documents. Your options for searching this database are as follows.

   a. Search in Citation Hypertext: The citation hypertext is the text in the hotspot of an HTML file—the clickable portion that links to another resource.

      With this selection, you'll find the URLs in the database that match your search criteria, and you'll be given links to the documents that cite (refer to) these URLs. In this way, you can use this searching mode to find patterns of citation in the Web.

   b. Search in titles of citing documents: This option will give you a list of "hits" on the strings within the titles of the citing documents.

   c. Search in names of URLs: With this option, you'll obtain all the URLs in the database that contain your search string and links to the documents that cite these URLs.

   d. Search in names of citing documents: This option refers to the names of the URLs (filename, directory name, host name, or other identifiers in the URL) of the citing documents.

The home page of the Worm itself contains some examples of some search possibilities. Here are some different examples that illustrate the power of the Worm:

1. Find all the HTML pages that have the word "Environment" in their title.

   Solution:

   a. Start from the Worm's home page (Figure 19.10).

   b. Select this search option: "1. Search only in Titles of citing documents."

   c. In the Keywords box, enter environment.

   d. Click on Start Search.

   e. Sample results are shown in Figure 19.11.

FIGURE 19.11.

Worm Search results for Title Environment.

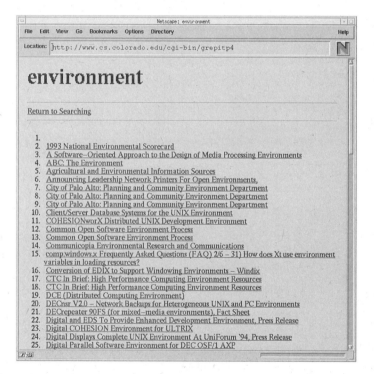

2. Find all the HTML pages that have the string apc.org in their URL. (For this search, the user would have to have as a starting point the knowledge that apc.org is the domain of Association for Progressive Communications / Institute for Global Communications, which is active in environmental and other related issues.)

   a. Start from the Worm's home page (Figure 19.10).

   b. Select this search option: "2. Search in Names of Citing Documents."

   c. In the Keywords box, enter apc\.org (you need the \ in order for the Worm to recognize the "." in the apc.org domain name.).

d. Click on Start Search.

e. Sample results are shown in Figure 19.12.

FIGURE 19.12.

Worm Search results for apc.org.

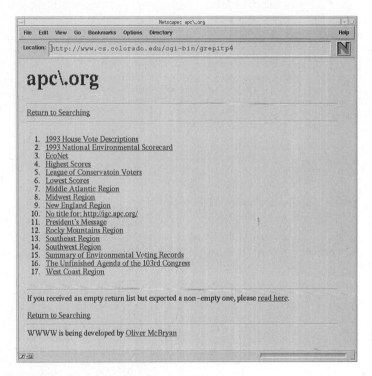

3. Find all references to "acid rain" (in that order) within the hotspots (e.g., the citation hypertext) of all the documents in the Worm's database.

a. Start from the Worm's home page (Figure 19.10).

b. Select this search option: "3. Search all Citation hypertext."

c. In the Keywords box, enter acid.*rain. The .* sequence between the words acid and rain indicates that the Worm will allow any amount of intervening text.

d. Click on Start Search.

e. Unfortunately, this particular search for "acid rain" did not return any results. Searching for the word "rain" in citation hypertext yields the results shown in Figure 19.13.

4. Find all Web pages that refer to apc.org.

a. Start from the Worm's home page (Figure 19.10).

b. Select search option: "4. Search in all Names of Cited URL's."

c. In the Keywords box, enter apc.\org.

d. Click on Start Search.

e. Sample results are shown in Figure 19.14.

FIGURE 19.13.

Worm Search results for rain *in hotspots.*

FIGURE 19.14.

Worm Search results for citations of apc.org.

WebCrawler

Like the Worm, the WebCrawler finds references to URLs on the Web and makes the resulting database that it builds available for searching. Unlike the Worm, however, the WebCrawler makes indexes of the *contents* of documents it finds, in addition to URLs, hotspot text, and titles like the Worm.

The WebCrawler was developed by Brian Pinkerton. Its home page is at URL http://webcrawler.com/ and is shown in Figure 19.15.

The WebCrawler, like the Worm, Lycos, and Harvest, returns a set of links that match a given keyword search. Here are the WebCrawler's important features:

- It records not only URLs starting with http (like the Worm) but all other protocols—Gopher, FTP, and others (like Lycos and Harvest).

- Its search pattern is for words, not strings. This means your search on the words electronic frontier will turn up matches for any of those two words anywhere on a page. (The Worm requires consecutive occurrences of words in hotspots, not anywhere on a page.)

- You can set a Boolean AND function for searching by setting the switch on the Crawler's panel toggle to the On position for "and" function. (If the button is pushed in, all the words in your search string must be on the page in order to produce a successful hit).

- Its output is arranged by a "score" in which resources judged to be the best (through the indexing algorithm of the Crawler) are listed first.

Since the WebCrawler indexes the contents of documents, in addition to the information that the Worm collects, the Crawler is a powerful search tool. The flip side of this is that the Crawler must work harder in order to perform this total text search of all documents in the Web and at the Web's edge (in Gopher space, FTP space, or other protocols accessed from some HTML file). The Worm, collecting less information, can travel lighter than the Crawler, but it knows less about the URLs it finds.

As an illustrative example of the Crawler, we'll enter this search string in its query box:

```
acid rain damage
```

We leave the "and" toggle key set to On, and the default matches number set to 35.

We get the results as shown in Figure 19.16.

FIGURE 19.16.

WebCrawler search for
acid rain damage.

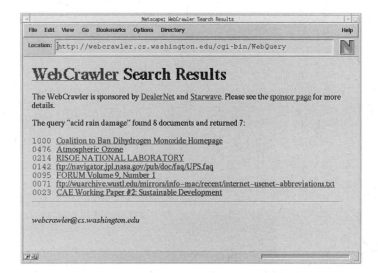

JumpStation

The JumpStation, developed by Jonathon Fletcher, references information on the Web by document title or header, although extensions of this are in the works for the JumpStation. The JumpStation's home page is at `http://www.stir.ac.uk/jsbin/js`, and its search form is shown in Figure 19.17.

The beta version (not yet available) of the JumpStation will count the occurrences of words in the document, remove references to common words such as "and," "a," and "the," and use this index of words and occurrences in the document as a way of determining the "subject" of the document. The beta JumpStation also will make use of the header and title tags in HTML documents. In this way, the JumpStation, like the Crawler and the Worm, attempts to cull out important keywords from documents to perform a search. The beta version of JumpStation is also expected to have a "server scanner" service, which will allow you to search the URL database by a partial name of the server you are interested in.

Netscape: The JumpStation Search Page
File Edit View Go Bookmarks Options Directory Help
Location: http://www.stir.ac.uk/jsbin/js?search
The JumpStation Search Page
The JumpStation is a Form for finding other World Wide Web Pages. Please refer to the front page for more information. Please send comments and criticisms to the address at the bottom of this page, both are welcomed.
Please note that the best results are obtained by entering short words (or partial words).
Enter Search Word :
Search type: Title
Press here to submit the query, or reset the form.
Return to front page
Copyright (C) 1993 by Jonathon Fletcher
jonathon@japan.sbi.com

FIGURE 19.17.
The JumpStation search form. Copyright © 1993 by Jonathon Fletcher. Printed by permission.

The RBSE Spider

The RBSE (Repository Based Software Engineering) Program Spider, developed by David Eichmann, works like many of the spiders described, roaming the Web collecting URLs. The search form for the RBSE spider is at URL `http://rbse.jsc.nasa.gov/eichmann/urlsearch.html`, and its front page is shown in Figure 19.18. Its unique features are as follows:

- It indexes the full text of HTML documents.
- It traverses links that have patterns of `.html` and `http://` in them.
- It uses an Oracle database for storing references.
- It uses a version of WAIS technology to present the results to the reader.

THE RBSE Spider accepts as input a set of search keywords that are part of a URL or a word in an HTML document. It will return pages that fit this search pattern, arranged in descending "relevance"—the higher the score, the more relevant the document.

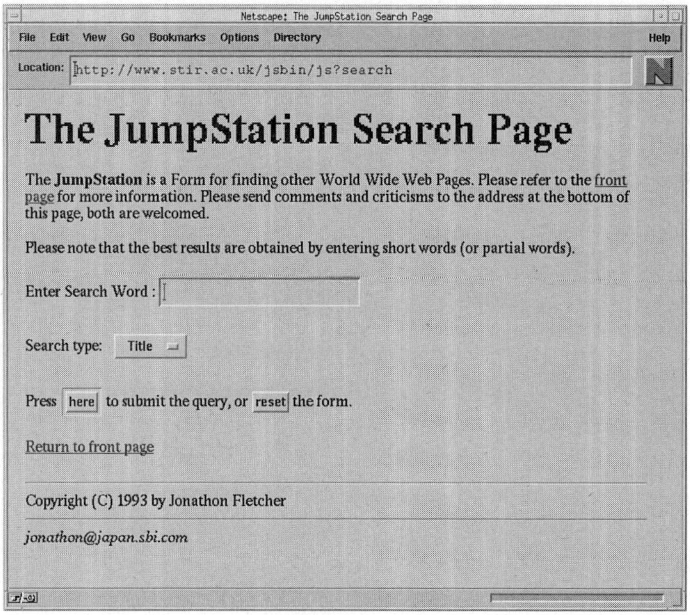

FIGURE 19.18.

The RBSE Spider search form. Courtesy of Dr. David Eichmann, Assistant Professor of Software Engineering, University of Houston–Clear Lake.

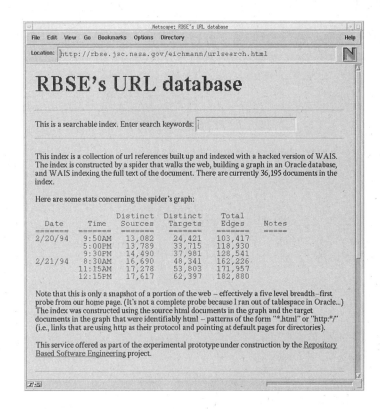

NIKOS—The New Internet Knowledge System

NIKOS (The New Internet Knowledge System) organizes information into large pools of URLs organized by topic. Its URL is `http://www.rns.com/cgi-bin/nikos`, and its front screen is shown in Figure 19.19.

To use NIKOS, you type in a topic name. If the topic name is recognized, it will retrieve items from the database matched with that topic. Otherwise, a search will be done against the URLs in the database for matches to that topic name. James Aviani, NIKOS developer, says that this scheme is useful because it takes very little space to run. Keywords in the actual text of the resources are *not* indexed, like in the WebCrawler. Rather, NIKOS is useful for finding starting points, not necessarily for Web searches. Because NIKOS travels light, it can travel often and can cover a lot of the Web.

FIGURE 19.19.

The NIKOS search form.
Courtesy of James Aviani.

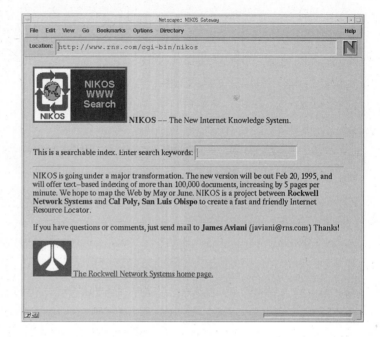

More Spiders

Spiders are extremely useful in finding information in the Web—so useful, in fact, that many new ones are in development. Check out the list of active spiders at the URL `http://web.nexor.co.uk/mak/doc/robots/active.html`.

Indexes

While all the spiders described herein have the same characteristic of being *automated* Web-searching facilities that look through the Web, there are other resources that can help you find items on the Web based on keyword patterns found in handcrafted lists and compilations of resources. The following subsections outline some tools and resources that you can use to pull out information from collections of URLs. These resources also include some unification of many searching mechanisms into forms-based tools. These are not true spiders but are interfaces to URL collections that behave similarly to the interfaces to the databases of URLs generated by spiders. Their purpose, just as with the spiders, is to help users find specific resources in the Web.

CUI W3 Catalog

The CUI W3 catalog is a collection of URL references built from a number of handcrafted HTML lists (Figure 19.20). The CUI W3 Catalog (`http://cuiwww.unige.ch/cgi-bin/w3catalog`) periodically scans these lists and produces a database of the URLs and hotspot texts in them. The CUI W3 forms interface enables a user to query this database for keyword patterns.

FIGURE 19.20.

The CUI W3 Catalog document set.

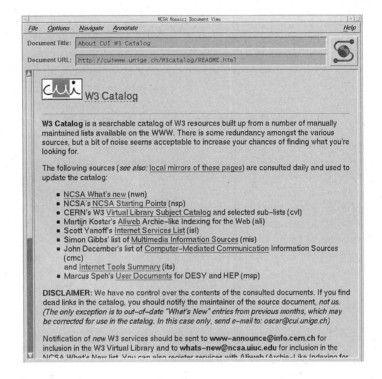

The limitation of the CUI W3 Catalog is that it depends on human-made documents for information about resources. However, it is still very useful, because these lists, although potentially limited in coverage and accuracy, can help in very focused kinds of searches. Thus, the searches for information related to the content covered by the lists shown in Figure 3.6 can be very helpful.

Yahoo Index

We've already talked about Yahoo as a subject tree in Chapter 18. In addition to being a great tree, Yahoo is also a very useful index to Web documents. Yahoo is a "hotlist" style subject tree of Web resources. It rose rapidly in size and prominence during 1994 and 1995. Yahoo, as of February 1995, included links to over 28,000 URLs. Yahoo's home page is at URL `http://www.yahoo.com/` and is shown in Figure 19.21.

Besides access to hundreds of categories of Web pages, Yahoo also offers a search form (Figure 19.22) that you can use to search its database.

For example, a search for `acid rain` yields results as shown in Figure 19.23.

Thus, Yahoo's search engine, like that of the CUI W3 Catalog, searches documents that are part of a handcrafted set of index lists, not the result of a Web spider's crawl. As such, Yahoo's database may be smaller, but its links tend (in general) to be more high-level and useful.

FIGURE 19.21.

*Yahoo, a guide to WWW.
Copyright © 1994, 1995
David Filo and Jerry Yang.
Printed by permission.*

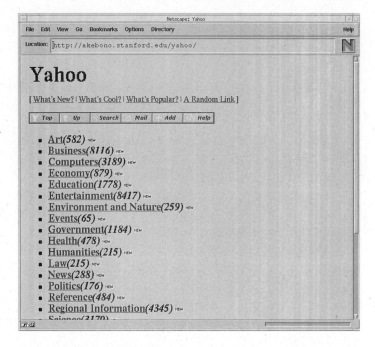

FIGURE 19.22.

The Yahoo search form.

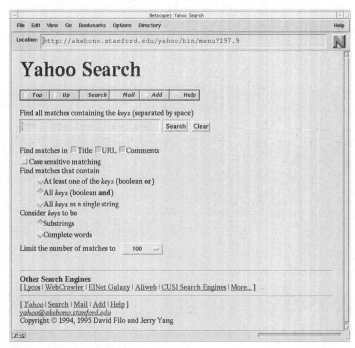

FIGURE 19.23.

Yahoo search for acid rain.

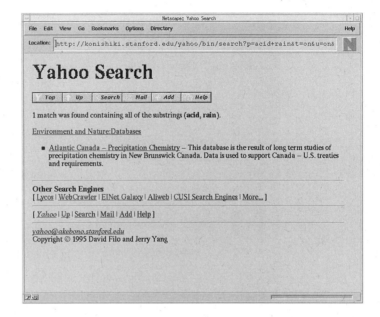

ALIWEB

The name ALIWEB stands for "Archie-like indexing for the Web," and it attempts to do for the Web what Archie intended to do for FTP space. Archie, along with its ability to collect the names of directories and files at FTP sites, has a facility associated with it that allows for maintainers of files to describe those files. Done by hand, this feature never proved as successful as the automated activity of Archie. ALIWEB seeks to do this for the Web, and it seems to be more successful, with its more appealing forms-based interface to collect information from developers. ALIWEB should not be confused with Web-based interfaces to Archie and ArchiePlex. ALIWEB is an index to Web resources, while the Web-based Archie interfaces (ArchiePlex) index FTP space.

ALIWEB's home page is at `http://web.nexor.co.uk/aliweb/doc/aliweb.html`. The way ALIWEB works is that people write index files in a specific format and store these files on their server. They inform ALIWEB about these files and ALIWEB regularly retrieves these files and creates a database from them. The result is a fairly up-to-date database of available resources.

Unified Search Engines

We've talked about several spiders and catalogs that index resources on the Web. You might be wondering if there is some place where you can easily access a list of them. The answer is yes. These collections of keyword-based search tools (sometimes called *unified search engines*) exist in several places, as follows:

■ The Meta index (Figure 19.24) at `http://cuiwww.unige.ch/meta-index.html`

- Martijn Koster's CUSI, `http://web.nexor.co.uk/public/cusi/cusi.html`, which includes a link to a list of CUSI-like services, `http://web.nexor.co.uk/public/cusi/doc/list.html`

- Twente University's External Info at `http://www_is.cs.utwente.nl:8080/cgi-bin/local/nph-susi1.pl`

The Meta Index, shown in Figure 19.24, is a typical example of a unified search engine.

The Meta Index serves as an interface to many different indexes through a forms interface. These collected search engines are useful, both because they give a one-stop approach for keyword-oriented searching and because they help in building an awareness of the kinds of tools on the Web for such searching, including links to the home pages of the tools themselves, so that the user can choose which index would be best as a place to search.

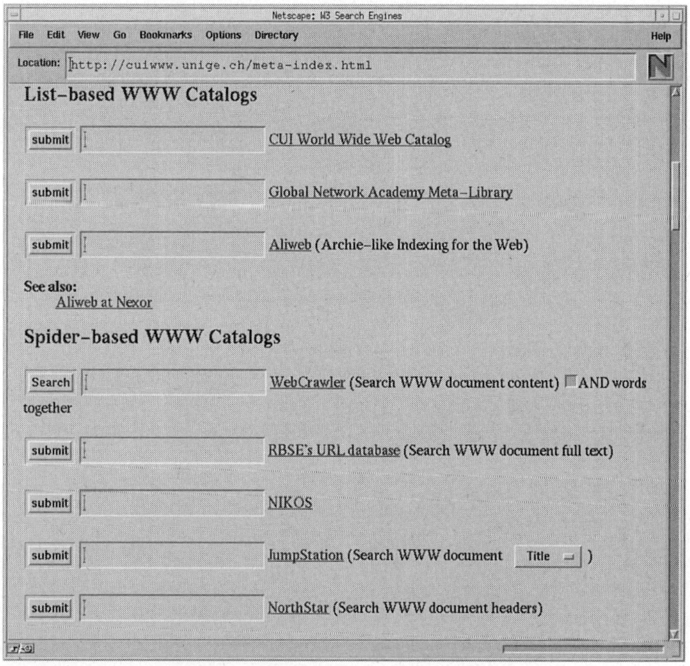

FIGURE 19.24.

The Meta Index search form.

Tips and Techniques for Using Spiders

We've talked about several spiders and indexes that are useful for finding information based on keyword searches on the Web. All of these tools have their strengths and limitations, but overall they are some of the most useful tools on the Web for finding specific information. Using these tools takes some getting used to, however. The following are some tips and techniques for making the best use of these tools:

1. **Know the limitations of the spider or index that you are using.** In this chapter I've briefly covered the strengths and weaknesses of currently available spiders. There will be more spiders (and all spiders evolve over time), so you'll need to keep abreast of developments. If one spider yields poor results, try another. Some spiders, because of the areas they usually walk on the Web or because of their diet, might seem to have more resources in your fields of interest than others. (Perhaps specialized spiders will develop that will be known for their capability to walk through specific subject-oriented areas of the Web.)

2. **Be respectful and patient of the spider developers and databases.** Spiders, if not properly behaved, can run rampant on the Web, which may cause administrators to ban spiders from their hosts, neutralizing the spiders' function as a helpful resource-searching tool for the Web. Therefore, be patient with a spider administrator—don't pressure him or her to walk a spider. Assure yourself that the spider's developer and administrator follows "Guidelines for Robot Writers," `http://web.nexor.co.uk/mak/doc/robots/guidelines.html`, written by Martijn Koster, Jonathon Fletcher, and Lee McLoughlin.

3. **If you get extensive and useful search results from a spider, save the results to an HTML file on your local directory (in HTML).** This is necessary because, in most cases, you will not be able to save the search results as a URL reference in your hotlist.

4. **Be flexible in your search strategies.** Sometimes a subject-oriented approach can yield results, as well as surfing methods (discussed in Chapter 21) or machine-oriented methods we'll talk about in the next chapter.

Spiders of the Future

The spiders we have examined thus far—Lycos, Crawler, the Worm, the Harvest WWW Home Page Broker—are all different species. They can't talk to each other; and, although they aren't outright hostile towards each other, they don't share. Lycos' collects its own database, of the Web, as does the Crawler, the Worm, and the Brokers. But they are all trying to do the same thing: explore the Web for information. But what if they could all use the same database? In sharing the responsibility, collectively, could they to do a better job? Lycos, with its massive database, experiences large numbers of hits, making it difficult for users to query its database during peak Web usage hours. The Harvest WWW Broker scours the Web looking for many of the same things that Lycos looks for—so why do this twice? Moreover, the Web is getting larger every minute. Can a single spider possibly keep up? Can the current spiders survive in a rapidly growing Web?

The WebAnts project approaches these problems by attempting to create cooperating Web walkers (ants) with distributed databases. These cooperating ants can then each work separately, coordinating which regions of the Web to scour. The results are distributed on several servers, so that one spider database doesn't get hit so much (with requests for information) and users can retrieve information. The home page of the WebAnts project (`http://thule.mt.cs.cmu.edu:8001/webants/`) is shown in Figure 19.25.

FIGURE 19.25.

The WebAnts project home page. Courtesy of John R. R. Leavitt.

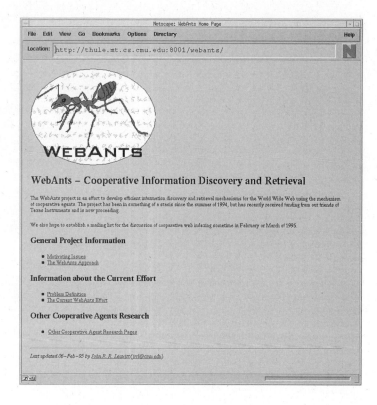

The Web will inevitably host new crawlers and spiders that will be stronger, faster, and smarter in order to survive the dynamic, massively expanding Web. Projects such as WebAnts may be the future of crawler/spider development. Prototype ants should be ready in the spring of 1995, and the first searchable indexes should be available by autumn. The Web will probably never host only a single species of spider. There is too much divergence in the way people use information for that to ever happen. In fact, in the interests of electronic biodiversity, the Web probably shouldn't support a spider monoculture (having only a single species of spider) or even a dominant species; it should encourage a diversity of searchers that grow stronger and more intelligent and that fit well into particular niches and information needs of users.

Navigator's Check

Finding a specific resource in the enormous information space of the Web is a difficult task. Spiders can help, but the conflict between searching broadly (finding out about a lot of things) and searching deeply (finding a lot about anything you look at) will necessarily remain unresolved. Some spiders, such as the Worm, collect specific text that is set apart by the tags in HTML documents. Others, such as Lycos, Harvest WWW Broker, and WebCrawler, search more deeply and make indexes of the entire contents of documents.

In addition to spiders, you can use other indexes to search through URL collections for patterns of keywords. However, these indexes, sometimes relying on handcrafted lists or manual maintenance of information, also have their limitations.

Some keys to using spiders and indexes effectively are as follows:

- Understand that finding information on the Web is a complex task and that no spider or index has infallible knowledge of the Web.

- Be aware of major spiders and spider collections. Use a variety of spiders in performing searches.

- For the spiders that seem most helpful to you, learn the details of their searching-pattern options and how they work. Attempt to answer these questions (abbreviated from a list earlier in the chapter):

  1. How does the spider feed/eliminate waste?

  2. How often does the spider walk?

  3. Is the spider caged?

  4. Can the spider leave the Web or touch its edges?

  5. Does the spider behave?

  6. What does the spider know?

  7. How can you communicate with the spider?

- Keep up with developments in new spider species such as WebAnts. Watch for spiders to evolve into stronger, smarter, and faster searching tools.

Machines: Space-Oriented Searching

20

by
John December

Although the subject- and keyword-oriented searching methods described in the previous two chapters might help you locate what you want in most cases, another challenge is to find resources based on the notion of distinct "spaces."

Spaces can be defined as groups of servers or sites that are related to each other, whether geographically, conceptually, or by protocol. In Chapter 16, "At the Edge of the Web," we looked at how information spaces exist at the Web's edge. In this chapter, we'll visit each of the major information spaces of the Web itself and examine what Web-based resources exist that can help a navigator find the server machines in these information spaces. We'll examine Web pages that can help you locate specific machines in geographical space as well as look at some search techniques that treat "space" in a less obvious way.

Naturally, a primary definition of "space" on the Web relates to geography. After all, servers in information spaces exist in an actual physical location. Using maps representing the earth's geography or using lists of locations organized by country, region, state, and city, a Web navigator can locate particular information servers based on geography or can "visit" a geographic location in cyberspace and discover what servers exist there. The skilled navigator also can find information and resources (which may be located anywhere physically) that relate to a particular geographic region. There are several Web collections that organize this kind of "tourist" information.

Still another notion of space involves "home page" space, or "directory space." Certainly, you could use keyword-searching (and even subject-oriented searching) methods to locate home pages of individuals; but in this chapter, we'll look at some webs that are specifically defined to help you get in touch with other people more directly.

Information Spaces

An information space can be defined as the set of all information worldwide that is available on servers of a particular protocol. For example, Gopher space consists of all the information and files on publicly available Gopher servers worldwide. Each information space then presents its data in its own format, and each information space can be thought of as being defined by the collection of all servers of that type. To search information spaces by these server machines, we want to find a "monster" list of all the servers in each information space. (These lists are called monster lists because they are often extremely long.)

FTP Space

There is a monster list of publicly accessible File Transfer Protocol (FTP) sites worldwide at `http://www.info.net/Public/ftp-list.html`. (Warning: This file is very large—over 100KB—and could cause some browsers to crash.) This list is a Web version of the FTP-list Usenet FAQ files maintained by Perry Rovers at `ftp://rtfm.mit.edu/pub/usenet-by-group/news.answers/ftp-list/`. Figure 20.1 shows the top of the Web version of the monster FTP site list.

Figure 20.2 shows sample entries from this list. Each site annotation gives information about the kinds of files found there as well as the subject matter. Therefore, a Web navigator might use this FTP monster in conjunction with a Find command in a Web browser as a way to find specific subjects at FTP sites or particular server names.

FIGURE 20.1.

The monster Web FTP list. Copyright © 1995 Infonet Services Corporation. All rights reserved. Printed by permission.

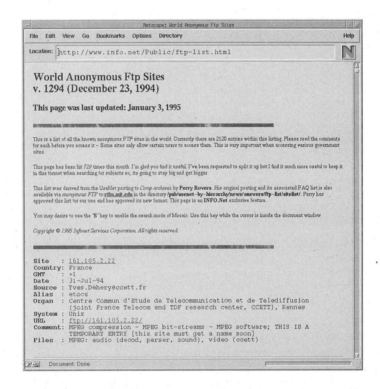

The example entry shows typical information that you might need to know in searching for or using anonymous FTP servers. You can find out the local time of the server (important to identify off-peak times for transferring files), as well as a summary of some of the subject matter found at the site.

Gopher Space

We've already talked about Gopher in Chapter 16, "At the Edge of the Web." You can browse a monster list of Gophers by geographic region from the Minnesota Gopher (gopher://gopher.micro.umn.edu/) by selecting "Other Gopher and Information Servers." By tradition, most Gophers offer a similar option to search Gopher space through a geographic breakdown.

Many campuswide information systems have been implemented as Gophers, as these institutions quickly adopted Gopher as "the next generation" of information-delivery tools after many

FIGURE 20.2.

A sample entry in the monster Web FTP list.

libraries adopted Telnet. Certainly, there are more libraries now using Gopher, and many universities and libraries are migrating to the Web. You can use this "space migration" phenomenon to judge where in cyberspace you would be most likely to find a particular institution's information server. Many new commercial ventures are going directly to the Web, and most new systems built after 1994 seem destined for the Web. Some older library systems still use Telnet or Gopher. If spiders never learn to leave the Web entirely, you may see more information providers leave Gopher space because their information won't be indexed by important forms of searching tools available on the Web.

Telnet Space: Hytelnet

We've already talked about Hytelnet in Chapter 16. Hytelnet also organizes Telnet-accessible resources by geography (as well as subjects). Hytelnet, developed by Peter Scott, is particularly useful for services that adopted online technology early—such as libraries and community-based Free-net systems—because Telnet is a widely available interface for dial-up modem users. Hytelnet's list of "Other Telnet-accessible resources," at URL `http://www.cc.ukans.edu/hytelnet_html/SITES2.html`, shown in Figure 20.3, gives you an idea of what to expect in Hytelnet space.

FIGURE 20.3.

Other Telnet-accessible resources.

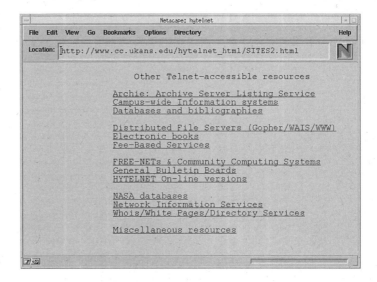

WAIS Space

We've also already visited WAIS space in Chapter 16. Figure 16.18 shows a partial listing of the WAIS directory of servers provided by WAIS, Inc. (`http://www.wais.com/`). WAIS, Inc., maintains the WAIS directory of servers, listing all the known publicly accessible WAIS databases in the world. This list, however, can't be interpreted by geography or server machine name, but rather by database name. Because WAIS databases organize information by indexes, you can search through WAISGATE (`http://server.wais.com/waisgate-announce.html`) for databases that are likely to contain the subjects or keywords you're looking for.

Web Space

Web space can be organized according to machine name. However, the list of Web servers at CERN (`http://www.w3.org/hypertext/DataSources/WWW/Servers.html`) is organized by geography (Figure 20.4). (See the section later in this chapter on geographic-space searching of the Web.)

Matthew Gray created a Web robot (the World Wide Web Wanderer) to travel through the Web and create a database of WWW sites (Figure 20.5). His list organizes Web space by server name. The interface to this list at `http://www.netgen.com/cgi/comprehensive` will help you find particular Web servers based on domain names.

FIGURE 20.4.

List of Web servers.

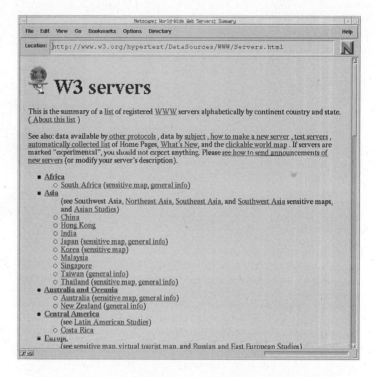

FIGURE 20.5.

Matthew Gray's Web server interface. Courtesy of Matthew Gray, Chief Technologist of net.Genesis Corp. of Cambridge, MA.

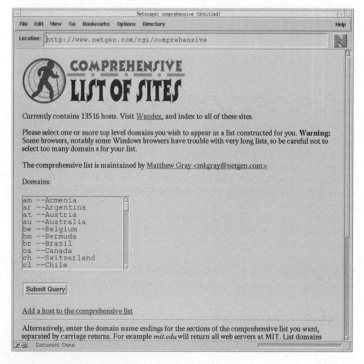

Figure 20.6 shows the result of querying the database for a particular domain (in this case, .fr for France). Although this makes the database roughly organized by geography (in the case of domain names ending in country names), the resulting list as shown in Figure 20.6 includes only a listing of Web server names in the .fr domain, not an organization by geography within this domain.

Searching by domains is very useful, for example, when you want a list of all servers for the government servers (domain names ending with .gov). Using Gray's list of Web servers, you can obtain such a list, and the server names listed can give you a clue as to the government agency sponsoring the server.

FIGURE 20.6.

Web Servers in the .fr domain. Courtesy of Matthew Gray, Chief Technologist of net.Genesis Corp. of Cambridge, MA.

Both the WWW Server List and Matthew Gray's server list are very useful ways to look for known Web servers as well as discover new ones as they arrive on the Web.

Geographic Spaces

As we've seen, perusing long lists of server names is not necessarily the best way to search an information space. Frequently, if you are looking for a particular Web server, you'll know its geographic location. There are a variety of Web applications that you can use to view Web resources organized in graphical maps and geographically organized listings of servers.

The Virtual Tourist

Let's say you are interested in the country of Turkey and you want to get an idea of what Web sites are in the country. A Web spider search (see previous chapter) might turn up references to Turkey, but not necessarily to just information related to the country of Turkey. Further, let's say you don't really want to look at just a text-based list or find isolated instances, but you'd rather see the "lay of the land" of Turkey in cyberspace.

There is a tool for exactly this purpose, called the Virtual Tourist, developed by Brandon Plewe. The URL of the Virtual Tourist is `http://wings.buffalo.edu/world`, and its front page is shown in Figure 20.7. The Virtual Tourist works in conjunction with the CERN WWW Server list (`http://www.w3.org/hypertext/DataSources/WWW/Servers.html`).

The Virtual Tourist accomplishes several things. First, it serves as a visual interface into the geographic distribution of World Wide Web servers. Second, it gathers information about many geographic regions. Third, it does all this through a cooperative system of hypertext documents that is voluntarily developed. Fourth, it effectively employs the graphical information maps feature available through Mosaic. By clicking a symbol or boxed region, the user obtains more information about that region. In this way, the Virtual Tourist accomplishes much.

FIGURE 20.7.

Virtual Tourist front page.
Courtesy of Brandon Plewe.

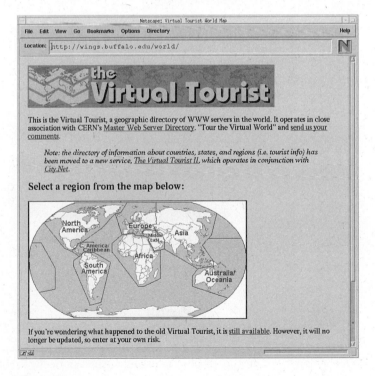

Let's continue our exploration of Turkey. By clicking the box over the Middle East on the world map (Figure 20.7), we obtain the Middle East map (Figure 20.8).

FIGURE 20.8.

Virtual Tourist Middle East.

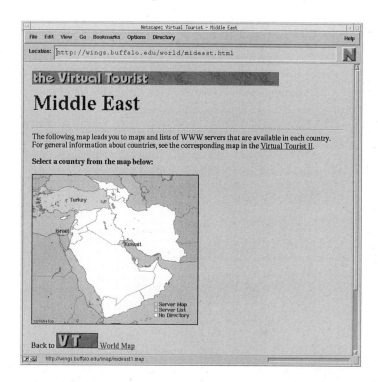

Note that in Figure 20.8 there are several choices for Turkey: the resource map, a resource list, and country information. The resource map gives a visual perspective of the layout of cyberspace in Turkey. The results are shown in Figure 20.9.

Notice how the Turkey map differs slightly in style from the Middle East map, a difference that allows for expressive variation in how administrators at individual sites want to represent their region, while still retaining the functionality and intent of the Virtual Tourist itself. The Turkey map shows the locations of Web sites that have registered with the developer of the map shown. It quickly gives an idea of locations in the region where you might find Web servers. Let's examine the link labeled METU on the Turkey map. Clicking on the square next to the label METU, we obtain Figure 20.10.

FIGURE 20.9.

Turkey map.

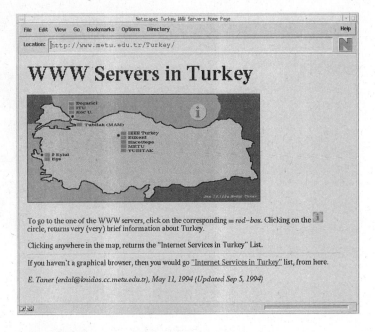

FIGURE 20.10.

Middle East Technical University home page.

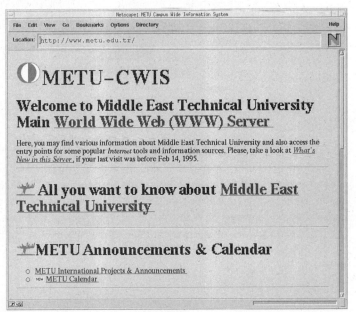

This page gives us a launching point for more information about Middle East Technical University. Although we might have found this same home page with a Web spider (as well as hits for each word in the name of METU), we might not have been able to locate other contextual information (such as neighboring Web servers) so easily. Moreover, the graphical map interface is fun to use. If you want to browse a hypertext (non-graphical) list of Web servers, you can open URL `http://www.w3.org/hypertext/DataSources/WWW/Servers.html`. This list gives you links to many of the country maps shown throughout the Virtual Tourist as well as a means to scan keywords or phrases easily (using Mosaic's File | Find In Current command).

The Virtual Tourist II/City.Net

Like the Virtual Tourist, City.Net presents information about geographical locations by using clickable maps. But whereas the Virtual Tourist I provides information about WWW sites and other network servers, City.Net (Virtual Tourist II) focuses on tourism and information about specific cities. Figure 20.11 shows the Virtual Tourist II/City.Net front page (`http://wings.buffalo.edu/world/vt2/`).

FIGURE 20.11.

Virtual Tourist II/City.Net home page. Copyright 1994–1995, City Net Express. All rights reserved. printed by permission.

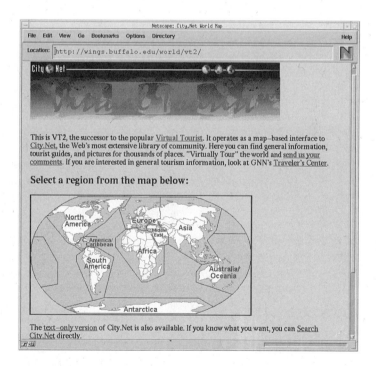

Notice that the front page of the Virtual Tourist II (VT II) is much like VT I. To show the difference, however, let's focus on the same region of the Middle East we previously visited via VT I. Clicking the Middle East section of the map in Figure 20.11, we obtain Figure 20.12.

FIGURE 20.12.

Virtual Tourist II/City.Net Middle East page.

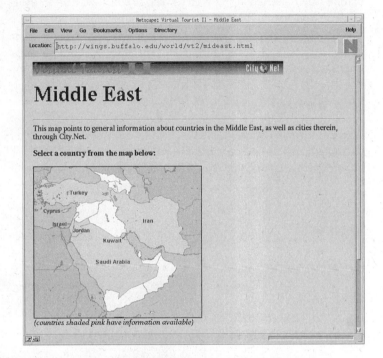

Notice how this Middle East page is slightly different from Figure 20.8. Instead of listing Web and other information servers, the VT II focuses on city and tourist information. Choosing the country of Turkey from the map in Figure 20.12, we obtain Figure 20.13.

Again, comparing Figures 20.9 and 20.13, we see the difference between the VT 1 and VT 2 more dramatically. In Figure 20.13, we have a listing of city and country information, some from online references sources such as the CIA Factbook for Turkey. Choosing a particular city, Istanbul, from Figure 20.13, we get a page that is still on the VT II/City.Net server, giving us the available jumping-off points for information about Istanbul (Figure 20.14).

FIGURE 20.13.

Virtual Tourist II/City.Net Turkey page.

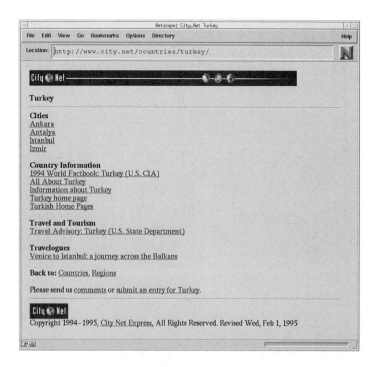

FIGURE 20.14.

Virtual Tourist II/City.Net Istanbul, Turkey page.

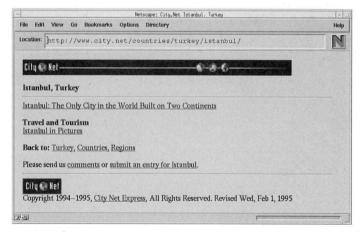

Choosing the link "Istanbul: The Only City in the World Built on Two Continents," we obtain an information page about Istanbul, Turkey, written by Melih Ozbek (Figure 20.15). Note that this information is hosted on the server at Middle East Technical University. Therefore, VT II/City. Net serves as an elaborate "switching web" that takes you to information about geographic regions worldwide, often to information developed and maintained by people in that region.

FIGURE 20.15.

Virtual Tourist II/City.Net Istanbul, Turkey, information page.

CityLink

Like VT II/City.Net, CityLink gathers geographical information about locations in a web with clickable maps as "switching points." CityLink focuses on U.S. cities. Its home page (http://www.neosoft.com/citylink/) is shown in Figure 20.16.

CityLink also develops material for cities. For example, from CityLink's front page, we can choose the link for St. Louis, MO, as shown in Figure 20.17 (http://www.neosoft.com/citylink/st-louis/default.html).

The St. Louis page from CityLink offers a wealth of information in the standard format that CityLink uses for other city information pages: what to see and do, where to stay and eat, where to shop, and how to get more information.

FIGURE 20.16.

The USA CityLink Project. Copyright © 1995, Blake & Associates, Internet Marketing Consultants. Printed by permission.

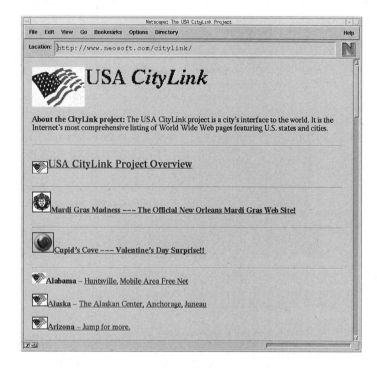

FIGURE 20.17.

CityLink St. Louis page. Copyright © 1995, Blake & Associates, Internet Marketing Consultants. Printed by permission.

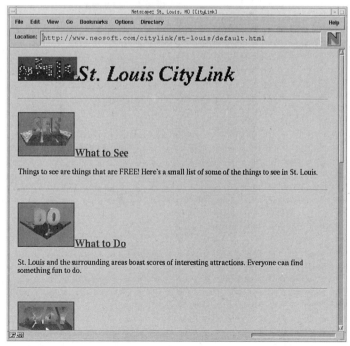

Web Navigation Tools and Techniques

Part III

People Space

Just as geographic directories like the Virtual Tourist I and II, City.Net, and CityLink have organized geographic-based information about servers and tourist information, so too is there a need to create directories to help you find specific people in cyberspace. Although keyword- and even subject-oriented searching methods might be just right for getting in touch with people (through common interests tied to keywords or subject-oriented resource collections), it's useful to be able to search for a particular person or a person with particular interests in directories that collect home pages or in "white pages" directories. In the following sections, we'll look at "phone-book" style directories as well as collections of home pages that will help you search "people space" from the Web.

Directory Servers

One kind of people space searching involves trying to track down individuals using "directory services." There are a variety of "white pages," electronic directory services based on various schemes with names such as whois and X.500. The page at `http://honor.uc.wlu.edu/directories.html` is an entry point into a collection of directory servers. Part of the breakdown of directory servers by name is shown in Figure 20.18.

FIGURE 20.18.

Directory of white pages servers by name.

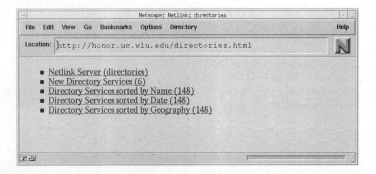

Another collection of useful reference information is located on the Yaleinfo gopher at `gopher://yaleinfo.yale.edu:7700/11/Internet-People`. (Figure 20.19.) This resource collection includes links to "CSO Phone Books," a collection of white-pages directories based on a variety of data formats. To use this service, you locate the "phone book" of the organization of the person you seek, and then you can search the list using a first name and a last name or with a wildcard.

In general, there is no simple way of finding a person on the Net by using the Net itself; often you'd be better off to contact the person directly by telephone! However, directory services are improving. As an experiment, you might try to locate yourself in the directory services described here. You might be surprised at how difficult it is.

Netfind

Still another way to search for people is through Netfind. Figure 20.19 includes a link to a Telnet connection to Netfind. Netfind's Web interface provided by Nova University at `http://www.nova.edu/Inter-Links/netfind.html` is shown in Figure 20.20.

FIGURE 20.19.

Resources for finding people on the Net.

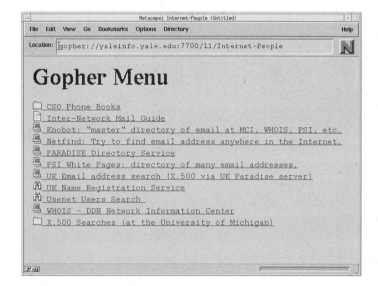

FIGURE 20.20.

Web interface to Netfind. Courtesy of Nova University.

Like a Web spider, Netfind searches the whole space of directory servers and returns a list of "hits" that match your keyword-search pattern. For example, I used Netfind to search for my entry at Rensselaer Polytechnic Institute. Figure 20.21 shows the results from using Netfind to locate `december rensselaer`. `rennsselaer` is used as the key to search for servers; `december` is used as the key to find users.

FIGURE 20.21.

Results of searching `december rensselaer` using Netfind.

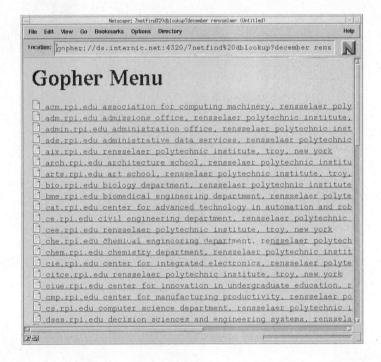

Figure 20.21 illustrates one of the difficulties of using Netfind. The long list of hosts matching the keyword "rensselaer" include machines located at Rensselaer Polytechnic Institute (and also some machines in Rensselaer, IN). But which one does my account reside on? Clicking the first entry shown in Figure 20.21, for the `acm.rpi.edu` domain name, the local chapter of the Association for Computing Machinery, I get no results, because I do not have an account on that machine domain. In fact, of the 69 machine domain-name entries on the returned list, I have accounts on only three of them. Someone searching for me would be hard-pressed to guess which machine would lead to a success. In general, however, databases such as Netfind can be useful, especially if you are willing to spend some time weeding through the results or if you have a pretty good idea of the server machine name. Ideally, each institution would have a central "white pages"

phone-book server implemented for all the machine domains at that institution. (In fact, many institutions do maintain such a resource for some domains, as listed in an experimental X.500 phone book that is contained in a menu entry within the CSO Phone book directory of servers.) From a single phone book, you could look through the entire white pages for an institution rather than using the machine domain-oriented searching method Netfind offers.

Community of Science

Although white-page, phone-book servers can help you locate people at institutions or on particular machine domains, you still may want to browse collections of home pages. One collection of home pages called the Community of Science, at `http://cos.gdb.org/`, offers users a way to connect with researchers and scientists with similar interests. Figure 20.22 shows the home page of the Community of Science server.

FIGURE 20.22.

The community of Science Web Server.

The Community of Science server offers an interface that you can use to search for researchers with a particular expertise specified in a Forms interface (Figure 20.23).

FIGURE 20.23.

A forms interface for the Community of Science Web Server.

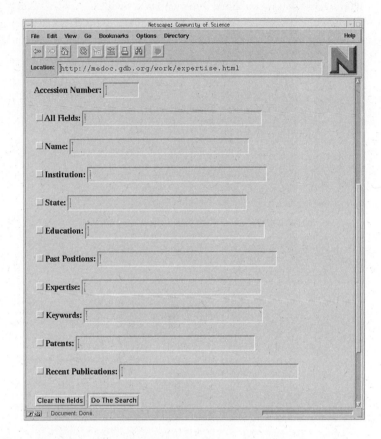

The Community of Science server offers similar forms-based searching for inventions, facilities, and funding opportunities. By providing this system, the Community of Science server helps you gain contacts through the Web.

Who's Who on the Internet

Unlike the Community of Science server, the "Who's Who on the Internet" web (http://web.city.ac.uk/citylive/pages.html) shown in Figure 20.24, doesn't organize its entries based on an extensive format or fill-in form. Instead, "Who's Who" gathers links to personal home pages and a brief description of the page for use in a searching service.

FIGURE 20.24.

Who's Who on the Internet. Copyright © 1994, 1995 Kirk Bowe. Printed by permission.

The keyword-searching mechanism for "Who's Who" allows you to search through the database of keywords that individuals give when they register their home page. "Who's Who on the Internet" is part of the WWW Virtual Library, and it is growing rapidly in size and coverage. In this directory you'll find students and teachers, people in industry, and Web enthusiasts from many interesting categories.

WHO's On-line

Like the Community of Science server, the WHO's On-line server (`http://www.ictp.trieste.it/Canessa/whoiswho.html`) gathers information and links to home pages of people involved in professional, academic, educational, and scientific pursuits (Figure 20.25).

The WHO's On-line database organizes individuals by profession and/or activity and provides a keywords index that users can search. You can also search all the profession databases at once (consisting of keywords that users supply when registering with WHO's On-line) through a single interface. Once you find links that match, you'll be given a list of links to the matching pages.

FIGURE 20.25.
WHO's On-line. Courtesy of E. Canessa.

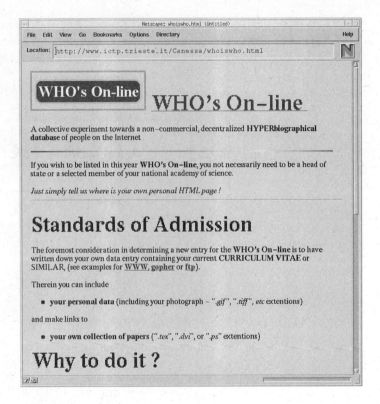

Home Page Collections

The "Who's Who on the Internet" database described previously is part of the WWW Virtual Library. There are other collections of personal pages that are more informal or grew as part of other activities. These collections include the following:

- *Personal Pages Worldwide:* This is a large collection of university, K–12, and commercial home-page collections worldwide. You'll be able to follow links in this collection, for example, to pages for the graduate students at Caltech or the Reece High School (Australia) 7th grade. (`http://www.utexas.edu/world/personal/index.html`)

- *Netizens:* This is a service provided by O'Reilly & Associates as part of its Global Network Navigator. This collection of home pages grows as people voluntarily add pointers to their pages. The collection is organized by name and by date of entry. (`http://nearnet.gnn.com/gnn/netizens/index.html`)

- *Galaxy's Net Citizens:* This is a collection of individual pages, guides, collections, and other directories of home pages. (`http://www.einet.net/galaxy/Community/Net-Citizens.html`)

- *World Birthday Web (WBW):* This isn't a formal "home page" registry, but rather a fun service. You can register your home page (or just your name if you don't have a home page) in a database organized according to the day of the year you were born. (See Figure 20.26.) Created by Tom Boutell, this service is a fun way to meet others who share your same birthday or just sample home pages (`http://sunsite.unc.edu/btbin/birthday`).

FIGURE 20.26.

World Birthday Web.
Courtesy of Tom Boutell.

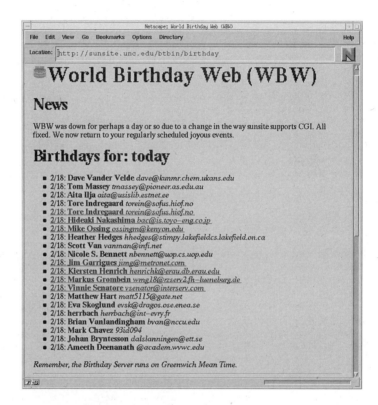

- *People section from Yahoo:* Along with the many subject and topic branches in the Yahoo tree is one for personal home pages. The Yahoo entries are sorted alphabetically. Since the individual entries are also part of Yahoo's database, you can search for home pages (by the name of the person) using the search mechanism of Yahoo. The Yahoo collection includes many individual pages, with some entries for collections or groups of people (such as Geek Houses) (`http://www.yahoo.com/Entertainment/People/`).

Locating Organizations

Locating specific organizations on the Web or Internet can be difficult without a guide. You could use keyword or subject-oriented searching methods to try to find the organization, and you might also find the organization through individual listings in white-pages servers like those described previously. However, there are now "yellow pages" that have been developed on the Web to help put you in touch with companies and organizations more quickly. The World Wide Yellow Pages are at http://www.yellow.com/. (See Figure 2,27.)

FIGURE 20.27.
World Wide Yellow Pages.

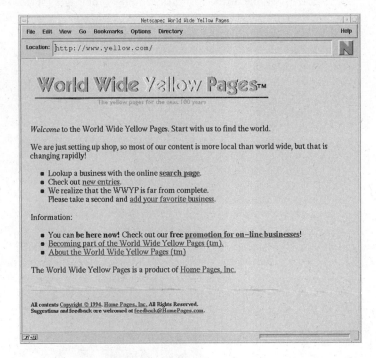

The World Wide Yellow Pages gives you a way to search for businesses that advertise within it. Based on the entries, you can perform keyword searches or search for entries by subject heading (much like categories in the paper yellow pages), company name, or company location.

Other business/organization directories include

- *Open Market's Commercial Sites Index:* Lists commercial services and products. You can search the directory by keyword or by alphabetical listings. This is a free service (that is, the listing is free) provided by Open Market, Inc. (http://www.directory.net/).

- *The Internet Business Directory:* Lists a variety of businesses and includes a form for keyword search of listings (http://ibd.ar.com/).

Navigator's Check

We've covered a variety of ways that you can search for machines in information spaces for servers, information related to geographical locations, and individual people and organizations. However, there is no simple and universal way to locate a given machine, person, or organization on the Web. Instead, there are a variety of tools and catalogs that are likely to lead to what you need. You can use all these methods within your repertoire of Web navigation skills, along with the keyword- and subject-oriented searching methods described in the previous chapters. This diversity of portals into the Web underscores the Web's flexibility in presenting information. In the next chapter, we'll explore a creative and subjective way to search for information on the Web: the phenomenon known as surfing.

Surfing: Finding the New and Unusual

21

by
John December

So far we've covered some major ways to find information on the Web and at its edges: navigating through trees for subject-oriented information, using spiders to find keyword information, and employing space-oriented searches for machines, geographic locations, and people. All these are valuable searching and navigating methods and may truly yield what you want. However, the Web isn't always neat and tidy. As you've seen, spiders are imperfect, and every hand-crafted resource index is imperfect. Until the development of advanced artificial-intelligence searchers (smart spiders) that can efficiently and intelligently scour the Web and the Net for resources, you'll have to use the most powerful intelligence agent available—you.

In this chapter, I ask you to drop your spiders, machine lists, and subject trees—and to learn how to surf instead. If discovering the new and the quirky is something you want to do anyway, surfing might be your thing. The term "surfing," as used here, refers to the experience of encountering information and communication in cyberspace in nonlinear (and sometimes illogical) ways.

There are some practical reasons for learning how to surf:

- To keep up with new and developing tools that will help you use the Net more effectively
- To build your awareness of resources and activities in your field of study or area of interest
- To experience serendipity—a rare moment when you find something very useful among the large volume of information on the Net
- To stay current in your awareness of what is out there as well as possible on the Net
- To develop your awareness of the state of Net information quality in your area of interest

Surfing is an active, wide-ranging navigation activity that requires you to not rely on any single software tool or list, but rather to employ your personal insight and feel for the Net. You can't surf by just clicking down lists of resources, although that activity is a part of surfing. You can't surf by just using spiders, trees, or space maps of the Net, although you will use all of those searching techniques and skills while surfing. Surfing means crawling and running along the links of the Web and beyond its edge, into the trees of Gopher space, the archives of FTP space, and the scores and lists of WAIS responses. Although other means of searching rely on your analytic and logic skills to find resources, surfing involves using your intuition—a feeling that can only develop over time in a holistic experience of a network's resources and the people behind it. The philosophy of surfing draws on the principle that you might not know what you want on the Web, but you'll know it when you see it.

Introduction to Surfing

The key to surfing is to integrate the available searching methods with your own intuition and judgment. Surfing involves working subjectively from a logically acquired set of information using skills that are both analytical and physical. Surfing involves the feeling you have when you are encountering networked information and communication. Even if you do not have all the usual senses or physical capabilities, you can develop what you have in order to experience the Net. When you surf, you take network-access techniques that are acquired through language, logic, and analytic reasoning and turn them into intuitive responses and muscular reactions, much the way a tennis player practices a serve over and over, both to perfect it and to make it automatic and available in the dynamic flow of a competition.

This may sound like I'm advocating a very strange approach to finding and experiencing network information. But you don't have to change your life or abandon all reasoning. You only need to be open to a different way of interacting with the people and resources on a network. Moreover, in this "guide to surfing," you can pick and choose from among the techniques described here. Choose what works best and seems right for you.

Initial Considerations

When surfing, you might become physically, emotionally, and mentally taxed. You'll encounter large amounts of information rapidly and make quick judgments about where your attention and concentration should go next. Carpal tunnel syndrome and other physical ailments are realistic concerns, particularly if you use repeated physical actions to perform a task. (You should consult a physician if you experience any pain or discomfort when using a keyboard, mouse, or computer monitor.)

You'll need to keep track of the time of day you surf and the amount of time you spend. If you share resources, don't tie up the computer. Surfing is not necessarily a waste of time, but you will be spending many hours at the keyboard and encountering many, many information sources you don't want or need; therefore, use good judgment about the resources you tie up. Moreover, you might find that you lose track of time when you are accessing large amounts of information. (You might consider setting an alarm so that you don't overdo it!) Late nights and weekends are usually off-peak usage hours for Web access at your local site, although these same times may be peak hours somewhere else on the Web. Surfing during your local off-peak times will usually help minimize the drain on the network while giving you better responses. (And don't forget that limiting the amount of time you spend online will save you money.)

Coping with Information

Many people find that the large amount of information they encounter on the network is daunting. If you are a new user, you'll need to develop skills to quickly skim through hypertext. You should read in detail only those resources and pages that are the most valuable to you. Without skills to cope with large amounts of information, you'll suffer information overload and waste your time on irrelevant information. Your goal is not to read everything, but rather to discover what's out there and to become current in your particular area of interest. Here are some tips to avoid information overload:

1. **Pace yourself.** Only *you* know how much computer interaction you can take. If you know that an hour's worth is going to give you a headache or frustrate you, it's probably best not to push yourself beyond that. You will become more adept at surfing when you you are rewarded with valuable information, not when you push your tolerance limits.

2. **Don't read everything.** While you'll need to use the navigation skills we talked about in Chapter 15, "Browser Operations," and you'll need to pay attention to the indicators on your browser while going through the Web, don't feel compelled to read all the text on the screen. In my own classes, I've seen many students start at the top of a screen and read down. This is not necessarily the best strategy. We'll talk about specifics in the next section, but be aware that surfing does not necessarily mean reading all of the text on the screen word-for-word.

3. **Pay attention to the information's space, texture, and cues.** While encountering networked information, ask yourself the following:

   - What information space is this? (Gopher, FTP, WAIS, HTTP.) The answer to this question will help you perform the basic navigation skills we talked about in Chapter 15.

   - What is the information's texture? By texture I mean the media composition and organizational structure of the information. Hypertext in HTML is one identification of a media texture. Another example of a media texture is a Gopher or FTP menu that has many multimedia icons (for sound, binary files, graphics, movies). Besides medium, another aspect of texture is information structure: Do you see many symbols for directories or directories and files? Still another aspect of information texture is interconnections: Are you at the home page of a much larger set of connected documents? Or are you at a document buried deep in a web? This texture information gives you immediate clues about the site's organization as well as what kind of material you'll find there. If you've just come into a site and the texture of what you see is varied (many different icons for directories, text files, graphics files all mixed together), you may have stumbled into the "back closet" where you'll expect to see very little orientation or explanatory information. In contrast, you might reach the "front door" of a site, with "About this server" or "README" links immediately apparent.

   - What navigation cues can you see immediately? For example, in hypertext, can you see links back to a "front" or home page? If you are at an FTP site, do you see a file folder for "Parent directory"? If you are on a Gopher, can you see any menu entries for orientation information? What navigation cues (links back to home, links to parent directories, links to README files or orientation information) can you see? Are you at the home page for a group of documents?

   - What information cues can you see immediately? What text appears in the Document Title window on the front panel of the Web browser? What does this title mean to you? What does the URL tell you about the host and resource type?

What does the heading information in the document tell you? Is there a clearly stated purpose for the resource you are looking at?

4. **Travel light.** Avoid saving information or files until you are sure you want them. If you consider a resource potentially valuable, put a reference to it on your hotlist. I've often encountered students who want to print every page they find interesting. This perhaps comes from being attuned to print and wanting to "feel" information in a familiar medium rather than on the computer (which, to a new user, may seem a capricious barrier between themselves and the information). At first, you may feel a need to print screens and save files to your home disk. There may even be good reasons to do so. (Resources can disappear or their network connections become lost.) However, as you gain experience, you'll feel more confident that you will be able to track down a resource again, perhaps by using a spider. By traveling light, you'll save disk space, time, resources, and attention, and you'll also free yourself to move on to new resources.

5. **Move on.** Surfing represents the discovery phase of encountering information. You should certainly spend some time while surfing contemplating the value and meaning of what you find, but you shouldn't get bogged down in any one particular site. Avoid the tendency some new users have to consider the first site they find on a particular subject to be the definitive one. The composition of sites and the quality of "definitiveness" changes dynamically. In a manner of hours or minutes, a developer at one site might add valuable resources another site doesn't have. In fact, you can't consider any information on the Web to be static.

The point of this advice on coping with information overload is to increase your ability to sift through large volumes of data. This will increase the probability that you'll find valuable resources with the quantity and quality of data you desire.

Equipment

Not everyone has high-speed connections to the Internet that offer rapid access to resources, particularly graphics. If you have a slow Internet connection, you should consider turning the graphics capability off on the Web browser main panel. Also, you'll have to access the network during off-peak hours. A slow Internet connection also means that you'll pay closer attention to the texture of information you find; you might need to avoid graphics and movie files or be more selective in the ones you do access.

Outlook

Unlike the previous chapters, in which I've discussed searching in terms of an "indexing mode" (by subject, by keyword, by space), the goal for surfing is not necessarily to find information according to an indexing mode, but rather to encounter information for its own sake. You might possibly encounter information just for the purpose of building awareness, or with the intent of grabbing URLs and references within hypertext so that you can later navigate more carefully using other techniques.

Skills

In order to encounter large amounts of information using a Web browser, you'll need to have good basic navigation skills (see Chapter 15) as well as good file-management skills. You should know how to save and manage files in directories, as well as know the basics of navigating in your computer's operating system.

Surfing

Now that you're prepared with an awareness of how to cope with information overload and special considerations for the equipment you need, let's look in detail at some surfing techniques. I'll describe some general procedures that you can use in any situation and also provide examples to illustrate specific techniques. We'll start by looking at preparations you can make and then some ideas for choosing your starting point for surfing. Then we'll look at how you can use these starting points to encounter more information.

Preparations

Find a comfortable place to work with the computer. Often it is helpful to have an environment in which you won't be distracted and you can concentrate fully. You might consider turning off any incoming message icons (like a mailbox icon) that may be on your screen and image loading on the Web browser.

You'll also want to have an e-mail communications program available and links to your favorite spiders, trees, or machine lists in your hotlist.

Starting Points

Your first goal is to get started in a process of encountering information. Although you don't need to have a specific mode of information discovery in mind when you start, you need to have some link that will take you to entry points, either in the form of a list of resources or the results of a spider search.

Here are some techniques to generate starting points:

1. **"What's New" pages:** There are a variety of "What's New" pages on the Web that offer ways to discover new resources. Some of the major sources of "What's New" information are

   a. **Yahoo's What's New:** This is an amazing treasure-trove of very current new listings. Whereas pages like Netscape's What's New page and Mosaic's What's New page (see subsequent listing of sites) sometimes experience quite a backlog of listings, Yahoo's database (Figure 21.1) offers hundreds of new listings daily (with updates coming sometimes three times daily). Because, of course, all of these "What's New" entries for Yahoo are also in Yahoo's database, you can search for keywords through Yahoo's search mechanism.

FIGURE 21.1.

The What's New resource from Yahoo. Copyright © 1994, 1995 David Filo and Jerry Yang. Printed by permission.

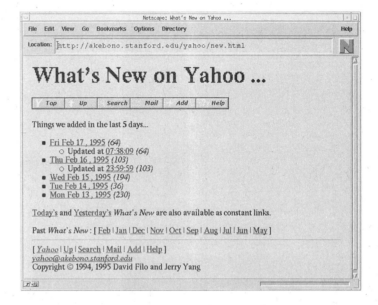

b. **webNews:** As part of a project, Studies in Information Filtering Technology for Electronic Resources (SIFTER), the Department of Computer and Information Sciences at the University of Alabama at Birmingham offers a very useful service for finding out about new resources, events, and news of the Web called webNews. You can find webNews off the UAB-CIS Web home page (`http://twinbrook.cis.uab.edu:70/Home.80`) or at `http://twinbrook.cis.uab.edu:70/webNews.80`. Figure 21.2 shows the opening screen for webNews.

webNews is a great place to start learning about new events and resources on the Web, and its interface offers a variety of ways to search its archives. First, webNews offers a chronological list of articles from Usenet newsgroups (for example, `comp.infosystems.www.announce` and other groups related to the Web and the Internet). There is also a "Hyperdex" which allows you to search a list of keywords to locate articles from webNews that relate to that term. Each article includes hyperlinks for URLs listed within it as well as hyperlinks to cross-indexed terms. The webNews Dendronomicon is meant to be a "tree of terms," breaking up the collections of articles by keywords into a large branching tree of related words. The webNews interface also enables you to search for keywords in the database of articles. Overall, webNews is a surfer's delight; it culls out the major announcement articles from Usenet and indexes and cross indexes them to the point that you can browse by subjects, keywords, or the many branching cross-indexes webNews supplies.

FIGURE 21.2.

webNews. Courtesy of R. L. Samuell, Department of Computer and Information Sciences, University of Alabama at Birmingham.

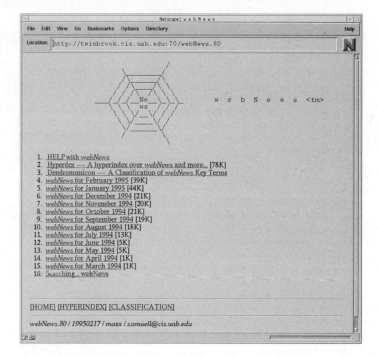

c. **Net-happenings:** Net-happenings is a mailing list and also a newsgroup (`news:comp.internet.net-happenings`) that serves to disseminate a wide variety of information about the Internet, its resources, tools, information, and events. You can search the Net-happenings database on the Web `http://www-iub.indiana.edu/cgi-bin/nethaps/`. From that page, you'll also be able to examine the archives by posting type.

d. **Newsgroup `comp.infosystems.www.announce`:** This is a moderated newsgroup dedicated to providing information about new Web resources. You can read articles in this group at `news:comp.infosystems.www.announce` or read the group's charter on the Web at `http://www.halcyon.com/grant/Misc/charter.html`. This is a particularly useful "What's New" service since it usually has a fairly short turnaround time between the information provider submitting the entry and when it appears. Also, the moderators of the newsgroup enforce a standard format and rules (see charter) that make the newsgroup easier to read.

e. **What's New (NCSA Mosaic):** When Mosaic was developed, its creators started an HTML page entitled, "What's New with National Center for Supercomputing Applications (NCSA) Mosaic." Begun as a simple service to help the Web community, it grew in popularity to become one of the most accessed documents on the Web and won the "Most Important Service Concept" in the "Best of the Web '94" contest. Because of this award and the popularity of Mosaic's "What's New," many more information providers have created "What's New" pages of their own.

The What's New with NCSA Mosaic page is now operated by NCSA and Global Network Navigator. Its URL is `http://www.ncsa.uiuc.edu/SDG/Software/Mosaic/Docs/whats-new.html`.

The above "What's New" pages serve Web-wide audiences. If you're interested in new resources in this context, these pages are good starting points.

There are specialized "what's new" pages, particular to specific servers, that can benefit you. A technique to find these pages is to use a Web spider to locate the phrase "What's New." If you know you want to surf in a particular subject area, examine the "What's New" page on servers that you know will give you the best coverage for that subject. How do you know which servers will give you the best coverage? You can examine the results of a WebCrawler search for keywords in your area of interest.

2. **Personal Home Pages:** The plethora of links on the Web makes individual perception valuable, and the personal home pages of people that share your interest often contain links to new resources and information, sifted by their tastes and judgment. These personal home pages may give you excellent jumping off points into the Web. There is no central "white pages" for the Web, although there are several initiatives being developed to collect home pages. (See Chapter 20, "Machines: Space-Oriented Searching," for a discussion of how to locate home pages in "People space" on the Web.)

A spider search for the keywords "home page" (and perhaps further words in your area of specialty) will yield both personal home pages of individuals as well as collections of home pages. Finding such a Web community devoted to your area of interest may be a gold mine for interesting personal home pages.

3. **Institutions:** As you explore the Web, you'll find that the Web servers of institutions (academic, commercial, nonprofit) contain just the links you want to have for exploring the Web. However, the caveat here is that institutional Web servers vary in information maintenance and development activities. You'll have to explore these institutional pages (obtained through any of the search techniques we've talked about so far) to find out which ones develop links to new resources most consistently. If you find institutional links with good new Web information coverage in your area of interest, these may be good surfing starting points.

4. **Language strategies:** To find sites with a particular (cultural, scientific, or information) orientation, use your knowledge of language conventions of that community to locate resources. For example, if you are looking for information about youth activities on the

Web (actually a very well-represented topic with the large proportion of younger people using the Web), use spider searches for title terms like "cool sites" or "fun sites." Use search terms for specialized vocabulary of that community or culture. Search for keywords that serve as language markers (words or phrases that uniquely identify members of a community) or terms that distinguish one community from another.

5. **Guessing:** This technique is one of the least likely to succeed, but its payoff can be great. Let's say that you want to find out about a new company called XYZ Corporation. You suspect they probably have a Web server. You could do a spider search, but if no spider has yet visited the XYZ corporation's server, its page will not show up in any database. A scan of the What's New Mosaic Page (through the CUI Catalog mentioned in Chapter 19, "Spiders and Indexes: Keyword-Oriented Searching") might also yield a match, or a search of a geographical listing of Web servers. Let's say these don't yield a match. What do you do?

   Try opening the URL http://www.xyz.com. You'll get an error message if the server does not exist or if the server's public access to files is turned off. If you are lucky, you'll see the home page for XYZ company neatly appear in the browser display window.

6. **Random searching:** This technique is perhaps the least likely to yield good information, but it can be used as a creative way to build your awareness of the kinds of resources you might be looking for and the possibilities for Web communication and expression.

> **NOTE**
>
> Yuval Fisher has created a page with "not exactly a thousand" points that connect to URLs in far-flung places. (Figure 21.3.) This is about as random as you can get. In addition to Yuval Fisher's "A Thousand Points of Sites," there are now a variety of "random generators" to throw you somewhere on the Web. See Yahoo's listing of these at http://www.yahoo.com/Reference/Indices_to_Web_Documents/Random_Links/.

Other (nearly) random ways to enter the Web:

- Comprehensive lists of Web servers, generated from spiders. Find these lists by doing a spider search on "web sites." (See the Web server lists, mentioned in Chapter 20, for the Web and other information spaces.)
- Try a Worm title search (so that the order of the words matters) on web sites in addition to doing a WebCrawler search.
- Use the Virtual Tourist or CERN's Web server list as starting points.

Another way to find (nearly) random sites to explore is to look for free-for-all pages. These pages developed out of early applications of the HTML Forms facility for allowing people to add links to a page. The resulting free-for-all pages grow very rapidly, as they are a shared, public space for announcing new resources. You'll find several free-for-all pages, and their contents will often be oriented to a particular outlook or area of interest. These lists serve as a kind of public wall on which hypergraffiti in the form of links are placed. Because these are often unmoderated (unlike many "What's New" postings), the tone of the entries is far from "official."

7. **Spider search:** Use your favorite spider (Chapter 19) to generate a list of resources that match your keyword search terms. Use this list as a "base" for delving into the Web and finding new resources in your area.

FIGURE 21.3.

*A Thousand Points of Sites.
Courtesy of Yuval Fisher.*

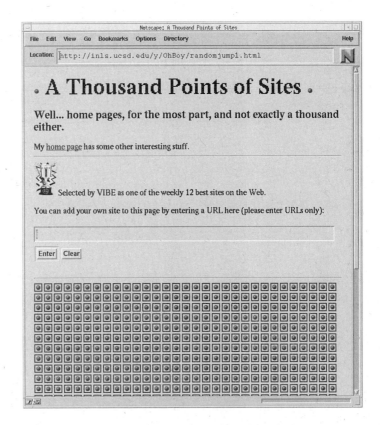

The preceding techniques are specific ways to generate starting points. Like other activities in surfing, there is no single technique that will always yield the results you want, nor is there a comprehensive list of logical procedures to find the best starting points. You'll surely develop your own techniques, but remember: Generating starting points for surfing is not the same as simply applying search strategies; rather, it involves integrating and extending your current awareness of what the Web does and could potentially offer.

Into the Web

Using one of the start-up techniques that were just described, and armed with the advice given earlier for coping with information overload, you're ready to start surfing. Because all sessions are different, I'll use an example to illustrate, and then I'll cover more general techniques and tips.

Here's the example: Let's say I'm interested in the subject of "cyberspace"—what people are doing, why they are doing it, and what artifacts, communication, and information exist there. This is a huge subject area, but it is an area of study in which I need to keep current, particularly with regard to new Web resources. I'll go through a step-by-step session in which I add to my current knowledge of what is out there.

- Starting point: I know that "What's New" pages contain a gold mine of new applications of cyberspace tools like the Web, and these are interesting in themselves as objects of study, but I'd like to scan the Web for new developments or thought in the study of cyberspace. There's no single institution that studies cyberspace in all its details; therefore, I won't select an institutional Web sever as a jumping-off point. Rather, I'll use the Harvest WWW Home Page Broker to generate a list of possible resources. Using the Broker, I search for documents containing the keyword "cyberspace." I also set the "verbose display" OFF and set the maximum number of matched lines to 100. This gives me a relatively compact base of results to explore.

  I use the word "cyberspace" as my keyword because I know it is a marker in the community of people who study online communication. In the Broker's query box, I enter

  ```
  keywords = cyberspace
  ```

  Figure 21.4 shows the top items from my search; Figure 21.5 shows the bottom items.

- I immediately look over the list that I've generated.
  1. I quickly judge the size of the search results by glancing at the scrollbar on the Web browser panel. I did get many results. A quick look at the bottom of the list (Figure 21.5) shows that I've reached the maximum number of hits at 100. This tells me that my search for the single keyword cyberspace might be too broad—there's probably many more hundreds of pages in Web space that feature the word "cyberspace." Therefore the size of my results doesn't feel "right"; I've probably found many pages that I don't need or that contain incidental uses of the word "cyberspace."

     Because the spider uses an indexing system to assign "scores" to retrieved resources, I know that the documents that are likely to be my best matches are at the top of the list.

  2. I look over the top titles in the list (Figure 21.4). The Description lines showing the titles of the document are helpful because they give me a clue about the use of the word "cyberspace." None of the top six results surprises me. (I'm already familiar with GNN's I-Media Center, which is shown). So I scan down the 100-item list for something to catch my eye.

FIGURE 21.4.

Harvest broker search results for "cyberspace."

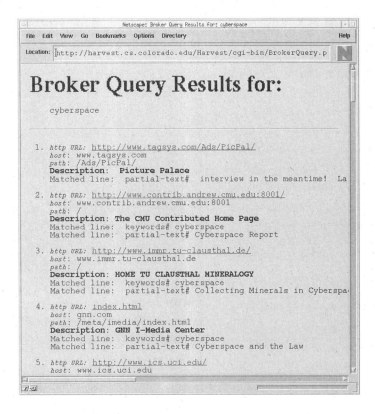

3. I see references to Internet and Web documentation. I'm not necessarily trying to build my awareness of that area of cyberspace now, so I mentally "shade out" those titles on the list.

4. I look for any odd items that are unusual in terms of what I've seen before or in the title displayed.

   The first resource that seems interesting is %BEGIN OUTPUT

   ```
   20. http URL: http://rt66.com/
       host: rt66.com
       path: /
       Description: Rt66 WEB Server
       Matched line:  keywords# cyberspace
   ```

   This piques my curiosity—mainly because of my interest in metaphors that people use for cyberspace. Route 66, a U.S. highway. is culturally significant in American history. I'm wondering what an online equivalent of it might be. So I choose the link and see the server in Figure 21.6.

FIGURE 21.5.

Harvest broker search results for "cyberspace."

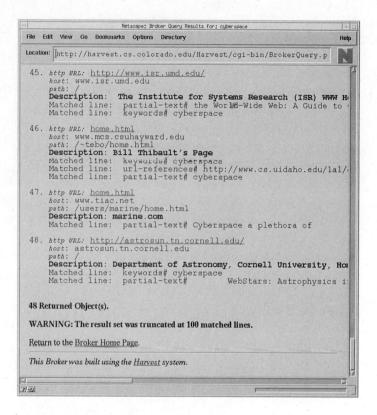

The Route 66 server is interesting in that it uses the highway metaphor for a public-access dial-up system in New Mexico. I know that the `Matched line: keywords# cyberspace` entry that got me to Route 66 was only an incidental use of the word "cyberspace." This could be interesting from a language point of view if I were interested in pursuing more metaphors for cyberspace.

5. I continue down the list. I see many entries such as

```
28. http URL: http://131.111.84.120/
              host: 131.111.84.120
              path: /
              Description:  Jamie Cope's WWW Home Page
              Matched line:  keywords# cyberspace
```

which I know are personal home pages (see the title). I continue down the list, looking instead for major collections or applications that might be using the term "cyberspace" in a non-incidental way.

FIGURE 21.6.

Route 66 WEB Server.

The next entry that catches my interest is

```
38. http URL: http://www.quiknet.com/
              host: www.quiknet.com
              path: /
              Description: This is QuikNet WWW's Homepage
              Matched line:  keywords# cyberspace
```

This seems like it might be another service like Route 66. In fact, the server name, `www.quiknet.com` clues me into this. I know I won't expect to see an academic discussion of cyberspace. In my mind, having seen Route 66, I wonder what QuikNet is all about. I click on the link and get Figure 21.7.

I can see that I'm in another kind of Web access service. The science-fiction rendering of QuikNet's World Wide Web Center gives me the idea that I could compare this vision of cyberspace with Route 66's. The contrast is very interesting. Route 66 uses an old cultural "highway" metaphor; QuikNet uses a "space/transit" metaphor. This is an example of the kinds of connections that can come about while surfing. In fact, this connection makes me want to collect more examples of cyberspace visions and to examine how people envision cyberspace and how access to it is sold. Naturally people don't label their pages "visions of cyberspace" or anything like that, so my search strategy of looking for the single word "cyberspace" is probably a good one for this purpose.

FIGURE 21.7.

QuikNet, Inc. Web server. Copyright © QuikNet, Inc. 1994. All rights reserved. Printed by permission.

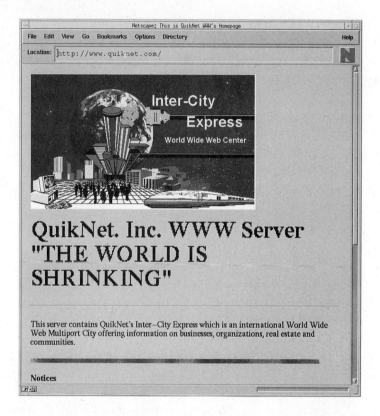

6. I check out QuickNet's page some more, placing it on my hotlist. I also back up and re-enter Route 66's page to place it on my hotlist. Now there is a quasi-purpose to my surfing session, arising out of what I've found. In fact, I find several more sites that fit this category, as follows:

```
39. http URL: http://www.eastgate.com/
    host: www.eastgate.com
    path: /
    Description: North Shore Access Home Page
    Matched line:  keywords# cyberspace
```

```
54. http URL: http://www.j51.com/
    host: www.j51.com
    path: /
    Description: TZ-Link - Public Access Internet in New York
    Matched line:  keywords# cyberspace


59. http URL: http://america.net/
    host: america.net
    path: /
    Description: Connect Atlanta!
    Matched line:  keywords# cyberspace


91. http URL: http://cyberspace.com/
    host: cyberspace.com
    path: /
    Description: CyberSpace: Home Page
    Matched line:  keywords# keywords{21}:      cyberspace
```

At this point, I know I'm not truly finding every Internet access provider, only those that have used the word "cyberspace" in a Web page and who were among the first 100 entries returned by the Harvest Broker that I used. I'm satisfied that I can proceed with my surfing session, taking the "curl" that I've discovered—the idea generated by the juxtaposition of the Route 66 imagery versus QuikNet's Web Port. Expanding on this theme, I quickly enter the entries 39, 54, and 59 and enter them in my hotlist. Later, I'll need to revisit each and perhaps formulate more strategies for analyzing this information.

The entry for cyberspace.com intrigues me—a domain devoted to the word "cyberspace." Clicking on the URL given in the list, though, I get the error:

```
ERROR
Requested document (URL http://cyberspace.com/) could not be accessed.
The information server either is not accessible or is refusing to serve
the document to you.
```

This seems a bit odd. I would doubt that a whole domain would go away. Opening a UNIX window, I use the whois command to do a quick check on the domain:

```
~ (34) whois cyberspace.com
[No name] (CYBERSPACE2-HST)      CYBERSPACE.COM       199.2.48.12
CyberLink Communications, Inc. (CYBERSPACE2-DOM)     CYBERSPACE.COM
The InterNIC Registration Services Host contains ONLY Internet Information
(Networks, ASN's, Domains, and POC's).
Please use the whois server at nic.ddn.mil for MILNET Information.
```

This is a registered domain. My hunch is that the URL given may have been from a spider crawling on some early references to the server, particularly since it is missing the www at the start of it (a common convention). I open the URL `http://www.cyberspace.com` and see Figure 21.8.

FIGURE 21.8.
CyberSpace home page.

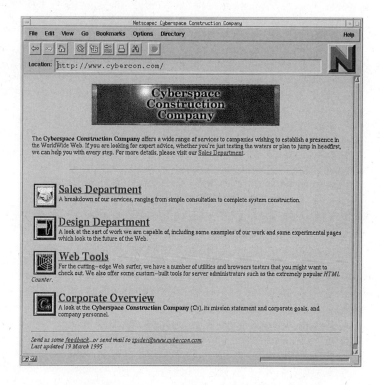

I have located another Internet provider service using "cyberspace" as its theme. I add it to my hotlist. Searching through the rest of the entries down to the 100th in the list (Figure 21.5), I'm satisfied that I've found some interesting examples of how cyberspace is portrayed and access to it is sold. At this point, if I'd like to search for how Internet access providers portray the spaces they sell access to, I should go to a tree and find listings of providers (this will help me get over the restriction of needing the word "cyberspace" on the home page of the service).

7. I decide to go to Yahoo (`http://www.yahoo.com/`) to continue surfing, following the theme of "cyberspace." I know I'll be able to follow branches of Yahoo down to lists of Internet Access/Presence providers, but before doing something logical like that ;-), I want to try out a hunch. I use Yahoo's search form to search for occurrences of the word "cyberspace" in its database. My gut feeling is that such a comparison would be interesting. Because Yahoo is a tree, it would tend to have

fewer entries matching "cyberspace" in it, but its entries should, in general, be more "finished" in the sense that they serve as an entry in a subject tree, making them more likely to be works intended for larger distribution and use (as opposed to many of the home page matches as found through the spider).

Yahoo's search results for "cyberspace" are in Figure 21.9. The list shows that I found 98 matches.

FIGURE 21.9.

Yahoo search results for "cyberspace."

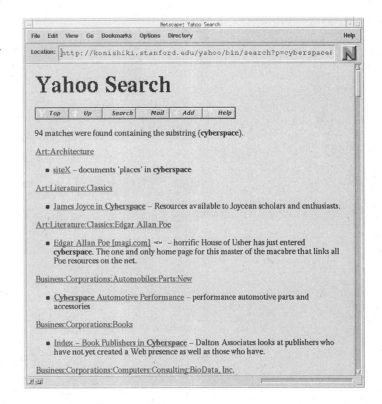

Scanning down this list, I see some entries that were in the spider results (`http://www.cyberspace.com`, for example). However, the list has entries that seem to include a conscious (or self-conscious) use of the word "cyberspace." For example, the entry

```
Entertainment:Television:Shows:Comedies:Brady Bunch
                    Nick at Nite's Buncha Brady - brings the classic TV
                family of the '70s into cyberspace.
```

at URL `http://nick-at-nite.viacom.com/` doesn't really relate to cyberspace but represents a "Brady presence" on the Web. I do find an entry that expands my idea of what I might find in Yahoo related to cyberspace:

```
Regional Information:States:Ohio:Cleveland:Internet Presence
Providers:Cyberspace Construction Company
        Cyberspace Construction Company
        Cyberspace Construction Company FTP Server
```

I click this entry and get Figure 21.10.

FIGURE 21.10.

Cyberspace Construction Company.

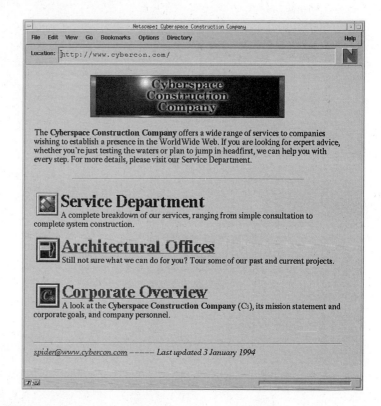

The Cyberspace Construction Company isn't in the same category as an Internet access provider, but it touches on the same issue, and even its home page implies a "material" metaphor for cyberspace.

8. I can quickly proceed to Yahoo's categories for Internet presence providers by clicking the subject heading above the entry for the following:

```
Business:Corporations:Internet Presence Providers:Cyberspace Development
        Cyberspace Development FTP Server
        Cyberspace Development Gopher
```

This takes me to a page for Cyberspace Development. Clicking the heading of that page brings me to Figure 21.11.

FIGURE 21.11.

Yahoo's list of Internet Presence providers.

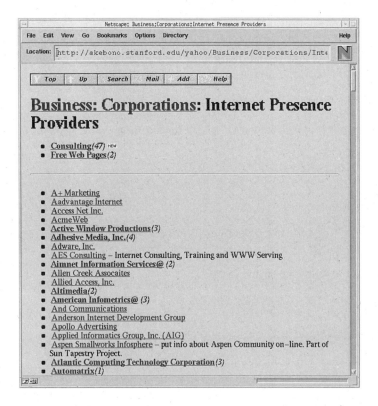

Using this list as a base, I can continue surfing, this time concentrating on gathering interesting representations of online cyberspace.

You can see from the preceding account that

- I move as efficiently as possible, making use of cues about space (what information space is it), texture (media form, structure, and organization), and others, such as navigational and information/cues.

- I employ a base—a single Web page, list, or spider search results to return to several times after delving down its branches. If I find another base while searching, I may abandon the original one (although I often end a surfing session by clicking the Back button many times), and re-encounter bases further up the windows history list.

- I use my hotlist to store promising entries, not passing final judgment as to the value of the resource, but gathering links that I will later go through as part of a regular hotlist and web-weaving maintenance session. In the hotlist maintenance session, the hotlist itself serves as a base.

■ I let my interests and intuition, not always logic, guide me in my search. Through experience, I know right away when I see a novel way of presenting information on the Web or a novel kind of information on the Web. This prompts me to look further. By making mistakes and also finding valuable things, I build my awareness.

■ I don't stick to one spider or one tree, and I may make the same search query in several different trees. If I would have continued the above example, I would have done a Lycos search on "cyberspace," as well as checked out the Galaxy tree and compared the results.

■ I let the purpose and goal of my surfing change as I find more information. When I started in the preceding sample session, I didn't have a purpose in mind, other than to find resources about cyberspace. Finding an interesting comparison (Route 66 versus QuikNet), I set out in a direction to find more pages to expand this theme. I might use a variety of basic searching methods (keyword, subject, space), but I always use my intuition and subjective interest of the moment to guide my search.

Tips

The previous section described a sample session of using a variety of methods to search for information. There's no typical surfing session—and the actual technique relies on previous awareness and accumulated understanding. Here are some specific tips that may help you build this awareness:

1. Have a set of regular pages that you check, possibly including the following:

   ■ "What's New" pages

   ■ Your favorite spider search

   ■ Your favorite subject tree links

   ■ Home pages of people who have similar interests

2. Collaborate with others on locating, identifying, and reviewing network resources. You may work out a shared resource database among a group of people with interests similar to yours. You can use this as a regular way to collaborate.

3. Surf regularly. Set aside a time period in which you regularly sweep through your starting points. Remember, allow for new and unique resources to come to your attention through "What's New" pages. Find out how often your favorite spider walks and recheck its database for matches against phrases you've used before.

4. Build your own mental model of the Web and its resources. You might try to sketch it graphically or create a verbal or hypertext map of resources important to you. Try not to duplicate existing collections of resources, but to point to them through your own links.

Advanced Surfing Techniques and Topics

Although the above general method of surfing should help you encounter new Web information of interest to you, there are other advanced methods for surfing that might also help you.

Surf Among Like Minds

In Chapter 18, we've already seen how well the Web binds information together. But the Web also binds like minds; the people who hold an interest in a particular subject can usually find their contributed information and ideas referenced on a single page, or as part of collections of information on a given topic. As a Web surfer, you can take advantage of this confluence of minds by seeking out the people behind the information and following connections these people make in their own personal information spaces—in their home pages or in the resource collections they create. You'll find that you can learn a great deal from people who are interested in the same topic you are, and your connections made this way can broaden your own knowledge. Ideally, through collaboration with others, you can increase the knowledge available on your topic of interest.

Here's some practical tips for the technique of "surfing like minds":

1. **Seek out subject-oriented collections of home pages.** We've seen in Chapter 20 how there are several home page collections that enable you to query by keyword. Use these search engines to create a home page list to use as "base" for surfing.

2. **Seek out meta centers.** An ideal meta center would be a web that is devoted to the study of a particular subject or topic, which integrates a range of activities for its participants—not only Web-based collections of resources, but "white page" collections of people and their interests as well as other activities like discussion lists or real-time chat areas. These meta centers can serve as gathering places for like minds and the basis for learning more and increasing your connections in a subject area.

3. **Check out the personal page of the information providers.** The information provider often (ideally, should be) very well-versed in the information presented on the Web pages. Connections on his or her personal page usually reveal still further information about the subject.

Free Associate: The Web as Metaphor Builder

Part of the core nature of the Web is the way people can use it to link related information. Hypermedia on the Web, however, can be much more than simply an switching mechanism meant to sift a reader through information. Instead, the Web, when used in its most expressive form, can be more like a poet fusing ideas and images using fresh metaphors. The juxtaposition of the "yellow wood" and the speaker's sense of choice in Robert Frost's poem "The Road Not Taken" is no accident—the poet Frost juxtaposes a vivid sensory image (the "yellow wood") with a complex human emotion (wondering what to do). The crisp leaves of the woods, the path that is untrodden, draw the reader down a clearer road giving a sense of "rightness" and closure, a sense of a choice in which the speaker finds comfort, as echoed in the speaker's closing line, "and that has made all the difference."

So, too, does the Web offer the surfer choices in a tangle of links that no human being could ever exhaust in a lifetime. The diversity of Web design, depth and richness of information, uniqueness of links, and subjective and aesthetic value of the information on the Web make it impossible to create an algorithm to find the truly meaningful. Instead, one way to surf is to free associate, to use the Web as an analogical thinking tool. The goal is to find meaning in associations and to create new meaning by new associations. Hypermedia is a wonderful medium to express these associations.

Analogies and metaphor depend on a delicate balance between the representation of the objects compared and the "stuff" that emerges from their comparison. For example, if A ("yellow wood") and B ("I have to figure out where I'm going") rub together in a poem to create C ("I'll take that untrodden path there"), the reader has to somehow grasp all of A, B, and C in his or her mind at once. In hypermedia terms, the substance of objects A and B must be salient enough in the user's mind so that an associated C can emerge from them with some force of meaning. In more concrete terms, a Web page with some content evoking ideas A and B might have a link to C within these explanations. A user surfing this Web page might, after perceiving the gist of A and B, choose the link to C and gain the power of C's association with A and B. The representation A and B range from "black" (content in the form text and images explaining A and B in detail) to "blue" (composed largely of hyperlinks to other information sources). The trick for the web creator is to balance the black and the blue of A and B with the black/blue balance of C to create meaning through association. For Web surfers, the analogical aspects of hypermedia can be a boon: By following the next link that "comes to mind" when encountering information on a Web page, surfers can form new ideas and information can come into focus with a new significance.

Here's some practical advice on analogical Web surfing:

1. Start with a page that is neither all "black" (composed of text without any hyperlinks) nor "blue" (composed entirely of links such as a resource list or a spider search result).

2. From this "black-and-blue" page, gain an awareness of all the ideas represented. Read background information, delve into the links, but keep returning to the page until you understand its main points.

3. Look at the blue parts of the page and consider how they relate to what is in the "black." Follow the first hyperlink that seems to pop into your mind after knowing the page pretty well. Ideally, the black-to-blue transition will bring a new idea or thought into focus for you.

Read Dead Trees/See It on TV!

The Web's popularity has rocketed knowledge of the Internet's Web as a communications medium into popular culture and mainstream media coverage. Now, it is not unusual for general paper-based publications like *Newsweek* or *The Wall Street Journal* to include URLs in their articles (and for advertisers to include a Web address in ad copy). So it may be that you find a new Web resource URL encoded in paper media at your newsstand or library even before you find it on the Web. Paper publications that regularly mention URLs include *Newsweek's* Cyberscope column, and (of course) the raft of Internet and computer-related magazines at newsstands. Because you'll want to discover new URLs related to your area of interest, you might watch for similar "Web surfing" columns appearing in your favorite print magazine or newspaper geared to what you want to discover. If you copy a URL by hand from paper, remember to copy it exactly and carefully.

ANNOUNCING URLS IN OTHER MEDIA

If you supply a URL that will be printed in a paper publication, be sure to double-check it in a browser (and also ask to proofread the copy before printing). Ideally, whenever you supply URLs to readers on paper, supply the shortest possible URL you can give them to reach the information. This decreases the chance of errors and cuts down somewhat on the likelihood of the URL of the resource changing. In most cases, if you have your own Web server, you can give your server name, `http://www.company.com`, and tell the user in general where to look on the server for the specialized information (for example, "See the New Music page on our Web server for direct links to the latest CD releases" rather than saying: "Open the URL `http://www.company.com/new-releases/CD/hot/announce.html`").

If you mention a URL on television, it would probably be a good idea to back up the vocalization with a graphic showing the URL exactly. In vocalizing the URL, one approach is to shorten the reference to the server name, rather than trying to stumble over pronouncing `http://`. For example, if you are announcing the Web server at `http://www.company.com`, you could say, "[Company Name] announces its new Web server at `www.company.com`." Web surfers will realize that the complete URL includes the `http://` at the start of it (because you said "Web server"), so there is no need to vocalize `http://`. However, in the graphic, show the complete URL: `http://www.company.com`, so that the dozing viewer suddenly recognizes a Web reference being displayed. Showing the `http://` is particularly important if the company uses a server name without the `www` starting convention; just showing `company.com` onscreen will confuse the reader—not knowing if it is a Gopher, e-mail, or FTP address.

As a consumer of non-Web media that may refer to URLs, you might find out if your favorite non-Web information source provides a Web support site. This may be most likely of computer magazines and major media outlets (`http://www.cbs.com`) or paper books such as this one (`http://www.rpi.edu/~decemj/works/wwwu.html`). A support web may contain the URLs mentioned in the paper or other media listed in a Web page, so that you don't have to copy or remember the URLs. A Web support site can also immediately convey the latest on updates or changes to the resources mentioned.

Find Your Electronic Tribe

We've already seen the power of discovering the home pages of people who are interested in a particular area during our subject, keyword, and space-oriented searching forays into the Web. The one Web tradition that weaves people powerfully to the information they create is the personal home page. By surfing for these home pages, you'll find that they are often one of the richest sources of new, creative, and expressive information on the Web. Finding all the people who are in your Web "tribe," those who share your same interests or pursuits, can be difficult. You can use the methods from the previous chapter to find directories of people to search for interests. You could also use keyword and subject-oriented searching methods to locate pools of information related to your area of interest on the Web. However, through these methods, you might only find the information providers—the people who set up the big collections that get listed in trees. Where's the rest of your tribe?

The solution to finding people who are interested in your pursuits lies in following the associative links from home pages on the Web. You can do this by taking advantage of a not uncommon practice among web weavers—to list, within their personal information spaces in their home page or personal web, links to others as well as to pools of information. The practice of listing other people on one's home page creates "web cliques"—threads in the Web that lead from one person to another, evoking their relationships in circuits and branches of links. By listing the people who also share your interests on your own home page, you can continue the weaving of tribes.

To locate electronic tribes, seek out major home page collections and then use any keyword-searching mechanism provided by that collection to find people who share your interest. If a specialized directory of people interested in your area exists, you've hit a gold mine. If not, you might consider starting your own listing of people in your tribe. Eventually, by listing yourself within home page directories, you'll also connect with other people on the Web, and get connected into multiple and overlapping associations among people.

Navigator's Check

We've seen how surfing integrates our other searching methods—trees, spiders, and spaces—into a process of seeking and trying out links. Surfing relies heavily on your awareness of the structure of the Web, finely tuned navigation skills for using your browser, the use of particular searching techniques, and your personal tastes, interests, and associations. Surfing might be the least likely form of activity to yield useful results; but, without surfing as a technique within your repertoire, you won't be able to find new resources easily, make new connections, or see what can be possible.

As a general guide to surfing, remember the following:

- Have a set of starting points that you regularly check, including "What's New" pages, as well as subject trees in your area and the home pages of institutions and individuals.

■ Based on your starting points, arrive at (possibly through a spider search) a page with the "right" number of links on it. Use this page as a base for exploring the links leading off it.

■ Abandon the base page for a new base as soon as you find a page that exceeds the value of the first base.

■ Work this pattern recursively; save all promising links in your hotlist.

■ At a later time, go through your hotlist and examine the links more carefully for relevance and value; share the valuable links with people who have interests similar to yours.

■ Consider using advanced searching techniques to find new associations in the analogic nature of the Web and discover new resources in the home pages of members of electronic tribes.

Elephants: Putting It All Together and More

22

by
John December

No, *elephants* are not another kind of creature that roams the Web. In this chapter I use elephants (the real kind) as the topic for an information search of the Web and Net. Our search will employ the navigation techniques and critical skills we've covered so far and will demonstrate their flexibility in real-world applications.

Searching for Elephants

We've already talked about how the Web and the Net are not necessarily a good source for peer-reviewed academic, research, or other kinds of official information. Such rigorously reviewed information can best be found in a (paper-based) library (although, gradually, more of this kind of material is making its way to the Web). What the Net *can* do is to help you gain awareness of collections, people, and institutions that may point you to other useful resources (on the Net or off it). Indeed, the associative, context-generating nature of Net information, particularly typical of the Web, may be the ultimate power of the Net—its capability of bringing you into contact with the people and resources directly involved in the detailed study of a subject.

All the search strategies we've talked about in this part of the book won't help you discover everything there is to know about elephants. Only a small fraction of the available information and resources about elephants is on the Net. Further, we've already seen how the Net tools for even finding what's on the Net are imperfect. Moreover, the Net itself isn't a "black box" where questions go in and answers come out, but rather a collection of resources behind which are people—imperfect or passionate, knowledgeable or naive, helpful or cynical. Therefore, don't look on our search through the Net as simply a process of encountering data; people constructed the Web, and the human aspect of the resource pool may represent the most valuable connection you make.

Having said this, let's use our elephants example to illustrate both the value and the pitfalls of finding Net information about a topic. Let's say your situation is as follows: You are gathering information about elephants for an audience of high-school sophomores. You're not exactly sure what kind of resources you want—there are no set information requirements you must fill—but you know you generally want to find the following:

■ **Context information:** Everything from geographic and climate data about the places where elephants live to political and social issues related to elephants' interaction with people.

■ **Specific information:** Material about elephants themselves—what they eat, their life cycles, status of species endangerment, social groups, etc.

■ **The role of elephants in human activities:** For example, information about circus elephants and elephants as workers.

■ **Artistic or literary works that involve elephants.**

You know you want more information than just this, but you're not sure what that might be (although you'll know it when you see it). Let's assume also that you have good library skills, you're on good terms with your reference librarian, and that you'll be able to locate authoritative sources of information to verify Net resources whenever the nature of the information requires a close check for accuracy. Situations that require close checks could include the following: when the Net information you find will be used in research, in formal academic contexts, or any other situation where the accuracy of the information is paramount or when you have a "gut feeling" that such a check is necessary. You'll find that some kinds of information don't need such a thorough check. For example, if you find a photograph that purports to be of an elephant, you can judge for yourself whether it really is an elephant. (You can also verify the kind of elephant that is represented in the image, if that is important.)

Starting Points

I've mentioned how the Net is a powerful way for you to make connections with people of specific interests and expertise. Don't take this close connection to experts as an excuse not to do the Web-work of finding out information on your own, particularly the basic facts about your subject. You might "listen in" on an electronic-mail discussion group devoted to a particular specialty, but the nature of e-mail is such that the participants are not usually discussing basic, core information about their specialty.

STARTING AT THE WRONG PLACE

It is worth repeating: Before you consult the experts, do your homework. The following electronic-mail message originally appeared in a discussion group called comp.risks, which is devoted to discussing risks to the public welfare from computers and the users of them. The discussion group that is mentioned in this post, BIOSPH-L@UBVM.BITNET, is a discussion list, distributed through electronic mail, that is devoted to issues related to the biosphere.

Getting information from discussion groups

by

Dan Yurman (dyurman@igc.apc.org)

Perhaps one disturbing trend as more people use Internet is the practice by college students of using subject matter listservs as sources of first resort for information they should be looking up in their university library.

Every year BIOSPH-L@UBVM.BITNET, a list dealing with environmental issues, is flooded with ill- expressed questions that should not be addressed to the list. These include questions such as "what is hazardous waste," etc. Another which came up today was a question which could be answered by using the Statistical Abstract of the US or any World Almanac, etc. Last year a hot debate erupted when a graduate teaching assistant at a major, dare I say, top 10, Eastern

university, assigned a class of undergraduates to use Internet to seek information on research paper topics. The TA did not instruct the students to use the
library first and then pose well formulated questions to the net. BIOSPH-L was
flooded with questions on basic environmental science.

Both the TA and the students were outraged by the complaints they received from
list readers who objected to being asked fundamental questions that ought to be
dealt with by the students themselves. The root cause appears to be neither the
TA nor the students had any idea who was at the other end of the line. All they
saw was a computer that should be giving them answers. What was said to them
repeatedly is this. The courtesy issue is that traffic on BIOSPH-L is voluntary.
If you want people to take the time to answer your questions, indicate you have
done some legwork on your own and have a genuine problem looking for additional
information. Otherwise, you are soaking up volunteer resources which could be
better used to meet needs not answered elsewhere. Also, neither the students nor
the TA took kindly to suggestions that if they absolutely insisted on using
computer terminals instead of (gasp) books, that there are online services which
for a fee will gladly give them the information they want.

If going directly to experts is not the best place to start, what is? I suppose our ideal find would be
an "Elephant Home Page" or the "Elephant Meta Center" on the Web—an integrated presentation of resources and discussion on the many aspects of elephants, put together and maintained
collaboratively by experts in the field. How might we find such a thing?

- A subject search might not be the quickest way. Elephants are often treated as a subtopic within larger areas of knowledge, such as the environment or biology. Because we
  want to find out more about elephants than just their biology and environment, a
  subject-based approach may throw us into too many different subject trees, which would
  be laborious to search exhaustively.

- A keyword-oriented search seems like a good start. The word "elephant" probably
  wouldn't be used in too many other contexts, so the number of false hits we could get
  might be low.

- A space-oriented search might not be a bad idea, either. Where do elephants live? Are
  there institutions in that geographic area with collections of information about elephants? (One thing to keep in mind here is that the knowledge center for elephants
  might not be based in the same geographic region where elephants live.)

- Surfing probably isn't the way to start. We are trying to improve our awareness of Net resources about elephants, but we've no base to start from. We don't yet know of any starting points for surfing (What's New pages, free-for-all pages) that are specialized enough to yield good results. Surfing from these specialized pages for elephants is out for now.

Based on our options, it looks like a keyword search would be a good start. For this kind of search, we can choose from a selection of spiders. (See Chapter 19, "Spiders and Indexes: Keyword-Oriented Searching.") Do we know of a specialized spider, perhaps an environmental or biological one? Our ideal would be an elephant spider, a spider that crawls on webs where elephant-related information is usually found. As of now, we really don't know of one. The spiders we do have and their pros and cons are as follows:

- Spiders that collect information from titles in HTML documents. Pro: This spider travels lighter, perhaps covers more ground. Con: The term "elephant" has to be somewhere in the title of the document.

- Spiders that contain full-text indexes of Web pages. Pro: Any occurrence of the word "elephant" in the document will be a hit. Con: Any occurrence of the word "elephant" in the document will be a hit. Spiders that do this kind of searching can't travel as far.

Although a full-text spider search may represent a smaller part of the Web, it seems more likely to lead us to relevant resources. A title search might yield something only if the word "elephant" is in the title field of the HTML document. (A great page to find might have a title such as "All About Elephant Resources on the Web.")

Spider Searches for Elephants

Let's start with a Harvest WWW Home Page Broker search for elephants. Using the search command, with verbose OFF and the number of returned objects set to 100, we use the following search string:

```
keywords = elephant
```

We get the results shown in Figure 22.1.

Our results didn't produce a great deal of hits (only four). None of them, based on the descriptions on the page, seem to be promising.

FIGURE 22.1.

*Harvest WWW Broker
search results for elephant.*

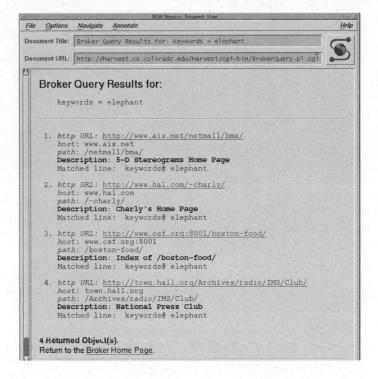

Let's use the WebCrawler to do a full-text search of Web documents in its database. After entering the keyword **elephant** in the input box of the WebCrawler, we get the results shown in Figure 22.2.

Some entries in the list look more promising than others. Remember, the word "elephant" appears in these resources, and the ones at the top have a higher score, so these are judged (by the indexing system the WebCrawler uses) to be more relevant. This list is essentially a base from which we can use surfing techniques to examine other areas that seem interesting or relevant.

A quick scan of the list shows the following entries:

■ "Protection Summaries." This seems promising. Placing my cursor over the hotspot, I see that the URL is http://ash.lab.r1.fws.gov/cargo/protect.html. The gov in the host name indicates it is probably a U.S. government source. I'm not sure to what domain fws.gov refers. My guess is "Fish and Wildlife Service." If so, this could be a very authoritative source. I click its hotspot and get the page in Figure 22.3.

This looks like a good information source. I place a reference to this on my hotlist. The page refers to the "Cargo of Conservation booklet," which might be a lead on a government document to find.

FIGURE 22.2.

WebCrawler search results for the keyword elephant.

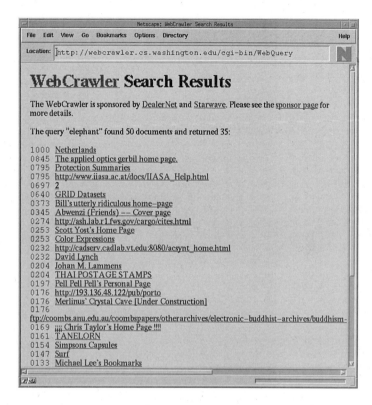

FIGURE 22.3.

Protection Law Summaries.

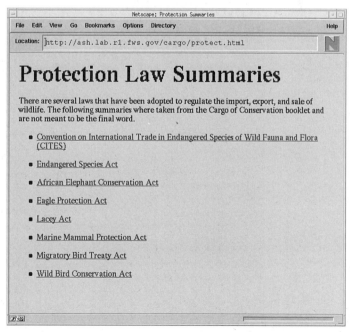

Moreover, the "African Elephant Conservation Act" looks like a great specific source. I click this link to find a narrative describing the act itself (a summary, not the actual legislation). This summary is written for the level of my audience. I save the reference to it on my hotlist and quickly scan the document for any other links. There are none. I click the Back button. On the "Protection Law Summaries" page, the "Convention on International Trade in Endangered Species of Wild Fauna and Flora (CITES)" looks like good information, but I don't want to stray too far from information specifically about elephants. I've saved a link to this "Protection Law Summaries" page in my hotlist for detailed examination later.

On the "Protection Law Summaries" page, I begin to wonder if there are higher-level pages on the same Web server. There are no navigation links to them, but I see from the URL that I'm in a subdirectory called `cargo`. I wonder what is at the top level for this host. I open the URL `http://ash.lab.r1.fws.gov/` and find I'm at Figure 22.4.

FIGURE 22.4.

Forensic Science Web Server.

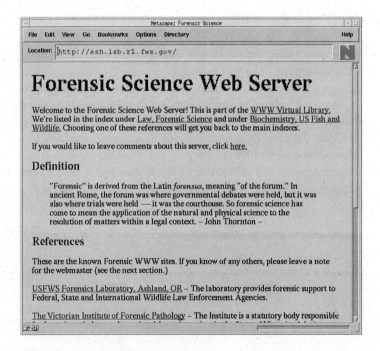

The title throws me off a bit. Forensic science? But the narrative at the top of the page helps me realize that I'm now in CERN's Virtual Library subject tree. This particular page, as the narrative states, is part of "Law, Forensic Science" and "Biochemistry, US Fish and Wildlife." I don't understand the connection, although I suppose biochemistry has a great deal to do with forensic science. The link to "Biochemistry, US Fish and Wildlife" is promising as more background information. I click it and see that I'm in the "Biosciences" page for CERN's Virtual Library subject tree, as shown in Figure 22.5.

FIGURE 22.5.

The World Wide Web Virtual Library: Biosciences.

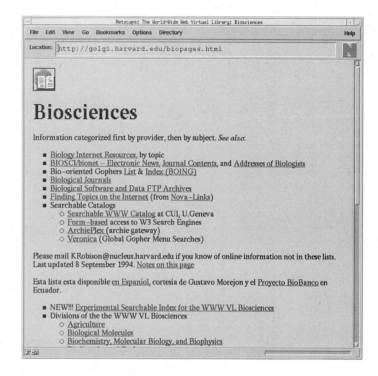

I feel I'm straying from my specific interest in elephants, although I'm finding good background information. In fact, this Biosciences page looks as if it could be a good source to retain for surfing after I exhaust some other possibilities back on the WebCrawler results page. After scanning down the Biosciences list quickly to see if anything such as "All about elephants" jumps out at me, I save a reference to the page on my hotlist and hit the Back button until I'm back at the WebCrawler search-results page (Figure 22.2).

At this point, I feel that I've obtained some good links to general biological information that I can search through later to find references to elephants. But I really want to get more specific. I look at the WebCrawler search results with the idea of finding something very particular to elephants. I try the following:

■ "Netherlands." This is the very first entry in the WebCrawler results, the most likely (according to the WebCrawler's algorithm) to lead to my best match. Clicking the title, I get Figure 22.6.

At first, I don't know what the purpose of this page is, nor where the word "elephant" could occur in it. Using the Find function in the Web browser, I discover the following entries:

```
Pink Elephant DCMS Ltd (Organization)
    Pink Elephant Education & Development bv (Organization)
    Pink Elephant Finance bv (Organization)
```

```
Pink Elephant Industry bv (Organization)
Pink Elephant Nederland BV (Organization)
Pink Elephant Public Sector bv (Organization)
```

FIGURE 22.6.

Netherlands.

Clicking the links leading from these entries, I find entries that show names and addresses. I decide I need more context to figure out what this directory is. Back at the first page (Figure 22.6), I click the link at the top, "The World," and see that I'm in an X.500 directory service, a type of "white pages." (See Figure 22.7.)

Obviously the "Pink Elephant" organizations must be related to some agency or business. From links within the service, though, I can tell nothing about the function of these organizations. I click the Back button enough times to return to the WebCrawler results in Figure 22.2.

■ Scanning down the WebCrawler search results, I find similar incidental or nonsignificant uses of the word "elephant" in several other links. However, I do find something serendipitous at the entry "2" shown in Figure 22.2. I'm curious why a page would have a title of "2," so I click it. (Logic would say that I should exhaust all identifiable entries first.) I find I'm in the home page for Chaffee Zoological Gardens in Fresno, California (See Figure 22.8.)

FIGURE 22.7.

X.500 white-pages directory service.

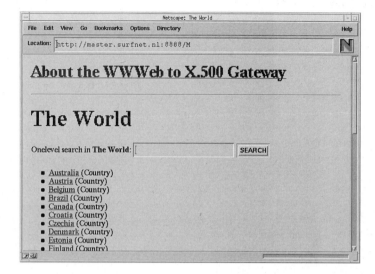

FIGURE 22.8.

Chaffee Zoological Gardens Web page.

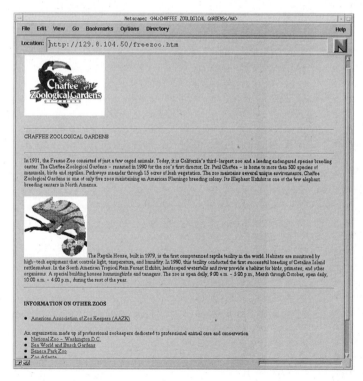

Scanning this page, I find no specific information about elephants (other than their incidental mention in the text). However, at the bottom of the Chaffee page, I find links to other zoos and the American Association of Zoo Keepers (AAZK) and links to zoos: the National Zoo in Washington, D.C., Sea World and Busch Gardens, Seneca Park (New York) Zoo, and Zoo Atlanta. What better place to find elephants than at a zoo?

■ Using the Chaffee list of zoos as a base, I follow links to each zoo page in search of something specific about elephants.

The American Association of Zoo Keepers (AAZK) (Figure 22.9) has some great information on animals. I save a link to the page in my hotlist.

FIGURE 22.9.

American Association of Zoo Keepers page. Courtesy of Herbie Pearthree.

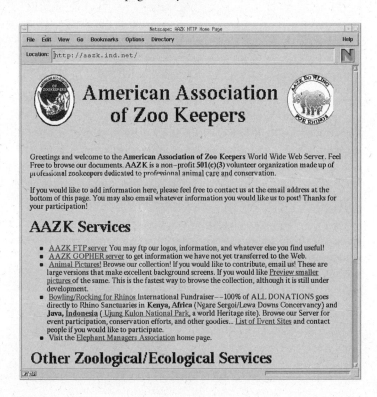

Before leaving the AAZK site, I look into their archive of animal pictures. It's a goldmine of animals! In the Safari folder, I find two pictures of elephants: elephant.african.calf (55KB) and elephant.african.jpg (85KB). I save the URL of the picture archive on my hotlist. Just before I leave the AAZK, I scan down the links and find perhaps what I was looking for: The Elephant Managers Association (EMA) (Figure 22.9) at http://aazk.ind.net/ema/emahome.html.

FIGURE 22.10.

Elephant Managers Association page. Courtesy of Terry Polk. EMA site is made possible by Herbie Pearthree and the American Association of Zoo Keepers WWW server.

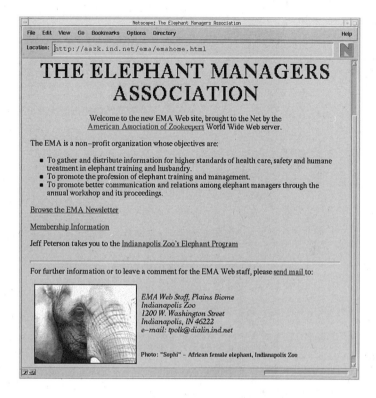

The EMA page looks like the closest thing to an "Elephant Meta Center." One link on its page is to The Elephant Managers Association Newsletter, which includes past issues. Articles in the newsletter include field reports, interviews, and regional reports that are detailed and written by experts. I save a link to this source in my hotlist, because it should form the basis for some detailed readings about elephants for my audience.

Another link from the EMA page includes one to the Indianapolis Zoo's elephant program, which looks like another great lead. I place the EMA page on my hotlist. I quickly check out the Indianapolis Zoo material, eventually finding "A Day with the Elephants" (Figure 22.11).

I'm ecstatic that I've found such a great source. "A Day with the Elephants" includes separate pages with pictures that show the entire day in the life of an elephant in Indianapolis. Perhaps this is a bit "young" for my audience, but I save this material on my hotlist.

FIGURE 22.11.

A Day with the Elephants.
Courtesy of Terry Polk.

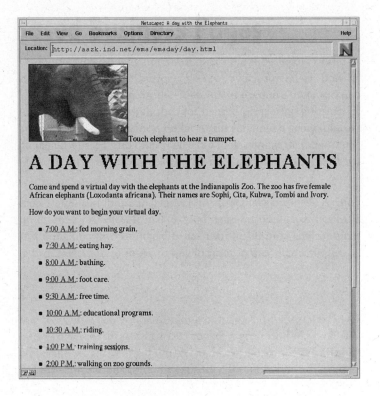

■ Enthused by my finds, I decide to look for more zoos. Clicking the Back button, I get back to the Chaffee list of zoos (Figure 22.8). I try the link to the National Zoo (a gopher, but the link doesn't work). At the Sea World/Busch Gardens web (`http://www.bev.net/education/SeaWorld/homepage.html`), I find teacher's guides and an animal-information database. I check through these, but don't find any specific elephant information. (Of course, Sea World probably is not the best place to look for elephants.)

I try the link to the Seneca Park Zoo Web. Its home page (`http://www.memo.com/rochester/todo/sights/zoo/zoo.html`) is shown in Figure 22.12.

There is a picture of an elephant on the Seneca Park Zoo page, so I click it, and I get a larger version of the same picture. I save this page on my hotlist.

At Zoo Atlanta (`http://www.gatech.edu/3020/zoo/home-page.html`) (Figure 22.13) I find another goldmine of information about elephants, including a 2.6-minute movie about elephants and an 8KB sound file of elephants.

FIGURE 22.12.

Seneca Park (New York) Zoo. Courtesy of Edward Avila.

FIGURE 22.13.

Zoo Atlanta.

The Zoo Atlanta web also includes links to other leads: a Smithsonian exhibit and links to the following:

- The Electronic Zoo, a collection of animal-related computer resources (`http://netvet.wustl.edu/0n:\e-zoo.htm¦/`). This is a large collection that includes subject-oriented Internet resources, Telnet sites, FTP archives, electronic publications, Usenet newsgroups, gophers, and Web sites about animals. I save this on my hotlist, as it could be the best source for background information.

- LaTrove University School of Zoology, (`http://www.zoo.latrobe.edu.au/`), which includes links to animal/nature GIF files, biology servers, and the Tasmania Parks and Wildlife Service.

At this point, I'm pretty happy with what I've found. Later, I'll go over the entries on the hotlist. In particular, the Elephant Managers Association could be a good source for e-mail addresses of experts in elephants. To supplement my searching, any good library would have an encyclopedia entry for elephants that would give me more basic facts and keywords to use in spider searches. The realization that zoos are a great place to find elephant information piques my interest to find more zoos. I use Yahoo to search for `elephant` and then `zoo` in its database. The search for `elephant` turns up nothing, but I find many unrelated links from the `zoo` search in Yahoo: Kalamazoo College, Zootopia (Yale Undergraduate Computing Facility—Zoo), plus the zoo pages I've already visited previously. I also find Yahoo's entry for Science: Museums and Exhibits: Zoos (`http://www.yahoo.com/Science/Museums_and_Exhibits/Zoos/`), which contains the zoos I've visited, so I'm satisfied I've visited the major online zoos.

I could continue to collect related information by surfing more spider-results pages and the links from them. However, I'll take another approach and try to go where the elephants live (not counting Indianapolis).

A Space-Oriented Search for Elephants

After searching through the Web's links for subject and keyword information, I've decided to try to find elephants using the Virtual Tourist II maps of geographically organized regional information resources. I open the URL for the Virtual Tourist (shown in Figure 20.11 in Chapter 20). Now my problem is to determine where elephants live in the world. At this point, it might be helpful to consult a basic encyclopedia article to identify geographic regions where elephants live. Working from the Virtual Tourist II, I try the sector of the map including India. I click the world map until I obtain Figure 22.14.

This looks like a good set of information. By focusing on one country where elephants live, I may get an idea of their interaction with people. I save the link to this page on my hotlist. I take a look at the India information page (Figure 22.15).

FIGURE 22.14.

Information about India from City.Net. Copyright 1994–1995, City Net Express. All rights reserved. Printed by permission.

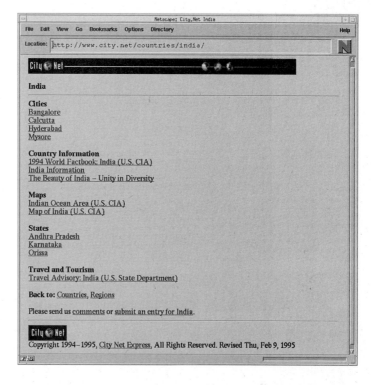

FIGURE 22.15.

Information about India. Courtesy Dinesh Venkatesh. Initial concept and creation by Sridhar Venkataraman.

The India information page contains a good selection of links. In the Tourism link, I find many links, including the "Rec.travel Guide to India (1993 June, version 1.0)," part of the Usenet newsgroup hierarchy, rec.travel, FAQ archive. Kaye Stott is the editor of this document at URL ftp://ftp.cc.umanitoba.ca/rec-travel/asia/india/india-guide, and I use the File | Find In Current operation to locate a reference to elephants, as follows:

```
Urban traffic in India is a miasma of vehicular and non-vehicular traffic, including
such diverse things as cars, semis, motor-rickshaws (three-wheeled taxis), bicycle-
rickshaws, motor scooters, elephants, goats, dogs, children, chickens, bearers, push-
carts, camels, buses, etc.
```

This is a vivid description of how elephants interact with people in India, another lead. I save the URL in my hotlist. I can continue to use the methods shown above to find information about elephants. Although I've not found the "Elephant Home Page," I have found some links that perhaps I could use to start putting one together.

Other Searches: Background and Experts on Elephants

The other side of a subject search involves getting background material for any particular topic. Determining what background material is available for a topic is a skill that you can develop by using the techniques described here to locate specific subject-oriented collections. Your body of knowledge about what kind of reference and background material is available will grow as you learn more about the Net. I know that I could get weather and climate information, political information, and perhaps some more specific statistics about elephants. I could locate even more picture archives containing images of elephants. I could also locate discussion lists that may cover some of the detailed environmental issues related to elephants. So far, in the small search segment I've completed, I've found the following:

- A description of specific legislation related to elephant protection.
- A link to the Elephant Managers Association, perhaps the closest thing to an "Elephant Meta Center," which includes the current and past issues of its newsletter, offering detailed accounts of field and regional reports on elephants.
- A link to a day in the life of an elephant at the Indianapolis Zoo.
- Links to elephant pictures, movies, and sounds.
- A rich source of information about India, a country where elephants are found.

Navigator's Check

You can see from this example that searching the Net is not a substitute for a library or the skills of a good reference librarian. On the Net, certain topics that may seem at first glance to be fairly basic lead one on a chase throughout network links to try to locate information that might easily be found in a general reference work. The preceding example, however, did show us that we can locate some specific (and very useful) background information. Applying more of the techniques we've covered in this part, you would be able to put together even more links. In this process of discovery, keep the following techniques and tips in mind:

1. Use background information that you can obtain from "traditional" general sources, such as encyclopedia articles and books, to guide you to a list of keywords, subjects, and world locations to search for information.

2. Use this background information to generate a series of keyword, subject-oriented, and space-oriented searches on the Web. Use techniques of surfing to go quickly through large amounts of information to find the nuggets you want.

3. Keep track of these nuggets of valuable URLs on your hotlist. During the course of your search, you may run across people who are interested in the same topic; contact them and collaborate on building a web page or a meta center around your topic. For more detailed information about creating HTML documents and webs, see Part V, "Weaving a Web."

PART

IV

Exploring the Web

Business and Commerce

by
Neil Randall

23

When you look at the World Wide Web today, it's hard to believe that, not very long ago, business activity on the Internet was strictly forbidden. When the first edition of this book went to press, the Web was still dominated by academic and research entities, but business and commercial sites have grown at such a rapid pace over the intervening year or so that it's doubtful this is still the case. Or, if it is, it has become increasingly clear that the business interests will soon take center stage, eclipsing just about everything else in their efforts to use the Web as a promotion or sales tool. Not everyone would suggest that this is a good thing; but whether we like it or not, the Web, like the Internet itself, is very quickly becoming a commercial medium.

A commercial presence is one thing, but whether the Web ever becomes a commercially *driven* entity is the question foremost in many Net-watchers' minds. So far, it hasn't, at least not to the degree that alarm bells ring in the minds of those who fervently hope that it won't. The Web was initiated as a communications medium for the exchange of scientific research, and it remains a vital community, nurturing a range of scholarly endeavors. Its development has been driven by the needs of the academic community, in both its traditional and experimental facets. In meeting these needs, the Web has emerged as both a database service and a multimedia communications tool, because these are the two foremost requirements for scientific and research organizations.

But the needs of business are different from those of the scientific and academic communities, and it's important to understand a bit about why the Web is becoming such an appealing commercial domain. Because they were already on the Internet for a variety of reasons, including research and development, business became interested in the Web almost as soon as it appeared. A hypermedia environment available to the entire world offered all sorts of commercial potential because it enabled appealing, interactive access. Given that the much-touted, much-maligned, much-misunderstood information superhighway sought to provide precisely this kind of access, as the Web's capabilities became manifest the interests of business grew accordingly.

The race to cash in on the Web began in earnest when Mosaic for X appeared and turned some of the promises of the Web into reality. Businesses started utilizing the Web for purposes such as marketing, customer service, product information, and ordering. Today, commercial activity on the Web has increased to the point where new companies are adding Web pages daily, and a What's New page for commercial sites (`http://www.directory.net/dir/whats-new.html`) is being updated almost as often as NCSA's famous What's New page for the entire Web. Put simply, business activity on the Web is exploding.

Given the current efforts and successes at making the Web fully secure for the transmission of such things as classified data or credit-card information, it is inevitable that the Web will evolve into a commercially driven medium. Nobody knows exactly what this will mean for the structure of the information environment; but keep in mind that in the world of business and commerce, shared research and development is rarely allowed, let alone encouraged. This is not to label business as the enemy of Web development; it's simply to recognize that the priorities of business and academia are essentially different from one another.

Obviously, we'll just have to wait and see. Just as obviously, you'll discover as you navigate the growing number of commercial sites that we won't have to wait very long. My own view of these developments is an optimistic one, a feeling I share with several long-time Internetters with whom I've talked. The scenario goes like this: Commercial activity will go a long way towards paying for the Internet, making it less costly for the rest of us, and the explosion of interest this activity causes will assist rather than hinder the growth of the Net as a viable global-communications tool. But then again, I generally believe in a *Star Trek* future rather than a *Neuromancer* one, so you can judge this prognostication however you see fit.

> **NOTE**
>
> This chapter introduces you to the variety of business and commercial sites on the Web. No attempt has been made at comprehensiveness. Instead, I have focused on a representative sampling of these sites, trying to point out the ones that are the most typical, the most detailed, and the most creative. From this sampling, you'll get a good indication of the range of activity in this area.

Finding Business and Commercial Sites on the Web

With all the commercial activity on the Web, what's needed is a Web page that provides the links necessary to access the main players. There are other ways of finding Web information than by accessing a central directory page (see Part III, "Web Navigation Tools and Techniques"), but using the Web's search tools shouldn't be necessary for something this obvious. And besides, it's often more useful to browse than to search, especially if you don't know exactly what you're looking for.

Fortunately, a few pages have appeared to help you find the business information you need. Others exist in addition to the ones described here, but the two shown here are easily accessible and reasonably well organized. You can take your pick, or try both.

List of Commercial Services on the Web (and Net)

Open Market's Commercial Sites Index (http://www.directory.net/) serves an invaluable function. Here, on a series of alphabetically organized HTML pages, you will find thousands of links to businesses, business services, nonprofit organizations, and sites that gather several businesses together. For a businessperson investigating how other companies are using the Net, this is an invaluable page from which to start.

The site offers two ways of finding what you want. First, you can click the "alphabetical listings" link, which will take you to a page displaying the letters of the alphabet. From here you click on a letter, and you'll retrieve a page showing all the organizations whose names begin with that letter. A much more efficient way of accessing information about a particular topic is to type what you're looking for in the Search box. You can do this by company name or product, or any you can use other keyword you wish. For an example, try "chocolate," "bicycles," "software," or "Canada" to get a sense of how this works. It's quite powerful.

FIGURE 23.1.

Commercial Sites Index main page.

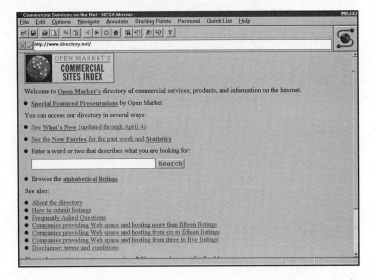

The main page also offers a link to the equally useful What's New in Commercial Services on the Web page. (See Figure 23.2.) Updated frequently, this page offers a look at recent entries onto the page, organized in the same manner as NCSA's extremely popular What's New page, by date. The main page is worth turning to on a regular basis.

FIGURE 23.2.

What's New page from the Commercial Sites Index.

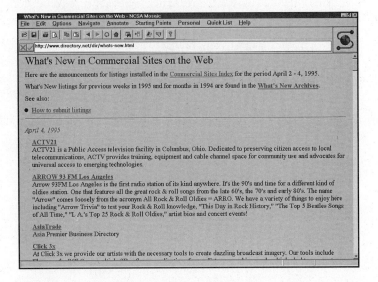

Interesting Business Sites on the Web

An aptly named collection of links out of Rensselaer Polytechnic Institute (`http://www.rpi.edu/~okeefe/business.html`), Interesting Business Sites on the Web doesn't pretend to be all-inclusive. Instead, as the home page illustrates in Figure 23.3, its stated function is to be a "relatively small" listing that covers "most of the exciting business uses of the Web, plus some reasonable international and industry coverage." And that's what it does. There's a link to the Pick of the Month, which is always worth visiting, and internal links (that is, links within the same page) to several companies. This is an excellent companion site to the much more expansive Commercial Sites Index, and between the two of them you can't go very far wrong.

FIGURE 23.3.

Main page for Interesting Business Sites on the Web.

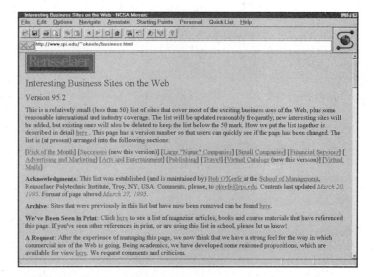

SPRY City

Another page directing Web users to business sites is SPRY, Inc.'s Spry City (`http://www.spry.com/sp_city/sp_city.html`). A completely redesigned home page for the old NetAccess site (featured in the first edition of this book), Spry City features listings of everything from education sites to art and theater sites, but its business area remains strong.

Concentrating in its initial stages on links to players in the computer industry, Spry City now offers links to large corporations, small businesses, financial-information sites, legal-information sites, career sites, and so forth. Unfortunately, the Business Center retains its earlier problem of not offering even a small blurb of information about each company. (See Figure 23.5.) This would provide useful information for seeking the products you want.

This leads to another design suggestion for the future of Spry City: providing a product index as well as a name index. For any site that seeks to provide useful information about one particular industry, such product and service indexes are almost necessary. Sometimes, certainly, users look for a specific firm, but just as often users are searching for companies that produce specific kinds of products.

FIGURE 23.4.

The Spry City main page, offering link to Business Center.

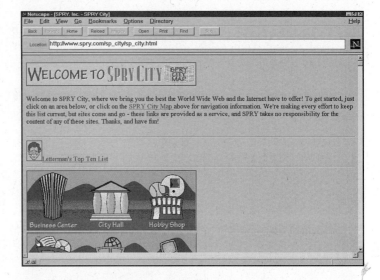

FIGURE 23.5.

A small portion of the business listings in Spry City.

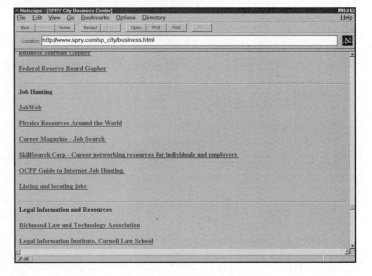

Special-Interest Business Sites

This section looks at the growing number of Web pages aimed at specialized markets. Here we see the World Wide Web being used as an inexpensive means for small businesses to make their products known to more potential buyers than would be possible in any other way besides full-scale, mass-media advertising. (And in mass-media advertising, there's no guarantee that anyone will actually pay attention.)

Are companies now using the Net for advertising, an activity once frowned upon by the Internet community at large? Yes, blatantly. But while these Web pages suggest the possibility that one day the Net will be saturated with the electronic version of direct-mail advertising, there is no pressure for anyone to access these sites. If you wish, you can avoid them completely. Yet if even one of them fulfills a hobby or gift-buying need, you'll be glad you have access to them.

Auto Pages of Internet

The worlds of cars and computers have a lot in common. Car owners are just as critical of other people's machines as computer owners are, and both groups want nothing less than the best, the fastest, and the most technologically advanced. They also want the machine that will afford them the most prestige. However, there is at least one fundamental difference: Computer owners don't routinely polish up their old Altairs and Apple IIs and parade them around at antique computer show to the oohs and ahs of admiring onlookers.

The Auto Pages of Internet home page (`http://www.clark.net/pub/networx/autopage/autopage.html`) offers a place on the Web for people to advertise their classic or exotic cars and motorcycles for sale. As shown in Figure 23.6, the page has links to Exotic Cars and Classic Cars, and links further down provide access to car dealers and manufacturers, articles and reviews of interest, and pages explaining how to advertise on the AutoPages Web site (and even how to earn a commission by soliciting advertising). As a business, this is the equivalent of a specialty buy-and-sell paper, and the fact that it's so focused in scope is precisely what makes it interesting. Hobbyists and collectors will find themselves accessing the page regularly.

Figure 23.7 shows the top of the Exotic Cars page. Each of the links provides information about the cars, including contact names and prices. As of this writing, these pages were only in the beginning stages of development. It's easy to foresee a web page about each car, which would offer interior and exterior views, a look under the hood, and perhaps even an audio file so the potential buyer could listen to the purring of the engine.

FIGURE 23.6.

The Automobile Sellers home page.

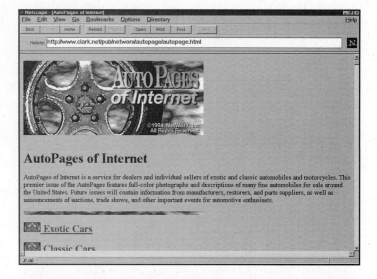

FIGURE 23.7.

The AutoPages Exotic Cars page, with links to information about specific cars.

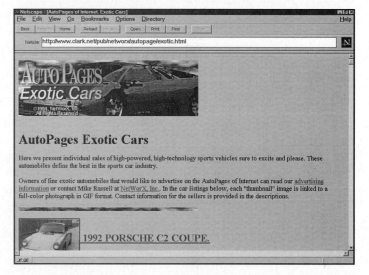

Condom Country

One of the most interesting designs on the Web is Condom Country (http://www.ag.com/condom/country), whose home page is shown in Figure 23.8. Far from a simple novelty (which is what probably draws the bulk of its first-time visitors), this site demonstrates what thoughtfulness, humor, and a good user-interface design can accomplish when conducting business through the Web. Even the means by which the page designers warn users that they might be offended is well considered, and if you want privacy rather than online ordering (which isn't secured), you can have that, too.

FIGURE 23.8.

The home page for Condom Country.

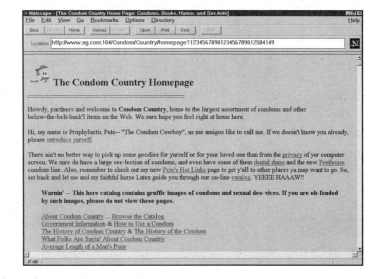

Condom Country was one of the first sites on the Web to make use of the "shopping basket" idea. After you establish an account with the company—which you can do either through the Web or via telephone—you look through their product selection (there are graphics of several of the products) and order the ones you want while you browse. You can select any quantity of any item, and the site adds the total to your shopping bag. At any time, you can check your shopping bag, removing items if you no longer want them. Once you've decided you have all you need, simply click the Check Out button and verify your order.

Several Condom Country ideas have since been incorporated into other sites that offer products for sale.

InContext Systems

InContext Systems is a Canadian firm that produces software for document creation (including Web design). They hired a creative advertising agency to give their Web site maximum impact. The result is a multi-page, in-depth site that combines the design quality of *Wired* magazine with a genuine attention to usability. Despite its graphical orientation, the site doesn't take much longer to retrieve than many other sites, because the graphics have been limited to a sensible size (including 8-bit rather than 16-bit versions) whenever possible. The home page, at `http://www.InContext.ca/` (see Figure 23.9), demonstrates the site's creative design approach.

In Figure 23.10, we see an internal page at this site. This is the first page of a fairly lengthy document, and it demonstrates some of the site's many strengths. First, each page is designed to fit comfortably on a single screen of a user's monitor. This is a far superior design to the standard idea of offering long pages that force the user to scroll down several times. Second, the document looks and reads like a magazine article, complete with columns and margin art. Third, to reinforce the magazine concept even further, this document continues on the next page (and several pages after that) by means of a hyperlink consisting of the last few words of each page. In other words, you read to the end of the page and then click to "turn" to the next page.

FIGURE 23.9.

The eye-catching design of InContext Systems' home page.

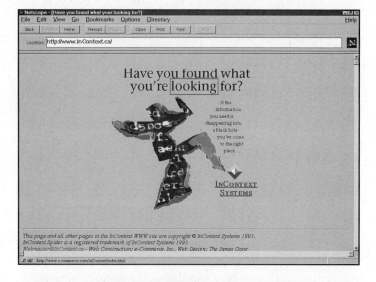

FIGURE 23.10.

An internal magazine-style page from InContext.

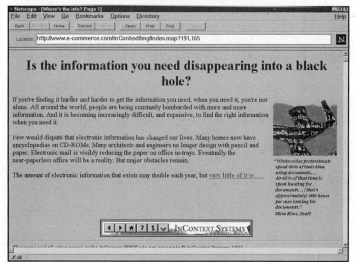

Arctic Adventours

Given the fact that the tourism industry caters to people who are interested in travel and who often travel to exotic places around the globe, the Internet seems a logical venue for posting materials about travel. So far a few tour operators have jumped on the bandwagon, including Norway's Arctic Adventours (http://www.oslonett.no/data/adv/AA/AA.html). Two of Arctic Adventours' are shown in Figures 23.11 and 23.12.

There's not a huge amount of information on these sites, but then again, there isn't much in most tour catalogs. Links point to separate pages about specific tours, where you can find the details you need in order to determine if you're interested. A nice touch is the link to the yacht Arctic Explorer, and another good link is to the GIF images from various parts of the world. Because of the GIFs, the information loses little of the visual appeal it would have in a glossy printed version, although the GIFs take much longer to download than they would to glance at in print.

Figure 23.12 shows one of the indexes of downloadable picture files available from this site. Many of these are quite large, but if you're looking to build an archive of superb Arctic scenery photos, and if you have the patience to download them, you'll find some superb shots here. And many of these are actual tour photos, as well, so there's a sense of authenticity.

FIGURE 23.11.

Arctic Adventours' main page, offering glimpses of their offerings.

FIGURE 23.12.

Index of downloadable graphics files.

Large Corporations on the Web

Web use by large corporations is a topic of considerable interest as we approach the second half of the '90s. Large businesses today see the Net as a very real tool for attracting, serving, and maintaining customers and clients. Predictably, however, they're approaching the Net very cautiously, partly because of security issues and partly because no concrete figures exist to suggest how many people can be reached this way. Because of both concerns, the tendency is to direct funding elsewhere—and in corporations, an unfunded project is a nonexistent project.

This is not to suggest that corporations have not already begun some major online activities. A quick scan of the Commercial Sites Index demonstrates that large companies are beginning to assert an Internet presence. While many of these are computer companies (such as Digital Equipment, Hewlett Packard, and Silicon Graphics), other types of businesses are coming onto the Web as well.

If corporate America determines that a Net presence can be profitable, we can expect the Web to experience an explosion of big-business activity—to the extent that the balance of Internet activity will be swung in business's favor. This is something that the larger Internet community is extremely wary of.

CommerceNet

CommerceNet is among the more significant business sites on the World Wide Web, although it is perhaps not as important as it was before the advent of security-capable commercial browsers and servers. Page through CommerceNet's directories and you'll find some Fortune 500 giants, and although the site hasn't developed as quickly as was first expected, it can't be ignored as an indication of things to come.

CommerceNet (`http://www.commerce.net/`) is a consortium, a project jointly sponsored by a number of corporations to take advantage of the Internet's vast promise. From the home page (see Figure 23.13) through the individual pages (even in their continually "under construction" state), it's clear that these sites will bear little resemblance to the product-information pages we saw among the small companies discussed previously in this chapter. The promise here is for fully developed, fully operational sites, using the World Wide Web not only as a means of generating awareness but also as a means of transacting real business in real time.

It has taken months for important things to happen on CommerceNet, and there's still a sense that its true importance has yet to be realized. The biggest stumbling block, as always, is security; but given the release of some important server products, with built-in data encryption and other security technologies, this is a problem with available solutions. A problem that is perhaps more difficult to solve is convincing companies to actually offer something users will want to spend money on. While a host of corporations support the Web as a means of giving and receiving information, it's still not a proven marketplace, and as a result, resources are not being pumped into it.

FIGURE 23.13.

The CommerceNet home page, with full graphics interface.

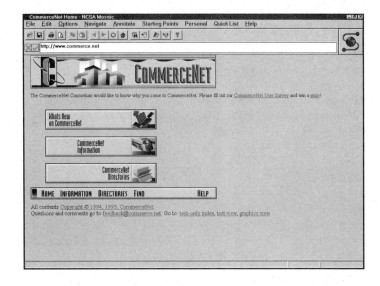

The home page demonstrates the graphic nature of CommerceNet, although it's clear from the subhead that a text view is also available. The design works as a series of pushbuttons, and it works well. Figure 23.14 shows a similar interface from a subsequent page.

FIGURE 23.14.

CommerceNet's directories, with links to participants and partners.

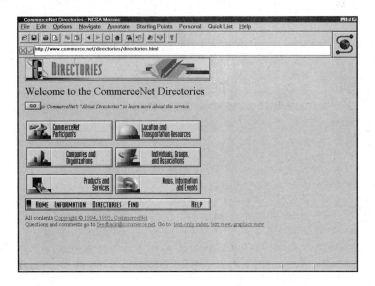

Canadian Airlines International

The Canadian Airlines International site on the Web (`http://www.CdnAir.CA/`) demonstrates more of the Web's promise, but it also shows how far the Net still has to go to be an effective business tool. Here we have access to a good range of useful information about the airline, including flight and departure schedules. Eventually we'll be able to use this site to order airline tickets and to make rental-car, hotel, and tour reservations.

The problem is, you can already do all this on the commercial online services. So while this site is ahead of many in its efforts to provide services, it's still way behind the less-glamorous, competing technologies. Indeed, it's *years* behind in a number of ways. Of course, this is true of just about all Web-based ordering activities; we've been able to shop on CompuServe or America OnLine for a long time.

So let's not get carried away. Indeed, let's ask why so very little has happened at this site and others since the first edition of this book was published. At the same time, let's keep in mind the complexities that arise from the Web's size, its growth rate, and its stupendous problems with security and interactivity. (This isn't just a couple of computers joined together, remember.) With those considerations in mind, we can see the potential of the Canadian Airlines site while we remark on the clean design and the orderly interface. Figure 23.15 makes this abundantly clear.

FIGURE 23.15.

The Home page for Canadian Airlines International, with link to flight information.

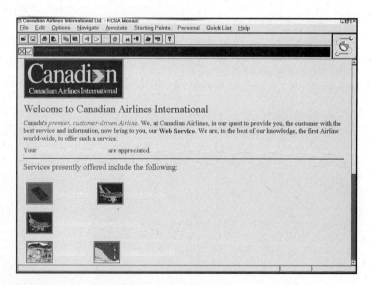

Figure 23.16 shows one way the Web can help make information extremely accessible. You can click any continent on the gorgeously rendered map and be given a closer view of that continent, with information about the destinations. Start merging this with reservation information and you have something very real to build on.

FIGURE 23.16.

A page with a clickable map to details on Canadian Airlines destinations.

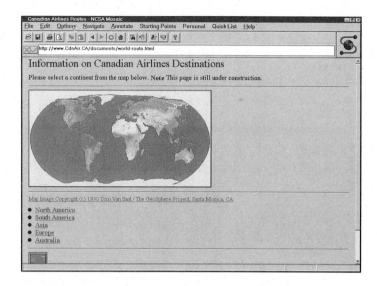

Lockheed Martin Missiles & Space

As the home page displayed in Figure 23.17 shows, Lockheed Martin Missiles & Space (`http://www.lmsc.lockheed.com/`) specializes in space systems, missiles, and other high-tech products. The company earns its income primarily through Defense Department contracts (the civilian space-missile market is extremely limited these days), and that probably has a lot to do with why the home page offers an immediate link to the Public Information Office and transcriptions of recent press releases. One imagines that Lockheed spends a fair amount of time and money on public relations, and the Web is a useful tool in this regard.

The site doesn't offer a great deal of information beyond the standard p.r. and some technical details, but it is a good example of a corporation using the Web to education the public about its activities and projects. If you've ever wondered about the companies that land those lucrative defense contracts, give this page a look.

The design of the home page is straightforward, with appropriately iconic custom bullets and easy-to-understand links. Clearly, the page is meant for viewing through high-speed connections, however (the graphics take forever to download across a modem), and this seems a bit strange given the public focus of the information. (In other words, don't forget the little guys, Lockheed.) Figure 23.18 shows the accessible Lockheed press releases page, and although it is not notably designed, it's quite functional.

FIGURE 23.17.

The Lockheed home page, with press releases and company info.

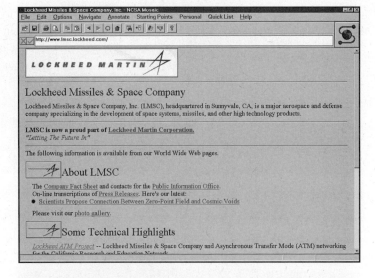

FIGURE 23.18.

The Lockheed page for access to company press releases.

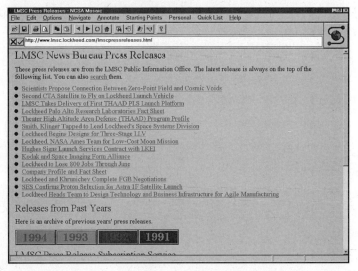

Bank of America

A participant in the CommerceNet initiative, Bank of America has hit the Web with a series of pages that show significant potential. The home page (http://www.bankamerica.com/) consists of a huge clickable map in the form of a large, colorful logo. It offers no concession to text-only users while it clearly demonstrates the financial activities that will be possible from this site in the near future.

Somewhere along the line, Bank of America customers will be able to make payments of various types over the Web, first by filling in the check-like blanks and then clicking the Paper Check, ACH Payment, or Wire Transfer buttons. Here we see a solid use of the HTML fill-in form, with the arrows signifying selection menus. It takes little imagination to see how we might turn to this or a similar page in the future and make the transactions from our computers. (As of this writing, this is the result of clicking *any* of the icons.)

The stumbling block, once again, is security. At this stage in the Web's existence, services such as those proposed here by the Bank of America simply can't happen. But let the Web security gurus get their act fully together—and a lot of money is being spent by CommerceNet and others to make this happen—and you might find yourself Web-banking before too long. While making payments this way might not seem too exciting, directing your investments certainly does.

Hewlett Packard

Hewlett Packard, like several other computer companies, has developed an extensive corporate site on the Web, one that clearly demonstrates the Web's potential in the areas of technical support and customer service. Shown in Figure 23.19 is the HP SupportLine home page (`http://support.mayfield.hp.com:80/support/`), which loads with the large imagemap graphic that contains the buttons you need to traverse the site. This map is clearly and colorfully designed and extremely easy to understand, and it fits with the theme of the HP access pages throughout the site. For modem users, four of the items are accessible from the links at the bottom of the page.

FIGURE 23.19.

The HP SupportLine home page.

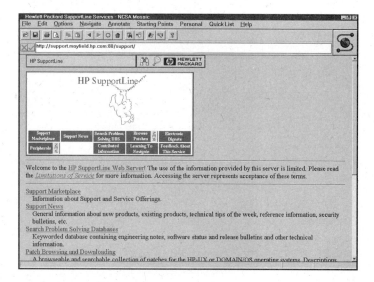

This is a well-organized FTP site, fully accessible from the Web, that demonstrates the extent to which corporation can use the customer and technical services potential of the Net. It's not hard to imagine HP's customers, especially MIS staffers, coming to rely on this page from the time they install new HP products until the day they exchange them for others.

Nor is this anywhere near the full extent of the material available from this site. Press releases, question-and-answer sessions, educational items, and other support elements are here as well, and the HP customer is advised to check it out frequently. (See Figure 23.20.) The Hewlett Packard site is one of the most impressive business sites available.

FIGURE 23.20.

The HP Peripheral Anonymous FTP Site page with links to technical information.

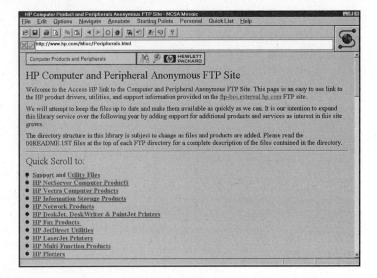

Digital Equipment

Very similar in scope to Hewlett Packard's site is Digital Equipment's extensive and highly useful area (http://www.digital.com). Like HP, Digital leads off on its home page with a clickable imagemap (Figure 23.21), a somewhat overlarge graphic that continues Digital's science-fiction theme from their previous—and much more graphical—Web offering. From this graphic you can navigate anywhere on Digital's site, and there's a very great deal to see.

If you're a Digital customer, or at least thinking of becoming one, you'll want to explore several of the pages offered from this initial graphic. Of particular interest are the featured sites with the large logos, the extensive reading room, and the useful directory of services. The link to new technology and research will show you directions in which the company is headed, while the link to customer periodicals will let you spend some quiet moments on the Web reading.

One notable feature, becoming popular among computer companies on the Web, is the software patches page, which is accessible through the support area and which leads to the page displayed in Figure 23.22. The Patch page offers Digital's customers downloadable files that contain software patches (corrections)—an immensely useful feature for anyone in charge of installing and maintaining Digital equipment. Digital offers a huge amount of technical information on these pages, including technical reports and documentation, along with educational items. From a customer- and technical-service perspective, this is another impressive Web business site.

FIGURE 23.21.

Digital Equipment's main page, with large graphic and clickable display.

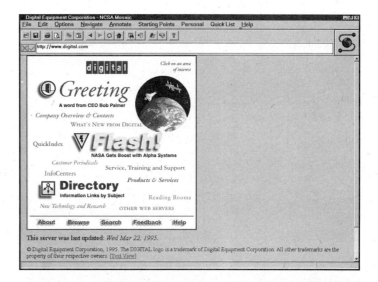

FIGURE 23.22.

Digital's patch page.

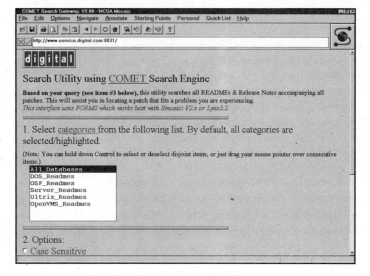

Compaq Computer Corporation

It's hardly surprising that the computer companies seem to be leading the way in using the Web to present information about products and customer service, and it's always valuable to look at what these companies are doing if you want to see some of the Web's potential. One of the latest to make their way to the Web is Compaq, whose home page at `http://www.compaq.com` (shown in Figure 23.23) is available in either a full-graphics (extremely modem-hostile) or a full-text version, with nothing left out of the latter. From here you can get information about individual products or product lines, and you can access the customer-service area as well.

FIGURE 23.23.

Compaq Computer Corporation home page.

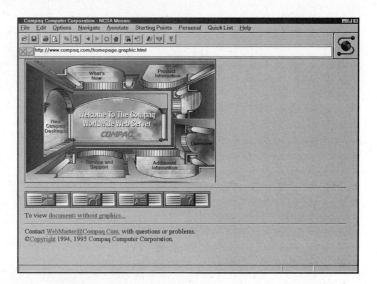

As with computer companies such as Digital Equipment, Silicon Graphics, and Hewlett-Packard, Compaq's customer-service pages (see Figure 23.24) feature technical information, answers to questions, and an archive of downloadable software. If you have a Compaq PC, you'll want to check the drivers and ROMPaqs frequently to make sure you're completely up to date.

Toronto-Dominion Bank

One of the first Canadian banks on the World Wide Web, the Toronto-Dominion Bank offers a series of pages (`http://www.tdbank.ca/tdbank/`). With links to a series of investment services, RRSP details, downloadable software, and even a library, the home page (see Figure 23.25) demonstrates the kind of commitment necessary for a business to make the Web work for them.

The link to the T-D Library proves useful as well. Here you can read or retrieve articles about mortgages, newsletters about business, press releases and speeches by T-D officials, and economic and quarterly reports. None of this is information you couldn't get by just walking into your local branch, but since banking is moving away from that model, providing this material on the Web is a worthwhile thing to do.

FIGURE 23.24.

Compaq's downloadable files page.

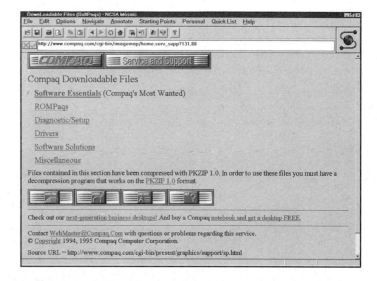

FIGURE 23.25.

The home page for the Toronto-Dominion Bank.

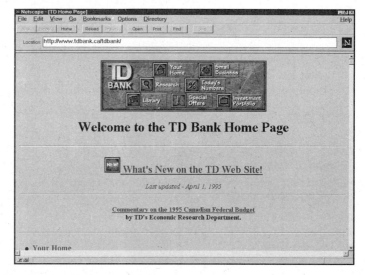

Dun & Bradstreet

Dun & Bradstreet is a venerable presence in the financial-information community, and the fact that they have established pages on the Web suggests that they're aware of the Net's potential for financial organizations. As is evident from the company's home page (http://www.dbisna.com/, shown in Figure 23.26), this site includes links to several important resources for financial information and services. This site has changed dramatically since the appearance of the first edition of this book.

The site is divided by issues rather than products, with a slightly confusing imagemap at the top of the screen containing what's-new information and details for new users. From that point, it's a matter of deciding which issue you want to deal with and clicking from there. Figure 23.27 shows the opening page of the Market Your Business Globally link, with further links to useful details.

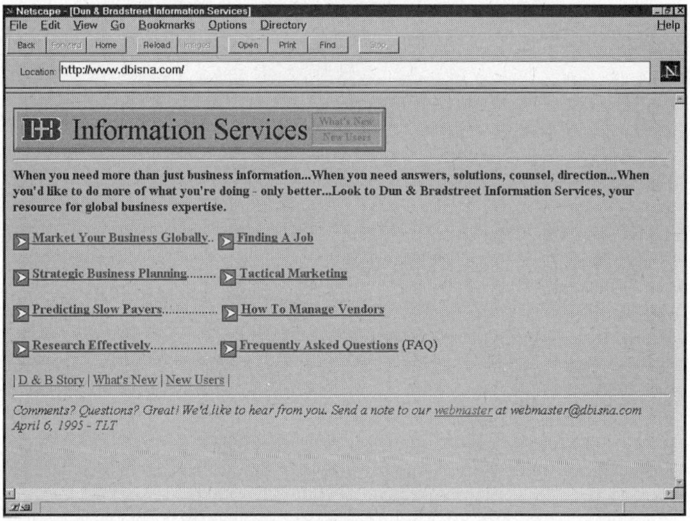

FIGURE 23.26.

A clickable diagram from Dun & Bradstreet's information page.

FIGURE 23.27.

The Marketing Your Business Globally sub-page from the D&B site.

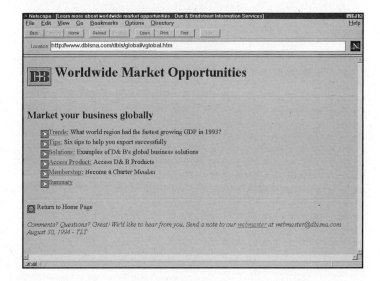

Federal Express

Located at `http://www.fedex.com/`, the Federal Express pages are part of the CommerceNet initiative. At this point, it's not possible to call FedEx for a package pick-up over the Web, but it's definitely possible to track a package that you've already sent with them. The home page, shown in Figure 23.28, shows the somewhat meager offerings of this page, which primarily break down to a what's-new page and a shipment-tracking page. If you're interested, you can check out the company's availability as well, but you could do that by simply calling their toll-free phone numbers instead. Even the what's-new page is less than wonderful, consisting primarily of press releases at this stage in its development.

FIGURE 23.28.

The Federal Express home page.

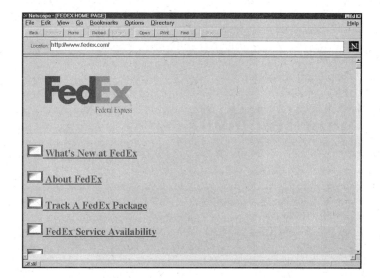

What makes the site valuable is the ability to track your packages. Figure 23.29 shows the tracking page, a very simple one-field, fill-in form. All you need do is enter your airbill number, and you'll be provided with the scan information for that package. Again, this is only a way of getting the same information you could obtain by calling the company directly, but sometimes this way is much faster.

FIGURE 23.29.

*A shipment-tracking form
from a FedEx site.*

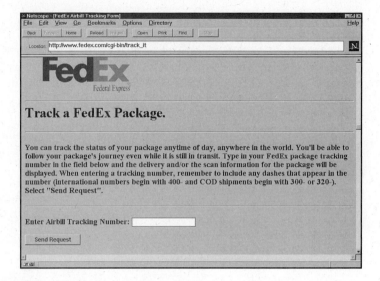

Industrial Malls

Large companies can afford to establish their own Internet connections. Small companies, for the most part, cannot. For that reason, we're seeing an increasing number of "industrial malls" coming into operation on the World Wide Web. Like a real industrial mall, the principle behind these "e-malls" is that one company owns and maintains the structure, collecting rent from the tenants and providing them a space. Rather than a building, of course, the e-mall landlord owns and maintains a full Internet connection, renting disk space and bandwidth to the tenants for a setup fee, a monthly fee, and, in some cases, a page-design fee as well. The possibilities are varied, depending on the site.

The advantage for the tenants is that they obtain an Internet presence without the significant cost in both equipment and labor of installing their own connections. They don't have to worry about system upgrades, hard-disk failures, UNIX arcana, or anything else. They just assert their presence, pay for the amount of e-space they take up, and display their wares to 20 million Internet users. The disadvantages are that they don't have the freedom to develop full Internet integration into their company's daily activities, and they don't have unique URL addresses (although this isn't always true). But since most Web users point-and-click their way onto a site rather than type in the actual URL, this latter point probably doesn't matter that much.

Expect industrial malls to increase in both number and quality. This is an obvious entry point onto the Web for a great many businesses, and not just small ones.

Downtown Anywhere

As the home page shown in Figure 23.30 says, Downtown Anywhere (`http://www.awa.com/`) is "conveniently located in central cyberspace." It's structured according to the town metaphor, with a main street, a library and newsstand, and just about everything else you'd find in a downtown. The idea behind the site is to collect a wide variety of businesses and services in one spot, creating not just an industrial mall but a virtual town, and the early development of this site ought to lend some credibility to the possibility of future success.

FIGURE 23.30.

Downtown Anywhere's home page with links to a commercial page.

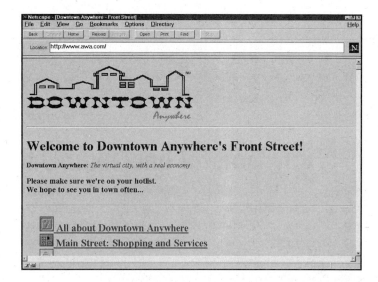

This is an exciting site. Browse it for a while, and you start to feel a sense of "town-ness" building up. (Of course, it helps to first experience the "static-ness" of some other mall sites.) Inevitably, the strength of the town is only as strong as its inhabitants, but that's true of real towns as well. Not everything in Downtown Anywhere is going to attract your immediate attention, but the concept certainly should.

After a truly enticing home page, the interior pages seem comparatively drab, however. Main Street, shown in Figure 23.31, looks no different from any other hastily developed collection page on the Web, and clicking several of the links reveals that the site is in its very early stages. Considering what the site's designers did with the home page, Main Street (which should be the one fully developed attraction) just doesn't cut it from the standpoint of aesthetics. It's functional, but it should be much more. Still, it's a site that's well worth watching.

FIGURE 23.31.

Main Street from the Downtown Anywhere site.

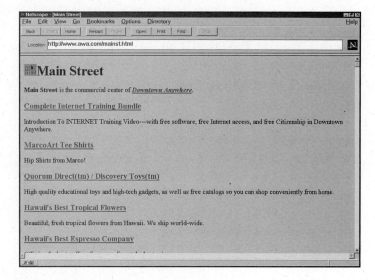

BizNet Technologies

Unlike Downtown Anywhere, BizNet Technologies (`http://www.biznet.com.blacksburg.va.us/`) has organized its tenants around the metaphor of the shopping mall. The concepts are similar, but when the metaphors are fully developed, the two sites will end up with very different atmospheres. So far, however, the sites appear alike, but this is hardly surprising; interface designers have always been much better at coming up with metaphors than developing them fully. Still, the shopping mall is a metaphor you'll run into frequently on your Web travels, so it's worth exploring here.

The home page (Figure 23.32) is clear and attractive. It is brief (this will change as more stores are added), and the logo is clever and appealing. (It omits Antarctica, but that's probably acceptable.) One of the interesting points about this site is that it's not just a collection of shops. Instead, it mixes a flower shop with an apartment site and two other not-completely predictable tenants (Durability, Inc., and Home Technologies, Inc.), a combination that makes you want to start browsing to see the differences. Apartment blocks in particular are very rare on the Web.

Inside, the client pages are varied and are usually interesting. There are some weak sites (but then, there are weak stores in any mall), but for the most part this is a site worth visiting. Figure 23.33 shows the list of BizNet clients and demonstrates the variety of business on the site.

NetMarket

Among industrial malls on the Web, NetMarket (`http://www.netmarket.com/`) is unique. Not only is it designed to house a variety of businesses (which isn't unique at all), it is also structured so that you open an account that covers all the offerings in the mall itself. Establish the account, and you can go shopping inside any of NetMarket's stores (which were few at the time of this writing). This is an extremely interesting idea because it encourages e-shoppers to stay in that particular mall for all their shopping needs. Rather than establish accounts with each individual store, you only need one in order to begin shopping. (This is potentially dangerous from a personal-finances standpoint, of course, but such is the nature of credit-card shopping.)

FIGURE 23.32.

BizNet's home page, including links to a variety of businesses.

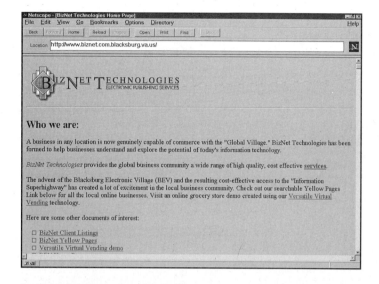

FIGURE 23.33.

BizNet Technologies' list of clients.

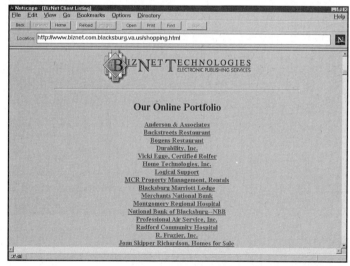

Figure 23.34 shows the HTML form in the account-creation page. Note that you can create your account fully over the Net, or you can call or write NetMarket to arrange the account otherwise. Note also that your account is active as soon as you send the form. That means you can impulse shop until you drop. At this stage, it's probably not a good idea to send credit-card information through the Web, but if you're interested in doing so, why not contact NetMarket and see what they have to say?

FIGURE 23.34.

A NetMarket account setup form with fill-in radio buttons.

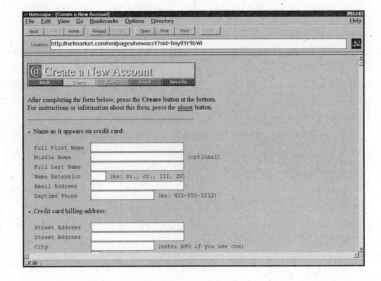

Inside NetMarket, the most fully developed site (as of this writing) is Noteworthy Music Compact Discs. Their home page (Figure 23.35) displays the colorful pushbutton interface common throughout NetMarket, and its options are intriguing. Cleverly, the store offers either a browsing or a searching choice, including complex searches. You have the option of a multimedia display as well, an extremely promising idea for CD buyers.

Figure 23.36 shows the extent of Noteworthy Music's site. Below the Page button you can see that this is the first of 775 pages! Surely this is a CD-buyer's dream, a fact that is confirmed by the running purchase total displayed immediately below the top menu. The idea here is to browse or search for what you want, clicking on the button beside the item to select it, then watching your dollar total increase until you're satisfied you have the items you want and have spent the money you can afford. Then you can finish the transaction. Noteworthy's interface takes some getting used to (practice a few times before actually launching an order), but it's powerful.

This is a very interesting site, and probably a harbinger of the future.

The Internet Plaza

One of a growing number of virtual malls on the Web, the Internet Plaza offers an attractive opening imagemap at `http://plaza.xor.com/` (Figure 23.37) that divides the service into the standard business areas of a town. Included here are the leasing office, which gives you information about how to get onto this service, and a Monthly Feature, which encourages users to return to the Plaza at least once per month.

FIGURE 23.35.

Noteworthy Music's main menu with links to order forms.

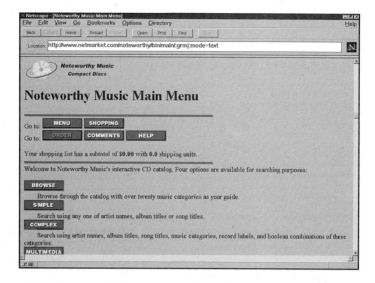

FIGURE 23.36.

Noteworthy Music's browsable and searchable catalog of CDs.

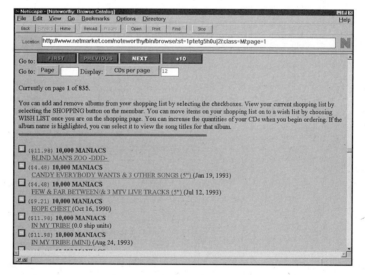

FIGURE 23.37.

The home page for the Internet Plaza, with strong imagemap.

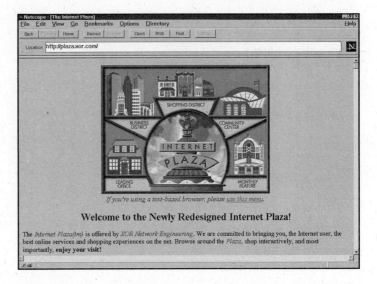

A number of good offerings are available from the Plaza, including a very good site from Alamo Rent A Car. As Figure 23.38 demonstrates, this site features forums in which users can offer their own opinions about travel issues, a collection of maps to help you plan your vacation, and lists of travel tips and other "fun" items. Of immediate use to travelers is the online vehicle-reservation page, which consists of a fairly elaborate form in which you specify your needs. As of this writing, the page was a working prototype, but it gives you an idea of how easy booking a car should be in the future.

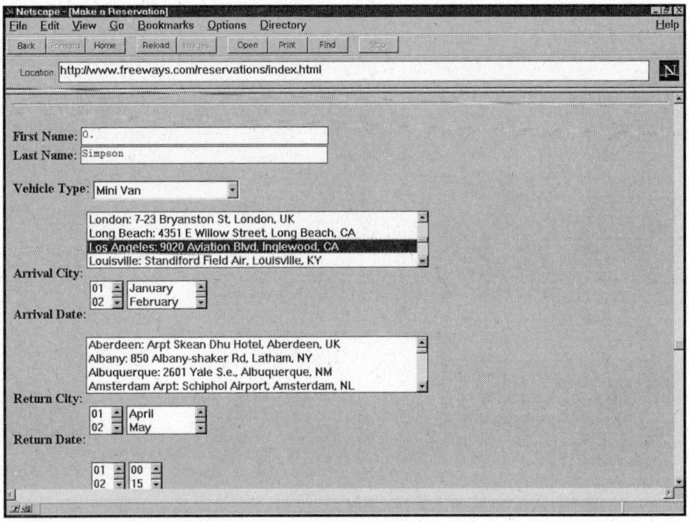

FIGURE 23.38.

The vehicle-reservation form from Freeways—Alamo Online.

The Internet Shopping Network

The Home Shopping Network has been such a success on cable television that it comes as no surprise to see a version offered over the Internet. There's no question which version is superior. Instead of staring at your screen while hunks of cheap jewelry and commemorative plaques work their way past you, with the Internet Shopping Network (http://www.internet.net/) you can move straight to your chosen interest area and see what the service has to offer. Figure 23.39 shows the main directory, with buttons for different product types and a list of "hot deals."

FIGURE 23.39.

The Internet Shopping Network's main directory.

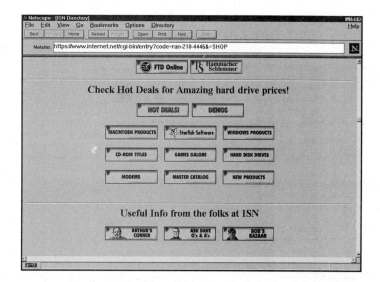

Once into ISN, you can order easily and quickly, using a secured Web site that stores your credit-card information. If you wish, you can download software demos from the site, and you can also read computer-product reviews from the industry publication *InfoWorld*. Figure 23.40 shows one such review, and several others are available. All in all, ISN is growing nicely, and sometimes their hot deals really are hot.

FIGURE 23.40.

InfoWorld product review from ISN.

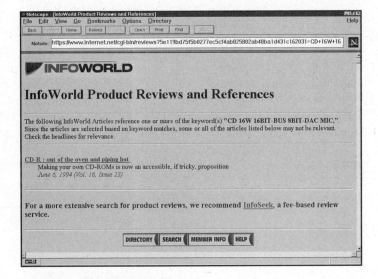

internetMCI

As if Internet "founder" Vint Cerf needed any more pats on the back ("founder" is in quotations because Cerf wouldn't call himself that), his new internetMCI (http://www.internetmci.com/) service has all the makings of a superb piece of Net-based business. Figure 23.41 shows the home page of the new service—an attractive design with a reasonably sized imagemap as the main interface.

FIGURE 23.41.

The home page for the internetMCI service.

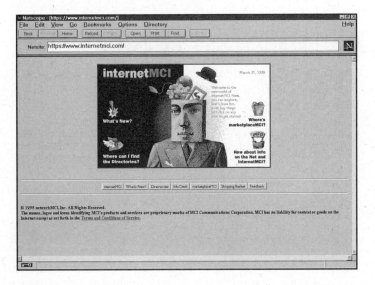

From this page, you can easily click to any of the service's offerings. One of these, important to the future of shopping on the Web, is marketplaceMCI, a virtual mall from which you can make secure credit-card purchases. (See Figure 23.42.) The site makes use of an increasingly popular idea, the virtual shopping basket, which keeps track of your purchases as you make your way through the marketplace. You use the online shopping basket the way you'd use a real-world one: Check to see what you've decided to buy, removing anything you no longer want, and compute the grand total.

FIGURE 23.42.

internetMCI's Marketplace, with links to secure credit-card purchases.

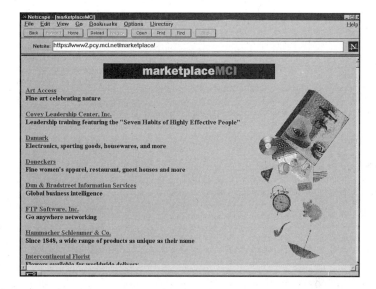

MCI has been an important participant in e-mail services, and internetMCI should prove to be equally important in the area of business on the Web.

OfficeMax

One of the stores that sells merchandise from marketplaceMCI is the office-equipment retailer OfficeMax. Its home page and all subsequent pages are consistently and cleanly designed. One of the selections from this page leads to product selection. This page (`https://www2.pcy.mci.net/market/omax/html/2100.html`), identical in graphic design to the home page, can be seen in Figure 23.43.

FIGURE 23.43.

The Products Selection page from OfficeMax.

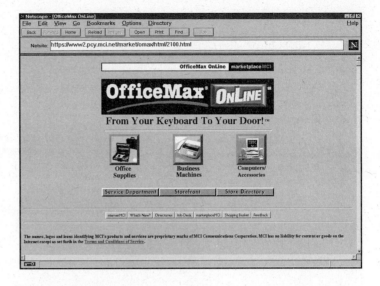

Clicking the Office Supplies button moves you to the products page shown in Figure 23.44. Several things are noteworthy here. First, the page uses graphic-alignment tags as an alternative to the standard vertical list of items. Second, the three long buttons near the bottom of the page are consistent across all OfficeMax pages, demonstrating a concern for ease of use that the other sites on the Web are only now beginning to demonstrate. Third, the page tells you, in the top left, that other pages from this area are available. To access them, click the arrow on the left side of the top graphics; this is another nod to usability. Finally, splitting the site into easily downloadable pages does two things: It means that no single page is too large even for modem users, and it means that products won't get "lost" by loading below the immediately accessible display area of most PCs.

FIGURE 23.44.

The first of several displays of office machines in OfficeMax.

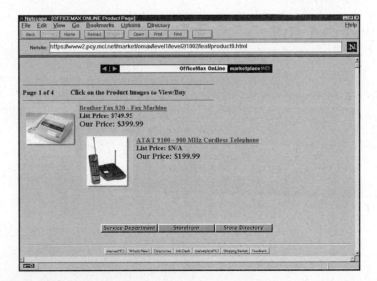

Business Services on the Web

As businesses develop a Web presence, so do the corresponding business-support services. One of the most prevalent services, as you might expect, are the Internet site providers; but I've foregone a discussion of those in favor of two less obvious examples. The following two sites demonstrate that the nature of Web-based business services is yet to be determined, but eventually we can expect the same range of services over the Net that we have in the non-Net world. There's one problem: The Net as it now exists is extremely public, and many business-service companies project an image that suggests they deal with a very elite (that is, very big business) clientele.

Capital One

Much of the current focus of business on the Web is on the possibility of paying for merchandise by credit card. Not long ago, it wasn't a good idea to send your credit-card information over the Web, because lack of security meant the information could be stolen by just about anyone with the know-how. With the advent of servers offering data security, however, such as the well-known Netscape Netsite server, the possibility of Web-based credit-card purchases now exists, and it's not likely to go away.

The problem is, not everyone has a credit card. So it was only a matter of time before someone would make it possible to use the Web to obtain a card, in order to make credit-card purchases available to as many Web users as possible. That's the role of Capital One, whose home page is shown in Figure 23.45 (`https://www.capital1.com/CapitalOne/c1-application.html`). From this page you can apply for a Visa card by using secured fill-in forms, and if you don't already have one (or if you want another), it's well worth a try.

FIGURE 23.45.

The Capital One home page, with a credit-card application link.

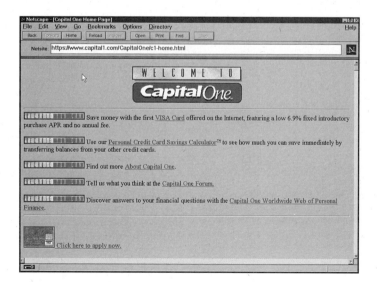

Figure 23.46 shows the application form for your credit card, which is surprisingly simple to fill out. But applying for a card isn't the only feature at this site. Included here is a forum for discussing Capital One's services and a page of links to personal-finance information. Capital One isn't a one-stop financial service, but it has the potential to be so.

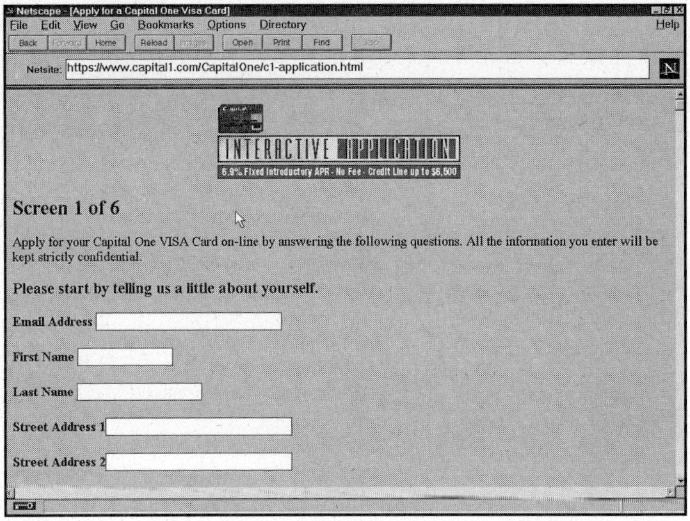

FIGURE 23.46.

The Capital One credit-card application.

PAWWS

PAWWS stands for Portfolio Accounting World Wide from Security APL, but that's not important. Much more interesting is the fact that PAWWS offers a set of useful utilities and services over the Web that are designed to help you with money management. Another of the growing number of secure Web sites, PAWWS (`https://pawws.secapl.com/`) is an investor service with a number of interesting and appealing features. Figure 23.47 displays the PAWWS home page.

You can open different kinds of accounts with PAWWS, depending on what you want to do. (No, it's not free). When you have your account and password, you log in to The Source information service to make use of PAWWS' services. This log-in is seamless across the Web—you don't see a separate Telnet screen or anything of the sort.

Of particular interest in PAWWS is the excellent design of the pages. The imagemap on the opening screen is a bit large for comfortable modem use (although it's far from the worst offender), but all pages are clear and even concise, to the point where it's rarely necessary to scroll. Such clean design is a rarity on the Web. Figure 23.48 displays the mutual funds buy-and-sell page.

FIGURE 23.47.

The home page for the PAWWS financial services area.

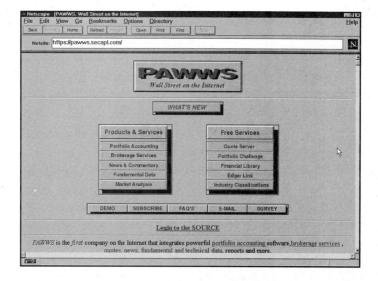

FIGURE 23.48.

The mutual-funds ordering and selling page from PAWWS.

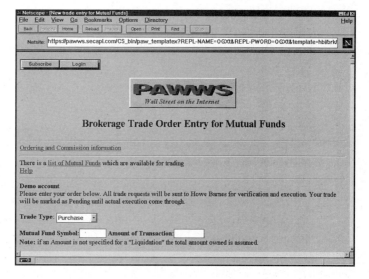

Quote.Com

If you're continually reviewing your financial position and you need up-to-the-minute details about your portfolio, you'll probably find Quote.Com (`http://www.quote.com/`) an indispensable resource. Appearing on the Web in the last quarter of 1994, Quote.Com became an immediate sensation because of its range of services and because it was among the first services on the Web that wasn't actually free. You could get limited access to the full-service line-up for no charge, but if you wanted to get serious about tracking financial activity over the Web, you would pay on a monthly basis. Quote.Com's home page is shown in Figure 23.49.

FIGURE 23.49.

The Quote.Com home page, featuring a large clickable map with blanks for future services.

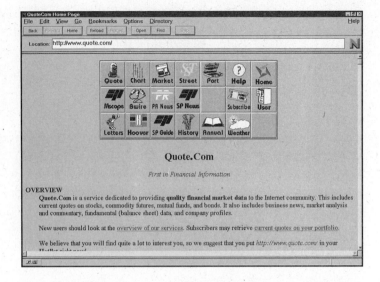

A free subscription entitles you to five quotes per day from a list of over 20,000 items on U.S. domestic exchanges. A $9.95 basic monthly subscription raises the number of daily quotes to 100 and provides you with some balance-sheet information for specific stocks. Another $14.95 gets you Standard and Poor's MarketScope; other subscriptions provide additional services. You can even get a Weather Subscription, which gives you trading advice based on weather reports from Freese-Notis.

Figure 23.50 displays the form used for the standard quote request. You can search for the ticker, futures, index, or street symbols if you don't know them, and you can track your portfolio only. Fill in the user name and password (established when you open your account), and Quote.Com will deliver your information immediately over the Web.

This is an important site that demonstrates some of the Web's potential for offering easy-to-use services and continually updated information.

Corporate Agents, Inc.

Corporate Agents (http://www.corporate.com/) is an example of a business service designed to appeal to small businesses or individuals wanting to start or expand a business. The purpose of the company is to help its clients incorporate. Incorporating is a good idea for many businesses for a variety of reasons, yet it's a process that, for the uninitiated, seems awash in legal technicalities. What makes Corporate Agents' site an especially clever one is that it uses the democratizing effect of the Internet as a way of illustrating its point that incorporating is neither all that difficult nor necessarily all that expensive. In other words, it's a service that seems especially suited to the Net itself, which has thousands of small-business or would-be small-business users.

FIGURE 23.50.

*Quote.Com's fill-in
form for quotes.*

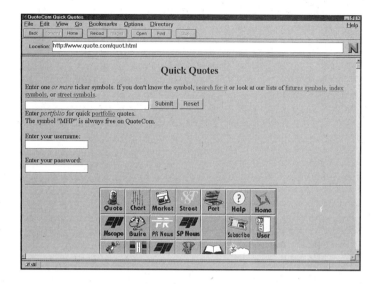

The home page is sparse but easy to follow, although the logo should probably be redone for Web purposes. The crucial links for many users are called Why Incorporate and Incorporation Fees, and these are nicely emphasized right up front.

You can order the company's actual products: "corporate kits" that, although you do not order them over the Web itself. The page's image is taken from the middle of the page, and it shows a picture of the kit and a bulleted list of what's in the kit. It would be a good idea if some of the items themselves were given a fuller explanation (or perhaps a link to a separate information page).

Graphics Visualization and Usability Center

Although sparsely developed at this stage, we can expect more from the Graphics Visualization and Usability Center (`http://www.cc.gatech.edu/gvu/user_surveys/survey-09-1994/`) in the future. We can also expect similar sites to pop up across the Net. What business continually needs is detailed demographic information so that it can track and target potential customers, and because of its chaotic nature, the Internet does not easily yield such information. This lab's home page offers a very brief look at who's using the Net, and although it's only very generally useful, it provides some insights on its own. (The relatively small percentage of users in the 36–50 age range strikes me as extremely odd.)

Clearly, this is interesting material. Just as clearly, business needs much more of it, and in much finer detail, across a much larger range of sampling categories. While not constituted as a business service *per se*, this center's Web offerings demonstrate the need for such sites. It's also an intelligent site; from this graph alone, the center is likely to receive consulting requests from major clients, and that's something many centers and labs are looking for. In other words, this page might act as a teaser for business users to contact the center and contract for more information.

Municipality-Based Business Pages

We've seen a virtual downtown on the Web, so why not a real one? One subcategory of the industrial mall is the municipality-based collection of business sites, of which several are now appearing on the Web. While it's true that shopping on the Web doesn't require users to know where they are geographically (that's one of its pluses), the idea behind presenting information about businesses in real communities is that the business dollar is still very much geographically based. In some cases, these municipality-based sites offer travelers a look at what they can expect when they visit that location. The site also shows businesses who their corporate neighbors will be if they move there.

Keep in mind that one of the most significant municipal tasks is to attract new business. As more and more businesses develop an Internet presence, it makes good sense for municipalities to attract these businesses by demonstrating that the municipality has a strong business environment. That might be a big factor in a firm's decision to move to one location rather than another.

Businesses in Utah

Utah doesn't immediately spring to mind when you're thinking of major business states, so the Businesses in Utah site (`http://www.utw.com/UtahBusi.html`) makes a great deal of sense. The home page shows that the state's businesses are aware of the Net and have developed at least some Web presence, although some of the explanations could be expanded for more immediate interest. Still, one of the links is to the world-famous WordPerfect Corporation, and this is an obvious place to start browsing.

There are many WordPerfect pages available. One, for example, is an information page for users of WordPerfect for UNIX. (One of the strong design touches is the 3-D buttons at the top of the page.) This page is nothing more than a product information document—there are no patches or bug-fixes available—but it's useful in demonstrating what other information WordPerfect provides. Expect this site to improve dramatically in the near future.

One company can gain presence by being associated on the Web with a large company. Appearing with WordPerfect on the Utah business home page is a local Orem company, Computer Recyclers. Although the logo could be better scanned, it's attractive, and the large links are clear and unambiguous. The fact that a browser on the Utah page can switch from a large corporation to a small local business makes Web presence a particularly attractive proposition for the latter.

Quadralay Corporation, Austin, Texas

Some states have taken a far stronger initiative than others in getting the information superhighway up and running, and Texas is one of the most aggressive. Among the most noteworthy Net sites in the state is the one for its capital, Austin (`http://www.quadralay.com/www/Austin/Austin.html`), developed by Quadralay Corporation and sporting some of the most interesting business-related information on the Net.

The Austin home page has links to information about universities, the county, and the state capital, and with a well-structured set of links to a wide variety of businesses, organizations, and interests further down the page.

One of the links leads to the Austin Business page has more than the usual assortment of information. Central to this page, of course, are the companies that have developed an Internet presence, but this page also features organizations "dedicated to helping Austin-based businesses," an important consideration for any firm browsing the Web and thinking of making a move.

Also available here are details about Austin's economy and employment possibilities. Another link offers information about the Texas Capital Network, which provides a very clear indication of how actively Austin is seeking to attract new businesses into the area. This is a very well-developed site and one that is frequently updated. It's probably the best example on the Web of a municipality's support of its business community.

Explorer's Check

Even from the small sampling of business and commerce sites presented in this chapter, it's easy to see the potential of Web-based commerce, whether from the standpoint of customer service or for full-scale product browsing and ordering.

The next year will see an explosion of commercial activity on the Web, as businesses in greater numbers come to realize the Web's potential for advertising, marketing, public relations, and sales.

Niche products and services, international business ventures, and fully developed support sites will spring up continually in 1995 and beyond, to the extent that we will find ourselves doing business on the Web in ways that we can scarcely begin to envision now.

The Web isn't likely to replace many existing business venues, but it will certainly add to the potential means of conducting global and local commerce. As a resource, it's simply too large and too cheap for the business sector to ignore.

Entertainment and the Arts

24

by
Neil Randall
and
Carrie Pascal

This chapter, if truly unleashed, would be huge, unruly, and guilty of some of the sheer frivolity and silliness that characterizes some of the entertainment and arts activity on the Web itself. Presented in the next few pages is a glimpse, *and only a glimpse*, of the extraordinary variety of fascinating sites accessible through even casual browsing, a variety that is increasing with each passing week. At the rate the category of Entertainment and the Arts is growing, there's almost no doubt that future editions of this book will be forced to split them into two categories. As it is, they're shoehorned into one, and the two are growing a tad displeased with one another's company.

Still, in many ways they belong together, and no less on the Web than in real life. In real life (whatever that is, exactly), many people turn to the arts for entertainment, and the arts find themselves increasingly in the position of having to entertain to stay alive. On the flip side, the entertainment industry depends on the arts for many of its ideas, much of its validity, and no small portion of its leading personnel.

On the Web, the arts sites and the entertainment sites are linked by the fact that they represent the Web's most creative efforts. Yes, you can find some superbly designed sites in the other chapters in this book, and all throughout the Web, but if you want to experience the true potential of the Web, turn to the entertainment and/or arts sites and work your way through them. Besides, they're fun and sometimes even educational, something that computers should try to achieve more often.

Still, there's a problem. The first edition of this book stated that, so far, very little is available on the World Wide Web that isn't available on other media, and in better formats. Despite the huge number of arts and entertainment sites that have appeared on the Web over the past eight or nine months, that criticism still holds. Collections of great art dot the Web, but nothing available so far even begins to approach the pleasure of visiting a museum, paging through a well-designed art book, or experiencing similar collections on CD-ROM. The Web should be a place for artists to congregate and display their works in progress, but even this has barely begun to occur (at times for obvious reasons of financial exigency, but not always). And where, it might be asked, is the Net's great promise of collaboration, something we might expect to be rampant? It's out there, as this chapter will show, but in very small doses.

And so with entertainment. Although the Web allows the kind of interesting, "on the site" activity that occurred during the Woodstock '94 festival, then during subsequent festivals and even over the MBONE with the Rolling Stones, too few entertainment designers have shown true creativity—true design excellence—in what they have to present. Several interesting archives exist, and many things on the Web are entertaining without necessarily meaning to be so, but in very few places are we seeing the kind of around-the-world, join-in-the-fun type of activity that seems so natural for a global network. Where are the creative and inventive games? Where are the contests, the trivia diversions, the collaborative ventures, the coffee-shop chats, the next-to-live bands? Where are the plays we might visit, the books we might interact with, the...well, you get the idea.

What's a bit mystifying about all of this is that artists and entertainers have always been among the first to bend technology precisely to their needs and wants. The arts often venerate the past, but artists fully realize that new technologies allow them to make their statements, construct their worldviews, offer their insights, or simply display their talents in a host of new ways. The entertainment industry has historically taken any promising technology and similarly co-opted it for the sake of mass interest, a tendency of which television is only the most obvious example. (It was originally supposed to be of primary interest to educators, let's remember.)

This is not to say there isn't a significant commitment to entertainment and the arts on the Web today; it's a suggestion, instead, that the efforts so far have been surprisingly conservative, backward-glancing, and tentative. If you're an entertainer or an artist and you're reading this right now, consider this a plea to use the Net to its fullest. You have a point to make, and there's now a new way of making that point. And many of us around the world are glued to the set, waiting.

It's safe to say by this time in mid-1995 that the World Wide Web has demonstrated a very strong potential for entertainment and arts designers and aficionados alike. But there's still too little that's truly dazzling to keep us actively tuned to new sites. What's apparent, however, is that all this is about to change. Activity on the Web has begun to reach the critical mass necessary for an artistic and/or entertainment revolution of sorts, and we can expect this to happen over the next year. Like business, entertainment and the arts are about to go over the edge. Somewhere. Somehow.

For now, we have a huge selection of everything from very bad to very, very good. Here we look at only a tiny sample, because this book, unlike the Web, has a page limit.

The Arts Projects

Any number of ways present themselves for detailing information on the Web about the arts. We could start with a guided tour of the museums and the archives, or we could launch immediately into a display of some of the Web's more interesting "weirdness." Instead, we'll head somewhere in between, opting for a good beginning collection of activity and moving outward.

ANIMA

One of the best sites for beginning an Internet arts expedition is found in *ANIMA*, an acronym for the Arts Network for Integrated Media Applications. Part of the often-creative `wimsey.com` series of pages out of Vancouver, ANIMA offers not only resources of its own, but a solid basis for further exploration. Figure 24.1 shows part of the ANIMA home page (`http://wimsey.com/anima/ANIMAhome.html`), with colorful links to a range of fascinating (and not-so-fascinating) material.

FIGURE 24.1.

The ANIMA home page, leading to a number of different artistic sites.

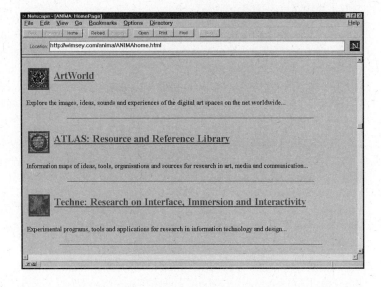

The links, in fact, are ANIMA's real strength. All links are to other pages on `wimsey.com` and demonstrate how committed this site is (or at least has been) to scouring the Web in search of items of artistic and artistic/theoretical interest. The first significant link is to ArtWorld, a highly personalized page—in many ways clumsily and even unattractively designed—that provides a huge range of options for the artistic traveler. One such page of links is shown in Figure 24.2; we'll visit a few of these links later. Although this page has little to recommend it from the standpoint of sheer design (perhaps ironically, given its origins), it demands recognition through its function as gateway to the Web's artistic wonders and blunders.

FIGURE 24.2.

A series of artistic links from the pages of ArtWorld.

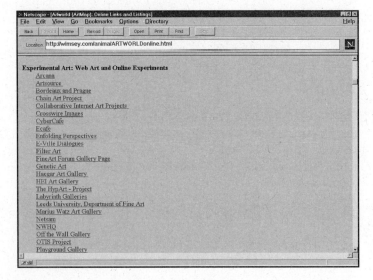

Yet another ANIMA subpage is *ATLAS*, the Arts and Technology Resource and Reference. The issues raised here deal with the importance of technology to the arts, and also, of course, with the problems that accompany the association. From links to sites and essays dealing with the electronic media, electronic literature, computer interfaces, and technology and social issues, this site can commandeer hours of your reading time. Figure 24.3 shows links to some of these issues. A page that is somewhat similar, and just as interesting, is the link to Techne: Interface, Immersion and Interactivity Research.

Finally in ANIMA, we have *NEXUS: Network Projects by Artists*. Although this page (see Figure 24.4) isn't anywhere near as full of exciting and inspiring art projects as you'd hope, what appears at this site is precisely the kind of activity the Web needs much more of from the artistic community. Here we see artists at work, displaying what they've done and what they've found themselves capable of doing by using the technology. They comment on the technology, demonstrate collaborative approaches, and so on; here, again, you could spend a good deal of time. Not all of this is well-designed, but that's not exactly the point. It's ideas we're after here, and ideas we get—even if some of them are off a bit into left field.

FIGURE 24.3.

Part of the ATLAS home page.

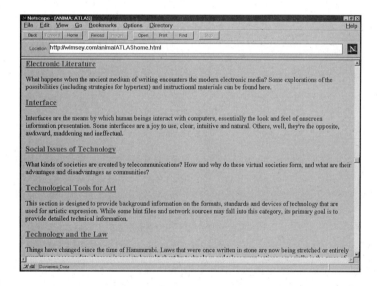

FIGURE 24.4.

Some of the projects in the NEXUS home page.

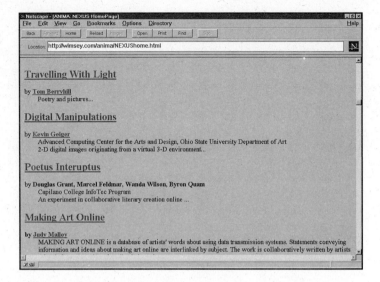

The real criticism of ANIMA is that it doesn't change often enough. Even so, from here you can see the arts on the rest of the Web, so at the very least it's an excellent place to begin.

The OTIS Project

Coming to us from the well-known `sunsite.unc.edu` site is the OTIS Project, an online gallery and collaboration project (`http://sunsite.unc.edu/otis/otis.html`). *OTIS* stands for Operative Term Is Stimulate, and for the most part that's exactly what it does. Some of the material isn't worth a repeat visit, but that applies to all galleries, digital or physical. What's important is that the project is going on, and that it seems to be thriving quite well. OTIS's home page (see Figure 24.5) shows the obvious artistic bent of its contributors (each of the bars represents a separate page or series of pages). For those with slower connections, the OTIS directory is available without inline images at `http://sunsite.unc.edu/otis/schmotis.html`.

The first link from the home page takes us to the OTIS Gallery. Here we find nothing but a long list of links to further pages (see Figure 24.6), but what a list! Pick a medium, any medium, and see what the gallery has to offer. For me, Morphs, Jewelry, Math-art, and Collaborations were must-sees; I only wish this page offered a better indication of what lies behind each link. In the case of jewelry, for instance, no artwork existed at all, and the same held true for morphs; there was, however, an invitation to submit your own art for the category, which is, after all, the point. And the etchings link, like the paintings link and others, takes you to a collection of JPEG and GIF files available for downloading, but nowhere is there a guide to the size of these files. Trust me; they're not small. Still, a few hours spent downloading some selected items will give you a very strong collection, and this is only one site on the Net.

FIGURE 24.5.

The OTIS Project home page.

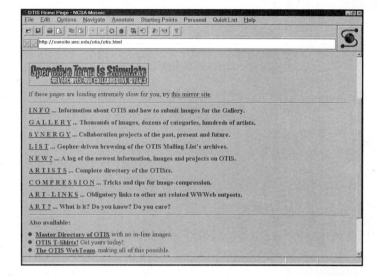

FIGURE 24.6.

The various media from the OTIS Gallery.

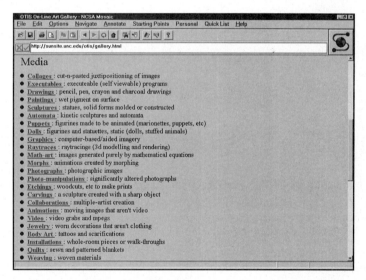

Perhaps the most interesting area of the OTIS site is the collection of collaborative art projects called Synergy. The purpose behind the project is, as its home page points out (see Figure 24.7), exactly what the Net should be good for. One person starts a picture/drawing/construction, usually by offering an overall concept with very little detail, and anyone from the Net is free to add to the overall idea or contribute details or even offshoots. Eventually the picture is completed, at which time another picture on the same theme is begun, or the artists start another Synergy project entirely. So far, the results have ranged—predictably—from the bizarre through the terrible and the intriguing, but the idea itself remains continually appealing.

FIGURE 24.7.

The Synergy home page, with links to details about the collaborations.

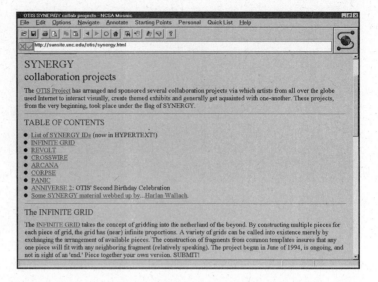

Using sheer morbidity as a guideline, let's look at one of the Synergy collaborations in a bit more detail. This one is called CORPSE, the idea being to assemble an entire corpse from body parts contributed by other artists. Figure 24.8 offers links to rules of contribution, thumbnail sketches, and (below the figure) to various attempts at corpse assembly. The results, which I've decided not to display in this chapter, are extremely mixed but always at least interesting.

FIGURE 24.8.

The CORPSE project from OTIS Synergy.

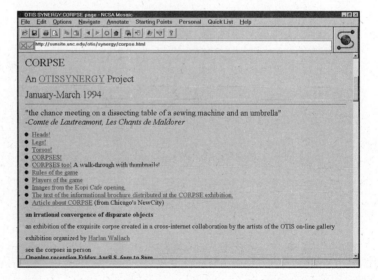

Kaleidoscope

Another project site for artists is Kaleidoscope (http://kspace.com/), whose home page (see Figure 24.9) is subtitled "Where Independent Artists Sell their Work to the World." In fact, a stroll through this site reveals that there are indeed pictures of works of art offered for sale; although no forms accompany the site, instructions exist for ordering. The most interesting design approach for the site, however, lies with its home page. A colorful, unusual, clickable "map" takes you to whichever section of the wheel you choose, and as you can see, the artistic possibilities are endless. As of this writing, however, some of the categories were underdeveloped.

Cyberkind

Another opportunity for collaborative art, or at least the unusual presentation of art, exists in the literary world. Figure 24.10 shows the home page for Cyberkind, subheaded "prosaics and poetics for a wired world." Here, as you might expect, are literary works of a variety of types, and one of the more attractive logos on the Web. The page is clear and well-designed, and if you have literary material of the kind this site is after, you should consider contacting the editor about submissions.

All sites of this kind offer extremely mixed reading (and viewing), but Figure 24.11 demonstrates the type of activity well-suited for Internet-based literary demonstration. "The Complex, Adaptive, Dynamic, Autocatalytic, Multicultural Hypertext Poem" is a title you won't easily find in your local bookstore, especially because the hypertextuality is important to this particular concept. For poets, in fact, the Web offers an opportunity to reach thousands more people than would normally buy a book of poetry anyway. Given the high price of printed books today, and the fact that almost nobody makes a living writing poetry, it wouldn't be surprising to see more poets start publishing on the Web. If the idea is experimentation, or simply an expanded audience, why not?

FIGURE 24.9.

The Kaleidoscope home page, with the clickable wheel.

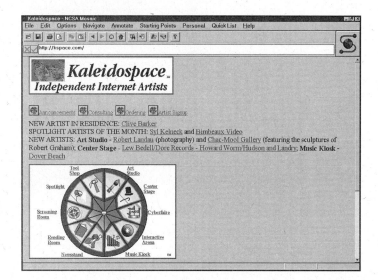

FIGURE 24.10.

Cyberkind's home page with guidelines for aspiring writers.

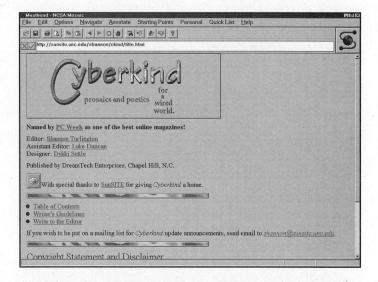

FIGURE 24.11.

One literary venture from the Cyberkind site.

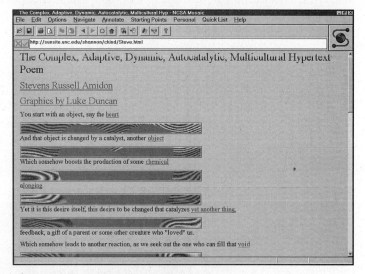

The Arts: Museums and Galleries

Of course, what would an arts medium be without galleries? Traditionally, galleries have benefited the arts community in one major way: They provide a place for works of art to be on permanent or temporary display to the public. Their assumption is that people will actually want to look at works of art, an assumption that appears to be correct, if the fact that many are still open is any indication. Galleries also provide a place (sometimes) for artists to present new works of art, and consequently a place where the public can watch for new artistic developments. The arts community has raging debates about the role of even real-world galleries, but those outside that community who are interested in art for any reason rarely question the galleries' usefulness, perhaps even necessity.

Each of the preceding project sites is also a gallery. Here, however, we'll look at the more traditional style of gallery: the art museum. In these galleries, each of which has a real-world counterpart (that is, an actual building) outside the Net, works are displayed not as a means to find additional contributors, but rather because either the artists are dead or, if still alive, their work is deemed of public interest (by the gallery, society, or whoever). The function of the World Wide Web in this context is to provide a means for users around the world to visit these galleries, albeit in a limited way. In fact, the online versions of some of these galleries operate essentially as an advertisement for the real galleries, a means of building awareness. For the first gallery discussed in this section, however, this isn't the case.

art gallery

Names don't get much less pretentious than this one, and in fact it nicely blends the contributors' gallery of the OTIS type with the traditional gallery of the Louvre type. (See the upcoming section, "The Louvre.") Maintained entirely by one person, as many Web galleries are, the art gallery (`http://heiwww.unige.ch/art/`) features a limited selection of works along with commentary, and the inevitable links to other art sites on the Web, as shown in Figure 24.12.

FIGURE 24.12.

The art gallery home page, with links to a variety of displays.

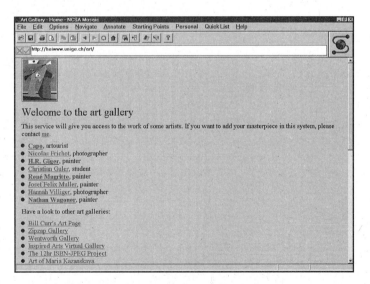

One of the links is to an exhibit of works by Rene Magritte, and here we see the impressive collection of holdings of this gallery. All of the links shown in Figure 24.13 (and this is only a portion of the full page) are to further pages that display the work of art and offer commentaries about it. Whereas the OTIS gallery offers downloadable graphics files, these are viewable on the Web itself, a solution that is instantly more attractive. The problem with downloads is that they demand external viewers (in most instances) and often hard disk space (even when they're not permanently stored), and they simply don't fit with the spirit of navigating and viewing that the Web offers. This is a good site.

FIGURE 24.13.

Links to the specific art works of Rene Magritte.

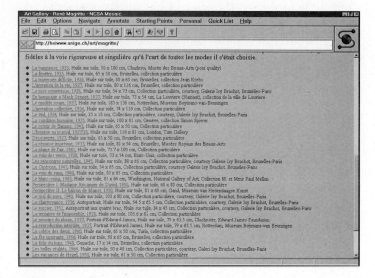

Krannert Art Museum

Our first real-world gallery is the Krannert Art Museum, physically located at the University of Illinois at Urbana-Champaign (which, perhaps not incidentally, is also the home of NCSA), and electronically available at

```
http://www.ncsa.uiuc.edu/General/UIUC/KrannertArtMuseum/KrannertArtHome.html
```

As Figure 24.14, the home page, makes clear, the function of the Krannert Web site is to introduce long-distance viewers to the museum and to offer a sampling of some of the treasures contained in the real building. A very sharp map of the museum is available, as well as an extremely useful list of educational resources.

Figure 24.15 shows a typical exhibit from the Krannert site. Here, three samples of the museum's collection of twentieth-century art are given (relatively) small representations, and clicking on the links downloads a larger version. Like the rest of the Krannert Museum, this is a well-designed page: clear, colorful, and highly accessible. The limited amount of information is actually a plus, because the tendency of Web pages is to cram rather than present. Still, having only three works on display is a bit disappointing and might have the negative effect of suggesting that the museum itself is poorly stocked.

FIGURE 24.14.

The Krannert Art Museum home page.

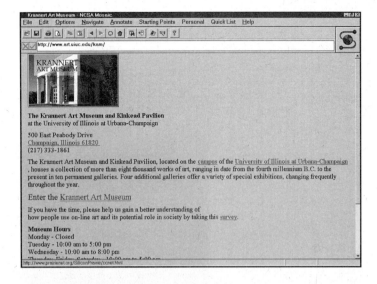

FIGURE 24.15.

The Twentieth-Century Art page from the Krannert Museum.

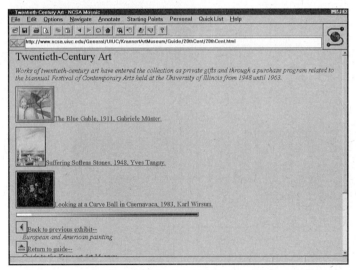

The Louvre

No art museum in the Western world has the prestige of the Louvre, and it's nice to see its presence on the Web (`http://www/cnam.fr/louvre/`). It's even nicer to see that the site is well-designed and maintained, because it would be wrong to expect anything less of an institution like this one. Of course, the nicest thing of all would be to be able to sit back and tour every item in every exhibit in every room of the real museum, something that wouldn't likely even make a dent in the potential attendance at the place. In fact, it might even entice visitors who wouldn't otherwise come to see it.

What we have in this site is a fractional sampling of the material available in the museum itself. Figure 24.16 is the home page, which clearly states that three exhibits are currently being offered. Of these, strangely enough, the tour of Paris might well be the most complete, but the two internal exhibits are at least worth seeing.

FIGURE 24.16.

The Louvre home page, with links to a tour of Paris.

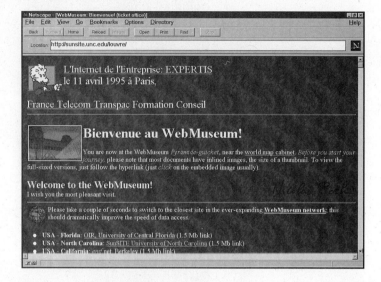

Figure 24.17 offers an introduction to the Famous Paintings exhibition. Again, a well-developed page with attractive and modem-friendly small inline graphics leads us in an uncluttered fashion through the offerings. This page demonstrates the importance of a clear and uncomplicated entrance to a Web site, and it's almost as if the Louvre knew something about building accessibility. At any rate, all items are appealing, but keep in mind that they're definitely limited in what they display thereafter.

A click on the Impressionism category leads to a small but worthwhile list of artists, including the Dutch painter/printmaker Johan Barthold Jongkind. Here is an example of the use of the Web to spur interest in an item that physically exists. One look at Jongkind's "The Church of Overschie," even at this size, makes you realize first that you have to see it in order to appreciate it fully; and second, that you want to see it to grasp what appears to be superb effects of color and texture. The text of the page—especially the French text—makes the real site all that much more appealing.

FIGURE 24.17.

The entry to the Famous Paintings exhibition at the Louvre.

FIGURE 24.18.

A sample work of art from the Jongkind display at the Louvre.

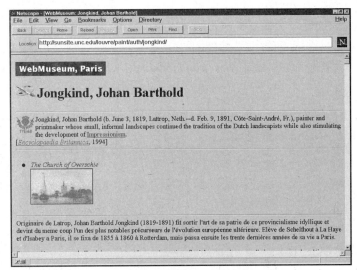

The Arts: Publications and Collections

There are so many arts-oriented sites on the Web worth visiting that it would require an entire book, rather than a single chapter, to capture them all, even at this early stage of the Web's career. Here we'll look at a sampling of other efforts, which I've lumped under the category Publications and Collections. These are indicative of the kind of material available for the diligent searcher, but I've not chosen them because they're necessarily representative. Right now, there's really no such thing as a representative collection of sites, because designers are putting forth a considerable effort to be creative and remain individualistic. Still, they demonstrate some important trends.

Verbiage—Short Fiction

Verbiage (`http://sunsite.unc.edu/boutell/verbiage/index.html`) is an electronic publication specializing in short fiction. A no-nonsense, easy-to-navigate site, it includes about 10 pieces of short fiction per issue. You can access either the current issue, or any back issue, although no actual dates are apparent. You also can submit fiction; a link from the Verbiage home page tells you how to do so. As for the material, it's very Generation X-ish. Many pieces seem ridden with angst and may leave you heavy of heart, although there are a few lighter pieces. If you find the content not to your liking (or if you find you can't devour it fast enough), you can mail comments to the authors with the click of a mouse button. These e-mails might appear along with the fiction, so make sure you want to send them, although inclusion is at the editor's discretion.

CBC Radio

The Canadian Broadcasting Corporation has a reputation for being anything but "with-it," but you wouldn't know it by looking at their Web site (`http://radioworks.cbc.ca`). Here we have not only information about the nationwide (in Canada) radio network, but also lists of products available for ordering and a link to a fascinating area called Illustrated Audio (a necessity if the Web is to fulfill its communicative potential). Figure 24.19 displays the CBC Radio home page, with links to specific tools that allow you to play audio files on your machine.

FIGURE 24.19.

The CBC Radio Trial home page.

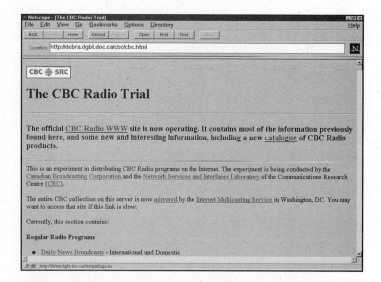

From the sample radio programs link on the CBC home page, you arrive at Figure 24.20, which offers links to several representative CBC programs. While several of these are of interest to many people (although admittedly The Idea of Canada might have limited appeal), the best-known of the bunch is unquestionably Quirks and Quarks, a science-explanation program. Clicking any of these links takes you to a page offering downloadable audio files, each containing a sample of a particular show. Some are several minutes long (and thus take an extremely long time to download), but others are shorter and more instantly accessible.

FIGURE 24.20.

Internal site page for CBC Radio pages.

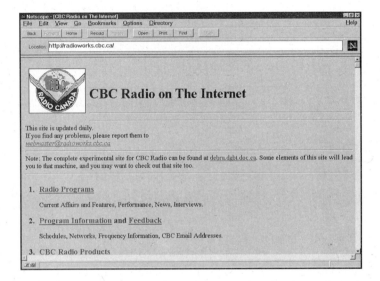

J.R.R. Tolkien

The next two sites demonstrate how one solitary fan of a given artist can simultaneously fuel a passion for that artist's works and make a huge amount of valuable information available to a worldwide community at the same time. Figure 24.23 (`http://www.lights.com/tolkien/rootpage.html`) is a truly impressive page, featuring links to just about anything you could possibly want to know about the author of *The Lord of the Rings* and a host of other material, and it clearly represents hundreds of hours of searching, compiling, and presenting.

Another fan site exists at (`http://www.cs.indiana.edu/hyplan/awooldri/Xanth.html`). Similar to the Tolkien pages, this site deals with the Xanth novels of Piers Anthony. It is somewhat less complete than the Tolkien site, but equally impressive in its display of sheer labor. In both cases, very clearly, that labor is a labor of love.

FIGURE 24.21.

The J.R.R. Tolkien home page, with links to newsgroups and many other sites.

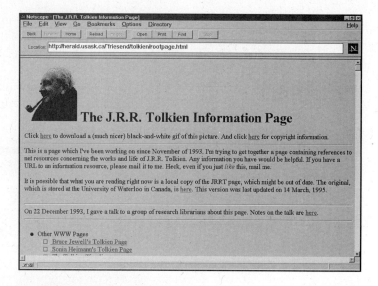

Entertainment: Television

Well, why not? Television and the World Wide Web are linked, of course, especially as the multimedia nature of the Web begins to kick in. Given enough bandwidth, and high enough speeds, the Web has the potential to become part of the promised interactive television technology that's been bandied about for the past several months, and I suspect it won't be an extremely long time before Web sites are used as supplemental activities for TV programs. Is there any doubt that right now, in 1995, a Web site that featured outtakes, fill-in episodes, trivia contests, and interviews with the cast members of *Melrose Place*, *Friends*, *ER*, or *Frasier* would be an immediate success? The age group is right, the familiarity with computers is right, and the Web is almost as hyped as the shows. Newsgroups about these and other shows—everything from *The Simpsons* through *My So-Called Life* and *Party of Five* and just about everything else— are already hugely popular, and they offer nothing but text and opinions.

Whether we'll see television-style programming over the Web, the way we're seeing magazine-style publishing, remains to be seen. Just don't be surprised, given the possibility of such ventures as the Internet Multicasting project, to find Web "stations" listed beside the real stations in the *TV Guide*. Not this year, certainly, but who knows what the latter half of this decade might bring? And who knows, additionally, whether the decade will be exciting or terrifying?

The Lurker's Guide to *Babylon 5*

Babylon 5 has garnered a loyal following partly because of its similarities to and important departures from *Star Trek*. As far as entertainment archive information is concerned, the Lurker's Guide to *Babylon 5* (`http://www.hyperion.com/lurk/lurker.html`) is probably the most impressive on the Web. The home page (see Figure 24.22) is clear and free of (often) unattractive lists, and it leaves no question of what's available on the site.

FIGURE 24.22.

The Babylon 5 home page.

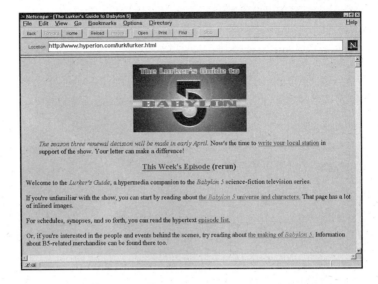

What the home page doesn't do is demonstrate the richness of what's behind the links, because any viewer (except the absolutely most knowledgeable) will find information he or she may not have known. Figure 24.23 displays a series of links that begin to show the amount of material available, and this, while enticing, isn't anywhere near the most attractive of the lot. Other pages offer pictures and information about the actors and their careers, and still other pages offer still other details about other aspects of the show—well worth examining if you're thinking of putting together a worthwhile archive. If nothing else, this site shows how much sheer work is involved.

FIGURE 24.23.

The Making of Babylon 5 page.

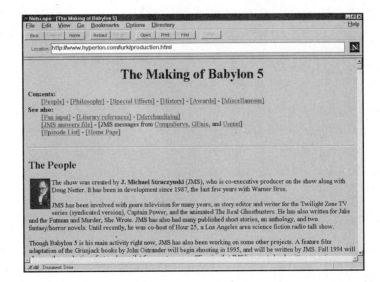

Star Trek: The Next Generation

And, of course, where would any self-respecting global network be without its requisite share of *Star Trek* material? Beginning with a (perhaps inevitable) picture of the *Enterprise*, the home page for *Star Trek: The Next Generation* (http://www.ee.surrey.ac.uk:80/Personal/STTNG/), shown in Figure 24.24, offers a clear structure and equally clear links. If you're a fan of the now-completed but forever-to-be-rerun series, or even if you're just a casual viewer or someone trying to construct a similar site, this one is worth visiting. One of the problems, however, is that there's surprisingly little good material on the Net about any of the *Star Trek*s, other than copious text files about aliens and starships and endless discussions about the possibilities of warp-factor travel and the like, and this site suffers in that way. But that's hardly its own fault.

FIGURE 24.24.

Star Trek: The Next Generation home page.

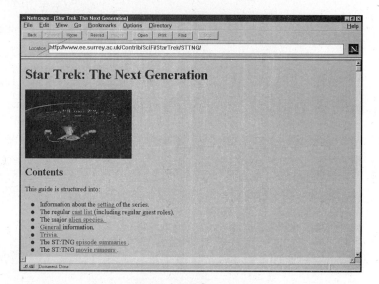

Star Trek Voyager

Star Trek material has been on the Internet since the beginning, and the popularity of the Next Generation series brought even more material. Lately, Paramount Pictures itself has been trying to capitalize on the *Star Trek* popularity, opening Web sites for the *Star Trek: Generations* movie (now closed) and, hardly unexpectedly, for the new series, *Star Trek Voyager*.

This effort, at http://voyager.paramount.com (and shown in Figure 24.25), takes you through an interactive voyage with the USS *Voyager*. You start off as an amnesiac visitor awakened in Sick Bay by the Emergency Holographic Doctor, who tells you that you must learn about the USS *Voyager* in order to recover. To do so, make use of your PADD—Personal Access Display Device (hey, is this legitimate *Star Trek* terminology?), which can be activated in graphics mode or, for those with a slow connection (or little patience), in text mode.

Keep weaving, and you'll learn about the latest *Voyager* mission (that is, this week's episode), Starfleet personnel, the *Voyager*'s technical details, and so on. And, of course, you're only cured after you've visited every site at the link.

A nice example of promoting a TV show over the Web, and one that'll make you wish we all had faster connections to the Net so we could be given even more.

FIGURE 24.25.

Home page for the official Star Trek Voyager site.

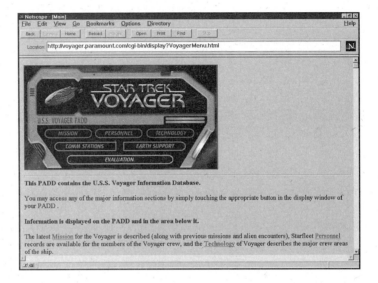

FOX Broadcasting

The Fox network might take its lumps, but it has some of the most frequently watched shows of all by what's known as the "Gen-X" crowd: *Beverly Hills 90210, Melrose Place, The X-Files, The Simpsons, Animaniacs,* and so on, they're all the rage on college and university campuses around North America. And here we have it: a Fox Broadcasting site (`http://www.eden.com/users/my-html/fox-list.html`). It's not an "official site" (one developed by Fox), but at this point few sites are. Like most, this one's constructed by a fan, and like most it represents hours of devoted work. If you're a fan of Fox programming in general, you'll spend more time than you can afford seeing what's here. The home page, shown in Figure 24.26, offers links to several Fox programs.

This site isn't much to look at; because it is so widely accessed, its author removed the graphics that once accompanied each show's title in order to economize on retrieval time. However, it's still a great archive, and much faster if you access it in the middle of the night.

FIGURE 24.26.

Web page from a fan of Fox's TV line-up.

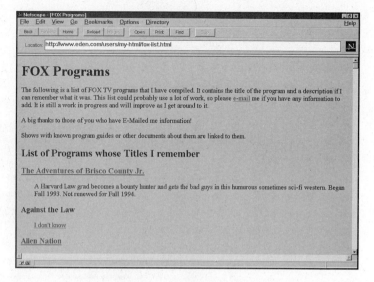

Who knows which Fox program is the most popular among these, but The X-Files page (see Figure 24.27), at `http://www.rutgers.edu/x-files.html`, is as richly detailed as any being offered. In addition to a sound icon that lets you hear the program's theme music, there's an episode guide, a FAQ, two FTP sites, a collection of related art and fiction, a survey, and fan club information. The page is indicative of many fan pages in demonstrating that you're likely to meet people with common interests all over the Net, and any *X-Files* fan will find at least some happiness here.

FIGURE 24.27.

Fan home page for The X-Files.

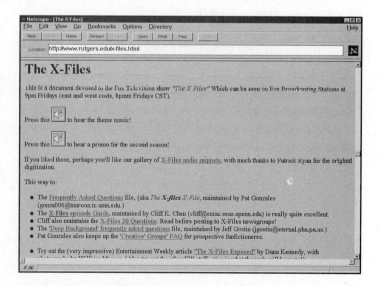

The Simpsons

Of course—it had to happen. America's favorite TV family, now the Web's favorite TV family, none other than the four-fingered, blue-haired (some), Springfield dwellers are featured in *The Simpsons* page, at `http://www.digimark.net/TheSimpsons`. The site (shown in Figure 24.28), although well-designed overall, requires a substantial amount of surfing to uncover some of its best qualities. The home page contains the expected information, such as episode summaries and character sketches, but it would have been nice to see other favorite details, such as "Stupid Homer Quotes," "Bart's Crank-Call Names," and "Famous Voices that have Guest Spoken on The Simpsons." A show like this—replete with subtle humor and intertexts—deserves an equally well-thought-out site, and this isn't quite it. However, the site is continually updated to include links to other Simpsons sites on the Web, none of which is all things to all fans, but when taken together satisfy most requirements.

In the meantime, this site provides additional interesting information on its own, including, under Guides and Lists, a link to a Detailed Floor Plan of the Simpsons' Household. Here you can discover that the Simpsons' home is architecturally impossible (or at least that it's sometimes modified through the practice of artistic license). Also available is information regarding an ongoing debate about the actual location of Springfield, which is, after all, one of the most common city names in the USA (and which is also probably the point). If you're a Simpsons fan, there's lots on the Net to choose from, and this page isn't a bad place to start.

But set your sights there quickly. Fan sites are under almost continual threat from the official owners of the products being featured, and by the time you read this, the Simpsons site and several others might no longer be around.

FIGURE 24.28.

The Simpsons Archive home page.

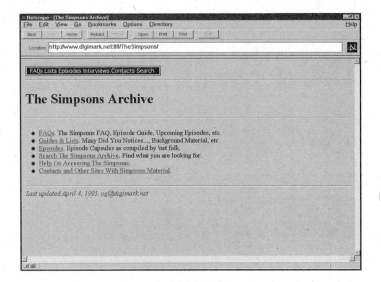

Entertainment: Movies

Movies survived the onslaught of television and are starting to capture this new medium (the Web) as well. An increasing number of sites are featuring movie databases, fan support, actor information, and so forth, for movies both past and present. The Web seems to be a natural place for this activity to occur, because movie fans tend to be more active than television fans, (movie fans usually have to leave the house to see or rent the flick of their choice), and the Web promotes activity as well. Movie fans also tend to crave additional information about their favorite films, actors, or directors, perhaps even more than fans of other media.

Cardiff's Movie Database Browser

Undoubtedly one of the most extensive and well-thought-out sites on the web, Cardiff's Movie Database Browser can be found at `http://www.cm.cf.ac.uk/Movies/`. The site is in need of some redesign, so read it carefully to make sure you're clicking in all the right places, but from the standpoint of content it's phenomenal (it's shown in Figure 24.29).

You can search on just about anyone or anything in the television/movie industry; whether you choose titles, actors, directors, or dates, you'll probably end up with more information than you bargained for. For example, try a title search on *Silence of the Lambs*. You'll learn its year of release (1991), genre (thriller serial killer/psychoanalysis), filming location (Pittsburgh), running time (118 minutes), and predecessor (*Manhunter*, made in 1986, a.k.a. *Red Dragon: The Pursuit of Hannibal Lecter*). You'll also be provided with a point-and-click interface to information on all the movie's cast members and production staff (check out Jodie Foster's bio: It's superb). Still thirst for more? Also available are the plot summary, quotes from the script (like Dr. Lecter's famous, "I'm having an old friend for dinner"), movie trivia, soundtrack information, and reviews from the newsgroup `rec.arts.movies`.

FIGURE 24.29.

A sample page from the Cardiff Movie Database.

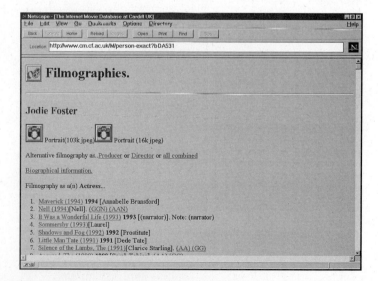

If that isn't enough, you get a chance to vote for any movie you want in a variety of categories (see Figure 24.30); an entire ratings database is maintained in these packages of the combined and ongoing ratings of all users. You could easily spend hours on the ratings system alone, both contributing to it and reading it, and if you're a movie fan you'll find this place endlessly fascinating. Don't access it right before a pressing appointment.

FIGURE 24.30.

The voting form from the Cardiff Movie Database.

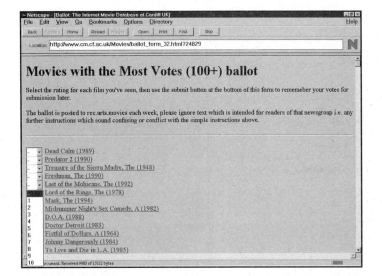

Entertainment: Sports

Not surprisingly, several Web sites offer sports-related pages. During the 1994 World Cup, an official site offered advance information such as schedules and ticket availability, and during the course of the tournament, updates were available as well. This was also the case during the 1994 Winter Olympics in Lillehammer, Norway, with an official Norwegian site featuring medal results and standings, graphics, and news material about the games. Look for a huge amount of detailed Web-based information about the 1996 Summer Games in Atlanta as well. This is only natural for events such as these; they appeal to all the world, and that's what the Internet attracts.

But there's room on the Web for more than just worldwide interests. The New York Rangers have a home page, as do several other sports clubs, and the Canadian Football League (which has now expanded into U.S. cities) also has an official site. There's no reason for minor leagues and minor teams not to have sites as well, as the cost of renting Web space is extremely small considering the benefits that a well-maintained site can offer in public relations and fan information. Statewide or interstate competitions could benefit as well; the name of the game is getting the word out and offering interested people continual updates on what's transpiring. In the case of major sports events, such as the World Cup, the European Cup, the Super Bowl, the Stanley Cup playoffs, or the World Series, Web sites can help maintain fan enthusiasm and satisfy fan obsession.

World Wide Web of Sports

The World Wide Web of Sports (`http://tns-www.lcs.mit.edu/cgi-bin/sports`) offers links to a variety of professional and amateur sports. As the home page (see Figure 24.31) shows, the format is brief but clear, and the information provided useful but hardly mesmerizing. Being able to get video highlights from yesterday's basketball games requires two things—a high-speed Internet connection and the actual playing of basketball games—and it would be nice to have full box scores and revised rosters.

FIGURE 24.31.

The NBA Basketball section of the World Wide Web of Sports page.

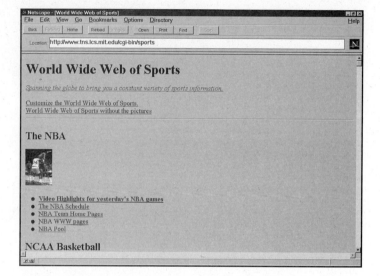

One of the more interesting features in this site is shown in Figure 24.32. Here, you can create your own HTML page that bypasses links to sports you're simply not interested in. This is interactive webbing at its height, allowing you not just to bookmark the pages you want to visit but in fact to change the ones you find. Expect more of this from similar sites in the future.

FIGURE 24.32.

The Create Your Own Sports Page site.

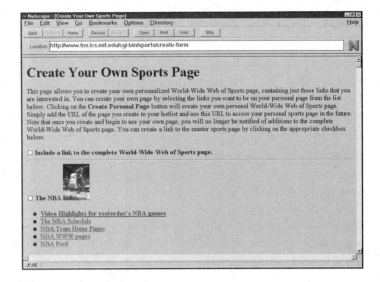

Entertainment: Music

It stands to reason that the World Wide Web is becoming a hot resource for information about music of all kinds. Music is, after all, a primary interest for many people, and among one specific category of Web users—university and college students—it is often the primary pasttime as well. Music lovers have formed mini-communities on the Net in the form of newsgroups, and now the Web takes the possibilities to even greater levels.

Newsgroups, after all, are mostly discussion. The Web, however, offers multimedia. For music fans, this means not only text, but graphics, sound, and video as well. Music sites offer information about new, upcoming, and established artists, bands, and even symphonies, but they offer much more than just written information. At many sites you can view and download photographs, and at a growing number of others you can click on (or download) sound files containing samples of the artist's work. There's no reason clips of videos can't be included as well, and we can expect to see these very soon.

What's new since the first edition of this book is the establishment of Web pages by the recording companies themselves. Sony, Warner Brothers, Geffen, and others have sites, designed—as you would expect—to help sell their artists' work. But the main attraction to the Web for music fans tends to be the sites created by fans of the artists, because here we see a much more "real" giving of information and ideas. These abound, and their quality is often unexpectedly high.

The Classic CD Home Page

Music lists abound on the Web, with compilations of the latest CDs, the best American CDs, the best country albums of all time, John Doe's personal favorite collection, African tribal beats—the list goes on. But many of these pages are simply a bunch of titles thrown together in a text file, and, generally, copyright protection prohibits the page maintainers to allow you to listen to any clips. But a growing number of high-quality music pages exist, and they're not hard to find.

If you're a fan of classical music, have a look at the Classic CD home page, shown in Figure 24.33 (`http://www.futurenet.co.uk/music/classiccd.html`). This page, of course, includes a list of "The Best of Classical Music," but also contains more interesting features, such as a beginner's guide to classical music and an extensive history of classical composers, ranging from medieval times through the Renaissance and Restoration periods, right up to the contemporary era. You can also read about the popularization of classical music such as the use of classical compositions in television commercials, so the next time you're watching a car commercial and you want to know where the music came from, you'll have a place to find out.

The Classic CD Home page is, in fact, a subset of the Futurenet pages, another interesting site to visit (`http://www.futurenet.co.uk/index.html`). This online service, provided by the British magazine-publishing company Future, offers several Web zines, covering material such as music (hence Classic CD), computing, video games, outdoor activities, and crafts.

FIGURE 24.33.

The Classic CD home page.

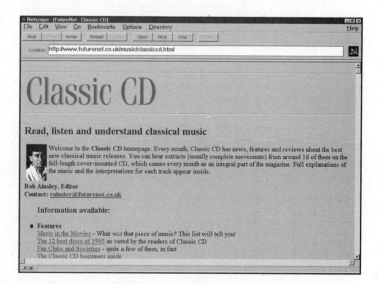

The Rolling Stones

To drum up a bit more interest in their 1994 Voodoo Lounge tour, Mick and the boys sat down at their 386 clones and cranked out some HTML code for the world to see (they were going to hire someone, but their bank accounts have been dipping into the low hundred-millions lately). The result is the Stones' official Web site shown in Figure 24.34 (`http://www.stones.com`)— "official" meaning that the site can offer Stones paraphernalia for a price, and can use Stones logos without getting into trouble. This site boasts a *lot* of tongues. Everywhere you look, there seems to be an image of a tongue, so if you're queasy about these organs, you might want to turn inline images off when you head in this direction. Then again, you already knew that about the Stones.

The site also contains some useful information. Tour dates for 1995 are included (although no one has gotten around to deleting the '94 dates), you can hear sound samples from the Voodoo Lounge collection (assuming your computer can play sound), and you can link to a set of pictures, although many of the faces are unrecognizable and the images take a long time to download. Two features in the works include a contest to win Stones merchandise (we're hoping to see a Charlie Watts Reclining Rocker and a Keith Richards Wrinkle Remover), and a link to actual live concert footage. This latter item is interesting: The Stones did a short live set over the Web in 1994, making use of the technologies known as MBONE, but you needed some very expensive equipment and access to see it. With the coming of higher-speed ISDN lines and faster multimedia computers, more of this kind of activity will start to appear.

FIGURE 24.34.

The official Rolling Stones home page.

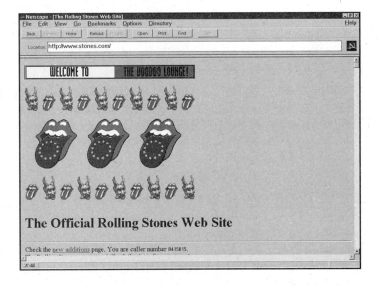

Internet Underground Music Archive

The Internet Underground Music Archive (`http://www.iuma.com/`) has received a considerable amount of press already, but a quick look at what's available here will demonstrate that the attention is worthwhile. The home page, displayed in Figure 24.35, shows the various buttons you can select, including information about live broadcasts over the Net itself. The Music Archive is devoted to the presentation of independent bands, and as a result it's an excellent place to keep in touch with the "real" music that's happening in the world of rock and blues.

FIGURE 24.35.

The Internet Underground Music Archive home page, with links to bands and labels.

The live broadcasts are available only over the MBONE, for which you need an extremely high-speed connection and, typically, a good UNIX workstation. But you can keep in touch with the events by logging onto the site, so if you're interested you won't miss anything crucial. Figure 24.36 shows a page with broadcast information.

So what can you get through the IUMA? Tons, as it turns out. This site has sponsorship from high-powered computer and music companies, to the degree that it's able to offer information and even samples from a wide range of labels and artists. And not only can you download parts of songs, you can get entire songs and, in the case of the Quagmire label, there's even a full 16-song album available for download, in either excerpt or complete song format. Of course, the entire album means about 50MB of downloading (don't try this at 14.4Kpbs or slower), but you're doing it song by song so it's not such a bad thing. What a superb idea, though, for those who consider buying new material once in a while but are unsure about what's good.

FIGURE 24.36.

IUMA information about a particular live MBONE broadcast.

Entertainment: Games and Interactivity

If there's one area where the Internet has been surprisingly weak, that would be the games department. Yes, MUDs (Multi-User Dialogs, text adventure games available through telnet) are a fact of Internet life, but although some people find them addicting and some designers are using them for very worthwhile purposes, they hold utterly no appeal for a wide range of users. One reason is that they're text-only (with a few very limited exceptions), and in a world of colorful, highly graphical computer games this is less than acceptable. Anyone who's spent even 20 hours a year for the past three years trying out even one hot new game each time knows that text games aren't even available any more. Graphics, sound, and full multimedia are the hot ticket items, and gamers will settle for nothing less.

Obviously, the Web is too young and too slow to offer anything approaching even the most rudimentary graphic games. It's not too young or too slow to offer interactive gaming, but there's virtually nothing available. This is surely a resource (both creative and financial) just waiting to be mined.

In the meantime, the Web has proven adept at offering support for players of existing games, and at least a couple of examples of interactive fiction. A few examples are explored here.

Fantasy and Other Role-Playing Games

If you're a role-playing fan, you'll want access to this extremely attractive gaming page (`http://www.acm.uiuc.edu/duff/index.html`). As the home page demonstrates (see Figure 24.37), the site offers pointers to items of interest to players of AD&D and other role-playing games, including

information and archives about mailing lists and newsgroups. The Boris Vallejo painting is a perfect attention-getter from this crowd—Vallejo is the artist against whom all other fantasy artists are judged—and the clear contents and purpose of the page make it highly accessible.

FIGURE 24.37.

The Fantasy and Other Role-Playing Games home page.

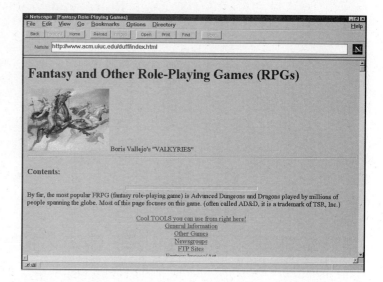

Of particular interest to those collecting the work of Vallejo and his colleagues is the Fantasy Art link. Figure 24.38 offers a very attractive group of sample graphics files that can be downloaded from one specific archive, with a pointer to a second. Also of interest to HTML designers is the designers' candid comments about the tribulations of trying to construct a useful page. Not only do the comments add to the personal element (important in hobby pages), they also encourage interaction.

FIGURE 24.38.

Fantasy Art page from the RPG site.

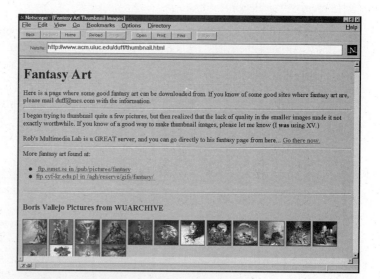

Myst and ShadowRun

Figures 24.39 and 24.40 show a recent trend on the Web that has the potential to be extremely useful to gamers. These pages offer support and guidance for players of two particular computer games, of the same nature found in the forums of online services such as GEnie or America Online. The Myst page (`http://www.best.com/~rdc/roger/myst.html`), in fact, operates as a mini-hint guide, and it's easy to see how a page like this could prove invaluable for those stuck at a particular point (in most adventure games, this happens at least two or three times). There's no money in it for the author, but there isn't for those who post hints and tips to the commercial online forums, either. That's not the point.

The Myst home page makes use of large font sizes for its main questions. Although the size is perhaps too large for good aesthetics, it more than accomplishes its goal of drawing attention to the purpose of the page and simultaneously avoiding the problem of too much white space on pages with limited content. The ShadowRun home page, shown in Figure 24.40, builds its appeal around the idea of comprehensiveness; anyone interested in the ShadowRun game (`http://www.ip.net/shadowrun`) will find this page a starting point to a variety of Internet activities.

FIGURE 24.39.

Home page for the popular Myst adventure game.

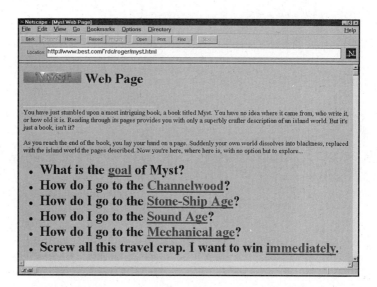

The value of pages like this is that they promote community among game players. Computer gaming by its nature (for now, at least) is a solitary activity, and there are so many games available that it's often difficult to find anyone nearby who plays the same game you do. But there's certain to be a group of people somewhere on the Net who share your interest, and these pages help you find them.

FIGURE 24.40.

Home page for resources about the ShadowRun game.

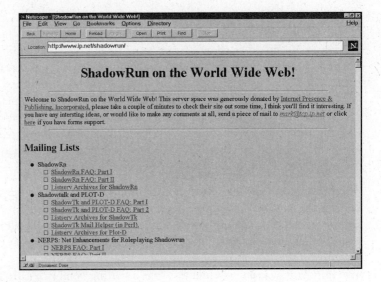

The Doomsday Brunette

Somewhere in our youth, most of us encountered the reading phenomenon known most popularly as "choose your own adventure." The idea was to read a page, then make a decision about what the character should do next. Instructions at the bottom of the page then told you what page to turn to, based on your decision, and the story proceeded from there. All in all, you'd make a few dozen decisions by the time the story ended, and if you ended up with an unsatisfying ending you just started over and decided differently.

Multiple-path novels found a new home with the Macintosh after the introduction of HyperCard. In fact, they proliferated. *The Doomsday Brunette* (`http://zeb.nysaes.cornell.edu/ddb.cgi`) is the same kind of novel, a hypertext-based multiple-path story found on the World Wide Web. Actually, as its author makes clear on the home page (see Figure 24.38), the full version of the story is available for download as an MS-Windows hypertext program, one that allows you to read through the first three chapters before asking for a few bucks to go on. (The beginning of Chapter 1 is shown in Figure 24.39.) Publishing this shortened version on the Web does two things: first, it gets readers hooked; second, it lets non-Windows users give it a try as well (and, presumably, they can ask that it be released for their own platform).

The importance of this endeavor is that it represents the kind of fiction that the Web makes entirely possible. Second, it represents a way for new authors to get published, without the huge barrier of going through a print publisher, who won't usually offer first-time authors anything approaching real money anyway. There's no reason why such a publishing venture couldn't be profitable, and it's a superb way of trying out experimental fiction.

FIGURE 24.41.

The Doomsday Brunette home page.

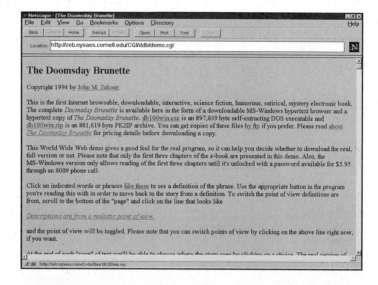

FIGURE 24.42.

Chapter 1 from The Doomsday Brunette.

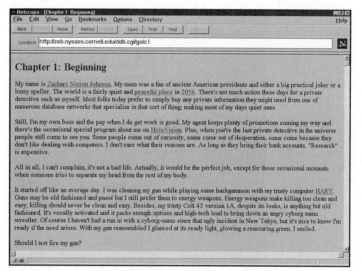

Entertainment: The Afterlife

Elvis lives! At least, he does on the Internet. The Elvis home page (`http://sunsite.unc.edu/elvis/elvishom.html`) was designed and is maintained by Andrea Berman, who has been quoted as saying she does *not* believe Elvis is alive (we know differently, don't we?), but thought it would be a neat idea to pay tribute to him with a home page. (See Figure 24.43.) The Elvis home page received considerable press when Elvis Presley Enterprises' lawyers sent Ms. Berman a letter warning her to remove the Graceland CyberTour component of the site immediately because of

copyright infringement (thereby proving that lawyers are indeed capable of learning new technologies if it means additional fees). Ms. Berman complied, and also posted a copy of the letter she received. You can link to the text version from the home page. As of early April 1995, you can also take another Graceland tour (just under the gun for inclusion in this book).

When you visit the page, be sure to jump to the guest book, which you can "sign" to indicate that you've visited. You can also view the doghaus Collection, (displayed in Figure 24.44)—a list (with accompanying images) of Elvis toiletries and souvenirs. The collection includes such memorabilia as Elvis salt-and-pepper shakers, Elvis cookbooks, Elvis shades (of only the "sunglasses" genus, unfortunately), and Elvis neckties. Apparently, Elvis sightings have appeared all over the Internet, and this page contains links to many of these as well. (There is, we want to make clear, no truth whatsoever to the rumor that Elvis himself has been posting to the `alt.cheeseburger` newsgroup. It's only an impostor… it's only an impostor…)

FIGURE 24.43.

The Elvis Presley home page, with the new Graceland tour.

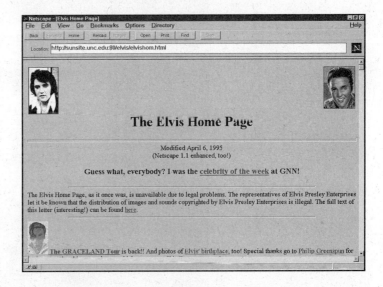

FIGURE 24.44.

The doghaus Collection, for those with too few Elvis items around the house.

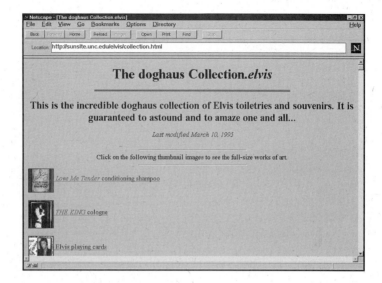

Creatures of the Night on the Vorld Vide Veb

This collection is designated "for vampyres only," but those of us who prefer grape juice can probably sneak a peak anyway. The site at `http://www.vampyre.wis.net/vampyre/index.html`, shown in Figure 24.45, offers a substantial amount of vampire-related information, trivia, and fiction. Puns abound—for example, you are told to check out "similar veins of interest" if you "thirst for more" than you have already seen. And you might want to take the two vampire tests, determining your vulnerability level—that is, the likelihood that you will have your neck bitten by a vampire—and your probability level (the likelihood that you might actually be a vampire). The site also hosts a collection of vampire stories; clicking a link called Walpurgisnacht will lead you to several not-so-pleasant tales, formatted into several hyperlinked chapters in an effort to mimimize scrolling. The Vampire Writings Index comprehensively lists vampire-related books, magazines, and anthologies, and the Vampire trivia section contains some interesting—albeit weird—information, such as diseases thought to be related to vampires. Even if Wimsey (who maintains the site) doesn't necessarily believe in vampires, this site makes a pretty convincing argument that they exist.

FIGURE 24.45.

Home page for Creatures of the Night on the World Vide Veb.

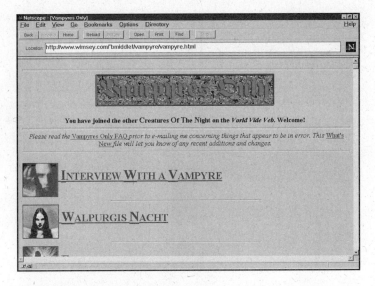

And if You're *Still* not Satisfied

This chapter has provided links to a substantial variety of pages dealing with entertainment and the arts, but you might well have different interests, and you're certainly going to want to discover your own sites. The Web, with its ever-increasing range of features, lets you do this. Two sites—the Roulette Wheel site and the Useless Pages site—provide further opportunities for you to "click'n'see."

The Useless Web Pages site (`http://www.primus.com/staff/paulp/useless.html`) was created by someone who thought that personal CD collection Web pages were useless, and who therefore compiled them into one big page (useful, huh?). The site gained so much popularity that people began submitting their own sites, asking the maintainer to include them for their uselessness. The site now hosts links to at least 100 pages, most of which really do question the Web's function. Currently, for example, you can link to a page that finds your birthday in the number pi; for instance, you enter 260173—day/month/year, and the site finds that sequence of digits in the infinite decimal places of pi. You can also select and vote for your favorite Ken doll hairstyle, view Dutch traffic signs, read about fish and whale regurgitation (no—really!), and return to your youth to play Ask the Magic 8-Ball. At the very least, visit this site when the pressure's getting to you.

For a more random (but only sometimes more useful) starting point for your surfing, try spinning the Web's roulette wheel at `http://kuhttp.cc.ukans.edu/cwis/organizations/kucia/uroulette/uroulette.html`). The site is simple, yet intriguing. Just click on the large roulette wheel (you can't miss it) and you will connect to a site randomly selected by the server. But beware: You might link to a site that no longer exists, or of course to an infinitely boring site, but you can always go back and try again. You may want to use this site outside of business hours; it takes quite a while even at the best of times, especially if it randomly takes you to a graphics-laden page. And no betting allowed, although that's something worth adding in the future. (Twenty bucks says my site takes longer to retrieve than yours.)

Explorer's Check

This has been a brief tour through a portion of the growing number of entertainment-related pages on the World Wide Web. The pages are indicative of the kind of entertainment activity occurring on the Web, and although you will be able to add several references of your own within hours after starting to browse the Web, the basic idea remains that entertainment on the Web is largely an underdeveloped area.

There are plenty of sites available, and plenty of variety as well, but only in a few cases are the sites as useful as a good entertainment book or CD-ROM. On the other hand, they're cheaper (unless you pay by the hour, perhaps), so for that reason alone they're worth visiting. For highly specific entertainment information, however, the Web is not the best choice of media.

Education, Scholarship, and Research

25

by
John December

Historically, one of the strengths of computer networks has been the ability to bring people together. Educators such as those at the Open University in the United Kingdom and the New School for Social Research in the United States have long recognized this and have used computer networks for education. While scholars still debate the value and proper application of online learning, the Web creates information spaces and communication opportunities that represent a wide range of activities.

This chapter presents some examples of how the Web can be used for education and to awaken students' minds to the excitement of learning. Other examples show how educators have created webs to reflect their activities, projects, and resources.

Next, this chapter surveys how scholars can use the Web to share ideas, collaborate on research, and develop materials for their students. Like many information systems before it, the Web has its limitations and weaknesses. A primary weakness is that there is still relatively little educational material available through the Web. However, the examples shown here demonstrate a remarkable richness in innovation and creativity. By exploring these, you can develop enthusiasm for the process of learning beyond the physical walls of the classroom.

Motivating Students to Learn

Although a traditional classroom relies on a single teacher to provide students with a glimpse into knowledge, the Web can offer direct connections between knowledge producers and students. The following example describes the JASON project, an effort to involve students in exploration. It is just one illustration of how many educators can collaborate to create an online learning environment that extends from the classroom to the world.

In 1985 Dr. Robert D. Ballard (now Director of the Woods Hole Oceanographic Institution's Center for Marine Exploration) and a research team discovered the wreck of the *R. M. S. Titanic* on the floor of the North Atlantic Ocean. In order to photograph the vessel's interior, the team designed a submersible robot called Jason. In 1989, due to the success of the Jason and the curiosity of school children who wanted to know how his team discovered the Titanic, Dr. Ballard founded the JASON project. In 1990, the JASON Foundation for Education was formed "to excite and engage students in science and technology and to motivate and train their teachers." (See Figure 25.1.)

In the JASON Web (http://seawifs.gsfc.nasa.gov/scripts/JASON.html), Dr. Robert Ballard talks about the project's purpose: "[To] excite young people in the fields of science and engineering by involving them in the excitement that we as scientists and engineers enjoy...[to] involve them in moments of discovery...[to] take young people to interesting research sites and let them participate in live exploration" (http://seawifs.gsfc.nasa.gov/JASON/JASON6/ballard_purpose.au). One feature of the JASON project is *telepresence*, in which scientists, using remote sensing devices, involve others in the process of discovery. The JASON Project home page (Figure 25.1) serves as a clearinghouse for information about the project, as well as tutorials and information for participants.

FIGURE 25.1.

The JASON Project home page. Courtesy of the JASON Project.

Designed for students in grades four through twelve, the JASON Project material offered through the Web page provides an overview of past and future expeditions. These expeditions involve the use of telepresence, the technology of the JASON submersible robots, as well as in-class activities and observations at many sites throughout the world. Figure 25.2 shows the page providing an overview of the 1995 expedition to "Island Earth," the environment of Hawaii.

The Web materials on this overview page place the voyage in context—linking it to information on the Web related to Hawaii's natural features such as background material about the origins of planets, volcanoes, and other natural features. The home page for the voyage, shown in Figure 25.3, links to additional material.

This additional material provides specific information about Hawaii, demonstrating the strength of the Web to contextualize a project by bringing together diverse information sources. In this way, the JASON Project Web creates an excellent set of preparatory materials that teachers can use to familiarize themselves and their students with what they will experience during the telepresence phase of the expedition. While the JASON Project Web is not the focus of the expeditions, the background material, information, and specific guides the JASON Web offers support the entire project—making it visible and accessible to still more students world-wide.

FIGURE 25.2.

The JASON Projects Island Earth overview. Courtesy of the JASON Project.

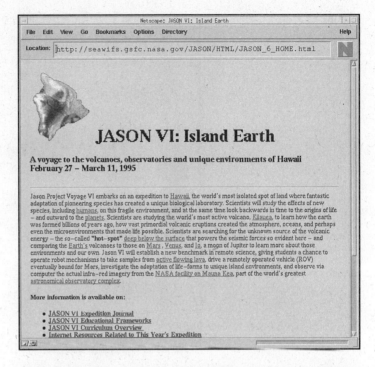

FIGURE 25.3.

The JASON Project Island Earth home page showing links to additional material. Courtesy of the JASON Project.

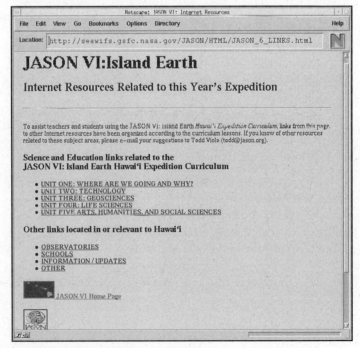

Schools on the Web

Although specific projects such as JASON demonstrate how the Web can be used to support educational projects, other applications of the Web show how schools can build webs to provide information to their own students and teachers, as well as to connect their site to the larger world of the Web.

While electronic mail, real-time text conferencing, and online tutorials have been used in the education community for several years, the Web brings a unique aspect to these online efforts by helping educators create information spaces that present the "face" of a school to anyone on the Web who ventures in for a visit. This section describes several school webs and surveys the kinds of information that have been created.

Hillside Elementary School

Hillside Elementary School is located in Cottage Grove, Minnesota, in the southeast section of the Minneapolis-St. Paul area. In March 1994, sixth-grade students at the school began work on their own web, as part of a joint project between the University of Minnesota's College of Education and Hillside. The Hillside home page, `http://hillside.coled.umn.edu/`, is shown in Figure 25.4.

FIGURE 25.4.

The Hillside Elementary School home page. Courtesy of Hillside Elementary School and Stephen E. Collins.

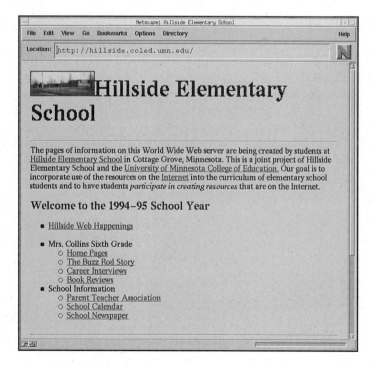

The goal of the Hillside web is to foster the use of the Internet in the curriculum by helping students access the Web for information as well as create their own information. As part of this work, a teacher at the school, Chris Collins, created an Internet Research Project Assignment, in which the students had to locate and use references to Web resources for a research paper. Mrs. Collins also provided the students with a "JumpPage" listing various Web documents for references to HTML, Web searching tools, and resource lists.

The sixth-graders produced a variety of reports on subjects ranging from Antarctica to weather, each incorporating links to Web resources. In addition, each student created his or her own home page, as well as helped Mrs. Reid's third-grade students create their own home pages. Announced on the "Mosaic What's New" page (`http://www.ncsa.uiuc.edu/SDG/Software/Mosaic/Docs/whats-new.html`), their project attracted a great deal of attention in the spring of 1994, logging between 500 and 1,000 connections per day during the week after it was first announced.

The long-term goals of the teachers at Hillside are to document their work and to share their experience through their Web server so that others might build on their efforts. Hillside provides a directory to other elementary schools on the Web at `http://hillside.coled.umn.edu/others.html`.

The Virginia L. Murray Elementary School

Like at Hillside, the teachers at Virginia L. Murray Elementary school in Ivy, Virginia, (`http://pen1.pen.k12.va.us:80/Anthology/Div/Albemarle/Schools/MurrayElem/`) worked with a nearby college of education to develop a Web server. Working with the Curry School of Education at the University of Virginia, along with a grant from Albemarle County, the Parent-Teacher Organization, and money from the school's budget, the school established an Internet connection in February 1994. The top of Murray Elementary's home page is shown in Figure 25.5. The home page contains links to class pages and the library, as well as local resources such as a Mosaic tutorial written by graduate students in the Curry School of Education and a tutorial written by Theresa McMurdo and Jason Mitchell for fourth- and fifth-grade students called "How Light Works." By providing links to local sources, the Murray school can share resources that other schools may find valuable. By linking to resources on the Web itself, the Murray school creates relationships beyond its own walls.

FIGURE 25.5.

Virginia L. Murray Elementary School home page. Courtesy of Virginia L. Murray Elementary School.

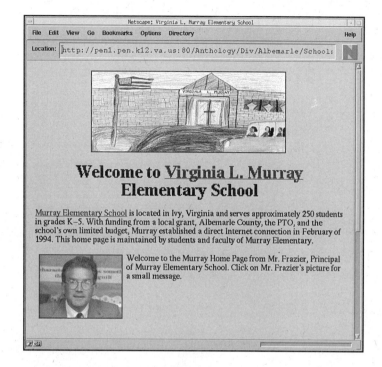

Thomas Jefferson High School for Science and Technology

Thomas Jefferson High School for Science and Technology in Alexandria, Virginia, was founded in 1984 as a special magnet school (a school that receives a special designation within a school district for excellence in a range of subjects). Although students at Thomas Jefferson excel at the school's offerings in science and technology, they share a wide variety of interests, and these interests are reflected in their web (http://boom.tjhsst.edu). (See Figure 25.6.)

The Jefferson Web was originally run by a student administrator, Nathan J. Williams, who trained his teacher, Donald W. Hyatt, in the summer of 1994 and then left to start school at MIT. The Jefferson web presents a wide variety of information about the school, including reference information for students, and it records happenings (News Items) accessible from links on the home page.

The Thomas Jefferson Web includes extensive information about its technology labs, particularly its Computer Systems Laboratory, including detailed descriptions of its educational focus on Artificial Intelligence, Computer Architecture, Supercomputer Applications, Computational Physics, and Computer Systems Research. Links within several of these categories provide detailed course descriptions, including statements of objectives and assignments. For example, the page for the Artificial Intelligence course is shown in Figure 25.7.

FIGURE 25.6.

Thomas Jefferson High School for Science and Technology home page. Courtesy of Nathan J. Williams.

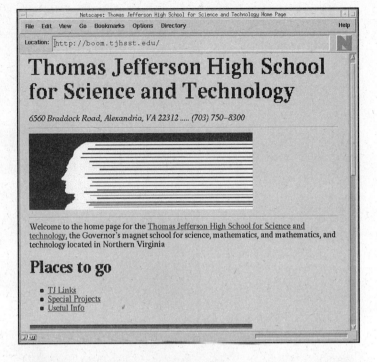

FIGURE 25.7.

General Description page for the Artificial Intelligence course at Thomas Jefferson High School for Science and Technology. Courtesy of Phyllis T. Rittman.

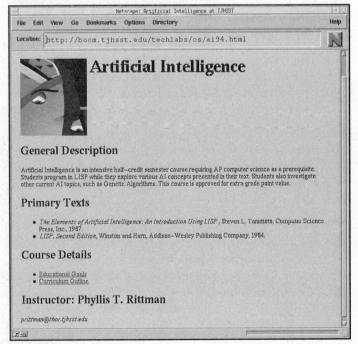

As shown in Figure 25.6, Thomas Jefferson's front page contains links to information about its Geoscience department as well as to home pages of people at the school. The front page also contains a link to a database that keeps track of alumni of the school by class year. In this way, the Thomas Jefferson Web page functions not only as an information space for its current students, but as a gathering-point on the Web for its alumni—relationships that may yield additional connections and ideas to increase the information and knowledge that the Thomas Jefferson web can offer.

Claremont High School

Claremont High School in Claremont, California, is another high school with a web. Its home page, `http://www.cusd.claremont.edu/`, is shown in Figure 25.8.

The Claremont web contains links to information and resources at Claremont High School, such as links to resources related to its academic departments, information resources about the Internet, and reports about the web server. Like the Thomas Jefferson web, the Claremont web provides a mix of resources and links that help students at the local school make sense of the Internet as well as locate information to support their education at the school.

FIGURE 25.8.

Claremont High School WWW home page. Courtesy of Claremont High School.

Patch American High School

Patch American High School, located in Vaihingen, a small section of Stuttgart, Germany, provides education to family members of the United States European Command (US EUCOM). The school's Web server and other technology programs are part of the U.S. Department of Defense's Dependents Schools Program, offering education to over 100,000 students on U.S. military bases in 19 countries world-wide. The Patch American High School web was the first high school web in Europe and offers a detailed look at how the Web can support education, help students, and create an online information system to help learning and inform the general Web public.

FIGURE 25.9.

Patch High School WWW home page. Courtesy of Bill Dyer, Patch American High School.

The top of Patch's home page is shown in Figure 25.9. The school web offers information that helps people learn about the high school and its programs as well as its unique setting as an American high school in Germany. Highlights of the web include

- "A Look at Stuttgart:" A narrative about the history of Stuttgart, with detailed maps and photographs. A nice touch is including links to the current day and time in Stuttgart as well as the current European weather map. Also included are "tours" of sights in Stuttgart, including the Mercedes-Benz Museum and the Porsche Museum (Figure 25.10).

FIGURE 25.10.

Patch High School Porsche Museum. Courtesy of Bill Dyer, Patch American High School.

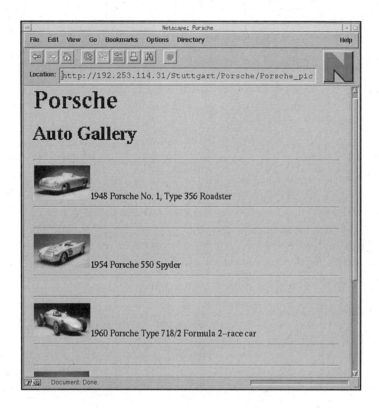

■ "WWW Interactive Project on Berlin:" This includes information and perspectives about the state of Germany five years after the fall of the Berlin Wall. This project is being done in collaboration with 10 Defense Department schools, 10 European schools, and 10 U.S. schools. Patch High School's exhibit, "D-Day: The World Remembers," is part of this exhibit, a multimedia presentation including text, pictures, sounds, and movies about D-Day.

■ A wide range of information about academics (a student art gallery, German language and culture information), as well as clubs, and multi-curricular projects, such as the "Berlin Wall Falls" exhibit as part of the WWW Interactive Project on Berlin.

■ A collection of virtual field trips to Stuttgart, Augsburg, Maulbronn Abbey, and the Patch Barracks.

Patch High School's web demonstrates how online information can give students a chance to learn multimedia skills, share information, collaborate with other students and schools, and learn more about their community's place in history. Part of the power of a web such as Patch's is in how its links can make connections that can serve as jumping-off points for further learning and collaboration. For example, the Patch web includes links to "partner schools," such as the

Realschule Renningen school's home page as well as alumni of Department of Defense Dependent Schools. Thus, the web that the students, teachers, and administrator's create is not necessarily the full body of knowledge that the students study, but rather an information system that helps make public relationships and projects that are just part of the products of learning.

Smoky Hill High School

Smoky Hill High School is located in Aurora, Colorado. Smokey Hill's web (`http://smokywww.ccsd.k12.co.us/`), shown in Figure 25.11, has particular strength in its assortment of student-developed publishing online. The *Smoky Hill Express* student newspaper (Figure 25.12) offers a detailed look at school events, news, sports, as well as opinions and viewpoints of the students. The students also put together a newsletter, *Smoky Hill Signals,* which gives a detailed look at school activities and news with announcements of upcoming events (such as the "Principal's Coffee," a time for students to meet informally with the principal of the school). There is also a Technology Newsletter for the school, surveying the user of computers, the Internet, and lectures and computer labs.

FIGURE 25.11.

Smoky Hill High School home page. Courtesy of Kevin M. Dougherty, Smoky Hill High School.

Smoky Hill's web also includes student home pages and student projects, including an effort to explore how information technology fits into a global society. The Smoky web demonstrates how a school can put Web technology in the hands of students so that they can explore their own issues through online publishing and other projects.

FIGURE 25.12.

Smoky Hill Express student newspaper. Courtesy of Kevin M. Dougherty, Smoky Hill High School.

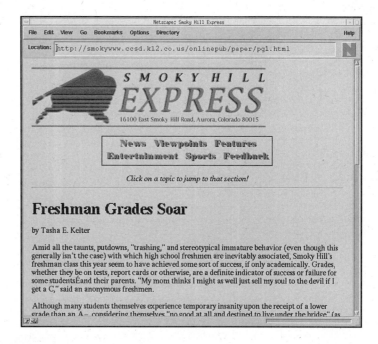

Community Colleges

While the elementary and high school webs described in the preceding sections provide information for students and educators located at a single campus, other academic institutions serve a more dispersed and diverse student population. One such example is the Maricopa Community College District in Arizona, the second-largest multi-college community-college system in the United States. Established in 1962, Maricopa serves the needs of a varied student population with an average age of 30, of whom 80 percent are employed, 50 percent with full-time jobs. Maricopa schools offered more than 180,000 credit hours during the 1993-94 academic year. This student population requires high-quality, relevant education that can flexibly help them succeed academically while maintaining busy lifestyles.

The Maricopa Center for Learning and Instruction (MCLI) operates a web that provides a set of links, bringing together information to support its active academic community and linking together the Gophers and other information servers that individual institutions within the Maricopa Community College District operate. The Maricopa web links offices, departments, and campuses within the district and has been recognized as a model for "motivating, infusing, and promoting innovation and change in the community college environment" (http://www.mcli.dist.maricopa.edu/). CAUSE, the association for managing and using information technology in higher education, and Novell, Inc. presented Maricopa with the 1993 CAUSE Award for Excellence in Campus Networking, citing Maricopa's "exemplary campus-wide network planning, management, and accessibility" (gopher://cause-gopher.colorado.edu/00/awards/networking/1993-net-award-winners.txt). The top of MCLI's home page, http://www.mcli.dist.maricopa.edu/, is shown in Figure 25.13.

FIGURE 25.13.

The home page for the Maricopa Center for Learning and Instruction. Courtesy of Maricopa County Community College District, Arizona, Alan Levine.

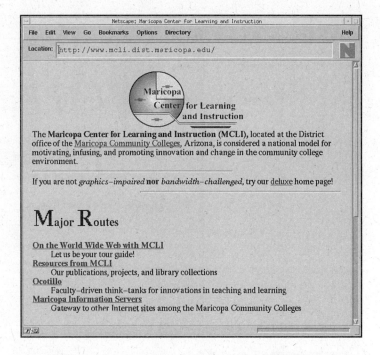

The front page provides links to a wide variety of Web and Internet orientation information as well as more pages to information about Maricopa's publications, projects, library, and campuses. These links furnish a wealth of information about Maricopa's educational offerings. MCLI's publications offered through links in its web include the *Labyrinth,* focusing on instructional technology, and the *Forum,* covering teaching and learning methodologies. A project called Ocotillo, deriving its name from a plant indigenous to Arizona whose branches reach up and out, is a "think tank" that reports on issues such as emerging technologies, information literacy, intellectual rights, and technology-based training. These reports, available in the Maricopa web, provide valuable resources that relate how Maricopa deals with these issues while utilizing technology for education.

The MCLI web also contains links to information about the Library and special projects such as Learning English Electronically, as well as links to Gophers, such as MariMUSE, a Gopher of the Learning Collaboratory located at Phoenix College, which supports education through access to resources, faculty directories, and links to individual colleges and centers. (See Figure 25.14.)

The Maricopa web demonstrates how a diverse collection of many campuses can combine to create an information space to support education as well as explore the uses of educational technology.

FIGURE 25.14.

Links within the Maricopa Center home page. Courtesy of Maricopa County Community College District, Arizona, Alan Levine.

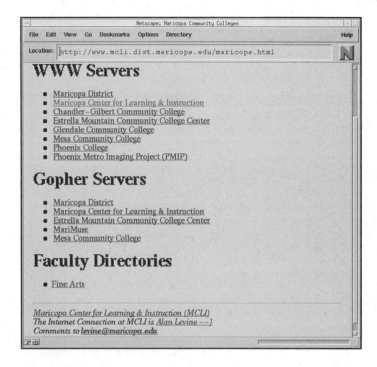

Colleges and Universities

The number of colleges and universities with home pages is large and growing very quickly. As of August 1994, Mike Conlon's page of American Universities at http://www.clas.ufl.edu/CLAS/american-universities.html has more than 480 entries, and Christina DeMello's page of American and International colleges at http://www.mit.edu:8001/people/cdemello/univ.html lists more than 1,000 college-level webs world-wide. In Chapter 27, "Communication, Publishing, and Information," campuswide information systems are discussed as an example of organizational communication. This section focuses on selected college course material created for the Web.

Online Course Information

The University of Texas at Austin maintains a collection of pointers to course material (much of it college-level) used for instruction at http://www.utexas.edu/world/instruction/index.html. The offerings include material in more than 42 subjects, including Anatomy, Archaeology, Architecture, Art and Art History, Astronomy, Biochemistry, Biology and Botany, Chemical Engineering, Chemistry, Communication, Computer Science, Finance, History, Language Lab, Management Information Systems, Mathematics, Medicine, Nuclear Engineering and Engineering Physics, Physics, Psychology, and Religious Studies.

The material in this collection varies in depth and coverage. Most of the web pages offering course information simply point to ASCII or other notes files used in the course, and no course listed was delivered solely through the Web without face-to-face, teacher-student interaction.

A Computer-Mediated Communication Course

One course web from the Texas-Austin collection, at `http://www.rpi.edu/Internet/Guides/decemj/course/cmc.html`, is shown in Figure 25.15. The graduate-level course, Computer-Mediated Communication (CMC), was taught at Rensselaer Polytechnic Institute by Dr. Teresa Harrison. Participants investigated the nature of CMC's impact on interpersonal, work, and societal contexts. The students also were exposed to some technologies and skills necessary to take part in CMC on the Internet and visited an IBM groupware facility.

FIGURE 25.15.

Computer-Mediated Communication course web.

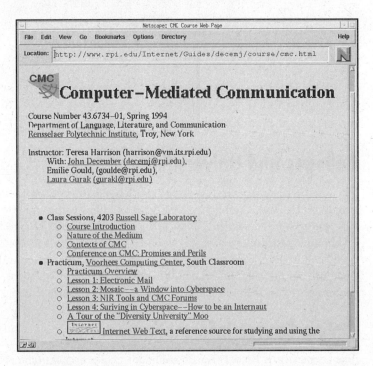

The CMC course web's front page provides the information found on many college syllabi: instructor's name, course number and location, and an outline of the course contents. Links on the page allow the student to browse a hypertext version of the syllabus. In cases where required readings were available online, links were made from the syllabus directly to these readings. The front page also links to the lessons used in the practicum portion of the course, in which the students use workstations to access various Internet resources. The text for this online portion of the course, Internet Web Text, URL `http://www.rpi.edu/Internet/Guides/decemj/text.html`, shown in Figure 25.16, links the student to Internet resources, including orientation material, guides, reference information, browsing and exploring tools, subject- and word-oriented searching tools, and information about connecting with people.

By providing both course and study information, the CMC course web shows how a web can be used both as an information system and a learning tool.

FIGURE 25.16.

Internet Web Text.

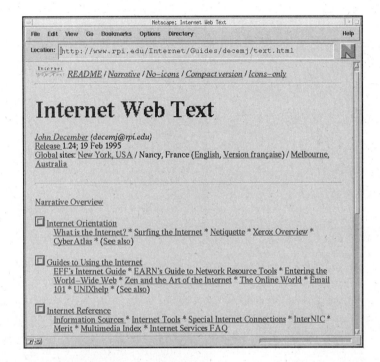

A Management Information Systems Course

Another example of a course web is Brian Butler's undergraduate Management Information Systems course that was taught in the summer of 1994 at Carnegie Mellon University. Figure 25.17 shows the online information page for the course (http://www.gsia.cmu.edu/bb26/70-451/). This page links the student to a variety of information, not just the course outline, the syllabus, and schedule, but to final exam study hints, lecture notes, and course readings when they were online. The instructor also provided links to assignment questions, with the answers provided after the students turn in the assignment. The exam, study questions, and assignment solutions also contain links to the relevant lecture notes. For example, Figure 25.14 shows exam answers, with links to the relevant lectures.

FIGURE 25.17.

*Online Information page for
a Management Information
Systems course at Carnegie
Mellon University. Courtesy
of Brian Butler.*

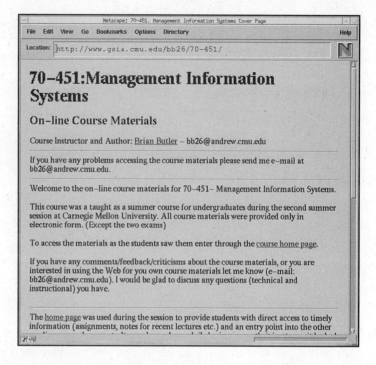

According to the instructor and author of this course material, Brian Butler, this web provides
students with access to course materials and also prompted him to prepare the exam shown in
Figure 25.18. The MIS course web is a good example of how course materials can be provided
through a web. Direct student-teacher interaction plays a part in learning, but a web such as that
shown for the MIS course, as well as the others shown in this section, can help a busy student
access current course materials. Placing these materials on the Web, the instructors help expand
and extend the context of the information they present; the classroom ceases to be provided only
in a particular physical space at a particular time, and the sources of information and instruction
materials are not supplied only by the instructor.

FIGURE 25.18.

MIS exam answers with links to relevant lectures. Courtesy of Brian Butler.

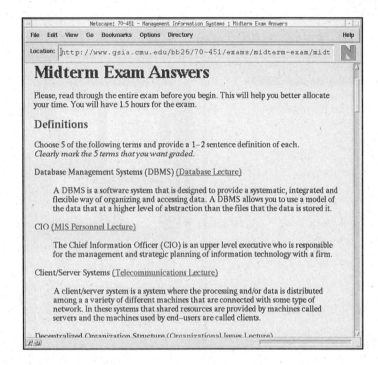

A Composition Lab and Course

The Computer Writing and Research Lab (CWRL) in the Division of Rhetoric and Composition at the University of Texas at Austin provides a view into how educators can create a web of information surrounding a particular area of teaching. In the case of the Writing and Research Lab, of course, student composition skills are the focus. CRWL's home page (http://www.en.utexas.edu/), shown in Figure 25.19, offers a view into this information structure. The lab's web is organized around multiple views—from student-centered resources (such as online writing dictionaries and style guides) to instructor resources (hypertexts and hypermedia information, as well as online courses and syllabi). The lab also publishes a journal, *The Electronic Journal for Computer Writing, Rhetoric and Literature,* and provides links to a large collection of completed student projects created as a result of classes at the CWRL.

FIGURE 25.19.

Computer Writing and Research Lab home page. Courtesy of the Computer Writing & Research Lab Division of Rhetoric and Composition of the University of Texas at Austin.

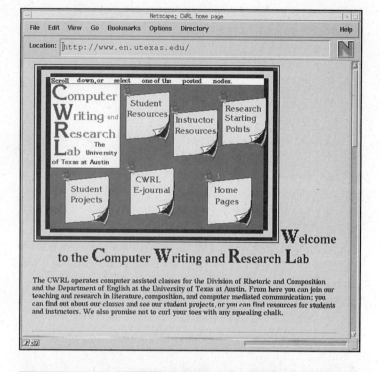

FIGURE 25.20.

Computer Writing and Research Lab instructor resources. Courtesy of the Computer Writing & Research Lab Division of Rhetoric and Composition of the University of Texas at Austin.

The CWRL's instructor resources (Figure 25.20) show more specifically how the Web can be used to support instruction in composition. For example, Daniel Anderson's course in composition (`http://www.en.utexas.edu/~daniel/syllabus/syl.html`), shown in Figure 25.21, illustrates how a Web can support student writing.

FIGURE 25.21.

Web page for Daniel Anderson's course in composition. Courtesy of Daniel Anderson.

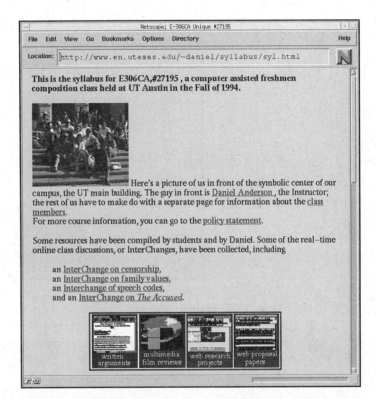

Daniel Anderson's composition web is organized around four course units:

■ *Written arguments:* In this unit, students present arguments and critique those of others. As part of the classroom exercises, the instructor used an electronic, real-time discussion forum to encourage students to state their views online. The transcript of these discussions are provided as text in the course web, so that students can use this as a basis for recalling the class discussion. The instructor used a similar discussion forum for more exchanges on other topics. Then, linking to the transcripts of these exchanges, along with other resources on the provided on the web, the instructor provided students with an assignment to write an "arguable claim."

■ *A multimedia film review:* In this unit, students were expected to create a film review in hypermedia. The instructor provided students with links to resources on the course web as resources to complete the reviews (Figure 25.22).

FIGURE 25.22.

Multimedia film review resources. Courtesy of Daniel Anderson.

- *Group web research projects:* In this unit, students work in groups to create web pages that explore issues such as the environment, foreign relations, technology, and campus issues. For each week, the instructor provides a hypertext page that gathers the online resources to help students with a particular stage of their projects (for example, to select a topic and to format the presentations).

- *Research proposal papers:* The final unit the course web supports are the student research paper proposals. By building on links created in the earlier part of the course (such as the group projects developed in the third unit), the instructor links together the previous work of the class and shows—through the course web—how the units lead to helping the students express themselves in text as well as hypermedia.

Course webs such as Daniel Anderson's are more than just syllabi; they're an ongoing part of a course, growing as students participate and creating a central "information store" that the students can access at any time. The completed course web—Daniel Anderson's class took place in the fall of 1994—serves as a model for other instructors to consider for their own courses.

Tutorial Modules

In addition to information that supports an educational institution or a particular course, there are many webs that contain detailed tutorial and materials for learning. These webs delve into very specific topics to help students grasp a concept or learn information. Unlike the course webs described previously in this chapter, these tutorial modules are examples of the Web being used to teach students particular content.

A Tutorial Module: The Knee

Michael L. Richardson at the University of Washington has prepared Anatomy Teaching Modules (`http://www.rad.washington.edu/AnatomyModuleList.html`), which guide the user through normal knee anatomy and normal distal thigh anatomy. (See Figure 25.23.) The first module, Normal Knee Anatomy 1, takes the reader through a discussion of knee anatomy (Figure 25.24).

FIGURE 25.23.

University of Washington Anatomy Module List. (Copyright Michael L. Richardson, M.D. Reprinted by permission.)

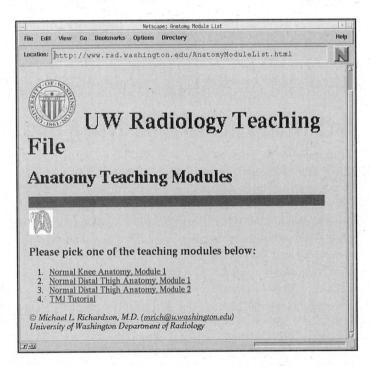

The Normal Distal Thigh Anatomy 1 lesson includes images as well as a movie showing the operation of the distal thigh. These modules use a combination of graphics and text to help students learn. While similar materials (excluding the movie) could be presented in a book, the Web version can be customized and immediately updated by the instructor and is accessible worldwide, available to anyone who would like to learn.

FIGURE 25.24.

*Normal Knee Anatomy 1.
(Copyright Michael L.
Richardson, M.D. Reprinted
by permission.)*

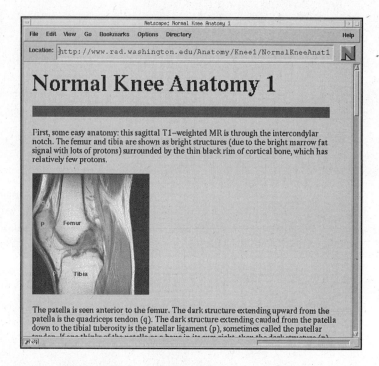

An Interactive Training Module: A Frog Dissection Kit

The Lawrence Berkeley Laboratory in California, in work sponsored by John Cavallini of the U.S. Dept. of Energy's Energy Research Division, Office of Scientific Computing, has created a virtual frog that can be dissected online. This online "frog" was created as part of the Whole Frog Project, which provides high-school biology students with a tool for exploring a frog's anatomy using high-resolution MRI imaging and 3-D surface and volume rendering software. As a result of this work, the project has created not only a useful tool but also has demonstrated the value of computer-based, 3-D visualization and whole-body, 3-D imaging as a curriculum tool. The Whole Frog Project home page, at http://george.lbl.gov/ITG.hm.pg.docs/Whole.Frog/Whole.Frog.html, links into a preview of the Frog Dissection Kit as well as tutorials. Figure 25.25 shows the interactive program with the frog's skin still on. (This is the Netscape version using the graphical information map feature as well as HTML Forms; a version that can be used for Windows is also available.)

By clicking the image of the frog near an edge, the student can alter the position of the frog—changing the view to a side or bottom view, for example. By using the selector bar (currently set to Skin in the preceding figure), the student can open up the view of the frog to see inside the skin through a window or remove the skin entirely. (Figure 25.26 shows the frog with no skin.) The kit offers the students a variety of ways to focus on particular organs and systems. By selecting the checkboxes at the top of the menu, a student can remove selected organs. For example, Figure 25.27 shows the frog with the skeleton, nerves, and intestines removed.

FIGURE 25.25.

Frog Dissection Kit. (Copyright 1994 by Lawrence Berkeley Laboratory. Reprinted by permission.)

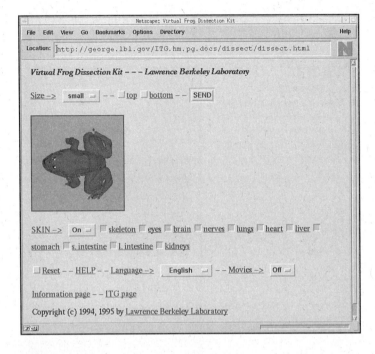

FIGURE 25.26.

Frog with no skin. (Copyright by Lawrence Berkeley Laboratory. Reprinted by permission.)

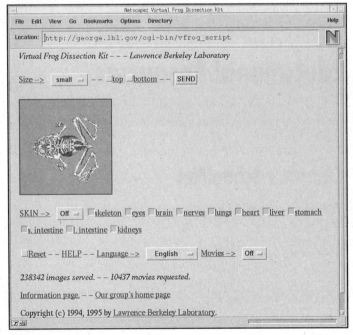

The online virtual frog is valuable both as an educational resource—giving students an interactive program for learning—and as a model for using graphics for this kind for education.

FIGURE 25.27.

Frog with selected items removed. (Copyright 1994 by Lawrence Berkeley Laboratory. Reprinted by permission.)

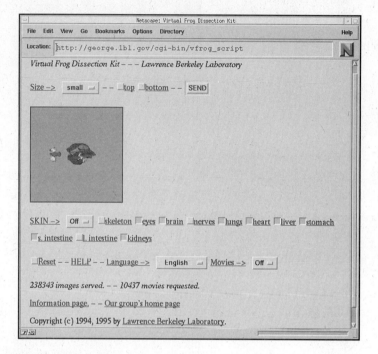

Educational Resources

In addition to webs that support information for and about education offered at schools, a wide variety of online resources is available to support educators. In this section, you'll explore some major collections.

Canada's SchoolNet

Seldom does an entire country have as bold an initiative as Canada's—to link all of Canada's more than 16,000 schools to the Internet as quickly as possible. SchoolNet is the name for this project, and its home page is at `http://SchoolNet.Carleton.ca/english`. (The English-language version is shown in Figure 25.28.)

FIGURE 25.28.

Canada's SchoolNet.
Courtesy of Dan Martin, Le
Groupe de soutien du Reseau
scolaire canadien.

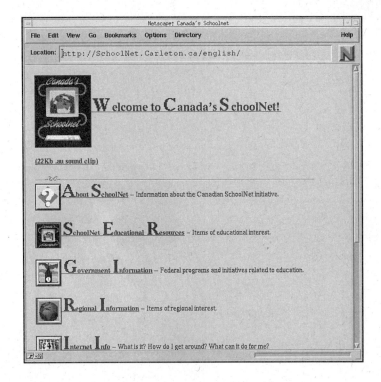

The overall objectives of the SchoolNet project are to increase the educational opportunities for all students, to disseminate resources and education through online communication, and to stimulate learning primarily through information technologies. SchoolNet's web is just one part of the overall project and contains an exceptionally large collection of educational resources on Canada's history, native people (Figure 25.29), the Canadian space program, and educational camps in Canada.

The SchoolNet web also connects students to Canadian Government information—a tour of Parliament Hill, the Canadian Open Government web at `http://debra.dgbt.doc.ca:80/opengov/`, and the National Atlas Information Service (NAIS), a comprehensive collection of geography information about Canada. Students and educators using the Web can access regional information, such as webs for the governments of Ontario, New Brunswick, and British Columbia. The SchoolNet web also collects "utility" information, such as Internet information, links to other educational resources in a variety of subjects, and a list of Canadian schools with Web sites.

SchoolNet represents a national initiative to collect and disseminate information online about education. One benefit of webs such as SchoolNet is in the example it sets. It provides motivation for all schools to join the Internet and make use of (rather than duplicating) the resources that the SchoolNet web gathers. The links in SchoolNet—to Canadian government information, other schools, and to resources on the Web world-wide—help educators find information to them that can be relevant in building their own specialized webs.

FIGURE 25.29.

Canada's Native People.
Courtesy of Dan Martin, Le
Groupe de soutien du Reseau
scolaire canadien.

The United States Department of Education

The U.S. Department of Education's web (`http://www.ed.gov/`), shown in Figure 25.30, offers a wide variety of both administrative and resource information to educators. The government information (such as links to administrative information about the Department, greetings from the current Secretary, and mission statements) provides educators with current background information about current national educational goals.

The Department's web also offers "specialized views" into the information on it:

- *A Teacher's Guide:* This gives a comprehensive overview of all the services and resources available. These include special programs, National centers for specific areas, and contact information.

- *A Researcher's Guide:* This presents an overview of the department for people who are engaged in research in education, either for the government or for another institution. This guide summarizes sources of information and gives contact information about available research data sets, as well as research services and resources.

FIGURE 25.30.

*U.S. Department of
Education web.*

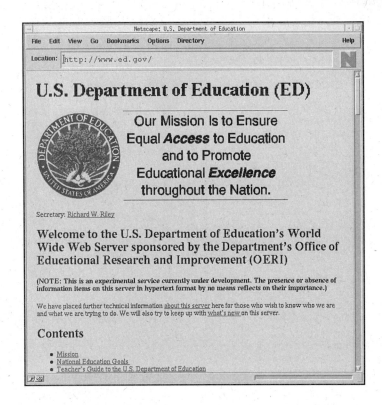

The Education Department's web also links to a great deal of background and supporting information about initiatives such as GOALS 2000, family involvement, the Education Technology Initiatives, and elementary and secondary education. Like Canada's SchoolNet web, the U.S. Department of Education web serves as both a "switching station" to guide users to appropriate information as well as a "clearinghouse" for information about education.

AskERIC K-12 Information

AskERIC is a service providing information for K–12 educators. Part of the ERIC (Educational Resources Information Center) Clearinghouse on Information and Technology, AskERIC is a project funded by the U.S. Department of Education.

Based at Syracuse University and sponsored by the schools of Information Studies and Education, AskERIC's Virtual Library connects teachers to resources through a variety of online means (e-mail, FTP, and Gopher, as well as the Web). AskERIC also provides connections to Network Information Specialists (NIS), who can answer questions from K–12 staff related to education. The overview portion of AskERIC Virtual Library's home page, `http://eryx.syr.edu/Main.html`, is shown in Figure 25.31.

FIGURE 25.31.

The overview portion of the AskERIC Virtual Library home page.

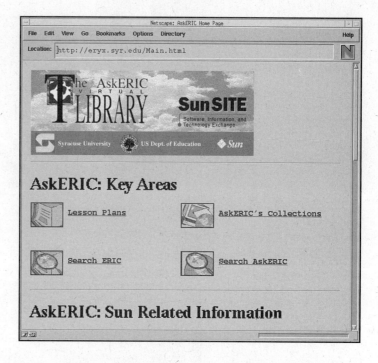

The AskERIC Virtual Library (AEVL) gives K–12 educators automated access to more than 700 lesson plans, archives of Listserv discussions, and pointers to Internet services. The Collection page (Figure 25.32) includes indexes, remote reference sources, and related Web sites. The AskERIC web also links to specific lesson plans. For example, Figure 25.33 shows the front page for the NASA SIR-C Education Program.

SIR-C stands for Spaceborne Imaging Radar-C, a type of imaging radar produced by the Jet Propulsion Laboratory for the National Aeronautics and Space Administration (NASA). SIR-C will be onboard Space Shuttle flights, and the SIR-C educational (SIR-CED) program's goal is to involve middle-school and high-school students in an experience of discovery and learning, with the benefit of helping students improve math, science, and geography skills. The teacher's guide for the program includes a special unit on spaceborne imaging radar, and computer and in-class activities (Figure 25.34).

Written exercises in the lesson plan involve students in exploring data collection aboard the space shuttle's Earth Observing System as part of lessons on concepts in remote sensing. Part of the goal of these lessons is also to spark students' interest about the environment. Put together by people at the Jet Propulsion Laboratory (Anthony Freeman, JoBea Way, and Ellen O'Leary) as well as teachers in the Los Angeles Unified School District (Kathleen Crandall, David Gunderson, and Robert Veas), the program combines excellent teaching with exciting content. AskERIC itself is in development—don't be surprised if AskERIC's web looks different than pictured here—in a research and development effort to support the Virtual Library and the NIS services. Efforts are underway to create new resources as well as a new virtual interface. The ultimate goal is to have a seamless, intuitive, point-and-click interface that will help guide educators to the resources and answers they need.

FIGURE 25.32.

The AEVL collection page.

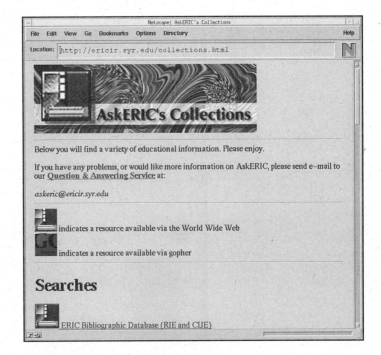

The AskERIC system thus combines a source of help for teachers in K–12 through a virtual library with Network Information Specialists available for answers and a research-and-development program aimed at improving the contents and interface of AskERIC's offerings.

FIGURE 25.33.

The front page for the NASA SIR-C Education Program.

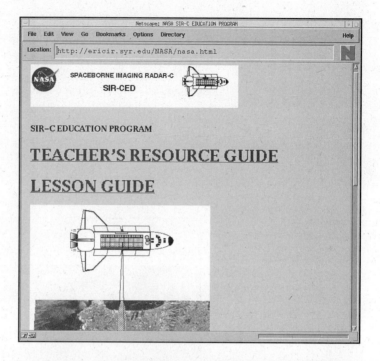

FIGURE 25.34.

The table of contents page for the SIR-CED Teachers Guide.

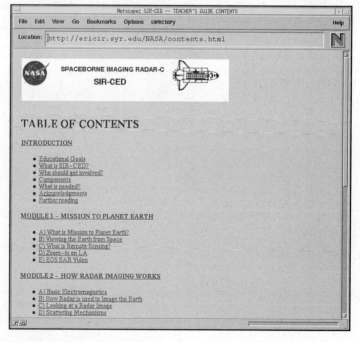

The DeweyWeb

Like AskERIC, the DeweyWeb at the University of Michigan is a project to both provide information and facilitate communication. DeweyWeb accomplishes this by providing links to resources as well as a computer-mediated communication activity called Interactive Communications & Simulations (ICS) World Forum.

Figure 25.35 shows the top of the DeweyWeb's home page, `http://ics.soe.umich.edu/`. The work on the DeweyWeb extends work that has been done with the World School for Adventure Learning, Indiana University, ICS at the University of Michigan, and the International Arctic Project.

FIGURE 25.35.

DeweyWeb home page.

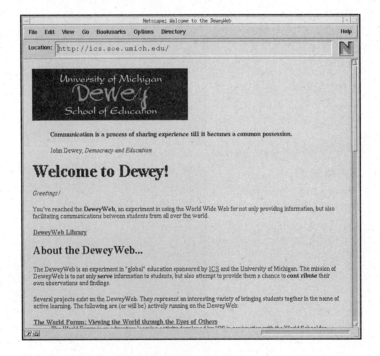

One ICS Forum involves school children around the world in tracing the training activities of the International Arctic Project in preparation for a trip across the Arctic. This project is called "Journey North." Figure 25.36 shows the home page for this project.

Journey North helps students learn more about the Arctic, including the environment, wildlife, and culture. The web links to "Arctic Bites," a collection of writings relating to the Arctic, information and news about the 1994 International Arctic Project team, and a "Wild Adventurers" section where students can report their own observations of wildlife (Figure 25.37).

Thus, the DeweyWeb, like JASON and many of the other projects described here, illustrates how both information and hands-on involvement can excite students to learn.

FIGURE 25.36.

The Journey North home page.

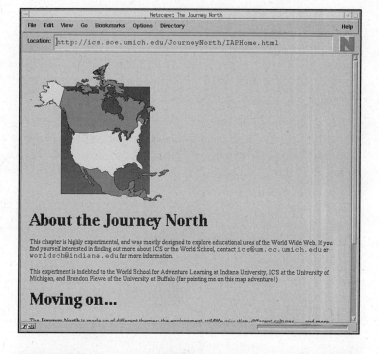

FIGURE 25.37.

Tracking the Journey North page interactive map.

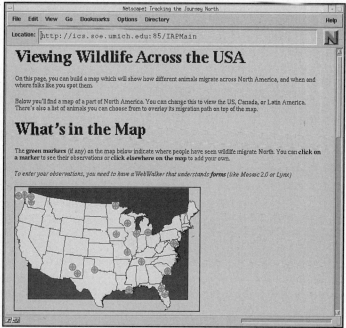

Educational Online Sources Help and Pointers for Information

With a goal of creating a centralized resource for information about education, Educational Online Sources (EOS) has grown a vast web of information for educators (Figure 25.38, `http://netspace.org/eos/main_image.html`).

FIGURE 25.38.

The Educational Online Sources home page.

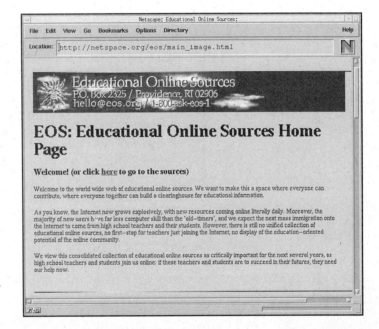

The goal of EOS, according to Joel Parker Henderson, is to help teachers grasp concepts and skills necessary for primary and secondary educators, to consolidate resources and information, and to provide basic information about how to use the Internet. These goals address the need for providing annotated citations of educational sources in FTP, Gopher, mailing lists, and webs (Figure 25.39). EOS includes collections of webs, a Gopher, a file list, educational Gophers, Usenet newsgroups, Internet guides, and subject-oriented resources.

FIGURE 25.39.
*Educational Online
Sources web list.*

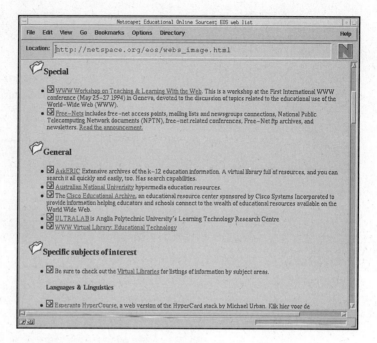

Web 66

Route 66 was a fabled and well-traveled highway linking Chicago and Los Angeles in the United
States. Using that storied highway as a metaphor, Web 66, a project of the University of
Minnesota's College of Education, helps educators and students set up Internet servers and find
resources on the "highway" of the Web. Web 66's home page, `http://web66.coled.umn.edu/`, is
shown in Figure 25.40. This web's offerings include an "Internet Server Cookbook," which gives
instructions on how to set up various Internet servers. Web 66 also offers large collections in the
following areas:

■ **Resources**

 SharePages: These can be downloaded and used on your own server, such as a search
 engine meta-page.

 What's New: New information and services on Web 66

 WWW Schools Registry: An imagemap that guides you to school Web servers throughout
 the U.S., Canada, and the world (Figure 25.41). When the Hillside Elementary WWW
 server went on the Web on March 12, 1994, there were only four K–12 WWW sites. By
 March 1, 1995, the Web 66 School Registry listed 121 Elementary schools and 228
 secondary schools, for a total of 349 sites world-wide.

FIGURE 25.40.

Web 66 home page. Courtesy of Stephen E. Collins.

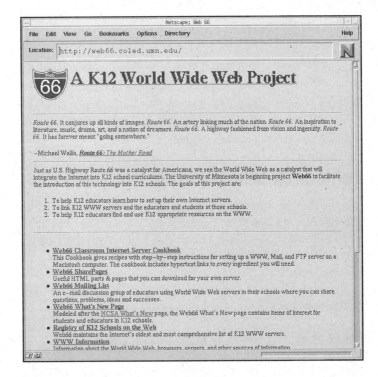

FIGURE 25.41.

Web 66 WWW schools registry. Courtesy of Stephen E. Collins.

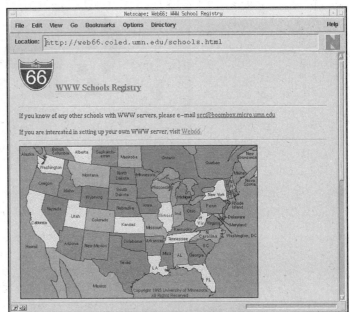

- **Discussion**

  Web 66 Mailing List: A discussion forum for educators using the Web.

  WebMaster Ramblings: A presentation of pointers to the ins and outs of developing and serving information on the Web.

Web 66 is a rich resource for educator information not only for the local (Minnesota) schools, but for all schools. Its imagemap interface to schools on the Web is unique, as is its "cookbook" guidance for creating an Internet server.

Latitude28 Schoolhouse

The Latitude28 Schoolhouse (`http://www.packet.net/schoolhouse/Welcome.html`; home page shown in Figure 25.42) is a privately sponsored project to help disseminate education materials to students of all ages. The Schoolhouse maintains a database of useful links to educational resources on the Web. The subject areas include art, civics and government, games, mathematics, reading, and science. The mathematics section, for example (Figure 25.43), includes links to major Web resources that can engage students in a variety of scientific areas—from astronomy and space to Paleontology.

FIGURE 25.42.

Latittude28 Schoolhouse home page. Copyright 1995 OpenNet Technologies, Inc., All Rights Reserved. Printed by permission. Courtesy of OpenNet Technologies and Kurt Long.

FIGURE 25.43.

Latittude28 Links to Web resources. Copyright 1995 OpenNet Technologies, Inc., all rights reserved. Printed by permission. Courtesy of OpenNet Technologies and Kurt Long.

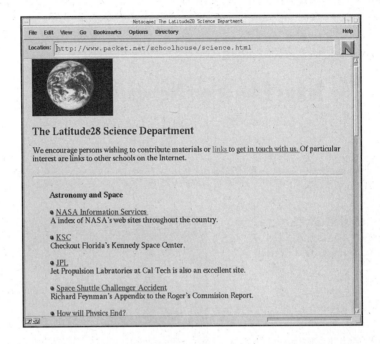

Latitude28 is maintained by OpenNet Technologies and supported by sponsors—including The National Gold Exchange, CTS International, and The artists at ARTWHERE Clothing, as well as PacketWorks, which provides the Web server. This arrangement of private support for online information for students opens up possibilities for businesses to contribute and students to benefit.

The Global Schoolhouse Project

The Global Schoolhouse at `http://k12.cnidr.org/gsh/gshwelcome.html` offers online "classroom" resources linking students and educators world-wide with a variety of multimedia tools. Funded in part by the National Science Foundation, the project connects students to the Internet and classroom applications that allow them access to resources and communication. The goals for the project are as follows:

- To demonstrate how the Internet can be used as a classroom environment for research and collaborative learning
- To help students learn more about information and active learning
- To develop online systems for training and support for teachers in Internet technology
- To demonstrate Internet tools and connectivity in classroom settings
- To foster relationships among business, government, schools, and the education community for ongoing integration of technology into classrooms

The Global schoolhouse web offers a large collection of supporting information for these goals—including resource tips, mailing list information, tools, training, technical support, and listings of teachers and projects.

The Texas Education Network

The Texas Education Network, or TENET, is a Texas-based initiative to advance education state-wide through a communications infrastructure. TENET's home page, `http://www.tenet.edu/`, is shown in Figure 25.44. TENET's web is organized around a "Central Station," providing links to resources such as K-12+ servers; academic resources; and library, computer-lab, and field-trip information.

FIGURE 25.44.

The Texas Education Network (TENET) home page. Courtesy of Gayle Gaston, The Texas Education Network.

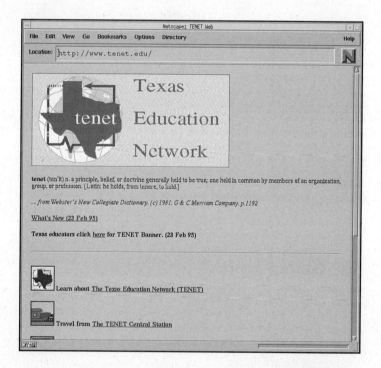

TENET also provides information to the State Networking Project, a nation-wide effort among schools in the K–12 community to explore and establish strategies for applying information technologies to learning. Links to Texas information, such as the TEA (Texas Education Agency) Web and the vast array of educational projects that the TENET administrators regularly add to the web (a sample list shown in Figure 25.45), make the TENET web a rich source of educational information. The TENET web demonstrates how a state-wide web can augment national webs in education (such as the U.S. Department of Education's Web) and provide a valuable, growing resource base for information.

FIGURE 25.45.

TENET What's New information. Courtesy of Gayle Gaston, The Texas Education Network.

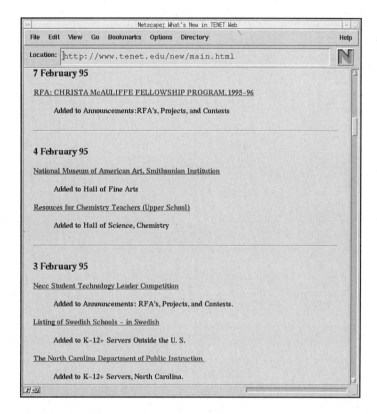

Scholarship and Research

Human knowledge has accumulated over centuries through the careful work of scholars who create, critique, and disseminate information and research. These scholars, working through a continual process of interchange with peers, experts, and students, require communication in order to generate and evaluate new knowledge. While traditional forums for scholarship, such as paper-based journals and in-person conferences and gatherings, have been used for centuries, scholars today have adopted the power of the Net to fulfill many of their needs.

Net-based scholarship is a routine part of the lives of many scholars today. This has come about through the widespread use of computer networks for electronic mail as well as the demonstrated propensity of networked communication to foster communities of people interested in specialized knowledge. The plethora of Usenet newsgroups, electronic-mail–based discussion, and the wide number of subject-specific Net and Web resources are testaments to this phenomenon. Part of this power to create communities of interest lies in the ability of the Web and Net to draw people together who are geographically dispersed, yet share the same passion for an area of study.

Tools such as the Web provide the means to create shared resources in a different way than electronic mail or other Net-based means for communicating and sharing information. While electronic mail discussions or archives of files often require compartmentalized development, Web structures can expressively present and evoke ideas and foster cooperation and collaboration. The hypermedia links that the Web makes possible facilitate interchange and shared development in a way that other networked information delivery systems, such as electronic mail, file transport protocol, or Gophers, do not. The Web opens doors to hypermedia as well as networked communication that can be shaped to meet the needs of an audience through text layout, design, and rhetorical devices. (See Part V, "Weaving a Web.") Moreover, by integrating the views of Internet resources (Chapter 16, "At the Edge of the Web"), the Web also provides a platform for gathering information from a diverse set of Internet protocols. This integrative and collaborative nature of Web communication holds great promise for future scholarship on the Web.

This section explores some sample resources and organizations devoted to enhancing online scholarship. These examples range from the Jeffersonian idea of an "Academical" Village to organizations that foster information-sharing, research, and learning online.

These organizations and resources attempt to fulfill a challenging mission: to help scholars search for information, communicate and collaborate with colleagues, analyze information, disseminate findings, and prepare curriculum and instruction. With increasing opportunities on the Web to pursue these activities, scholars can exchange ideas at many different levels of formality ranging from chance and serendipitous connections struck on an electronic mail discussion list or on a Web-based communication forum (see Chapter 27) to the more formal exchanges in peer-reviewed electronic journals. By assisting in this scholarly communication, the Web itself may help bring about Thomas Jefferson's dream of a community of scholars exchanging ideas and working together, as you'll see in the first example.

Jefferson Village Virginia, An Electronic Academical Village

Thomas Jefferson's idea for a society in which people work and learn in an integrated environment, sharing interdisciplinary ideas and growing in understanding, may be happening on the Web. The University of Virginia in Charlottesville has created an "Academical Village." The home page for this village (`http://jefferson.village.virginia.edu/home.html`) is shown in Figure 25.46.

Unlike Jefferson's village based on geography, the Institute for Advanced Technology in the Humanities (IATH) at the University of Virginia in Charlottesville uses technology to support humanities-related scholarship. Founded in 1992 with a grant from IBM as well as support from the University, IATH's web now supports a range of holdings, including publications, research reports, a magazine (*Postmodern Culture*), and technical reports to support humanities scholarship.

FIGURE 25.46.

The home page for the Institute for Advanced Technology in the Humanities at the University of Virginia. Courtesy of the University of Virginia.

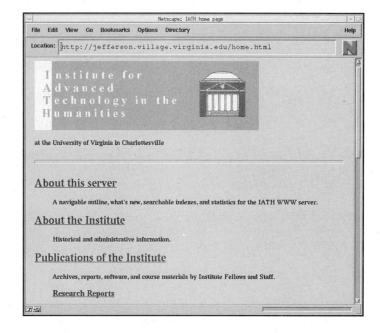

The research report holdings range from hypertext reports such as Mike Gorman's report on "Bell's Path to the Telephone," to "Noun Classification in Swahili," by Ellen Contini-Morava. The Rossetti Archive (Figure 25.47) contains many writings and pictures of Dante Gabriel Rossetti (its goal is to eventually contain Rossetti's complete works) in a hypermedia web, `http://jefferson.village.virginia.edu/rossetti/fullarch.html`.

The Rossetti Archive illustrates the depth of coverage that a Web-based hypermedia archive can offer; it includes images of paintings, drawings, and designs, texts of poems and fragments, commentary, prose works and fragments, manuscripts, and translations. The IATH, through institutional support and the commitment of scholars, has developed a web with the potential to enrich all who venture into it. Because the Web transcends geography, politics, and culture, people worldwide can make use of the collection of knowledge in Jefferson Village.

Coalition for Networked Information

While the University of Virginia's Jefferson City web focuses on a specific area (humanities scholarship), the Coalition for Networked Information (CNI) focuses on promoting the creation and dissemination of networked information in all scholarly disciplines. CNI's home page located at `http://www.cni.org/CNI.homepage.html`, is shown in Figure 25.48.

FIGURE 25.47.

The D.G. Rossetti Hypermedia Archive. Courtesy of the University of Virginia.

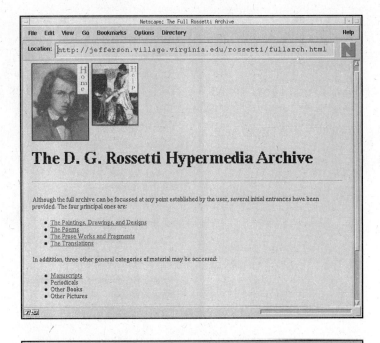

FIGURE 25.48.

The home page for the Coalition for Networked Information. Courtesy of Craig A. Summerhill, Coalition for Networked Information.

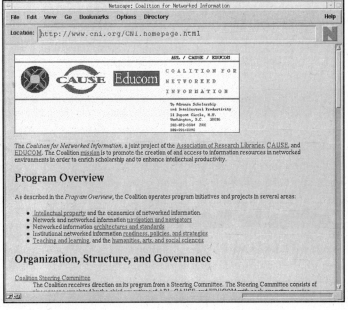

CNI is a collaborative project—which is often a hallmark of valuable collections—among a group of information-related organizations: the Association of Research Libraries, CAUSE (the association for the management of information technology in higher education), and EDUCOM (a consortium of higher education institutions to facilitate information resources for teaching, learning, and scholarship). CNI's home page contains links to information about

- Intellectual property
- Projects dealing with networked navigation and navigators
- Architectures and standards for networked information
- Networked information policies for institutions
- Teaching and learning
- Links to other services provided by participating organizations: Association of Research Libraries, CAUSE, and EDUCOM

CNI's work includes initiatives to explore important issues for making networked information available and useful to all scholars.

The Scholarly Communications Project

As CNI works to foster the use of networked information, the Scholarly Communications Project at the Virginia Polytechnic Institute and State University works to provide scholarly materials through electronic communication. The home page of the Scholarly Communications Project, shown in Figure 25.49, is located at `http://borg.lib.vt.edu/`. Begun in 1989 as an effort to pioneer the electronic dissemination of scholarly materials, the Scholarly Communications project today includes publishing the following:

- Electronic journals, including the *Journal of the International Academy of Hospitality Research, Community Services Catalyst,* and the *Journal of Technology Education*
- Abstracts of the print quarterly *International Journal of Analytical and Experimental Modal Analysis*
- Research data of the *Journal of Fluids Engineering*

The project develops electronic editing skills and provides participants with a means to experiment in various display formats on the Internet. The project offers texts through ASCII at an FTP site, through Gopher and WAIS, and through the Web.

FIGURE 25.49.

The home page for the Scholarly Communications Project of Virginia Polytechnic Institute and State University. Courtesy of Virginia Polytechnic Institute and State University.

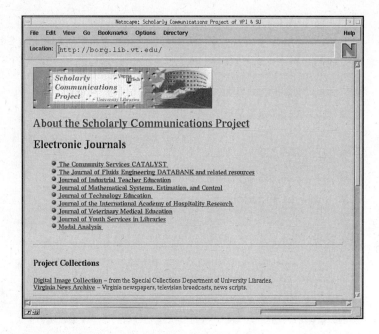

Fostering Specialized Scholarly Connections

In-person meetings, conferences, and symposia have long been forums for scholars to meet and exchange ideas. These meetings, however, have required scholars to physically relocate to be in touch with other scholars. These in-person connections are invaluable because interpersonal dynamics and the shared experience of a conference bring participants together. Many participants might consider the "connections" made at a scholarly conference as important as (or even more important than) the information transmitted. Fostering similar kinds of "connections" in online environments is an important part of scholarly activity on the Web. This section examines some organizations and resource collections that bring scholars together.

University of Waterloo Scholarly Societies Collection

Many scholarly societies have recognized the value of networked information and communication for their membership and have created online forums. However, how does a scholar find an organization of interest? One way could be to use keyword- or subject-oriented searching methods. (See Chapter 18, "Trees: Subject-Oriented Searching," and Chapter 19, "Spiders and Indexes: Keyword-Oriented Searching.") However, a comprehensive, professionally maintained collection can serve the needs of a scholar or interested student much more efficiently.

The University of Waterloo Library has created such a collection of pointers to scholarly societies. The Waterloo collection facilitates access to electronic resources maintained by scholarly organizations, as defined on the Waterloo web at `http://www.lib.uwaterloo.ca/society/overview.html` as "organizations in which membership is determined by scholarly credentials, not by the existence of a contract of employment or of visitation rights, as in the case of a research centre."

The Waterloo collection lists almost 100 organizations that have Web pages, Gophers, or FTP archives providing information for members or the public. Figure 25.50 shows the holdings of the Web pages collection of scholarly societies.

The University of Waterloo's collection serves a valuable service because it acts as a central branching-off point for scholars seeking to find organizations in a particular field of interest. It also provides an excellent means to locate authoritative information for a particular subject area, as many societies also maintain resource collections in their members' area of expertise.

FIGURE 25.50.

Web pages of Scholarly Societies with subject area listing. Courtesy of The University of Waterloo Library.

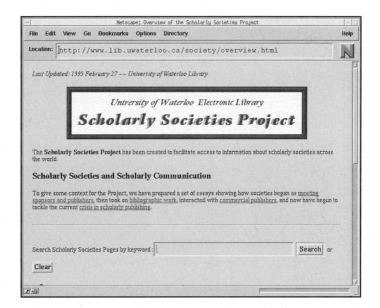

The Communication Institute for Online Scholarship

The Communication Institute for Online Scholarship (CIOS) is a nonprofit organization codirected by Timothy Stephen and Teresa Harrison, both associate professors of communication at Rensselaer Polytechnic Institute in Troy, New York. The goal of CIOS is to facilitate communication-related scholarship through the use of computer and information technologies.

CIOS operates Comserve, an online service for scholars interested in human-communication research. Begun from an idea by Timothy Stephen and Teresa Harrison for scholarly electronic communication in 1985, Comserve today serves a community of thousands of users at more than 50,000 e-mail addresses in 80 countries. Comserve functions as a resource library, a news service, an electronic "white pages," a computer conferencing system, a database of journal indexes, and a distributor of electronic announcements and surveys. The philosophy guiding Comserve is to provide high-quality services for communications scholars with as much distributed responsibility as possible. The emphasis for Comserve's growth and development is to continue to improve the quality of the scholarly discussion taking place as well as to increase the value of the materials stored in Comserve's resource library.

Comserve provides both a model for scholarly online communication and a forum for studying online scholarly interaction. Since Comserve provides a full range of services to meet scholarly needs for communication and resource sharing, it can give other scholarly organizations some direction in designing Net- or Web-based forums for interaction. Comserve also facilitates the study of online communication itself, through its hotline discussions focused on the study of computer-mediated communication, as well as through its resource library holdings, communication-journal indexes, and an online journal related to the study of communication.

The full range of Comserve's services is available through electronic mail. For more information send the message Send Comserve HelpFile to Comservc@Vm.Itc.Rpi.Edu. The CIOS Gopher is at gopher://cios.llc.rpi.edu/.

The Centre for Networked Access to Scholarly Information

Although efforts to increase scholarly interaction world-wide often have great impact, local efforts can also show success in helping scholars make use of networked information and communication. The Centre for Networked Access to Scholarly Information (CNASI) at the Australian National University Library aims to deliver online information to the University's academic community (Figure 25.51). The efforts of CNASI (http://snazzy.anu.edu.au/) include

- A Campus-Wide Information System (CWIS)
- An Electronic Library Information System at Australian National University (ELISA)
- Daily Reuters Newsbriefs
- Developing electronic resources in the area of Asian Information through the cooperation of the National Library and the Research School of Social Sciences
- Establishing a national network of centers for teaching resource materials
- Establishing a central gateway to access all Australian Gophers
- Creating a directory of Australian electronic mailing lists
- Providing access to course materials to students
- Developing links to network information materials, government information, and electronic journals

FIGURE 25.51.

The home page for the Centre for Networked Access to Scholarly Information. Courtesy of Tony Barry.

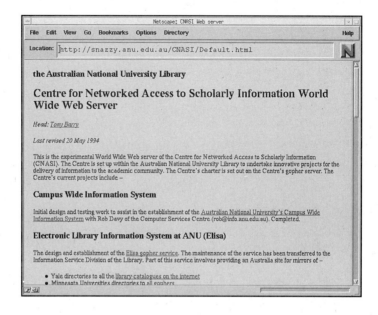

Although the CNASI web and related Gophers are still under development, its current state demonstrates the potential scope of how university-wide access to networked resources can be developed.

Brown University's Institute for Information Research and Scholarship

The Institute for Information Research and Scholarship (IRIS) was established in 1983 at Brown University to explore the ways computing technology can be used for research and teaching. Now absorbed into Brown's Computing and Information Services department, IRIS provides hypertext materials in a variety of specialized areas. One example is the The Religion in England web, (`http://www.iris.brown.edu/iris/RIE/Religion_OV.html`), developed as part of an IRIS project to provide contextual information for a course in English literature. Developed by a team of authors—David Cody, George P. Landow, Anthony S. Wohl, Robert Aurellano, and David B. Stevenson—the web offers a very rich set of background information on all aspects of religion in England (Figure 25.52). David B. Stevenson converted its Storyspace (a Macintosh-based hypertext system) version to the Web.

The depth and richness of the contextual information offered by the Religion in England web is an example of what can be done for a specialized use. The value of the Web-based version of this hypertext is that this web can be freely used by students and scholars world-wide to gain an understanding of religion in England.

FIGURE 25.52.

The Religion in England web. Courtesy of David Stevenson.

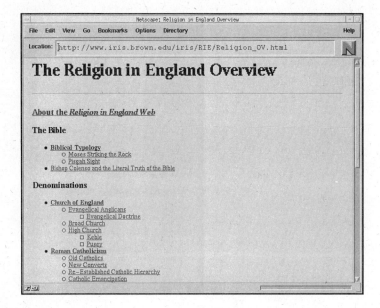

Explorer's Check

The Web can serve as a tool for scholars and educators to not only express their ideas but to also share their knowledge within a community of scholars and students. Elementary and secondary schools as well as community colleges and universities have all joined the Web with information and instructional material.

Organizations such as the Coalition for Networked Information foster the use of networked information in education and research through innovative and authoritative collections of information and guidelines on important issues and topics.

Specialized forums such as Jefferson Village Virginia, the Scholarly Communications Project, and the Communication Institute for Online Scholarship foster scholarship in broad areas of interest by creating forums and structures to disseminate, create, and critique knowledge.

At the local level, scholars can develop webs to support specific needs. Australian National University's Centre for Networked Access to Scholarly Information and Brown University's Institute for Information Research and Scholarship demonstrate webs that support a local need and at the same time serve to inform and educate all students on the Web.

Through the pioneering efforts of these online organizations, scholars can continue to build structures that fully explore the potential of the Web for communicating, sharing information, and creating scholarly communities.

Science and Technology

26

by
John December

Because the Web was invented by CERN (http://www.cern.ch), an organization that is part of an active scientific community (see Part I, "Introduction to the World Wide Web"), it is no surprise that science and technology subjects are well represented on the Web. This chapter describes webs that present science and technology information for public and professional education as well as for direct use in research. The capability of the Web to expressively convey multimedia information through a graphical browser such as Mosaic is well demonstrated among these examples, with many webs using hypermedia to inform and educate the user.

These webs also illustrate the value of having *domain experts* (people with expertise in the knowledge domain represented by the web) involved in developing web information. Systems of peer-review and quality checks are essential to providing reliable web information, and many of these webs show exceptional involvement by domain experts. Moreover, these webs illustrate the way specialized science webs can serve the public well through the collective efforts of several organizations.

The first section explains how OncoLink, a service for disseminating information about cancer, provides not only an excellent service for practitioners in the field, but also serves the public by providing accurate information about this important topic. Many organizations already strive to educate the public through materials and courses, often provided for free. The Web facilitates the dissemination of detailed, up-to-date educational materials that utilize the expressive power of hypertext and multimedia on a global scale.

Many of the webs described in this chapter were still in their infancy (less than a year old) when they appeared as shown here. The developers will surely have increased the offerings on these webs since the time of this writing. You can find many more webs covering scientific subjects in the "Science" section of one of the subject trees discussed in Chapter 18. In my narrative of each web, I'll stress various aspects of the information contained in the web itself. Therefore, my description is not a complete guide to the total offerings in each web, but rather it highlights significant aspects and special needs that each web meets.

OncoLink: Quality Information for Specialists and Patients

Oncology is the study of cancer, and comprehensive, up-to-date educational information is critical for the treatment of patients, the education of health-care professionals, and the development of the field of oncology itself. The University of Pennsylvania's Cancer Center meets this need through OncoLink, a multimedia, Web-accessible oncology resource. Supported by the Radiation Oncology Department and founded by E. Loren Buhle Jr., Ph.D, and Joel Goldwein, M.D., OncoLink was the first multimedia cancer-resource collection established on the Internet. For its excellence, OncoLink earned the International Best of the Web Award for Best Professional Service in 1994. Its home page (http://cancer.med.upenn.edu/) is shown in Figure 26.1.

FIGURE 26.1.

OncoLink home page. Copyright © 1995, The Trustees of the University of Pennsylvania, courtesy of E. Loren Buhle Jr., Ph.D.

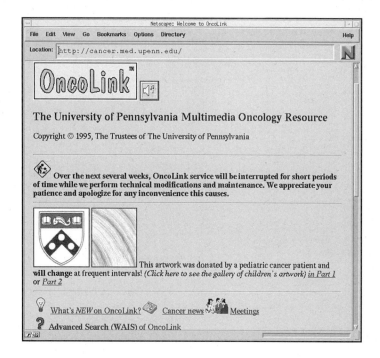

OncoLink supports a wide variety of information for

- The rapid collection and dissemination of information related to oncology
- Education for health care personnel
- Education for patients, families, and the general public

Although many information webs provide a variety of links to outside resources, OncoLink's stress is on developing high-quality, well-organized, peer-reviewed information pertinent to the field of oncology and its specialties. OncoLink offers information in several general categories:

- Specific diseases, such as breast cancer, ovarian cancer, cervical cancer, and gestational trophoblastic disease
- Specialties within oncology such as pediatric (Figure 26.2), gynecological, and radiation (Figure 26.3)
- Patient support and information; for example, psychosocial support (Figure 26.4), cancer FAQs, and topical information on subjects such as smoking, pain, and prevention
- News such as meeting and conference announcements
- Pointers to cancer-related Internet information
- Administrative information

Within each category, accessible from the home page, other web pages offer a variety of information. Figure 26.2 shows the top of the Pediatric Oncology page, and Figure 26.3 shows the top of the Radiation Oncology page.

FIGURE 26.2.

The Pediatric Oncology page. Copyright © 1995, The Trustees of the University of Pennsylvania, courtesy of E. Loren Buhle Jr., Ph.D.

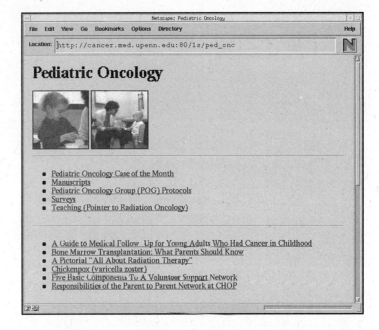

FIGURE 26.3.

The Radiation Oncology page. Copyright © 1995, The Trustees of the University of Pennsylvania, courtesy of E. Loren Buhle Jr., Ph.D.

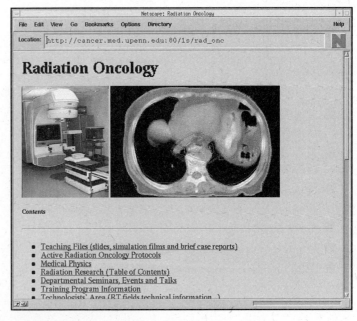

The individual page designs make good use of techniques to package information into distinct conceptual categories. The pages also illustrate how graphics can be used to add information as well as visual appeal to a page, without being obtrusive. Because OncoLink's information is also accessible via Gopher, the images might not be available to all users (including those with nongraphical Web browsers). OncoLink's design takes this into account by not providing important information solely through graphics. For example, on the Psychosocial Support page, shown in Figure 26.4, images add an element of beauty to a page that can help ease a patient into information that otherwise might look cold and impersonal on a computer screen.

OncoLink's users are worldwide, and a group of seven cooperating editorial advisors reviews the information provided. The audience for OncoLink includes physicians, health care workers, patients, and the public. As a provider of important information to this audience, OncoLink developers very responsibly include disclaimers acknowledging the limitations of Web information, stating that the information is for informational purposes, does not imply University of Pennsylvania Cancer Center endorsement, and is not a rendering or substitute for medical services and care. This disclaimer is important, because it reveals the necessary limitations of Web-based information itself: It does not replace appropriate medical care but rather provides information in order for patients and providers to obtain and experience quality care.

FIGURE 26.4.

The Psychosocial Support page. Copyright © 1995, The Trustees of the University of Pennsylvania, courtesy of E. Loren Buhle Jr., Ph.D.

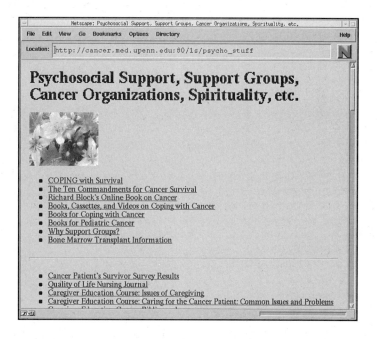

OncoLink has experienced great popularity, and the statistics offered about its use demonstrate extensive access. OncoLink was announced via Usenet on March 7, 1994. Between its official announcement and July 31, 1994, users accessed OncoLink an approximate average of 3,000 times per weekday and 1,000 times per day on the weekend. Moreover, accesses were from more than 45 countries (see Figure 26.5), although the majority (52 percent) were from the United States.

The global reach of OncoLink shows that it not only meets a unique need for the users but also facilitates connections for the developers, establishing relationships that might grow over time among international researchers. These relationships might, through feedback and involvement, improve the quality of information on the OncoLink web.

FIGURE 26.5.

OncoLink use. Copyright © 1995, The Trustees of the University of Pennsylvania, courtesy of E. Loren Buhle Jr., Ph.D.

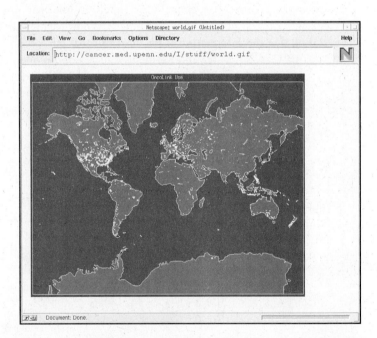

OncoLink's authoritative, comprehensive collection of oncology information, combined with a peer-review process to ensure the highest quality information and packaged in a good web design, makes OncoLink an excellent example of how the Web can be used for advancing and explaining science.

The European Space Information System: Multinational Scientific Information

There are many challenges that arise when presenting scientific information from a variety of sources to a variety of audiences dispersed worldwide. The European Space Information System (ESIS) web demonstrates that a high-quality information system to support researchers and developers can be created and maintained.

The European Space Agency (ESA) consists of 14 member states: Austria, Belgium, Denmark, Federal Republic of Germany, Finland, France, Ireland, Italy, the Netherlands, Norway, Spain, Sweden, Switzerland, and the United Kingdom, and Canada (as a participating member). The diversity of languages and cultures, as well as the complexity of the science involved in space research, challenges information providers to present timely, accurate information to support scientists and researchers. Figure 26.6 shows the ESA's home page (`http://www.esrin.esa.it/htdocs/esa/esa.html`).

FIGURE 26.6.

European Space Agency home page. Courtesy of ESRIN DPE/I.

As part of the complex task of keeping members informed as well as providing the space science community access to scientific data, images, and resources, the ESA provides information through the ESIS web shown in Figure 26.7 (`http://www.esrin.esa.it/htdocs/esis/esis.html`).

The ESIS web provides extensive links to astronomical databases and catalogs, a space science bibliography (including a forms interface), a space physics catalog and datasets, and a space physics bibliographical service.

FIGURE 26.7.

European Space Information System home page.

A partial listing of the astronomical databases illustrates the wide variety of information:

- SIMBAD: Information on individual astronomical objects, at the Centre de Donnees Astronomique de Strasbourg, France
- STARCAT: European Coordinating Facility for European Use of the Hubble Space Telescope and the European Southern Observatory and Space Telescope, in Garching bei Muenchen, Germany
- Canadian Archive Data Centre in Victoria, B.C., Canada
- Villafranca Satellite Tracking Station data, near Madrid, Spain

The ESIS web utilizes several kinds of graphical interfaces to guide the user through this data. For example, Figure 26.8 shows the view of the interface available for the system itself. Figure 26.9 shows the ESIS Imaging Application interface.

The ESIS web provides further links to services for space physicists (the ESISBIB bibliographical service shown in Figure 26.10), as well as links on the Web to space research sites and other space agencies.

The ESIS also offers reprints of publications, a newsletter, and a user's guide.

FIGURE 26.8.
Overview of ESIS.

FIGURE 26.9.
ESIS Imaging Application.

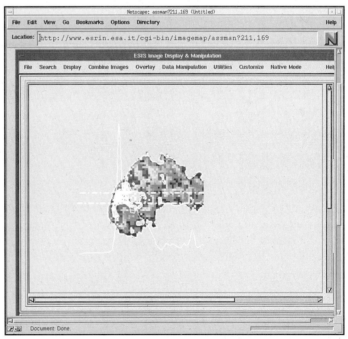

The ESIS is a good example of how a community of scientists from diverse organizations can cooperate to share valuable scientific information, not only for their own benefit, but for the benefit of the wider scientific community as well. In this way, the ESIS web itself serves as a focal point for sharing space science information, and fostering connections and associations that can enrich the progress of science itself.

Netscape: ESISBIB
File Edit View Go Bookmarks Options Directory Help
Location: http://www.esrin.esa.it/htdocs/esis/esisbib.html
ESISBIB: ESIS Bibliographic Service Version 2.5
ESIS
European Space Information System
The SIMBAD Object Search will be made available in the next release
WARNING: ESISBIB is currently being updated. Please bear with us
Searchable Fields
Title:
Journal:
Date:
Author:
Affiliation:
SIMBAD Ref.:
Keywords:
Document: Done.

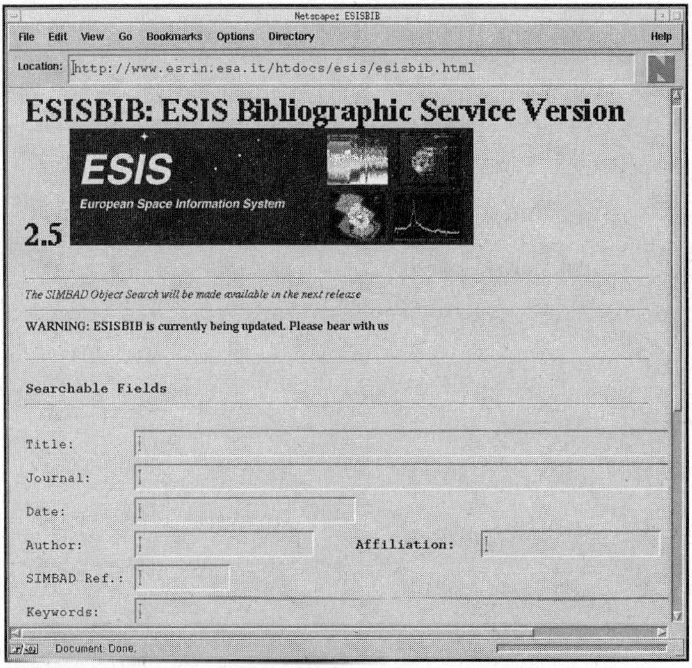

FIGURE 26.10.
The ESISBIB Bibliographical Service.

Institute for Telecommunication Sciences: Science in Service to People and Government

While the mission of ESIS is multinational and draws on many kinds of databases from multiple sources, other scientific webs provide information from more localized sources. The Institute for Telecommunication Sciences (ITS) is a U.S. Government research and engineering organization. As such, it has special requirements to serve its employers (the U.S. taxpayers) as well as the government agencies it serves through the work it performs.

The ITS is part of the National Telecommunications & Information Administration (NTIA) (`http://www.ntia.doc.gov/`), which in turn is part of the U.S. Department of Commerce (`http://www.doc.gov/`). The goal of the Department of Commerce is to promote U.S. business and trade, and as part of this work, the Department of Commerce calls on the NTIA to advise the President on telecommunications and information policy matters and to present these policies before Congress. In cooperating with other federal government agencies, NTIA also contributes to the United States' initiative to develop the Information Infrastructure Task Force (IITF), chaired by the Secretary of Commerce. Within the context of these government relationships, the Institute for Telecommunication Sciences (ITS) serves NTIA with research and engineering to promote an advanced telecommunications and information infrastructure. The ITS also serves as a focal point for helping federal agencies, state and local governments, and corporations and organizations solve telecommunications problems. The ITS home page (`http://www.its.bldrdoc.gov/its.html`) is shown in Figure 26.11. In its mission to serve as a research and engineering arm of the NTIA, ITS works in areas such as the following:

- Radio-spectrum use analysis
- Telecommunication-standards development
- Telecommunication-systems performance and planning
- Applied research (for example, radio-wave modeling)

The goal of ITS is to benefit the public and private sectors through its products (engineering tools, standards, research results) and services (training for industry and government users). Reflecting this purpose, the ITS web offers organizational information (a breakdown of the divisions and groups is shown in Figure 26.12) and access to files and programs—for example, computer models of high-frequency propagation.

FIGURE 26.11.

The Institute for Telecommunication Sciences home page.

Figure 26.13 shows Integrated Networks Group's group-level web offering links to projects on which the people in the group are working and to home pages of people in the group.

Moving one step down again, following the link to the BATMAN project, you'll see another detailed web summarizing this project.

FIGURE 26.12.
The Institute for Telecommunication Sciences divisions.

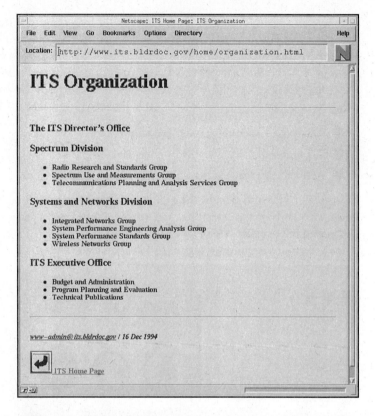

FIGURE 26.13.
The ITS Integrated Networks Group.

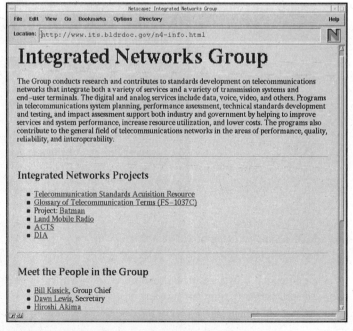

The BATMAN (Boulder Asynchronous Transfer Mode Advanced Network) project is a technology trial of asynchronous transfer mode (ATM), a type of computer communication in which units of data, called *cells,* are exchanged independently from source to receiver. The value of this page is that it serves as a focal point for the project as well as the cooperating organizations and participants. The page provides general information for the public. (See Figure 26.14.)

FIGURE 26.14.

ITS BATMAN home page.

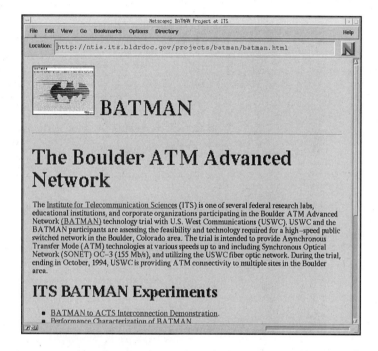

The ITS BATMAN page points to a BATMAN page at the University of Colorado, one of the participating institutions. From the ITS BATMAN page, you can obtain specific technical information, such as a diagram showing an overview of the BATMAN network topology (Figure 26.15). By combining selected technical information, such as that shown here, with a good set of administrative and contact information, the ITS web serves both the public and private sectors as an information source for government engineering and research in advanced telecommunications. In this way, the ITS web shows particular attention to organizational information needs—an important aspect in complex government, university, and corporate interaction.

FIGURE 26.15.
BATMAN network topology.

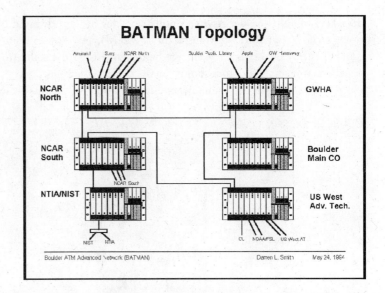

Artificial Life Online: Breaking New Ground in an Emerging Discipline

The webs examined so far deal with scientific subjects that have a long history and body of research, but the Web can be especially helpful in disseminating information about an emerging field and discipline. A web in a (relatively) new field of scholarly inquiry can broaden the range of information people can access and serve as a gathering point for scholars interested in the discipline.

Artificial Life Online, developed by Chris Langton and Scott D. Yelich, is a forum for people interested in the study of an emerging area of research. The Artificial Life web text states that artificial life is "[re-created] biological phenomena [made] from scratch within computers and other 'artificial' media" (http://alife.santafe.edu/alife/alife-def.html).

The study of artificial life thus attempts to synthesize systems that act like living things, as opposed to the traditional biological approach of analysis (taking apart or examining living organisms to analyze how they work). Although artificial life study aims to create advances in the understanding of biology, it also can be applied to complex systems that have many interacting parts—such as computer networks, nanotechnology, and industrial assembly. Figure 26.16 shows the home page of the Artificial Life web.

FIGURE 26.16.

Artificial Life Online home page. Courtesy of Christopher G. Langton.

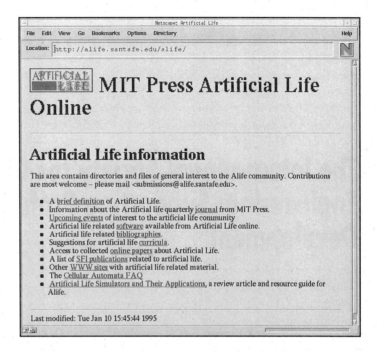

The developers of the Artificial Life web have created many features to support scholarly communication, including the following:

- Information about *Artificial Life,* a quarterly journal from MIT Press (text not online)

- Links to Usenet discussion groups that examine related issues (including links to local information at the Santa Fe Institute)

- Software available via FTP, including "Cellsim," a cellular automation simulator; "Polyworld," an artificial world for studying evolution, and "Echo," an ecological simulation

- A bibliographic database, including entries from the First Alife Workshop

- Curriculum materials, such as suggestions for Artificial Life courses and syllabi contributed by educators in the field

- An archive of papers by authors who want to gather comments

- A list of upcoming conferences, seminars, and other events of interest to the Artificial Life community

- Links to WWW resources related to Artificial Life

This extensive offering supports a variety of ways for scholars to contribute and discuss ideas. Besides the Web-accessible offerings, Artificial Life Online also sponsors discussion lists and Usenet newsgroups. The offerings on the Artificial Life Online web comprise a range of communication, from formal publications (the *Artificial Life* quarterly) to informal discussions (mailing list and Usenet newsgroups) to review processes (paper review area). The Artificial Life BBS thus gathers a community of scholars around an emerging discipline, educates interested outsiders, and provides a focal point for further research and discovery.

The International Society for Optical Engineering: Supporting Professional Development

The International Society for Optical Engineering (SPIE) is a nonprofit association of professionals working in the optical sciences. The goals of SPIE are to advance research, education, and applications. The SPIE web "brings the latest technological breakthroughs to the doorstep of individuals and organizations all over the world" (`http://www.spie.org/web/member_guide/about_spie.html`). The SPIE web's home page is shown in Figures 26.17 and 26.18. The SPIE web offers a variety of information to support its membership in a rapidly changing field. The Membership Guide for SPIE states: "Keeping abreast of the latest developments in optics, electro-optics, and optoelectronic engineering has always been a challenge. Today, rapid changes throughout the industry make this challenge even more imperative" (`http://www.spie.org/web/member_guide/individual_member.html`).

With more than 11,500 members in 64 countries, SPIE is truly worldwide and multidisciplinary, with organizations supporting SPIE in education, industry, medicine, and government. Each year SPIE sponsors more than 200 technical conferences and meetings and offers more than 400 courses in conjunction with technical meetings, some of which are broadcast live over the National Technological University satellite network. SPIE also publishes more than 200 conference proceedings a year, 30 books, a refereed technical journal (*Optical Engineering*), and *OE Reports*, an industry newspaper.

With this range of activities, a web supporting its members must have the breadth to cover the concerns of a diverse, geographically dispersed community while at the same time covering each topic with enough depth to justify the work of creating and maintaining the web itself. SPIE's membership includes industry and academic researchers, educators as well as students. Because the web server is publicly accessible, SPIE's web audience also includes the general Web public who may be seeking expert information in the field of optical engineering.

What makes the SPIE web a good example of a professional-society web is the variety, depth, and breadth of information it provides. For example, Figure 26.19 shows a collection of engineering-standards information.

FIGURE 26.17.

The SPIE home page. Courtesy of Brian J. Thomas, SPIE.

FIGURE 26.18.

The SPIE home page. Courtesy of Brian J. Thomas, SPIE.

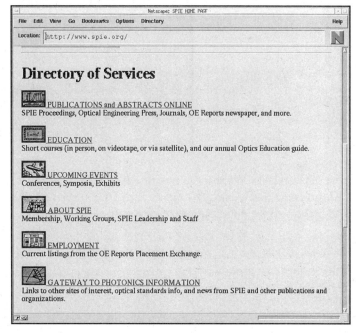

By maintaining this collection of online standards, the SPIE web simplifies the information retrieval process for researchers while presenting an excellent overview for students.

Another example of the SPIE web's depth and breadth is the contact information it offers. The SPIE web provides an Optics Education directory online. This directly lists more than 200 college and university programs in North America and the world, published with assistance from the Lawrence Livermore National Laboratory and Control Optics Corporation. This guide is comprehensive, and its presentation on the SPIE web serves as an invaluable contact resource for students. The SPIE web also includes a complete listing of corporate members as a bridge from SPIE to industry.

FIGURE 26.19.

The SPIE Optical Standards collection. Courtesy of Brian J. Thomas, SPIE.

The SPIE web also offers a gateway to information resources on the Net related to the optics industry, as well as a database of more than 20,000 abstracts available for searching by scholars and researchers for noncommercial purposes.

By providing a range of services, the SPIE web demonstrates how a scholarly society web can support scientific research for a diverse and widely dispersed community. Indeed, the SPIE web itself serves as an important focal point for the organization, serving as SPIE's "front door" on the Web.

The Cornell Theory Center: Pioneering Research and Education

The U.S. National Science Foundation (NSF) (`http://www.nsf.gov/`) supports four advanced scientific computing centers: the Cornell Theory Center (`http://www.tc.cornell.edu/`), the National Center for Supercomputing Applications (`http://www.ncsa.uiuc.edu/General/NCSAHome.html`), the Pittsburgh Supercomputing Center (`http://pscinfo.psc.edu/`), and the San Diego Supercomputer Center (`http://www.sdsc.edu/`). These centers began collaborating in 1992 under the framework of a MetaCenter for Computational Science and Engineering (`http://www.tc.cornell.edu/MetaCenter/`). The MetaCenter builds on each Center's strengths and unique resources to provide scientists access to diverse, high-performance computing technologies, technical support, and training. The MetaCenter also works with other institutions through MetaCenter Regional Alliances, which are funded by NSF. The National Center for Atmospheric Research (NCAR) also participates in MetaCenter projects (`http://http.ucar.edu/metapage.html`).

As a part of the national MetaCenter, the Cornell Theory Center (CTC) at Cornell University in Ithaca, New York, offers a wide range of resources for research, computation, and education. Figure 26.20 shows CTC's home page and illustrates how its web is designed.

FIGURE 26.20.

The Cornell Theory Center home page. Copyright © 1995 by Cornell University. Used with permission from the Cornell Theory Center.

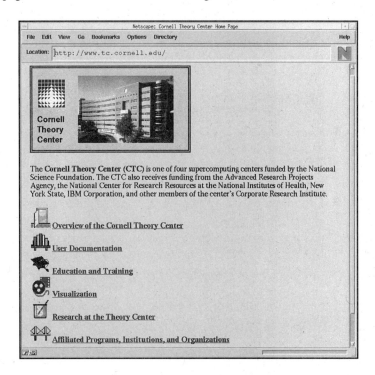

CTC's web reveals a wealth of information about its pioneering research, educational programs, and computing resources. It reflects how the work of a scientific research organization can be presented well using hypertext. The web covers

■ **Research:** CTC supports researchers in a broad spectrum of scientific and engineering fields, ranging from economics to epidemiology and from astrophysics to applied engineering. The CTC also conducts research in various fields of computational science, as well as in software development, visualization, and parallel computing. The CTC web reflects this diversity and range in its online publications, which include full hypermedia science reports such as "Acetylcholinesterate: Nature's Vacuum Cleaner," and technical reports such as "How Parallel Programming Tools are Used." The Technical Reports web page features a searchable index, abstracts, and in some cases, the full content of reports. The CTC web also offers its Science Report, *Discovery*, Research Abstracts, and a bibliographic database of publications and other works by researchers who have used CTC resources.

CTC highlights specific research projects through its web pages. For example, Figure 26.21 shows a project to simulate fabric draping (`http://www.tc.cornell.edu/Visualization/animations/Fabric/`). This research was done by Bijian Chen and Muthu Govindaraj of the Department of Textiles and Apparel at Cornell University with visualization work by Catherine Devine of the CTC. This research and web exhibit demonstrate a concrete example of a synthesis of work from various fields—mathematical modeling, rendering, and animation—and present the results in a hypertext display. Ultimately, this research in draping can help in computer-aided design of apparel and better insights into apparel assembly processes. The figure shows part of the exhibit, showing a simulation of how a tablecloth "falls" over a table. An MPEG movie as well as detailed graphics of this demonstration are also available.

■ **Computing:** The CTC offers high-performance computing resources for researchers nationwide, including a 512-processor IBM POWERparallel System 9076 SP2 that is capable of a peak speed of 136 Gigaflops. The CTC web provides details about its system and how researchers can request access.

■ **Education:** The CTC supports educational programs and offers a wealth of materials online. With a focus on high-performance computing for the exploration of scientific problems, the CTC web offers the following types of information:

> *Resources for Scientists, Researchers, and Users:* Includes online workshop materials for training researchers in using the CTC's computational resources, including tutorials and sample programs. CTC offers a repository of shared expertise and custom programs for IBM's Visualization Data Explorer (DX) and runs a Smart Node program to disseminate information about supercomputing and expertise.

Resources for Undergraduate and Graduate Students: Includes the Supercomputing Program for Undergraduate Research, in which undergraduates explore computational science at Cornell. Other programs include visualization programs with IBM's DX for teaching computer graphics.

Resources for K–12 Students and Educators: Includes Kids on Campus, a computer day for elementary students to visit the Cornell campus as part of NSF's National Science and Technology Week. As an example of web-based information, the CTC Math and Science Gateway provides science and mathematics resources for secondary school students (`http://www.tc.cornell.edu/Edu/MathSciGateway/`, Figure 26.22). The Math and Science Gateway was created by Caroline Hecht, Kathy Barbieri, Helen Doerr, and Tony Gonzalez-Walker and provides links to information in a wide range of subjects, from astronomy to computing, mathematics, and physics. The information includes lesson plans and software.

FIGURE 26.21.

The Fabric Drape Model from Cornell Theory Center. Copyright © 1995 by Cornell University. Used with permission from the Cornell Theory Center.

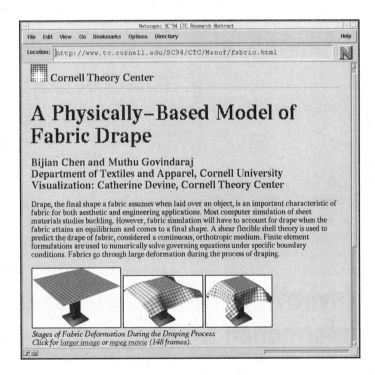

FIGURE 26.22.

The Cornell Theory Center Math and Science Gateway. Copyright © 1995 by Cornell University. Used with permission from the Cornell Theory Center.

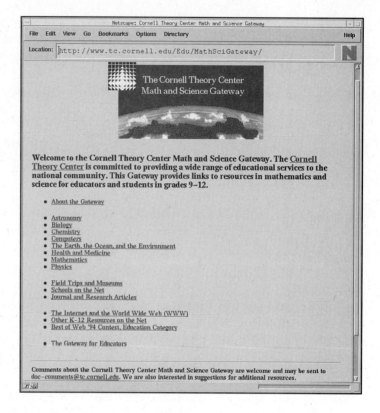

The CTC helps researchers, educators, and students find connections among the complexities of computational science and technology. The CTC's web reflects the interdisciplinary work of this center and the power of the Web to bring together information from a wide range of expertise. Through links in the MetaCenter, anyone interested in advanced computing can tap into the wealth of knowledge at CTC and at the other national Centers as well.

EnviroWeb: Communicating Environmental Information Globally

The EnviroLink Network is an online service to disseminate environmental information world-wide. Reaching more than a half-million people in more than 98 countries, EnviroLink services are free. Started in 1991 by Carnegie Mellon University freshman (now EnviroLink Director) Josh Knauer, EnviroLink comprises an online environment including Telnet, Gopher, and Web access, and comes closest to being the "metacenter" for gathering and disseminating environmental information such as that featured in the search examples in Part III, "Web Navigation Tools and Techniques" of this book. Figure 26.23 shows the EnviroWeb's home page (`http://envirolink.org/`).

FIGURE 26.23.

The EnviroWeb home page.
Copyright © 1991–1995
The EnviroLink Network
(phone (800)328-7211).
Used by permission. Courtesy
of Josh Knauer, Director.

Linking to all its online services, the EnviroWeb offers an extensive collection to EnviroLink projects, resources, and information about environmentally friendly products. The Virtual Environmental Library project illustrates well the depth of this web. The Library includes links in environmental topic areas such as activism, government, organizations, publications, and products. For example, the products link includes the "Internet Green Pages®," a listing of businesses with Internet connections that have shown environmental and social responsibility. The environmental organizations entry in the library presents a comprehensive list of environmental organizations on the Internet, with links to the organizations' online information.

EnviroWeb also disseminates specific environmental information, such as "Action Alerts" about specific issues, organizing information, activism, and legal resources. It hosts the Sustainable Earth Electronic Library (SEEL), a collection of educational material about preserving the environment such as the *South Florida Environmental Reader* (Figure 26.24).

In addition, EnviroWeb hosts the "EnviroArts Gallery," a collection of essays, music, sounds, photos, and other art that evokes the environment and relationships with it. By providing a range of environmental information in a variety of online forums, the EnviroWeb demonstrates how the global reach of information can be used to promote saving the Earth.

FIGURE 26.24.

The South Florida Environmental Reader. *Copyright © 1991–1995 The EnviroLink Network (phone (800)328-7211). Used by permission. Courtesy of Josh Knauer, Director.*

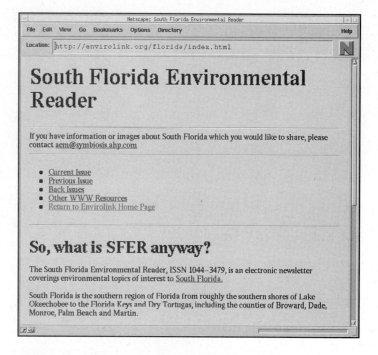

Woods Hole: Views from the Deep

Woods Hole Oceanographic Institution (`http://www.whoi.edu/`, Figure 26.25) at Woods Hole, Massachusetts, is a private, nonprofit corporation dedicated to exploring the frontiers of ocean science and research. Its facility at Woods Hole supports research in a variety of areas, from acoustic telemetry to seafloor samples, to ocean bottom and multichannel seismology.

One example of a lab at Woods Hole is the Deep Submergence Laboratory (DSL). The DSL focuses on unmanned explorations of the deep-sea floor; DSL engineers explored the *Titanic* using remotely operated vehicles, including Medea/Jason (used in the JASON project, described in Chapter 25). Figure 26.26 shows the DSL home page (`http://www.dsl.whoi.edu/`).

The DSL web offers connections to an assortment of undersea still images (Figure 26.27), as well as movies documenting the work of the remote vehicles. One movie, for example, shows the sonar imagery of the under-ice canopy from the Arctic Ocean. The 273KB MPEG file gives the user a glimpse of conditions on the deep-sea floor.

The DSL web demonstrates how the Web can deliver the wealth of knowledge from laboratories in very direct and visually dramatic ways.

FIGURE 26.25.

Woods Hole Oceanographic Institution home page. Courtesy of Julie Allen, Computer and Information Services, Woods Hole Oceanographic Institution.

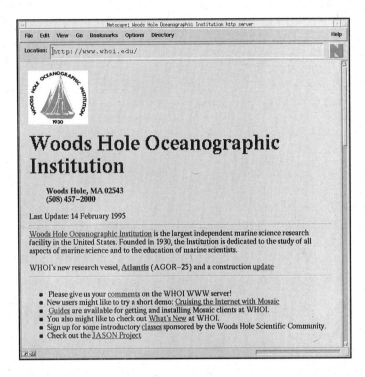

FIGURE 26.26.

The Deep Submergence Laboratory home page. Courtesy of Ken Stewart.

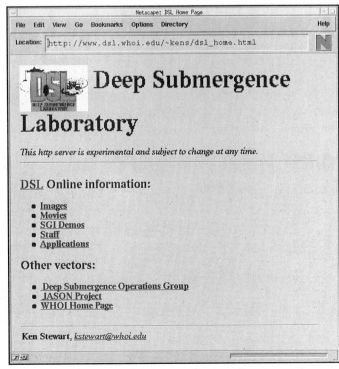

FIGURE 26.27.

The Deep Submergence Laboratory images. Courtesy of Ken Stewart.

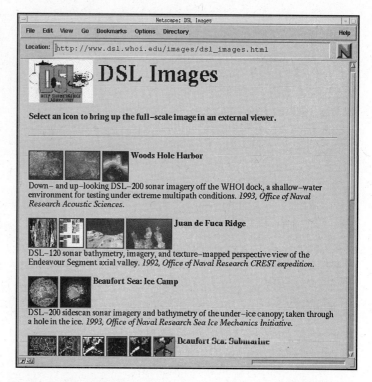

A Wealth of Knowledge from Laboratories

Besides efforts such as the preceding examples that involve multinational efforts to bring scientific and research communities together, there are webs that highlight the accomplishments of a single laboratory or research center. Through their webs, these labs offer a wealth of knowledge to interested researchers, potential participants, and the general public. From the examples in this section, you'll see how these webs are a rich source of unique information on the Web.

QUEST Protein Database Center

QUEST (QUantitative Electrophoresis STandardized) Protein Database Center is a U.S. National Institutes of Health biomedical-research technology resource. Located in Cold Spring Harbor (New York) Laboratory (CSHL), which provides services in addition to core research, the QUEST web's goal is to support the "construction and analysis of Protein Databases" (http:// siva.cshl.org/index.html). The home page for the QUEST web (http://siva.cshl.org/) is shown in Figure 26.28.

FIGURE 26.28.

The QUEST home page. Courtesy of QUEST Protein Database Center, Cold Spring Harbor Laboratory.

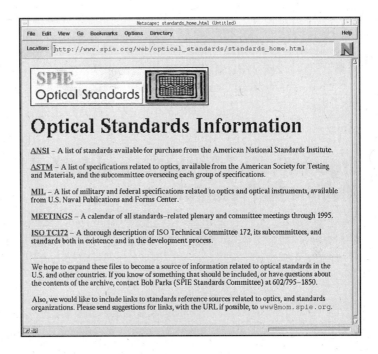

The QUEST web provides a detailed glimpse into protein research. For example, Figure 26.29 illustrates the image representation of a 2-D Gel Protein Database for a rat protein.

FIGURE 26.29.

Rat Protein Database. Courtesy of QUEST Protein Database Center, Cold Spring Harbor Laboratory.

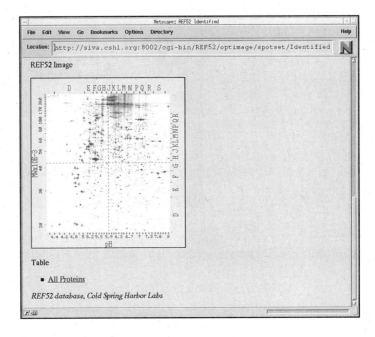

The QUEST web also provides

■ Links to software for analysis and comparison of protein patterns

■ Links to other related databases in Switzerland and at the Laboratory of Mathematical Biology, National Cancer Institute

The QUEST web is a good example of a single lab providing access to an extensive database of information through a graphical interface on a specific subject.

Ergonomics in Telerobotics and Control Laboratory: Multimedia Presentations

The Ergonomics in Telerobotics and Control (ETC) lab is part of the Human Factors Laboratories at the University of Toronto's Department of Industrial Engineering. The researchers of ETC lab (home page, `http://vered.rose.utoronto.ca/`, shown in Figure 26.30) work in a variety of areas, including telerobotics, virtual reality, and other perception- and display-related projects.

FIGURE 26.30.

The Ergonomics in Telerobotics and Control Lab home page. Courtesy of Human Factors Laboratories, University of Toronto Department of Industrial Engineering.

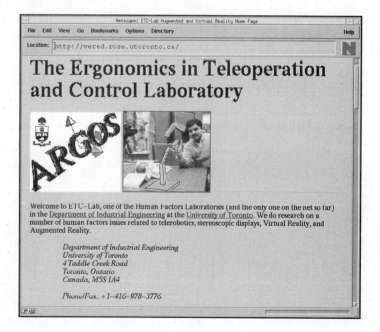

One project of the ETC lab is "Input/Manipulation in 3-D Environments." This project has a page containing important reference information for the project itself (Figure 26.31).

FIGURE 26.31.

Input/Manipulation in 3-D Environments. Courtesy of Shumin Zhai, Human Factors Laboratories, University of Toronto Department of Industrial Engineering.

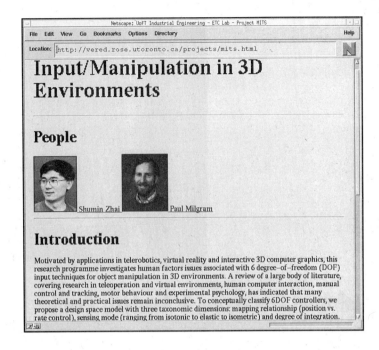

The developers of the ETC web use multimedia to illustrate the projects of the lab. The Input/Manipulation in the 3-D Environments page links to the home pages of the scientists working on the project as well as to information about the project itself—in the form of PostScript papers and MPEG movies of project demonstrations. A frame from the movie *Virtual Robotic Control* is shown in Figure 26.32. By viewing these movies, a user can get an idea of how the projects operate in a way not easily available with a textbook.

The ETC lab, like the Cold Spring Harbor Lab already mentioned, explains scientific work to the public and interested researchers, using innovative techniques for graphics and multimedia. The web pages for the labs are like an "open" lab tour always available to those who are interested, expanding public knowledge, drawing the attention of researchers, and creating relationships with researchers in these fields worldwide.

FIGURE 26.32.
A frame from the movie
Virtual Robotic Control.

Infrared Processing & Analysis Center

Another scientific laboratory with a web is the Infrared Processing & Analysis Center (IPAC), operated by the California Institute of Technology, Jet Propulsion Laboratory under contract to the National Aeronautics and Space Administration (NASA). IPAC's home page, `http://www.ipac.caltech.edu/`, is shown in Figure 26.33. The goal of IPAC is to perform the intensive processing NASA requires for infrared astronomy investigations as well as contribute scientific expertise on infrared imaging projects to the astronomical community. In pursuit of these goals, IPAC offers a variety of information through its web. Online User Services include resources and tools for observation planning, astronomical catalog scanning, sky atlas retrieval, and data processing services by e-mail. Also available are an archive for the Infrared Astronomical Satellite and Infrared Space Observatory tools. Project information is available for the 2 Micron All Sky Survey (to complete a map of the entire sky in near-infrared wavelengths), the Infrared Astronomical Satellite, the NASA/IPAC Extragalactic Database, the Astrophysics Data System, and the Midcourse Space Experiment (MSX). Another area contains links to news and information from the staff, bulletins, and the IPAC newsletter. These services provide a unique collection of detailed information about infrared imagery.

The Bulletins area of the web contains links to ongoing or special astronomical events. For example, the Supernova 1992bu in NGC 3690 was discovered in 1992 at NASA's Infrared Telescope Facility on Mauna Kea, Hawaii. The team of researchers from IPAC, CalTech, and the University of Hawaii provides a discussion of images of the supernova (Figure 26.34).

Another example of IPAC's offerings is the Infrared Sky Survey Atlas (ISSA) Postage Stamp Service, a tool to retrieve two-degree areas of the sky from the Infrared Sky Survey Atlas. Figure 26.35 shows the web page for the interface to the server.

FIGURE 26.33.

The Infrared Processing & Analysis Center home page.

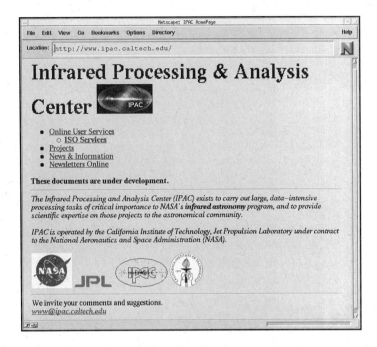

FIGURE 26.34.

Supernova 1992bu in NGC 3690 images.

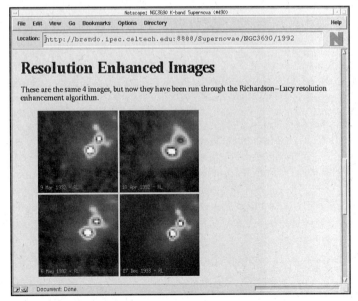

By entering the name of an object or a position, the user can retrieve an infrared image of the sky. This service, along with IPAC's extensive information on infrared astronomy, makes its collection a valuable part of the rich resources about astronomy that are available online.

FIGURE 26.35.

ISSA Postage-Stamp Service.

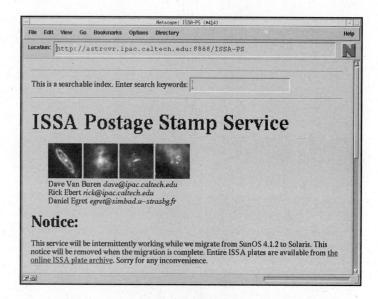

The MEMS Information ClearingHouse WWW Home Page

The Information Sciences Institute (ISI) at the University of Southern California is a research facility of the School of Engineering focusing on information-processing research and advanced communication systems (`http://www.isi.edu/`). As part of the ISI's projects, the Microelectromechanical Systems (MEMS) Information ClearingHouse was established by the U.S. Advanced Research Projects Agency's Electronic Systems Technology Office (ESTO). The goals of the MEMS Information ClearingHouse are to create information systems and perform basic research in technology products and processes (`http://esto.sysplan.com/ESTO/`). The MEMS home page (`http://mems.isi.edu/mems`) is shown in Figure 26.36.

Microelectromechanical systems include micro-devices (such as sensors and actuators) that are arranged into large collections to form an overall microdynamic system (`http://esto.sysplan.com/ESTO/MEMS/`). The clearinghouse offers information and interaction about MEMS in a variety of formats, including a discussion group (e-mail), a quarterly newsletter, and information archives (Figure 26.37). These archives offer a detailed set of information for research relevant to MEMS.

# Chapter 26

FIGURE 26.36.

The MEMS Information ClearingHouse WWW home page.

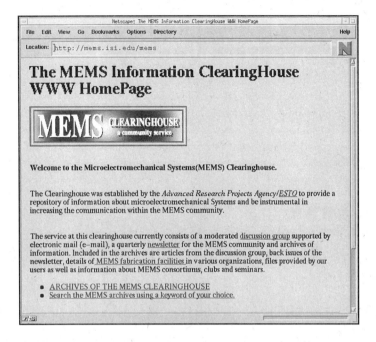

FIGURE 26.37.

MEMS Information ClearingHouse Information Archives.

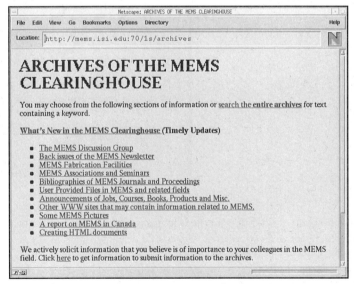

Gateway to Antarctica: Ongoing Explorations and Knowledge

In 1992, the International Centre for Antarctic Information and research (ICAIR) was established to serve as a central location for the collection and use of scientific and environmental information on Antarctica and the Southern Ocean. ICAIR is an independent organization within the Royal Society of New Zealand and is a joint initiative between New Zealand, the United States, and Italy. As part of its mission, the ICAIR collects and presents a variety of databases, geographic information systems, and remotely sensed imagery. The ICAIR web, called "Gateway to Antarctica" (http://icair.iac.org.nz/), is shown in Figure 26.38.

FIGURE 26.38.

Gateway to Antarctica.

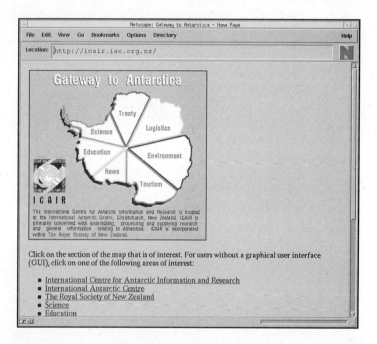

The ICAIR web offers a variety of links (as shown in the figure) to major information sources about Antarctica. For example, the science page links the user to information sources such as the contents pages from issues of *Antarctic Science*, the *Antarctic Address Book* (listing contacts of people who are interested in Antarctica), and a variety of reports and map catalogs. (For an example, see Figure 26.39.)

FIGURE 26.39.

Catalog of Ross Sea area coverage.

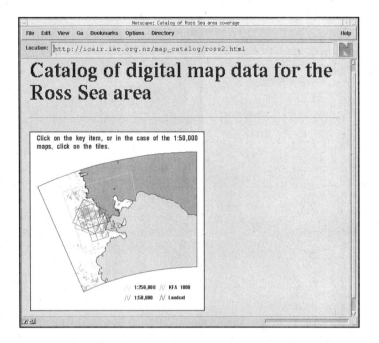

In addition to scientific information, the ICAIR web provides information to place the entire region in the context of international treaty information, logistic information for expeditions, and even tourism information such as a visitor's introduction to Antarctica and its environment. By showing leadership in collecting, reviewing, and presenting comprehensive information about the Antarctic, the ICAIR web demonstrates how an international organization can cooperate to provide accurate, up-to-date information about its area of speciality that can benefit the larger Web community.

WebElements: A Science Information Server

Although many of the preceding webs provide detailed views of very complex, team-produced science and technology, there are many opportunities for the individual researcher to contribute to science information on the Web. Dr. Mark J. Winter of the Department of Chemistry at the University, Sheffield (in England) has prepared a web called "WebElements" (`http:// www2.shef.ac.uk/chemistry/web-elements/web-elements-home.html`), shown in Figure 26.40.

Although not an official service of the university itself and still under development (as the web page states), the WebElements page demonstrates how a single individual can provide a useful interface to scientific information on the Web. By clicking a symbol shown in the figure, the user can get a page containing information about the element. Small, focused efforts like WebElements can add to the scientific offerings on the Web. With appropriate peer review and fact-checking, such services have the potential to enable other developers to draw upon them for advancing science itself.

FIGURE 26.40.

WebElements. Courtesy of Dr. Mark J. Winter, Department of Chemistry, The University, Sheffield.

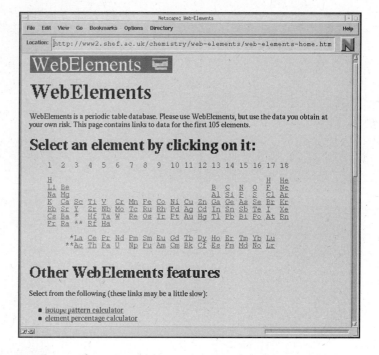

Explorer's Check

Because many scientific organizations were early adopters of World Wide Web technology, the offerings on the Web in the fields of science and technology are unusually abundant. Ranging from multinational efforts to coordinate access to information from a wide variety of databases such as the European Space Information System to the focused collection of peer-reviewed information about a field of knowledge like OncoLink, scientific information on the Web, in fields and specialties for which it exists, is often deep and rich. Groups such as the International Society for Optical Engineering draw professionals together to increase knowledge in a field. Other organizations such as the Institute for Telecommunication Sciences create webs serving the public interest for research and engineering.

Laboratories share their wealth of knowledge through webs that enable other scientific researchers to access databases and information sources. Webs such as Artificial Life Online create a forum for scientists to participate in developing new areas of knowledge. Although the work of scientific organizations is extensive and impressive, there are many opportunities for individuals to create focused webs to disseminate scientific information.

Communication, Publishing, and Information

27

by
John December

The Web is essentially a communications medium, making it possible for organizations, individuals, and groups to connect in a variety of ways. The applications discussed in the other chapters in this part reflect this; they all show examples of the Web as a communications tool. This chapter, however, focuses on Web communication in more detail, presenting applications in various contexts—individual, group, organizational, mass publishing, and specialized areas such as surveillance and information. These examples illustrate the flexibility of the Web as well as the ingenuity of people who mold and use it to fit their needs.

The communication categories *individual*, *group*, and *mass*, although useful guidelines to the scope of the communication contexts discussed here, are not necessarily clear-cut on the Web. Whereas traditional notions such as what distinguishes a mass publication from an individual one can shape our expectations about Web information, the Web itself can blur or break these expectations: An individual's home page might attract a larger audience than does a mass publication such as an online newspaper. Similarly, the boundaries of organizations can blur. Whereas organizations can provide very specialized information spaces, people can collaborate and provide similar or the same information, creating their own organizations on the Web.

Individual Communication

The tradition of having a personal *home page* is just that—a tradition. Although there's no technical reason why a person must have a page describing himself or herself, the practice of having one has evolved with the development of the Web. The origins of providing personal information over the network include the `.plan` files offered through the `finger` command; however, the personal home page allows a far more expressive and flexible format than does a `.plan` file.

A person creates a home page in the same way any other HTML page is written. (This is explained in Part V, "Weaving a Web.") The user makes a home page publicly available through a means that may vary from server to server, based on technical issues as well as administrative policy.

The information found on home pages varies widely, and reflects the diversity and personalities on the Web. There are no set formats, no one style or substance to include. In this section, four examples illustrate a variety of approaches to providing a web page that expresses one's personality.

Jane Patterson's Home Page

The first home page example is Jane Patterson's, shown in Figure 27.1.

Jane has created links to express her identity within the context of her work at her university (links to Willamette) as well as to other pages that outline her academic, artistic, and political interests. This extensive collection of links is a more thorough presentation than a typical home page, and it indicates the richness possible. Through personal home pages, people can network (a practice by which people grow a set of relationships in order to share information, resources, experiences, and advice) in a new way.

FIGURE 27.1.

Jane Patterson's home page.

For example, Jane's page contains a link to "My REAL Hotlist," the places on the Web she often visits. This helps people who share some of Jane's interests get connected with even more resources that may interest them. Also, *network friendship circles* can become expressed through links on home pages; for example, Jane has a link to Eric "Tilt" Tilton, a person with whom she works on a hypertext Principia Discordia project.

Ellen Spertus's Home Page

Ellen Spertus's home page is another example. Through links to the projects, individuals, and organizations connected to her work, she has created an intricate and very detailed personal information space. Part of her home page is shown in Figure 27.2.

Ellen's home page illustrates how a personal web page is frequently a treasure-trove of material related to an area of expertise or study. (See Chapter 18, "Trees: Subject-Oriented Searching.") Ellen's page illustrates how her contributions to knowledge in her fields of expertise augment the Web itself. For example, a link on her home page from the term "superscalar" to the free online dictionary of computing (http://wombat.doc.ic.ac.uk/) includes a definition that she contributed (http://wombat.doc.ic.ac.uk/?superscalar).

FIGURE 27.2.

Ellen Spertus's home page.

Michael Witbrock's Home Page

Michael Witbrock's home page conveys his personality, identity, and creativity through a balanced design and creative use of graphics. Figure 27.3 shows his "Fabulous Sepia Home Page."

Michael's page contains references—both personal and professional—that convey his interests. This set of links creates an information (and also a social) space that expresses humor ("talk to our cat"), professional accomplishments ("Publications"), and the context in which he works ("SCS [Carnegie Mellon's School of Computer Science] home page"). Thus, Michael's page, like Ellen's and Jane's, shows personal places of interest as well as specific knowledge, information, and works that he has created.

FINGER: AN EARLIER "PERSONAL BROADCAST" SERVICE

Just like the personal information available on a home page on the Web, users of UNIX systems have made use of the features of the `finger` protocol to provide a personal set of information for retrieval by any user on demand. A user can make `finger` information available by creating a text file called `.plan` in his or her home directory and making this file readable to anyone. When someone uses the command

`finger user@host.dom`

where `user@host.dom` is the electronic mail address of the fingeree, the contents of the `.plan` file are displayed to the fingerer.

It's a good idea to carefully consider what personal information you want to give out through `finger` (or your Web home page); remember, it is available *globally.*

FIGURE 27.3.

Michael Witbrock's Fabulous Sepia Home Page.

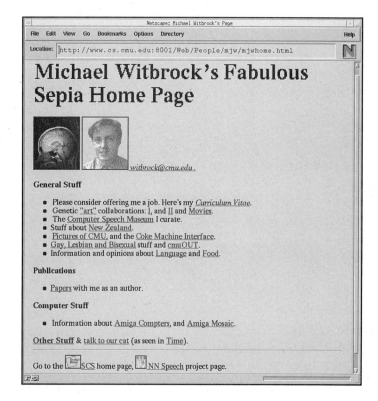

bianca's Shack

Whereas many home pages express a fairly conservative view of life, others adopt a very expressive, artistic view, and thus provide a gathering point for a culture or subculture. Figure 27.4 illustrates bianca's Shack, a collection of musings and art about a wide range of subjects. The figure shows the graphical information map interface. (See Chapter 34, "Advanced HTML Features.")

According to Chris Miller, a participant in bianca's Shack, the page exists as a jumping-off point on the Web for "artists, hackers, poets, and minstrels dedicated to making the Internet a happy and open place, where everyone may always be at play in the streams."

FIGURE 27.4.

bianca's Shack.

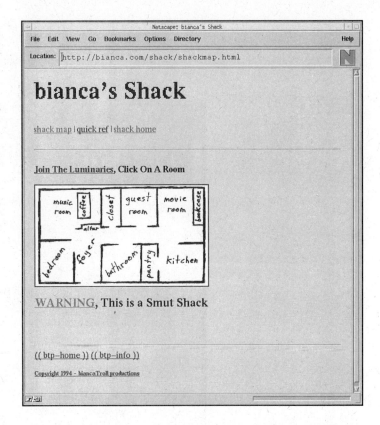

As these four examples illustrate, the individual communication expressed through the home page varies in style and content. The Web has an enormous potential to give people a means for creativity and self-expression. Home pages can open up the genius of individuals to everyone on the Web.

Group Communication

Whereas personal home pages represent the life and view of individuals, there are many other pages that groups of people use to communicate and form group identities. Many of these pages make use of the *interactive Forms* (see Chapter 34) a process of "interactive webbing" by which people can contribute to a common space for network-distributed hypermedia writing.

Hypergraffiti Walls—Free for All

Perhaps the forerunner of applications of interactive webbing was a page called Free for All, offered originally on the NCSA (National Center for Supercomputing Applications) web. Free for All was an HTML page allowing users to add any URL and a brief explanation for it. The contributors of these URLs had the ability to remain anonymous while posting (so that readers of the page would not necessarily know who posted what to the link), and the tone of the page quickly became graffiti-like with a wide range of entries. The page also grew very large, so that as of summer 1994, it was not available on its original server. Since then, other Free for Alls began operating; you can locate them through a spider search. (See Chapter 19, "Spiders and Indexes: Keyword-Oriented Searching.") Use the keywords `free for all` or `graffiti wall`.

Web Interactive Talk

Whereas hypergraffiti can create group communication on one level (in which each participant contributes just a link in a sequence of links), other systems for adapting to the Web for group communication have been developed. One is *World Wide Web Interactive Talk* (WIT), `http://www.w3.org/hypertext/WWW/WIT/User/Overview.html`. WIT was originally developed by Ari Luotonen and Tim Berners-Lee following the first international World Wide Web conference in Switzerland.

In WIT, a user can contribute a new proposal for discussion or respond to an existing proposal within the context of a list of topics in a discussion area. Although similar to other discussion systems such as Usenet or mailing lists, WIT differs in at least one important aspect: The contributions do not "evaporate" after the user submits them because they are not distributed through a propagation scheme. Rather, the postings are stored on the computer hosting the discussion area(s). Using this feature, the goal is to create a permanent knowledge base in which the same topic is not introduced time and time again. This important difference between WIT and both Usenet and mailing lists could possibly change the kind of communication taking place. For more discussion on this topic, see Chapter 49, "Conferencing on the Web."

Jay's House: Melding a MOO with the Web

A group communication system called a MOO provides chances for lively talk and interchange. The term *MOO* stands for MUD Object Oriented. The term *MUD* stands for Multiple User Dimension/Dialogue/Dungeon and is a term for a class of computer programs that enable users to traverse and build a text-based virtual world.

A MOO is a variant of a MUD that borrows ideas about its structure and operation from a computer software-engineering technique known as *object-oriented* programming, in which software components are considered to be objects consisting of encapsulated data (nouns) and operations that can be performed on that data (verbs). In a MOO, everything is an object—even the inhabitants—and object-oriented concepts such as inheritance provide builders in a MOO with ways to create still more objects.

The corridors and links of a MOO are lively with conversations and objects, in a world made of text. Builders in a MOO must rely on their skills with words to create imagery. Although most MOOs are not connected to the Web (most are available for use through special client software or through Telnet access), there's a MOO called Jay's House that has nestled some of its functions into the Web.

The Web entrance for Jay's House MOO (JHM) is at `http://jh.ccs.neu.edu:7043/`. This entrance provides links to helpful information about JHM and some views of the goings on of the JHM itself.

For example, from the Web entrance for JHM, you can

- Look at the objects in The Big Book of Objects
- View the help system
- See who's currently logged into JHM
- View background materials, including papers and other information about JHM

Although the Web entrance for JHM allows you to see many features of JHM, true interactivity is still available only through a MOO client or a Telnet session. However, JHM demonstrates a truly intriguing possibility—the first steps toward integrating the lively real-time interactions possible in a MOO with the Web.

Organizational Communication

Applications using interactive webbing lead to intriguing structures, but an organization that needs to communicate information to its members requires less interactivity and more information and usability. An organization needs to inform its members to support their activities, to create a sense of belonging in the group, and to communicate to others what that group is all about. The next section covers some Web applications that organizations use to reach their members.

Campus-Wide Information System

Colleges have the mission to provide for the educational development of students and to support staff, faculty, and all others involved in the life of the college. A college community is a whole world unto itself, with a great variety of information needs ranging from building locations, library hours, course offerings, departments, and other information about the academic and support community.

A type of system for delivering information for a university or college called a *Campus-Wide Information System* (CWIS) has developed out of this need. Telnet and Gophers were the systems of choice for many initial CWISs , and today Gophers still meet many needs for information. However, the development of the Web has brought many CWIS developers to Web-space. Polly-Alida Farrington maintains a list of CWISs at `http://www.rpi.edu/dept/library/html/cwis/cwis.html/`, including links to Gopher, Telnet, and Web-based CWISs.

One example of a CWIS is St. Olaf College's Web Server, `http://www.stolaf.edu/`, shown in Figure 27.5.

FIGURE 27.5.

The St. Olaf College home page.

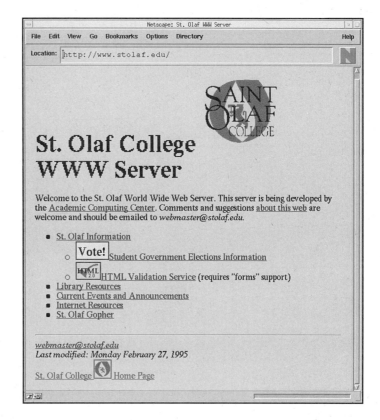

St. Olaf's CWIS offers a rich set of information to support its campus community. From links on the front page, you can reach the services shown in Figure 27.5. Information about St. Olaf, the library, current events, and resources, as well as St. Olaf's Gopher-based CWIS. St. Olaf's CWIS also offers the following:

- An interactive campus map (see Figure 27.10), `http://www.stolaf.edu/stolaf/stolaf/map/`, showing the buildings on campus and offering text, audio, or picture information to describe each building.

- A complete course catalog, `http://www.stolaf.edu/stolaf/catalog/courses/`, with hypertext links to current class and lab schedules.

- A special collection of U.S. State Department Travel Advisories and Consular Information Sheets, `http://www.stolaf.edu/network/travel-advisories.html`. St. Olaf is the designated Internet and BITNET distribution point for this information, so it is among St. Olaf's unique offerings.

- A hypertext interface to its library catalog interface, `http://www.stolaf.edu/library/unofficial_pals.html`.

- A complete presentation, including the full audio, of the St. Olaf Choir's signature piece, "Beautiful Savior," `http://www.stolaf.edu/stolaf/depts/music/stolaf_choir/`.

FIGURE 27.6.

St. Olaf's campus map.

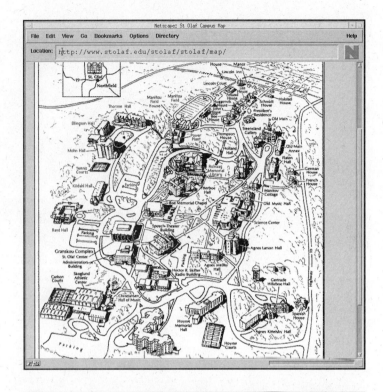

FIGURE 27.7.

St. Olaf's choir.

Through a collection of unique resources and "standards" (customary information that many colleges offer), St. Olaf's CWIS supports the current campus community, potential staff and students, and even alumni who want to find out what's going on at the campus.

A Commercial Organization—MathWorks, Inc.

A commercial organization shares many of the interests an academic organization has—to provide information and support connections among people. In the case of a commercial organization, however, these connections include those among customers, employees, and the general public. A commercial organization's web often provides many of the same functions as an academic CWIS, but with some differences—most notably a focus on product support and *domain* (the subject area in which the commerce is conducted) information to a geographically dispersed audience.

MathWorks, Inc. (`http://www.mathworks.com/`) produces MATLAB, a scientific and engineering software tool. As shown in Figure 27.8, MathWorks's home page offers links to

- What's New notice
- Product information
- MATLAB forum—a collection of resources useful to customers
- Contact information

FIGURE 27.8.

The MathWorks, Inc., home page.

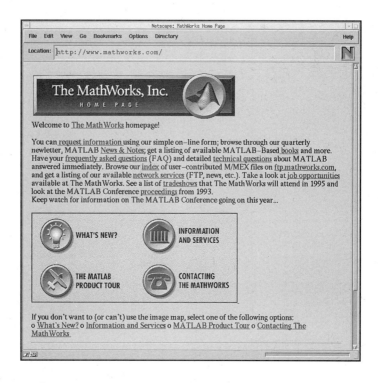

Like the St. Olaf CWIS, the MathWorks web provides an extensive set of links and pages. Unlike the St. Olaf web, however, which addresses the concerns of people located within a geographic region, the MathWorks web seeks to address a worldwide audience of customers, potential customers, and employees.

To accomplish this, MathWorks provides a graphical interface that serves throughout its web to guide the user to information about the company as well as its products and services. Because MATLAB is a scientific visualization tool, the MathWorks web also hosts a MATLAB Gallery that contains exemplary applications of MATLAB.

FIGURE 27.9.

The MATLAB Gallery.

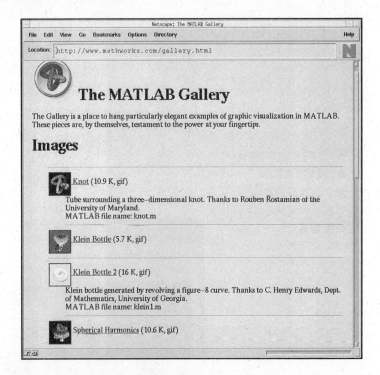

Because MATLAB runs on workstations that also often support Web browsers for X, customers using MATLAB can use a session of a Web browser to learn more about the product and its applications online.

A Nonprofit Organization—The Computer Professionals for Social Responsibility (CPSR)

The Computer Professionals for Social Responsibility (CPSR) (http://www.cpsr.org/home) is an alliance of information-technology professionals who are concerned about public policy issues dealing with information technology. Unlike a campus CWIS or a commercial web, CPSR's members are not all located in the same place geographically. Therefore, the CPSR web functions as a critical tool to provide information for its members who are spread throughout the world.

FIGURE 27.10.

The Computer Professionals for Social Responsibility home page.

CPSR's web, therefore, delves deeply into both organizational information about CPSR and issues of interest to CPSR members or potential members. Moreover, since CPSR's web also functions to serve part of its mission to provide public information on critical issues, its holdings in many areas are quite extensive. For example, its Gender and Minority Issues directory contains extensive links to online resources. (See Figure 27.11.)

The CPSR web, like the MATLAB web, reaches its geographically dispersed constituents with relevant domain information. Whereas a campus CWIS can draw on cultural artifacts and activities from the physical world its members inhabit, the dispersed organization must create an entirely virtual world and thus create an information space that, for the users, becomes the organization.

FIGURE 27.11.
The Computer Professionals for Social Responsibility Gender information.

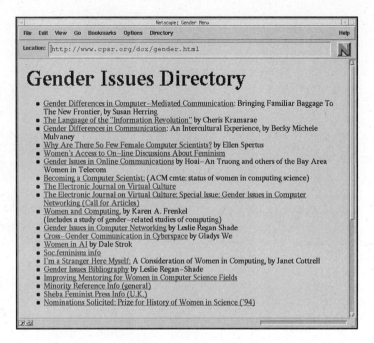

Publishing

Although the Web might blur the distinction among communication contexts—individual, group, and mass—the intent of many Web offerings is to reach a large audience. Although mass communication through the Web is still an emerging practice, publishers of paper-based information have crossed over to the Web. In many cases, the result of this crossover is an online publication that continues some print traditions and conventions. Another aspect of mass communication involves supporting off-Web activities such as radio broadcasting and product sales. This section explores examples of several of these forms of Web-based publishing.

A Newspaper—The *Palo Alto Weekly*

The *Palo Alto Weekly* is a twice-weekly, free newspaper distributed in the Palo Alto, California area. Covering events of local interest such as land use, community policing, government, and education, as well as features such as health and fitness, sports, and arts and entertainment, the paper serves its communities with a variety of information. The home page of the Web version of The *Palo Alto Weekly* is shown in Figure 27.12.

Chapter 27

741

FIGURE 27.12.

The Palo Alto Weekly *home page. (Copyright 1994 Embarcadero Publishing Company. All rights reserved. The* Palo Alto Weekly *and the* Weekly *logo are registered trademarks of Embarcadero Publishing Company. Other trademarks or registered trademarks are the property of their respective owners. Reprinted by permission.)*

Internet Distribution Services, Inc. provides the Web services for the paper, and the offerings through the Web include an index and links to back issues as well as the full text of the current issue. Aside from distributing the text through the Web, the paper itself contains no unusual Net-references or interaction (no hypertext links in the Web-version text, for example). In this way, *Palo Alto Weekly* demonstrates simultaneous publication on paper and on the Web.

A Zine—Cyberkind

Unlike *Palo Alto Weekly*, there are many publications intended for mass, public use that exist solely on the Web with no paper equivalent. John Labowitz maintains a list of online magazines (or *zines*—a term used to describe a small or self-published periodical, particularly network-based ones, although the term now encompasses many periodicals, some of which involve extensive professional and commercial involvement) available on the net at `http://www.ora.com:8080/johnl/e-zine-list/`. The origins of zines go far back before the start of the Web, growing out of the early use of bulletin board systems and electronic mail. People realized that they could be publishers by creating content that appeals to a wide audience and distributing that content through informal and formal channels, including electronic mail and/or computer bulletin board systems.

Although early zines consisted of basic ASCII text, Web-based versions have sprung up, exploiting the possibilities offered by hypertext in both the design of the magazine itself and in the articles. Although *Palo Alto Weekly* uses many hypertext features in its Web presentation, it uses none within the text of its articles. In contrast, one example of an online magazine, *Cyberkind*, shown in Figure 27.13, uses hyperlinks in both its design and content.

FIGURE 27.13.

Cyberkind *home page.
(Logo and design Copyright
1994 by Dykki Settle. Table
of contents graphic and
separator line design
Copyright 1994 by Luke
Duncan. Reprinted by
permission.)*

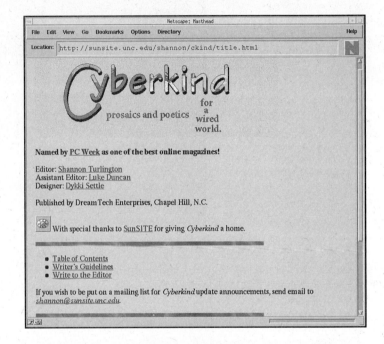

Edited by Shannon Turlington, *Cyberkind* offers a mix of nonfiction, poetry, and fiction that has some relation to cyberspace or online discourse. The result is a publication with a unique appeal, available Web-wide to anyone would like to read or contribute.

FutureNet—A New Face in Publishing

FutureNet is part of the online work of *Future Publishing*, a successful (paper) magazine publishing enterprise in Britain. *Future Publishing*, like many other paper-based publishing enterprises, is starting to realize that paper is not the only way to reach customers. FutureNet represents its effort on the Web, and provides access to content selected from *Future Publishing*'s more than 37 specialist consumer magazines and other material prepared for the Web. Figure 27.14 shows FutureNet's home page (http://www.futurenet.co.uk/).

FIGURE 27.14.
FutureNet home page.
(Courtesy of Karl Foster.)

FutureNet's web offers a wide range of content in computing, music, games, outdoors, crafts, and other consumer interest areas. For example, the computing section gives access to the individual magazines in that category, subscription information, plus samples of content. The whole of certain issues of some magazines are online—for example the premier issue of the magazine *.net.* (See Figure 27.15.)

FutureNet is not the only Web-based effort at magazine publishing by paper-based publishers. Time-Warner's electronic publishing Web efforts (`http://www.timeinc.com/time/universe.html`) include support pages for its paper *Time* magazine and full text of its Web-based *Pathfinder* (`http://pathfinder.com`), among others. *Hotwired* (`http://www.hotwired.com/`) is the Web counterpart of the popular paper magazine, *Wired.* You can find more Web-based publishing information in Yahoo's (`http://www.yahoo.com/`) sections on Business-Corporations-Publishing and Business-Corporations-Magazines.

Online Publishing—Electric Press

Whereas paper-based publications and zines can reach a mass audience with news, opinion, features, and other traditional journalism content, other Web services work to present services and products to build presence on the Web and support widespread attention to a particular customer's content as the focus of a web. For example, the Electric Press (`http://www.elpress.com/`, home page shown in Figure 27.16) offers a range of products and services to create business opportunities on the Web.

FIGURE 27.15.

.net magazine home page.
(Courtesy of Karl Foster.)

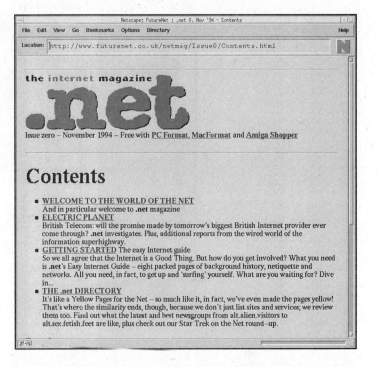

FIGURE 27.16.

The Electric Press home page.

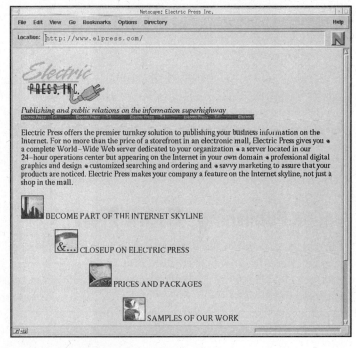

Distribution of mass information has long been supported by advertisers—in the case of free community (and most other) magazines, advertising is the main source of revenue. Operating within the context of the Web, developers have recognized the widespread "free" nature of Web information and use a model of providing customers directly to advertisers through attractive information and interaction.

The Electric Press is an example of an organization that provides specific products and services to (potentially) bypass the journalism content and directly link an advertiser to customers to offer information "advertisements" through a Web server or other network communication. This same model of direct advertiser-customer connection can be seen in many commercial Web applications. (See Chapter 24, "Entertainment and the Arts.")

Internet Multicasting Service—Talk Radio and More

Internet Talk Radio is a service of the Internet Multicasting Service (IMS), a nonprofit corporation based in the National Press Building in Washington, D.C., IMS serves the Internet community currently with two channels of online sound distribution files: Internet Talk Radio (science and technology coverage) and Internet Town Hall (public affairs). IMS is not really a radio station in the traditional sense (it does not broadcast over the air), but it publishes sound files that you can download and listen to. You can get sound files of previous programs as well as access libraries of sound files. IMS is perhaps most famous for its Internet Talk Radio program (`http://town.hall.org/radio/index.html`) shown in Figure 27.17. This page gives you access to the current developed programs as well as past programs.

FIGURE 27.17.

The Internet Talk Radio home page. (Courtesy of Carl Malamud.)

746

The IMS web also provides a unique glimpse into real-world places such as the "Digital Deli" section, which provides you access to places such as the menu from the Red Sage restaurant in Washington, D.C., complete with sound greetings from the hostess and audio clips describing what's on the menu. (See Figure 27.18.)

FIGURE 27.18.

Menu at the Red Sage restaurant in Washington, D.C. (Courtesy of Carl Malamud.)

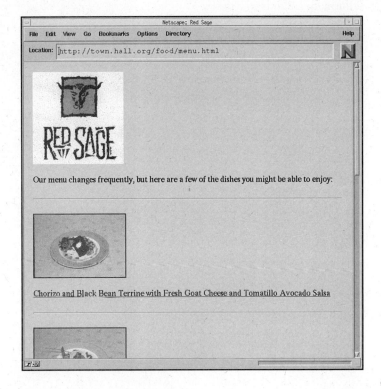

You read more about IMS at the FAQ `http://town.hall.org/radio/faq.html`. From there, you can find out more about sound files, distribution, and other sites where you can listen to more Internet Radio, and perhaps get into desktop radio broadcasting yourself.

Supporting Radio Broadcasting—Canadian Broadcasting Corporation (CBC)

The Canadian Broadcasting Corporation's Radio services, working with the New Broadcast Services Laboratory of the Communications Research Centre (CRC) (`http://www.crc.doc.ca/`) in Canada have created a Web page (see Figure 27.19) containing links to supporting information as well as the full sound recordings about CBC broadcasts (`http://radioworks.cbc.ca/`).

FIGURE 27.19.

The CBC Radio home page.

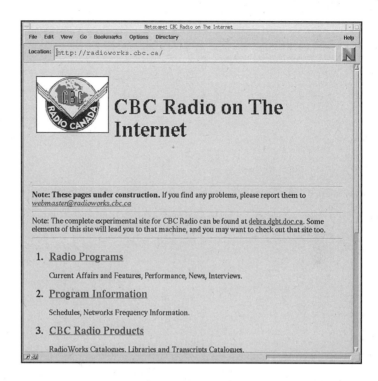

CBC's Radio Trial is the first presence of a national broadcaster on the Internet, and its offerings at its Web site are extensive. The collection includes popular, general-interest programs such as "Quirks and Quarks" (a science program), "Basic Black" (featuring people with unusual activities), and "Sunday Morning" (CBC's flagship current-affairs program). The CBC's web links users to audio files of segments of each program, program schedules, and information about how to order supporting products such as transcripts and recordings.

A new product offered on CBC's web is Illustrated Audio, a synchronization of text and image that gives images a sound track and defines a new file format (.Ia, illustrated audio). Thus, the CBC has innovatively moved beyond just sound to merging pictures and images and making these available to a global audience on a demand basis—a different model than just broadcast radio. CBC's whole effort demonstrates the power of the world's first broadcast mass medium to move into the world's newest.

Supporting Television Broadcasting—CBS, Inc.

CBS Television was the first major U.S. television network with an official Web page (although "fan" pages collecting information from other networks and many particular programs have been on the Web for a while). The CBS web (http://www.cbs.com/) supports its broadcast programs, offering information about its programs as well as other projects. The CBS home page is shown in Figure 27.20.

FIGURE 27.20.

CBS Television home page. (Copyright 1995. CBS, Inc. All Rights Reserved. Printed by permission.)

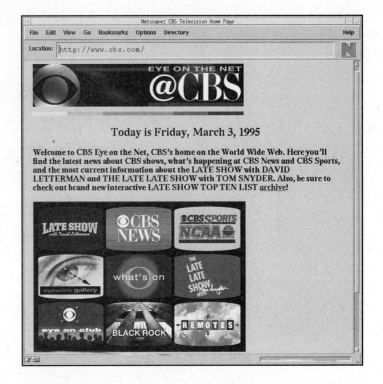

As part of its offerings, the CBS web includes links to major programs. For example, "Late Show with David Letterman" now has an official home page. (You can see an unofficial Letterman page at http://bingen.cs.csbsju.edu/letterman.html.) The CBS page for Letterman (see Figure 27.21) includes information about upcoming guests and the staff of the show, as well as the signature comedy piece from the show—the Top 10 lists.

The CBS web also provides some information about CBS and its efforts to interact more with its audience. The Black Rock page (see Figure 27.22) gives a glimpse into these activities. ("Black Rock" is the informal name for CBS's imposing black granite headquarters building on West 52nd Street in New York City.)

FIGURE 27.21.

The Late Show with David Letterman home page. (Copyright 1995. Worldwide Pants, Incorporated. All rights reserved. Printed by permission.)

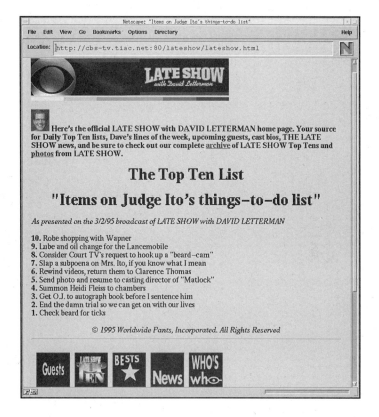

By combining television schedules and other "official" information plus some of the most popular "teaser" information circulating on the Internet (Letterman's Top 10 lists are among the most popular items circulated online), the CBS web shows how a broadcaster can begin the process of including the Web as part of its media delivery options.

FIGURE 27.22.

Black Rock home page. (Copyright 1995. CBS, Inc. All rights reserved. Printed by permission.)

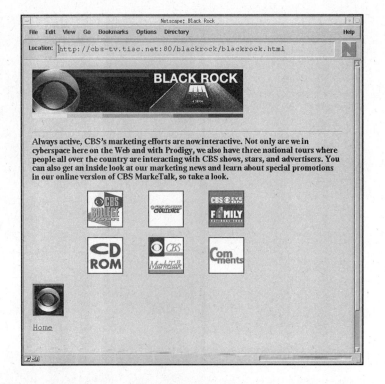

The Macmillan USA Information SuperLibrary—Supporting Readers Online

Macmillan Publishing USA created a "SuperLibrary"—a collection of information about books, computers, reference materials, and software that supports readers as well as the whole Web community. Macmillan Publishing USA (a Simon and Schuster company, the publishing arm of Viacom) consists of several divisions offering books under a variety of imprints. One division, Macmillan Computer Publishing, the world's leading computer book publisher, offers books under the imprints Brady, Hayden, New Riders, Que, Que College, Sams, and Sam.net (this book's imprint). The Macmillan SuperLibrary web (http://www.mcp.com, Figure 27.23) supports this extensive publishing enterprise by reaching the readers of (and potential customers for) their books right on the Web.

FIGURE 27.23.

The Macmillan USA Information SuperLibrary home page. (©1995, Macmillan Publishing USA, a Simon and Schuster Company.)

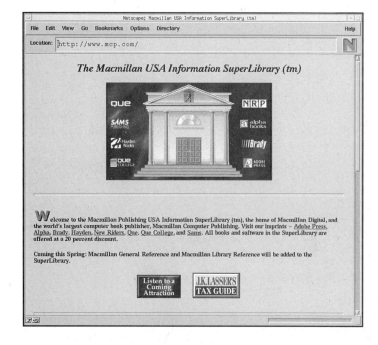

FIGURE 27.24.

The Macmillan USA Information SuperLibrary home page. (©1995, Macmillan Publishing USA, a Simon and Schuster Company.)

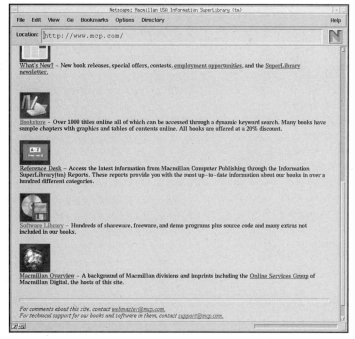

Figure 27.24 shows the bottom of the SuperLibrary web, illustrating the main sections of the web:

■ A newsletter offering information about new books, press releases, special offers, and contests. This newsletter includes features such as the "Author Talk" column in which Macmillan authors talk about their work. (For example, see `http://www.mcp.com/general/news1/jdec.html` for an article about the genesis of the first edition of this book.)

■ A full bookstore, offering access to information pages for individual titles. You can scan the database by keyword, so you can quickly find the book you need. Each book has a home page (see Figure 25.25 for the home page for the first edition of this book) where you can access a table of contents listing plus sample chapters. Watch for online discounts on book purchases.

FIGURE 25.25.

The World Wide Web Unleashed *(first edition) book home page. (© 1995, Macmillan Publishing USA, a Simon and Schuster Company.)*

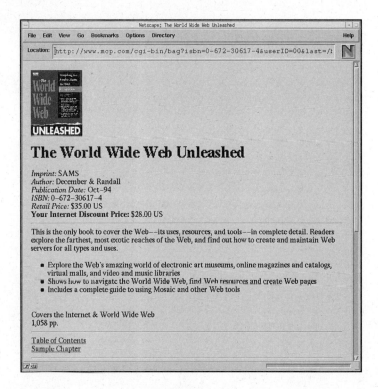

■ A reference desk (see Figure 26.26) giving access to a full range of reports, reference articles, and back issues of the SuperLibrary Newsletter. For example, you can subscribe to free reports on dozens of subjects ranging from databases to desktop publishing.

FIGURE 27.26.

The Macmillan USA Information SuperLibrary Reference Desk. (© 1995, Macmillan Publishing USA, a Simon and Schuster Company.)

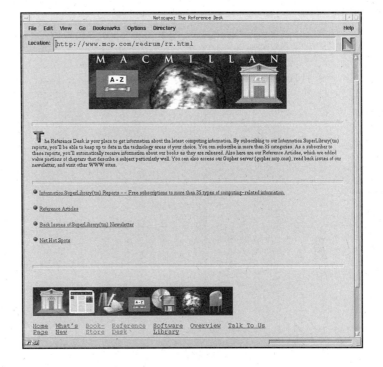

- A software library (see Figure 27.27) giving you access to shareware and demonstration programs, plus extras and other materials featured in Macmillan books. (FTP access is also available through `ftp://ftp.mcp.com`.) Application areas include word processing, games, programming, Internet, and multimedia. For example, you can access a variety of Internet software library applications and files at `http://www.mcp.com/softlib/Internet/`.

- An overview of Macmillan, explaining the different divisions (including Macmillan Digital USA, developers of the Macmillan web) as well as links to author home pages and other links to the people behind all the books and information offered by the SuperLibrary.

The Macmillan web offers an array of support services for readers, computer enthusiasts, and potential book buyers, as well as keyword searching mechanisms so that customers can find the books they need, communication opportunities to contact the people at `mcp.com` or authors (through e-mail or Web pages), and the delivery of the latest information and updates through the newsletter, reference desk, and software library. Macmillan's web—by fostering these author-reader, customer-company, and customer-information relationships, demonstrates the power of the Web to create a strong online presence for a book publisher.

FIGURE 27.27.

*The Macmillan USA
Information SuperLibrary
Software Library. (© 1995,
Macmillan Publishing USA,
a Simon and Schuster
Company.)*

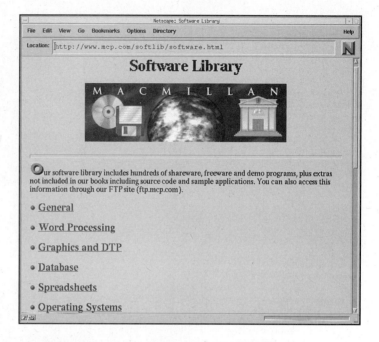

Surveillance and Remote Manipulation

The preceding applications for communication deal in varying degrees with the size of the audience intended for the communication. This section deals with a specialized kind of communication—surveillance—and how it can be used for remote sight, manipulation, and temperature sensing.

Sight—Spy on Dennis Gannon, Research Director of the Center for Innovative Computer Application

Dennis Gannon is director of CICA (The Center for Innovative Computer Applications at Indiana University, http://www.cica.indiana.edu/). In the spring of 1994, he had a new workstation installed in his office, equipped with a small camera on the top of it. One of the graphics programmers at CICA, without telling Dennis, hooked up the camera to a screen-capture program and added it to the "What's New" page for CICA, without going into Dennis Gannon's office. The result allows anyone with a graphical browser to "spy" on Dennis Gannon, as well as other CICA Celebrities, as shown in Figure 27.28.

Subsequently, the graphics programmer let Dennis in on the joke—and the page remained on the CICA web. This application provides a demonstration of an innovative application: remote sensing via the Web. Normally, Web users expect to encounter text and graphics and perhaps animations, movies, or sound files, but the Web itself can be used to extend the human senses. There are other applications similar to the CICA camera that "spy" on areas of a campus or a coffee pot. (See the next section, "Beverage Surveillance.")

FIGURE 27.28.

Spy on Local CICA Celebrities.

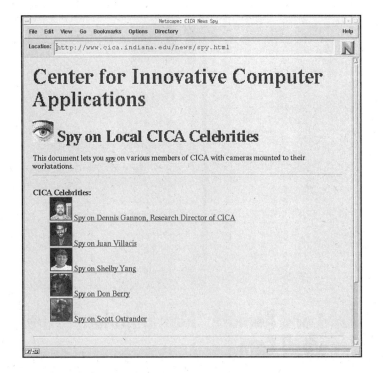

Temperature—The Roof of the Engineering Center at the University of Colorado

The Web can also extend your sense of temperature—at least through a numerical temperature readout. Oliver McBryan created an application (see Figure 27.29) that connects a remote sensing device to a Web page.

While the statement "Click here, then touch the middle mouse button, to feel the current temperature" is a humorous addition—or perhaps a challenge along the lines of the finger-vending machine interface in the specification for the `finger` protocol (see the next section, "Beverage Surveillance"); the temperature sensor, along with similar applications on the Web, extends the bounds of what can be communicated across networks.

FIGURE 27.29.

University of Colorado Engineering Center roof temperature. (Courtesy of Oliver McBryan.)

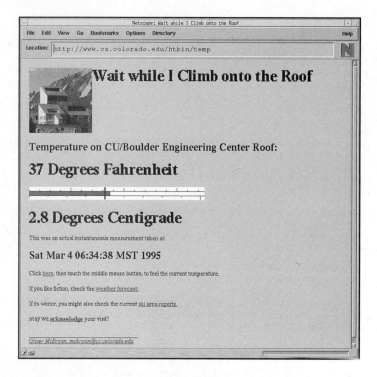

Sight and Remote "Manipulation"—The Rome Lab Snowball Cam

The United States Air Force's Rome Laboratory (`http://www.rl.af.mil:8001/`) is one of the nation's premiere laboratories for research into C4I (command, control, communications, computation, and intelligence) technologies. People at the Rome Lab delve into cutting-edge projects in intelligence, reconnaissance, surveillance, photonics, electromagnetics, and many other fields. The Rome Lab's motto is, "Where Visions Become Reality," and its home page (Figure 27.30) offers a good glimpse of the serious research that takes place there.

While the defense community looks upon the Rome Lab as an outstanding C4I research facility, users of the Web know the Rome Lab as the home of the Snowball Cam. Extending the ideas and technologies of remote viewing via the Web, plus remote manipulation, the Rome Lab Snowball Cam is a unique application of the Web (`http://www.rl.af.mil:8001/Odds-n-Ends/sbcam/rlsbcam.html`).

FIGURE 27.30.

The Rome Laboratory home page. (Courtesy of the Rome Laboratory, U.S. Air Force.)

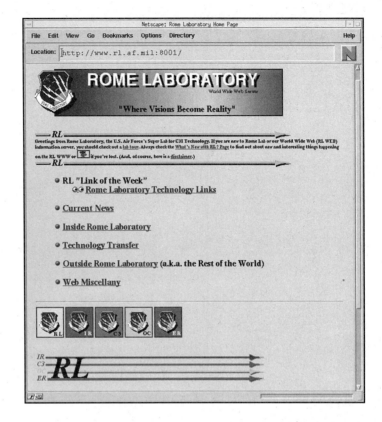

The Snowball Cam allows users to throw simulated snowballs at the occupants of a computer room at the lab. No physical snowballs or any other projectiles are thrown, but a simulated hit is shown as a result of the user selecting one of three snowball icons on the Snowball Cam home page. The hit is shown superimposed on the scene in that computer room—along with whatever occupants may be in that room at the time. The example shown in Figure 27.32 is from the Snowball Cam hall of fame (which offers free parking as well as an international wing). This shot is called, "That's gonna leave a mark," and was thrown by Dave Farrier from the computer host `lsptppp35.epix.net`.

FIGURE 27.31.

The Rome Lab Snowball Cam home page. (Courtesy of Scott Gregory, Rome Laboratory.)

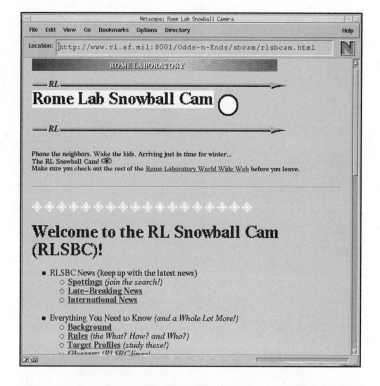

FIGURE 27.32.

Snowball Cam hall of fame shot by Dave Farrier. (Courtesy of Scott Gregory, Rome Laboratory.)

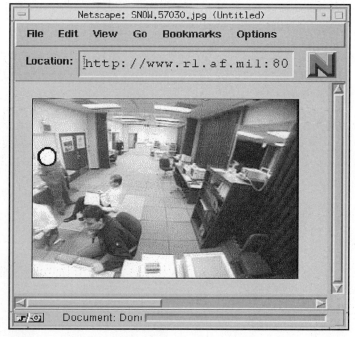

The Snowball Cam, although a light-hearted exercise, builds the skills and creative abilities of the Web developers who invent applications such as this. Through similar surveillance and remote manipulation, these creative Web developers continue to open new possibilities for communication on the Web. For more glimpses of other devices, see Yahoo's list at `http://www.yahoo.com/Computers/Internet/Interesting_Devices_Connected_to_the_Net/`.

Beverage Surveillance

Just as Web home pages have some origins in the `.plan` files offered by the `finger` protocol, so do applications for Web surveillance. A connection for an interaction between the `finger` protocol and vending machines was specified in the Network Working Group's RFC (Request For Comments), a document that specified an Internet Activity Board standard for a protocol for the Internet community. RFC 1288, "The Finger User Information Protocol" by D. Zimmerman, includes this statement on page 7: "Vending machines *should* respond to a {C} request with a list of all items currently available for purchase and possible consumption. Vending machines SHOULD respond to a {U} {C} request with a detailed count or list of the particular product or product slot. Vending machines should *never never ever* eat money."

Obviously, this specification was provided in jest, a humorous turn to an otherwise (to casual readers at least) dry technical specification. But graduate students and computer scientists (some of whom can be quite literal-minded) have implemented the `finger` command to operate as specified. There are a variety of Internet-accessible vending machines on the Net. For example, checking on the machine at Carnegie Mellon University, `finger coke@g.gp.cs.cmu.edu` (equivalent to URL `gopher://g.gp.cs.cmu.edu:79/0coke`), we can see the state of this machine:

```
Login name: coke          In real life: Drink Coke
Directory: /usrg1/coke        Shell: /usr/cs/bin/csh
Last login Tue Nov 15 13:50 on ttyv8 from PTERO.SOAR.CS.CMU.EDU
Mail is forwarded to coke@L.GP.CS.CMU.EDU
Plan:
Thu Sep 29 17:33:39 1994
M&M validity: 0   Coke validity: 0 (e.g. da interface is down, sorry!)
Exact change required for coke machine.
  M & M            Buttons
 /――\      C: CCCCCCCCCCCC............
 ｜   ｜     C: CCCCCC...... D: CCCCCC......
 ｜** ｜     C: CCCCCC...... D: CCCCCC......
 ｜*****｜      C: CCCCCC...... D: CCCCCC......
 ｜*****｜          C: CCCCCC.....
 \――/          S: CCCCCC.....
  ｜     Key:
  ｜      0 = warm; 9 = 90% cold; C = cold; . = empty
  ｜      Leftmost soda/pop will be dispensed next
```

Extended to the Web, this idea can lead to another kind of beverage surveillance: coffee. The

Trojan Room Coffee Machine at http://www.cl.cam.ac.uk/coffee/coffee.html (see Figure 27.33) provides the user with a way to get a real-time view of the amount of coffee in the pot. While obviously only useful to members of the research lab, its operation extends the interaction between the Web and machines, providing a view of how the Web itself can extend one's senses.

FIGURE 27.33.

The Trojan Room coffee machine. (Courtesy of Daniel Gordon.)

Weather

Whereas surveillance for pictures of beverage levels and other "spy" cameras make for interesting exercises in linking the Web to the larger world, other applications of remote sensing are particularly useful. For example, real-time weather forecasts and reports have long been made available over the Internet, mostly through text interfaces. With the widespread development of graphical browsers, current weather imagery—satellite cloud cover images, forecast maps, and digital radar summaries—has been made available over the Net.

Charles Henrich at Michigan State University has developed an Interactive Weather Browser, weaving together many existing weather data sources into an easy-to-use Web interface. Figure 27.34 shows the front page.

FIGURE 27.34.

The Interactive Weather Browser. (Courtesy of Charles Henrich.)

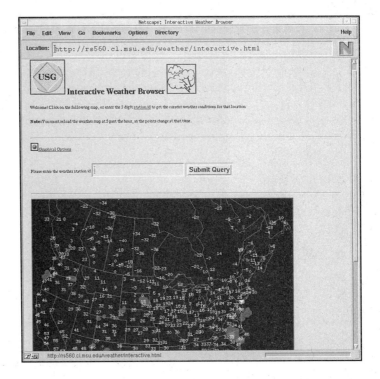

The Interactive Weather Browser enables a user to view the current conditions map as well as obtain a National Weather Service forecast for a weather station by entering the station's name or by clicking the current conditions map. Although these weather services are offered in different forms in other areas of the Net and Web, Charles Henrich's Weather Browser brings these together in an easy-to-use Forms interface. The result is that the user can access the remote sensing devices available to the National Weather Service through the Web.

Information

Communication being at the heart of the purpose of all webs, the dissemination of information is part of any web. There are webs and organizations, however, that focus specifically on information itself (for example, the Coalition for Networked Information mentioned in Chapter 25, "Education, Scholarship, and Research").

Networked Information Discovery and Retrieval

The Clearinghouse for Networked Information Discovery and Retrieval (CNIDR) was created in 1992 by a three-year grant from the National Science Foundation (NSF) for the purpose of fostering the coordination of networked information tools so that they are compatible and consistent. CNIDR also educates and supports NSF investigators in the use of networked information-retrieval tools and participates in standards development with the Internet Engineering Task Force and the Coalition for Networked Information The CNIDR home page, `http://cnidr.org/`, is shown in Figure 27.35.

Within the CNIDR web, more information is available about CNIDR projects. These efforts are to make information more available, easier to retrieve, and more organized on several information systems:

- The Web
- Wide Area Information Server (WAIS) and freeWAIS
- Gopher
- Archie

Thus, CNIDR is an example of an organization that is organized around the study of information itself, and its web is a natural outgrowth of its work.

FIGURE 27.35.

Clearinghouse for Networked Information Discovery and Retrieval.

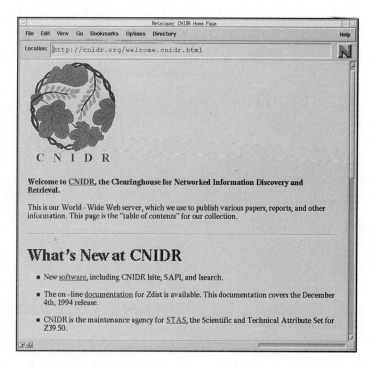

The U.S. Library of Congress Web

Libraries are information treasure-troves, and many libraries now offer some Web-based services. The United States Library of Congress has a web that contains links to not only the online information catalog of the library, but also to online exhibits and collections. (See Figure 27.36.)

The links shown in Figure 27.36 provide the user with the ability to view exhibits that otherwise might have required a trip to Washington, D.C. to see. These multimedia exhibits include popular Web destinations, including "Scrolls From the Dead Sea" and "The Vatican Library." In this way, the Library of Congress web demonstrates how libraries contain not only written texts, but cultural expressions in multimedia forms.

FIGURE 27.36.

The U.S. Library of Congress home page.

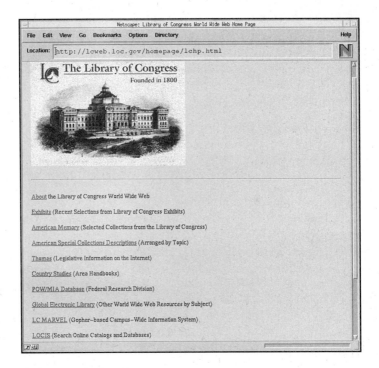

Explorer's Check

Communication is one of the oldest activities of humans, so it is no surprise that people continuously adapt and shape technology to achieve communication with each other. In fact, many observers of networked communication note that people taking part in online communities and groups is one of the recurrent aspects of online activity and that the pull of people toward each other is often far stronger than interest in information and data. Moreover, many would argue that the impact of online human communication on shaping our culture is far more profound than the technical details of the tools and conduits themselves.

In this chapter, you've seen how individuals can create their own online "personas" in the form of hypertext home pages, linking their personal work with other works and thus creating elaborate information and social spaces that establish points of departure for others who may share similar interests. The interactive forms feature opens up new possibilities for people to contact each other, to create online hypergraffiti, to create virtual communities, or to provide interfaces with communication systems such as MOOs.

Organizations have a special need to communicate information and at the same time create a sense of community through shared information. Campus-Wide Information Systems provide these links in academic settings. Commercial and nonprofit organizations also solve their problems in keeping their geographically dispersed memberships informed and motivated through their webs.

On the Web, new possibilities open for mass communication. Publishing can take the form of a direct translation of a print publication to a web. Another option is to provide asynchronous access to synchronous mass media, such as the online archives of CBC's radio programs. Online zines can create a whole medium that has no offline equivalent by making full use of the Web's features in both design and content.

People can create "sensory doorways" glimpsing real-time conditions or scenes in places all over the world. These applications range from demonstration exercises such as the Trojan Room coffee machine and other remote sensing exercises to valuable applications such as Charles Henrich's Weather Browser.

Like communication, information itself is at the heart of all webs. Organizations such as the Clearinghouse for Networked Information Discovery and Retrieval work to increase the interoperability and use of tools to discover and retrieve information in online systems. As such, their web provides a wealth of information about supporting information itself. Other information organizations' libraries—also exploit the power of the Web to disseminate information widely. The U.S. Library of Congress, continuing its role as an information storehouse, uses the Web to make its exhibits available to still wider audiences. These examples show how the Web can be applied to communication in varying contexts. Still in its infancy, Web communication is potentially a very rich future activity, mainly as a result of the genius of individuals working out ways to contact each other and to extend what they can know through the Web.

Government and Communities

by
John December

28

National governments have recognized information and telecommunications technologies as sources of wealth in their economies. Initiatives to develop computer and communications networks, such as the networking project by the United States Defense Advanced Research Projects Agency (ARPA) in the 1970s, eventually can lead to global communication networks (for example, the Internet). At the community level, people are also developing information and communications systems, such as Free-Nets, to link together people and valuable community information. The result of these government and community networking initiatives is an increasingly dense mesh of networks at all levels—community, state, region, nation, and world.

This chapter surveys webs that support national (and global) information infrastructure plans as well as government and community information. Although these webs are not necessarily the information infrastructure called for in national plans, the webs themselves demonstrate possibilities for and government commitment to advanced forms of information delivery. This chapter presents examples of the range of government information available on the Web, including pages from international organizations, government agencies, and a U.S. Senator. Finally, some community-based information systems demonstrate how people are creating ties with each other and the world.

National and Global Information Infrastructure Initiatives

Many nations and economic regions are taking active steps to create national information infrastructures, including the European Community, Japan, Singapore, Canada, and the United States. This section looks at some web sites that governments have established to disseminate information about their national infrastructure initiatives.

A Global Information Infrastructure

Vice President Al Gore has not only worked to develop an information infrastructure for the United States, but he has also supported a similar infrastructure for the world—the Global Information Infrastructure, or GII. As part of their efforts to bring about the cooperation necessary for a GII, Al Gore and Secretary of Commerce Ron Brown, as well as Larry Irving, Arati Prabhakar, and Sally Katzen prepared a document, "The Global Information Infrastructure: Agenda for Cooperation." Available on the Information Infrastructure Task Force server (http://ntiaunix1.ntia.doc.gov:70), the top of this report is shown in Figure 28.1. (The artwork for the cover was donated by artist Peter Max.)

The goals of the GII, as articulated by Al Gore at the Buenos Aires World Telecommunication Development Conference in March 1994, are to encourage private investment and competition, provide open access to users and information providers, create flexible regulation, and ensure universal service (http://ntiaunix1.ntia.doc.gov:70/0/papers/speeches/

`032194_gore_giispeech.txt`). World leaders met again to discuss the GII in February 1995 in Brussells and also at the G7 economic summit in Halifax, Canada, in late June 1995. The Web information supplied by individual countries, as shown below, may be just the nascent stages of what a full GII may be. For more information on the GII, see Computer Professionals for Social Responsibility collection of information at `http://www.cpsr.org/dox/global.html`.

FIGURE 28.1.

Global Information Infrastructure Agenda for Cooperation.

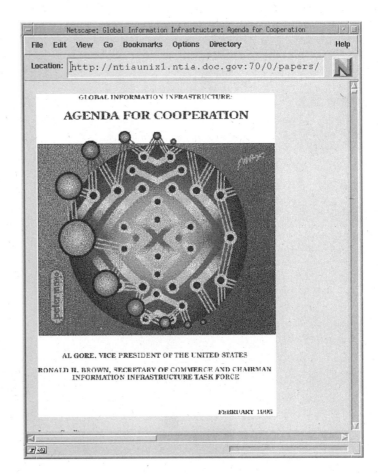

Canada

The Canadian government has developed plans to develop an Information Highway national infrastructure that builds on Canada's existing strength in information technologies. In a video conference speech to the "Powering up North America Conference" in February 1994, the Minister of Industry, John Manley, described a vision for a Canadian information infrastructure that would improve communications in the country as well as spark economic growth (`http://debra.dgbt.doc.ca/isc/Canadian.Information.Highway/manley.speech.feb.2.1994`). Canada's goal is to create an infrastructure that will "give all Canadians access to the employment, educational, investment, entertainment, health care and wealth-creating opportunities of the Information Age" (`http://debra.dgbt.doc.ca/isc/Canadian.Information.Highway/Building.Canada's.Info.Infrastructure.April94.txt`). This ambitious plan will bring together the academic, government, cultural, and community wealth of Canada through networked communication and information access.

Figure 28.2 shows the home page for the Electronic Document Distribution of Industry Canada (`http://debra.dgbt.doc.ca/isc/isc.english.html`), which makes information about Canada's plans available over the Web.

FIGURE 28.2.

Industry Canada.

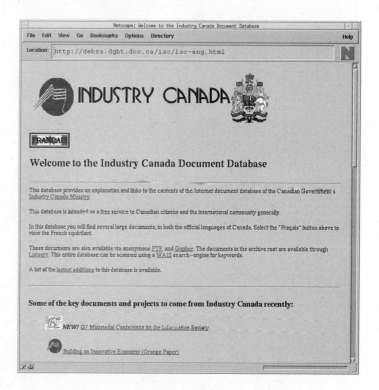

The Industry Canada web also offers many detailed documents describing Canada's infrastructure plans, including links to

- Technology Networking Guide, a directory guiding Canadian companies to develop information technology
- An archive of news releases related to the infrastructure efforts

■ Gazette notices listing information about telecommunications regulations and legislation from the Communications sector of Industry Canada

By gathering information about their information infrastructure initiative and delivering it over the Web, the Canadian government helps all citizens of Canada access these plans in a manner that is very much in keeping with the ultimate goals of the Canadian Information Highway initiative itself.

I'M EUROPE

Begun in 1994, the Information Market-Europe (I'M EUROPE) Web server provides information about the European Union, programs, and research and development projects related to European initiatives for information infrastructure. The I'M Europe web was developed by the European Commission, Directorate General (DG) XIII Telecommunications, Information Market and Exploitation of Research, and Directorate E-Information industry and market and language processing groups. This web is part of the DG XIII's mission to support "the establishment of a European single market in electronic information creation, retrieval and storage" (`http://www.echo.lu/dg13/en/dg13tasks.html`). Figure 28.3 shows the home page of this web (`http://www.echo.lu/`).

FIGURE 28.3.

Information Market—EUROPE home page. Courtesy of Stig Marthinsen, European Commission, Directorate General XIII Telecommunications, Information Market and Exploitation of Research, Directorate E-Information industry and market and language processing.

The I'M EUROPE web offers detailed information about:

- The European Union: the full text of the "Bangemann Report," a report prepared by a request from the European Council, which outlines the issues for a global information infrastructure.

  An action plan for Europe's information society (a followup to the Bangemann Report) outlining issues and recommendations for a European information infrastructure.

- The European Parliament: fact sheets (Figure 28.4) and further reports on Europe's plans for information infrastructure.

FIGURE 28.4.

European Parliament fact sheets. Courtesy of Stig Marthinsen, European Commission, Directorate General XIII Telecommunications, Information Market and Exploitation of Research, Directorate E-Information industry and market and language processing.

- European Union programs related to the information market, including the Information Market Policy ACTions (IMPACT) Programme.

- The Information Society INFO2000 document, outlining how Europe's information and multimedia industries can be stimulated.

- ECHO, the European Commission Host Organisation, a non-commercial service to provide free access to databases in all European community languages.

- Community Research and Development Information Service (CORDIS), an initiative of Directorate-General XIII, D-2 for information about research and technological development activities of the European Union.

The I'M EUROPE web melds a great deal of information about how the European Union is approaching the challenge of developing a European information infrastructure. What Europe's role will be in shaping the GII is not known, but the document "Europe's way to the information society: an action plan," adroitly observes the competitive nature of developing national information infrastructures: "The race is on at global level, notably the U.S. and Japan. Those countries which will adapt themselves most readily will set *de facto* technological standards for those who follow" (`http://www.echo.lu/eudocs/en/com-asc.html`).

Japan

GLOCOM (`http://www.glocom.ac.jp`) is the Center for Global Communications at the International University of Japan in Tokyo. A research center focusing on the impact of computer-based communication, GLOCOM examines a wide range of issues, including Japanese government information policy. GLOCOM's web contains a report on Japan's plans for information infrastructure, shown in Figure 28.5 (`http://www.glocom.ac.jp/NEWS/MITI-doc.html`).

FIGURE 28.5.

Japan Program for Advanced Information Infrastructure.

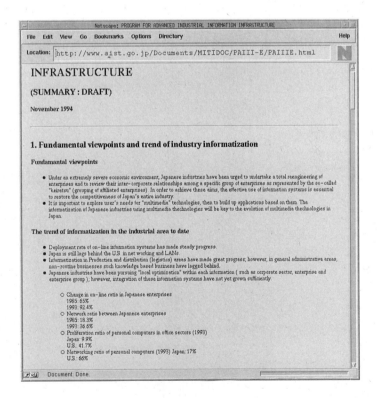

Japan's plan for information infrastructure, like the plans of other nations, acknowledges a shift in economic activity from manufacturing to intellectual activity and articulates a vision of a comprehensive government program to promote information technology. The May 1994 report (Figure 28.5) on the GLOCOM web offers a detailed statement of the program. Japan's plan pays particular attention to a future "Advanced Information Infrastructure Society." According to the plan, people in this information society will "ultimately be able to obtain and process information from anywhere in the world no matter where they are located, through a variety of media, and to easily transmit their own information to any point in the world."

Other key webs related to Japan's initiative include

- Communications Research Laboratory, Koganei, Tokyo (`http://www.crl.go.jp/`)
- Nippon Telegraph and Telephone Corporation (`http://www.ntt.jp/index.html`)
- Stanford U.S.-Japan Technology Management Center (`http://fuji.stanford.edu/`)
- Internet Initiative Japan, Inc. (`http://www.iij.ad.jp/`)

Singapore

The National Computing Board (NCB) of Singapore has a vision for an "intelligent island," an intensive, country-wide information technology (IT) infrastructure intended to improve the quality of life and create competitive business advantages for Singapore. Figure 28.6 shows an information page about this plan called "IT2000."

FIGURE 28.6.

Singapore Information Technology 2000.

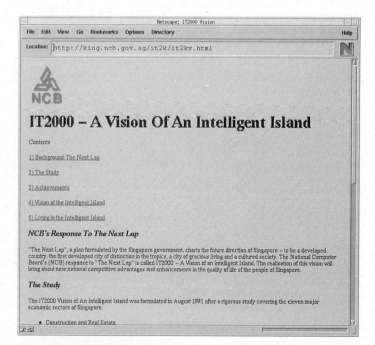

The IT2000 plan is comprehensive, aimed at interconnecting "computers in virtually every home, office, school, and factory" (`http://king.ncb.gov.sg/it2k/it2kv.html`). The framework for the development includes integrating legal and technical policy and standards with infrastructure (networks and services) to support applications (Figure 28.7).

FIGURE 28.7.

Singapore NII framework.

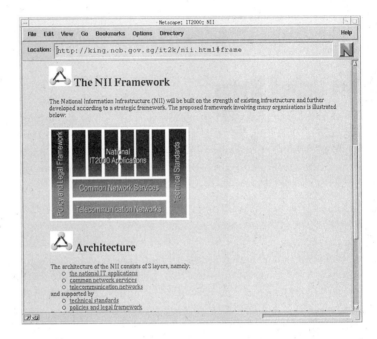

Singapore's framework is more comprehensive and requires greater government involvement and top-down planning than many other national plans. Although the United States' plan (below) focuses on a few key areas such health care, education, libraries, and government information, the Singapore plan targets a larger range of economic sectors (`http://king.ncb.gov.sg/it2k/it2kv.html#study`):

- Construction and Real Estate
- Education and Training
- Financial Services
- Government
- Healthcare
- IT Industry
- Manufacturing
- Media, Publishing, and Information Services
- Retail, Wholesale, and Distribution

- Tourist and Leisure Services
- Transportation

Thus, the Singapore plan reaches farther into all the sectors of the national economy than many other national plans. Sandy Sandfort, writing in *Wired* (1.4), speculates on the outcome of Singapore's ambitious plan: "Perhaps a cosmopolitan, more robust Singapore will emerge, or maybe it will be consumed. What does seem clear is that the information technology bell cannot be unrung."

The United States

The United States has taken an aggressive approach to developing a National Information Infrastructure (NII). President Clinton, in his 1994 State of the Union message, stated the goal of working "with the private sector to connect every classroom, every clinic, every library, and every hospital in America to a national information superhighway by the year 2000" (http://ntiaunix1.ntia.doc.gov:70/0/papers/documents/state_of_union.txt).

While efforts for national communications networks were underway decades before—with the development of the forerunners to the Internet, ARPAnet, as well as growth and development of communication technologies—the Clinton Administration has made networked communication a national goal. Through the leadership of Al Gore, first as a Senator, then as the Vice President, a National Information Infrastructure Agenda has been developed that seeks to create "a seamless web of communications networks, computers, databases, and consumer electronics that will put vast amounts of information at users' fingertips" (http://ntiaunix1.ntia.doc.gov:70/0/papers/documents/nii_agenda_for_action.txt).

The National Information Infrastructure Act (H.R. 1757) was passed in July 1993 and is an extension and acceleration of the High Performance Computing Act (P.L. 102-94) of 1991. To support this effort online, the Information Infrastructure Task Force (IITF) has developed a web server (http://iitf.doc.gov/), shown in Figure 28.8.

The IITF web contains links to a variety of supporting information, as shown in the Figure 28.8. Since it is a government-oriented server, it contains a large selection of documents, testimony, speeches, and reports revolving around the legislative efforts to create a national information infrastructure. For example, a portion of the executive summary of a report called "Framework for NII SERVICES" is provided, which outlines some issues about how NII services will be provided. Figure 28.9 describes relationships and roles that might emerge in a U.S. NII. Other information in the IETF web includes summaries and transcripts of hearings that have been held to debate and discuss how a national infrastructure might develop. The IETF web is part of other major webs related to the U.S. NII project, including the following:

- The National Coordination Office for High Performance Computing and Communications (http://www.hpcc.gov/)
- U.S. Department Of Commerce (http://www.doc.gov/)

FIGURE 28.8.

US Information Infra-structure Task Force.

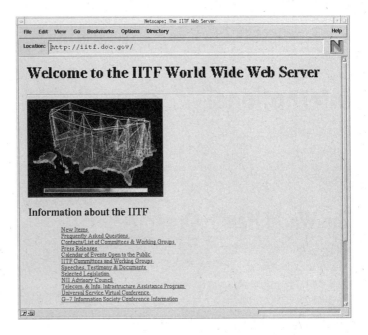

- The Digital Information Infrastructure Guide, "a collection of information about projects and organizations working on the development of the NII" (http://farnsworth.mit.edu/diig.html)

- National Information Infrastructure Testbed (http://www.niit.org/niit/)

FIGURE 28.9.

National Information Infrastructure relationships.

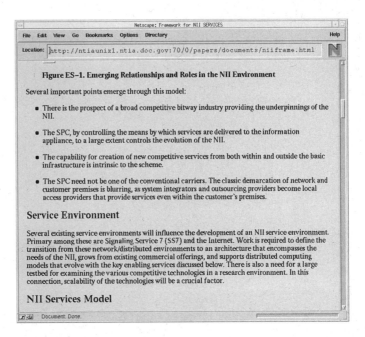

Although the U.S. NII project is not specifically focusing on the Web as a basis for an NII, the use of the Web illustrates how timely and valuable information about information infrastructure can be delivered online.

International

Besides national governments, a range of international organizations use the Web to deliver information to the general public as well as members. These webs are particularly valuable when current, detailed information is needed from an organization that may be distributed across the globe.

The World Health Organization

The goal of the World Health Organization (WHO) is "the attainment by all peoples of the highest possible level of health" (http://www.who.ch/WHOis.html). As part of this broad mission, WHO directs and coordinates international health work, promotes technical cooperation, and assists in emergencies. WHO advances disease-prevention work, the improvement of living and working conditions, health services, and education. Headquartered in Geneva, Switzerland, WHO also proposes and makes recommendations about health policy and promotes international standards for food and other substances. The WHO web is shown in Figure 28.10 (http://www.who.ch/).

FIGURE 28.10.

*The World Health
Organization home page.*

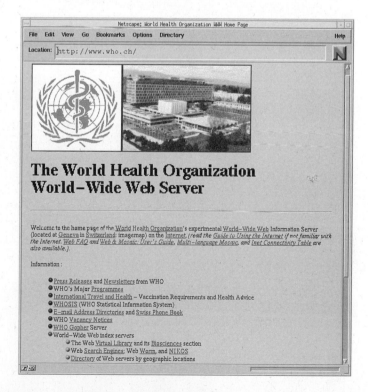

The WHO web offers a wide variety of information, general web links, and a link to the WHO Gopher and related organizations (for example, the World Bank). The WHO web offers access to a variety of informational publications online, including the following:

- Press releases (for example, An Update on the Cholera Strain in Rwanda 25 July 1994)
- Several newsletters
- Environmental health
- Influenza
- AIDS
- WHO library Digest for Africa

Figure 28.11 shows a page linking to descriptions of WHO's major programs.

FIGURE 28.11.

World Health Organization major programs.

The information on the WHO web is very specific—including not only background information, on Acute Respiratory Infections and Diarrheal Disease Control for example, but detailed bibliographies and ordering information for WHO publications on these subjects.

The WHO web demonstrates how an international organization with a complex mission can create an information system to disseminate useful information to the public and to serve as an information and education system for any user.

The World Bank

The World Bank is an international agency that lends money to poor countries for development, finances private sector projects, advises governments and businesses on investment, and promotes foreign investment ("The World Bank Home Page," `http://www.worldbank.org/`). The home page is shown in Figure 28.12.

FIGURE 28.12.

World Bank home page. (Copyright the World Bank. Reprinted by permission.)

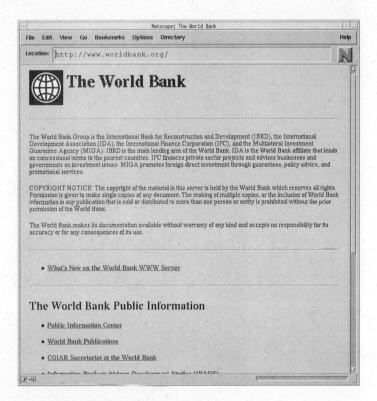

The World Bank's web provides an offering of public information as well as descriptions of World Bank publications that are for sale. The public information center on the World Bank web is one aspect of a new policy of the bank, approved in August 1993, which makes operational information available to the public that had previously been restricted to official users. This public information includes items such as

- Economic reports
- Environmental information
- Assessments and analysis
- Data sheets
- Global environmental facility document

■ Environmental documents

■ National environmental action plans

■ Project information, policy papers, and reports

These links include searchable indexes as well as many detailed information sheets; environmental datasheets, for example, include more than 500 documents. By creating a single web source for their documents, the World Bank's web can truly serve all interested people worldwide by providing access to detailed and current information.

Government Information

National government plans for information infrastructure are just one part of the government information offered through the Web. In the United States, for example, many federal agencies and offices have web servers. Figure 28.13 shows a partial list of agency webs from the Federal Information Exchange, Inc., a private company operating several multi-agency information services. This section uses two example webs to illustrate federal information on the Web—a government agency and a legislator.

FIGURE 28.13.

U.S. Federal webs.

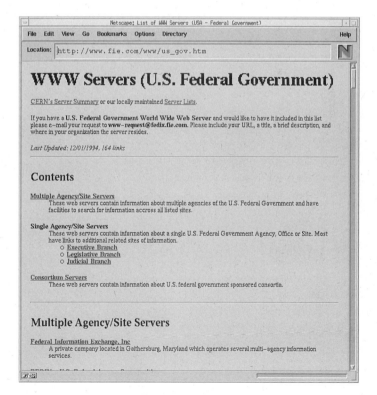

FedWorld Information Network

FedWorld is a service operated by the National Technical Information Service (NTIS) since November 1992. Besides its Web server (`http://www.fedworld.gov`), FedWorld also offers a Telnet connection at `telnet://fedworld.gov`.

FIGURE 28.14.

FedWorld Information Network home page.

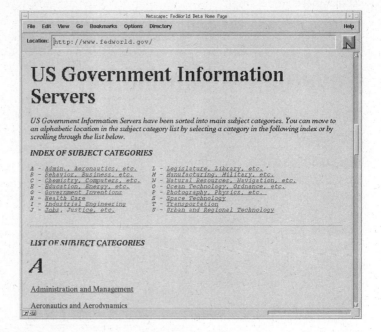

FedWorld's aim is to provide links to government information sources. This list is separated into categories (as shown in Figure FEDW.1). FedWorld serves as a one-stop source for government information in all these areas. For example, its category for Legislative Branch, Congress, Committees (`http://www.fedworld.gov/legislat.htm`) links you to the Congressional and Executive Office webs mentioned previously.

The United States White House

The United States White House deployed a Web server in the fall of 1994, offering "An Interactive Citizen's Handbook" detailing life at the White House and other information. The White House home page (`http://www.whitehouse.gov/`) offers a glimpse into the executive branch of the U.S. government—the First Family, tours, publications, and other background information.

Although the information is not as nitty gritty as some other independent political Webs (such as PolicyNet at `http://policy.net/`), the White House web nonetheless establishes the U.S. executive mansion's branch in cyberspace.

On the White House web, you can learn more about the First Family, as well as see (and hear) the First Feline (Socks the Cat), as shown in Figure 28.15.

FIGURE 28.15.

Family life at the White House.

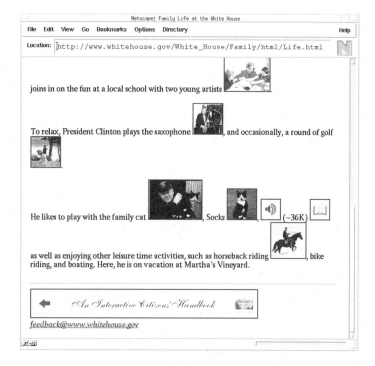

More significantly, the White House web gives online reference information about the White House executive offices, including home pages for the President, Vice President, First Lady, and Mrs. Gore. Cabinet information includes home pages for each of the 14 departments (Figure 28.16).

The individual Cabinet Department pages link to their respective Web servers. Another page on the White House web links to independent federal agencies and commissions (such as the CIA and the Consumer Product Safety Commission). By combining executive office information with links to federal agencies, the White House web offers a valuable online information source.

FIGURE 28.16.

The President's Cabinet.

The United States House of Representatives

While the Thomas web focuses on legislative information, the United States House (`http://www.house.gov/`) has its own web (Figure 28.17). The House web also offers information about the legislative process, and its "Tying It All Together" page (`http://www.house.gov/Tying_it_all.html`) is particularly effective in presenting this process through hypertext. (Law-making is, by its nature, often non-linear.) Figure 28.18 shows a section from the "Tying It All Together" document.

The House web's strength lies in the detailed breakdown it presents about House schedules, who's who in the House (contact information for committees, members, and leadership), as well as educational resources and visitor information (including maps and information about how you can see the House Floor proceedings from the gallery in Washington). You can also find out which House members have published their own Web pages at `http://www.house.gov/MemberWWW.html`. Note that the House developed a Web server before the Senate (although it was Senator Edward Kennedy from Massachusetts who had the first Web page, described in the next section).

FIGURE 28.17.

The United States House of Representatives home page.

FIGURE 28.18.

A Section from "The Legislative Process—Tying It All Together."

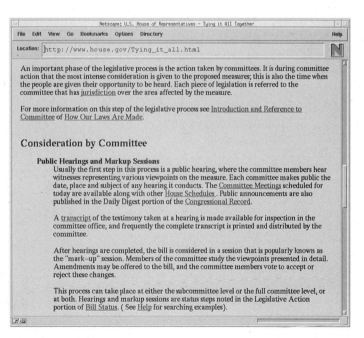

The Thomas Legislative Information System

The United States Library of Congress (`http://www.loc.gov/`), in conjunction with the U.S. Congress, provide the Thomas Legislative information system on the Web (`http://thomas.loc.gov/`). Figure 28.19 shows Thomas' home page. The Thomas web links the user with a wide range of information—perhaps most notably the complete text of the Congressional Record as well as legislation and U.S. codes. The Congressional Record is a published account of debates, proceedings, and other activities of the Congress. Published daily, the Congressional Record offers a very detailed insight into the goings-on of the Congress.

Figure 28.20 shows the form that you can use to search the Congressional Record for keywords.

The Thomas web also has an exceptionally wide array of information about the legislative process, including "How Our Laws Are Made," a detailed account of how Congress develops legislation through committees and legislative processes. The Thomas web also links to other government information sources, particularly those on the Library of Congress web's Global Electronic Library. (See `http://lcweb.loc.gov/global/globalhp.html`.)

FIGURE 28.19.

The Thomas Legislative Information home page.

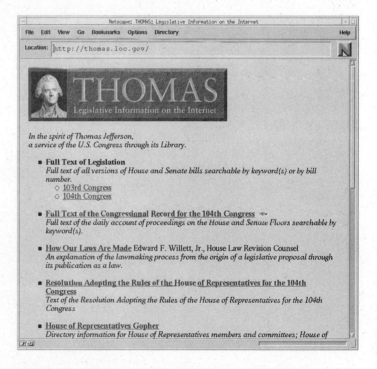

FIGURE 28.20.

Search form for the U.S. Congressional Record.

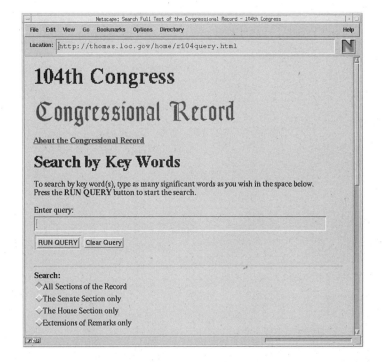

A Sample Federal Agency—U.S. Department of Transportation

As shown in the list in Figure 25.13, there is a wide variety of U.S. government agencies with web servers. As an example, the U.S. Department of Transportation (DOT) offers a web, http://www.dot.gov/, as shown in Figure 28.21. The U.S. DOT web contains a wide variety of material about the agency, including

- DOT TALK, a forum for learning more about DOT in the form of a newsletter; includes full text of past issues
- DOT information links, including a list of operating agencies (Federal Aviation Administration, Federal Highway Administration, and so on), budget, and financial information
- The DOT telephone directory

FIGURE 28.21.

U.S. Department of Transportation web.

The DOT thus can serve both its employees (the many people working in DOT's operating agencies) and its employers (the American taxpayers) by providing links to agency and government information. Moreover, the DOT web is just one part of DOT's overall strategy to use information technology throughout its operations. The DOT web, still under development when shown in the preceding image, will eventually contain more links about the agency and easier access to information so that citizens anywhere can use it.

U.S. Senator Edward Kennedy

Senator Edward Kennedy (D-Mass) was the first United States senator with a web page. Eric Loeb and John C. Mallery at the Artificial Intelligence Laboratory of Massachusetts Institute of Technology developed the page as part of the Intelligent Information Infrastructure Project. The top of Senator Kennedy's page (http://www.ai.mit.edu/projects/iiip/Kennedy/homepage.html) is shown in Figure 28.22, and another section illustrating more information available about legislation and the commonwealth itself is in Figure 28.23.

FIGURE 28.22.

The Senator Edward Kennedy home page.

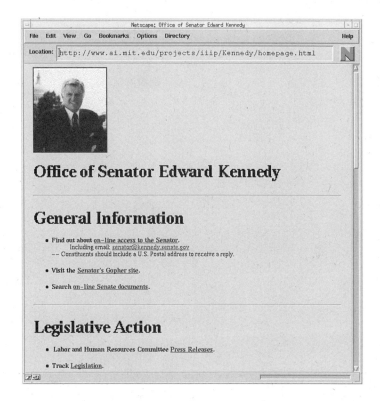

Senator Kennedy's web contains an excellent collection of information for his constituents and other people who might be interested in the U.S. political process. The United States Senate itself has a Gopher, and the web gives a pointer to the Senator's Gopher menus. Besides legislative and budget information and press releases, the web links to important information for the citizens of Massachusetts:

- Press releases from the senator's office that highlight important developments and issues about Massachusetts and New England
- A Web resource map of Massachusetts (created by the UMass Astronomy Department), showing graphical information maps to Internet resources in the commonwealth (as part of the Virtual Tourist, discussed in Chapter 20, "Machines: Space-Oriented Searching")
- A variety of World Wide Web links to other links of interest to Massachusetts citizens, and other U.S. infrastructure and government information

By combining links specific to the senator's record and activities with information sources relevant to citizens, the Kennedy web offers constituents a way to keep track of government activities that is far more flexible and detailed than any noninteractive news source.

FIGURE 28.23.

Senator Edward Kennedy's web site.

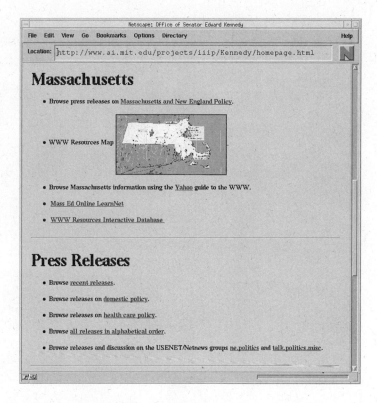

Community Networking

Like national governments and international organizations, regional and metropolitan communities need to provide information structures for their citizens. People have been developing community-based networking for more than a decade—the first community network was Dr. Tom Grundner's public health information bulletin board "St. Silicon's Hospital and Information Dispensary," in Cleveland, Ohio in 1984. This service eventually developed into the Cleveland Free-Net. In 1989, the National Public Telecomputing Network (NPTN) was formed to help other communities form similar networks (ftp://nptn.org/pub/nptn/nptn.info/basic.guide.txt).

Today, community networks extend across the world, with many offering connections through Telnet, Gopher, and the Web. Peter Scott (the creator of HYTELNET) maintains a Free-Nets home page (Figure 28.24) that offers a variety of links to Free-Nets as well as background information on them.

The rest of this section highlights some networks that support communities.

FIGURE 28.24.

The Free-Nets home page.
Courtesy of Peter Scott.

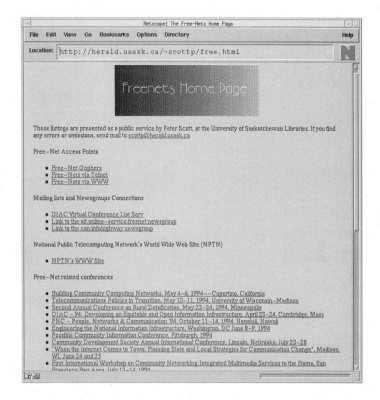

The Silicon Prairie

As part of a collaboration between the National Center for Supercomputing Applications (NCSA) and the Champaign (Illinois) County Chamber of Commerce, Alaina Kanfer and Gordon M. Taylor of NCSA created a web to demonstrate how information about a community can be presented. Figure 28.25 shows the front page of "The Silicon Prairie," Champaign County, Illinois (http://www.prairienet.org/SiliconPrairie/ccnet.html).

The Champaign County web offers information about its natural and cultural attractions as well as community information. For example, links on the "Living in Champaign County" page connect a user to the University of Illinois at Urbana-Champaign as well as to a brief history of the county. The web also offers community profiles, travel information, and detailed information about the county. The Champaign web describes plans for Prairienet (Champaign County's Free-Net) to link all county citizens to information. Another development, the Champaign County Network (CCNet), will offer webs related to organizations and individuals.

FIGURE 28.25.

Champaign County web page.

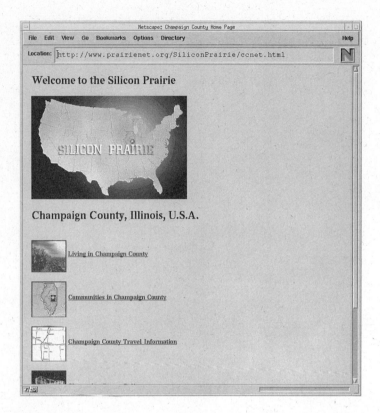

St. Petersburg, Russia

The 1994 Goodwill Games brought a great deal of attention and activity to the city of St. Petersburg, Russia, and the St. Petersburg's web (`http://www.spb.su/`) grew out of this attention (Figure 28.26).

The St. Petersburg web offered detailed information about the progress of the Goodwill Games while they were being held there in 1994. Other information includes the full text of *The St. Petersburg Press*, the city's English-language daily newspaper covering news as well as the culture and lifestyle of St. Petersburg's restaurants, shops, transportation, and other tourist attractions. The web also contains "St. Petersburg Pictures Gallery" (Figure 28.27), which shows a variety of scenes.

FIGURE 28.26.

*St. Petersburg, Russia
home page.*

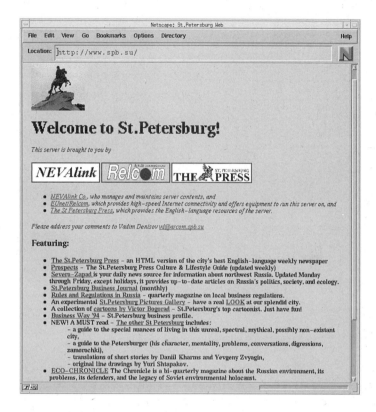

By using St. Petersburg's web, particularly the picture gallery and the detailed cultural guide offered by the St. Petersburg Press, you can get a unique glimpse into a city with a long history. While the St. Petersburg web does not offer all the connections that older Free-Nets might offer (it doesn't have online conferencing and discussion areas), it nevertheless demonstrates how a city can increase its connections to the world, leveraging the attention of a popular event held there into more publicity for the city itself.

FIGURE 28.27.

St. Petersburg picture gallery.

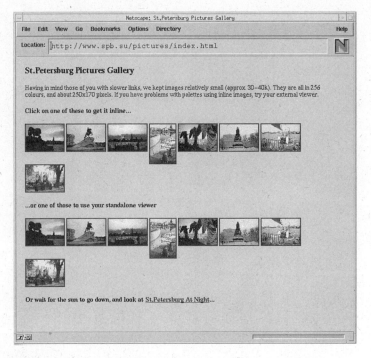

San Carlos, California

The city of San Carlos is located in the San Francisco Bay Area of California. As part of the Association of Bay Area Governments (ABAG), San Carlos has developed the web shown in Figure 28.28 (http://www.abag.ca.gov/abag/local_gov/city/san_carlos/schome.html).

The San Carlos web links citizens to information about

- What's new on the San Carlos web: Including back issues from the 1994 "What's New" pages
- City overview information: Overview of the San Carlos Online project and web server statistics
- City Hall information: A letter from the mayor and a report about disruptions from a local construction project
- City Clerk and Council information: The FAQ list for the city, county election returns, election returns from the Secretary of State, State of California election server
- Economic Development and Housing: Affordable housing information—information about property for lease
- Finance information: The business license rules and rates
- Fire Department: Fire safety tips and department news
- Parks & Recreation: The FAQ about the parks, job openings in the parks, and park services

- Public works information: The FAQ for the Public Works Department
- Technology and Telecommunications: League of California Cities—Model Telecommunications Policy, San Carlos Telecommunications Policy
- Transportation: Bay-Area Rapid Transit (BART), CalTrain, and SamTrans fares and schedules
- Airport: West Valley Flying Club
- Business: Restaurants, real estate, and restaurant reviews
- Schools: Workshops, programs, and the San Carlos Charter School
- Other government resources
- Local newspapers

FIGURE 28.28.

San Carlos, California home page. (Copyright 1995, The City of San Carlos. The City of San Carlos Seal, the City motto "The City of Good Living" and "San Carlos On Line" are trademarks of the City of San Carlos. All rights reserved. Reprinted by permission.)

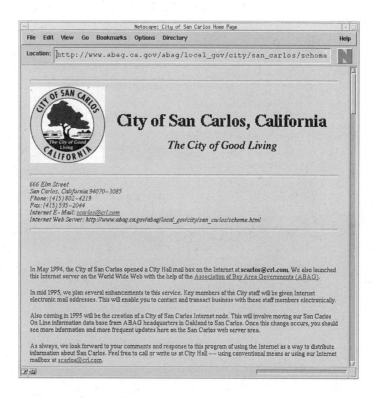

Begun in May 1994 and still under rapid development, the San Carlos web is an example of what a city can do to connect its citizens to information. The links under development on the home page show the potential for even more detailed information. For example, a link in the Business links area is to a company called Bay Area Model Mugging (BAMM), a company offering a range of classes in self-defense techniques. By providing information at this level of detail, a citizen can rely on the community web for up-to-date and detailed information, and a remote user can gain a good idea of the community itself.

Boulder Community Network

The Boulder Community Network (BCN) web was launched in July 1994 as a project involving many of Boulder, Colorado's educational, civil, and corporate organizations, including Apple Computer and the University of Colorado at Boulder. BCN offers a variety of links relating to "Information Centers" regarding many aspects of city life (see Figure 28.30), `http://bcn.boulder.co.us/`. The goal of BCN is to gather community information important to citizens and at the same time ensure that all citizens have access to this information.

According to Ken Klingenstein, Director, University of Colorado Computing & Network Services, the web is a work in progress. The process of BCN's growth will include not only increasing the information offered, but also adding a research agenda in cooperation with the Schools of Journalism and Mass Communication, Computer Science, and Sociology. Scholars in these departments will investigate the impact of computer-mediated communication and delivery of information on the community. As the vision statement for BCN points out, Boulder offers a combination of advanced technology institutions that can serve as a testbed for a community of the future (`http://bcn.boulder.co.us/bcn/vision.html`). By providing links to information about these plans on the Web and tying the web to the research process of local academics, the Boulder Community Network is poised to both invent and understand the future.

FIGURE 28.29.

The Boulder Community Network home page.

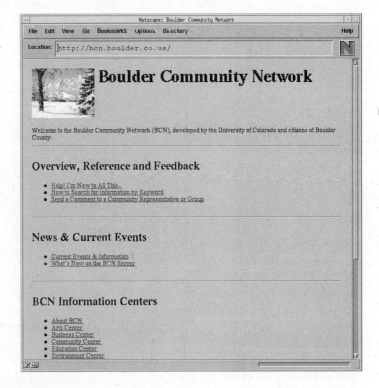

LibertyNet

LibertyNet presents a wealth of online information about the Delaware Valley (Philadelphia and New Jersey) area of the United States. LibertyNet provides access to users in the Delaware Valley. While not a FreeNet, LibertyNet is a non-profit organization with the goal of offering regional network communications and information to citizens for free or for a modest fee. The LibertyNet web (`http://libertynet.org/`) shown in Figure 28.30 offers users access to a wide variety of information about the community and institutions.

FIGURE 28.30.

LibertyNet home page. Courtesy of LibertyNet, Nathan Gasser.

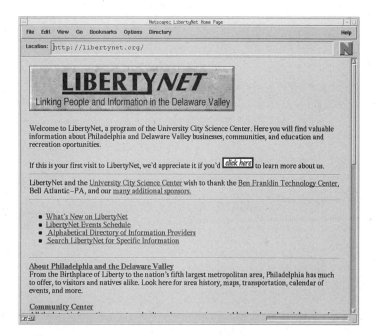

LibertyNet's main categories of information are

- Philadelphia/Delaware Valley information: Information about the city of Philadelphia attractions and culture (for example, Figure 28.31, the home page of the Philadelphia Museum of Art), including maps and movies, how to use the public transportation, and events

- A community center focusing on the neighborhoods, communities, and counties, with information about human services, non-profit information, employment, and special interest organizations for arts, culture, religion, and community service

- A medical center providing information about health, insurance, and preventative medicine

- A business and economic development center providing information on business associations, jobs, and other development opportunities

■ Other centers focusing on education, government, recreation and entertainment, Internet information, and LibertyNet administration

FIGURE 28.31.

The Philadelphia Museum of Art home page. Courtesy of LibertyNet, Nathan Gasser.

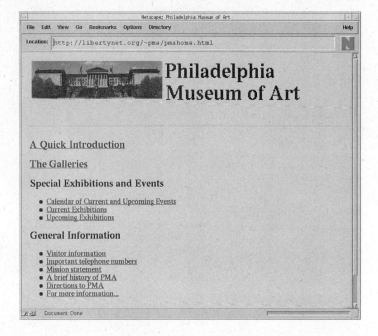

LibertyNet, like many networks across the country, performs many services at once: First it connects citizens in its region to the Internet at low or no cost; second, it provides a web of information to these citizens so that they can find resources and information in their community; and third, LibertyNet provides its information to the Web as a whole, so that students, potential visitors, former residents, and anyone on the Web can find more about the Delaware Valley area by looking at an information web created by citizens living there.

Blacksburg Electronic Village

Blacksburg Electronic Village (BEV) in Virginia is a cooperative effort to create a comprehensive information infrastructure to support an entire community. Using the strength and talents of the partners in the program—Virginia Tech, Bell Atlantic, and the Town of Blacksburg, Virginia—the project attempts to create a "critical mass" of users so that people can and will use electronic means to interact and gather information. Figure 28.32 shows the home page of BEV (http://www.bev.net/BEVhome.html).

FIGURE 28.32.

The Blacksburg Electronic Village home page.

As an electronic village that reflects the activities of a real community, the offerings on the BEV web include features that you would expect to find in a community—such as links covering aspects of education, health, government, and cultural activities, as well as support information for using the BEV web. The Community Square, for example, provides links to local attractions and activities, such as a restaurant guide, local organizations, and general interest information. In the Village Mall area, you can find out the weekly specials and look at the menu of restaurants such as Backstreets (Figure 28.33), and even obtain a coupon for specials on pizza and calzone from the Backstreets home page.

The BEV web's goal is to provide an information infrastructure that can support many information needs a citizen might have. For example, in addition to the links mentioned previously, the BEV web includes information about the following:

- Movie schedules at local cinemas
- Bus schedules
- Recycling drop-off points
- Supermarket specials

FIGURE 28.33.

Backstreets Restaurant home page.

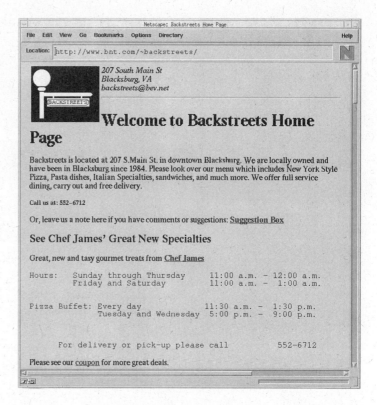

The Blacksburg plan takes community networking to a very detailed level. The goal of the developers is to develop a "community of the future" in which the routine use of networked information and communication will increase the quality of life, expand educational and business uses of the Web, and create an online system for citizens to participate more effectively in civic activities.

Statewide Networks

Many states now support efforts to provide a central Web server that brings together individual Web servers throughout the state. South Dakota and North Carolina were both early adopters of Web technologies to create a statewide information infrastructure. South Dakota's web presents strength in legislative and tourism information. North Carolina's web reflects the intense technological activity in its Research Triangle area.

South Dakota

South Dakota has developed a web that meets the need for a state-level information system. The front page of the graphical version of the South Dakota web, located at `http://www.state.sd.us`, is shown in Figure 28.34.

FIGURE 28.34.

The South Dakota web page.

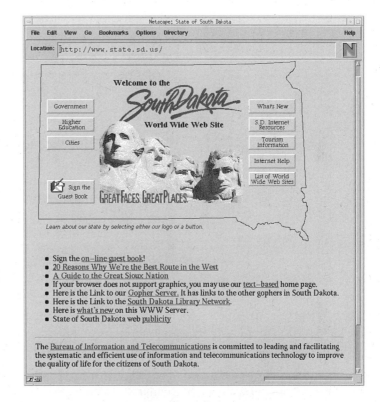

The South Dakota server offers a good collection of government information, with a graphical interface to information about branches and offices. (For example, Figure 28.35 shows the State Executive Branch Hierarchy.)

By clicking a box within the diagram, the user can obtain a description of the office or department. Similar diagrams show the judicial and legislative branches of the South Dakota government.

FIGURE 28.35.

South Dakota Executive Branch.

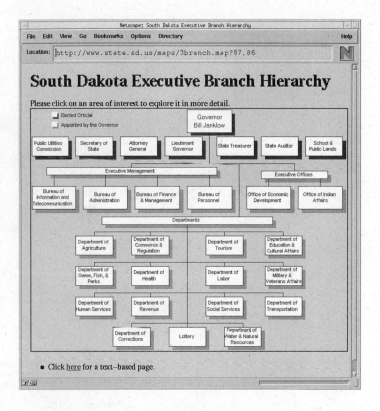

The web also has a tour of the Capitol Complex in Pierre, complete with a map and pictures of the buildings and features. There's also a collection of information about the state's attractions, such as one of its most famous, Mount Rushmore National Monument (Figure 28.36).

Other tourism information includes the Crazy Horse Memorial, Oahe Dam, and natural features and activities in the state. By combining extensive government, education, and tourism information, the South Dakota web accomplishes on a statewide level what many community-based networks are striving to accomplish—an information system that helps residents by providing important information for their lives as citizens and as life-long learners, and which presents a best "face" to the larger world on the Web.

FIGURE 28.36.

*The Mount Rushmore
National Monument.*

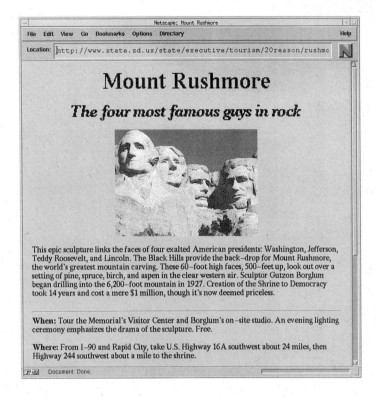

North Carolina

The state of North Carolina has adopted networking as one of its strengths. North Carolina's home page, http://www.sips.state.nc.us/, is shown in Figure 28.37.

The North Carolina web includes a link to the North Carolina Information Highway server (http://www.ncih.net/), which is the state's major initiative to link the state's institutions to the Internet. North Carolina has an exceptional collection of Web servers, as shown in Figure 28.38, particularly the inset for the Research Triangle Area of the state.

North Carolina's web links to government information servers—webs for services ranging from the state library to government offices such as the Department of Public Instruction and the Employment Security Commission.

FIGURE 28.37.

The North Carolina home page. Courtesy of the State of North Carolina.

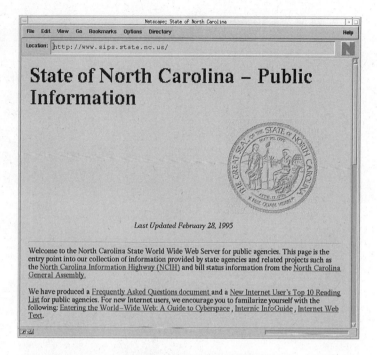

FIGURE 28.38.

W3 Servers: North Carolina. Courtesy of Jinny Crum-Jones.

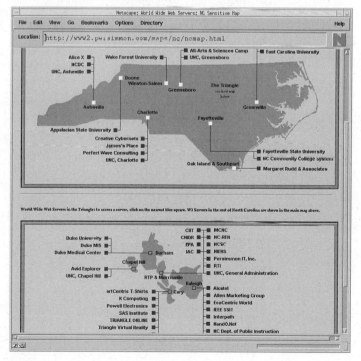

Explorer's Check

Just as people throughout history have collaborated to create governments at the local, regional, and national levels, governments and communities today create webs to support the needs and interests of citizens. National governments have recognized information as a valuable resource not only for economic wealth but also as a way to supply information to citizens about a variety of topics. Many countries now are developing initiatives for national infrastructures to increase the use of information technology by citizens. Using a variety of approaches, Canada, Japan, Singapore, and the United States supply webs of information that support these plans.

International organizations have recognized the Web's power to supply detailed information for a worldwide constituency on demand. Both the World Bank's and the World Health Organization's webs illustrate the value of Web-delivered information.

At the federal, state, and local levels, governments and communities have created webs to enrich and inform their citizens. South Dakota's web shows how a web can provide extensive information for a state's citizens and at the same time inform and attract others to the state. At the community level, a range of activities has been occurring for more than a decade—Free-Nets to support community information at a variety of levels of detail, including the ambitious plan of Blacksburg Electronic Village to provide a complete information infrastructure for its citizens.

PART

V

Weaving a Web

Communication Processes on the Web

29

by
John December

The Web is a very new medium for communicating with other people. However, this novelty doesn't mean that you have to reinvent the art of creating a message and structuring its content to reach a particular audience through the Web. Instead, you can draw on a large body of knowledge about crafting information from the ancient art of discovering the means of persuasion (rhetoric) and the relatively modern field of technical communication. These fields, rooted in static or noninteractive media such as paper, film, or recorded sound, can enrich the process of weaving a web.

> **NOTE**
>
> The term *web* with a lowercase *w* is used here to refer to the local hypertext you create, in order to distinguish from the *Web,* the collection of all hypertext publicly available on servers worldwide.

Borrowing some ideas from disciplines such as computer software engineering and user-interface design, this chapter outlines a web-weaving methodology that addresses the dynamic nature of Web communication.

This chapter covers some of the implications of the Web's transformation of the information development process. It reviews how the Web changes communication processes involving *mediated* communication (that is, communication that employs an object—such as paper, a graphic, a screen display, a user interface, or a computer network—to convey a message). It explores some of the characteristics of Web communication that set it apart from traditional forms.

This chapter begins with a review of how Web communication is different from other forms of mediated communication. It then gives an overview of what these changes hold for a new process of information development and communication on the Web.

How Is the Web Different from Other Communication?

Communicating on the Web is different from communicating through paper-based means such as brochures, reports, letters, memos, and other documents because it involves a different kind of *encoding* process (that is, how you create it using hypertext) as well as a different kind of *decoding* process (that is, how users perceive it through network-distributed browsers and servers). While it is beyond the scope of this chapter to enumerate all of these differences, those related to web weaving will be described.

> **NOTE**
>
> The preceding paragraph doesn't use the term *reader* because the Web includes multi-media as well as hypertext, and the experience styles of the users of the Web (as you saw in Part III, "Web Navigation Tools and Techniques") aren't necessarily best described by the term *reading* as well as by the term *using* information.

No longer constrained to a single physical object such as a piece of paper, Web communication becomes independent of time and space constraints, and is limited only by the interface (for example, a browser such as Mosaic) working in conjunction with the distribution mechanism (for example, a computer network). The user is also less constrained because he or she has more choices for interaction with the universe of information available on the Web than with a paper-based form of communication.

Web communication differs from communication in traditional media in the following ways:

- Web communication involves different *space and time constraints,* taking on a different *form,* and employing a different *delivery* mechanism than traditional media.

  For example, when you receive a paper memo in your in-basket, you might first pile it with all the other things you must deal with: reports, electronic mail, meetings, voice mail, postal mail, express mail, and so on. All of these kinds of communication compete for your attention in terms of the space and time they occupy. The memo on your desk is more likely to get your attention than the one in the bottom drawer of your filing cabinet or the one that arrived last week. In addition, these forms of communication compete in terms of what form and delivery mechanism they employ. A brightly packaged express mail letter (a special form of communication) usually commands more attention than a plain manila envelope, particularly when you must sign for the express mail (a special form of delivery).

  On the Web, however, the user chooses the time and space for communication. The form of the communication's display (how the hypertext file will be shown, in terms of font and appearance) is set by the user's browser, and the delivery mechanism is the same for all information—along the hypertext links of the Web itself. While access to information on the Web is constrained by awareness of it and the skills necessary to retrieve it, all information is potentially equally accessible. For example, is the 1948 company report in a storage room equally accessible to you as the memo sitting on your desk today? If delivered over the Web, that 1948 company report becomes not only more accessible to you but to any number of other users at the same time.

  The form of the Web itself—hypertext—is different from the linear flow of print on paper. Whereas memos and other communications offer themselves as separate objects, branches off a hypertext document can link to and thus relate one document or piece of a document to another, resulting in contextual relations among documents. Links from Web documents can be to hypermedia resources, interactive documents, or information delivery systems.

■ Web communication takes place within a context much larger than a single site or organization, involving social and cultural structures shaped by traditions, shared meanings, language, and practices developed over time.

The Web, like many other forums for computer-mediated communication on networks, has rapidly created specialized information and communication spaces. On computer networks, social and information spaces exist that are, by tradition, set aside for particular purposes. Behavior in these spaces is governed by collective agreement and interaction, as opposed to a single organization's rules of operation.

Community norms developed on networks inhibit advertising in noncommercial spaces. Just as going to a public place and shouting "Buy my widgets!" could be done, this is a method of advertising that may bring derision, particularly if it disturbs the decorum (or other chaos :)) the people in that public space had been previously enjoying. Although there may be no "Net cops" monitoring what is said and done, inappropriate communication risks invoking the wrath of a community. In contrast, the same widget seller in the market bazaar (or the Web-equivalent virtual mall) would be welcomed, because the users going into that marketplace know that they will see ads. The enthusiastic widget seller may be eagerly approached by those looking for very good widgets.

Examples illustrating appropriate and inappropriate advertising demonstrate the developed sense of community responsibility and tradition that has evolved over time in networked communities. Web traffic occurs in the context of these traditions. In contrast, the inter-office memo and the internal report exist within a closed environment—closed not just by proprietary considerations, but by the space and time limits inherent in the paper memo as a communications medium. This is not to say that there are no private, proprietary spaces on the Web. Indeed, an organization or individual would not even have to link the hypertext to the Web, and servers can support restricted access via passwords and machine names. However, a local community can still evolve on private, internal webs, and display all the cultural and psychological effects that have been occurring in computer-mediated communication systems for decades—community building, socioemotional interactions, evolving social practices, and conflicts.

Since communication on the Web exists within a larger community, the information provider must cope with the relationships arising from these connections. Web communities evolve over time, and relationships may cross national, cultural, language, and space and time borders. The challenge for this larger Web community is to negotiate the norms for individual interactions appropriately.

■ Web communication is dynamic. Traditional information development practices have long recognized the iterative nature of the process of creating and delivering information. Web communication, however, involves not only iterative development, but offers a delivered artifact that is conceptually and physically very different than that in traditional media. Web communication need not be fixed in its delivered form and exists within an information flux.

When you write a report, you often go through the processes of copyediting, revising, reviewing, user testing, and revising again. Eventually, the deadline clock ticks, and there is a final form that the information takes. Although changes can be made—and there are very possibly second, third, and more editions of the work created—the sense by all parties involved is that the work is "completed" when it is etched into a medium, such as paper, a CD-ROM, a computer disk, or video tape.

On the Web, hypertext links, the multiple interactions with and among users, and the changing Web information universe all mark the Web as a medium attuned to flux rather than to stasis. Although you can create a web and deliver it to the world through a Web server, your job as an information developer is not done—in fact, it is just starting. You must not only manage the technical operation of your server, but also feedback from users and your web's place in the constant flow of new information introduced on the Web. In managing this change—since keeping track of document versions is not built into Web servers—you may also need to develop archiving procedures if you want to keep track of incremental changes.

Although the implications for how the Web changes communication go beyond even considerations of space, time, form, delivery methods, context, and information dynamism, these issues are enough to raise your awareness of how the Web medium differs from traditional media. The full implications of this change for our society and culture as a whole are still being worked out; we are still living through these changes as well as creating more of them.

A Traditional Information Development Process

The characteristics of Web communication described above—changes in space, time, and form relationships, as well as a shift in expectations about information context and change—necessitate a change in the processes people use to develop information for the Web.

Perhaps in high school you learned a process for composing an essay using a three-part model—an introduction, a body, and a conclusion. Such a model, evolving through thousands of years of human experience with written texts, serves as an information development method that can still be effective today in many situations. While the relationship between web information and its user is different from that between printed text and its reader, composing webs can involve many of the principles gleaned from centuries of experience in shaping communication.

One field on which you can draw for ideas about web composition and design is the field of technical communication. Practices and methods of technical communication developed in the twentieth century as a result of increased industrialization and knowledge specialization. Today, the need for computer documentation, descriptions of technological innovations, and legal and environmental documentation fuel the need for many forms of technical communication.

One way you can view technical communication is as a set of processes involving information development. These processes occur within a problem domain and yield specific products, such as a finished report or document.

Figure 29.1 shows the processes, products, and techniques of a technical communication model.

FIGURE 29.1.

The technical communication process.

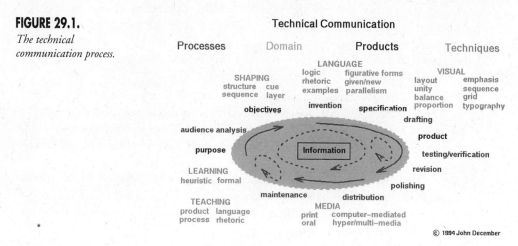

© 1994 John December

These processes operate within an information domain. For example, your information domain might be from the field of banking, or, more specifically, the information needed to operate an automated teller machine. In such a case, your challenge might be to accomplish a specific purpose, such as instructing customers how to use the machine to make a deposit, withdraw money, or check on an account balance. Based on this purpose, you can state information objectives such as the following:

- To inform the customers how to identify themselves and their accounts
- To present the deposit, withdrawal, and balance options, including variations and combinations such as savings, checking, and loan accounts
- To accept the customer's choices for interaction
- To give the customer feedback concerning the transaction process
- To conclude the transaction with the appropriate result—whether it is cash in the drawer, a balance slip printed, or some error condition

Based on the objectives for the automated teller machine information, you can then create a specification for how this information should take shape. Should you display the information on the screens of the machine? Should you provide a poster next to the machine with the information on it? Will you write a brochure explaining the machine that you will send to all customers? This specification answers these questions about the form and the medium of the information. This specification can get very detailed about the form of the information, including exact sizes, type fonts, and other details.

Continuing the automated teller machine example, consider how you might develop the information that will be displayed on the video screen of the machine. You need to develop a detailed statement of exactly what you want your information to accomplish. Once you get this exact statement, you'll move on to the phase of designing the information product (an individual screen display) itself. In this design process, you can weigh all your options for how the screens should look, and how the user will interact with them. These options include the screens' sequence, contents, wording, and appearance. Developing this information, you can draw on design principles such as layout, typography, and other considerations.

In the automated teller machine example, you eventually must create all the *products* of the information development process—the purpose statement, objectives, specification, and design. In creating these products, you'll employ a variety of processes. First, the purpose and objectives themselves were influenced by a thorough understanding of audience (the users of the machine). What do people care about when using an automated teller machine? Do they want to know the bank's reputation? The total cash on hand in its vaults? Common sense and knowledge of the audience help answer these questions. The act of coming up with a purpose statement requires some idea of audience and an understanding of what that audience wants to and needs to know.

The transition from having objectives defined and making specifications for information to achieve these objectives involves a process of invention, of coming up with creative ideas to accomplish a goal and solve a problem. For example, how can you let a user know that he or she has inserted the bank card into the machine backwards? How should you handle the user's request for how much money he or she wants from the account? These kinds of questions, derived from the objective statements, determine the information specifications. For example, your objective to accept the customer's choices for interaction (whether to make a deposit, a withdrawal, or to check on the account balance) might take on an additional specification, such as "to take the user's choice for interaction through a numeric keypad on the automated teller machine."

With the processes and products leading up to the specification of the automated teller machine information, you can now draft a final product. Since this example involves using a machine—rather than a brochure or paper report—your actual design must involve experts in the mechanics and operation of that machine. You must know how to encode the commands to achieve a particular effect or screen display and how to decode inputs from the user—the buttons the user pushes on the machine—into information the system can accept and use.

When your initial design is complete, obviously you want to test it—first, with some tests in your own lab, and then with tests by real customers in mock situations (some customers might wince at risking their own bank balances in an untested new system). Based on this testing, as well as verification that all your objectives have been met, you can polish the result, or even restart the process of audience analysis, invention, drafting, and design. When you have a final form for the automated teller machine that meets your objectives, you can distribute and then maintain the system.

How the Web Transforms the Information Development Process

The automated teller machine example in the preceding section has many characteristics similar to a development and design process that can be used to weave a web. The example emphasizes user interactivity, user interface design, and human-computer interaction issues. Is this same model of information development appropriate for weaving a web? Yes and no. The traditional technical communication process matches web weaving in the following ways:

- A traditional information development process often recognizes the importance of understanding the user's needs, perceptions, abilities, and ways of interacting with the information.

- A traditional information development process employs an iterative, even cyclical, approach in which specific products are created by processes, employing techniques to shape information.

The traditional technical communication process does not match web weaving for the following reasons:

- The Web offers unique space and time possibilities.

- Web messages have a form and delivery largely determined by the user's equipment and options not under the total control of the information developer.

- Web information is often extremely dynamic and exists within a larger information and social context.

An Information Development Process for the Web

How can you create a development process for the Web, drawing from techniques of information development processes based largely on static mediated communication? This is not an easy question to answer. However, you can develop information for the Web by using an information development process that relies on your knowledge of the Web's unique characteristics while at the same time using a basic design and development process similar to that used by many technical communicators, writers, designers, and software developers.

This section previews a web-weaving methodology that serves as the basis for the next chapters in this part. These chapters cover the planning, analysis, design, implementation, and development processes for weaving a web. Although these processes might seem like an encumbering amount of work to go through, a well-designed web has a far greater value than one that is hastily put together, particularly if your web is for business or professional communication. For casual web developers, the methodology can still help to illuminate possibilities for structuring information and techniques to improve the overall effectiveness of a web.

An Overview of a Web-Weaving Methodology

Figure 29.2 illustrates a methodology that can be used to develop webs. At first glance it seems similar to Figure 29.1 (which is a more traditional technical communication methodology). The web-weaving method contains many of the same elements, but web-weaving processes are more open ended because the final product (an operating web) is often not as permanently fixed as traditional media.

FIGURE 29.2.

A web-weaving methodology.

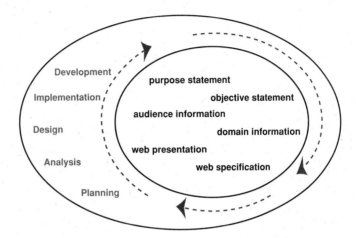

In the example, automatic teller machines were installed and occasional checks were made to make sure they were working correctly, but a web is often never completed. (Many webs offering a static set of information can often have large sections that remain stable, however.) The traditional technical communication approach, although recognizing the need for review, revision, maintenance, and re-release of information products, eventually stops because of the encoded nature of the medium; etched in paper or even in the workings of an automated machine, the information becomes "set," and there is no further development. Web information exists in the constant flux of the global Web, is used by new users with new kinds of browsers, and often involves much user–developer interaction. Therefore, web weaving often requires that the processes performed on information elements are continuously done.

Moreover, web elements themselves are subtly changed from elements in a traditional communication process. While the traditional approach to technical communication saw audience analysis as a crucial part of shaping information, the web-weaving methodology recognizes audience information as an intrinsic element of the web itself. Information about an audience must be gathered, planned for, analyzed, designed, and implemented in the information presentation itself. In a web, audience information plays a crucial role in publicity and user feedback. Thus, all processes in web weaving depend on audience information.

These web elements and processes are interconnected, and decisions web weavers make rely on these interconnections. As such, there is redundancy in the methodology. If any one element or process is weak, another stronger element or process may be able to compensate. For example, a good implementation can sometimes make up for a bad design. A good objective statement can make up for a poor purpose statement. The goal is not to have these weaknesses, but to counter the inevitable problems that result.

The rest of the chapters in Part V go into the details of this web-weaving methodology. The following are the elements:

■ *Audience information:* A store of knowledge about the target audience for the web as well as the actual audience who uses the information. This information includes the audience's background, interests, proclivities, and all details helpful to shaping the information to suit the users' needs. All this information may not be complete at any time during the web-weaving process; only a store of information will develop over time. The audience information may be very useful and accurate at one time; it may then pass out of currency as different users start accessing the web.

■ *Purpose statement:* An articulation of the reason for and scope of the web's existence. At all times during web development, a web weaver should have a succinct purpose statement for the web. This statement might be in general terms, such as "to create a presence for our company in cyberspace" or it may be very specific, such as "to provide information about our company's new line of modems." This purpose statement itself is dynamic—over time, an organization that started a web to "establish presence in cyberspace" may want to make that web serve another, more specific, purpose. A succinct statement of this purpose, at whatever level of generality, serves as a guidepost for the web-weaving processes.

■ *Objective statement:* Flows from the purpose statement and defines what specific goals the web should accomplish. For example, an objective statement based on the purpose used in the preceding paragraph—"to provide information about our company's new line of modems"—might include a statement of the modems the company offers and what kind of information should be given (pictures, prices, schematics, and so on). Like the audience information and purpose statements, the objective statement is dynamic, and it may become apparent later in web weaving to define still others. Therefore, the objective statement will change as the purpose of the web changes, but also as the information about the audience changes. For example, it may be that the audience looking at the modems might be suddenly very concerned about display buttons on the devices themselves. In that case, an objective might be created to include pictures of modems in the web itself.

■ *Domain information:* A collection of knowledge about the subject domain the web covers, both in terms of information provided to users of the web and information the web weavers need. For example, a web offering modems for sale might also necessarily draw on a variety of information about the use, mechanics, principles, and specifications for modems. While not all this information would necessarily be made available to the users of the web, this domain knowledge may be essential for the web developers to have. Often, this domain knowledge makes a good complement to the information the web already offers. For example, a modem manufacturer with a good collection of modem facts might find that interested buyers visit that web for technical information about modems and, in the course of the visit, be informed of a company's products.

■ *Web specification:* As in the automated teller machine example, the specification statement describes, in detail, the elements that will go into a design. The specification statement lists what pieces of information will be presented as well as any limitations on the presentation. For example, one part of a specification might state that the picture of the modem must be placed on the same hypertext page as a link to an order form. The specification, as with all the other elements of the web, may be in constant flux.

■ *Web presentation:* The means by which the information is delivered to the user. The presentation is the result of design and implementation processes that build on the web specification. In these processes, creative choices are made among design and presentation techniques to achieve the web specification as well as considerations for efficiency, aesthetics, and known web usage patterns.

From this list of the elements involved in the web-weaving methodology, you can see that there are many interactions and relationships among them. In fact, all of the elements depend on the best information being available about the other elements in order to be successful. For example, a web weaver needs to know if the objective is to sell modems or educate people about modems if he or she is designing a particular piece of a web. Similarly, the elements interact with the *processes* of the methodology.

The processes of the methodology are the following:

■ *Planning:* This is the process of choosing among competing opportunities for communication so that overall goals for the web can be set. These goals include anticipating and deciding on targets for the audience, purpose, and objectives for the information. Planning is also done for domain information through a process of defining and specifying the supporting information that must be collected, how it will be collected, and how the information will be updated. A web planner anticipates the skills called for by the web specification as well as the skills needed for constructing particular parts of a web. For example, if a specification for a design calls for using a forms (a feature supported by HTML) interface, the web planner needs to identify the need for web implementors to have these skills. The web planner also anticipates other resources needed to support the operation and development of the web. For example, if user-access statistics will be gathered, the plan for the web must account for the need to procure and install a web statistics program.

■ *Analysis:* This is a process of gathering and comparing information about the web and its operation in order to improve the web's overall quality. An important operation is one in which a web analyst examines information gathered about the audience for its relevance to some other elements or processes in web weaving. For example, information about the audience's level of technical interest can have a great deal of impact on what information should be provided to a user about a particular product or topic. Similarly, analyzing the web's purpose in light of other new developments, such as the contents of a competitor's web, must be an ongoing process. An analyst weighs alternatives and gathers information to help with a decision in the other processes of planning, design, implementation, or development.

- *Design:* In this process, a web designer builds on the web's specification and makes decisions about how a web's actual components should be constructed. This process involves taking into account the web's purpose, audience, objective, domain information, and specifications. A good designer knows how to achieve the effects called for by the specification in the most flexible, efficient, and elegant way. However, because it relies so heavily on the other processes and elements in web weaving, the design process is not more "important" than any of the others, but it requires a thorough grounding in implementation possibilities as well as knowledge about how particular web structures affect an audience.

- *Implementation:* This is the process of actually building the web itself using HyperText Markup Language (HTML) (or improvements on it). The implementation process is perhaps most like software development because it involves using a specific syntax for encoding web structures using a formal language in computer files. Although there are automated tools to help with the construction of HTML documents, a thorough grounding in HTML as well as an awareness of how designs can best be implemented in HTML enriches the web implementor's expertise. (See Chapter 37, "HTML Editors and Filters," for more information.)

- *Development:* This is the process of making sure that the other processes continue and that the web itself is being presented well to the World Wide Web. The web development process involves directing the analysis of audience information, usability, and use patterns; publicizing the web's availability and purpose; monitoring usage; and making sure that the planning and design processes continue for new conditions and information.

While this methodology for weaving a web won't work flawlessly in all situations, it can serve as a basis for looking at the issues of web weaving. You may find that the actual processes and elements you use are some variation on these. Being aware of what elements and processes are involved in web development is key: Once you are aware of what you might face, you can most flexibly grow a successful web.

Weaver's Check

When you weave a web, you are making paths through the tangle of links that make up the Web. Unlike the linear paths that paper books present to readers, hypertext paths in a web give the user a different experience of space and time constraints, form and delivery methods, context, and information flux, than do traditional forms of mediated communication. The key in weaving a web is to meet the user's needs.

A web-weaving methodology, like traditional communication or composition methodologies, employs a set of elements and processes for creating and shaping information. Web weaving involves processes of planning, analysis, design, implementation, and development, as well as elements including audience information, purpose and objective statements, domain information, web specification, and web presentation. A web-weaving methodology uncouples the processes from the communication elements more than in a traditional process. The Web-weaving methodology described here results in a final product—an operating web—that can be considered to have a life cycle with periods of change and growth rather than a final static form.

The next chapters explore each of the processes of web weaving described in this chapter.

Planning a Web

30

by
John December

Frequently great things can be done without a plan. Sometimes, well-planned things meet with dismal failure. Often, well-planned projects are successful. Although planning a web is not required, a well-planned web can help web weavers meet their goals and improve the quality of the information they provide.

The previous chapter described the differences between Web information and traditional forms. These differences make planning an important part of web weaving.

This chapter first looks at what you can and cannot plan for when weaving a web. Then it looks in detail at how to plan for the six key elements of web weaving: audience information, purpose statement, objective statement, domain information, web specification, and web presentation. As you will see in this chapter, this process of planning a web is incremental (moves in small steps) and is cyclical (moves in cycles).

What You Cannot Control

In weaving a web and making it available to the public to freely browse, there are a range of factors over which you have no control. The first step of the planning process is to recognize these factors and consider how they will affect your particular web. The factors over which you have no control include user behavior, browser display, links into your web, and what's behind the links out of your web.

User Behavior

You cannot control how the user is going to access and use your information. You might assume that the user will enter your web at its "front" or "top" page, but it is possible to link into your web at any arbitrary point given its URL. While your intent may be to guide your user down a series of pages in your web, as shown in the left picture of Figure 30.1 (the wine bottle model), users can actually enter your web at any arbitrary link (the pin cushion model in the right side of Figure 30.1).

FIGURE 30.1.
A user can enter your web at an arbitrary point.

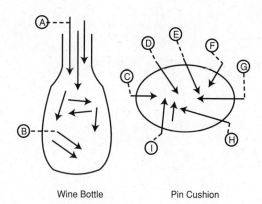

Wine Bottle   Pin Cushion

This means that you must take this arbitrary linking to your web into account during planning, as well as in the other processes of weaving: analysis, design, implementation, and development (as described in detail in later chapters). During the planning stage, it is possible to *intend* to build a web with a different entry pattern than the pin cushion model. In fact, it is often possible to shape general user behavior toward a wine bottle model by using the right navigational cues, web publicity (the process by which you make your web and its features known), and other design features. At the planning stage, it is important to identify what model of user behavior you are aiming for and state it explicitly. While you can't control user behavior, an explicit statement of how you would like a user to access your web serves as a guide in later processes and elements in web weaving.

Just as you can't control a user's entry point into your web, you cannot shape the user's path through it. While navigational cues and the links you make available will guide the user on a likely path through your web, the planning process of web weaving cannot make explicit assumptions about what this entry point is or how the user will traverse the information.

It is important to note that not being able to control a user's entry point or path through your web is not necessarily an undesirable feature. In fact, many would say that this is precisely the power and benefit of hypertext—the user can follow links based on his or her interest or thought process.

The User's Browser and Display

As described in Part II, "Web Browsers and Connections," there are a wide variety of browsers available to view the Web. In planning a web, you must recognize that you might not know what kind of browsers your users will have. Moreover, new browsers are in development, and future browsers are certain to provide more and different features than the ones presently available.

Therefore, different users, based on their browser's operation, will experience your web differently—from an ASCII display of your web (in Chapter 14, "Web Structure and Spaces") to a hypermedia experience with Mosaic (Figure 14.3). Therefore, in planning for your web, you need to think about what kinds of information will be essential. For example, if you place important or essential information in a graphics file, not all browsers will support that display, and the information will be lost to some users.

Just as you might not know what browser the users of your web will have, you can't control exactly how information is displayed in a browser. This is a very big change from traditional desktop publishing, in which every aspect of font style and size, alignment, and other layout features can be carefully controlled. In fact, such control and fine-tuning has been a big part of a desktop publisher's job for a long time.

However, the HyperText Markup Language (HTML) works on a completely different philosophy for presenting information. HTML is a *markup* language, which means that the *structure* of a document is marked with tags. For example, an ordered list starts with the tag <OL>, each item in the list is preceded by <LI>, and the list ends with </OL>. Thus, the *meaning* of the text is marked within the HTML document, rather than the appearance.

Some say that this separation of content from display frees the writer to concentrate more on producing good content than worrying about how it looks. (HTML is thus said to be a presentation-independent language.) This same feature disappoints others, however, who are fond of presentation-dependent tools such as WYSIWYG (what-you-see-is-what-you-get) word processors.

HTML is covered in more detail in Chapter 33, "Implementing a Web: Basic HyperText Markup Language (HTML)," and Chapter 34, "Advanced HTML Features." For the planning process, you must recognize that the tags in an HTML document define the structures of a document but do not define how these structures are displayed. For example, in some browsers, the ordered list is normally displayed with Arabic numerals, starting from 1, in a vertical list slightly indented from the previous list. However, a browser could be designed that reads the same HTML file and displays the same ordered list with Roman numerals and the list items arranged in a block paragraph form.

In fact, there is no reason why future browsers may not have preferences whereby the user can control how ordered lists are displayed. Moreover, font style and size, while controlled to some degree by HTML tags that suggest different levels of headings, are ultimately under control of the browser. In the Mosaic browser (Chapter 15, "Browser Operations"), the user can alter the appearance of text by choosing from four different fonts in three different sizes each. In other browsers, such choices are not possible.

Links Into and Out of Your Web

In the course of weaving a web, you may make many links to other resources on the network that you don't control. In so doing, realize that resources often move, making the link no longer valid (the link is then said to be *stale*). A user following a stale link from your document will encounter an error message and not get the information you had originally intended for him or her to access, thus degrading the experience of the user in your web.

Realize that you can't control this. Even if a link isn't stale, an error message might result when a remote computer host is down temporarily. Users should realize that this is an unavoidable aspect of web navigation (Part III, "Web Navigation Tools and Techniques"). While you may have relied for a long time on a particularly beneficial resource to be available to your web's users, that resource may eventually go away, leaving a stale link and information missing from your web.

Not only can a link you create from your web to an outside resource go stale, but it can also change in unexpected ways. This can be particularly troubling when you are linking to resources created by people for very informal reasons (for example, a school project or a hobbyist's project).

For example, you may have linked to a very nice photograph of a train at a remote site, a photograph key to your web's information content. The hobbyist who made that photograph available, unless by an agreement with you, is under no obligation to forever offer a picture of a train through that link. It may be that the hobbyist changes the image at that link every month. Next month, your users retrieve a photograph of a tree. This example helps you see how link maintenance and coordination is an important part of web weaving, and that the planning process involves recognizing that remote resources might not always be stable or readily accessible.

Just as you can't control what resources exist at the links out of your web, you cannot control the links into your web. When publicly available, any link in your web—any URL that resolves to an HTML page that you provide—can be used in any other work on the Web. (You can make a statement explicitly forbidding these links, but this kind of restriction is rarely done on the Web and itself may be considered a breach of "community tradition.")

Someone linking to your web could misrepresent its purpose or content, perhaps unintentionally. For example, while your web might be "The XYZ Company's Modem Products," someone at a remote site might identify your link as a "instructions for hooking up to a computer bulletin board." You can track down references to your web by using a Web spider (Chapter 19, "Spiders and Indexes: Keyword-Oriented Searching"), and you will often be able to correspond with anyone who may have misinterpreted the meaning or purpose of your web; you can't, however, control all links into your web.

While this benign case of a misunderstanding of your web's purpose may be something you can easily fix, it is not clear if you will be able to suppress or stop malicious references or links to your web. The legal issues involved are not worked out.

For example, you might run across someone who describes your modem products web as "the lamest modems made" or even maliciously spreads your web's URL among large groups of people, with instructions to "click on this link until the server crashes." The latter case is a bit more clear-cut; there are explicit rules of conduct that most users, at least at institutional sites, must follow, and these often include rules against intentionally damaging any equipment. Moreover, the commonly held set of traditions on the Net itself would definitely prohibit maliciously crashing a server.

However, another view is that the user who makes the comment "the lamest modems made" about your web may be simply exercising his or her freedom of speech, and there might be nothing you can do about it. In actual practice, you'll find that links into your web will be made in good faith, and you will be able to clear up any misinterpretations of your web's purpose.

What You Can Control: Planning

Now that you've surveyed some of the major factors that you cannot control in web weaving, it's time to look in more detail at the specific elements that your plan should cover.

The purpose of planning is to choose among competing opportunities, options, and choices. Specifically, you need to plan particular aspects of each of the web-weaving elements: audience information, purpose statement, objective statement, domain information, web specification, and web presentation. This chapter goes into detail about how planning works for each of these elements.

Audience Information

Part IV, "Exploring the Web," presents a large number of ways the Web can be used in many contexts. The applications in Part IV along with navigation skills in Part III can help you consider what you want to do in your web. Creating effective communication, particularly mediated communication, requires that you plan what you want to communicate to whom. Information about the target audience for your information is crucial for creating successful communication. In fact, many would consider information about your audience to be your most precious resource.

Knowing your audience is important because it, like the purpose statement, helps shape the whole information content of your web as well as its "look and feel." If you do not have a specific audience in mind for your web, a specific audience will use your web, and their experience of it may be positive or negative as a direct result of the choices you make about the way you present your web. A web influenced by accurate information about its intended and actual audience should have a higher probability of successfully communicating its intended message and information.

Excellent planning for audience information involves two steps: defining your audience and then defining the information that it is important to know about that audience:

1. **Define your target audience.** In a simple statement, describe the audience you want to reach with the information in your web. For example, you may want to reach "scholars who are interested in geology." Although this statement is simple, it serves as a valuable guide for developing many of the other elements in web weaving. A plan to reach the audience "everyone interested in science" is a very broad one. Although a web that reaches this audience might be successfully created, it may be an unrealistic audience planned for a new web.

   One technique for helping you define your audience is to generate a cluster diagram. Draw a diagram, such as the one shown in Figure 30.2, in which you show overlapping circles representing different audiences that you might target, as well as their relationships. For example, you might be interested in reaching just professors at universities who are geologists, or any scholar (someone seriously pursuing the academic study of a subject at a high level).

   Draw ovals to represent the audiences and their relationships (such as overlapping or inclusion). Also show related audiences—even if you might not want to reach them—as a way of explicitly defining who you might *not* want to reach. For example, Figure 30.2 shows a large oval for students. You might not plan to reach grade-school and high-school students, but you might include them in your diagram in order to show their relationship to members of your target audience. For example, many scholars may teach younger students. As such, some of your target audience (geology scholars) may have an interest in gathering and developing material for younger audiences or issues involved in teaching.

FIGURE 30.2.

*A cluster diagram
of an audience.*

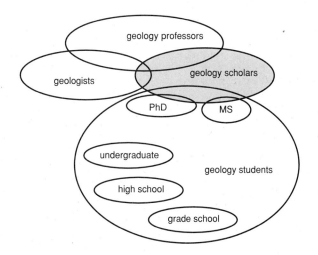

Continue this clustering process until you've zeroed in on what you can say is the specific audience you want. Maybe you'll decide after looking at this diagram that you want to target only professional geologists who are also geology professors. Thus, the cluster diagram helps you more carefully define your target audience. Note that you can target multiple and overlapping audiences, not just a single group.

2. **Define information you will need to know about the audience.** Based on your audience description, what information about them would be useful? For example, if you plan to reach scientists interested in geology, what characteristics of these scientists are important to you? Educational level? Area of specialization? Personal characteristics such as age, height, and weight? For some purposes and some audiences, different information will be important. For example, weight and height information might be important if you are trying to sell the scientists clothing or equipment for their research that depends on their body characteristics. Otherwise, such information might be totally irrelevant. The key is to identify the *relevant* information about your audience in the planning stage. In later stages, you'll use this list as a basis for gathering information and analysis.

Since the planning process itself is incremental and continuous, you might find that you don't know exactly what information about your audience will be important later on. You can use the cluster diagram you made to generate characteristics of that audience. With your target audience shaded to help you focus on it, generate lists of your audience's characteristics, concerns, and activities. (Figure 30.2 shades the geology scholars audience.) Write down this list as quickly as you can, including entries without judgment about the relevance of that entry.

Here's an example:

Geology scholars—characteristics:
        highly educated
        interested in earth processes
        skilled in critical thinking

Geology scholars—concerns:
funding for projects
publishing findings
getting the right equipment
teaching
valid research methodologies
locating related publications

Geology scholars   activities:
attending conventions
conducting research
communicating with the public
teaching
gathering samples
serving in industry roles

Continue these lists until you've included just about everything you can think of that relates to your audience's characteristics, concerns, and activities. Some items may naturally fall into several categories; notice that "teaching" showed up both as a concern and an activity.

The next section shows how planning for your purpose helps you select the audience information you intend to gather and maintain. After defining your purpose, you can return to these lists and choose which of these items is relevant or important for the purpose you've defined. The set of characteristics you select as important will serve as the database of audience information you are concerned about collecting and maintaining.

Purpose

The statement of purpose serves as the driving force throughout web weaving. The purpose helps you choose what information about your audience you must gather and maintain, and it influences the form of your web's presentation. Not having a succinct purpose statement for why the web is operating in the first place makes it very hard for web designers to choose among techniques to present information. Without a statement of purpose, web analysts have no basis for evaluating if the web is operating effectively. Moreover, a web without a clear purpose often carries a cloudy message to the user—upon entering, the user will wonder "What is this for?" And have no clue as to an answer.

To define your purpose, you need to make a statement about what you want your web to do, which identifies the following elements:

■ **The subject area.** What area of knowledge serves as the context for what your web conveys? This area of knowledge does not have to be a traditional Library of Congress subject classification (such as geology or biology). It might be "information about the odd-bearing division of XYZ Industries."

- **The audience.** Your purpose statement contains the audience identification within it. This audience identification is a part of the purpose statement because so much of the "What are we doing?" question about your web revolves around the specific audience you are trying to reach.

- **The level of detail at which information is presented.** Your purpose might be, for example, "to provide a comprehensive overview of geology for geology scholars" or it might be more specific, such as "to present basic reference material about geology for geology scholars." This level of detail influences how much domain information you will need to gather and maintain.

- **The user's expected benefit or response.** What will users of your web gain from it? The purpose statement might include the phrase "in order to keep current in the field of geology," "in order to keep up with current developments," or some combination of these kinds of statements.

As you can see from this list, planning the purpose statement forces you to make many decisions about the message you want your web to convey. A well-formed purpose statement serves as a touchstone for all the other web-weaving processes and elements. Indeed, the purpose statement itself may play a very important role as one of the first pieces of information about your web that is presented to users.

Here are some actual purpose statements that contain many of the points in the previous list. Notice that the more complete the statement of purpose is, the easier it is for a user to answer the question "What is this for?"

- "This information server (`ftp.arpa.mil`) provides selected information about the activities and programs of the Advanced Research Projects Agency (ARPA). It initially contains information provided by the Computing Systems Technology Office (CSTO) and associated information about the High Performance Computing and Communications Program. Additional capabilities will be added incrementally to provide additional information."
  —from the *ARPA home page,* URL `http://ftp.arpa.mil/`

- "The purpose of this center is to serve the needs of researchers, students, teachers, and practitioners interested in computer-mediated communication (CMC). This center helps people share resources, make contacts, collaborate, and learn about developments and events."
  —from the *Computer-Mediated Communication Studies Center,* URL `http://www.rpi.edu/~decemj/cmc/center.html`

- "This project is intended as a demonstration vehicle to show how information useful for teaching and learning about business telecommunications and data communications may be effectively shared over the Internet."
  —from the *Distributed Electronic Telecommunications Archive (DELTA) home page,* URL `http://gozer.idbsu.edu/business/nethome.html`

■ "The purpose of this server is to provide access to a wide range of information from and about Japan, with the goal of creating deeper understanding about Japanese society, politics, industry, and, most importantly, the Japanese people."
—from the *Center for Global Communications home page*, URL `http://www.glocom.ac.jp/index.html/`

Objective Statement

Once you have planned for the purpose of the web, who the audience is, and what you need to know about the audience, you need to combine all this information to arrive at a specific statement of web objectives. As such, an objective statement is much more specific and lengthy than a purpose statement. An objective statement makes clear the specific outcomes and information that will implement the stated purpose of the web. Thus, the objective statement expands on the general descriptions given in the purpose statement. However, an important difference exists: While the purpose statement stays the same, the objective statement may change as new information about the domain or audience becomes available.

A phrase in the purpose statement such as "to provide access to a wide range of information from and about Japan" (Center for Global Communications home page, URL `http://www.glocom.ac.jp/index.html`) could be implemented with a variety of specific objectives. The objectives could include showing Japanese cultural information, geographical and climate information, and selections of online Japanese publications. While the purpose statement says "here is what we are going to do," the objective statement says "here is the information that will do it."

Unlike the purpose statement, the objective statement need not necessarily be written on the web's home page. Instead, an objective statement is "behind the scenes" information that guides the development of other elements in web weaving.

For example, from the statement of purpose given for the Computer-Mediated Communication (CMC) Studies Center, the statement "help people share resources" can be used to generate a set of specific objectives as follows:

Purpose: Help people share resources

Objective: Provide a list of resources with links to the following:
Major online collections of CMC-related material
Bibliographies
Academic and research centers related to CMC
Online journals

Over time, this objective statement may change by expanding to include links to other kinds of forums for subjects related to CMC. Also, changes in the objective statement may require that features are removed from the web.

Planning the objective statements gives you a head-start on another web-weaving element: domain information.

Domain Information

Domain information refers to information and knowledge about the subject area of the web, including both online and offline sources of information. Domain information includes not only information that will be presented to users of the web, but it includes all information and knowledge the weavers of the web need to know in order to do a good job.

Therefore, the collection of domain information serves as an "information store" from which both the developers and users of the web will draw. It may be that the purpose of the web itself is to provide an interface to this information store; or it might be that this information store is only incidental to the purpose of the web and plays only a supporting role as background information for the developers. In either case, planning for domain information is essential. These are steps for planning for domain information:

1. **Define what domain information is necessary for the weavers to know and what information will be provided to users.** Are there specialized databases to which you must gain access? Is there an existing store of online material that will serve as a basis for user information? What kind of background in the discipline do weavers of the web have to appreciate and understand in order to effectively make choices about information content and organization? What other material might be needed, either by the users of the web or by the developers?

2. **Plan for the acquisition of domain information.** Once the information store is defined, how can it be obtained? For example, is there a large collection of information files easily accessible? Or is there a paper-based information source that the web developers should read or a course they should take before trying to build the web? For example, developers working in creating a web about geology should have some appreciation for the topics and subdivisions of the field in order to make judgments about how information should be presented.

3. **Plan for updating and maintaining the information.** It is not enough to define and acquire a database. If it is time-dependent information, when will it lose its usefulness? How will it be updated? Who will update the information? What will be the costs of this updating and maintenance?

The degree of attention paid to domain information acquisition and maintenance varies a great deal according to the purpose of the web itself. For example, a web that purports to be an interface to current satellite imagery of the earth's clouds must necessarily have constantly updated domain information. In contrast, a web for information about British literature might require updates as new knowledge is formed, but not on an hourly or minute-by-minute basis.

Web Specification

The web specification is a refinement of the objective statement in more specific terms, adding a layer of constraints or other requirements. These requirements may restrict or further describe in detail what the web will offer and how it will be presented.

The web specification, for example, takes the objective statement "to provide links to bibliographies in the field" and makes it specific—with a list of the URLs that will be provided. The specification statement can also characterize limitations on the information and its presentation, such as "no more than 10 bibliographies will be listed on the resources page; if more are required, a separate bibliographies page will be made."

The specification, however, doesn't dictate how the web should look (which is the goal of the web design process). Rather, the specification acts as a guidebook for the designers and implementors who will create the actual files of the web itself. The specification should completely identify all resources (for example, links; web components such as forms or graphical image maps; other resources such as sound, image, movie, or text files) that should (or can) be used in the web.

Similar to how the objective statement can change while accomplishing the same purpose, the specification statement can change while accomplishing the same objective. (For example, the URL to a resource required by an objective statement might change.)

The major issue in planning for the specification is to make sure that the people developing the web have the tools, training, and time necessary to weave the web according to specifications. For example, one part of the specification could state that a customer can order a product by using the Forms feature of HTML. In such a case, the planning process must identify the ability to build these forms as a skill web implementors must have.

The web specification can also *exclude* specific items. For example, the specification may state that the Forms feature of HTML is *not* to be used (because many browsers do not support Forms) or that no graphics are to be used. Thus, the specification acts as a list of "building blocks" and "tolerance limits" that can satisfy the objective statement for the web.

Web Presentation

Although the audience definition, purpose and objective statements, and domain information are most closely associated with the planning process of weaving a web, the development of a web's presentation must also be planned.

The web's presentation is the whole "look and feel" of the web, along with its actual implementation. Web designers planning for the web's presentation rely heavily on the web specification statement as a basis for making choices.

Planning for a web presentation involves verifying that resources are and will be available to support the files on the server that comprise the Web. Therefore, the person planning for the web's presentation must work closely with the web server administrator (sometimes called the *webmaster*) whose duties include allocating space or setting any special file or directory permissions so that the web presentation can be implemented.

Web planners also anticipate needs for the web's presentation by doing the following:

■ Generating a set of possibilities for the web presentation based on current or possible specifications. These possibilities might include sample HTML pages or, if the specifications allow, graphical image maps or forms to help the user interact with the information.

■ Planning the work schedule necessary to implement the web according to specifications, including how much time it will take to implement and test web pages, verify links, and implement changes based on new specifications.

■ Creating and maintaining a pool of generic web components (for example, common web page layouts or forms to serve as templates for web implementation).

■ Creating a mockup of the web based on an initial specification. This mockup could be quickly created from generic web components and offer a rapid prototype to be used in the other web weaving processes.

While the web implementors working on the web's presentation are the ones to actually write HTML files, the implementors aren't the "authors" of the web itself. As you can see from this chapter and Chapter 29, "Communication Processes on the Web," there are many processes involved in weaving a web. Whether it is one individual involved or a whole team, all weavers take part in creating an effective web.

Weaver's Check

It may seem like a lot of work, and you might rather just dive into writing HTML before planning, but taking the time to plan a web can raise the probability of a web's success. Thinking about and anticipating issues of audience, purpose, objective, domain information, specification, and presentation can lead to the creation of a web that best conveys an intended message and may save time and energy in the long run.

A web weaver cannot control many factors of a web: user behavior, the user's browser and display, and links into or out of the web. A web weaver can make efforts to ensure that web-weaving processes work together continuously and involve each of the six elements of a web (audience information, purpose statement, objective statement, domain information, web specification, and web presentation). During the planning process, a web planner must pay attention to the following:

■ Defining the web's intended audience and important characteristics about the audience.

■ Formulating a purpose statement that identifies the web's subject area, intended audience, level of detail, and expected user benefits or response.

■ Making an objective statement that specifically tells *how* the web's purpose will be accomplished by enumerating the resources and information.

- Defining the web's specification—a complete enumeration of the specific resources that will accomplish the objectives and any restrictions or special circumstances, including identification of special skills, tools, or resources needed by the web developers.

- Identifying the domain information necessary to support the information the web serves to the users as well as to support developers, including planning for acquiring and updating this information.

- Planning for the web's presentation by verifying that a Web server is available that has enough space for the expected web size, planning the time table for implementation and the resources needed, anticipating needs by developing or acquiring a generic set of web components, and making a mockup of the web based on the specification.

- The planning process may never stop. The intended audience for the web, its stated purpose, objective, domain information, specification, and presentation could change, thus requiring a revisit to all of the web's elements affected by the planning process.

A well-done planning process can keep a web fine-tuned and always ready for growth, change, and improvement. The next chapters look at the roles of other processes involved in web weaving and how they build on the work done in planning to continuously improve the web.

Plan Worksheet

Target Audience

1. Definition

   One-sentence statement:
   More complex description:
   Cluster diagram:

2. Information about audience

   Characteristics:
   Concerns:
   Key concerns based on purpose definition (below):

Purpose

1. Subject area:

2. Audience (defined previously):

3. Level of detail:

4. User's expected benefit/response:

5. Succinct purpose statement:

Objective Statement

1. Specific goals to accomplish the purpose:

2. Restrictions:

Domain Information

1. Information necessary:

   a. Web team:

   b. Information served:

2. Acquiring information:

3. Updates and maintenance:

Specification

1. Limitations on information:

2. Limitations on media:

3. Resources (for example URLs; web components such as forms or graphical image maps; other resources such as sound, image, movie, or text files) that should and can be used in the web's design:

Presentation

1. Look and feel possibilities:

2. Work schedule:

3. Skills required:

4. Components:

5. Mockup web:

Analyzing a Web

31

by
John December

Whether your web is already operating or you have just planned it, you might ask yourself: "Is the web accomplishing (or will it accomplish) the planned objectives?" You can answer this question through a process of analysis, in which you gather information about your web's elements (audience information, purpose and objective statements, domain information, web specification, and web presentation) and compare it with information about how users have used or will use your web. The analysis process also involves gathering information about other webs that may be accomplishing a similar purpose or reaching a similar audience. When done in conjunction with the other people involved in the other web weaving process, analysis serves as a check of the web's overall quality and effectiveness. Web analysis seeks to uncover the answers to the following questions:

Is the web accomplishing its stated purpose and meeting its planned objectives?

Is the web operating efficiently?

Are the intended benefits/outcomes being produced?

While a definitive answer to these questions might be impossible to obtain at all times, web analysis can serve as a check on the other weaving processes. This chapter looks at how you can go through web analysis at any time during your web's development. This analysis process involves gathering information and comparing it to feedback from users, server statistics, and information about your web's elements.

Analyze the Web's Elements

Figure 31.1 shows an overview of information useful in analysis. In the figure, the web's elements are in rectangles, and supporting or derived information is in ovals. Key checkpoints for analysis are shown in dashed circles, labeled A through E. At each checkpoint, the web analyst compares information about the elements or information derived from the web elements to see if the web is working or will work effectively.

The information about the web elements and derived information will vary in completeness depending on how far you are into actually implementing the web. You can obtain information about the web elements from the results of the planning, design, implementation, or development processes. If you've just started the planning process, you can analyze the checkpoints for which you have information. You can obtain the derived information through examining web statistics. Ideally, you'll be able to observe representatives from your intended audience as they use your web. If you don't have a working web ready, these audience representatives may give feedback on a mockup of your web, its purpose statement, or a diagram of its preliminary design.

The key to the analysis process is that it is meant to check the overall integrity of your web. Results from the analysis process are used in other processes to improve the web's performance. For example, if analysis of the web's domain information shows that it is often out-of-date, the planning process would need to be changed to decrease the time between updating the domain information. The analysis process on the web's elements helps all processes of web weaving work correctly and efficiently. The following sections go through each of the analysis checkpoints shown in Figure 31.1.

FIGURE 31.1.

The Web's elements must work together to meet objectives.

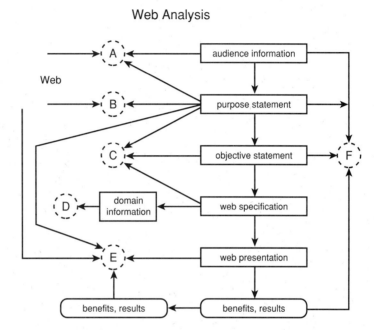

Web Analysis

Does the Audience Exist on the Web for the Given Purpose? (Checkpoint A)

Before spending too much time in the planning process defining and describing a target audience, you should check first to see that this audience could make use of your web at all. While the interests of all the people who use the World Wide Web is growing increasingly diverse, a routine check of the Web's demographics or contents may tell you something about the size of the audience you want to reach.

Up-to-date, accurate demographics of Web users are difficult to obtain (mainly because getting this information is a complicated task). Moreover, even an up-to-date demographic profile of *current* users may not say anything about the massive number of people who are beginning to use the Web. Therefore, comparing a description of your target audience with any demographic statistics should be done with caution, and only gives you a "rough feel" about whether the audience you seek is out there. The Graphics, Visualization, and Usability Center at Georgia Tech (URL http://www.gatech.edu/pitkow/survey/) has compiled a good collection of demographic statistics.

Without demographic statistics, the other way to see if your audience is on the Web (or the Net) is to check for subject-oriented information resources and forums that are interest items of your audience. (Chapter 18, "Trees: Subject-Oriented Searching," details how to locate subject-oriented resources.) For example, if your target audience is geologists, what online information already exists that shows geologists as active on the Web and the Net? You can do the following to find out:

- Search subject-oriented trees for resource collections related to geology.
- Locate institutions—academic, commercial, or research—that are involved with geology.
- Check Usenet newsgroups and FAQ archives to see what geologists are active on the Net.
- Check to see if there is an online mailing list devoted to geology.
- Check to see if professional societies or publications in the field of geology offer an online forum or information service.

You can interpret the results of your check of demographic statistics or Net resources related to your subject in two ways. First, if you find nothing, it might mean that your audience has made no forays into the Net—no newsgroups, no mailing lists, no online collections of resources at major institutions. Based on this, you could decide that your web would therefore fill a great need for this audience. In contrast, you might conclude that this particular audience is not interested in online communication at all. To decide which of these two alternatives is more accurate, you should consult representative audience members. Check with people you know in the field, and ask them, "What if you had an online system for information and communication?" Because online electronic mail discussion lists have been around longer than many network communication forums, an online mailing list that your target audience uses can be a good source of information about that audience's interests.

Another aspect of this analysis of audience information is to make sure that the purpose for your web is one that meets the audience's patterns of communication, or at least patterns that they are willing to engage in.

For example, you may find that certain audiences are not willing to have a publicly available forum for discussion and information because of the nature of their subject matter. For example, computer security systems administrators might not want to make detailed knowledge of their security techniques or discussions publicly available on a web server.

Certainly, private businesses or people involved in proprietary information may not want to support a web server to share everything they know. However, it may be that these same people would be interested in sharing information for other purposes. For example, computer security administrators might want to support a site that gives users advice about how to increase data security on computer systems. Thus, the web's purpose statement must match the audience's (or information provider's) preferred restrictions on the information. Current technology can support password protection or restricted access to Web information, so that specific needs for access can be met.

Through a check of the audience, purpose, and communication patterns for that audience, you can quickly detect logical problems that might make a web's success impossible.

For example, if your web's purpose is to teach new users about the Web, you might have a problem if your audience definition includes only new users. How can new users access your web in the first place? In this case, it may be that you should redefine your audience to include web trainers as well as the new users they are helping. This more accurate audience statement reflects the dual purpose of such a training web—getting the attention, approval, understanding, and cooperation of trainers as well as meeting the needs of the new users. By having an accurate audience statement, all the other processes in web weaving, such as design and development, can work more efficiently because they take the right audience into account.

Is the Purpose Already Accomplished Elsewhere on the Web? (Checkpoint B)

Just as you don't want to reach an audience that doesn't exist, or target an audience for a purpose they don't want to achieve, you don't want to duplicate what is being done successfully by another web. Checkpoint B is the "web literature search" part of the analysis: "Is some other web doing the same thing as what you want to do?" "What webs out there are doing close to the same thing?" These questions should be asked at the start of web development as well as continuously during the web's use. New webs and information will be developed all the time, and someone else may develop a web to accomplish the same purpose for the same audience as yours.

To find out if someone has built a web for a specific audience and purpose, use the subject- and keyword-oriented searching methods of Chapter 19, "Spiders and Indexes: Keyword-Oriented Searching." You might also try "surfing" for a web like yours or for information related to your audience and purpose. (See Chapter 21, "Surfing: Finding the New and Unusual.") During this process, save these links; if they are relevant to your audience and purpose, they become part of the domain information on which your own web's developers and users can draw.

The other benefit of this web literature search is that you can find webs that may be accomplishing the same purpose for a different audience. These webs may give you ideas about the kinds of information you want to provide for your audience. Also, you may find webs that reach the same audience but for a different purpose. These webs can give you useful background or cognate information that you could include as links in your own web. If you find a web that reaches the same audience for the same purpose you are considering, you can consider collaborating with the developers and further improve the information.

Do the Purpose, Objective, and Specification Work Together? (Checkpoint C)

One of the most important elements for the integrity of your web is the purpose, objective, and specification triad. These three elements spell out why your web exists and what it offers. The purpose statement, as you saw in the last chapter, serves as the major piece of information that your potential audience will read to determine if they should use your web. If the purpose statement is inaccurate, the audience might not use your web when they could have benefited from it, or they might try to use your web for a goal they will not be able to accomplish.

The check of the purpose-objective-specification triad is to make sure that something wasn't lost in the translation from the purpose (an overall statement of *why* the web exists) to the objective statement (a more specific statement of *what* the web will do) to the web specification (a *detailed enumeration* of the information in the web and constraints on its presentation).

It may be that during the development of the specifications, a piece of information was added that has no relation to the stated purpose. Or it might be that some aspects of the stated purpose are not reflected in the specification at all.

One way to do this check is to make a diagram that traces the links from the purpose statement to the objective statement to the specifications, both top-down and bottom-up. For example, Figure 31.2 shows how a purpose can be matched to specific objectives. Each objective gives rise to specifications for the web. From the bottom up, every specification should be traced to an objective and each objective to some aspect of the purpose.

The diagram shown in Figure 31.2 is incomplete in that the specifications would include a list of *all* URLs used in the web as well as a more complete specification of the database. Figure 31.2 shows just the categories for this specification information. When filled out completely, however, every URL and component of the specification should be traced back to an objective and each objective traced back to the purpose statement. If there is a mismatch, more planning must be done to restate the purpose, objectives, or specification so that they all match.

FIGURE 31.2.

The Web's purpose, objectives, and specification must work together to accomplish the same aim.

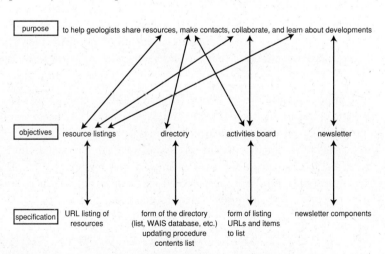

Is the Domain Information Accurate? (Checkpoint D)

The quality of the domain information you serve from your web and use in the web's development affects the users' perceptions of your web's overall quality. Inaccurate or incomplete information will hinder web developers as well as lead to dissatisfaction by your web's users. The domain information must be checked to make sure that it is accurate, updated, and complete. Periodic checks can be made according to the nature of the domain.

Recall from the definition given in Chapter 29, "Communication Processes on the Web," that there are two kinds of domain information: the information your web developers need to understand enough to plan, analyze, design, implement, and develop the web; and the domain information that your web provides to its users. Remember also that domain information of the first type need not be located on the Net at all—it may include textbooks or courses that the web developers use as a means of getting up to speed in the area of knowledge the web covers. This kind of domain information can also serve as reference information throughout the course of web weaving.

Verifying the accuracy, currency, and completeness of the domain information is a difficult task because you must have adequate knowledge of the subject matter to make a judgment about the veracity of all domain information. While the verification of off-Net resources such as books and courses can be evaluated according to the judgment the domain information analyst uses for similar offline materials, the Net information included in the first type of domain information and all the second type of domain information can be checked through a process of Net-access and retrieval.

The following is the process for checking Net-accessible domain information. For domain information provided to developers but not users of the web (the first type of domain information, which is Net-accessible), check the web page provided to developers in the same manner as described in the following list:

1. **Verify the freshness of links.**

    If the web is operational, use the links provided in the web itself to ensure that the links are not stale or the resource has not moved.

2. **Check the accuracy of the information.**

    If the web purports to respond with the correct solution to a problem given a set of inputs (for example, a physics problem answered through a Forms interface), have a set of conditions that lead to a known result. Test the web to verify that it yields the same answer, and vary the test cases you use.

    Use reliable and authoritative sources, where available, to verify the new information added in the web since the last analysis. If necessary, contact the developer of that information and discuss his or her opinions of the information's accuracy.

    In the case of databases, make sure that they are as current as they possibly can be. This is crucial, for example, if your web serves out time-dependent data such as earthquake reports. If you are not getting a direct feed from an information provider who supplies the most current information, check to make sure that the most current reports or data have been downloaded to the database that you use in your web.

3. **Check the completeness of the information.**

    Compare all specifications to items in the database. Are there any specifications calling for information that is currently missing?

Check locations on the Net (using methods of navigation described in Part III, "Web Navigation Tools and Techniques") to locate more current or reliable domain information.

Check locations on the Net to find other domain information that might be helpful as background to developers. Also look for information that could be part of the objective statement of the web.

4. **Check the appropriateness of the information.**

Is the information at the right level of detail? Are the web weavers getting the right level of information for their work? Are the web's users given the right amount of information, or is there an "information overkill" or an oversimplicity in what is offered?

Is any of the information not appropriate for serving or providing to your users or to the Web community at large? Is any of the information unethical, illegal, obscene, or otherwise inappropriate? Check links to outside information to verify that users will not encounter inappropriate material. Clearly, for outside sources of information, you will be limited in your ability to control inappropriate information. Include this check in your analysis process to make decisions about what outside links you want to use.

Is the Web Presentation Yielding Results Consistent with the Web's Design and Purpose? (Checkpoint E)

In this checkpoint, your goal is to determine if your web, based on server statistics or feedback from users, is being accessed consistently with how you want it to be used. One part of this consistency is to find out if the web server's access statistics show any unusual patterns. Your web server administrator should be able to provide you with a listing of your web's files and how many times they have been accessed over a given period of time. While this file access count is a simple measure of usage of your web, using it may reveal some interesting access patterns.

For example, a check of your web's files might show the following access pattern over the past 30 days:

File	Number of Accesses
top.html	10
about.html	9
overview.html	1,000
resources.html	800
people.html	20
newsletter.html	8

This shows a fairly uneven distribution of accesses in which a single file is accessed many times (the 1,000 shown here for overview.html). Compared to the small number of accesses to a "front door" (top.html) of your web, this pattern shows a problem unless this imbalance was intended. Also, the statistics show the newsletter isn't getting read very much, while the resources are being accessed quite a bit.

In order to interpret your web's access statistics, ask yourself these questions:

- Does the overall pattern of accesses reflect the purpose of the web?

- Does the pattern of access indicate a "balanced" presentation, or are some pages getting disproportionate access? Does this indicate design problems? (See the next chapter.)

- If the web's "front door" page isn't getting very many accesses, this could indicate problems with the publicity about your web.

Another aspect of verifying your web's consistency of design and purpose is to see that it is listed and used in appropriate subject indexes related to the subject of your web. Do you find links to your web on home pages of people working in your field? Is the general reputation for your web good? You can find answers to these questions by doing web spider searches to find what pages on the web reference your pages. Check major subject trees to see if your web is represented in the appropriate categories. Much of this analysis of your web's "reputation" is useful in the development process. (See Chapter 39, "Developing a Web.")

Another aspect of your web's design efficiency is access time. Go through the pages on your web and time how long the retrieval takes. Pay particular attention to pages that are large or pages that contain many inline figures. Consider how long it would take users at remote sites or with slow connections to download these pages. Your local access time may often be much shorter than for your audience, so that a long local access time required to download a page may indicate a still longer access time for the remote audience. Report this information to the designers and implementors.

Also, check your web using several different browsers. If your web has been viewed with Mosaic, try Lynx and see how it appears. You may discover that some HTML features have to be adjusted for use in an ASCII browser such as Lynx. Report problems with the display of the web in various browsers to the designers and implementors so that they can adjust the HTML used in the web.

Do the Audience Needs, Objective, and Results of Web Use Correspond to Each Other? (Checkpoint F)

It is very important that you determine whether your audience's needs are being met by your web. To do this, you must compare the audience information (your audience's needs and interests) with the objective statement and the intended and actual benefits and results from your web. Information about the actual benefits and results of your web's use will be the most difficult to come by. There are several methods, however, that may help you get a view of the effects of your web:

- **Ask users**. Design and distribute a survey. This could be done using the Forms feature of HTML if you are willing to use features not found on all web browsers. You could distribute the survey by e-mail to a random sample of users (if such a sample can be constructed from either a listing of "registered" users or derived from web access logs).

Include in this survey questions about user satisfaction. Are the users satisfied that the web meets their needs? What else would the users like to see in the web? How much do users feel they need each of the features your web offers?

■ **Survey the field.** Is your web used as a standard reference resource in your field of study? This is similar to the analysis performed at Checkpoint E, but rather than just focusing on the occurrence of links in indexes and other web pages, you need to analyze your web's reputation in the field of study or business as a whole. Do practitioners generally recommend your web as a good source of information?

■ **Are you accomplishing your purpose**? Are there outcomes occurring that you specifically stated in your purpose? For example, if one phrase of your purpose is to "foster research in the field," is there any evidence to support this? Is there research published that was sparked by the interactions your web fostered? If you have a commercial web, how many sales can you say the web generated? Determine some measure of your purpose's success and apply it during the analysis process.

Another way to look at Checkpoint F is to ask the broader question: Is the web doing some good? Even though your web may be under development and its objectives have still not truly been met, is there at least some redeeming value of your web? What benefits is it offering to your specific audience or even to the general public? For example, a commercial site that also provides some valuable domain information is performing a public service by providing education about that topic.

Another approach is to conduct research using theory and methods from the fields such as Computer-Mediated Communication, Computer-Supported Cooperative Work, Human-Computer Interaction or other disciplines that can shed light onto the dynamics of networked communication. These fields may yield theory that you can use to form testable hypotheses about how your web is working to meet users' needs, foster communication, or effectively convey information.

The key to Checkpoint F is to make sure that the other checkpoints—A through E—are working together to produce the desired results. You'll notice that Checkpoints A through E in Figure 31.1 each touch on groups of the web's elements. Only Checkpoint F spans the "big picture" questions: Are the *people who use your web* (audience information) getting *what they need* (purpose, objective, benefits/results) from it?

Weaver's Check

You can analyze your web to determine its communication effectiveness. This process of analysis involves gathering information about your web's elements and supporting information to make sure that your web does the following:

■ Attempts to reach an audience that has and will use Web access (Checkpoint A)

■ Contributes new information (accomplishes goals that haven't already been attained) (Checkpoint B)

- Is self-consistent (its purpose matches its objectives and specifications) (Checkpoint C)
- Is correct (the domain information it presents is accurate, up-to-date, and complete) (Checkpoint D)
- Is accessed in a balanced manner, both in terms of its own files and in terms of outside links into it (Checkpoint E)
- Is accomplishing objectives that meet the needs of its intended audience (Checkpoint F)

Designing a Web

32

by
John December

As a Web navigator, you've probably used webs that seemed to have *the right stuff*—information was at the right level of detail and the arrangement of pages and links guided you quickly to what you needed. While a positive web experience depends a great deal on your subjective preferences, a web designer can create a web *look and feel* that can increase the probability that most users will have a positive experience in a web. Because all users are different in their abilities and tastes, it is impossible to design a web that meets all user needs. Using the web weaving processes and elements, combined with an understanding of users' web experiences, a web weaver can create an effective design for a specific audience and purpose.

A web's design includes its look and feel and takes into account all the elements of web weaving—audience information, purpose and objective statements, domain information, and web specification—and combines these to produce a description of how the web can be implemented. Web implementors then use this design and the web specifications to create a working web.

A web designer makes many choices about how to best achieve the effects called for by the web specification. The web designer also draws on a repertoire of techniques for packaging, linking, and cueing information utilizing one or more design methodologies. Throughout this process, the web designer is sensitive to a user's experience of the web's information space, texture, and cues. There are very practical issues involved in designing—such as considerations for inline images and graphics, how much to put on a single page, and what should be linked and what should not. Over time, a web designer gains a sense of judgement and experience on which he or she draws—ultimately making web designing an art in itself.

The design process, however, is just one process in the interlocking web-weaving processes. A successful web requires that all processes and all elements work together. Thus, we'll see in this chapter how designing a web draws on the elements that the other web-weaving processes have helped develop.

Figure 32.1 illustrates how the web design process takes information from all elements of web weaving and combines them to produce a look and feel design that is then used by the implementation process to create a working web. By separating the design from the implementation process, information about the web's structure and operation can be cast in a hypertext language-independent form. That is, while the design process is influenced by knowledge of what is possible in the target design language, its product can be implemented in any language that can capture the features used in the design. In this way, this design process can be used with successors or alternatives to the widely used HyperText Markup Language (HTML).

This chapter first reviews the experience of a web user, emphasizing many of the aspects of user experience described in Part III, "Web Navigation Tools and Techniques," but from a design perspective. This review is meant to highlight how this design process is essentially *user-centered*—that is, it draws on audience information and the designer's understanding of how people navigate in webs.

FIGURE 32.1.

The web design process combines web elements.

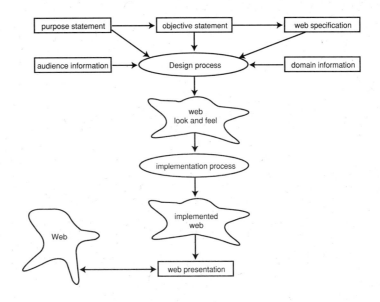

Following the review of user experiences of a web, some basic design methodologies are described—top/down, bottom/up, and incremental/in-time. These terms should be familiar to people who develop software, as they take their inspiration from software engineering. In web designing, there is not necessarily one methodology that should be followed throughout the web design or implementation process, particularly as the design process—like all the other processes of web weaving—can continue even after the web is deployed and used. Instead, the designer should be aware of the different design methodologies and be prepared to flexibly use any one of them at various times during the process of web design.

Aside from having a set of design methodologies to flexibly draw upon, the designer should also have a set of techniques for packaging, linking, and cueing information. The nature of hypermedia demands a strong attention to the user's experience of space, texture, and cues. The best way to manipulate the user's experience is by judiciously packaging the information in the right amounts on pages and in sections of pages, linking these pages to support the user's needs, and cueing the user to information and navigation aids.

Throughout this chapter, you'll see how the design process itself works with each of the elements of web weaving to produce a look and feel for the web. Because this chapter is more of a survey of design issues than a case study, you'll see this design process in a more sequential form in the hypothetical case study in Chapter 40, "Putting It All Together: A Case Study."

Principles and Goals

Throughout the design process, try to keep the following principles in mind:

1. **Meet the user's needs.** The web is not built for the personal taste of the designers, the convenience of the implementors, or the whims of the planners. Rather, the web serves the audience for which it is designed. Meeting the needs of the users is the first priority for the web.

2. **Efficiently use resources.** In designing and implementing a web, select features that meet the user's needs with the least amount of space, access time, graphics, and long-term maintenance requirements. That is, aim for web features that are efficient to operate, elegant to use, and easy to maintain.

3. **Create a consistent, pleasing, and efficient look and feel.** The design of the web should aim to give the user impressions on all its pages that reflect a common organization and consistent visual cues. Each page of the web should cue the user to the web's identity and page purpose. The web's overall appearance should help the user accomplish his or her objectives through interfaces which strike a balance between simplicity and completeness, and aim for an aesthetically pleasing appearance.

You'll now look more closely at specific issues a designer needs to consider in order to weave a web consistent with these principles.

User Experience

The idea of developing any product in a *user-centered* manner—that is, one in which the needs, interests, characteristics, abilities, knowledge, skills, and whims of the user are central in the whole process—may not seem like a radical idea. After all, a web is meant for users to find information and accomplish specific objectives. Not all web designers, however, are sensitive to the role of the user. In fact, because user information is often difficult to plan for and analyze (see Chapter 30, "Planning a Web," and Chapter 31, "Analyzing a Web"), it is often overlooked. Moreover, the idea of the user is not as simple as it may seem. Who is the user of your web? Your web planning process should have produced a good set of audience information—a definition of the audience and an enumeration of audience characteristics.

In moving to the design process, however, it helps a designer to be aware of the needs of any general web user. In Chapters 17 through 21, we saw how in navigation, a user needs to look at specific things when encountering a display in his or her browser window. The user asks, "What is this? What is it made of? What is it for? What can I do with it? How do I get what I want?" The user is not concerned with the fine points of the web's design. Instead, the user is concerned with getting his or her job done correctly and efficiently. Therefore, this review of a user's general experience helps the designer become more aware of the perceptive qualities of web information—what I call information space, texture, and cues.

Information Space

The eager Web navigator clicks quickly on a link, looks over the display in the browser, and asks, "What is this?" One of the fundamental pieces of information that a Web navigator needs to know when encountering a new display on his or her browser is: What information space is this? Have I entered a Gopher? An FTP site? A WAIS session? A Web server?

While this information is not necessarily crucial to the *semantic* or meaning of the web, the kind of information space you present to the navigator immediately establishes *user expectations* about how to navigate and even what kind of information might be found at that site. For example, a Gopher information space presents menus of information, each entry of which may be another menu, a link to a document, a link to a search, or a link to a Telnet session. This information structure sets up user expectations about *navigation*. At the same time, through traditions and practices (that do change over time), a user gains expectations about what *kinds* of information Gophers often present. A user of a Gopher might expect to encounter tree-like information: subject catalogs and organizational or campuswide information systems (although not exclusively, but these are very common applications of a Gopher).

Therefore, the web designer must make choices—within the web specifications—about what information spaces will be presented to the users and how these information spaces should be presented. Often, the web specifications require that an existing information system be used in the web, such as an FTP site that already contains most of the files of information to be presented to the user. It may even be that the web specifications call for integrating other spaces into the web, such as a Gopher server. The key for the designer is to contemplate the user's experience of these spaces individually and how they can be used in combination. Specifically, a web designer should consider the following:

1. **Difference in space interface:**

   As shown in Chapter 16, "At the Edge of the Web," the appearance of the information spaces at the edge of the Web differ. The user who encounters an FTP site through a Web browser such as Mosaic has a different experience than seeing that same information through a web or a Gopher. As such, this difference can have a big impact on the look and feel of your web. A designer should examine the web specification and enumerate the different spaces it requires. It may be that none are specified, in which case the designer could make the choice to serve all information through the web. The designer should also, however, consider the needs of the users: Will someone need to access this same information through an FTP session? The answer to this question requires input from the planning and analysis processes, and, if FTP access is required, it should be stated in the web specification. A good designer, however, is aware of issues raised by the information spaces used in the web.

2. **Space overload:**

   If web developers decide to include different types of information spaces in the web, such as several FTP sites and several Gophers, the designer needs to consider how this variety might be best integrated to create a consistent look and feel. The web designer might object if such a variety would lead to space overload or to too many information systems with disparate styles of interfaces in the web. The benefit of a browser like Mosaic is that, although the information spaces at the edge of the web are different, Mosaic provides consistent functionality in each (point-and-click mechanism, similar graphical representation). Combined with the uniformity the browser itself brings (displays all spaces in same typeface, uses same symbols where possible), a designer may judge that a number of different spaces in the web will still meet the users' needs. In other words, the final decision comes down to the characteristics of the users: Are they concerned with a uniform appearance? Do they have experience using an existing information space for the same purpose? For example, do they already use a Gopher or FTP space, or will a variety of information spaces detract from their experience of the web?

3. **Space transitions:**

   If multiple information spaces are to be used in the web, consider how transitions between them are designed. A transition to an FTP space, if the users are not familiar with using one, might be a bit daunting. In an FTP space observed through a Web browser, the textual cues may be dramatically reduced. Consider what level of transition would be right for your users, ranging from none to a transition page that explains the use of the FTP, Gopher, or other information space.

4. **Web layers over spaces:**

   As a designer, you may decide to put a web layer over an information space by preparing a web page that contains links into the information space. This allows greater flexibility for describing the information. The drawback is that implementation and maintenance of these web layers can be expensive. If there are only a few links, this may be a good way to link to the information space while retaining the expressive possibilities of the web.

Figure 32.2 illustrates how a web layer can be designed on top of an FTP space.

FIGURE 32.2.

A web layer over an FTP space.

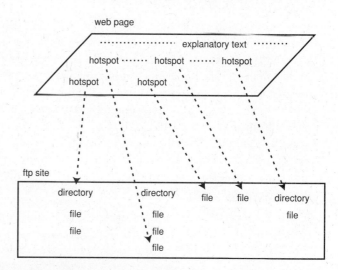

The figure shows how the links from the web page's hotspots can be made into the directories or specific files at the FTP site. The benefit of this layering is that you can include explanatory text, placing the meaning of the files at the FTP site within the context of the meaning of the information presented on the web page. Notice, though, how this linking requires a coordination of the web page with the structure of the FTP site, requiring more links than if just one link were made to the FTP site. This requires an increase in implementation time as well as maintenance.

Information Texture

Just as web users gain a great deal of cues from the kind of information space they are in, they must pay attention to the information's *texture*. In this section, I'll first define three aspects of information texture and then discuss specific strategies the designer can consider with regard to them.

Information texture refers to the medium in which the information is encoded, the structure of the information, and the connections to and from the information. Just as the user of a web looks quickly to find cues about the information space he or she is in, so too does the user look for cues about information texture. By examining cues of media type, information structure, and connections, the user quickly gets a handle on how to extract information.

Media type is one aspect of information texture. A user entering an FTP site, for example, might encounter a long list of files which display a variety of media types—graphics, a movie, text files, and directories, for example. This variety (or uniformity, in the case of all the same kinds of media presented to the user) is the media type, which is one aspect of the information's texture. A quick look at the possible graphical symbols at an FTP site or a Gopher, for example (see Figure 16.3) quickly sets up a set of user expectations about *what* will be found there and the *interface* required to sense that information. A user entering a long list of sound files, for example, knowing that his or her sound player is not hooked up to their web browser, knows immediately that the site contains information that he or she cannot use.

Another aspect of information texture is information structure. Structure is the overall organization of the information within the display of the browser. The structure could be characteristic of an information space, such as the list of files at an FTP site, a menu from a Gopher, or it might be an ordered or unordered list within an HTML file. Structure is the pattern by which the information is presented. Simple structures, like lists or menus, are immediately recognized by the user.

Other structures, such as the complex interspersing of paragraphs, ordered and unordered lists, figures, and forms using HTML may be more difficult at first for the user to perceive. In either case, the structure of the information sets up expectations in the user about how to deal with the information. If the list shown on the browser display is numbered, and it continues down the page, a user quickly forms the expectation that the rest of the list will be available by using the scrollbar. In more complicated structures that are possible in webs, the structure of the information, although more expressive, might include paragraphs and lists, and the user might not know what to expect on the rest of a page or on other pages.

Just as media type and structure contribute to the information's texture, so do the connections that are either explicit or implied. The media type and structure contribute to information about connections. An FTP site listing, for example, often includes a folder at the top of the list with the label "parent directory" next to it. This folder is a connection, and it sets up in the user's mind the knowledge that the information he or she is presently encountering is possibly connected to some other information (hierarchically "up" in the case of FTP sites). In the case of a web, these connections might be to pages that are either more general or more specific in information content than the page the user is presently viewing. Moreover, the user wonders, "Where in the hierarchy (in the case of FTP sites or Gopher menus) am I?" or "Where in the mesh (in the case of webs) am I?" The connections to this other information, revealed by cues (see next section), can have a great impact on setting up a user's expectations about how to deal with the information shown.

Based on the previous discussion of information texture, the designer can appreciate some factors of the user experience while encountering information. The information texture sets up user expectations about *what* has been found and *how* to deal with it. As a designer, the following specific strategies might help in dealing with the way a user perceives information texture:

1. **Media type:**

   What matters to the user most, the media type of the information or the content conveyed? Some users might want to locate all sound files on a web. Other users only want relevant information presented as it relates to meaning, with media type flagged (a symbol shown to alert the user of the media type for a link in the web). As a designer, your user's needs will dictate how you choose to arrange resources according to media type.

2. **Information structure:**

   What degree of guidance do your users require to make use of the information? A list of items conveys less context information than a narrative paragraph but is more to the point, particularly if the user knows exactly what the list is for and what each item on the list means. As a designer, in creating web pages, you'll constantly need to balance expressiveness with terseness.

3. **Connections:**

   When does the user need the information? In the case of introductory or help information, how can you place it so that it is easily available at the major web entry points as well as at other appropriate places? How can you place a web page at exactly the right spots in a web so that its meaning is enhanced by connections to other pages? These are the main issues dealing with connections you face as a designer. The answer, of course, lies in the user's needs:

   - How often would the user need to see this information?
   - When would the user need to see this information?
   - Why would the user need to see this information?

   These questions can help you determine the placement of pages within a web.

Cues

While information texture is often the first thing a user might notice on entering a web, cues are the next part of a user's experience. While information space and information texture have set up expectations in the user about "Where am I?" "What is this?," cues are the features in a web that say to a user, "Here is what this is" (information cues) and "Here is how you get there from here" (navigation cues).

Information cues are the features of the text or graphics on a web page that help the user know the page's purpose, intended audience, contents, and objective. In other words, information cues help the user know what the page is for and what it contains. Notice that in our discussion of the user's experience, we've not yet talked about the user encountering the substance of the information's content yet. We're still at the stage of helping the user get oriented. A careful presentation of information cues can get the user oriented quickly, and thus enable the user to more efficiently use the information.

Some examples of information cues are the following:

The title of the document (both as it appears in the "Document Title" window on the Mosaic browser and the words that appear most prominently at the top of the page). The user expects some sort of meaningful title in document—a holdover perhaps from encountering print. A meaningful title that conveys the purpose, audience, and objectives for that web page serves well to orient the user. For example, a title such as "Business Divisions of XYZ Industries, Listed by Region" immediately helps the user know what to expect on that page.

The sponsoring organization. Who created this web? Is it an official web server for an organization or a web put out by an individual?

A statement of purpose. This can flow directly from the purpose and objective statements. During design, however, you will need to customize the level of detail and the wording of the statement to be appropriate to your audience's needs on each page. I'll cover this more in the later section in this chapter about applying the design process to the purpose and objective statement elements.

A statement of objective. Similar to the statement of purpose described above, the objective statement can flow directly from the prepared objective statement, customized for the level of detail and audience needs.

A hint at the contents. Sometimes this can take the form of a list (even a hypertext list) of what the page contains. It is not necessary, however, (nor desirable all the time) to do this. A well-worded paragraph that gives a narrative of the web's contents might be best.

Headings. The use of well-worded, prominently placed headings can enable a user to quickly scan a page to get an idea of the contents. These headings should carry specific meaning, such as "An Overview of XYZ Products" as opposed to "Section One."

In writing headings, seek parallelism in phrasing. For example, your top-level headings might read as follows:

Opening the URL
Printing the Document
Exiting the program

Notice how each of the headings starts with the same "*-ing*" verb form. Compare this to

URL opening
Printing the Document
How to exit from the program

This mismatch in phrasing lacks the consistency of the previous set of headings.

The maintainer of the document. Users will find errors, have questions, or want to otherwise give feedback about the content of a document. The maintainer's address often appears at the bottom of the page with at least an e-mail address given and possibly a link to his or her home page. The maintainer might also provide comment boxes or other features to explicitly seek feedback.

While information cues help a user make sense of a page's purpose and contents, navigation cues help the user do the following:

- Understand where the page fits into the larger web
- Learn how to leave the page or web quickly
- Find out how to obtain further information

There are a variety of navigation cues that can help a user move through a web. All cues need not be present on each page of a web, but these cues should be easily available to the user:

- Links to home pages—links to the top or home page of your web. These help the user who is lost to get back to the beginning to start over. The presence of these links helps users who have entered your web by some other method than the top (see Figure 30.1 in Chapter 30) to reach the front page. When used in a consistent title bar or foot bar on the page (see the upcoming Design Techniques section), the presence of your home page link acts as a marker to help identify each page as a part of your web.

- Links to related pages in your web. One of the benefits of hypertext is that you can offer choices to your user about what to encounter next. A well-chosen selection of links to information in your web (or outside of your web) that relates to the information on a given page adds this "associative dimension" to the page's topic.

- Links to help/indexes/README pages. In many places throughout your web, it is helpful to create links to indexes, help pages, or README pages that help a user understand where they are in your web and what other information they can get. A link to a help or index page can play a part in a consistent title bar or foot bar on all the pages of your web (see the upcoming "Design Techniques" section).

- Expert links. These are "fast track" links that help a user who is familiar to your web to quickly go to featured resources, bypassing introductory or explanatory pages.

Design Methodologies

While there is no one way to weave a web, you can choose among a variety of approaches. No one way will necessarily work best all the time; therefore, you might even consider varying the approaches while developing the same web.

Top-Down

If you have a good idea about what your whole web should contain, a top-down method of design might be best. In the top-down methodology, you start with a front or top page (often called the "home" page) for your web and work branching off from there. You might even create prototype "holder" pages that contain only minimal information but hold a place for later development in the web.

The benefit of the top-down approach is that you can develop your pages according to one central theme or idea. That is, you have a good chance to affect the look and feel of the whole web very powerfully because all pages are designed according to the top page look and feel. A good way to do this is to design a set of templates for types of pages in your web and use these during the implementation process.

Bottom-Up

If you don't have a good idea of what the final web will look like (or even exactly what it will do), but you know how specific pages will look and work, it might be that working from these specific pages to the top page is the way to proceed. This is particularly true if you already have existing pages as a result of the development of some other web or service.

If you have no pages from which to start, you can begin by designing *leaves*—pages that accomplish specific objectives—and then linking them together through intermediate pages to the top page. The benefit of this design is that you are not constrained by the style of a top page in the leaf pages. Instead, you design the leaf pages in exactly the right style based on their function. Later, you adjust the pages to create a common look and feel for the whole web.

Incremental/In-Time

Similar in ways to both the top-down and bottom-up approaches, the incremental/in-time approach develops pages "just in time" when they are needed. It may be the case that an initial top page is needed and so are specific leaf pages that implement particular objectives. These are created and linked together with the understanding that, later, intermediate pages may be added. This works well if you want to very quickly have a working web that will grow incrementally, rather than being deployed all at once.

Design Techniques

Designing a web and dealing with the issues raised in the last section about user experiences and design methodologies require a designer to employ a variety of techniques to achieve particular effects. These techniques have to do with shaping information for user's needs and abilities and expressing a consistent look and feel for the whole web. Like many aspects of web weaving, design techniques are an art in themselves, and having a good repertoire of them increases your value as a web designer.

Package Information in the Right-Sized Chunks

Humans can process only so much information at a time. Helping your users process information is your overall challenge as a web designer and a specific task in your design is to package or "chunk" information in pieces that do not overwhelm your users. As a general guideline, the number of pieces of information to have in the user's attention at any one time is five, plus or minus two. While you'll have to judge what constitutes an information "piece" and decide exactly what constitutes the field of "a user's attention," the key idea is to chunk information as follows:

- So that the amount of information on any one page doesn't overwhelm the user.

- So that you can create reusable pages; that is, if each page you create accomplishes one specific purpose, it can be a useful link throughout the entire web for that purpose. In this way, you can flexibly include a page of information in as many places as appropriate to the user's needs, but only create that information once.

- So that you can focus the user's attention. The chunks of information, when created around ideas, concepts, and ways of thinking familiar to your users, will help a user focus on one topic at a time and build his or her knowledge incrementally.

How can a designer do this chunking? There are several techniques. As a first step for all of these techniques, the designer must gather the documents that represent the information to be presented in the web. This information should be listed in detail in the web specifications (created by the planning process) and reflected in the objective statement. Information to be served to users and useful to designers should be in the store of domain information.

Here is a clustering technique to arrive at packages of information for a web:

1. Start with a copy of the objective statement for the web. Circle the nouns in the objective statement.

2. Using a simple graphics drawing program, type in the circled nouns and move them until related ones are close together. Define this *relatedness* in terms of the user's perspective. Ideally, you would know how the user thinks about the information your web will provide. Does a user think in terms of subjects or topics (the subject categorization of the nouns) or in terms of processes (what you do with the nouns)? Try both arrangements and show each version to a representative user, asking "Which clustering of words

is most useful to your work (the work that the web intends to support)?" The benefit of hypertext is that you may be able to implement both views of the same information.

3. In the word cluster diagram, draw more nested circles around the words that relate. In the case of a topic-oriented clustering, this can proceed along a hierarchical breakdown of the topic. In a process-oriented clustering of words, this can be done by grouping nouns that the same processes act upon. After all words are in at least one loop (even if there is just one phrase in each loop), group loops together by drawing lines around related groups. For example, Figure 32.3 shows how the nouns given in the (partial) objective statement in Chapter 30 are clustered.

Computer-Mediated Communication (CMC) Studies Center

Purpose: To help people share resources

Objective: To provide a list of resources with links to major online collections of CMC-related material, bibliographies, academic and research centers related to CMC, online journals, and other resources

Note in the figure that the "online journals, online resources, and online bibliographies" group is also grouped with "research center home pages." This reflects, at the level of clustering shown, a separation of what the web offers into *people, activities,* and *resources.* A different clustering could have been done—the list of people grouped with the online resources and the research center home pages grouped with the list of activities. This would have reflected a research/activities and resources slant to this information (with people looked upon as resources, possibly in supporting or informational roles).

4. Continue clustering until you draw a final loop around all the clusters. This final loop acts to show that the clustering diagram is "finished" and no other clustering can be done.

FIGURE 32.3.

An information cluster diagram.

Your clustering diagram now can serve as a map to breaking down your web into packages. A *package* is a web page or group of web pages that are closely related, as defined by the above clustering process. Eventually, each package must be defined as a web page or set of web pages. One simple transformation from a cluster diagram to packages is to make each loop a package. In other words, if we had a loop around the three outer loops shown in Figure 32.3, we would have the following packages:

1. A package with links to a list of people, activities, and resources
2. A package containing a list of people
3. A package containing a list of activities
4. A package ("list of resources" from 1) containing links to online resources, online journals, and online bibliographies
5. A package containing online resources (from 4)
6. A package containing online journals (from 4)
7. A package containing online bibliographies (from 4)

You can see how this cluster method works even with a simple example to give you a quick way to create a preliminary set of packages of information. The next step is to transform packages to pages:

1. A simple transformation is to make each package a page, paying close attention not to overload any given page. Based on Figure 32.2, you would obtain seven pages, described in the preceding list.

   To ensure that no page gets overloaded, for each page, estimate the total number of *kinds* of links and how much of each. For example, the list of people page might contain just one kind of link—to a personal home page. Let's say there's 50 people on the list. That would mean that this page contains 50 links to personal pages plus other navigation or information links (say there are five of these). This yields 50 instances of one kind of link and five instances of navigation links. This is not necessarily an unmanageable combination for a single web page. However, if there were 500 people in the directory, it might be a problem to put the whole directory on one page. The main issue is scalability. The directory could grow to a page size that will cause performance problems. The design decision at this point might be to include the preliminary listing, but then to investigate using a database or other lookup scheme for the lists of people.

2. A better transformation might be to create a page for every noun in the cluster diagram and a page for every package that has more than one noun phrase in it. Using this method for Figure 32.2, a total of nine pages would be made: six pages would be created for each noun phrase, and three pages would be created to handle links to the following:

   A page linking to the online bibliographies, journals, and resources pages

   The page linking to the page described in 1, above (online pages), and the research center home pages page

A page linking to the page described in 2, a list of people page, and a list of activities page

Link Pages Together

Once you have a set of pages, you need to design how they will link together. The cluster diagram showing packages and pages is a good start toward seeing how these links might be made. The following methods will yield an initial linking of pages that can be built upon using some other linking techniques (see index, title bar, and foot bar methods). To get an initial link diagram, do the following:

1. Link pages in a hierarchy determined by the nesting of packages shown in the cluster diagram. Link pages within the same package together. For example, using this method, we can link the nine pages generated by the second method shown above for package>page breakdown. Figure 32.4 shows the initial link diagram using this method. The benefit of this scheme is that the hierarchy of pages helps guide a user through the information. The downside is that the user must follow a particular path to reach a page—a path that might be several links long from the home page.

FIGURE 32.4.

The link by package hierarchy.

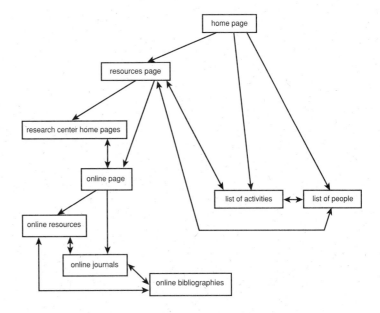

2. Create pages for only the *leaves* of the package hierarchy shown in Figure 32.3 (that is, only pages generated from the noun phrases in the objective statement) and link every one of them to each other. This creates a nonhierarchical web, in which all the pages of information called for by the objective statement are available to every other page. For webs with a small number of total pages, this might work well; for large webs, the number of links required will grow large very rapidly as the number of pages increases.

Figure 32.5 shows a nonhierarchical link of all the leaf pages of Figure 32.3. The benefit of this structure is that all pages are just one link away from any other page. The downside is that there is no information hierarchy to help the user cope with the link choices from any given page, and that this technique is not scalable (requiring many links for large webs).

There are obviously many more variations of these linking schemes, but the two directions above—linking for hierarchy and total (nonhierarchical) linking—have their advantages and disadvantages. Other methods for linking include the following:

1. *By need:* In a test situation, give representative users a problem (a set of questions or an "information hunt" type of exercise) that they solve by using the information given in the web pages. Observe the order in which the users access the pages in search of information to solve the problem. Based on these observations of user access, link the pages together based on minimizing the number of links a user must typically traverse to solve the problem.

FIGURE 32.5.

Completely linking all leaf pages.

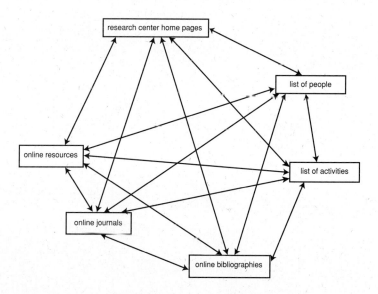

2. *By association:* Have representative users rank how closely each of the pages relate to each other (for example, on a scale of 1 to 5 with 5 being a strong association). Provide double links between pages with association scores over the average for all links (or use some other criterion that generates something short of a complete, double linking of all pages).

Specify Overall Look and Feel with a Universal Grid

Besides the package, page, and link diagrams, the web designer can make several other products to help express the look and feel for the web. One of these diagrams is a universal grid for the entire web, a diagram that sets out the function and arrangement for text, cues, and links on any given page.

For example, a universal grid is shown in Figure 32.6.

The purpose of the universal grid is to create a template to give all pages of the web a uniform look. This uniform look helps the user of the web know what cues to expect where on each page. Notice how the universal grid shown in Figure 32.6 doesn't specify exactly what has to go into the footer and header for each page; this could vary according to the purpose for each page or type of page.

FIGURE 32.6.

A sample universal grid.

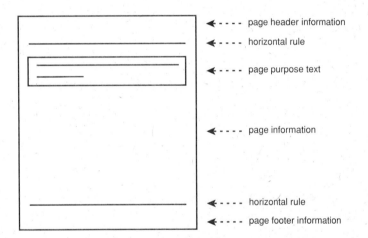

◄ - - - - page header information

◄ - - - - horizontal rule

◄ - - - - page purpose text

◄ - - - - page information

◄ - - - - horizontal rule

◄ - - - - page footer information

Use Repeated Icons

Another technique for creating a unified look and feel for the web is to use repeated icons to represent classes of information or an icon representing the web itself. These repeated icons could be specified in the universal grid. For example, Figure 32.7 shows the universal grid from Figure 32.6 with a repeated web icon (an icon that represents the whole web) and a repeated topic icon (an icon that represents the particular topic this page addresses) in the header information.

These repeated icons help the user gain a sense of consistency in all the pages from this web. The topic icon helps cue the user to the purpose of the page. Because these icons are repeated, the user benefits because the browser loads a given icon only once, and then can use it (without reloading) on any other page in the web. In this way, repeated icons can give the web a strong sense of identity for each page. This is particularly important when a pin-cushion access pattern (Figure 30.1 in Chapter 30) is expected for the web; the repeated icons help let the user know where he or she is.

FIGURE 32.7.

A sample universal grid with repeated icons.

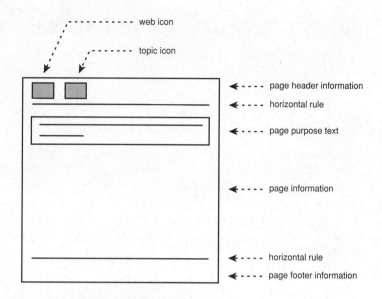

Create and Use Web-Wide Navigation Links

Just as repeated icons provide the user with information cues on each page, navigation cues and links can help the user move through an entire web.

One technique for creating a web-wide navigation link is to make an index page that links to every page of the entire web. For webs with a large number of pages, this can clearly create problems, but the concept is to provide a central point for the user to locate a page that he or she knows is in the web somewhere but can't remember how to get to it. An index page is particularly important for webs linked using a hierarchical technique (Figure 32.4). For example, the index page for the web in Figure 32.4 is shown in Figure 32.8.

FIGURE 32.8.

An index page for a hierarchically linked web.

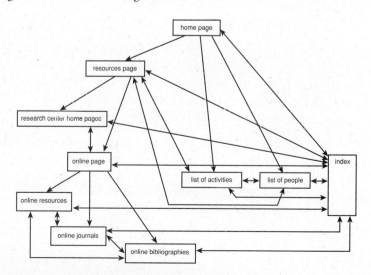

Given that an index page is created, the index itself then can become part of the universal grid, either in the title bar or in a foot bar. Local or specialized indexes of pages within the same package could also be created and placed on pages within the same package.

Another web-wide navigation link might be to the top or home page for the entire web. Often, the web icon itself can serve as this link. When you place this link on the universal grid, the home page for the web can be just one link away from any page in the web. Just like the other elements of the universal grid, these repeated navigation links can help a user make sense of an arbitrary web page, particularly in pin-cushion access patterns.

Use Web Elements for Information Cues

Within each page of your web, look for opportunities to use the audience information or purpose and objective statements for explanatory or information cues. For example, you've carefully planned which audience you are targeting for your web in the planning process. Why hide this information from the user? An explicit statement of the target audience, written with the appropriate wording for a particular web page, can help the user immediately see if he or she is right for the information on that page.

The purpose statement is perhaps the web element you'll draw on the most in providing information cues to your user. Purpose statements can serve as a powerful "mission statement" for communicating the web's intent with users. Since every page of the web reflects its purpose, you'll find that every page can contain a variation of the purpose statement that is specific to the function the given page is serving.

Similarly, the objective statement can be put to use on pages worded for the right level of detail and serve as an important information cue for the user. For example, one objective statement might be

"To list online bibliographies in the field of geology."

This can translate directly to introductory text at the top of the page that meets this objective:

"This page lists online bibliographies in the field of geology."

While not all translations between web elements and information cues used in the web design will be as easy or mechanical, the web designer should take full advantage of the store of wording and language in these elements.

Design Problems

Although the previous techniques can help you create a consistent look and feel for your web, there are specific problems that can detract from a web's design. These include problems with a lack of navigation and information cues ("the page from outer space"), a page with large access time required or with an overly complex information texture and structure ("the monster page" and "multimedia overkill"), a page with an uneven information structure ("the uneven page") and problems with linking ("meaningless links") in pages. All these design problems *may* lead to problems; there are exceptions where many of these same effects I critique here may play an integral role in effectively accomplishing a purpose. The key is that these design problems are issues that web designers should be aware of, not as iron-clad rules or formulas. Moreover, every designer may create one of these problems at one time or another, such as a page evolving over time, accumulating links until it gradually becomes a "monster." Rather, these are issues to consider when designing (or analyzing) a web.

The Page from Outer Space

One of the most frustrating things you may find as a web navigator is a page like the one in Figure 32.9.

FIGURE 32.9.

The page from outer space.

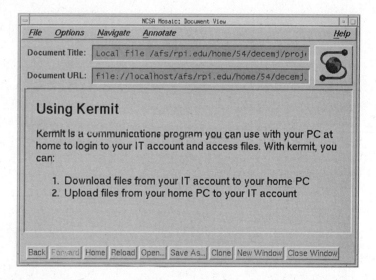

The page is well-written: it has a descriptive heading, it includes a narrative that guides you through its main points about using kermit. However, a navigator who enters this page would have many questions: Who wrote this page? Why? What web is it a part of? What does "IT" stand for?

The page shown in Figure 32.9 has no information cues, not even a <TITLE>, to cue the user to the purpose of the page. Since there are no links on the page, we can't easily locate the home page for this web (a navigator would have to use the technique of opening a URL consisting of just the beginning part of the URL for this page). The information on this page—apparently instructions about what kermit can do—is contextless, and therefore of little use. Moreover, a navigator coming into this page has *no easy way* to find out the answers to the above questions; the page has no links, no context, no cues. Hence the phrase "the page from outer space."

Avoid creating pages that have no cues. You generally cannot assume the user will encounter your web according to the wine bottle model of access (Figure 30.1 in Chapter 30). Moreover, you're not taking advantage of the power of the Web itself if you treat the information on each page as just a "slab" of text with no links to other context, information, or navigation cues. Most importantly, you're closing off user interaction and feedback. A user encountering the page in Figure 32.9 would have no contact point for even asking the above questions. On the other hand, there's no need to provide links to every conceivable scrap of information related to the topic of the page. The key is to balance the number of cues versus completeness of information. As a rule of thumb, ask yourself what a user would do to get more information from a given page. There should be at least one cue or link on that page to help them at some level, even if it is a link to the home page.

Variations on the "page from outerspace" include home pages that give information that has little meaning in a global context. For example, you might see the following as a title for a page:

"Department of Physics home page"

What university? What country? What continent? Although the skilled navigator can (usually) obtain the answers to the questions by looking for clues in the URL, the designers of this page apparently did not realize that their page reaches a global audience.

Although it's usually not necessary to qualify a geographic location as: "Department of Physics, Delta University, Delta, Mississippi, USA, North America, Earth," as a designer, you should have some sense of how many cues to give in order to help a user place your information in the global context of the Web. Don't assume that your organization, city, or state name is recognized worldwide. Often, qualification to the country level is enough.

The Monster Page

Just as the "page from outer space" had too few cues to help the user effectively place the information in context, so too can a page get too cluttered with links, graphics, lists, and other effects. There are two major problems with cluttered pages:

1. **Access time:** If there are many inline images, or there is a great deal of text on the page, the access time for that page can be enormous. (Read about my own monster page and my redesign of it in Chapter 45, "Challenges for Web Information Providers.")

2. **Information overload:** If you put too much information on a single page, the user simply will not be able to cope with it. The physical limits of the browser display will by default chunk the information on the page into screenfuls of information accessible by the scrollbar or other system in the browser. Rather than having the browser chunk the information the designer should determine these chunks. There are situations, though, where a long list of similar items is best browsed in one long list and any breakup of the information would be arbitrary.

The strength of hypertext is that information can be chunked into pages, so that these pages can then be encountered by users according to their need. The "monster" page, with its overabundance of links and cues, creates too much noise for the user to pick out the essential information.

Multimedia Overkill

New designers using the facilities of a browser such as Mosaic often include many inlined images as well as links to graphics, sounds, movies, or other multimedia files. When not needed, this multimedia overkill can lead to the same problems associated with the "monster page" discussed previously. The multimedia used in a web must play a key role in accomplishing an objective that directly meets a user's need. Chunking links to these resources, just like chunking links among pages, can be done using the cluster diagram and packaging techniques outlined above.

Another issue related to multimedia overkill is using the same graphics in several different places in a web without using a link to the same graphics file, which requires that the Web browser must reload the image every time it is used. If you use a repeated image in a web, link to the same file (same URL) every time you include it on a page. By doing this, the Web browser can load the file just once and display it on many other pages in the web.

The Uneven Page

An uneven page is one that contains information at vastly different or incongruous levels of detail. For example, Figure 32.10 shows the home page of the ABC University's Information Technology Department. The design and context information is adequate—a link to the university's home page is given, a link to an index is shown, and the page is signed by the webmaster.

The items in the list given on the page, however, are very incongruous—"Faculty Directory" seems on the same level of importance as "Research Programs" and "IT Department's Mission." But the next two links—"How to Use Kermit" and "CS 101 Final Grades"—seem to be at some other level of detail.

A page often becomes uneven through a process of iterative accumulation of links. The webmaster in the case of the ABC IT Department probably added links as they were developed. This unevenness, however, weakens the coherence of the page—the user begins to wonder what this page is supposed to accomplish. Naturally, a page reflecting a deliberate "grab bag" or collection of links would display this unevenness. Usually, unevenness can be a problem on major home pages or pages that have a specific, often high-visibility, purpose in the web. Every time you add a link to a page, ask if it fulfills the purpose of that page or in some other way helps the user with that information.

FIGURE 32.10.

An uneven page.

```
┌──────────────────────────────────────────────────────────┐
│ ─                   NCSA Mosaic: Document View          ▫ □│
│  File   Options   Navigate   Annotate                  Help│
├──────────────────────────────────────────────────────────┤
│ Document Title: │ABC University's Information Technology Depar│ ⬡
│ Document URL:   │file://localhost/afs/rpi.edu/home/54/decemj/│ ⬡
├──────────────────────────────────────────────────────────┤
│                                                            │
│   Index / ABC University Home page                         │
│                                                            │
│   Welcome to ABC University's Information                  │
│   Technology (IT) Department                               │
│                                                            │
│   ABC University, Alpha–Beta, NY 12345                     │
│                                                            │
│       ● Faculty Directory                                  │
│       ● Research Programs                                  │
│       ● IT Department's Mission                            │
│       ● How to Use Kermit                                  │
│       ● CS 101 Final Grades                                │
│                                                            │
│                                                            │
│   webmaster@it.abc.edu                                     │
│                                                            │
├──────────────────────────────────────────────────────────┤
│ Back  Forward  Home  Reload  Open...  Save As...  Clone  New Window  Close Window │
└──────────────────────────────────────────────────────────┘
```

Meaningless Links

Just as links can be uneven, they can also fail to add any meaning to the information presented. Of course, any stale link fulfills this criterion, but stale links shouldn't be intentionally designed into a web.

One manifestation of a meaningless link is a "vacuous" link that takes the user to a resource or document with no apparent connection to the meaning conveyed on the original page. Every link should somehow extend the meaning of a page. The link in the following sentence:

```
Welcome to <a href="abc.html">ABC</A> University's Home Page</A>
```

from the term ABC to the file abc.html should contain some background or historic information about the University's name (because the link was made to "ABC" as opposed to "ABC University's Home Page"). If this link is to a special project by the page designer or some other unrelated or unpredictable subject, the link is vacuous.

Another form of vacuous link is a sentence such as

```
For more information, click <a href="info.html">here</A>.
```

The hotspot, here, has no meaning within the sentence. A better choice might be

```
You can get <a href="info.html">more information</A>.
```

Another kind of meaningless link is the trivial link, in which a link is made to some resource or document that relates to the original page, but only trivially in the given context. For example, you might find this sentence on the home page of ABC University:

```
Welcome to ABC University's Home <a href="page.html">Page</A>
```

If the link from Page to the file page.html is to a dictionary definition of the word *page,* it is a trivial link because the information isn't essential in the context of a university's home page. In the context of a narrative about Web vocabulary and terms, this same link (from "page" to a definition of the term) might be essential.

Another kind of meaningless linking occurs when a designer creates a web with very small chunks and excessively links these chunks together. This creates a mesh of pages, and each page carries very little context and content. This requires the user to traverse a great number of pages in order to accumulate meaning or context. This is the opposite of the "monster page" effect and represents hypertext taken to an extreme. In some cases, however, this effect is highly desired, such as in hyper-art, hyper-fiction, or hyper-poetry, where the medium of hypertext may be stretched to its limit. As a general rule, though, each page should accomplish a specific, self-contained purpose, so that the user has a feeling of attaining a goal rather being left with a need to follow still more links.

Weaver's Check

Designing a web involves considering the user's experience and meeting the user's needs by shaping information. In doing this, a designer strives to follow the principles and goals of a user-centered web design process to weave a web that works efficiently and is consistent and aesthetically pleasing.

The web designer understands a user's experience of information space, texture, and cues, and uses design techniques to package and link information in a way that best meets a user's abilities and needs. The designer can approach the overall process of web design in a top-down, bottom-up, or in-time/incremental methodology. The web designer uses a variety of techniques to specify the look and feel of the web—through a cluster diagram showing web packages and pages, through a link diagram, or a universal grid for an overall pattern for page development.

There are many problems a weaver may unintentionally create in the process of web design: a page with no accessible context ("the page from outer space"), a page with an overabundance of information texture or information ("the monster page"), a page with too many multimedia effects, particularly inline graphics ("multimedia overkill"), an uneven page with items at inconsistent levels of detail, and meaningless links that distract from the user's ability to gain useful information.

The overall process of web design involves both acquired skills in information design and also acquired experience in design problems and their solutions. No web design is flawless, but the task of the web designer should be to always strive to improve a web's design to better meet the needs of users.

Implementing a Web: Basic HyperText Markup Language (HTML)

33

by
John December

All Web browsers must recognize a version of HyperText Markup Language (HTML) called Level 0. On top of Level 0 HTML, there are specifications for additional language constructs that not all browsers may recognize. Level 1 HTML includes Level 0 constructs plus HTML features for character formatting and inline images. Level 2 HTML includes all Level 0 and 1 constructs plus features such as forms that only certain Web browsers understand. Level 3 HTML, still under development, includes lower-level HTML features plus figures, tables, mathematical equations, stylesheets, and other features for the control of layout.

In brief, the HTML levels are as follows:

Level 0:

The minimum set of tags that make up an HTML document and that all browsers recognize.

Level 1:

Level 0 tags plus tags for character formatting and inline images.

Level 2:

Level 0 and Level 1 tags plus Form tags.

Level 3 (proposed):

Level 0, 1, and 2 tags plus extensions for figures, tables, mathematical equations, stylesheets, and other features for the control of layout.

> **NOTE**
>
> The complete specification for HTML at all levels is still being developed by working groups at the Internet Engineering Task Force (`http://www.ietf.cnri.reston.va.us/home.html`) in cooperation with the World Wide Web Consortium (`http://www.w3.org/hypertext/WWW/Consortium/Prospectus/`). This chapter (and the next chapter) represents the best information available and the state of practice as of this writing. For further information and updates, consult the online information resources listed at the end of this chapter.

By recognizing the level of HTML compliance, you can be assured that the HTML you write using tags in this chapter will be recognized by most browsers. Most modern browsers recognize up to Level 2; and many recognize higher-level HTML and extensions. Competition among browser manufacturers will continue to pressure them to support all standard constructs as well as advanced (and possibly non-standard) HTML features.

This chapter presents a detailed tour of basic HTML (Level 0 and Level 1). First, I describe the purpose of HTML and why a browser-independent (also called presentation-independent) markup language helps developers. Then I present the details of HTML Levels 0 and 1, demonstrating how different features of HTML express the structure of a document.

This chapter fits into the overall web-weaving processes described in Chapter 29, "Communication Processes on the Web." Once you've developed a design for a web, the next step is to implement the design in HTML. After this chapter's coverage of Level 0 and 1 HTML, the next chapter, "Advanced HTML Features," we'll look at some features of Level 2 and higher HTML as well as extensions to HTML; Chapter 35, "Gateway Interface Programming," covers tools that can help you create HTML files; and in Chapter 36, "Creating Imagemaps," we'll explore how to implement a specific web design in HTML. Chapter 36 covers HTML Imagemaps in detail, and Chapter 35 covers Forms/common-gateway interface programming.

You'll find that the tasks involved in writing basic HTML documents are really not overly complex. In practice, however, the coherent design and operation of a web is far more complex than just creating HTML files (in the same way that typing skills are merely one aspect of composing an effective document).

The Purpose Behind HTML

HTML, similar to a computer-programming language, requires you to express your thoughts in a specific structure in order for the "computer" (in this case, the hypertext browser) to understand. While HTML is not as complicated as some computer-programming languages, writing HTML requires that you follow specific rules to "tag" or "mark" the parts of your document. This marking distinguishes HTML from free-form prose or text created in a word processor. The whole idea of marking up a text to express its structure represents a very different approach from the What-You-See-Is-What-You-Get (WYSIWYG) word processing that is employed in many desktop systems. In WYSIWYG word processing, you concentrate on a document's appearance. Using HTML, you concentrate on the document's structure.

(We'll see in this chapter, however, that some browsers support extensions to HTML that are not yet part of the HTML standards—thus enabling some browser-dependent features to creep into HTML expressions and causing HTML to become the "layout" language it was never meant to be. However, this chapter, covering Levels 0 and 1 HTML, constitutes a core set of HTML constructs that you should feel confident about using in any browser.)

There are tools that help you create HTML documents in a WYSIWYG manner, as covered in Chapter 35. However, it is important for you to first familiarize yourself with HTML itself, particularly if you will work extensively on developing HTML files.

Why Worry?

Why would you want to worry so much about a document's structure, when a WYSIWYG word processor can show you—right away—what a document looks like? The answer lies in the relationship between HTML and all the possible hypertext browsers that might read it. (See Part II,

"Web Browsers and Connections.") Using HTML, you carefully define the structure of a document so that any browser can read it and display it in a way that is best for that browser. For example, we've seen how the HTML file in Chapter 14, "Web Structure and Spaces," can be displayed in a graphical Web browser (refer to Figure 14.3) and Lynx.

The result of this browser-independent characteristic of HTML is that it enables developers to express their thoughts in a structure that any Web browser will be able to interpret and display. This makes it possible to develop information in HTML and not have to create a separate version of it for the Lynx browser and another for Cello and still another for Netscape or Mosaic. Can your word processor do this—read a document from any other word processor? Not usually. When you share a document from your word processor with a friend, probably the first thing you ask is, "Can you read my files?" With HTML, you'll never have to do that; any Web browser will read your (Level 0) HTML files.

The Good News

Not only will your HTML files be compatible with any browser, but they will be in plain ASCII text—that is, text which does not have control characters or embedded binary codes—so that you can easily look at an HTML file, e-mail it, or edit it in any plain ASCII text editor.

Another benefit derives from the markup philosophy of HTML. HTML is defined by Standard Generalized Markup Language (SGML), an international standard (ISO 8879) for text-information processing. SGML itself is a meta-language (a language to define languages). The goal behind SGML is to help format information online for efficient electronic distribution, search, and retrieval in a way that is independent of the appearance details of the document. Without having to worry about the details of a document's appearance, the writing and production of documents can be expedited. An organization can have a store of reusable "chunks" of information that can be deployed into any publication easily. It is like having an "information store" expressed in terms of its structure, so that an "information displayer" can translate this store of information into any format. For example, ordered lists in HTML are defined by tags, not by a series of numbers, so that while one browser could display this list using Arabic numerals, another could use Roman numerals. HTML thus serves as an expression of information in its raw form, without a consideration for formatting, and this separation leads to many efficiencies.

Remember Web spiders (Chapter 19, "Spiders and Indexes: Keyword-Oriented Searching")? Some spiders couldn't work very well without HTML tags, because they look for tags that mark the document's title, headings, or the hotspots in the hypertext. Without a standard labeling scheme for these pieces of a document, spiders wouldn't know where to look. HTML facilitates this kind of information indexing; and, as the universe of HTML documents grows on the Web, this information search-and-retrieval process will play a larger role in making information usable.

The Bad News

Although HTML might sound great at this point, offering so many benefits, the bad news (at least according to some people) is the way an HTML document looks. For example:

```
<HTML>
   <HEAD>
      <TITLE>Telecommunications Resources</TITLE>
   </HEAD>
   <BODY>
      <H1>Some Telecommunications Resources</H1>
      <HR>
      <UL>
         <LI><A HREF="http://gozer.idbsu.edu/business/nethome.html">DELTA</A>
             Distributed ELectronic Telecommunications Archive-teaching and
             learning about business telecommunications and data communications
         <LI><A HREF="telnet://ntiabbs.ntia.doc.gov">NTIA</A> National
             Telecommunications and Information Administration (USA)
      </UL>
      <HR>
      <ADDRESS>
         <A HREF="http://www.rpi.edu/~decemj/index.html">John December</A>
         (<A HREF="mailto:decemj@rpi.edu">decemj@rpi.edu</A>)
      </ADDRESS>
   </BODY>
</HTML>
```

The < and > symbols that seem to dominate an HTML file are the beginnings and endings of the tags that mark a document's structure. At first glance, an HTML file looks confusing; it's hard to pick out the actual content of the document from all the tags used to define the document's structure. With an understanding of what these tags do, however, you'll quickly find that the tags mark things that you are already familiar with: titles, headings, paragraphs, and lists. Once you know the meaning of the tags, the meaning of the document's structure becomes clear, although the document's appearance in any browser cannot be determined solely from the HTML file.

Parts of an HTML (Levels 0 and 1) Document

We've seen how HTML employs tags to mark a document's structure. All the < and > symbols in an HTML document are part of these tags. A tag is a sequence of characters that starts with a < and ends with a >. The following sections introduce you to the basics of tags used in HTML for elements and entities. Read these sections to get a feel for the major tags and some examples of tags that are available. Following this section, I'll present Level 0 and Level 1 HTML summaries that will give you a more detailed and complete list for reference.

Elements

An HTML document consists of elements that mark the document's structure. We'll first look at the definitions of these elements before we look in detail at how they are used in HTML documents.

The labels in these elements are case-insensitive; that is, a browser will interpret the word TITLE the same as title or Title within an element. Some elements, such as the one for a paragraph break, <P>, are expressed by just one tag (one set of < and >). Others, such as the title element, <TITLE>, employ a corresponding tag to mark the end of the title, using the same label with a / (forward slash) before it: </TITLE>.

There are three types of elements: head, body, and graphics. The following list uses some of the more common instances to illustrate these types:

1. **Head elements:** Head elements are used to mark properties of the whole document, such as the title, links to indicate the relationship of one document to another, and the base URL of the document. This information is not displayed as part of the document itself but rather is information about the document that is used by browsers in various ways. The following is an example:

   ```
   <TITLE>Selected Telecommunications Resources</TITLE>
   ```

2. **Body elements:** Body elements are used to mark text in the body of the document. Unlike the head elements, all these marks (if recognized by the browser, of course) lead to some visual expression in the browser. Some body elements are as follows:

   a. **Headings:** Used to mark divisions of a document. Up to six levels of headings are supported.

      Examples:

      ```
      <H1>The Purpose Behind HTML</H1>
      <H2>The "Good" News</H2>
      <H2>The "Bad News" News</H2>
      ```

   b. **Anchors:** Used to mark the start and end of hypertext links. These links may refer to other documents or resources on the Net (through using URLs within the link) or to parts of the document itself.

      Example:

      ```
      The <A HREF="http://www.w3.org/hypertext/WWW/
      MarkUp/Tags.html">Elements of HTML</A>
      are head, body, and graphics.
      ```

   c. **Paragraph marks (<P>):** Defines a paragraph break. Don't use a <P> to provide any other kinds of breaks, such as between text and headings or between text and lists. These necessary breaks and spacings are handled by the browser operating on the heading and lists elements.

Example:

```
The paragraph mark usually can be expressed by a browser in any way.
Usually, though, a browser will skip a blank line between paragraphs.<P>
```

d. **Line breaks (`<BR>`):** Indicates the start of a new line. Without a `<BR>` mark, all text—even if you leave a blank space in the HTML file—will run together in a paragraph. (HTML is thus said to be "whitespace insensitive," (all extra spaces, tabs, and line breaks are ignored) except for use in specific tags, such as `<PRE>`, discussed forthwith.) Use `<BR>` when you want a line break, such as in a postal mailing address (see the following example), or when you want to start a new line without an intervening space (which `<P>` will do).

Example:

```
The HTML Institute<BR>45 General Square<BR>
Markup, LA 70462<BR>
```

e. **Horizontal rule (`<HR>`):** Indicates that the browser should create a long line, one adjusted to go across the width of the display window. Typically, a text browser will render this with a series of underline characters. Graphical browsers such as Mosaic and Netscape render an <HR> as a "shaded" horizontal rule.

f. **Address tags:** `<ADDRESS>` and `</ADDRESS>` are used to indicate authorship of a document. Within the address, the links to an author's home page might be given.

Example:

```
<ADDRESS><A
HREF="http://www.home.edu/~ima/index.html">I.
M. Author</A></ADDRESS>
```

g. **Blockquote style:** Used to mark text quoted from another source.

Example:

```
<BLOCKQUOTE>
Nick stood up. The rail tracks, where he could see them curve off in the
distance, disappeared in a heavy mist. He lost his fishing pole, the
sandwiches he had taken from Seney, the knife he had found on the streets
of Cadillac, and all hope that he'd make it to Two Heart before dark.
</BLOCKQUOTE>
```

h. **Lists:** Can be definition lists (glossaries), unordered lists, ordered lists, menus, and short lists. Entries in the lists are marked with a `<LI>` (List Item) tag.

Example (unordered list):

Lists can be

```
<UL>
<LI>Definition Lists (Glossaries)
```

```
<LI>Unordered Lists
<LI>Ordered Lists
<LI>Menus
<LI>Short Lists
</UL>
```

Example (ordered list):

An html document consists of

```
<OL>
<LI>Head elements
<LI>Body elements
<LI>Graphic elements
</OL>
```

Example (definition list):

A definition list, or glossary has these parts

```
<DL>
<DT>The term
<DD>what is to be explained in more detail by a definition
<DT>The definition
<DD>The longer explanation of the term, which
may include several lines of text.
</DL>
```

Example (menu):

A menu has

```
<MENU>
<LI>Smaller paragraphs
<LI>Typically one line an item
<LI>Typically less space between items as compared to an unordered or
ordered list
<LI>The same appearance as an unordered list in some browsers
</MENU>
```

Example (short list):

A short list can be arranged in columns across the page, although not all browsers
do this

```
<DIR>
<LI>Eggs
<LI>Fish
<LI>Meat
<LI>Grains
</DIR>
```

i. **Preformatted text:** Text that you want to have displayed in a fixed-width font, with spacing preserved.

Example:

```
<PRE>
```

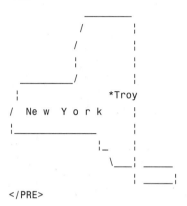

```
</PRE>
```

j. **Character formatting:** Elements that enable you to use physical styles such as bold, italics, fixed-width, or underlines. You also have the option to use logical styles to indicate emphasis, a computer code example, a citation, and so on.

Examples (physical styles):

```
<B>Bold</B>
<I>Italics</I>
<U>Underline</U>
<TT>Fixed-width</TT>
```

Examples (logical styles):

```
<STRONG>Strong emphasis, often same as bold</STRONG>
<VAR>A variable name</VAR>
<CITE>A citation</CITE>
```

3. **Graphics:** Capable browsers will display inline graphics (graphics imbedded in the display of the HTML page). Browsers that don't support graphics will still read a reference to an online image and display the word IMAGE or a string defined in the graphics element (using the ALT attribute, described forthwith). The SRC=" " part indicates the source of the image, which could be any URL on the network. For example:

```
<IMG SRC="xyz-logo.gif">XYZ Industries
```

For browsers that can't display images, use the ALT=" " label to help the user know the meaning of the image, as follows:

```
<IMG SRC="xyz-logo.gif" ALT="XYZ Logo">XYZ Industries
```

4. **Entities:** There are also entities that can be used in HTML documents to represent special characters. For example, you might have wondered how you could possibly write

the less-than symbol (<) in an HTML document, since < indicates the start of an element. You make a < with the sequence < in HTML, an ampersand followed by lt (for "less than").

Other entities include the following:

```
&gt; (greater than)
&amp; (ampersand)
&quot;(double quote)
```

You also can represent special characters, such as the Icelandic-thorn symbol, þ. See URL http://www.w3.org/hypertext/WWW/MarkUp/ISOlat1.html for more entities.

An HTML Document Layout

To make an HTML document, you include the following in a file:

- Head elements: Information about the document
- Body elements: The content of the document itself

It is a good idea to wrap these parts in tags that mark the start and end of the head and body. Then wrap this up inside tags marking the start and end of the HTML code itself:

```
<HTML>
<HEAD>
head elements go here
</HEAD>
<BODY>
body elements go here
</BODY>
</HTML>
```

HTML Tag Summaries

Now that we've explored the basic elements, entities, and layout of an HTML document, let's look at an enumeration of the features of Level 0 and Level 1 HTML. For the typical user, a careful separation of Level 0 and Level 1 tags isn't all that necessary. Most browsers support up to at least Level 1 HTML (and most up to Level 2 HTML), but such a separation may be useful for reference as well as to see the progression of the HTML language.

HTML Level 0 Tag Summary

The following HTML source file is written using HTML Level 0 constructs. First, the HTML source file is shown. Then the rendered version (in Netscape) is shown in Figures 33.1 through 33.3. Figures 33.4 through 33.11 show the character entities that you can use in HTML to produce special characters.

```
<HTML>
<!-- Level 0 HTML Tag Summary -->
```

```
<!-- The minimum set of elements and entities which make up an HTML
     document and all Web browsers recognize. -->
<HEAD>
    <TITLE>Level 0 HTML Tag Summary</TITLE>
    <BASE Href="http://www.rpi.edu/~decemj/pages/level0.html">
</HEAD>
<BODY>
<I>HTML Tag Summary:
    <B>Level 0</B> /
    <A Href="level1.html">Level 1</A> /
    <A Href="level2.html">Level 2</A> /
    <A Href="level3.html">Level 3</A> /
    <A Href="levele.html">Extensions</A>
    </I>
<HR>

<H1>Level 0 HTML Tag Summary</H1>

An HTML document consists of text and tags that mark the structure
of the document.  Elements in an HTML document are marked by
the tags &lt; and &gt.  Some elements have both a start and
end tag:  e.g., &lt;TITLE&gt; and &lt;/TITLE&gt;.  Other elements
use only a single tag:  e.g., &lt;P&gt; (the paragraph element).
Some elements have <I>attributes</I>, which are
qualifications of the element's meaning or optional parameters
for that element.
<P>

A Level 0 HTML document can include the following elements
with the attributes shown.  In this document,
the elements are listed in all capital
letters (e.g., TITLE), and  the attributes are indicated by initial
capital letters (e.g., Href).  In order to benefit from the information
in this document, view both its HTML source as well as its rendered form
in a Web browser.  The elements and entities are explained in the list
below as well as demonstrated here in appropriate locations
(e.g. HEAD elements are demonstrated only in the HEAD of this document;
and I don't demonstrate the heading (H1...H6) within the list of elements).
<P>

Note that the different brands of browsers vary in how they render
these features.  The intent of HTML is that the browser designers have
a "basic set" of features that they should implement, so that their browser
renders these HTML constructs <I>some</I> satisfactory way.

<A Name="Structure"><H2>HTML structure and comment elements</H2></A>

<UL>
<LI>HTML:
    The HTML element identifies the file as
    containing HTML elements.  Only
    HEAD, BODY, and comment elements that should go inside the
    HTML element start and stop tag.

<LI>comment:
    You can include a comment anywhere within
    an HTML document; comments can cross several lines of text.
    <!-- start a comment with and end it with -->
```

```
</UL>

<H2>The HEAD and related elements</H2>

<UL>
<LI>HEAD:
    The HEAD element brackets a set of unordered descriptive
    information about a document.   Elements within the HEAD
    element include: TITLE, BASE, ISINDEX, and NEXTID.

<LI>TITLE:
    Every HTML must have one title element which
    identifies the contents of the document.
    The title may not contain anchors, paragraph elements, or
    highlighting.  Choose a title which is descriptive
    outside the context of your document's context, as
    the title is commonly used to identify a document
    in navigation and indexing applications (e.g., hotlists
    and spiders).

<LI>BASE:
    The BASE element can be used to record the
    URL of the original version of a document when
    the source file is transported elsewhere; the base element
    has one attribute, Href, which is used to
    define the base URL of the document.  Partial
    URLs in the document are resolved by using this
    base address as the start of the URL.

<LI>ISINDEX:
    This element marks the document as searchable—the
    server on which the document is located must have a
    search engine defined that supports this searching.

<LI>NEXTID:
    This element is used by text generated software
    in creating identifiers; its attribute, N, is
    used to define the next identifier to be
    allocated by the text generator program.  Normally,
    human writers of HTML don't use this element; and
    Web browsers ignore this element.

</UL>

<H2>The BODY and related elements</H2>

<UL>
<LI>BODY:
    The BODY element's start and stop tags mark the
    content of an HTML document—within the body, you'll
    find links, text, and other formatting and
    content information that is not appropriate
    for the descriptive information found in the HEAD.

<LI><A Name="Anchor">A:</A> this is the anchor element which is
    used as the basis for linking documents together.<BR>
```

```
    Attributes:
    <UL>

    <LI>Href: this attribute identifies the URL of the
        hypertext reference for this anchor in the
        form Href="URL", where the URL given will
        be the resource which the browser retrieves
        when the user clicks on the anchor's hotspot.
        For example:<BR>
        <A Href="http://www.w3.org/">W3O</A><BR>
        will take the user to the World Wide Web's home.

    <LI>Name: this attribute creates a name for
        an anchor; this name can then be used within the
        document or outside of the document in anchor
        to refer to  the portion of text identified by the name.
        For example:<BR>
        <A Name="AnchorName">Text can have a named anchor.</A><BR>
        <A Href="#AnchorName">You can jump to that anchor within
            the file in which it is named...</A><BR>
        <A Href="level0.html#AnchorName">
            ...or from another file (perhaps on a remote host).</A><BR>
    </UL>
    Note that an anchor can have both the Name and Href
    attributes:<BR>
    <A Name="W3O-reference" Href="http://www.w3.org/">W3O</A><BR>

<LI>character blocks: these are elements that help you
    "chunk" text in lists or blocks.
    <UL>

    <LI>PRE: this element sets up a block of text which will
        be presented in a fixed-width font, with spaces as
        significant.<BR>

        <PRE>
    PRE's one attribute, Width, lets you
    specify the width of the presentation.
    You can use <A Href="#AnchorName">anchors</A>
    and <I>character formatting</I> within PRE, but not
    elements that define paragraph breaks
    (e.g., headings, address, the P element, etc).
        </PRE>

    <LI>BLOCKQUOTE: this brackets text that is an extended
        quotation from another source.
        <BLOCKQUOTE>
        A typical rendering of a BLOCKQUOTE is to provide extra
        indentation on both sides, and possibly highlight
        the characters in the BLOCKQUOTE.
        </BLOCKQUOTE>

    <LI>UL (LI):  The UL element:
        <UL Compact>
        <LI>Brackets an unordered list of items.
        <LI>Employs the LI element to mark the elements.
        <LI>Is rendered using bullets to start items.
```

```
    <LI>Can have the Compact attribute  (example in this list)
        to suggest to the Web browser to keep the items in
        the list close together.
    </UL>

<LI>OL (LI): The OL element:
    <OL>
    <LI>Brackets an ordered list of items.
    <LI>Employs the LI element to mark the elements.
    <LI>Is rendered using a numerical sequence.
    <LI>Can have the Compact attribute.
    </OL>

<LI>MENU (LI): The MENU element:
    <MENU>
    <LI>Brackets an more compact unordered list of items.
    <LI>Employs the LI element to mark the elements.
    <LI>Is rendered using bullets to start items.
    <LI>Can have the Compact attribute.
    </MENU>

<LI>DIR (LI): The DIR element:
    brackets a list of items which are at most 20
    characters wide. The intent is that a browser can
    render this in columns of 24 characters wide.
    DIR can use the Compact attribute.
    <DIR>
    <LI>ITEM A.
    <LI>ITEM B.
    <LI>ITEM C.
    <LI>ITEM D.
    </DIR>

<LI>DL (DT, DD): A definition list, or glossary has these parts:
    <DL>
    <DT>A term:
    <DD>a detailed explanation of a term.
    <DT>Another term:
    <DD>an explanation of a term, which may include several
        lines of text.
    <DT>Can have the Compact attribute.
    <DD>Use the element &lt;DL Compact&gt; as the start of the list.
    </DL>

<LI>ADDRESS:  this element brackets ownership or authorship
    information, typically at the start or end of a
    document (see the end of this document for an example).

</UL>

<LI><A Name="Formats">character formatting:</A> these are elements
    that allow you to format characters in a document.  These
    are called <I>physical</I> elements because they dictate the
```

```
    appearance of the text rather than the semantic intent of
    the words (contrast with <A Href="level1.html#Formats">Level 1's
    logical elements for character formatting.</A>)
    <UL>
    <LI>B:  <B>Marks bold text</B>
    <LI>I:  <I>Marks italic (or underlined) text</I>
    <LI>TT: <TT>Marks teletype (fixed width typewriter) text</TT>
    </UL>

<LI>headers:
    H1, H2, H3, H4, H5, H6:
    these are elements you can use to create an information
    hierarchy in your document.
    Don't use these to take advantage of the possible variations
    in appearance in browsers, but only use them to mark the
    logical structure of your document.

<LI>separators
    <UL>
    <LI>HR: Horizontal rule, divides sections of text.
    <LI>P: this element signals a paragraph break.
    </UL>

<LI>spacing
    <UL>
    <LI>BR: This element forces a linebreak.<BR> Typically, this
        is used to represent postal addresses or text<BR>
        (like poetry) where linebreaks are significant.
    </UL>

<LI>character sets
    <OL>
    <LI>ascii characters: an HTML document can, of course, contain
        all the keyboard characters such as a-z, A-Z, 0-1,
        and !@#$%^&*()_+-=¦\{}[]:"~;''<>?,./

    <LI>entities: since some characters (e.g., < > & ")
        are used within HTML to create tags, so some browsers
        don't render them; you can use
        special entities within documents to represent these characters:
        <OL>
        <LI>Less than sign: &amp;lt = &lt
        <LI>Greater than sign: &amp;gt = &gt
        <LI>Ampersand: &amp;& = &amp
        <LI>Double quote sign: &amp;quot = &quot
        </OL>

  <LI>iso-latin1: You can represent a set of ISO Latin character entities;
      See <A Href="http://www.rpi.edu/~decemj/pages/iso-latin1.html">
      ISO Latin 1 character entities (Table)</A>.

  <LI>numeric characters: You can use numeric codes to represent
      characters; See
```

```
        <A Href="http://www.rpi.edu/~decemj/pages/codes.html">Numeric
        code references in HTML (Table)</A>.
    </OL>
</UL>

Copyright &#169 1995 by John December.  All rights reserved.
<HR>

<ADDRESS>
<A Href="http://www.rpi.edu/~decemj/index.html">John December</A>
(<A Href="mailto:decemj@rpi.edu">decemj@rpi.edu</A>) / 15 Mar 95
</ADDRESS>

</BODY>
</HTML>
```

FIGURE 33.1.

*HTML Level 0 Summary
rendered in Netscape for X
(page 1).*

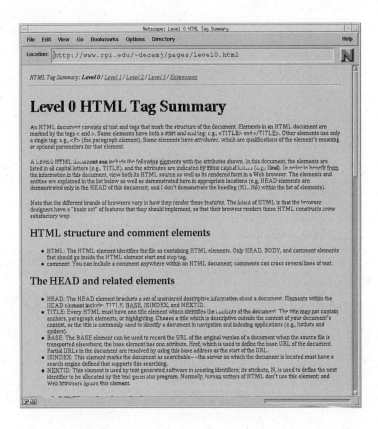

FIGURE 33.2.

HTML Level 0 Summary rendered in Netscape for X (page 2).

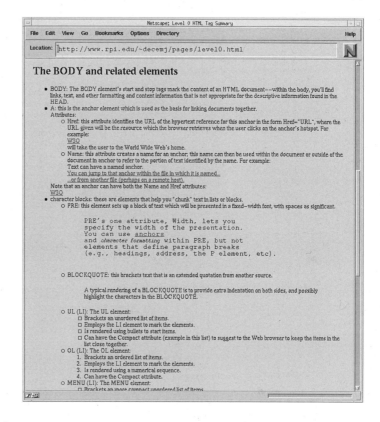

FIGURE 33.3.

HTML Level 0 Summary rendered in Netscape for X (page 3).

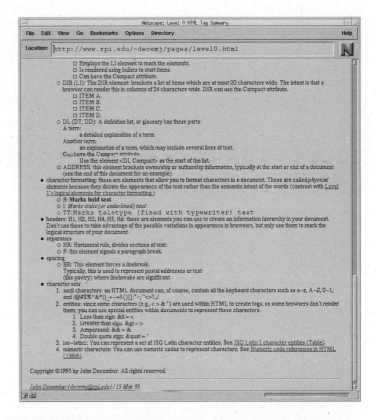

NOTE

In using any of the character or numeric code entities, be sure to include a semicolon (;) between contiguous characters. If you leave the semicolon out, the browser won't know what entity you refer to. For example use `fran&ccedil;aise` for "française," not `franc&ccedilaise`. (Otherwise the browser will try to find a `&ccedilasie` entity.) With spaces between the entities, the references with or without the colons will work: `&ccedil;` and `&ccedil` will both represent a c with a cedilla.

FIGURE 33.4.

ISO Latin Character entities (page 1).

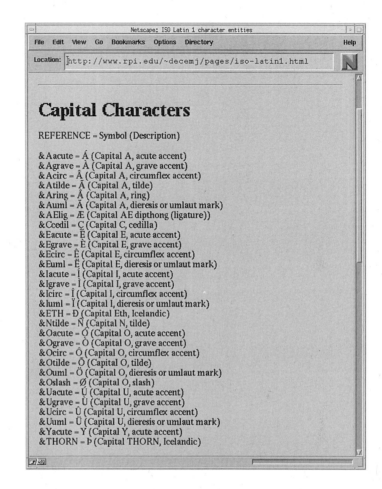

FIGURE 33.5.

ISO Latin Character entitites (page 2).

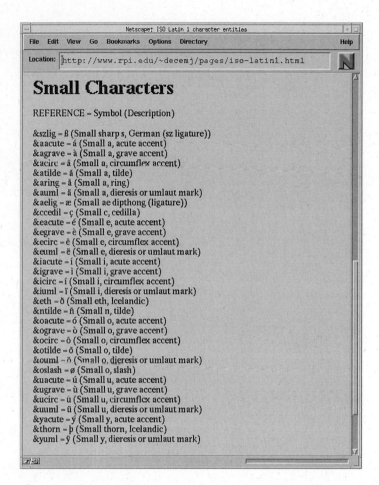

FIGURE 33.6.

*Numeric code entities
(page 1).*

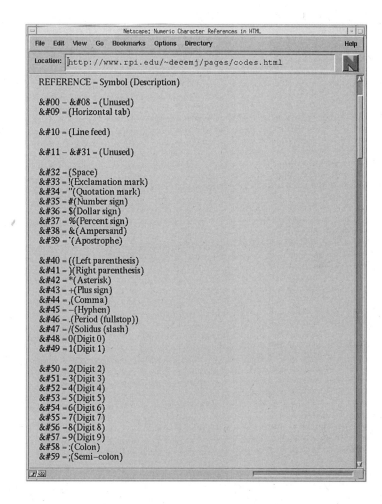

FIGURE 33.7.

*Numeric code entities
(page 2).*

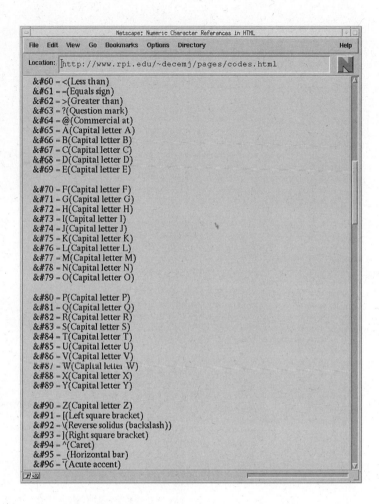

FIGURE 33.8.

*Numeric code entities
(page 3).*

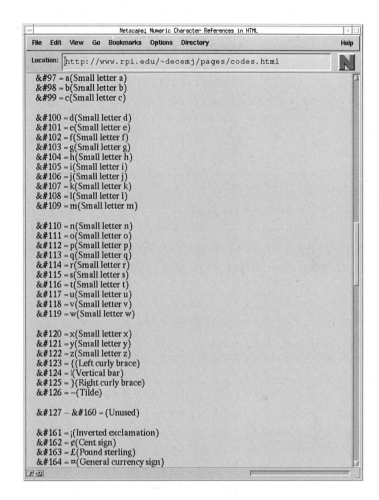

FIGURE 33.8.

Numeric code entities (page 3).

FIGURE 33.9.
*Numeric code entities
(page 4).*

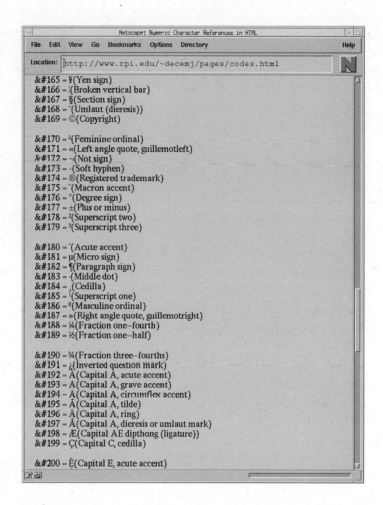

Netscape: Numeric Character References in HTML

File   Edit   View   Go   Bookmarks   Options   Directory   Help

Location: http://www.rpi.edu/~decemj/pages/codes.html

```
&#165 = ¥(Yen sign)
&#166 = ¦(Broken vertical bar)
&#167 = §(Section sign)
&#168 = ¨(Umlaut (dieresis))
&#169 = ©(Copyright)

&#170 = ª(Feminine ordinal)
&#171 = «(Left angle quote, guillemotleft)
&#172 = ¬(Not sign)
&#173 = -(Soft hyphen)
&#174 = ®(Registered trademark)
&#175 = ¯(Macron accent)
&#176 = °(Degree sign)
&#177 = ±(Plus or minus)
&#178 = ²(Superscript two)
&#179 = ³(Superscript three)

&#180 = ´(Acute accent)
&#181 = µ(Micro sign)
&#182 = ¶(Paragraph sign)
&#183 = ·(Middle dot)
&#184 = ¸(Cedilla)
&#185 = ¹(Superscript one)
&#186 = º(Masculine ordinal)
&#187 = »(Right angle quote, guillemotright)
&#188 = ¼(Fraction one–fourth)
&#189 = ½(Fraction one–half)

&#190 = ¾(Fraction three–fourths)
&#191 = ¿(Inverted question mark)
&#192 = À(Capital A, acute accent)
&#193 = Á(Capital A, grave accent)
&#194 = Â(Capital A, circumflex accent)
&#195 = Ã(Capital A, tilde)
&#196 = Ä(Capital A, ring)
&#197 = Å(Capital A, dieresis or umlaut mark)
&#198 = Æ(Capital AE dipthong (ligature))
&#199 = Ç(Capital C, cedilla)

&#200 = È(Capital E, acute accent)
```

FIGURE 33.10.

Numeric code entities (page 5).

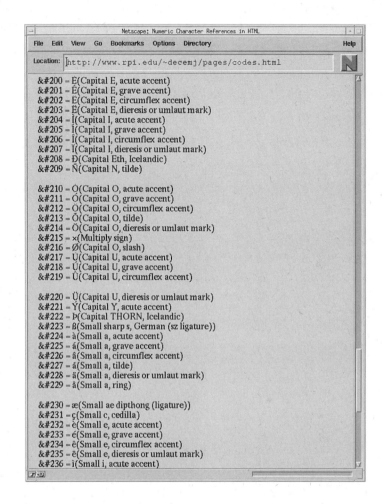

FIGURE 33.11.

*Numeric code entities
(page 6).*

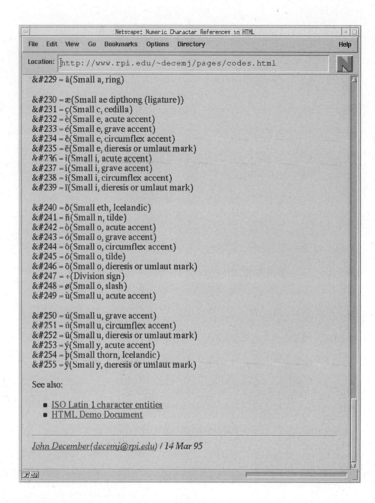

HTML Level 1 Tag Summary

The following HTML source file is written using HTML Level 1 (which includes Level 0) constructs. First, the HTML source file is shown. Then the rendered version (in Netscape) is shown:

```
<HTML>
<!-- Level 1 HTML additions -->
<!-- Features such as character formatting and images
     that not all browsers may recognize. -->
<HEAD>
    <TITLE>Level 1 HTML Tag Summary</TITLE>
    <BASE Href="http://www.rpi.edu/~decemj/pages/level1.html">
    <LINK Href="mailto:decemj@rpi.edu" Rel="made">
    <META Http-equiv="Reply-to" content="decemj@rpi.edu (John December)">
    <META Name="IndexType" Content="Listing">
</HEAD>
<BODY>
```

```
<I>HTML Tag Summary:
    <A Href="level0.html">Level 0</A> /
    <B>Level 1</B> /
    <A Href="level2.html">Level 2</A> /
    <A Href="level3.html">Level 3</A> /
    <A Href="levele.html">Extensions</A>
    </I>
<HR>

<H1>Level 1 HTML Tag Summary</H1>

A Level 1 HTML document can include the following elements
and attributes in addition to
<A Href="http://www.rpi.edu/~decemj/pages/level0.html">Level 0 elements
and attributes</A>.  Within this document,
the elements are listed in all capital letters;
the attributes are indicated by initial capital letters.
In order to benefit from the information in this file, view both
its HTML source as well as its rendered form in a Web browser.
The tags are explained in the list below as well as demonstrated in this
file.  In many cases, some of the attributes described here are
rarely used (or supported) by Web browsers.  For the most part, I've
tried to illustrate the more popularly-used constructs within this
document as a guideline.  This is particularly true with HEAD and
related elements.

<H2>HTML structure and comment elements</H2>

Level 1 specifies no additions in this category over
<A Href="level0.html#Structure">Level 0's structure features</A>.

<A Name="Head"><H2>The HEAD and related elements</H2></A>

<UL>

<LI>LINK: this element is used to define a relationship between the
    document and other objects or documents.  A link element can indicate
    authorship or indicate the tree structure of a document.<BR>

    Attributes:
    <UL>

    <LI>Href: this identifies the document or part of
        a document to which this link refers

    <LI>Name: this is a way to name this LINK as a possible
        destination for another hypertext document

    <LI><A Name="Rel">Rel:</A> describes the relationship defined by
        this LINK, according to the possible relationships as defined by the
        <A Href="http://www.w3.org/hypertext/WWW/MarkUp/RegistrationAuthority.html">
        HTML Registration Authority</A>'s list of
        <A Href="http://www.w3.org/hypertext/WWW/MarkUp/Relationships.html">
        relationships</A>

    <LI><A Name="Rev">Rev:</A> Similar to Rel, above, but the Rev attribute
        indicates the <EM>reverse</EM> relationship as Rel.  For
        Example, the LINK with Rel="made" indicates that the
```

Href attribute indicates the URL given in the Href
is the author of the current document. Using the Rev="made"
link indicates that the <EM>current document</EM>
is the author of the URL given in the Href attribute.

   <LI>Urn: This indicates the Uniform Resource Name of
      the document; the specification for
      <A Href="http://www.w3.org/hypertext/WWW/Addressing/Addressing.html">URN
      and other addressing</A> is still in development.

   <LI>Title: This attribute is <EM>not</EM> to be used
      as a substitute for the TITLE attribute of the document itself,
      but as a title for the document given by the Href attribute
      of the LINK element. This attribute is rarely used or supported by
      browsers, but may have value for cross referencing the
      relationships the LINK element defines.

   <LI>Methods: This attribute describes the HTTP methods the
      object referred to by the Href of the LINK element
      supports. For example, one method is searching; a browser
      could thus use this Methods attribute to give information to
      the user about the document defined by the LINK element.

   </UL>

<LI>META: The META element is for recording information about
   the document itself (meta information) that is not defined
   by other elements. This information should be useful in
   indexing the document.

   Attributes (see the header of this document for typical examples):
   <UL>

   <LI>Http-equiv: This attribute connects this META element to
      a particular protocol response which is generated by
      the HTTP server hosting the document.

   <LI>Name: This attribute is a name for the information in
      the document—<EM>not</EM> the title of the document
      (which should be defined in the TITLE element) but a
      "meta name" classifying this information.

   <LI>Content: A "meta name" for the content associated with
      the given name (defined by the Name attribute) or the
      response defined in Http-equiv.

   </UL>

</UL>

<H2>The BODY and related elements</H2>

<UL>

<LI>anchors: A: Level 1 adds more attributes for anchors as defined
   in <A Href="level0.html#Anchor">Level 0's anchor attributes</A>


```
        Attributes:
        <UL>
        <LI>Title: This attribute is for the title of the document
            given by the Href attribute of the anchor.  A browser
            could use this information to display this title before
            retrieving it, or to provide a title for the Href document
            when it is retrieved (e.g., if the document is at a Ftp
            site, it will not have a title defined).

        <LI>Rel: Defines the relationship defined from
            the current document to the target (Href document).
            See <A Href="#Rel">the discussion of the Rel attribute</A> in
            the LINK element, above.

        <LI>Rev: Defines the relationship defined from the
            target (Href document) to the current document.
            See <A Href="#Rev">the discussion of the Rev attribute</A> in
            the LINK element, above.

        <LI>Urn: This indicates the Uniform Resource Name of
            the target (Href) document; the specification for
            <A Href="http://www.w3.org/hypertext/WWW/Addressing/Addressing.html">URN
            and other addressing</A> is still in development.


        <LI>Methods: Provides information about the functions the
            user can perform on the Href object.  Similar to described
            above for Title, this information might be useful for the
            browser to display in advance.

        </UL>

<LI><A Name="Formats">character formatting:</A>  Level 1 defines several
    additions for logical elements over <A Href="level0.html#Formats">Level
    0's physical elements for character formatting</A>. <BR>

    <UL>

    <LI>CITE: Marks a citation of a book or other work:
        <CITE>The Mona Lisa</CITE>.

    <LI>CODE: Used to mark computer language source code; often
        rendered as monospace type:

        <CODE>
        Note that the CODE element's rendering does not
        keep the line breaks that the PRE element does.
        </CODE>

    <LI>EM: Used to mark <EM>emphasis</EM>, typically rendered the
        same as the physical tag for <I>italics</I> or as underlined
        text.

    <LI>KBD: Used in computer instructions to mark text the user
        enters on a keyboard; typically rendered as
        <KBD>monospaced text</KBD>.
```

```
        <LI>SAMP: Used to delimit a sequence of characters that are
            to be rendered as is ("sample" text): <SAMP># @ % * !</SAMP>.

        <LI>STRONG: Used to mark strong emphasis; often rendered the
            same as the physical <B>bold</B> element.

        <LI>VAR: used to mark a variable used in computer code,
            equations, or other work.  A <VAR>variable</VAR> is
            typically rendered in <I>italic</I>.

        </UL>

    <LI><IMG Src="http://www.rpi.edu/~decemj/images/stats.gif"
            Alt="statistics sphere"
            Align="middle"> images (IMG): The IMG element allows
        you to insert a graphic image into the document at the location
        of this element tag ("inline images").

        <UL>

        <LI>Src: This attribute indicates the source file of the image.

        <LI>Alt: You can define a string of characters that will be
            displayed in non-graphical browsers.   The IMG element
            can be used in Level 0 documents if this Alt attribute
            is given.

        <LI>Align: this attribute sets the positioning relationship between
            the graphic and the text that follows it; values include:
            <UL>
            <LI>top: the text following the graphic should be aligned with
                the top of the graphic.
            <LI>middle: the text following the graphic should be aligned with
                the middle of the graphic.
            <LI>bottom: the text following the graphic should be aligned with
                the bottom of the graphic.
            </UL>

        <LI>Ismap: this attribute identifies the image as an image map,
            where regions of the graphic are mapped to defined URLs.
            Hooking up these relationships requires knowledge of
            setting an imagemap file on the server to define these
            connections.

        </UL>

    </UL>
```

```
Copyright &#169 1995 by John December.  All rights reserved.
<HR>

<ADDRESS>
<A Href="http://www.rpi.edu/~decemj/index.html">John December</A>
(<A Href="mailto:decemj@rpi.edu">decemj@rpi.edu</A>) / 15 Mar 95
</ADDRESS>

</BODY>
</HTML>
```

FIGURE 33.12.

HTML Level 1 Summary rendered in Netscape for X (page 1).

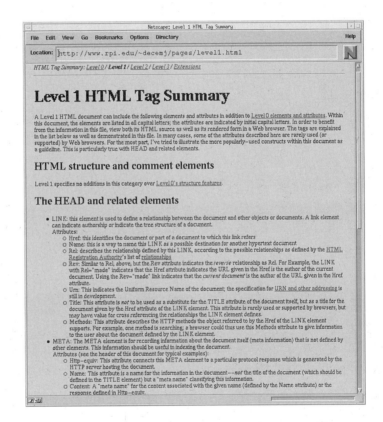

FIGURE 33.13.

HTML Level 1 Summary rendered in Netscape for X (page 2).

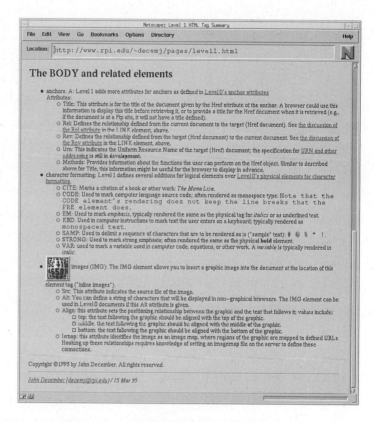

Expressing Yourself in HTML: The Basics

Now that we've covered the basic elements, entities, and layout of an HTML document, and you've seen an enumeration of Level 0 and Level 1 HTML, let's go through an example of how you can express yourself in basic HTML. In order to help you see what you can do, I'll first review what you can't do in basic HTML and what people often have a hard time doing.

What You Can't Do and the Tough Stuff

As a user of HTML, you'll start to want to do some things that might not seem all that complex for a text-formatting language; there are, however, some things that basic HTML can't do:

- Make tables
- Include mathematical equations
- Include an external HTML file
- Specify multiple columns of text or graphics
- Embed a movie into a document

Some of these features are expected to be included in later enhancements of HTML.

Writers of HTML will also find that some things seem to create more errors than others. We'll cover all these in detail in a moment, but it may help you to know the following is usually the toughest stuff for people to learn:

- Making sure that the < and > all match up when composing an anchor. For example:

```
The <A HREF="http://www.w3.org/hypertext/WWW/MarkUp/Tags.html">Elements of
HTML</A> are head, body, and graphics.
```

  Notice how the anchor starts with <A and ends with </A>, and what's in between are the HREF label, the URL of the resource, and the hotspot for the hypertext. Missing just one of the ", >, <, or / symbols will cause an error.

- Verifying that many browsers will read the HTML file without problems. In developing HTML, you'll find that some browsers are forgiving in that they let you get away with small errors in your HTML code. Another browser might not be as forgiving, so it is a good idea to check your HTML code in at least one other browser than the one you're using for development.

- Linking to other documents using relative links. When you write an HTML document, you can refer to other HTML files that are located on your server by using relative links within your HTML. For example, if you are writing the top HTML document (`top.html`), and you are referring to the index document (`myindex.html`) that is located in the same directory, you can link from top.html to myindex.html as follows:

```
<A HREF="myindex.html">Index</A>
```

  Anyone who links to your top document, perhaps from a distant host, will use the link

```
<A HREF="http://your.host.com/Project/top.html>Top Document</A>
```

  When this user clicks the Index hotspot, the reference to myindex.html will be resolved to be the URL

```
http://your.host.com/Project/myindex.html
```

  even though you had only used `myindex.html` in your HTML document. This is called relative naming (or relative addressing or linking).

Getting Started: The Basics

Because there are certain tags that you will have in all HTML documents, it is a good idea to make a template for yourself (create a file called template.html) that contains all the basics, as follows:

```
<HTML>
   <HEAD>
      <TITLE>title</TITLE>
   </HEAD>
   <BODY>
      <ADDRESS>your name (your email address)</ADDRESS>
   </BODY>
</HTML>
```

Now let's put some information onto this template and step through some of the most commonly used HTML structures.

1. **The title:** Think up a good one. As we saw in looking at spiders in Chapter 19, the title is often used as an identifier of your HTML document on the Web. Therefore, your title should be meaningful outside of the context of your document's contents (but not be overloaded with every conceivable buzzword to grab a spider's attention). For example, your document might be the overview for your company's products. Using the title Overview, however, won't have any meaning to anyone else who might come across this title. The title Overview of XYZ Industry Product Line, instead, will have more meaning to anyone seeing your document's title in a spider list.

   Put the title between the <TITLE> and </TITLE> brackets in the <HEAD> of the document:

   ```
   <TITLE>Overview of XYZ Industries Product Line</TITLE>
   ```

   Remember, this title does not show up in the document's representation in a browser. You'll have to repeat the document's title, if desired, in the text itself (possibly as a heading).

2. **Headings:** The six levels of headings give the opportunity to create an information hierarchy within your document. As such, the heading elements are used to indicate semantic hierarchy, not necessarily to take advantage of the varying sizes of type that the headings might offer in some browsers. Therefore, you should attempt to use these headings in sequence, starting with Level 1 <H1>, and continuing to <H6> in step sizes of 1 (that is, not jumping from heading 1 to heading 6). If you find you are tempted to violate this rule (that you want to use a high-numbered heading to take advantage of the type-display change in graphical browsers), remember that not all browsers will support a type-size change—so that while your Mosaic users see small type with <H6>, your Lynx users are seeing the same-sized type as with heading <H1>.

   Similar to the title, the headings too should be as descriptive as possible, particularly because there are some spiders that use heading information as a means to index your document's content.

   The very first heading you put in a document could reflect the purpose of the document itself. For example, continuing with our XYZ Industries example, the first heading in our document might be XYZ Industries Product Line. We put this as a major heading as follows:

   ```
   <H1>The XYZ Industries Product Line</H1>
   ```

   Since this entire page is devoted to the XYZ Industries Product Line, we wouldn't normally put another <H1> header on the page. We might include <H2> and <H3> headers for information one or two levels down from the product-line description. You'll find, however, that the nature of hypertext gives you the opportunity to avoid this nesting of parts within the same HTML page. Therefore, you'll find it uncommon to have many layers of headings on a page. If you find yourself nesting information to many levels of headings, you should consider breaking up the document into several HTML pages.

3. **Paragraphs:** The text that you type into an HTML file outside of any of the elements marked off by the < and > tags will be placed into paragraphs. Only the <P> tag marks the end of a paragraph, no matter how many blank lines or intervening spaces there are. Moreover, most browsers "chew up" any extraneous white space between words, so that you won't be able to "format" your text using spacing. (Use preformatted text, <PRE>, for this).

So after your heading, you can explain a little bit about XYZ Industries product line, like this:

```
Founded in July 1994, XYZ Industries has rapidly become a world leader in
HyperWidget and Odd-Bearing Machine (OBM) technologies. <P> XYZ's product line
includes industry standards such as the HyperWidget 2000 and OBM 411, as well
as such innovations as the Alpha-class HyperWidget line that allows hyper-
window mapping on VR (<A HREF="http://guinan.gsfc.nasa.gov/W3/VR.html">Virtual
Reality</A>) helmets or displays. With XYZ's products, you can be assured of
the highest quality and state-of-the art design. <P>
```

Notice in the preceding example, I used only a <P> to break the paragraphs. For readability in my HTML source file, I might have placed a blank line between the paragraphs, but it would not have been required. Note also, that the line breaks in the HTML source file don't matter. The browser will break lines and wrap lines of text based on how wide the display area for the text is, not based on the HTML source (unless a <BR> was used).

4. **A list:** Lists provide a very useful way to focus a user's attention on a series of items. As described previously, you have a variety of choices for lists. Generally, you'll use a sequential list for steps or directions that must be done in a particular order, or for a list of counted items.

Since we want to impress the potential customers about the wide range of products that XYZ Industries offers, we'll use a numbered list to emphasize the quantity of items shown:

```
The XYZ products currently available for sale and delivery are:
<OL>
<LI>OBM 411, 412, 413, and 440
<LI>HyperWidget 2000, 2000A, 2000A-XL, and 2000A-XL-G
<LI>Alpha, beta, gamma, and delta class HyperWidgets for VR applications
</OL>
```

You can quickly change a list that is ordered to an unordered list by changing the starting tag from <OL> to <UL> and the ending tag from </OL> to </UL>.

5. **A link:** Looking over what you've written about XYZ Industries' products, you might notice that you've used many highly technical terms and jargon that might be company- or industry-specific. For example, the term VR was defined (as virtual reality) but not explained. As we saw in the previous two chapters, what you need to explain largely depends on your audience's knowledge and interests. Assuming that an educated customer would be reading about XYZ's product lines, you wouldn't necessarily have to go into great detail about every term. However, if you do want to provide a way to help a user who wants to find out more about a topic, a link is a very useful way to connect information—in fact, this is the heart of writing hypertext.

To help the user who is interested in finding out about virtual reality, let's make a link from the phrase "virtual reality" in our document to a page that presents a large selection of resources for virtual reality at the URL `http://guinan.gsfc.nasa.gov/W3/VR.html`. Note that, as discussed in the previous chapters about planning and analyzing a web, we need to take special care when we link to resources outside of our web, paying attention to link freshness and appropriateness.

To make the link in our text, we have to modify a few lines:

```
Alpha-class HyperWidget line that allows hyper-window mapping on VR (<A
HREF="http://guinan.gsfc.nasa.gov/W3/VR.html">virtual reality</A>)
```

Notice that the basic form of making a link is

```
<A HREF="URL">Hotspot</A>
```

where URL is the Uniform Resource Locator for the document, and Hotspot is the explanatory text for the link that is usually highlighted (or underlined) in the browser.

Getting Started: Some Flairs and Details

In the previous section, we've done the most common things you'll do in an HTML document—set up the heading and body tags, given the document a title, put in a heading, written some paragraphs, created a list, and put in a link. There are a few other flairs that you can put in your document to add visual cues—things to draw and focus the user's attention. These include small images and horizontal lines, as well as details like a link to your home page in the address of a document, a revision link in the head of the document, and comment lines in the HTML source code:

1. **A logo:** Our page for XYZ Industries, while providing an overview of products, seems a little dry. One flair you can add is a small logo or inline image in the document. First, you need to create the logo itself with tools on your computer and create a file in a graphics format that can be recognized by the browsers you expect your users to have. A common type of graphics file that works is a GIF (Graphics Interchange Format) file. Also, keep in mind, of course, that browsers that cannot display inline graphics won't show the logo.

Once you have the XYZ industries logo created (in file xyz-logo.gif in the same directory as your HTML page), add the following line just below the `<BODY>` element:

```
<IMG SRC="xyz-logo.gif" ALT="XYZ Logo"> XYZ Industries
```

The inline image element `<IMG>` will bring the image in the file given directly into the text of the document. We've also added text to the right of the logo to identify the full name of the company. Note also that we've used the `ALT=" "` option to include a descriptive title that will be displayed in browsers which do not support graphics. This is important because otherwise, the users of these browsers will just see the word `IMAGE` and might wonder what they're missing.

2. **Horizontal lines:** Just as the fine lines going horizontally across the top of a page in a magazine serve to bracket the text visually for a pleasing appearance, so too can you create horizontal lines in your HTML pages to help bracket text. The key is not to over-use these lines but to use them selectively to help guide the reader's attention in your document. If you find yourself making too many horizontal lines, you should consider making separate pages out of the regions on the page you're marking off with the horizontal lines.

   Let's add horizontal lines just after the logo:

   ```
   <IMG SRC="xyz-logo.gif" ALT="XYZ Logo"> XYZ Industries
   <HR>
   ```

   and just after the end of our product list:

   ```
   The XYZ products currently available for sale and delivery are:
   <OL>
   <LI>OBM 411, 412, 413, and 440
   <LI>HyperWidget 2000, 2000A, 2000A-XL, and 2000A-XL-G
   <LI>Alpha, beta, gamma, and delta class HyperWidgets for VR applications
   </OL>
   <HR>
   ```

   The two horizontal lines created by `<HR>` serve to bracket the body of text that contains the page's main information, with the header being the logo and the signature being the address at the bottom of the page. In this way, this organization corresponds closely with a letter style, in which a company logo starts off the letter, a signature ends it, and the content of the letter is bracketed in between.

3. **Your address:** An address for the developer of the page is important to have; what if there were an error in the page or if a customer actually wanted to buy a OBM 411? Without a contact address at the bottom, it would be hard for a customer to make contact. Note that a contact address is not required in an HTML document, and it could come at the top or bottom (or anywhere) in a page.

The contents of the address can be the name of the developer for the page or an organizational unit's name and e-mail address. There also can be a link to a home page for that person or organizational unit.

```
<ADDRESS><A HREF=="http://www.xyz.com/units/cc.html">Corporate
Communications</A> (<A HREF="mailto:cc@xyz.com">cc@xyz.com</A>)</ADDRESS>
```

Note that a link was made in this address to the home page for corporate communications at the URL http://www.xyz.com/units/cc.html and that we've used the "mailto" link to provide a quick way for users to send a letter.

4. **Revision link:** Similar to the tradition of signing a page so that users can contact the developers, so too is including a revision link in the header of the document a valuable (but not necessary) detail. The revision link is made as follows:

```
<HEAD>
<TITLE>Overview of XYZ Industries Product Line</TITLE>
<LINK REV="made" HREF="mailto:cc@xyz.com">
</HEAD>
```

This will direct anyone who wishes to find out more about the revision of this document to contact cc@xyz.com. While this same information is included in the ADDRESS element, its inclusion in the HEAD element (which is not actually displayed) makes it accessible to browsers that recognize the special function of the LINK REV element. (For example, in the Lynx browser, hitting the "c" key will set up an e-mail session in which you will send e-mail to the address given by the LINK REV="made" element).

5. **Comments in the HTML code:** Just as the ADDRESS and LINK REV elements add important contact information and documentation to your HTML file, so too can you add comments to your source code itself. While comments are not required (as well as not displayed) in the browser, they can add significant value to your work by providing background and administrative information, labeling the information so that developers know who wrote it, why, and any special considerations for it. You bracket each comment within <!---- and ---->. For example:

```
<!---- Author:    M.U. Langdon (mul@xyz.com) ----
<!---- Dept:      Corporate Communications ---->
<!---- Date:      15 Mar 95 ---->
<!---- Purpose:   overview of XYZ products-->
<!---- Comments: check with Sales to get the latest enumeration of model
numbers. ---->
```

The XYZ Industries Product-Line Page

Now that we've gradually added HTML code to the XYZ Industries product page, let's look at the whole page with our changes:

```
<HTML>
<!-- Author:    M.U. Langdon (mul@xyz.com) -->
<!-- Dept:      Corporate Communcaitions -->
<!-- Date:      15 Mar 95 -->
<!-- Purpose:   overview of XYZ products-->
<!-- Comments:  check with Sales to get the latest enumeration of model numbers. -->
<HEAD>
   <TITLE>Overview of XYZ Industries Product Line</TITLE>
   <LINK REV="made" HREF="mailto:cc@xyz.com">
</HEAD>

<BODY>
<IMG SRC="../images/xyz-logo.gif" ALT="XYZ Logo"> XYZ Industries

<HR>

<H1>The XYZ Industries Product Line</H1>

Founded in July 1994, XYZ Industries has
rapidly become a world leader in
HyperWidget and Odd-Bearing Machine (OBM) technologies.
<P>
XYZ's product line includes industry standards
such as the HyperWidget 2000 and OBM 411, as well as such innovations as the
Alpha-class HyperWidget line that allows hyper-window mapping on
VR (<A HREF="http://guinan.gsfc.nasa.gov/W3/VR.html">virtual reality</A>)
helmets or displays.  With XYZ's products,
you can be assured of
the highest quality and state-of-the art design. <P>

The XYZ products currently available for sale and delivery are:
<OL>
<LI>OBM 411, 412, 413, and 440
<LI>HyperWidget 2000, 2000A, 2000A-XL, and 2000A-XL-G
<LI>Alpha, beta, gamma, and delta class HyperWidgets for VR applications
</OL>

<HR>

<ADDRESS> <A HREF="http://www.xyz.com/units/cc.html">Corporate Communications</A>
(<A HREF="mailto:cc@xyz.com">cc@xyz.com</A>)</ADDRESS>

</BODY>
</HTML>
```

Figure 33.14 shows the page displayed in Netscape, and Figure 33.15 shows it displayed in Lynx. Note how the displays differ, yet the same logical structure is expressed.

FIGURE 33.14.

The XYZ Industries Product Line page (Netscape for X).

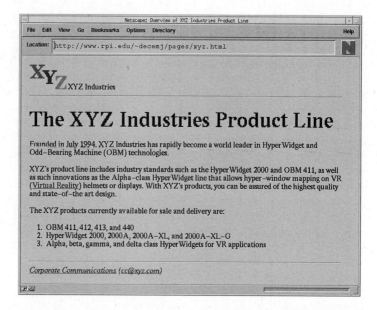

FIGURE 33.15.

The XYZ Industries Product Line page (Lynx).

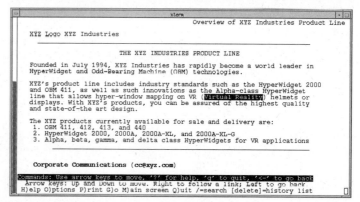

More HTML Features

While our XYZ Industries product page illustrates many common features of HTML, there are a some features that deserve a closer look because of their complexity and their special uses.

Anchors

We've already seen one kind of anchor that links a hotspot in your text to another document somewhere out on the Net:

```
Alpha-class HyperWidget line that allows hyper-window mapping on VR (<A HREF="http://
guinan.gsfc.nasa.gov/W3/VR.html">virtual reality</A>)
```

Another kind of anchor links a hotspot in your document to another place in your document (for example, if you want to allow the reader to jump quickly to another section). At the hotspot, make your link as follows:

```
You can find more about this same topic
at the <A HREF="#JUMP-TO-NAME">Jump Spot</A> later in this
document.
```

Notice that instead of a URL after HREF=", I included a "# and a string of characters JUMP-TO-NAME". At the point in your document that is the destination for this jump, make an anchor like this:

```
<A NAME="JUMP-TO-NAME">some text here</A>
```

This will allow users of your document to jump from your hotspot to the portion of the text marked by the destination anchor. As we'll see below in our detailed look at HTML Level 0, the keyword NAME is an attribute of the anchor (<A>) element that allows you to create these "anchors" where you can "jump into" a document.

A variation on this anchoring occurs when the document is at a remote place. In your own document, you can jump to this specific place in the remote document like this:

```
You can find more information about
of
<A HREF="http://www.zippy.com/products.html#COOL-STUFF">Zippy Products</A>.
```

Notice that I've included the full URL of the document and then I used #COOL-STUFF to mark the anchor point in that document where I want the user to jump. Somewhere on the Zippy products page (http://www.zippy.com/products.html) there must be something like this:

```
The Zippy product line includes lots of <A NAME="COOL-STUFF">cool stuff.</A>
```

If there is no anchor named "COOL-STUFF" in the destination document, the browser will jump to the top of that page. It is okay to put an anchor in an HTML element, such as <H1>The <A HREF="http://www.xyz.com">XYZ Industries</A> Product Line</H1>.

But do not put an HTML element in an anchor, such as <A HREF="http://www.xyz.com"><H1>The XYZ Industries Product Line</H1></A>.

The reason for this is that the HTML specifications prohibit an HTML element placed in an anchor; semantically it doesn't make sense (because an anchor should be a hotspot, not a list, heading, or other element).

Nesting

You can nest lists—for example, these regions of the U.S. and representative states and cities:

```
<UL>
<LI>East
   <OL>
   <LI>New York
       <MENU>
```

```
            <LI>White Plains
            <LI>Latham
            </MENU>
     <LI>Delaware
     </OL>
<LI>Great Lakes
     <OL>
     <LI>Michigan
         <MENU>
         <LI>Troy
         <LI>Escanaba
         </MENU>
     <LI>Wisconsin
     </OL>
<LI>Midwest
<LI>Plains
<LI>West
</UL>
```

But don't try to nest physical or logical character highlights:

```
<B><I>The House of the Seven Gables<I><B> is a great book.
```

The preceding won't necessarily give you bold italics (although some browsers, such as Netscape, now support such an accumulation of character formatting).

Logical Versus Physical Tags

The tags used for character highlights (bold and italics) are either physical or logical. Physical tags define the appearance of the characters, like this:

```
<B>Bold</B>
```

```
<I>Italics</I>
```

```
<U>Underline</U>
```

```
<TT>Fixed width</TT>
```

Logical tags define the meaning of the characters that are highlighted:

```
<STRONG>Strong emphasis, often same as bold</STRONG>
```

```
<VAR>A variable name</VAR>
```

```
<CITE>A citation</CITE>
```

You'll notice that the physical tags go against the HTML and SGML philosophies of marking the meaning and structure rather than the appearance. However, the existence of the physical tags is an acknowledgment that bold, italics, and other forms of character highlights are meaningful in certain contexts. The logical tags provide an alternative means to mark the semantic meaning of the character highlights. For example, the logical tag style uses `<STRONG>...</STRONG>` to indicate emphasis rather than `<B>...</B>`. These logical alternatives help you achieve an appearance-independent HTML file. However, one problem with logical tags is that a tag's appearance might not correspond to the context in which it is used. For example, a

`<CITE>Citation</CITE>` tag is typically rendered in italics. This may be fine for many contexts. However, it may be that citations within your discipline or field of study should always be marked by quotation marks around the cite (short stories or poem titles, for example). Therefore, the logical tags in many cases provide a useful alternative to the physical tags and should be used where possible. But in situations where the rendering of the characters is important—such as where a particular physical style is required—you'll have to use a physical tag.

Nicks and Cuts

Whenever you develop an HTML page, spend some time examining it in several different browsers. Often, particularly when working with links to graphics displayed by Mosaic, you'll find marks and irregularities in the display. One example is a "nick" that can occur when making a logo a hotspot. For example, you may make a logo a hotspot as follows:

```
<A HREF="xyz.html"><IMG SRC="xyz-logo.gif"> </A> XYZ Industries
```

However, some browsers (such as Mosaic) interpret the space between the `<IMG SRC="xyz-logo.gif">` and the end of the anchor, `</A>`, in a way that causes a nick to appear in the display, as shown in Figure 33.16. The nick is a small line between the logo and the label `XYZ Industries`. Taking out the space will remove the nick.

FIGURE 33.16.

A nick in an icon hotspot (magnified).

Similarly, "cuts" can appear under other conditions in specific browsers. For example, if you include a physical tag such as `<I>` within a hotspot, such as `You can find more about this same topic at the <A HREF="#JUMP-TO-NAME">Jump <I>Spot</I></A> later in this document.`

You'll find that some browsers display a cut or discontinuity in the display of the anchor line in `Jump Spot`. While curing all nicks and cuts is not crucial to a successful HTML document (and it actually goes against the philosophy of HTML itself to not worry about a browser display), sometimes fine-tuning your HTML can help make its appearance more pleasing in your target browser. If you find an unusual display in your browser, it might even be an indication that you are misusing some aspect of HTML, and the browser can't determine a satisfactory way to resolve your error.

Weaver's Check

HyperText Markup Language (HTML) is a way to express information and ideas in hypertext. Based on a philosophy of marking up the meaning of a text rather than its appearance, HTML gives you a great deal of flexibility in defining semantic structures in your document but discourages attempts to manipulate the appearance of your text in any particular browser.

HTML itself is written in ASCII text files following a specific format for elements and entities. Head elements identify information about a document such as its title that are not displayed directly in a browser. Body elements such as headings, lists, block quotes, preformatted text, and physical and logical character highlights mark the structure of a document. Graphics elements allow you to imbed inline images in a document. Entities are special characters that you can have displayed in most browsers.

To create HTML files, it's a good idea to make a template to hold the basic tags to mark the head, body, and address parts of a document. Based on this template, you can add headings, paragraphs, lists, and links. You can improve the appearance of an HTML file with horizontal rules and inline images. You can help document an HTML file through comments, the address element, or a revision link in the head of the file.

There are fine points to making anchors, nesting elements, and creating physical and logical tags that can help you in special situations or when you're struggling with the structure of your document. Finally, a careful examination of a document in a variety of browsers can reveal some display anomalies—nicks and cuts—that can be cured by removing spaces or fixing errors in the HTML itself.

We've seen how writing in HTML, although conceptually fairly straightforward, requires a concentration on syntax and fine points that might make it difficult to routinely produce such text. (However, there are tools to assist you in preparing HTML code. See Chapter 35.) Also, you'll find that the basic HTML covered in this chapter doesn't do everything you want. The next chapter provides an overview of advanced features and extensions of HTML (Level 2 and higher).

KEY HTML INFORMATION SOURCES

■ "A Beginner's Guide to HTML," from the National Center for Supercomputing Applications:

`(http://www.ncsa.uiuc.edu/General/Internet/WWW/HTMLPrimer.html)`

■ HTML information from the World Wide Web Consortium:

`(http://www.w3.org/hypertext/WWW/MarkUp/HTML.html)`

- Web Lint forms interface: a service to check your HTML files for faulty syntax or other errors, sponsored by UniPress W3 Services:

  (http://www.unipress.com/web-lint/)

- "WWW Names and Addresses, URIs, URLs, URNs," from the World Wide Web Consortium:

  (http://www.w3.org/hypertext/WWW/Addressing/Addressing.html)

- Drafts of Internet Engineering Task Force:

  Check for information from the HTML working group.

  (http://www.ietf.cnri.reston.va.us/home.html)

- "Quality, Guidelines & Standards for Internet Information Resources," from the Coombs Computing Unit, Research Schools of Social Sciences & Pacific and Asian Studies, The Australian National University:

  (http://coombs.anu.edu.au/SpecialProj/QLTY/QltyHome.html)

Advanced HTML Features

34

by
John December

The basic HTML covered in Chapter 33, "Implementing a Web: Basic HyperText Markup Language (HTML)," constitutes a language set that just about every Web browser will recognize. (Level 0 is mandatory for a Web browser; most browsers will also recognize Level 1 HTML.) Above this "basic HTML," the development of graphical browsers such as Netscape and Mosaic have inspired new features for HTML that extend hypertext in a profound way: by adding features that provide more ways to build interactivity into hypertext. These features include Forms and graphical imagemaps (also sometimes known as graphical information maps), both of which are supported by most modern graphical Web browsers—including current versions of Netscape and Mosaic, but not necessarily other Web browsers. Both Forms and imagemaps are useful for collecting information from users, as well as for implementing new methods of interactive Web-based communication.

This chapter presents an introduction to Forms and imagemaps as well as an overview of Levels 2 and 3 HTML and extensions to HTML. Level 2 HTML includes specifications for Forms.

Techniques, practices, and tools for developing Forms and imagemaps are still under development. For more information, consult the tutorials given in the "Key Resources" section at the end of this chapter. Information for the discussion about Forms and graphical imagemaps in this chapter comes from the following documents:

- "Graphical Information Map Tutorial," from NCSA, originally written by Marc Andreessen (`http://wintermute.ncsa.uiuc.edu:8080/map tutorial/image-maps.html`).
- "The Improved Imagemap Script," from NCSA (`http://hoohoo.ncsa.uiuc.edu/docs/setup/admin/Imagemap.html`).
- "Mosaic for X Fill-Out Form Support" (`http://www.ncsa.uiuc.edu/SDG/Software/Mosaic/Docs/fill-out-forms/overview.html`).

A Quick Introduction to Forms

Forms are features that elicit responses from the user through a graphical user interface consisting of fill-in blanks, buttons, checkboxes, and other features to get input from the user. After the user fills in Form values, the entries can be used by an arbitrary script (a list of commands for a computer to perform) or a separate computer program created by the implementor. In this way, a Form can interface with any other program the implementor designates, such as another database, an accounting program, or a program to handle a user's order for a product.

This section focuses on the HTML aspects of forms, rather than on the implementation of scripts or programs to handle the output. (These scripts and programs vary widely based on the application and the script or program language; see Chapter 30, "Planning a Web.")

The Form Tag

A Form tag is used in an HTML document just like any other element. A Form tag looks like this:

```
<FORM ACTION="URL" METHOD="POST">Form contents</FORM>
```

where URL is the query program or server to which the contents of the fill-in fields of the Form will be sent. METHOD identifies the way in which the contents of the form are sent to the query program. Mosaic documentation suggests always using the form POST because it allows for the form contents to be sent to the query program in a data structure as opposed to being appended to the URL. The Form itself is defined in the area where the words "Form contents" are.

Form contents and the possible tags are described in the following sections.

Tags in a Form

There are a variety of tags that can be used within a Form to provide interfaces for user response. The following description gives a quick narration through popular tags. See the HTML Level 2 tag summary given in the section later in this chapter for more details.

1. **The INPUT tag:** The INPUT tag is the basic way to get input from the user in a variety of situations. These situations include asking for a user's name (when an exhaustive list of possibilities is not desirable) and also when a strict enumeration of user choices is possible (for example, a user's gender). Here's an example input tag that queries the user for a name (using text):

   ```
   <INPUT TYPE="TEXT" SIZE=40 NAME="NAME">
   ```

   An INPUT tag can have various values for TYPE, including the following:

   TEXT (shown previously) is used for any alphanumeric string entry.

   NUMBER causes the input to be read as a number. PASSWORD causes the text to be read as an alphanumeric string but with the characters displayed as stars when entered.

   CHECKBOX enables the user to toggle a single button on or off.

   RADIO enables the user to choose to toggle on exactly one button out of a set of buttons.

   SUBMIT refers to a pushbutton that causes the current Form to be submitted to the query program.

   RESET clears all values that a user might have entered in the Form and sets them to their default settings (a way for the user to start over).

   The SIZE portion of the INPUT tag determines how wide a box or input area is displayed.

The NAME portion of the INPUT tag designates the variable name that will be used in the data structure sent to the query program. This name is then used to pull the value of the user's response from the data structure.

The VALUE field is used to specify default values.

For example:

```
<INPUT TYPE="NUMBER" NAME="quantity1" VALUE="12" SIZE=5>
```
will set the default value for this entry to 12. That is, the user might change this value, but upon entry to the form and after a RESET, the form's value will be set at 12 (and a 12 will be displayed in the input area).

2. **The SELECT tag:** Like the INPUT tag, the SELECT tag is for querying the user for values. The basic structure of a SELECT tag is as follows:

```
<SELECT NAME="select-menu" SIZE=2 MULTIPLE=2>
<OPTION> View the product.
<OPTION> Call for help.
<OPTION> Request a catalog.
<OPTION> Exit this form.
</SELECT>
```

In the SELECT tag, the following conventions apply:

NAME designates the symbolic name for use in the data string submitted to the query program.

SIZE, if missing or set to 1, will make the SELECT tag an option menu (displayed with all the options shown). If SIZE is 2 or more, the number of options indicated by SIZE will be shown in a scrollable list.

MULTIPLE sets the number of options that can be chosen from the list.

3. **The TEXTAREA tag:** This tag is used to allow the user to enter several lines of text. An example TEXTAREA tag is `<TEXTAREA NAME="comments" ROWS=4 COLS=30></TEXTAREA>`.

The attributes of the TEXTAREA tag are the following:

NAME is used to identify the text in the data structure sent to the query (or other) program.

ROWS are the number of vertical rows displayed for user entry.

COLS are the number of horizontal columns displayed for user entry.

A Sample Form

Let's put all this together and construct a sample form.

Here's the HTML code:

```
<HTML>
<HEAD>
<TITLE>Example Order Form</TITLE>
</HEAD>
```

```
<BODY>

<H1>Order Form</H1>

Please fill out the following form.
<P>

<FORM METHOD="POST" ACTION="http://hoohoo.ncsa.uiuc.edu/cgi-bin/post-query">
Your Name: <INPUT TYPE="TEXT"  size=32 NAME="NAME"><BR>
Customer Number: <INPUT TYPE="NUMBER" size=10 name="CUSTOMER-NUMBER"><BR>
<P>

Size?
<INPUT TYPE="radio" name="SIZE"  value="S">S
<INPUT TYPE="radio" name="SIZE"  value="M">M
<INPUT TYPE="radio" name="SIZE"  value="L">L
<INPUT TYPE="radio" name="SIZE"  value="XL">XL<BR>
<P>

<SELECT NAME="select-menu" SIZE=2 MULTIPLE=2>
<OPTION> View the product.
<OPTION> Call for help.
<OPTION> Request a catalog.
<OPTION> Exit this form.
</SELECT>
<P>

<TEXTAREA NAME="comments" ROWS=4 COLS=30></TEXTAREA>
<P>

<INPUT TYPE=submit value="Order Product">
<P>

<INPUT TYPE=reset  value="Cancel Order">
</FORM>
<P>

</BODY>
</HTML>
```

Figure 34.1 shows the appearance of this Form.

When the Form is filled in by the user and the user presses the SUBMIT button ("Order Product"), the results are sent to the demonstration query program (at http://hoohoo.ncsa.uiuc.edu/ cgi-bin/post-query). The results are shown in Figure 34.2. This test server is provided by NCSA developers to echo the data structure submitted by a POST query. The developer could develop his or her own program that would use the Form values in some other way.

FIGURE 34.1.

A filled-in Form.

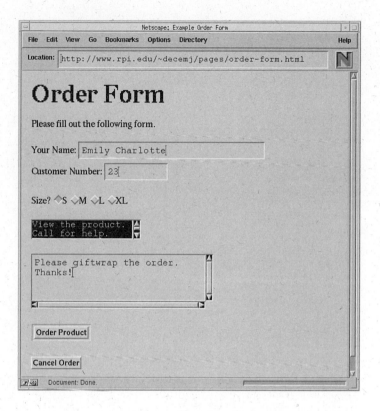

FIGURE 34.2.

Form results.

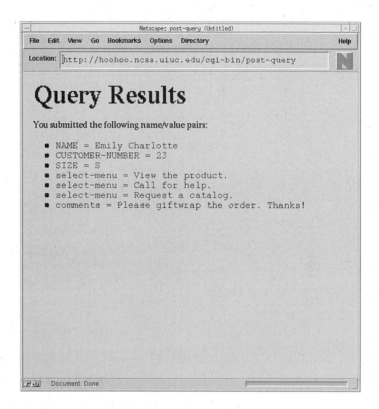

Another Form Example: A Survey

The following Form example illustrates most of the popular Form elements. Instead of sending its output to an "echo" program, this example illustrates a popular application of a Form as a survey instrument. The HTML code is shown here. The Action attribute of the FORM element is a program that echoes the status of each form element sent to the address defined in the "address" input variable. Notice how the "address" and "subject" input variables are hidden, and they have fixed values as set in the Form; no user input changes affect the Form:

```
<HTML>
<!-- Level 2 HTML Form Example -->
<HEAD>
    <TITLE>LEVEL 2 HTML Form Example--User Survey</TITLE>
    <BASE Href="http://www.rpi.edu/~decemj/pages/form.html">
</HEAD>
<BODY>

Please complete this user survey.

<HR>
```

```
<FORM Method="POST"
     Action="http://madoka.its.rpi.edu/cgi-bin/mailform">

     <INPUT Type=hidden Name="address" Value="decemj@rpi.edu">
     <INPUT Type=hidden Name="subject" Value="Level 2 HTML Form response">

     Your age in years:
        <INPUT Type=text Name="user-age" Size="2">

     Your gender:
        <INPUT Type=radio Name="user-gender" Value="male">Male
        <INPUT Type=radio Name="user-gender" Value="female">Female
        <BR>

     Check all the names of the people listed whom you have heard about or know:<BR>
        <INPUT Type=checkbox Name="user-knows" Value="Marc Andreesen">Marc Andreesen
        <INPUT Type=checkbox Name="user-knows" Value="Lisa Schmeiser">Lisa Schmeiser
        <INPUT Type=checkbox Name="user-knows" Value="Al Gore">Al Gore
        <INPUT Type=checkbox Name="user-knows" Value="Boutros Boutros Ghali">Boutros
        Boutros-Ghali
        <BR>

     What is your favorite Web browser?
     <SELECT Name="favorite-web-browser">
        <OPTION>Arena
        <OPTION>Cello
        <OPTION>Chimera
        <OPTION>Lynx
        <OPTION>MacWeb
        <OPTION>Mosaic
        <OPTION Selected>Netscape
        <OPTION>SlipKnot
        <OPTION>Viola
        <OPTION>Web Explorer
        <OPTION>None of the above
        </SELECT><BR>

     Guess the secret password: <INPUT Type=password Name="user-password"><BR>

     Enter your personal motto:<BR>
     <TEXTAREA Name=user-motto rows=2 cols=40></textarea><BR>

     When you are done with the above responses, please submit this form
     by clicking on your current geographic location on this map:<BR>

     <INPUT Type=image Src="http://www.rpi.edu/~decemj/images/world.gif"
            Name="user-image-location" Align=bottom><BR>

     <INPUT Type=submit Value="Send this survey">

     <INPUT Type=reset  Value="Cancel this survey">

</FORM>

Thank you!
<HR>
```

```
<ADDRESS>
<a href="http://www.rpi.edu/~decemj/index.html">John December</a> (<a
 href="mailto:decemj@rpi.edu">decemj@rpi.edu</a>)
/ 17 Mar 95
</ADDRESS>

</BODY>
</HTML>
```

Figure 34.3 shows the Form itself filled out as an example. Notice how the graphic image acts as the Send key for this Form. If the user does click on the Send This Survey button, the geographic coordinates will not show up.

FIGURE 34.3.

Survey Form filled out.

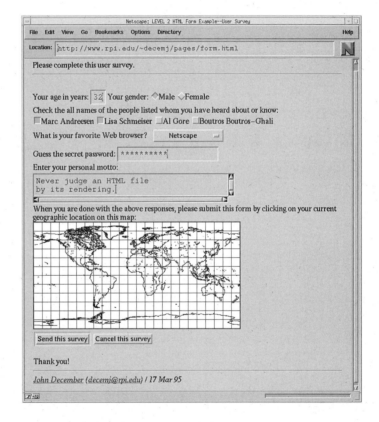

The results of the Form as an e-mail message are shown in Figure 34.4. Notice how the sender is totally anonymous. I know that the message I received is one from the Form because it has the fixed title "Level 2 HTML Form response."

Each variable in the Form is repeated on a separate line with its setting on the line below. The map coordinates are given in pixels from the upper-left corner of the image: 143 pixels across from the left side of the image, and 64 pixels down from the top of the image.

I could use this information to get a geographic breakdown of my user base.

FIGURE 34.4.

*Survey Form results
as e-mail.*

```
─                          xterm
~ (66) m
Mail version UCB 5.5.1 Fri May  7 16:16:55 EDT 1993.  Type ? for help.
"/tmp/mail.decemj": 1 message 1 new
>N  1 nobody                Wed Mar 22 01:58  29/780   "Level 2 HTML Form res"
& t
Message 1:
From nobody Wed Mar 22 01:58:18 1995
From: "Sun's nobody" <nobody>
Date: Wed, 22 Mar 1995 01:59:51 -0500
Message-Id: <199503220659.BAA24639@madoka.its.rpi.edu>
To: decemj@rpi.edu
Subject: Level 2 HTML Form response

user-age:
32
user-gender:
male
user-knows:
Marc Andreesen
user-knows:
Lisa Schmeiser
favorite-web-browser:
Netscape
user-password:
fishheaven
user-motto:
Never judge an HTML file
by its rendering.
user-image-location.x:
143
user-image-location.y:
64

& []
```

A Quick Introduction to Imagemaps

Just as HTML Forms are a way to elicit input from the user, so too are graphical information
maps (imagemaps). While Forms provide a template for information that the user fills in, the
graphical imagemap is a way for a user to respond through graphics. Essentially, a graphical
imagemap provides a way for any part of an arbitrary image (in a graphics file) to be linked to a
set of URLs. A common application is in point-and-click maps (Figure 34.5) that enable you to
find out information about a particular area or building.

Because every pixel on an imagemap can be a link, you can create very rich and intricate interfaces to information using imagemaps.

To use a graphical imagemap, you must have several elements in place that might require the
same technical skills employed in setting up the Web server itself. You must have the following:

1. An HTTP server installed and operating.
2. Write privileges to the conf/imagemap.conf file. (The server administrator would have to
   give you these permissions if you aren't the server administrator yourself.) For security
   reasons, users aren't often allowed access to this file. See the workaround illustrated in
   the "My world" imagemap example shown below.
3. The "imagemap" program compiled in the cgi-bin directory of the server. (See http://
   hoohoo.ncsa.uiuc.edu/docs/Overview.html.)

FIGURE 34.5.

A clickable campus map.

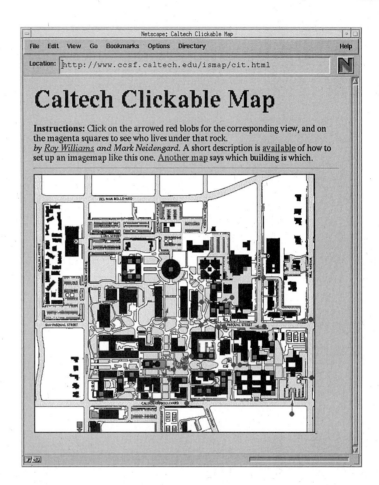

Once these elements are in place, the steps are as follows:

1. Create an image. There are a variety of drawing and painting tools available. A typical extension for the image file is Graphical Interchange Format (GIF). Other inline-image formats include JPEG, xbm, and xpm. For example, your image file might be info.gif.

INTERLACED AND TRANSPARENT GIFS

You can use the technique of creating interlaced GIFs in imagemaps (or any other GIF graphics that you make) to create a different download pattern for your graphics. An interlaced GIF file will appear first in "rough" Form and then get clearer as the rest of the image is downloaded. Interlaced GIFs thus help your users see a big picture faster, rather than having to wait for the entire graphic to download in a falling curtain.

Another effect is the transparent GIF, where a designated background in the GIF image disappears into the background color of the browser window.

You can obtain the source code for the shareware program GIFTOOL from Home Pages, Inc., at `http://www.homepages.com/tools/` to create interlaced (as well as transparent) GIF images.

You can find a collection of images to use in imagemaps at `http://www.yahoo.com/Computers/Multimedia/Pictures/`.

2. Create an imagemap file. This file specifies what URL will be opened as a result of a user clicking on a region of your image.

   The general format of this imagemap file is as follows:

   ```
   default default-URL

   rect URL UL-corner LR-corner

   poly URL POINT1 POINT2 POINT3 .... POINTN
   ```

   where `default-URL` is the resource that is opened if the user clicks any region not designated in one of the other lines of the file.

   The keyword `rect` identifies each line as a rectangle. The URL after `rect` is the resource that will be opened if the user clicks the image in the rectangle bounded by the upper left corner (`UL-corner`) coordinates (given in x,y pairs in pixels) and the lower-right (`LR-corner`) coordinates.

   The keyword `poly` identifies a polygon; using this you can trace around areas on your image that you want to associate with a particular URL.

   Note: You can quickly find the pixel coordinates on an image by using the xv viewing program or some similar graphics program on your computer.

3. Put a line in the `conf/imagemap.conf` file like the following:

   ```
   infomap:/yourhome/yourdirectory/info.map
   ```

   `infomap` is the symbolic name recognized by the server as the name of your map. After this name, the full pathname of your imagemap file (relative to the `conf/imagemap.conf` file) is given.

4. Add a reference to your map in an HTML file, for example:

   ```
   For more information, click on part of the image below:
   <A HREF="http://yourhost.domain/cgi-bin/imagemap/infomap">
   <IMG SRC="info.gif" ALT="IMAGE MAP" ISMAP></A>
   ```

A Sample Imagemap: *myworld*

Let's put together a sample imagemap using the particular situation on my system.

Since I'm just a user (not an administrator) on the computer system I use, I don't have access to the conf/imagemap.conf file of the server.

The webmasters for my system, however, have provided a way for me to create and use imagemaps by providing a remote image "link" script on a server on our system. The resulting arrangement is very similar (from an imagemap author's perspective) to the preceding scheme, and it is completely the same for people using the resulting imagemap.

Here's how I create my imagemap (using a Sun workstation):

1. I use a drawing program, xpaint, to create an image, called myworld.gif (Figure 34.6). For this imagemap, my goal is to create a graphical version of some information from my home page, linking images (instead of links) to resources or information I've created. I use the clipboard feature of the xpaint drawing program to import existing graphics and other icons from my works into my imagemap picture. I put this image file, called myworld.gif, in my images subdirectory. I use the GIFTOOL program (described previously) to interlace this image.

FIGURE 34.6.

The "my world" image.

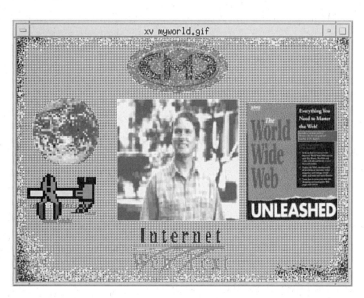

2. Using the xv program, I determine the boundary points for the regions of my picture. After each region, I list the URL corresponding to the image regions:

```
default http://www.rpi.edu/~decemj/index.html
rect http://www.rpi.edu/~decemj/works/wwwu.html 294,82 413,255
rect http://www.rpi.edu/~decemj/cmc/center.html 125,5 280,70
rect http://www.rpi.edu/Internet/Guides/decemj/icmc/top.html 10,71 111,158
```

```
rect http://www.rpi.edu/Internet/Guides/decemj/itools/top.html 10,159, 112,237
rect http://www.rpi.edu/Internet/Guides/decemj/text.html 129,231, 282,298
rect http://www.rpi.edu/~decemj/pages/jd.html 130,78 283,224
poly http://www.rpi.edu/~decemj/sound/beverage.au 1,240 46,277, 35,287 72,303
1,303
```

Note that I don't necessarily have to link these graphical regions to another HTML page. In the last line, I've created a "secret" place on my imagemap, corresponding to the lower-left corner of the picture, which links the user to a sound file.

I call this map file `myworld.map`, and I put it in my maps subdirectory.

3. I create an HTML file that will be the page that serves my imagemap to users. This page will refer to the two main pieces I've created in steps 1 and 2: the picture for the imagemap (`myworld.gif`) and the map file (`myworld.map`).

In this HTML file, I use standard header and footer information. The key line, however, is the anchor of the following form:

```
<A Href="MAP"><IMG Src="GIF" Ismap></A>
```

In this anchor, *MAP* is the URL that connects the special server "imagemap gateway" to my mapping file (`myworld.map`), and *GIF* is the URL of my picture (`myworld.gif`). Here's the HTML file:

```
<IITML>
<HEAD>
   <TITLE>John December World Map</TITLE>
   <LINK REV=made HREF="mailto:decemj@rpi.edu">
</HEAD>
<BODY>
<HR>
<A Href="http://madoka.its.rpi.edu/cgi
-bin/remoteimage/~decemj/public_html/maps/myworld.map">
<IMG Src="http://www.rpi.edu/~decemj/images/myworld.gif"
Ismap></A>
<P>
<HR>
<address> <a href="http://www.rpi.edu/~decemj/index.html">John December</a>
(<a href="mailto:decemj@rpi.edu">decemj@rpi.edu</a>) / 17 Mar 1995</address>
</BODY>
</HTML>
```

I name this HTML file `myworld.html`, and I place it in my pages subdirectory.

4. I test it out my imagemap by opening the URL of my imagemap page at `http://www.rpi.edu/~decemj/pages/myworld.html`. Figure 34.7 shows the result. I test out each of the main links corresponding to the visual cues in the imagemap as well as the "secret" sound in the lower-left corner of the picture.

FIGURE 34.7.

The "my world" imagemap.

HTML Tag Summaries

Level 2 HTML

Now that we've explored imagemaps, let's look in detail at their specification in a Level 2 HTML Tag summary. The following is the HTML source; Figures 34.8 through 34.12 show the rendering of this in a browser.

```
<HTML>
<!-- Level 2 HTML additions -->
<!-- Features (Forms) that not all browsers may recognize. -->
<HEAD>
    <TITLE>Level 2 HTML Tag Summary</TITLE>
    <BASE Href="http://www.rpi.edu/~decemj/pages/level2.html">
</HEAD>
<BODY>
<I>HTML Tag Summary:
    <A Href="level0.html">Level 0</A> /
    <A Href="level1.html">Level 1</A> /
    <B>Level 2</B> /
    <A Href="level3.html">Level 3</A> /
    <A Href="levele.html">Extensions</A>
    </I>
<HR>

<H1>Level 2 HTML Tag Summary</H1>

A Level 2 HTML document can include the following elements
and attributes in addition to <a href="level0.html">Level 0</a> and
<a href="level1.html">Level 1</a> elements and entities.
```

In this document, the elements are listed in all capital letters;
the attributes are indicated by initial capital letters.
In order to benefit from the information in this file, view both
its HTML source as well as its rendered form in a Web browser.
The tags are explained in the list below as well as demonstrated in this
file.

<H2>HTML structure and comment elements</H2>

Level 2 specifies no additions in this category over
<A Href="level0.html#Structure">Level 0's structure features</A>.

<H2>The HEAD and related elements</H2>

Level 2 specifies no additions in this category over
<A Href="level1.html#Head">Level 1's head features</A>.

<H2>The BODY and related elements</H2>

<H3>Forms</H3>

Forms are used to present an interface consisting of fill-in-the
blank boxes, checklists, radiobuttons, or other features to
gather input from a user.   The FORM element brackets
an input data form; the elements INPUT, SELECT, OPTION,
and TEXTAREA are used to set up areas within the Form for input.
Here is a <A Href="form.html">sample form</A> that illustrates
these elements and attributes.

<UL>

<LI>FORM: delimits the start and end of a data input form.
    Forms can't be nested although there may be several
    in each document.

    Attributes:
    <UL>
    <LI>Action: This attribute specifies the URL of the
        program or script which accepts the contents of
        the form for processing.

    <LI>Method: this attribute indicates the variation in
        the Forms-handling protocol which will be used.
        A popular method is POST.
    </UL>

<LI>INPUT: This element is used for collecting information
    from the user.

    Attributes:
    <UL>
    <LI>Align: This attribute is used only with the image
        Type (see list below). Possible values are
        "top," "middle," and "bottom," and define the
        relationship of the image to the text following it.

```
<LI>Maxlength: this attribute sets a maximum number
    of characters that can be entered in the
    field.

<LI>Name: this is the symbolic name that is used in
    transferring the output from the Form.

<LI>Size: specifies the field width as displayed to
    the user.

<LI>Src: Used to define the source file for the
    image used with Type image.

<LI>Type:
  <UL>
  <LI>checkbox: This is used for gathering data that
      can have multiple values at a time.

  <LI>hidden: This is for values that are set by the
      form without input from the user.

  <LI>image: An image field can be used in submitting the Form:
      when the user clicks on the image, the Form is submitted,
      and the x and y coordinates of the click are transmitted.

  <LI>password: This is a field in which the user enters text,
      but the text is not displayed (could appear as stars).

  <LI>radio: Used to collect information where there
      is one and only one possible value from a set of
      alternatives.

  <LI>reset:  This is used to reset and clear the Form.

  <LI>submit:  This button is used to submit the Form.

  <LI>text:  This is used for a single line of
      text; this uses the Size and Maxlength
      attributes.  For multiple lines, use TEXTAREA (below).
  </UL>

<LI>Value: This sets the initial displayed value of the field
    or the value of the field when it is selected (the radio
    button type must have this attribute set).

</UL>

<LI>SELECT: this element allows a user to choose
one of a set of alternatives.  The OPTION element is used
to define each alternative.<BR>

  Attributes:
  <UL>

  <LI>Name: The logical name that will be submitted and associated
      with the data as a result of the user choosing select.
```

```
        <LI>Multiple: By default, the user can only make one selection
            from the group in the SELECT element.  By using the
            Multiple attribute, the user may select one or
            more of the OPTIONs.

        <LI>Size: specifies the number of visible items.
            If this is more than one, the visual display will be
            a list.

        </UL>

<LI>OPTION:  This element occurs only within the SELECT element (above) and
    is used to represent each choice of the SELECT.<BR>

    Attributes:
    <UL>
    <LI>Selected: indicates that this option is initially
        selected
    <LI>Value: If present, this is the value that will be returned
        by the SELECT if this option is chosen; otherwise,
        the value returned is that set by the OPTION element.
    </UL>

<LI>TEXTAREA: This element is used to collect multiple lines
    of text from the user; the user is presented with a scrollable
    pane in which text can be written.<BR>

    Attributes:
    <UL>

    <LI>Name: The logical name that will be associated with the
        returned text.

    <LI>Rows: The number of rows that will be displayed (note
        the user can use more rows and scroll down to them).

    <LI>Cols: The number of columns that will be displayed
        (the user can use the scrollbar to move through more
        columns if written).

    </UL>
</UL>

Copyright &#169 1995 by John December.  All rights reserved.
<HR>

<ADDRESS>
<a href="http://www.rpi.edu/~decemj/index.html">John December</a>
(<a href="mailto:decemj@rpi.edu">decemj@rpi.edu</a>) / 14 Mar 95
</ADDRESS>

</BODY>
</HTML>
```

FIGURE 34.8.

*Level 2 HTML Tag
Summary (page 1).*

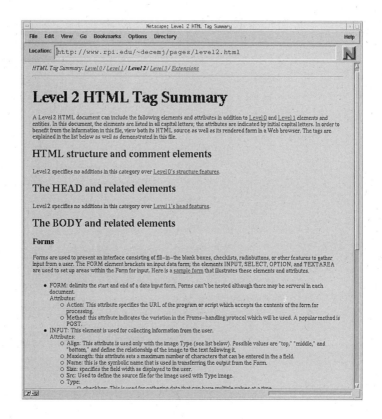

FIGURE 34.9.

Level 2 HTML Tag Summary (page 2).

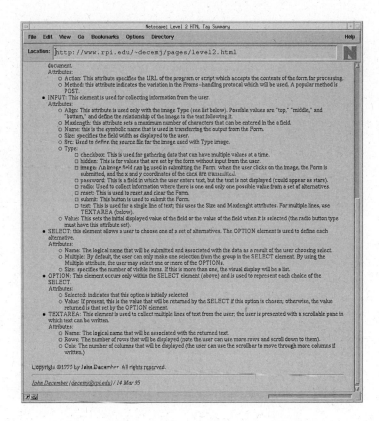

Level 3 HTML

```
<HTML>
<!-- Level 3 HTML additions summary -->
<!-- Main additions: more LINK Rel attribute values; tables;
     mathematical expressions -->
<HEAD>
    <TITLE>Level 3 HTML Tag Summary</TITLE>
    <BASE Href="http://www.rpi.edu/~decemj/pages/level3.html">
    <LINK Href="http://www.rpi.edu/~decemj/pages/level2.html" Rel="Previous">
    <LINK Href="http://www.rpi.edu/~decemj/pages/levele.html" Rel="Next">
</HEAD>
<BODY>
<I>HTML Tag Summary:
    <A Href="level0.html">Level 0</A> /
    <A Href="level1.html">Level 1</A> /
    <A Href="level2.html">Level 2</A> /
    <B>Level 3</B> /
    <A Href="levele.html">Extensions</A>
    </I>
<HR>

<H1>Level 3 HTML Tag Summary</H1>
```

The specification of Level 3 HTML is still largely in development, so
this document should be considered a brief <EM>glance at what may come</EM>
for HTML Level 3. Only a selection of the current proposed elements are
shown here; and not all attributes of each are shown. <P>

When completely defined, the Level 3 specifications will be additions over
the <a href="level0.html">Level 0</a>, <a href="level1.html">Level 1</a>,
and <a href="level2.html">Level 2</a> elements. In this document, the
Level 3 elements listed are in all capital letters; the attributes are
indicated by initial capital letters. In order to benefit from the
information in this file, view both its HTML source as well as its
rendered form in a Web browser. The tags are explained in the list
below as well as demonstrated in this file. <P>

For more information, see
<a href="http://www.hpl.hp.co.uk/people/dsr/html/CoverPage.html">HyperText
Markup Language Specification Version 3.0</a> or
<a href="http://www.w3.org/hypertext/WWW/Arena/tour/start.html">The HTML
3.0 Hypertext Document Format</A>.

<H2>HTML structure and comment elements</H2>

Level 3 specifies no additions over <A Href="level0.html">Level 0</A>,
<A Href="level1.html">Level 1</A>, or <A Href="level2.html">Level 2</A>.

<H2>The HEAD and related elements</H2>

<UL>
<LI>LINK:
    Extensions to the Rel attribute; Rel can be used to define a
    series of values for browser toolbar or other buttons:
    <UL>
    <LI>Rel = Home; defines the home page link relative to this document
    <LI>Rel = ToC; table of contents link
    <LI>Rel = Index; an index
    <LI>Rel = Glossary; the glossary of terms
    <LI>Rel = Copyright; the copyright statement
    <LI>Rel = Up; the parent document
    <LI>Rel = Next; the next document to visit in a "tour"
    <LI>Rel = Previous; the previous document in a "tour"
    <LI>Rel = Help; a link to a help document or service
    <LI>Rel = Bookmark; a link to a list of key links for the document
    <LI>Rel = StyleSheet; a stylesheet to control the rendering
               of the current document
    </UL>

<LI>STYLE: This element provides a way for the author of a document to
    define rendering information which will override client defaults
    and LINKed style sheets. Its one attribute, Notation,
    specifies an entity identifying an SGML description of the style.

</UL>

<h2>The BODY and related elements</H2>

<UL>

<LI>most BODY elements can use these attributes:

```
    <UL>

    <LI>Id: an SGML identifier used for naming parts of the document
        in style sheets; also can be used as the target for a hypertext
        link; Id values must be unique within a document.

    <LI>Lang: An ISO (International Organization for Standardization)
        abbreviation for the human language used in
        the text (e.g., "en.uk" for English as spoken in the United
        Kingdom).  The first part of the code is the language as
        defined in ISO 639.  The second part of the code is the two-letter
        country code from ISO 3166.  This can be used by browsers to
        select from among a variety of choices for the document.

    <LI>Class: This attribute defines an element as a particular
        kind of text sequence that can be then used in style sheets.
        The class designation can also be used in searching.

    <LI>Background: This attribute can specify the image tile to
        appear in the document background.

    </UL>

<LI>BODY elements:

    <UL>
    <LI>DIV: used with the Class attribute to represent containers, or
        sections, of a document.  For example, the Banner should
        be rendered in a browser so that it is always "on screen":<BR>

        &lt;DIV CLASS=Banner&gt;Company Confidential--do not disseminate&lt;/DIV&gt;

    <LI>TAB: used to control horizontal positioning.  Attribute
        "Id" to define a tabstop; attribute "To" to move to a
        tabstop:
        <PRE>
        This is the stop &lt;TAB Id=T1&gt; where the tab &lt;BR&gt;
        &lt;TAB To=T1&gt;will move the text.
        </PRE>
        rendered as:
        <PRE>
        This is the stop where the tab
                        will move the text.
        </PRE>

    <LI>A: anchors: more attributes:
        <UL>
        <LI>Md: specifies a message digest (cryptographic checksum)
            for document defined by Href.
        <LI>Shape: used within figures to define regions corresponding
            to a link to the document defined by Href.
        </UL>

    <LI>information typing elements
        <UL>
        <LI>DFN: the defining instance of a term
        <LI>Q: a short quotation
        <LI>LANG: the (human) language currently defined
        <LI>AU: the name of an author
```

```
        <LI>PERSON: names of people
        <LI>ACRONYM: acronyms in the document
        <LI>INS: inserted text (e.g., when documents are amended)
        <LI>DEL: deleted text (e.g., when documents are amended)
        </UL>

    <LI>font style elements
        <UL>
        <LI>BIG: big print relative to current font
        <LI>SMALL: smaller print relative to current font
        <LI>SUB: a subscript
        <LI>SUP: a superscript
        </UL>

    <LI>FIG: used to define figures with captions; example:
        <PRE>
        &lt;FIG Href="map.gif"&gt;
            &lt;CAPTION&gt;Map to My House&lt;/CAPTION&gt;
            &lt;CREDIT&gt;C. B. Boese&lt;/CREDIT&gt;
        &lt;/FIG&gt;
        </PRE>

    <LI>TABLE: used to define tables; example:
        <PRE>
        &lt;TABLE Border&gt;
            &lt;CAPTION&gt;August Standings&lt;/CAPTION&gt;
            &lt;TR&gt;&lt;TH ROWSPAN=2&gt;&lt;TH COLSPAN=2&gt;Totals
            &lt;TR&gt;&lt;TH&gt;Wins&lt;TH&gt;Losses
            &lt;TR&gt;&lt;TH ALIGN=LEFT&gt;White Sox&lt;TD&gt;22&lt;TD&gt;55
            &lt;TR&gt;&lt;TH ALIGN=LEFT&gt;Tigers&lt;TD&gt;84&lt;TD&gt;8
        &lt;/TABLE&gt;
        </PRE>

        Would be rendered, for example:

        <PRE>
                    August Standings
            /-------------------------------\
            |             |       Totals     |
            |             |------------------|
            |             | Wins  | Losses|
            |-------------------------------|
            | White Sox |  22   |   55   |
            |-------------------------------|
            | Tigers    |  84   |    8   |
            \-------------------------------/

        </PRE>

    <LI>MATH: to represent mathematical expressions.  For
        example, the integral from a to b of f(x):
        <PRE>
            &lt;MATH&gt;&int;_a_^b^{f(x)} dx&lt;/MATH&gt;
        </PRE>


    </UL>

</UL>
```

FIGURE 34.10.

*Level 3 HTML Tag
Summary (page 1).*

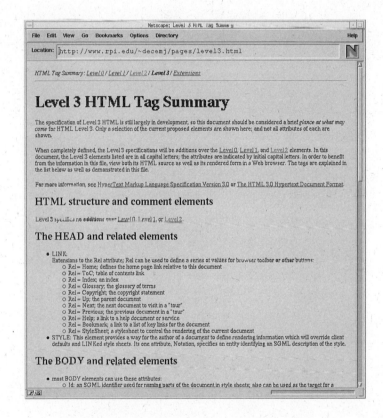

FIGURE 34.11.

Level 3 HTML Tag Summary (page 2).

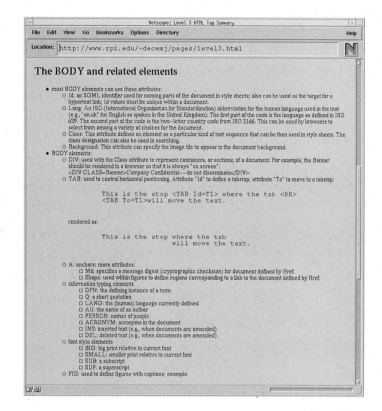

Weaving a Web

Part V

FIGURE 34.12.
Level 3 HTML Tag Summary (page 3).

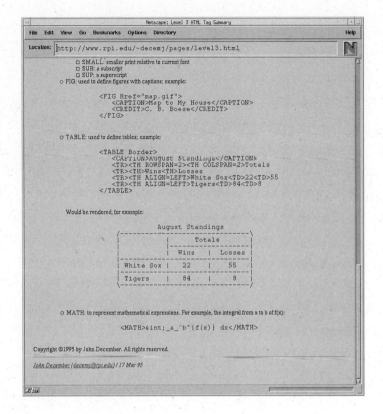

Extensions to HTML: Netscape

```
<HTML>
<!-- HTML extensions from Netscape -->
<!-- Features such as BLINK, font changes, CENTER, etc,
     that not all browsers may recognize. -->
<HEAD>
    <TITLE>HTML Extensions Tag Summary--Netscape</TITLE>
    <BASE Href="http://www.rpi.edu/~decemj/pages/levele.html">
</HEAD>
<BODY>
<I>HTML Tag Summary:
    <A Href="level0.html">Level 0</A> /
    <A Href="level1.html">Level 1</A> /
    <A Href="level2.html">Level 2</A> /
    <A Href="level3.html">Level 3</A> /
    <B>Extensions</B>
    </I>
<HR>

<H1>HTML Extensions Tag Summary</H1>

This list summarizes the extensions
```

```
<A Href="http://www.netscape.com/">Netscape</A> has made
to HTML.   <P>

The elements shown here are in all capital letters;
the attributes are indicated by initial capital letters.
In order to benefit from the information in this file, view both
its HTML source as well as its rendered form in a Web browser.
The tags are explained in the list below as well as demonstrated in this
file. <P>

For more information, see
<A Href="http://www.netscape.com/home/services_docs/html-extensions.html">
Netscape Navigator Extensions to HTML</a>

<H2>HTML structure and comment elements</H2>

Netscape makes none over <A Href="level0.html">Level 0</a> HTML.

<H2>The HEAD and related elements</H2>

Netscape adds:

<UL>
    <LI>ISINDEX attribute Prompt to specify the message a
        user sees for a searchable index.  Example:
        Prompt="Enter keyword(s)."
</UL>

<H2>The BODY and related elements</H2>

<UL>
<LI>HR: attributes added:
    <UL>

    <LI>Size=number: how think the line should be.   Example:
                    <HR Size=5>

    <LI>Width=number¦percent: the width of the line, either
        expressed as width in pixels (number) or a relative
        width as a percent of the current display width
        (not page width, see this example). Example:
                    <HR Width= 33%>

    <LI>Align=left¦right¦center: the alignment of horizontal
        lines that are less than the full width of the page.
        Example:
                    <HR Width= 10% Align=Right>

    <LI>Noshade: turns off shading to create a solid bar.
    </UL>

<LI>UL: attribute added:
    <UL Type=square>
    <LI>Type=disc¦circle¦square
    </UL>

<LI>OL: attribute added:
    <OL Type=I>
```

```
      <LI>Type=A¦a¦I¦i¦1: A = capital letters; a = small letters; I = capital
         roman numerals;  1 = numbers (default)
      </OL>

<LI>LI: attribute added:
   Unordered list:
   <UL>
   <LI Type=disc>Type=disc
   <LI Type=circle>Type=circle
   <LI Type=square>Type=square
   </UL>
   Ordered list:
   <OL>
   <LI Type=A>Type=A
   <LI Type=a>Type=a
   <LI Type=I>Type=I
   <LI Type=i>Type=i
   <LI Type=1>Type=1
   </OL>

<LI>OL(LI): attribute added:
   <OL>
   <LI Value=6>Value: changes the displayed value for the list item
   </OL>

<LI>IMG: attributes added:
   <UL>
   <LI>Align=left¦right¦top¦texttop¦middle¦absmiddle¦baseline¦bottom¦absbottom

      Examples:

      <IMG Src="http://www.rpi.edu/~decemj/images/stats.gif" Align=left>
      left aligned image
      <BR Clear=left>

      <IMG Src="http://www.rpi.edu/~decemj/images/stats.gif" Align=right>
      right aligned image
      <BR Clear=right>


   <LI>Width=value Height=value; width and height of the image in
      pixels; speeds up processing if given

   <LI>Border=value; thickness of the border around images

   <LI>Vspace=value; Hspace=value; controls the blank space
      above and below (Vspace) and to the left and right (Hspace)
      of an image
   </UL>

<LI>BR: attribute added:
   <UL>
   <LI>Clear=left¦right¦all: used in conjunction with image placement (see
      examples above) to flush text to clear the left or right (or both)
      margins

   </UL>

<LI>NOBR: (NO BReak).
   <NOBR>All text placed between the start and end of the NOBR
```

```
       element will not have line breaks inserted. </NOBR>

<LI>WBR: (Word BReak)
       <NOBR>Within a NOBR element, you can define where a line break <WBR> should
       be made</NOBR>.  Outside of the NOBR element, <WBR>WBR is a hint,
       (use BR to force a linebreak).

<LI>FONT Size:
         <FONT Size="1">Y</FONT><FONT Size="2">o</FONT><FONT Size="3">u</FONT>

         <FONT Size="4">c</FONT><FONT Size="5">a</FONT><FONT Size="6">n</FONT>

         <FONT Size="7">c</FONT><FONT Size="6">h</FONT><FONT Size="5">a</FONT>
         <FONT Size="4">n</FONT><FONT Size="3">g</FONT><FONT Size="2">e</FONT>

         <FONT Size="1">t</FONT>
         the font size in sizes from 1-7 or
         <FONT Size="+1">u</FONT><FONT Size="+2">s</FONT><FONT Size="+3">e</FONT>

         <FONT Size="+4">+</FONT>

         <FONT Size="+5">o</FONT><FONT Size="+6">r</FONT>

         <FONT Size="-1">-</FONT>

         <FONT Size="-2">t</FONT><FONT Size="-3">o</FONT>

         <FONT Size="-4">c</FONT><FONT Size="-5">h</FONT>
         <FONT Size="-6">a</FONT><FONT Size="-7">n</FONT>ge relative
         to the current base size (default 3).

<LI>BASEFONT SIZE: changes the current base font size (default of
       3 to another size in the range 1-7.

<LI>Font accumulations of attributes:<BR>
         <I>Italic font can accumulate <TT>typewriter and <B>bold</B></TT></I><BR>
         Compare that to: <I>italic,</I> <TT>typewriter</TT>, and <B>bold</B>.

<LI>CENTER: <CENTER>centers text</CENTER>

<LI>BLINK: <BLINK>creates blinking text</BLINK>

<LI>entities:<BR>
       <UL>
       <LI>&amp;reg = &reg (Registration mark)<BR>
       <LI>&amp;copy = &copy (Copyright mark)
       </UL>

</UL>

Copyright &#169 1995 by John December.  All rights reserved.
<HR>

<ADDRESS>
<a href="http://www.rpi.edu/~decemj/index.html">John December</a>
(<a href="mailto:decemj@rpi.edu">decemj@rpi.edu</a>) / 14 Mar 95
</ADDRESS>

</BODY>
</HTML>
```

FIGURE 34.13.

*HTML Netscape Extensions
Tag Summary (page 1).*

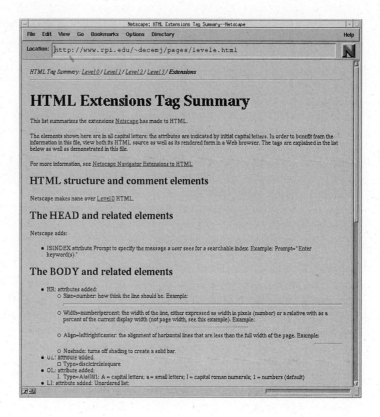

FIGURE 34.14.

HTML Netscape Extensions Tag Summary (page 2).

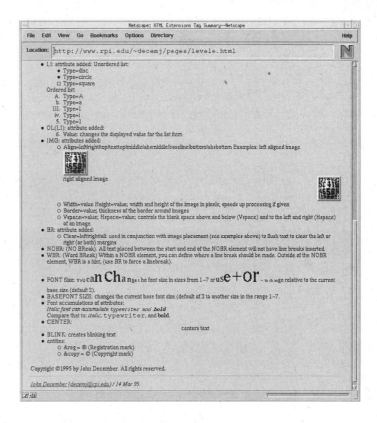

950

Weaver's Check

Some features that graphical Web browsers can access are not available to other Web browsers, but they provide very useful methods for interacting with users. The Forms interface allows the developer to create a Form—complete with checkboxes, fill-in slots, scrollable text entry, and other features. Once the user enters data and clicks the feature designated as the SUBMIT button, the values in the Form are sent to a query (or other) program created by the developer.

Graphical imagemaps are another way to get information from a user. Instead of the static template that a Forms interface presents, a graphical imagemap allows the developer to map any geometric region of an inline image to a particular URL. In this way, graphical imagemaps help developers create user-friendly, point-and-click interfaces.

KEY RESOURCES

- Cyberweb, a resource collection for Web information providers and users (`http://www.charm.net/~web/`)

- "MapMarker [a tool for clickable imagemaps] Home Page," by Peter Murray-Rust (`http://www.dl.ac.uk/CBMT/mapmarker/HOME.html`)

- NCSA Mosaic Tutorials (`http://www.ncsa.uiuc.edu/SDG/Software/Mosaic/Docs/mosaic-docs.html`)

- Yahoo-HTML section (`http://www.yahoo.com/Computers/World_Wide_Web/HTML/`)

Gateway Interface Programming

35

by
John December
and Laura Lemay

The *Common Gateway Interface* (CGI) is the key to connecting the Web with other software and databases. CGI—true to its name—is a *gateway* (to databases, programs, executable files, scripts, and so on). With CGI, you can enable a user to look up items in a database, execute a program, or exchange information through an interface with other software.

This chapter covers the basics of CGI, providing you with an overview of the concepts involved, specific programming practices, some examples, and a list of pointers to further information that can be found online. Developments and techniques in the area of CGI have developed relatively recently. This chapter should give you an overview of the concepts necessary to understand CGI and develop some basic knowledge of it. With this foundation you can look at how your particular server supports CGI and use online information to brush up on the most current techniques and practices.

Because gateway programming as it applies to the Web has evolved its practices from UNIX-based versions of CERN and NCSA Web servers, this chapter heavily reflects this bias (and also includes some UNIX and Perl scripts in examples).

TERMINOLOGY

A *script* is a file of commands that, when run from an operating system prompt, are executed. Scripts for UNIX include C-shell, Korn shell, and Bourne shell, as well as Perl and Python. Users of MS-DOS should be familiar with BAT files, which are also scripts, under this definition.

A *gateway program* is either a script or an executable file written for use with a Web server's gateway interface. A gateway program might be any executable entity, including compiled computer programs in languages such as C or C++.

CGI stands for Common Gateway Interface and is the method used for interfacing external programs with NCSA and CERN Web servers. Other kinds of interfaces are being developed for other platforms and servers (other types of gateways).

Gateway Program Uses, Operations, and Security

Gateway programs work with a variety of HTML structures, including hypertext links, ISINDEX search boxes, and Forms. Most commonly, as this chapter outlines, you can handle ISINDEX and Form requests using gateway programs. You also can use gateway programs to execute filters for formatting documents *on the fly* (for example, so that you can have just one format of a manual on your system and generate the HTML (or other formats) for the manual pages according to user requests rather than storing all of the different formats for all of the pages). You also can create gateway interfaces between the Web and WAIS or Archie databases, or use the output of Forms to allow the user to append information onto an existing HTML file (for example, comments, annotations, or new files/web structures defined by the user).

Programming with gateways for many kinds of Web servers (NCSA and CERN, for example) requires that you have write access to the /cgi-bin/ (or other directory as defined in the configuration files) on the server. Because this could be a security concern, if you are just a system user (as opposed to systems administrator), for your Web server, you will probably not be able to enter and edit programs in CGI-defined areas on the server. Gateway programs may also create vulnerability in your server; clever users can execute scripts with different arguments than the script expects, opening up the possibility for security problems on your system. You should consult your server documentation in detail for the operation and security issues of gateway programs.

For details on security issues, see

- *Making your setup more secure:* An explanation of issues for NCSA server administrators (`http://hoohoo.ncsa.uiuc.edu/docs/tutorials/security.html`).

- *Writing secure CGI scripts:* Security issues for gateway programmers (`http://hoohoo.ncsa.uiuc.edu/cgi/security.html`).

- *NCSA httpd server-side includes:* Describes issues with regard to NCSA httpd (`http://hoohoo.ncsa.uiuc.edu/docs/tutorials/includes.html`).

Another issue concerning gateway program execution is CPU time. When a gateway program operates, of course, it uses time on the Web server or some other host defined by the program. Placed on the open Web for public use, a gateway program with considerable execution time can easily cripple a server with requests. Gateway programmers often use techniques for executing gateway programs on different hosts than the Web server or the server that originally presented the user with a choice for the gateway program. For example, the Lycos system (`http://lycos.cs.cmu.edu/`) uses a load-balancing scheme for user requests and execution to avoid overload because of its high popularity.

Another cost in gateway programming is in training and skills. Gateway programming requires the ability to create either scripts or executable programs in the languages mentioned above (UNIX shell scripts, programming languages like C or C++). This chapter won't go into the details of all of these languages, but will give you a flavor for very basic programming with UNIX shell scripts and then point you to online documentation on Perl, a very popular script language for use with gateway programming. Programming the fine details of gateway programs requires that you be very familiar with one of these programming languages. This chapter, however, will simply outline some examples that you should be able to understand, even if you just have a casual knowledge of UNIX shell programming.

Gateway Programs in a Nutshell

A programmer creates a gateway program and places it in the /cgi-bin directory of the server (for NCSA and CERN Web servers). A user of a Web page selects the gateway program URL as part of using a Web page link, Form, or ISINDEX query box. In response to the user request, the gateway program executes and returns the results to the user. These general relationships are shown in Figure 35.1.

FIGURE 35.1.

General relationships in gateway programming.

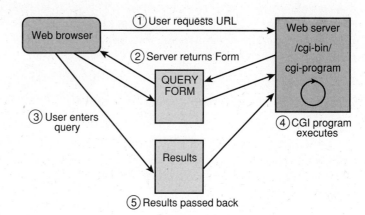

The basic procedures for gateway programming and use are the following:

1. Gateway program setup.

   a. The gateway programmer creates a gateway program. This gateway program could be any script (for example, a UNIX shell script or a Perl script) or an executable program (that is written in C or C++).

   b. The gateway programmer or Web administrator makes the gateway program available for execution by the Web server. For NCSA and CERN servers, this is done by placing the program in the /cgi-bin/ directory of the server (or in a directory specified in the server configuration files).

   c. The gateway application programmer creates a link to the gateway program on a Web page. The gateway program's URL is used as the link in the anchor. For example, if the gateway program is called test.pl (the pl extension here indicating a Perl script), the URL for the program is

   ```
   http://www.server.com/cgi-bin/test.pl
   ```

   The application programmer includes the anchor

   ```
   You can <A Href="http://www.server.com/cgi-bin/test.pl">test the Perl
   script program</A>.
   ```

2. Gateway program use.

    a. The user selects a link that activates the gateway program. As shown in the anchor shown in 1(c) above, the link between the gateway program and the user activation of it is through a HTML anchor.

    b. The user's request for the URL of the script is passed to the Web server. Because of the placement of the script in the Web server's /cgi-bin directory (CERN and NCSA) (or because of the filename extension for other kinds of Web servers), the Web server executes the script (as opposed to just passing the text of the script back to the user's browser for display).

    c. The *output* resulting from the gateway program's execution is passed to the user's browser and displayed according to the formatting statements defined in the output.

Note that the fundamental difference between a user accessing a gateway program and a regular HTML file is that the gateway program is *executed* and the *output* is passed back to the user's browser.

In the next two sections, we'll look more in detail at gateway programming, this time using a specific "nutshell" example.

Gateway Program Example Setup

For our example, we'll use a simple UNIX Bourne shell (sh) script as our gateway program. Our program will simply echo the current date and time on the Web server.

Here's the script written in the UNIX Bourne shell (we'll cover why this has to be in this format later in this chapter):

```
#!/bin/sh

        echo Content-type: text/plain
        echo
        /bin/date
```

We put these code lines in a file called showdate. This file is our gateway program, so we have to verify that it is indeed executable. Normally, a UNIX file isn't executable until the execute permission is set for that file. We can do this at the UNIX prompt ($) by

```
$ chmod +x showdate
```

It's a good idea to test the gateway program before presenting it to users, so we'll check our showdate program at the UNIX prompt:

```
        $ showdate
        Content-type: text/plain
        Thu Apr  6 07:55:14 EDT 1995
```

The script echoes the line `Content-type: text/plain`, a blank line, and then the current date. The line `Content-type: text/plain` informs the browser the kind of data to be displayed. In this case, the data is "plain text"—just the current date and time currently on the Web server.

Let's say our Web server's name is `www.server.com`. Our next step is to place the showdate script (if it isn't there already) in the `/cgi-bin/` directory. Therefore, the URL to this script is `http://www.server.com/cgi-bin/showdate`.

Gateway Program Example Execution

An application developer (who could be a different person than the gateway programmer who created and tested the showdate script above) now can use the showdate script in an HTML page. Here's a very short page, at the example location `http://www.server.com/local/about.html`-

```
<HTML>
      <HEAD>
            <TITLE>About Our Web Server</TITLE>
      </HEAD>
      <BODY>
            <H1>About Our Web Server</H1>

            Our Web server is a NCSA server.  Physically,
            it is located in heart of the Hypermedia Valley,
            on Third Street in Troy, New York.
            For reference, you can check the
            <A Href="http://www.server.com/cgi-bin/showdate">local
            date and time</A>.
      </BODY>
</HTML>
```

The application programmer makes this page, `http://www.server.com/local/about.html`, available to any user, as part of any web. Once the user clicks the "local date and time" hotspot, that URL request is sent to the Web server. The Web server executes showdate and the output:

```
Content-type: text/plain

Thu Apr  6 08:06:59 EDT 1995
```

is sent to the user's browser for display. The user's browser "knows" only that it is receiving output which has a type "`text/plain`," and displays the date:

```
Thu Apr  6 08:06:59 EDT 1995
```

in the browser display (not the `Content-type: text/plain` header information). In the next section, we'll look at some gateway programming specifics, examining how the header and body portions of the gateway program output need to be formatted.

Gateway Programming Specifics

The basics of gateway programming include knowledge of a script or programming language as well as the ability to format the output of the gateway programs in a specific way. Other skills needed include knowing how to implement interactivity (getting information from the user through Forms), creating special output formats, and dealing with environment variables.

Formatting the Output

The output of a gateway program execution is data formatted in a particular way with a header and a (possibly empty) body. It consists of the following:

1. Output description (header)

   Each script needs to describe the information that will be displayed in the user's browser. This information is sent in the header of the script output. There are many types of headers, but the major three are Content-type, Location, and Status.

   a. Content-type. As in the above nutshell example, "Content-type" is used to describe the format of the file you are sending back to the user. These formats are defined by MIME (Multi-purpose Internet Mail Extensions). For more information on MIME, see the MIME FAQ at `http://www.cis.ohio-state.edu/ hypertext/faq/usenet/mail/mime-faq/top.html`. For an NCSA server, the file `/conf/mime-types` lists the kind of MIME types the server can accept.

   Common content types include

   Content-type: `text/html`
   Content-type: `text/plain`
   Content-type: `image/gif`
   Content-type: `image/jpeg`
   Content-type: `application/postscript`
   Content-type: `video/mpeg`

   A longer list of MIME types is shown in Table 35.1. In this table, the x- prefix for the content-type indicates that the extension is not considered a standard type and may change or be defined otherwise by other users.

Table 35.1. MIME types.

Content-Type Keyword	File Type(s)
application/mac-binhex40	hqx
application/octet-stream	bin
application/oda	oda
application/pdf	pdf

continues

Table 35.1. continued

Content-Type Keyword	File Type(s)
application/postscript	ai eps ps
application/rtf	rtf
application/x-mif	mif
application/x-maker	fm
application/x-csh	csh
application/x-dvi	dvi
application/x-hdf	hdf
application/x-latex	latex
application/x-netcdf	nc cdf
application/x-sh	sh
application/x-tcl	tcl
application/x-tex	tex
application/x-texinfo	texinfo texi
application/x-troff	t tr roff
application/x-troff-man	man
application/x-troff-me	me
application/x-troff-ms	ms
application/x-wais-source	src
application/zip	zip
application/x-bcpio	bcpio
application/x-cpio	cpio
application/x-gtar	gtar
application/x-shar	shar
application/x-sv4cpio	sv4cpio
application/x-sv4crc	sv4crc
application/x-tar	tar
application/x-ustar	ustar
audio/basic	au snd
audio/x-aiff	aif aiff aifc
audio/x-wav	wav
image/gif	gif
image/ief	ief
image/jpeg	jpeg jpg jpe

Content-Type Keyword	File Type(s)
image/tiff	tiff tif
image/x-cmu-raster	ras
image/x-portable-anymap	pnm
image/x-portable-bitmap	pbm
image/x-portable-graymap	pgm
image/x-portable-pixmap	ppm
image/x-rgb	rgb
image/x-xbitmap	xbm
image/x-xpixmap	xpm
image/x-xwindowdump	xwd
text/html	html htm
text/plain	txt pl
text/richtext	rtx
text/tab-separated-values	tsv
text/x-setext	etx
video/mpeg	mpeg mpg mpe
video/quicktime	qt mov
video/x-msvideo	avi
video/x-sgi-movie	movie

b. Location header. This is a second type of header you can have in the output of a gateway program. The Location header is used to load another document to the user's browser rather than executing a script. The form is

```
Location: URL
```

where *URL* could be the full URL of a document or a relative pathname to that document. When a Location header is encountered and the URL is local, the Web server sends the document at the given URL to the user's browser. If the URL is remote, the server sends the location header to the browser which is responsible for fetching that URL transparently to the user. In either case, the Web server does *not* execute this remote URL.

c. Status header. This is a third type of header for a gateway program's output. The status header is used to pass back a code to the user's browser. For example, one status code is 204, for No Response. A header to transmit this code to the user's browser would be

```
Status: 204 No Response
```

This should tell the browser to do nothing as the result of the query. (More status codes are shown in Table 35.2.) For further information, see `http://www.w3.org/hypertext/WWW/Protocols/HTTP/HTRESP.html`.

Table 35.2. Status codes for HTTP.

Code	Indication
2xx	**Success**
200	OK; the request was fulfilled.
201	OK; following a POST command.
202	OK; accepted for processing, but processing is not completed.
203	OK; partial information—the returned information is only partial.
204	OK; no response—request received but no information exists to send back.
3xx	**Redirection**
301	Moved—the data requested has a new location and the change is permanent.
302	Found—the data requested has a different URL temporarily.
303	Method—under discussion, a suggestion for the client to try another location.
304	Not Modified—the document has not been modified as expected.
4xx	**Error seems to be in the client**
400	Bad request—syntax problem in the request or it could not be satisfied.
401	Unauthorized—the client is not authorized to access data.
402	Payment required—indicates a charging scheme is in effect.
403	Forbidden—access not granted even with authorization.
404	Not found—server could not find the given resource.
5xx	**Error seems to be in the server**
500	Internal Error—the server could not fulfill the request because of an unexpected condition.
501	Not implemented—the sever does not support the facility requested.
502	Server overloaded—high load (or servicing) in progress.
503	Gateway timeout—server waited for another service that did not complete in time.

After the header line (Content-type, Location, or Status) you must have a blank line before the body. You can't mix content types that don't make sense. For example, it wouldn't make sense to mix Content type and Location, but it's normal to send both Status and Content type. (The server will set a default status of 200 OK for you.)

2. Output Data (body)

For Location and Status headers, the body of the output will be blank.

For Content-type headers, the rest of the output is the text you want displayed to the user, in the format identified in the Content-type field of your header. Therefore, you'll create HTML output data if you have Content-type: `text/html`. If you are using Content-type: `application/postscript`, the data that follows should be a PostScript file. In our nutshell example, we had Content-type: `text/plain`, so we didn't have to use any HTML tags or other formatting marks.

Interactivity

Our nutshell example showed the basic setup for a gateway program that didn't use much information from the user (only that he or she wanted to know the local time at the Web server). In this section, we'll go over a basic method for interactivity using the ISINDEX HTML element. There are two forms for adding interactivity to a gateway program: document-based queries and Forms-based queries.

Document-Based Queries

Document-based queries using gateway programs utilize three elements:

- The ISINDEX element located in the `<HEAD>` of the HTML file.
- Special query URLs the browser generates (using the ? symbol).
- Arguments selected or input by the user and passed to the gateway program.

On a first call to a document-based gateway program, no arguments may be passed, indicating that a default page should be passed to the user. This default page can contain introductory information for the gateway program. In the HEAD of this page, the ISINDEX element is placed:

```
<HEAD>
     <ISINDEX>
</HEAD>
```

This ISINDEX element turns on the browser "searching" mode, in which the user is presented with a box for input. The user enters a string in this box and then presses Enter (or selects some other submit button). As a result, the browser requests the same URL as before except that now the URL includes the search string at the end followed by a question mark. For our example, let's say that the gateway programmer creates a UNIX script called `datasearch` and places it at `http://www.server.com/cgi-bin/datasearch`. This script allows a user to search for strings in a database at `http://www.server.com/data/animals.dat`. Here are the script contents:

```
#!/bin/sh
#----------------------------------------------------------
# Example script to demonstrate very simple database lookup.
#----------------------------------------------------------

echo Content-type: text/html
echo

echo "<HTML>"
echo "<HEAD>"
if [ $# = 0 ]
then
  echo "    <TITLE>Database search</TITLE>"
  echo "    <ISINDEX>"
  echo "</HEAD>"
  echo "<BODY>"
  echo "<H1>Database search</H1>"

  echo "This page will help you search for strings in the database."
  echo "In the field, enter any part of an animal type to search for."
else
  echo "    <TITLE>Results of searching for \"$*\" in the database.</TITLE>"
  echo "</HEAD>"
  echo "<BODY>"
  echo "<H1>Results of search for \"$*\" in the database.</H1>"
  echo "<HR>"
  echo "<PRE>"
  grep -i "$*" ../data/animals.dat
  echo "</PRE>"
fi
echo "</BODY>"
echo "</HTML>"
```

The first time a user calls up the `datasearch` script, the first part of the script is executed (the text bracketed by `if [ $# = 0 ]` (indicating no arguments were passed to the script) and the `else`. The following output is sent to the user's browser:

```
Content-type: text/html

        <HTML>
        <HEAD>
            <TITLE>Database search</TITLE>
        <ISINDEX>
        </HEAD>
        <BODY>
        <H1>Database search</H1>
        This page will help you search for strings in the database.
        In the field, enter any part of an animal type to search for.
        </BODY>
        </HTML>
```

The user can read the introductory information and type in some string to look for. Let's say that the contents of our `animals.dat` database are

```
        fish-gold 3.23
        goat-billy 5.57
        pig 4.27
        fish-cod 3.80
```

```
        fish-salmon 3.95
        cat-house  3.97
        goat-mountain 4.17
        cow 3.79
cat-alley  1.17
```

Let's say that the user enters `fish` in the input box. The URL `http://www.server.com/cgi-bin/datasearch?fish` will be sent to the Web server. The script `datasearch` will be executed with `fish` as the argument. Because the `datasearch` script now has an argument, it performs the search defined in the `else` portion of the script and passes the results back to the user's browser as

```
Content-type: text/html
```

```
        <HTML>
        <HEAD>
           <TITLE>Results of searching for "fish" in the database.</TITLE>
        </HEAD>
        <BODY>
        <H1>Results of search for "fish" in the database.</H1>
        <HR>
        <PRE>
        fish-gold 3.23
        fish-cod 3.80
        fish-salmon 3.95
        </PRE>
        </BODY>
        </HTML>
```

Notice that the heart of the search engine is just the command

```
grep -i "$*" ../data/animals.dat
```

The `grep` command is a UNIX command to search for and extract all of the lines matching a particular string in the file `../data/animals.dat`. The `-i` option makes this search case-insensitive, and the `"$*"` argument indicates the entire phrase that the user had entered. The rest of the output in the `datasearch` script is just HTML elements to set up the web page.

Forms-Based Queries

We talked about Forms in Chapter 34, "Advanced HTML Features," so you can refer to that chapter to see the options for making buttons, text input areas, and other user-interface features. The main concept about Forms important for gateway programming is that information in the Forms is encoded in name/value pairs—so that if you have a text area with the name of "comments," the value of this text field is the text comments that the user has entered (if any). When used in conjunction with gateway programs, Forms are the second type of query available in gateway programming (the other being the document-based queries used with the ISINDEX element).

Using Forms-based queries involved the following steps:

1. You must choose a method for submitting information to the gateway program. Two choices are

a. GET. Similar to document-based queries, a GET submission encodes the information (value/name pairs) into the URL and then assigns the set of these value/name pairs to the environment variable on the server called QUERY_STRING (environment variables are listed in the next section). The gateway program on the server can then pick out the name/value pairs of the variables from this QUERY_STRING.

b. POST. The name/value pairs from the Form are passed directly to the gateway script through standard input. This is often the preferred method of operating with Forms-gateway scripts. The reason why POST is preferred is that GET uses the UNIX shell to assign the values to the environment variables. A UNIX shell is limited in the number of characters it can handle at a time, so a Form with a lot of data could cause a loss of data. In the POST method, there are no limits (as all data is passed through standard input, a way of transferring information in a "stream" without limits). The rest of this chapter focuses on POST methods.

2. You must create a Form. Forms structures are outlined in Chapter 34.

3. You must connect the Form to the gateway program. You connect the Form to the gateway program through the line:

```
<FORM Method="POST" Action="http://www.server.com/cgi-bin/testform">
```

The FORM element announces the start of the Form. The attribute Method identifies the Method (the recommended is POST). The Action attribute identifies the URL (which could be a relative pathname) of the gateway program to be called upon execution of the Form.

4. You must write a gateway program. Your gateway program interprets the information from the Form, decoding the name/value pairs for use in its processing. There are many publicly available tools for handling this decoding process. Using cgiparse, a program that comes with the CERN/HTTPD distribution, you decode the input from a Form like this:

```
CGI=/usr/local/bin/cgiparse
eval '$CGI -init'
eval '$CGI -form'
```

This script decodes the information from the Form and creates environment variables, one for each name and one for each value in the name/value pairs. Each variable name will have the prefix FORM_ prepended to it. For example, if you have a name in the Form called userid, the environment variable set by cgiparse will be FORM_userid. Note that cgiparse is a very limited decoder, appropriate perhaps best for short examples—its use in long Forms also risks information loss. Also, cgiparse doesn't handle multiple names in a Form, but only reports the name/value pairs for the last pair corresponding to a name. Check out some more advanced parsing programs in the online collections listed at the end of this chapter.

Let's put together the above steps into a simple example. Here's the Form. (For our example, let's say it is stored in http://www.server.com/doc/testform.html.)

```
<HTML>
<HEAD>
    <TITLE>Test Form</TITLE>
</HEAD>
<BODY>
<H1>This is a test</H1>
<FORM Method="POST" Action="http://www.server.com/cgi-bin/testform">
Enter your test phrase: <INPUT NAME="test-phrase">
 <P>
 <INPUT Type=submit Value="Send the Test Phrase">
 <P>
 <INPUT Type=reset  Value="Cancel the Test">
 </FORM>
</BODY>
</HTML>
```

This code will present the user with the Form shown in Figure 35.2.

FIGURE 35.2.

Test Form.

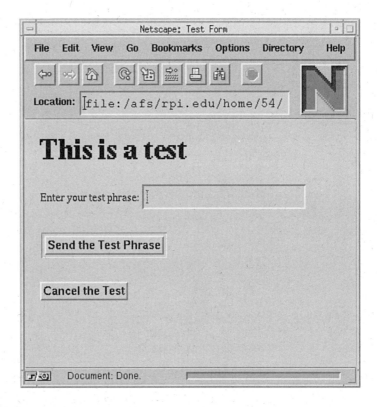

The next step is to write the testform script, make it executable, and place it at `http://www.server.com/cgi-bin/testform`. For this example, we'll use the `cgiparse` program to decode the name/value pairs from the Form.

```
#!/bin/sh
     CGI=/usr/local/bin/cgiparse
     eval '$CGI -init'
     eval '$CGI -form'
```

```
echo Content-type: text/html
echo

echo "<HTML>"
echo "<HEAD>"
echo "<TITLE>"
echo "Test Form Results"
echo "</TITLE>"
echo "</HEAD>"
echo "<BODY>"
echo "<H1>Test Form Results</H1>"
if [ ! -z "$FORM_test-phrase" ]; then
        echo -n "Your test phrase was: "
        echo $FORM_test-phrase
else
        echo "You didn't enter a test phrase!"
fi
echo "<P>"
echo "<A Href=\"http://www.server.com/doc/testform.html\">Return to test
form</A>
echo "</BODY>"
echo "</HTML>"
```

Here's how our example works:

1. The user has the page http://www.server.com/doc/testform.html in his or her browser.

2. Seeing that this is a test Form, the user enters a string in the box shown in Figure 35.2.

3. The user clicks on the Send the Test Phrase button (alternately, the user could have pressed Enter in most browsers).

4. The connection from the Form to the gateway program at http://www.server.com/cgi-bin/testform causes that program to execute.

5. The testform program operates. The testform program sends its results in HTML, so that the output is displayed as a Web page. If the user had not entered a phrase, the statement You didn't enter a phrase is displayed. If the user had entered a phrase, its value is echoed back to the user. A link at the bottom of the page is given to return to the Test Form.

Gateway Program Environment Variables

Passing information from the gateway program to the browser is done through environment variables. These environment variables are set when the server accesses the gateway program as a result of the user query. Table 35.3 summarizes these. You can see these variables set for your browser in a test script provided by NCSA at http://hoohoo.ncsa.uiuc.edu/cgi-bin/test-cgi. An example later in this chapter will show how you can access these environment variables in a Perl script.

Table 35.3. Environment variables for use in gateway programs.

Variable Name	Description
AUTH_TYPE	The protocol-specific authentication method used to validate the user. It is set when the server supports user authentication.
CONTENT_LENGTH	The length of the content as given by the client.
CONTENT_TYPE	The content type of the data for queries that have attached information (for example, as HTTP POST and PUT).
GATEWAY_INTERFACE	The CGI specification revision of the server. Format: CGI/revision.
PATH_INFO	Path information, as given by the user request.
PATH_TRANSLATED	The translated version of PATH_INFO, with the path including any virtual-to-physical mapping to it.
QUERY_STRING	The information following the ? in the URL when referencing the script (using GET).
REMOTE_ADDR	The IP address of the remote (user's) host making the request.
REMOTE_HOST	The name of the host making the request (user host).
REMOTE_IDENT	This variable is set to the remote username as retrieved from the server (if the HTTP server supports RFC 931 identification).
REMOTE_USER	This is set to the username if the HTTP server supports RFC 931 identification and the script is protected.
REQUEST_METHOD	The method by which the request was made (for example, GET, HEAD, POST, and so on).
SCRIPT_NAME	A pathname of the script to execute.
SERVER_NAME	The server's hostname, DNS alias, or IP address as it would appear in self-referencing URLs.
SERVER_PORT	The port number where the request was sent.
SERVER_PROTOCOL	The name/revision of the information protocol.
SERVER_SOFTWARE	The name/version of the information server software that answered the request.

Gateway Programming Topics and Techniques

As you develop skills in gateway programming, you'll be able to refine your techniques and extend your ability to include interactivity in your webs. This section includes a few tricks that will help get you started in developing these techniques.

Keeping State Variables from One Form to the Next

A Forms-based query for gathering user output will work well, as long as you don't ask too many questions—the form can get unmanageably long. You also might want to ask the user different questions based on his response to other questions. In either case, you'll want to carry the variable states over from Form to Form so that the information in the variable settings attached to the specific user doesn't get lost. You can do this using the hidden input data type in the Forms. The idea is to carry over any variables set in earlier Forms to subsequent Forms with a line like this:

```
<INPUT Type=hidden Name="variable-name" Value="variable-value">
```

For example, let's say your initial Form is (the same as in our previous example, but with a new gateway program) nextform:

```
<HTML>
      <HEAD>
         <TITLE>Test Form</TITLE>
      </HEAD>
      <BODY>
      <H1>This is a test</H1>
      <FORM Method="POST" Action="http://www.server.com/cgi-bin/nextform">
      Enter your test phrase: <INPUT NAME="test-phrase">
       <P>
       <INPUT Type=submit Value="Send the Test Phrase">
       <P>
       <INPUT Type=reset  Value="Cancel the Test">
       </FORM>
      </BODY>
      </HTML>
```

Based on what the user types in as the test phrase, you might want to send him or her to another set of branching pages. So, your nextform program might read

```
#!/bin/sh
CGI=/usr/local/bin/cgiparse
eval '$CGI -init'
eval '$CGI -form'
echo Content-type: text/html
echo

echo "<HTML>"
echo "<HEAD>"
echo "<TITLE>"
echo "Test Form Results"
echo "</TITLE>"
echo "</HEAD>"
echo "<BODY>"
echo "<H1>Test Form Results</H1>"
if [ ! -z "$FORM_test-phrase" ]; then
        echo -n "Your test phrase was: "
        echo $FORM_test-phrase
        echo -n "<INPUT Type=hidden Name=\"test-phrase\" Value=\""
        echo $FORM_test-phrase
        echo "\"><P>"
        echo "Now, enter the secret password"
```

```
            echo "<FORM Method=\"POST\" Action=\"http://www.server.com/cgi-bin/
             secretform\">"
            echo "Enter the secret password: <INPUT NAME=\"secret\">"
            echo "<INPUT Type=submit Value=\"Try the secret\">"
            echo "</FORM>"
  <P>
  <INPUT Type=submit Value="Send the Test Phrase">
  else
            echo "You didn't enter a test phrase!"
  fi
  echo "<P>"
  echo "<A Href=\"http://www.server.com/doc/testform.html\">Return to test
   form</A>
  echo "</BODY>"
```

In the above Form, if the user enters some test phrase a new Form is generated, with the user's test phrase set as a hidden variable, asking him to enter a secret password. In this way, you can *cascade* Forms, carrying over name/value settings from previous Forms as hidden values. Note that the user can find out these hidden values by viewing the HTML source code of the Form (which is possible on a non-secure server), although the values won't be displayed on the Form itself.

Gateway Programming and Perl

Perl is a script programming language that is very popular for programming gateway programs. See the online Perl manual at http://www-cgi.cs.cmu.edu/cgi-bin/perl-man.

Here's a quick way to start programming in Perl, showing how you can echo the environment variables shown above.

1. First, find the path to Perl on your system so you can identify your script as a Perl script. At the UNIX prompt ($), enter

   ```
   $ which perl
   ```

   Your system should respond with a pathname, typically

   ```
   /usr/local/bin/perl
   ```

2. Create a script file with the first line set to #! plus your path to Perl; for example:

   ```
   #!/usr/local/bin/perl
   ```

3. Create a Perl script (let's call our example test.pl):

   ```
   #!/usr/local/bin/perl
      # Test Perl script
      print "Content-type: text/plain\n";
      print "SERVER_SOFTWARE is set to $ENV{'SERVER_SOFTWARE'}\n";
      print "SERVER_NAME is set to $ENV{'SERVER_NAME'}\n";
      print "GATEWAY_INTERFACE is set to $ENV{'GATEWAY_INTERFACE'}\n";
      print "SERVER_PROTOCOL is set to $ENV{'SERVER_PROTOCOL'}\n";
   print "SERVER_PORT is set to $ENV{'SERVER_PORT'}\n";
   ```

4. Test the Perl script (verify that the script is executable).

5. Install the Perl script in /cgi-bin/.

6. Have a user test the Perl script (the output for this will be similar to that shown above for http://hoohoo.ncsa.uiuc.edu/cgi-bin/test-cgi).

Gateway Programming and Databases

NCSA provides some CGI programs that will help you interface to WAIS (Wide Area Information Server) databases. See the distribution code in the directory ftp://ftp.ncsa.uiuc.edu/Web/ httpd/Unix/ncsa_httpd/cgi/. The file is named wais.tar.Z in that directory. You can find more about WAIS and WAISGate (another gateway program for WAIS) at WAIS, Inc's. server at http:// /www.wais.com/.

A Sample Perl Gateway Program: A Calculator

Alan Richmond is the webmaster behind an extensive collection of HTML/CGI/WWW resources at http://WWW.Stars.com/. He's prepared an interesting demonstration program, a Perl script that implements a calculator. (Note: As Alan points out in his opening comment header, this is not meant to be a *practical* calculator, but a good *illustration* of how a Perl script can work as a gateway program.)

Figure 35.3 shows the visible part of this calculator in Lynx, showing the sum 4+3 in the display. (Note: the calculator uses tables, which your Web browser may not render.)

```
#! /usr/local/bin/perl
    #
    #    /\ /\           CyberWeb SoftWare: Internet Information Systems
    # -{-<*>-}-      World-Wide Web          <URL:http://WWW.Stars.com/>
    #  __\/_\/
    # Author :      Alan Richmond
    # File   :      WebCalc.pl
    # Purpose   :      A Demonstration of HTML Table/CGI/Perl Features.
    # Comment   :      Only a demo of WWW/CGI/Perl features,
    #                  NOT a practical application!
    #
    # The buttons are arranged for compatibility with Lynx or other
    # browsers that may number their links: the link numbers coincide
    # with the numbers on the buttons. Actually it doesn't work too
    # well with Lynx anymore; maybe I'll fix it one day..
    # Each button is a hyperlink to this CGI program.
    #
    # The operators [+-*/=] are encoded as [pmtde] as some (e.g. +)
    # will get mangled on the way here.. more elegant would be real
    # URL-encoding, but this will do for now.
    #
    $home = "/home/web/public_html";

    require "$home/cgi-bin/cgi-lib.pl";

    &ReadParse    (*input);
```

```
    @info  = split        (/\//, $ENV{'PATH_INFO'});

    $title = "WebCalc";
    $calc  = "/cgi-bin/web-exe/Calc";

    print "Content-type:       text/html\n\n";      #        MIME type.

    $e     = $info[2];             #        current expression
    $x     = $info[3];             #        equals flag
    $      = $info[4];             #        button label

# If      the button is an operator
    if     ( /[pmtde]/ ) {         #        [+-*/=]
#
#          then the expression will be evaluated

        if     ( $e =~ /[^\dpmtd\.]/ )     {

#              if there is nothing other than digits & operators

            $e = $_ = "";
            $d =   "Invalid characters";      # possible break-in?
            goto          Print;
            }
        else   {
#              Decode operators

            $e     =~ s,p,+,;
            $e     =~ s,m,-,;
            $e     =~ s,t,*,;
            $e     =~ s,d,/,;

#              The result becomes the new expression.

            $e     = eval($e);  #      Calculate!

#              Trap eval() errors.
            if     ( $@ ) {
                $d = $@;
                $e = $_ = "";
                goto Print;
                }

# The flag serves to indicate that the current expression was just
# previously the result of the equals operator, so digits should not be
# appended but start a new number.

            if     (/e/)  {   $_ = ""; $x = 1;      }
            else          {   $x = 0;               }
            }
        }
    elsif  ( /c/ )         {

#       Clear current expression.

        $e = $_ = "";
        }
    elsif  ( $x ) {
```

```
#        Digit following a prior = operator: clear current expression
#        to start a new number.

         $e = "";
         $x = 0;
         }
# If the button is a digit then it is appended to the expression.
  $e       .=       $_;

# Prepare to display the result: decode operators.

  $d       = $e;
  $d       =~ s,p,+,;
  $d       =~ s,m,-,;
  $d       =~ s,t,*,;
  $d       =~ s,d,/,;
  if       ( $d eq "" ) {        $d = 0;                 }
Print:
# The next HTML display is generated with appropriate
#        arguments written into the hyperlinks.

  print <<EOT;
<!DOCTYPE HTML "-//IETF//DTD HTML 3.0//EN">
<HTML><Head>
  <Title>        $title </Title>
  <Base  href="http://WWW.Stars.com/.">
</Head>
<Body  background="/Icons/blue_paper.gif">
<center>
<table    border width=75%>
  <tr>
    <td colspan=5 align=right> <h1> $d
  <tr>
    <td align=center> <a href="$calc/$e/$x/1"> <h1>1</a>
    <td align=center> <a href="$calc/$e/$x/2"> <h1>2</a>
    <td align=center> <a href="$calc/$e/$x/3"> <h1>3</a>
    <td align=center> <a href="$calc/$e/$x/4"> <h1>4</a>
    <td align=center> <a href="$calc/$e/$x/5"> <h1>5</a>
  <tr>
    <td align=center> <a href="$calc/$e/$x/6"> <h1>6</a>
    <td align=center> <a href="$calc/$e/$x/7"> <h1>7</a>
    <td align=center> <a href="$calc/$e/$x/8"> <h1>8</a>
    <td align=center> <a href="$calc/$e/$x/9"> <h1>9</a>
    <td align=center> <a href="$calc/$e/$x/0"> <h1>0</a>
  <tr>
    <td align=center> <a href="$calc/$e/$x/."> <h1>.</a>
    <td align=center> <a href="$calc/$e/$x/p"> <h1>+</a>
    <td align=center> <a href="$calc/$e/$x/m"> <h1>-</a>
    <td align=center> <a href="$calc/$e/$x/t"> <h1>*</a>
    <td align=center> <a href="$calc/$e/$x/d"> <h1>/</a>
  <tr>
    <td align=center> <a href="$calc/$e/$x/c"> <h1>C</a>
    <td align=center> <a href="$calc/$e/$x/e"> <h1>=</a>
    <td align=center    colspan=3> <h1><i>WebCalc
  </tr>
</table>
EOT
```

FIGURE 35.3.
WebCalc displayed in Lynx.

Client-Side Programs

The gateway programs described in the preceding sections worked through the client (Web browser), sending the Web server a request to run a program on the Web server. There is another variation—client-side programs—that involve commands sent from the Web server to the Web client to execute programs. Obviously the implications of this could be devastating for security—a naive client could receive a command from a Web server to wipe out all of the files on the client computer!

Here is an example of a server-side gateway program that initiates a client-side application:

```
#!/bin/sh
echo "Content-type: application/x-client-exe"
echo
echo "#!/bin/sh"
echo
echo "xterm -display $DISPLAY -e /usr/local/bin/rn alt.internet.services"
echo
```

Note that this script uses the Content-type `application/x-client-exe`. This is the content-type appropriate for a script that a client should execute. Note that the subtype name `x-client-exe` could be any name that starts with a prefix x. The client needs to be told how to handle this type of input, however. To do this, you add the line

```
application/x-client-exe:    /bin/sh %s
```

to your Web browser's configuration file (for example, `mailcap` file for Mosaic). This line tells your browser how to handle any document of the `application/x-client-exe` type—simply to execute the document using the Bourne shell. In the above example, this would launch an xterm (terminal) session in which the Usenet newsreader rn will be invoked, starting with the newsgroup `alt.internet.services`. Be sure to check your Web browser configuration files for any `application/x-` MIME types. Make sure you understand what these types do.

NOTE

Here are some collections of information about gateway programming available on the Web:

■ The Web Developer's Virtual Library

Alan Richmond put together this extensive collection of HTML/CGI/WWW resources. This service includes the "Ask Dr. Web" service, linking you to 16 WWW experts around the world. This is a must-visit site for any HTML developer (http://WWW.Stars.com/).

■ A CGI Programmer's Reference: a compendium of information for gateway programmers, including a FAQ, a survey of browser characteristics, a listing of existing gateways, and reference manuals. Developed by M. Hedlund (http://www.halcyon.com/hedlund/cgi-faq/).

■ Group Cortex CGI Center: These pages point to reference information about CGI. Developed by Group Cortex (http://www.netweb.com/cortex/resources/cgi/).

■ CGI Documentation: A guide to CGI from NCSA (National Center for Supercomputing Applications) by Rob McCool (http://hoohoo.ncsa.uiuc.edu/cgi/).

■ Yahoo Index: This is the Computers-World Wide Web-CGI section from Yahoo (http://www.yahoo.com/Computers/World_Wide_Web/CGI___Common_Gateway_Interface/).

■ Perl/HTML page: A collection of information and resources for using Perl in conjunction with gateway programs, developed by Meng Weng Wong (http://www.seas.upenn.edu/~mengwong/perlhtml.html).

■ The University of Florida Perl Archive: This includes a large collection of information about learning Perl (http://www.cis.ufl.edu/perl/).

■ Perl scripts: Useful Perl scripts for dealing with WWW (http://iamwww.unibe.ch/~scg/Src/Scripts/).

Gateway Programming Check

Common Gateway Interface is the key to creating interactivity in your web. Skills and permissions to program and use CGI often place it outside of a Web-beginner's range, as the permissions normally include having write access to the /cgi-bin/ directory and the skills required include the ability to create programs in UNIX scripts or other programming languages. However, given these permissions and skills, a gateway programmer can create interactivity within webs. On the most basic level, this interactivity could involve a simple data return in response to a user request (such as the simple showdate script shown as a nutshell example in this chapter).

Other levels of interactivity include using document-based queries through the ISINDEX element and Forms-based queries using HTML Forms constructs.

There are many variations on how gateway programming can be done. Techniques and practices vary by server type, programming language used, and the details of the specific application. This chapter gave you an overview of gateway programming to get you started in tapping a great potential for interactivity on the Web.

Creating Imagemaps

36

by
Brandon Plewe

The power of the World Wide Web is plain to see from the chapters of this book. It provides access to information around the world in a good-looking, easy-to-use manner. One of the most powerful and popular features of the Web is its *interactivity*—its capability to let the user communicate with the server. This two-way communication takes place primarily in two types of WWW information: fill-out forms, which are discussed in Chapter 34, "Advanced HTML Features," and imagemaps.

Imagemaps, also known as interactive graphics, clickable images, and hot images, are to graphics what hypertext is to documents. In an imagemap, different parts of the image are *linked* to other places on the World Wide Web. When the user points to that part of the image, she is transported to another document, just like a normal hypertext link. Thus, imagemaps combine the navigational power of HTML with the freedom of graphic design.

This tool was originally invented in May 1993 by Kevin Hughes, then of Honolulu Community College, as a way to implement an interactive campus map (`http://www.hcc.hawaii.edu/hccinfo/hccmap/hccmap2.html`). He had to alter Mosaic and his HTTP server himself to get it to work, but the idea quickly caught on, and support for this feature has been a standard part of most WWW software ever since.

Some Sample Imagemaps

Today most commercial servers, as well as many others, use imagemaps to produce high-quality home pages; many people are also using them in unique interactive services to enable the user to find and display information. A few examples of the common types of applications are shown in the following figures.

Figure 36.1 shows the Virtual Tourist, at the State University of New York at Buffalo (`http://wings.buffalo.edu/world/`). The service consists of maps of the world and continents, as well as the United States, as shown in the figure. The map is *clickable*, meaning that the user can point to a state or country, and an action will take place. In this application, another page showing the WWW servers in the respective state or country is displayed.

A more common application is to use imagemaps as a navigational tool, as shown in Figure 36.2. In this case, the designer creates an entirely graphic home page, including the organization logo, and a series of buttons to represent the various information resources that make up the service. Although this demands more resources to accomplish the same objective as a normal HTML document, it gives the designer full control to create a professional look for the service's initial entry point.

FIGURE 36.1.

An imagemap: the Virtual Tourist.

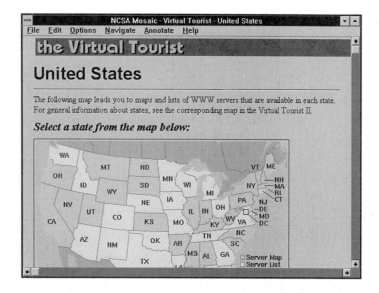

FIGURE 36.2.

The imagemap as a navigational tool.

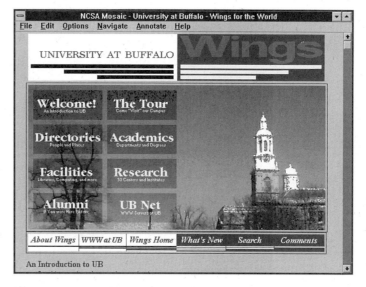

A third application of imagemaps is the *button bar*, as shown at the bottom of Figure 36.3. The button bar is a horizontal image that appears at the top or bottom of all pages in the service and contains labels or icons that represent common tasks a user may want to do at any time, such as searching the service's information or returning to the home page.

FIGURE 36.3.

*The imagemap as
a button bar.*

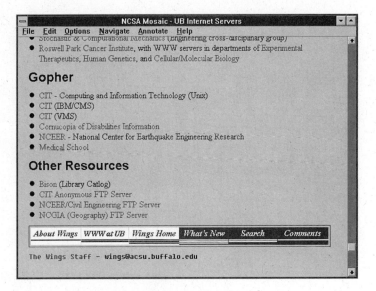

How to Do It

Now let's put together an interactive application using an imagemap. The following procedure generally applies to all brands of HTTP servers; however, some of the details vary widely among software packages and hardware platforms. This chapter will cover the basic procedures for several of the more popular server programs, but it is best to consult your respective manual for detailed information. Even if your software is not mentioned here, the overall process will probably still apply.

Getting Started: The Preliminaries

Before you can start doing interactive graphics, you need to make sure that your WWW server will support the imagemap features. If you are placing your documents on a school or company machine along with other contributors, this might mean nothing more than asking the server administrator. He or she will also likely have documentation that is tailored to your particular installation, in which case you might not need this chapter at all.

If, on the other hand, you don't have it so easy, you will need to find out on your own whether your server will support imagemap features. Following is a list of several of the popular HTTP server packages, and the status of imagemap modules for them, including URLs for more complete documentation.

■ **NCSA HTTPD (UNIX)**. Requires a CGI module, `imagemap`, which is delivered with the package but must be compiled separately. More info at: `http://hoohoo.ncsa.uiuc.edu/docs/setup/admin/NewImagemap.html`.

- **CERN/W3O HTTPD (UNIX).** Requires a CGI module, `htimage`, delivered in the Utilities package (`cern_httpd_utils_x.x.tar.Z`), which is in the same directory as the server software. More info at: `http://www.w3.org/hypertext/WWW/Daemon/User/CGI/HTImageDoc.html`.

- **Windows HTTP, by Robert Denny.** Imagemap support is built into the package (distribution also contains documentation).

- **HTTPS (Windows NT) from Edinburgh University.** Imagemap support built in. More info at: `http://emwac.ed.ac.uk/html/internet_toolchest/https/imgmap.htm`.

- **MacHTTP (Macintosh), from BIAP Systems.** Requires a separate CGI module, which is not delivered with the software. There are two third-party programs available: MacImageMap, by Lutz Weimann (`http://weyl.zib-berlin.de/imagemap/Mac-ImageMap.html`), and MapServe, by Kelly Campbell (`http://www.spub.ksu.edu/other/machttp_tools/mapserve/`).

Those with separate imagemap programs may require some work to install the modules. The home pages listed should include installation instructions.

The First Step: Drawing the Image

When everything is operational, you're ready to start work. The first task is to create the image that will be displayed. This image is under your complete control and could be anything from a photograph, to a graphic showing menu choices, to a geographic map. This image can be created using any ordinary raster graphics (often termed *photo-editing* or *paint*) package. Although different browsers support a variety of image formats, it is best to save the image in GIF format, which is the only one supported by all browsers. After you have created the image, place it where it can be accessed via a URL (that is, in your Web document space).

Creating the Configuration File

There is no way for the computer to intuitively see what areas on the image are "hot," let alone to where they point. Your second step is to give it this information. This is normally done by making a text file (normally called a *configuration file* or *mapfile*) that tells the server about the imagemap. Generally, there are three pieces of information required for each hotspot:

- **Shape of the hotspot.** Common shapes include rectangles, circles or ellipses, arbitrary polygons, and points. Also called the *method*.

- **Coordinates.** This is the location of the hotspot, given in x and y pixels from the top left of the image. There could be one (for example, points and circles, the latter also requiring a radius), two (for example, rectangles and ellipses), or more for polygons (one for each vertex). To find these coordinates, you need to use a graphics program that will show the coordinates of the cursor as you move the mouse across the image (most programs can do this). As you move the cursor to each needed point, you can record the x and y coordinates shown on the screen.

■ **Uniform Resource Locator.** This is the full address of the item to which the hotspot points. Some, but not all, servers also allow relative URLs and references using # (subdocument names) and ? (queries).

In the configuration file, there is one line for each hotspot, containing these three fields. However, there is no standard syntax, and the files may vary considerably between different brands of HTTP servers. The following sections describe each format, with comparable sample code.

NCSA Style

NCSA Style is the most common format, used in NCSA HTTPD (UNIX), Windows HTTPD, MacImageMap (with MacHTTP), and MapServe (with MacHTTP). There are three standard shape codes: RECT(angle), CIRCLE, and POLY(gon). The syntax is as follows for each shape (case is not important in the style code):

```
RECT URL x,y x,y
```

Where the top left and bottom right corners are given.

```
CIRCLE URL x,y x,y
```

The center and a point along the edge, respectively.

```
POLY URL x,y x,y x,y ...
```

The coordinates for each vertex.

Some of the servers also support other shapes:

```
POINT URL x,y
```

A single point (NCSA, MacImageMap, MapServe).

```
ELLIPSE URL x,y x,y
```

Ellipse (WinHTTPD). Coordinates are the upper left and lower right of the bounding rectangle.

```
CIRC URL x,y x,y
```

Ellipse (MacImageMap). Same syntax as ELLIPSE.

```
OVAL URL x,y x,y
```

Ellipse (MapServe). Same syntax as ELLIPSE.

For example, the following is the imagemap file that would be used with the home page image shown earlier in Figure 36.2:

```
default http://wings.buffalo.edu/sorry.html
rect http://wings.buffalo.edu/general/overview.html 10,10 140,63
rect http://wings.buffalo.edu/tour/ 150,10 280,63
```

```
rect gopher://wings.buffalo.edu/hh/directories 10,73 140,126
rect http://wings.buffalo.edu/academic/department/ 150,73 280,126
rect http://wings.buffalo.edu/services.html 10,136 140,189
rect gopher://wings.buffalo.edu/hh/faculty/research 150,136 280,189
rect gopher://wings.buffalo.edu/hh/alumni 10,199 140,252
rect http://wings.buffalo.edu/other.html 150,199 280,252
```

CERN Style

Used in the CERN HTTPD (UNIX), it supports the same three shapes. It has a slightly different syntax, with the coordinates (in parentheses) preceding the URL:

```
RECT (x,y) (x,y) URL
CIRCLE (x,y) r URL
```

where r is the radius in pixels.

```
POLY (x,y) (x,y) (x,y) ... URL
```

Here is the same configuration file as above, but in CERN format:

```
default http://wings.buffalo.edu/sorry.html
rect (10,10) (140,63) http://wings.buffalo.edu/general/overview.html
rect (150,10) (280,63) http://wings.buffalo.edu/tour/
rect (10,73) (140,126) gopher://wings.buffalo.edu/hh/directories
rect (150,73) (280,126) http://wings.buffalo.edu/academic/department/
rect (10,136) (140,189) http://wings.buffalo.edu/services.html
rect (150,136) (280,189) gopher://wings.buffalo.edu/hh/faculty/research
rect (10,199) (140,252) gopher://wings.buffalo.edu/hh/alumni
rect (150,199) (280,252) http://wings.buffalo.edu/other.html
```

HTTPS (Windows NT)

This server uses a format similar to CERN, but without the parentheses or commas. It supports the same three standard shapes:

```
RECT x y x y URL
CIRCLE x y r URL
POLY x y x y x y ... URL
```

The order of the hotspots is important, as they are evaluated in order. For example, if two hotspots happen to overlap, and someone points in the overlapping region, the hotspot of the two that appears first in the file will be chosen.

There is also a *default* given, which is the URL that will be retrieved if the user points to the image but misses all of the hotspots. It is not required; but if it is not included, the user will usually be presented with an unfriendly error message. This line is generally placed at the beginning of the file, and has the following syntax (although this may be slightly different in some servers):

```
DEFAULT URL
```

The location and filename of this configuration file are usually not important, as long as it is somewhere in the server's WWW document space. Some servers have restrictions, however:

- HTTPS requires that the filename have a .map extension.
- MapServe (1.0) requires that the config file be in the same directory as the mapserve script. A newer version was in testing at the time of this writing that was supposed to allow the file to be anywhere.

An Easier Way

Obviously, this step is the most difficult of the entire process. Finding the coordinates can be a very time-consuming process, especially if there are many polygonal hotspots as in the imagemap at the beginning of the chapter in Figure 36.1. Fortunately, there are tools available, called *imagemap editors*, that can aid you in this process. These programs load the image you created in step 1, and enable you to "draw" the hotspots on top of them (although they are invisible to the user), entering the respective URL for each one. It then saves the finished configuration file. The following are some popular imagemap editors:

- Mapedit (UNIX/X, Windows) by Thomas Boutell. Supports NCSA and CERN formats (http://sunsite.unc.edu/boutell/mapedit/mapedit.html).
- WebMap (Macintosh) by Rowland Smith. Supports NCSA and CERN formats; it works well with MacImageMap and MapServe (http://www.city.net/cnx/software/webmap.html).

> **NOTE**
>
> Some server modules, namely MacImageMap and older versions of NCSA HTTPD (1.3 and earlier), require an intermediate step. These programs need to know the names of all available imagemaps they serve, which are entered into a global configuration file (usually called `imagemap.conf`). See the MacImageMap documentation (http://weyl.zib-berlin.de/imagemap/distribution/README.html) for detailed instructions. The other servers are able to recognize imagemaps from their URLs (shown in the next section), and decode them automatically.

Making the HTML Document

This is the easiest of the three steps. To make your new imagemap "live," you need to put it in an HTML document. This is done with the following simple construct:

```
<A HREF="imap-URL"><IMG SRC="image-URL" ISMAP></a>
```

The `<IMG>` element displays the image at `image-URL`, whereas the `<A>` element links it to the imagemap config file at `imap-URL`. Whereas the image could be anywhere accessible via a valid

URL, the `imap-URL` depends on the server module (as well as your local installation), and generally follows these constructs:

NCSA HTTPD (1.4+)

`http://host.domain/cgi-bin/imagemap/path/filename`

Where `http://host.domain/path/filename` is the URL that would normally point to the map config file.

CERN HTTPD

`http://host.domain/cgi-bin/htimage/path/filename`

With same meaning as above

Windows HTTPD

`http://host.domain/cgi-win/imagemap.exe/filename`

HTTPS

`http://host.domain/.../filename.map`

The path isn't important as long as the filename has a .map extension

MacImageMap

`http://host.domain/imagemap/imagemap.cgi$mapname`

Where `mapname` is the name given in the global config file (mentioned in the note box earlier).

MapServe

`http://host.domain/path/mapserve.cgi$filename`

Where *path* is the path to the script.

The ISMAP attribute of the `<IMG>` element in our simple construct is important, in that it tells the browser to return the coordinates of the user's mouse click (as opposed to a normal hyperlinked graphic, such as an iconic button, in which the entire graphic is a single link and location is unimportant).

For example, the image in Figure 36.2 (which resides on a CERN server) would be referenced with the following HTML code:

```
<A HREF="http://wings.buffalo.edu/cgi-bin/htimage/maps/homepage">
<IMG SRC="http://wings.buffalo.edu/images/homepage.gif" ISMAP>
</A>
```

The Gory Details

If you're interested, here is a brief description of what is going on when you use imagemaps. If not, skip to the next section. Basically, the imagemap gets used in the following process:

1. The user points to a spot on the image.
2. The browser sends a request for the imagemap with the given coordinates—that is, `imap-URL?x,y`.

3. The HTTP server recognizes the requested URL as an imagemap and sends the pertinent information (coordinates and `config` filename) to the imagemap script.

4. The imagemap script reads the config file and finds a match.

5. Rather than send back a real HTML document, the module returns a simple header, known as a *redirection*, containing the URL of the selected hotspot: `Location: URL`

6. The browser sees this response and issues a new request for the correct document. From here on, everything is the same as in a normal HTTP request.

Design Tips

As you create your imagemap applications, please keep in mind the following suggestions. They will help you build more easily and widely usable pages.

- **Image design.** The image you create for your page can be anything you want. However, remember that for most applications, the purpose is not to impress people by your graphics prowess, but to produce an easy-to-use service. Thoughtfully consider your users, and how best to design your image to benefit them.

- **Limitations of browsers.** Although you may have a high-resolution, true-color monitor, many people don't. If you make a huge image, people with smaller screens will have to scroll around, and they will likely not come back. If you use 16 million colors, with very subtle color changes conveying important messages, the image will likely be invisible on screens with 16 or 256 colors (let alone monochrome). A good limit is 600×350 pixels, using about 50 unique colors (you can usually get away with 100 colors on a photo and keep acceptable quality). Most importantly, remember that many users are on terminals that don't have graphics support at all. If your imagemap will convey an important message (such as a navigational menu on a home page), include the equivalent information in normal HTML, either on the same page or as a separate document. Respect for others' computer capabilities will bring them back.

- **Memory size.** Remember that the larger your image is on the disk, the longer it takes (and the more frustrating it is) for users to download. 60–70KB is a good upper limit on most images (unless more is absolutely necessary). Two things affect the size of a GIF image: physical size (see above) and complexity. Complexity can be reduced by using fewer colors and having larger sections of constant color.

- **Appearance of hotspots.** It is important that your image convey its purpose to users simply and clearly. This means two things: first, the areas that are linked need to be made apparent. Users are likely to point to anything on the image that looks like it might go somewhere. You can use background color and shading, outlines, or a 3-D "button" motif to make the "hot" areas look "hot." You also can shade the labels or icons in hot areas in brighter colors, to emulate the method in which hypertext links are shown in the rest of the document. Your alternative is to make everything in the image go somewhere (including the title), but this might not always be meaningful.

The other implication of this requirement is that the contents of the hotspot are clear as to where it is pointing. Take care to choose icons and text that convey their meaning unambiguously. For example, a large question mark as an icon may mean "search" or "help" or "more information." Although text labels may not be as pretty, they can often be much more understandable than any icon. Using them thoughtfully and effectively will make your image immediately clear to almost anyone.

Alternative Interactive Graphics

The interactive graphics concept is not limited to imagemaps. It can be used (albeit with more difficulty) in a wide variety of other applications. As the `<A href=URL><IMG ISMAP></A>` construct sends a normal-looking query (such as `URL?x,y`), the destination URL can be a non-imagemap CGI script that is able to do something with the coordinate. This enables you to build an application that might look like an imagemap, but is much more powerful, such as a drawing application that plots a point on the image at the requested coordinates.

Interactive graphics can be included in forms as well. The following element will place an image in a form that works much the same as an imagemap:

```
<input name="xxx" src="image-URL" type=image>
```

When the user points to a spot on the image, the entire form is immediately submitted, including the parameters `"&X=x&Y=y"` where the latter x and y are the actual coordinates. Thus, coordinate data can be processed by the CGI script along with the rest of the form data.

An example of this advanced usage is shown in Figure 36.4, which is a page from the Tiger Mapping Service from the U.S. Census Bureau (`http://tiger.census.gov/` (written by the author of this chapter). In this page, the clickable image is combined with a form consisting of desired parameters, including instructions on what to do with the mouseclick. The script must not only combine the parameters in this case, but convert the x and y coordinates to latitude and longitude, before taking the prescribed action.

FIGURE 36.4.

A page from the Tiger Mapping Service.

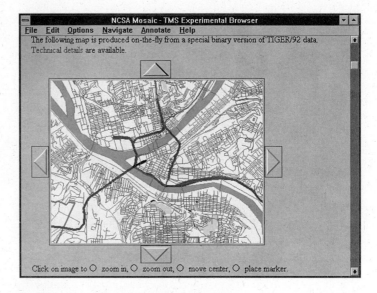

The Future of Interactive Graphics

Although the process described in this chapter is not terribly difficult, it can often be unwieldy for both the designer and the user. Maintaining several imagemaps, each containing several links, can be very time-consuming, even when using editors, because three separate files (image, `config` file, and HTML document) have to be maintained. It is also quite inefficient, because an imagemap query requires four HTTP messages (the imagemap request, the redirection reply, the true document request, and the document transfer) instead of the two used in a normal hypertext link. This makes the link act more slowly, and therefore less interactively.

There are several proposals being worked on for better implementing interactive graphics; two of the more likely are discussed now.

HTML Imagemaps

This approach, planned as part of the upcoming HTML 3.0 specification, attempts to cut down on the network traffic by having the browser do all of the work. The coordinates for the hotspots are encoded as part of the HTML document, inside the new `<FIG>` element (which replaces `<IMG>`) in a format like the following (which would be used for the image in Figure 36.2):

```
<FIG SRC="http://wings.buffalo.edu/images/homepage.gif">
 <P>Select one:
 <DL>
  <DT><A HREF="/general/overview.html"
     SHAPE="rect 10,10,140,63">Welcome!</A>
   <DD>An introduction to UB: its history and mission
  <DT><A HREF="/tour/"
     SHAPE="rect 150,10,280,63">The Campus Tour</a>
   <DD>Come "visit" our campus
```

```
<DT><A HREF="gopher://wings.buffalo.edu/hh/directories"
   SHAPE="rect 10,136,140,126">Directories</a>
 <DD>Help in finding people and places on campus
<DT><A HREF="/academic/department/"
   SHAPE="rect 150,73,280,126">Academics</a>
 <DD>Top-notch departments and degree programs
<DT><A HREF="/services.html"
   SHAPE="rect 10,136,140,189">Facilities</a>
 <DD>Libraries, computing services, and more
<DT><A HREF="gopher://wings.buffalo.edu/hh/faculty/research"
   SHAPE="rect 150,136,280,189">Research</a>
 <DD>Exhibits of work done by faculty and in our 50 centers
<DT><A HREF="gopher://wings.buffalo.edu/hh/alumni"
   SHAPE="10,199,140,252">Alumni Relations</A>
 <DD>Information for those of you who used to be part of us
<DT><A HREF="http://wings.buffalo.edu/other.html"
   SHAPE="150,199,280,252">UB Net</A>
 <DD>WWW and other information services on campus
 </DL>
</FIG>
```

In this example, the body contained within <FIG> will be displayed if the image isn't (eliminating the need to create a second page for non-graphics users). Notice that each <A> element has a SHAPE attribute. This defines the hotspot for the image when it is displayed.

When the user points to the image, the coordinates are processed by the browser, which retrieves the proper URL without having to ever go back to the server. This method can be much simpler than the current method, as you need to deal with one less file (the map config file). However, it can become unwieldy if more than eight to 10 hotspots are used, as so much code has to go into a normally textual document. Its best niche will be in the relatively simple graphical menus and button bars.

For more information, see the figures section of the draft HTML 3.0 specification at http:// www.hpl.hp.co.uk/people/dsr/html/figures.html.

Built-In Imagemaps

In this style, the hotspots are an integral part of the graphic file itself. This capability is being included in several proposals for new formats, especially object-based graphics (as opposed to raster graphics such as GIF) such as the Simple Vector Format (http://www.niiip.org/svf/) and Virtual Reality Modeling Language (http://vrml.wired.com/). In the software used to create the graphic, URLs could be attached to any visible object (such as a rectangle or a piece of text), automatically making it live. "Invisible objects" could also be created, for hotspots with no visual representation. In the WWW, the imagemap would be transported to the browser as part of the file. Once there, the browser would read it and process clicks itself, as in the previous example.

The biggest advantages of this approach are: hotspots are associated with actual image objects (necessary if the user can zoom and pan to browse the drawing); large numbers of hotspots can be created without the overhead of drawing separate hotspot objects; and creating imagemaps could be an integral part of commercial graphics software. However, no compatible software will likely exist for a while, and this approach cannot be done manually, as can today's method (that is, editing a file with a generic text editor). Even with software, it would be much more work for simple imagemaps, and unlike the other two styles, it couldn't be altered on-the-fly, as in some dynamic graphics applications now on the WWW.

The built-in approach will probably be best suited to interactive applications involving very complex graphics, such as architecture, engineering, and mapping.

In the future of the Web, all three approaches will probably coexist, with each being appropriate for various applications. Although the current system will continue to work for most imagemaps, the HTML imagemap will work well for the simplest applications, whereas the vector, built-in imagemap is used with sophisticated graphics.

Together, interactive graphics tools give WWW designers the ability to give their pages a professional appearance. Judging by their growing popularity, it is clear that we could be coming to a point where there will be two "flavors" of the World Wide Web: one like the current system, based on a document metaphor; and a second, entirely graphics oriented, built of interconnected "slides" rather than "pages." Perhaps each will use its own viewer/browser, or perhaps the Web will be able to integrate them together much better than it does now, giving users the best of both worlds: the solid information of the document side and the visual appeal of the graphics side.

HTML Editors and Filters

37

by
Thomas Boutell,
Laura Lemay,
and
David Randall

Faced with the task of creating HTML (HyperText Markup Language) documents, it is natural to wish for an easy, friendly way of creating them. If you have a large number of existing documents, you probably want a straightforward way to convert them to HTML without rewriting them; this is the purpose of HTML filters. Fortunately, HTML filters, which are discussed later in this chapter, are fairly numerous.

When creating new documents, one might expect a *WYSIWYG* (What You See Is What You Get) environment, in which you can immediately see the final appearance of your work. After all, word processors have provided such features for years.

But now the reality: Although there are plenty of HTML editors that claim to make your task easier, few of them succeed. Some editors attempt to provide a WYSIWYG environment, and a few attempt to help you write correct HTML documents, but only a small number of products make a credible showing in all three categories: ease-of-use, WYSIWYG environment, and the creation of correct documents that look good within many different browsers.

There is also a much smaller group of editors that attempt to be even remotely WYSIWYG. An even smaller assortment actually attempts to help you write correct HTML documents. Fortunately, there are a few products that make a credible showing in all three categories.

As has been discussed in earlier chapters, HTML documents consist of a collection of tags in angle brackets, such as <EM> for emphasis and </EM> to close it. Learning to follow these tags is relatively easy, as their names are fairly intuitive, but memorizing all of them and keeping the order straight is more work than you might want to do by hand.

All HTML editors provide convenient tag-insertion menus and button bars, but editors *should* be able to insert closing tags for you and make sure that your document follows the HTML standard. Unfortunately, though, most of the presently available editors are essentially text editors with pretty buttons provided to insert tags. They do nothing to help structure your document, and in most cases their only WYSIWYG feature is the ability to invoke Mosaic or another browser as a WYSIWYG previewer.

You might feel the need to point out that you can create such a collection of macros yourself using your favorite word processor, and you'd be correct. Some of the best editors are macro packages for Microsoft Word and WordPerfect (under the Microsoft Windows and Macintosh environments), and for the Emacs editor (under UNIX).

BEFORE YOU FETCH THESE PACKAGES...

Anonymous FTP sites and URLs are provided for each package described in this chapter, but remember that Internet sites are subject to rapid change. Also remember that sites often are overloaded by too many attempts to retrieve the same package. Before obtaining one of these packages from the URL provided, make an effort to locate it at a site near your own by using the Archie program that is available from nearly all Internet sites (such as any UNIX shell account provider you might use).

Non-WYSIWYG Editors

Most standalone HTML editors for Microsoft Windows or for the Macintosh have no WYSIWYG features. They do, however, attempt to provide other benefits. The following section describes several such editors for a variety of platforms.

HTML Assistant

One of the most popular editors for Microsoft Windows is HTML Assistant, available by anonymous FTP from `ftp.cuhk.hk` in the directory `pub/www/windows/util/htmlasst.zip`. HTML Assistant is essentially a text editor dressed up with buttons that can insert the more commonly used HTML tags. (See Figure 37.1.)

FIGURE 37.1.

HTML Assistant.

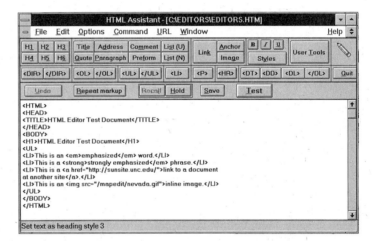

Perhaps its best feature is the ability to automatically instruct your World Wide Web browser to load or reload the document, providing a preview capability. HTML Assistant also has good online help.

In addition, this editor helps the user construct URLs, providing a history of frequently linked-to URLs and a menu of the usual access methods (`http:`, `ftp:`, and the like) to construct links more quickly.

An important disadvantage: HTML Assistant cannot open files larger than 32K in size. This restriction makes it impossible to open large HTML files, such as the WWW Frequently Asked Questions (FAQ) list, which was used as a test document.

HTMLed

HTMLed for Microsoft Windows is a newer package, available by anonymous FTP from `ftp.cuhk.hk` in the directory `pub/www/windows/util/htmled10.zip`. Much like HTML Assistant,

HTMLed is a gussied-up text editor with convenient buttons for the insertion of HTML tags (see Figure 37.2). However, HTMLed lacks many of the features of the latest versions of HTML Assistant. HTMLed has no capability to assist in building anchors (except for a history capability), and no online help.

FIGURE 37.2.

HTMLed.

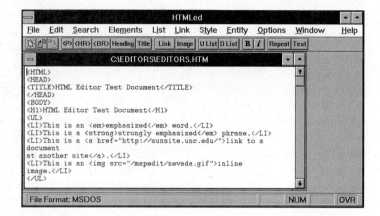

The strongest feature of HTMLed could be a conversion facility provided for *intelligently* inserting tags at the beginnings and ends of lines in a particular portion of the document (see Figure 37.3). This makes it easy to convert a plain ASCII text document into a reasonable HTML document.

HTMLed does attempt, in a very limited way, to encourage good HTML style by inserting both opening and closing tags when elements are inserted from its toolbars. It has other interesting macros, such as one that creates the following commonly seen structure:

```
<TITLE>The title text</TITLE>
<H1>The title text</H1>
```

Unfortunately, this is not correct HTML. The title tag should be within the `<HEAD>` tag at the beginning of the document, and the `H1` tag should follow later within the `<BODY>` tag.

In addition, HTMLed has the same problem as HTML Assistant: it cannot open large files. Worse, it does not produce a clear error message when failing to do so.

Products such as HTML Assistant and HTMLed are essentially stopgaps. What they truly reveal is the need for editors that actually understand HTML to a significant degree and help the user to create correct documents. The more the editor knows about HTML, the more it will be able to help you.

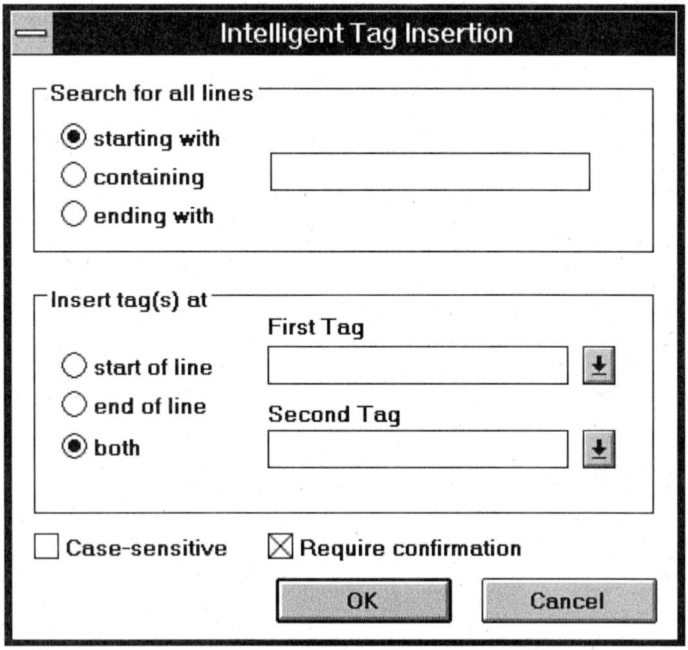

FIGURE 37.3.

HTMLed intelligent tag insertion.

```
┌─────────────────────────────────────────────┐
│ ─     Intelligent Tag Insertion              │
├─────────────────────────────────────────────┤
│ ┌─Search for all lines──────────────────────┐│
│ │  ◉ starting with      ┌──────────────────┐││
│ │  ○ containing         │                  │││
│ │  ○ ending with        └──────────────────┘││
│ └───────────────────────────────────────────┘│
│ ┌─Insert tag(s) at──────────────────────────┐│
│ │                      First Tag             ││
│ │  ○ start of line     ┌──────────────┐ ┌─┐ ││
│ │  ○ end of line       └──────────────┘ └↓┘ ││
│ │  ◉ both              Second Tag            ││
│ │                      ┌──────────────┐ ┌─┐ ││
│ │                      └──────────────┘ └↓┘ ││
│ └───────────────────────────────────────────┘│
│  ☐ Case-sensitive    ☒ Require confirmation  │
│            ┌────────┐      ┌────────┐         │
│            │   OK   │      │ Cancel │         │
│            └────────┘      └────────┘         │
└─────────────────────────────────────────────┘
```

HTML.edit

HTML.edit is a freeware HTML editor for the Macintosh. HTML.edit is available by anonymous FTP at most common Macintosh archives such as sumex or its various mirrors (try the Gopher archive at gopher://catfish.lcs.mit.edu, for example). HTML.edit is written in HyperCard, and behaves much like a HyperCard stack, but does not require the HyperCard program in order to run.

HTML.edit is quite complete, allowing you to insert most HTML tags (including <HTML>, <HEAD>, and <BODY>) into a simple text file. Inserting links is particularly easy; HTML.edit allows you to easily create both links to other documents and anchors within the current document.

In addition to the standard HTML tags, HTML.edit also contains an automatic indexing feature (for easily creating linked Table of Contents listings), a command for inserting paragraph (<P>) tags at the end of every paragraph in the selected text (which makes converting plain text files particularly easy), and a window of special characters (diacriticals and other entities) where, when you click on a character, the appropriate HTML code for that character is inserted.

The biggest problem with HTML.edit is its interface. It opens with an index page (card) that lists several files and includes buttons for saving, deleting, and editing files. (See Figure 37.4.)

FIGURE 37.4.

HTML.edit Index Card.

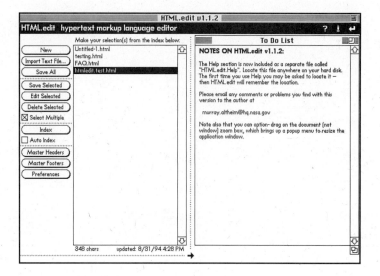

The relationship between the files in the list and the HTML files on the disk was somewhat confusing. The lists were entirely different. A quick read through the online help file cleared up the confusion: The index card enables you to create a system of HTML files (sort of like a project in Think C, or a Book file in FrameMaker), and easily create links between them (the files in the index appear in a menu for inserting links). To have a file listed in the index page, you must import it into HTML.edit first.

The cards for actually editing HTML files are slightly more straightforward, but are littered with extra buttons and menus whose effects are mysterious and confusing (see Figure 37.5). The window itself is divided into three parts: a header, a body, and a footer. The header and the footer are one line wide, and it was difficult to figure out how to resize them without reading the help. There are also buttons and menus everywhere: a toolbar with pull-down menus, a set of navigation buttons along the button edge, and several other clickable items whose effects were not immediately apparent. Once again, after reading the online help, things were much clearer.

The help for HTML.edit implies that when you import an HTML file into HTML.edit, the HTML tags in that file are parsed and errors are pointed out. Several intentional, grievous errors to the sample file were made (closing a `<STRONG>` tag with `</em>`, leaving off a closing tag for an anchor `</a>`, and creating a mythical tag `<ruff>`). HTML.edit imported the file with not a single complaint. It did, however, recognize and correct a `<TITLE>` tag in the `<BODY>` section, and moved it to the `<HEAD>` section.

Like HTML assistant and HTMLed, HTML.edit has a limit on the size of imported files (30KB), imposed by the HyperCard engine. The online help does provide a "cheat" for getting around the limit by putting parts of the file in the header and footer windows.

FIGURE 37.5.

HTML.edit editing windows.

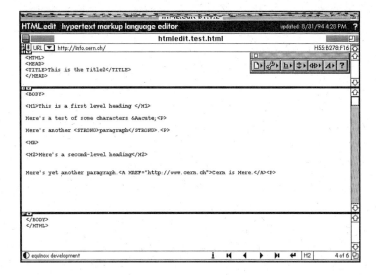

Simple HTML Editor

Simple HTML Editor (SHE), for the Macintosh, is freeware, and is available by anonymous FTP from `ericmorgan.lib.ncsu.edu`, in `/Public/simple-http-editor.hqx`. SHE is a HyperCard stack and requires the HyperCard program to run (see Figure 37.6).

The interface is simple: an HTML menu allows the insertion of many popular HTML tags including titles, heading tags, paragraphs, comments, rule lines, links, and character formatting (it does not provide document tags such as `<HTML>`, `<HEAD>`, or `<BODY>`).

There is also a small tool palette that allows you to insert tags by selecting icons. Most of the menu items (and palette icons) require some amount of text to be selected before SHE imports the tags.

You can import files into SHE by using the Open... menu item. Be forewarned, however, that SHE has a size limit on imported files that it does not tell you about. Worse, when you try to import larger files (such as the Frequently Answered Questions file), SHE silently cuts off any portion of the file that exceeds the limit. No error or warning message is ever produced; you just find out when you get to the end of the scrolling window that the end of your file is missing.

SHE is acceptable for small, simple files, but the functionality is limited. HTML.edit is more general and comprehensive for editing HTML files on the Macintosh.

FIGURE 37.6.

SHE.

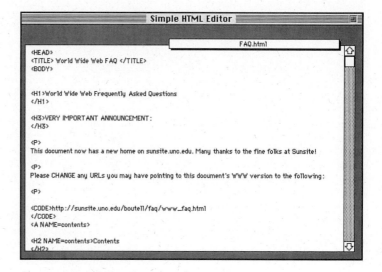

Extensions for Alpha and BBEdit

Alpha and BBEdit are two popular text editors for the Macintosh, and both have extensions available that allow insertion of HTML tags into the file you're editing, enabling you to use the powerful capabilities of a general text editor as well as insert HTML tags. Alpha is a shareware programmer's text editor; BBEdit's interface is friendlier, but is a commercial application (there is a freeware "lite" version with fewer capabilities).

The BBEdit HTML extensions (and the freeware version of BBEdit as well) are available by anonymous FTP at most common Macintosh archives such as sumex or its various mirrors (try the Gopher archive at `gopher://catfish.lcs.mit.edu`, for example). See Figure 37.7 for an example of the HTML menu in BBEdit after the extensions have been loaded.

The Alpha HTML extensions (and the Alpha editor) are available by anonymous FTP at `cs.rice.edu`. As of Alpha version 5.92b, the HTML extensions have been incorporated into the main Alpha release. For earlier versions of Alpha, get the file `html.0.14.sit.bin` from the `Alpha/contrib` directory on `cs.rice.edu` (`ftp://cs.rice.edu/public/Alpha/contrib/html.0.14.sit.bin`).

See Figure 37.8 for an example of the HTML menu in Alpha after the extensions have been loaded.

FIGURE 37.7.
BBEdit.

FIGURE 37.8.
Alpha.

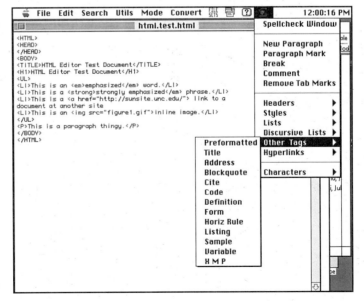

Near-WYSIWYG Editors

A truly WYSIWYG HTML editor is impossible. This is because there are many different browser packages, including the Windows, Macintosh, and UNIX flavors of Mosaic and many others such as Chimera (for X11), Cello (for Windows), and Lynx (for text environments such as DOS and UNIX shell accounts). Each browser has its own idea of how to display HTML text, and its own formatting conventions.

What's more, even if all of your readers were to use the same browser, they still wouldn't see the same thing. Many users change the font settings, window size, and other attributes of their browsers to suit their personal taste.

Many of the worst documents on the Web try to assume that text will wrap at a particular point on the line, or that every user will have a particular font size, or that a convenient bug found in one browser will also exist in every other browser. When using near-WYSIWYG editors, be sure to remember that if your document depends on the exact window width, font size, or other idiosyncrasies of your browser, it will probably look terrible on another user's display.

Near-WYSIWYG features are a great help, because they enable you to see at a glance whether you have turned on <em> (emphasis, *italic* on most browsers), <strong> (strong emphasis, **bold** on most browsers), <H1> (header one, very large on most browsers), and the like. They also enable you to see at a glance how deeply you have nested list elements (such as an unnumbered list, displayed with bullets for each item on most browsers). But it is just as well that they do not match browser displays exactly, as it would be a mistake to assume that the display of every user's browser will precisely match that of your editor.

CU_HTML

CU_HTML is a template package for Microsoft Word for Windows that provides an impressive, near-WYSIWYG environment for creating HTML documents. (Both Word 2.0 and Word 6.0 are supported. At the time of this writing, the Macintosh version of Word is not supported.) CU_HTML can be obtained by anonymous FTP from `ftp.cuhk.hk` in the directory `pub/www/windows/util/cu_html.zip` (see Figure 37.9).

CU_HTML is quite useful for creating new HTML documents and immediately seeing the results. Because it is a template package, it works within Microsoft Word, which ensures a full-featured editing environment; but as it provides several DLLs of its own, it is capable of things that most standalone editors can't even handle, including inline image display. (The inline images do have to reside on your file system, but this is quite often the case. Inline links to outside images cannot be easily created, however.)

CU_HTML provides a collection of styles that allow header levels 1 through 6, emphasis, strong emphasis, addresses, and the like. CU_HTML also provides a small toolbar of frequently used operations, such as the creation of links.

FIGURE 37.9.
CU_HTML.

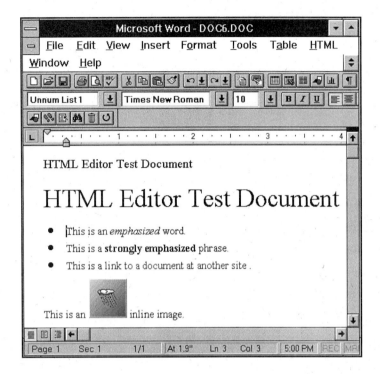

Link creation with CU_HTML is most elegant when the document you are linking to exists on the same system. In that case, you can take advantage of the File dialog box provided to seek out the file to which you want to link. In the case of links to documents located on other servers, CU_HTML is actually less elegant than HTML Assistant, as it does not provide the convenience of a history of frequently used URLs.

CU_HTML and Existing Documents

The greatest weakness of CU_HTML is that it cannot be used to edit existing HTML documents. CU_HTML documents continue to exist in the Word for Windows DOC format, side by side with HTML versions that are exported, one-way, from the system. As with the other editors, it was not possible to effectively edit a large existing HTML document, the WWW FAQ List. Re-creating every tag in an existing document is not an acceptable price to pay for a WYSIWYG environment.

If you will be creating new documents or converting ASCII documents, and already have access to Word for Windows, CU_HTML is worth careful consideration. If you have a large collection of existing HTML documents, or expect to inherit one, you will probably want to look elsewhere.

ANT_HTML

ANT_HTML is also a template package for Microsoft Word for Windows. Much like CU_HTML, ANT_HTML provides a near-WYSIWYG authoring environment. ANT_HTML, however, differs in several respects. It can be obtained by anonymous FTP from `ftp.einet.net` in the directory `EINet/pc` (see Figure 37.10).

ANT_HTML has most of the same advantages and disadvantages as does CU_HTML; it cannot edit existing HTML documents, but has strong capabilities for creating new ones. Like CU_HTML, ANT_HTML can handle inline GIF images, but it does not provide DLLs for this; instead it requires that you acquire appropriate filters for the images you want to insert.

ANT_HTML has stronger documentation and a more comprehensive toolbar than does CU_HTML, providing buttons for most of its operations instead of just a few. Also, it makes a point of inserting both opening and closing tags when an element is inserted.

FIGURE 37.10.
ANT_HTML.

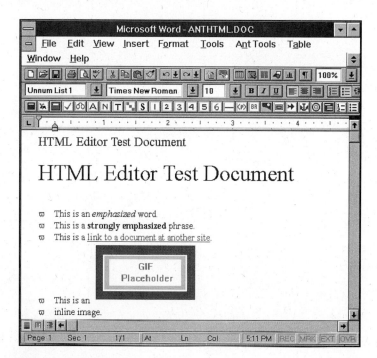

ANT_HTML and Existing Documents

Like CU_HTML, ANT_HTML cannot be used to edit existing HTML documents in a WYSIWYG fashion. Unfortunately, this is not easily understood from the documentation, and considerable time was lost trying to convert the Frequently Asked Questions document to take advantage of the styles ANT_HTML provides.

As with CU_HTML, if you will be creating new documents or converting ASCII documents and already have access to Word for Windows, ANT_HTML is worth careful consideration. Although ANT_HTML puts more functionality on the button bar and does a better job with nested lists, CU_HTML is preferred because of its superior display. Neither package, though, is suitable for editing existing HTML documents.

Softquad HoTMetaL—Above the Crowd

The strongest editor as of this writing is Softquad HoTMetaL, which is available for both Microsoft Windows and Sun SPARC (UNIX) systems. (It is likely that it will be available for other UNIX platforms by the time you read this.) HoTMetaL is a commercial product, but the entry-level version is freely available by FTP; the commercial version, HoTMetaL Pro, has more features and should be available for purchase in the immediate future. HoTMetaL is available from anonymous FTP from `ftp.ncsa.uiuc.edu` in the directory `/Web/html/hotmetal/Windows`.

Unlike CU_HTML, HoTMetaL is a standalone program and does not require a word processor. Softquad is truly remarkable in that it provides both a reasonably-close-to-WYSIWYG display and a good sense of the structure of your HTML document. What's more, it actively encourages good HTML style by only allowing you to insert tags where they are legal. For instance, your entire document must be enclosed in an `<HTML>` tag, and the `<TITLE>` element must be enclosed in a `<HEAD>` tag.

These requirements might seem like nit-picking, but in actuality they are very worthwhile because they make it possible for future clients to request only certain portions of your document in much less time, and also because they allow your documents to be examined by SGML-supporting programs. (HTML is a particular case of SGML, a more general language for describing markup languages like HTML. Most HTML documents don't comply with the SGML DTD, or rule set, that formally defines HTML.)

> **NOTE**
>
> In Figure 37.11, Display of tags is turned on. This can be toggled on and off freely; tags need not be displayed all the time.

The Word for Windows-based packages do have some advantages over HoTMetaL; note that the GIF image in the above document is not visible. But HoTMetaL's capability to ensure that you insert only the tags that make sense at a particular point outweighs the disadvantages.

FIGURE 37.11.

Softquad HoTMetal.

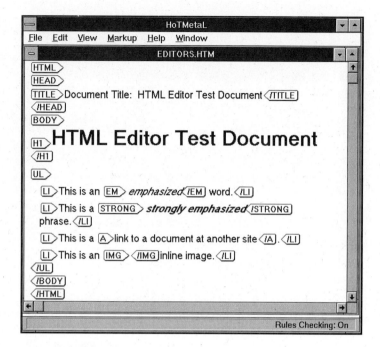

Existing Documents and HoTMetaL

The greatest disadvantage of HoTMetaL at this time is its inability to load many older docu-ments that do not conform closely to the official rules of HTML. In practical terms, this means that most documents cannot be loaded, or they can only be loaded with a *relaxed rules file*, which HoTMetaL automatically tries when the strict rules fail.

When you attempt to load an older document into HoTMetaL using the strict rule set, you will probably receive a message saying that your document is not fully compliant, and specifying a line number (which in my experience is not always correct) where the first violation of HTML takes place.

It was hoped that HoTMetaL would be suitable to edit the World Wide Web FAQ (Frequently Asked Questions list). Unfortunately, it was impossible to open it with the strict rule set *or* the relaxed rule set. It is certainly true that it would be possible to load the document if it were com-pletely compliant with the rules, but bringing it into compliance is something one would like to be able to do with the editor!

As an example, see Figure 37.12, which contains the error message that HoTMetaL produced for the first version of the editors.htm file shown in Figure 37.11. In the first version of the file, I had attempted to close a <STRONG> tag with an </EM> closing tag (the correct tag is </STRONG>).

You might ask, "So why can't it load the document anyway, show me where the errors are, and let me fix them?" It should be possible, but as of this writing HoTMetaL can't do it. The HoTMetaL authors have stated that this feature will be available in HoTMetaL Pro (at least in the commercial version). HoTMetaL Pro will also include a cleanup program that attempts to fix problems with old HTML files before they are imported. Nonetheless, for the creation of new documents, HoTMetaL is tough to beat.

FIGURE 37.12.

HoTMetal error message (refusal to load file).

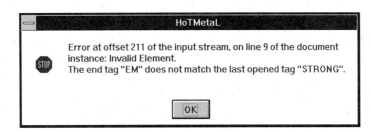

> **HoTMetal**
>
> Error at offset 211 of the input stream, on line 9 of the document instance: Invalid Element.
> The end tag "EM" does not match the last opened tag "STRONG".
>
> OK

HTML Editor

HTML Editor for the Macintosh is an interesting combination of a non-WYSIWYG text editor that simply inserts tags and a WYSIWYG editor that allows you to see what your text might look like in its final form. HTML Editor is available by anonymous FTP at cs.dal.ca in the file /giles/HTML_Editor_1.0.sit.hqx. The documentation is available as a separate file at ftp:// http://dragon.acadiau.ca:1667/~giles/HTML_Editor/Documentation.html. (See Figure 37.13.)

HTML Editor is shareware, and at $25 is a bargain, given its capabilities.

HTML Editor allows you to insert tags into text using menus, buttons, and command keys. It includes a rather complete set of HTML tags, and any missing tags can be specified in a User Tags window. When you insert a tag, the tag text itself appears in a light gray color (if you have a monochrome monitor, there is no color difference); when you type, the text you enter is in an appropriate format for that tag. For example, Headings (<H1>, <H2>, and so on) are in a larger font and boldface (see Figure 37.13). The default formatting appears to be Mosaic-like, but HTML Editor allows you to change the styles for each tag and then reapply those new styles across the document.

You can preview the text you have written, either within HTML Editor using the Hide Tags button or by selecting the Mosaic button, which loads the browser of your choice (Mosaic by default; it can be customized through the Preferences... dialog box). Or at least, that is the theory; it didn't seem to work reliably.

Opening existing HTML documents is straightforward, and there are no file-size limits that were discernible. You have a choice in the Preferences dialog box of whether to *auto-style* the text you are importing; with auto-style turned on, the HTML tags are turned on and the text is formatted in appropriate ways. Turning auto-style off imports files much faster, but they appear in all the same font.

It was possible to import the Frequently Asked Questions file with auto-style turned on, and although the translation took many minutes, the result was accurate and impressive.

FIGURE 37.13.

HTML Editor.

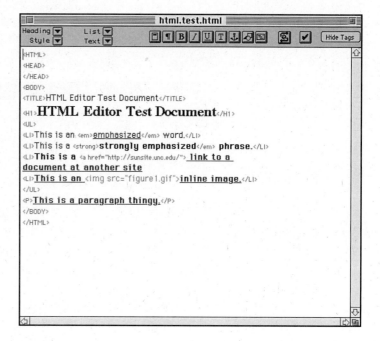

Like HoTMetaL, HTML Editor did not understand how to handle the file with errors in it. However, it did do HoTMetaL one better: it loaded the file, and simply skipped over the erroneous tag that closed a . Or rather, the style skipped over the tag; the tag was still included, which made for quick debugging of the text.

The only quibbles with HTML Editor are that it doesn't have document tags such as <HTML>, <HEAD>, and <BODY> (although you can easily specify those in the User Tags window), and it doesn't have printing capabilities (but printing is promised in a later version).

tkWWW

tkWWW is a combined World Wide Web browser and editor based on the Tk/Tcl toolkit. As such, it currently runs only on UNIX systems with the X Window System, but ports of the Tk/Tcl toolkit to Microsoft Windows and the Macintosh are well on the way (see Figure 37.14).

The Tk and Tcl packages can be obtained by anonymous FTP from ftp.cs.berkeley.edu in the directory /ucb/tcl; tkWWW itself can be obtained by anonymous FTP from harbor.ecn.purdue.edu in the directory /pub/tcl/extensions as the file tkWWW-*.tar.Z, where * is the latest version number. Version 0.12 was evaluated (note that this is still a beta version).

tkWWW is another near-WYSIWYG editor, and because it is also a browser, it can lay claim to a certain degree of true WYSIWYG. If you create a page with tkWWW as an editor and then view it with tkWWW as a browser with the same font settings and window size, you will indeed see exactly the same thing. (However, tkWWW is not a terribly impressive browser from a visual standpoint. It's unlikely many will abandon Mosaic in favor of tkWWW for general web-surfing purposes.)

FIGURE 37.14.

tkWWW.

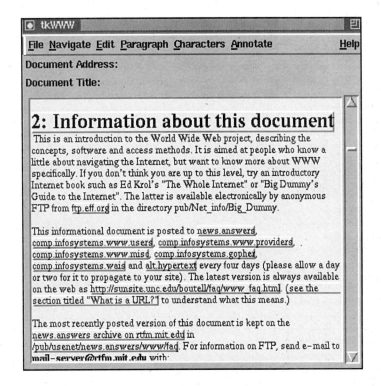

tkWWW stacks up well, feature for feature, when compared to other HTML editors. Unlike HoTMetaL, tkWWW does not enable you to see the structure of your document directly. Instead, it insulates you completely from the HTML, a valid approach in its own right.

In HoTMetaL, when you create an HTML document it ensures that you do so by the rules; you remain aware of the tags throughout the process. In tkWWW, you create a document by selecting list items, text styles, and the like from menus and observing the visible results, and tkWWW outputs correct HTML when you save the document. The HoTMetaL approach ensures that you have full control over your document, but requires more knowledge; the tkWWW approach is very user-friendly but can lead to surprises if you attempt to simply make the document look correct on the screen rather than using meaningful styles.

Unlike most editors discussed so far in this chapter, tkWWW could load the Frequently Asked Questions document. Unfortunately, it could not save that document. Instead, it produced a blank error message and offered a stack trace of its code.

To be fair, tkWWW is still in beta test. It did load, save, and edit a smaller test document.

htmltext

htmltext is an HTML editor based on the Andrew Toolkit. As such, it runs on UNIX systems with the X Window System. Ports to Microsoft Windows and the Macintosh are not expected in the near future (see Figure 37.15).

This editor is available by anonymous FTP from `ftp.cs.city.ac.uk` in the subdirectory `pub/htmltext`. If you do not have a system for which a binary is provided (at the time of this writing a binary for SunOS 4.1.X was available), you will need to obtain the Andrew Toolkit as well; Andrew is available as part of the contrib tape of the X11 distribution (which is available by anonymous FTP from many sites). Use Archie to locate a site near you.

htmltext is quite similar to tkWWW in its capabilities. Both are near-WYSIWYG, and both take the approach of insulating the user from the actual HTML tags.

If you define WYSIWYG as *looks like it will look in Mosaic*, htmltext is decidedly the closest thing to WYSIWYG available at this time. The htmltext display looks very much like that of the X Window System version of Mosaic. (Note that because there are many other browsers, and even many possible font settings for Mosaic, it is not generally a good idea to depend on this resemblance.)

Like tkWWW, htmltext places the features of HTML in a set of menus and enables you to work with the document in a word processor-like manner. Unlike tkWWW, however, htmltext has the full power of the Andrew Toolkit behind it, which means that many traditional word processing features are available, including spell checking. Also unlike tkWWW, htmltext can display inline images if they are located on the same system.

This is both a blessing and a curse, because the Andrew Toolkit, fully installed, requires between 70 and 100MB of disk space to build. There is a binary standalone version of htmltext available for SunOS 4.1.X that requires only a few megabytes, but some features are disabled due to the absence of the rest of Andrew. (This binary version was used in our evaluation, however, and no significant frustrations were encountered.)

Like tkWWW, htmltext can load the Frequently Asked Questions document. Unlike tkWWW, it can also save it.

Unfortunately, however, htmltext does not appear to fully understand nested lists. Nested lists were used to create an outline at the beginning of the Frequently Asked Questions document. But when the document is saved with htmltext, the resulting HTML is incorrect; in areas where lists are nested, seemingly random portions of the text are missing. It is difficult to be certain what htmltext is objecting to in the document.

Also, the highest level of list is not properly opened and closed. This is probably done to exploit the coincidence that some versions of Mosaic will display a flush-left list when the list is not actually opened, but it is not correct HTML and it definitely shouldn't happen to a document that dealt correctly with lists when it was loaded.

FIGURE 37.15.

htmltext.

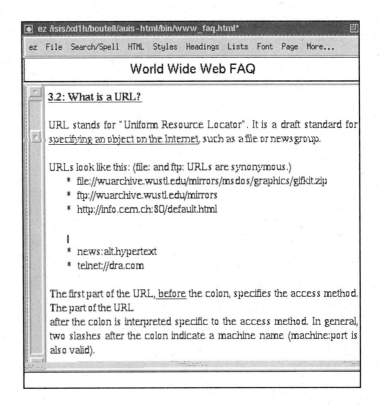

htmltext is an impressive editor, one very suitable for simple tasks. Until its list-handling features improve, however, it will not be suitable for large documents such as the Frequently Asked Questions document. Nonetheless, htmltext came closer than most editors evaluated to being able to handle that task.

Converting Your Document's HTML Filters

While HTML editors have a long way to go, HTML filters are quite well-developed. A sizable number of filters have been created to convert from existing formats such as WordPerfect, nroff/troff, RTF (Rich Text Format), and TeX to HTML.

In some cases, you might find that conversion is an ideal solution, and that you don't want to create HTML documents directly. Given the state of HTML editors, this is a possibility worth considering.

Converting from WordPerfect

WPTOHTML is a collection of WordPerfect macros that convert from WordPerfect versions 5.1 and 6.0 for DOS to HTML. It is available by anonymous FTP from oak.oakland.edu in the directory SimTel/msdos/wordperf, as the files wpt51d10.zip and wpt60d10.zip.

At the time of this writing, a conversion package from WordPerfect 5.2 for Windows was not available.

Note, however, that WordPerfect can read and write RTF (Rich Text Format), which can also be converted to HTML (see the next section).

Converting from Microsoft Word

See CU_HTML and ANT_HTML, described previously in the WYSIWYG editors section, for two good ways of transforming Word for Windows documents into HTML documents.

For a more automatic form of conversion, see the section on Rich Text Format, immediately following. (Microsoft Word can load and save RTF as well as the normal DOC format.)

Converting from RTF (Rich Text Format)

RTFTOHTML is a utility that converts files in RTF to HTML, preserving styles as well as links to other documents. RTFTOHTML binaries are available for Macintosh and Sun SPARC platforms, and source code is also available in order to build it for your own system if you have access to a compiler. RTFTOHTML is available by anonymous FTP from `ftp.cray.com` in the directory `src/WWWstuff/RTF`.

The Macintosh version of RTFTOHTML also includes a sample template file for Microsoft Word that contains a set of styles that match the HTML tags (see Figure 37.16). Like CU_HTML and ANT_HTML's templates, this provides an excellent way to write HTML documents on the Macintosh and allows them to be easily converted.

FIGURE 37.16.

The RTFTOHTML style sheet for Microsoft Word.

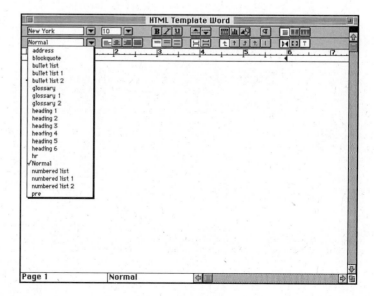

Converting from FrameMaker

`fm2html` is a set of scripts for UNIX systems, written mostly in Perl, that convert files written in FrameMaker to HTML. The fm2html package was written by Jon Stephenson von Tetzchner at Norwegian Telecom Research and is available by anonymous FTP at `bang.nta.no:/pub/ fm2html.tar.v.0.n.m.Z`.

The conversion from Frame document to HTML is quite sophisticated. fm2html includes mechanisms for converting hypertext links into HTML links and tables into preformatted text, and even translates imported images into GIF files (with the GhostScript and PBM filter programs installed). A 30-page FrameMaker file was translated with 10 imported PostScript graphics, tables, and several internal links using this filter, and the results were excellent.

Although `fm2html` is only available for UNIX, versions of FrameMaker exist for many different systems (including the Macintosh and Windows), and the files are binary-compatible across platforms. If you have access to a UNIX system with which to do the final translation, you could easily write your documents on any platform for which you had FrameMaker.

Converting from TeX and LaTeX

LaTeX (a variant of TeX) is a common format on UNIX systems, and is much more expressive than HTML in many ways. Converting it to HTML is a tough job. There is, however, an excellent package for this that succeeds amazingly (some would say to the point of overkill).

LATEXTOHTML does a very thorough job of converting LaTeX to HTML, even to the point of creating inline images for LaTeX equations. You can obtain LATEXTOHTML by anonymous FTP from `ftp.tex.ac.uk` in the directory `pub/archive/support/latex2html`, but the authors specifically request that you attempt to locate a copy closer to your site using the Archie file-finding program (installed at virtually all Internet sites). LATEXTOHTML requires that your system have an up-to-date version of the Perl script language installed.

VULCANIZE is a simpler program, also in Perl, that takes care of most nonmathematical LaTeX documents in a more straightforward manner. You can obtain VULCANIZE via the Web (URL is `http://www.cis.upenn.edu/~mjd/vulcanize.html`). Complex mathematical LaTeX documents cannot be converted without a more sophisticated package such as LATEXTOHTML, but most documents simply don't fall into that category. In the words of the author, Mark-Jason Dominus, "for a program that doesn't work, it is remarkably successful."

ADDITIONAL SOURCES OF INFORMATION

For additional information about HTML editors and filters, consult CERN's collection of tools for generating HTML (URL is `http://info.cern.ch/WWW/Tools/Overview.html`).

You also can consult NCSA's list of filters and editors (URL is `http:// www.ncsa.uiuc.edu/SDG/Software/Mosaic/Docs/faq-software.html`).

Summary

For those hoping to create World Wide Web documents dynamically in an elegant WYSIWYG environment, the future has not quite arrived. On Windows PCs and UNIX systems, Softquad HoTMetaL comes very close to the goal, but is still too frustrating for those who want to edit existing documents. On the Macintosh, HTML Editor does an excellent job. The other editors are even more disappointing, though still useful in their present form. On the Macintosh, however, the exceptional HTML Editor comes very close to the mark, failing only in the area of document tags such as <HTML>, <HEAD>, and <BODY>.

HTML filters, on the other hand, are in good shape, although they do tend to require UNIX systems or at least software with a UNIX background (with which PC users might be unfamiliar). In the future, as more and more Web servers are installed on PCs, we will probably see one-piece conversion programs for Microsoft Windows and the Macintosh.

With the growing acceptance of HTML and the World Wide Web technology, however, there is little doubt that the capability to read and write HTML will soon make an appearance in mainstream word processors themselves. IntelliTag, an SGML editing package, is already available for WordPerfect; it won't be long before WordPerfect and Word both come with HTML capability as standard equipment.

In the meantime, the authors of HoTMetaL for Windows and UNIX, HTML Editor for the Macintosh, and other products like them have an opportunity to create superior solutions tailor-made to the needs of World Wide Web information providers.

Implementing a Web Design

38

by
John December

If all the processes of web weaving operate well together, and you've mastered the skills to write HTML, you're ready to implement a web design. To do this, you'll need the products of the design process—the look and feel diagrams; the package, page, and link chart; the web specification—as well as information from the other processes of web weaving, including audience information, the purpose and objective statements, and domain information.

As an implementor, your challenge is to turn the design into a working web. To do this, you'll need to be fairly organized and have excellent knowledge of HTML and the computer system on which your web will be developed and deployed. You'll also need excellent writing skills, talent for layout and design, and a sense of how the audience uses and thinks about the information you're presenting.

In this chapter, we'll go over a sample web implementation. First, we'll start off with some general considerations for setting up the web. Then, we'll go through a step-by-step process of creating a prototype web. Throughout this chapter, we'll use the "ElectricMarket," an imaginary Web department store as an example.

A SEMINAL HYPERTEXT ARTICLE

Vannevar Bush's article, "As We May Think," which appeared in the July 1945 issue of *The Atlantic Monthly* has inspired generations of hypertext designers and implementors.

Denys Duchier has created a hypertext version of this article, reproduced with the permission of *The Atlantic Monthly,* which is available at URL
`http://www.csi.uottawa.ca/~dduchier/misc/vbush/as-we-may-think.html`.

General Considerations

In implementing a web design, you'll not only create files of HTML, but you will work with people—web planners, analysts, designers, developers, and users. You'll also have to be on good terms with your webmaster (the person who is responsible for the deployment and maintenance of your web server).

You'll need to recognize that your work, like the work of the other processes in web weaving, may never end as long as the web is deployed. Therefore, you'll need to develop your own system to deal with the multitude of changes in design that inevitably occur in a good web. You'll have to be aware of the latest methods for maintaining directories and files on your computer system as well as be responsible for backups and coordinating with the webmaster for your web's security.

You'll need to compose text to explain features of your web. Often, you'll be able to use wording from the audience information, purpose and objective statements, or other web-weaving products generated from the planning and design processes. You'll often need to customize this prose to guide the user through the specific situations occurring in the pages you'll implement.

Working with People

Although much of your time as web implementor will be spent constructing HTML files, you'll also work with other people. Even if you are the sole weaver of your web—the planner, analyst, designer, implementor, and developer—you'll still need to work with representatives from a very important group: the users of your web. Without a representative user, or at least a close analysis of their characteristics and a good understanding of them, a web can get off base and miss meeting their needs. The analysis process of web weaving (Chapter 31, "Analyzing a Web") is a means to check that audience needs are being met on the "big picture" level. As implementor, you'll be intimately concerned with minute decisions about the construction of hypertext—the placement of hotspots, links, and composing specialized features such as Forms or graphical information maps. Although a good web designer should have created a look and feel for the web, and the web specification should be able to be implemented without any problems, there will still be decisions you will have to make. It is impossible to fully specify every last detail of a web. In fact, the only record of this set of minute decisions is the web itself.

Therefore, it is important that you keep lines of communication open and operating with the following individuals:

■ **Web planners**

What do you know about the audience that might help the planners identify or meet their needs better?

Are there parts of the design that you know are not meeting the needs of the audience or are extraneous to the purpose or objective of the web?

What are the planners considering for the future? This information may help you anticipate future directory or file requirements or other future requirements that you might begin to implement as prototypes.

Do you feel that some parts of the purpose or objective of the web have not been expressed in the web specification or design?

What skills do you need to implement the web itself? Are there specialized skills or resources that you don't have?

■ **Web analysts**

What performance problems are you aware of in the web's design (many images on one page, huge pages, problems with interfaces to databases)? You can inform the web analysts to pay particular attention to these areas of the web for timing and user feedback.

What are the patterns for web use? Consider how you can help the analysts interpret the file use statistics. Do you know of a particular page that seems to be either under- or overused considering its purpose?

What overall performance concerns do the web analysts have? For example, if the purpose of the web is to get orders for products, is the number of orders low? Do you know this may be because the order form, for example, is implemented in a manner that makes it difficult to use? What other aspects of the implementation might be causing problems or dissatisfaction in users?

■ **Web designers**

What aspects of the web design are impossible or awkward to implement?

What design decisions haven't been considered or specified with sufficient detail for you to implement?

What issues of look and feel or linking in the web design do you think need to be changed or modified?

What overall concerns do you have about how the web design is meeting the purpose and objective of the web?

■ **Web developers** (web development is covered in the next chapter)

What suggestions do you have for publicity and timing of web announcements and public releases?

What features of the web do you feel need to be brought more to the attention of users?

What problems do you see with the current way web development (publicity, inputs to the planning analysis and design processes) is being done?

■ **Audience representatives**

Do you have access to a pool of representative audience members for testing your web's implementation? The analysis processes should involve a detailed study of the results of your web's use. Direct feedback from users in how you've implemented a web feature can also be very valuable.

Could you use the Forms capability of HTML to include response forms or comment boxes for eliciting user feedback?

As implementor, you'll often be the one to get e-mail from users (because of a stale link or a problem with your web). What sense do you get about the user's overall satisfaction with the web based on this feedback? What suggestions or comments might you pass on to planners, designers, and developers?

Overall, you'll find that the people-processes in implementing a web can be as complex—if not more so—than developing the HTML itself. This should not be a great surprise. After all, the web you weave is created and used by people, and people are notoriously inexact and changing. In all these interactions, keep your patience and listen: your interpersonal communications skills in eliciting constructive criticism will be a major factor to help you implement the web in the best way possible.

Planning Your File and Directory Structure

Essentially, you weave a web from files of HTML. There may be just one file, or there may be hundreds. In either case, you should be sensitive to issues of file naming and source code control. After all, if the users can't find or access the files, the web isn't useful.

■ Have a consistent, stable server name. Work with the webmaster to create a publicly known name for your server that can remain constant, even though the actual machine that supports the server may change. For example, a name like

```
www.company.com
```

is a good one, since it uses a common convention: the string www in front of the company's network domain name (company.com). A poor choice would be something like

```
unix5.its.itd.td.company.com
```

Not only is the name long and not descriptive (maybe too descriptive since it reflects the company hierarchy all the way down to the web server machine). What if the web server is moved from the unix5 machine to the unix6 machine? You don't want to have to tell all your users to change their hotlists or web pages to accommodate the name change. Instead, choose a name for your web server that is descriptive and can remain constant.

■ Organize your files in a way that is consistent but allows for growth. Just as you don't want your users to have to change their URL references to your web because of a server name change, don't force them to change their URLs because of changes in directory structure.

Plan your directory structure so that it can remain stable, even as other projects are added to your server. For example, don't put all the files for the very first web project you have in the top-level directory of your web server. This will cause a crunch later on when you add other projects.

So, for example, instead of the first project (for example, the "star" project) having the home page

```
http://www.company.com/star.html
```

consider

```
http://www.company.com/star/home.html
```

where the directory name you use (in this case, star) is a short, descriptive name of the project itself. At the project level, you can use the structure of the web design (the package, page, and link diagram) as the basis for a directory structure. Above the project level, if you know that your server will contain a great deal of information besides projects, consider

```
http://www.company.com/projects/star/home.html
```

which will leave room for

```
http://www.company.com/projects/delta/home.html
```

```
http://www.company.com/documents/catalog/home.html

http://www.company.com/services/orders/home.html
```

and other development. Although it's not impossible to change naming schemes, it's best to design an extendible naming scheme at the start. Naturally, you don't want to go to the other extreme and have a labyrinthine directory structure such as

```
http://www.company.com/projects/new/info-tech/startups/tuesday/morning/star-
project/home-directory/home.html
```

■ Consider using a source code control system, such as SCCS (Source Code Control System) on UNIX platforms to maintain configuration control over files, particularly if your web is large or there are many web weavers. Source code control systems have facilities for maintaining information to regenerate previous versions of files. So if you have to go back to a previous version of your web, you're prepared. Systems of source code control can also keep track of who makes changes to files and when. The whole process of web design, implementation, and management may be amenable to such tools. Use them where it makes sense. For small projects, these tools may create far too much overhead for them to be beneficial. For large projects, they may be essential to keep track of the many changes made in the web files.

Composing Text and Page Layout

You'll need some writing ability to implement a web. Not only will you need to know how your audience uses language, but you'll need to know how they think about the information you're presenting. In many cases, you'll be able to "steal" wording and text right from the purpose and objective statements, audience information, and domain information. With just a bit of change, this text can serve different purposes in the web implementation.

For example, each web page should have enough text to cue the user to the purpose of the page and how it's used. This text should be aimed at the needs of the user for that particular page—a customized statement of purpose, a concise overview of what information is on that page, and instructions for using the information. The designer might not have specified this language down to the wording level, but this language is important. Use a spell checker and proofread the text for grammar and syntax errors.

Although the look and feel diagrams from the design process should set goals for the overall appearance of each page, the implementor still will make many decisions about the details of each page layout. The implementor should make use of the following guidelines in creating a page:

■ Keeping in mind that you can't control how any particular browser may display your HTML file, work with the features of HTML to create, as much as possible, a grid pattern to suggest an information hierarchy. To reveal the grid pattern for a page design, draw vertical lines on the left side of the start of every element on the page. Figure 38.1 shows the grid pattern for a sample look and feel design.

FIGURE 38.1.

Gridline pattern on a page.

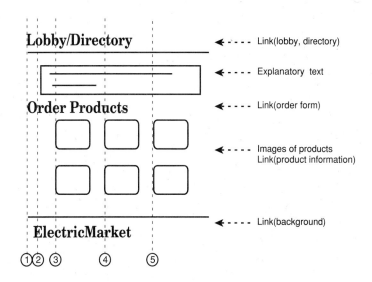

Note in this sample that there are five gridlines. The gridlines identify where the user sees vertical alignment, and this alignment implies equal functionality and purpose. Do the five gridlines on the page show an equal level of purpose?

Gridline 1 seems to indicate the headers at the first level of information—the "Lobby/Directory" and "Order Products" are cues to the reader about major functions.

Gridline 2 seems extraneous. Why slightly indent the label for "ElectricMarket?" Moving this label over to align with gridline 1 will reduce the number of gridlines by one and thus simplify the information hierarchy of the page. The explanatory text can be moved to the left, to gridline 1. Because it is set off from the "Lobby/Directory" labels by a horizontal line and the "Order Products" label by a change in font size, the indentation to gridline 2 is an extraneous emphasis of the functional difference.

Gridlines 3, 4, and 5 function only to separate the images of products. However, the placement of the products implies an information hierarchy. What products are listed first? Are the products on the same row similar? Are the products on the same gridline similar? The implementor might suggest to the designer that if the present arrangement of products has no meaning (that is, the gridlines aren't conveying different categories of products), the products could be arranged in a vertical list or on separate pages. The downside of using a vertical list is that the list of products consumes a great deal of page real estate, so the user might not be able to see all the items on the same screen. The answer to what to do about these gridlines lies in the users. How do the users want to see the products? By category? In one big list? Does the arrangement on the gridlines confuse them?

Gridlines thus reveal the information hierarchy implied in the arrangement of the elements on the page. Most browsers do an excellent job of interpreting HTML and aligning text along gridlines. You should check how several browsers handle a page. Each browser may make different alignments, but by choosing appropriate (reflecting semantic structure) HTML features consistently (lists, horizontal lines, paragraphs, and line breaks), you can influence an information hierarchy.

■ Use typographic changes to focus a user's attention. On a page, photographs, drawings or icons, and particularly color, will very quickly grab the user's eye. Next, bold headings, large letters, and page features with empty space around them will catch the reader's attention. On a page, where do you want the user's attention to go? The diagram in Figure 38.1 shows the guide links to the "Lobby/Directory" as very dominant on the page. Are the "Lobby/Directory" links central to the purpose of the page, or are they just navigation links?

Browsers display letters and fonts differently. Be aware of how the major browsers — your users—are most likely to use your pages. Look at the pages through different browsers. Locate the areas of the page where the dark/light contrasts caused by the typography or the color in images draw the user's eye. Are these the areas of the page that best reflect its purpose? If not, adjust the page elements by toning them down: make the font smaller, eliminate a diagram or a photograph or make the text smaller. Use the high-contrast elements to guide the reader's attention to the most important parts of the page.

■ Use a given/new information chain to compose text and present information on a page. While hypertext allows nonlinear reading of a web, each web page (at the surface level) still presents a linear set of information for the user. To deal with the information on a page, the user might apply the convention: start at the top and left, read to the right and down. (Many Western cultures use these conventions, but people from other cultures may have a different reading pattern. Also, surfers might not read a page like this; see Chapter 21, "Surfing: Finding the New and Unusual.")

At the prose level, take advantage of reading sequence by using an *information chain*— taking the reader from a point they know to new information. For example, if someone on the street asks me where the library is, I might say the following:

Starting from this corner, go east until you reach Second Street.

Turn north along Second Street until Congress Street.

Just north of Congress, you'll find the library.

In each sentence of these directions, I link a place the listener knows to a new place, and I repeat this new place as the known place in the next sentence.

Used with expressive variation, the information chain technique, used at the sentence as well as paragraph and page level, can help guide your user through information.

■ Use parallelism in phrasing and information wherever possible. Just as you used the gridlines to match up information at the same level of importance or functionality, use parallel phrasing to match information in lists and headings. In lists, use entries in all the same grammatical form. For example,

Products include

- apples
- oranges
- bananas

rather than

Products include

- four bags of apples
- some oranges
- banana

- Use a consistent voice when addressing the user. If you've made a decision to use direct address, be consistent. For example, the instructions at the top of a page for resources might be

  "This page contains links to well-known resources in the field of Astronomy. You can access these resources by following the highlighted links in the list. If you have suggestions for more links, or have questions, please contact the page developer at the address given at the bottom of this page."

  Rather than

  "This page contains links to well-known resources in the field of Astronomy. *The user* can access these resources by following the highlighted links in the list. If *you* have suggestions for more links, or have questions, the page developer at the address given at the bottom of this page *can be contacted... .*"

  This second example shows some inconsistency. At one point the user is referred to in third person ("the user can access") and then addressed directly ("If you have any suggestions..."). Finally, the writer uses passive voice ("the page developer....can be contacted") in which the agent of the action implied in the sentence (the person doing the contacting) is not explicitly mentioned.

- Adopt an appropriate tone for your prose and other features. If your web is meant for professional use, avoid "cute" diagrams or colloquialisms. Every part of your web conveys something about its purpose and its developers. While helping the user feel relaxed and even entertained can help the effectiveness of the web, too many "fun" additions can make the users take your web less seriously than you might have intended. On the other hand, the lack of graphics or human elements can make a web seem very dry and not the expression of a vibrant, active information community. A good way to adopt an appropriate tone is to notice how the audience members themselves talk about the information covered by the web. Also note the tone of supporting or background literature (part of the domain information).

Implementing a Design

Now that we've reviewed some general considerations about naming files and directories and shaping information and prose, let's delve into implementing an example web design.

For our example, we'll assume that we've been given design information about ElectricMarket, an innovative Web-based department store. So far, only a portion of the ElectricMarket web has been designed, but you're told to implement a prototype.

Gathering Information

The first step in implementing a web design is to gather the following information:

1. Design information—look and feel of package, page, and link diagrams

   Look and feel diagrams: You are given one for a generic page (Figure 38.2), one for a department page (Figure 38.3), and one for a product information page (Figure 38.4).

   Package, page, and link diagram. (Figure 38.5)

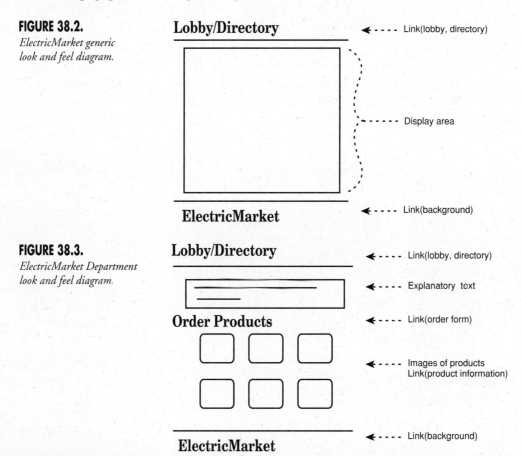

FIGURE 38.2.
ElectricMarket generic look and feel diagram.

FIGURE 38.3.
ElectricMarket Department look and feel diagram.

FIGURE 38.4.

ElectricMarket product information look and feel diagram.

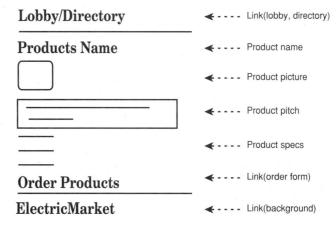

FIGURE 38.5.

ElectricMarket package, page, and link diagram.

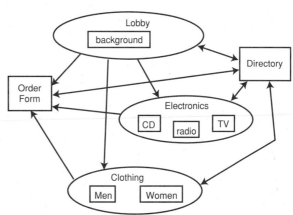

2. Audience information

   Target audience: younger net surfer with disposable income; old enough to have a credit card

   Important aspects about audience: interested in new gadgets, personal electronics, new clothing styles; willing to buy products over the Net

3. Statement of purpose

   "The purpose of the ElectricMarket is to attract buyers interested in electronics and clothing products and to solicit sales of these products."

4. Objectives

   ▪ To attract the attention of potential buyers to the ElectricMarket web

   ▪ To inform users of the products available

   ▪ To reach a sales volume that justifies the cost of web deployment and development

   ▪ To achieve customer satisfaction and get feedback on what we should offer in our product line

5. Domain information—a variety of collections

   Product information: all specs on products

   Buyer profiles: information from past studies and profiles of target audience members

   Company background: mission statement, history, and product lines

   Materials from competitors' catalogs and webs

6. Web specification—limitations on web information

   Company background: Wording from current paper brochure "About ElectricMarket, Inc." condensed to 100-300 words, no current stock or profit information

   Department offerings: List products from different departments on separate page

   Product presentation: Pictures no smaller than 2cm × 2cm, no larger than 4cm × 4cm

   Product information available at `ftp://ftp.em.com/products/`, data that should be displayed: size, color, price, catalog number

Designing a Directory and File Structure Tree

After you've gathered the previous information, you're ready to start planning the web. The first step is to plan how you will organize the files and directories to hold the ElectricMarket project. Based on the package, page, and link diagram, you can create a structure as shown in Figure 38.6.

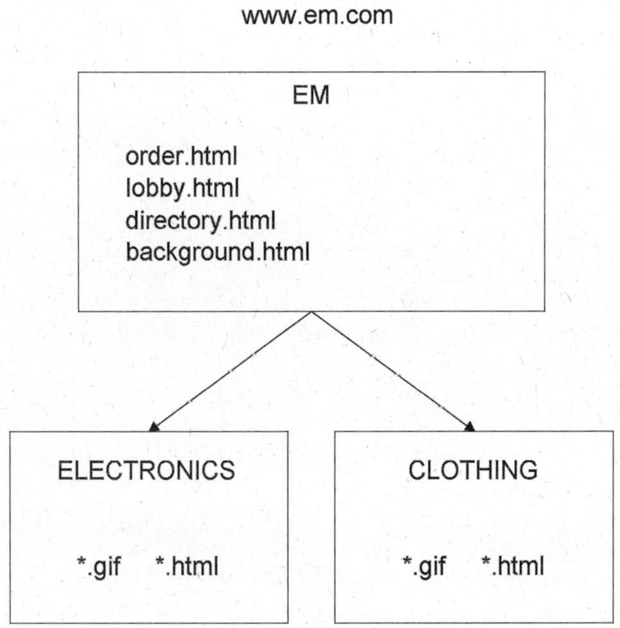

FIGURE 38.6.

ElectricMarket directory structure.

www.em.com

EM

order.html
lobby.html
directory.html
background.html

ELECTRONICS

*.gif   *.html

CLOTHING

*.gif   *.html

Making Templates

Based on the look and feel diagram shown in Figure 38.2, 38.3, and 38.4, you can construct a template that will help start the implementation of each page of the web.

First, a template like the following can serve as a basis for the whole look and feel of all the other pages:

```
<HTML>
<!— Author: K.C. Deemark (kcd@em.com) —>
<!— Dept: Web Weaving —>
<!— Date:   11 Jul 94 —>
<!— Purpose:  overall look and feel template for ElectricMarket —>
<!— Comments:  bring to next meeting for approval. —>

<HEAD>
<TITLE>ElectricMarket—Page Title</TITLE>
<LINK REV="made" HREF="mailto:kcd@em.com">
</HEAD>

<BODY>
<A HREF="../lobby.html">Lobby</A> / <A HREF="../directory.html"> Directory</A>

<HR>

<H1>Page Title</H1>
page explanation / overview / salespitch
<P>

page information
page information
page information
page information
page information
page information
page information
page information

<HR>

<ADDRESS> <A HREF="../background.html">ElectricMarket</A></ADDRESS>

</BODY>
</HTML>
```

This universal template appears through the Mosaic for X browser as shown in Figure 38.7. Notice how the features as displayed in Mosaic differ from the "look and feel" sketch in Figure 38.1.

FIGURE 38.7.

The ElectricMarket universal template viewed through Mosaic.

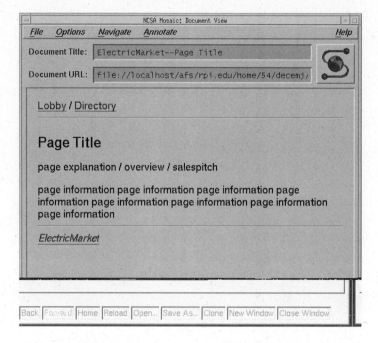

By copying the universal template to a new file, you can modify it to create a department template. Based on the department look and feel diagram, you can make a department template as follows:

```
<HTML>
<!— Author: K.C. Deemark (kcd@em.com) —>
<!— Dept: Web Weaving —>
<!— Date:   11 Jul 94 —>
<!— Purpose:   look and feel template for ElectricMarket —>
<!— Comments:  bring to next meeting for approval. —>

<HEAD>
<TITLE>ElectricMarket—DEPT(page name)</TITLE>
<LINK REV="made" HREF="mailto:kcd@em.com">
</HEAD>

<BODY>
<A HREF="../lobby.html">Lobby</A> / <A HREF="../directory.html"> Directory</A>

<HR>
page explanation / overview / salespitch /
page explanation / overview / salespitch /
page explanation / overview / salespitch /
page explanation / overview / salespitch /
<P>

<H1><A HREF="../order.html">Order Products</A></H1>
<P>

<A HREF="product.html"><IMG SRC="product.gif" ALT="PRODUCT NAME"></A>
```

```
<A HREF="product.html"><IMG SRC="product.gif" ALT="PRODUCT NAME"></A>
<A HREF="product.html"><IMG SRC="product.gif" ALT="PRODUCT NAME"></A>
<BR>
<A HREF="product.html"><IMG SRC="product.gif" ALT="PRODUCT NAME"></A>
<A HREF="product.html"><IMG SRC="product.gif" ALT="PRODUCT NAME"></A>
<A HREF="product.html"><IMG SRC="product.gif" ALT="PRODUCT NAME"></A>
<BR>
<A HREF="product.html"><IMG SRC="product.gif" ALT="PRODUCT NAME"></A>
<A HREF="product.html"><IMG SRC="product.gif" ALT="PRODUCT NAME"></A>
<A HREF="product.html"><IMG SRC="product.gif" ALT="PRODUCT NAME"></A>
<BR>

<HR>

<ADDRESS> <A HREF="../background.html">ElectricMarket</A></ADDRESS>

</BODY>
</HTML>
```

Next, make a template for the individual product page information:

```
<HTML>
<!— Author: K.C. Deemark (kcd@em.com) —>
<!— Dept: Web Weaving —>
<!— Date:   11 Jul 94 —>
<!— Purpose:   look and feel template for Product Information, ElectricMarket —>
<!— Comments:  bring to next meeting for approval. —>

<HEAD>
<TITLE>ElectricMarket—DEPT/PRODUCT NAME</TITLE>
<LINK REV="made" HREF="mailto:kcd@em.com">
</HEAD>

<BODY>
<A HREF="../lobby.html">Lobby</A> / <A HREF="../directory.html"> Directory</A>

<HR>

<H1>PRODUCT NAME</H1>

<IMG SRC="product.gif">
<P>

product explanation / salespitch /
product explanation / salespitch /
product explanation / salespitch /
product explanation / salespitch /
<P>

<UL>
<LI> Uses: use, use, use, use
<LI> Sizes: S, M, L, XL
<LI> Colors: Red, Green, Blue, Indigo
<LI> Catalog Number: 123-456-789
<LI> Price: $123.45
</UL>

<H1><A HREF="../order.html">Order Product</A></H1>
```

```
<HR>

<ADDRESS> <A HREF="../background.html">ElectricMarket</A></ADDRESS>

</BODY>
</HTML>
```

Implementing Major Pages

Now that you've developed templates for many branches of the web, you should consider interacting with other web weavers, particularly the designers and the planners, to make sure that your look and feel corresponds to what they had in mind. This is important because, as described above, your web implementation is based on a copy-and-modify method. You'll copy a root template (the universal template) and then add variations to it to create templates for other major web page types. If you have a mistake or error in the universal template, it will cascade down to all the files you've made using it as a base. Ideally, you could develop or use some automated or computer-aided tool for web design and implementation to help you with this work. Otherwise, work carefully with the files you have.

At this point, it would be a good idea to implement the other major pages for the web and then construct a working prototype of the web for further approval from other web weavers. As such, you should implement these with just prototype or initial information filled in. Later you'll carefully craft the necessary wording and make the real links. The goal is to create a working prototype for generating feedback from the other web weavers as well as possibly from representative audience members.

You can implement the Lobby as follows:

```
<HTML>
<!— Author: K.C. Deemark (kcd@em.com) —>
<!— Dept: Web Weaving —>
<!— Date:   11 Jul 94 —>
<!— Purpose:   Prototype Lobby for ElectricMarket —>
<!— Comments:  bring to next meeting for approval. —>


<HEAD>
<TITLE>ElectricMarket—Lobby</TITLE>
<LINK REV="made" HREF="mailto:kcd@em.com">
</HEAD>

<BODY>
<A HREF="directory.html"> Directory</A>

<HR>

<H1>Welcome to ElectricMarket</H1>

page explanation / overview / salespitch /
page explanation / overview / salespitch /
page explanation / overview / salespitch /
page explanation / overview / salespitch /
<P>
```

```
<UL>
<LI><A HREF="DEPT/dept.html">Look at Electronics</A>
<LI><A HREF="DEPT/dept.html">Look at Clothing</A>
<LI><A HREF="order.html">Order Products</A>
</UL>

<HR>

<ADDRESS> <A HREF="background.html">ElectricMarket</A></ADDRESS>

</BODY>
</HTML>
```

The Directory:

```
<HTML>
<!— Author: K.C. Deemark (kcd@em.com) —>
<!— Dept: Web Weaving —>
<!— Date:   11 Jul 94 —>
<!— Purpose:   Prototype Directory for ElectricMarket —>
<!— Comments:  bring to next meeting for approval. —>

<HEAD>
<TITLE>ElectricMarket—Directory</TITLE>
<LINK REV="made" HREF="mailto:kcd@em.com">
</HEAD>

<BODY>
<A HREF="lobby.html">Lobby</A>

<HR>

<H1>ElectricMarket Directory</H1>

<UL>
<LI><A HREF="lobby.html">Lobby</A>
<LI><A HREF="DEPT/dept.html">Electronics</A>
<LI><A HREF="DEPT/dept.html">Clothing</A>
<LI><A HREF="order.html">Order Products</A>
</UL>

<HR>

<ADDRESS> <A HREF="background.html">ElectricMarket</A></ADDRESS>

</BODY>
</HTML>
```

The order form is as follows:

NOTE

This order form is for illustrative purposes. It is not advisable to either solicit or provide credit card numbers in a form where encryption and other security measures have not been implemented.

```
<HTML>
<!— Author: K.C. Deemark (kcd@em.com) —>
<!— Dept: Web Weaving —>
<!— Date:   11 Jul 94 —>
<!— Purpose:   Prototype Order Form for ElectricMarket —>
<!— Comments:  bring to next meeting for approval. —>

<HEAD>
<TITLE>ElectricMarket—Order Form</TITLE>
<LINK REV="made" HREF="mailto:kcd@em.com">
</HEAD>

<BODY>
<A HREF="directory.html"> Directory</A>

<HR>

<H1>Order Form</H1>

page explanation / directions / salespitch
<P>

<FORM METHOD="POST" ACTION="http://www.em.com/cgi-bin/orderscript">
Your Name:        <INPUT TYPE="TEXT" size="40" NAME="NAME"><BR>
Customer Number: <INPUT TYPE="TEXT" size="40" name="CUSTOMER-NUMBER"><BR>
<P>
Product Catalog Number?
<INPUT TYPE="TEXT" size="30" name="CAT-NUMBER"><BR>
Number to order? <INPUT TYPE="number" name="QP1" size="8"><BR>
Size?
<INPUT TYPE="radio" name="SIZE"   value="S">S
<INPUT TYPE="radio" name="SIZE"   value="M">M
<INPUT TYPE="radio" name="SIZE"   value="L">L
<INPUT TYPE="radio" name="SIZE"   value="XL">XL<BR>
Color?
<INPUT TYPE="radio" name="COLOR" value="Red">Red
<INPUT TYPE="radio" name="COLOR" value="Green">Green
<INPUT TYPE="radio" name="COLOR" value="Blue">Blue
<INPUT TYPE="radio" name="COLOR" value="Indigo">Indigo<BR>
<P>


Your Credit card:
<INPUT TYPE="radio" name="CARD-TYPE" value="EMCard">ElectricMarket Card
<INPUT TYPE="radio" name="CARD-TYPE" value="AMEX">American Express
<INPUT TYPE="radio" name="CARD-TYPE" value="Visa">Visa
<INPUT TYPE="radio" namc="CARD-TYPE" value="Discover">Discover
<INPUT TYPE="radio" name="CARD-TYPE" value="Mastercard">Mastercard<BR>
Card number: <INPUT TYPE="number" name="CARD-NUMBER" size="36"> <BR>
Expiration date (dd/mm/yy): <INPUT TYPE="text" name="CARD-EXPIRE" size="8"><BR>
<P>

<INPUT TYPE=submit value="Order Product">
<INPUT TYPE=reset  value="Cancel Order">
</FORM>
<P>
```

```
<HR>

<ADDRESS> <A HREF="background.html">ElectricMarket</A></ADDRESS>

</BODY>
</HTML>
```

And, finally, the background information for the company is as follows:

```
<HTML>
<!— Author: K.C. Deemark (kcd@em.com) —>
<!— Dept: Web Weaving —>
<!— Date:   11 Jul 94 —>
<!— Purpose:   Prototype Background for ElectricMarket —>
<!— Comments:  bring to next meeting for approval. —>

<HEAD>
<TITLE>ElectricMarket—Background</TITLE>
<LINK REV="made" HREF="mailto:kcd@em.com">
</HEAD>

<BODY>
<A HREF="directory.html"> Directory</A>

<HR>

<H1>ElectricMarket</H1>

page explanation / overview / salespitch /
page explanation / overview / salespitch /
page explanation / overview / salespitch /
page explanation / overview / salespitch /
<P>

<H1><A HREF="lobby.html">Go to ElectricMarket Lobby</A></H1>

<HR>

<ADDRESS> <A HREF="background.html">ElectricMarket</A></ADDRESS>

</BODY>
</HTML>
```

Making a Prototype

Link the templates you've generated according to the package, page, and link diagram (Figure 38.5). You'll create a web as shown in Figures 38.8 through 38.12.

FIGURE 38.8.

Prototype lobby.

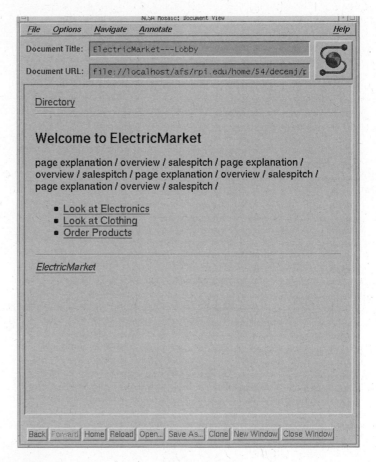

Testing Your Prototype

Ideally, once you've generated the prototype, you'll test it on the following individuals:

- Yourself—Click through the web and see how things work. Try a simple task that you know users would probably do (find the page for a certain product, for example). The look and feel diagram and the package, page, and link diagrams never really capture the experience of an actual working web. Ask yourself the following:

  How does this work together?

  Is there any page that seems unneeded?

  Do you feel that the web conveys the sense of a consistent, coherent design?

  Take your concerns to the designer and solve problems associated with your implementation.

- Designers—Have the designer who created the look and feel and other design products go through the prototype with you. What opinions do they have about how the web looks, and how the major pages fit together?

FIGURE 38.9.

Prototype directory.

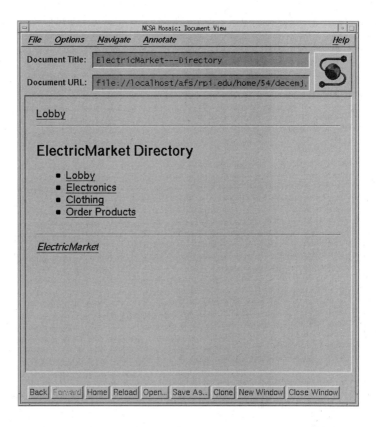

■ Other weavers—Check with the planners, analysts, and developers of the web. What suggestions do they have based on seeing the prototype?

■ Representative audience members—If possible, have a member of the target audience go through the prototype web. Elicit any comments you can from them. It may be that the prototype is too rough for the audience member to be able to say exactly how they feel about it, but observe how the audience member navigates through the prototype. Identify the problems they have. These comments can help you quickly identify areas where you might have to provide additional guidance and information.

Continuous Implementation

Once you've built and demonstrated a prototype and gained some comments from other web weavers and audience members, you can continue implementation based on these results. It may be that the comments from the prototype may even lead to a redesign. More likely, some parts will be redesigned while the implementation of other parts of the web can go forward. Remember, the redesign of the web will probably be more or less continuous over the deployed life of the web. As an implementor, you'll need to adjust to a process of change and growth in the web.

FIGURE 38.10.

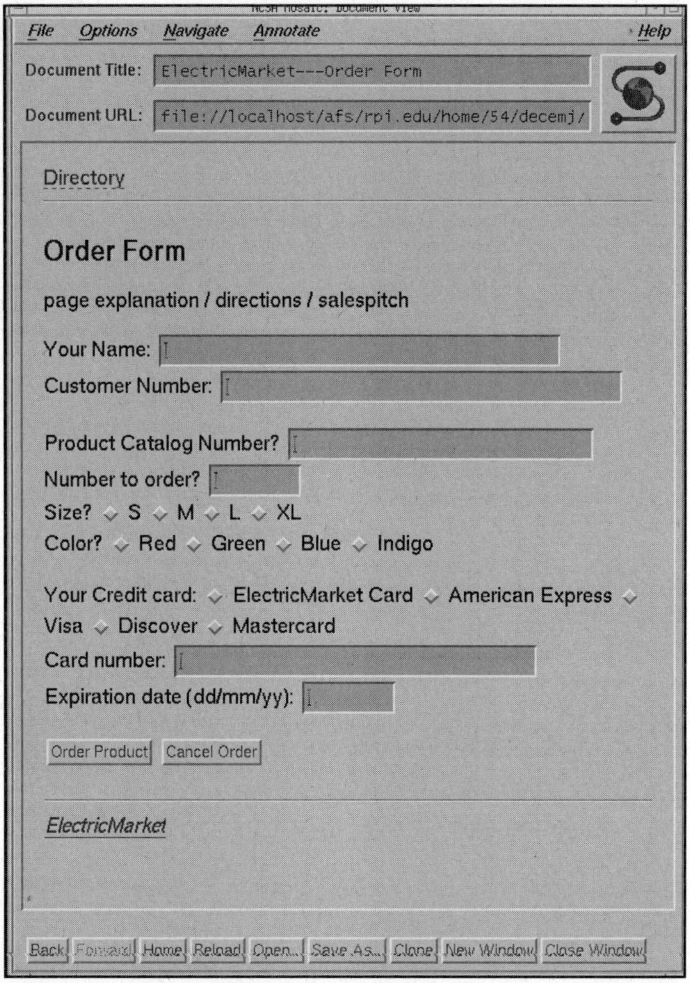

Prototype order form.

NCSA Mosaic: Document View

File   Options   Navigate   Annotate   ·Help

Document Title: ElectricMarket---Order Form

Document URL: file://localhost/afs/rpi.edu/home/54/decemj/

Directory

Order Form

page explanation / directions / salespitch

Your Name:

Customer Number:

Product Catalog Number?

Number to order?

Size? ◇ S ◇ M ◇ L ◇ XL

Color? ◇ Red ◇ Green ◇ Blue ◇ Indigo

Your Credit card: ◇ ElectricMarket Card ◇ American Express ◇ Visa ◇ Discover ◇ Mastercard

Card number:

Expiration date (dd/mm/yy):

[Order Product] [Cancel Order]

ElectricMarket

[Back] [Forward] [Home] [Reload] [Open...] [Save As...] [Clone] [New Window] [Close Window]

Continue to implement areas of the web, always seeking feedback as described above for the prototype. In a way, the web itself is always an "evolving prototype." As implementor, the key is to continue to craft HTML files and keep track of changes to design (particularly when it affects all files such as changes in the look and feel of the universal template).

In the long term, you'll have to be concerned with web maintenance, both the maintenance of the HTML features as well as the information (wording) in the files themselves:

1. Work closely with the web analyst to detect stale links. If possible, use automated programs to do this.

FIGURE 38.11.

Prototype department page.

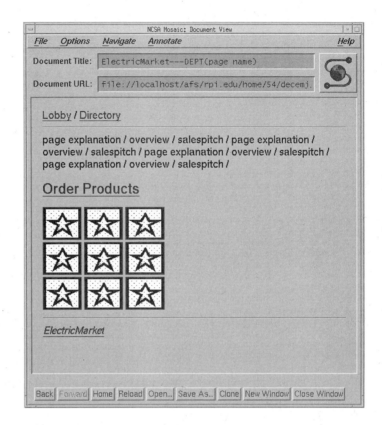

2. Routinely check the web pages for any updates you need to make in the wording and presentation of the information. This can be particularly crucial if web planners make a major change in the target audience or purpose of the web.

3. Routinely check the web's access statistics. (The webmaster should be able to set up a program to collect these.) Look for links that show up in the error logs for the server; they may be stale or malformed links.

4. If you must change the name of a file, provide a link in the old file's name for a period of time with a "link moved" notice, and provide users with a link to the new file. Using a carefully designed directory and file-naming plan, you should be able to avoid many of these "link moved" notices.

5. Continue to build your store of knowledge about HTML (and its extensions) and identify new ways to implement the web's design more efficiently.

FIGURE 38.12.

*Prototype product
information page.*

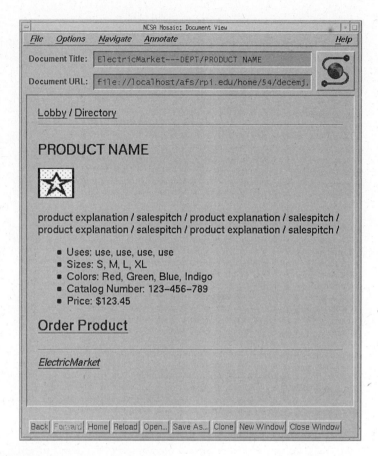

Weaver's Check

Implementing a web is a demanding part of web weaving. As implementor, you must work closely with others—the web planners, analysts, designers, and developers.

Working with HTML files and directories is also part of a web implementor's job. Plan a stable, extensible structure for the Web server's name, directories, and files. Use configuration control systems, when appropriate, to keep track of changes and alterations in the web's files and templates.

In creating individual web pages, consider general principles for presenting information: grid; typography; given/new information chain; and consistent, appropriate voice and tone.

If you're just starting a web, first gather all the information you can from the other processes and web elements: look and feel diagrams; package, page, and link diagrams; audience information, purpose and objective statements; domain information; and web specification.

Building a web prototype is the next step in implementing a new web. Create templates based on the look and feel diagrams for the whole web and as well as templates for pages that serve other functions. Link these pages based on the package, page, and link diagram to create a web prototype.

Test the prototype yourself, and then seek comments from web designers, planners, analysts, and developers. If possible, have a representative audience member look over the prototype web and comment on it.

You'll continuously implement the web; change and growth are characteristic of good webs. Develop a process of implementation and testing and open communication with other web weavers and representative audience members. Fine-tune the web so that it best expresses its design and accomplishes its overall objectives.

Implementing a web is very challenging; it draws on your technical abilities to create and manage a complex system of HTML files, your expressive capabilities with language and design elements, and your communication skills in asking for and receiving feedback to continuously improve the web.

Developing a Web

39

by
John December

If you weave a web, will they come? Will your web server statistics rise long after your grand opening? Will users' hotlists include your URL? Will your target audience find increasing levels of satisfaction with your web? The answers to these questions lie in how you promote, improve, and grow your web. The constantly changing needs of your users make keeping a web current, accurate, and relevant an enormous challenge.

As a web developer, your work will involve keeping the general Web public and your web's users informed about the purpose and offerings of your web. You'll need skills in public relations, interpersonal communications, mass communications, and listening. The need for continuous web development arises from the dynamic environment in which web information exists. New resources, new information, and new forums for communication come into existence all the time. These changes alter the context in which your users experience your web. If you don't grow your web and continue its development, your web will inevitably lose value to your audience.

This chapter presents some strategies for developing a web, including techniques for publicity, attention to quality, and continuous development.

Publicity

The users and potential users of your Web experience information overload. Every moment, new services and information become available on the Web, some of which grabs your audience's attention. Making your web known to the Web public at large is a difficult task. There's no central "What's New Page" to announce a new web to the world (although NCSA's "What's New" page serves this purpose to a large degree). Moreover, there are few subject-related "What's New" pages, so someone interested in what you have to offer might not easily come across your Web.

There are, however, strategies you can take to publicize your web. This publicity has several goals:

- To inform the general Web public as a whole of the existence of your web and what it has to offer

- To attract the interest of your target audience members and let them know about how your web meets their needs

- To educate your current web users of new developments on your web

The work you've done in composing purpose and objective statements and gathering audience information will be key to the success of web development. You'll draw on the wording of your purpose and objective statements to create publicity statements for the Web (Web releases), and you'll draw on your audience information to know where to place these Web releases. In the sections to follow, I'll describe strategies for reaching a variety of Web audiences. I'll start out with the most general audience and then describe how to focus on the narrower audience you are trying to reach with your web. Finally, I'll review how you can keep publicity and information flowing to your current web users. Before we look at how you can create Web releases, however, we need to review their timing.

Publicity Timing

No one likes to go into a brand-new shopping mall that still has sawdust and equipment spread all over. Similarly, your audience won't have a good experience if you announce your web's "grand opening" too soon. As a web developer, you'll need to work closely with other web weavers, particularly the web implementors and planners, to decide when your web is ready to "go public." Before this time, the web implementor and web master must make sure that the general public cannot access the files that comprise your web on the server. (The web server itself will often have to go public for testing before your web's public release.)

One of the most intense times for your web will be just after Web-wide announcements of its availability. This initial wave of interest will bring Net surfers, the curious, indexers, resource aficionados, and a variety of others to your web for a first look. Don't announce your web publicly until you're ready to make a good first impression. When your web is "ready" is a subjective judgment. Remember your web is never "done," so you'll have to decide what web objectives must be met before public release and have the web in place and well-tested before this public release.

In the following sections, we'll look at how to create and disseminate general (Web-wide) and targeted (focused to a specific Web audience) publicity. Your goal is to implement a series of periodic announcements that catch the attention of Web-wide and targeted audiences. The basic techniques for doing this include writing announcements at varying levels of detail and releasing them to appropriate forums.

Timing and content issues are a part of this dissemination process. You don't want to release so much periodic publicity that you saturate the audience's attention for your web. This may happen if the audience sees a release from your web every time some minimal change occurs. Use more frequent publicity for more specific audiences. For general audiences, announce only the "big stuff." Another technique is to use a resource on your web that has proven to be a popular item as "teaser information" that can help draw attention to your web's publicity.

General Web Releases

Reaching a Web-wide audience to announce your new web, or updates to it, is not easy. Despite the enormous demand for such a service, there are few services on the Web that offer up-to-date, widely recognized "What's New" announcements for a Web-wide audience.

There are several reasons for reaching a Web-wide audience. First, you want to announce your web as part of the whole Web itself, to allow the whole Web community to benefit from or use the information you provide. Second, reaching a general audience for your announcement might be a key way to reach your target audience or to spark an interest in your subject by a member of the general Web audience. Third, the general announcement serves as a public announcement of your Web's availability so that indexers and other Web-information gatherers can then evaluate your Web and place it within their web indexes and resource lists.

There are several considerations in creating a general web release:

■ **Audience.** The ultimate audience for your web, of course, is the audience you've defined and analyzed in the web weaving processes covered in the previous chapters. However, in creating a general web release, step back from this audience just a bit and focus on explaining your web's purpose and offerings from a general point of view—from a context outside of your web.

For example, in the previous chapter we looked at a sample design for ElectricMarket, an imaginary web-based department store. The audience for ElectricMarket are those who are interested in buying the products offered: electronics or clothing. We'll talk about how to target this specific audience in the next section on focused web releases, but for a general web release, you need to focus not just on your target audience but on any Web user.

■ **Commercial or noncommercial.** Just as discussed in Part III, "Web Navigation Tools and Techniques," the Web is a community of people, not a neutral collection of machines and software. As part of Web community traditions, there are places set aside for commercial activity and acceptable ways to advertise. These usually involve the following:

> Designated marketplaces—virtual malls and directories that are clearly labeled or intended to be commercial

> Commercial "What's New" lists and sponsored advertising in other webs

> Commercial asynchronous text discussion or information lists, such as commercial newsgroups or company-sponsored mailing lists

The key is to *not* place a commercial advertisement where the standards of the Web community don't allow it. Many places on the Web welcome commercial announcements (such as NCSA's "What's New" page). Observe the information outlet for a while to see whether commercial announcements are placed there or ask a moderator or frequent participant in the forum what would be appropriate.

■ **Appropriate forum.** Just as commercial advertisements are not acceptable—by Web community standards—where they don't belong, so too are nonrelated announcements in a subject-specific information or communication forum. For example, there are a variety of subject-specific web indexes (see Chapter 18, "Trees: Subject-Oriented Searching") as well as subject-specific newsgroups and mailing lists. Choose only the most appropriate forums for announcements. You'll be using subject-specific forums for focused web releases (next section). For general web releases, make sure that the forum you choose is intended for general Web audiences.

■ **Purpose.** Describe your purpose in terms that appeal to the average person on the Web. For the ElectricMarket example from the previous chapter, a general announcement could describe the web as a new, innovative shopping web and as a place to find out more about new products in electronics and the latest fashion trends.

- **Tone, depth, length, and content.** General web releases should be very brief. In large forums like NCSA's "What's New" page (described later), the guidelines call for a concise paragraph and stipulate the format of the entry. Follow the guidelines of the forum closely.

  Adopt a tone and choose details that will attract the attention of a general audience, as opposed to an exhaustive list of what your web has to offer. Choose only the major links of your web to include in your announcement, rather than including links to many pages. These extra links clutter the announcement, and you may unintentionally place users too deep in your web, bypassing the introductory pages you've carefully designed and built.

  For example, the ElectricMarket's general announcement might read as follows (this example is hypothetical; the URL won't access a web):

  *The `<A HREF="http://www.em.com/EM/lobby.html">ElectricMarket</A>`,
  a new, innovative shopping web, is now open. The ElectricMarket
  offers a wide variety of the latest electronics and fashions
  for the discriminating shopper, complete with product images
  and detailed specifications.*

  This announcement doesn't go into too much detail of exactly what electronics are offered or what other features the store has. Rather, it mentions keywords to catch the attention of a Web user who is interested in shopping or electronics or clothing products. A spider reading your announcement will catch the important key words: market, shopping, electronics, and fashion.

Once you've developed a well-worded general web release that appeals to a general Web audience, you need to choose some forums that will disseminate this release.

Some Web-based outlets include the following:

- Moderated Web forums.

  NCSA's "What's New," URL `http://www.ncsa.uiuc.edu/SDG/Software/Mosaic/Docs/whats-new.html`

  The InterNIC's "Scout Report" URL `http://www.internic.net/scout-report/`

- Unmoderated Web forums. "Free for Alls" (locate these by a Web spider search for "free for all").

  These are lists of hypertext, in which you can add items at will (usually through Forms). Because they are essentially unmoderated and often run by individuals on a very informal basis, the tone of these lists can vary from serious to scatological. Obviously, you'll need to decide if the tone of this list is appropriate for your web's announcement. Frequently, you'll only be able to add a short title and a short description.

Let's look in detail at one of the major outlets for general web releases—the "What's New" page at the National Center for Supercomputing Applications (NCSA), URL `http://www.ncsa.uiuc.edu/SDG/Software/Mosaic/Docs/whats-new.html`. This page won a 1994 "Best of

Web" award for Most Important Service Concept. Brandon Plewe, who coordinated the contest, wrote about the NCSA "What's New" page: "Probably the single most accessed page on the Web, this service has helped unknown thousands keep up with this fast-moving virtual world." The NCSA page quickly rocketed to popularity because it met a need; people want to know "what's going on" and learn about new developments and resources.

NCSA's page has also grown in popularity because it is located at a centrally-known place (for Mosaic users) and is moderated. Although originally meant just to carry information about Mosaic, the service quickly included announcements for a Web-wide audience, and now serves as a gathering point and common-experience base for Web users (just like watching major network newscasts. ("Did you see that on the CBS News last night?" "Did you see the latest in 'What's New'?")

Located at the home of Mosaic, the page has at least a cachet of being "official," although no claims are made about the announcements or links contained on the page. It is moderated through a process of electronic mail: you send an announcement to the address shown on the top of the page, following a suggested set of guidelines (URL `http://www.ncsa.uiuc.edu/SDG/Software/Mosaic/Docs/submit-to-whats-new.html`). These guidelines include a request for a one paragraph, concise announcement in the third person, with no headers, inlined images, or bold text.

There are other forums that are often appropriate for general web releases:

- Net-happenings mailing list. To subscribe, send e-mail to `listserv@is.internic.net` with the body, `subscribe net-happenings YOUR NAME`. You'll receive e-mail about the list and how to submit items to it.

- NewNIR-L—announcements of new Network Information Retrieval and Online Public Access Catalogue Services. To subscribe, send e-mail to `listserv@itocsivm.csi.it` with the body `subscribe NEWNIR-L YOUR NAME. Archive: http://www-chem.ucdavis.edu/nir/nirwww.html`.

- Usenet `Comp.infosystems.announce`—announcements of new WWW sites or information services.

- New Commerce—"What's New in Commercial Services on the Web (and Net)," URL `http://tns-www.lcs.mit.edu/commerce/whatsnew.html`.

- "Meta-List of What's New pages"—`http://www.seas.upenn.edu/~mengwong/whatsnew.list.html`, by Meng Weng Wong.

- Infobank's collection of "What's New" lists—`http://www.clark.net/pub/global/new.html`.

Focused Web Releases

As part of the publicity for your web, general announcements are great for spreading the word about the existence of your web and possibly catching the attention of the audience you are targeting. However, focused web releases also should be part of your overall strategy to seek out your specific audience.

Instead of wording your announcement for a general audience as for a general web release, instead, write a focused web release with your audience's greater knowledge of the subject in mind.

For example, the ElectricMarket announcement would read as follows:

```
The <A HREF="http://www.em.com/EM/lobby.html">ElectricMarket</A>
a new, innovative shopping web, is now open. The ElectricMarket
offers a wide variety of the latest electronics—including
watch tvs, CD-ROM viewers, personal digital assistants, and
a full range of personal area network (PAN) supplies.
You can also check out the latest fashion trends, from the
Webs of Europe to the far-East.
You'll find detailed product specifications, including
images, sounds, and motion videos. While shopping, you
can get helpful advice on our in-store
<A HREF="telnet://moo.em.com/">MOO</A>, and
access a <A HREF="wais://wais.em.com/">WAIS database of
fashion reviews</A>.
```

This announcement provides specific keywords to grab the reader's attention. Its increased detail would be too much for a general audience but would engage the attention of an audience interested in electronics, particularly the ElectricMarket's strength in personal electronics.

There are many ways to find outlets for focused web releases:

Subject-specific indexes (see Chapter 18)

Subject-specific Usenet newsgroups and mailing lists

Professional organizations and societies

Individuals involved in indexing network resources

Current Web Releases

Not only do you have to keep the general public and your potential audience informed, you'll also need to provide information to your web's users about what is new on your web.

The best way to do this is to create your own "What's New" page and keep a link to it prominently displayed on your web's home page or in its index.

You can craft the wording of these current web releases to be more specific than either the general or focused web releases. You can assume that your readers have some familiarity with your web and also very strong interest in the details of a new service or feature of the web. Naturally, you'll post current web releases more frequently than general or even focused web releases. A current web release, for example, might be placed on your web's "What's New" page to announce even a minor change in a resource, or the addition of a set of new links. You shouldn't send minor changes to Web-wide "What's New" services like NCSA's "What's New." Minor changes are usually only appropriate for your web's own "What's New" page.

Quality

The user's experience of your web is the indicator of your web's health. If the user gets the information he or she needs, you're doing your job. Maintaining a web at a high level of service, however, is not easy. You'll need to make an effort to keep your web relevant to your audience's needs as well as accurate and complete.

To develop the quality of your web, use results from the analysis process. Examine the contents of your web's access statistics files and look for patterns. Are the files that are currently getting high access appropriate to your web's purpose? You also can contact users directly and find out how they are using your web—either through a survey form (or comment box) on your web or through a voluntary e-mail list.

A successful web can build on its success. The key to making a web successful is recognizing the dynamic nature of the Web as a communications medium, and carefully attending to the intricacies of the web-weaving processes.

Here are some specific things you can do:

- **Usability testing**

  Laboratory: Invite a sample of audience members to use your web to accomplish a specific objective. For example, your web might provide a list of resources related to your web's field of specialization. Devise a series of test questions that draw on your web's information. Use these items as test questions and observe how your audience uses your web to attempt to find these resources.

  Field: Observe audience members in their own settings as they use your web. This might be difficult, particularly if your users are geographically dispersed. This may be more feasible for studies of "company" webs, in which there are groups of co-located users.

- **Feedback**

  If a voluntary registry of users is available, send a survey to a random sample of users and ask about their overall levels of satisfaction and use of your web. Note: when your users voluntarily register, inform them that they might receive such a survey.

  Provide a Forms interface to elicit user feedback. (Note how this is a self-selected means of getting feedback versus a direct questionnaire sent to a sample of users as suggested previously.)

- **Iterative analysis**

  The analysis checkpoints for your web defined in Chapter 31, "Analyzing a Web," serve as a way to examine the overall integrity of your web. As a web developer, work closely with the web analyst (you might even be the same person!) to improve on these checkpoints and possibly add more. Devise other checks and tests, particularly for issues that are giving you trouble, such as a large database or low use of a resource that is identified as critical in your web.

Continuous Development

Because the information space in which your web operates constantly changes, as does as the domain information that you present in your web, you'll need to recognize that deploying and operating a web involves continuous development. You usually can't just set up a web and then let it run. The amount your web changes will depend on your users' needs, the nature of the domain information, and other factors such as the growth of competitive webs.

Here are some specific strategies for continuous development:

- **Keep all web weaving processes going.** Make sure that the people working on the planning, analysis, design, and implementation processes are communicating, working together, and continuously striving to improve the web for the greater good of the user.

- **Keep abreast of publicity outlets.** New outlets to explain or announce your web will develop all the time. Keep track of new developments in "What's New" pages as well as subject-oriented resources related to your web.

- **Keep informed of similar or competitor's webs.** New webs will come into existence that may share your web's purpose and audience. Examine how these webs work; if appropriate, you might consider collaborating with another web so that you each might focus on a specialization and share the results.

- **Keep abreast of your audience's professional societies, trade shows, conventions, periodicals, related Web resources, and changing interests.** You may have to do this through off-Web channels (on the Net) or print magazines, journals, and newsletters. Know what your audience is involved with and how their interests and pursuits are changing.

- **Build your web's reputation for quality, comprehensiveness, and user service.** Do this through a continuous process of defining what these issues mean in terms of your web's goals. For example, what does your web's objective statement define as "comprehensive"? Consider how you can integrate these issues into the planning and analysis processes.

- **Aggressively meet your defined audience's needs and purpose.** Explore ways to offer new services using innovative delivery methods before other webs do rather than merely follow the norm.

Weaver's Check

A web developer's concerns are for both public relations as well the overall excellence of the web. A developer should release web publicity at appropriate times and in appropriate forums, worded for the level of interest of the audience. General web releases reach a Web-wide audience and are usually placed in "What's New" pages or submitted to mailing lists. Focused web releases try to reach the specific audience that the web addresses, through specialized or topic-related forums. Current web releases inform the web's current users and can be offered through a "What's New" page specific to the web.

Besides publicity, a web developer is concerned with the web's quality and continuous improvement. Keeping the other web-weaving processes (planning, analysis, design, and implementation) operating and the people involved in these processes communicating is a big part of web development. A web developer also looks for opportunities to expand the web's service offerings or to suggest improvements for design or implementation. Working closely with the web analyst, a web developer can identify areas of the web that may lack publicity and educate the users about these features.

A web developer works with the whole web-weaving team to help ensure that the web continuously improves in quality and value and is represented well to the whole Web.

Putting It All Together: A Case Study

40

by
John December

For the first time in human history, individuals and organizations can be instant global publishers through the Web. With this opportunity, vast quantities of information will be disseminated on top of the flood of information and communication already flowing on the Net and in other media.

Web information will add to this information flood both in terms of quantity and in terms of the *kind* of information disseminated. Web communication takes place in an environment where all information is potentially equally accessible. The Web's information space is in flux because of a continuous stream of new information, and existing information constantly changes in its relationships with other information. Thus, developing information and communication on the Web challenges web weavers to adopt new skills and new methodologies to take advantage of the exciting possibilities.

Because of the Web's information dynamism, the web weaving methodology outlined in the previous chapters occurs in a much more complex way in the real world than was described in the chapters. In my own work, I switch very quickly from web analysis and planning to implementation and design—not necessarily in a neat order or with clean breaks between work on processes and web elements.

Developing complex information structures with networked hypermedia requires a methodology that has flexibility and change built into it, and I attempt to evoke these qualities in this hypothetical case study.

This chapter presents the case of the Kappa Company (an imaginary organization), describing how a team of its information developers weaves a web, starting from an inspiration from the company's president.

How you weave your web for your organization or your personal use will vary widely based on what you want to accomplish. However, the case of Kappa is typical: an enthusiastic beginning followed by a process of fits, starts, and surprises.

The Kappa Company Web

The example for this chapter is an imaginary company that offers—according to one of its brochures—*integrated solutions for today's business problems.* In other words, Kappa does whatever is necessary with products and services to meet customers' needs. Kappa develops and sells business software and training courses, and analyzes customer needs for information and online services. They're a natural candidate for adopting Web communication.

Kappa—in business for five years—has 100 employees, and although it has experience in analyzing online communications services for its customers, it does not have expertise with the Web. The president of Kappa, Anne Smith, is interested in moving onto the Web and recently attended an international conference on Mosaic and the Web. Returning to Kappa headquarters with enthusiasm, President Smith calls Lynn Jones, a key information developer in the company. Lynn is the sole person in the company dedicated to developing information *about* Kappa—information for company reports, publicity, company brochures, and proposals. In the short time since the company started, Lynn has created or overseen the design of all the information about Kappa presented to prospective clients.

President Smith's corner office is on the 33rd floor of Kappa headquarters, overlooking a compact but rapidly growing downtown in a sunny, midwestern city. Lynn has no idea why the president called her in and is concerned about possible cutbacks or "right-sizing." But as soon as Anne and Lynn sit down at the window alcove, Lynn knows that it's not bad news; the lore of Kappa is that Smith never delivers bad news at the alcove.

President Smith tells Lynn, "This information highway thing, we need to get on it."

Lynn appears puzzled. Knowing the president had gone to the Web conference, Lynn suspects that this has something to do with that.

President Smith shrugs her shoulders as if surrendering to some inevitable point and says, "We need to build a Mosaic server."

To Lynn, it makes sense now. Mosaic's alluring view into the Web—probably prevalent at the conference—easily seduces. Lynn understands the president's error in the term *Mosaic server* but also recognizes the genuine interest the president has. Lynn nods her head to show she understands. President Smith continues. "We need the global reach—the flexible way we can provide information about ourselves to attract clients, inform people about what we do, and understand the medium itself so that we might be able to advise our clients on how to use it. We need to have a presence on the Web."

Lynn says, "I'd be glad to do it."

"Great, You have all the budget you need." President Smith stands up and says, "I have a meeting."

Lynn knows this is her cue to get moving.

Putting a Team Together

Now all Lynn needs to do is obtain the equipment and software and the Internet connections, and make a server. Right?

Well, not exactly. Because Lynn is an information developer, she knows that what content will be on the Web server will be crucial to accomplishing the goals of establishing a Web presence.

The skills of the talented people who obtain the hardware and install the software and network connections to get a Web server operational is crucial. Without them, there would be no Web server. Similarly, without excellent content, there would be no reason why anyone would use a web from the Kappa Company.

Lynn pulls a team together—a mix of software, hardware, and Kappa product experts—people who know how to work with hardware and software, along with people involved directly with the potential audience of the web, including a sales representative, an account manager, and a customer service person.

Setting Goals

In their first meeting, the team brainstorms what the web server could possibly do—what "a presence on the Web" could mean. Writing down as many ideas as possible on the whiteboard in the conference room, the team generates and then synthesizes ideas. They arrive at the following list:

Goals for Web Server

Information for prospective customers
Information supporting current customers
Kappa services and products catalog
Background information about Kappa

These goals imply reaching an audience that members of the team know: potential and existing customers. The team knows information about Kappa that they can use to reach these customers now: information about products, services, company background, and even the sales pitches to potential customers.

Lynn has a collection of brochures, company reports, and full access to all company information. The sales representative, Karen, explains that she sees a trend in Net-literate customers showing increasing interest in the Web and knows some customers who are developing their own webs, either directly in their business or as part of their own interests and hobbies.

The customer service representative, Mark, has many stories about what people want to know—the continued questions that prospective customers always seem to ask on the 800 phone number they use for sales and support.

The people with technical knowledge of the hardware and software necessary to bring the web server into operation know all the issues about networks and security.

After the first meeting, the web server developers (the webmasters) want to work on their own to create an operational server. Still keeping the lines of communication open, Lynn sets the webmasters free, allowing them to dedicate their time to getting the necessary hardware and software up and running.

With the rest of the team, Lynn needs to get an idea of what content could be possible. Lynn, several other information developers, and a graphic designer at Kappa will acquire skills in Web navigation (see Part III, "Web Navigation Tools and Techniques") and learn HTML by reading some books (see the previous chapters of this part). They'll install and use Web browsers (see Part II, "Web Browsers and Connections") to experiment on their own. They'll also spend time getting familiar with Web applications (see Part IV, "Exploring the Web").

Learning

After a few weeks, the initial enthusiasm seems drowned in a sea of new terms and concepts—URLs, spiders, Gopher, Mosaic, Lynx, HTML. The team members have spent time searching for subjects and keywords, surfing, and researching their competitors' webs.

President Smith, however, seems a bit confused. She's spent tens of thousands of dollars on the project, but when she visits the cubicles of the team members, she sees only the bright graphics of web pages like the "Late Night with David Letterman" home page (URL `http://bingen.cs.csbsju.edu/letterman.html`) or the "Star Trek" page (URL `http://www.cosy.sbg.ac.at/rec/startrek/index.html`). Once in a while, she sees small, jerky MPEG movies of people on bicycles or scientific visualizations of gas jets on a team member's computer monitor.

The developers seem entranced—surfing through colorful pages on webs covering every conceivable subject and making their own home pages with photographs and lists of their hobbies. The Kappa web server isn't public yet, so these pages aren't being provided to anyone worldwide, but President Smith begins to wonder if the Web is a very expensive waste of time.

President Smith asks Lynn for a written plan for how the "Mosaic server" (no one has corrected President Smith yet) is going to benefit the customers of the company. Moreover, she asks Lynn how they could possibly make money on information that they will be *giving away for free* on a public web. And not only giving it away for free to potential customers, but to all their competitors as well. President Smith warns, "Our competitors will be able to see, in intimate detail, exactly how we are serving our customers, enabling them to steal our market share even faster."

The Planning Process

Lynn calls a meeting of the web team and brainstorms more specific goals. The team members' immersion in what the Web has to offer has raised their awareness of many kinds of webs. They've honed their skills in navigating the Web (see Part III) and in writing and designing with basic HTML (Chapter 32, "Designing a Web," and Chapter 33, "Implementing a Web: Basic Hypertext Markup Language (HTML)"). They're actually very anxious to get started with a public web. One of the team developers has already created a "Kappa Home Page" and wants to make it available for public use right away.

Lynn senses that it's time to start planning exactly what their web should do before the force of the team's enthusiasm pushes them into deploying a web too soon. They also need to address President Smith's very serious concerns about making money from something (information) that they will give away for free.

Lynn calls the team together and again brainstorms all aspects of their web: what should go in it, and what should not.

Gradually, they see a pattern emerging. They recognize that just because the Web offers a wide range of possible ways to communicate: hypermedia, movies, graphics, interactive Forms, and graphical information maps, they're not obligated to implement a particular feature just to display the technology. Moreover, just because they *could* present all kinds of information about the company and its inner workings, they don't have to. It seems obvious to Lynn that they, as a team, can carefully plan what information goes public and what does not—a balancing of choice that Lynn has always been familiar with in the many reports and presentations she's designed.

President Smith, seeing the vast amounts of information on demonstration webs, might have assumed a web would, somehow by its own volition, "suck up and serve out" all the information a company might have to offer. Lynn knows they have choices, and that, given the President's mood and the team's enthusiasm, it is time to start making those choices.

Lynn opens the meeting by asking, "Why are we building this web?" Through a process of discussion, the team comes up with some answers:

- To help customers make better use of our products
- To reach customers who might be interested in our company
- To attract customers to buy our services and products
- To inform our own employees about our products and services
- To have a Web "presence"

Although this list seems to be getting at why they are building the web, Lynn still wonders what all this *means,* particularly that last point. What is a "Web presence"? Pressing on this point, Lynn helps the team elaborate on the meaning of "Web presence":

> To tell potential customers what products we have, just as we do now in the paper catalogs and brochures that we distribute. The advantage the Web can give us is global reach and no marginal cost increases for each electronic catalog distributed via the Web.

> To let customers know our company, so that someday they may have us in mind when they need us, just as we are doing now in our print ads and television commercials. The advantage of the Web is that its information is customer-driven: through the Web's hypertext, the customer selects the information and level of detail he wants.

> To help current customers see what other products we offer and to provide them with specific information they can use on demand. We're doing this to some degree with our sales calls, but the Web offers a more flexible way for customers to find this out. Satisfied with our initial products and services, they can link to our home page and find out more about what we have to offer.

> To use the Web as a locus for doing business, much as the downtowns of cities formed because of the ease of communication with other businesses and proximity to business services, support information, and supplies. The Web is evolving as a place where business needs can be met. A presence on the Web also means that our customers can include a link on their own web pages with a hotspot that says, "Here is where we bought our business software for project X." These links foster and continue relationships. Without a Web presence, we do not even show up within the larger context of Web information—in the indexes, lists, and directories on the Web or in any Web spider search. Our Web presence is just one more form of communication. No company

today would question having a phone (although the Web may change this) or a fax machine (it might change this, too). The Web and the Internet are part of an infrastructure for communicating and doing business, for providing the customer the means to acquire the information they want when they want it rather than relying on face-to-face or voice communication at mutually agreeable times and places.

Lynn is now satisfied with how the team has defined the reasons for going onto the Web. They've mentioned specific benefits in terms of how things have been done (such as business contacts through sales calls, advertisements, and customer information through 800 numbers) and in terms of what new things are possible (most notably, the idea of the Web presence leading to new kinds of relationships through hypertext links).

Now Lynn pushes the team to explore what content they could possibly create to address these issues. What kind of information could we provide? To whom? Why? The team arrives at several points:

> We can provide on the Web all the information we are presently giving away—promotional brochures, annual reports, product catalogs, and all other supporting company material. We can do this on the Web for the same reason we are now in print: to inform our customers about what we can offer. Our competitors have access, in one way or another, to this information already. Online, we can have an opportunity to help a potential customer see our total company, rather than the limited view a sales catalog might bring. They can see our products and services as a total plan to help them meet their needs.

> Our web will serve not just as a marketplace where we know our customers will often visit, but as a communication and information space. We'll include a contact e-mail address and ways for our customers to give us direct feedback. Also, we'll provide valuable information to the Web as a whole. We could do this by providing information in our area of expertise. For example, we can provide techniques and tips for using our products in specific business applications or information about other resources on the Net that our customers might often need.

> Our web can serve as a visible focal point that conveys important information about our company in a way that no paper source can. Current and prospective employees can find out about our products, company background, and current activities in one central location. Paper sources quickly go out of date or become unavailable, while our web's information can be updated instantly.

Lynn is happier with the results of this meeting but is still concerned. It seems as if there's a great deal of talk, but not enough specifics. Highbrow philosophies of new frontiers in communication sound great, but the reality is that they must decide what is going to go in the HTML files served out on their web and that those files must be able to demonstrate *cost recovery* (in other words, pay their way) in terms of increased sales. At the next meeting, Lynn intends to bring a plan worksheet and prompt the team to become more specific about the purpose and objective for the web server. Meanwhile, Lynn realizes she needs to placate President Smith before the web project itself is canceled.

An Answer for President Smith

Lynn visits President Smith the afternoon after the planning meeting. On the overhead projector in the president's office, Lynn puts up her first chart:

- Information fosters relationships
- Relationships bring us customers

Smith's brow furrows, and she says, "I've been president of this company for five years and now you tell me we're in the business of *relationships*? I should read fewer books by Tom Peters and more by Leo Buscaglia?"

Lynn looks again at the chart. "No," she says. "We want to build a web that can help us keep in contact with current and potential customers in many of the ways we're doing already, only our web could bring us a global audience. The information we provide about Kappa's products can be the most current and comprehensive available."

"OK," President Smith says. "I can see that—our catalog all over the world at the speed of light. But where's the value in the information we serve out on our web? Are we going to charge the customers to access it because it's a more convenient way to order?"

Lynn knows that the discussion could quickly devolve into an endless debate over charging policies on networks—pay-per-view versus flat rates versus free access. Lynn looks directly at President Smith and quickly says. "The information we give away in our web has no value to us or anyone until it leads to a relationship."

"There's the word 'relationship' again," Smith says, "I'm not going to pay for ten color workstations and two hundred person hours a week for relationships."

"But you will pay for a team of five salespeople on the road," Lynn says.

"Well," Smith says, "that's how we get our orders. That's where the money comes from."

"...and $10,000 a year for print ads and $500,000 a year for internal documentation and reports and thousands a month for phone service and FAX numbers and office rent...."

"You're giving me the *it's a part of doing business* line—I don't buy it. You can't tell me that providing color workstations for everyone is just a way of doing business."

Lynn began to wonder if the project might be canceled. Not only did they not have a clue about what would be served out on the web, but the president herself was losing faith in the project. All the collaboratively-brainstormed points on the white board in the conference room seemed to fade, seemed less important than this direct challenge—the president of the company wondering why tens of thousands of dollars had already been spent for something that hadn't shown any results.

"Where are our customers?" Lynn asks.

Anne Smith leans forward, straining her eyes to see Lynn. She hesitates and then says, "Out there...," and gestures toward the large picture window overlooking the boxy towers of downtown, with its late-'80s, slick-tech architecture that the city residents regarded with considerable pride. It *looked* like a serious downtown, a place where business people on their lunch hour could wander on the street among hotdog vendors and the swirl of briefcased salespeople—a flow that didn't change very much over the years but still seemed the highlight of many workers' days.

"How are they going to find us?" Lynn's voice was lower, almost a whisper.

Anne lowered her voice, matching Lynn's in a mock-whisper, "Our address is printed on all our sales literature: 21 North Water Street."

"That's not our address anymore," Lynn said.

"Did I miss something, Lynn?" the president asked.

"Our address is kappa.com."

"Lynn," Anne said, straightening up in her chair, "I've always respected your work. You develop all the print, radio, and television materials that explain our company to the public and customers; you direct the product catalog and the sales brochures. You've even scripted the presentations that sales representatives give to customers. You know how we communicate in every medium we use. You know this isn't a starship—we're not talking about some journey into cyberspace."

"Our customers are using online communication."

"I know," Anne said. "I developed the procedures for analyzing our customer's needs for online news, information, and stock quotes. I know online services. That Mosaic server you want to build is very different."

Lynn brightened. "The server is very different. It can give our customers—both current and potential—a way to gain updated and comprehensive information about us on their own terms any time they want to."

Lynn paused. President Smith seemed weary with the whole subject.

Lynn continued, "We've always met our customers on their terms and become part of their way of doing business. We don't question the need for phones, advertisements, or fax machines because our customers have them. The Web server can be a part of this same information and communication infrastructure. It's not going to work miracles. It would be unfair to judge it in any other way than as a medium for communication, and its success will depend on how we use it, not on any of its inherent properties."

President Smith looked at Lynn and back at the chart still beaming onto the screen from the overhead projector.

Lynn continued, "We want spiders to find us and intelligent agents to know us. We want to be able to be distinguished in a new medium that breaks from the one-way media like print or TV and involves the user in shaping information. We want our company to be a part of the relationships our customers will choose to have. Our customers are using the Web in increasing numbers. Our potential customers are out there, increasing traffic on the Web by hundreds of thousands of percent in a year."

Lynn paused, sensing that nothing she had said was convincing President Smith.

"Okay," Smith said, "go ahead with the server for now. Once you get an initial operational web, I'll take a look at it. I'll invite a group of customers to give it a try, and I'll watch them. Then we'll go from there."

A Plan Worksheet

Lynn and her team, after going over the details of possibilities and brainstorming what they want to do on the web, carefully write down a plan by filling in a web planning worksheet.

PLAN WORKSHEET

Kappa Web Team

Plan A

TARGET AUDIENCE

Discussion: While our ideal audience will be customers ready to buy our products and services, we recognize that Web surfers and the curious may use our web, and we won't discourage this. Moreover, our long-term goal will be to include support for an increasingly wider audience: employees (current, prospective, and past), investors, business partners, and other people with key relationships to our company. However, our initial plan will be to reach a specific, targeted audience whose needs our sales team and customer service representatives know well: potential clients interested in the business applications we develop and sell.

1. Definition

    One-sentence statement: Potential customers identified by our sales team as likely prospects for buying our products and services

    More complex description: These customers are

    - In a business with little or no in-house software development or consulting support (they have a need for our products/services)
    - Willing to take part in advanced forms of technology and interfaces (have an existing set of equipment, people, and skills involved in modern communication, such as computers, networks, and some computer-mediated communication)

■ Either already have and use an Internet connection and one or more Web browsers or are willing to have our sales staff assist in installing and providing some training in their use

Cluster diagram. Figure 40.1 (shown at the end of this worksheet) illustrates the overlapping possible audiences for the web. We'll target the shaded portion—those who are web literate or willing to try and who are identified by our sales staff as likely customers or past customers. We'll also target Web indexers, including spiders, agents, or people concerned with gathering or cataloging information on the Web.

2. Information about audience

Characteristics

■ Technology adopters

■ Results-oriented

■ Need rapid communication for products and services

■ Need updated, comprehensive product support information

■ Want current and comprehensive sales and promotional literature

Concerns

■ Value and quality in products and services

■ Meeting their own business needs/customer needs

■ Reliable, trustworthy partners

Key concerns based on purpose definition (to follow)

■ Product information is current, complete, and correct

■ Customer support will be continuing and reliable

■ Security and privacy will be ensured and respected

PURPOSE

1. Subject area: Kappa company current software products and services

2. Audience (defined previously)

3. Level of detail: Equivalent to sales literature we already provide to customers, giving full details of what we sell, can develop, or services we provide. This does not, of course, include customized services or products or proprietary products (products developed for a company and sold exclusively to them).

4. User's expected benefit/response: Ideally, sales. But just as we recognize that developing customers means spending time to inform them about what we can do, we understand that what we serve on our web may help keep our name in the customer's mind for the next time they need our products or services.

5. Succinct purpose statement:

To provide potential customers with a comprehensive collection of information about Kappa products and services.

OBJECTIVE STATEMENT

1. Specific goals to accomplish the purpose:

   Provide a comprehensive and current product catalog

   - All current software products, including demos when available, detailed reviews, and documentation
   - Software development team capabilities

   Present a services list

   - Business areas in which we have strength and have succeeded in the past
   - Willing customers can provide case studies

   Provide free domain information

   - A well-checked, authoritative guide to technologies in which we excel
   - Background information in our areas of expertise

2. Restrictions:

   No proprietary information about our own customers or Kappa itself (President Smith will clear all information).

   Tone of web should be low-key—not heavily "sales," but more informative/helpful to potential customers, even providing a good collection of useful information for free.

DOMAIN INFORMATION

1. Information necessary:

   Web team: All members know Kappa's operations, products, and services well. Sales and customer service representatives will do a series of presentations on customer needs and concerns. Existing background, sales, and other information—on paper and online—will be gathered and placed in a central library.

   Information served: Existing electronic version of product and services catalog will be translated to HTML. A database of company background information and domain information to be given away (see objective statement) will be gathered.

2. Acquiring information:

   Kappa employees who are directly involved in creating domain information used will be trained in HTML. The most authoritative and complete version of all information for this project will be the one on the web.

3. Updates and maintenance:

   As part of regular duties, people supplying domain information will keep it continuously updated with the most current available information.

SPECIFICATION

1. Limitations on information:

    Proprietary (see objective) restrictions

    Competitive—President Smith will meet regularly with sales representatives and other web team members to evaluate any information that may be too valuable to serve out on the web.

    Appropriate legal and ethical considerations—Information will be presented according to all copyright and other laws and will represent the best interests of the company in fostering good customer relations by following Web customs and practices, including considerations for multicultural communication.

2. Limitations on media:

    Initial web will provide text and graphics; multimedia will be incorporated according to customers' needs.

    Forms support will not be used until such time when security measures are in place; our current 24-hour 800 telephone number will be offered to customers to place orders.

3. Resources:

    List of in-house URLs: sales; company background; and product, service, and domain information directories will be established on the server.

    Outside links will be evaluated for background domain information.

PRESENTATION

1. Look and feel possibilities:

    A fairly conservative overall look, focusing mostly on providing useful content that meets customer needs, with graphics playing a role to enhance information and navigation.

2. Work schedule:

    We'd like to deploy an in-house prototype for invited customers to evaluate with President Smith in three to five weeks; we'd like to hook up our web to the Web in three months.

3. Skills required:

    Web planning, analysis, design, implementation (basic HTML), and development

4. Components:

    Web designers and implementors have already developed some candidate components

5. Mockup web:

    A mockup web that demonstrates functionality and "look and feel" will be operational for a review by the President in three weeks.

FIGURE 40.1.
*Kappa audience
cluster diagram.*

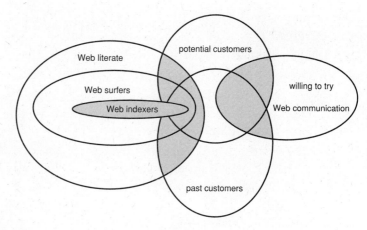

Preliminary Analysis

After the initial confusion, now it all seems too easy to Lynn and her team. They've created a written plan, and President Smith seems placated, at least for three more weeks until they have a mockup web operational. But is the plan sound? Will this web be successful? Because there is no operational web, only a limited amount of analysis can be done (see Figure 31.1 in Chapter 31). Lynn and her team identify the analysis that can be done based on the web plan so far:

- Is the web attempting to reach an audience that has and will use Web access (Checkpoint A)?

- Is the web contributing new information (accomplishing goals that haven't already been done) (Checkpoint B)?

- Is the web self-consistent (that is, its purpose matches its objectives and specification) (Checkpoint C)?

Lynn assigns Jack, a member of the web team who had seemed particularly adept at finding Web resources and surfing the web, to be web analyst. Jack's first tasks are to analyze checkpoints A, B, and C for their proposed web. Jack will find out more about where their target audience "hangs out" on the Web and the Net and locate any existing webs that may be supplying similar information. He'll continually work with the web planners, designers, and implementors to make sure that the web's purpose, objectives, and specifications match. He'll coordinate with the web developer to identify problem areas in the web or opportunities for other publicity outlets. Jack spends time surfing the Web to find out about current Web offerings and similar Web audiences. At the same time, he gathers useful background domain information.

A Preliminary Design

Jose, the graphic designer on the web team, doesn't know HTML. But he knows the layout and design of the existing product catalog well; he developed it for Lynn. Lynn assigns him the task of web designer, and Jose spends time at his personal computer using a drawing program to create sketches that can be used as a basis for the appearance of web pages. Jose's knowledge of layout and design principles helps him articulate a professional look for the pages. Although his sketches can't be implemented directly (he still struggles to adjust to the non-WYSIWYG nature of HTML and web browsers), the sketches give all the web team members a sense of having something concrete to look at and critique.

Jose also spends a great deal of time navigating and exploring the Web itself (see Part III and Part IV), and he gains a sense of what kinds of structures and layouts are possible, while at the same time retaining his own aesthetic vision for the Kappa web—that is, not being swayed by some of the poor web designs he finds. He even interacts with some webmasters, making constructive suggestions for improving their web's appearance, and they appreciate his insights.

Jose's concept for the universal grid for the Kappa web is in Figure 40.2, and he spends time with Karen, Mark, Lynn, and other team members asking for comments as well as how this universal grid can be used to generate grids for other types of information: the product catalog, the domain information page, and so on.

FIGURE 40.2.

The Kappa universal grid.

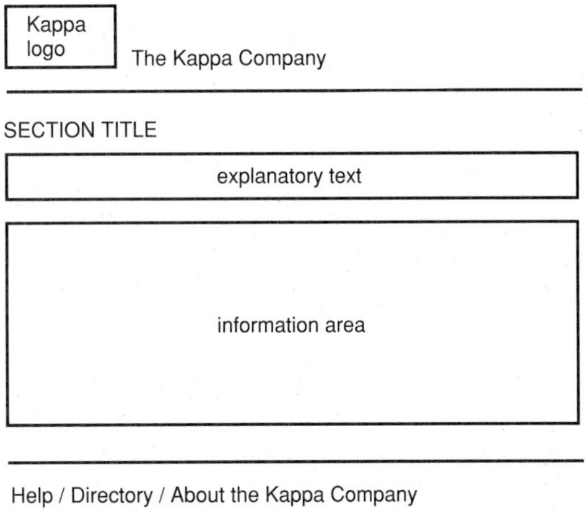

```
┌──────┐
│ Kappa │
│ logo  │    The Kappa Company
└──────┘
───────────────────────────────

SECTION TITLE
┌─────────────────────────────┐
│        explanatory text       │
└─────────────────────────────┘

┌─────────────────────────────┐
│                               │
│                               │
│         information area      │
│                               │
│                               │
└─────────────────────────────┘
───────────────────────────────

Help / Directory / About the Kappa Company
```

Jose also works from the written plan and drafts an introductory statement for the Kappa home page:

"This is the home page for Kappa, a diversified company offering products and services for networked business information systems worldwide. From links on this page, you can find out more about our company, products, and the field of business communications."

More Tasks for Team Members

Lynn is pleased that team members now can independently produce information for the web. She assigns Jack, the web analyst, to also develop the store of domain information by identifying scholars and other people on the Web who maintain business information related to Kappa's products. Jack asks each if they would be willing to allow the Kappa web to link to their pages.

Lynn assigns Holly and Bill to be web implementors. Both have shown a keen ability to compose in HTML. Holly had already made a preliminary home page for Kappa, and her personal home page is extensive, with links to where she had gone to school and worked before, as well as links to Web resources she likes. Bill has been a software developer with Kappa for three years, and his ability to manage collections of files and directories is well-known among the Kappa software team.

In addition, she assigns Karen to work with Jose in the web design. Karen has an M.S. in technical communication, and she has developed her own web on her Macintosh at home. She knows many customers who have developed their own webs as a hobby. Both Karen and Jose will work closely with Holly and Bill to work out ideas for what could be possible and what can be done.

Lynn spends some time surfing the Web herself—finding potential outlets for Web-wide and focused web releases—as well as getting a feel for the culture and customs she encounters. She notices that President Smith's visits to the cubicles of the web-weaving team are becoming more frequent. Lynn looks up one morning to see Smith standing quietly behind her, looking at the Tango Server (URL `http://imtsun3.epfl.ch:8000/tango/`) in Lynn's Mosaic browser. Lynn senses it will be best to have a prototype completed soon.

Moving Toward a Prototype

The team members increase the specificity of their plans to include the actual URLs that Jack, Bill, and Holly have designated as repositories for domain information. Jose and Karen have a large set of story boards showing screen designs for the Kappa web. They show these to President Smith, and she says she likes seeing something concrete, but seems impatient, as if the story boards were somehow a small consolation for the talent, time, and money she's spending on the web. In the course of explaining to Smith why they can't precisely control the appearance of their web in the many different browsers that their audience might have, Jose very diplomatically explains that they're creating a "Web server," not a "Mosaic server." Smith squints a bit and seems disappointed that they're not going to be able to guarantee that each customer will look at their web through Mosaic. Smith vividly remembers the colorful displays at the conference and wonders if they will be able to appeal to the customers through the dull text in nongraphical browsers.

After another meeting of the whole web team, in which they look through all the story boards defining the look and feel of the web, including Karen's package, page, and link diagram (Figure 40.3), they decide to start implementing a prototype.

Holly and Bill design a directory structure and make templates that implement the look and feel designs. The web team members seem more excited one afternoon when they all gather in Holly's cubicle to see the working prototype, with all links working to prototype pages (the home page is shown in Figure 40.4).

Bill works out a translation scheme to turn their current products catalog to an HTML-like format that can easily be converted to correct HTML. This enables the team to quickly offer a great deal of content on their web: descriptions of their entire line of software products.

FIGURE 40.3.

The Kappa package and link diagram.

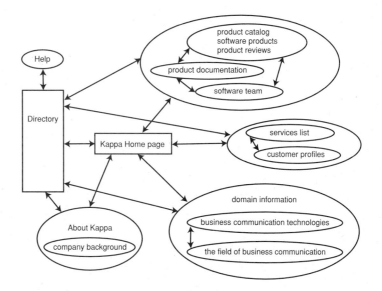

FIGURE 40.4.

The Kappa home page.

After several weeks of moving through the processes of planning, design, analysis, and implementation, Lynn finds that they have a prototype web with at least as much content as their existing sales brochures. They've more branches to add in the background domain information section, but they have completed all the product pages. The services list is the same as they offer customers now, but more current than the paper copies in circulation.

A Prototype

In a meeting with President Smith at Holly's cubicle, the web team members watch while President Smith uses the Kappa web. She's impressed by how much information is available—a complete catalog of the company's business software products as well as all the information that they normally provide to customers through sales brochures.

"I'm impressed," President Smith says, "Do you think the customers are going to use this?"

"I think so," Lynn says. "It's already the most current and comprehensive source for information about our products."

"What do you mean?" President Smith asks.

Lynn explains, "We've included pages about our two newest software products—PANMate (Personal Area Networks interface to local area networks) [Figure 40.5] and Cygnus14 (spreadsheet)."

Lynn continues, saying, "These two products won't show up in our paper catalog until the next quarterly printing, and those catalogs probably won't be widely circulated for six months."

President Smith squints and clicks again on the screen for PANMate (Figure 40.5). She knew that this should be one of their hottest selling items; no one else has ever marketed PAN-LAN interface software. Their sales force is out there now, she thought, spreading the word at the speed of airplanes and rental cars, while the web she's looking at could deliver current information to customers immediately.

"Let's get on the Web with this now," says President Smith.

Development

Lynn knows that the web team will have to work carefully on their web before deploying it, despite the pressure to release it right away. Already, salespeople want to know when Kappa's home page will be ready so that customers can link to it. Lynn holds more planning sessions with the web team, and meets with Jack about his continued analysis of the web's integrity. Lynn talks more with Karen and Jose about design ideas and with Holly and Bill to check that they have the skills and equipment to do the implementation correctly.

FIGURE 40.5.

Kappa's PANMate product page.

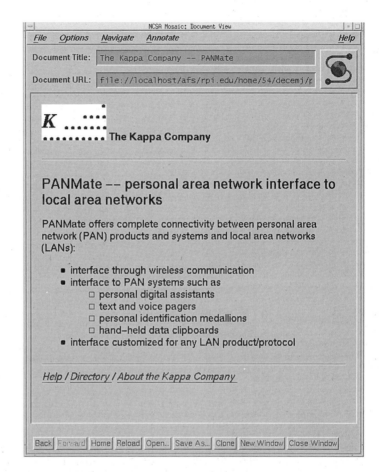

President Smith invites a focus group of customers to Kappa headquarters to use and view the prototype web. One long-time customer in the group, actually a good friend of President Smith's, tells her, "I didn't realize your company offered so many products and services." Later, Smith tells Lynn to connect the Kappa web to the Web and to announce it to the world.

Lynn had already crafted general and focused web releases. She'd tracked down some outlets for Web-wide releases as well as some places she could place announcements to reach their target audience. Lynn places a full-page print ad in a well-known business communications trade journal (Figure 40.6).

Lynn hopes the ad will catch the attention of the Web-literate and perhaps catch the attention of those who might be interested in knowing what Kappa is doing. Lynn smiles to herself, knowing the ad will perhaps rankle their competition just a little bit.

FIGURE 40.6.
Kappa's print ad.

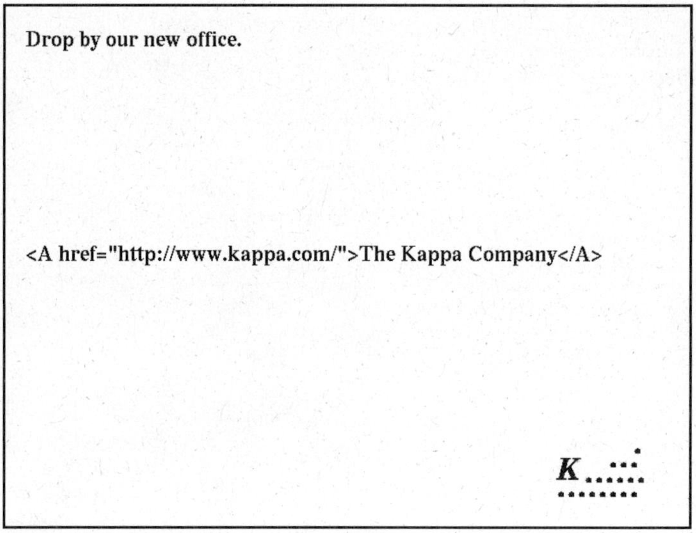

Drop by our new office.

<A href="http://www.kappa.com/">The Kappa Company</A>

K .....

Weaver's Check

Weaving a web is not a simple exercise. Although you can quickly get an HTML page up and running on a server, a carefully crafted web, one designed to accomplish a set of objectives for affecting a specific audience, is a complex task.

Web weaving requires people skills as well as technical skills in communication and shaping information. A group of people—or even a single individual—can employ an iterative, incremental process of creating audience information, objective and purpose statements, a web specification, and a web presentation through processes of planning, analysis, design, implementation, and development.

The imaginary narrative describing the Kappa Company's experience might not be comparable to your situation, but you'll probably face many of the same issues. These issues include identifying and understanding the people you want to reach with your web, more precisely stating why you want to reach them, and defining your web's content. You'll be under pressure from whomever is funding your work (or yourself if you're doing your own web) to justify spending time and talent on creating something that's essentially just ephemeral electric transmissions throughout a patchwork of worldwide networks. A well-done web, however, can extend the range of your communication. With the increasing number of individuals, businesses, schools, and universities using the Web, you'll be able to communicate with more people, more flexibly, and with greater impact.

VI

PART

Setting Up and Administering a Web Server

Managing a Web Site: Planning, Implementing, Installing, and Updating

41

by
Neil Randall
and
Karin Trgovac

HTTP: What Happens When Somebody Clicks?

Part VI of this book offers a low-level view of the World Wide Web. To understand what setting up a server entails, it's necessary to understand the client–server interaction in at least some detail. The first step is to look at what Web serving actually means—that is, what occurs between the user's mouse click and the display of your document on that user's monitor.

Most Internet resources are based on the client–server relationship, which basically works in the following way. A client—the software employed by an individual user who wants a specific piece of information—sends commands via a common language or protocol (protocols have names such as HTTP, FTP, and Gopher) to a server—the software run by an individual or group who provides information on the network. Some of the protocols (FTP and Telnet, for example) maintain a virtual link between the client and server until the session is finished. HTTP (HyperText Transfer Protocol) is a *connectionless* protocol, meaning that there is no continual virtual connection; a client issues a command, and the server executes it immediately. Consequently, HTTP is also a *stateless* protocol; it does not retain any information about a client's prior session(s) or state. Each request is made on an as-is basis.

HTTP is not a difficult or complex protocol. Then again, neither are most protocols. The principle behind a client–server protocol is simply that the client must communicate with the server, which in turn will typically acknowledge the communication and respond in a manner befitting the initial communication. If that initial communication is to request a file retrieval, then it's up to the server to send the file out over the network to the client. HTTP is very much about file retrieval, and the stages of this process are relatively few. Over the Internet, HTTP is dependent on the more fundamental TCP/IP protocol suite, which essentially allows the client and the server to contact each other in the first place. HTTP determines specifically what that contact is supposed to accomplish (that is, the serving and retrieving of Web documents). But you could establish HTTP as a protocol on a non-TCP network, with a fairly small degree of difficulty, if you wanted to run a local Web instead of a Web accessible through the Internet.

There are essentially four sequential elements to the HTTP transaction: *connection, request, response,* and *close.* Each is discussed briefly here. Note that you can watch the entire process take place on the status bar of most browsers. You'll see some variation of the following:

```
Connecting to http://www.xxx.xx/...
Connected with www.xxx.xx ...
Awaiting response
Transferring path/filename.html ...
Done
```

This is nothing more than the browser telling you exactly which stages of the transaction it's moving through. This is extremely valuable information, especially given the high possibility of the connection not being made properly or consistently.

Connection

In this stage, the client attempts to connect to the server (actually to the server software running on the remote machine). On the Internet, the connection attempt occurs whenever the user either types in or clicks on a URL, thereby commanding the client program (that is, the Web browser) to move out onto the Net, locate the correct machine, and establish a connection with it. When the connection is made, the client software recognizes it and moves to the request stage.

Request

In this stage, with the connection in place, the client (that is, the browser) sends a request out to the server program for a specific action to be performed. This request, in its full state, includes the information outlined in the following sections.

Request Method

There are several possible request methods: *Get, Head, Post, Put, Delete, Link,* and *Unlink.* For the purposes of this short summary of HTTP, only the first four are particularly important.

A *Get* request, as its name suggests, is for retrieval of an entity, typically an HTML document. The document itself is actually specified in the Request-URI portion of the request, and this request can state that the entity is to be retrieved only if it has been modified since the specified date. This latter possibility is the reason for the configuration item in recent browsers that allows you to check if a cached document has been changed and then to retrieve the new version if it has been.

The *Head* request method is exactly the same as the Get method, except that the client is asking to be sent only the header information of the entity, not the item's actual content. The server will send full URL information, the date of most recent modification, and so forth. You can see this at work in browsers that have an "information about document" type of feature, which yields a window showing details about the document but not the actual document itself. Obviously, this is a faster request method.

Post is the opposite of Get. Here, the browser's request is that the server accept the attached information (entity) and store it in the appropriate manner. The Post method is used when you send e-mail through the browser, when you post a newsgroup message through the browser, and when you submit a filled-in form. It can also be used for extensive database operations, although few of these have appeared on the Web as yet.

Put is very similar to Post, except that it gives the sender greater control over what happens to the item (entity) being sent to the server. With Post, the information is received by the server and routed to whatever location the server's software dictates. In a Put request, the server *must* apply the received data to the item specified by the sender, without re-routing. For the most part, information sent over the Web is done so through the Post rather than the Put method, because doing so allows the server software to be set up more flexibly, and the request to be handled at the server's discretion.

Request-URI

URI stands for Universal Resource Identifier, and it specifies to the server the exact resource against which to apply the request. In the most common request method, Get, the Request-URI identifies the document to be retrieved. When you click a hyperlink labeled `http://www.company.com/service/courses.html`, the Request-URI is usually just `/service/courses.html` and specifies what document at location `www.company.com` is to be retrieved. There's no need to specify the machine and the domain name in the request, since the connection will already have been made to that machine when the request occurs.

Request Header Fields

The request header fields contain further information to convey to the server. This is where various character sets are established, where coding mechanisms are stated, and two important features: Authorization and From. The Authorization feature allows the possibility of restricting access to Web documents (thereby requiring account names and passwords), while the From feature sends information such as e-mail address. Much of this information is set up in the Configuration panels of your browser.

Response

The real action of World Wide Web browsing occurs in the response stage. Here, the server software attempts to fulfill the client's request. It responds to the client in the form of a status line, including the important version information, and other information about the server and the data.

The response is considerably simpler than the request. In the *status line*, the response lists the version of HTTP being used and the three-digit status code that tells the client how the response was understood and attended to. The $1xx$ series of codes (not currently used) offers particular kinds of information. The $2xx$ series gives successful acceptance information. The $3xx$ codes mean that further actions are necessary, perhaps in the case of a redirected document, whereas $4xx$ and $5xx$ codes indicate an error of some kind. Naturally, there are more of the last two types than the first three, since nobody's interested in why something worked, only why it didn't.

Close

In the *close* element of the transaction, the connection between client and server is terminated. Generally speaking, each transaction begins with the client establishing a connection, and it ends

Managing a Web Site: Planning, Implementing, Installing, and Updating

Chapter 41

1075

with the server closing down the connection after performing the requested action. The HTTP specifications don't require the isolation of each transaction, however, and both the client software and the server software must be designed to handle instances of unexpected or premature closings. These are initiated by users when they click the Stop button of their browser, if they lose their network connection (that is, the modem hangs up), or even by a power failure shutting down the client software. Each time a close takes place, the current transaction is ended, although (especially in the case of the Stop button) the client software might have received enough data to display it in partial form. This explains the Transfer Interrupted message at the bottom of a stopped message in some browsers. (Version 1.0 of Netscape for Windows attempted to close transactions prematurely under certain circumstances, but it didn't do so successfully, meaning the user waited in limbo.)

Understanding the URL

Perhaps the best way to understand what happens at a Web site is by breaking down a URL (Uniform Resource Locator), which constitutes the address of a Web site. Let's look at a hyperlink with the syntax URL `http://department.institution.org/pubdocs/johnson/neatstuff.html`. The `http:` in the address tells the server that an HTTP request is being initiated. `department` is the name of the machine at the domain `institution.org` (this isn't necessarily strictly true, but it's frequently so), and in fact is the machine running the Web server software. When a user clicks that hyperlink, the browser initiates a connection to `department.institution.org` then sends a Get request for the URI `/pubdocs/johnson/neatstuff.html`. In other words, the user wants the browser to retrieve and display the file `neatstuff.html` that is in the directory `johnson`, which is in turn in the parent directory `pubdocs`.

In order to communicate the information contained in the requested document back to the client, the server employs an Internet standard called MIME (Multipurpose Internet Mail Extensions). MIME defines how material other than straight ASCII text is to be sent between Internet machines. Valid content types for MIME include text/HTML (HTML stands for HyperText Markup Language, the primary authoring language for Web documents), image, video, audio, and applications. When the server returns the requested document, it precedes the data with a MIME header containing bits of information about the data, including the content type. These headers allow the Web client or browser to interpret the information it receives and display it to the user. In your browser software, this information is necessary in order to activate the viewers or players you have set up to accommodate those types of files.

In addition to serving Web documents, Web servers also have the capability to act as gateways between clients and other networked information resources, such as a relational database. Using the Common Gateway Interface (CGI—another Internet standard), the Web server invokes a CGI script in which it takes information provided by the client (usually from a fill-out form that appeared in the client's browser), manipulates it according to the script, and then returns an HTML document to the client. This process, while allowing for powerful database searches and dynamic

Web documents, also creates several security concerns, but it should nonetheless be part of your overall Web security strategy.

A good Web server will also allow for the logging of Web activity. Monitoring which documents are the most requested and keeping track of which Internet addresses are using the server are important activities within a successful Web site. Web servers can also monitor and regulate the user base; the software can specify that unauthenticated users cannot access any or all of the Web site, and in some cases the authentication method allows for the establishment of accounts that allow certain users (such as credit-card buyers) into non-public areas of the server. These abilities are important for keeping a Web site secure.

It's Analogy Time

Except for a brief passage very early in this book, *The World Wide Web Unleashed 1996* has been primarily concerned about what you can find on the Web, not how to make Web material available. Part V, "Weaving a Web," discussed in detail the concepts behind designing a Web site and authoring the Web pages that go along with it, but that's only part of the solution. An even more basic question remains: How do you make your Web pages available to the world?

Let's start with an analogy. If you're already knowledgeable about how network servers work, this analogy won't do much for you. But it's always useful to keep the non-virtual world in mind when you're designing things for computers, and your Web server is special in that it allows access from anywhere on the planet. So here goes…

Think of your Web server as a McDonald's (okay, so it's a bit strained). As the manager of this store, you want to see lots of satisfied customers. That means, quite simply, that hundreds of people must walk through your door every day, receive their orders promptly and efficiently, and leave the store satisfied. Making sure this happens is primarily a matter of planning, which is the basis for establishing a Web server as well. Staying with the McDonald's idea for the time being, let's see how this happens.

First, you need content. In the case of the restaurant, that means burgers, fries, and shakes, and in the case of the Web it means documents. Now, you can set up a Web server without any documents on it, but that would be much like a burger joint that had no food (which some would argue applies to McDonald's, but never mind…). Still, as a Web administrator the content isn't really up to you, so you shouldn't have to worry about it. In fact, there'd be no reason to set up a Web server in the first place if you had nothing to serve. Still, it's worth keeping in mind: If your organization decides it wants to be up on the Web, start with the simple question, "What do we have that we want people to see?"

Assuming content is in place, the next step is getting the stuff you need to let service happen. There's money, of course, and it's a primary consideration for both the McDonald's franchisee and the server owner, but what do you need the money for? In the case of the restaurant, you need a store, and in that store you need equipment such as grills and cash registers and plastic tables and soda dispensers. In the case of Web management, you need a computer, and in that computer you need hard drives and network cards and operating systems and server software.

Fine. Now you have everything you need to get started. What's next? Well, there are some decisions to be made. Your restaurant can only seat so many people, so you have to determine how many people you want to be serving at any one time. This decision will have a bearing on how many grills and deep-friers you need, how many cash registers you make available, and so on. Notice that, in the burger establishments, these things differ from place to place. McDonald's, which serves up standardized fare and tries to push through as many customers as possible simultaneously, operates multiple cash registers and serving personnel. Other outlets that cater to individual tastes typically have fewer simultaneous orders—often, in fact, only one. But the McDonald's model is closer than the others to the networking model, which is why we'll stick with it. Other choices to be made include the speed at which you want your customers served, the hours you want the store open, and how you intend to deal with issues of security, both internal and external.

On your Web server, you'll want to decide how many simultaneous users you want to have access to your documents. This decision will substantially affect your choice of computer and your choice of network type. You'll also want to determine the speed at which you'll serve up your documents, and this affects the speed of your connection to the Internet. Another decision—and a major one—has to do with security. If your organization is running an internal network, security has always been a consideration, but now you're asking potentially millions of users to come in and take a look at what you're offering as well. There's no guarantee everyone who visits your Web site won't also want to dig into your company's crucial data files, and while the vast majority of users would have no idea how to go about doing this, it takes only one to cause a great deal of damage.

At some point, you have to stop planning and get your enterprise going. As soon as you do, you'll notice that various elements need fine-tuning or rethinking. In the McDonald's case, this has to do with demand proving to be less or more than expected, with the resulting restructuring of hours, personnel, and so forth. Staff might need to be increased, decreased, or reassigned. Quality of content might need reassessment and replacement. You might be experiencing some unexpected security concerns. And so on…

For your Web server, similar rethinking or tweaking occurs. You'll find that the number of users requesting your documents might be far more or far less than you planned. Your network might be straining with the bandwidth, or it might be largely unused. Your server software might need upgrading or replacing, depending on whether it's been performing its duties correctly. The content of your documents might be mediocre, and you'll need to spend some time redesigning. And you might be experiencing security problems, a fact that will raise alarms.

End of analogy. The point is that a Web server must be *planned* and, once implemented, *managed*. That might seem obvious, but most server problems are the result of misplanning or mismanagement, not technical foul-ups. Now, back to the non-analogous discussion of what these things do.

Decisions, Decisions

For a Web site to be accessible by users with an Internet connection and a Web browser, you need to place your information on a Web *server*. A Web server is a computer that runs special software designed specifically to answer requests for documents made by Web clients (that is, Web browsers). The computer itself can be anything from a mainframe to a standard PC, but typically a Web server is a UNIX machine specially configured to store Web pages and make them available over the Net. The Web documents (HTML files, as well as graphics and other multimedia files) are stored on that computer's hard drive, and the server software basically allows outside users to retrieve the files for display in their own browser software.

First, then, you need a computer. Of course, you might already have one, in which case you can probably turn it into a Web server simply by acquiring the server software. You don't need a computer dedicated exclusively to the task of Web serving, but if you plan to build an extensive Web it's often recommended, primarily for the sake of security. But more on this later.

Server software is available for all the major hardware platforms: UNIX, VAX, Macintosh, Windows NT, Windows, and OS/2. We'll examine several server packages here. The major difference among the packages is that some are completely free, whereas others cost money. Commercially available Web server software is a recent phenomenon, and most computers you access are almost certain to be running free software instead. Both CERN and NCSA have software available for the price of a download, whereas companies such as Netscape Communications have broken into the commercial server market, offering full support and enhanced features (particularly in the area of data security).

So let's say you have a UNIX workstation and server software. You also have a data connection with which users can access your server. Typically this means you have a connection to the Internet through an Internet provider (or the phone company), and if you're in an organization that has a local area network (most Web servers are connected internally to LANs), you're likely to be running your system through a connection such as Ethernet. Even with all this in place, is that all you need to get going? Is publishing on the Web yours to command?

Hardly. More than anything else, setting up a Web server demands planning. It's one thing if you have a Windows NT or Apple Macintosh server, and you're supplying your materials through a 28.8Kpbs modem connected to a 24-hour phone line (you can usually do this for about $250 per month or so), because in that case you're in charge of the server, the content, and the design of the Web itself. But if you're a systems administrator in a company, the reason you're establishing a Web server in the first place is because a variety of people want to put their materials up on the Web; you're no longer wholly and exclusively in charge.

As a result, you'll have decisions to make. Who gets to write HTML pages? Who gets permissions to place documents in server directories? What happens if you need to change directories for specific departments or users? How do you track usage and document retrievals? What about security? Do you let outside Web surfers come straight into your server directories, or do you

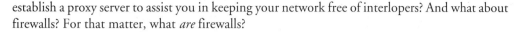
establish a proxy server to assist you in keeping your network free of interlopers? And what about firewalls? For that matter, what *are* firewalls?

These are just some of the questions you'll have to answer before embarking on the fascinating journey of "serving up the Web." If you're already a systems administrator in a large organization, you've probably already thought of them, and in that case the following section will do little more than remind you of things you already know. But if you're in a smaller organization, and you think you'd rather set up your own server than rent space on someone else's (this is an option, and is discussed later in the chapter), this section of *The World Wide Web Unleashed 1996* should at the very least help you begin the process.

But it won't do everything for you. This is a relatively short section—intentionally so. The one central fact about setting up and maintaining a Web server is that no two servers are identical. Especially in the UNIX world, with its myriad flavors and configurations and systems variables, anything that purports to be all-inclusive would be entirely misleading. UNIX stations by themselves vary enough, let alone when you connect a LAN and the Internet to them, plus whatever permutations of the system you've developed over years of tweaking and perfecting. What this section provides, therefore, is a basis for continuing. If you need to know more, the best bet is to contact the hardware and software companies and let them come in to show you their wares. Take what they say with a healthy grain of salt, but then again you already know how to do that.

Network Connections

Your first decision about running a Web server lies in choosing the appropriate type of network connection. Your machine—the designated Web server—must have a reachable Internet address. Actually, this isn't quite true. Your server need only be accessible by your intended audience, which doesn't have to be Internet users at all. If you only want to serve documents on your LAN, you can certainly do that, and it's still called a web. But that's a subject for another book, because the reason you're reading this is your interest in the *World Wide Web*, not just any web. Still, it's worth knowing, because you might find it useful to establish a local web before venturing into the area of full access from the Internet.

Of primary concern is the speed and bandwidth of your line. It's safe to assume that you get what you pay for, and what you can pay varies greatly. Although Internet connections range from a 2.4Kbps dial-up connection to a 45Mbps dedicated T3 line, to operate a Web server you should be prepared to spring for a (minimum) 56Kbps line, because anything less will frustrate your would-be users considerably. It's possible to assign your Web to a 28.8Kbps modem, or even a 14.4 version, but few people will access your site more than once if you do (they'll receive your documents far too slowly). A 56Kbps line or higher—which means a leased line or an ISDN connection—can handle the traffic on a moderately busy site, and if you need to upgrade, talk to your telco about a 128Kbps ISDN connection. If, down the road, you find your site becoming immensely popular, you should consider getting a 1.54Mbps T1 line to handle the additional accesses, especially if you're basing a substantial portion of your business dealings on your web.

There's one further crucial decision, although it's not likely to be one you can change if it's already in place. This is the nature of the local area network from which you want your Internet connection to flow. In all likelihood, your Ethernet or Token-Ring network (or whatever other kind your organization operates) is the one you'll have to work with; this means you'll need to plan your connection to the Internet accordingly. You'll need the appropriate hardware—routers, connections, and so forth—to make the link to the Net possible, and several companies can give you the consulting help you need on this decision. The number and quality of commercially available products designed to perform precisely this type of activity are increasing constantly, and it's well worth checking with your network specialists, your local network resellers, and the pages of computer publications to discover what these are.

UNIX and Windows and Mac, Oh My!

If you have a computer, chances are you can find Web server software to run on it. That goes for UNIX workstations, rather obviously, but it also applies to Macintoshes, PCs with Windows NT or even Windows 3.1, PCs running OS/2, and even larger machines running VMS. Without question, the most advanced and persistent designs of server software have occurred on UNIX, primarily because UNIX servers constitute by far the bulk of machines that connect networks to the Internet. Furthermore, much of the software for UNIX is available free over the Net itself, another hallmark of this powerful platform. Recently, commercial server software—complete with technical support and a few other perks—has begun to appear as well.

In many cases, you'll have no choice about which platform to use for your Web server. Whatever equipment you currently have will be what you're expected to use. So if you have an OS/2 network, you'll probably be forced into the limited area of OS/2 server software, and the same goes for the Macintosh and Microsoft Windows. What's encouraging, however, is that the limitations for these platforms don't mean low quality. Nor does it mean there won't be more software available soon. Commercial interests are developing server software for Microsoft Windows (both NT and Windows 95 environments), with Macintosh development slightly behind. And from the looks of it, OS/2 users will have a choice as well.

Web server software is available for several different platforms. They all have their advantages and disadvantages. Single-user systems (for example, a Macintosh or a PC running Windows) are machines that were never intended to function as network servers. Although they will do the job for a Web server, it is best that these machines operate as dedicated Web servers only, partially because of security reasons and partially because they're prone to crashing (although the new 32-bit operating systems should help). UNIX systems are designed as solid, stable, multi-user systems, which is why UNIX has become the *de facto* operating system of the Internet itself.

Hardware presents a concern, but not very much more than for a standalone station. For a PC running Windows, you should have a 486 with at least 8MB of RAM. 16 is strongly recommended; anything up to 64 will help, especially as you move to Windows 95. For a Macintosh, you need at least a 68040 with the same RAM recommendations for the PC. You must also consider storage space on your system. Ideally, you should start off with 1GB of hard disk space.

There are multiuser systems that can run on an Intel-based PC. Both native OS/2 as well as Windows NT will make stable server environments. Linux (a public domain UNIX for PCs) and NeXTstep are also solid networking environments. For these environments, you should have at least 16MB RAM, and the more the better.

Historically, the environment of choice on the Internet is a UNIX workstation. Almost any of the workstations which are currently on the market (including IBM's RS6000, Sun Microsystem's Classic, and Hewlett Packard's Gecko) will function well as a server. For a UNIX workstation, you should have at least 4GB of storage space, and as much RAM (starting at about 24MB) as you can afford.

Despite the inevitable development of server software for microcomputers, and the fact that packages like WebSite and eventually Netsite will be readily available for them, you should almost certainly go with the UNIX environment at this point, if you're given a choice. The software choices are strong, the user community is helpful and plentiful, and there's tons of support on the Net itself as far as configuration files, sample installation procedures, and advanced methods and tools are concerned. Furthermore, there are a growing number of combined hardware/software solutions for full Web service appearing in the product listings of the major workstation suppliers. Silicon Graphics, for example, offers a series of products called WebForce, designed expressly as World Wide Web servers for small to medium-sized businesses. Similar products are available or under development from Sun Microsytems, Digital Equipment, and Hewlett Packard as well.

No matter which system you use, *strongly* consider allocating one computer to the exclusive task of serving documents. This doesn't necessarily mean Web documents only, although if you're planning an extensive Web, or if you're planning to rent space to clients for their own Web use, a dedicated Web server would be ideal. You can use the same machine for serving Gopher documents and as a public FTP station (if you want to), and for that matter this machine could serve documents to internal users as well. Obviously, running a dedicated server means additional costs, and this means it isn't normally done except in the largest organizations. But from the standpoint of security alone, the idea has some very real benefits; it's simply easier for a knowledgeable hacker/cracker to break into accounts and files on one machine than across a network of machines. You can build firewalls, make use of proxy software, purchase the new breed of "smart" routers for network connection, and so forth. There are, of course, disadvantages to the dedicated server idea, but they have to do mostly with the problems of adding an additional machine to *any* network.

If you're not able to dedicate a server to your web, or if you're simply looking to get things going and worry about dedicated service later (after determining the web's importance to your organization, for instance), the available Web servers are able to accomplish sophisticated security and directory management on their own, with only a minimal number of setup headaches.

Web Administration

We've touched on this already, but it can scarcely be stated too often: A successful Web site requires a commitment of human resources. In other words, you need people to run a Web, and these people need training—or a great deal of practice—in how to do it well. Which isn't to say that the systems gurus currently in charge of your network aren't good enough; in fact, they're probably exactly the right people for the technical part of the task. Just make sure that keeping the Web going isn't something simply added to their job descriptions on the spur of the moment. This is your *public* face, after all, something available to millions of people all over the world, and the last thing you want is a hastily conceived site with out-of-date or technically poor service.

After you've set up your site and got it functioning, someone (or some team) is going to have to provide continual administration. This task is essential to an effective and popular site. There must be someone available who can respond to user queries, analyze the access logs to see if there are any problems with a specific part of your Web, provide guidance to system users setting up their own pages, and so on. In order to keep your site running smoothly, some person or group must be designated to perform these tasks. They certainly don't all have to be performed by one individual (for example, you could have one person who advises members of your organization on how to provide their own Web pages, one person who is the recipient of e-mail queries from outside users, and so on), but it is best if these tasks are designated before you have your server installed. Thorough planning of your Web site is important.

Here are just two of the items a thoughtful server setup will include. To prevent everyone who contributes a Web page from setting up their own set of graphics for standard items like bullets and logos, you should consider setting up one directory on your server where you put all your images and that you allow all users to reference. This enables your users to share icons, buttons, bars, or whatever they want, and will conserve disk space (you won't have 100 copies of the same blue button in everyone's public_html directory). Another is to ensure that large files, such as those in PostScript, are stored in compressed format on your drive. Either the browser itself or a freely available program can decompress the file, and your valuable disk space will be saved. Two simple things to accomplish, but they should be put in place as the site is designed—don't wait to do it later. That's a small part of what we mean by the need for advanced planning.

Web Designer—Editor in Chief

Even if you have the best systems administration staff on the planet, however, there's another side to Web administration that must be dealt with: design. The Web has developed an unofficial title for the staff (often a single person) who does the organization's Web work. That title is "Webmaster," and as you navigate the Web you'll notice it used at many sites (there's also "Webslave," but that's a tad less professional, even if true). Usually, however, it denotes the systems person who keeps things running, rather than the person or group who designs the materials, administers regular updates, tracks user feedback, and so forth. Why? Because most organizations don't *have* that person or group in place.

You wouldn't think of sending out a company report, newsletter, product brochure, or even press release without assigning the responsibility for producing the document to a professional communicator and/or designer. Often, in fact, this work is farmed out to agencies, precisely because you have nobody internally who either can or has the time to do it themselves. Why, then, would you even consider establishing a Web site intended for viewing by the world without using a similarly professional approach? True, HTML design and publication are both easier and less resource-consuming than traditional paper-document design and production, but your Web site makes your statement to a huge number of people, and you want to make sure that statement is the correct one. If you have a publications group, consider turning the design of the Web over to them. But do so only after they've researched the Web and its design possibilities, and only when they're comfortable dealing with the differences between Web design and paper design. One of these differences is in speed of updating, which in many Web cases must be weekly or even faster.

Designing Web sites is covered in Part V. But setting up a Web server and building a Web site are *not* mutually exclusive processes, especially in the planning stages. What's needed is site design from the standpoint of both design and service as soon as you decide to get into the game. Everything from the number of documents to the number of files to be made available via FTP, to the number of graphics included in the documents, to the number of people who will actually be contributing Web pages, impacts the initial configuration of the server software itself.

Security Issues

If you intend to serve Web documents to the vast Internet community, you *must* develop a security plan. Although a detailed security analysis is beyond the scope of this book, primarily because it will vary according to the server software you choose and the network guidelines currently in place in your organization, there are a few basic concerns that are common to any server setup and that we can address here. Most of these issues are not just Web security concerns, but larger networking ones as well. In the case of the Web, you're inviting users from around the globe into your system, and not all of them will be trustworthy. Whether for the sake of industrial espionage, or simply because it's "fun," there will be users who try for access beyond the Web documents you're making readily available.

First, determine the data on your network that needs to be kept secure. You've probably already thought of this, and configured your network to protect them, but allowing public access is a good reason to reevaluate the entire strategy. At the very least, you'll want to keep outside users away from the internal user directories, as well as from the directories containing sensitive data such as financial, accounting, research, and planning information. For all information, evaluate the data to which you *will* allow access, and determine where the potential risks in that information being altered lie. Perhaps several people are responsible for providing the information. Meet with them and discuss their concerns.

After evaluating the potential security breaches of your information, formulate an official security policy regarding the provision of this information on your Web site. Define who controls the information and who should have access to the system for the sake of adding or altering existing information. When you have defined the policy, publicize it to your organization, ideally at the same time you introduce the establishment of a Web site (and thereby provide details and even training). Also keep in mind that, as research shows, more security breaches are initiated from inside an organization than from outside. If necessary, retrain your staff in areas such as effective selection and protection of passwords and the safe transferring of files. Also, particularly if your organization is a large one, inform your staff of the possibility of physical intruders (not just virtual ones). Some corporations and organizations have been duped by individuals who walk in, sit down at an unattended computer and start typing away, or by individuals who claim to be security consultants but who do not, as it turns out, have any dealings with your organization.

If your data concerns are extensive, consider investing in "firewall" technologies. *Firewalls* act as a barrier between your network and external networks such as the Internet (or, for that matter, between more than one internal network). Through various filtering methods, a firewall enables you to restrict the traffic that passes through it. For example, you can configure your firewall to allow only those machines having official registered domain names to access your information, and many other methods of firewalling are available as well. Firewalls as a complete issue are beyond the scope of this book; speak with your systems consultants about the possibilities.

Each of the Web servers discussed in the following chapters has various security measures built in, from user authentication to specifying which files can be served. Consider your security needs (as well as your platform, technical, and budget restrictions) and select the server that will protect your information. Even the popular, freely available server software is becoming increasingly sophisticated about issues of security.

Moving to a New System

Hardware doesn't last forever; neither do URLs. There might come a time when your Web site has to move from your current machine to another, and your machine name may change. Given that everything in your server setup points to specific directories, and therefore so do your publicly announced URLs, this scenario can be a nightmare. Among the best solutions is to ensure that when you set up your site, the machine has an "alias" such as www.domain assigned to it (for example, www.company.com or www.public.org), and then use this name when making internal references to your machine. This will make things much easier if you ever have to move, because all pointers are to the alias rather than the actual locations of the server and document files. Aliasing is a feature provided by UNIX itself, and is available within the server software you obtain.

If you are a division of a larger organization, make sure that you confirm with the organization which name to use. The organization as a whole may have already claimed www.organization_name and want you to use www.division.organization_name. It is important that your Web site follow logical hierarchies, and this is one of them. Web users have certain expectations when they browse through Web sites. They expect them to be well-organized. As far as domain names themselves are concerned, that's a separate issue. You must apply for a domain name, and your Internet service provider can help you with that.

Summary

Establishing a Web server is not a monumental task in itself. The challenge lies in managing and developing it. Since the primary purpose of the Web site is to enable your organization's employees to publish information ("publish" used to mean "to make public"), it's only natural that at least some of these employees will want to seize the opportunity and publish early and often. If you have no organizational strategy for the direction of the Web, you'll also have none for its technical structures, those involving hardware, software, security, and directory access. Planning counts, as it does with any system that puts your organization's information front and center, especially one that makes that information available to millions of users around the globe.

Selecting Server Software

42

by
Neil Randall
and
Karin Trgovac

UNIX

Currently, the UNIX environment has the most variety in Web servers. UNIX was the environment of choice for so long on the Internet that most Internet resources are originally written in UNIX (or a variation) and then ported to other platforms. The UNIX versions still retain the old-world charm of an earlier, much less friendly era of surfing. Consequently, the installation processes and configuration files described in the following sections might seem nonsensical; that's because they are (to all but the UNIX sysop). If you have never computed in UNIX before, if the mention of vi, grep, and other strange beasts of UNIX-speak make you cringe, do not expect to go out, buy a workstation, and have your server up and running over your coffee break.

> **NOTE**
>
> For an online overview of Web servers see
>
> `http://www.info.cern.ch/hypertext/WWW/Daemon/Overview.html`
>
> as well as Paul Hoffman's WWW Servers Comparison Chart at
>
> `http://sunsite.unc.edu/boutell/faq/chart.html`

As discussed in Chapter 40, there are many issues to consider in setting up a Web server; UNIX increases the number of these issues, particularly security concerns (exponentially!), but it also makes those concerns solvable. The following discussion of UNIX servers will give you a taste of what is available to you. If you're interested, talk to people at your home site, on the Web. UNIX folks are always eager to lend a hand. If you are a UNIX guru, well, chances are you know pretty much everything we've stated below, but a refresher course—as well as a look at other servers than the one you use now—never hurt anyone.

CERN HTTPD and NCSA HTTPD

The two most popular Web server software packages are CERN's http daemon (CERN HTTPD 3.0), the original Web server written by Web founder Tim Berners-Lee; and NCSA's HTTPD daemon (NCSA HTTPD 1.2), written by Rob McCool. These two servers share several characteristics that make them very popular, but there are a few key differences.

Both CERN's and NCSA's HTTPD can be executed either as stand-alone or under the Internet Services daemon (inetd). If it is configured as stand-alone, the server is started when the system is booted and then continues to run. If it is configured to run under the inetd, the server is not activated until a specific request is made. The latter type of configuration is suitable only if the traffic on a server is very light, because every time a request is made, the server must run an initialization sequence. This takes time and can lead to delays in processing requests, and it also consumes enormous amounts of CPU cycles (that is, it takes activity bandwidth) on the serving computer. Both CERN and NCSA recommend running in stand-alone mode; in fact, the developers almost insist on it.

CGI 1.1 scripts, used for any number of purposes but most visibly for processing the information sent by the user through browser fill-in forms, are supported by both CERN's and NCSA's HTTPD. Each HTTPD package comes with some script examples, including gateways to the `finger` command and the UNIX `cal` (calendar) command. Clickable imagemaps as well as forms are supported by both.

Users on UNIX systems that are running HTTPD can designate their own directories for HTTP access. Requests that come as `http://hostname/~username/` are mapped to the subdirectory `public_html` of that username. Both the CERN and NCSA servers have security features that permit the restriction of what the user is able to serve from his or her directory, most notably CGI scripts. The problem with CGI scripts is that they're capable of reaching out beyond the server directories, and they're capable of damaging the directories in which they reside. They must be treated with considerable caution by Web administrators, and many current administrators propose not letting users develop CGI scripts at all. If you're starting from scratch, this last option seems the wisest route, at least until your users have a real need for producing their own scripts.

The two versions of HTTPD take different approaches to security. CERN's default setting is to deny access to all files in the Web hierarchy unless specified otherwise in the configuration files. In other words, users cannot modify Web files unless given specific permission to do so. The NCSA HTTPD is the opposite; it allows access to *all* files unless specified in the configuration file, an arrangement more suited to a small, UNIX-savvy development staff than an extensive in-house network of users with extremely varying technological capabilities. NCSA does allow configuration to prohibit access by a specific domain name, however, whereas CERN has no such provision. Both can prohibit access by IP name. Both CERN's and NCSA's HTTPD allow the creation of user groups, and both can allow access to files by group name instead of merely individual name.

The CERN HTTPD has the unique feature of being able to function as a proxy server. A *proxy* is an HTTP server that usually runs on a firewall machine (a machine that functions as a security barrier between the Internet-at-large and a smaller, self-contained network). The proxy makes requests for information on behalf of the machine inside the firewall. It receives a request from an internal machine, ships the request out, waits for the response from outside the firewall, collects it, and returns it to the inside machine.

A proxy can also cache (store) documents. This is useful if the internal network clients make several requests for the same documents. In such cases, the proxy will have stored the first request and can then simply pass on the stored document for subsequent requests. Consequently, network access time is highly reduced. This caching feature also makes the CERN server attractive to those clients who are not behind a firewall. The proxy server can be designated for a specific group of clients. It can store popular documents, again cutting down on network time and costs.

NCSA's HTTPD server-side includes the ability to include the output of commands, or of other files on the server, in the HTML documents that are returned to the client. If the requested document has a special extension (the extension is defined for the server in the configuration files; a common example is .shtml), the server treats it differently than a normal .html document. The server parses the document, looking for the includes within the document. Typical includes are the current date, the date of last modification of the file, and the size of the file.

Server-side includes also can provide a powerful interface to CGI scripts. For this reason, there are some key security issues surrounding the use of server-side includes. NCSA cautions against their use, particularly within user directories. The designers are currently rewriting this part of that organization's HTTPD; information about security issues with server-side includes is available at

http://hoohoo.ncsa.uiuc.edu/docs/tutorials/includes.html.

Both types of HTTPD are available as precompiled binaries for several UNIX platforms. Check http://info.cern.ch/hypertext/WWW/Library/User/Platform/Platform.html (CERN) and http://hoohoo.ncsa.uiuc.edu/docs/setup/PreCompiled.html (NCSA) to see if your system is listed. If it is, follow the instructions for downloading and installing; if not, you will have to download the source. For CERN you will have to compile the source code as well as the World Wide Web Library of Common Code. NCSA requires you to compile the server, the scripts, and the support programs. There is extensive documentation for both of these processes at the URLs listed in the beginning of this paragraph.

CERN's and NCSA's configuration files are quite similar in both content and layout; however, CERN includes all of its configuration information in one file, whereas NCSA has four different configuration files (server config file, resource config file, access config file, and types config file). A *configuration file* consists of directives and comments about those directives. It is also possible to include blank lines to make the file more easily readable by a human being. *Directive statements* are case-insensitive; one directive per line is allowed, followed by the data that is specific to that directive. Comments in the configuration files are preceded by a hash (#) symbol to indicate that they should be ignored by the server.

For those individuals who are on UNIX, but might not be entirely familiar with the editing and installation of configuration files, Enterprise Integration Technologies Corporation (EIT) has created a WebMaster's Starter Kit that walks you through the basics of Web server installation on UNIX. The URL is http://www.eit.com/wsk/doc/. The WebMaster Kit builds upon NCSA's HTTPD. It has added some new directives that allow you to customize such elements as the error messages. It also comes with an automatic server monitor with restart feature and request prioritization.

> **NOTE**
>
> Part of the CERN HTTPD Installation Guide—from http://www.w3.org/hypertext/WWW/Daemon/User/Installation/Installation.html
>
> Getting the program:
>
> Often you don't need to compile the server yourself; precompiled binaries are available

for many UNIX platforms. If there is no precompiled version for your platform, or if it doesn't work (e.g., the name resolution doesn't work), you should get the source code and compile it yourself. There is special instructions if you are installing under VMS.

There are many precompiled versions available in the subdirectory corresponding to your machine architecture.

The server is also available as `WWWDaemon.tar.Z` from our source archive. Please note that you also need the WWW Library of Common Code in order to compile the server. The Library is available as `WWWLibrary.tar.Z`.

Compilation:

Uncompress and untar the distribution tar files:

```
uncompress WWWDaemon.tar.Z
tar xvf WWWDaemon.tar
```

and

```
uncompress WWWLibrary.tar.Z
tar xvf WWWLibrary.tar
```

The compilation and linking of the server is done using the `BUILD` script which figures out what platform you are using. If you have built earlier versions of the CERN software and you already have a WWW directory then it is very important that you do the following

```
cd WWW
make clobber
./BUILD daemon
```

in order to make sure that all new code is built. If not, then go to the newly created WWW directory, and give the `./BUILD daemon` command:

```
cd WWW
./BUILD daemon
```

If you encounter problems during compilation or you don't have the compiler which the `BUILD` script uses, then please read the section on how to modify the `BUILD` script.

Executable HTTPD appears in directory `../WWW/Daemon/sun4` (if you have a Sun4 machine), or in another subdirectory corresponding to your machine architecture.

Configuration File:

HTTPD requires a `./Config/Overview.html` configuration file, the default configuration file is `/etc/HTTPD.conf`. If this doesn't suit you, you can specify another location to it using the -r option:

```
HTTPD -r/other/place/HTTPD.conf
```

Sample configuration files are available from

`*directory cern_HTTPD/config` inside the binary distribution, or

> * under `WWW/server_root` inside the source code distribution.
>
> If this is missing, you can get them from the distribution file `server_root.tar.Z`
>
> If you have all your documents in a single directory tree, say `/Public/Web`, the easiest way to make them available to the world is to specify the following rule in your configuration file:
>
> `Pass/*/Public/Web/*`
>
> This maps all the requests under the directory `/Public/Web` and accepts them.
>
> The default welcome document (what you get with URL of form `http://your.host/`) is now `Welcome.html` in the directory `/Public/Web`.

GN and WN

GN and WN are significantly different from the CERN and NCSA server software. GN and WN were both written by John Franks of Northwestern University and are available through the URL `http://hopf.math.nwu.edu/`. GN can interpret both HTTP and the Gopher protocol, allowing two different types of information resources to access the same data set. WN can be used if only HTTP is desired.

GN/WN's unique approach to serving Web documents functions as an enhanced security feature. WN serves only documents that are specified in the server's `index.cache` file, a flat database that indicates which files have explicit permission to be served. The default on WN is not to serve a file; if WN receives an HTTP request for `/dir/welcome.html` and `welcome.html` is not listed in the `index.cache` of directory `dir`, the file will not be served. This is a different approach to security than other UNIX servers take; the standard is to serve all documents in the Web hierarchy unless it has been explicitly indicated that they are not to be served.

In general, if you are running a server designed for extensive public access to multiple files, and especially if those files will be altered by potentially several people at your site, the GN/WN approach might not be practical. But if your plan is to keep strict control over the documents that will be made available to the public, and you want no chance of someone happening upon a document by simply guessing filenamcs, GN/WN can be a powerful ally. Much depends on the purpose of your Web site, and the discussion should be part of your initial Web strategy-planning sessions.

WN also has built-in search capabilities for the documents that are indicated in the `index.cache`. By formulating a search request via a URL (for example, `http://server/dir/search=title`), WN will search the `index.cache` files in `dir` to see if any of the titles match the search term. An HTML document will then be returned. WN also supports keyword (strings in HTML headers), user-supplied field, context, and range searches as part of its regular features.

GN and WN are available according to the GNU public license at the previous URL. Also available is complete documentation on installation, configuration, and troubleshooting, as well as addresses for the Usenet and mailing lists that offer support for GN/WN. Interestingly, the designer offers a logo for those interested in why they might adopt his software. At the bottom of his overview (`http://hopf.math.nwu.edu/docs/overview.html`), he writes: "WN—for those who think the Web should be more than a user-friendly version of FTP." That says more about the philosophy behind his Web server software than any explanation ever could.

> **NOTE**
>
> Introduction to GN by Author John Franks—from `http://www.ncsa.uiuc.edu/SDG/Software/Mosaic/Notes/gn-1.0-release.txt`
>
> GN Release 1.0 (no longer beta)
>
> A Free Multi-protocol Server for Gopher and HTTP
>
> FEATURES: (* means new in version 1.0)
>
> ■ HTTP support—GN now serves two protocols gopher and HTTP, the protocol used by WWW clients. GN recognizes the protocol from the request and responds appropriately. This allows the use of WWW browsers like Mosaic in their native mode. The 1.0 release supports HTTP/1.0 and fixes several bugs in GN-1.0beta (*)
>
> ■ Per Directory Access control.
>
> ■ Support for structured files.
>
> ■ Support for compressed files.
>
> ■ Built-in menu hierarchy searches.
>
> ■ Free for any use, commercial or otherwise! (GNU license)
>
> ■ Capability to decouple menus from filesystem.
>
> AVAILABLE BY ANONYMOUS FTP:
>
> FTP to: `ftp.acns.nwu.edu`
>
> Get file `pub/gn/gn-1.0.tar.Z`
>
> OR VIA GOPHER:
>
> Server: `hopf.math.nwu.edu` port 70
>
> Get file: `gn-1.0.tar.Z`
>
> You can also browse the source and documentation here.
>
> GN is a gopher/HTTP server, which is written in C and runs under UNIX. It is freely available for any use, commercial or otherwise. The software is freely redistributable under the terms of the GNU public license. There is good documentation—three man pages and an extensive installation and maintenance guide.

GN has "per directory" access control. You can have different access (by IP address or subnet) to every directory if you want to. You don't need to run different servers on different ports to have different levels of access!

GN supports the standard text and binary types, including sound and image. Index types include programs (or shell scripts) which return "virtual directories" and also "grep" type searches. GN runs only under inetd. See the man page for details.

Starting with release 1.0, the GN sever is becoming a multi-protocol server. It will accept either gopher requests or HTTP requests and respond appropriately. To the maintainer this takes place automatically with no action necessary on his or her part. For those interested in migrating from gopher to HTTP this is a very easy way to make the transition.

For those not familiar with it, HTTP stands for HyperText Transfer Protocol and it is the underlying protocol used by WWW (World Wide Web) browsers such as the Mosaic family or Cello. Gopher and HTTP each have some advantages not shared by the other. Making GN a multi-protocol server is an attempt to let us have our cake and eat it too. To see this in action try gopher://gopher.math.nwu.edu/ with a gopher client and http://gopher.math.nwu.edu/ with a WWW client and compare the two. This is one server with one data directory.

One of the biggest advantages of HTTP is in the presentation layer provided by the NCSA Mosaic browsers. With GN release 1.0 or later it is a fairly trivial matter to put nicely formatted text or images in any of several formats into menus viewed by Mosaic. Gopher client users will not see the images. The text can be converted to type 'I' or omitted at the GN maintainer's discretion. The inlined images in documents available from HTTP servers are more than just a cute feature. They add functionality which is just not available from gopher. For example, there is a server which provides a campus map in text about the campus and has the feature that if you click a building you get a new document describing the building and containing a photo of it. A Michigan State server offers a campus map with the feature that clicking on a location in it gives an enlarged map of that area. These are not GN servers but these features could be implemented using GN 1.0.

On the other hand gopher has some advantages too. At present the gopher protocol is much more widely used if you count the number of servers. Measured by network traffic the difference is smaller. Also gopher has Veronica indexing. Indexing is somewhat harder for HTTP servers.

As of release 1.0 the interactive forms facility has been withdrawn from GN. The intent is to replace it in a future release with a mechanism for doing forms which is compatible with what is being done with other servers. For GN what this will mean is a single simple form syntax which will result in GN using ASK blocks when serving a gopher+ client and HTML+ forms when serving an HTTP client, This should be done in a way that is transparent to the maintainer.

Plexus

Plexus is a public-domain HTTP server that was written in the Perl scripting language by Tony Sanders. It is available at `http://www.bsdi.com/server/doc/plexus.html`. Plexus is a highly configurable server, which makes it desirable for those administrators who want to be able to extend security features as well as gateways to such features as the `finger` and `archie` commands. It is also a desirable possibility for anyone well-versed in Perl, because changes can be made to fit the particular situation.

Plexus supports the new HTTP 1.0 and the older HTTP 0.9 protocols (as do the others). Currently, it does not support Gopher protocols, which let you serve Gopher directories to the Web (both CERN and NCSA do support the Gopher protocols). If you're into streamlining your own server, you'll appreciate Plexus's dispatch routines for setting up different types of supported protocols.

Plexus's limitations show through in a few areas. Although the GET and HEAD request methods are supported, there is no support for PUT and only a minimal amount for POST. Obviously, then, Plexus would be largely unsuitable if your interest lay in serving large numbers of fill-in forms containing extensive data sets.

But there are several strong elements to this server as well. An easily configurable bookmark icon gives users a graphical item that looks like a book for moving forward and backward through the Web. A useful directory browser can be set to return an alphabetically arranged listing of items in the requested directory if the originally requested filename doesn't exist. Furthermore, directory searches are possible using regular Perl expressions (meaning they can be both complex and powerful), and this search will yield lists of documents adhering to the search as well as the title information from these documents. Access can be controlled by both IP address filtering and by restricting access to directories, and is simple to configure. Finally, Plexus is very good at image decoding, allowing some advanced work with imagemaps; and user familiarity with Perl allows the fairly simple additions of gateways to `finger`, `calendar`, and others. Advanced gateways are readily available on the Web for searches through ArchiPlex (a form for searching `archie` databases).

THE PLEXUS CONFIGURATION FILE

(By Plexus author Tony Sanders—from `http://www.bsdi.com/server/doc/Configuration.html`.)

plexus [-c config] [-d topdir] [-i ¦ -I sockfd] [-l log] [-p port] [-P pidfile] [-D diag]

-p port specify port to open (/etc/service name or number) Without -i or -I plexus will start in daemon mode, [-p port] is only useful in this mode.

-d topdir Override default directory (/usr/local/www)

-c config Override default config file (server/plexus.conf)

`-l log` Override default log file (`log`)

`-P pidfile` Override default pid output file (`plexus.pid`)

`-D diag` Specify diagnostic output file (`enable debug`)

`-i` Use `stdin`/`stdout` (e.g., running under `inetd`)

`-I sockfd` Use specified socket (mostly for server restarts)

Plexus contains the main loop that accepts incoming HTTP connections and forks a process to handle the transaction. The main server can continue to accept other connections while the child processes the request in the background. The child vectors though the associative array %method, defined in plexus.conf , to one of the method routines (e.g., GET is handled by &do_get).

If started as a normal user, the default port is $http_userport and is defined in `plexus.conf` . It can be changed on the command line using the `-p` option. When started as root, it will open the standard HTTP port which defaults to $http_defaultport from `plexus.conf`. However, the port assignment can be overridden either on the command line using the `-p` option or in `/etc/services` by adding a line for the `http protocol` e.g.: `http 80/tcp`. Command-line options always override internal defaults.

Topdir defaults to `/usr/local/www` , the config file defaults to `server/plexus.conf` , and the log file defaults to `log` .

Plexus also assumes that perl lives in `/usr/bin/perl`. If this is not the case, then it's best if you create a symlink for it. If you can't do that, then you will need to edit a bunch of files. To get the list run, `find . -type f -print ¦ xargs grep -l /usr/bin/perl` from the top level Plexus source directory.

site.pl

One of the first things you need to do is configure the `site.pl` file. This file contains all the platform-dependent code. It helps if you have installed your standard system header files using Perl's h2ph. The only config option in `local.conf` that affects this file is locking, which is set in `local.conf`. It should be set to either flock or fcntl ; the default is flock.

plexus.conf

Next, you should make sure all the settings in `plexus.conf` agree with your local system configuration. There shouldn't be much need to change this file unless you are adding new features. The notable exceptions are $http_chroot, which controls whether or not to chroot to the top of the tree; $http_user and $http_group which define the user and group to switch to if started as root; and $hostname, which should contain your fully qualified domain name (it defaults to `/bin/hostname`).

```
local.conf
```
Contains settings for various system parameters including which files to load, directory mapping, format translations, and file-extension-to-content-type mappings. This file is not a perl script. It is designed for ease of use and flexibility.

Verification

After you install the files, test the server from the command line using the following command: `/usr/local/www/server/plexus -i -l /dev/tty -D /dev/tty`. This will log all information to your tty. You can type your request directly from the keyboard (e.g., `GET /HTTP/1.0`).

Finally, run plexus in server mode using the following command: `/usr/local/www/ server/plexus -D /dev/tty &amp;`. Once plexus is running, test it using your browser. If you run plexus as root, it opens port 80; if you are running it as a normal user, it opens port 8001.

Macintosh

For those operating in the Macintosh environment, the most popular server is MacHTTP 2.0, written by Chuck Stotton and now available from BIAP Systems Inc. at `http://www.biap.com`. You can download the software for a 30-day trial period, after which time you must either register it or discontinue its use. The cost to license ranges from $50 if you're planning to allow no Internet access (that is, a local server) to $100 for full commercial use (hardly exorbitant).

The installation, like most Mac software installation, is quite straightforward. You simply download it to your machine, Un-Stuffit, and launch it like any other Macintosh program. The package comes with help documentation in the form of HTML files. You can access these by pointing a browser to `http://your.server`. After reading through the document, you can customize the software, setting changes such as number of simultaneous users and restricting access by IP address as required.

MacHTTP 2.0 enables the serving of not just HTML files (the standard Web document), but several varieties of binary files, such as GIF and JPEG graphics files. Perhaps more importantly, but not implemented nearly as often, the server software enables Web authors to embed AppleScripts into their documents under certain conditions—a powerful feature that lets you draw on HyperCard and other applications to make your Web documents more inclusive and worth visiting. Version 2.0 of MacHTTP supports CGI (Common Gateway Interface) applications and scripting, enabling you to further integrate applications outside the server software itself.

This is a powerful and well-supported server package. If you want to run your Web from a Mac, it's also the most well-developed package available for that platform. And commercial support, especially at the reasonable price, is nothing to shudder about.

OS/2

If you want to run a Web server under OS/2, you can use GoServe, a combination WWW and Gopher server written by Mike Cowlishaw of IBM UK Laboratories, or OS2httpd, written by Frankie Fan.

GoServe

GoServe can be downloaded from `http://www2.hursley.ibm.com/goserve/`. It is provided according to IBM's OS/2 Employee Written Software program and is available free of charge subject to the terms of the agreement available at `http://www2.hursley.ibm.com/goserve/license.txt`.

Assuming that you have IBM's TCP/IP already running, GoServe is easy to install and use; there are no configuration files to tweak. Download GoServe to your machine in a directory (for example, `D:\GOSERV`). In an OS/2 window, unzip the file into a different directory (such as `D:\GOHTTP`). After changing the current directory back to the original directory (`D:\GOSERVE`), start up GoServe with the parameter `http` (that is, `start goserve http`). You should then see a GoServe window. For further information about troubleshooting, filter commands, and other options, see GoServe's reference documentation at `http://www2.hursley.ibm.com/goserve/goserve.doc`.

GoServe does not support CGI scripting on its own. It can, however, be used in tandem with Don Meyer's GoHTTP. (A version of GoHTTP is bundled with GoServe; updates are available at `http://w3.ag.uiuc.edu/DLM/GoHTTP/GoHTTP.html`.) With the combination of these two packages, GoServe can transfer files with HTTP/1.0 headers, support fill-in forms with external scripts (including the POST request method), and support multiple CGI directories (essential if CGI scripts come to be a major part of your Web operations). In addition, the programs can be used together to support imagemaps at a sophisticated level, "CIRCLE" areas on HTML pages, and authentication by directory or by specific access by groups or users.

OS2HTTPD

OS2HTTPD, a native OS/2 Web server, is a port of the NCSA httpd 1.3. It is available at `ftp://ftp.netcom.com/pub/kf/kfan/web2-104.zip` and requires IBM TCP/IP for OS/2 Base Kit 2.0 or later. After you download it to the `root` directory of your machine, you should unzip it using the `-d` option to preserve the directory structure. You will end up with the whole package being in `\os2httpd`. To start the server, open an OS/2 window, change to `\os2httpd\bin`, and type `os2httpd` to start the daemon.

Although not all of the features of NCSA HTTPD are included in OS2HTTPD, it's close. Extensive forms and CGI scripting are supported, and OS/2's flexible directory structure makes maintenance and configuration relatively simple. For now, the GoServe/GoHTTP combination is probably the more complete package, but as OS2HTTP continues its development toward a full implementation, it should overtake GoServe/GoHTTP before long.

Microsoft Windows

If you want to run a server under Windows 3.1, you have a couple of choices: SerWeb and NCSA's HTTPD for Windows (also referred to as Win-HTTPD). SerWeb is currently no longer under development. According to its home page (`http://riskweb.bus.utexas/www.html`), SerWeb is fairly primitive, offering no forms or logging support. It is stressed that if you choose to use SerWeb, you should not use your machine for anything else. Because it is an *orphan* program, it won't be covered here.

NCSA HTTPD for Windows

The other alternative for the Windows environment, and a far stronger alternative at that, is NCSA's httpd for Windows, created by Robert Denny. Win-HTTPD is available from `http://www.alisa.com:80/win-httpd/` for a 30-day free trial after which a registration fee (for commercial use) is required.

FTP the software from `ftp://ftp.alisa.com/pub/winhttpd/whttpd14.zip` (access between 6:00 p.m. and 6:00 a.m. Pacific Time). After downloading, create a directory on your hard drive (assuming c:) called `c:\httpd` and unzip the file (use the `-d` option on PKUNZIP to preserve the directory structure). There will then be an information file in `c:\httpd\htdocs`, which you can read with your browser as a local file. After you have read through it and the accompanying checklist, you will be ready to start the server.

The most recent version is 1.4. This server includes most of the features of the UNIX NCSA httpd server (see following section). Highlights are numerous. Win-httpd supports up to 16 simultaneous connections, and it fully supports the GET, HEAD, and POST request methods. The package contains a dual-mode CGI interface, with a script interface using a DOS virtual machine, and a Windows CGI interface with form field decoding.

Win-HTTPD's directory support is strong. The directory indexes can be annotated with HTML links and readme files, useful for people who either stumble onto your Web site or who access it for the first time (and special instructions are desirable). In compiling the directory index, Win-httpd automatically extracts title strings from the HTML documents to provide usable descriptions. Furthermore, directory indexes generated by the server use icons to represent document types, conforming to the formatting of the current CERN and NCSA servers. The server also allows URL aliasing and redirection to enable document collections to be mapped to a virtual directory structure.

By the time this book appears, Win-HTTPD will have become a commercial product. O'Reilly & Associates will release it as WebSite, a 32-bit product designed for Windows 95 or Windows 3.1 with the Win32 extensions. Included in the package, according to the information available at `http://gnn.com/gnn/bus/ora/news/c.website.html`, are the full server itself, a copy of Enhanced Mosaic 2.0, a 350-page documentation book, and a program called WebView. WebView will let you view your directories graphically, and it enables you to enhance images in Web documents through a graphical editor. In addition, you can view multiple Web directories simultaneously in separate windows, and you can make use of *wizards* to help you create common Web documents.

Windows NT

HTTPS is an HTTP/1.0 server that runs as a Windows NT service; it was written by Chris Adye as part of the European Microsoft Windows NT Academic Centre (EMWAC). Three versions are available: one for Intel-based systems, another for MIPS processors, and a third for DEC Alpha. You can download the server from `ftp://emwac.ed.ac.uk/pub/https/`. Hypertext information is available at `http://emwac.ed.ac.uk/html/internet_toolchest/https/contents.htm`. This site includes a full manual that walks you through installation (and deinstallation), configuration, and use. There is also a solid troubleshooting section.

This server is relatively limited in features, but it's a good stepping stone to the commercial product, Purveyor. HTTPS's features include support for HEAD, GET, and POST request methods, CGI scripts and HTML fill-in forms, full directory browsing (which can be disabled for security reasons), and imagemaps. It also allows users to search local WAIS databases.

HTTPS is a freeware version of Process Software's Windows NT commercial WWW server, Purveyor, which lists at $1,995.00 (US). Information about Purveyor is available at `http://www.process.com/prodinfo/purvdata.htm`. Purveyor is available now for Windows NT, and will be released later in the year for Windows 95 servers. It comes complete with HTTP, FTP, and Gopher proxy support, basic authentication support, and access control by group, username, or IP filtering. It installs and configures through a graphical interface, but configuration should be simple. Full documentation and technical support are provided by the company, rather nice to have if you're having trouble getting your server to serve in the middle of the night.

Summary

The simple fact about servers for a Macintosh, Windows, or OS/2 environments is that setting them up is extremely easy. As long as you have the Internet connection and your machine has a dedicated and unique IP address, you can establish your machine as a Web server, with very little difficulty. For both Mac and Windows, all you need do, practically speaking, is to download the software, install it, set your directories, and start serving your Web. The flexibility of the UNIX packages might not be there, and complex scripting and imaging capabilities remain primarily the province of the UNIX server software, but Mac and Windows server software is enjoying an increasing amount of developmental activity and will soon be able to match its UNIX counter-part, especially with the 32-bit operating systems fully in place. OS/2 development remains largely up to its growing number of non-professionals, but IBM itself (which seems highly committed to the operating system) will likely introduce fully supported server software shortly.

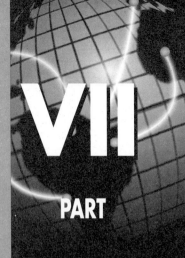

VII

PART

New Technologies

Java and HotJava

43

by
John December

The World Wide Web has transformed the online world. No longer constrained to just text-only information systems, users of the Web have a great deal of choices for selecting and viewing information. However, while the Web's system of hypertext gives users a high degree of selectivity, hypermedia opens up many options for new kinds of sensory input a user might receive. Using the Web, you can access information, graphics, text, or even videos. However, the Web lacks true interactivity—real-time, dynamic, and visual interaction between the user and appli-cation.

The new Java language from Sun Microsystems brings this missing interactivity to the Web. With a Java-enabled Web browser—such as Sun's HotJava—you can encounter animations and in-teractive applications. Java programmers can make customized media formats and information protocols that can be displayed in any Java-enabled browser. Java's features enrich the com-munication, information, and interaction on the Web by enabling users to distribute executable content—rather than just HTML pages and multimedia files—to users. This distribution of ex-ecutable content is the power of Java.

With origins in Sun's work to create a programming language to create software that can run on many different kinds of devices, Java evolved into a language for distributing executable content through the Web. Today, Java brings new interest to Web pages through applications that can all give the user immediate feedback and accept user input continuously through mouse or key-board entries.

In this chapter, I first present a description and definition of Java and explore what Java brings to Web communication. Then I present a brief "armchair" tour of some examples of what Java can do.

What Can Java Do?

Java animates pages on the Web and makes interactive and specialized applications possible. Fig-ure 43.1 illustrates how the software used with the Web can support a variety of communication. With hypertext, the basis for information organization, you can select what information to view. Programmers can create special kinds of Gateway programs that use these files of hypertext on the Web as interfaces. When you use a Web page with such a gateway program associated with it, you can access databases or receive a customized response based on a query. But Java's executable content brings the opportunity for a hypertext page to involve you in continuous, real-time, and complex interaction. This executable content is literally downloaded to your computer so that it can run an animation, perform computation, or guide you through more information at remote network sites.

FIGURE 43.1.

The Web's software supports selectivity, display, computation, and interactivity.

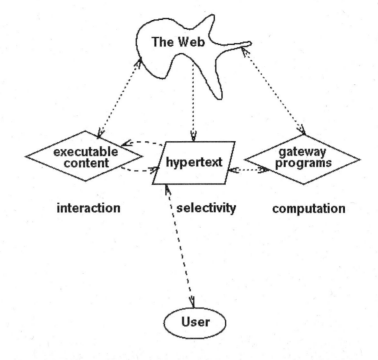

A METAPHOR FOR JAVA

One metaphor for hypertext is that it offers a visually static page of information (which can include text, graphics, sound, and video). The hypertext page can also have "depth" where it contains hyperlinks connecting to other documents or resources.

Java transforms this static page metaphor into a more dynamic one. The information on a Java page on the Web does not have to be visually static or limited to a predefined set of ways to interact with users. Users encountering Java programs can take part in a wider variety of interactive behavior, limited only by the imagination and skill of the Java programmer. Java thus transforms a hypertext page into a stage, complete with the chance for actors and players to appear and things to happen. And, instead of the user being in the audience, you as a user of a Java-enabled Web browser are actively a part of the activity on this stage. With Java, you can take part in changing what transpires and react to it, which makes you more actively involved in shaping the information content delivered on the Web.

Java thus brings Web pages alive through animation and a higher degree of interaction than what is possible through gateway programming alone.

What Is Java?

The name *Java* stands for the programming language developed by Sun Microsystems that is used to create executable content that can be distributed through networks. Used generically, the name Java stands for a set of software tools used to create and implement executable content using the Java programming language. One key software tool is the special browser that can interpret Java-generated code. The browser, called HotJava, was developed to showcase the capabilities of the Java programming language.

HotJava has the same capabilities as most Web browsers, but is additionally capable of interpreting and displaying Java's executable content. So while HotJava can display any page on the Web, a Web browser that does not recognize Java can't display the Java executables. Thus, the HotJava browser "sees" the Web plus more—applications written using Java. As described in the following section on Java's origins and future, Java capability is expected to be integrated into future versions of other Web browsers.

JAVA'S HOME

Sun Microsystems, the developers of Java, provide a one-stop collection of information about Java on the Web at `http://java.sun.com/`. This site includes a full range of the latest information on Java and Java-enabled browsers. Links from this site take you to detailed announcements, release information, documentation, and links to Java demonstrations.

When you download HotJava, the browser, you can also get a set of Java language development tools.

What Is Executable Content?

Executable content is a general term that identifies the important difference between the content a Java-enabled Web browser downloads and the content a non-Java-enabled browser can download. Simply put, in a non-Java Web browser, the downloaded content is defined in terms of Multipurpose Internet Mail Extensions (MIME) specifications, which include a variety of multimedia document formats. This specification of content is made so that it can be *displayed* in the browser or in a helper application (to display multimedia such as images, sound, and video). The result is that the user chooses and then observes content.

A Java-enabled browser also downloads content defined by MIME specifications and displays it. However, the key difference is that a Java-enabled browser recognizes a special hypertext gat called

<CODE>*APP*</CODE>. When you're downloading a Web page containing APP, the Java-enabled browser knows that a special kind of Java program called an *applet* is associated with that page. The browser then downloads a file of information that describes the execution of that applet. This file of information is written in what are called *bytecodes*. The Java-enabled browser interprets these bytecodes and runs them as an executable program on the user's host. This downloading and execution happens automatically, without requiring the user to request it.

So when surfing the Web with a Java-enabled browser, you might find not only all the hypertext content that the pre-Java–age Web offered, but also animated, executable, and distributed content. Moreover, this executable content can include instructions for handling new forms of media as well as information protocols.

How Java Changes the Web

Java profoundly changes the Web because it brings a richness of interactivity and information delivery not possible using previous Web software systems.

Figure 43.2 illustrates the technical difference between Java's interactivity and hypertext selectivity and gateway programming. The figure illustrates how gateway programming allows for computation and response but not in real-time.

FIGURE 43.2.

Java interactivity is based on executable content downloaded to the user's computer.

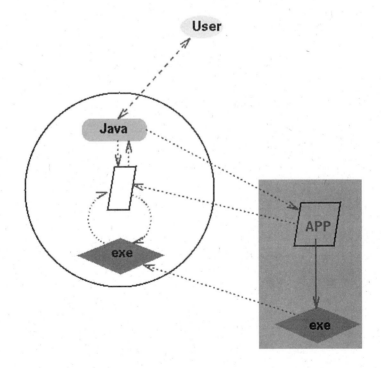

Java Origins and Direction

According to Michael O'Connell's feature article on the origins of Java in the July 7, 1995, issue of *SunWorld Online* (http://www.sun.com/sunworldonline/swol-07-1995/swol-07-java.html), the development of Java began at Sun Microsystems in California just as the World Wide Web was being developed in Switzerland in 1991. The goal of this early development team including Java creator James Gosling was to develop consumer electronic products that could be simple and bug free. What was needed was a way to create platform-independent code and thus allow the software to run on any central processing unit (CPU).

As a starting point for a computer language to implement this platform independence, the development team focused first on C++. However, the team could not get C++ to do everything they wanted in order to create a system to support a distributed network of communicating heterogeneous devices. The team abandoned C++ and developed a language called Oak (later renamed Java). By the fall of 1992, the team had created a project named Star 7 (*7), which was a personal handheld remote control.

The development team was incorporated as FirstPerson, Inc., but then lost a bid to develop a television set–top box for Time-Warner. By the middle of 1994, the growth in the Web's popularity drew the team's attention. They decided they could build an excellent browser using Java technology. With a goal of bringing their CPU-independent, real-time programming system to the Web, they built a Web browser.

The browser, called WebRunner, was written using Java and completed early in the fall of 1994. Executives at Sun Microsystems were impressed and saw the technology and commercial possibilities that could result from a new browser: tools, servers, and development environments.

On May 23, 1995, Sun Microsystems, Inc., formally announced Java and HotJava at SunWorld '95 in San Francisco.

Java's Current Status and Timeline

For the most current information on Java's releases, see Sun Microsystem's Java site at http://java.sun.com/.

Java/HotJava timetable:

- San Jose, California, April 11, 1995: Netscape chairman Jim Clark and Sun CEO Scott McNealy reaffirmed their working relationship and promised more news at SunWorld '95.

- San Francisco, California, May 23, 1995: At SunWorld '95, Netscape announced that it will license Sun's Java programming language for its Netscape Navigator browser.

- Summer 1995: Java and HotJava in alpha stages of development. Alpha release for Sun Solaris 2.3, 2.4, and 2.5 SPARC-based. Alpha release also for Microsoft Windows NT.

Ports underway for Microsoft Windows 95, and MacOS 7.5. Ports are underway in third-party projects for other platforms and operating systems, including Windows 3.1, Amiga, NeXT, Silicon Graphics, and Linux.

- Summer 1995: Sun Microsystems sponsored an applet programming contest to encourage the development of excellent applets. Winners were announced on the HotJava home page (`http://java.sun.com/`) in September, 1995.

- Fall/winter 1995: Java technology to be integrated into Netscape browsers (see `http://home.netscape.com/`).

Java Future Possibilities

Java technology can be deployed in embedded systems—such as in consumer electronics, such as handheld devices, telephones, and VCRs. Mitsubishi Electronics has been working to use Java technology in these devices.

The association of Netscape and Sun Microsystems should bring Java technology into Netscape browsers by late 1995. With Netscape's widespread installed base, the use of Java in applications could very rapidly increase.

Sun Microsystems also plans to license its Java technology to other Web browser manufacturers, online service providers, and software developers. The market for third-party object and tool libraries for Java is expected to take off. Software layers on top of Java will enable developers to use more sophisticated tools to create applications.

Illustrations of Java's Potential

Java is a new programming language, and programmers outside of Sun Microsystems are just beginning to explore its potential. However, you can see Java in action now. The rest of this chapter shows you examples of the basic kinds of activity Java can support, emphasizing the unique way Java enables the distribution of executable content.

Animation

Java's applications put animated figures on Web pages. Figure 43.3 shows a still image of Duke, the mascot of Java who tumbles across a Web page displayed in the HotJava browser. Duke tumbles across the page, cycling through a set of graphic images that loop while the user has this page loaded in the HotJava browser.

Animation isn't limited to cartoon figures, however. Pages can have animated logos or text that moves or shimmers across the screen. Java animations also need not just be a decorative pre-generated figure, but can be a graphic that is generated based on computation. Figure 43.4 shows a wave form drawn based on a mathematical equation.

FIGURE 43.3.

Tumbling Duke, mascot of Java. (Courtesy of Arthur van Hoff, Sun Microsystems.)

FIGURE 43.4.

A graph generated as a result of a mathematical formula. (Courtesy of Arthur van Hoff, Sun Microsystems.)

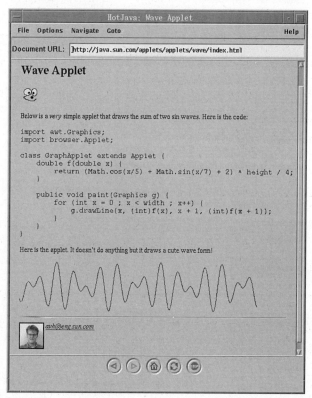

Interaction

While the animations shown can be static images that are drawn or generated, or animated images that can behave according to a pre-set algorithm (such as the tumbling Duke in Figure 43.3), animation can also be made interactive, where the user has some input as to its appearance. Figure 43.5 shows a three-dimensional rendering of chemical models. Using the mouse, you can spin these models and view them from many angles. Unlike the source code for the graph applet shown in Figure 43.4, of course, the source code for the chemical modeling is more complicated. To the user, however, the chemical models seem three dimensional, giving an insight into the nature of the atomic structure of these elements like no book could.

FIGURE 43.5.

Three-dimensional, manipulatable chemical models. (Courtesy of Sun Microsystems.)

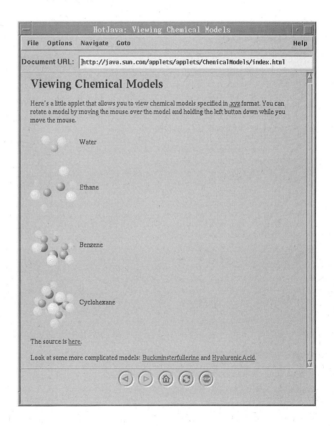

The chemical models in Figure 43.5 respond to user clicks of the mouse. Another variation on this animation involves providing the user with a way to interact with an interface to enter data and get feedback. The crossword puzzle example in Figure 43.6 is an excellent example of this. This application works just like a paper puzzle, except that the user enters guesses using the keyboard. Using the mouse to place the cursor in any square, a highlighted bar as well as the clue window at the top of the puzzle show the current word the user is guessing. Correct letters are displayed in black and incorrect letters are shown in red. In Figure 43.6, 40 across is highlighted, and the clue is shown in the window at the top. The letter *K* in 40 across is incorrect, as the letters of 26 down are in red (not distinguishable in the black-and-white image shown in this book) to indicate an incorrect guess. This feedback gives the user an advantage for guessing that a paper crossword puzzle could not do. The resulting application is an excellent demonstration of how Java can create an interface for user interaction and immediate feedback.

FIGURE 43.6.

Interactive crossword puzzle.
(Courtesy of Carl W. Haynes III.)

Another variation on interactivity is real-time interactivity. Figure 43.7 shows an interactive application that involves moving graphics that the user manipulates. This is the game of Tetris, in which you try to line up the falling tile shapes to completely fill the rectangle. Using designated keys for playing, you interact with the interface to steer the falling shapes. This Tetris implementation demonstrates the possibilities for arcade-like games using Java technology.

FIGURE 43.7.

The Tetris game. (Courtesy of Nathan Williams.)

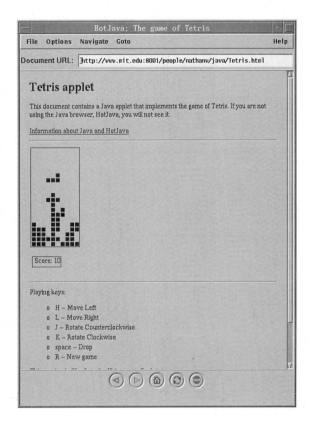

Interactivity and Computation

The crossword puzzle and Tetris game described in the previous section demonstrate how interactivity and animation can work together. Both applets customized their animated output based on user input, so both applets were actually performing computation. However, an example that shows this computational ability in more concrete terms is in Figure 43.8, a simple spreadsheet.

This spreadsheet works in much the same manner as the crossword puzzle, but emphasizes that the computational possibilities can allow users to have an environment in which to work instead of just a puzzle to solve. The spreadsheet shown allows you to change the contents of any of the 24 cells (A1 through D6) by replacing its label, value, or formula. This is just like a real spreadsheet, which is more of an environment in which the user can work than a fixed game such as the crossword puzzle. This subtle difference is a profound one: Using Java, a user can obtain an entire environment for open-ended interaction rather than a fixed set of options for interaction—opening up the Web page into a Web stage.

FIGURE 43.8.

*A simple spreadsheet.
(Courtesy of Sami Shaio,
Sun Microsystems.)*

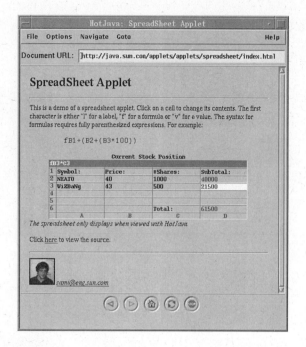

Distributed Applications

The oscilloscope shown in Figure 43.9 operates in a HotJava browser and allows the user to manipulate its settings. The result is an application something like the chemical models but with continuous independent feedback to the user. Once the settings are made, the oscilloscope displays the lissajous figures that show the waveform of the electrical signals. This application shows animation, interaction, computation, and continuous display based on user settings. The result is that a user has essentially downloaded an oscilloscope remotely.

Just as the user can download an oscilloscope, so can a user download a "kit" for doing almost anything. Figure 43.10 shows a makeover kit that demonstrates the possibilities with Java. This kit allows the user to select a color and a brush style and then paint on the face provided in the kit. This very simple paint application shows how the user can build something with a Java page.

FIGURE 43.9.

An oscilloscope. (Courtesy of Hugh Anderson.)

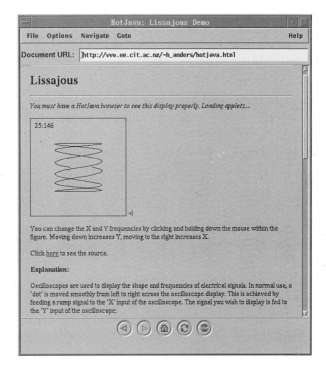

FIGURE 43.10.

A makeover kit. (Courtesy of George Coates Performance Works.)

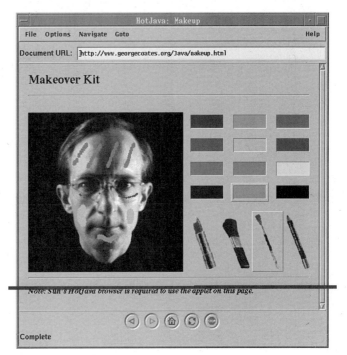

Communication

The preceding examples demonstrate many informational, animation, and computational applications of Java. Another application area is communication among people. Carl W. Haynes III has implemented a simple Java-based chat system, shown in Figure 43.11. This system allows you to log in to this Web page and type sentences that are seen by others who are viewing that page. The text you type is visible to all others who have the page displayed in their Java-enabled browser. This results in a group chat system similar to that implemented in a Telnet, Internet Relay Chat, or MU* systems.

FIGURE 43.11.

A Java-based chat system. (Courtesy of Carl W. Haynes III.)

Of course, communication takes place all the time on nearly all Web pages through text or other media. But a Java-enabled browser can also display multimedia. Figure 43.12 illustrates a simple speaking clock—you can retrieve the current time as sound in response to a mouse click on the clock display.

Java can also be used to support mass communication in new ways. The *NandO Times* is a Web-based news service that has been very innovative in news delivery on the Web. Using Java, this news agency now provides a tickertape of headlines across its front page. The text under the NandO banner in Figure 43.13 scrolls continuously to show the world, national, sports, and political top stories at the moment. The four pictures under the labels for these categories also change, giving a "slide show" that is very effective in displaying new information without requiring the user to select it for viewing. This transforms the Web into something people can watch to get new information.

FIGURE 43.12.

A speaking clock. (Courtesy of Arthur van Hoff, Sun Microsystems.)

FIGURE 43.13.

Headline feed on NandO Times. *(Courtesy of* NandO Times.*)*

Similarly, Figure 43.14 shows how current information feeds can act as surveillance for specific activities. The figure shows a test of ESPNET's SportsZone Live Scoreboard, showing the current scores of games in progress. As the scores change, this display changes, so that the sports-minded can keep up with the current games and scores. Like the *NandO Times* news feed, this sports feed changes the Web into something to watch in addition to something to interact with.

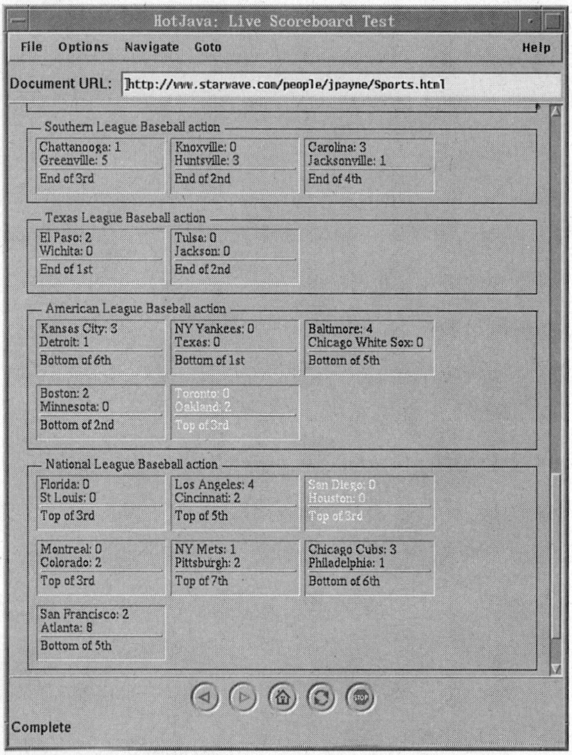

FIGURE 43.14.

ESPNET SportsZone Live Scoreboard. (Courtesy of Jonathan Payne, Starwave Corporation.)

Applications and Handlers

In addition to applets like the ones shown here, Java programmers can also create applications, or standalone programs, that don't require the Java-enabled browser to run. (The HotJava browser itself is such an application, written using Java.) Applications could thus conceivably be new browsers or interfaces that interact with other network or local resources.

Another kind of software program available with Java is a *handler*. A protocol handler enables a Java programmer to specify how a Java browser should interpret a particular type of protocol. The HotJava browser knows how to interpret the Internet protocols such as HTTP, FTP, Gopher, and others because of the browser distribution code. But if new protocols are invented, a Java programmer can specify how they should be handled by creating a protocol handler.

Another type of handler is a content handler. This handler translates a particular specification for a file type based on MIME. This content handler will specify how the HotJava browser should handle a particular file type. By creating a specification in a content handler, all Java-enabled browsers will be able to view this special format.

The handlers and applications that Java makes possible have the potential to dramatically extend what can be browsed on the Web. No longer will information developers have to be concerned about making sure their users have the proper software to view a particular type of file or handle a new kind of protocols. The protocol and content handlers, like the executable content Java makes possible as applets, can be distributed as needed to requesting Java-enabled browsers.

What Java Might Make Possible

The previous examples illustrate only some of the potential of Java. A few of these examples are "toy" demonstrations meant to show the possibilities of Java. What kind of communication might Java foster? The *NandO Times* example shows an innovative application for providing information in a way that allows you to sit back and observe rather than selecting hypertext links.

Java opens up a new degree of interactivity and customizability of interaction for the Web. Earlier Web development techniques of creating pages and linking them together will still be necessary in a Java-flavored Web. However, Java creates possibilities for richer kinds of content to be developed. The user can interact with and change the appearance of a Web page along with the state of a database using a Java-enabled browser. Thus, Java profoundly changes the texture of the Web in the following ways:

- **Java creates places to stop on the paths of the Web**. A well-done Java application on a single hypertext page can engage a user for a long time. Rather than just text, sound, images, or videos to observe, a Java page can offer a place to play, learn, or communicate and interact with others in a way that isn't necessarily based on going somewhere else on the Web through hyperlinks. If the hypertext of the Web are like paths, the Java pages are like the towns, villages, and cities to stop on these paths and do something other than just observe or "surf."

- **Java increases the dynamism and competitiveness of the Web**. Just as new browser technology prompted Web developers to create still more applications and pages to exploit these features, so too does Java technology promise a new round of content development on the Web.

- **Java enriches the interactivity of the Web**. Java's interactivity is far richer, more immediate, and more transparent than the interactivity possible through gateway programming. Gateway programming still should have a role in Web applications, just as page design and multimedia presentation will still play a role. However, Java's interactivity brings new possibilities of what can happen on the Web. With Java, transactions on the Web can be more customized, with immediate, continuous, and ongoing feedback to the user.

■ **Java transforms the Web into a software delivery system.** Java's essential design as a language to deliver executable content makes it possible for programmers to create software of any kind and deliver it to users of HotJava browsers. Rather than having to focus on the interface, the Java programmer focuses on the interaction desired and lets the built-in features of the graphics take care of the rest of the implementation. The result is that very simple programs like the drawing and spreadsheet applications can be created quickly and distributed worldwide.

The true potential of Java to transform the Web is still in its initial stages. New potential applications for commerce, information delivery, and user interaction still await the imagination and skill of future Java developers.

Summary

Java is a programming language designed to deliver executable content over networks. A user or programmer should know what kinds of interaction Java can make possible and what its true potential can be: enlivening the Web, enriching the display of information in the form of animation and interactive applications:

■ Java enriches the interactivity possible on the Web. Rather than making just informational content possible, Java can support interactive content in the form of software that can be downloaded and run on any computer host with the Java interpretation environment installed.

■ Java was developed from ideas about platform-independent executable code. Sun Microsystems researchers have developed Java to be a powerful programming and information delivery system for use with the Web.

■ Java makes animation, interaction, computation, distributed applications, and new forms of communication possible. Through protocol and content handlers, Java has the potential to make new formats and new protocols available for use on the Web.

■ Java transforms the Web into a software delivery system where users have things to do rather than just places to go. Java may change the surfing behavior of Web users into playing and learning behavior in new interactive environments.

VRML on the Web

44

by
Adrian Scott

Virtual Reality Modeling Language, or *VRML,* is a way to describe virtual worlds on the Web, just as HTML describes Web pages. Soon, having a home page on the World Wide Web won't be enough. You'll need your own home world (home.wrl) as well!

In this chapter, you learn what Virtual Reality Modeling Language is, what it looks like, what you can do with it, and how it works. You also look at designing a VRML site and what kinds of business models can work for VRML creators. At the end of the chapter is a VRML resources section with pointers to URLs relating to information, software, examples, and converters.

The goal of virtual reality is to create an immersive experience so that you feel you are in the middle of a separate virtual world. Virtual reality generally relies on three-dimensional computerized graphics plus audio. Virtual reality uses a first-person outlook. You are moving about in the virtual world, rather than controlling a computer-generated figure moving around in the world.

Whereas HTML is a mark-up language, VRML (pronounced *ver-mul*) is not. In this chapter, you look at a simple world described in the standard VRML ASCII text representation, plus screen shots of what those worlds actually look like using a VRML browser. To start off, Figure 44.1 shows VrmLab by Jeff Sonstein of the New College of California.

FIGURE 44.1.

VrmLab, a virtual world described using Virtual Reality Modeling Language.

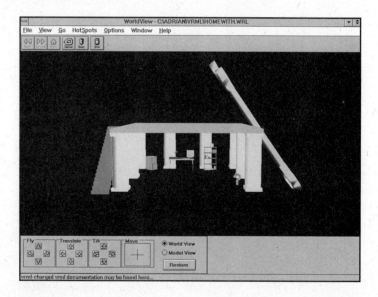

What is a VRML browser? A VRML browser is to VRML what a standard browser such as Mosaic is to HTML. The VRML browser loads in a virtual world described in VRML and then *renders* it, drawing a picture on your computer screen in three-dimensional graphics, and enables you to roam through the virtual world. You can select links in the virtual world that can take you to other worlds, or any other URL, such as an HTML page or a GIF image.

Your VRML and standard WWW browsers communicate so that when you select a link to an HTML file from a virtual world, your standard WWW browser loads in that URL. Conversely, when you select a link to a VRML file from your standard WWW browser, the WWW browser recognizes the MIME type and passes the URL or VRML file over to your VRML browser. In the future, you may see added capabilities in VRML browsers; they may be able to render an HTML page without your having to switch to the standard WWW browser.

You can send VRML files using the HTTP servers you use for your current HTML Web sites. In the future, you may see new kinds of servers with special capabilities suited to virtual reality applications, or they may be a part of HTTP NG, a future version of HTTP.

So what might your home world look like? You might have a three-dimensional figure of yourself or even of your living room (real or virtual?!). If you like windsurfing, you might have a windsurfer in some waves, linked to a map of your favorite windsurfing spots. Or you could have an art sculpture floating in mid-air.

History of VRML

At the first World Wide Web conference in 1994, Tim Berners-Lee (developer of the World Wide Web concept) and Dave Raggett of HP organized a session known as a "Birds-of-a-Feather" (BOF) session to discuss virtual reality and how it could be applied to the Web. Excitement took off rapidly with the creation of an e-mail list for discussion of what was then called Virtual Reality Markup Language.

Because VRML isn't an SGML language and because of its graphical nature, the word *Markup* was later changed to *Modeling*, although you can still find references to *VR Markup Language* floating around the Net. Memes are hard to kill.

The initial BOF meeting included several people who were working on 3D graphical interfaces to the Web. The e-list grew and grew: Within a week, over 1000 members were on the list. The list moderator is Mark Pesce, one of the prime architects of VRML. Pesce announced the goal of having a draft version of the VRML specification ready for the Fall 1994 WWW Conference.

Rather than reinvent the wheel, the list members wanted to choose an existing technology as a starting point. Several proposals were put together. You can still see these proposals at the VRML repository Web sites. Eventually (try getting agreement among that many people!), the list chose the Open Inventor ASCII File Format developed at Silicon Graphics (SGI).

A subset of this format with extensions for WWW hyperlinks came to form VRML's birthday suit. Gavin Bell (from SGI) adapted the format for VRML, with input from the list members. SGI allowed the format to be used in the open market, and also put a parser into the public domain to help VRML gain momentum.

After the draft specification of VRML 1.0, the list members looked at what changes might be needed. Around this time, I joined the list. The list members considered the complexity of various enhancements and the desirability of having them available. We decided that text was pretty important. Without a text node, you would have had to create a huge file describing all the text letters as polygons. Thus, the AsciiText and FontStyle nodes were introduced. In addition, changes were made to the LevelOfDetail node, and it was renamed LOD. The three credited authors of the VRML 1.0 specification are Gavin Bell of SGI, Anthony Parisi of Intervista, and Mark Pesce, the list moderator. Other major contributors are Chris Marrin of SGI and Jan Hardenbergh of Oki Advanced Products.

Introduction to Creating VRML Worlds

To give you a feeling for what VRML looks like, you can use Wanna-Be Virtual World Factory, a simple Web-based publicly accessible VRML authoring tool (`http://www.virtpark.com/theme/vwfactez.html`). Just fill out a Web-based HTML form, as shown in Figure 44.2.

FIGURE 44.2.

Creating a simple VRML world with the Wanna-Be Virtual World Factory.

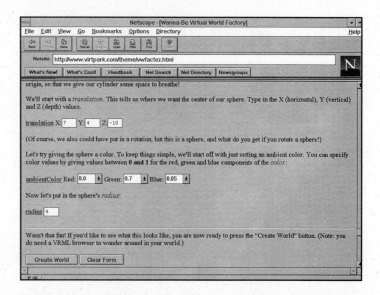

Listing 44.1 shows the listing of a VRML file created with Wanna-Be Virtual World Factory.

Listing 44.1. A VRML file created with Wanna-Be Virtual World Factory.

```
#VRML V1.0 ascii
# Created with the Virtual World Factory (TM)
#   from Scott Virtual Theme Parks
#
#   http://www.virtpark.com/theme
#   theme@netcom.com
#
Separator {
    Separator {
        Cylinder {
            radius 4
            height 2
```

```
        }
    }
    Separator {
        Translation {
            translation 3 5 7
        }
        Material {
            emissiveColor 0.15 0.45 0.85
        }
        Sphere {
            radius 4
        }
    }
}
```

If you load this world into your VRML browser and wander around, you see the example shown in Figure 44.3.

FIGURE 44.3.

Wandering in a VRML world created with Wanna-Be Virtual World Factory.

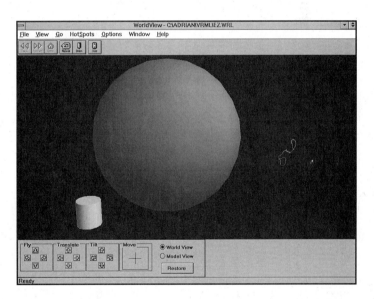

The MIME type for VRML is x-world/x-vrml. If you haven't convinced your Web site administrator to add the VRML MIME type to your Web server yet, you can set up a simple CGI script that starts out with the following line (in Perl):

```
print "Content-type: x-world/x-vrml\n\n";
```

After that, you can have the script print out the rest of your VRML world.

As you learned in Listing 44.1, a VRML world starts off with the first line:

```
#VRML V1.0 ascii
```

Anything after a # in a line of a VRML script is considered a comment. For transmission purposes, comments can be stripped out of a VRML file before it is transmitted across a network. If you want anything like a copyright or other information to get to the viewer, you should use an INFO node. However, at the current time, none of the HTTP servers have been configured to strip the comments out, so you can be a bit sloppy in the near future.

Each VRML world consists of one node. Typically, that one node is a Separator node, which includes a grouping of various nodes inside it. Nodes can represent shapes such as cubes and cones, properties such as colors and textures, or groupings. Nodes can also give World Wide Web references, such as hyperlinks or inline worlds, similar to HREFs and inline graphics in HTML (maybe they should be called in-space worlds).

As an example, the Material node is a property node that enables you to assign colors and transparency properties. One day at home, I was helping my dad paint our house. My dad was excited about the paint roller extender he had put together to reach the top of the house. I remarked, "Gee, Dad, I could make one of those in VRML."

He responded, "Yes, you could probably paint the whole house in VRML."

"Yes," I answered, "just one Material node and the job would be done." This really happened, and I retold the story to the www-vrml e-list. Of course, although making the Material node for changing the color would be easy, I also would have to create the house in VRML, using Cubes, IndexedFaceSets, and so on.

For a detailed description of VRML nodes, refer to the VRML specification at `http://www.hyperreal.com/~mpesce/vrml/vrml.tech/vrml10-3.html`. A VRML-enabled HTML version of the spec is at `http://www.virtpark.com/theme/vrml/`.

What You Need (Browsers, Hardware, Internet Access)

The minimal setup for experiencing VRML is a computer and VRML browser software. An Internet connection is necessary to download worlds. However, you can view VRML worlds stored on a computer disk without an Internet connection. Actually, when I started out creating VRML software, I didn't even have VRML browser software, so I had to use wetware (my imagination) to visualize how my VRML worlds might look.

A basic VRML setup includes a 486/50 computer with 8MB RAM, VRML browser software such as WebSpace or WorldView, and an Internet connection over a 14.4Kbps modem. This setup gives you only basic performance because the first versions of the VRML browsers are CPU hogs and complicated, uncompressed VRML worlds can take up as much as 500KB (which takes awhile to transfer over a 14.4Kbps Internet connection).

Serious VRML creators may want to move toward a UNIX workstation and a T1 connection. However, to create VRML worlds, all that you need is a text editor and knowledge of the VRML specification.

The first browsers available are WebSpace from Silicon Graphics (`http://www.sgi.com/Products/WebFORCE/WebSpace`) and Template Graphics (`http://www.tgs.com/~template`) and WorldView from Intervista (`http://www.hyperreal.com/intervista`).

To go beyond the basic system setup, you can get into fancy input and output devices. Head-mounted displays, or HMDs, bring virtual worlds closer to your eyes by displaying the worlds on two small screens that are part of glasses you wear. Some HMDs block out the outside world or enable you to see through the display so that your virtual world can overlay the real world. Prices on head-mounted display devices are dropping into the $500–$700 price range where they will start to become commonplace.

Head tracking devices can figure out which direction you are facing and relay this information to the browser to change your orientation.

Using a 3D mouse, you can move around in the three-dimensional virtual world, just as a standard mouse enables you to move around in two dimensions. Another input device is the data glove. However, data gloves are not yet user-friendly, nor are any great applications available for them yet. In general, 3D input devices are not yet mature, so many people may still be happy using keyboard/mouse combinations. Some of the recent input and output devices for virtual reality are the 5th Glove from Fifth Dimension Technologies and the "i-glasses!" HMD with tracking from Virtual I/O. As the VRML browsers develop, you'll see expanded support for advanced input and output devices.

Using the Browsers

After you download a VRML browser from the Internet (see the resources section for URLs at the end of this chapter) and install the browser, you are ready to get started.

Both browsers come with some simple worlds that you can load into the VRML browser to get started. After you get familiar with the navigation commands, you can start moving around the Web.

In the main navigation mode, you use a combination of the keyboard and a mouse to move around. For example, in WorldView from Intervista, you can use the arrow keys. The Up and Down keys move you forward and backward. The Left and Right keys let you rotate to the left or to the right. You can also use the mouse to click on directional arrows on the screen.

VRML Site Design

To design a VRML site at Scott Virtual Theme Parks, for example, you take the following steps:

1. Identify the goal of the site.
2. Identify participants.
3. Create wild ideas for site possibilities, including multiuser interactivity, sound, and behaviors.
4. Consider bandwidth and rendering concerns of participants.
5. Plan the range of site configurations.
6. Design the overall framework of the site.
7. Create actual VRML objects.
8. Integrate into the completed site.
9. Perform the initial testing and refinement.
10. Test with amateur users and assess site goal achievability and refinement.
11. Continue improving and redesigning the site.

In the following sections, you look at these steps in detail.

Identify the Goal of the Site

Identifying the goal of the site is the most important step for any VRML or HTML site. If it's a commercial site, is the goal to build name recognition or actually sell a product? For a political site, is the goal to win votes or register voters? Without clear goals, Web sites end up being little more than a show of what technology can do. To have a successful site, you first need to figure out what being successful means to you. VRML sites should be more than fancy 3D worlds.

Identify the Participants

For the second step, identifying the participants, note that I don't write *audience* or *viewers* here. In the immersive experience of virtual reality, everyone at your site is part of your world. Companies have experienced how easy it is to offend *Netizens* (Net denizens/citizens) with overly commercial pitches. With VRML, the emotions are raised to a higher level. Therefore, you want to know whom you're creating this site for. What are their desires, values, attitudes, and concerns?

Create Wild Ideas for Site Possibilities, Including Multiuser Interactivity, Sound, and Behaviors

At the beginning, you'll want to create wild ideas without regard for the current limitations of technology. What is your world about? What should it feel like to wander around your world? What kind of amusements would participants like?

Consider Bandwidth and Rendering Concerns of Participants

You'll find two key bottlenecks for networked VRML: bandwidth and rendering speed. Therefore, you should think about the technological limitations of your participants. Will they be dialing up from 14.4Kbps modems? Will they have fast UNIX graphics workstations or just 486 PCs?

It's important not to limit yourself too much by these considerations because technology is advancing so quickly that concepts of slow and fast are continually changing.

Plan the Range of Site Configurations

Based on the previous steps, you should have some idea of what you want from your site. Now you can think about what kind of site configurations you want. Do you want different versions (different file sizes) for participants on different bandwidths? Do you want a version of your world with complicated texture-mappings for users with advanced graphics capabilities?

Design the Overall Framework of the Site

Now is the time to lay out an overall framework or foundation for your site. You can design on paper, in a CAD package, or even in VRML. At this step, you're just developing an outline, saying "the house is here," without creating the whole house. This way you get an idea of what the experience of being in your world will be like, without having to get it fully completed.

At this stage, you might use common objects to create a quick draft. For instance, you might have the file house.wrl lying around in one of your directories. Although eventually you want to have an intricate house in that location, you can use this one as a WWWInline in the meantime.

Create Actual VRML Objects

Next, you can create the actual VRML objects to populate your world. You can use CAD packages together with file format conversion software, use VRML authoring tools, or even write VRML by hand with a text editor.

Integrate into Completed Site

At this stage, collect all the objects and the framework together to bring your world into virtual existence. For example, you might have started out designing your framework and objects in a CAD software package. At this stage, you can edit the files after converting them to VRML. You insert special VRML features such as the hyperlink nodes WWWAnchor and WWWInline, plus the special LOD node giving VRML information on switching between different objects at different distances. You also can run scripts to optimize file sizes at this point.

Perform the Initial Testing and Refinement

At this stage, you want to make sure that the basic world works and that the world can be accessed through the various combinations of bandwidth and rendering speeds your participants may have.

Test with Amateur Users and Assess Site Goal Achievability and Refinement

If you're designing a site where you're expecting thousands of accesses daily and you want the site to represent your product, it's worth testing the site with amateur users. Ad campaigns and feature films generally take this step, but people don't think of trying this procedure with Web sites. The first, simple way of testing is just to e-mail the URL to a few friends and ask what they think. Depending on who your friends are, having them test your site can be a start.

To get a comprehensive look at what people think of your site, gather several VRML-neophytes in a room and set them loose in your world. Observe closely where they go first and when they get a confused look in their eyes. You might even want to videotape the session so that you can review it later. You can get more feedback on your site this way, more than you'll get from waiting for people to say something or e-mail feedback.

Continue Improving and Redesigning the Site

Rather than set your site loose and forget about it, you should update your site with new information and approaches. Together with this step, you'll also want to get continued feedback on your site. A standard way to get feedback on Web sites is to include an HTML feedback form that generates e-mail to the Webmaster.

For you CGI-diehards, you can follow this sophisticated, subtle way to get data on people going through your site. You can approach this challenge by developing CGI programs that tag a person when he or she first enters the site. Then you can pass the ID number along through the QUERY_STRING environmental variable. You can log the ID number, time and date of access, and file accessed. This way you get some kind of feeling for how long a person stays in a particular VRML world and your site overall. You can also create CGI programs to log when a person selects a link to a different site. This method can give you piles of data, so the challenge becomes interpreting the data.

Authoring Tools and Converters

Trying to create a VRML world by hand in a text editor can take quite awhile, and may give you a headache as you try to spatially imagine your world. Many tools are becoming available to ease VRML world development. You can use either of two categories of tools: authoring tools or converters.

Authoring tools are software packages that enable you to create worlds described in VRML. The HTML equivalent is software programs such as Hotmetal and HTML Assistant. Hopefully, VRML authoring tools enable you to develop and test your worlds in 3D. Most VRML authoring tools are still in preliminary versions, although you can expect to see an explosion of these tools in the near future. Some that have been announced include Virtual Home Builder from Paragraph, G-Web from Virtual Presence, Virtual World Factory from Scott Virtual Theme Parks, and EZ3D from Radiance. For the latest authoring tool information, the best bet is to check the VRML repository Web sites.

Converters enable you to create a world using CAD software and then translate a file from the 3D file format into the VRML format. Converters exist, or are being developed, for formats such as DXF, 3DS, OFF, and IV. Also available are commercial converter programs, such as Interchange from Syndesis, that convert between many 3D file formats; they support or are planning to support VRML.

You may encounter a problem with converters, however: They tend to generate huge, inefficient VRML files. In addition, the files may not be true, up-to-spec VRML. Currently, many .wrls that are not real VRML are on the Net. Many of them are in SGI's Inventor File Format, where people have just renamed the .iv file to .wrl and added a VRML file header. To make matters worse, the first versions of WebSpace from SGI and TGS enable you to load these non-VRML files, so you often don't realize that the files are not true VRML.

Optimizing Virtual Reality on the Web

In addition to converters, people have been developing Perl scripts to optimize converted worlds. Typically, running a converter creates a very inefficient, big VRML file. The scripts attempt to trim down the file size to make the world more usable. For example, one technique is to trim the number of decimal places on values. Therefore, you should understand what an optimized script does before using it. If you are creating a medical or architectural world where precision is important, you can get in trouble if the script you use affects the accuracy of the placement of objects.

Creating efficient and effective VRML worlds is quite different than using a standard CAD package, so I think a niche will develop for VRML-specific authoring tools. In addition, you'll see that the CAD packages include an "export" capability that enables people to save or convert their files in VRML format.

As part of working with the Interactive Media Festival, James Waldrop developed a script that reduces file size by about 75 percent. One file was reduced from 2.3MB down to 570KB. Information on the script is located at `http://festival.arc.org/vrmltools/datafat.html`. It's important to understand what this script does before you use it because the special optimizations it performs may or may not be appropriate for your world.

Using this script and gzip compression, James Waldrop, Mark Meadows, and others with the Interactive Media Festival (`http://vrml.arc.org`) managed to compress their files by 94 percent.

File sizes of 1.4MB to 2.3MB shrunk down to 88KB to 126KB. The 2.3MB file represented the first floor of an arts center. The files came from using the 3DS to VRML converter. Some of the techniques they used were

- Turning infinitesimal numbers like 3.9e-09 into 0
- Trimming off long decimal expansions (for example, trimming 3.4567890 to 3.456)
- Getting rid of white space
- Getting rid of unnecessary normal information (for example, VRML Normal nodes)

Figure 44.4 shows what the trimmed files from the Interactive Media Festival look like.

FIGURE 44.4.

The Interactive Media Festival in VRML.

The main compression method used for VRML is *Gnu zip*, also known as *gzip* in UNIX. A gzipped filename looks like home.wrl.gz. Using gzip, you can compress a VRML file down to about 30 percent of its original size. The HTTP server can transmit the gzipped file with appropriate MIME type, and the VRML browser uncompresses the file after it receives it.

Rendering Speed

The techniques discussed in the preceding section are useful for optimizing transmission time for users with low-speed network connections. The other main area for optimization is in rendering speed. These two concerns, transmission and rendering speeds, are sometimes at cross-purposes because improving rendering speed can sometimes result in a larger file.

Three important techniques for optimizing rendering time are the use of cameras, rendering hints, and levels of detail. Another concern is when to use texture maps.

Use of Cameras

In designing your HTML-based Web sites, you've probably found occasion to use anchors within a page, particularly inside a long document. The same kind of capability exists within VRML. Cameras represent viewpoints from which the user can start. If a VRML file doesn't contain a camera, the VRML browser starts you from a default position (0,0,1) and orientation.

If you have cameras in your world, using the PerspectiveCamera or OrthographicCamera nodes, you can start viewing from various preset viewpoints. If you have the following camera in a file called sample.wrl, for example, you can go into the world from that viewpoint by going to the URL `sample.wrl#LongView` (this feature is not implemented in the first versions of many VRML browsers):

```
DEF LongView PerspectiveCamera {
    position 100 500 100
    orientation -1 -5 -1 0
    focalDistance 500
}
```

It gets exciting when you can use these cameras like stepping stones to hop and skip through a world. In a virtual world without cameras, to get from point A to point B you need to go along a path of points in between them. That's fine if you have a maxed-out graphics workstation.

If you're using a computer that can barely render the world, however, moving point by point could take forever. An ergonomic design gives you camera viewpoints with hyperlinks to other camera viewpoints using the WWWAnchor node. This way, you can jump from one camera to the next, so traveling 100 meters takes only a few seconds rather than half an hour.

Rendering Hints

As well as cameras, VRML provides the ShapeHints node to help optimize rendering of polygonal faces. Using the ShapeHints node, VRML enables you to tell the rendering engine in the VRML browser that several polygons are solid or have convex faces. It also tells when to generate smooth edges or creased edges when the polygons intersect.

Levels of Detail

If an object is far in the distance or isn't something you're focused on, your eye doesn't give you much detail. If you're wandering around a virtual world, you want your limited computing power focused on important objects. One of the ways to accomplish this in VRML is to use the LOD node. The LOD node enables you to view different representations of an object from different distances. When you are far away from a building, you might just see a huge block. As you get closer, the floors and windows gradually become visible. Then as you zoom in, you can see and hear pigeons hanging around in ledges of the building.

Texture Maps

Texture maps are like wallpaper—they provide a pattern that is draped on an object, which can simulate rough surfaces like mountains, even though the underlying object might have flat surfaces. Texture maps provide a high degree of realism, but they are computation intensive. For fast movement around your virtual world, you may want to skip texture maps. Here, as in other design considerations, the question is how much value your texture map can add, given the extra computing power it requires. At the same time, texture maps are easy candidates for the preferences section of VRML browsers. Browsers probably have an option that enables you to turn off texture mapping, just as standard WWW browsers let you turn off inline images.

CGI and VRML

If you are a CGI guru, you've probably already thought up all kinds of applications for CGI and VRML. I've postulated that static HTML is dead, and all HTMLs should be generated on the fly by advanced CGI scripts. VRML is the next frontier for CGI fun.

Although bandwidth and rendering considerations remain bottlenecks for complex VRML, CGI can play a part in easing the bottlenecks. For instance, VRML users can fill out an HTML form on which they give information about the speed of their Internet connection and the CPU power of their rendering machine (the rendering machine is the computer that the VRML browser is running on), such as the form in Figure 44.5. Alternatively, you could have an introductory VRML world where people select a link to the relevant version of the complete world.

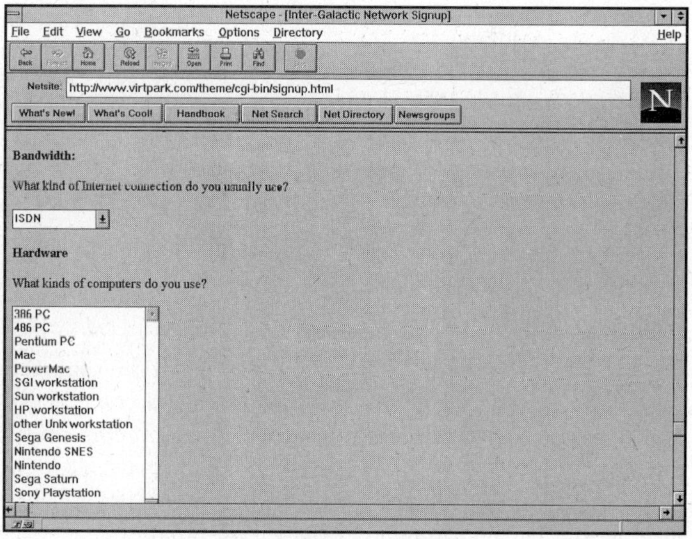

FIGURE 44.5.

A sample HTML form for setting bandwidth and rendering settings.

Using the HTML form, your CGI scripts can tailor subsequent worlds so that they are optimized for that configuration. Unless you have a high-power workstation, you don't want to send those people a pile of texture-mapped worlds. If they are running on a 14.4Kbps modem connection, you might send them a simplified version of your house, with doors that are flat. If they have a T1 connection, you can send them the version of your house that includes all the door handles and detailed ridges on doors. The information on bandwidth and rendering settings can be passed through the QUERY_STRING and PATH_INFO environmental variables (through URL encoding).

If you are working on a world populated by many people, your CGI script might represent those people by a sphere (head) and a cube (body) for bandwidth-impaired users. Users on a high-bandwidth connection could receive all the person-specific features, such as hairstyle and hair coloring. A simple idea of a low-bandwidth multiuser world is shown in Figure 44.6.

FIGURE 44.6.

A version of a prototype multiuser environment from Scott Virtual Theme Parks that is tailored to low-bandwidth users.

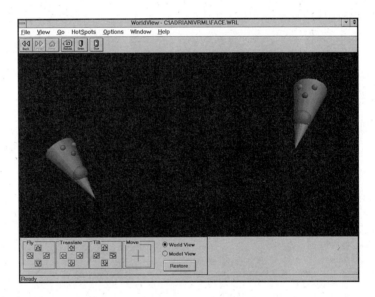

An advanced CGI program can simulate multiuser interactivity or effects such as gravity. However, the users would have to keep getting updates by repeated clicking or client-pull/server-push methods.

A VRML feature that cries out for CGI programs is the map field of the WWWAnchor node. You use the WWWAnchor node to create hyperlinks in VRML, much like the `<a href="">` tag in HTML. You can have a map setting on your WWWAnchor by using `map=POINT`, which inserts the space coordinates after the URL in the format "?x,y,z". Thus, you might have the following node:

```
WWWAnchor {
        name "http://www.virtpark.com/theme/cgi-bin/home.wrl"
        map POINT
```

```
      Cube {}
}
```

Selecting the Cube while you are located at the coordinates (5,14,–100) would then call the URL "http://www.virtpark.com/theme/cgi-bin/home.wrl?5,14,-100".

The 1.1 version of VRML will most likely add new maps, such as TEXTURE and POINTORIENTATION. TEXTURE would give the s,t coordinates of where you are on the texture, like an HTML imagemap. POINTORIENTATION would give the POINT information as in the preceding example, and also include the orientation of the viewer (what direction he or she is facing) when selecting the link.

Other CGI/VRML applications could include VRML searches, ID tagging, a VRML Web index, and randomized links. Users could enter text messages through an HTML form that is then processed into the inside of a balloon over their heads in a multiuser virtual world.

Hacks for Advanced VRML Within 1.0

Three nodes in VRML are best suited to creating neat worlds: WWWInline, LOD, and Switch.

WWWInline loads in a VRML file and renders it. Technically, a WWWInline does not have to be a VRML file—it can be any URL. At this point, what the VRML browser does with non-VRML URLs is undefined. A fun, legal VRML world could have itself inlined inside it ad infinitum—like the following fractal (which may crash your computer because your browser probably cannot handle self-referential VRML):

```
#VRML V1.0 ascii
#  inside.wrl
Separator {
  Sphere { }
  Scale { scaleFactor 0.5 0.6 0.7 }
  Translation { translation 1 1 1 }
  WWWInline { name "inside.wrl" }
}
```

One of the nice things about WWWInlines is that a good VRML browser caches the file in your local disk storage space. So, instead of grabbing this file over the Internet each time, it should just reload the file from memory. A nice hack based on this is to have a several-megabyte VRML file for a background in a multiuser game. Then you can send updates containing the new positions of characters, while using the WWWInline of the large file for the background.

The LOD node is the most fun of all because it switches between different VRML nodes based on the viewer's distance from the LOD node's center. Although this capability is intended to enable you to switch between different levels of detail, you don't need to worry about that. You could use it to hide a secret world far away from the center of your world that appears only when people go close to it.

As another example, consider this LOD node that lets a monster catch a person by "boxing" him or her in with a sphere. This example works only if your VRML browser does not permit collisions:

```
LOD {
    range [ 0.2, 0.5, 0.8 ]
    center 50 50 50
    Separator {
        WWWInline { name "monster_has_caught_you.wrl" }
        Sphere { radius 0.2 }
    }
    WWWInline { name "monster_has_almost_caught_you.wrl" }
    WWWInline { name "monster_grabs_at_you.wrl" }
    WWWInline { name "monster_is_relaxing.wrl" }
}
```

The Switch node defines different nodes that you can switch between. However, the VRML specification does not include a determination of how a VRML browser does this switching. This situation may be taken care of when behaviors arrive in VRML 2.0.

You also can have extensions to VRML. Some virtual world creators have used this capability to add simple animations, using Open Inventor's syntax. However, extensions may not be rendered by all VRML browsers—only by those that are programmed to understand the extensions.

Another hack relates to setting the units or scale of your world. The standard unit for length in VRML is meters. An easy way to change the scale is to surround all your objects with a Scale node. Just do a scaling of 10^(−10), and then you're creating molecules in angstroms.

The Future of VRML—Version 2.0 and Beyond

The four main enhancements expected for version 2.0 of Virtual Reality Modeling Language are interactivity, behaviors, 3D sound, and multiuser capability.

Interactivity

In an interactive virtual world, you can open doors and watch them slowly open. You can move around the furniture in your apartment. Or hit the snooze button on your twitching, ringing alarm clock after you get pulled out of a dream virtual world back into your home virtual world (a virtual world within a virtual world!).

Designing this level of interactivity into VRML will be a challenge. It also will increase file sizes significantly.

Behaviors

Version 1.1 of VRML may include some limited capacity for animations. In version 2.0 and beyond, you should be able to create behaviors so that objects have a minimal life of their own. Besides having some limited movements, such as a windmill turning, you may create objects that affect each other; for example, when Don Quixote tries to joust with the windmill, his horse shies away, or else the windmill shreds the tip of his lance.

Creating behaviors could be chaotically exciting. Have you ever seen hypnotist magicians on television? One day, I saw a hypnotist create a whole set of dependent behaviors in a group of hypnotized people and then set them loose. One person was continually creating imaginary sandcastles on the stage. Each time he got one theoretically finished, another person would walk through it. Another person, seeing this behavior, would shout. A person hearing the shout was programmed to put on a tie (on top of other ties he was previously wearing). All in all, total havoc.

Now imagine this wildness going on in your virtual world, with sound floating around, hyperlinks that appear and disappear, and other people wandering around too. Wow!

To get involved in VRML behaviors, check out the VRML behaviors e-list information at the end of this chapter.

Sound

3D sound gets very interesting and brings in a whole range of new possibilities. Sound has been a key feature in creating good immersive environments. In fact, people experimenting in virtual reality have found that small improvements in sound improve the immersive experience, as perceived by the user, more than small improvements in graphics quality.

You can experiment with all kinds of exciting methods for deploying sound as it applies to VRML worlds. For example, you might create soundproof rooms for privacy. You also might create virtual bugging, in which you can listen to conversations in soundproof rooms. Sound transmitted at lower frequencies can be used to simulate vibrations (like earthquakes). Or imagine various sound encoding and transmittal schemes used in real life. You could end up with virtual cellular phones and radio stations. And the frequency range that you perceive might not be the standard human range. For example, you might be in a game in which you are a dog. In that case, you perceive sound frequencies only within a dog's hearing range. And who knows, maybe sound transmitted by human characters would be unintelligible—unless they knew how to speak dog language.

Multiuser Capability

Imagine playing football with a group of people in a virtual world in cyberspace. Or imagine designing a new product with them. For these applications, you need to have a multiuser capability in your virtual world. In the future, hopefully, VRML will allow support for multiuser worlds. It is currently possible to create some basic multiuser worlds using intensive CGI programming.

In the future, we may see a range of server software emerge for adding multiuser functionality to virtual worlds. Some of the issues that must first be tackled include logging who is currently in the world; this capability includes killing off *vampires*, which means being able to detect when people have stopped being involved even if they have not explicitly sent a message to the server saying that they are signing off. Also, in some worlds you may want collision detection, to prevent two avatars (cyberspace representations) from existing in the same space. In addition, you need a way to hand off avatars to other servers if someone chooses a hyperlink to another world. Other considerations include how a person's avatar is created, how it is logged and transmitted, and what rules it may need to follow in various worlds.

In addition, copyright issues may become important. If you're Batman, for others to see you as Batman, they need to download a file or data that is a representation of Batman. They could thus potentially save that file, use it in their own worlds, or modify it as well. These are *bastard worlds*, the illegitimate children of other worlds. You might create a corporate VRML site for an automobile manufacturer, for example, when somebody comes along, spraypaints virtual graffiti on the showroom cars, kicks the tires in, and posts the new version on his or her own Web site.

Other VRML 2.0 Issues

Other issues that will be important to the development of VRML in the future are forms and browser modes. After reading the HTML and CGI sections of this book, you may be a die-hard forms fan. Currently, no facility is available in VRML for inputting information besides the map=POINT field of the WWWAnchor node, which transmits the current position. Thus, VRML world designers have to provide links to HTML forms. VRML might develop a forms-like facility or else include the capability to have inline HTML forms in worlds. The latter approach is better by not reinventing forms; however, the whole inclusion of the expanding HTML specification within VRML would require complicated coding, and the 2D HTML would stick out like a worn-out photo in the 3D world. For instance, just think of a SELECT field in an HTML form. Wouldn't it be appropriate in virtual reality for the options to stick out in 3D?

If you're creating a special kind of world, you might want the VRML browser to enter a special mode. For instance you may require some kind of gravity, where people stick to the ground. Also, you might want hyperlinks or interactive items selected in a certain way. You might want a link selector to be a machine gun as in the game DOOM. Or you might want a lasso that you spin around an anchored object and use to pull yourself in.

Business Models for Virtual Reality on the Web

The big question among business people is "How can we make money on the Net?" VRML opens up new business models and possibilities on the Net. They include shopping worlds, virtual theme parks, marketing efforts, and group communication.

At its crudest, virtual reality on the Web can include shopping worlds, three-dimensional stores. Initial attempts will probably focus on the earth-bound metaphors of the shopping mall, as initial HTML Web pages have done. Advanced attempts will dismiss old metaphors and will also take advantage of interactivity to generate excitement about buying a product. Imagine *The Price is Right* TV show in virtual reality. Or imagine an exciting, glamorous auction, where it turns out that all the other bidders are computer-generated automatons.

Virtual theme parks encompass all forms of entertainment models. Users might play in a huge, multiplayer game, represented by avatars (3D bodies in VR). Or small groups might buy $30 tickets for an hour-long group adventure on a special server that gives them an overwhelmingly emotional, high-bandwidth experience. Users might subscribe on a monthly basis to basic games or worlds they can enter and in which they can interact.

As in HTML, probably the first area of business in VRML will focus on marketing. VRML provides marketers with new kinds of capabilities to appeal to emotions and abstraction. In HTML's text-intensive environment, the standard approach has been to give a great deal of detail and information. In the world of VRML, marketers and advertisers will instead attempt to create powerful virtual worlds that affect users' feelings and the thoughts they attach to products.

Group communication can develop into an important area for business as VRML develops into the 3D equivalent of e-mail. With VRML, businesses can have long-distance meetings that have the benefits of videoconferencing (representing people by avatars), yet in a lower-bandwidth environment. To develop this capability, avatar software will have to have some basic capabilities to represent personality, such as through facial expressions.

Another related possibility is *MBVWA*, or *Management by Virtually Wandering Around*. Management journals emphasize the benefits of managers wandering around to see what's going on in their factory or organization. Doing so can be difficult if the facility you want to visit is in another country. An advanced VRML application could let a manager "virtually wander around" an office in another country. The manager might even be able to see inventory stock and items moving around the factory, through a VRML representation of the factory or a video camera interface.

You also could apply this concept to network administration. Network administrators are challenged with looking after huge numbers of computers at one time. Network administration software is starting to use two-dimensional graphics to help network administrators keep a handle on all the information associated with their computers. Imagine a VRML approach to this situation, where the user is in the middle of a virtual world populated by computers. When the computers have problems or break down, they start moving toward the user at the center of the world at a speed related to the severity of the computer problem and importance of the particular computer. If the user (network administrator) isn't fixing the computers quickly enough, the computers surround the user. The user can't move until he or she fixes the computers. However, the user could call for help and have a second person come in to help fix the computers. The computers would move toward the user most likely to be able to fix their problems (or in some cases, they might run away from both!). The color and shape of the representation of the computers also could be based on other relevant data, such as how long the computer has been down. The same model could be applied to managing telecommunications networks, air traffic control, or strategic defense systems.

Virtual reality has been successfully applied to stock market and portfolio management in the past. With VRML, WWWInline nodes can link in data from many sources. You also can use LOD nodes so that the closer you move to the representation of a certain financial instrument or derivative, you get more and more information, plus additional hyperlinks to other sources of information and intelligence.

Another market that may open up through VRML is the video game market. The new game platforms, such as the Sega Saturn, Sony Playstation, and Nintendo Ultra64, are essentially small systems optimized for rendering 3D worlds. Browsers can be developed for these systems (something Scott Virtual Theme Parks is looking at), modems can be attached to the game systems, and then the users can go wandering around the Internet through VRML.

In most of this chapter, I've made the assumption that all the VRML worlds will be transmitted over the Internet. However, that's not necessarily the case. Diskettes and CD-ROMs containing VRML files can be created with a few purposes in mind. They could be a database of commonly used objects, such as streetlamps, chairs, and tables, that could be accessed by other worlds as inline worlds. Or they could just be static, highly detailed worlds for a person to wander around in. What is really exciting is to distribute background worlds that can be used as inline objects in CGI-dependent interactive adventures. The nice thing about the CD-ROM and disk distribution model is that consumers are used to paying for these media.

Scott Virtual Theme Parks is creating a variety of content that includes several of these concepts. Participants either pay or qualify by questionnaire for membership in the Inter-Galactic Network, which allows access to software like Virtual World Factory and basic access to virtual theme parks like Monkitaka and Macrosück. Revenue will be generated through subscription fees and targeted advertising. Additional fees (tickets) will permit access to higher-level experiences similar in emotional level to amusement park rides. CD-ROMs will be sold for PC and videogame system platforms to lessen limitations of bandwidth.

Business is going to fall in love with virtual reality on the Web. This new technology will also raise the playing field, with increased costs required to develop excellent Web sites.

Go Forth and Create Virtual Worlds

The explosion of interest in the World Wide Web has been incredible. VRML promises to ramp this exponential growth up to a new level of interactivity and feeling.

At the same time, highly detailed VRML worlds will be limited to users of advanced computers and high bandwidth connections in the short term. In the short term, the Web will also be littered with poorly constructed, inefficiently designed VRML worlds.

As VRML moves into its 2.0 version, virtual reality on the Net will become as commonplace as HTML is today. Interactivity, animations, and behaviors will enliven virtual worlds with personality and attitude.

Businesses will take advantage of virtual reality on the Web, starting with marketing efforts and graduating to original content.

VRML Resources

In the ever-changing world of VRML, the Internet is probably the best place to find the latest information. Yet finding the starting points for this information is often a challenge. Here are some pointers to VRML resources to help get you started.

General VRML Information

General information on the Web includes the basic information on VRML, questions people usually ask about VRML, and what products and tools are available.

VRML Repositories on the Web

The three main repositories for VRML information are the following:

> `http://www.sdsc.edu/vrml/` includes information on various VRML tools, software, and example applications. This repository is the most up to date.

> `http://vrml.wired.com/` includes an archive of the VRML e-list.

> `http://www.eit.com/vrml/` features the public domain VRML artwork files.

In addition, to find VRML worlds relating to various subjects, use Serch, which is a database of VRML links, sort of like a VRML version of Yahoo, the HTML Index. Serch can be accessed in VRML, `http://www.virtpark.com/theme/cgi-bin/serch.wrl`, or in HTML, `http://www.virtpark.com/theme/cgi-bin/serch.html`. VRML creators will want to add their worlds to Serch.

FAQ (Frequently Asked Questions) Web Pages

The main VRML FAQ is maintained by Jan Hardenbergh and is located at `http://www.oki.com/vrml/VRML_FAQ.html`. The FAQ includes information on configuring your HTTP server to transmit the MIME types for VRML and compressed VRML.

Yukio Andoh has translated the FAQ into Japanese, at `http://www.anchor-net.co.jp/rental/andoh/vrml/vrmlfaq.html`.

VRML Specification

The Version 1.0 specification for Virtual Reality Modeling Language is at `http://www.hyperreal.com/~mpesce/vrml/vrml.tech/vrml10-3.html`.

A VRML-enabled version of the spec is at `http://www.virtpark.com/theme/vrml/`.

VRML Browsers

Intervista's WorldView VRML browser runs on various Microsoft Windows operating systems and will soon be out for other platforms such as the Macintosh (`http://www.hyperreal.com/intervista`).

Template Graphics Software produces the WebSpace VRML browser for platforms other than SGI (`http://www.tgs.com/~template`).

Silicon Graphics WebSpace is a VRML browser for SGI machines only (for non-SGI machines, see TGS above); it's located at `http://www.sgi.com/Products/WebFORCE/WebSpace/`.

Paper Software, Inc., has produced WebFX, a VRML browser that works within standard WWW browsers (`http://www.paperinc.com`).

SDSC (the San Diego Supercomputer Center) is developing a VRML browser for SGI/UNIX machines, with source code available free for non-commercial use (`http://www.sdsc.edu/EnablingTech/Visualization/vrml/webview.html`).

Other browsers in development are NetPower (`http://www.netpower.com/`), VRweb from IICM, NCSA, and the University of Minnesota (`http://vrml.wired.com/arch/1739.html`), Geomview (`http://www.geom.umn.edu/software/geomview/`), and WIRL from Vream (`http://www.vream.com/vream/index.html`).

Newsgroups

The e-list had a huge discussion about what a VRML newsgroup should be named. When all the votes came in, `comp.vr.vrml` was the most popular. However, it may take some time to get this newsgroup set up, as it requires the creation of the vr subhierarchy in the `comp.` realm. An `alt.vrml` newsgroup may also pop up.

E-Lists

The main e-list for discussion of VRML is the unmoderated www-vrml list. Expect a minimum of 30 messages a day on this list; it's not for the faint-hearted. For information, e-mail `majordomo@wired.com` with the message info `www-vrml`. A digest version also exists; it concatenates the daily messages into one message. E-mail `majordomo@wired.com` with the message info `www-vrml-digest` for more information. Because of the volume of postings to the www-vrml list, you should read the list for a day or two before posting so that you can get a feel for what's discussed. And if you have questions like "When will such-and-such browser be available?" try the FAQ or VRML repositories mentioned in this section first. If you have problems with a VRML browser, e-mail the relevant company.

Two other VRML e-lists exist. They are the vrml-modeling and vrml-behaviors lists. The vrml-behaviors list is starting to get busy as people propose ideas for behaviors in VRML 2.0. For information, e-mail listserv@sdsc.edu with the message info vrml-modeling or info vrml-behaviors.

An e-list about business applications and models for virtual worlds is vworlds-biz. E-mail listserv@best.com with the message info vworlds-biz.

Software

The QvLib parser is a program that parses VRML files. An SGI version is at ftp://ftp.sgi.com/sgi/inventor/2.0/qv1.0.tar.Z and a Windows NT version is at http://www.omnicode.com/~omar/. Old versions corresponding to Pre-1.0 VRML specification drafts are available for LINUX, IRIX, Sun, NT, and Mac at ftp://ftp.vrml.org/pub/parser/.

Mark Pesce has created the VRMLint tool for WinNT 3.5, by repackaging the readtest tool from qvlib; it's available at http://sky1.net.org/~mpesce/vrml/readtest.exe.

Authoring Tools

Virtual World Factory from Scott Virtual Theme Parks is a Web-based, platform-independent authoring tool at http://www.virtpark.com/theme/factinfo.html. The 2.0 version uses HTML forms. The 3.0 version will just use VRML. The freeware version, Wanna-Be Virtual World Factory, is located at http://www.virtpark.com/theme/vwfactez.html.

Home Space Builder (from Paragraph) is a VRML-compatible authoring tool for PCs; it's located at http://www.us.paragraph.com/whatsnew/homespce.htm.

PORTAL (from Inner Action Corporation) is a tool for building VRML worlds, running on Microsoft Windows operating systems. You can find it at http://www.well.com/user/jack/.

WRLGRID from the SDSC generates tile or grid geometries in VRML format. It's available at http://www.sdsc.edu/EnablingTech/Visualization/vrml/.

Radiance software is developing Ez3d-VR, a VRML authoring tool. You can find it at http://www.radiance.com/~radiance.

Converters

DXF2IV converts DXF files to Open Inventor format (what VRML is based on). It's available at ftp://ftp.sgi.com.

Interchange for Windows from Syndesis Corporation (`syndesis@beta.inc.net`) translates more than 30 3D file formats, and the new version supports VRML.

OBJ2WRL and TRI2WRL convert Wavefront obj (object) files and Alias tri (triangle) files to VRML, from the SDSC. You can find them at `http://www.sdsc.edu/EnablingTech/Visualization/vrml/`.

Object File Format (OFF) to VRML is located at `http://coney.gsfc.nasa.gov/Mathews/Objects`. OFF is an ASCII format for indexed 3D polygons. The specification and sample objects are available at `ftp://avalone.chinalake.navy.mil/`.

Keith Rule has added VRML output support to his freeware converter, wcvt2pov. It's located at `http://www.europa.com/~keithr ftp://ftp.povray.com/pub/povray/utilities/wc2pov26.zip`.

Interesting VRML Web Sites

`http://vrml.arc.org/` is the home of the Interactive Media Festival.

`http://www.vrml.org/vrml/` contains simple VRML models.

`http://www.lightside.com/3dsite/cgi/VRML-index.html` contains several VRML-related links.

`http://www.virtpark.com/theme/home.wrl` is the home world of Scott Virtual Theme Parks.

The CAVE is at `http://www.ncsa.uiuc.edu/EVL/docs/html/CAVE.overview.html` and `http://jaka.eecs.uic.edu/dave/vrml/CAVE/`.

You can build your own cell membrane at `http://bellatrix.pcl.ox.ac.uk`.

You can find Step-by-Step Origami at `http://www.neuro.sfc.keio.ac.jp/~aly/polygon/vrml/ika`.

An interactive application that enables you to move around objects through the use of HTML forms and CGI is available at `http://andante.iss.uw.edu.pl/viso/vrml/colab/walk.html`.

Fractal lovers can check out a page on VRML fractals at `http://kirk.usafa.af.mil/~baird/vrml`.

Related Resources of Interest

Java is an effort by Sun to create a secure language for transmitting applications along the Web (`http://java.sun.com/`).

GopherVR is a virtual reality representation of gopherspace for UNIX workstations and XWindows primarily. You can find it at `gopher://boombox.micro.umn.edu/11/gopher/Unix/GopherVR` and `ftp://boombox.micro.umn.edu/pub/gopher/Unix/GopherVR`.

Dive is a multiuser virtual reality system that includes many VRML 2.0-level features, such as behaviors and interaction. It is available for the Solaris, Sunos, and Irix operating systems. The creators expect to add a VRML interface in the future. You can find it at `ftp://ftp.sics.se/pub/dive/dive-3.0-beta.tar.Z`.

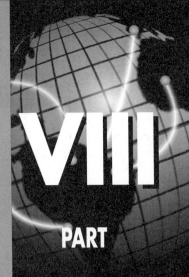

PART

VIII

Whither the Web: Trends and Issues

Challenges for Web Information Providers

45

by
John December

Developers are producing reams of information on the Web, and users are accessing it at a breakneck rate. Web traffic on the National Science Foundation (NSFNET) backbone (just one conduit for exchanging Internet packets) increased from a monthly transfer total of 78 megabytes in December 1992 to 1,056,081 megabytes (over 1 *terabyte*) in July 1994. It would be cliché to call this an "information explosion." However, this rapid growth in Web utilization raises questions: What is the meaning of all this "information" being transmitted so feverishly? How do we make sense of it and improve information quality? Although there certainly has been a dramatic increase in activity, traffic, servers, and data—raw "stuff"—on the Web, a correspondingly dramatic increase in the kinds of information that facilitates knowledge and wisdom has yet to be seen.

Without effective tools and methodologies for gathering, evaluating, managing, and presenting information, the Web's potential as a source of knowledge could be lost. In an increasingly thin soup of redundant, inferior, or incorrect information, even the smartest Web spiders won't be very effective. A flood of information unfiltered by the processes of peer review and collaborative input can overwhelm users—and can obscure the value of the Web itself. The Web certainly needs new technical means of information discovery and retrieval—indeed, the use of intelligent spiders, worms, robots, and ants is crucial to making sense of the Web. The Web will also need new protocols, tools, browsers, hypermedia interfaces, and software. But along with these tools for information discovery and delivery, we must develop information-shaping capabilities—skills to select and present information on the Web. These information-shaping capabilities cannot be based on machine intelligence alone. Human wisdom, judgment, and aesthetics must play a part in improving the quality of Web information.

In this chapter, I first explore the growth in Web activity in terms of the increased amount of traffic, information, and Web servers. I then survey the growing diversity of Web communication, a pattern of growth that dramatizes the need for better information quality. Next, I describe some lessons I've learned through my experiences in gathering, managing, and presenting Internet information. Finally, I discuss information quality as it relates to Web developers and users.

Web Growth

An extensive user community has developed on the Web since its public introduction in 1991. In the early 1990s, the developers at CERN spread word of the Web's capabilities to scientific audiences worldwide. By September 1993, the share of Web traffic traversing the NSFNET (National Science Foundation Network) Internet backbone reached 1 percent. On December 8, 1993, John Markoff reported on Mosaic on the front page of the business section of *The New York Times*. Around the same time, Mecklermedia's Internet World '93 conference and exposition in New York City featured colorful views of the Web through NCSA's Mosaic, the first version of which had been released just a few months earlier. By January 1994, the Web comprised 2.6 percent of NSFNET backbone traffic. The concept of Web growth, however, includes more than just the increase in traffic. Web growth can also be seen in terms of the number of servers and the increasingly various kinds of information offered.

Growth in the Number of Web Servers

Matthew Gray, writing in his Web page "Growth of the World Wide Web" (URL `http://www.netgen.com/info/growth.html`), reports a dramatic increase in the number of servers. Using his "World Wide Web Wanderer" (W4) program, Gray found the results shown in Table 45.1.

Table 45.1. Increase in Web servers.

Date	Number of identified Web servers
Jun 1993	130
Sep 1993	204
Oct 1993	228
Nov 1993	272
Dec 1993	623
Mar 1994	1,265
Jun 1994	3,184
Dec 1994	11,576
Mar 1995	15,768

Gray notes that this W4 survey does have limitations, and these figures are only representative of what W4 could find. However, these figures give a good snapshot of the rapid growth in the number of Web servers—one part of the "information explosion" on the Web. Each server represents the work of one or more administrators (webmasters) as well as people who provide information in large or small local webs on each server. Each of these servers, then, is potentially a large source of even more information, analogous to television stations that are ready to broadcast to the masses. Thus, the June 1994 figure is like a world with more than 3,000 channels. Moreover, by August 1994, the SG-Scout (`http://www-swiss.ai.mit.edu:80/~ptbb/SG-Scout/SG-Scout.html`) robot had located over 7,000 Web servers.

Growth in Web Traffic

Along with an increasing number of Web servers, there have been dramatic increases in Web traffic. According to NSFNET backbone statistics (URL `ftp://nic.merit.edu/nsfnet/statistics`), during the first several months of 1994, the Web's share of NSFNET backbone traffic increased from 2.6 percent in January to 6.1 percent in June; in March it surpassed Gopher in terms of bytes transferred. (Note, however, that this is a limited measurement of traffic, exclusively measuring traffic over the NSFNET backbone. Other estimates still place the Web behind

Gopher in terms of traffic; see `http://www.cc.gatech.edu/gvu/stats/NSF/merit.html`.) This is significant because Gopher, just a year earlier, was ahead of the Web. In January 1993, Gopher's share of the backbone was 0.8 percent (the Web's was 0.002 percent), and by June 1993, Gopher was at 1.61 percent (with the Web at 0.515 percent). The Web thus has overtaken Gopher—an information system that had reached wide popularity and had a large base of deployed information before the Web became so popular. This "byte ratings" race on the NSFNET backbone, shown in Table 45.2, dramatizes the pull the Web has for information and traffic.

Table 45.2. WWW traffic over NSFNET backbone (in megabytes/month).

Month/Year	WWW Traffic	Gopher Traffic
Dec 92	78	34,247
Jan 93	122	43,238
Feb 93	512	60,897
Mar 93	3,613	79,024
Apr 93	8,116	89,074
May 93	17,298	103,870
Jun 93	35,701	111,881
Jul 93	48,728	139,006
Aug 93	50,779	148,795
Sep 93	75,401	198,096
Oct 93	122,174	250,785
Nov 93	172,340	291,133
Dec 93	225,443	309,691
Jan 94	269,129	374,681
Feb 94	347,503	396,066
Mar 94	518,084	480,690
Apr 94	671,950	517,625
May 94	799,163	555,708
Jun 94	946,539	567,479
Jul 94	1,056,081	555,089

The preceding statistics illustrate a dramatic increase in Web traffic. The *daily average* number of Web bytes exchanged in July 1994 (34,067 megabytes) exceeds the *monthly* total for May 1993. Also notice that there was a slight *decrease* in the number of Gopher bytes transferred from June to July 1994.

Growth in Web Information Variety

While there's no quantifiable way to characterize the variety and extent of Web information available, it is possible to gain a qualitative sense by examining the "What's New With NCSA Mosaic and the WWW" page at URL `http://www.ncsa.uiuc.edu/SDG/Software/Mosaic/Docs/whats-new.html`.

The NCSA "What's New" page is a good indicator of the growth of the variety, quantity, and extent of information provided through the Web, particularly that which resulted from the development of Mosaic. The "What's New" page's archives go back to June 1993. The June 1993 page had 26 entries (11,426 bytes). A typical entry from that month is the following:

```
June 25, 1993

A Web server has been installed at the Centre Universitaire
d'Informatique of the University of Geneva. Information
about various research groups at the CUI is available, as
well as a number of other experimental services.
```

Six months later, the December 1993 page had 124 entries (40,750 bytes), including not only such institutional offerings as the following

```
December 10, 1993

A new Web server is online at the Nippon Telegraph and
Telephone Corporation, in Tokyo, Japan, serving
Japanese information. This server contains documents in
Japanese, as well as notes on Japanese encoding
methods and WWW browsers that can display Japanese.
```

but also more informal information, such as this:

```
December 10, 1993

The first ice hockey team on the Web!
```

```
December 26, 1993

A J.R.R. Tolkien information page is now online at
University of Waterloo.
```

By June 1994, the "What's New" page included 297 entries (146,684 bytes), and it included more specialized webs such as the following:

```
June 29, 1994

The protein H-Bond analysis software, HBPLUS, now has a WWW page.
```

```
June 27, 1994

For lovers of plastic arts a page on stone sculpture from
Zimbabwe has been placed on the Web. See these pages on
Shona Sculpture! There also is a list of exhibitions on the
subject. These pages are regularly expanded as new
information becomes available.
```

These entries illustrate the trend during the spring and summer of 1994 toward increasingly specialized webs. In many cases, these webs exist on institutional and organizational web servers that had been previously announced or were recently developed.

Also, during the early part of 1994, subject trees continued to flourish. Established subject-oriented webs such as CERN's Virtual Library (URL `http://info.cern.ch/hypertext/DataSources/bySubject/Overview.html`) continued to grow, while newcomers like Yahoo (URL `http://www.yahoo.com`) grew at an astounding rate. According to Yahoo developer Jerry Chih-Yuan Yang, Yahoo started in March 1994 with about 100 links. It then grew as shown in Table 45.3.

Table 45.3. Yahoo database growth.

1994 date	Number of URL Links
Mar (start)	100
May 9	1666
Jun 1	2823
Jun 15	3607
Jul 11	5479
Jul 23	6121
Aug 5	7337
Aug 11	8265
Aug 17	8566

Now, there are 34,978 links.

Therefore, along with an explosion in the number of Web servers and traffic, there has been an expansion in content—both in terms of amount and diversity—with many institutional "official" webs as well as informal, entertainment, and individual webs growing in the numbers of the links they contain. Older subject trees such as CERN's Virtual Library operate according to a more conservative model involving distributed moderators (people who oversee development of an individual topic page within the virtual library) and have grown steadily during this same period. However, some informal, single-site trees (exemplified by Yahoo) have grown very rapidly.

Challenges from Growth for Information Providers

With all this growth—in Web servers, traffic, and information—what are the major issues facing providers of Web information? Because an information provider's first concern should be the information user's needs, information discovery and retrieval tops the list of concerns. Web spiders (as discussed in Chapter 19, "Spiders and Indexes: Keyword-Oriented Searching"), particularly newer spiders such as Lycos (URL `http://lycos.cs.cmu.edu`) and systems such as Harvest Brokers (URL `http://www.town.hall.org/brokers/www-home-pages/query.html`), help solve parts of the information discovery and retrieval problem. Subject-oriented webs (see Chapter 18, "Trees: Subject-Oriented Searching") also assist users who want to browse information according to subject.

But other issues related to the user's needs arise *after* the user discovers and retrieves information—issues of content and presentation. With the rapid growth of the Web, the user can no longer easily browse alternate or multiple sources for the same or related information; the Web information space has become "saturated"—that is, there is so much information that a human being can't adequately compare the value of available information sources on a particular subject or topic. Along with saturation, the rapid growth in the Web's information space has led to a kind of information "pollution": redundant, erroneous, or poorly maintained information that can obscure other information.

This is not to say that Web growth has created no valuable information nor imply that there can ever be a universal standard for information quality. Parts III and IV of this book highlight many webs that are genuinely valuable. Information saturation and pollution, much like the noise in Usenet, are an offshoot of growth that is diverse, distributed, creative, and chaotic development. The goal of information developers is not to eliminate this "noise" on a global scope or to crush creative expression; this would lead to unacceptable levels of control, censorship, a loss of diversity, and the undue dominance of certain kinds of information over others. Information-space saturation can lead to competition among information providers, and this competition can drive web weavers to improve information quality in order to attract users.

So while saturation and pollution are issues that information providers should consider, the goal is not to seek out or eliminate offending webs or to excoriate particular web weavers. The diversity of information and views on the Web does not inherently qualify as pollution or saturation. Rather, pollution and saturation occur when individual information providers don't meet their users' needs or interests. The challenge is for information providers to best define—according to the needs of their users—the content and presentation methods that define quality information. This may include eliminating web structures and information that other webs already offer (thus reducing redundancy) or correcting erroneous or poorly presented information. In Part V, "Weaving a Web," I propose a methodology web weavers might use to achieve this process of meeting user needs and continuously improving a web.

Although information spaces such as traditional media (TV, radio, newspapers) exhibit the characteristics of saturation and pollution, these are not as troublesome because of editorial and institutional control. For example, there's a great deal of news during a single day, and I don't have time to sort it all out and decide what is important (saturation) or correct (pollution). Therefore, I choose various media—such as a network's evening-news broadcast or a weekly news magazine—to select and filter that information for me. So while I won't monitor wire reports or C-SPAN during the day, I can depend on Dan Rather or Bernard Shaw to provide a daily selection of what happened that is important. I choose information sources based on my previously developed trust of their work.

On the Web, however, there's no Dan Rather. Web information providers must become aware of the nature of their medium. For instance:

■ **Surface cues are gone on the Web.** All Web information is presented equivalently through a browser. Cues that might indicate quality or value (production values in a television broadcast, paper and print quality in a magazine) are gone. Individual Web browsers transform HTML files using a specified mechanism—so the surface cues about quality don't come from the interface. Instead, as covered in Part V and as discussed later in this chapter, the design of webs and arrangement of information in the HTML file are the main contributors to perceptions of quality differences. It is as if everyone had the same television production team, but they could only change the content and arrangement of the information to differentiate their show from others.

■ **Web information providers don't face scarcities in presentation media.** While scarcities of resources and time in print and broadcast media lead to traditions of editorial selection and control, Web publishers don't often face similar time or resource constraints for dissemination (unless, of course, due to disk size or other constraints). The 22 minutes Dan Rather fills each night forces a selectivity (and a corresponding simplification) of content. On the Web, without constraints, information providers are not necessarily compelled to be selective about providing information. Like cheap, suburban land, Webspace can thus fill with banalities.

■ **Web information encounters different patterns of peer review.** Voices of experience are not always heard on the Web. Unlike the peer review processes formal scholarly work often undergoes, the traditions for Web information review are not mature. Often, Web information can encounter a maelstrom of comment and critique similar to what a Usenet FAQ list faces. In other cases, collaborators or experts in a field or topic assist in reviewing and correcting Web information. In still other cases, "peer review" has little meaning: personal information (home pages), artistic expressions, and other information on informal webs (opinion, descriptions, product information, and so forth) doesn't necessarily require close critique aside from accuracy checks to be valuable. Moreover, measures of value and "correctness" gained from traditional media can't be applied to a medium that is highly dynamic and, by its nature, is *always* incomplete.

The challenge for information providers is to be aware of these issues arising from Web growth and the dynamic nature of Web information. Providers should consider how their information can do the following:

■ Meet user needs

■ Cue the user about the level of quality and completeness

■ Filter out noise and redundancy as the result of review or critique where appropriate

As a rule of thumb, an institutional imprimatur is useful for ensuring quality. (This is similar to the concept of the "trusted information source" described earlier for encountering news.) For instance, I might seek out the Web page of a university or government research center for information related to a particular topic. This information is made more valuable because specialists and experts maintain it.

Other challenges for information providers go beyond these considerations of information-space saturation and pollution. These challenges involve the details of implementing specific information structures and of developing *processes* for gathering, selecting, and presenting online information. To illustrate these issues, in the next section I discuss some lessons I've learned from my experiences in providing information.

A Case Study: Tracking Internet Information Sources

Through my work providing information about the Internet and other forms of computer-mediated communication (CMC), I've gained insights into many issues facing information providers. My experience includes developing a list of "information about information." In this list (URL `http://www.rpi.edu/Internet/Guides/decemj/icmc/top.html`), I have attempted to organize and present information sources describing the Internet and computer-mediated communication technologies, applications, information culture, discussion forums, and bibliographies. In this section, I describe my experience and discuss some lessons I've learned.

Background

In May 1992, I began an independent study project (as part of doctoral work at Rensselaer Polytechnic Institute) investigating the Internet and how it can be used for communication. As part of this project, I located information sources about the Internet itself. I listed these resources and posted the result to `alt.bbs.internet` (the only Usenet newsgroup at that time with the word "internet" in its address). I received some comments and feedback, and I added items to the list as a result of suggestions and further searches of the network. I tried to organize the list so that it would be easy to read, listing Internet descriptions, information services, electronic publications, societies and organizations, newsgroups, and bibliographies. After further revision, I placed the list on my university's FTP site and posted an announcement of its availability and updates to `alt.internet.services` (a newsgroup formed after `alt.bbs.internet` people grew tired of having non-Internet BBS-related items posted to their group). Over the next year, I continued to gather information from mailing lists and my own use of Archie, FTP, Gopher/Veronica, WAIS, and the Web.

The reason for my approach in developing a list of information about information was that I found many useful documents describing the Net that were available over the Net. Rather than duplicating these efforts, my goal was to develop a list summarizing where I could obtain further information sources. I could then use my list to obtain information to help people become familiar with the Internet, or as a tool to define areas to examine in the field of CMC. The process I used to develop this information has evolved over the years and has taught me a great deal about the elements of site development, including information discovery and selection, presentation formats, usability and design, information quality, and the context in which I should present my list to others.

Gathering Information Discovery and Selection

I've noticed a similar pattern for information space development throughout my work with Internet information. File transfer protocol, Telnet, Gopher, and the Web all created new information spaces, yet the ways these spaces became populated with information were similar:

1. Developers introduced an information presentation protocol or system.

2. Users contributed information to the resulting information space, leading to the following problems:

    a. Information space saturation: A plethora of information servers and an abundance of content. This abundance grows to such a degree that the space can't be encountered without information layering or filtering through handcrafted indexes or other guides to the spaces.

    b. Information space pollution: Redundant, erroneous, or poorly maintained information becomes replicated throughout the space, obscuring other information.

3. Developers created tools to automatically traverse the space and glean information about resources. The result of this automated gleaning is a database that can be queried through a keyword or other indexing scheme.

4. With increased visibility of the available resources, redundancy decreased and specialization increased. Specialized information servers, often under the guidance of experts in the subject area of the information, created new levels and standards for quality. Often, lists or indexes of information servers also contributed greatly to this process. (For example, the well-known Gopher called Jewels now showcases specialized gophers, discouraging duplication and encouraging specialization.)

The preceding pattern occurred with FTP (with Archie as the automated indexer), Gopher (Veronica), and the Web (Spiders).

By observing and making use of this information-space life cycle, I have tried to locate the updated and authoritative source for all the information I present. For example, during the summer and fall of 1992, I made use of Archie to locate directories describing the Internet. In release 1.0 of my list (23 May 92), I had three entries for descriptions of the Internet, as follows:

```
o INTERNET DESCRIPTIONS ANONYMOUS FTP HOST  FILE OR DIRECTORY/
~~~~~~~~~~~~~~~~~~~~~~ ~~~~~~~~~~~~~~~~~~~~ ~~~~~~~~~~~~~~~~~~~~~~~~~~
Zen & Art of Internet  ftp.cs.widener.edu  pub/zen/
```

```
NWNet Internet Guide      ftphost.nwnet.net    nic/nwnet/user-guide/
Hitchhikers Guide         ftp.nisc.sri.com     rfc/rfc1118.txt
```

I later was able to add more (from release 1.50, 01 Aug 92):

```
o INTERNET DESCRIPTIONS  ANONYMOUS FTP HOST   FILE OR DIRECTORY/
~~~~~~~~~~~~~~~~~~~~~~~~  ~~~~~~~~~~~~~~~~~~~~  ~~~~~~~~~~~~~~~~~~~~~~~~~
New User's Questions     ftp.nisc.sri.com     fyi/fyi4.txt
Hitchhikers Guide        ftp.nisc.sri.com     rfc/rfc1118.txt
Gold in Networks!        ftp.nisc.sri.com     rfc/rfc1290.txt
Zen & Art of Internet    ftp.cs.widener.edu   pub/zen/
Zen ASCII version        csn.org              pub/net/zen/
Guide Internet/Bitnet    hydra.uwo.ca         libsoft/guide1.txt
NSF Resource Guide       nnsc.nsf.net         resource-guide/
NWNet Internet Guide     ftphost.nwnet.net    nic/nwnet/user-guide/
SURANet Internet Guide   ftp.sura.net         pub/nic/infoguide.*.txt
NYSERNet Internet Guide  nysernet.org         pub/guides/Guide.*.text
CERFNet Guide            nic.cerf.net         cerfnet/cerfnet_guide/
DDN New User Guide       nic.ddn.mil          netinfo/nug.doc
AARNet Guide             aarnet.edu.au        pub/resource-guide/
```

Using Archie, coupled with a growing awareness of the duplication of resources in FTP space, I searched for the "definitive" editions and versions of each document. I eventually identified major FTP repositories for Internet information that offered well-maintained collections. As these sites changed and evolved, I added additional pointers to my list. Gradually, I began to see more redundancy at FTP sites—many administrators would copy an entire set of documents to their site. As these documents evolved into later additions, many outdated copies would remain online. By monitoring newsgroups, I gained information about new information as well as updates to existing documents. Where possible, I focused on collecting links to well-maintained FTP sites, such as those maintained by people with an interest in having a good collection, such as at Network Information Centers (NICs).

After discovering a resource, I evaluated it for possible inclusion in my list. Before the development of information-space-searching tools such as Veronica and Web Spiders, I had to rely on newsgroups and mailing lists to discover information sources. After the development of space-searching tools, I could be more selective about which sources to include because I knew the space-searching tool itself was available for users to find sources in the space. I used Veronica to glean gopherspace, and I used spiders to search the Web. (The World Wide Web Worm, the first widely used spider, was available in March 1994.)

After searching tools were introduced for each space, I knew a user should be able to locate sources based on any given keyword. This fact led me to redefine the purpose of my list. For example, one section in my list included electronic journals, services, and publications:

```
o JOURNAL/SERVICE   Subscribe with email to    Body of letter
~~~~~~~~~~~~~~~~~~~  ~~~~~~~~~~~~~~~~~~~~~~~~~~~  ~~~~~~~~~~~~~~~~~~~~~
Comserve           comserve@vm.ecs.rpi.edu     Send Comserve Helpfile
EJC/REC            comserve@vm.ecs.rpi.edu     Directory EJCREC
EJournal           listserv@albnyvm1.bitnet    subscribe ejrnl YourName
Netweaver          comserve@vm.ecs.rpi.edu     Send Netweave Winter91
RFCs               rfc-info@isi.edu            help: ways_to_get_rfcs
```

A user could create such a list by keyword searches of a database of mailing lists. But how would the user know which keywords to use? Moreover, the process of locating these addresses and resources, if repeated, would be laborious. Thus, I began to realize that another value of my list was that it collected semantically related specialist information that could not be easily generated by using an information space-searching tool.

The information-space life cycle also caused me to reevaluate the value of my list in other ways. Early in an information space's life cycle, when just a few servers exist, a handcrafted index into the information isn't necessary, as users could, in a relatively short period of time, become familiar with resources. Later, as the space fills with information, a list becomes more valuable as a reminder of where the major or definitive information sources are. When the information space fills to the point where space-searching tools are developed and used widely, indexing instances of resources and documents in that space becomes less necessary.

However, as the information space matures, space saturation and pollution start to set in. The space-tool searches turn up many duplicate or out-of-date entries, so that a handcrafted index which carefully lists the most authoritative collections or updated editions becomes more important. Finding these accurate collections became my goal as each information space matured.

Table 45.4 shows the changing contents of my list at various release dates. (There were incremental releases between the ones shown here.)

Table 45.4. Number of entries in Information Sources List.

FTP			EMAIL	USENET	TELNET	GOPHER	HTTP	PAPER
Release 1.00	23 May 92	20	5	7	0	0	0	
Release 1.50	01 Aug 92	75	12	17	0	0	0	14
Release 2.00	19 Jan 93	120	21	27	0	0	0	21
Release 2.50	10 May 93	188	41	31	0	0	0	25
Release 3.00	03 Nov 93	303	85	36	20	41	13	44
Release 3.14	01 Dec 93	317	107	36	23	47	40	48
Release 3.20	22 Jan 94	340	148	37	38	60	101	49
Release 3.25	11 Feb 94	319	156	37	32	180	649	64
Release 3.62	21 Aug 94	363	209	37	42	191	764	67

Release 3.00 was the first in HTML and other formats, and it was the release in which I first listed resources in Gopher, Telnet, and HTTP. Release 3.62 marked the start of a major shift in my efforts toward consolidating references in my list. Note the slowed expansion of FTP, e-mail, and Gopher entries in the later releases.

I see a strong trend now toward specialized, Web-based collections of information that are collaboratively maintained by experts in the field. The Web offers more expressive possibilities than Gopher, a more uniform interface than Telnet sessions, and the capability to integrate information from a variety of protocols (Gopher, Telnet, FTP, and so on). Most importantly, the Web, because it is based on hypertext, encourages linking to specialized information rather than reinventing or duplicating it. Thus, my goal now is to locate higher-level, well-maintained collections in my area of interest. At the same time, I try to remember that many of the users of my list don't use the Web for information retrieval, and thus I try to list non-Web sources of information as well. However, I see the best resources gradually moving to the Web along with the best collections that integrate many resources in multiple protocols. Therefore, I see an inevitable shift toward a greater proportion of Web-based information sources in my list.

Information Formats, Usability, and Design

With the growth of my list, I've made changes in its format and design. My early list included a short name for the resource, followed by its location at an FTP site or e-mail address. I distributed my list as an ASCII file, using a scheme for formatting the information into three columns, with dividers to help the user distinguish between sections, subsections, and divisions of the information:

```
Section -1- THE INTERNET AND SERVICES
=======================================================================
This section lists information about the Internet, services available
on it, and topics related to computer networking.

o INTERNET DESCRIPTIONS ANONYMOUS FTP HOST FILE OR DIRECTORY/
~~~~~~~~~~~~~~~~~~~~~~~~ ~~~~~~~~~~~~~~~~~~~~ ~~~~~~~~~~~~~~~~~~~~~~~~~~~~~
New User's Questions    ftp.nisc.sri.com    fyi/fyi4.txt
Hitchhikers Guide       ftp.nisc.sri.com    rfc/rfc1118.txt
Gold in Networks!       ftp.nisc.sri.com    rfc/rfc1290.txt
```

In the fall of 1993, several people asked if I had an HTML version of my list. Kevin Hughes (at that time at Honolulu Community College) created a version of my list in HTML, which he had generated using a C program. Although I had not planned for it, my list's fairly consistent format made it possible for him to write software to scan and translate my list into HTML. However, I realized that my list could be improved by making my format more consistent to accomplish this (and other) translations.

Based on the idea that I wanted to create a *database* for my list's information, from which I could then generate a variety of formats, I devised a simple markup system for the "raw" data. Using this system, I marked the entries in my list by semantics. For example:

```
#SECTION INTERNET

#SUB-SECTION Introduction

#SUB-SUB-SECTION Motivation
```

```
#FTP "Gold in Networks!:a description of gold nuggets in the network, by J. Martin"
%HOST nic.merit.edu  %FILE documents/fyi/fyi_10.txt %CHECKED 02-Oct-93

#HTTP "Internet: a column about the Internet from the Magazine of Fantasy and
Science Fiction, Feb 1993, by Bruce Sterling" %HOST www.lysator.liu.se
%PORT 7500 %FILE etexts/the_internet.html  %CHECKED 25-Mar-94

#SUB-SUB-SECTION Overviews

#FTP "Hitchikers Guide: describes the Internet (circa September 1989), by Ed Krol"
%HOST nic.merit.edu  %FILE documents/rfc/rfc1118.txt %CHECKED 11-Oct-93

#FTP "Surfing the Internet: a narrative of what the Internet has to offer, by
Jean Armour Polly" %HOST nysernet.org
%FILE pub/resources/guides/surfing.2.0.3.txt %CHECKED 11-Oct-93

#FTP "What is the Internet?: by Krol and Hoffman" %HOST nic.merit.edu
%FILE documents/fyi/fyi_20.txt %CHECKED 11-Oct-93
```

I wrote a Pascal program to use this marked-up version of my list as data and then generated HTML, LaTeX (typesetting language), and text versions of my list. Figure 45.1 illustrates this multiformat generation process.

FIGURE 45.1.

*Information Sources
List generation.*

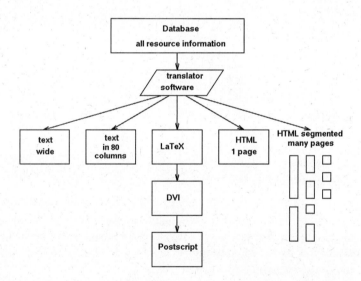

Using my translation program, I could easily generate an ASCII list in a format similar to what I had previously been offering my users:

```
|-----------------------------------------------------------------------------
* Section -2- INTERNET
|=============================================================================
o Introduction
- Motivation
Gold in Networks!:     ftp nic.merit.edu      documents/fyi/fyi_10.txt
Internet:              http www.lysator.liu.se :7500/etexts/the_internet.html
```

```
- Overviews
Hitchikers Guide:        ftp  nic.merit.edu    documents/rfc/rfc1118.txt
Surfing the Internet:  ftp  nysernet.org      pub/resources/guides/
                                              surfing.2.0.3.txt
What is the Internet?: ftp  nic.merit.edu    documents/fyi/fyi_20.txt
```

The HTML version of the list proved to be very useful, as it not only listed the resources but also gave the user the links to retrieve the resources through hotspots in the document.

As my list grew, however, a serious usability problem arose. The size of the list, particularly in its HTML form (one very large page) caused problems with some Web browsers (crashing them). Therefore, during the summer of 1994, I modified my translation program to also create a "segmented" hypertext version (Figure 45.2).

FIGURE 45.2.

Segmented hypertext version.

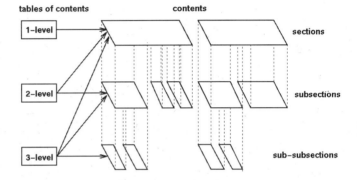

This segmented version divides the file into various-sized "chunks": sections, subsections, and sub-subsections (which had already been marked in the database file). Using automatically generated tables of contents at one, two, or three levels, users can retrieve just the part of the document they need. This dramatically reduces the amount of download time for a user. Moreover, the separation of the list into files of varying sizes allows the users to select the amount of information they want to encounter. This change was essential for the continued usability of the document itself. The list's size before segmentation was over 150KB, requiring large amounts of time to download as well as frustrating the user with information overload.

Improving Content

In the course of improving my processes for information retrieval, selection, and presentation, I've also developed processes for improving various aspects of my list's contents. Content considerations include:

- **Accuracy of sources:** In the early days of widespread use of the Net, any information about how to use it or understand it was welcome. Today, the variety of information sources requires me to seek out only those sources that are most accurate and usable for my list. The dynamic nature of the Net and the plethora of alternate operating systems, tools, and configurations makes it impossible to check each source for accuracy. However, I've kept informal track of which sources have proven to be reliable in the opinion of others and through my own checking. In some cases, particularly with very new and emerging tools and resources, there may be only a single source of information available. Later, as other information is developed, I try to point to resources that are accurate, high-level, and appealing to a variety of audiences (beginners, advanced users, administrators).

■ **Link freshness:** Because Net resources constantly change, keeping the links updated in my list is an ongoing task. Ultimately, I would like to have tools or methods to automatically verify the existence and location of a resource at a given URL. Through an interface to such a tool, I could verify or correct links in my database automatically. Without such a tool, I rely on user reports as well as periodic manual sweeps through my list in order to verify links. I've also developed a sense of which links will be more stable than others. (Older institutional and organizational links are often more stable as opposed to those developed by individuals or those that are relatively new.)

■ **Reducing redundancy:** I seek to link to high-level, stable, comprehensive information sources for the topics I cover. A positive trend in this direction is the development of topic-specific collections of information. For example, I now don't have to offer a wide selection of links to information about developing HTML files. Instead, I can link to a few good collections, including WWW & HTML Developer's JumpStation (URL `http://oneworld.wa.com/htmldev/devpage/dev-page.html`), maintained by Barry Raveendran Greene of the Johns Hopkins University Applied Physics Lab, and WebWeavers, (URL `http://www.nas.nasa.gov/RNR/Education/weavers.html`), a collection of links to assist web weavers, maintained by Chris Beaumont. Some redundancy in my list helps users see alternate views of the same information. However, once an information source appears to have surpassed other similar sources for accuracy, completeness, and usability, I'll tend to list just that resource, particularly when it collects and organizes links to other instances of information that I can eliminate from my list.

■ **Improving annotations:** My database format allows for a short name for a resource and an optional longer description. This longer description gives me the chance to add value to the information by providing a good description of the resource. Oscar Nierstrasz (when he was at the Centre Universitaire d'Informatique (CUI), l'Université de Geneve) included my list as a source in the CUI Web Catalog (URL `http://http://cuiwww.unige.ch/w3catalog`), so I am aware of how these descriptions play a role in making this catalog more valuable.

■ **Providing alternate views:** I've created other hypertext guides to provide higher-level and alternate views into my list. By developing the Internet Web Text (URL `http://www.rpi.edu/Internet/Guides/decemj/text.html`), I've tried to layer the abundance of information so that newer users can encounter it in a variety of ways and in smaller "chunks." By providing information in narrative, list-oriented, and graphical formats, I hope to provide users with a variety of ways to learn about the Internet.

Expanding the Context and Activity

I've recognized that my list of information sources is just one part of developing my understanding in this area of study. Therefore, I've entered another stage that can be vitally important in developing online information—gathering a community of people interested in the information itself. The tradition of Usenet FAQs is very rich because participants share and build elaborate information artifacts in the context of a group identity. (For example, there often seems to be a strong sense of community and group ownership of a FAQ.) On the Web, subject-specific information doesn't necessarily rise directly out of such group forums.

With this need to gather a group of peers, I've created a Web-based forum for sharing information and connecting with other people interested in computer-mediated communication (URL `http://www.rpi.edu/~decemj/cmc/center.html`). The Computer-Mediated Communication Studies Center (Figure 45.3) includes a resource collection, a directory of people interested in CMC, a list of activities, and a publication, *Computer-Mediated Communication Magazine.*

By expanding the context in which I develop my list, and by gathering experts interested in the same field, I'm starting to make the important transition from information to knowledge.

Lessons Learned

In developing my CMC Information Sources list, I've learned the following lessons that may be useful to other information providers:

1. It is possible to develop and maintain a handcrafted index to Internet resources with these benefits:
   a. The list adds value over what could otherwise be easily obtained (either through another list or index or through space-searching tools).
   b. The list is continuously updated and improved in terms of selectivity, usability, design, and content.
   c. The list is offered in a variety of formats.
2. A single database combined with a translator program is essential to providing multiple formats of a list. It would be far too difficult for me to create and maintain the individual files required for the segmented hypertext version. I would not even attempt to make a single LaTeX version of the file by hand.
3. In order to develop a successful list, the list maintainer should do the following:
   a. Keep aware of current developments in Internet resources.
   b. Become knowledgeable in the domain area represented by the field of study of the list. The maintainer should also rely on domain experts to help advise on the significance and value of information sources.
   c. Be available and accessible for comments from users and domain experts and timely maintenance of the list (based on these comments).

d. Provide leadership/vision toward making the list serve the interests of the users by seeking out opinions and testing the information frequently.

e. Ask for and acknowledge the assistance and collaboration of others in shaping the information in the list.

f. Actively seek and install new resources, links, or information presentation methods in the list.

g. Provide periodic publicity and announcements about the list to appropriate online discussion forums and indexes.

h. Seek a replacement when no longer able to develop the information in the list or when absent for an extended period.

FIGURE 45.3.

The Computer-Mediated Communication Studies Center.

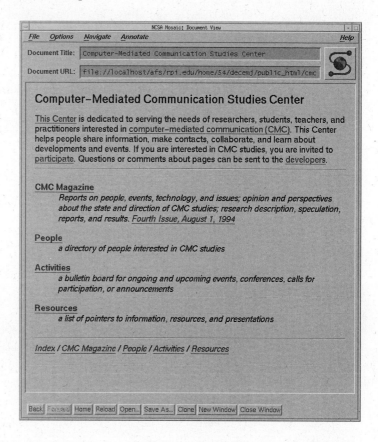

4. A resource list exists within a larger context in which its value as information can be used to create or develop knowledge (and eventually wisdom). To accomplish this, a resource list should be presented and used within a community of people interested in the information, in order to facilitate critical review as well as suggestions to improve it.

5. A resource list's ultimate value lies in the judgment and care of the list maintainer. Annotation becomes very important; and, as the information spaces that the list points to become saturated and polluted, the judgment about what to leave out becomes even more important. Eventually, the list maintainer relies on others who create more focused and specialized collections of information to provide excellent destinations as links.

6. It is important to recognize the limitations of Web-based information. In most academic disciplines, important journals, books, and other scholarly materials are still on paper. Net-based information should recognize this and point the user to appropriate paper-based resources.

Toward Web Information Quality

Based on the preceding discussions, this section presents an approach toward defining *quality* in Web information.

Toward a Notion of Web Information Quality

Quality is a difficult term to define for a particular domain or product. The concept of total quality management, derived from W. Edwards Deming's principles, includes ideas such as continuous improvement and multidisciplinary responsibility for improving a product.

Information quality has much in common with product quality. Like a physical product, information should meet users' needs (satisfy the customer). Implementing this principle in specific information-development practices and web-design features, however, is not so easily achieved, as the needs of the users can vary greatly from application to application. However, the following is a preliminary statement for Web-information quality:

> Quality as a goal for Web information involves a continuous process of planning, analysis, design, implementation, and development to ensure that the information meets user needs in terms of both content and interface.

Thus, quality is more a process of continuous improvement rather than a set of the characteristics of a finished object (a web). Due to the dynamic nature of Web information and the context in which it exists, any outward sign of a web's quality can change over time even if the web itself doesn't change. In Part V, "Weaving a Web," I describe a methodology for weaving a web using a user-centered, continuous process emphasis, with the goal of building up information so that it can lead to knowledge. An information developer can view quality as emerging from processes. However, more specific characteristics for the quality of products resulting from these processes can be stated. Quality Web information meets the following criteria:

■ **The information is correct.** Within its stated scope, purpose, and the context of its presentation, Web information should give the user cues as to its purpose, scope, and status. Developers should ensure that the information presented in the web stays consistent with these stated characteristics. For example, OncoLink (see Chapter 26, "Science and Technology") is peer-reviewed, and it functions in a specific role within the medical community (not as a substitute for professional medical care). In other words, Web information must not only be factually correct, but it should also include cues that help the user know the web's particular definition and scope of "correctness" as well as appropriate use.

- **The information is accessible.** While information presented with a web, when viewed with multimedia equipment, can present a rich experience for the user, web developers must ensure that these "bells and whistles" don't make important information inaccessible to some users. Web developers should know their audience's requirements, but they need not abandon the use of graphics or sound to conform to the least capable browser. However, if significant segments of the target audience do not have multimedia capabilities (or want such features), the web should be designed so that important information is not masked behind features the users can't or won't access.

- **The information is usable.** From the functional perspective, the web should deliver the information that users need with a minimum amount of clutter, in a design that captures the information and takes full advantage of hypertext. This means that text is not in one monstrous file (as my CMC information sources file was before I "segmented" it). Rather, the pages in the web should aim to capture a single unit of user attention. It should not have so little information that the user has to sort through multiple links in the web to find meaning, nor should it have so much information that the user is overwhelmed by a single page.

- **The information is understandable.** The web should contain cues and employ composition principles that build and shape meaning. Web developers can use techniques that are used in print and other media: audience analysis, rhetorical devices (for example, parallelism, analogies), and technical communication techniques (for example, chunking information, cueing the reader, ordering information). Hypertext is not constrained to being linear; however, in local doses and at surface layers, hypertext is linear prose. Hypertext can be thought of as text that is not constrained in a single expressive object (such as a web) or confined to a single perspective. Web-based hypertext is *unbounded* text that derives meaning from its links, which branch into Webspace. Making meaning at a local level within hypertext, however, still involves crafting prose (or using visual or aural elements) to create meaning. To do this, a developer needs to use effective composition principles (as opposed to forcing a user to "construct" meaning by decoding unorganized pieces of information).

- **The information is meaningful.** Within its stated scope and context of presentation, a quality web should somehow reach for a significance beyond itself, a meaning that can help a user form new relationships among units of information. From these new relationships, new knowledge or insights may form. For example, Le WebLouvre (URL `http://mistral.enst.fr/~pioch/louvre/louvre.html`) is an online art gallery, containing online exhibits and a tour of Paris. While the "information" presented by art is not as obviously useful as scientific information in webs, it nonetheless functions as art does in our culture—evoking a feeling of human identification such as emotion or association. Thus, "meaning" is not purely a transfer of information content, but rather something that emerges as a result of encountering the information. A web should not merely present information but assist users in analyzing and interpreting that information within a larger context. In fact, this contextualizing aspect of meaning is one of the strengths of the Web itself.

What Information Providers Need to Increase Quality

The Web has the potential to help people articulate and arrange information more expressively than any other information-delivery system in history. In order to tap into this potential, and to ensure and develop notions of quality such as those outlined earlier in this chapter, the following methodologies and tools for information providers might be developed in the future:

- Tools to assist in web design and implementation.

- Automated tools for maintaining HTML files or for creating and enforcing web "look-and-feel" design decisions.

- Automated tools for web maintenance (to verify link freshness) and to assist in other tasks of web development.

- Higher-level languages that articulate web constructs and structures above the HTML level, capturing notions of inheritance (from object-oriented design methodologies), packaging (module concept from procedural programming languages), and information-shaping (from rhetoric, composition, and technical-communication techniques).

  These higher-level languages might include a logical level over Uniform Resource Locators (or Identifiers) that captures abstraction in naming. For example, a link to a national Network Information Center (NIC) could be expressed as a generic term within an anchor that is instantiated in a web-generation scheme to an appropriate URL specific to a given parameter (for example, yielding a specific link for a European web, another link for an Australian web).

- Automated tools to help a designer evaluate a web's performance, with accesses by page (perhaps graphically represented) to alert web designers to how the web's information is actually being used. (See WebViz's approach to this at `http://www.gatech.edu/pitkow/WebViz/WebViz-html/WebViz.html`.)

- Methodologies to support web planning, analysis, design, and development.

- Techniques for web-usability testing.

- Methods for web audience analysis.

- Techniques for information presentation that help a diverse audience of users find different "ways into" or views of a body of information.

While some of the preceding tools and methods might involve computer-assistance or automation (for example, link-freshness checks), the key element in successful webs is human intelligence and judgment. A management system for information providers should thus include automated procedures along with ways for information providers to contribute judgment and knowledge. For example, in information discovery, hand-crafted indexes are costly in terms of time, but they can lead to valuable results for specialized uses. While automated methods (WAIS, Veronica, Archie, WWW Search engines) can scan a large amount of information, the raw search results can bewilder an inexperienced user. Combining human judgment with the strength of automated tools may ultimately lead to more powerful ways to gather and shape information.

Finally, web-information providers need an information-literate audience. Information literacy includes the ability to access, evaluate, and use networked information in the pursuit of a goal. Helping a user gain this literacy and to progress from merely *using* information to gaining knowledge involves presenting the right information at the right time in the right context. Often, web developers can do this by providing a variety of ways to access, view, and understand the continually changing resources on the Internet.

What Information Providers Can Do to Increase Quality

The growth of Web information challenges information providers to increase quality in the areas outlined in the following sections.

Improving Content

- Draw on domain experts to judge and critique information and to suggest content development and improvements.
- Have authoritative sources, along with fresh links to those sources.
- Promote collaboration in developing content.

Improving Presentation

- Use techniques to cue users about the purpose, offerings, status, and usability of web information.
- Use HTML design techniques that exploit the power of hypertext. Break up information into manageable pieces or chunks. Use links to refer to concepts and information rather than reproducing it.
- Ensure that graphics, multimedia, and other features serve the best interests of the users. This includes minimizing them when necessary and including them when appropriate.

Improving Discovery

- Keep aware of subject-oriented collections as well as indexes on the Web. Publicize the web's information so that it is included in appropriate indexes and subject trees.

■ Be aware of schemes for spider indexing. Design document hotspots, titles, and other features to provide the best information for spiders.

■ Provide your web's information within the context of its intended audience so that your users (and potential users) know your web's offerings and are aware of new developments.

Promoting Innovation

■ Aim for innovative techniques in your web's presentation and content that will meet your users' changing needs.

■ Experiment with nontraditional modes of expression to exploit new hypermedia features and techniques

■ Adjust your web-development processes to allow for new ideas, approaches, and techniques, so that creativity can flourish.

Summary

If there were only a few Web resources, users could easily find and compare them to identify the most useful ones for their needs. However, with an increasingly large and diverse universe of Web servers, traffic, documents, and audiences, even smart Web spiders can't identify the resources that are correct, complete, or most useful for a given purpose.

The Web itself is a means of *expression*, not just a conduit for delivering information. The challenge for Web information providers is to increase the quality of information they deliver—in terms of both its content and its method of presentation. Web-information providers must continually examine the processes by which they gather, present, and improve their web's information.

By refining skills and techniques for gathering and presenting information and tapping into the wisdom of experts for critical review, web-information providers can engage in a continuous process of quality improvement. Methods for presenting web information can be derived from such fields as technical communication, rhetoric, and composition. Web-information providers can also draw on concepts and practices from software engineering in order to develop new design and implementation techniques. Automated tools and higher-level hypertext languages can provide more abstract levels above HTML, so that larger units of information and web structure can be articulated. Ultimately, the challenge for a web-information provider is to acknowledge the dynamic nature of information on the Web and recognize that information quality is not just a set of outward characteristics or design decisions but a part of a continuous process in which content and presentation are adjusted to meet user needs. Webs that more completely articulate information so that it can become knowledge are critical to the Web's continued growth.

Surveying the Web

46

by
James E. Pitkow

Most of us at one time or another have been asked to participate in a survey of some sort. Whether we received a phone call asking us to answer a few questions, or opened a piece of mail with printed questions and predefined choices to choose from, the notion is the same: Someone somewhere wants information from us. This concept of attempting to answer some or all of the basic five questions—who, what, when, where, and how—is at the heart of surveying. Electronic surveying is a new and exciting research area, especially given the opportunity for surveys to utilize Web technologies. This chapter provides the reader with an understanding of the basic issues involved in surveying and applies them to a survey on a very pertinent subject: the Web itself.

The Basics of Surveys

Sampling, which refers to the manner in which observations are gathered for a population, is one of the most important elements of surveying. When a population is large, making observations on all members of that population (a census) usually becomes impractical, if not impossible. Web users are a good example of a population that would be difficult to sample completely. When the surveyor is presented with these kinds of populations, sampling methods that randomly select members for participation are the next best alternative.

Random samples enable surveyors to make generalizations and inferences about the entire population based on the smaller, sampled population. Such random samples can produce results with an identifiable level of confidence. For the sake of this discussion, "confidence" refers to the reliability of a statement or the strength of one's conclusion based on that statement; "generalizations" refers to statements made from the sampled populations that apply to the entire population; and "inferences" combine two or more facts to form new statements. So, when members are chosen from a population in a non-determined (random) manner, estimations about the whole population can be made with some degree of certainty. Typical forms of off-line random sampling include randomly dialing phone numbers, randomly selecting addresses and drawing evenly distributed numbers from a hat.

Alternatively, when non-random sampling methods are used, conclusions made about the sampled population *may* or *may not* be true about the entire population. The problem is that unless certain characteristics are known about the entire population, the extent to which the non-random sample matches the real population is indeterminable. Thus, no corrective measures can be applied to the data and the non-random sample merely represents information about the members who participated.

Although the statistical basis for the strength of random sampling is beyond the scope of this chapter (for those interested, please look up the Central Limit Theorem in your favorite statistics book), it makes sense intuitively. For example, if one sets out to determine characteristics of Usenet news readers but only samples Usenet news posters, conclusions made about the posters may or may not apply to Usenet readers, because some people read newsgroups and never post. Granted, some users read *and* post—which is exactly the point! Unless we know the ratio of readers to posters and how readers and posters typically differ, the data we collect only applies to posters. Therefore, nothing can be said about the readers with any determinable level of confidence.

Data Representation and Loss

Traditional surveys usually involve methods such as direct mailings and phone-based polling. With such surveys, the responses by participants (also called respondents or users) must somehow be collected and translated from their initial form to a form that is suitable for analysis. Mailings and phone-based surveys typically use paper as the primary medium for capturing responses and use statistical computer packages for analysis. Several problems can occur during the translation from one medium (paper) to another (electronic). These problems can include human errors as well as those that result from automated processing (such as SAT's fill-in-the-circles forms). Although these translation errors can be treated as "noise" within the data and usually do not significantly effect the results, the translation process can be eliminated altogether by electronic media.

Analysis

Once the sampling method is determined and the data is collected, analysis of the results can take place. The types of analysis that the surveyors perform are directly tied to the type of data collected. The intent of this section is to provide an overview of the types of analysis that are commonly performed.

Descriptive statistics typically report the total number of responses per observation, the average (mean), the range (minimum and maximum), the variance (how spread out the data is), percentages, etc. These analyses only apply to the sampled population. Inferential statistics attempt to draw conclusions about the entire population based upon the sample. Typical inferential statistics include confidence intervals, z-test, t-tests, ANOVAs (ANalysis Of VARiance), linear regressions, and Chi-Square analyses. Finally, when more than one sample exists for a population, comparisons between the populations can be performed using modifications to the statistical procedures.

Biases and Confounds

Even when random sampling is used, other problems can occur with the method of collecting data. Two factors that effect the validity of the sample are *self-selection* and *estimation bias*. Self-selection occurs when a member of the population has the option whether or not to participate. The problem is that the members who choose to participate may be different than those who choose not to participate. Thus, the characteristics of the participating and non-participating populations *may* or *may not* be different. This reduces the strength of any statements made about the sampled population.

Interestingly, almost all modern surveys suffer from self-selection. For example, if users hang up the phone, they have chosen not to participate; if users do not return the survey via postal mail, they have chosen not to participate. These are all forms of self-selection, since they involve a choice by the respondent not to participate.

Estimation bias results when a user is asked to approximate or judge the value of a certain quantity. For example, if I ask you to tell me the percentage of females in your organization, you would most likely have to estimate this quantity (unless your organization made this information available to you based upon actual employee records). Note that users could be asked to estimate values that they themselves might know—for instance, how many hours per day do you do this activity. Psychological experiments show that the estimation of values is not highly reliable, particularly when individuals are asked to estimate values for large groups of people or to produce precise values.

The Challenges of Electronic and Web Surveying

Electronic surveying in networked environments such as the Internet is a new and exciting field. This section discusses electronic surveying and Web surveying, and some of their existing problems.

Most electronic surveys have either solicited participation via postings to UseNew newsgroups, electronic mailing lists, or electronic mailings to individuals. Each of these options offers different degrees of intrusion, with the former being the least intrusive and the latter being the most intrusive (whether these techniques are more or less intrusive than traditional surveying techniques such as phone and mail-based surveys is debatable). These forms of electronic surveys typically require that the respondent fill out the survey and send the results via e-mail to the surveyor. After a form is received, the surveyor can process the results electronically, because the information is already in digital form. There might be some difficulty in getting the values for each question automatically, because respondents can place answers anywhere and provide a myriad of spellings and abbreviations.

Web surveying also relies upon some method of notifying the user that the survey is underway, though this can be done by placing links on heavily accessed pages. The area Web surveying really wins is in the point-and-click method, wherein respondents can fill in answers. This eliminates much of the overhead incurred by the user having to type in answers in addition to having to e-mail the results to the surveyor. After the results are received by the surveyor, the data can be automatically processed because many, if not all, of the questions have a fixed set of possible answers. This constraint is achieved by either using checkboxes or radio buttons. Answers that require text entry are to be avoided.

The "How Many" Questions...

The question that everyone asks but that no one convincingly answers is "How many WWW users are there?" The larger, related question is, of course, "How many people are on the Internet?" The reason this question is difficult to answer is that currently there is no global registration mechanism for the Web (let alone for the Internet). Basically, to accurately determine the total number of users, you need to count all users. Perhaps this could be achieved via a census (complete population surveying), as is periodically practiced in certain countries.

The Web equivalent to a census is sending a survey to every machine with Web access (also know as *spamming*). The sampling methodology must allow for multiple submissions from the same machine as well as exclude multiple submissions from the same person on different machines, and it must allow enough time for everyone to eventually log on to a machine to obtain the survey and fill it out. This is not a very practical approach, and it suffers from self-selection problems.

Alternately you could use random sampling of machine names, let's say in Europe, and calculate the percentage of those users that use the Web. Unfortunately, you have the self-selection issue as well as difficulty in drawing conclusions about the Web population based on the sampled population, because users in Europe *may* or *may not* be different from users in the U.S., India, Africa, and elsewhere. See the problems? Because there is no global registration for all users, self-selection biases and the random sampling of sub-populations reduce our ability to make strong statements about the entire population. These are the some of the same problems we would face in determining the number of Internet users.

Nonetheless, electronic surveying of distributed computer environments is a new and exciting field of research that offers solutions to existing problems (albeit while raising new problems). As the field matures and more surveys are conducted and analyzed, a better understanding of the electronic surveying of distributed computer environments will inevitably result.

GVU's WWW User Surveys

The next two sections of this chapter cover the WWW User Surveys conducted by the Graphics, Visualization & Usability (GVU) Center, a research lab of Georgia Institute of Technology's College of Computing. The reasons behind the surveys as well as what makes them unique are discussed, along with pointers to the freely available online results. Access to all the information cited below is available via URL :http://www.cc.gatech.edu/gvu/user_surveys/.

The surveys are run every six months, for a month starting April 10 and October 10 each year (please use the above URL for accessing). Because of the commitment of the surveying team (Mimi Recker, Colleen Kehoe, Laurie Hodges, and myself) and GVU to the Web community, the results of our analyses and collected datasets are free. Furthermore, in hopes of global involvement, we readily welcome new questions and the improvement of previous questions from other interested researchers.

The First Survey: The Pilot Study

The surveys were initially conceived with two intentions: 1) to demonstrate the Web as a viable surveying medium, and 2) to characterize and chart the changes of the Web's user population. As you'll see, both goals have been accomplished. The latter goal is particularly important from a usability perspective in that an understanding of the basic questions about Web users—the who, what, where, when and how—can aid in the development and direction of Web technologies. It also has the pleasant side-effect of providing much sought-after data for academic and commercial Web ventures.

The Methodology

The first survey was run for a month during January 1994. The questions on the first survey were separated into five categories or questionnaires: General Demographics, HTML Authoring, HTTP Servers, Mosaic Specific, and WWW Browser Usage. The participants in the survey were asked to fill out only those surveys that applied to their WWW use. Surveys were filled out via the use of FORMs that enabled point-and-click responses to questions; text entry was also permitted on several questions. On the server side, software was used to log the users' responses to files.

Sampling was accomplished via non-random methods. At the time (and still to this day), no global broadcasting mechanism existed to notify all Web users of events. Our approach was to announce the survey via as many methods as possible without spamming. Specifically, several periodic announcements were made to WWW-related Usenet newsgroups, and a entry was made on NCSA's "What's New Page" and CERN's WWW Home Page.

The Questions

The usual demographic questions concerning age, occupation, education, and so on were asked in the first questionnaire. Broad categories were used when the number of options exceeded reasonable screen space. For example, the question about the user's location allowed the user to choose from continents and not individual countries within continents, because this would easily take several screens to present all the choices. Additionally, the survey asked computer-specific questions about the number of hours of computer use per week and the user's primary WWW browser.

For the HTML authoring portion of the survey, we sought to get a handle on how difficult or easy HTML was to learn and use. Similarly, questions that inquired about the extent of the user's HTTP knowledge and ease of server operation were asked in the HTTP questionnaire. The Mosaic-specific portion attempted to address and evaluate the role of NCSA in such areas as support and online documentation. Finally, the WWW Browser Usage questionnaire focused on what users do with their browsers.

The Results

In short, over 1,300 users responded to the survey. The typical user was a 21–30 year old male professional from the United States with computer experience. The complete results and analyses can be found online via the URL `http://www.cc.gatech.edu/gvu/user_surveys/`.

The Problems

Fortunately, the First WWW User Survey was a pilot study, because there were numerous problems. First, because non-random sampling techniques and self-selection biases occurred, no conclusions about the entire Web user population could be made (although this was not—and still is not—our intent). Another problem was that NCSA's X Mosaic was the only FORMs-compliant browser that was available for the duration of the sampling period. This helps explain the high proportion of UNIX respondents. Duplicate submissions were not handled directly by the surveying software but rather required post-hoc identification and manual removal. Each user did not have a unique ID across all questionnaires, which prevented answers from the General portion from being compared to the answers in other questionnaires for the same user. For example, we could not determine the average age of HTTP server operators. (This is a side effect of HTTP's stateless protocol.) Also, questions that were not filled out (whether intentionally or by mistake) were not re-asked. This resulted in the loss of data points for certain questions by certain users, which interfered statistically with some analyses. While the list of difficulties is indeed lengthy, we gained tremendous insight and understanding of the issues involved with surveying the Web user populations via Web technologies.

The Second Survey: Getting More of the Picture

Given the dynamic nature of the Web's growth, any data collected about the user population is sure to be out-of-date within months of collection. In order to maintain data about current users as well as the community's positive response to the First Survey's results, a second survey was conducted from October 10, 1994 through November 16, 1994. It was also decided that GVU would run the surveys every six months as public server to the Web community. This interval would not irritate users with often-running surveys but would be timely and capture data about the user population.

The Methodology

Essentially, the methodology employed for the first survey was used for the second survey (this survey started October 10, 1994). Survey announcements were made periodically to WWW- and Internet-related Usenet newsgroups and to WWW-based e-mail lists (such as www-talk), and our efforts were augmented by some limited coverage in Web-related magazines, positions on NCSA's and CERN's pages, and an announcement at the Second International WWW Conference. The underlying survey software was rewritten to help correct several of the problems with the first survey.

User Identification

Each user was asked to enter one word (ID) to be used for internal identification purposes. This ID was used in combination with the user's machine address to track users' responses across questionnaires. This also enabled maintenance of specific state information, such as which portions of the survey each user had completed. Additionally, code was added that re-asked unanswered questions.

Adaptive Questioning

An additional feature that was added to the second survey was adaptive questioning. (The idea was suggested by John Mallery at the First International WWW Conference.) Adaptive questioning refers to the capability of the surveying software to ask questions based upon previous responses. For example, in trying to determine the country/state where the user was located, a list of over 100 options would have to be presented to the user. But via adaptation, two sets of questions could be asked—the first providing a broad location choice (for example, the Middle East) followed by the second question providing a list of *only* Middle Eastern countries. Thus, with two questions, a fine granularity of data could be obtained. Additionally, from the user's perspective, the process of responding to the question is simplified, because the user does not need to search through large numbers of irrelevant country/state names.

The Questions

The questions from the first survey were redesigned and refined for the second survey. The Mosaic Specific section was dropped, and the HTML Authoring and HTTP Server sections were collapsed into one section. Additional demographic questions were also added to the General section. Thus, the user was presented with three questionnaires to complete. Additionally, a pre-test of consumer-based questions was added to the survey (developed by Sunil Gupta of the University of Michigan's Business School). These questionnaires addressed Web users' purchasing behaviors and preferences.

The Results

Over 4,000 users responded to the survey, 2.6 times the number of responses from the First survey. Fortunately, most major computing platforms had FORMs supporting Web browsers publicly available, thus resulting in a more even distribution across computing platforms. The average age of the respondents was 31 years old, and 90% were male. 73% were from the U.S. and

23% from Europe. The average income was computed as $54,000 (U.S.). The primary reasons that were cited for using their Web browsers (predominately Mosaic, because Netscape products were released only towards the end of the sampling period) were browsing and entertainment. (Please see URL `http://www.cc.gatech.edu/gvu/user_surveys/` for more complete coverage of the results as well as access to the collected datasets.)

The Problems

As with the first survey, the second survey had non-random sampling and self-selection problems. Additionally, duplicate submissions by a single user were accepted, with the most recent submission's responses being used for analysis. Our software did not get explicit user consent for this form of overwriting previous answers.

Other smaller-scale, Web-based surveys that employed similar sampling methodology (see the previously referenced URL for a list of other Web surveys) report similar means and percentages on key demographic information. The process of comparing the surveys (also called triangulating the data) helps increase our confidence level in the data on the Web-user population.

The Third Survey: Tracking Users Through Time

The response by the Web community, as well as the popular media, to the Second Survey was quite strong. In keeping with our survey's every six-month agenda, GVU's Third WWW User Survey is scheduled to run from April 10, 1995, to May 10, 1995.

Tracking User IDs

New to the third survey is the capability of tracking users from the second survey. This will provide longitudinal analysis of how certain users' preferences and usage patterns change over time. In attempting to make sure that the users are who they claim to be, we have implemented a type of challenge-response mechanism into the surveys. For all the users who participated in the second survey, certain questions will be asked, such as age and location, that the user must answer correctly before being allowed to re-enter the surveys using that ID. Once in, certain demographic questions will have default values already selected, based upon their answers to the same questions on the second survey, in order to facilitate response efficiency. This and other mechanisms will hopefully keep the already-surveyed users coming back.

How many users will participate in the third surveys? How many will be return users? No one knows, but it will be really exciting to find out.

Summary

This chapter provided an overview of the basics of surveying and discussed the new frontier of electronic surveying via the Web. This chapter presented the results and methodology for the GVU Center's World Wide Web User Surveys (and their shortcomings). All results are freely available to the public from URL http://www.cc.gatech.edu/gvu/user_surveys/. Although the definitive answer to the "who's out there" question remains beyond current reach, GVU's periodic surveys provide needed and sought-after data points about Web users.

The Future of Web Commerce

47

by
Andrew Dinsdale

Can any of us predict how the World Wide Web will look and be used in five years? At current growth rates, it is inevitable that the Web will become a popular medium for entertainment, information, education, and business; but how far away are we? Laying the cables to allow millions of users to connect to the Web and funding the research and development needed to make the Web a more effective medium will cost millions of dollars, yen, pounds, and deutsche marks. Therefore, the future of the Web will depend on commercial involvement and acceptance.

Science-fiction authors such as William Gibson (*Neuromancer*) and Neal Stephenson (*Snow Crash*) have described a so-called "cyberspace" or "virtual world." The Web is a tangible incarnation of the global communities depicted in these fictive works. We can use e-mail to communicate with friends and colleagues all over the world, partake in synchronous discussions in MUDs (Multi-User Domains, text-based meeting places), and connect to server computers without the need for high-level computer-science studies. The possibilities appear endless, and these new virtual worlds will certainly include a virtual marketplace.

The function of a marketplace is to bring together buyers and sellers. There must be methods of bringing goods to market and encouraging buyers to attend, there must be a place to meet, and there must be a transaction system. Organizations are complex; they depend not only on interactions between departments but also on interactions with interested parties in the larger world, including suppliers, consumers, and the media. Web technology enables a new system of interaction and provides the latest marketplace.

Over the last year, an unprecedented number of companies started using the Internet to communicate internally and with the public. The electronic press release, e-mail-based customer support, and "Net-Presence" have become almost commonplace. The Web is a new medium for companies to bring information to those who need it, and it provides a virtual space for meetings and transactions to be performed. Web sites contain fill-in forms that function such as a 1-800-ORDER-NOW phone number; ordering takes place within the same medium that brought the message. Simultaneously, the Web is the promotional tool, the ordering device, the communication method, and the "place." Already the virtual world will allow computer-mediated education, entertainment, and shopping. Soon doctor's visits and banking may be possible. It is inevitable that many events from real life (RL) will soon take place in this virtual reality (VR), or so we are led to believe. A year ago, the idea of a global virtual marketplace was almost vaporware. (*Vaporware* is the term applied to not-yet-developed software and hardware.) Although we have come a long way in a short time, the real marketplace potential of the Web is far from reality. In a few years, we might look back at the current attempts at net-marketing and think of them as alpha tests. Yes, there is already a place to meet; those with browsers can be encouraged to attend (if they know the URL); and with a Web form you can order from electronic storefronts. Business associates can collaborate and work via e-mail, and multimedia files can be moved around the network with great ease. But there are many potential pitfalls and problems that need to be solved before the Web becomes a true marketplace.

This chapter introduces some of these problems and demonstrates how they will effect the development of a commercially driven Web. Some potential solutions are offered, but the primary aim here is to promote discussion and an awareness of the problems.

Web Browsing for the Masses?

Netscape, Mosaic, and other browsers are becoming popular, but not every PC user has access to the Web. The major online companies, such as Prodigy, CompuServe, and America Online, are all making efforts to incorporate the Web into their portfolio of services, but for many users access to the TCP/IP pipes is difficult. The lowest common denominator of Internet access is an e-mail address, and even though Web traffic (measured in *packets*) is increasing at an alarming rate (see `http://www.cc.gatech.edu/gvu/stats/NSF/merit.html`), e-mail will remain the *de facto* standard of online communication for many years to come. A problem facing those at the forefront of Web commerce is the complexity inherent in accessing the Web. Fortunately, access has become much easier over the past few months.

The major ingredients for Web access are a TCP/IP connection, a TCP/IP stack running on a PC or workstation, and a Web browser. Internet connections are becoming much cheaper, falling some 30 percent over the past year as more providers enter the market. Access to an IP connection is now commonplace in almost all corners of the U.S., as well as throughout the world.

In both the Mac and Windows worlds, new and improved products enable surfing on the Web from office LANs and home computers. Macintosh now ships MacTCP with its System 7.5 operating system, and Windows 95 (as well IBM's OS/2 Warp) incorporates Winsock as a major feature. Peter Tattam's Winsock has been upgraded, is easier to use, and features an internal PPP dialer. For those on non-TCP/IP networks, Proxy connections to the Web are now possible, enabled by a variety of products. Companies controlling incoming and outgoing packets with so-called firewalls can still let users surf the Web by using proxy servers such as CERN's (`http://www.w3.org/hypertext/WWW/Daemon/Status.html`).

The most important piece of the puzzle is the Web browser. Computer manufacturers are including browsers in software bundles, and commercial versions of the father of all browsers, Mosaic, are easier to install as well as faster and more robust. Plug-and-play Net access can be had with such products as Spry's Internet-in-a-Box and Netmanage's Chameleon. The popular Netscape browser is a novice's dream. It is installable from a self-extracting file for both Mac and Windows, it is user-friendly, and offers built-in links to up-to-date Net directories such as Yahoo (`http://www.yahoo.com`) and Lycos (`http://lycos.cs.cmu.edu`). Further, the major online services—Prodigy, America Online, and CompuServe—are offering their customers very easy-to-run Web browsing utilities, which the user can access just as with any of the other services.

The development of user-friendly Web browsers is an important step, because the Net can be a hard phenomenon to understand, and computer phobes are scared enough of even the simplest applications. (Of course, the user's education level is crucial; the generation raised on Nintendo and with computers in the classroom will not face the same obstacles as older users.)

Other important developments include Twinsock (`http://ugsparc0.eecg.utoronto.ca/~luk/tsfaq.html`) and The Internet Adaptor (`http://marketplace.com/tia/tiahome.html`)—products that allow those with standard UNIX shell accounts to access the Web via "pseudo-SLIP" connections. SlipKnot achieves a similar aim by offering Microsoft Windows a shareware graphical

Web browser to users with a dial-up shell account (`http://www.interport.net/slipknot/slipknot.html`). Such products will enable thousands of users to run graphical interfaces such as Netscape and Mosaic, without a privileged and expensive TCP/IP account.

A Shift in Focus: From the Academic to the Commercial

The domain-naming system classifies each node on the Internet into one of several categories: `.com`, `.edu`, `.org`, `.gov`, and `.mil` in the United States; other countries are identified by a two-letter country code, such as `fr` (France) and `de` (Germany), with subdomains identifying the nodes category `.co.uk` (for commercial sites in the United Kingdom), and so on. This system enables names to be used (instead of a series of IP address numbers) to identify hosts on the Net. The `.com` (for commercial) domain now accounts for approximately 50 percent of registered domain names on the Net. This is a dramatic shift, because the Internet was an academic environment until only a few years ago (a time when a vague regulation limited commercial use of the tax-funded NSFnet).

This shift is also reflected in the development of browsers and servers. We owe the development of the Web to CERN, a major physics research center in Geneva, Switzerland; and we owe Mosaic to NCSA, part of the University of Illinois. But the future of Web tools now lies with commercial companies. The huge commercial potential of the Web has encouraged many new software manufacturers to take up the challenge. The software product with the biggest impact has been Netscape. Netscape is free to download and to test (`ftp://ftp.netscape.com`), but commercial users must buy a licensed copy. The licensed copy has a commercial focus and features a suite of products emphasizing commercial use of the Net. The NetSite server, for instance, features high-end security provisions enabling secure transactions. Like other commercial navigators, such as Spry's Air Mosaic, the commercial version of Netscape Navigator is fast and efficient. This kind of industrial strength makes a Web browser a viable tool for business.

For users of Mosaic, the NCSA home page was the most common point of entry to the Web. Links and starting points built from there had a distinctly academic focus: the Web, according to the developers of Mosaic, was a virtual research library. Today, when a user runs Netscape, it takes him or her to the Netscape Web server. Here one can read about Netscape's products and services, and many of the external links relate to setting up shop on the Internet: how to author HTML, how to set up servers, and so forth.

Setting up shop is further enabled by the plug-and-play Internet servers being developed by major computer companies, such as SUN's Netra, Silicon Graphic's WebFORCE line, BSDI, Net-ready DEC Alphas, or even easily configurable PowerMACs running MacHTTP (`http://www.biap.com`).

These provide real alternatives to CERN and NCSA UNIX-based HTTPD servers, alternatives that even a kid could use (`http://catweb.novi.k12.mi.us`). These machines enable a company to serve documents and communicate to the world.

The true power of CGI scripts and third-party add-ons that give the server an application layer are also being realized. Examples of this include online ordering, user authentication, and the ability to link existing databases to the Web. This gives the Web the capability to incorporate new and unforeseen sources of information. The way the Web is developing, it appears that any information you need to collect, maintain, and distribute can be encompassed into your own Web site through a hypertext link and relatively simple programming. Duplicity of effort will thus be reduced; accounting and reporting mechanisms such as databases will be turned into communicative tools.

To check out the kinds of businesses that are already online (and you may be surprised), go to Open Market's Commercial Site Index at `http://www.directory.net/` and look up a company name or a service offering. (See Figure 47.1.)

FIGURE 47.1.

http://
www.directory.net/.

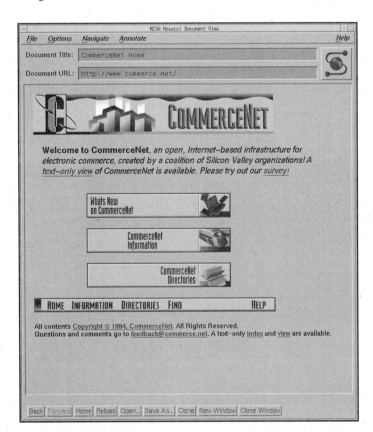

Caution: Construction Ahead—
Expect Delays

A major consideration in the growth of the Web is its potentially insufficient bandwidth. As Web use increases, the current network backbone, or infrastructure, may not be sufficient for the demand. Already there have been instances of online overload. In 1994, when NASA offered .GIF files of Jupiter's encounter with the comet Shoemaker-Levy 9, traffic on the Internet was brought to a standstill (inspiring the metaphor of the Info-Highway traffic jam). The Web as currently configured is not amenable to the movement of simple files. When the average home user dials in to access the Net, it is at a modem speed of 9,600 or 14,400 bits per second—a speed too slow for downloading pictures, let alone multimedia presentations. But who is going to upgrade the Internet to support a true and virtual marketplace—and who is going to pay for it? These issues are more apparent now that the NSFnet has "gone away"—its void being filled by ANS (owned by America OnLine), MCI, Sprint, and MFS.

The momentum to improve the infrastructure necessary for a virtual world has been building for a number of years. These moves are akin to the building of the telegraph and railroads of the nineteenth century. The creation of a true I-Way will undoubtedly be achieved through a marriage of private companies with public agencies and utilities. The global nature of the Web will make the construction even more complex. In the United States, the Clinton-Gore administration has certainly committed a lot of energy and time to the development of a National Information Infrastructure plan. As planned, the Net will allow for information and entertainment delivery; it will be a medium that allows online shopping, game playing, libraries, news, banking, telecommuting, and education. One sure thing we can predict is that whatever is planned and no matter how many "lanes" are created, eventually the traffic on the I-Way, as with real-life highways, will be congested. The current growth of the Internet is incredible. The number of Web sites supposedly doubles every 54 days (over 30,000 as of April '95), and the InterNIC is currently receiving 700 requests for IP addresses and domain names per day.

This will certainly be the case if the I-Way backbone and the Web model form the basis of the game, edutainment, and video-on-demand projects currently under development by IBM, the Baby Bells, and Silicon Graphics, as well as promised by AT&T commercials. High-speed transmission lines and improvements in data compression necessary to transmit a movie through the Internet undoubtedly are in the future. The current compression standard that shrinks bite-sized movies and small sound files is not sufficient for the proposed uses of the I-Way; pundits predict personal ISDN and tie-ins with cable television as potential technological fixes.

Control of the Web

Another question for the future of the Web is who governs such an international network, sets the rules, and mediates the debate over policy. Future development and funding of the Web may depend on the answer.

The Web is primarily a communications medium. Other communications media, such as television, telephone, and postal mail, have fair-use and censorship rules laid down by statute and by cultural tradition. In the United States, where freedom of speech and of the press is protected, there are legal limitations imposed on "hate speech" and pornography. Could domestic censorship laws cover the international Web? The Net is already perceived by the general public as anarchistic. X-rated discussion groups flourish there, and servers could easily be established to promote racist rhetoric and criminal activity. How can this be controlled? Could a governing body monitor all sites?

The issue of Net control could fill several books, and those who are most vocal in the debate consider the Net to be something worth protecting. Organizations such as the Electronic Frontier Foundation and Electronic Messaging Association have recognized that the legal provisions of the real world do not transfer well to the digital one. The U.S. Government's attempt to place a tappable encryption device (the Clipper chip) on all telecommunications media was opposed by civil-liberties activists as an attack on privacy. In a virtual world, transactions could be monitored remotely, allowing many potential abuses of power. A recent piece of legislation would have made network carriers responsible for the contents of all transferred data. This proposal was subsequently watered down, but the control issue still remains.

Copyright protection for electronically transmitted material is another hotly debated issue. Digitized materials become tangible assets on the Web. Even though sites running Web servers can ensure that only paying customers have access to certain pages, what will prevent the contents from being illegally reposted and copied? Electronic publishers and application developers might be reluctant to sell digitized products if the threat of online piracy is too great. A related copyright issue is the ownership of electronically altered materials. If an image (or sound or source-code file) is downloaded from the Net, altered, and sold, is the original creator owed anything? Further, a case exists in which the creator of a commercial Web site, after spending hours creating Web pages and GIFs, and placing mpegs online for his customers' pages, found that another site had downloaded all of his work (typos included) and put them online on behalf of another customer in the same field.

On a micro or company level, control of Net usage could become a big issue. With all the potential information flying around, customers and workers will need to deal with information overload. E-mail often produces a new level of internal and external communication activity, combining business and personal uses. Employees subscribing to only a few e-mail lists may receive 100 or more messages per day, which could result in an awful lot of unproductive time. Add to this the lost business hours due to employees Web-surfing, playing in MUDs, and reading alternative newsgroups, and it's clear that companies will need to monitor the Net's effects on employee productivity. There are ways to limit or filter e-mail, and some companies have had to close down internal mail systems altogether so that real-life work gets done.

Transactions and Network Security

One of the most important factors pertaining to the development of commerce on the Web is the transaction system. Customers and sellers are already aware of the risks of real-world creditcard fraud; stolen carbon copies of transactions, unscrupulous shop assistants; even someone looking over your shoulder can lead to your credit-card number being used by a criminal. Even giving out credit information when ordering by mail and telephone is a scary thought to many. Transactions on the Web have their own type of risks, because transferring data via e-mail or WWW forms is not (with a few exceptions) absolutely secure.

Placing sensitive and personal information online and transferring it to a server is probably as safe as any method of credit transaction, but the perception is otherwise. Electronic information is readily moveable and relatively easy to access; movies such as *WarGames* and *Sneakers* have suggested the havoc that a wily *cracker* can create. Data cracking and telecommunications technology go hand-in-hand, and many security experts understand that a determined hacker can be the most effective perpetrator of credit-card fraud.

Cryptographic methodology (or crypto) means little to the general public; the mathematical encoding and decoding of messages is often considered something from the realm of spies. But a crypto technique known as *public key encryption* seems to offer a solution for data security that may become commonplace in the near future. Educating the public about this technique will be a challenge unto itself, but the following few paragraphs will suffice for our purposes here.

In the 1970s, a computer scientist named Whitfield Diffie developed a crypto system for which a secure channel was not necessary. In the Diffie system, everyone has two keys: a *public* key that can be widely disseminated and stored, and a private, *secret* key. The sender uses the recipient's public key to produce an encrypted text; the recipient turns this text back into plain text using the private (secret) key. The sender's *digital signature* can also be checked. This would have been encrypted using the sender's secret key; the recipient would use the sender's public key to decrypt the signature. Three researchers used this system to construct the Rivest-Shamir-Adleman (RSA) system, which allowed for the safe passage of keys and messages in a method more robust than any previous scheme.

Current examples of secure transactions using crypto can be seen in the relationship between Netscape's browser and its NetSite Commerce Server using the Secure Sockets Layer protocol (SSL). Upon connecting to a secure site, the browser and server initiate an exchange of keys that sets up a secure channel (http://home.netscape.com/info/security-doc.html). MCI's virtual catalog Web site requires the use of a secure client called *InternetMCI Navigator*. CommerceNet is advocating a security system developed by RSA, NCSA, and Enterprise Integration Technologies. New WWW forms will allow the contents to be encrypted using various methods, including public key, providing a secure communication mechanism between client and server. (At the time of this writing, a demo was available at `http://www.commerce.net/information/examples/demo/cl.secure/cl.info.html`.)

Unfortunately, the deployment and acceptance of such encryption methods is affected by a U.S. Government embargo. The export of American crypto technology is restricted due to its "munitions" applicability. This restriction is certainly detrimental to the creation of electronic commerce in the United States and suggests that the solutions to the "secure channel" problem will come from elsewhere while the United States will be left behind. Governments should be working with the financial institutions to develop regulations and printing "net cash" certificates, not formulating policies to paralyze the virtual marketplace. This embargo (along with the complexity of crypto technology) may necessitate alternate solutions.

Employing crypto and various net/digi-cash initiatives as the solution to this problem is not enough. Educating or convincing Web customers that tools such as Secure Mosaic really are secure will be a public-relations job. Developing robust crypto is important, but most of our trust in such systems will derive from the reputation of the companies involved. The Bank of America and major credit-card companies are working on such systems, and in the next few years an accepted method of digital cash transfer should be in place. At present, this author will continue to use the Web to find solutions to specific problems, to learn about new products, and even to make purchase decisions based on what is learned there. However, the final stage—the actual purchasing—is best handled by traditional methods.

As highlighted above, setting up a Web server is becoming easier, and more and more companies see the dramatic effect that e-mail and leveraging the Web's resources can have. Hooking up a LAN to an environment that is akin to the Wild West, however, has some serious security implications. The platform of choice for most Internet services is UNIX. Connecting a UNIX host to the Internet allows the transfer of e-mail and other IP packets (such as HTTP, FTP, and Telnet) to and from the company network—but at the risk of exposing the network. It is possible to limit the risks; probably the safest route is a firewall—normally a dedicated machine running security software to control incoming and outgoing packets. These can prove expensive and difficult to manage. Among its suite of products, one innovative Internet provider—Netrex, `http://www.netrex.com/`—offers secure connections by maintaining and configuring a firewall at its end of the pipe. Working with the customer, the company develops an access policy to limit the types of connections and packets that can make it to their customers' LAN or WAN. Other options include using encryption and running freely available tools such as COPS (Computer Oracle and Password System), ISS (Internet Security Scanner), or SATAN (System Administrators Tool for Analyzing Networks, `http://www.cs.ruu.nl/cert-uu/satan.html`) to demonstrate the holes a hacker could exploit. A truly determined and experienced hacker may still find a way into a host if the information contained therein is valuable enough. Some say the only safe network is an unconnected one, but many companies are still willing to take the risk.

FIGURE 47.2.

*https://
order.netscape.com/
order.html.
https is HTTP
secure. Notice: Blue
Line indicates a secure
site.*

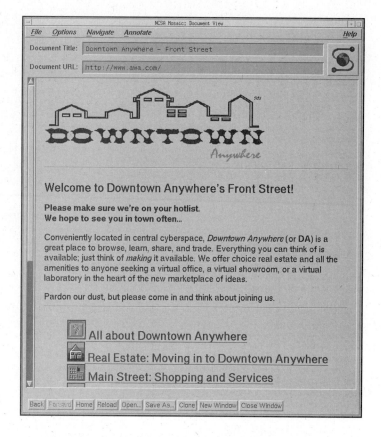

Discussion of these issues is heated in a number of online forums, and many people have concluded that the Web offers an opportunity for a new form of transaction based on strong and unbreakable encryption. (In a particular transaction, the communication could be three-way and instantaneous between the buyer, seller, and credit company/cyberbank.) A related security issue is that with information in the electronic form, it will become easier to move vast databases of sensitive information around, making the risks of industrial espionage, invasion of privacy, and employee theft even greater. Thus, if Web commerce is to become a reality, unbreakable and easy-to-use crypto and security tools are a necessity.

Commercial Interests in Communications Technology

A question in many boardrooms and on all of our lips is quite simply, "Who is going to pay for all this?" One method often mentioned is Pay-Per-View/Use (PPV), which further emphasizes the need for a safe transaction system. Theoretically, the multimedia ability of the Web allows text, graphics, sound, and motion to be downloaded. The Web will one day allow the movement of *virtual products*, so you will read your daily newspaper online, buy and transfer digitized music to disk, get copies of computer games and programs, and transfer other information to your client for personal use. Customers might simply pay for what they get or subscribe to the online *New York Times*, the online Columbia Digitized Music Club, or the Nintendo Games Server.

An examination of the history of communications technology demonstrates the connection between commercial interests and the development of the media. The invention of the printing press allowed the development of newspapers; soon advertising space was being sold, which helped build revenue for the publishers, helped improve coverage and print quality, and helped reduce the cover price. These improvements combined to boost readership. The cycle continued: greater circulation led to increased revenues, better newspapers, and more advertising revenue. The story of radio is similar, and the early advertisers enabled the creation of programming that became part of the American culture. (Even before radio-show sponsorship, the manufacturers of crystal sets had applied for, and been granted, licenses to broadcast. Thus, selling the hardware, even then, depended on the presence of software.) The development of television is even more vivid in our memories, and the relationship between commercialization and the media's content is undeniable.

To sell the medium of television, manufacturers needed killer applications: sitcoms, special effects, sports, and events such as the Super Bowl and NASA moon landings. These applications are intertwined with commercial interests via ads, messages, and sponsorships.

But the virtual marketplace of the traditional broadcast media is one-way. Even the home-shopping channels with their telephone ordering systems are part of the traditional broadcast model. The consumers have no say in what products they can learn about, and they can only learn as much as is broadcast to them. The potential of the World Wide Web is to make a marketplace where communication is two-way and where users have a free choice as to what merchandise they examine.

The broadcast model is not congenial to corporate communications. Corporations cannot exercise editorial control over how their public-relations are handled by the independent media. And the broadcast model does not allow organizations to have direct, two-way contact with key elements of their target audience: the government, shareholders, suppliers, and customers. To accomplish such contact, companies use the telephone, mass mailings, and personal visits; but producing feedback or communication from these constituencies requires additional effort and expense, such as customer surveys and toll-free support lines.

Businesses are starting to see the Web as an alternative to traditional media. Commercial interests, then, should be driving the Web and building the infrastructure, tools, and policies to aid in its development. The Web, if built to its true potential, will become a place where power is not tied to geographic location or the control of raw materials, but to ideas and knowledge. It is in the best interests of companies to get involved—not simply because it is trendy but because the Web offers some real solutions and profit-making possibilities. Those companies that take advantage of the Web will reap the benefits, especially as more potential consumers get on board.

Becoming part of this virtual marketplace is relatively easy. Many organizations already have a computing guru somewhere in their ranks, so setting up a dedicated server should be a possibility. An alternate route is to establish a connection to one of the virtual malls, Web cities, or Net-presence services. (Any organization with an eye on the Web should peruse the page called Interesting Business Sites on the Web, located at URL http://www.rpi.edu/~okeefe/business.html.)

All other media developments were funded and created with advertising dollars and commercial interests in mind. It is not much of an exaggeration to say that the mass media itself is a creation of the advertising industry. The Net, so far, is the exception and has developed very well without commercialization. In fact, the Internet culture is aghast at obvious sales pitches, as was demonstrated when two immigration lawyers tried to sell their services by e-mailing messages to thousands of Net users.

As currently configured, there is no real room on the Web for mass advertising. Only the so-called "Net presence" is accepted, and that will not sell 400 million cans of cola. So far, the American advertising industry has not become seriously involved with the development of the National Information Infrastructure or entered into collaborations with the computer, telephone, and cable companies involved in hard-wiring the Web and developing the applications. The advertising and promotions industries could offer valuable input at this early stage, input that would influence the commercial direction of the I-Way. Certainly commercial involvement could reduce the cost to the consumer and subsidize a PPV system; further, advertising billings could pay for development of the backbone. It is clearly in the best interests of the advertising, public relations, and communication industries to get involved; their futures might depend on it.

Companies need to consider the Web as a viable part of a promotional and communication strategies, and a marketing awareness needs to be added to existing Web sites. It is not surprising to learn that many Web sites have been established by MIS personnel with no input from marketers. The Web can be treated as a combination of a customer-relations hotline, a public-relations outlet, a sales tool, and an advertising medium. Information and documentation contained in Web pages needs to be consistent with the content, messages, and images used in other promotions. The Web should become an integral part of the promotional mix. It will soon be the norm to include e-mail addresses and even URLs in advertisements, sales literature, and business cards.

Encouraging Participation

The future of Web commerce depends on educating decision makers about the inherent advantages of the system. PC sales will remain high—placing computers in many homes—and over the next few years almost all computer owners will be accessing the Net. In 1993, the media hyped up the promise of 500-channel interactive television. The popular press was full of stories about mergers between cable, computer, and telephone companies. Although some experiments have taken place, and set-box/server technology may one day deliver entertainment to our homes, the topic has fallen into disfavor with the media, and the hype has turned into a backlash.

Likewise, media coverage of the Internet, especially relating to business on the Net, has promised much and raised short-term expectations a little too high. It now appears that companies are waiting for the Internet to deliver. The media often accelerates the diffusion of new ideas and new technologies, but in the case of the Net, it appears that the blind are leading the blind; few reporters really know what's going on, and those who do are usually writing for special-interest publications. Within the popular media, we are only very recently seeing articles explaining how to get connected or how to use the Net. (See URL `http://www.dserv.com/~andrew/business.html` for a thorough introduction to getting started in Net-based business.)

News stories suggest that doing business on the Net will allow companies to reach 30 million literate, wealthy, educated professionals via an e-mail message. Unfortunately for the marketers, that is far from the truth at this time. Expectations for the future of the Net have been running too high, and a media backlash might result if it fails to live up to anticipations. One thing that might be overlooked in the backlash is that the Net, unlike interactive TV, is already a tried-and-tested medium of communication. Eventually, with current growth rates, a virtual marketplace on the Web will have a healthy customer base.

Toward Virtual Reality

The convergence of telecommunications and microprocessing has brought us the World Wide Web. Two different technological revolutions—started by Charles Babbage (inventor of the analytical engine, the precursor to the computer) and Guglielomo Marconi (the father of radio) have merged to create a new industry characterized by complex new possibilities and even more complex problems. Computer-mediated business is now functionally possible, and a virtual world is within our grasp. Gibson's vision of cyberspace is perhaps closer than we realize as virtual meeting places become accepted in business and social life.

The interface for most Web GUIs and MUDs is static as well as 2-D and text-reliant, but software such as Meeting Place will soon give a graphical front-end to these worlds. Animation and interactive CAD/CAM applications are now possible with SUN's HotJava Web browser (`http://java.sun.com`), and almost real-time audio is made available by Progessive's "Real Audio" system, `http://www.realaudio.com/`. Further, virtual reality (VR) researchers are working on a VR Markup Language (based on the principles of SGML, HTML, and VR) that will produce a 3-D view of the Web (`http://www.sgi.com/Products/WebFORCE/WebSpace`). The same technology used by the Web will be transformed into a 3-D networked cyberspace that VRML browsers can attach to. According to Chris Hand, VR researcher at De Montfort University, England, "There can be no doubt that in five years time, a proportion of international business transactions will take place in 3-D virtual worlds on the Net. When that happens, [Neal Stephenson's] *Snow Crash* will follow in the footsteps of Musashi's *Book of Five Rings* as the latest Wall Street strategy guide." (For more about graphical meeting places, see URL `http://sunsite.unc.edu/cmc/mag/1994/sep/meetme.html`.)

Before this potential can be realized and virtual worlds on the Web become a reality, many obstacles need to be overcome. There needs to be a solid, high-bandwidth infrastructure, secure transmission and online storage of information, and an acceptance and understanding of this new media by consumers and the business community. Solutions to some of the problems will come from the computer-engineering field and perhaps from dedicated management consultants. Many answers will be found by experimental organizations learning from their bruises. It is possible that companies are holding back because they do not understand the technology or because they are watching the other brave and learning from the others' mistakes.

Participating in this new medium may seem risky, but when decision makers are educated enough, high-profile companies will go online. Some companies may be unwilling to commit venture dollars to the relatively anarchistic, unconstructed, and uninhabited virtual world because of security concerns. But just as pioneers such as Sears managed to reach new markets via the new media of mail order more than 100 years ago, new benchmarks for the Web are being set as companies like Sears and MCI go online, legitimizing the existence—and ensuring the future—of the virtual marketplace.

Challenges for Web Publishers

48

by
John December

Publishing—the process of making a work or information available and known publicly—has remained one of the key processes for transmitting human knowledge. Technologies for publishing have included the human voice, pictograms, alphabets, paper, mass-printed works made on printing presses, and electronic media, including television, radio, and now, global computer networks. Although technologies have changed, many needs for publishers and consumers have not changed—the need for accurate and timely material to publish, the consumer's need for access to publications, and the author's need for reward and intellectual property protection. The Web brings even more, newer needs to publishing, needs that arise from the unique nature of the Web as a medium, its possibilities for content, and the relationships it fosters among people and information.

Web publishing exists within a historical context of media evolution as well as within the changing trends and practices in publishing institutions. Still another context for Web publishing is within the communities of people involved in the creation and consumption of all Web hypermedia, and the specialized needs and interests of people in these communities. As we've seen in other chapters of this book, the Web makes possible new relationships in these contexts and transforms others, creating new space-time patterns for the distribution of works, and makes possible the creation of new works that are composed of unbounded hypertext and hypermedia. As Web technologies enable people to create these new kinds of works, new questions about the needs of publishers, consumers, and authors will arise. These questions include concerns about a range of issues related to online and Internet communication that are still being debated—such as security, authenticity, copyright, and intellectual property.

In this chapter, I focus on the unique challenges the Web brings to publishing in terms of media, content, and relationships. I'll begin by examining the meaning of publishing on the Web—defining the products and processes and noting the Web's media characteristics. Then I'll examine the theme of negotiation as a way to approach Web publishing. Negotiation is a key concept because it relates to a defining characteristic of the Web—its capability to foster relationships.

What Publishing Means on the Web

Modern notions of publishing rely heavily on commerce as a touchstone for significance and quality. Indeed, publishing brands such as "CBS Broadcasting," "Macmillan Computer Publishing," and "Pocket Books" are carefully developed and jealously guarded, because information sellers, authors, and consumers use these brands as a guideposts for choosing media to consider for consumption. These brands are developed over years and decades of careful production and publicity, and entry into the publishing arena at the level of national brands in books and television is extremely expensive and difficult. As a result, a new publisher faces the material expense of building the physical production and distribution facilities as well as the extremely difficult task of building a team of talented people to create content. The result of this high-entry barrier is that when an offline publisher presents something for sale, the consumer is reasonably assured (or carefully seduced to believe) that the product is of good quality and worth watching or buying—the expense of its production and distribution demand it.

So whereas the brands of offline publishing marry material scarcity and distribution costs to implications of value, the online world obliterates both material scarcity and distribution limitations, disconnecting notions of value from these factors. With the Web, anyone can become a global publisher and add to an information space that today is fairly choked with new material of widely varying quality. Therefore, on the Web, no longer can just the power to create and broadcast messages to large numbers of people across large distances be a measure of information quality.

Not only is global reach not necessarily a marker of quality, but it isn't even a guarantee of effectiveness in communication. Information spaces on the Net, and in particular on the Web, have become saturated and are rapidly becoming polluted with redundant, incorrect, or "junk" information. This late-stage saturated information space requires aggressive skills in Web publishing to create and promote quality information. Future "intelligent agents" may filter this thinning information soup to attempt to create meaning for the user, but even the most intelligent agent can't transform junk information into value. Instead, the key to Web publishing will be the work of intelligent humans—authors, editors, and publishers—to create works of significance, intelligence, and value, and to make these works widely known.

Therefore, publishing on the Web doesn't hinge so much on the mechanics of it—people can easily learn HTML and a methodology for weaving webs. (See Part V, "Weaving a Web.") Instead, the tough challenge for Web publishers lies in managing a Web work's dynamic life cycle and negotiating its relationships with the information, communication, and interaction communities on the Web and the Net. For paper works, this "role negotiation" involves placing a book in a bookstore or on a library shelf, as well as marketing and promotion. The paper work's reputation then rises or falls based on the reputation it gains as a fixed object within personal, academic, or professional environments. People judging paper works do so largely outside of the context of the work's creation and delivery; authors and editors are rarely available at a bookstore for discussion, and a paper work is often far removed from situations and contexts that gave rise to it. Thus, the paper work's media characteristics as an object bound by space and time force it to "free float" in the larger context of human activity.

In contrast, Web works are tied to the context of the Web and the relationships that the links into and out of the work foster. Instead of being free-floating, a Web work may be linked to other Web works, and other Web works can link to it. The resulting mesh contextualizes a Web work—links from the work to the authors' home pages, links from user pages to the work, and links in indexes and spider databases to the work. Some of these links indicate value (when people link to a work they consider is good), whereas other links are simply for reference; an entry in a spider database simply indicates existence and is not a marker for a work's quality. However, all links help define the reputation of a work on the Web, as well as the possible routes to it, and the creation of a work plus the negotiation of these links is the main challenge of a Web publisher.

Figure 48.1 summarizes how a paper and Web work differ in time/space and context bindings. A paper work is bound in space and time (paper copies of a work occupy one point in space/time) yet is free-floating within the contexts of its use. (People can take a paper work anywhere, far from connections to its authors or editors, and with no direct connections even to other texts.) In contrast, a Web work is unbound in time/space (unlimited numbers of copies are available worldwide at any time), yet can be deeply bound within the context of hyperlinks made from it (links out) and links made to the work (links in).

FIGURE 48.1.

A Web work and a paper work have different time/ space and context bindings.

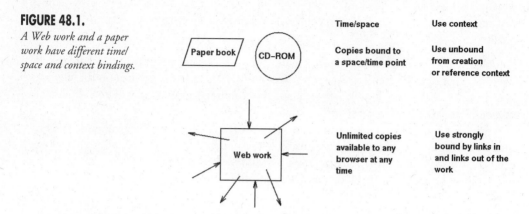

Based on the preceding discussion, we can state a definition for Web publishing:

> Web publishing involves the processes of creation, acquisition, development, editing, distribution, and promotion of information or communication content (products) on the World Wide Web for the purpose of negotiating the reputation of these products within communities of consumers.

Web publishing thus involves being an information provider as well as an editor, judge, and promoter. The key in this definition is negotiation. For commercial Web publishers such as *Hotwired* (see Figure 48.2), this process of negotiating involves creating interest among a particular group of Web users to draw attention to commercial sponsors (selling not content, but the eyes and ears of the audience to the advertisers), such as to ZIMA in Figure 48.3. *Hotwired* has the additional task of promoting its paper-based counterpart, *Wired* magazine. Therefore, *Hotwired*'s goal for acquiring and developing content is for information that is significant for its audience, and that creates a unique cultural "persona" for their web, drawing the attention and interest of individuals in the target Web communities.

In the next sections, we'll examine the Web's medium, content, and relationships. We'll explore how Web publishing is largely a process of negotiating connections among consumers to content, as well as from consumer to consumer, with the content as the context for interaction.

FIGURE 48.2.

Hotwired.

FIGURE 48.3.

An advertisement in Hotwired.

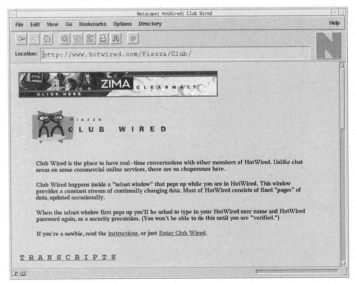

Negotiating the Medium

The product of Web publishing, a web, is a set of hypertext pages that is considered to be a single work or a *site* for a collection of similar or related works. A web has some inherent qualities as media with regard to time, porousness, dynamism, interactivity, and competitiveness. A Web work is

■ *Unbound in space-time:* Unlike paper works that are bound by space (replicated copies each occupy a particular point in space-time), Web works are accessible regardless of the physical location of the server or browser. (Of course, the server and browser must have Net or local network access.) Web works are generally available any time (barring network or server disruptions) to anyone with a browser, and the user can retrieve an arbitrary number of copies.

■ *Porous:* Web text is *unbounded* text—text that can extend, augment, or continue its meaning through links to other texts located throughout the Web and Net; any page of a Web text can be linked to or from another Web work. Moreover, a well-designed web doesn't consist of just one "monster" page, but a series of connected pages, each of which can serve as an entry point to the whole web. This unbounded nature of a web differs from the model of a paper book. In a paper book, pages exist in a bound order with no possibilities for recombination (except through physical destruction of the book). A web is like a paper book with its spine torn away, and all its pages free-floating among all the pages of similarly "exploded" books. Figure 48.4 shows how Web pages exist in a "cloud" of hypertext on the Web, and each page is a possible entry or exit point for the work; whereas a paper book's pages permit examination only in their bound form.

FIGURE 48.4.

A web is more porous than a paper book.

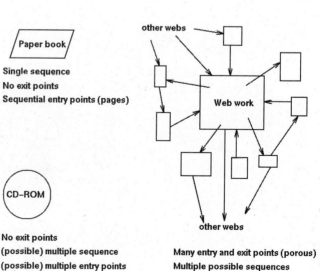

Paper book

Single sequence
No exit points
Sequential entry points (pages)

CD–ROM

No exit points
(possible) multiple sequence
(possible) multiple entry points

other webs

Web work

other webs

Many entry and exit points (porous)
Multiple possible sequences

■ *Dynamic:* A paper book is fixed at its time of printing; there are no possibilities for changing the content of a delivered text. In contrast, Web pages are continually changeable; pages of a Web text can be updated on a regular basis, and the link relationships and the pages included in a work can be altered or even generated on the fly. In its intended use, pages of a Web text are never actually "obtained" by the user permanently (except if printed or saved), but only downloaded into the browser's current memory cache. In contrast, a book buyer "owns" the pages he or she purchases, but those pages remain fixed in their printed form.

■ *Interactive:* The Web has features that permit users to construct their own path through information (with features such as hyperlinks, Forms, imagemaps, and hotlists) and to more easily contact or find more about authors, editors, and distributors (e-mail addresses, home pages). The result is that a Web user has a far greater choice when encountering material than does someone watching television (who can only change channels, not redirect the storyline of a program) or reading a book (he or she can flip and skip pages but not reveal further depths of information other than what's on the surface text). The Web doesn't guarantee interactivity (some web designs don't incorporate it), but interactivity is a possibility; the basis of the Web as a system for associative linking reinforces user control.

■ *Competitive:* Competition for attention among Web works happens all in the same arena—the open Web, with public trees and spiders, as well as branded content providing the navigational landmarks. This situation isn't too different from competition among television shows appearing in the *television space*—the set of all channels available to a viewer. However, the competition among Web works is further flattened because each web is delivered in the same form—in HTML—and is available to anyone on the Web (in contrast to local or cable television, or books that might be distributed only to certain stores in certain cities). So without production quality differences or distribution advantages, the only way for one web to distinguish itself from the next is through excellent design and content. This situation is like a ballroom dance where all the dancers of the same gender look the same (are physical clones) and are dressed in identical clothing. The participants can seek a dance partner only by distinguishing themselves by that which is not physical—such as by personality or intellectual qualities and character. This "flattening" of the Web's visual competitiveness only changes when some developers become more skilled in content development, design, and promotion; as Web space becomes saturated, users rely more on *branded content* to serve as a guidepost for content choices. The result is that the competition for attention on the Web is fierce—particularly in the early saturation stage of the Web's life cycle—when there are so many pages on so many servers one human cannot traverse them all.

The key for Web publishers is to use each of these characteristics to their advantage in publishing works on the Web. Techniques to do this are still evolving, but here is an overview of practices:

■ *Time-space practices:*

a. Because space is irrelevant in distribution, unique content that is locally produced becomes highly valuable. This might seem to be a contradiction—why would local material be valuable when global distribution is possible? The answer lies in the economics of scarcity; in the scope of a global environment, local information is a very small portion of the whole information space. Being very rare, well-done local information becomes very valuable. For example, community-based networks that give a rich, extremely detailed view of the geographically based communities they represent are "authoritative sources" for that locale, and often no one else in the world could give such a detailed view of that area. Thus, in negotiating the characteristic of space, Web publishers can focus locally (develop rare, unique information) and distribute globally (publish it in a very wide space where this information is rare and therefore valuable).

b. Around-the-clock potential for access, like the irrelevancy of space, establishes another Web publishing principle:

Time is an effect to shape meaning and content, not just an arbitrary stop/start marker. Instead of a time block set arbitrarily for broadcasting new content (for example, the Letterman Show on CBS at 11:35 p.m. EST each night), the Web enables a round-the-clock broadcast of information (for example, the Letterman home page on `http://www.cbs.com/`). Without an arbitrary time block for new content to appear, Web publishers have the opportunity to set a new rhythm of change and flux for their published works. A daily or hourly update of some information, and a less frequent change for other information, might be the right combination to affect users.

■ *Porousness practices:* Many publishers might be uncomfortable with a highly porous medium like the Web, when any one page of a work could be appropriated or linked within the context of another. Moreover, links out of a work could always lead the user far off into the Web, perhaps permanently away from the original work. However, a work that subverts the natural porousness of Web hypertext is often either a "monster page" or a poorly designed web with poor information-chunking and page design. The appropriation of a single web page is not a negative effect; a well-designed individual page can always draw the user back to the larger context of the work in which it exists through information and navigation cues and links. Similarly, links out of a web may expand, extend, or suggest comparisons—and these are essential parts of creating meaning with hypertext. Therefore, a Web publisher often works best in encouraging porous design and use of a published web.

■ *Dynamism practices:* As described in Part V, web weaving is often a continuous process. A dynamic web adds value to the same or similar information that could be supplied on paper. Similar to the concept of time as a means to achieve meaning, so too can dynamism play a role in expressions on the Web. Rates of change in a web's information can be set to best meet a user's particular needs for a given purpose.

■ *Interactivity practices:* Although Forms and imagemaps allow Web publishers to solicit feedback from users, the whole force of a web need not always be to include maximum (or even any degree of) interactivity. Hypermedia might enable a user to "write" the end of a novel—but who wants to write the end of a novel? Interactivity practices are still emerging on the Web—database lookups using Forms, feedback from users with Forms, and imagemaps for information mapping or hypertext selection are some of the present applications of interactivity in Web publishing.

■ *Competition practices:* Just as competition among offline organizations often fosters rising levels of quality and excellence to attract users, the Web's highly competitive nature can pressure excellence in Web publishing. For non-fee webs, a user can very easily click away to another location if the current web isn't fitting his or her needs. A Web publisher may need to view competition itself as a resource—as a way of identifying weak aspects of a web or as an indication that the publishing activity requires collaboration with other similar webs, to form coalitions to provide higher levels of integrated value to users.

Negotiating Content

The content of a published web, just like the qualities of a web, can differ from (and also share some characteristics with) traditional media. A web's content can

■ *Involve collaborative structures:* Often, large webs are the process of collaboration in different forms. For example, a Web-based "hypergraffiti" board (using interactive Forms to enable a user to place any message or URL on a particular Web page) could be part of a "published" web. A more common way of collaborating on a large web is through distributed development and maintenance. A good example of this is the World Wide Web Virtual Library (`http://www.w3.org/hypertext/DataSources/bySubject/Overview.html`), where branches and leaves of the subject tree are maintained by practitioners in that topic.

■ *Foster user-to-user activity and connections:* Traditional paper-based publications involve one-way distribution of text, but also can include reader feedback in the form of letters to the editor or other contributed material. Web publications open up more possibilities for interactions among readers. For example, *Hotwired*, *Wired* magazine's online counterpart, includes connections to an online real-time text discussion server, ClubWired (`telnet://chat.hotwired.com:2428`). ClubWired is a forum for author or other Net personality interviews, as well as a place that users can log in anytime and take part in discussions in channels on the talk area, such as Cafe Wired, Hotwired Central, and the Amphitheater (where guest interviews are conducted). This real-time, user-directed activity adds a dimension over the traditional, one-way text. Another example of connecting users to each other is Global Network Navigator (GNN)'s Netizens collection (`http://gnn.com/gnn/netizens/index.html`). Users can register their home page in this collection, and the collection itself is listed on GNN's home page. The result is that the users of *Hotwired* or GNN view those publications not just as places to retrieve information, but as forms for making contacts and interacting with other users.

■ *Encourage Interactivity:* Just as *Hotwired*'s ClubWired fosters interactivity at the user level, Web publication often give the opportunity for users to make comments or annotate selected content in a publication. For example, some publications use the interactive Forms in HTML to solicit input or comments from users that can then be attached directly to the web page.

Another aspect of interactivity is the ease with which users of a Web publication might be able to contact the authors and publishers, either through e-mail or by viewing Web pages. Although paper-based publications can encourage this (listing phone numbers or postal mail addresses), the ease of online communication makes reader-to-author or reader-to-publisher interaction more likely.

■ *Bind a work within context of social/cultural activities on the Web: Hotwired*'s ClubWired creates a social dimension for both *Hotwired*'s text and other one-way (broadcast) content. ClubWired also expands the reputation of its paper counterpart (*Wired* magazine) as a cutting-edge publication serving as a mouthpiece of the "digital generation." In a much subtler way, all Web publications, through the associative nature of linking, can bind themselves to the larger social or cultural expressions of a special interest group on the Web. For example, music enthusiasts can access Time, Inc.'s, *Vibe* (http://www.timeinc.com/vibe/) and catch the latest news about urban music or American youth culture. A survey of the Lycos spider database (http://lycos.cs.cmu.edu) turned up more than 600 references to *Vibe* on Web pages.

Negotiating Relationships

As I have described, the Web's media and content characteristics intermingle in many respects and share common themes: associations and linking, user choices, and publishers' choices for determining and developing content. Within these interactions, the theme of *relationships* also plays a profound role—the basis of the Web as a system for associative linking marks it as a medium filled with relationships. These relationships often are revealed in the links of a web, in the connections from a web to its creators, or in the links that users of a work make from their own work to a published web. All of these relationships must be negotiated: consumer-product relationships need a model for monetary transactions; author-user relationships require means for efficient communication; and user-to-user relationships need some context and purpose for adding value to a published work.

Models for Commercial Web Publishing

Trying to make commerce the central focus of a published Web work could very possibly fail. *Commodification* (the process of making a commodity out of something) as the driving force behind a web design may fragment the experience of a web into a series of transactions instead of a seamless experience driven by user interest, curiosity, and whims. Instead, other models for Web commerce may develop:

- *Pay-access models:*

    Pay-per-view model: A user pays for just the web pages or multimedia files downloaded, not the entire publication.

    Pay-for-acquisition model: Just as a user picks up a magazine at a newsstand or receives it by subscription, so too might a user on the Web either pay for access to an entire work (through a password system or a subscription e-mail system). Note how this model increases the salience of the entire publication as context, whereas the pay-per-view model emphasizes the value of individual segments of the publication.

    Pay-for-context model: This is another step up in granularity level from the pay-per-view and pay-for-acquisition models. Instead of paying for access to just a publication, the user pays for access to a broader context of activities surrounding that publication; for example, not only to the Web-based magazine (such as *Hotwired*), but for access to the user-to-user interaction areas (ClubWired) and other communication and information that forms a larger community or context for the publication. This model is close to the one-price amusement parks, where the user pays a single fee and can enjoy any attraction of the park for no further charge.

- *Free-access models:*

    No advertisements: This model provides the publication entirely for free without advertisement or product endorsement. Typical use might be for academic journals or special-interest publications oriented to highly motivated and specialized audiences with few alternative channels for their specialized interests.

    Advertisements: This model is similar to typical current free throwaway paper publications; advertising pays for all of the content, and the publication circulates as widely as possible.

    Sponsored: In this model, a single commercial interest pays for a publication and gains advertising/prestige or other customers for its commercial interests through this sponsorship. One example of this is a commercial entity hosting a Web publication that is often used (for example, The Internet Business Center sponsors Hobbes' Internet Timeline to draw traffic to its server, `http://tig.com/IBC/Timeline.html`).

    Product placements: Just as products are subtly placed within movies as advertisements, hotlinks to commercial products and sites can be placed within published webs focusing on related (or unrelated) activities or entertainment. (For example, the Stoli Vodka "coloring book" at `http://www.stoli.com/` is a small model of this.)

- *Service models:*

    Support-service: The commercial interest creates a free service (the published content) that adds value to their services provided for money (for example, Federal Express's package-tracking service at `http://www.fedex.com/`).

Information-service: The commercial interest creates publications that guide users in making the most out of, or selecting, their products (for example, Saturn automobiles at `http://www.saturncars.com/`).

Models for Author-User Relationships

The monetary relationships involved in transactions of most commercial products often also delimit user expectations about interactions with authors or producers of a work. A customer who sees the movie *Forrest Gump* for $7.50 doesn't expect to have any further interaction with the movie's creators or actors. Because the Web can bind a web publication within the context of communication and interaction with its creators, however, Web users may have different expectations. An author is more accessible on the Net, making more feedback (and perhaps better works) possible.

Most significantly, Web publishing can blur the distinction between author and user. With interactivity and with published Web works bound tightly in the context of their use in Web communities of interest, the users of works may play a major role in extending, maintaining, and developing meaning, turning the Web publisher into a more of a supplier of resources and infrastructure for the users to create new content.

Future Challenges

Considering these negotiations a Web publisher must balance—among media, content, and relationships—the fundamental challenge remains to carve out valuable meaning for others to use. Changes in technology, and perhaps more importantly social communities and contexts for Web use, will play a great role in shaping the future of Web publishing.

In specific, the future for Web publishers involves

- *User challenges:* Web publishers need to ensure that there are a large number of motivated and educated users who have the Net and Web literacy skills to make use of the medium of the Web. This is analogous to the book and newspaper publishers' special interest in literacy, both as a social good in itself and as a means to ensure interest in and use of their products.

- *Medium challenges:* A Web publisher needs to create an identity and a niche within a medium that might stubbornly resist many features that foster success for paper-based publications. Where commodification of entire issues of magazines makes sense for paper publications, Web use and Net traditions might resist these models. Commodification of any publication implies a self-sufficiency and boundaries that are antagonistic to the porous nature of Web hypermedia. So although the Web may continue to stubbornly resist commodity model, it might foster instead a contextual, community model for distribution, access, and payment.

- *Legitimacy challenges:* Whereas material scarcity and distribution expense often implied legitimacy (the view that an expensively produced publication implies that it has high-quality content), markers for legitimacy and reputation on the Web may be harder to achieve. The fluid nature of information value and currency could easily shift reputations rapidly among Web publishers. However, just as with paper publishing institutions, longevity, consistency, and a strong presence in the medium may provide the best avenue to achieving legitimacy.

- *Authorship challenges:* Just as the Web might shift relationships so that users can become authors, so too might it obliterate or weaken the notion of an individual author. In fact, the connected Web itself has no single author, and a Web publication linked extensively to other Web works draws on the work of many other authors. Paper works foster boundaries and authorship; Web works push at the edges of both.

- *Practice challenges:* Although Marshall McLuhan cautioned against using new media in old ways, it is naive to think that a new medium *necessarily* implies new practices devoid of connections with the old. The Web as a medium blends writing and design, technical communication, associative linking, analogic thinking, and hypermedia possibilities. All of these activities involve shaping meaning—something humans have been doing for millennia. Moreover, all human communication takes place in a social context, and human social practices strongly determine the success of the Web, not only the inherent properties of the technology (for example, witness the repeated failure of the picture phone despite the decades-long hype about it). Humans have adopted media for communication for millennia and have adapted new practices and expressions for each, powerfully drawing from the social practices, traditions, and needs of the time. In other words, Web publishers are challenged to remain unblinded by technology, and attend to the larger context of online activity meeting human needs.

Web Publisher's Check

Unlike content fixed in a paper book or CD-ROM, the content of a web can exhibit unbound time-space characteristics, porousness, dynamism, interactivity, and competitiveness. Using these characteristics to the best advantage, a Web publisher must negotiate the content of a web and its relationships with users. A web's content often fosters collaborative relationships among users and producers/authors. Within these relationships, Web publishers have options for commercial publishing, introducing advertisements or connecting consumers to producers in ways that intersect the paths a user follows when interacting with a web. Models for commercial commerce include pay-access, free-access, and service models. In the end, Web publishers are challenged to transcend practices that merely treat publishing as a commodification of content, but balance the information, communication, and interaction needs of people in online communities.

Conferencing on the Web

49

by
David R. Woolley

Bianca's Smut Shack is definitely one of the most happening spots on the Web. Alongside music reviews and tips about fun things to do in Chicago is a "room" where you can converse with the surly troll who lives atop Bianca's dresser. The troll likes to ask prying personal questions and responds mostly with insults. You can also sign the guest book, leaving your name, e-mail address, and favorite recipe. Or if you're feeling more scatological, you can step into Bianca's bathroom and read the graffiti left by other visitors. If you want to add your own anonymous pearls of wisdom, just choose a wall and let loose. Because HTML is available, you can spice up your message with large type or italics, or even include active links to other Web pages.

Although graffiti boards like Bianca's are fun, they're not of much practical use. But they do offer a key feature that lies at the heart of all online conferencing systems: the ability to post a message in a public place for others to read. Conferencing has been available on the Internet for years in the form of Usenet newsgroups. When support for forms input was added to HTML, it opened the door to conferencing on the Web.

What do I mean by "conferencing"? It's an overworked term, but it will have to do until something better becomes generally accepted. For my purposes, *conferencing* is a form of group discussion that uses text messages stored on a computer as a medium for communication. Usenet newsgroups, CompuServe forums, message boards on America Online, and Lotus Notes discussion databases are all examples. I'm *not* referring to real-time video or audio conferencing, nor to facilities like CompuServe's CB Simulator or America Online's chat rooms, which instantly relay typed messages between participants who are online at the same time.

Graffiti boards offer little structure for the posted messages. Each new message is simply tacked on to the top (or bottom) of the page. In this sense, these Web pages resemble the early electronic bulletin board systems that began to pop up in the late seventies and early eighties. It is possible to write a message responding to an earlier posting, but because it is just tossed into a big pot along with unrelated messages, with no connection between the original message and the reply, it's difficult to carry on an extended conversation.

For true conferencing, some structure is essential. In particular, the system must support *threading*, the ability to sequentially read the messages that make up one discussion. You need to be able to read all the way through the conversation about where to get the best sushi in Boise without having celebrity gossip and announcements about used stereo equipment for sale mixed in. Several conferencing systems now evolving on the Web offer such threading. But how much structure do you need?

WIT: The Perils of Too Much Structure

W3 Interactive Talk makes for a nice acronym, but it's something of a misnomer. It sounds like a chat system akin to CompuServe's CB Simulator. In reality, WIT is a highly structured conferencing system designed for group decision making.

WIT was a quick hack by Ari Luotonen of CERN, who put it together in a few days immediately following the WWW '94 Conference. Participants of the conference desired a way to carry on prolonged group discussions about technical issues related to Web development.

The weaknesses of Usenet and mailing lists for such a purpose are well known. Mailing-list discussions have no inherent structure at all, making it difficult to maintain more than one or two threads of conversation. In a Usenet newsgroup, a message can be posted specifically as a response to another message, but the overall structure tends to be rather chaotic. Also, Usenet messages typically disappear within a week or two, leaving no permanent record of what points have been raised and what issues have been settled.

By contrast, a WIT discussion takes the form of a permanent, continuously expanding hierarchical tree. The tree can branch out indefinitely, but the top three levels of the hierarchy have specific purposes and are labeled accordingly:

- **Topic:** An issue to be resolved
- **Proposal:** A statement up for discussion, related to a topic
- **Argument**: An argument for or against a proposal

Arguments are also called *articles*; the two terms are used interchangeably. There can be arguments to arguments, and arguments to arguments to arguments, and so on. Any participant can start topics and write proposals or arguments.

When you enter WIT, you see a welcoming message describing the purpose of the discussion area, followed by a list of topics. Selecting a topic takes you to the page for that topic. Topic, proposal, and argument pages all have a few things in common: a title, the date, the author's name, and text. They differ, however, in what appears in the text. A *topic page* lists only the proposals associated with the topic. But a *proposal page* shows the entire tree of arguments branching off of the proposal. An icon next to each argument indicates its type: a white checkmark for an agreement, a red X for a disagreement. (See Figure 49.1.) An *argument page* is similar to a proposal page, except that only the portion of the tree branching off of that particular argument is displayed.

The list of checkmarks and Xs can give you a quick sense of how a proposal is being received without requiring you to read all of the arguments. Looks can be deceiving, though: An agreement to a disagreement (are you still with me?) shows up as a white checkmark, although it argues *against* the proposal!

Of course, as soon as WIT was released, the structure of WIT itself became the most popular subject of discussion. One problem that has been noted by many participants is that each article is forced to either agree or disagree. What if you want to add a pertinent comment that does neither? What if you agree with some points of a proposal and not with others? Some people suggested adding a third button next to Agree and Disagree, labeled Other or Idea.

FIGURE 49.1.

A WIT proposal.

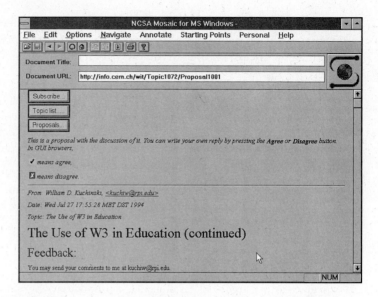

Another problem is that every branch off of a topic is labeled a *proposal*. But some topics need to branch into subtopics rather than into proposals. One participant suggested that, in addition to proposals and arguments, there might be questions, answers, merits, demerits, summaries, categories, qualifiers, and reframes. Another suggested that proposals be broken down into subproposals called *points*. Yet another asked for a way to rank arguments on various scales, such as serious to humorous, or friendly to flaming.

The limitations imposed by WIT's structure become immediately apparent when you start to use it for a discussion. Most of the suggestions for improving it center on extending the structure to accommodate a wider variety of comments. Yet the more classifications that are added, the more confusing and harder to use the system becomes. Deciding exactly where to place a response and how to categorize it becomes a major chore. And inevitably, arguments develop over such choices ("That's not a summary, that's a new proposal!"). Eventually, either the system will collapse under its own weight, or the participants will begin to ignore the structure and use it however they please.

Because WIT was implemented so quickly, a lot of obviously needed features were left out. For example, navigation between messages is rudimentary, and there is no good way to find messages written since your last visit. But even with improvements in these areas, WIT's structure will make it awkward for general-purpose conferencing.

HyperNews: The Next Usenet?

Along with WIT, HyperNews was one of the first conferencing systems to appear on the Web. Like WIT, HyperNews uses a hierarchical tree structure, but it's a simpler structure with only two types of messages: base articles and responses. (See Figure 49.2.)

The creator of HyperNews, Daniel LaLiberte, hopes that it will evolve into a next-generation replacement for Usenet. One of Usenet's biggest problems is its redundancy: Each widely distributed newsgroup is replicated on countless news servers around the world, consuming huge amounts of disk space. Consequently, messages must be thrown away quickly to make room for new ones. This, in turn, leads to another kind of redundancy, as people repeatedly ask the same questions and hash out the same issues. Rather than building a repository of knowledge, Usenet is forever locked into a cycle of destroying and re-creating the same knowledge time and time again.

FIGURE 49.2.

A HyperNews discussion.

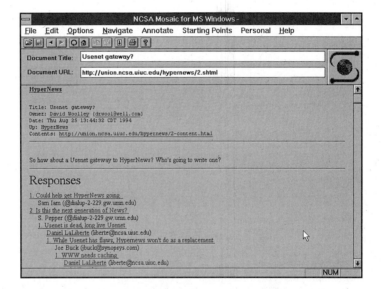

A HyperNews discussion does not rely on such massive replication. It can exist on a single server yet still be available worldwide through the Web. Because each HyperNews server only needs to host a few discussions, it should be possible to keep messages for a much longer time, perhaps forever.

LaLiberte's vision extends beyond conferencing. HyperNews, or something like it, could be used as a structure for organizing vast amounts of information. For the purposes of finding a particular piece of information, HyperNews would appear as a hierarchical tree with general subject areas near the top and finer divisions of knowledge farther down. But because lateral connections between documents are also possible, the true structure would be a constantly evolving web. Some areas of the web would be mostly discussion, whereas others would be mostly static information, but responses would be possible anywhere. LaLiberte has some innovative, yet-to-be-implemented ideas regarding discussions, such as allowing a message to be linked as a response to multiple articles, and the ability to snip off a subtree of responses and attach it somewhere else in the web.

This is an ambitious concept, to say the least, and LaLiberte does not claim to have solved the myriad of thorny issues it raises. I am less convinced than he of the value of keeping everything forever. Do we really need to save every byte posted to `alt.mcdonalds.ketchup` for the benefit of our children's children?

The next version of HyperNews will allow users to subscribe to specific articles, so they will be notified by e-mail when new responses are posted. This could be useful in keeping slow-paced discussions alive, but when a discussion becomes very active it would quickly become a burden both to the participants and to the HyperNews server hosting the discussion.

Although HyperNews holds interesting possibilities, the current implementation is a bare-bones system at about the same early stage of development as WIT—that is, not ready for prime time.

LaLiberte recently joined NCSA, where he is applying many of his ideas to an annotation system that will let readers leave comments for the owners of Web documents. Flexible access controls will allow an owner to accept annotations either from the general public or from a specified group of people only, and determine whether annotations are visible to others. If visitors are able to read and respond to annotations by other people, annotation begins to blur into conferencing.

HotWired and The Gate: The Flow of Conversation

HotWired burst on to the scene in October, 1994. HotWired's hype overplayed their innovations a bit: They trumpeted *HotWired* as the first Web site to offer conferencing, ignoring the fact that WIT and HyperNews were there several months earlier. Nonetheless, *HotWired* was the first *commercial* site to support conferencing.

HotWired calls its conferencing system *Threads*. What distinguishes Threads from most other conferencing software is that it presents each discussion as a single stream of text, rather than as a collection of discrete messages. In this, its design was obviously influenced by PicoSpan, the UNIX-based conferencing software used on the WELL.

The WELL was born in 1985, and by the early 1990s had gained a reputation as perhaps *the* place to find intelligent conversation online. In terms of membership, it is dwarfed by services like CompuServe and America Online, but the WELL's renown and influence are far out of proportion to its size. Many WELL adherents attribute its success in large part to the way PicoSpan structures conversations.

In Threads (as on the WELL), a topic consists of an initial message followed by a linear string of responses. There is no branching within a topic, as there is in Usenet and HyperNews. Each new response is attached to the end of the topic, rather than to a particular prior response. While reading, you can scroll through an entire topic without having to press a key or click a button to move from message to message. As a result, reading a topic in Threads feels more like following a "real life" conversation than it does in most other conferencing systems.

On the Web, there is an additional reason to design conferencing software this way. When you request a Web page, there is usually a noticeable delay while the server is contacted. A document can be transmitted very quickly once the connection is made, but still, the delays in moving from one page to another can be frustrating. Transmitting an entire topic as one document minimizes the number of separate transactions the client must make with the server. So there are fewer delays while reading messages, making the experience much more pleasant.

Threads does not keep track of what you have read, but it does let you filter messages so as to see only those written since a certain time. Unfortunately, the only way to specify the "since" cutoff is in hours. Quick, how many hours since 8:00 p.m. last Tuesday?

Threads has other design problems as well. Within a conference, the topic list displays the full text of the first message in each topic. This makes the topic list itself look like a conversation, which is very disorienting. Also, the term "thread" is used to refer to what most systems call a conference or forum, and that is confusing to anyone familiar with other conferencing systems. "Thread" usually refers to a single conversation within a conference.

In the spring of 1995, Threads gained a cousin when San Francisco's two daily newspapers, the *Chronicle* and the *Examiner*, jointly opened a Web service called The Gate. The Gate's conferencing system is also modeled after the WELL. That's no surprise, given that it was created by John "Tex" Coate, who was the WELL's conferencing manager for six years.

The Gate's conferencing is not as glitzy as Threads, nor does it offer as many ways to sort, filter, and view messages. But this might actually be a benefit. Whereas navigation in Threads can be confusing, navigating The Gate is straightforward. The Gate is less cluttered with buttons and features, yet it offers one crucial feature that Threads lacks: It remembers what you have read and shows only the messages that you haven't yet seen. The biggest problem with The Gate is its performance; moving from page to page seems to take forever.

Although both Threads and The Gate suffer from flaws, they are the first Web-based conferencing systems that display a conversation as a continuous flow. It would be good to see this become a standard feature of conferencing software.

WebNotes: A Solid Foundation

WebNotes represents a very different approach to implementing conferencing on the Web. A product of OS TECHnologies Corporation, based in Townsend, Massachusetts, WebNotes is the first commercially marketed conferencing software for the Web. It is also the most robust and feature rich.

What distinguishes WebNotes is that it is not a stand-alone system, but an interface to a client–server conferencing system. In a *client–server* system, the client is a piece of software running on a user's computer, and the server software typically runs unattended on a centrally located computer, responding to requests by clients. The key to a client–server application is the definition of a *protocol*, or common language, through which a client can access or update information stored on a server. It is a way of achieving platform independence: The server doesn't care what hardware or operating system the client is running on, and the client doesn't care what platform the server is using, as long as both client and server speak the same language. The World Wide Web itself is based on this concept, and it could never have achieved such phenomenal success otherwise.

The particular client–server software that WebNotes is built upon is a full-featured conferencing system called NetNotes, also made by OS TECHnologies. NetNotes is not the first conferencing system to use a client–server design. Lotus Notes, DEC Notes, and most other conferencing systems used in the corporate world are based on client–server technology.

A typical use for NetNotes is to allow employees of a company to communicate over a local area network. But with an Internet connection and the WebNotes add-on, a NetNotes server is capable of inexpensively hosting discussions among participants around the world. NetNotes client software is currently available only for Windows and the Macintosh, but WebNotes in effect allows any Web browser to act as a NetNotes client.

In terms of features, WebNotes/NetNotes is unmatched. It keeps track of what you have read, an essential but rare feature among Web conferencing systems. Navigation is both flexible and easy. The server includes a high-speed search engine, enabling you to quickly find messages by author, keyword, or other criteria. The user interface is highly configurable to accommodate individual preferences.

The only features of NetNotes not available through the Web interface are conference host privileges and the capability to attach binary files (executable programs, spreadsheet files, and so on) to messages. The plan is to implement binary file attachments as soon as the HTML 3.0 specification is established. One use for this feature might be to embed an image in a message. As for host privileges, they will have to wait until standards are in place for secure transactions on the Web. A conference host can delete messages posted by other people, change access privileges, and do other things that could wreak havoc on a conference. With security on the Web as lax as it is today, it would be dangerous to allow these functions to be performed over the Web.

WebNotes is not only a better performer than any other Web conferencing software available today, it is built on a foundation that is interoperable with other platforms, and that will allow it to evolve along with the rapidly changing technology of the Web.

What About Usenet?

You might be wondering why not just make Usenet available through the Web?

That's certainly possible. Two different approaches have been taken: building a newsreader into a Web browser, and creating a Usenet gateway on a Web server.

Netscape Navigator is an example of the first approach. It has a built-in newsreader that is adequate for occasional browsing, but lacks many of the capabilities found in traditional, full-featured newsreaders. Mosaic's newsreader is even more primitive: There is no threading, and it doesn't allow you to post messages.

The Forum News Gateway takes the second approach. It is a server-based gateway developed by the Geometry Forum at Swarthmore College. The gateway accesses a newsgroup on demand and converts each article to HTML for display. Each user's personal subscription files, which keep track of which articles have been read, are stored on the server—a big advantage for people who use more than one computer to read news (at work and at home, for instance). The gateway is easy to use, and has some nice features such as the ability to highlight or kill (skip) articles about a certain subject or by a certain author. Unfortunately, it is painfully slow. This is mainly because it is written in Perl and is implemented in such a way that it can handle only one request at a time, so the server tends to bog down when a number of users are reading news at the same time. At this point, the Forum News Gateway is a good prototype, but it would need to be completely rewritten before it could be a viable product.

In any case, it will not be possible to make the best use of the Web's capabilities through Usenet. For instance, a Usenet message could contain HTML formatting and hypertext links, but it would be readable only by other Web users. To anyone using a standard newsreader, the HTML codes would look like garbage.

Furthermore, Usenet suffers from some fundamental problems, particularly the massive replication of data discussed earlier. It is also lacking in access controls and host tools for managing discussions. (The Usenet concept of a moderated newsgroup is too blunt an instrument of control and precludes fast-paced discussions.) Usenet is probably not the right model to carry forward into the future.

HyperMail

Mailing lists have long been used for online discussions. E-mail does have certain advantages. It is the lowest common denominator of Internet services, and therefore reaches more people than any other avenue. And e-mail messages simply show up in your mailbox; you don't have to go looking for them.

On the other hand, e-mail is not organized by topic. Threading is difficult or impossible, because not all mailers supply enough information to associate a reply with another specific message. Even when they do, most mail-reading programs do not display messages as threaded topics. Nevertheless, mailing lists remain popular, and there have been some efforts to create Web interfaces for them.

HyperMail is one such interface. It was designed as a way to browse an archive of e-mail messages through the Web. It does so quite successfully, allowing you to sort messages by date, author, or topic and thread. Threading is often haphazard, but it works as well as can be expected.

Time-Warner uses HyperMail for discussions at their Pathfinder Web site. They have added extensions to HyperMail, making it possible to post messages to a discussion through a Web form.

What Makes a Good Conferencing System?

Ask 100 experienced conferencers what makes a good conferencing system, and you'll get 100 different answers. As with any kind of software, people tend to like whatever they are used to. For instance, some swear by GUIs, others swear at them. But almost anyone who conferences regularly will readily point out flaws in their own favorite system.

There is no single perfect solution for all people and all purposes. But having used a variety of systems over the past 20 years, I think I can make a few generalizations about what seems to work well:

Separate conferences for broad subject areas. This is a nearly universal feature. Whether the discussion areas are called conferences, forums, newsgroups, or notesfiles, they provide a basic level of organization. Besides focusing on different subjects, different conferences often have very different atmospheres and social conventions. People become "regulars" only in the conferences that most interest them.

Threaded discussions within conferences. This sometimes takes the form of a tree structure, in which each topic is the starting point for a branching tree of responses. For example, Usenet, HyperNews, and WIT use this structure. But although a hierarchical tree is a good way to organize static information, it does not work as well for conversation. It is easy to get lost in the tree, and it's often hard to figure out where to attach a response. Discussions tend to fragment and dissipate. I prefer a star structure, in which each topic has a simple chain of consecutive responses attached to it. This form is easily understood by most people because it closely resembles real-life conversation. WebNotes and HotWired's Threads are examples of systems that use a star structure.

Informative topic list. A reader should be able to easily see a list of the topics in a conference. At minimum, the list should show each topic's title and some indication of the amount of activity in the topic: the number of responses, date of the last response, or both. The topics should be sortable both by topic start dates and by last response dates.

Respect for the integrity of topics. A reader should always be able to go back to the beginning of a topic and follow it all the way through to the most recent responses. Of course, it is necessary to clear out obsolete material to avoid clutter (and because nobody has infinite disk capacity), but pruning should be done by deleting entire topics after they have fallen into disuse. Some systems (notably Usenet and CompuServe) throw away older messages even if they are part of an active discussion.

Support for both frequent readers and casual browsers. A browser wants to choose a conference manually and scroll through the list of topics, dipping in here and there, moving backward or forward sequentially through topics, returning repeatedly to the topic list. A frequent reader wants to cycle automatically through a customized list of conferences, skipping topic lists entirely and getting immediately to the new, unread messages. Most conferencing systems are biased toward one type of reader or the other; few support both well.

Search and filter tools for readers. A reader should be able to search messages by date, author, or keyword. Word searches on both topic titles and message texts should be possible. Frequent readers should also have tools for controlling what they see; for example, a way to "forget" topics so that any subsequent responses are skipped automatically.

Access control. Both public and private conferences are useful in different situations. A conference host or moderator should have flexible control over who can access the conference and what level of access each participant has. For example, it should be possible to give some participants read and write permission, others read only, and others no access. This, of course, runs counter to a widespread anarchist sentiment on the Net. Anarchy is marvelous—the Web might never have evolved without it—but being unable to have private discussions among chosen friends or colleagues is just a different form of tyranny.

Host tools. The host of a conference should have good tools for managing topics: for example, weeding out obsolete topics, archiving those that are worth saving but no longer active, and moving a divergent thread of a topic to a new topic of its own.

Speed. Frequently used functions such as advancing to the next message should require only one keypress or pointer-click and should happen instantly when selected. If the system is slow or cumbersome, people simply won't use it much.

What I have laid out here is an ideal. No conferencing software that I know of excels at everything. The systems that have been successful are those that do some of these things well enough to capture a critical mass of enthusiastic users, who then provide the content and culture that attracts others.

Why Conference on the Web?

The capabilities that the Web has to offer are enough to make a veteran conferencer salivate.

For years we have been shackled to plain ASCII text. People have responded creatively to ASCII's limitations, inventing customs like smileys :-) to express emotions and *stars* for emphasis, and even creating gigabytes of ASCII art (imagine a full-page picture of Snoopy cursing the Red Baron here). Some will bemoan the passing of this era, but the expressive capabilities of HTML text far surpass those of plain ASCII. Many sizes of type! Real italics! Bold text! And so on.

The Web's multimedia capabilities will add another dimension to conferencing. Many of us have long dreamed of including pictures and sound in our messages, and the Web will finally make this possible. Some of the uses will be trivial: ASCII smileys will give way to full-color smiley cartoons. Some uses will be annoying (imagine every instance of LOL—Net shorthand for laughing out loud—being replaced with a recorded laugh track). But there are many situations in which a picture really is worth a thousand words.

Hypertext links embedded in messages offer endless possibilities. One obvious application is to make the author line of every message an active link to the author's home page. This would eliminate the need for the long signatures often attached to Usenet articles, which add clutter and disrupt the flow of conversation. Links can reduce the need for quoting earlier messages as well. Instead of copying the text of the message, one could just include a link to it.

Links could also be used to post a message in two or more conferences in which it is relevant. For Usenet readers, this probably brings up hateful images of *spamming*—the posting of identical messages to every newsgroup in the world. But if a message is *linked* to multiple conferences rather than replicated, you will only see it once. If it appears again in another conference, the software will recognize that you have already seen it and skip over it.

There are practical reasons to use the Web for conferencing, also. There is an expanding plethora of Web client and server software to choose from, supporting a wide variety of hardware. Much of it is free. No proprietary system is likely to match the Web in terms of universality of service.

One of the Web's great strengths is that it provides a common user interface for Internet utilities like FTP, Gopher, and WAIS. It is natural to extend this to conferencing as well. People should be able to reach everything the Internet has to offer without leaving the familiar environment of their Web browser.

Finally, a conferencing system on the Web can be designed to scale well. Since the data can be distributed across any number of servers, there are no inherent limits to growth.

Issues and Challenges

There are a number of problems to be solved before most of today's Web-based conferencing systems will be ready for heavy use. Following are a few of the most vexing ones:

What's new? Regular readers of a conference want to see only the new messages added since their last visit, so the system must keep track of what each reader has seen. Either the client or the server could do this, and it's not clear which is the better choice. Web servers are designed to be *stateless*; that is, they simply respond to each request as it arrives and do not keep track of what clients are doing. Requiring the server to remember what messages have been sent to each client violates the spirit of the Web's design. On the other hand, client software is not "aware" of the distinction between a conferencing system and any other Web document.

Uploading. Users need to be able to upload existing files into the conferencing system, rather than always having to type messages into a Web form.

Images in messages. Although the ability to include images and sound into messages is one of the most exciting features Web-based conferencing has to offer, it might also be one of the most difficult to implement. A message containing an HTML reference to an existing image is no problem, as long as the image is already available on some Web server. But how can a user get a *new* image to the server? Ideally, the user should be able to draw a picture with her favorite paint program, drag it into a document editor with the mouse, type a message, and click the Send button. But this would require much more sophisticated HTML document editors than exist today, as well as coordination between the Web server, the Web client, and the document editor.

Limiting HTML. It seems natural to let users include HTML markups in their messages, yet this poses a problem. If users are allowed complete freedom with HTML, they can write messages that are visually disorienting to readers, or that interfere with the functioning of the conferencing software. The display must be formatted so that structural elements of the system, such as message headers and navigation buttons, cannot be confused with the content of messages. Exactly how much formatting freedom to allow in messages is a difficult design issue.

Maintaining focus. Web sites have no obvious boundaries, and the temptation to surf is strong. It's easy to click a hypertext link and find yourself wandering right off to another continent. If users can embed active links in their messages, it could be difficult to keep readers involved in a conversation long enough to follow it through to the end and add their own two cents. As we gain experience with Web-based conferencing, we might find that conversation is more successful if hypertext links are limited to a few specific applications, such as referring back to an earlier response.

Speed. This is crucial not just for conferencing, but for any highly interactive application. For users without a high bandwidth connection, the Web can be agonizingly slow when moving from one page to another. Using the Web at 14,400bps feels about the same as using an ordinary dial-up BBS at 2400bps. Much of the sluggishness is built into the Web's architecture; it was designed for shipping files around the world, not for quick response to keys. Netscape has introduced some changes in Web client technology that speed up navigation considerably: displaying each page as it is being received, and aborting the transmission if the user selects any link. Yet performance remains a major problem. Conferencing involves skimming over a lot of stuff to find the most interesting nuggets, so you need to be able to move around quickly.

Where to from Here?

Although Usenet has its problems, there will likely be continued efforts to integrate it into the Web, simply because the trend has been for the Web to incorporate more and more of the Internet. Newsreading capabilities of Web browsers probably will improve, although they might never match the features of traditional newsreaders. More Usenet-to-HTML gateways similar to the Forum News Gateway are likely to appear as well. But a more promising approach might be to create a gateway between Usenet and another Web conferencing system, such as HyperNews. Such a gateway would automatically copy all messages from a newsgroup into a Web-based system, and vice versa. This could give the Web system a running start but would not tie it permanently to the problematic Usenet architecture.

It's not difficult to create a simple conferencing system on the Web using a scripting language like Perl. WIT was the first of this variety, and there must be at least a dozen such systems today. These are fine for casual use, but they tend to be slow and lack many capabilities that are essential for long-term, heavy-duty conferencing,

WebNotes represents a trend with more potential. Makers of commercial conferencing software are hurrying to build Web interfaces to their products. WebNotes is the first such system to hit the market, but others will follow. Meanwhile, work is moving forward on Web systems for voting, annotation, and other types of collaborative projects that have the potential to evolve toward conferencing.

The Web continues to evolve rapidly, chaotically, and unpredictably. But it's safe to say that the Web will be a popular platform for conferencing. The promise it holds is too great to ignore.

Resources of Interest to Readers

Bianca's Smut Shack: `http://bianca.com/btp/`

WIT: `http://www.w3.org/hypertext/WWW/Discussion`

HyperNews: `http://union.ncsa.uiuc.edu:80/HyperNews/get/hypernews.html`

HotWired: `http://www.hotwired.com/`

The Gate: `http://sfgate.com/`

WebNotes: `http://webnotes.ostech.com/`

Forum News Gateway: `http://forum.swarthmore.edu/forum.news.gateway.html`

HyperMail: `http://www.eit.com/software/hypermail/hypermail.html`

Pathfinder: `http://www.pathfinder.com/`

List of collaborative Web projects: `http://union.ncsa.uiuc.edu:80/HyperNews/get/www/collaboration.html`

Computer-Mediated Communication Studies Center (index of people, activities, and resources related to CMC): `http://www.rpi.edu/~decemj/cmc/center.html`

Conferencing on the Web (links to many Web conferencing sites): `http://freenet.msp.mn.us/people/drwool/webconf.html`

Challenges for Web Navigators

50

by
John December

What is the Web? A cloud of hypermedia? An expanding mass of unbounded text that users pursue at whim, guided by landmark trees, spiders, and branded content? A maturing information space, moving quickly through stages of population to saturation and pollution? A tangle of links that eventually no one will be able to traverse completely? The Web shares many characteristics implied by these questions—and because of its essence as a medium for associatively linked, dynamic information, the Web challenges those who would try to navigate its links today.

TERMINOLOGY

A *Web navigator* is a person who uses a World Wide Web browser to search for, discover, view, or retrieve information from the Internet.

Pollution, in the context of online information, is defined here as erroneous, out-of-date, or otherwise invalid or unreachable information (see stale or broken link, next definitions).

A *stale link* on a Web page is a URL reference that does not or will not resolve to an existing resource, because the resource has moved or is no longer available. This does not include temporarily inaccessible resources (which are broken links).

A *broken link* on a Web page is a URL reference that is either stale (see previous definition) or syntactically malformed, misspelled, or otherwise preventing access to a resource or a Web page. Resource inaccessibility could be temporary. A broken link might be fixed.

Branded content is a Web resource or information that is provided by a particular Web publisher under a known name or imprint (a brand).

In order to make sense of its tangle of links, Web navigators need to develop skills, applications, landmarks, and tools to effectively locate content. These skills involve browser operations as well as searching techniques, as outlined in Part III, "Web Navigation Tools and Techniques." Still another area of Web knowledge involves the life cycle of information spaces in general, and the Web's life cycle in particular, and how to use this information to anticipate challenges for navigation. This chapter focuses on describing and speculating on the evolution of the Web, stressing changes in its information-space resources and structures. I first define an information space and propose a model for the stages through which information spaces typically progress. Then I discuss a navigator's needs during each of these stages. I will describe the Web's past and present and speculate on the Web's future. Finally, I'll survey how features of future Web browsers might help navigators and identify major Web landmarks that should help a navigator as Web space inevitably evolves and grows. The reader should be cautioned that the discussion and life cycle model presented here is highly speculative—particularly in its predictions. The exact course of events for the Web is, of course, unknown.

The Life Cycle of Information Spaces

I use the term *information space* for all of the information or communication accessible through a particular type of server. For example, all of the information available on Gopher servers constitutes *Gopher space*. I define *Web space* as all the publicly available content available on World Wide Web servers. Web space has grown—from an estimated 7,500 servers in August 1994 (see `http://www-swiss.ai.mit.edu:80/~ptbb/SG-Scout/SG-Scout.html`) to more than 15,000 servers by March 1995 (see `http://netgen.com/cgi/comprehensive`). No one knows how many pages there are on these thousands of servers in Web space. The Lycos spider (`http://lycos.cs.cmu.edu/`) held more than 2.5 million unique URLs in its database as of March 1995.

However, a Web navigator should not just be concerned about the size of an information space, but about the information structures and the quality of the information in it. To gain an understanding of structure and quality, a Web navigator must first understand the evolution of an information space as it is defined, grows, and becomes mature.

Information-Space Evolution

An information space is similar to an organic system that has a life cycle of birth, growth, maturity, and obsolescence. Like organic systems, information spaces often grow rapidly, starting with a slow growth curve that, when a critical mass of material exists, rapidly becomes very steep, and then levels off as the space becomes mature. Here is a seven-stage model of evolution that identifies stages in an information space's life cycle. Each stage's definition describes key activities and events that mark transitions from one stage to another. Particular activities, such as peer review, for example, may occur at any stage; what is key in these definitions is the intensity and importance of these particular activities as present in particular stages.

1. **Definition**

    When an information space is defined using a particular protocol (typically employing a client/server model for information retrieval and delivery), an information space is born. As soon as the first information provider makes information available using the information system, the second stage of the information space begins—population.

2. **Population**

    A period of growth in which users (typically through servers) provide information for retrieval by users. During this period, the space is still relatively "young"—the pioneer adopters of the technology are learning to deliver information in this format, and the base of users is relatively small, often consisting of information providers or specialists. When the number of information providers, information content, and users reaches a point of critical mass, the space enters the next stage, growth.

3. **Growth**

    This is the period in which the critical mass of users, content, and information providers built up in the population stage fuels rapid growth in the amount of content in the information space. Early adopters of the technology use the information space to deliver and access content. The number of non-specialist users increases. During this stage, the totality of the information provided in the space can be traversed by a non-expert user. When the amount of information becomes so great that a non-expert user cannot traverse the entire space, the information space enters its fourth stage, saturation.

4. **Saturation**

   In this period, the information space contains so much information that no human being can process it without secondary works (indexes such as trees in Web space) or tools (searching mechanisms such as spiders in Web space). The number of new servers, users, and information grows so virulently that spiders and trees can become difficult to construct, maintain, and operate. Users face a bewildering amount of choices. As the saturation continues and the information space ages, the space shows significant levels of pollution—redundant, inaccurate, or obsolete information. When this occurs, the information space enters its fifth stage, maturity.

5. **Maturity**

   In this period, the information space remains dynamic and useful to users as well as to information providers despite considerable pollution. Means for indexing, filtering, layering, and guiding users through information structures thrive. Systems evolve for reducing pollution, or winnowing out valuable information from the space through branded (commercial) content services, formal or informal peer review, or the activities of information communities (for example, Usenet news FAQs). When the growth rates for new information provided in the space slow, and when the levels of traffic in the information space decline, the space enters its next stage, advanced age.

6. **Advanced age**

   This is the period in which the information space is used less and less, and when little or no new information is provided in the space. Maintenance of information-filtering tools and services becomes increasingly expensive. Users show little interest in learning the tools and techniques of the space as the benefits accessing of the information become reduced. Levels of pollution increase rapidly. When pollution increases to the point when it is growing more rapidly than information is being added to the space, the space is in its final stage, obsolescence.

7. **Obsolescence**

   This is the period when users of the space gain very little benefit from information because of extremely high pollution levels. Indexing or filtering services are useless against grossly out-of-date or incorrect information. No new browsing or information-providing tools are created for the space. The space might become so polluted that information providers "shut down" services offered in the space, shrinking it to a terminal state that doesn't expand or contract further, consisting only of rogue servers that refuse to "give up the space," or abandoned, zombie-like servers that are left inexplicably operating yet unmaintained.

All information spaces might not be doomed to complete this entire life cycle—a space might stabilize and remain mature indefinitely, or perhaps "heal" back from advanced age to maturity.

Needs for Navigators in Each Information-Space Stage

For navigators, each stage of the information-space life cycle gives rise to a particular set of needs. Often, particular kinds of tools and techniques for navigation will develop according to the stage of the information space. Let's revisit each life cycle stage and look at the needs and tools navigators need (and which usually develop).

1. **Definition**

   Key events: protocol definition (including server addressing scheme development), client/server software construction.

   Navigator needs: knowledge of how client software will be available.

   Environment for navigator: there is no information in the space yet.

   Dangers: lack of consensus on standardization of protocol could stall evolution at this level indefinitely.

2. **Population**

   Key events: pioneer servers enter space; extremely early content development often exhibiting naive/amateur design; beginnings of user documentation.

   Navigator needs: specialist knowledge to operate client; a list of servers; accessible (technical) documentation on protocols.

   Environment for navigator: not very much content is available; content that is available is often focused on one field or subject area; an exhaustive search of servers is the primary searching technique; there is close communication/contact among protocol, server, and client developers.

   Dangers: lack of content, poor quality content, or poor client user interfaces could keep critical mass of users from forming.

3. **Growth**

   Key events: critical mass (a user base of sufficient size whose growth is self-sustaining) fuels interest by non-specialist information providers, non-enthusiast users; there is much growth in the number of servers.

   Navigator needs: server list organized by organizational scheme—geography, for example; rudimentary subject trees of servers specialized to particular areas.

   Environment for navigator: non-specialist users disappointed with lack of complete information; server list organized by geography; rudimentary special-interest lists for specialized subject and topic location.

   Dangers: extreme specialization of a large part of the information space toward a particular subject area could stifle information diversity and level off new user growth.

4. **Saturation**

Key events: extremely rapid growth in servers, information, and users. Alternate browsers developed.

Navigator needs: keyword-searching mechanisms, scalably extendable subject trees (as opposed to linear lists of resources); layered information; annotated guides to information resources; paper books about the space.

Environment for navigator: rapid growth fuels excitement, attention, and more growth; bewildering rate of new information introduction; subject trees, keyword-searching mechanisms, server directories develop more extensively; extremely rapid growth in subject catalogs, many of them redundant. In later stages of saturation, rapid shifts in completeness, accuracy, and authority among subject trees and indexes; rapid population of keyword-searching databases; rapid changes in secondary tools (client helper applications, information-structuring tools, guides and applications for organizing space). Techniques to deal with high traffic volume.

Dangers: rapid changes in techniques for organizing space or delivering information (for example, nonstandard structures in commercial clients) could segment the open space into noncompatible regions. Rapid growth in tools, resources, and applications could hobble documentation and training efforts, so that trainers inevitably are providing obsolete information, with only specialists having current knowledge. Virulent subject tree growth could obscure valuable works in the information space and make pollution more salient to users.

5. **Maturity**

Key events: client *shakeout*—emergence of standard or popular clients; subject tree shakeout—emergence of dominant trees and keyword searching systems, with attendant die-off of incomplete or aborted trees or keyword mechanisms developed during saturation. Emergence of branded content; keyword-searching mechanisms continue fierce competition; routine "cross-media" discussion/coverage of information space (for example, popular press routinely covers activities and developments in the information space).

Navigator needs: skills in choosing best client software for needs; mastery of major searching mechanisms; more extensive annotated information; peer-reviewed information; more specialist information; specialized books about the information space; user information for very new and beginner-level users. Disciplinary "MetaCenters" to assist in specialist information review and structuring. Techniques to deal with high traffic volumes.

Environment for navigator: stable growth in information; information communities form to provide more filtering and peer review services; major landmarks stabilize; growth in kinds of information slowed, while continuing steady growth in the amount of information offered. Growing salience of specialized and specialist-provided information.

Dangers: emergent dominant trees and keyword searchers lull users into trusting them too much—lack of indexing diversity could threaten access to information space, obscuring fresh information; rising levels of pollution could affect smaller trees and keyword-searching services. Increased commercial content could stifle creativity and amateur activity. Lack of coordination among subject experts could hasten the spread of pollution.

6. **Advanced age**

Key events: stabilization in the number of servers; shakeout of pollution in subject trees and keyword-searching databases could actually reduce the amount of indexed resources to less than during maturity.

Navigator needs: very complete keyword- and subject-search tools with aggressive anti-pollution methodologies; developed skills for dealing with pollution, downed servers, unavailable content; specialized searching services.

Environment for navigator: Rising levels of pollution lessen value of information space, increasing maintenance costs, particularly for specialized uses; servers are taken offline; resource collection abandonment; stable or declining levels of traffic.

Dangers: Creeping pollution in the space threatens usefulness of entire space. Lack of diversity in subject trees and keyword mechanisms could threaten indexing of entire space if these resources don't have aggressive methodologies for eliminating pollution from databases. Maintenance costs for hand-crafted resources by specialists could discourage peer review efforts.

7. **Obsolescence**

Key events: rapid depopulation of the space; "switchoff" of most servers; levels of pollution reach extreme levels.

Navigator needs: lists of nonpolluted/less-polluted information stores.

Environment for navigator: extent of pollution makes most regions of the space unusable; few resources of value; low levels of traffic.

Dangers: Changes in underlying communication protocols could eliminate the space entirely.

The Past, Present, and Future Stages of the Web's Evolution

The preceding scenario for the progress of information-space evolution can be used as a model for what might happen to the World Wide Web.

Figure 50.1 shows my projection for the Web's progress through its life cycle stages with (rough) dates for the transitions among stages, and the events that force the start of each stage.

Currently, the Web is entering a late saturation stage—no human being could possibly traverse or evaluate all the possible choices for Web destinations. Dominant trees and spiders are emerging, and users are beginning to rely heavily on trees and spiders as well as branded content to navigate or to make choices about what to access. Older, smaller trees are "dying out" with the growth of the "big trees" like Yahoo (`http://www.yahoo.com/`). Branded content is just starting to emerge, as well as more extensive specialist-created information sources.

FIGURE 50.1.

Estimated Web progress through its information-space lifecycle.

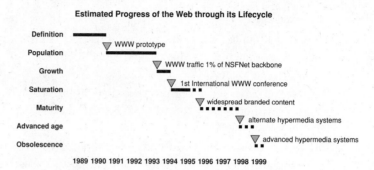

Estimated Progress of the Web through its Lifecycle

Definition
Population — WWW prototype
Growth — WWW traffic 1% of NSFNet backbone
Saturation — 1st International WWW conference
Maturity — widespread branded content
Advanced age — alternate hypermedia systems
Obsolescence — advanced hypermedia systems

1989 1990 1991 1992 1993 1994 1995 1996 1997 1998 1999

How will the Web grow in the future? What will the Web navigator need to have to stave off the effects of a mature or advanced-age Web? In the near term, I speculate that several "ages" will come into play for Web navigators. Figure 50.2 summarizes the approximate sequence of these ages through the saturation and maturity stages of the Web's life cycle.

My guesses for the ages of the Web in Figure 50.2 are

- **Growth Stage**

  Age of Trees: The growth of subject-based trees of information, in particular the WWW Virtual Library (`http://www.w3.org/hypertext/DataSources/bySubject/Overview.html`), marked the start of information organization during the growth stage of the Web.

  Age of Spiders: As the information space of the Web filled, the trees were not satisfactory to locate all information, and some keyword mechanism had to be developed; the World Wide Web Worm (`http://www.cs.colorado.edu/home/mcbryan/WWWW.html`), released in March 1994, was one of the first major keyword-searching mechanisms for the Web. As the Web moved into its saturation stage, the number of kinds of spiders increased rapidly.

A PRESATURATION-STAGE SPIDER

The WWW Worm, the earliest major Web spider, was launched in March 1994, two months before the point at which I fix the start of the Web's saturation stage (May 1994).

# Chapter 50

FIGURE 50.2.

Estimated near-term ages of the Web through its saturation and maturity stages.

Growth Phase

Age of Trees	WWW Virtual Library
Age of Spiders	WWW Worm

Saturation Phase

	Lycos
	virulent tree growth
Age of Big Trees	Yahoo
	tree "shakeout"
Age of Ants	WebAnts

Maturity Phase

Age of Smart Spiders	technical standards stabilized
Age of Smart Crawlers	spider wars
Golden Age of Content	crawler "shakeout"
	Metacenters
	major intellectual investment
	Branded Content
	major commercial activity
Age of Technology Flux	
	Technology expansion
	Advances in networked hypermedia
	Advances in networked virtual reality

■ **Saturation Stage**

Spider Age continues: More agile and smarter spiders develop early in the saturation stage of the Web, including Lycos (http://lycos.cs.cmu.edu/) and the WWW Harvest Broker (http://harvest.cs.colorado.edu/). These two spiders, particularly Lycos (having the largest database), begin to become dominant among all spider species. Other spiders die out, as their databases are not as large or are filled with stale or polluted links.

Age of Big Trees: In the early saturation stage, there are many (redundant) subject-tree representations of resources. This virulent tree growth continues until a small number of trees begins to dominate the information space. Yahoo (http://www.yahoo.com/) has begun to dominate the subject-trees in Web space, because it offers many (more than 35,000 as of March 1995) entries in an elaborate subject list. The popularity of Yahoo discourages the growth of the smaller and developing trees, and there is a *tree shakeout*—the smaller trees either are destroyed by their creators or they die out as their branches become polluted and stale. Only big trees (such as Yahoo, WWW Virtual Library, and Galaxy) survive.

Age of Ants: Keyword-searching mechanisms that use distributed methods (for example, WebAnts, `http://thule.mt.cs.cmu.edu:8001/webants/`) become necessary during the latter part of the saturation stage of the Web. So many new resources are being added that it takes a distributed approach to index them all.

■ **Maturity Stage**

Age of Smart Spiders: Rising levels of pollution require that spiders must use some form of filtering when delivering answers to users; otherwise the user is bewildered with an extremely large number of responses to a query, and many responses contain pointers to erroneous information. As a result, spiders employ *artificial intelligence* (AI) methods to become smart. The competition among the species of smart spiders occurs as each uses differing AI methods to perform this filtering.

Age of Smart Crawlers: A more general (or spider/ant hybrid) species of keyword-indexing system arises, perhaps out of distributed systems like WebAnts and Harvest (`http://harvest.cs.colorado.edu/`). These crawlers incorporate AI filtering techniques to cope with rising levels of pollution in the information spaces. Some species of crawler will be more successful in this, and there will be a crawler shakeout in which one or two species will dominate and the older species will die out.

Golden Age of Content: With the stabilization of technical standards (server software, HTML, and its upgrades) and with mature navigation resources and tools (Big Trees, Smart Crawlers), the resulting information infrastructure encourages the rise of major collaborations among academics and practitioners in many fields to create true Meta-Centers (collaborative, multi-organizational, multi-protocol collections of information and knowledge). The ascendance of branded content and major commercial activity ensures that excellent content gets rewarded; the result is a flourishing in diversity and quality of content.

Age of Technology Flux: As a result of new networked communication technologies for hypermedia or virtual reality, the Web's standards must be expanded. Superior systems for global networked communication as alternatives to the Web could create a massive *space migration* from the Web to this superior space (making the Web obsolete); or the Web could integrate these new technologies to change and grow, perhaps pushing the Web back into a secondary saturation phase as information providers take advantage of new protocols that interoperate with the Web.

Tools and Techniques for the Future

With the progress of the Web through its life cycle, how can a Web navigator adjust? Because a Web navigator relies first on the browser software, advanced browsers will be a first step, allowing for more customization and increased ease, agility, and flexibility.

Second, the rise of specialized, peer-reviewed content—the golden age of content that I outline above—should usher in a stable time when a navigator needs only a few landmark/survival links related to his or her own interests as jumping-off points for new information. In contrast, during the early saturation stage of the Web, a typical navigator's hotlist would be choked with new and interesting sites, many of them haphazardly organized.

In the following sections, I outline some issues for browser development and navigation landmarks that might help future Web navigators.

Dream Browsers

An ideal Web browser would meet all of a navigator's needs (outlined in Chapter 15, "Browser Operations") and would do so in an agile, flexible way, allowing for extensive user customization.

My ideal advanced Web browser (see Figure 50.3) would have

- **Customizable hot buttons.** The current Netscape browser includes a series of (factory-installed) Net Directory buttons. Customizable hot buttons would enable a user to define button labels and designate the associated URLs for these buttons. Another row of "application hot buttons" could be established based on the contents of the HTML page displayed in the browser (similar to the HTML LINK element's "Rel" attribute in current proposed Level 3 HTML specifications).

- **A variety of hotlists.** Current browsers allow only a single hotlist. Netscape's current bookmark facility (see Chapter 15) allows the list to be segmented, but an ideal Web browser would enable a user to have up to (say five) separate hotlists that he or she could label, based on subject or some other scheme (like the subjective value of the items in each of the hotlists).

- **Hit metrics.** Because a Web browser can keep track of what URLs it encounters, this information could be compared to the URLs in a user's hotlist collection or, alternately, a history file to reveal the resources the user has "hit" the most, organized in a sorted list by the number of hits; and the resources the user has hit chronologically, either between two dates or the most recent.

Landmark/Survival Links

As the Web moves into its stages of late saturation and maturity, although the number of resources will still continue to grow wildly, major structures for organizing these resources should merge and stabilize them. These structures include the "Big Trees" such as Yahoo, which act as giant hypertext switching stations to information in the leaves of the tree maintained by experts. Multi-organizational MetaCenters should arise, which will integrate Web resources and knowledge into a coherent, single web, providing important information-filtering and peer-review functions on the information. So as the Web grows, a Web navigator should learn to identify and collect those major landmark links that are important for his own interests or studies.

FIGURE 50.3.

A dream browser.

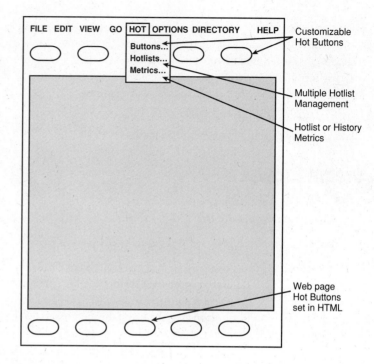

The categories of these links a navigator could choose presently are

I. General Navigation

    a. Keyword: Spiders and Indexes

        1. Lycos (`http://lycos.cs.cmu.edu/`)

        2. Harvest WWW Broker (`http://harvest.cs.colorado.edu/`)

        3. W3 Search Engines (`http://cuiwww.unige.ch/meta-index.html`)

    b. Subjects: Trees

        1. Yahoo (`http://www.yahoo.com/`)

        2. WWW Virtual Library (`http://www.w3.org/hypertext/DataSources/bySubject/Overview.html`)

        3. Galaxy (`http://www.einet.net/galaxy.html`)

    c. Spaces:

        1. Virtual Tourist I (`http://wings.buffalo.edu/world/`)

        2. CERN WWW Server list (`http://www.w3.org/hypertext/DataSources/WWW/Servers.html`)

        3. Virtual Tourist II (`http://wings.buffalo.edu/world/vt2/`)

    d. Reference:

        1. Internet Web Text (`http://www.rpi.edu/Internet/Guides/decemj/text.html`)

        2. Merit (`ftp://nic.merit.edu/`)

II. Specialist

Choose pages from major subject trees (listed above or in Chapter 18, "Trees: Subject-Oriented Searching") that pertain to your subject/interest area(s). Identify (if any) the major MetaCenter in your area(s) of interest.

III. Utility: orientation and general reference materials

    a. WWW FAQ (`http://sunsite.unc.edu/boutell/faq/www_faq.html`)

    b. W3 Consortium (`http://www.w3.org/hypertext/WWW/Consortium/`)

    c. Internet Tools Summary (`http://www.rpi.edu/Internet/Guides/decemj/itools/top.html`)

A WEB SURVIVAL CARD

If you were stuck on a desert island, what links would you take?

I created a Web Survival Card that lists key information for connecting to the Web and gaining more information about it. My card contains this information:

Access:

    Mail message HELP to agora@mail.w3.org
    Telnet to `telnet.w3.org`
    Anonymous ftp to `ftp.w3.org`
    Gopher to `gopher.w3.org`

Orientation:

    W3 Consortium (`http://www.w3.org/`), WWW FAQ (`http://sunsite.unc.edu/boutell/faq/www_faq.html`)

Navigating:

    `http://www.yahoo.com/`
    `http://www.einet.net/galaxy.html`
    `http://lycos.cs.cmu.edu/`
    `http://wings.buffalo.edu/world/`

You can retrieve a PostScript version of my Web Survival Card from the handouts section of the index at `http://www.rpi.edu/~decemj/works/wwwu/index.html`.

Future Navigator's Check

One key to gaining insight into the future challenges and needs for Web navigators is to understand the evolution of information spaces. The Web has passed through a period of definition and growth, and is rapidly moving through a stage of saturation. Eventually, stabilization of the Web's security and HTML protocols might foster a mature phase and a golden age of content. In this stage, branded content and specialist MetaCenters will serve as guideposts for navigators. Future Web browsers could incorporate more features for customization, and a Web navigator might look forward to a time when major resource collections stabilize into a manageable handful of links.

The Web: Essential Technology or Trivial Pursuit?

51

by
Neil Randall

The Web's Serious Nature

The World Wide Web, like the Internet itself, was conceived and designed as a technology for serious applications. The Net's purpose, as documented in any number of books and articles, was to keep open the communications channels necessary for the defense of a nation. The Web was designed to provide a means by which members of a scientific community could access the findings of their colleagues easily and thoroughly, a function different from the Net's in degree but not in kind. Whether or not either design team foresaw the trivial use to which their projects would eventually be turned is unknown, but it is highly unlikely. When one is thinking of the survival of a nation or the dissemination of scientific knowledge, newsgroups about Barney and Web pages displaying traffic citations rarely come to mind.

In many ways, the Web retains its serious origins. By "serious," I don't mean solemn (although they're obviously not mutually exclusive), I simply mean something closer to "worthwhile." Inevitably the question arises, "Worthwhile to whom?," but it's one I will leave unanswered. I'll merely take it on faith that we all recognize worth when we see it, and that we know the difference between the serious and the trivial. The point is that an increasing amount of activity on the Web has crossed precisely into the realm of the trivial, and the real question becomes: "How far in this direction can it afford to go?"

Origins of Trivia

North American culture—Western culture, in fact—has a rich and relentless history of turning technologies to trivial purposes. This tendency has been examined in detail by philosophers, sociologists, and social critics alike, most of them taking the stance that this is ultimately a negative process. One of the most vocal recent critics of our love affair with high technology is Neil Postman, whose *Amusing Ourselves to Death* raised a considerable stir in the late eighties, and which remains today a book very much worth reading. (Postman himself has become practically a parody of himself in recent writings and appearances, but that doesn't diminish the thought-provoking arguments of that book.) The fundamental thesis of *Amusing Ourselves to Death* is that we have openly accepted and readily embraced a technological lifestyle that ultimately allows only the trivial and the ephemeral, and that the influence of this lifestyle is so strong that there seems no way of reversing the process.

Much as it's tempting to answer Postman with a smirk and a knowing "Lighten up, Neil," a few minutes of contemplation render his arguments difficult to ignore. The single most ubiquitous multimedia technology in our lives is television, and while it has its moments of brilliance and wonder, such moments are very few and very far between. One July night in 1969, it's true, we all sat glued to the set as a human being stepped onto the surface of a world that was not our own, but on another summer night, this time 25 years later, what kept us at the set was a white van being escorted down a freeway by an unbelievably large contingent of police. In between, for every Watergate trial there were a thousand *Full House* and *Saved by the Bell* episodes, for every Berlin Wall destruction there were fifty thousand *Wheels of Fortune*. Trivia reigns, and pointlessness is rampant. Entertainment has come to mean *mindless* entertainment, and the result has been the almost inevitable phenomenon known as channel surfing. If nothing matters, everything is as important as everything else.

In many ways, I disagree with Postman. He allows no place for the significance of global communication that the Internet makes possible—a significance that exists no matter how many unnecessary responses we might receive to a one-liner posted on a mailing list. After the publication of my previous book, *Teach Yourself the Internet: Around the World in 21 Days*, I was contacted by readers in Norway, England, Malaysia, Singapore, Australia, and New Zealand, all within the span of two weeks; and this is significant communication, nontrivial communication, if only because it happened at all. Recently I was deluged with e-mail from various parts of the globe on another Internet matter, and that, too, was significant. And that's just e-mail. If I consider the Web, and the resources now available to me that I could not get in any other way, or at least I *would* not get in any other way, I have no choice but to conclude that this is communication of an extremely important kind. Potentially, at least, the Net—and through it, the Web—is a technology that does not trivialize.

But there are signs that the Web is following the path of television, from once-promising communications and education medium to a medium that encourages and applauds the dissemination of ephemera and inconsequentia. There are signs, in other words, that the Web has lost control of its future, and that it will become, increasingly, little more than a trivial pursuit. It might be less passive than television, and it might be more difficult to master, but those things alone don't make it worthwhile. In the rest of this chapter, I examine this trend and its implications.

Early in its history, accessing the Web was somewhat like accessing a well-stocked research library. What was available were studies, discussion papers, proposals, and screen after screen of information about research institutes, universities, and the Internet itself. Today, a Web session is less like browsing a research library than poring through the shelves of an extremely well-stocked magazine store. In such a store (which number distressingly few), you'll find magazines on every topic imaginable, and the styles will range from the scholarly to the effectively nonliterate, from the profound to the puffy, from the consequential to the trivial. Stores like this are exciting for anyone who craves information, and the Web today offers a similar range of material. The research reports and technical discussion papers are still there, but so are the details about university programs, the galleries of experimental art, the tours of cities and tourist attractions, the articles about social injustice, and the archives of *M*A*S*H* and *Married with Children*. And, just like in the bookstore, you can hop from one to the other with impunity and without guilt. That's what it's there for.

The Web as an Entertainment Medium

The question that faces the Web of the future is When does it stop being a well-stocked anything? When does it turn its back on its origins in research, and even on the fascinatingly eclectic entity it has become? When does the seriousness—the consequentiality—disappear, and when will it all be given over to the trivial? When, in other words, will the Web be an entertainment medium only?

Impossible? Hardly. Throughout the twentieth century, almost all major technologies have begun with a focus on significance but have become, in varying degrees, purveyors of entertainment. And not just entertainment, but *mindless* entertainment, primarily. Television in its infancy was seen as a tool for education and other serious information; its early history is punctuated with predictions that it would remain relatively undeveloped, that it had no real chance of capturing radio's audience, that it would find its chief use in the schools but not the homes. These predictions, obviously and dramatically, were wrong. The microcomputer in its infancy was seen as a smaller version of the data processing machines that were changing the face of research and business, but were doing little for the average person, and until the introduction of the Commodore VIC-20 (and later the Atari 400), there was little to change that initial perception. Earlier, radio itself changed from an information source to an entertainment medium, until by the end of the 1950s there was little on the radio but popular music and popular talk.

Whatever these technologies had once been, for any number of reasons they were changed into entertainment technologies. The microcomputer is the least changed of the three because it has also become a leading force in business, industry, and even government, but there's no question that the growth of multimedia has once again raised the possibility of a whole-scale entertainment revolution. And telephony, which has always blended the twin possibilities of consequentia and trivia, has allied itself with the computer in the development not only of online services, but of the thing known today as the information superhighway. The superhighway is touted as being the most important communications development in the past several decades, perhaps in history, but even the early perceptions suggest that it might be little more than a conduit for the ordering of entertainment and other unnecessary products. It will be overtaken, say the pundits, by the inevitability of mass entertainment.

Which brings us back to the World Wide Web. As perhaps the first real indication of what the superhighway might be like, the Web represents an opportunity to get it right. Coexisting right now are research, business, artistic, community, and entertainment interests alike, in much the same way as they coexist in information technologies such as libraries. But libraries are far different from bookstores, another information technology; very few bookstores offer anything approaching a balanced selection, because the emphasis in book popularity is increasingly on entertainment, whether it takes the guise of the mediocre best-seller or the ubiquitous self-improvement genre. Much as we like to encourage people to read, the fact is that there's no real qualitative difference between reading most best-sellers and watching most dramatic or comedic programs on television. They're all part of Theodore Sturgeon's "95 percent of *anything* is junk," and there's nothing intrinsically wrong with them. The problem is that they squeeze out the rest of the stuff because people become unaware that anything else exists. Or, once aware, they have no idea how to approach it.

The Web as an Information Medium

The year 1994 will go down in Internet history as, among a few other things, the year the Web hit the big time. But the explosion of interest has not necessarily been kind to the Web's actual "product." At this stage, it exists primarily *not* as a medium for depth of knowledge, but rather as a platform for breadth of information. And information, as we well know, has little to do with knowledge itself. We have information from the universities about graduate programs and research activities, but rarely do we have access to anything more than a cursory glance at the substance of the institution's activities in these areas. We have superbly designed pages from government institutions like NASA, but what we're presented with is often the stuff of coffee-table books, excellent for acquiring broad overviews but useless as a research base for anyone even halfway through secondary school. Yes, we have hordes of details about government bills and proceedings, but that's information we could quite easily get anyway (albeit not as conveniently). And, more importantly, we're seeing business using the Net for superficial marketing, and folks using the Net as a personal medium for publicly showing their hobby horses.

The keyword in many of these activities is "superficial." To be sure, there's plenty of room for the superficial, but one of the great dangers of our time is that *everything* is given a superficial treatment. Except for the truly dedicated, nobody bothers with in-depth analysis, because in-depth analysis is never required of us. Human resources people rely on canned psychological tests for their hiring of personnel, rarely bothering to question whether the specialists with a deep understanding of these tests would consider them valid. Science is presented to us in popular formats in an attempt to make it accessible to everyone, when in truth many scientific concepts can be comprehended only with years of specialist training. Newspapers like *USA Today* demonstrate that in-depth reporting is simply pointless, and so on and so on. The problem is not that the superficial is bad—it's not, and it can at least create awareness—but rather that, after a time, the superficial is regarded as the only knowledge needed. The board game *Trivial Pursuit* demonstrated quite clearly that we respect a person's knowledge of inconsequentia much more than a specialist's depth of understanding, and *Trivial Pursuit* was a game precisely for its time.

The Web Creates Awareness

So am I being Neil Postman here, decrying all this for the sake of a return to the old days? To a degree, sure, except that the old days hold neither appeal nor interest for me. They weren't any better, no matter what Postman and others suggest. People have always sought the trivial; they just didn't have as much of it as we have today. Our explosion of visual media has ensured that trivia proliferates, and we've reached the stage where it is both unavoidable and treasured. It's only natural, of course, that trivia will possibly overtake the World Wide Web as well.

What I want to reiterate, however, is that trivia itself isn't the problem. When recognized for what it is, trivia is harmless or even helpful. It does, I repeat, create awareness. The problem lies, once again, in our tendency to equate trivia with knowledge, and thus to value the overview, the summary—in short, the superficial. Most Web sites today have very little actual substance. A glossy home page offers links to one or two other pages within the site, and these quite typically offer a brief amount of information. The home page also offers links to other sites on the Web, and thus acts as a launching pad for further exploration of the topic, whether or not the remote sites are related to the content of the home page in any meaningful way. A few hours of following these links rarely yields anything that will sustain interest. Imagine a book offering nothing but tables of contents and abstracts, along with some graphics, and you have a pretty good idea of what the Web tends to be like.

But the Web hasn't gone completely over the top yet. Not by a long shot. Through a well-designed Web site you can gain access to FTP archives, where you can often find sustained analyses or studies of the topics in question, usually in the form of a PostScript, TeX, or other word processing or spreadsheet file type. Download it, and you have substance. Some Web sites offer page after detailed page of information, so much that reading everything will build an awareness of the topic (or the company or the program) that takes you far beyond the superficial. Even some entertainment sites offer in-depth looks at the subject matter, and thus become endlessly visitable if that's your area of interest. The good sites are out there, and they're well worth exploring.

But much of what appears on the NCSA What's New Page is of interest only to the person who mounted the site in the first place. Next time you access this site, the Scout Report, the Commercial Sites list, or any other page that collects a wide range of new sites, spend a couple hours exploring as many links as you can. Take note of which links initially grabbed your attention, and then, after accessing them, how many were ultimately disappointing. I'm willing to bet that at least 80 percent of everything you visited was less than it could have been, and that even if the page said "Under Construction," you're not likely to head back there again. Too many Web pages seemed designed as one-time appearances rather than continually developing presences, and too many are simply experiments to see if anyone will bother navigating to them.

The danger in all of this is that the growth of trivia on the Web will mean that its initial purpose will be lost. That purpose, you'll recall, was to provide a means for people to acquire knowledge and improve expertise in a manner and at a speed never before possible. By its very hypertext/hypermedia nature, the Web offers the opportunity to present information in a way that users can glean what they need from one site and then effortlessly find additional information from other sites. At its best, the Web already does this, acting like an almost endless book on the topic in question, one in which you don't have to return to the library to follow the footnotes and learn even more. Or, to use a different analogy, it's a means of moving from one televised feature about a topic to twenty others on the same topic, all without moving from your chair. Even entertainment sites can make use of this idea by stocking their sites with rich collections of material and pointing clearly and usefully to other repositories of relevant information. Many such sites are currently "under construction," but many are just as clearly not. The fear of Web-watchers everywhere is that the first group will never get constructed, while the second will go forth and multiply simply because construction isn't an issue.

Summary

If the Web becomes as trivial as television—and there is nothing in history that has sustained that level of inconsequentia for so long and with such success—then it will be abandoned by the people who could make the best use of it. In all likelihood, the abandonment has already begun. The signs are clear that the next eighteen months or so will see an explosion of purposeless home pages leading nowhere, or informational "teasers" that exist only to pique interest in something that is explored no deeper. If the Web were not an active medium, one that required an actual decision to move from one site to the next, this explosion of trivia would not matter. But to ask people to choose a site, only to insult them when they arrive, is not just stupid, it's a crime against the promise of the Web itself. Perhaps we'll see the next generation of browsers include the kinds of filters that will warn of these sites in advance, but it's far more reasonable to assume that we'll be spending hours of our own precious time sifting through them ourselves. The greatest danger of all is that sifting through the trivia will become the central, and the accepted, World Wide Web activity.

Challenges for a Webbed Society

by
John December

52

There are subtle, complex changes taking place in human communication, thought, and relationships within online communication and information communities. The Web is part of these changes, enabling new forms of communication and information delivery, and fostering new associations among people. One challenge for our society is to grapple with the questions raised by these changes. How might our culture, society, and communication patterns change as a result of widespread Web use?

In this chapter, I approach these questions by focusing on specific ways the Web alters communication, thought, and society, and on what issues arise from such changes. For people involved in the task of installing Web servers and for users trying to make sense of browsers and HTML, the Web may seem to consist only of a set of technical details, protocols, and network connections. However, communication on the Web, like human communication over computer networks for the past several decades, displays characteristic human qualities, including emotional, chaotic, surprising, and at times passionate or mundane exchanges. The Web illustrates how the inevitable pull of human beings toward each other in any communication system alters relationships, the way people think, and what they expect from communication.

The Scope and Extent of Web Transformations

Although the Web has changed the face of networked information dissemination dramatically over the past years, it is a much larger question whether the Web has or will ever change our society and culture significantly. The use of any communication technology evolves in the context of broader societal change, in ways so subtle that we may never be able to detect them.

Predictions

Many inventions in human history were thought to be the ultimate catalysts for sweeping social change: The telegraph would eliminate wars, the telephone and television would bring democracy and education to the people, and computer-mediated communication would transform society as Hiltz and Turoff envisioned in *The Network Nation: Human Communication via Computer* (Reading, MA: Addison-Wesley, 1978).

So the idea that the Web is *the* technology that will transform our culture must be tempered by noting the hollow predictions about earlier technologies. Humans often utilize technology in far too complex and quirky ways for neat predictions to come true.

While not always far-reaching in their effects on society, technologies have gradually and subtly changed communication patterns, relationships, and expectations. With 24-hour cable news, we expect to see a dramatic or important event as it happens. With global telecommunications, we expect to reach nearly anyone worldwide by telephone. Participants in global computer-mediated communication forums like Usenet expect to communicate with other people interested in very specialized discussion topics. Like Marshall McLuhan's vision of a global village, the electronic landscape today binds us together with connectivity we expect to access instantly.

So while the Web may fail to live up to any prediction that it will radically alter our lives immediately, its qualities as a communication technology may have some effect on future expectations and communication patterns. Also, the Web already offers unique features—interactivity and one-to-many broadcasting capabilities—that set it apart from previous communication media. The Web fulfills several "niches" within the communications landscape like few technologies before it and offers a new set of expectations about information that break the traditions of linear print.

The Web Fulfills a Dream and Fills a Gap

Vannevar Bush, in a landmark article called "As We May Think" in the July 1945 issue of *The Atlantic Monthly,* described his vision of a device for helping the human mind cope with information. Bush observed that previous inventions expanded human abilities to deal with the physical world, but not floods of information and knowledge. Observing that the human mind works by association through "some intricate web of trails carried by the cells of the brain," Bush proposed a device he called a *memex,* which could augment the human mind through "associative indexing." Bush's vision was for a system of information which could link documents in "trails" that could be saved and shared with others.

The Web fulfills Bush's dream of a memex in many respects. While a "universe" of knowledge is still evolving on the Web, the hypertext "trails" on Web pages are associative indexes that people save and share. The Web can link information in useful ways, giving rise to new insights—a transformation of information to knowledge that Bush described in terms of applications in law, medicine, chemistry, and history. An HTML version of Bush's article, developed by Denys Duchier, at URL `http://www.csi.uottawa.ca/~dduchier/misc/vbush/as-we-may-think.html,` contains links to several applications that fulfill Bush's predictions.

The Web offers other correspondences to many features of Bush's memex. There are "trails" within the subject trees of information on the Web that connect extremely useful documents and resources. Web browser hotlists serve as "trails," where people record their stops of interest along paths through the Web. As Bush predicted for his memex, there are many people on the Web today "who find delight in the task of establishing useful trails through the enormous mass of the common record." The Web's basic structure rests on Bush's principle of associative indexing, and the flourishing of information on the Web in the last few years demonstrates its potential as a "universe of documents."

In addition to fulfilling many needs identified by Bush for human intellectual activity, the Web also fills a "media gap" identified by Tetsuro Tomita. In his essay, "The New Electronic Media and Their Place in the Information Market of the Future," (in *Newspapers and Democracy: International Essays on a Changing Medium,* A. Smith, editor, Cambridge, MA: MIT Press, 1980), Tomita observed a pattern in the way traditional communications methods were used to reach audiences. Methods such as letters, telegrams, and conversation reach a very small audience in amounts of time ranging from immediate (telephone) to several days (a letter). Mass media such as radio and television, newspapers, books, and movies reach very large audiences in times ranging from immediate (radio, television) to weeks (magazines) to months (books). But the middle range—audiences of 10 to 10,000 people reached within times ranging from immediate to a day—is a gap filled by few traditional media. This is too small an audience for mass media and too large an audience for personally controlled (traditional) media. Yet this is the audience and time delay gap that many forms of computer-mediated communication fill, including the Web.

The Web offers immediate delivery of information to specialized audiences. There are many examples of webs that draw audiences in the range of Tomita's media gap. In fact, these audiences are what the Net seems to support in abundance. Specialized groups in Usenet and specialized webs do not necessarily appeal to massive audiences (in the 100,000 to millions range), but to quirky, specialized groups of hundreds or thousands of people. Before the invention of computer networks, an individual could not easily seek out several hundred others interested in a specialized hobby or area of interest, when those people were spread worldwide. No traditional media offered a personally available means to accomplish this; but the Web does, and filling this "media gap" is certainly a contributor to its popularity and growth.

Changes in Communication Characteristics

As part of fulfilling the needs identified by Bush for a system of associative thought and by Tomita for reaching specialized audiences in the media gap, the Web alters many characteristics of communication:

1. **Time and space constraints.** Like many forms of computer-mediated communication (CMC), the Web provides a way for users to create communication artifacts that can be accessed by anyone at any time. The benefits of this asynchronous communication are

   ■ People don't need to be co-present in order to exchange a message.

   ■ People can communicate with and associate online with others based on interest rather than geography.

2. **Power and communication control.** The power of the press lies with those who own a press. On the Web, everyone with the necessary skills owns a press.

   Dissemination of ideas on a mass and medium scale is no longer filtered through organizations and institutions but can come directly from individuals. Net and Web-based magazines (zines) (URL http://www.meer.net/~johnl/e-zine-list/index.html) can flourish rapidly or die quickly based on the ambition or interest of their publishers.

   Even without the label *zine,* all web pages serve as *publications* that anyone can access. On the surface, this is a dramatic shift from institutions as holders of the publishing key. However, the cacophony of voices on the Net generates "noise," causing users to seek guidance according to signposts—institutionally sponsored or established commercial publishers, or web pages that have grown reputations for various purposes.

   The Web can shatter institutional control over knowledge (which relies on geographic proximity of members and boundaries on knowledge dissemination), and give control to individuals and ad hoc, online groups.

3. **Expressive possibilities.** The Web offers expressive possibilities that no other information space has provided before. The Web's text is unbounded—not constrained to a single artifact or work—but can include links deep into other works by other authors. Web text, therefore, can be never-ending, finding continuing associations into the texts it links into and from texts that link to it.

4. **Relationships among people and information.** Paper texts reference each other. In fact, this is the basis for scholarly works and the "great conversation" of literature. However, the association on paper is referential (in the form of a citation, excerpt, or summary of the other work) rather than associative (a live "link" directly to the other work). Moreover, a paper reference is bounded (cast in the medium and space of the referring text) rather than unbounded (changing the user's focus of attention entirely into the space of the referred text via a hypertext link).

Associative linking fosters relationships among people in addition to relationships among information. Experts in a particular field create pools of knowledge on their home page. When other people link into these pages, cliques of experts form. These cliques might be based on information, hobbies, interests, culture, or political leanings. The result is that "electronic tribes" can form that meld cooperatively, linking people in associations that could not be possible any other way. For example, related information from a subject page in CERN's Virtual Library (URL `http://info.cern.ch/hypertext/DataSources/bySubject/Overview.html`) reveals collections of experts, institutions, and organizations all interested in a particular subject or topic. This linking creates visibility and associations among participants.

Through links, the Web reveals relationships among information and people. Unlike the linearism of text that integrates ideas in a single form, the Web relies on creating linked relationships among disparate pieces of information to build meaning. Unlike the ephemeral, synchronous communication spaces of Internet Relay Chat and MU*s, where text-based conversation flows and is usually never recorded, Web linking reveals relationships—and these links form a record of information relationships.

Issues and Challenges

As the Web alters communication and information patterns, the resulting change raises issues our society must face for individual, group, and societal responsibility. Moral and legal issues will arise in the areas of individual behavior, societal responsibility for issues of access and information literacy, and the new relationships, communication, and thought patterns the Web fosters.

Individual Behavior Packet Ethics

The current Internet/Web relies on an open-access model: Anyone can follow a public link in a web page and call up a resource, whether it is a 300-byte HTML file or a 1.8MB MPEG movie. While the relatively limited number of Web users today and adequate network bandwidth make this model feasible, its future is threatened if there are far more Web users without a proportional increase in bandwidth. Essentially, the problem relates to the "tragedy of the commons" situation: A commonly held resource (network bandwidth), when made freely available to all, sometimes results in users abusing the resource.

This issue is not yet a serious problem on the Web for several reasons. First, unlike a grazing commons for livestock, network bandwith is not consumed permanently, but only temporarily occupied. Second, advances in network technology have made more bandwidth available, and the bandwidth that exists is not needed all the time. Although popular Web servers are noted for their degraded performance during busy times, it is unlikely that all potential Web users will try access at the same time. In fact, the telephone system depends on this same principle: If everyone with a phone tried to make a call simultaneously, there would be "phone jams."

So while the aggregate behavior of users dispersed across a network often might not cause serious bandwidth problems today, widespread patterns of bandwidth-intensive individual behavior, in extreme cases, can. What about the user who heavily accesses graphics or movies on the Web? While there may be no laws to stop this user, an agreement between the user and the Internet service provider might restrict such activity. If the user violated this agreement, he or she could lose the account. However, on a much larger scale, enforcement and the definition of what is "overuse" is harder to pin down. Our society and sense of "etiquette" has only begun to address this and other issues about behavior in a public network space.

While Arlene H. Rinaldi's excellent Net Etiquette guide (URL `ftp://ftp.lib.berkeley.edu/pub/net.training/FAU/`) touches on many practical issues of personal behavior, larger questions remain that are not easily resolved or codified. For example, what about individuals who provide information that may be

- Illegal in some jurisdictions where it could be downloaded (for example, non-exportable encryption programs or information that is banned in a particular country or state)
- Offensive to others beyond mere disagreements, but violating cultural and community standards for offensiveness
- In violation of copyright laws or counter to Net traditions for information dissemination and intellectual property protection
- Intended to undermine or overthrow a government

Court cases may test these issues and prompt legislation. However, our laws and customs today aren't prepared to answer the issues these situations raise.

Societal Responsibility Access Issues

If the Web becomes a major form of communication for government, commerce, and education, how can we assure that everyone has access to it? Access is more than just physical; it means not only having the ability to use the hardware and software to access the Web, but having the knowledge (information literacy) to make use of the content. Today, we struggle to teach print literacy to people. What will the world be like when information literacy skills are needed in addition? Experts in communication today would be hard-pressed to even define Web information literacy, much less be prepared to create curriculum for a variety of educational contexts. At the same time, Web communication is here, and those who are skilled can take advantage of it.

Moreover, many initiatives for providing skills in networked communication focus only on physical access to networks and tools. Skilled people to set up the equipment and train people in Web-based communication is another, perhaps scarcer, resource. Networked communication today requires a fairly specialized set of skills. While the Web masks the details of some communication activities (like FTP commands or the details of a Telnet connection), it raises still more issues (for example, the fine points of HTML page design or the creation of a working browser form).

How will our society deal with a form of communication that requires such specialized knowledge on relatively expensive equipment? The U.S. Library of Congress has a Web server (URL `http://lcweb.loc.gov/homepage/lchp.html`), but whom does it serve? Can a society justify creating an elite information infrastructure, one that enriches only the privileged with the resources, skills, and knowledge to use it?

Human Relationships Balancing Online and Offline

If modern civilization obliterates safe public spaces for people to meet and freely interchange ideas, how will our society deal with such spaces formed only online? Will psychological dependence on networked communication create imbalances in offline relationships? Research in computer-mediated communication has not answered these questions with regard to Web-based communication, and answers won't necessarily come soon or easily (for example, the debate about television's impact on our society continues).

If network activity becomes a major form of human communication, people may associate more freely online because they are not slowed by geographical or temporal limits. How will our institutions (governmental, educational, and religious) change to accommodate these new associations? Institutions often act as a force to help people achieve a group identity, but if people can create their own group identity in the form of network-based alliances, how will this change offline institutions? What will happen to those institutions whose power and influence are usurped by groups performing the same function online?

Ultimately, the communication possibilities offered by the Web can't help but change human relationships. People no longer might identify with a physical neighborhood for companionship or advice; they can turn to a cyberspace neighborhood, based on mutual interests and association, as a source for support and information. (This has already happened for many people in many online communities.) Will this continue to erode physical public space? In the long term, the relationships the Web fosters will certainly continue to raise more questions as well as open up new ways for people to associate.

Summary

Like failed urban planning and architecture schemes, technology developed to transform society often falls flat. The Web, a technological invention that has spread through voluntary use, perhaps has an advantage over such inventions. Despite the rapid growth of Web traffic and activity, however, the significance of the impact of the Web on our society remains unknown.

There are several characteristics of the Web that may indicate its power to change our lives. The Web very closely fits Vannevar Bush's description of a tool essential for extending human thought. Similarly, the Web fits very well into Tetsuro Tomita's "media gap" of audiences and time constraints that traditional media do not reach. As a means of communication, the Web transcends time and space constraints; alters power and control; makes possible new, expressive styles; and creates new relationships among people and information.

Our society is just beginning to face issues that may have more serious impacts if Web use becomes more widespread. Individual and societal responsibilities for Web use, access, and training have not been defined; and the way Web-based communication alters human relationships has not yet been examined in detail. In the long term, human interaction online can't be planned or predicated any more than the growth of vibrant, exciting cities. Our society is only beginning to identify the changes the Web may have already brought to communication.

Appendixes

IX

PART

Web Reference

A

by
John December

This appendix lists some key online resources for finding out about and using the Web.

Introduction

Definition: The WWW is a global, distributed system for disseminating hypermedia resources through servers and retrieving hypermedia resources through browsers on global or local computer networks.

Overviews

The following is a list of locations where you can find general information about the World Wide Web:

■ WWW overview: Overview of the Web, from the World Wide Web Consortium (W3C) (`http://www.w3.org/`).

■ WWW info/EARN: What Is World Wide Web, a narrative introducing and explaining the Web, from European Academic Research Network Association (EARN) (`http://www.earn.net/gnrt/www.html`).

■ WWW Guide/Hughes: Entering the World Wide Web, A Guide to Cyberspace, by Kevin Hughes (`http://www.eit.com/web/www.guide/guide.toc.html`).

■ WWW-Yahoo: Computers-World Wide Web (`http://www.yahoo.com/Computers/World_Wide_Web/`).

FAQs

Following are two places where you can find FAQs about the World Wide Web:

■ WWW FAQ/Boutell: Frequently Asked Questions (FAQ) list and answers about the Web—covers user, provider, and general information; maintained by Thomas Boutell (`http://sunsite.unc.edu/boutell/faq/www_faq.html`).

■ WWW FAQ/CERN: Frequently Asked Questions on W3, by Tim Berners-Lee at CERN (`http://www.w3.org/hypertext/WWW/FAQ/List.html`).

Getting Connected

Access

- ■ WWW via e-mail: Obtain a web file (for example, http) via e-mail; URL = Uniform Resource Locator; send message body *www URL*; Use the message body HELP to get instructions (`mailto:agora@mail.w3.org Body: `*www URL*`).

- ■ WWW via Telnet: An example of using WWW via Telnet (to CERN) (`telnet://telnet.w3.org`).

- ■ WWW FTP info: Some information files about the Web; includes papers, guides, and draft specifications, from CERN (`ftp://ftp.w3.org/pub/www/`).

- ■ WWW Gopher info: Information files about the Web available via gopher (`gopher://gopher.w3.org/`).

- ■ Bootstrap: Information about gaining more information about and accessing the Web (`http://www.w3.org/hypertext/WWW/FAQ/Bootstrap.html`).

Software

The following are software packages available online that will help you better navigate the Web:

- ■ WWW Clients: A list of programs (Web browsers) that enable you to access the WWW, from CERN (`http://www.w3.org/hypertext/WWW/Clients.html`).

- ■ WWW Browsers/Yahoo: List from Yahoo, Computers-World Wide Web-Browsers (`http://www.yahoo.com/Computers/World_Wide_Web/Browsers/`).

- ■ WWW Browser source: Source code for a variety of Web browsers for different hardware platforms (`ftp://ftp.w3.org/pub/www/bin/`).

- ■ WWW Servers: A list of programs (Web servers) that enable you to provide information on the Web, from CERN (`http://www.w3.org/hypertext/WWW/Daemon/Overview.html`).

- ■ EIT WSK: Enterprise Integration Technologies Corporation's Webmaster's Starter Kit, a resource to help you install a Web server and optional extensions (`http://wsk.eit.com/wsk/doc/`).

Using the Web

Developing Information

■ CyberWeb: A resource collection for Web information providers and users; includes general information and links to various resources (`http://www.stars.com/`).

■ HTML Developer's: WWW + HTML Developer's JumpStation, maintained by SingNet and hosted by OneWorld Information Services (`http://oneworld.wa.com/htmldev/devpage/dev-page.html`).

■ WWW Weavers: A collection of links to assist web weavers; includes pointers to HTML resources, techniques, guides, and information, by Chris Beaumont (`http://www.nas.nasa.gov/NAS/WebWeavers/`).

Navigating the Web

The following locations are where you'll find lists of Web sites you might want to access.

■ WWW Servers/sites: A comprehensive list of WWW sites generated from a Web Wanderer program, by Matthew Gray (`http://www.netgen.com/cgi/comprehensive`).

■ WWW Servers/geo: A long list of registered WWW servers, listed geographically by continent and country (`http://www.w3.org/hypertext/DataSources/WWW/Servers.html`).

■ WWW Sites (CityLink): State and city Web sites (`http://www.neosoft.com/citylink/`).

■ WWW Sites (Virtual Tourist): A geographic map to aid in locating Web sites and other resources (`http://wings.buffalo.edu/world`).

■ Web Sites index: Index to WWW sites, by John Doyle (`http://herald.usask.ca/~scottp/home.html`).

■ Web Sites/Time: Timex World Time—shows time zones with current time and WWW sites in each (`http://www.timeinc.com/vibe/vibeworld/worldmap.html`).

■ WWW Spiders: Spiders are a class of software programs that traverse network hosts gathering information from and about resources (`http://www.rpi.edu/Internet/Guides/decemj/itools/nir-tools-spiders.html`).

■ WWW gateways: Interfaces between the WWW and other information or communication systems (`http://www.yahoo.com/Computers/World_Wide_Web/Gateways/`).

News and Discussion

- webNews: Announcements of new Web sites, services, and software (`http://twinbrook.cis.uab.edu:70/webNews.80`).

- WWW Conferences: International conferences on the Web, past and future (`http://www.w3.org/hypertext/Conferences/Overview-WWW.html`).

- WWW-Announce: Charter for the moderated Usenet newsgroup `comp.infosystems.www.announce` (`http://www.halcyon.com/grant/Misc/charter.html`).

- WWW-Announce: A moderated newsgroup announcing new WWW resources (`news:comp.infosystems.www.announce`).

- Web Newsgroups: A list of the World Wide Web discussion groups on Usenet (`http://sunsite.unc.edu/boutell/faq/newsgroups.html`).

Bibliography

- WWW Bibliography: Papers and articles about the Web (`http://www.w3.org/hypertext/WWW/Bibliography.html`).

Net Directory

B

by
John December

There are many online information sources that can help you learn more about the Net. The following listings contain descriptions of sources of information about the Internet, applications of the Net, Internet technology, and online culture. Each section will help you find more information about the Internet or will connect you directly to examples of how the Internet or World Wide Web can be used.

Each entry is of the following form:

- *Name*: *Description* (*URL*)

Where *Name* is a short name or title for the resource, and *Description* is a longer annotation describing the resource, and *URL* is the Uniform Resource Locator of the resource.

This list is a selection of annotated links from my list, "Information Sources: the Internet and Computer-Mediated Communication," (`http://www.rpi.edu/Internet/Guides/decemj/icmc/top.html`).

Internet

The Internet is a vast collection of resources, encompassing tens of thousands of cooperating organizations and tens of millions of users. This section provides you with information to find out more about the Internet on many different levels:

- Introductory information to orient you to what the Internet is and what is possible on it
- Collections of official Internet standards and technical documentation
- Training resources, collections, and courses
- Information about navigating the Internet, including guides and special collections
- Navigators and tools that help you find people or resources on the Internet based on a search by subject, keyword, information space, or list

Introduction

Overviews

- Gold in Networks!: A description of gold nuggets in the network, by J. Martin (`ftp://nic.merit.edu/documents/fyi/fyi_10.txt`).
- GlobalCenter Tour: A tour of the Internet from Global Village Communication (`http://www.globalcenter.net/gcweb/tour.html`).
- Hitchhikers Guide: Describes the Internet (circa September 1989), by Ed Krol (`ftp://nic.merit.edu/documents/rfc/rfc1118.txt`).
- Surfing the Internet: A narrative of what the Internet has to offer, by Jean Armour Polly (`ftp://nysernet.org/pub/resources/guides/surfing.2.0.3.txt`).

- What is the Internet?: By Krol and Hoffman
  (`ftp://nic.merit.edu/documents/fyi/fyi_20.txt`).
- Xerox Video: An Overview of the Internet and World Wide Web, by Xerox Palo Alto
  Research Center (`http://pubweb.parc.xerox.com/hypertext/wwwvideo/wwwvideo.html`).

Facts

- Internet Index: The Internet Index, a list of interesting facts about the Internet [Inspired
  by *Harper's Index*], by Win Treese
  (`http://www.openmarket.com/info/internet-index/current.html`).
- New User's Questions: Answers questions commonly asked by new users, by Malkin
  and Marine (`ftp://nic.merit.edu/documents/fyi/fyi_04.txt`).

History

- Internet Birthday: Happy 25th, Internet
  (`http://www.amdahl.com/internet/events/inet25.html`).
- Internet Future: Proposals for the future of the Internet
  (`mailto:Internet-drafts@nri.reston.va.us Body: help`).
- Internet History/ISOC: Internet Society's collection of Internet history
  (`gopher://gopher.isoc.org/11/internet/history`).
- Internet History: Master's Thesis, Henry Edward Hardy
  (`ftp://umcc.umich.edu/pub/users/seraphim/doc/nethist8.txt`).
- Internet Timeline: An Internet timeline highlighting some of the key events that helped
  shape the Internet as we know it today, by Robert H'obbes' Zakon
  (`mailto:timeline@hobbes.mitre.org`).
- Internet Timeline: Events in the history of the Internet by Robert H'obbes' Zakon
  (`http://tig.com/IBC/Timeline.html`).
- Netizen Anthology: The Netizens and the Wonderful World of the Net—an anthology,
  Ronda Hauben, Michael Hauben
  (`http://www.columbia.edu/~hauben/project_book.html`).

Collections

NICs (Network Information Centers)

- Acceptable Use: Directory of acceptable-use policies for many networks
  (`ftp://nic.merit.edu/acceptable.use.policies/`).
- DDN NIC: Network Information Center/Defense Data Network (`ftp://nic.ddn.mil`).

- InterNIC Telnet: Directory and Database Services Telnet Interface
  (`telnet://guest@ds.internic.net`).
- InterNIC FTP: FTP archives for InterNIC
  (`ftp://ds.internic.net/pub/InterNIC-info/internic.info`).
- InterNIC E-mail: Mail service to the InterNIC
  (`mailto:mailserv@internic.net Body: help`).
- InterNIC Gopher: Information server for Internet Network Information Center
  (`gopher://rs.internic.net`).
- InterNIC Web: Directory database (AT&T) and registration (Network Solutions)
  services (`http://www.internic.net`).
- InterNIC InfoSource gopher: (`gopher://is.internic.net/11/infoguide/`).
- InterNIC DS Web: Directory and Database Services Home Page
  (`http://ds.internic.net`).
- InterNIC Database Services (`ftp://ds.internic.net`).
- InterNIC Registry Services (`ftp://rs.internic.net/netinfo/`).
- Merit: Network Information Center (`ftp://nic.merit.edu`).
- Merit Gopher: Network Information Center (`gopher://nic.merit.edu`).
- SuraNet NIC: Southeastern Universities Research Association, Inc. Network
  Information Center (`http://www.sura.net/index.html`).
- SWITCHinfo: Swiss Network (`ftp://nic.switch.ch/info_service/`).

Series

- IEN Web: Internet Engineering Notes
  (`http://www.cis.ohio-state.edu/hypertext/information/ien.html`).
- FYI: For Your Information sub-series of RFCs about topics that relate to the Internet
  (`ftp://nic.merit.edu/documents/fyi/`).
- Internet Docs: Internet Documentation (RFCs, FYIs, and so on) from InterNIC
  (`http://ds.internic.net/ds/dspg0intdoc.html`).
- Internet Drafts: Draft documents to be submitted ultimately to the Internet Activities
  Board as RFCs (`ftp://nic.merit.edu/documents/internet-drafts/`).
- Internet Drafts Search (`http://web.nexor.co.uk/idindex`).
- Internet Handbook: A list of RFCs by subject and category
  (`ftp://sri.com/netinfo/internet-technology-handbook-contents`).
- STD: Internet Standards, subseries of notes within the RFC series that documents
  Internet standards (`ftp://nic.merit.edu/documents/std/`).
- RFC repositories: Repositories where RFCs are located
  (`ftp://isi.edu/in-notes/rfc-retrieval.txt`).

■ RFC: Request for Comments—A document series that describes the Internet suite of protocols and related experiments (`ftp://nic.merit.edu/documents/rfc/`).

■ RFC Web: Internet Request For Comments (RFC) in html (`http://www.cis.ohio-state.edu/hypertext/information/rfc.html`).

■ RFCs via mail: Request For Comments—documents about various issues for discussion, covering a broad range of networking issues (`mailto:rfc-info@isi.edu Body: help: ways_to_get_rfcs`).

Training

Collections

■ Beginner's Guides-Yahoo: Computers-Internet-Beginner's Guides entry from Yahoo (`http://www.yahoo.com/Computers/Internet/Beginner_s_Guides/`).

■ CBL: Computer-Based Learning Unit, The University of Leeds, United Kingdom (`http://cbl.leeds.ac.uk`).

■ DELTA: Distributed ELectronic Telecommunications Archive teaching and learning about business telecommunications and data communications (`http://gozer.idbsu.edu/business/nethome.html`).

■ HelpNet Archives: Reference base for new users to the Internet (`ftp://ftp.temple.edu/pub/info/help-net`).

■ Introducing the Internet: Merit's Directory of miscellaneous introductory Internet information (`ftp://nic.merit.edu/introducing.the.internet/`).

■ IETF/TERENA: Internet Engineering Task Force (IETF) Training Materials Catalogue (`http://coolabah.itd.adelaide.edu.au/TrainMat/catalogue.html`).

■ ITTI: Information Technology Training Initiative, a United Kingdom-wide initiative to provide training materials about or using Information Technology (`http://info.mcc.ac.uk/CGU/ITTI/ITTI.html`).

■ Matrix-WELL: Information about cyberspace networks (`gopher://gopher.well.sf.ca.us/11/matrix`).

■ MOREnet: Training materials from Missouri Research and Education Network (MOREnet) (`ftp://ftp.more.net/pub/nic/training`).

■ NETTRAIN archive: NETTRAIN (networking training) discussion list archives (`ftp://ubvm.cc.buffalo.edu/nettrain/`).

■ Nets and DB-MSU: Network and Database Resources (CWIS, gopher, electronic info) (`gopher://burrow.cl.msu.edu`).

■ NOCALL: Northern California Association of Law Libraries (NOCALL) and the Southern California Association of Law Libraries (SCALL) to encourage use of the Internet and provide training assistance to our members (`ftp://ftp.netcom.com/pub/loftus/buddies/home.html`).

- Schneider Bib: A bibliography of Internet Training Materials, by Karen Schneider (`ftp://alexia.lis.uiuc.edu/pub/training.bib`).
- Start Web: Where to Start for New Internet Users (in HTML), by James Milles (`http://www.law.cornell.edu/test/newusers.html`).
- Sunsite-UNC: Univ. of North Carolina's collection (`ftp://sunsite.unc.edu/pub/docs/about-the-net/`).
- Trainmat: Training Materials Gopher (`gopher://trainmat.ncl.ac.uk`).
- Trainpack: Repository of training and training-related materials (`ftp://ftp.ncl.ac.uk/pub/network-training/`).
- Venturing-Newfoundland: Memorial University of Newfoundland Venturing into the Internet collection (`gopher://cwis.ucs.mun.ca/11/Venturing%20into%20the%20Internet`).
- Wash Coll of Law: Net Training Materials, from Washington College of Law (`http://sray.wcl.american.edu/htm/training.htm`).
- Web Training: University of Toronto Instructional and Research Computing Group (UTIRC) World Wide Web home page, information about HTTP, HTML, and networked multimedia training and technology (`http://www.utirc.utoronto.ca/home.html`).
- Wheeler: Internet Training handouts, by Bill Wheeler (`ftp://s850.mwc.edu/nettrain/`).
- Yale: Internet Help (`gopher://yaleinfo.yale.edu`).

Resources

- Dir of Trainers/consultants: From the Internet Business Journal (`gopher://gopher.fonorola.net/00/Internet%20Business%20Journal/Directory_of_Trainers_and_Consultants`).
- Montsarrat: Training materials (basic and serious Internet) (`ftp://wilma.cs.brown.edu/pub/internet_course.tar.Z`).
- Net workbook: By Martin Raish (`mailto:listserv@bingvmb.bitnet` Body: GET NETKNOW NEOPHYTE BI-L).
- Newcastle/Tyne: Network Training Materials and Related Documentation (`ftp://mailbase.ac.uk/pub/lists/itli-networks/files/tms-list.txt`).
- Resources collection: Guides, lists, sites, and resources of interest and use to Internet Trainers, by Neil Enns (`http://www.brandonu.ca/~ennsnr/Resources/`).
- Start: Where to Start for New Internet Users, by James Milles (`ftp://sluaxa.slu.edu/pub/millesjg/newusers.faq`).
- VAX/VMS Networking: Beginner's Guide to Networking on the VAX/VMS, by Lucia Ruedenberg (`ftp://ftp.temple.edu/pub/info/help-net/vms-mail.guide`).

Exploring

- Beginners/Suarez: The Beginner's Guide to the Internet for DOS and Windows, by Patrick J. Suarez (`ftp://oak.oakland.edu/pub/msdos/info/bgi13a.zip`).

- DOS Internet Kit: Public-domain programs that enable Ethernet or serially connected PCs to access Internet services, by Dean Pentcheff (`ftp://tbone.biol.scarolina.edu/pub/kit/`).

- DOS Internet Kit Web: Public-domain programs that enable Ethernet or serially connected PCs to access Internet services, packaged as a kit, by Dean Pentcheff (`http://tbone.biol.scarolina.edu/~dean2/kit/kit.html`).

- Internet Cruise: A cruise of the Internet, computer-based tutorial for Internet navigators, DOS or Mac formats (`ftp://nic.merit.edu/resources/`).

- Internet Explorer's Kit: A hypertext system about the Internet for DOS, by Ernest Perez (`ftp://sunsite.unc.edu/pub/docs/about-the-net/libsoft/explorer.doc`).

- Internet Hunt: A game for learning about Internet resources (`ftp://ftp.cni.org/pub/net-guides/i-hunt/`).

- Internet Hunt Gopher: Hunt Questions, Results, and Comments (`gopher://gopher.cic.net/11/hunt`).

- Internet Navigating: Navigating the Internet Workshop List, by Richard J. Smith (`ftp://ubvm.cc.buffalo.edu/navigate/`).

Courses

- CMC: A graduate course in CMC with some network training components (`http://www.rpi.edu/Internet/Guides/decemj/course/cmc.html`).

- Compass in Cyberspace: Internet Training from John S. Makulowich (`http://www.clark.net/pub/journalism/brochure.html`).

- Courses/info tech: Courses related to social implications of information technology, list by Meng Weng Wong (`http://www.seas.upenn.edu/~mengwong/netsurf/otherclasses.html`).

- Gopherin: A course for cyberspace, by Jim Gerland and Rich Smith (via FTP) (`ftp://ubvm.cc.buffalo.edu/gophern/`).

- Internet Courses: Course Descriptions and Examples, by Neil Enns (`http://www.brandonu.ca/~ennsnr/Resources/courses.html`).

- Internet Resource: Internet Resource Discovery, Organization, and Design, by Lou Rosenfeld and Dr. Joe Janes, School of Information and Library Studies, University of Michigan (`http://http2.sils.umich.edu/~lou/60694.html`).

- Intro/Internet: one of several prototype classes and texts sponsored through the Globewide Network Academy (`http://uu-gna.mit.edu:8001/uu-gna/text/internet/index.html`).

- ISS 101: Internet survival skills, a course from Dr. Kenneth Hensarling (`http://kawika.hcc.hawaii.edu/iss101/101mods.html`).

- Gopherin course: Jim Gerland and Rich Smith's course about gopher (via gopher) (`gopher://wealaka.okgeosurvey1.gov/11/K12/GOPHERN`).

- LeJeune Course: Course materials and files, by Urban A. LeJeune (`ftp://pilot.njin.net/pub/Internet-course/`).

- Navigating: Navigating the Internet, workshop for teaching the Internet via e-mail, by Richard J. Smith (`gopher://jake.esu.edu/11/Help/net_stuff/training`).

- Navigating: Navigating the Internet workshop (`mailto:listserv@ubvm.cc.buffalo.edu` Body: `subscribe navigate` *YOUR NAME*).

- Navigating: An interactive workshop, by Richard J. Smith (`ftp://ftp.sura.net/pub/nic/training/`).

- Netsurf course: By Meng Weng Wong, covers social implications of information technologies (`http://www.seas.upenn.edu/~mengwong/netsurf/`).

- NITEC: NYSERNet (New York Education and Research Network) Internet Training and Education Center (`http://nysernet.org/nitec.info/`).

- Milles: An Introduction to Using the Internet at St. Louis University School of Law (`ftp://sluaxa.slu.edu/pub/millesjg/interlaw.txt`).

- Mining: Mining the Internet course, Central Michigan University's Computer Science 196 ($) (`mailto:34mjkeq@cmuvm.csv.cmich.edu`).

- Surfing: A course given at Florida State University on Internet use (`http://www.cs.fsu.edu/surfing.html`).

Tutorials for Specific Applications

- Ackermann tutorial: Internet Services and Resources for Computer Scientists, by Ernest Ackermann, Department of Computer Science, Mary Washington College, Fredericksburg, VA (`ftp://s850.mwc.edu/pub/tutorial`).

- Competencies: Competencies for Electronic Information Services, by John Corbin (`mailto:listserv@uhupvm1.uh.edu` Body: `GET CORBIN PRV4N6`).

- Discussion help: The art of getting help—guidelines for seeking help in discussion groups (`mailto:rrc request@weber.ucsd.edu` Subject: `archive send courtesy`).

- HTML Developer's: WWW + HTML Developer's JumpStation, maintained by SingNet and hosted by OneWorld Information Services (`http://oneworld.wa.com/htmldev/devpage/dev-page.html`).

- HTML FAQ: Hypertext markup language (`http://www.umcc.umich.edu/~ec/www/html_faq.html`).

- HTML info/CERN: HyperText Markup Language (HTML), Working and Background Materials, from CERN (`http://www.w3.org/hypertext/WWW/MarkUp/MarkUp.html`).

- Mosaic Web Index: An index to the National Center for Supercomputing Applications (NCSA) Mosaic online documentation and tutorials on the NCSA Web server (`http://www.ncsa.uiuc.edu/SDG/Software/Mosaic/Docs/web-index.html`).

- NIR/CMC Tools/December: A list summarizing Internet tools and computer-mediated communication forums; includes pointers to guides or information about each tool, by John December (`http://www.rpi.edu/Internet/Guides/decemj/itools/top.html`).

- Tutorial gateway: A filter for a CGI-compliant HTTP server that makes it slightly easier to develop tutorial-style questions for Web users (`http://www.civeng.carleton.ca/~nholtz/tut/doc/doc.html`).

- Unix Help: Nova University's Unixhelp for users (`http://alpha.acast.nova.edu/UNIXhelp/TOP_.html`).

- Unix Man Pages: HyperText interface to UNIX man pages, by Michael Fisk (`http://nmt.edu/bin/man`).

- Unix tutorials: A collection of UNIX and computer information, from East Stroudsburg University (`gopher://jake.esu.edu/11/Help/Tutorials`).

- URL: Curling Up to Universal Resource Locators, by Eric S. Theise (`gopher://gopher.well.sf.ca.us/00/matrix/internet/curling.up.02`).

- URL guide/NCSA: A Beginner's Guide to URLs, by Marc Andreessen (`http://www.ncsa.uiuc.edu/demoweb/url-primer.html`).

- Usenet and trn: An Introduction to Usenet News and the trn Newsreader, by Jon Bell (`ftp://cs1.presby.edu/pub/trn-intro/`).

- WWW Weavers: A collection of resources related to developing information on the World Wide Web, by Chris Beaumont (`http://www.nas.nasa.gov/NAS/WebWeavers/`).

- WWW talk/Maimone: Welcome to the World Wide Web! Tutorial slides by Mark Maimone, Carnegie Mellon Computer Science (`http://www.cs.cmu.edu:8001/afs/cs/usr/mwm/www/tutorial/index.html`).

- WWW talk/Musciano: An Introduction to the World Wide Web, Chuck Musciano, Corporate Information Management, Harris Corporation, September 2, 1994 (`http://melmac.corp.harris.com/www_intro/`).

- WWW talk/Wallach: The World Wide Web, Everything you've always wanted to know, but were afraid to ask, by Dan Wallach (`http://www.cs.princeton.edu/grad/Dan_Wallach/www-talk/talk0.html`).

- WWW talk/Berners-Lee: WWW Seminar, Transparency track, by Tim Berners-Lee , Robert Cailliau, CERN (`http://www.w3.org/hypertext/WWW/Talks/General/Transparencies.html`).

- X Tutorial: X Window System Tutorial, by David Marshall (`http://www.cm.cf.ac.uk/Dave/X_lecture/X_lecture.html`).

Navigating

Tools

- GNN's Tools: A list of tools and supporting documents, from Global Network Navigator (`http://nearnet.gnn.com/gnn/helpdesk/tools/index.html`).

- Internet Browsers: Sources for Internet Browsers and Client Software (`http://life.anu.edu.au/links/syslib.html`).

- Internet Tools/EARN HTML: European Academic Research Network Association Guide to Network Resources Tools in HTML (`http://www.earn.net/gnrt/notice.html`).

- Internet Tools NIR: A status report on networked information retrieval tools and groups, by Joint IETF/RARE/CNI Networked Information Retrieval Working Group (`ftp://mailbase.ac.uk/pub/lists/nir/files/nir.status.report`).

- Internet Tools/December HTML: HTML (segmented) version of a list summarizing Internet tools and computer-mediated communication forums, by John December (`http://www.rpi.edu/Internet/Guides/decemj/itools/top.html`).

- Internet Tools/December (text): A list summarizing Internet tools and computer-mediated communication forums, by John December (`ftp://ftp.rpi.edu/pub/communications/internet-tools.readme`).

- Internet Systems UNITE: A list of Internet tools and systems, by User Network Interface To Everything (`ftp://mailbase.ac.uk/pub/lists/unite/files/systems-list.txt`).

Guides

- AARNet Guide: Australian Network Sites and Resources Guide (`ftp://aarnet.edu.au/pub/resource-guide/`).

- AARNet User Guide: Australian Network User's Guide (`ftp://aarnet.edu.au/pub/user-guide/`).

- Argus Guide: The Internet Tools and Resources Guide (`http://argus-inc.com/Guide.html`).

- De Presno Guide Gopher: Full text of the Online World book by Odd de Presno (`gopher://wuecon.wustl.edu:10672/11/online`).

- De Presno Guide via FTP: A shareware book, 'The Online World' (long) (`ftp://ftp.eunet.no/pub/text/`).

- De Presno Guide via WWW (`http://login.eunet.no/~presno/index.html`).

- De Presno Guide via E-mail (`mailto:LISTSERV@vm1.nodak.edu` Body: `get tow where`).

- EFF's Guide: (formerly Big Dummy's Guide) written by Adam Gaffin for the Electronic Frontier Foundation (`ftp://ftp.eff.org/pub/Net_info/EFF_Net_Guide/`).

- EFF Guide Web: (formerly Big Dummy's) Guide in HTML, from the Electronic Frontier Foundation (EFF) (`http://www.eff.org/papers/eegtti/eegttitop.html`).

- EFF Guide Search: Search the (formerly Big Dummy's) Guide (`http://www.germany.eu.net/cgi-bin/eegfind.pl`).

- E-mail 101: Describes how to use e-mail as well as other Internet features, by John Goodwin (`ftp://mrcnext.cso.uiuc.edu/etext/etext93/email025.txt`).

- E-mail/access: Accessing The Internet By E-Mail, by "Doctor Bob" Rankin (`gopher://nisp.ncl.ac.uk/00/lists-k-o/lis-iis/files/e-access-inet.txt`).

- E-mail/Start: How to get initial Internet info via e-mail, by David Rosen (`http://www.scs.unr.edu/%7Ecbmr/net/start.html`).

- Entering/WWW: Kevin Hughes's guide to the Web (`http://www.eit.com/web/www.guide/`).

- Entering/WWW ftp: FTP site for Kevin Hughes's Web guide (`ftp://ftp.eit.com/pub/web.guide/`).

- HWGUIDE: A hypertext version of Noonan's Guide to Internet/Bitnet (`ftp://sunsite.unc.edu/pub/docs/about-the-net/libsoft/hwguide.txt`).

- InfoPop: A WINHELP (hypertext) guide to the Internet, CompuServe, BBS systems, and more, by Wally Grotophorst (`ftp://ftp.gmu.edu/library/`).

- Internet Companion (parts): A Beginner's Guide to Global Networking by Tracey LaQuey (`ftp://ftp.std.com/OBS/The.Internet.Companion/`).

- Internet Guide: A guide to Internet/Bitnet, by Dana Noonan (`ftp://sunsite.unc.edu/pub/docs/about-the-net/libsoft/guide1.txt`).

- Internet Tour: A Short, Semi-Guided Tour of the Internet, from Kapor Enterprises (`http://www.kei.com/internet-tour.html`).

- Internet Web Text: An index to the Internet's resources; links to orientation, guides, reference materials, browsing and exploring tools, subject and word-oriented searching tools, and information about connecting with people, by John December (`http://www.rpi.edu/Internet/Guides/decemj/text.html`).

- La toile d'araignée: French translation with European-oriented resources, by François Charoy, of John December's Internet Web Text (`http://www.loria.fr/~charoy/ToileInternet/text.html`).

- Library of Congress: A directory of Internet User Guides (`ftp://ftp.loc.gov/pub/iug/`).

- Meng's: Holistic Guide to the Internet, by Meng Weng Wong (`http://ccat.sas.upenn.edu/mengwong/guide.html`).

- Neophyte: Network Knowledge for the Neophyte, Stuff You Need to Know in Order to Navigate the Electronic Village, by Martin Raish (`ftp://hydra.uwo.ca/pub/libsoft/network_knowledge_for_the_neophyte.txt`).

- NSF Resource Guide: National Science Foundation Guide to Internet Resources (`ftp://ds.internic.net/resource-guide/overview`).

- NWNet Internet Guide: NorthWestNet's User Service Internet Resource Guide (`ftp://ftphost.nwnet.net/user-docs/nusirg/README.nusirg`).
- NYSERNet Internet Guide: New York State Education and Research Network Guide to the Internet (`ftp://nysernet.org/pub/guides/Guide.V.2.2.text`).
- SLAC: Introduction to the Internet—a narrative about the Internet from SLAC (Stanford Linear Accelerator Center), by Joan Winters (`http://slacvm.slac.stanford.edu/FIND/internet.html`).
- SURANet Internet Guide: Updated as `infoguide.MM-YR.txt` (`ftp://ftp.sura.net/pub/nic/`).
- SURFnet Guide: SURFnet is the Dutch academic network (`ftp://ftp.nic.surfnet.nl/surfnet/user-support/docs/training/`).
- WWW/Mosaic: User's Guide, by Craig I. Schlenoff (`http://elib.cme.nist.gov/fasd/pubs/schlenoff94.html`).
- Zen/Art of Internet: Zen and the Art of the Internet (1st edition), by Brendan Kehoe (`ftp://ftp.csn.org/pub/net/zen/`).
- Zen Web: Zen and the Art of the Internet (1st edition), by Brendan Kehoe, in HTML (`http://sundance.cso.uiuc.edu/Publications/Other/Zen/zen-1.0_toc.html`).

Collections

- GNN's Internet Helpdesk: From Global Network Navigator's (O'Reilly) (`http://www.ora.com/gnn/helpdesk/index.html`).
- Gopher Jewels: Internet Cyberspace-related gophers (`http://galaxy.einet.net/GJ/internet.html`).
- Hypermedia/Internet: Hypermedia and the Internet, by David Green (`http://life.anu.edu.au/education/hypermedia.html`).
- Info Deli: A collection of Net information, by Peter Kaminski (`ftp://ftp.netcom.com/pub/info-deli/bookmark.html`).
- Internet-Yahoo: Pointers to the subject classification Computers-Internet (`http://www.yahoo.com/Computers/Internet/`).
- NetCruiser: NETCOM On-Line Communications Services, Inc.'s online guide (`http://www.netcom.com/glee/cruiser.html`).
- NOSC Page: List of Internet-related sources, by Richard Bocker (`http://white.nosc.mil/internet.html`).
- Naval Research Lab: NRL Network Research Navigator, strong on technical aspects of networking (`http://netlab.itd.nrl.navy.mil`).
- The Net: Descriptions of how to access information through Mosaic/Web, by Robert Thau (`http://www.ai.mit.edu/the-net/overview.html`).

- Tractatus CyberNauticus: Information about the Internet and the Web, by Denys Duchier (`http://kaml1.csi.uottawa.ca:3000/tractatus.html`).

- Yale: General Overview of Worldwide Internet Resources (`http://www.cs.yale.edu/HTML/WorldWideWebTop.html`).

- U of TX: Internet Information Resources, from the University of Texas (`http://fiat.gslis.utexas.edu/internet/internet.html`).

Specialized Guides or Collections of General Interest

- Dern's Info: Daniel Dern's Internet Info, News and Views (`gopher://gopher.internet.com:2200/11/`).

- Agricultural Guide: Not Just Cows, by Wilfred Drew (`gopher://snymorva.cs.snymor.edu/hhGOPHER_ROOT1:[LIBRARY-DOCS.HTML]`).

- DDN New User Guide: Defense Data Network guide for new users (`ftp://nic.ddn.mil/netinfo/nug.doc`).

- Electric Mystics Guide: A Complete Directory of Networked Electronic Documents, Online Conferences, Serials, Software, and Archives Relevant to Religious Studies, by Michael Strangelove (`ftp://panda1.uottawa.ca/pub/religion/`).

- FidoNet Guide: The Big Dummy's Guide to Fidonet, by Michael Schuyler (`gopher://digital.cosn.org/11/Networking%20Information/Reference/The%20BIG%20DUMMY%27S%20GUIDE%20TO%20FIDONET`).

- Savetz Stuff: Kevin Savetz's Page o' Stuff, Internet-related resources and lists by Kevin Savetz (`http://www.northcoast.com/savetz/savetz.html`).

Navigators

- GNN: Global Network Navigator from O'Reilly (`http://gnn.com`).

- Hytelnet: Assists users in reaching Internet libraries, Free nets, CWISs, BBSs, and other information sites by telnet (`telnet://hytelnet@access.usask.ca`).

- Hytelnet web (`http://www.cc.ukans.edu/hytelnet_html/START.TXT.html`).

- Inter-Links: Internet resources, information, links, from Nova Southeastern University, in Ft. Lauderdale, Florida (`http://alpha.acast.nova.edu/start.html`).

- Netlink: Connects you with a wide variety of services, from Washington and Lee University (`http://netlink.wlu.edu:1020`).

- Washington and Lee: Explore Internet Resources (`gopher://liberty.uc.wlu.edu/11/internet`).

- WorldWindow: A service of the Washington University Libraries (`telnet://library.wustl.edu`).

Searching

New or Noteworthy

■ Archives: Summation of Announcements from WWW-ANNOUNCE, NET-HAPPENINGS mailing lists and `COMP.INFORSYSTEMS.WWW.*` newsgroups (`http://cair-archive.kaist.ac.kr:80/Archive/Announce/`).

■ Best of Web: A gallery of best of Web Award Winners (`http://wings.buffalo.edu/contest`).

■ Best of GNN: Global Network Navigator's Best of honorees (`http://gnn.com/gnn/wic/best.toc.html`).

■ Best of/PC Week: A collection of sites from *PC Week* Labs (`http://www.ziff.com/~pcweek/pcwbests.html`).

■ Cool/Day: Cool Site of the Day, from InfiNet (`http://www.infi.net/cool.html`).

■ Commerce New: What is new in commercial services on the Web (`http://www.directory.net/dir/whats-new.html`).

■ CUI W3 Catalog: Changes to the various W3 Catalog sources for the past week (`http://cuiwww.unige.ch/W3catalog/changes.html`).

■ CyberWeb New: Announcements for WWW Developers (`http://www.charm.net/~web/New.html`).

■ Fishnet: A weekly list of odds and ends of postings and information from the Internet (`http://www.cs.washington.edu/homes/pauld/fishnet/`).

■ GNN's WIC New: What's New with The Whole Internet Catalog, from Global Network Navigator, O'Reilly and Associates (`http://nearnet.gnn.com/gnn/wic/nunu.toc.html`).

■ InfoBank: InfoBank's collection of new lists (`http://www.clark.net/pub/global/new.html`).

■ Infobot: Hotlist database (`ftp://ftp.netcom.com/pub/ksedgwic/hotlist/hotlist.html`).

■ Infosystems—new: (Moderated) announcement of new information systems or resources (`news:comp.infosystems.announce`).

■ Infosystems index: What's New from `comp.infosystems.announce`, an index of articles from the newsgroup, by George Ferguson (`http://www.cs.rochester.edu/users/grads/ferguson/announce/`).

■ Info sys announce: Send announcements to this address (`mailto:infosys@msu.edu`).

■ Info sys admin: Send administrivia to this address (`mailto:infosys-request@msu.edu`).

■ Net happenings newsgroup: News about resources, information, happenings on the network (`news:comp.internet.net-happenings`).

- Net Happenings archive: Archive of a moderated mailing list that announces conferences, publications, newsletters, network tools updates, and network resources (`http://www-iub.indiana.edu/cgi-bin/nethaps/`).

- New index-Yahoo: Reference-Indices to Web Documents—What's New (`http://www.yahoo.com/Reference/Indices_to_Web_Documents/What_s_New/`).

- New Internet sites: Collection of links to new Internet Resources services (`gopher://liberty.uc.wlu.edu/11/internet/new_internet`).

- New Lists: New mailing lists announcements archive (`gopher://vm1.nodak.edu/11/Local%20LISTSERV%20Resources/NEW-LIST%20Project`).

- New sites: New Internet Resources (via Washington and Lee Law Lib) (`gopher://liberty.uc.wlu.edu/11/internet/new_internet`).

- Nova New: What's New on the Internet collection (`http://alpha.acast.nova.edu/misc/netnews.html`).

- Sites/Day-Yahoo: Reference-Indices to Web Documents—Sites of the Day entry from Yahoo (`http://www.yahoo.com/Reference/Indices_to_Web_Documents/Sites_of_the_Day/`).

- Useful/cool things: Daily showcase of one pointer to something useful on the Internet, and one pointer to something cool (`http://www.teleport.com/~lynsared/useful.html`).

- Web Announce: New resources about the World Wide Web, moderated newsgroup `comp.infosystems.www.announce` (`http://www.halcyon.com/grant/Misc/charter.html`).

- webNews: Announcements of new Web sites, services, and software, a service of the Department of Computer and Information Sciences at the University of Alabama at Birmingham, Studies of Information Filtering Technology for Electronic Resources (SIFTER) Research Group (`http://twinbrook.cis.uab.edu:70/webNews.80`).

- webNews search: A database of recent articles from Usenet news about the Web (`gopher://twinbrook.cis.uab.edu/7GO/webNews.70`).

- What's New/Gopher: What's new on known public gophers (gopher, telnet, wais) (`gopher://liberty.uc.wlu.edu/11/internet/new_internet`).

- What's New/Meta: A list of what's new pages, by Meng Weng Wong (`http://www.seas.upenn.edu/~mengwong/whatsnew.list.html`).

- What's New/Web: What's New With NCSA Mosaic; actually shows Web-wide new resources (`http://www.ncsa.uiuc.edu/SDG/Software/Mosaic/Docs/whats-new.html`).

- What's Cool/Web-Netscape: A "What's cool" page developed at Netscape communications (`http://home.mcom.com/home/whats-cool.html`).

- Yahoo New: What's New on Yahoo Hierarchical Hotlist (`http://akebono.stanford.edu/yahoo/new.html`).

Resource Lists

- ALICE: Annotated Listings for Internet and Cyberspace Explorers
  (`http://www.umanitoba.ca/ALICE/index.html`).

- Awesome List: A list of useful resources, by John Makulowich
  (`http://www.clark.net/pub/journalism/awesome.html`).

- CMC resources: Resources related to the study of Computer-Mediated Communication, from the CMC Studies Center (`http://www.rpi.edu/~decemj/cmc/resources.html`).

- Creative/Internet: The Creative Internet Home Page, a collection of fun and useful resources (`http://www.galcit.caltech.edu/~ta/creative.html`).

- Drakos List: Subjective Electronic Information Repository, by Nikos Drakos
  (`http://cbl.leeds.ac.uk/nikos/doc/repository.html`).

- Email Services: A list of services available via e-mail, by David DeSimone
  (`ftp://sunsite.unc.edu/pub/docs/about-the-net/libsoft/email_services.txt`).

- Exploring: Exploring the Internet, by Ed Kubaitis
  (`http://www.cen.uiuc.edu/exploring.html`).

- Freeside FAQ: Meng surfs the Internet
  (`http://www.seas.upenn.edu/~mengwong/fsfaq.html`).

- GNN's Internet Page: Internet information, from Global Network Navigator
  (`http://nearnet.gnn.com/wic/internet.toc.html`).

- Hot/Cool List: What's Hot and Cool on the Web, art/music/interesting emphasis
  (`http://kzsu.stanford.edu/uwi/reviews.html`).

- InfoBank: Information Bank's collection of Internet resources links
  (`http://www.clark.net/pub/global/front.html`).

- Internet-EIT: Enterprise Integration Technologies Web Resources
  (`http://www.eit.com/web/web.html`).

- Internet-Enns: A collection of resources that are useful to Internet trainers, as well as just about anyone else who is on the Net, by Neil Enns
  (`http://www.brandonu.ca/~ennsnr/Resources/`).

- Internet FAQ: Internet Services Frequently Asked Questions (FAQ) list for `alt.internet.services` Usenet newsgroup
  (`ftp://rtfm.mit.edu/pub/usenet/news.answers/internet-services/faq`).

- Internet Meta-Index: Internet Resources Meta-Index, from the National Center for Supercomputing Applications (NCSA)
  (`http://www.ncsa.uiuc.edu/SDG/Software/Mosaic/MetaIndex.html`).

- Justin's/Underground: Justin's Links from the Underground
  (`http://www.sccs.swarthmore.edu:80/jahall/`).

- MaasInfo Indexes: The index of indexes of Internet online files, by Robert Elton Maas
  (`ftp://NCTUCCCA.edu.tw/documents/Internet/MaasInfo/`).

- May List: Lists Telnet sites/services, by CC May
  (`ftp://aug3.augsburg.edu/files/bbs_lists/nal008.txt`).

- Planet Earth: Planet Earth home page, a list of things on the Internet, by Richard
  Bocker (`http://white.nosc.mil/info.html`).

- Power Index: from Web Communications, lists a variety of resources in many categories
  (`http://www.webcom.com/power/index.html`).

- Smith's BigFun List: Telnet, ftp, and other sites, by Jeremy Smith
  (`ftp://owl.nstn.ns.ca/pub/netinfo/bigfun.txt`).

- Spider's Web: A list of links to lists, Web/Net stuff, searchers, images, and references
  (`http://gagme.wwa.com/~boba/spider.html`).

- ThesisNet FAQ: A summary of academic resources pertaining to cyberspace
  (`http://www.seas.upenn.edu/~mengwong/thesisfaq.html#ftp`).

- Thousand/Sites: A Thousand Points of Sites, a random way (!) to encounter Web sites
  (`http://legendre.ucsd.edu/Research/Fisher/Home/randomjump.html`).

- Tong's Collection: Links to other sites, a miscellaneous collection of information and
  entertainment, by Andrew Tong (`http://www.ugcs.caltech.edu/~werdna/info.html`).

- Top Tens: From Internet Training and Consulting Services, resource lists that are picks
  of the Net and Web in Top-level resources, art, commerce, fun, Internet training, K-12
  education, library, Internet books and journals
  (`http://www.itcs.com/itcs/topten.html`).

- URouLette: A way to pseudo-randomly choose a URL to visit
  (`http://kuhttp.cc.ukans.edu/cwis/organizations/kucia/uroulette/uroulette.html`).

- Useless/WWW: 'America's Funniest Home Hypermedia,' a collection of strange, trivial,
  bizarre, unusual, and weird WWW pages, collected by Paul Phillips
  (`http://www.primus.com/staff/paulp/useless.html`).

- Yale Overview: General Overview of Worldwide Internet Resources
  (`http://www.cs.yale.edu/HTML/WorldWideWebTop.html`).

- Yanoff's Services List (ftp): Special Internet Connections (Internet Services List), by
  Scott Yanoff (`ftp://ftp.csd.uwm.edu/pub/inet.services.txt`).

- Yanoff List HTML: Hyptertext markup language version of Scott Yanoff's Special
  Internet Connections listing of resources by subject
  (`http://www.uwm.edu/Mirror/inet.services.html`).

- WWW/Internet: A collection of links to manuals and demos
  (`http://tecfa.unige.ch/info-www.html`).

Subjects

- CSOIRG Home Page: The Clearinghouse for Subject-Oriented Internet Resource
  Guides at the School of Information and Library Studies, University of Michigan
  (`http://www.lib.umich.edu/chhome.html`).

1282

- CSOIRG ftp: Subject-specific Internet Resource Guides collected by UMich (`ftp://una.hh.lib.umich.edu/inetdirs/`).

- CSOIRG gopher: UMich collection via gopher (`gopher://una.hh.lib.umich.edu/11/inetdirs`).

- CyberSight: Unique subjects on the Net (`http://cybersight.com/cgi-bin/cs/s?main.gmml`).

- CyberZine: A yellow pages user-friendly guide to Cyberspace (`http://cyberzine.org/index.html`).

- Galaxy: A service of EINet, a collection of information, searchable via index or by topic trees (`http://www.einet.net/galaxy.html`).

- GNN WIC: Global Network Navigator's Whole Internet Catalog, from O'Reilly and Associates (`http://nearnet.gnn.com/wic/newrescat.toc.html`).

- Gopher Jewels gopher: Subject-oriented gopher list (`gopher://cwis.usc.edu/11/Other_Gophers_and_Information_Resources/Gophers_by_Subject/Gopher_Jewels`).

- Gopher Jewels web: A collection of subject-oriented gophers (`http://galaxy.einet.net/GJ/index.html`).

- Gopher Jewels links: .links format (`ftp://usc.edu/pub/gopher/`).

- Gopher Jewels Info: Lists information available about Gopher Jewels (`mailto:listproc@einet.net` Body: `get gopher-lists.txt`).

- Gopher Trees: A collection of subject-oriented gopher trees (`gopher://burrow.cl.msu.edu/11/internet/subject`).

- Hyperdex: Hyperindex over webNews and more (`http://twinbrook.cis.uab.edu:70/hhyperdex.80`).

- INFOMINE: Resources covering a range of disciplines, by the Library of the University of California-Riverside (`http://lib-www.ucr.edu`).

- Internet at Large: Subject-oriented listing (`http://www.sdsc.edu/1/SDSC/Geninfo/Internet`).

- InterNIC Dir of Dirs: InterNIC's Directory of Directories, subject-oriented listing of registered Internet resources and services (`http://ds.internic.net/ds/dsdirofdirs.html`).

- IWT Narrative: Internet Web Text's narrative about subject-oriented searching (`http://www.rpi.edu/Internet/Guides/decemj/nar-subject.html`).

- Joel's List: Joel's Hierarchical Subject Index (`http://www.cen.uiuc.edu/~jj9544/index.html`).

- LOC/resources: U.S. Library of Congress code for classifying resources on the Net (`gopher://info.anu.edu.au/11/elibrary/lc`).

- LOC/VL: U.S. Library of Congress categorization of WWW Virtual Library (`http://www.w3.org/hypertext/DataSources/bySubject/LibraryOfCongress.html`).

- Mother/BBS: Mother of all BBSs, a project to allow users to add information to a subject tree, developed by Oliver McBryan (`http://www.cs.colorado.edu/homes/mcbryan/public_html/bb/summary.html`).

- Planet Earth: Richard P. Bocker created this web to collect a wide variety of Internet resources (`http://white.nosc.mil/info.html`).

- Study Carrels: Subject and Discipline-Specific Internet Resources, from North Carolina State University Library (`http://dewey.lib.ncsu.edu/disciplines/index.html`).

- Subject Lists: Resources Classified by Subject (LC Classification) (`gopher://info.anu.edu.au:70/11/elibrary/lc`).

- UMBC Web: University of Maryland—Baltimore County, exceptional Internet-based resources by subject category (`http://umbc7.umbc.edu/~jack/subject-list.html`).

- USENET FAQ Index: Forms-based gateway to Usenet FAQs, by INTAC (`http://www.intac.com/FAQ.html`).

- USENET Periodic Postings: List of Usenet periodic postings (`ftp://rtfm.mit.edu/pub/usenet/news.answers/periodic-postings/`).

- USENET repository: Collection of FA's and files from Usenet newsgroups (`ftp://rtfm.mit.edu/pub/usenet/`).

- USENET news.answers: A hypertext presentation of the answer lists posted in the news.answers newsgroup (`http://www.cis.ohio-state.edu/hypertext/faq/usenet/`).

- WAIS subject tree: A list of WAIS servers separated into subject areas (`http://www.ub2.lu.se/auto_new/UDC.html`).

- WAIS Servers: Directory of wide area information servers (`wais://cnidr.org:210/directory-of-servers?`).

- WAIS sources: A collection of WAIS sources (`gopher://liberty.uc.wlu.edu/11/internet/indexsearches/inetsearches`).

- Web of Wonder: Links to Web resources on various subjects, by Lance Weitzel (`http://www.digimark.net/wow/`).

- Yahoo: Yet Another Hierarchically Odiferous Oracle, an extendible collection of subjects (`http://www.yahoo.com/`).

- Yanoff List HTML: Hyptertext markup language version of Scott Yanoff's Special Internet Connections listing of resources by subject (`http://www.uwm.edu/Mirror/inet.services.html`).

- WWW VL: World Wide Web Virtual Library, a large hypertext collection of information organized by subject (`http://www.w3.org/hypertext/DataSources/bySubject/Overview.html`).

- WWW VL/LOC: The World Wide Web Virtual Library viewed as U.S. Library of Congress Classification (`http://www.w3.org/hypertext/DataSources/bySubject/LibraryOfCongress.html`).

Keyword

- Academic lists: Searchable index of academic e-mail conferences (`wais://munin.ub2.lu.se:210/academic_email_conf`).

- ALIWEB: Archie-Like Indexing for the Web, by Martijn Kosterrch (`http://web.nexor.co.uk/aliweb/doc/aliweb.html`).

- Archieplex: Archie via Web—access archie servers (search ftp sites) via the Web (`http://web.nexor.co.uk/archie.html`).

- CUSI: by Martijn Kosterrch interface; a forms-based interface into many indices, engines, and Web Spider databases (`http://web.nexor.co.uk/public/cusi/doc/list.html`).

- CUSI-R: Customizable Unified Search Index via Radio Buttons, by David Rosen (`http://www.scs.unr.edu/~cbmr/net/search/cusi-r.html`).

- Discussion groups: Search a list of discussion groups, Bitnet and Internet interest groups (Dartmouth list) (`http://alpha.acast.nova.edu/cgi-bin/lists`).

- External info: Collects some of the most useful search engines available on the WWW (`http://www_is.cs.utwente.nl:8080/cgi-bin/local/nph-susi1.pl`).

- Gloss: Glossary-of-Servers Server, a system to find data sources that match keyword queries (`http://gloss.stanford.edu`).

- Gopher Jewels Search: Search the Gopher Jewels (a collection of subject-oriented gophers) (`http://galaxy.einet.net/gopher/gopher.html`).

- GNA Meta-Library: Search the Globalwide Networking Academy (GNA) library of resources and information (`http://uu-nna.mit.edu:8001/uu-nna/meta-library/index.html`).

- Hytelnet search gopher: Given a keyword, returns Hytelnet entries (`gopher://liberty.uc.wlu.edu:3004/7`).

- Hytelnet Web search: Search all Hytelnet resource entries, via a web form, from Galaxy (`http://galaxy.einet.net/hytelnet/HYTELNET.html`).

- Infoseek: A keyword-searching service ($) over WWW pages, Usenet, computer magazines, newspaper newsires, press releases, company profiles, movie reviews, technical support databases (`http://ww.infoseek.com`).

- IWeb: Web search service, allows you to find resources matching a keyword query; allows you to contribute to the database by registering (`http://sparta.lcs.mit.edu/iweb/welcome.html`).

- JumpStation: Referencing the information available on the World Wide Web (`http://www.stir.ac.uk/jsbin/js`).

- NIKOS: An Internet Resource Locator (`http://www.rns.com/cgi-bin/nomad`).

- Shase: Virtual Shareware Library (`http://www.fagg.uni-lj.si/SHASE/`).

- WAISGATE: WAIS to WWW gateway, search WAIS databases through search terms (`http://www.wais.com/directory-of-servers.html`).

- Web Catalog/CUI: A collection of URL references built from a number of handcrafted HTML lists, from Centre Universitaire d'Informatique, l'Université de Génève (`http://cuiwww.unige.ch/w3catalog`).

- Web Search Engines: A meta-index of search engines on the Web, with a forms interface, from Centre Universitaire d'Informatique, l'Université de Génève (`http://cuiwww.unige.ch/meta-index.html`).

- Web Spiders info: Search the web for information about resources, collecting information into a database that can be queried; for example, Web Crawler, Web Nomad, Web Worm, RBSE database, Lycos (Araneida, Lycosidae, Lycosa), Harvest Brokers; entry from Internet Tools Summary (`http://www.rpi.edu/Internet/Guides/decemj/itools/nir-tools-spiders.html`).

- Web Spiders web: Wanderers, Spiders and Robots; includes list of known robots/spiders, guidelines, standard for robot exclusion, by Martijn Kosterrch (`http://web.nexor.co.uk/mak/doc/robots/robots.html`).

Spaces

- FTP Sites list: List of Internet sites accepting anonymous ftp, maintained by Perry Rovers (`ftp://rtfm.mit.edu/pub/usenet/news.answers/ftp-list/`).

- FTP Sites Web: Web interface to Perry Rover's FTP site monster list (`http://www.info.net/Public/ftp-list.html`).

- Gopher Sites: List of all gophers (long) (`ftp://liberty.uc.wlu.edu/pub/lawlib/all.gophers.links`).

- Telnet—Hytelnet/telnet: Access to the Hytelnet Service through telnet, by Peter Scott (`telnet://hytelnet@access.usask.ca`).

- Telnet-Hytelnet/WWW: Access to Hytelnet by Peter Scott, provided by the University of Kansas (`http://www.cc.ukans.edu/hytelnet_html/START.TXT.html`).

- WAIS Servers: List of Wide Area Information Servers (WAIS), by WAIS, Inc. (`http://www.wais.com`).

- WWW Servers/sites: A comprehensive list of WWW sites generated from a Web Wanderer program, by Matthew Gray (`http://www.netgen.com/cgi/comprehensive`).

- WWW Servers/geo: A long list of registered WWW servers listed geographically by continent and country (`http://www.w3.org/hypertext/DataSources/WWW/Servers.html`).

- WWW Sites (CityLink): State and city web sites (`http://www.neosoft.com/citylink/`).

- WWW Sites (Virtual Tourist): A geographic map to aid in locating Web sites and other resources (`http://wings.buffalo.edu/world`).

- Web Sites (City Net): Explore and browse resources by geography (continent, region, country, city) (`http://www.city.net`).
- Web Sites index: Index to WWW sites, by John Doyle (`http://herald.usask.ca/~scottp/home.html`).
- Web Sites/Time: Timex World Time—shows time zones with current time and WWW sites in each (`http://www.timeinc.com/vibe/vibeworld/worldmap.html`).

People

- Directory services: A collection of white pages servers to look up people (`gopher://gopher.nd.edu/11/Non-Notre%20Dame%20Information%20Sources/Phone%20Books—Other%20Institutions`).
- Finding people: A collection of resources to help you locate a specific person on the Net (`gopher://yaleinfo.yale.edu:7700/11/Internet-People`).
- Home Pages/directories: A collection of personal home pages lists and directories (`http://www.rpi.edu/Internet/Guides/decemj/icmc/culture-people-lists.html`).
- Knowbot: Provides a uniform user interface to heterogeneous remote information services (Internic Point of contacts, MCImail, x500 databases, finger, nwhois, and so on) (`telnet://info.cnri.reston.va.us:185`).
- Netfind: A simple Internet white pages user directory (`http://www.rpi.edu/Internet/Guides/decemj/itools/nir-utilities-netfind.html`).
- Netsearch: A database of companies and contacts (`http://www.ais.net:80/netsearch/`).
- Searching for People: e-mail addresses, phone books, from Washington and Lee (`gopher://liberty.uc.wlu.edu/11/internet/personsearches`).

Directories

- American Universities (`http://www.clas.ufl.edu/CLAS/american-universities.html`).
- CS Depts (`http://www.cs.cmu.edu:8001/Web/People/anwar/CS-departments.html`).
- CWIS Web: A listing of Campus-Wide information systems, by Polly-Alida Farrington (`http://www.rpi.edu/Internet/cwis.html`).
- Commercial List: List of Commercial Services on the Web, from Open Market (`http://www.directory.net`).
- Dartmouth Merged SIGL: Special Interest Group Lists (`ftp://dartcms1.dartmouth.edu/siglists/`).
- Electronic Conferences: Directory of Scholarly Electronic Conferences, by Diane K. Kovacs (`ftp://ksuvxa.kent.edu/library/acadlist.readme`).
- Electronic Conferences: Browse or search the Directory of Scholarly Electronic Conferences, by Diane K. Kovacs (`http://www.austin.unimelb.edu.au:800/1s/acad`).

- Electronic Conferences: Gopher presentation of the Directory of Scholarly Electronic Conferences, by Diane K. Kovacs (`gopher://info.monash.edu.au/11/Other/lists`).

- Electronic Journals/ARL: Association of Research Libraries Directory of Electronic Journals and Newsletters (`gopher://arl.cni.org:70/11/scomm/edir`).

- Electronic Journals/Strangelove: Directory of Electronic Journals and Newsletters, by Michael Strangelove (`ftp://ftp.cni.org/pub/net-guides/strangelove/`).

- Electronic Magazines/archive: An archive of various electronic magazines (`ftp://etext.archive.umich.edu/pub/Zines/`).

- Electronic Resources: Lists resources (CWIS, texts, guides, WWW, WAIS, etc.) by University of Waterloo Library (`gopher://watserv2.uwaterloo.ca/11/servers`).

- EZines List (ftp): Summary of electronically accessible zines, by John Labovitz (`ftp://ftp.etext.org/pub/Zines/e-zine-list`).

- EZines Web: Summary of electronic zines by John Labovitz (`http://www.ora.com:8080/johnl/e-zine-list/`).

- Finding Lists: How to find Listserv lists (`mailto:listserv@vm1.nodak.edu` Body: `get NEW-LIST wouters`).

- Freenets Home Page: Freenet information, presented as a public service by Peter Scott, at the University of Saskatchewan Libraries (`http://herald.usask.ca/~scottp/free.html`).

- Free Databases: A catalog of databases that are available without payment (`ftp://idiom.berkeley.ca.us/pub/free-databases`).

- InterActive Yellow Pages: by Lighthouse Productions—telephone-style yellow pages international directory (`mailto:tuna@netcom.com` Subject: `yellow pages` Body: *YOUR EMAIL ADDRESS*).

- IYP: InterActive Yellow Pages (`ftp://ftp.netcom.com/pub/tuna/`).

- InfoMagnet: Helps you find, join, search and participate in Listserv discussion groups on the Internet (`http://www.clark.net/pub/listserv/imag.html`).

- Internet Computer Index: Lists of PC, Macintosh, and UNIX-related resources (`http://ici.proper.com`).

- Internet Consultants: CommerceNet's directory of Internet consultants (products and services) (`http://www.commerce.net/directories/consultants/consultants.html`).

- Internet Trainers/consultants: (`gopher://gopher.fonorola.net/00/Internet%20Business%20Journal/Directory_of_Trainers_and_Consultants`).

- Interest Groups List: The Lists of Lists, a listing of special-interest group mailing lists available on the Internet (`ftp://sri.com/netinfo/interest-groups.txt`).

- Japanese: Key information sources on Japan currently available over the Internet (`http://fuji.stanford.edu/japan_information/japan_information_guide.html`).

- Library Access Script: A script to log in to online card catalogs (`ftp://sonoma.edu/pub/libs.tar`).

- Library Guide: Accessing online Bibliographic Databases, by Billy Barron and Marie-Christine Mahe (`ftp://ftp.utdallas.edu/pub/staff/billy/libguide`).

- Library Catalogs Noonan: A list of academic and public library catalogs online, by Dana Noonan (`ftp://sunsite.unc.edu/pub/docs/about-the-net/libsoft/guide2.txt`).

- Library Catalogs St Geo: Internet—Accessible Library Catalogs and Databases, Art St. George and Ron Larsen (`ftp://nic.cerf.net/internet/resources/library_catalog/`).

- NET-LETTER GUIDE: A newshound's guide to newsy periodicals available through the Internet (`mailto:higgins@dorsai.dorsai.org` Body: `SUBSCRIBE NET-LETTER`).

- Net Orgs: Outposts on the Electronic Frontier, International, Groups Supporting the Online Community (`ftp://rtfm.mit.edu/pub/usenet/news.answers/net-community/orgs-list`).

- Nonprofit Center: Supports and provides information about nonprofit organizations (`gopher://envirolink.org/00/.EnviroOrgs/.inc/.center`).

- Nonprofits: Nonprofit Organizations on the Internet, by Ellen Spertus (`http://www.ai.mit.edu/people/ellens/non.html`).

- Online books: Online books (`http://www.cs.cmu.edu:8001/Web/books.html`).

- Online bibs: Online Bibliographies and Journal Contents (`http://www.cs.cmu.edu:8001/Web/bibliographies.html`).

- Online journals: Online Journals (`http://www.cs.cmu.edu:8001/Web/journals.html`).

- Online libraries (`http://www.cs.cmu.edu:8001/Web/e-libraries.html`).

- PAML: Publicly Available Mailing Lists, a list of mailing lists available primarily through the Internet and the UUCP network, by Stephanie da Silva (`http://www.neosoft.com/internet/paml`).

- Patents: Patent searching by class/subclass, by Gregory Aharonian (`http://sunsite.unc.edu/patents/intropat.html`).

- Publisher's Catalogs (`http://herald.usask.ca/~scottp/publish.html`).

- Reference: Reference Resources via the World Wide Web (`http://vm.cfsan.fda.gov/referenc.html`).

- Reference-Yahoo: Reference section from Yahoo (`http://www.yahoo.com/Reference/`).

- Software downloads: Publicly available sites for software (`http://alpha.acast.nova.edu/downloads.html`).

- Technical Reports: Technical reports archive (`ftp://daneel.rdt.monash.edu.au/pub/techreports/`).

- UNCAT: The electronic catalog of uncataloged titles (businesses, nonprofit groups, trade associations, museums, and self-published authors), from Sapphire Press (`http://www.sapphire.com/UNCAT/`).

- Virtual Tourist: Geographical directory of WWW Information Services (`http://wings.buffalo.edu/world`).

- WAIS sources: A brief description of the content of many WAIS sources on the Internet, grouped into relevant categories (`ftp://kirk.bond.edu.au/pub/Bond_Uni/doc/wais/readme`).
- WAIS Directory of Servers: `wais://cnidr.org:210/directory-of-servers?`.
- WAIS Databases: A hypertext list (`http://kaml1.csi.uottawa.ca:3000/wais.html`).
- WWW Sites: Comprehensive list—a long list of WWW sites gathered through an automated program, Webwanderer, by Matthew Gray (`http://www.mit.edu:8001/afs/sipb/user/mkgray/ht/compre3.html`).

Services

- Anonymous post: (`mailto:anonymus+ping@tygra.michigan.com` Body: `help`).
- Anonymous post: (`mailto:help@anon.penet.fi` Body: `help`).
- Anonymous remail: (`mailto:remail@tamsun.tamu.edu` Subject: `remail help`).
- BITFTP: obtain files via anonymous ftp on Bitnet (`mailto:Bitftp@PUCC.Princeton.edu` Body: `help`).
- Correct Time/NBS: Tells National Bureau of Standards correct time (`telnet://india.colorado.edu:13`).
- Domain Name Lookup: Translate domain names to numeric IP address (`telnet://lookup@130.59.1.40`).
- Email FTP: Get files at anonymous ftp sites via e-mail. (`mailto:ftpmail@decwrl.dec.com` Body: `help`).
- Email Gopher: Use a gopher via e-mail (`mailto:gophermail@ncc.go.jp` Body: `help`).
- Email Gopher: Use a gopher via e-mail (`mailto:gophermail@calvin.edu` Body: `help`).
- Email Usenet: Post to newsgroup via e-mail (`mailto:hierarchy-group-name@cs.utexas.edu` Subject: *Your Subject Body: Your Contents*).
- FAXNET: Faxes via e-mail ($) (`mailto:info@awa.com` Body: `help`).
- FAX FAQ: How can I send a fax from the Internet?, by Kevin Savetz (`ftp://rtfm.mit.edu/pub/usenet/news.answers/internet-services/fax-faq`).
- HTML Validation (`http://www.cc.gatech.edu/grads/j/Kipp.Jones/HaLidation/validation-form.html`).
- IP address resolver: Given a site name, obtain its numerical IP address (`mailto:resolve@widener.edu` Body: `site` *SITE NAME*).
- Mail name server: Gives e-mail information about many e-mail names (for example, IP address given name) (`mailto:dns@grasp.insa-lyon.fr` Body: `help`).
- RFCs via mail: Requests For Comments—documents about various issues for discussion, covering a broad range of networking issues (`mailto:rfc-info@isi.edu` Body: `help: ways_to_get_rfcs`).

Applications

People use the Internet and the Web for many purposes and applications. Part IV of this book contains detailed discussions of some of these applications. The listing here includes examples of applications as well as pointers to information about Internet- and Web-based applications in the following areas:

- **Commerce.** Information about commerce on the Internet and the Web as well as resource lists to locate additional marketplaces.

- **Communication.** Information about applications for individual, group, organizational, mass, societal, surveillance, and scientific communication.

- **Education.** Resource lists and information about schools on the Net.

- **Entertainment.** Some example lists of fun resources.

- **Government.** Information about initiatives for national information infrastructures and pointers to information supplied by governments.

- **Information.** Dissemination, retrieval, and library applications.

- **Scholarship.** Information and pointers to organizations concerned with online scholarship.

Commerce

Information

- Advertising Blacklist: A compendium of advertisers who have misused Net access, compiled by Axel Boldt (`http://math-www.uni-paderborn.de/~axel/blacklist.html`).

- Advertising Guide: The Internet Advertising Resource Guide, maintained by Hairong Li, The Missouri School of Journalism; links to a large number of sources of information about Internet advertising, including collections and topics, studies, storefronts, and other information (`http://www.missouri.edu/internet-advertising-guide.html`).

- Advertising FAQ: Internet Advertising FAQ, by Strangelove Internet Enterprises (`mailto:interBEX1@intnet.bc.ca`).

- Advertising/marketing law: Emphasis on infomercials, home shopping, and direct-response TV; includes intellectual property and telemarketing, by Lewis Rose (`http://www.webcom.com/~lewrose/home.html`).

- Businesses: List of Commercial Services on the Web, from Open Market (`http://www.directory.net`).

- Business/Corporations: Lists of business and corporations on the Net (`http://www.yahoo.com/Economy/Business/Corporations/`).

- Business sites: Interesting Business Sites on the Web, by Bob O'Keefe at the School of Management, Rensselaer Polytechnic Institute (http://www.rpi.edu/~okeefe/business.html).

- Business uses: Commercial Use (of the Net) Strategies Home Page, by Andrew P. Dinsdale (http://www.dserv.com/~andrew/business.html).

- Canadian Business: Canadian Internet Business Directory (http://cibd.com/cibd/CIBDHome.html).

- Career Mosaic: High-tech companies offering career information (http://www.careermosaic.com/cm/).

- Commercial List: A directory of many commercial services on the Web (http://www.directory.net).

- Commercial Services: A list of telnet connections to many commercial information services, from The World (gopher://gopher.std.com:70/11/Commercial).

- Computer+Communications: Computer and Communication Company Sites on the Web, by James E. (Jed) Donnelley (http://www-atp.llnl.gov/companies.html).

- Entrepreneurs: Useful business information and services for entrepreneurs (http://sashimi.wwa.com/~notime/eotw/EOTW.html).

- FECRS: Fairfax Electronic Commerce Resource Center; Continuous Acquisition Lifecycle Support (CALS); enterprise integration, electronic commerce and business processing, re-engineering (http://www.ecrc.gmu.edu/index.html).

- Hermes: Research project on the commercial uses of the World Wide Web (http://www.umich.edu/~sgupta/hermes.htm).

- IBC: Internet Business Center is a World Wide Web server for information specifically related to business use of the Internet (http://www.tig.com/IBC/).

- IBD: Internet Business Directory, product/service information (http://ibd.ar.com).

- InterBEX: Business Exchange, selective content-oriented business information (mailto:interBEX-index@intnet.bc.ca).

- InterQuote: Continuously updating stock market information service (http://wwa.com/~quote).

- Internet info: Compiles information on the commercial activity on the Internet (mailto:info@internetinfo.com).

- Marketing/CMEs: Marketing in Computer-Mediated Environments Home Page, from Owen Graduate School of Management, Vanderbilt University, Nashville, TN, USA (http://colette.ogsm.vanderbilt.edu).

- MARTECH: Discuss MARketing with TECHnology tools, such as marketing via the Internet (mailto:LISTSERV@cscns.com Body: subscribe MARTECH *YOUR NAME*).

- MESCH: The Multi-WAIS Engine for Searching Commercial Hosts, enables you to search the databases of several commercial WWW providers (http://www.ip.net/cgi-bin/mesch).

■ Publications: Print Publications Related to Business Use of the Internet, from Tenagra (`http://arganet.tenagra.com/Tenagra/books.html`).

■ Stock Quotes: QuoteCom, a service dedicated to providing financial market data to Internet users (`http://www.quote.com`).

■ Thomas Ho: Favorite Electronic Commerce WWW resources, includes information sources, links to articles, economic development, service/presence providers (`http://www.engr.iupui.edu/~ho/interests/commmenu.html`).

■ What's New/Commerce: What is new in commercial services on the Web (`http://www.directory.net/dir/whats-new.html`).

Marketplaces

Lists of Marketplaces

■ Shop D Net: A list of virtual marketplaces, from Blake and Associates, Internet Marketing Consultants (`http://www.neosoft.com/citylink/blake/malls.html`).

Selected Instances of Marketplaces

■ CommerceNet: Internet-based infrastructure for electronic commerce, created and operated by a consortium of major Silicon Valley users, providers, and developers under Smart Valley, Inc. (`http://logic.stanford.edu/cit/commercenet.html`).

■ Digital's Emall: Digital Equipment Corporation's Electronic Shopping Mall (`http://www.service.digital.com/html/emall.html`).

■ eMall: WWW shopping and information (`http://eMall.com`).

■ IBC: Internet Business Connection, an electronic shopping mall and a service for companies that would like to promote their products or services on the Internet (`http://www.charm.net/~ibc`).

■ Internet Mall: Shopping on the Information Highway—a monthly list of commercial services available via the Internet (`ftp://netcom.com/pub/Guides/`).

■ Internet Shopping Network: Products from hundreds of vendors, along with query interface (`http://shop.internet.net`).

■ Sofcom: Home shopping, information providers, no-profits (`http://www.sofcom.com.au`).

Communication

Individual

■ CMC-Interpersonal: List of interpersonal tools for CMC (mail, talk) (`http://www.rpi.edu/Internet/Guides/decemj/itools/cmc-interpersonal.html`).

- Home Pages: A collection of personal home pages lists
(`http://www.rpi.edu/Internet/Guides/decemj/icmc/culture-people-lists.html`).

Group

- CCCC: Computerized Conferencing and Communications Center at New Jersey Institute of Technology (NJIT)
(`http://it.njit.edu/njIT/Department/CCCC/default.html`).

- CSCW Info: Computer-Supported Cooperative Work information (groupware), unOfficial Yellow Pages of CSCW (`ftp://gorgon.tft.tele.no/pub/groupware/`).

- CSCW Lab: Computer-Supported Cooperative Work laboratory at the Fraunhofer-Institut für Graphische Datenverarbeitung, Germany
(`http://www.igd.fhg.de/cscw-lab/`).

- CSCW pages: The Unofficial Yellow Pages of CSCW (`http://www.tft.tele.no/cscw/`).

- Collaborative Comm: Collaborative Networked Communication—MUDs as Systems Tools, by Remy Evard (`http://www.ccs.neu.edu/USER/remy/documents/cncmast.html`).

- Collaborative Design: Architecture and CAAD, Swiss Federal Institute of Technology, Zurich (`http://www.arch.ethz.ch/~dave/cmc-collab.html`).

- CRTR-U of CO: Collaboration Technology Research Group (group user interfaces, distributed editors, workflow systems, cooperative grown information systems), University of Colorado (`http://www.cs.colorado.edu/homes/carlosm/public_html/ctrg.html`).

- Collaboration: Workshop on Wide-Area Collaboration and Cooperative Computing
(`http://www.ai.mit.edu/projects/iiip/colab/workshop.html`).

- Communication Archive: Sunsite Communication archive—papers, logs, information, including April Fool's Page, maintained by David Barberi
(`ftp://sunsite.unc.edu/pub/academic/communications/`).

- Communication Archive Web: Sunsite Communication archive—papers, logs, information, including April Fool's Page, maintained by David Barberi
(`http://sunsite.unc.edu/dbarberi/communications.html`).

- Computer Network Conf: A Discussion on Computer Network Conferencing, by D. Reed (`ftp://nic.merit.edu/documents/rfc/rfc1324.txt`).

- Groupware Yellow Pages: Information resources, from Consensus
(`http://www.consensus.com:8300/GWYP_TOC.html`).

- Internet Citizen's Band: Internet group teleconferencing program
(`http://www.echo.com/~kzin/icb.html`).

- Internet Relay Chat (IRC): Real-time, many-many text discussion divided into channels
(`ftp://cs.bu.edu/irc/support/`).

- IRC FAQ: Internet Relay Chat Frequently Asked Questions and Answers
(`http://www.kei.com/irc.html`).

- ISO/IEC stds: Draft of standards on computer conferencing
  (`gopher://mars.dsv.su.se:70/0/iso-mess/gc/X.acc-First_CD.TXT`).

- MOO Papers: Pavel Curtis's collection of MU* papers
  (`ftp://ftp.parc.xerox.com/pub/MOO/papers/`).

- MUD info: Multiple User Dialogue/Dimension/Dungeon FAQs, Lists, Information, Collections, Servers, Archives, Newsgroups, by Lydia Leong
  (`http://www.cis.upenn.edu/~lwl/mudinfo.html`).

- MUD papers/Cherny: Gender- and discourse-related MUD papers, by Lynn Cherny
  (`http://bhasha.stanford.edu/~cherny/papers.html`).

- NCW: National Center for the Workplace (NCW) Gopher
  (`gopher://uclink.berkeley.edu:3030/1`).

- Project H: An ongoing computer-mediated collaboration, on a Comserve-sponsored hotline, of more than a hundred international researchers
  (`http://www.arch.su.edu.au/PROJECTH/index.html`).

- SHARE: A Methodology and Environment for Collaborative Product Development
  (`http://www.eit.com/projects/share/share/share-home.html`).

- Tools: A list of Internet tools for group communication
  (`http://www.rpi.edu/Internet/Guides/decemj/itools/cmc-group.html`).

Organizational

- Client/Server: Client/Server Coffeehouse, discussion about client-server systems in organizations (`http://www.onr.com/clients.html`).

- CORPS: Computing, Organizations, Policy, and Society, study of computerization in organizations, Information and Computer Science, University of California, Irvine
  (`http://www.ics.uci.edu/CORPS/`).

- CWIS List: Campus-Wide Info Systems list
  (`ftp://sunsite.unc.edu/pub/docs/about-the-net/cwis/cwis-l`).

- CWIS Paper: Campus-Wide Info Systems by Judy Hallman
  (`ftp://sunsite.unc.edu/pub/docs/about-the-net/cwis/hallman.txt`).

- CWIS Web: A listing of Campus-Wide Information Systems, by Polly-Alida Farrington
  (`http://www.rpi.edu/Internet/cwis.html`).

- Campus Net: Creating a Campus Network Infrastructure, by Steve Griffin
  (`ftp://gandalf.iat.unc.edu/technote/teknote4.txt`).

- Campus Net Bib: Creating a Campus Network Infrastructure—Bibliography
  (`ftp://gandalf.iat.unc.edu/guides/irg-15.txt`).

- IOS: Interorganizational Systems (IOS) WorldNet
  (`http://www-iwi.unisg.ch/iswnet/index.html`).

- OMT: Organization and Management Theory Division of the Academy of Management, to foster communication and to serve as an information resource to Organization scholars worldwide (`http://cwaves.stfx.ca/Subjects/Business/omt.html`).

Mass

Lists

- Campus Newspapers: Campus Newspapers on the Internet, by Jonathan Bell (`http://beacon-www.asa.utk.edu/resources/papers.html`).
- Internet news: Internet-accessible news, newspapers, TV, radio, press services, and publications, by C. Sam Sternberg (`ftp://ftp.shell.portal.com/pub/jshunter/news.html`).
- Commercial News/Web: A list of commercial news services on the WWW, by Gary Ritzenthaler (`http://www.jou.ufl.edu/commres/webjou.htm`).
- Communication Resources: Communications and Mass Media Resources, links, reviews, and resources for scholars and those interested in Journalism, Mass Media, and Communications Research, by Steve Brown (`http://www.jou.ufl.edu/commres/commhome.htm`).
- CyberNews: Student-run media connectivity, newswire on the Internet (`http://www.hmc.edu/www/people/teverett/cybernews/Home.html`).
- Daily business: Daily sources of business and economic news (`http://www.helsinki.fi/~lsaarine/news.html`).
- Electronic newspapers: by Steve Outing (`mailto:majordomo@marketplace.com` Body: `get online-news online-newspapers.list`).
- ENewsstand gopher: Information provided by U.S. magazine publishers (`gopher://gopher.internet.com`).
- GSN: Global Student News, a collaboration of student journalists, by Gary Ritzenthaler (`http://www.jou.ufl.edu/forums/gsn/`).
- Journalism/Comm schools: World Wide Web sites of interest to those in the fields of journalism and mass communications (`http://www.jou.ufl.edu/commres/jouwww.htm`).
- Journalism: Journalism List of Internet Resources, by John S. Makulowich (`ftp://rtfm.mit.edu/pub/usenet/news.answers/journalism-net-resources`).
- Journalism Directory: Internet Resources, by John S. Makulowich (`ftp://ftp.clark.net/pub/journalism/`).
- Media BBS: Media BBS List, broadcasting/journalism BBS list, by Mark S. Leff (`mailto:listserv@ulkyvm.louisville.edu` Body: `GET MEDIA BBSLIST`).
- Media List ftp: E-mail addresses of media outlets, by Adam Gaffin (`ftp://ftp.std.com/customers/periodicals/Middlesex-News/medialist`).

■ Media List list: E-mail addresses of media outlets, by Adam Gaffin
(`mailto:majordomo@world.std.com` Body: `subscribe medialist`).

■ Movies and TV: Nova's Movies and TV information
(`http://alpha.acast.nova.edu/movies.html`).

■ Periodicals: Electronic periodicals and journals
(`gopher://gopher.cic.net/11/e-serials`).

■ SPJ: Society of Professional Journalists (`ftp://ftp.netcom.com/pub/spj/html/spj.html`).

■ TV-film-video: Vortex's collection of materials, including Cable Regulation Digest
(`gopher://vortex.com/11/tv-film-video`).

■ TV Networks-Yahoo: Business-Corporations-Media-Television-Networks, entry from
Yahoo (`http://www.yahoo.com/Business/Corporations/Media/Television/Networks/`).

■ TV Schedules: The schedules of some television channels/shows
(`http://white.nosc.mil/television.html`).

■ Student Newspapers: High school and college newspapers online
(`gopher://blick.journ.latech.edu`).

■ Tools: A list of Internet tools for mass communication
(`http://www.rpi.edu/Internet/Guides/decemj/itools/cmc-mass.html`).

Application Areas

■ Amateur Radio: The World of Internet Amateur (Ham) Radio
(`http://www.acs.ncsu.edu/HamRadio/`).

■ Cable TV: Cable Television Laboratories, Inc.
(`http://www.cablelabs.com`).

■ Intelsat: The leading provider of satellite telecommunications services
(`http://www.intelsat.int:8080`).

■ Live TV: Demonstration consists of live video and audio using the vsdemo VuSystem
application that uses a live television source on the VuNet
(`http://tns-www.lcs.mit.edu/cgi-bin/vs/vsdemo`).

■ Satellite: The Satellite TV Page (`http://itre.uncecs.edu/misc/sat.html`).

Outlets

■ AP: Associated Press (`http://www.trib.com/news/AP.html`).

■ BBC Networking Club (`http://www.bbcnc.org.uk`).

■ C-SPAN: Cable-Satellite Public Affairs Network (`gopher://c-span.org`).

■ CBC Radio (`http://radioworks.cbc.ca`).

■ CBS (`http://www.cbs.com`).

■ ClariNet: Complete electronic newspaper delivered via Net
(`mailto:info@clarinet.com`).

- ITR: Internet Talk Radio (`http://www.ncsa.uiuc.edu/radio/radio.html`).
- Cyberspace Report: A public affairs radio show aired on KUCI, 88.9 FM in Irvine, California (`http://www.ics.uci.edu/~ejw/csr/cyber.html`).
- PBS: U.S. Public Broadcasting Service (`gopher://gopher.pbs.org`).
- Palo Alto Weekly (`http://www.service.com/PAW/home.html`).
- TV Net: Web Homes for Television and Cable Stations throughout the United States and the World (`http://cinenet.net/TVnet.html`).
- TV nets: Business-Corporations-Television-Networks, from Yahoo (`http://www.yahoo.com/Business/Corporations/Television/Networks/`).
- VOA: Voice of America (USA) (`ftp://ftp.voa.gov`).
- VOA gopher: Voice of America (USA) (`gopher://gopher.voa.gov`).
- Wired (`mailto:editor@wired.com`).

Societal

- Cyberpunk: texts for understanding technology and culture, from the English Server (`http://english-server.hss.cmu.edu/Cyber.html`).
- Friends + Partners: United States and Russia information and communication (`http://solar.rtd.utk.edu/friends/home.html`).
- Net Revisited: The Network Nation Revisited, a bachelor's thesis examining Hiltz and Turoff's predictions for CMC on societal change, by David Belson (`http://www.stevens-tech.edu/~dbelson/thesis/thesis.html`).

Surveillance/Remote Control

- Anthony's List: Internet-accessible machines for vending, temperature sensors, tele-operated machinery, equipment status, cameras/video, and others, by Anthony Anderberg (`http://www.dsu.edu/~anderbea/machines.html`).
- bsy's List: Internet-Accessible (non-Coke) Machines, connections to many surveillance and remote-sensing examples (`http://www.cs.cmu.edu:8001/afs/cs.cmu.edu/user/bsy/www/iam.html`).
- Camera in office: Spy on Dennis Gannon, Research Director of Center for Innovative Computer Applications (`http://www.cica.indiana.edu/htbin/camera`).
- Interesting Devices: Computers-Internet-Interesting Devices Connected to the Net, from Yahoo (`http://www.yahoo.com/Computers/Internet Interesting_Devices_Connected_to_the_Net/`).
- Robot: Robotic Tele-Excavation at the University of Southern California, Mercury Project, users tele-operate a robot arm moving over a terrain filled with buried artifacts (`http://www.usc.edu/dept/raiders/`).

■ Temperature: Temperature on CU/Boulder Engineering Center Roof (`http://www.cs.colorado.edu/htbin/temp`).

Scientific

■ CISTI: Canada Institute for Scientific and Technical Information—worldwide scientific, technical, and medical information (`http://www.cisti.nrc.ca/cisti/cisti.html`).

■ CAS: The Chicago Academy of Sciences (`http://www.mcs.com/~cas/home.html`).

■ CS Tech Reports: Computer Science Technical Reports Archive Sites (`http://www.rdt.monash.edu.au/tr/siteslist.html`).

■ EnviroWeb: Environmental information source on the Internet (`http://envirolink.org`).

■ NAS ftp: National Academy of Sciences (`ftp://ftp.nas.edu`).

■ NAS web: National Academy of Sciences (`http://www.nas.edu`).

■ NSF-USA: The National Science Foundation (NSF), United States (`http://www.nsf.gov`).

■ Science-Yahoo (`http://www.yahoo.com/Science/`).

■ SETN: The Science and Engineering Television Network, Inc., a nonprofit consortium of scientific societies, universities, laboratories, and corporations organized to foster the development of scientific communication in the medium of television (`http://www.service.com/stv/setncall.html`).

■ SPIE Web: Services from The International Society for Optical Engineering (SPIE) (`http://www.spie.org`).

■ Technical reports: List of science-research-technical reports, from Yahoo (`http://www.yahoo.com/Science/Research/Technical_Reports/`).

■ WATERS: Wide Area Technical Report Service, a WAIS-based technical reports repository (`http://www.cs.odu.edu/WATERS/WATERS-GS.html`).

Education

Major Tree Collections

■ Education-Galaxy: EINet Galaxy's collection of resources about education (`http://galaxy.einet.net/galaxy/Social-Sciences/Education.html`).

■ Education-WWW VL: WWW Virtual Library entry for education (`http://www.w3.org/hypertext/DataSources/bySubject/Education/Overview.html`).

■ Education-Yahoo: Education section from Yahoo (`http://www.yahoo.com/Education/`).

Other Collections

- AskERIC Web: Educational Resources Information Center, Clearinghouse on Information and Technology, federally funded collection of education-related resources (`http://eryx.syr.edu/Main.html`).

- Best for ed: A selection of the best of the Internet for educators (`gopher://info.asu.edu/11/asu-cwis/education/other`).

- BBN NSN: BBN's National School Network Testbed (`gopher://copernicus.bbn.com`).

- CALICO: Computer Assisted Language Instruction Consortium (`mailto:CALICO@Dukemvs.ac.duke.edu`).

- CAUSE gopher: Association for managing and using information technology in higher education (`gopher://cause-gopher.Colorado.edu`).

- Center/Excellence: Center for Excellence in Education, to help our best students and teachers keep the United States competitive in science and technology, and to nurture international understanding among potential leaders of many countries (`http://rsi.cee.org`).

- Chronicle web: ACADEME THIS WEEK, offers guide to contents of *The Chronicle of Higher Education* and all Positions Available ads, calendar of events, deadlines for grants, papers, fellowships, put out every Tuesday at noon EST (`http://chronicle.merit.edu`).

- Cisco: Education archive, lists a variety of resources about school connectivity to the Internet as well as resources on the WWW (`http://sunsite.unc.edu/cisco/edu-arch.html`).

- COL: Commonwealth of Learning, distance education techniques and associated communications technologies (`http://www.col.org`).

- CoVis: Learning Through Collaborative Visualization, Northwestern University (`http://www.covis.nwu.edu`).

- Cyberion City: Virtual environment built by schoolchildren (`telnet://guest@michael.ai.mit.edu`).

- CTC: Cornell Theory Center Math and Science Gateway, resources in mathematics and science for educators and students in grades 9-12 (`http://www.tc.cornell.edu/Edu/MathSciGateway/index.html`).

- DeweyWeb: Facilitating communication between students from all over the world (`http://ics.soe.umich.edu`).

- Distance Ed: `ftp://una.hh.lib.umich.edu/inetdirsstacks/disted:ellsworth`.

- Dr. E's Compendium: Dr. E's Eclectic Compendium of Electronic Resources for Adult/Distance Education, by J. H. Ellsworth (`ftp://ftp.std.com/pub/je/dre-list.txt`).

- NDLC: National (USA) Distance Learning Center (`telnet://ndlc@ndlc.occ.uky.edu`).

- Distance Ed DB: A database from the International Centre for Distance Learning at the United Kingdom Open University (`mailto:n.ismail@open.ac.uk`).

- Distance Ed DB: Contains full text of *Mindweave*, edited by Mason and Kaye (`telnet://icdl@acsvax.open.ac.uk`).

- Diversity U: Diversity University, an experiment in interactive learning through Internet (`telnet://moo.du.org:8888`).

- EdWeb-CPB: Corporation for Public Broadcasting, an online tutorial on education, technology, school reform, and the Information Highway (`http://k12.cnidr.org:90`).

- Education Gopher: Florida Tech's collection of educational resources (`gopher://sci-ed.fit.edu`).

- EOS web: Educational Online Sources, pointers for education (`http://www.netspace.org/eos/`).

- Educational Technology: The World-Wide Web Virtual Library—Educational Technology (`http://tecfa.unige.ch/info-edu-comp.html`).

- Education Technology Initiatives: Higher Education Funding Councils for England, Wales, Scotland, and Northern Ireland now support three major initiatives in the UK that are aimed at improving universities' awareness and use of technological innovations in teaching and learning (`gopher://gopher.csv.warwick.ac.uk/11/remote/other-remote/edu-tech`).

- Educator's Email: An Educator's Guide to E-Mail Lists (`ftp://nic.umass.edu/pub/ednet/educatrs.lst`).

- Educator's USENET: Ednet Guide to Usenet Newsgroups (`ftp://nic.umass.edu/pub/ednet/edusenet.gde`).

- Empire Schoolhouse: Empire Internet Schoolhouse, a selection of K–12 resources, projects, and discussion groups (`gopher://nysernet.org:3000/11/`).

- EnviroWeb: A project of the EnviroLink Network; sponsors many online environmental education initiatives (`http://envirolink.org`).

- ETB/NLM: Educational Technology Branch (ETB), part of the Lister Hill National Center for Biomedical Communications (LHNCBC) at the National Library of Medicine (NLM) (`http://wwwetb.nlm.nih.gov`).

- Exploratorium: A collage of 650 interactive exhibits in the areas of science, art, and human perception (`http://www.exploratorium.edu`).

- GENII: Group Exploring the National Information Infrastructure (`http://www.deakin.edu.au/edu/MSEE/GENII/GENII-Home-Page.html`).

- GNA: Globewide Network Academy, a nonprofit corporation affiliated with Usenet University; goal is to create a fully accredited online university (`http://uu-nna.mit.edu:8001/uu-gna/index.html`).

- High school/Internet: A case study of an east central Florida high school, by Michael Anthony Gallos to the Internet (`ftp://sci-ed.fit.edu/pub/Internet/study/`).

- HUB: Mathematics and science education (`http://hub.terc.edu`).

- IAT archive: Institute for Academic Technology ftp site
  (`ftp://gandalf.iat.unc.edu/user/home/anonftp/guides/`).

- iCDL: International Centre for Distance Learning, in the United Kingdom on the
  campus of the Open University, disseminating distance education information worldwide (`http://acs-info.open.ac.uk/info/other/ICDL/ICDL-Facts.html`).

- IKE: IBM Kiosk for Education (`gopher://ike.engr.washington.edu`).

- IKE Web: IBM Kiosk for Education (`http://ike.engr.washington.edu/ike.html`).

- ILT: Institute for Learning Technologies as part of the Columbia University Virtual
  Information Initiative (`http://www.ilt.tc.columbia.edu`).

- ILC-Southampton: Interactive Learning Centre, University of Southampton, United
  Kingdom (`http://ilc.ecs.soton.ac.uk/welcome.html`).

- Internet and Ed: By Noel Estabrook (`ftp://ftp.msu.edu/pub/education/`).

- IRD/Educators: Internet Resource Directory for Educators
  (`ftp://tcet.unt.edu/pub/telecomputing-info/IRD`).

- IT Connections: Instructional Technology Connections, by Martin Ryder
  (`gopher://ccnucd.denver.colorado.edu/h0/UCD/dept/edu/IT/itcon.html`).

- JASON: Introduces teachers to the world of telecommunicating
  (`telnet://topcat.bsc.mass.edu`).

- JASON Project web: A journey to the rain forest, caverns, Mayan ruins, and coral reef of
  Belize (`http://seawifs.gsfc.nasa.gov/JASON/JASON.html`).

- Jones Ed Nets: Jones Education Networks (Mind Extension University, Jones Computer
  Network) (`http://www.meu.edu`).

- K–12 Armadillo: Annotated directory of K–12 resources from Rice University
  (`http://chico.rice.edu/armadillo/Rice/K12resources.html`).

- K–12 Briarwood: Collection of K–12 resources of the Internet, including a Curriculum
  Database (`http://www.briarwood.com`).

- K–12 Gopher: CICnet's K–12 Internet gopher
  (`gopher://gopher.cic.net/11/cicnet-gophers/k12-gopher`).

- K–12 Info/CNIDR: Includes global schoolhouse project and Janice's K12 Cyberspace
  Outpost (`http://k12.cnidr.org`).

- K–12 List: List of K–12 Internet School Sites, by Gleason Sackman
  (`http://toons.cc.ndsu.nodak.edu/~sackmann/k12.html`).

- K–12 NASA/Langley: NASA Langley Research Center's HPCC K–12 Program
  (`http://k12mac.larc.nasa.gov/hpcck12home.html`).

- K–12 NASA/NAS: Pointers to online Educational Resources, by Chris Beaumont
  (`http://www.nas.nasa.gov/HPCC/K12/edures.html`).

■ K–12 Registry: WWW Schools Registry, from Web66/Hillside Elementary School (`http://hillside.coled.umn.edu/others.html`).

■ K–12 Web 66: Resources and information to facilitate the introduction of Web technology into K–12 schools (`http://web66.coled.umn.edu`).

■ Kenyon workbook: Workbook for Kenyon's Summer Institute on Academic Information Resources; emphasis on faculty and student exploration of information resources, communication, and collaboration, from Kenyon College, Gambier, Ohio (`ftp://ftp.kenyon.edu/pub/pub/e-pubs/workbook/`).

■ KidLink: Gopher aimed at 10- to 15-year-olds (`gopher://kids.ccit.duq.edu`).

■ Latitude 28: Latitude28 Schoolhouse, a privately sponsored project, designed to make educational materials accessible to students of all ages (`http://www.packet.net/schoolhouse/Welcome.html`).

■ Learning V: Learning Village, Internet access to schools, by National Public Telecomputing Network and Ameritech (`mailto:tmg@nptn.org`).

■ LRDC: Learning Research and Development Center at the University of Pittsburgh—thinking, knowing, and understanding in and beyond school (`http://www.lrdc.pitt.edu`).

■ NCSA education: National Center for Supercomputing Applications Education Program Home Page (`http://www.ncsa.uiuc.edu/Edu/EduHome.html`).

■ Maricopa: Center for Learning and Instruction, Maricopa Community Colleges, Arizona (`http://www.mcli.dist.maricopa.edu`).

■ MEU BBS: Mind Extension University Bulletin Board System (`telnet://bbs.meu.edu`).

■ Networking: Networking on the Network, an essay by Phil Agre (`mailto:comserve@vm.its.rpi.edu` Body: `send Profess Network`).

■ Networking: Networking on the Network, an essay by Phil Agre (`http://communication.ucsd.edu/pagre/network.html`).

■ NCET: National Council for Educational Technology Information Service (UK) (`http://datasun.ncet.org.uk`).

■ OISE Gopher: Ontario Institute for Studies in Education (`gopher://porpoise.oise.on.ca:70`).

■ Online LC: Mount Allison University's Online Learning Centre—tele-education (`gopher://pringle.mta.ca`).

■ Plugged In: A nonprofit group dedicated to bringing the educational opportunities created by new technologies to children and families from low-income communities, located in East Palo Alto, California (`http://www.pluggedin.org`).

■ Primary/Sec: Answers to Commonly Asked Primary and Secondary School Internet User Questions (`ftp://nic.merit.edu/documents/fyi/fyi_22.txt`).

■ Singapore-Ed: Ministry of Education (MOE), Singapore (`http://www.moe.ac.sg`).

- Teacher Education: Society for Technology and Teacher Education (STATE), the University of Virginia, and the University of Houston have collaborated to establish a Teacher Education Server on the Internet (`http://curry.edschool.virginia.edu/teis/`).

- TECFA: An academic team active in the field of educational technology at the School of Education and Psychology of the University of Geneva (`http://tecfa.unige.ch/tecfa-overview.html`).

- U.S. Dept of Ed gopher: United States Department of Education (`gopher://gopher.ed.gov`).

- U.S. Dept of Ed Web: United States Department of Education (`http://www.ed.gov`).

- USENET University: An online society of people interested in learning, teaching, or tutoring (`ftp://nic.funet.fi/pub/doc/uu/FAQ`).

- VOU: Virtual Online University, an online liberal arts university, using a virtual environment called a VEE (Virtual Education Environment) (`http://core.symnet.net/~VOU/`).

- WWW teaching: WWW for instructional use, a collection of course materials, from the University of Texas at Austin (`http://www.utexas.edu/world/instruction/index.html`).

Entertainment

Major Collections

- Entertainment-Yahoo: Entertainment section from Yahoo (`http://www.yahoo.com/Entertainment/`).

Selected Instances

- Coke Machines: bsy's List of Internet Accessible Coke Machines (`http://www.cs.cmu.edu:8001/afs/cs.cmu.edu/user/bsy/www/coke.html`).

- The Dominion: Sci-Fi Channel (`http://www.scifi.com`).

- Games: Games, FAQs, and other entertainment resources (`http://wcl-rs.bham.ac.uk/GamesDomain`).

- Interactive games: Zarf's List of Interactive Games on the Web (`http://www.cs.cmu.edu:8001/afs/cs.cmu.edu/user/zarf/www/games.html`).

- WWW/Sports: World Wide Web of Sports, Spanning the globe to bring you a constant variety of sports information (`http://tns-www.lcs.mit.edu/cgi-bin/sports`).

Government

Initiatives for Information Infrastructures

These government-sponsored initiatives and organizations to implement or support national or state information infrastructures.

- Canada: Industry Canada Ministry, Communications Development Directorate (http://debra.dgbt.doc.ca/.dtp/dtp.html).

- Europe: European Council report on specific measures to be taken by the European Community and the Member States for information infrastructures (http://www.earn.net/EC/bangemann.html).

- Europe/Info Market: I'M (Info Market)—Europe Home Page, information about Europe and the European electronic information market (http://www.echo.lu).

- France: Reseau National de Télécommunications pour la Technologie, l'Enseignement et la Récherche (http://web.urec.fr/docs/renater/renater.html).

- GII: Agenda for Cooperation, by Al Gore and Ron Brown (http://ntiaunix1.ntia.doc.gov:70/0/papers/documents/giiagend.html).

- GII Info: Global Information Infrastructure information from the Computer Professionals for Social Responsibility (http://cpsr.org/dox/global.html).

- Japan-MITI: Japan's Ministry of International Trade and Industry, program for advanced information infrastructure (http://www.glocom.ac.jp/NEWS/MITI-doc.html).

- Japan-MPT: Reforms toward the Intellectually Creative Society of the 21st Century (http://www.glocom.ac.jp/WhatsNew/MPT.html).

- Singapore-IT200: Information from the National Computing Board (NCB) of Singapore's Digital Media Centre (http://www.ncb.gov.sg).

- Singapore-ITI: Information Technology Institute (ITI), the applied R&D arm of the National Computer Board (NCB) of Singapore (http://www.iti.gov.sg).

- Singapore-NII SCAN: A publication of major NII policy trends around the world (http://www.ncb.gov.sg/nii/contents.html).

- USA-HPCC Web: The National Coordination Office (NCO) for High Performance Computing and Communications (http://www.hpcc.gov).

- USA-HPCC Gopher: The National Coordination Office (NCO) for High Performance Computing and Communications (gopher://gopher.hpcc.gov:70).

- USA-Info highway: Pointers to information about efforts to create information networks at government and private levels (http://ai.iit.nrc.ca/superhighway.html).

- USA-NII FTP: National Information Infrastructure (ftp://ftp.ntia.doc.gov/pub/niiagenda.asc).

- USA-NII BBS: The White House Information Infrastructure Task Force BBS (telnet://gopher@iitf.doc.gov).

- USA-NII Gopher: The White House Information Infrastructure Task Force BBS (`gopher://iitf.doc.gov`).

- USA-NII Dialup: The White House Information Infrastructure Task Force BBS (phone: 1-202-501-1920).

- USA-NII DIIG: The Digital Information Infrastructure Guide (DIIG) is a resource to facilitate the development of the National Information Infrastructure (NII) (`http://farnsworth.mit.edu/diig.html`).

- USA-NII Testbed: National Information Infrastructure Testbed (`http://www.esi.com/niit_top.html`).

- USA-NII Web: The White House Information Infrastructure Task Force Web (`http://iitf.doc.gov`).

- USA-NII Related: Related Efforts in the National Information Infrastructure (`http://www.acl.lanl.gov/sunrise/RelatedInfo/OtherProjects.html`).

- USA-NII-XIWT: USA's National Information Infrastructure Cross-Industry Working Team, a coalition of industry to define requirements for a national information infrastructure (`http://www.cnri.reston.va.us:3000/XIWT/public.html`).

- USA-North Carolina: North Carolina Information Highway (NCIH) home page (`http://www.ncih.net`).

Information Supplied by Governments

Government-sponsored or government-related information, particularly dealing with CMC issues.

Major Collections

- Government-Yahoo: A collection of links about government information, from Yahoo (`http://www.yahoo.com/Government/`).

Countries

- Canada: Open Government—information about the Canadian Federal government (`http://debra.dgbt.doc.ca/opengov`).

- Federal Info Resources: Documents from the Information Policy Branch, Office of Information and Regulatory Affairs, Office of Management and Budget of the U.S. government (`ftp://nic.merit.edu/omb/INDEX.omb`).

- Federal Govt: Federal Government Information on the Internet, by Maggie Parhamovich, Head, Government Publications, Dickinson Library, University of Nevada–Las Vegas (`gopher://una.hh.lib.umich.edu/00/inetdirsstacks/usfedgov%3aparhamovich`).

- Fedix: Federal Information Exchange, Inc., access to a wide variety of government data (`http://www.fie.com`).

- Fedworld: A system for government information (`telnet://fedworld.doc.gov`).

- Fedworld web: A gateway to U.S. Government information operated by the Department of Commerce's National Technical Information Service (NTIS) (`http://www.fedworld.gov`).

- Government-Galaxy: Page from EINet's Galaxy showing a large collection of government information (`http://www.einet.net/galaxy/Government.html`).

- GILS: Government Information Locator Service (`ftp://ftp.cni.org/pub/gils/`).

- Govt/Citizenship: Information about federal agencies, guides, policy, and other government information (`gopher://eryx.syr.edu`).

- Govt Information: Internet Sources of Government Information by Blake Gumprecht (`ftp://ftp.nwnet.net/user-docs/government/gumprecht-guide.txt`).

- Japan PM: Japan Prime Minister's official residence Web server (`http://www.kantei.go.jp`).

- U.K. CCTA: United Kingdom Government Centre for Information Systems (`http://www.open.gov.uk`).

- U.K. HM Treasury: United Kingdom Her Majesty's Treasury (`http://www.hm-treasury.gov.uk`).

- U.S. Govt Gophers: A collection of government gophers (`gopher://peg.cwis.uci.edu:7000/11/gopher.welcome/peg/GOPHERS/gov`).

- U.S. Govt Webs: List of WWW Servers (USA—Federal Government), from Federal Information Exchange (`http://www.fie.com/www/us_gov.htm`).

- U.S. NPR: U.S. National Performance Review (`http://www.npr.gov`).

- U.S. Patents and Trademarks: Includes Intellectual Property and the National Information Infrastructure issues (`http://www.uspto.gov`).

- U.S. House: U.S. House of Representatives gopher (`gopher://gopher.house.gov:70`).

- U.S. House: U.S. House of Representatives (`http://www.house.gov`).

- U.S. Senate: (`gopher://gopher.senate.gov:70`).

- U.S. Thomas: US Legislative Information (`http://thomas.loc.gov`).

- U.S. White House: (`http://www.whitehouse.gov`).

Policy

These pointers relate to public policy issues, government-citizen interaction, or legal issues.

- ACE: Americans Communicating Electronically (`gopher://cyfer.esusda.gov/11/ace`).

- CapWeb/Policy.Net: Political issues, campaigns, publications, and a guide to the United States Congress (CapWeb) (`http://policy.net`).

- Information Policy: Information Policy for Electronic Information Resources, by Mary Lou Goodyear (`mailto:listserv@uhupvm1.uh.edu` Body: `GET GOODYEAR PRV4N6`).

■ Intellectual Property: World Intellectual Property Organization (WIPO), includes Working Group on Intellectual Property Rights, a subgroup of the Information Infrastructure Task Force (`http://www.uspto.gov/wipo.html`).

■ International Trade: Network resources for legal research and education (`http://ananse.irv.uit.no/trade_law/misc/objective.html`).

■ Internet Economics Collection: A collection of documents that have to do with the economics of the Internet, information goods, and related issues, by Hal Varian (`http://gopher.econ.lsa.umich.edu/EconInternet.html`).

■ Internet Policy: What Should We Plan Given the Dilemma of the Network?, by G. Cook (`ftp://nic.merit.edu/documents/rfc/rfc1527.txt`).

■ MIT-RPCP: MIT's Research Program on Communications Policy (`http://farnsworth.mit.edu`).

■ Open Platform: Public Policy for the Information Age, EFF (`ftp://ftp.eff.org/pub/EFF/papers/Open_Platform/`).

■ Politics: A collection of electronic texts on miscellaneous political topics (`gopher://fir.cic.net/11/Politics`).

■ PPP: Political Participation Project, a research project at the MIT Artificial Intelligence Lab designed to explore how interactive media can be used to facilitate political participation; web includes collection of political sources, a bibliography, directory of grassroots organizations, and publications (`http://www.ai.mit.edu/projects/ppp/home.html`).

■ Tap Info: Reports on activities relating to federal information policy (`ftp://ftp.cpsr.org/taxpayer_assets`).

■ Telecom legislation: (`ftp://ftp.govt.washington.edu/legislation.telecom/`).

■ Telecom policy: (`http://www.ba.com/sites.html`).

■ Voters Telecom Watch: Monitoring important bills and alerting the public at crucial times in the life of a bill (`gopher://gopher.panix.com/11/vtw/vtwinfo`).

■ Warren Gopher: A collection of electronic newsletters distributed by Jim Warren on the subjects of political action and government access through the use of computer communications (`gopher://gopher.path.net:8102/1`).

Information

Dissemination and Retrieval

■ ACM/SIGIR: Association of Computing Machinery (ACM) Special Interest Group on Information Retrieval (`http://info.sigir.acm.org/sigir/`).

■ Agents, Intelligent: A collection of information about software information agents (`http://retriever.cs.umbc.edu/agents/`).

- Addressing: Uniform Resource Identifiers/Locators/Names (URI, URL, URN) (`http://www.w3.org/hypertext/WWW/Addressing/Addressing.html`).

- ArD: Database of published articles in the field of information systems (`http://www.zib-berlin.de/People/mueller/GNA/ISG/Services/ArD/`).

- ALMANAC: A service for multimedia document and information delivery and database functions (`mailto:almanac@oes.orst.edu Body: send guide`).

- Bibl-Mode: An Emacs Lisp package to keep track of information on the Net (`ftp://ftp.maths.tcd.ie/pub/bosullvn/elisp/`).

- CAIT-WUSTL: Center for the Application of Information Technology, part of the School of Engineering and Applied Science at Washington University in St. Louis (`http://www.cait.wustl.edu/cait/intro.html`).

- Carl/Uncover: Tables of contents and article-level access to over 16,000 unique multidisciplinary journals, reflecting the collections of selected CARL Systems and other libraries (`telnet://database.carl.org`).

- Cataloging Internet Res: Explores how to catalog electronic information, by Priscilla Caplan (`mailto:listserv@uhupvm1.uh.edu Body: get caplan prv4n2`).

- CATRIONA: CATaloguing and Retrieval of Information Over Networks Applications (`http://www.bubl.bath.ac.uk/BUBL/catriona.html`).

- CGI: Common Gateway Interface, a standard for external gateway programs to interface with information servers such as HTTP servers (`http://hoohoo.ncsa.uiuc.edu/cgi/overview.html`).

- CHAT: Conversational Hypertext Access Technology, natural-language interface (`ftp://debra.dgbt.doc.ca/pub/chat/`).

- CHAT: Natural language interface to information (`telnet://debra.doc.ca`).

- CIT: Center for Information Technology, a laboratory operated by Stanford University, the encoding, storage, communication, manipulation, and use of information in digital form (`http://logic.stanford.edu/cit/cit.html`).

- CIIR-UMass: Center for Intelligent Information Retrieval, University of Massachusetts, Amherst (`http://ciir.cs.umass.edu`).

- CNI FTP: Coalition for Networked Information (`ftp://ftp.cni.org/CNI/`).

- CNI Gopher: Coalition for Networked Information, promotes creation of and access to information resources in networked environments (`gopher://gopher.cni.org`).

- CNI Web: `http://www.cni.org/CNI.homepage.html`.

- CNI search: Coalition for Networked Information search server (`telnet://brsuser@gopher.cni.org`).

- CNI TopNode Project: Part of CNI's Directories and Resource Information Services Working Group (`ftp://ftp.cni.org/CNI/projects/topnode/`).

- CWI: Centrum voor Wiskunde en Informatica, Centre for Mathematics and Computer Science, Amsterdam, Netherlands (`http://www.cwi.nl/default.html`).

- CNIDR Web Page: Coalition for Networked Information Discovery and Retrieval Home Page (`http://cnidr.org/welcome.html`).

- CyberWeb: Useful information for information providers (`http://www.charm.net/~web/`).

- Data Research: Databases and information, some free (don't abuse free services) (`http://www.dra.com`).

- DIMUND: Document Understanding Information and Resources (`gopher://dimund.umd.edu`).

- DIMUND FTP: Document Understanding FTP Archives (`ftp://dimund.umd.edu/pub/`).

- Doc Center: Document Center, a hard-copy document-delivery service for government and industry specifications and standards (`http://doccenter.com/doccenter/home.html`).

- Electronic pub. info: Electronic Publishing information from the U.S. Library of Congress (`gopher://marvel.loc.gov/11/research/e`).

- Electronic pub. samples: Samples of electronic publishing (`http://www.elpress.com/samples/samples.html`).

- IAFA: Internet Anonymous FTP Archives Working Group (`ftp://archive.cc.mcgill.ca/pub/Network/iafa/charter`).

- Info Provider: Discussion of WWW and other servers from an information provider standpoint (`http://www.w3.org/hypertext/WWW/Provider/Overview.html`).

- Integrated Information: A Vision of an Integrated Internet Information Service, by Weider and Deutsch (`ftp://venera.isi.edu/internet-drafts/draft-ietf-iiir-vision-01.txt`).

- IIP: Intelligent Information Infrastructure Project, MIT Artificial Intelligence Laboratory (`http://www.ai.mit.edu/projects/iiip/home-page.html`).

- Interpedia: Mission is to be a primary source of information for Internet users, and a guide to many of the online resources available (`http://www.hmc.edu/www/interpedia/index.html`).

- IRLP: Internet Resource Location Project (`http://www.cs.colorado.edu/home/gc/cs/genbbb_wwww.html`).

- IRIS-Brown: Brown University's Institute for Information Research and Scholarship (`http://www.iris.brown.edu/iris`).

- IRTF: Internet Research Task Force Research Group on Resource Discovery (IRTF-RD) (`http://rd.cs.colorado.edu/~schwartz/IRTF.html`).

- ISI-USC: University of Southern California (USC) Information Sciences Institute (ISI) (`http://www.isi.edu`).

- ISRI-UNLV: Information Science Research Institute, University of Nevada–Las Vegas (`http://www.isri.unlv.edu`).

- ISWorld Net: Information systems web, sponsored by the Edwin L. Cox School Management at Southern Methodist University (`http://www.cox.smu.edu/mis/iswnet/home.html`).

- Library Special: Library special collections on the Internet (`ftp://vm1.nodak.edu/nnews/nnews.1993-10`).

- Lycos: A research program in providing information retrieval and discovery in the WWW, using a finite memory model of the Web to guide intelligent, directed searches for specific information needs (`http://lycos.cs.cmu.edu`).

- Mailbase: An enhanced electronic mailing-list service (`http://mailbase.ac.uk/welcome.html`).

- NIR Archives: Networked Information Retrieval (`ftp://mailbase.ac.uk/pub/lists/nir/`).

- NIR Gopher: Networked Information Retrieval Gopher (`gopher://mailbase.ac.uk`).

- OCLC Research: Toward Providing Library Services for CMC (`ftp://ftp.rsch.oclc.org/pub/internet_resources_project/report/`).

- OSS: Open Source Solutions, open sources, methods, and products; competitive in the Age of Information (`gopher://gopher.oss.net`).

- PCP: Principia Cybernetica Project (PCP)—the computer-supported collaborative development of an evolutionary-systemic philosophy (`http://pespmc1.vub.ac.be/RELATED.html`).

- Publishing: Advanced Publishing in the Web, by Terje Norderhaug (`http://www.ifi.uio.no/~terjen/WWWauthoring/abstract.html`).

- Quality: Quality and Standards of the Internet Information Resources (`http://coombs.anu.edu.au/SpecialProj/QLTY/QltyHome.html`).

- ResInfo: Working toward a basic operational framework necessary to implement a globally distributed information system (`http://www.hmc.edu/~jared/professional/resinfo/resinfo.html`).

- Resource Transponders: By Weider and Deutsch (`ftp://venera.isi.edu/internet-drafts/draft-ietf-iiir-transponders-01.txt`).

- Retrieval success: Successful stories of using the Internet for reference, by Karen Schneider (`ftp://mailbase.ac.uk/pub/lists/unite/files/internet-stories.txt`).

- Riddle: Rapid Information Display and Dissemination in a Library Environment (`ftp://ftp.cwi.nl/pub/RIDDLE/`).

- SIFTER-UAB: Department of Computer and Information Sciences at the University of Alabama at Birmingham (UAB), Studies of Information Filtering Technology for Electronic Resources (SIFTER) Research Group (`http://twinbrook.cis.uab.edu:70/AdPage.80`).

- Scout project: Approximate matching and probabilistic retrieval for multimedia and hypermedia applications (`http://fuzine.mt.cs.cmu.edu/scout/home.html`).

- SGML Open: A nonprofit, international consortium of providers of products and services, dedicated to accelerating the further adoption, application, and implementation of the Standard Generalized Markup Language (`http://www.sgmlopen.org`).

- SGML Review: A biased review of SGML, by Tim Berners-Lee (`http://www.w3.org/hypertext/WWW/MarkUp/SGML.html`).

- SIGNIDR: Special Interest Group on Networked Information Discovery and Retrieval (`http://www.wais.com/SIGNIDR/`).

- System comparison: Comparing issues in world-wide networked hypertext systems, by Arthur Smith (`ftp://snorri.chem.washington.edu/comparison_table`).

- UNITE Archive: User Network Interface To Everything (`ftp://mailbase.ac.uk/pub/lists/unite/`).

- UWI: UnderWorld Industries, nodes that want to share information with other UWI nodes (`http://zapruder.pds.med.umich.edu/uwi/uwi-info.html`).

- Web Publishing: The Web Communications Comprehensive Guide to Publishing on the Web (`http://www.webcom.com/html/`).

- Z39.50: Network Information Dissemination Standards (`http://www.research.att.com/~wald/z3950.html`).

Library

- Access: Catalogs and databases (`ftp://ftp.unt.edu/library/libraries.txt`).

- ALA: American Library Association (`gopher://gopher.uic.edu/11/library/ala/`).

- ALAWON archive: Files from American Library Association (`mailto:listserv@uicvm.uic.edu` Body: `send ala-wo filelist`).

- ALIX: Automated Library Information Xchange; Advice, opinion, and software by and for librarians; a service of the Federal Library and Information Center Committee, Federal Library Network (`telnet://alix.loc.gov:3001`).

- ARL Web: Association of Research Libraries Web server (`http://arl.cni.org`).

- BUBL gopher: The Bulletin Board for Libraries gopher (`gopher://bubl.bath.ac.uk`).

- BUBL Web: The Bulletin Board for Libraries Web server (`http://bubl.bath.ac.uk/BUBLHOME.html`).

- CARL: Access to UnCover and other indexes (`http://www.carl.org/carl.html`).

- Dialog: A service of Knight-Ridder Information, Inc. (`http://www.dialog.com`).

- Internet libraries: Various Internet material for librarians (`ftp://nic.funet.fi/pub/doc/library/`).

- LaUNCpad: Access various information services, from the University of North Carolina (`telnet://launch@launchpad.unc.edu`).

- LIS-Galaxy: Library and Information Science listing from Galaxy (`http://www.einet.net/galaxy/Social-Sciences/Library-and-Information-Science.html`).

- Library Resources: Library Resources on the Internet—Strategies for Selection and Use, Ed. Laine Farley (`ftp://dla.ucop.edu/pub/internet/libcat-guide`).

- Lib resources/Northwestern: Library resources on the Internet, from Northwestern University (`http://www.library.nwu.edu/DOCS/LibResources.html`).

- Lib webs: Library Information Servers via WWW, by Thomas Dowling (`http://www.lib.washington.edu/~tdowling/libweb.html`).

- LEXIS-NEXIS: Legal and news information (`http://www.meaddata.com`).

- OCLC: Online Computer Library Center, a nonprofit computer library service and research organization (`http://www.oclc.org`).

- Public Libraries: St. Joseph County (Indiana, USA) list of public libraries with Internet services (`http://sjcpl.lib.in.us/homepage/PublicLibraries/PublicLibraryServers.html`).

- RLG: Research Libraries Group, Inc., a not-for-profit membership corporation of universities, archives, historical societies, museums, and other institutions devoted to improving access to information that supports research and learning; includes access to Eureka (search system), RLIN (library support system), and Zephyr (Z39.50 services), databases, citation files, Ariel document delivery (`http://www-rlg.stanford.edu/welcome.html`).

- US LOC Marvel: United States Library of Congress, Marvel (Machine-Assisted Realization of the Virtual Electronic Library) (`telnet://marvel@marvel.loc.gov`).

- US LOC telnet: United States Library of Congress telnet access (`telnet://locis.loc.gov`).

- US LOC web: United States Library of Congress web (`http://lcweb.loc.gov/homepage/lchp.html`).

- WWW/Mosaic: The World-Wide Web and Mosaic—An Overview for Librarians, by Eric Lease Morgan (`http://www.lib.ncsu.edu/staff/morgan/www-and-libraries.html`).

Multiple

- 101 stories: Reprinted from 101 Success Stories of Information Technology in Higher Education; The Joe Wyatt Challenge, Edited by Judith Boettcher. A Project of EDUCOM's Educational Uses of Information Technology (EUIT) (`gopher://ivory.educom.edu/11/stories.101`).

- FARNET stories: Federation of American Research Networks (FARNet) descriptions of 51 Reasons for a National Information Infrastructure (NII) (`gopher://gopher.cni.org/11/cniftp/miscdocs/farnet`).

- Success stories: Internet Reference Success Stories, collected by Karen G. Schneider (`http://www.intac.com/~kgs/success/successcover.html`).

Scholarship

- CIOS: Communication Institute for Online Scholarship, a nonprofit organization for online communication scholarship; gopher server (`gopher://cios.llc.rpi.edu`).

- CNI: Coalition for Networked Information, a project of the Association of Research Libraries, CAUSE, and EDUCOM to promote the creation of and access to information resources in networked environments in order to enrich scholarship and enhance intellectual productivity (`http://www.cni.org/CNI.homepage.html`).

- IATH: Institute for Advanced Technology in the Humanities at the University of Virginia in Charlottesville, an effort to bring Thomas Jefferson's educational ideas of exchange across disciplines and integrated living and learning (`http://jefferson.village.virginia.edu`).

- IRIS-Brown: Brown University's Institute for Information Research and Scholarship; explores ways technology can be used for research, teaching, and learning (`http://www.iris.brown.edu/iris`).

- Scholarly Communications Project: Of University Libraries, Virginia Polytechnic Institute and State University, a project to pioneer electronic communication of scholarly materials (`http://borg.lib.vt.edu`).

- Scholarly Communication Reports: Quarterly Technical Reports (`ftp://borg.lib.vt.edu/pub/vpiej-l/reports`).

- Scholarly Societies gopher: University of Waterloo Library maintains links to gophers and other servers of scholarly societies (`gopher://watserv2.uwaterloo.ca/11/servers/campus/scholars`).

- Scholarly Societies web: University of Waterloo Library maintains links to gophers and other servers of scholarly societies (`http://www.lib.uwaterloo.ca/society/overview.html`).

- Scholarly Comm paper/Kahin: Scholarly Communication in the Network Environment Issues of Principle, Policy, and Practice, by Brian Kahin (`ftp://ftp.cni.org/CNI/projects/Harvard.scp/kahin.txt`).

- Scholarly Comm/Libraries: Published by The Association of Research Libraries for The Andrew W. Mellon Foundation (`ftp://ftp.cni.org/ARL/mellon/`).

- Scholarly Communication study: University Libraries and Scholarly Communication, A Study Prepared for The Andrew W. Mellon Foundation, by Anthony M. Cummings, Marcia L. Witte, William G. Bowen, Laura O. Lazarus, and Richard H. Ekman, November 1992 (`http://www.lib.virginia.edu/mellon/mellon.html`).

- Scholarly Publishing: Centre for Networked Access to Scholarly Information at Australian National University Library (`http://info.anu.edu.au`).

- Scholarly Publishing models: Model University Policy Regarding Faculty Publication in Scientific and Technical Scholarly Journals: A Background Paper and Review of the Issues (`ftp://sunsite.unc.edu/pub/docs/about-the-net/trln-copyright-paper`).

Technology

The technology of the Net involves a wide spectrum of telecommunications and computing equipment and software. This technology supports the infrastructure of the Net itself as well as the applications that run on it. This section provides pointers to information about computing, multimedia, virtual, network, and telecommunications technologies and resources.

Computing

- ACM Gopher: Association for Computing Machinery's gopher information server (gopher://acm.org).

- ACM Web: Association for Computing Machinery (http://info.acm.org).

- CACS-U of S LA: Center for Advanced Computer Studies, University of Southwestern Louisiana (http://www.cacs.usl.edu/Departments/CACS/).

- CPU Info Center: Central processing unit (CPU) information, includes press announcements, papers, machine information, by Tom Burd (http://www.ncsa.uiuc.edu/General/MetaCenter/MetaCenterHome.html).

- HPCC-NSE: High Performance Computing and Communication (USA) National Coordinating Office, National Software Exchange (http://www.netlib.org/nse/home.html).

- HPC Archive: London and South East Centre for High Performance Computing archive on high-performance computing, includes articles and facility to add articles (http://www.lpac.qmw.ac.uk/SEL-HPC/Articles/index.html).

- HPC-Southampton: University of Southampton High Performance Computing Centre (http://cs1.soton.ac.uk).

- HPCWire: The High-Performance Computing news and information service, covering workstations through supercomputers (telnet://hpcwire.ans.net).

- IEEE Web: Institute of Electrical and Electronics Engineers (http://www.ieee.org).

- Ohio Supercomputer: A state-funded computing resource, provides high-performance computing to scientists and engineers at Ohio colleges, universities, and companies (http://www.osc.edu/welcome.html).

- NCSA-USA: National (USA) Center for Supercomputing Applications (http://www.ncsa.uiuc.edu/General/NCSAHome.html).

- NMCCSE-USA: United States National MetaCenter for Computational Science and Engineering (http://www.ncsa.uiuc.edu/General/MetaCenter/MetaCenterHome.html).

- NPAC-Syracuse: Northeast Parallel Architectures Center Home Page, at Syracuse University, New York (http://minerva.npac.syr.edu/home.html).

- Pitt SCC: Pittsburgh Supercomputing Center home page (http://pscinfo.psc.edu).

- RICIS-Houston: Research Institute for Computing and Information Systems (`http://rbse.jsc.nasa.gov`).
- SDSC: San Diego Supercomputer Center (`http://gopher.sdsc.edu/Home.html`).
- SEI-CMU: Software Engineering Institute at Carnegie Mellon University (`http://www.sei.cmu.edu`).

Developing

- IEEE Tech: Portfolio of Emerging Technologies (`mailto:info.new.tech@ieee.org` Body: *anything*).
- NIMT-Ireland: National Institute for Management Technology, Ireland (`http://www.nimt.rtc-cork.ie/nimt.htm`).
- NIST-USA Web: National Institute of Standards and Technology WWW Home Page (`http://www.nist.gov/welcome.html`).
- NIST-USA Gopher: National Institute of Standards and Technology (USA) Gopher (`gopher://gopher-server.nist.gov`).
- NSF-USA Gopher: National Science Foundation (USA) Gopher (`gopher://stis.nsf.gov:70/11`).
- NTTC-USA: National Technology Transfer Center (`http://iridium.nttc.edu/nttc.html`).

Human Interaction

- ACM/SIGCHI: Association of Computing Machinery (ACM) Special Interest Group on Computers and Human Interaction (`gopher://gopher.acm.org/11[the_files.sig_forums.sigchi]`).
- HCIBIB: A mail-based retrieval system interface to a database related to Human-Computer Interaction (HCI) (`mailto:hcibib@bellcore.com` Body: query:).
- HCIBIB web: References to literature on human-computer interaction, including hypertext/hypermedia (`http://www.tu-graz.ac.at/CHCIbib`).
- HCI-Galaxy: Human-Computer Interaction page from EINET Galaxy (`http://galaxy.einet.net/galaxy/Engineering-and-Technology/Computer-Technology/Human-computer-Interaction.html`).
- HCI ftp site: Human-Computer Interaction (HCI) bibliography repository (`ftp://archive.cis.ohio-state.edu/pub/hcibib/`).
- HCI Index/deGraaff: Human-Computer Interaction Index web (`http://www.twi.tudelft.nl/Local/HCI/HCI-Index.html`).
- HCI Launching Pad: Human-Computer Interaction resources and pointers, by Keith Instone (`http://www.cs.bgsu.edu/HCI/`).

- HCS: Center for Human-Computer studies, at Uppsala University, Sweden (`http://www.cmd.uu.se`).

- HITL: Human Interface Technology Laboratory, the University of Washington, includes information on the Virtual Worlds Society and the Virtual Worlds Consortium (`http://www.hitl.washington.edu`).

- Ubicomp: Ubiquitous Computing—computing and communications available every-where to help people communicate and get information, information from Mark Weiser of XEROX PARC (`http://www.ubiq.com/hypertext/weiser/UbiHome.html`).

Multimedia

Audio

- CDM-NYU: New York University (NYU) Center for Digital Multimedia, a New York State Center for Advanced Technology, sponsored by the New York State Science and Technology Foundation (`http://found.cs.nyu.edu`).

- CERL: The CERL Sound Group (U of IL) (`http://datura.cerl.uiuc.edu`).

- Clips: Sites with audio clips (`http://www.eecs.nwu.edu/~jmyers/other-sounds.html`).

- Internet Sound: Various documents and programs having to do with sound (`ftp://ftp.cwi.nl/pub/audio/INDEX`).

- Internet Talk Radio: By Carl Malamud (`ftp://sunsite.unc.edu/pub/talk-radio/ITRintro.readme`).

- Internet Multicasting FAQ: FAQ for the Internet Multicasting Service (`mailto:info@radio.com` Body: send `FAQ`).

- Internet Multicasting WWW: Home page for the Internet Multicasting Service (`http://www.cmf.nrl.navy.mil/radio/radio.html`).

- Internet Talk Radio sites: (`mailto:sites@radio.com` Body: send `SITES`).

- IUMA: Internet Underground Music Archive (`http://sunsite.unc.edu/ianc/index.html`).

- MCRL-Ottawa: Multimedia Communications Research Laboratory at the University of Ottawa (`http://mango.genic.uottawa.ca`).

- MIDI: Musical Instrument Digital Interface (`http://www.eeb.ele.tue.nl/midi/index.html`).

- Multicast Backbone: Live audio and video multicast virtual network on top of Internet (`ftp://venera.isi.edu/mbone/faq.txt`).

- Mbone FAQ Web: Frequently Asked Questions (FAQ) on the Multicast Backbone (MBONE) (`http://www.research.att.com/mbone-faq.html`).

- Music Resources: `http://www.music.indiana.edu/misc/music_resources.html`.

- NeXT sounds: A collection of sound files for NeXT machines (`ftp://wuarchive.wustl.edu/pub/NeXT-Music/`).
- Say: Text to Audio (translate text to sound) (`http://www_tios.cs.utwente.nl/say/form/`).
- Sound Site: PC sound (`ftp://oak.oakland.edu/pub/misc/sound`).
- UnderWorld: Major source of sound information, repositories, music, and voice, by Jennifer Myers (`http://www.nd.edu/StudentLinks/jkeating/links/sound.html`).

Graphics

- ACM/SIGGRAPH: Association of Computing Machinery (ACM) Special Interest Group on Graphics (`gopher://siggraph.org`).
- AIG-Manchester: Advanced Interfaces Group (AIG) at the Computer Science Department at the University of Manchester (`http://www.cs.man.ac.uk/aig/aig.html`).
- CGU-Manchester: The Computer Graphics Unit—Research (`http://info.mcc.ac.uk/CGU/CGU-research.html`).
- CVU-GA Tech: Georgia Institute of Technology's Graphics, Visualization & Usability Center (`http://www.cc.gatech.edu/gvu/gvutop.html`).
- Scientific Visualization: Annotated Scientific Visualization URL Bibliography (`http://www.nas.nasa.gov/RNR/Visualization/annotatedURLs.html`).
- Thant's: Animation index (`http://mambo.ucsc.edu/psl/thant/thant.html`).
- Video: Demonstration of vsbrowser, a video file browser (`http://tns-www.lcs.mit.edu/cgi-bin/vs/vsbrowser`).
- ZGDV: Zentrum für Graphische Datenverarbeitung e.V., Computer Graphics Center (`http://zgdv.igd.fhg.de`).

Multi

- Bell Atl-CNM: Bell-Atlantic Center for Networked Multimedia, interactive multimedia applications over networks (`http://www.cnm.bell-atl.com`).
- File formats: Formats of graphics and sound files (`ftp://wuarchive.wustl.edu/pub/doc/graphic-formats/`).
- File formats: Graphics and sound file formats (`ftp://ftp.ncsa.uiuc.edu/misc/file.formats/`).
- GNN I-Media: Global Network Navigator's Interactive Media Center (`http://gnn.com/gnn/meta/imedia/index.html`).
- ICME-RPI: The International Center for Multimedia in Education at Rensselaer Polytechnic Institute, Troy, New York (`http://www.ciue.rpi.edu/index.htm`).

■ Media Lab: MIT Media Lab Home Page (`http://debussy.media.mit.edu`).

■ MICE: Multimedia Integrated Conferencing for European Researchers (`http://www.cs.ucl.ac.uk/mice/`).

■ Multimedia Index: Multimedia Information Sources, by Simon Gibbs (`http://viswiz.gmd.de/MultimediaInfo/`).

■ Multimedia Survey: A Survey of Distributed Multimedia Research, Standards and Products, by RARE (`ftp://ftp.ed.ac.uk/pub/mmsurvey/mmsurvey.txt`).

■ Multimedia Lab BU: Multimedia Laboratory at Boston University (`http://spiderman.bu.edu`).

■ NYU-Digital: New York University Center for Digital Multimedia (`http://found.cs.nyu.edu`).

■ Rob's Multimedia Lab: `http://www.acm.uiuc.edu:80/rml`.

■ Sunsite Multimedia: Multimedia presentations based on SunSITE (`http://sunsite.unc.edu/exhibits/exex.html`).

■ TNS Tech demo: Technology Demonstrations—multimedia (`http://tns-www.lcs.mit.edu/vs/demos.html`).

Hypermedia

■ ACM/SIGLINK: Association of Computing Machinery (ACM) Special Interest Group on Hypertext/Hypermedia (`gopher://gopher.acm.org/ 11[the_files.sig_forums.siglink]`).

■ Beyond Gutenberg: Hypertext and the Future of the Humanities, Yale University, New Haven, Connecticut, Thursday-Friday May 12-13, 1994 (`http://www.cis.yale.edu/htxt-conf/index.html`).

■ Bush, Vannevar: As We May Think, article from July 1945 issue of *The Atlantic Monthly* about hypertext (`http://www.csi.uottawa.ca/~dduchier/misc/vbush/as-we-may-think.html`).

■ H Hyperbook: A simple hypertext markup language (`http://siva.cshl.org/h/h.body.html`).

■ Hypermedia Lab-TAMU: Texas A and M Hypermedia Research Lab (`ftp://bush.cs.tamu.edu/pub/home.html`).

■ Hypermedia/Internet: Hypermedia and the Internet (`http://life.anu.edu.au/education/hypermedia.html`).

■ Hypertext resources: Lists of articles, systems, organizations, and resources, by Volker Zink (`http://www.uni-konstanz.de/FuF/Inf-Wiss/IW/hypertext_e.html`).

■ Hypertext systems: An Overview of Hypertext and IR systems and applications (`http://www.w3.org/hypertext/Products/Overview.html`).

- HTML Analyzer: Assist the maintenance of HyperText MarkUp Language (HTML) databases (`http://www.gatech.edu/pitkow/html_analyzer/README.html`).

- HTML DTD: 1986, Document Type Definition for the HyperText Markup Language as used by the World Wide Web application (HTML DTD) (`http://www.w3.org/hypertext/WWW/MarkUp/HTML.dtd.html`).

- HTML Specs: Hypertext markup language specs, by Tim Berners-Lee and Daniel Connolly (`ftp://www.w3.org/pub/www/doc/html-spec.txt.Z`).

- HTML Web: A collection of top-level information, from CERN, about hypertext markup language (`http://www.w3.org/hypertext/WWW/MarkUp/MarkUp.html`).

- Hypermedia Review: State of the Art Review on Hypermedia Issues And Applications, by V. Balasubramanian, Graduate School of Management, Rutgers University, Newark, New Jersey (`http://www.csi.uottawa.ca/~dduchier/misc/hypertext_review/`).

- Hypertext/rhetoric: Hypertext and the Rhetorical Contract, by Wm. Dennis Horn (`http://fire.clarkson.edu/horn/proposal-mla.html`).

- Hypertext terms: Glossary of terms from the WWW project, from CERN (`http://www.w3.org/hypertext/WWW/Terms.html`).

- MapMarker: A tool for creating clickable maps for HTML (`http://www.dl.ac.uk/CBMT/mapmarker/HOME.html`).

Virtual

- DIS: Distributed Interactive Simulation (`ftp://ftp.netcom.com/pub/frankc/dis.html`).

- Meme: Virtual world development system (`http://remarque.berkeley.edu/~marc/home.html`).

- Meta VE: Meta Virtual Environments (`http://www.gatech.edu/gvu/people/Masters/Rob.Kooper/Meta.VR.html`).

- MIT Media Lab: Access to Massachusetts Institute of Technology's Media Lab (`ftp://media-lab.media.mit.edu/access/`).

- MIT Media Lab—how to: How To Do Research In the MIT AI Lab (`http://www.cs.indiana.edu/docproject/mit.research.how.to/mit.research.how.to.html`).

- MIT TNS: MIT's Telemedia, Networks, and Systems Group (`http://tns-www.lcs.mit.edu/tns-www-home.html`).

- MSDL: Manchester Scene Description Language (`ftp://ftp.mcc.ac.uk/pub/cgu/MSD/scene-survey.tar.Z`).

- SUD: Single User VR Resources (`gopher://actlab.rtf.utexas.edu/11/SUD`).

- VR collection/Texas: `gopher://ftp.cc.utexas.edu:3003/11/pub/output/vr`.

- VR Page/Cardiff: `http://www.cm.cf.ac.uk/User/Andrew.Wilson/VR/`.

- VR Page/Chris Hand: Research, Papers, Archives, Events, User Groups and so on (`http://www.cms.dmu.ac.uk:9999/People/cph/vrstuff.html`).

- VR Page/Luke Sheneman: `http://www.cs.uidaho.edu/lal/cyberspace/VR/VR.html`.
- VR Web: Virtual Reality Web Page (`http://guinan.gsfc.nasa.gov/W3/VR.html`).
- VR Archive: Sunsite Virtual Reality archive—papers, information, maintained by David Barberi (`http://sunsite.unc.edu/dbarberi/vr.html`).
- VR Testbed: Open Virtual Reality Testbed Home Page (`http://nemo.ncsl.nist.gov/~sressler/OVRThome.html`).
- VSR: Virtual Shared Reality Project (`http://nfhsg3.rus.uni-stuttgart.de/virtual/index.html`).

Networks

Access and Connectivity

These documents help with gaining or finding out about access to networks.

- BBS Internet List: Zamfield's Wonderfully Incomplete, Complete Internet BBS List (`ftp://sunsite.unc.edu/pub/docs/about-the-net/libsoft/internet_bbs.txt`).
- Connecting to Internet: What Connecting Institutions Should Anticipate (`ftp://nic.merit.edu/documents/fyi/fyi_16.txt`).
- Connectivity-Yahoo: Computers-Internet-Connectivity (`http://www.yahoo.com/Computers/Internet/Connectivity/`).
- DLIST: A list of dedicated-line Internet providers, by Susan Estrada (`mailto:dlist@ora.com` Body: `Please send DLIST`).
- Freenet papers: Papers about network public access (`ftp://alfred.carleton.ca/pub/freenet/working.papers/`).
- FSLIST: The Forgotten Sites List of public-access Internet sites, by Louis Raphael (`ftp://freedom.nmsu.edu/pub/docs/fslist/`).
- GNET Archive: Bring the Net to lesser-developed nations and poorer parts of the world (`ftp://dhvx20.csudh.edu/global_net/`).
- Inet-Access FAQ: How to become an Internet service provider, an extremely detailed guide to procedures, equipment, hooking to the Net, agreements, software, fees, technical issues, marketing, legal issues, resources, by David H Dennis (`david@amazing.cinenet.net`) (`http://amazing.cinenet.net/faq.html`).
- Internet Access Guide: Access Guide to `introducing.the.internet`, by Ellen Hoffman (`ftp://nic.merit.edu/introducing.the.internet/access.guide`).
- Internet Access: Individual access to Internet, by James Milles (`ftp://sluaxa.slu.edu/pub/millesjg/internet.access`).

■ Internet Modem: Internet service providers in the United States accessible through dial-up connections from a personal computer, by Genevieve Engel (`ftp://dla.ucop.edu/pub/internet/dial-access`).

■ Internet Providers: All Providers Alphabetically (`ftp://sri.com/netinfo/internet-access-providers-alphabetical-listing.txt`).

■ Internet Providers Non-U.S.: Non-U.S. Internet Providers (`ftp://sri.com/netinfo/internet-access-providers-non-us.txt`).

■ K12 Access: Documents of California Education Network (CENet) Technical Planning Committee (`ftp://ftp.cc.berkeley.edu/k12/README`).

■ NIXPUB: Public/Open Access UNIX, by Bux Technical Services (`ftp://rtfm.mit.edu/pub/usenet/alt.bbs/Nixpub_Posting_(Long)`).

■ Network Startup: NSF-sponsored Network Startup Resource Center (`ftp://ftp.psg.com/README`).

■ PDIAL: The Public Dialup Internet Access List, by Peter Kaminski (`ftp://rtfm.mit.edu/pub/usenet/news.answers/pdial`).

■ PDIAL search: Directory provides information on service providers in Northern California, Southern California, and the United States. It was compiled from the Internet `pdial` listing (`http://www.commerce.net/directories/news/inet.prov.dir.html`).

■ PSGnet/RAINet: Networking in the developing world, low-cost networking tools, computer networking in general (`gopher://gopher.psg.com`).

■ RAIN: Rural Area Information Network (`telnet://visitor@rain.gen.mo.us`).

■ Registering on the Net: Transition and Modernization of the Internet Registration Service, by S. Williamson (`ftp://nic.merit.edu/documents/rfc/rfc1400.txt`).

■ Rural Nets/GAIN report: (`ftp://nysernet.org/pub/gain/final_report`).

■ Rural Nets: Rural Datafication Project (`mailto:rjacot@cic.net`).

■ Rural Datafication gopher: Information about the rural datafication project—Extending Information Highways for Education, Research, and Economic Development in the Great Lakes States (`gopher://gopher.cic.net/11/cicnet-gophers/ruraldata-project`).

■ Rural Datafication Web: Bring the power of the Internet to rural and otherwise underserved communities (`http://www.cic.net/rd-home.html`).

■ Service Providers: Network Service Provider WWW Servers (`http://www.eit.com/web/www.servers/networkservice.html`).

■ Slip Starter Kit: Help get started with making a SLIP connection with Windows 3.1, by Jean van Eeden (`ftp://aztec.co.za/pub/win3/Slip_Starter_Kit`).

■ Winsock: Windows and TCP/IP for Internet access, by Harry M. Kriz (`ftp://nebula.lib.vt.edu/pub/windows/winsock/wtcpip05.asc`).

Administration

- Domain Administration: `ftp://nic.merit.edu/documents/rfc/rfc1033.txt`.
- Domain Name surveys: `gopher://is.internic.net/11/infoguide/about-internet/domain-surveys/`.
- Domain Name Survey: An attempt to discover every host on the Internet by doing a complete search of the Domain Name System (`http://www.nw.com/zone/WWW/top.html`).
- Domain Names: `ftp://nic.merit.edu/documents/rfc/rfc1034.txt`.
- Host managers: `ftp://nic.merit.edu/documents/rfc/rfc1173.txt`.
- Internet Servers: Building Internet Servers, a collection of information and links from Charm Net (`http://www.charm.net/~cyber/`).
- SNMP: Simple network management protocol project group, at the University of Twente, the Netherlands (`http://snmp.cs.utwente.nl`).

Networking

- Amateur Radio Packet: Connects between Amateur Radio Packet (digital data stream) network and the Internet (`ftp://ftp.std.com/pub/hamradio/faq/packet.faq`).
- Andrew Consortium: A portable set of applications that runs under X11 (`http://www.cs.cmu.edu:8001/afs/cs.cmu.edu/project/atk-ftp/web/andrew-home.html`).
- ATM forum: Worldwide organization, aimed at promoting ATM within the industry and the end-user community (`http://www.atmforum.com`).
- ATM Research: Asynchronous Transfer Mode (ATM) Research at Naval Research Lab (`http://netlab.itd.nrl.navy.mil/ATM.html`).
- Bitnet Address: Get the Internet address of a Bitnet host that is also on the Internet (send e-mail to host with SHOW Alias) (`mailto:listserv@ubvm.bitnet` Body: SHOW ALIAS UBVM).
- Bitnet info: A large collection of documentation about Bitnet and EARN (`ftp://lilac.berkeley.edu/netinfo/bitnet/`).
- Bitnet intro: (`mailto:listserv@bitnic.educom.edu` Body: send BITNET INTRO).
- Bitnet nodes: A listing of BITNET (Because It's Time Network) nodes (`gopher://nak.berkeley.edu:4303/11/bitnet`).
- Bitnet nodes: Those Bitnet nodes that have Internet addresses (`mailto:listserv@bitnic.educom.edu` Body: get internet listing).
- Cell Relay: Cell-relay or broadband technologies (ATM/DQDB/SONET, etc.) including research papers, standards, product information, mailing list archives, and events (`gopher://cell-relay.indiana.edu/1`).
- Concise: Database about networks, networking tools, and projects (`http://www.w3.org:80/hypertext/DataSources/CONCISE/UserGuide/Overview.html`).

- Data communication—Yahoo: Computers-Networks and Data Communications (`http://www.yahoo.com/Computers/Networks_and_Data_Communication/`).

- Ethernet page: Resources related to the Ethernet (IEEE 802.3) local area network system, by Charles Spurgeon (`http://wwwhost.ots.utexas.edu/ethernet/ethernet-home.html`).

- FidoNet Gateway: How to use the UUCP/Fido-Net Gateway, by Lee Damon, Dale Weber, assisted by Lisa Gronke (`ftp://ftp.csn.org/pub/mail/internet.fidonet`).

- FidoNet News: Archives of the newsgroup `comp.org.fidonet` (`ftp://rtfm.mit.edu/pub/usenet/comp.org.fidonet/`).

- FidoNet Nodes: A list of systems with FidoNet (`ftp://genome.wi.mit.edu/wais-sources/fidonet-nodelist.src`).

- GOSIP: Government Open Systems Interconnection Profile (`ftp://%FILE/rfc1169.txt`).

- IBM's collection: Networking information, protocols, standards (`ftp://networking.raleigh.ibm.com/pub`).

- INET 93: Proceedings of the INET '93 conference (`ftp://mordor.stanford.edu/pub/inet93/`).

- International Connect: International Connectivity Table, by Larry Landweber (`ftp://ftp.cs.wisc.edu/connectivity_table/`).

- Internet Country Codes: FAQ about country codes (`ftp://rtfm.mit.edu/pub/usenet/news.answers/mail/country-codes`).

- Internet Domain Names: Relationship of Telex Answerback Codes to Internet Domains (`ftp://nic.merit.edu/documents/rfc/rfc1394.txt`).

- Internet + Networking-Galaxy: List of resources related to Internet and Networking from EINet's Galaxy (`http://galaxy.einet.net/Reference-and-Interdisciplinary-Information/Internet-and-Networking.html`).

- Internet Protocols: Listings of working groups and information about protocols—applications, Internet, next generation, network management, operational requirements, routing, security, and much more (`http://netlab.itd.nrl.navy.mil/Internet.html`).

- Internet Root Domain: Lists of Internet hosts (`ftp://ftp.rs.internic.net/domain/`).

- InterNetwork Mail: Methods of sending mail from one network to another, by John Chew and Scott Yanoff (`ftp://ftp.csd.uwm.edu/pub/internetwork-mail-guide`).

- Intro TCP/IP: Describes the Internet protocols (`ftp://nic.merit.edu/introducing.the.internet/intro.to.ip`).

- IP address resolver: (`mailto:resolve@widener.edu` Body: site *SITE NAME*).

- ISDN: The Combinet, Inc., Integrated Services Digital Network (ISDN) deployment database (`telnet://isdn@bbs.combinet.com`).

■ ISDN info/Bellcore: Collection of Integrated Services Digital Network (ISDN) information, from Bellcore (`ftp://info.bellcore.com/pub/ISDN/`).

■ ISDN info/Kegel: ISDN Page, a collection of pointers to resources about Integrated Services Digital Network (ISDN), including standards and discussions, providers, vendors, products, by Dan Kegel (`http://alumni.caltech.edu/~dank/isdn/`).

■ ISDN info/Pac Bell+ATT: Integrated Services Digital Network (ISDN) from Pacific Bell and American Telephone and Telegraph (`http://www.pacbell.com/isdn/isdn_home.html`).

■ Matrix info: Bitnet, FidoNet, fredmail, ARPAnet, ddn (`gopher://is.internic.net/11/infoguide/about-internet/other-networks`).

■ Matrix: Information about connected e-mail systems (Quarterman's Matrix) (`gopher://nkosi.well.sf.ca.us/11/matrix`).

■ Minitel: French Videotex terminal (Minitel) emulator, requires X11 terminal or simulator (`http://www.enst.fr/~meunier/english/minitel/`).

■ Network Research sites: A list of network researching sites (`http://netlab.itd.nrl.navy.mil/onr.html`).

■ Networking Overview: Overview of information available (`http://web.doc.ic.ac.uk:80/bySubject/Networking.html`).

■ Networking EINet: List of resources related to networking by EINet's Galaxy (`http://galaxy.einet.net/galaxy/Engineering-and-Technology/Computer-Technology/Networking.html`).

■ PSGnet/RAINet info: Networking in developing world, low-cost tools, networking in general (`gopher://rain.psg.com`).

■ NREN Information: Merit's directory of National Research and Education Network information (`ftp://nic.merit.edu/nren/INDEX.nren`).

■ NREN Recompetition: Contains information about the recompetition of the NSFNET backbone project (`ftp://nic.merit.edu/cise/recompete/INDEX.recompete`).

■ OneNet: A global network of Macintosh computers (phone: 415-948-4775).

■ Personal IP: PPP, MS-Windows, and other information and links about connecting with Internet protocols, from Charm Net (`http://www.charm.net/ppp.html`).

■ PCLT: PC Lube and Tune; informative introductory material on PC hardware, networks, and newer operating systems (`http://pclt.cis.yale.edu/pclt/default.htm`).

■ RSA info: Information on many cryptographic related topics (`ftp://rsa.com`).

■ SDSC Appl Net Res Group: Activities of the San Diego Supercomputer Center Applied Network Research group. (`ftp://ftp.sdsc.edu/pub/sdsc/anr/README`).

■ Sprintlink: FTP site for Sprint's networking activities (`ftp://ftp.sprintlink.net`).

■ Sprintlink Gopher: Sprint's internetworking activities and networking information (`gopher://ftp.sprintlink.net`).

- Wireless: The Wireless Opportunities Coalition, a group of organizations and companies seeking to expand wireless communications development, manufacturing, and use (`http://wireless.policy.net/wireless/wireless.html`).

Security

- Business Security: Security for Businesses on the Internet, by Marianne Mueller (`http://www.catalog.com/mrm/security.html`).
- CERT FTP: Computer Emergency Response Team at Carnegie Mellon Univ. (`ftp://cert.org/pub/`).
- CERT-DFN: Computer Emergency Response Team for the German Research Network (`http://www.cert.dfn.de/eng/`).
- Cryptorebel/Cypherpunk: Vince Cate's Cryptorebel and Cypherpunk page (`ftp://furmint.nectar.cs.cmu.edu/security/README.html`).
- CSC: Computer Systems Consulting, system security issues information (`http://www.spy.org`).
- DoD Security: Department of Defense Goal Security Architecture (DGSA) (`ftp://asc.dtic.dla.mil/pub/tafim/`).
- First: Forum of Incident Response and Security Teams (`http://first.org`).
- Hack/phreak: Resources, happenings, connections, from Randy King (`http://www.phantom.com/~king/`).
- Internet Security: GAO report on Computer Security (June 1989) (`ftp://nic.merit.edu/cise/gao8957.txt`).
- Internet Worm: A collection of papers about Internet security compromises (`ftp://nic.funet.fi/pub/doc/security/worm/`).
- NIST Security: U.S. National Institute of Standards and Technology (NIST) Computer Security Resource Clearinghouse (`http://csrc.ncsl.nist.gov`).
- SAIC: Science Applications International Corp, computer security (`http://mls.saic.com/mls.security.text.html`).
- Security index: Computer and Network Security Reference Index, by Rodney Campbell (`http://www.tansu.com.au/Info/security.html`).
- SHEN: A Security Scheme for the World Wide Web (`http://www.w3.org/hypertext/WWW/Shen/ref/shen.html`).
- Site Security: Site Security Handbook, FYI 8, guidance on how to deal with security issues in the Internet, eds. Holbrook, Reynolds (`ftp://nic.merit.edu/documents/fyi/fyi_08.txt`).

Statistics

■ IBC Stats: Internet Business Center's collection of Net statistics—shows lists of Net cities, states, Net Presence by industry, from The Internet Group (`http://tig.com/IBC/Statistics.html`).

■ Internet Charts/ISOC: Charts of traffic, connectivity, hosts, and so on from the Internet Society (`ftp://ftp.isoc.org/isoc/charts/`).

■ Internet Growth: Charts showing the Internet's past and projected growth, by Texas Internet Consulting (`ftp://tic.com/matrix/growth/internet/`).

■ Internet Growth/Lottor: Internet Growth (1981-1991) (`ftp://nic.merit.edu/documents/rfc/rfc1296.txt`).

■ Internet Stats/Demographics-Yahoo: `http://www.yahoo.com/Computers/Internet/Statistics_and_Demographics/`.

■ NSFnet stats: NSF Statistics about Internet use, from Merit (`ftp://nic.merit.edu/nsfnet/statistics/`).

■ NSFnet stats/GVU Center: Georgia Tech's Graphics, Visualization, and Usability Center NSFNET Backbone Statistics Page, includes graphs of statistics (`http://www.cc.gatech.edu/gvu/stats/NSF/merit.html`).

Maps

■ ARPAnet Map: An index of Interface Message Processors on the ARPAnet (circa 1986) (`http://web.kaleida.com/u/hopkins/arpanet/arpanet.html`).

■ Internet Maps (Many) (`ftp://ftp.uu.net/inet/maps/`).

■ Internet Maps (NSFNET) (`ftp://nic.merit.edu/maps/`).

■ Internet Maps (SuraNet) (`ftp://ftp.sura.net/pub/maps/`).

■ Internet/Matrix: Maps from MIDS (Matrix Information and Directory Services) (`gopher://gopher.tic.com/11/matrix/maps/matrix`).

■ Internet Topology-Yahoo: `http://www.yahoo.com/Computers/Internet/Network_Topology/`.

■ USENET Maps: Maps of Usenet news feeds/backbones (`ftp://gatekeeper.dec.com/pub/maps/`).

■ UUCP Maps: Unix-Unix Copy Protocol Map Data (`gopher://agate.berkeley.edu:4324/1uumaps`).

■ WWW Resource Maps: The Virtual Tourist, a collection of maps from all over the world to help you locate Internet sites and resources (`http://wings.buffalo.edu/world`).

Telecommunications

- ATP-LLNL: Advanced Telecommunications Program at Lawrence Livermore National Laboratory (`http://www-atp.llnl.gov/atp/`).

- Computer + Communications: InfoBahn, Global Information Infrastructure, Telecommunications, large resource collection of companies, media, organizations, programs and projects, standards, and Usenet groups and FAQs (`http://www-atp.llnl.gov/atp/telecom.html`).

- Computing + Telecom: World Wide Web Virtual Library entry for Communications and Telecommunications (`http://www.analysys.co.uk/commslib.htm`).

- CTR-Columbia U Web: Columbia University Center for Telecommunications Research (CTR) (`http://www.ctr.columbia.edu/CUCTR_Home.html`).

- Data Comm/Networking: Data Communications and Networking Links, by Don Joslyn (`http://www.racal.com/networking.html`).

- INT-France: Institut National des Télécommunications, France (`http://arctique.int-evry.fr`).

- ITC: International Telecommunications Center—telecommunications, data communications and networking; includes archives, information, software, product and employment information, sponsored by `telematrix.com` (`http://www.telematrix.com`).

- Tele/Communications: Information Sources about Communications and Telecommunications (`http://www.tansu.com.au/Info/communications.html`).

- Telecomm Archives: Files about telecommunications, from the Usenet group `comp.dcom.telecom` (`ftp://lcs.mit.edu/telecom-archives/`).

- TelecomInfo: From New York State Department of Education gopher (`gopher://unix5.nysed.gov/11/TelecommInfo`).

- Telecom Information Resources: Technical, economic, public policy, and social aspects of telecommunications—including voice, data, video, wired, wireless, cable TV, and satellite—are included (`http://www.ipps.lsa.umich.edu/telecom-info.html`).

- Telephone industry: Telephone Industry Information Page, a service of The Telephone Customer's Corner (`http://www.teleport.com/~mw/cc/tii.html`).

- TIS-Kansas: Telecommunications and Information Sciences Laboratory, University of Kansas (`http://www.tisl.ukans.edu`).

- US-FCC FTP: Federal Communications Commission (USA) (`ftp://ftp.fcc.gov`).

- US-FCC Gopher: Federal Communications Commission (USA) (`gopher://gopher.fcc.gov`).

- US-FCC web: Federal Communications Commission (USA) (`http://www.fcc.gov`).

- US-ITS: Institute for Telecommunication Sciences, USA government research and engineering laboratory (`http://www.its.bldrdoc.gov/its.html`).

- US-NTIA: National Telecommunications and Information Administration (USA) (`telnet://ntiabbs.ntia.doc.gov`).

- US-NTIA web: National Telecommunications and Information Administration (USA) (`http://www.ntia.doc.gov`).

- WilTel Library: Telecommunications Library, telecom business and technology, sponsored by WilTel Network Services (`http://www.wiltel.com/library/library.html`).

Culture

Although the Net is composed of a remarkable combination of hardware, software, and network connections, the most amazing thing about the online world is the cultural and social expressions that take place on it.

This section surveys online art, communities, language-related resources, people, and society. You'll find pointers to individual home pages as well as pointers to collections of papers about societal impacts and issues.

Art

- Art-Yahoo: `http://www.yahoo.com/Art/`.

- ANIMA: Arts Network for Integrated Media Applications (`http://wimsey.com/anima/ANIMAhomeF.html`).

- Art/images: A collection of art and images in several formats (ASCII, TIFF, GIF, JPEG) (`gopher://cs4sun.cs.ttu.edu/11/Art%20and%20Images`).

- Art/Net: Art on the Net; artists share and create works together on the Internet (`http://www.art.net`).

- ArtSource: A gathering point for networked resources on Art and Architecture (`http://www.uky.edu/Artsource/artsourcehome.html`).

- Artwork: OTIS project to collect online art (`ftp://sunsite.unc.edu/pub/multimedia/pictures/OTIS/`).

- ASCII Art: A FAQ about ASCII art, by Jorn Barger (`ftp://ftp.mcs.com/mcsnet.users/jorn/asciifaq.txt`).

- ASCII Art Bazaar: Collection of ASCII art and images, 12MB of information covering an estimated 24,000 art works from more than 3,300 contributions classified under 759 subject titles (`gopher://twinbrook.cis.uab.edu/1asciiarc.70`).

- ASCII Art collection: A collection of files showing images, fonts, and other ASCII art (`ftp://ftp.cs.ttu.edu/pub/asciiart/`).

- Cirque de la Mama: To bring works of art to people and to bring people to works of art (`http://lancet.mit.edu/cirque/cirque.html`).

- CIS-AH: Center for Integrative Studies—Arts and Humanities (`http://web.cal.msu.edu`).
- Electric Gallery: Presents naive and primitive art that is unique and famous throughout the world (`http://www.egallery.com/egallery/`).
- FineArt Forum: List of art-related Web resources (`http://www.msstate.edu/Fineart_Online/art-resources.html`).
- Free Art: Pages and the graphics, by Harlan Wallach (`http://www.mcs.net/~wallach/freeart/buttons.html`).
- NWHQ: New World Headquarters—free expression and the distribution of artistic ideas, independent artists supporting independent artists (`http://www.knosso.com/NWHQ/index.html`).

Community

Information

- Civic Networking: WWW Guide to Community Networking, by Catherine Kummer (`http://http2.sils.umich.edu/ILS/community.html`).
- Community Nets/McGee: Information about community networks, by Arthur R. McGee (`ftp://ftp.netcom.com/pub/amcgee/community/`).
- CPSR Community Net info: `http://www.cpsr.org/dox/community.nets.html`.
- Freenets Home Page: Freenet information, presented as a public service by Peter Scott, at the University of Saskatchewan Libraries (`http://herald.usask.ca/~scottp/free.html`).
- Freenet List/Gopher: `gopher://gopher.tamu.edu/11/.dir/freenet.dir`.
- Freenet List/Hytelnet: `http://www.cc.ukans.edu/hytelnet_html/FRE000.html`.
- NPTN: National Public Telecomputing Network (`ftp://nptn.org/pub/`).

Virtual

Some instances of virtual communities are as follows:

- Blacksburg electronic village: `http://www.bev.net`.
- CIAO!: British Columbia, Canada (`telnet://ciao.trail.bc.ca`).
- Cleveland Freenet: The world's first community Freenet (`telnet://visitor@freenet-in-a.cwru.edu`).
- Digital City: de Digitale Stad, Amsterdam, Netherlands (`telnet://dds.hacktic.nl`).
- EnviroFreenet: An online community of people who are concerned about the Earth (`telnet://envirolink.org`).

- Internet Town Hall: A service of the Internet Multicasting Service
  (`http://www.town.hall.org`).

- Oceania: The Atlantis Project; new country in development—you can get Constitution
  and Laws, passport info, free subscription to newsletter Oceania Oracle, and more
  (`http://oceania.org`).

- Silicon Valley: Silicon Valley Public Access Link Community Page
  (`http://www.svpal.org`).

- Virtual City: Virtual City Network Project (`http://virtual.net/VirtualCity/`).

Language

- ABU: L'Association des bibliophiles Universels
  (`http://www.cnam.fr/ABU/principal/ABU.v2.html`).

- ACW web: Alliance for Computers and Writing
  (`http://prairie_island.ttu.edu/acw/acw.html`).

- ALEX: Find and retrieve the full-text of documents on the Internet from such archives
  as Project Gutenberg, Wiretap, the On-line Book Initiative, the Eris system at Virginia
  Tech, the English Server at Carnegie Mellon University, and the online Oxford Text
  Archive (`gopher://www.lib.ncsu.edu/stacks/alex-index.html`).

- Babel: A glossary of computer-oriented abbreviations and acronyms
  (`ftp://ftp.temple.edu/pub/info/help-net/babel95a.txt`).

- Baylor etexts: (`ftp://ftp.byu.edu/pub/next/Literature/`).

- Book collection: Electronic books, reference, special collections
  (`gopher://psulias.psu.edu/11[_shelves]`).

- Citation: Bibliographic References for Computer Files in the Social Sciences, A Discussion Paper, by Sue A. Dodd
  (`ftp://ftp.msstate.edu/pub/docs/history/netuse/electronic.biblio.cite`).

- Computer Writing: Computer Generated Writing resources, by Marius Watz
  (`http://www.uio.no/~mwatz/c-g.writing/`).

- Computer Jargon search: Search the jargon file on WWW
  (`http://web.cnam.fr/bin.html/By_Searchable_Index?Jargon_File.html`).

- Computer Jargon: The Jargon File (the definitive compendium of hacker slang)
  (`ftp://aeneas.mit.edu/pub/gnu/jargon-README`).

- Computing Dictionary (gopher): The Free On-line Dictionary of Computing
  (`gopher://wombat.doc.ic.ac.uk`).

- Computing Dictionary (web): The Free On-line Dictionary of Computing
  (`http://wombat.doc.ic.ac.uk`).

- CMC Glossary: Compiled by Collins and Berge, from St. John's University
  (`gopher://sjumusic.stjohns.edu:1070/11/%40uni%3acmc.glossary`).

- CMT: The Center for Machine Translation (CMT) at the School of Computer Science at Carnegie Mellon University; advanced research and development in natural language processing, with a focus on multi-lingual machine translation (`http://www.mt.cs.cmu.edu/cmt/CMT-home.html`).

- CPET: Catalogue of Projects in Electronic Text (`ftp://guvax.georgetown.edu/cpet_projects_in_electronic_text/`).

- CSLI-Stanford: Center for the Study of Language and Information (CSLI), Stanford University (`http://csli-www.stanford.edu`).

- CTI-Oxford: Centre for Textual Studies, Oxford (`mailto:ctitext@vax.ox.ac.uk`).

- eText-Caltech: The eText (electronic hypermedia textbooks) group at Caltech (`http://www.etext.caltech.edu`).

- Electronic Text archive: Copy of archive services on `etext.archive.umich.edu` (`gopher://fir.cic.net/00/0-README`).

- Electronic Text: Catalogue of projects in electronic text, Center for Text and Technology (`ftp://guvax.georgetown.edu/cpet_projects_in_electronic_text/`).

- ETC-UV: Electronic Text Center—University of Virginia (`http://www.lib.virginia.edu/etext/ETC.html`).

- Electronic Word: Democracy, Technology, and the Arts, by Richard A. Lanham (`ftp://press-gopher.uchicago.edu/pub/Excerpts/lanham.txt`).

- Gutenberg Web Page: A project to give away online texts, hundreds of titles (`http://med-amsa.bu.edu/Gutenberg/Welcome.html`).

- Hacker's Dictionary: A searchable index of Hacker's Jargon (`http://iicm.tu-graz.ac.at/Cjargon`).

- Human: Human languages page, cataloging human-language resources and making those resources available to the Web community through a concise index (`http://www.willamette.edu/~tjones/Language-Page.html`).

- IBIC: Internet Book Information Center (`http://sunsite.unc.edu/ibic/IBIC-homepage.html`).

- Internet Glossary: Search a collection of Internet terms (`wais://pinus.slu.se:210/Internet-user-glossary?`).

- Internet Glossary: Internet-specific terms defined (`ftp://nic.merit.edu/documents/fyi/fyi_18.txt`).

- Internet Wiretap: Electronic books and information (`ftp://wiretap.spies.com/About/`).

- Internet Wiretap Gopher: Electronic books and information (`gopher://wiretap.Spies.COM`).

- ITK: Instituut voor Taal- en Kennistechnologie, Institute for Language Technology and Artificial Intelligence (`http://itkwww.kub.nl:2080/itk/itkhome.html`).

- Jargon: Jargon File Resources, browse or download the file in different forms (`http://www.ccil.org/jargon/jargon.html`).

- LETRS: Library Electronic Text Resource Service
  (`gopher://gopher.indiana.edu:1067/11/letrs/gopher`).

- Natural Language: Natural Language Software Registry, summary of the capabilities and sources of language-processing software available to researchers
  (`http://cl-www.dfki.uni-sb.de/cl/registry/ed_note.html`).

- OBI: Online Book Initiative (`ftp://ftp.std.com/obi/README`).

- Online books: An index of hundreds of online books, collections of online books and documents (`http://www.cs.cmu.edu:8001/Web/books.html`).

- OWL: Purdue Writing Labs' Online Writing Lab (OWL)
  (`mailto:owl@sage.cc.purdue.edu` Subject: `owl-request`).

- Oxford Archive: Oxford Text Archive (`ftp://ota.ox.ac.uk/ota/`).

- Post-Gutenberg Galaxy: The Fourth Revolution in the Means of Production of Knowledge, by Steven Harnad (`ftp://infolib.murdoch.edu.au/pub/jnl/harnad.jnl`).

- Scholar: Natural Language Processing On Line
  (`gopher://jhuniverse.hcf.jhu.edu/11/.HAC/Journals/.SCHOLAR`).

- Smileys (all): All the smileys in the known universe
  (`gopher://gopher.ora.com/00/feature_articles/universe.smiley`).

- Smiley Catalog: `telnet://help@twinbrook.cis.uab.edu:3399`).

- Smileys: A smiley server by David W. Sanderson
  (`ftp://ftp.uu.net/usenet/comp.sources.misc/volume23/smiley/part01.Z`).

- Writer's Resources: Internet Writer Resources, Compiled/Edited/Maintained by L. Detweiler (`ftp://rtfm.mit.edu/pub/usenet/news.answers/writing/resources`).

People

Aspects

- APA: American Psychological Association (`http://www.apa.org`).

- Cognitive/Psychological sources: Information sources on the Internet about academic programs, periodicals, network resources, and many other online resources, by Scott Mainwaring (`http://malia.stanford.edu/cogsci.html`).

- GA Tech—Cognitive: Cognitive Science at Georgia Tech
  (`http://www.cc.gatech.edu/cogsci/cogsci.html`).

- HCRL-Open U: Human Cognition Research Laboratory, The Open University, Milton Keynes, United Kingdom (`http://hcrl.open.ac.uk`).

- Webaholics: Resources that will get you hooked to the Web; includes a Forms interface to add entries to a Webaholics support group
  (`http://www.ohiou.edu/~rbarrett/webaholics/ver2/`).

Lists—Directories, Home Pages

Major General Collections

- Who's Who: Who's Who on the Internet, from CityLive! Magazine, part of the WWW Virtual Library (http://web.city.ac.uk/citylive/pages.html).

- GNN's Netizen's: Global Network Navigator's Internet Center Netizen's project, a directory of home pages written by GNN users (http://nearnet.gnn.com/gnn/netizens/index.html).

- People-Yahoo: Entertainment—People (Home Pages collection), from Yahoo (http://www.yahoo.com/Entertainment/People/).

Specialized Collections

- CMC People: People interested in the study of CMC, from the CMC studies center (http://www.rpi.edu/~decemj/cmc/people.html).

- COS: Community of Science, identify and locate researchers, inventions, and facilities at U.S. and Canadian universities by interest and expertise (http://cos.gdb.org).

- Communications Scholars: http://alnilam.ucs.indiana.edu:1027/sources/dirpage.html.

- DA-CLOD People Page: Distributedly Administered Categorical List Of Documents collection of personal home pages (http://schiller.wustl.edu/DACLOD/daclod?id=00008.dcl).

- Four11: Directory Services, a free and easy-to-use directory of online users and their e-mail addresses, from Four11 Directory Services (SLED) (http://www.four11.com).

- Houh's People: Henry Houh's List of People on the Web (http://tns-www.lcs.mit.edu/people/hhh/people.html).

- Home Page Publisher: Create/edit your own home page with its own URL, includes a collection of home pages (http://www-bprc.mps.ohio-state.edu/HomePage/).

- Internet People: Who's Who in the Internet, Biographies of IAB, IESG and IRSG Members (ftp://nic.merit.edu/documents/fyi/fyi_09.txt).

- Netpages: A phonebook-style directory for the Internet, from Aldea Communications, Inc. (ftp://ftp.sco.com/NetPages/).

- UT-Austin Personal Pages: A collection of personal pages worldwide, from the University of Texas at Austin (http://www.utexas.edu/world/personal/index.html).

- WBW: World Birthday Web; you can record your birthday and link to your home page, by Tom Boutell (http://sunsite.unc.edu/btbin/birthday).

- Who's Online: A collective database of non-commercial biographies of people on the Net (http://www.ictp.trieste.it/Canessa/whoiswho.html).

- WWPR: World-Wide Profile Registry (commercial) (http://snark.wizard.com/wwpr.html).

Society

■ ACM SIGCAS: Association for Computing Machinery (ACM) Special Interest Group on Computers and Society
(`gopher://gopher.acm.org/11[the files.sig_forums.sigcas]`).

■ Anonymity FAQ: Anonymity on the Internet
(`ftp://rtfm.mit.edu/pub/usenet/news.answers/net-anonymity/`).

■ CCH: Centre for Computing in the Humanities
(`gopher://alpha.epas.utoronto.ca/11/cch`).

■ Computer Underground: The Social Organization of the Computer Underground, an MS Thesis by Gordon R. Meyer
(`ftp://ftp.eff.org/pub/Publications/CuD/Papers/meyer`).

■ Coombs Papers: Science and humanities papers, bibliographies, directories, theses abstracts and other high-grade research material (`gopher://coombs.anu.edu.au`).

■ Culture/Tech: A collection of texts exploring the relationship of technology and culture
(`http://english-server.hss.cmu.edu/Cyber.html`).

■ Cyber-Culture-Yahoo: Society and Culture-Cyber-Culture
(`http://www.yahoo.com/Society_and_Culture/Cyber_Culture/`).

■ Cyber papers/EFF: Collection of cyberspace-related papers, from the Electronic Frontier Foundation (`ftp://ftp.eff.org/pub/Publications/CuD/Papers/`).

■ Cyberspace: The New Frontier, by The Laboratory for Applied Logic at the University of Idaho (`http://www.cs.uidaho.edu/lal/cyberspace/cyberspace.html`).

■ Cyberpunk FAQ: From the Usenet newsgroup `alt.cyberpunk`
(`ftp://rtfm.mit.edu/pub/usenet/news.answers/cyberpunk-faq`).

■ Cypherpunk Topics: Information pulled off of many sources, mostly `sci.crypt` and the cypherpunks mailing list
(`ftp://ftp.u.washington.edu/public/phantom/cpunk/README.html`).

■ Cypherpunks gopher: clipper, DC Nets, digital cash, protocols, other info
(`gopher://chaos.bsu.edu`).

■ Cypherpunks home page: PGP, remailers, rants, various crypto-tools, newspaper clippings, and a good deal of other things
(`ftp://ftp.csua.berkeley.edu/cypherpunks/Home.html`).

■ MetaNet Gopher: Management, organizational change and development, education, the arts and the humanities, the impact of technology on society, the future, law, health, the environment, public policy, reinventing government (`gopher://gopher.tmn.com`).

■ English Server: Examine the possibilities of collaborative, community-run communications (`http://english-server.hss.cmu.edu`).

■ Fourth World: Indigenous Peoples' Information for the Online Community
(`http://www.halcyon.com/FWDP/fwdp.html`).

- Future Culture: FutureCulture FAQ, or Cyberography, is maintained by Andy Hawks (`mailto:future-request@nyx.cs.du.edu` Subject: `send faq`).

- Future Culture: Information about Net culture, media, virtual communities, cyberpunk, memetics (`http://www.uio.no/~mwatz/futurec/`).

- Gender Issues: Gender Issues in Computer Networking, by Leslie Regan Shade (`ftp://alfred.carleton.ca/pub/freenet/93conference/leslie_regan_shade.txt`).

- Gender/Spertus: Ellen Spertus' Writings on Gender and Science/Engineering (`http://www.ai.mit.edu/people/ellens/gender.html`).

- Global/Women: Global Fund for Women, an international grantmaking organization (`http://www.ai.mit.edu/people/ellens/gfw.html`).

- Humanities: Ad Hoc Steering Committee of the National Initiative for Humanities and Arts Computing (`mailto:rre-request@weber.ucsd.edu` Subject: `archive send humanities`).

- IEEE SSIT: The Society on Social Implications of Technology (SSIT) of the Institute of Electrical and Electronics Engineers (IEEE) (`http://www2.ncsu.edu/unity/users/j/jherkert/index.html`).

- Internet demographics: A survey by Texas Internet Consulting (`ftp://ftp.tic.com/survey/`).

- McGee collection: Art McGee's collection on culture and society issues—Activism, African, community, development, gender, indigenous, Latin (`ftp://ftp.netcom.com/pub/amcgee/`).

- Net Ethics: Ethics and the Internet (`ftp://nic.merit.edu/documents/rfc/rfc1087.txt`).

- Net Etiquette Guide: By Arlene H. Rinaldi (`ftp://ftp.lib.berkeley.edu/pub/net.training/FAU/`).

- Net Rights/NRC: Rights and Responsibilities of Participants in Networked Communities, from the U.S. National Research Council, National Academy Press, National Academy of Sciences (`http://www.nas.edu:70/1/nap/online/rights`).

- Netizen Anthology: The Netizens and the Wonderful World of the Net—An Anthology, Ronda Hauben, Michael Hauben (`http://www.columbia.edu/~hauben/project_book.html`).

- Networking: Networking on the Network, by Phil Agre (`mailto:rre-request@weber.ucsd.edu` Subject: `archive send network`).

- Privacy: Archive about network privacy, from Usenet group `alt.privacy` (`ftp://rtfm.mit.edu/pub/usenet/alt.privacy/`).

- Privacy forum: Materials for the Privacy forum, including all Privacy Forum Digest issues and materials (`gopher://vortex.com/11/privacy`).

- SeniorNet: Senior citizens' network on America OnLine (voice) (phone: 415-750-5030).

- SeniorNet Profile: (`http://nearnet.gnn.com/gnn/bus/senior/index.html`).

■ Togethernet: Online information and communication network for sustainable planetary future (gopher://gopher.together.uvm.edu).

■ Usenet Oracle: (mailto:oracle@cs.indiana.edu Subject: help).

■ Women: Online writings and resources by/about/for women (http://www.mit.edu:8001/people/sorokin/women/index.html).

■ UWI Cultural Play: UWI's Web's Edge/UnderWorld Industries' Cultural Playground (http://kzsu.stanford.edu/uwi.html).

Organizations

These are organizations that relate to Internet (or computing) communications, telecommunications, or other related activities, through the fields of study they represent or through their activities and research.

Commercial

These are commercial organizations that deal with Internet, CMC, or computing, communications, telecommunications, or other related activities.

Lists

■ Access Providers—Yahoo: Internet Access Providers list from Yahoo (http://www.yahoo.com/Business/Corporations/Internet_Access_Providers/).

■ Applications—commerce:
(http://www.rpi.edu/Internet/Guides/decemj/icmc/applications-commerce.html).

■ Business-indices: Business-Corporations-indices, from Yahoo (http://www.yahoo.com/yahoo/Business/Corporations/indicies/).

■ Computer and Comm Companies: Computer and Communication Company Sites on the Web, by James E. (Jed) Donnelley (http://www-atp.llnl.gov/atp/companies.html).

■ Computer Companies: List from Web of Wonder (WOW), includes systems, consulting, hardware, software, other links
(http://www.digimark.net/wow/companie/computer/index.html).

■ DLIST: A list of dedicated line Internet providers, by Susan Estrada (mailto:dlist@ora.com Body: Please send DLIST).

■ Gray Pages: Information on business products and services through a Web interface (http://www.trinet.com/tgp/).

■ Ho, Thomas: Favorite Electronic Commerce WWW resources; includes information sources, links to articles, economic development, service/presence providers (http://www.engr.iupui.edu/~ho/interests/commmenu.html).

- Indices: Business-Corporations-Indices, from Yahoo (`http://www.yahoo.com/Business/Corporations/Indices/`).

- IAP Catalog: Internet Access Provider Catalog (indexed by area code/country code), from Network-USA (`http://www.netusa.net/ISP`).

- Internet Consultants: CommerceNet's directory of Internet consultants (products and services) (`http://www.commerce.net/directories/consultants/consultants.html`).

- Internet Providers: All Providers Alphabetically (`ftp://sri.com/netinfo/internet-access-providers-alphabetical-listing.txt`).

- Internet Providers Non-U.S.: Non-U.S. Internet Providers (`ftp://sri.com/netinfo/internet-access-providers-non-us.txt`).

- PDIAL: The Public Dialup Internet Access List, by Peter Kaminski (`ftp://rtfm.mit.edu/pub/usenet/news.answers/pdial`).

- POCIA: Providers of Commercial Internet Access (`http://www.teleport.com/~cci/directories/pocia/pocia.html`).

- WWYP: World Wide Yellow Pages (`http://www.yellow.com`).

- WWW Service: Companies providing various WWW services such as serving pages, authoring pages, and so on, by Mary E. S. Morris of Finesse Liveware (`ftp://ftp.einet.net/pub/INET-MARKETING/www-svc-providers`).

Providers

- POCIA: Providers of Commercial Internet Access (`http://www.teleport.com/~cci/directories/pocia/pocia.html`).

Following is a partial list of commercial organizations that provide Internet connectivity or access.

- America OnLine (phone: 800-827-6364)
- BIX (phone: 800-695-4775)
- CONNECT (phone: 408-973-0110)
- CompuServe (phone: 800-848-8199)
- CompuServe (`http://www.compuserve.com`)
- Delphi (phone: 800-695-4005)
- Delphi web (`http://www.delphi.com`)
- Dialog (phone: 800-334-2564)
- Dow Jones (phone: 800-522-3567)
- EUnet European Internet-related service organization (`http://www.eu.net`)
- GEnie (phone: 800-638-9636)

- INO: Intelligence Network Online, Inc. (`mailto:info@intnet.net`) *
- Japan-IIJ: Internet Initiative Japan Inc. (`http://www.iij.ad.jp`)
- MCI Mail (phone: 800-444-6245)
- MSEN: MSEN offers Usenet and Internet Connectivity (`gopher://gopher.msen.com`)
- Netcom (`mailto:info@netcom.com`)
- PCIX: Internet Service Provider, New England USA (`http://www.pcix.com`)
- PC-LINK (phone: 800-827-8532)
- PSI: Performance Systems International, dial-up Internet access (phone: 703-620-6651)
- PSI: Performance Systems International (`mailto:all-info@psi.com`)
- PSI Web (`http://www.psi.net`)
- Pipeline: NYC-based Internet gateway (`mailto:infobot@pipeline.com` Body: `help`)
- Prodigy (phone: 800-776-3449)
- Prodigy/Astranet (`http://www.astranet.com`)
- Software Tool and Die: The World, online service for dialup access to the Internet (`gopher://world.std.com`)
- TMN: The Meta Network (`mailto:info@tmn.com`)
- The WELL (`mailto:support@well.sf.ca.us`)

Consortia

- ACC: Alliance for Competitive Communications (formerly MFJ Task force) an *ad hoc* coalition of the seven regional Bell operating companies (`http://bell.com`).
- CIX Web: Commercial Internet Exchange (`http://www.cix.org/CIXhome.html`).
- IFIP gopher: International Federation for Information Processing, a multi-national federation of professional and technical organizations (or national groupings of such organizations) concerned with information processing (`gopher://ietf.cnri.reston.va.us/00/ifip/ifip.info`).
- IFIP web: International Federation for Information Processing, a multi-national federation of professional and technical organizations (or national groupings of such organizations) concerned with information processing (`http://www.dit.upm.es/~cdk/ifip.html`).
- IIA: Information Industry Association, 500 member companies in the generation, processing, distribution, and use of information (`mailto:iia.ipo@his.com`).
- NIIP: National Industrial Information Infrastructure Protocol Consortium (`http://www.niiip.org`).
- NIIT: National Information Infrastructure Testbed (`http://www.niit.org/niit/`).
- NIPDE: National Initiative for Product Data Exchange (`http://www.eeel.nist.gov/nipde/`).
- NOMA: National Online Media Association (`mailto:natbbs-request@echonyc.com`).

■ SGML Open: A nonprofit, international consortium of providers of products and services, dedicated to accelerating the further adoption, application, and implementation of the Standard Generalized Markup Language (http://www.sgmlopen.org).

■ Wireless: The Wireless Opportunities Coalition, a group of organizations and companies seeking to expand wireless communications development, manufacturing, and use (http://wireless.policy.net/wireless/wireless.html).

Developers

Lists

■ Comm+Media: Business-Corporations-Communications and Media Services, from Yahoo (http://www.yahoo.com/yahoo/Business/Corporations/Communications_and_Media_Services/).

■ Internet Consulting-Yahoo: Internet-Consulting, from Yahoo (http://www.yahoo.com/Business/Corporations/Internet_Consulting).

■ Internet Presence-Yahoo: Internet-Presence-Providers, from Yahoo (http://www.yahoo.com/Business/Corporations/Internet_Presence_Providers/).

■ WWW Consultants/Providers: (http://hanksville.phast.umass.edu/~bdelong/res/wwwexp.html).

Selected Instances

The following are selected instances of consultants/marketers/markets/advertisers related to computer-mediated communication.

■ DCI: Digital Consulting-computer/telecommunications conferences (for example, Distributed Computing World) (http://www.oec.com/DCI/index.html).

■ MIDS/TIC web: Matrix Information and Directory Services/Texas Internet Consulting, includes Internet information (http://www.tic.com).

■ Mecklermedia: Publishers of Internet books and conferences (phone: 800-MECKLER).

■ Mecklerweb (http://www.mecklerweb.com/home.htm).

■ PIPEX: The Public IP Exchange (http://www.pipex.net).

■ WAIS, Inc.: Interactive online publishing systems and services to organizations (http://www.wais.com).

Products

■ Cisco: Manufactures and sells multiprotocol routers (http://www.cisco.com).

■ Consensus: Software support for collaboration, including groupware (ftp://www.consensus.com:8300).

- DEC: Digital Equipment Corporation, Marketing Home Page (`ftp://gatekeeper.dec.com/info.html`).

- IBM: International Business Machines Corporation (`http://www.ibm.com`).

- ICI: Internet Computer Index, lists almost all of the Internet resources relating to PCs, Macintoshes, and UNIX systems (`http://ici.proper.com`).

- Microsoft: Research in fields of computer science that might be beneficial to Microsoft in the future (`http://www.research.microsoft.com`).

- Motorola: Wireless communications, semiconductors, and advanced electronic systems and services (`http://www.mot.com`).

- NCD: Network Computing Devices (`http://www.ncd.com`).

- NEC: `http://www.nec.co.jp`.

- Novell: `http://www.novell.com`.

- OCM: Online Computer Market; information about computer hardware, software, and services (`http://www.ocm.com`).

- RNS: Rockwell Network Systems, high-performance, standards-based networking equipment (`http://www.cmc.com`).

- TMC: Thinking Machines Corporation (`http://www.think.com`).

- RSA: RSA Data Security, Inc., world leader in cryptography (`http://www.rsa.com`).

- RTZ: RTZ software, Cupertino, California, real-time multimedia conferencing products (`ftp://ftp.netcom.com/pub/rtz/www/rtzhomepage.html`).

- SCO Web Page: The Santa Cruz Operation (`http://www.sco.com/index.html`).

- Silicon Surf: Silicon Graphics' SILICON SURF Home Page (`http://www.sgi.com`).

- Spry, Inc.: Applications for LANs, AIR Mosaic, NetAccess(a computer industry business directory for Mosaic users) (`http://www.spry.com`).

- Sun Home Page: Sun Microsystems distributed computing technologies, products, and services (`http://www.sun.com`).

- Sun Microsystems: Archives, Newsgroups and More! (`http://sunsite.unc.edu/sun/inform/sun-info.html`).

- VTLS Web Page: Automation solutions for libraries and other information centers worldwide (`http://www.vtls.com`).

- Wildfire Communications: Personal communication assistants for the mobile professional (`http://www.utopia.com/companies/wildfire/home.html`).

- Xerox PARC: Xerox Palo Alto Research Center (`http://www.parc.xerox.com`).

Telecom

Lists

- Telecom-Yahoo: Business-Corporations-Telecommunications (`http://www.yahoo.com/Business/Corporations/Telecommunications/`).

Selected Instances

- Ameritech (`http://www.ameritech.com`).
- AT&T (`http://www.att.com`).
- AT&T Research: Web server for AT&T Bell Laboratories Research (`http://www.research.att.com`).
- Bellcore (`http://info.bellcore.com`).
- Bell Atlantic (`http://www.ba.com`).
- British Telecom (`http://www.bt.net`).
- MCI (`http://www.mci.com`).
- MPT-Japan: Ministry of Posts and Telecommunications, Japan (`http://www.mpt.go.jp`).
- NTT-Japan: Nippon Telegraph and Telephone (`http://www.ntt.jp/index.html`).
- Pacific Bell (`http://www.pacbell.com`).
- Southwestern Bell (`http://www.sbc.com`).
- Sprint (`http://www.sprintlink.net`).
- Tampere: Tampere Telephone Company, Tampere, Finland (`http://www.tpo.fi`).
- US West (`http://www.uswest.com`).
- WilTel (`http://www.wiltel.com`).

Internet

These are organizations that work to develop the Internet.

- Internet WG: Internet working groups (`http://netlab.itd.nrl.navy.mil/Internet.html`).
- IEPG: Internet Engineering and Planning Group, a group of Internet service providers working together to promote a global Internet (`http://info.aarnet.edu.au/iepg/`).
- IETF ftp: Internet Engineering Task Force (`ftp://cnri.reston.va.us/ietf/`).
- IETF web (`http://www.ietf.cnri.reston.va.us/home.html`).
- IS: Internet Society (`http://info.isoc.org`).
- Merit: NSFNet Engineering (`http://rrdb.merit.edu`).

- W3C: the World Wide Web Consortium; supports the stable evolution of the World Wide Web and its protocols (`http://www.w3.org/hypertext/WWW/Consortium/`).
- Working Groups: Internet working groups (`http://netlab.itd.nrl.navy.mil/Internet.html`).

Network

These are consortia, collections of networks, or national or regional networking organizations or groups.

- EARN: European Academic Research Network (`ftp://ftp.earn.net`).
- EARN Web: `http://www.earn.net/welcome.html`.
- NEARnet: New England Academic and Research Network (`ftp://nic.near.net/docs/`).
- NYSERNet: New York State Education and Research Network (`ftp://nysernet.org/pub/resources/guides/`).
- NYSERNet web: New York State Education and Research Network (`http://nysernet.org/nysernet.html`).
- RARE: Reseaux Associes pour la Récherche Européenne, European research networks and users (`ftp://ftp.rare.nl/rare/`).
- RARE docs: Document store of Reseaux Associes pour la Récherche Européenne, European research networks and users (`http://www.rare.nl`).
- RIPE: Reseaux IP Europeen, ensures coordination to operate a pan-European IP network. (`ftp://ftp.ripe.net/ripe/`).
- RIPE Gopher: Reseaux IP Europeens, collaborative organization that consists of European Internet service providers (`gopher://gopher.ripe.net`).
- RIPE Web: Reseaux IP Europeens (`http://www.ripe.net`).
- SuperJANET: Super Joint Academic Network, an advanced, high-speed optical fiber network linking a large number of sites within the academic community (`http://gala.jnt.ac.uk`).
- SURAnet: Southeastern Universities Research Association Network (`ftp://ftp.sura.net/pub/README`).
- TARENA: Trans-European Research and Education Networking Association, international information and telecommunications infrastructure; formed from the merging of RARE and EARN (Oct 1994) (`http://www.terena.nl`).

Nonprofit

These are organizations that work to foster networking or advocate for issues related to CMC, communications, or technology.

- APT: Alliance for Public Technology, "A Washington, D.C.-based nonprofit, tax-exempt coalition of public-interest groups and individuals whose goal is to foster broad access to affordable, usable information and communication services and technology" (`http://apt.org/apt.html`).

- ASIS: American Society for Information Science (`mailto:asis@cni.org`).

- ASIS students: Web page for the Bay Area (San Francisco, USA) Student Chapter of American Society for Information Science, includes links to other chapters (`http://ranga.berkeley.edu/ASIS/asis-sc.html`).

- CCN: The Center for Civic Networking, applying information infrastructure to the broad public good (`mailto:ccn@civicnet.org`).

- CCN: Civic Network is an evolving collection of online resources dedicated to supporting civic life and civic participation (`http://www.civic.net:2401`).

- CCN Archive: `ftp://ftp.std.com/ftp/amo/civicnet/`.

- CIOS: Communication Institute for Online Scholarship, a nonprofit organization for online communication scholarship (`mailto:comserve@vm.its.rpi.edu` Body: `help topics associates`).

- CIOS gopher: Communication Institute for Online Scholarship, a nonprofit organization for online communication scholarship; gopher server (`gopher://cios.llc.rpi.edu`).

- CITS: Center For Information, Technology, and Society (`ftp://ftp.std.com/customers/nonprofits/CITES`).

- CIX: Commercial Internet eXchange Association, nonprofit trade association promoting communications services. (`ftp://cix.org/cix/README`).

- CIX Web: Commercial Internet Exchange (`http://www.cix.org/CIXhome.html`).

- CME: Center for Media Education; promotes democratic potential of electronic media (`mailto:cme@access.digex.net` Subject: `CME Sub`).

- CNI: Coalition for Networked Information; promotes creation of and access to information resources in networked environments (`ftp://ftp.cni.org/CNI/`).

- CNI Web: `http://www.cni.org/CNI.homepage.html`.

- CNIDR Web Page: Coalition for Networked Information Discovery and Retrieval Home Page (`http://cnidr.org/welcome.html`).

- CNRI: Corporation for National Research Initiatives, develop information-processing technology (`gopher://ietf.cnri.Reston.va.us`).

- CoSN: Consortium for School Networking; helps educators and students access information and communications resources (`mailto:cosn@bitnic.bitnet` Body: `Please send CoSN info.`).

- CoSN Gopher: Consortium for School Networking (`gopher://cosn.org`).

- CPI: Coalition for Public Information; information developers, providers, and educators dedicated to ensuring public access to the evolving electronic information infrastructure in Canada (`gopher://resudox.net:1994`).

- CPSR: Computer Professionals for Social Responsibility; alliance of computer professionals who discuss the impact of computer technology on society (`ftp://ftp.cpsr.org/cpsr/`).

- CPSR Gopher: Computer Professionals for Social Responsibility; alliance of computer professionals who discuss the impact of computer technology on society (`gopher://cpsr.org`).

- CPSR Web: Computer Professionals for Social Responsibility; alliance of computer professionals who discuss the impact of computer technology on society (`http://www.cpsr.org/home`).

- CREN: Supports low-cost access to worldwide electronic networking for education and research (`gopher://info.educom.edu`).

- CSD: The Center for Software Development (`http://www.center.org/csd/home.html`).

- CSF: Communications for a Sustainable Future (`gopher://csf.colorado.edu`).

- ECHO: European Commission Host Organisation (`telnet://echo@echo.lu`).

- EDUCOM: Dedicated to the study and access of information technology in higher education and integrating technology into learning and research (`mailto:inquiry@educom.edu` Body: `Please send EDUCOM info`).

- EDUCOM Gopher: `gopher://educom.edu`.

- EDUCOM Web: `http://educom.edu`.

- EFF: Public-interest organization to educate public about computer and communication technologies (`ftp://ftp.eff.org/pub/EFF/about-eff`).

- EFF Gopher: A gopher information server for the Electronic Frontier Foundation (`gopher://gopher.eff.org`).

- EFF Web Page: Electronic Frontier Foundation Web Page (`http://www.eff.org`).

- EMA: Electronic Messaging Association; foster the development and use of secure global electronic commerce (`http://www.ema.org/ema/ema-home.htm`).

- ENA: Electronic Networking Association; promotes electronic networking (`mailto:comserve@vm.its.rpi.edu` Body: `send Netweave Winter91`).

- FARNET: Nonprofit corporation to advance the use of computer networks for research and education (`ftp://ftp.farnet.org`).

- GNA: Globewide Network Academy, a nonprofit corporation, affiliated with the Usenet University; goal is to create a fully accredited online university (`http://uu-gna.mit.edu:8001/uu-gna/index.html`).

- HPCC Office: The National Coordination Office (NCO) for High Performance Computing and Communications (`gopher://www.hpcc.gov`).

- IANA: Internet Assigned Numbers Authority (`mailto:iana@isi.edu`).

- IATH: Institute for Advanced Technology in the Humanities (`http://jefferson.village.virginia.edu`).

- ICC: The International Center for Communications; link communities through technology (`http://www.ifi.uio.no/~terjen/cv/ICC/info.html`).
- IGC: Institute for Global Communications, improving global network communication and information exchange (`ftp://igc.org/README`).
- IGC Gopher: `gopher://igc.apc.org`.
- IRMAC: Information Resource Management Association of Canada (`telnet://freenet.carleton.ca`).
- IRVC: Institute for Research on Virtual Culture (`ftp://byrd.mu.wvnet.edu/pub/estepp/IRVC`).
- IRTS: the Internet Roundtable Society (`http://www.irsociety.com`).
- ISOC: The Internet Society; supports the development of the Internet and promotes education and applications (`ftp://ftp.isoc.org/isoc/`).
- ISOC Gopher: the Internet Society's information server (`gopher://gopher.isoc.org`).
- ISOC Web: the Internet Society's Web page (`http://info.isoc.org/home.html`).
- ISTE: International Society for Technology in Education (`mailto:ISTE@Oregon.uoregon.edu`).
- Kestrel Inst: A nonprofit computer science research institute; methods for incremental automation of the software (`http://kestrel.edu`).
- NIIT: National Information Infrastructure Testbed (`http://www.esi.com/niit/niit_top.html`).
- NPTN: National Public Telecomputing Network (`ftp://nptn.org/pub/info.nptn/`).
- OSF: Open Software Foundation (`http://www.osf.org:8001/index.html`).
- PD: Public Domain, Inc., a 501(c)3 nonprofit organization whose stated mission is to explore the interface between art, technology, and theory (`http://noel.pd.org`).
- WAENA: WideArea Educational Network (`mailto:jwmilton@waena.portal.com`).
- SEA: Society for Electronic Access (`http://www.panix.com/sea/`).
- UniForum: The largest vendor-independent association for open systems professionals (`http://www.uniforum.org`).
- USENIX: A forum for innovation and research in UNIX and modern open systems (`http://usenix.org`).

Standards

These are organizations that play some part in setting technical standards for telecommunications and networking.

- ACM-TSC: Association for Computing Machinery Technical Standards Committee (`http://www.cs.purdue.edu/homes/spaf/acm/acm-tsc.html`).

■ ANSI: American National Standards Institute, a U.S. clearinghouse for standards, member of ISO (phone: 212-642-4900).

■ ATIS: Alliance for Telecommunications Industry Solutions (phone: 202-434-8845).

■ CCITT: International Telegraph and Telephone Consultative Committee, a member of the ITU (phone: +41-22-995111).

■ CCITT Doc Retrieval: (mailto:teledoc@itu.arcom.ch Body: help).

■ Committee T1: ANSI (American National Standards Institute) accredited ATIS (Alliance for Telecommunications Industry Solutions) sponsored Committee T1 (Telecommunications); the focal point for developing U.S. positions for the ITU-T (formerly CCITT) (ftp://ftp.t1.org).

■ DISA: Data Interchange Standards Association, Inc. (http://www.disa.org).

■ ECMA: European Computer Manufacturers Association; computer and communications technologies (phone: +41-22-353634).

■ EIA: Electronic Industries Association; national trade association (phone: 202-457-4966).

■ IEEE Web: Institute of Electrical and Electronics Engineers (http://www.ieee.org).

■ ISO: International Organization for Standardization, a voluntary body of national standardization organizations (phone: +41-22-341240).

■ ISO web: International Organization for Standardization (http://www.iso.ch).

■ ISO info: International Organization for Standardization information, by Dr. Hiroaki Ikeda (http://www.hike.te.chiba-u.ac.jp/ikeda/ISO/home.html).

■ ITU gopher: International Telecommunication Union, a United Nations agency that coordinates telecommunications (gopher://info.itu.ch).

■ NIST-USA Web: National Institute of Standards and Technology WWW Home Page (http://www.nist.gov/welcome.html).

GLOSSARY

Add-ons General term encompassing viewers, players, and other multimedia additions to Web clients.

Amiga Mosaic Web client program for the Amiga computer (formerly from Commodore). Otherwise known as *AMosaic*. Unlike the other Mosaics, it is *not* distributed by NCSA.

Browser More common term for *client*.

Bulleted list List of items separated by large dots on a Web page.

Cello Popular Web client for Microsoft Windows. Cello is distributed through Cornell University's Legal Information Institute.

CERN The European Laboratory for Particle Physics where the World Wide Web project originated in 1989.

CERN Line Browser The first Web client, distinguished by the use of numbers where most clients show highlighted hyperlinks.

Chimera Web client for X Window System.

Clickable map   Unofficial name for *imagemap*. So called because to access a related URL, the user clicks the mouse when the on-screen pointer is positioned on a portion of the map (or graphic).

Client   Unofficially termed *browsers*, client software packages enable users to access and browse the World Wide Web. Clients can display HTML pages in their desired format.

DNS   Domain Name System. DNS errors occur when clients cannot determine the site of a requested Web document.

Document   Catch-all term for anything that appears in the main windows of a Web client. More specifically, a Web document is an HTML document that the client displays.

Editor   For the Web, a program that assists in the authoring of HTML documents. Typically it includes tagging and formatting macros.

Fill-in Forms   Specially designed section of HTML document that accepts input from users. Forms are typically used for user feedback, product ordering, or document searching.

Firewall   Areas of a computer file system protected against unwanted access by Web users.

Formatted text   Text included on a Web page that was formatted by another type of computer program (that is, not in HTML format), and is displayed by the Web client in that original format.

Forms   Short for *fill-in forms*.

FTP   File Transfer Protocol. A means to exchange files across a network. The set of all resources accessible through publicly available file transfer protocol sites is sometimes referred to as *FTP space*.

Gateway   A connecting point that translates different network e-mail protocols, thus enabling them to intercommunicate.

Gopher   A means for disseminating or discovering resources on the Internet through a menu interface. Menu items can be links to other documents, search utilities, or information services. The set of all resources publicly accessible through the Internet Gopher protocol is sometimes referred to as *Gopher space*.

Graphical browser   A Web client capable of displaying inline graphics, and that offers a mouse-based, point-and-click hypertext interface.

Graphics file   A file in graphics format that can be retrieved through the client's capabilities, but that usually cannot be displayed via the browser itself. Graphics files are typically viewed through an add-on or file viewer associated with the client.

Heading   An emphasized line or section in an HTML document. Several heading styles are available.

Helpers   Macintosh name for add-ons, viewers, and *players*.

Home page   Refers to a designated entry point for access to a local web. Also refers to a page that a person designates as his or her own "main page," often presenting personal or professional information.

Hotspot   A region within the display of hypertext that, when selected, links the user to another point in the hypertext or to another (possibly nonhypertext) resource.

HTML   HyperText Markup Language. The coding mechanism used to author Web pages. Web clients display HTML pages according to their coded format.

HTTP   HyperText Transfer Protocol. The Web's primary protocol. HTTP performs the request and retrieve functions necessary to display documents stored on remote computers.

Hyperlink   A hypertext link appearing as a highlighted number in a client's main window.

Hypermedia   An extension of *hypertext* that includes sound, graphics, and video as linking devices.

Hypertext   Term coined by Ted Nelson denoting text linked across a potentially unlimited number of information sources. One link takes the user to another document, which contains links to other documents (and so forth), and these documents can be located on any hypertext-capable system anywhere in the world. Hypertext is the basis of the World Wide Web.

Imagemaps   Formal name for *clickable maps*. Graphic elements that have two or more hyperlinks embedded into them, with each hyperlink offering an individual jump to a linked document. Frequently, imagemaps are in fact maps, but they can appear as any graphic. A medical tutorial, for example, could offer a graphic of the human body as an imagemap; users clicking on the heart area of the imagemap would be linked to a document or series of documents related to heart issues.

Inline image   Graphic that appears as part of the Web page. Inline images are coded into Web documents through the HTML language and load with the Web page itself. With most Web clients, inline images can be delayed or toggled off to improve retrieval speed.

Internet   A cooperatively run, globally distributed collection of computer networks that exchange information via a common set of rules for exchanging data (the TCP/IP protocol suite).

Jump   The act of retrieving a new document as the result of selecting a hyperlink. The term *jump* is used because the user is often accessing a different computer somewhere in the world, but no actual leaping about takes place, except for a change in URL addresses.

Knowbot   A *robot* that is programmed to acquire specific document references.

Line browser   Short for *CERN line browser*.

Link   A reference to another Web document, or another section of the same Web document. Links are typically highlighted when displayed in Web clients.

Lynx   The most capable nongraphical Web client, developed by the University of Kansas and available on many UNIX servers.

MacMosaic   Short for *NCSA Mosaic* for the Apple Macintosh.

MacWeb   Web client distributed by EINet for the Apple Macintosh.

MacWWW   Alternative (and seldom-used) name for the Web client *Samba*.

The Matrix   The set of all networks that can exchange electronic mail either directly or through mail gateways. This term was coined by John S. Quarterman in his book *The Matrix* (Digital Press, 1990).

MidasWWW   X Window System Web client developed by the Stanford Linear Accelerator Center.

Mosaic   Short for *NCSA Mosaic* or a licensed version distributed commercially.

Multimedia   Catch-all term for the integration of text, graphics, sound, animation, video, and communications technologies.

Navigation   The act of traversing the Web, or of moving among linked documents on a variety of computers. Navigation is a central topic in discussions of a hypertext system, because of the problem of getting "lost in hyperspace." Web clients typically offer navigation histories to help users find their way back along their hyperlink paths.

NCSA   The National Center for Supercomputing Applications located at the University of Illinois at Urbana-Champaign. Developers and distributors of *NCSA Mosaic.*

NCSA Mosaic   The most popular graphical Web client; available for the X Window System, the Apple Macintosh, and Microsoft Windows. NCSA Mosaic is licensed to several companies for commercial release.

The Net   An informal term for the Internet or some subset of *The Matrix,* with its specific meaning defined by the context of use. For example, a computerized conference via e-mail might take place on a BITNET host that has an Internet gateway, making the conference available to anyone on either of these networks. In this case, the developer might say, "Our conference will be available on the Net."

Numbered list   List of items separated by numbers on a Web page.

Page   HTML document displayed in a client's main window. It has completely undefined parameters, but typically a Web page is about 40–60 lines in length, including inline graphics.

Player   Software program capable of displaying sound or video files retrieved through a Web client. Players are separate programs from clients, with their functions and file associations specified in the client's configuration system.

Robot   Program that automatically traverses the Web looking for URL addresses. The results of the search are typically built as an HTML document.

Samba   The first graphical client for the Web, developed by CERN and still available today. Significantly lacking in features according to the standards set by today's graphical clients.

Site   File section of a computer on which Web documents reside. The term is typically used to refer to the specific organization that controls these documents (for example, the MIT site, or the AT&T site).

Sound file   Computer file containing digitized sound that can be retrieved by a Web client but can be heard only through *player* software associated with the client.

Spider   Program that traverses the Web automatically. Similar to *robot,* a spider creates a database of Web links.

Surfing   The act of navigating the Web. Surfing is typically used to denote jumping (see *jump*) from page to page using techniques to rapidly process (or disregard most) content in order to locate subjectively valuable or interesting resources.

Tag   Formatting code item within an HTML document.

Text-based browser   Web client used by text terminals. Typically UNIX based.

Title   The author-determined name of a World Wide Web page.

tkWWW   Graphical Web client for the X Window System.

URL   Uniform Resource Locator. The addressing system for Web documents.

Usenet   System for disseminating asynchronous text discussion among cooperating computer hosts. A Usenet newsgroup is a forum for discussing a particular subject, topic, or subtopic. Usenet is not a network, nor is it limited to distribution on the Internet, but is disseminated widely throughout The Matrix and beyond.

Video file   Computer file consisting of digitized video. A video file can be retrieved by a Web client but can only be heard through a *player* or *viewer* associated with the client.

Viewer   Software program capable of displaying graphics or video files retrieved through a Web client. Viewers are separate programs from clients. Their functions and file associations are specified in the client's configuration system.

Viola   Graphical Web client for the X Window System. Viola is part of an object-oriented programming language.

Wanderer   Program that automatically traverses the Web. Similar to a *robot*, its aim is to measure the growth of the Web.

web   A set of hypertext pages related to a particular topic or that might be located on a single host; a subset of the *Web*.

Web   Short for the World Wide Web.

Web server   Computer on which Web documents reside, and that runs HTTP software to permit Web transactions.

WinMosaic   Short for *NCSA Mosaic* for Microsoft Windows.

WinWeb   Web client for Microsoft Windows distributed by EINet. It is the Windows version of *MacWeb*.

World Wide Web   Distributed hypermedia system originating at CERN in 1989.

www   Little-used name for the *CERN Line Browser*.

WWW   Abbreviation for *World Wide Web*.

XMosaic   Short for *NCSA Mosaic* for the X Window System.

INDEX

The World Wide Web Unleashed, 1996

The World Wide Web Unleashed, 1996

The World Wide Web Unleashed, 1996

The World Wide Web Unleashed, 1996

The World Wide Web Unleashed, 1996

The World Wide Web Unleashed, 1996

X-Y-Z

Add to Your Sams.net Library Today
with the Best Books for Internet Technologies

ISBN	Quantity	Description of Item	Unit Cost	Total Cost
0-672-30737-5		The World Wide Web Unleashed, Second Edition	$39.99	
1-57521-041-x		The Internet Unleashed 1996	$45.00	
0-672-30685-9		Windows NT 3.5 Unleashed, Second Edition	$39.99	
1-57521-005-3		Teach Yourself More Web Publishing with HTML in a Week	$29.99	
0-672-30764-2		Teach Yourself Web Publishing with Microsoft Word in a Week	$29.99	
0-672-30586-0		Teach Yourself Perl in 21 Days	$29.99	
1-57521-004-5		The Internet Business Guide, Second Edition	$25.00	
0-672-30402-3		UNIX Unleashed (book/CD)	$49.99	
0-672-30529-1		Teach Yourself REXX in 21 Days	$29.99	
0-672-30705-7		Linux Unleashed (book/CD)	$49.99	
0-672-30719-7		Navigating the Internet with OS/2 Warp	$25.00	
0-672-30584-4		Networking UNIX	$35.00	
0-672-30549-6		Teach Yourself TCP/IP in 14 Days	$29.99	
❏ 3 ½" Disk		Shipping and Handling: See information below.		
❏ 5 ¼" Disk		TOTAL		

Shipping and Handling: $4.00 for the first book, and $1.75 for each additional book. If you need to have it NOW, we can ship product to you in 24 hours for an additional charge of approximately $18.00, and you will receive your item overnight or in two days. Overseas shipping and handling adds $2.00. Prices subject to change. Call between 9:00 a.m. and 5:00 p.m. EST for availability and pricing information on latest editions.

201 W. 103rd Street, Indianapolis, Indiana 46290

1-800-428-5331 — Orders   1-800-835-3202 — FAX   1-800-858-7674 — Customer Service

Book ISBN 1-57521-040-1

The MCP Forum on CompuServe

Go online with the world's leading computer book publisher!
Macmillan Computer Publishing offers everything
you need for computer success!

Find the books that are right for you!
A complete online catalog, plus sample
chapters and tables of contents give
you an in-depth look at all our books.
The best way to shop or browse!

➤ Get fast answers and technical support for
MCP books and software

➤ Join discussion groups on major computer
subjects

➤ Interact with our expert authors via e-mail
and conferences

➤ Download software from our immense
library:

  ▷ Source code from books
  ▷ Demos of hot software
  ▷ The best shareware and freeware
  ▷ Graphics files

Join now and get a free CompuServe Starter Kit!

To receive your free CompuServe Introductory Membership, call **1-800-848-
8199** and ask for representative #597.

The Starter Kit includes:
➤ Personal ID number and password
➤ $15 credit on the system
➤ Subscription to *CompuServe Magazine*

Once on the CompuServe System, type:

GO MACMILLAN

for the most computer information anywhere!

PLUG YOURSELF INTO...

MACMILLAN INFORMATION SUPERLIBRARY™

que · SAMS PUBLISHING · Hayden Books · que COLLEGE · NRP · alpha books · Brady · ADOBE PRESS

THE MACMILLAN INFORMATION SUPERLIBRARY™

Free information and vast computer resources from the world's leading computer book publisher—online!

FIND THE BOOKS THAT ARE RIGHT FOR YOU!

A complete online catalog, plus sample chapters and tables of contents give you an in-depth look at *all* of our books, including hard-to-find titles. It's the best way to find the books you need!

- **STAY INFORMED** with the latest computer industry news through our online newsletter, press releases, and customized Information SuperLibrary Reports.

- **GET FAST ANSWERS** to your questions about MCP books and software.

- **VISIT** our online bookstore for the latest information and editions!

- **COMMUNICATE** with our expert authors through e-mail and conferences.

- **DOWNLOAD SOFTWARE** from the immense MCP library:
    - Source code and files from MCP books
    - The best shareware, freeware, and demos

- **DISCOVER HOT SPOTS** on other parts of the Internet.

- **WIN BOOKS** in ongoing contests and giveaways!

TO PLUG INTO MCP: ➔

GOPHER: gopher.mcp.com

FTP: ftp.mcp.com

WORLD WIDE WEB: **http://www.mcp.com**

Home Page · What's New · Bookstore · Reference Desk · Software Library · Macmillan Overview · Talk to Us

What's on the Disc

The companion CD-ROM contains many of the shareware programs mentioned in the book and dozens of useful third-party tools and utilities.

Windows 3.1 Installation Instructions

1. Insert the CD-ROM disc into your CD-ROM drive.
2. From File Manager or Program Manager, choose Run from the File menu.
3. Type <drive>INSTALL and press Enter (<drive> corresponds to the drive letter of your CD-ROM. For example, if your CD-ROM is drive D:, type D:INSTALL and press Enter.)
4. Follow the on-screen instructions in the installation program. Files will be installed to a directory named \WWW96 unless you choose a different directory during installation.

INSTALL creates a Windows Program Manager group called WWW Unleashed 96. This group contains icons for exploring the CD-ROM. A guide to the CD-ROM program starts automatically once installation has been completed.

Windows 95 Installation Instructions

If Windows 95 is installed on your computer, and you have the AutoPlay feature enabled, the guide to the CD-ROM program starts automatically when you insert the disc into your CD-ROM drive.

> **NOTE**
>
> The guide to the CD-ROM program requires at least 256 colors. For best results, set your monitor to display between 256 and 64,000 colors. A screen resolution of 640×480 pixels is also recommended. If necessary, adjust your monitor settings before using the CD-ROM.

To learn how to use the Guide to the CD-ROM program, press F1 from any screen in the program.

Macintosh Installation Instructions

1. Insert the CD-ROM disc into your CD-ROM drive.
2. When an icon for the CD appears on your desktop, open the disc by double-clicking on its icon.
3. Double-click on the icon named Guide to the CD-ROM, and follow the directions that appear.